Publishers note.

I first heard Captain Beefheart and His Magic Band on John Peel's *Perfumed Garden* radio show when *Safe As Milk* was released, and was instantly converted. So was my erstwhile chum and Proper colleague, Paul "Bassman" Riley.

Our earliest opportunity to see the band live was at our fabled local venue "The Star Hotel" in home-town Croydon on 16th May 1968. Admission was 7/6 (seven shillings and sixpence). The tiny bar in the pub was a well-established venue on the circuit and artists appearing at the time included The Jimi Hendrix Experience, Graham Bond Organisation, John Mayall (Clapton/Green era), Cream, Jethro Tull, Fleetwood Mac etc., and we went there every week.

Almost opposite the pub was The Croydon Suite which was a notorious club for early skinheads and other less peaceful people! On our way to the gig we saw Captain Beefheart and the band in full regalia walking past the entrance of the *The Suite.* Under normal circumstances, any hippies taking such a risk would have come under fire. But the band just looked *SO* weird that they were left untroubled by the speechless onlookers. Reassuringly, we must have looked like "people" as Don asked me and Paul if we knew "The Star" because they had got lost wandering around Croydon.

It is difficult to describe the show because it was simply overwhelming in every respect. We sat in the front row chairs in a half-filled room and Don boomed at Paul "I REMEMBER YOU" then kicked off a thunderous set leaving us awestruck. Over the years and of the thousands of gigs I've seen, there have not been many that rival the impact of that memorable night.

I subsequently saw the band each time they toured England but didn't get involved with John French until he reformed The Magic Band and they performed at Glastonbury. He

told me he was writing a book about his time with Captain Beefheart. When I read the first few draft pages I wanted to publish it in order for him (and the others) to get some well-deserved credit for his considerable contribution to the unique and timeless body of work that has given me so much pleasure.

MM 1968

Thanks John. Miriam says a big thank you for *Bat Chain Puller* too!

Malcolm Mills. Chairman. Proper Music Group Limited. 2010

BEEFHEART: THROUGH THE EYES OF MAGIC

JOHN "DRUMBO" FRENCH

Exclusive distributors:
Music Sales Limited,
14/15 Berners Street,
London, W1T 3LJ.

Published by Proper Music Publishing Limited,
Gateway Business Centre,
Kangley Bridge Road,
London, SE26 5AN.

Every effort has been made to trace the copyright holders of the photographs in this book but one or two were unreachable. We would be grateful if the photographers concerned would contact us.

Editorials: Alan Price. Editorial assistance: Xtal Gwinn and David Rathborne.
Design and typesetting: Adam Yeldham at Raven Design.
Printed by The Gutenberg Press Ltd.

A catalogue record of this book is available from the British Library.

The views expressed in this book are of John French and the interviewees and not necessarily of Proper Music.

The author thanks: Bob Adams, Don Aldridge, Allison at ATP, Scott Amendola, Steve Backman, Bill Bamberger, Dick Barber, Barrie Barlow, Mike Barnes, James Bedbrook, Cristina Berio, Herb Bermann, Lisa Best, Beverley, Jim Bistany, Jimmy Carl Black, Dean Blackwood, Barbara Blair, Darlene Blair, Jesse Blair-French, Richard Blalock, Mark Boston, Matt Boudreaux, Karen Bradley, Thom Britt, Jeff Bruschelle, Craig Bunch, Daren Burns, Annabel Butler, Michelle Campbell, Duane Capizzi, Catherine Carey, Traci Carter, Miss Christine, Irwin Chusid, Danny Clifford, Herb Cohen, Scott Colby, Scott Collins, Chris Constable, Ry Cooder, Helen Cottage, Jeff Cotton, John Crosby, Greg Davidson, Joe Davies, John Defore, The Depot, Oliver DiCicco, Sharon Donovan, Hector Dorado, Richard Drexler, Harry Duncan, Brian Dunnagan, Roy Estrada, Jacqueline Falls, Merrel Fankhauser, Steve Feigenbaum, Eric "Kitabu" Feldman, Jim Fergueson, Harold Fields, Phyllis Flotre, Bruce Fowler, John Franklin, Donna French, Phill and Joyce French, Tom French, David French, Keith French, Toni French, Todd French, C. Michael French, Fred Frith, Chris Garcia, Ronny Gaye, Grant Gibbs, Don Giesen, Andrew Greenaway, Norman and Sharon Griffin, Mario Grossi, Kurt Gunzel, Total Gym, Daltan Hagler, Jerry Handley, Bill Harkleroad, Victor Hayden, Jerry Hayes, Laura Hemenway, Roberta Hesslegrave, Deborah Higgins, Colin Hill, Louis Hinkle, Robyn Hitchcock, Nick Hobbs, Mike Hoff, Barry Hogan, Keith Hollar, Andy Hollins, Mick Houghton, Eric Hovland, Elliot Ingber, Bob Irin, Billy James, Art Jarvinon, Gary Jaye, Shonna Marie Jones, Adam Jones, Chris Jones, Deborah Lee Jones, Mikole Kaar, Henry Kaiser, Anna Karatziva, Keith Kennedy, Mike and Barbara Kenny, Destiny Kincaid, Eric Klerks, Glan Kolotkin, Bob Krasnow, Dick Kunc, Dennis Ling, Tim Livingston, Les and Mickey Long, Rick Lonow, Pete Lovio, Gary Lucas, Jeff Lunk, Ian S. MacArthur, Niall Macaulay, Deanna MacLellan, Pastor Majeske and Carolyn, Micke Maksymenko, Gary Marker, Cliff Martinez, Lee Matalon, Cameron Maus, Danny McCullough, Gerry McGhee, Don McKay, Danny McKinny, Michael Melchione, Sergio Merino, Tim Meyer, Carl Meyerholtz, Louis Mills, Malcolm Mills, Colin Minchin, Marc Minsker, Doug Moon, Daniel Moore, Shannen Moore, Thomas Moore, Vic Mortensen, Lars Movin, Buell Neidlinger, Sean Newsham, Penny Nichols, Steve Nootenboom, John O'Donnel, Tom Odell, Robert Ormsby, Erik Palm, Dean and Julie Palmer, Miss Pamela, Grant Peden, John Peel, Richard Perry, Marty Prue, Pat Prue, John Ramsay, Richard Redus, Per-Christian Rekdal, Paul Riley, Cliff Roeher, Andrew Rogers, Christophe Rossi, Rova Saxophone Quartet, Julie Rubio, Ellen Rudnick, Wally Salazar, Bruce Schmidt, Steve Schneider, Don Schott, Jim Scimonetti, Carl Scott, David Sefton, Berthold Seliger, Shirley Selwood, Ulli Shafer, Sarah Shankland, Pat Shelton, Elaine Shepherd, Jim Sherwood, Michael Shore, Rui Silva, Dan Silver, Giovanni and Janine Simi, Tyler Simi, Mark Simms, Paul Smith, Richard Snyder, Rick Snyder, Johan Sundin, Tim Sutton, Irene Swenson, Pat Tagliaferro, John and Kerry Tanner, Toby Taylor, Jeff "Moris" Tepper, John Thomas, Eleanor Thomas, Mark Thompson, Richard Thompson, Michael Traylor, Art Tripp, Jay Tripp, Kitty "marimba" Tripp, John True, Phil Tynan, Jan Van Vliet, Arjen Veldt, Denny Walley, Chris Wangsgard, June Wangsgard, Ben Waters, Mary Wattenbarger, Guy Webster, Bob Weston, Nancy Whaley, Matty Whittle, Larry Willey, Robert Williams, Ted Williams, John Williams, Randy Wimer, Langdon Winner, Charlie Winton, Andy Woolliscroft, Bill Word, Ron Young, Frank Zappa, Gail Zappa, Moon Zappa, Zappanale, Jesus.

Special thanks to Matt Groening for selection of cover photo.

Dedicated to Alex "St. Clair" Snouffer, the guy who started it all.

CONTENTS

CHAPTER ONE:
MADNESS AND MOJAVE

"Cop out!" Van Vliet shouted at me. I cringed and moved quickly to my right as the sharp jagged point of the broomstick he was holding dug into the soft wood of the laundry shed wall at my back. The adrenaline caused my thoughts to flow at an incredible speed. In between each new lunge of the stick, a different phase of my 20 years of life came under review. I wondered, "is this similar to the sensation of those who have a near-death experience in which their life passes before their eyes?".

I studied the expressions on the faces of bassist Mark Boston and guitarists Jeff Cotton and Bill Harkleroad who stood in a semicircle behind Don. He had "ordered" them to push me back against the wall if I attempted to escape this dilemma, and they obeyed – just as I had in times past. They had all been in my shoes time after time and I in theirs. Guilt was written on their faces, just as it probably had been written on mine in recent times during their "turns." Similar scenes had been played out many times before, but this was more physical and violent than most.

"Where are you at, man? Why are you so selfish?" Don snarled, and another jab and another dance on my part to avoid the broomstick occurred. Was Don purposely avoiding actually hitting me in the abdomen with the sharp point? I wasn't sure, but it seemed he was bluffing. This was most likely just another attempt to humiliate one in front of the others - another of his ridiculous witch trials. I know, however, that I was feeling a great deal of fear, more than I'd ever felt. Whether this was real or a bluff, it was convincing enough for me.

A relatively normal day – if one day of recent months in this house could be called normal – would be comprised of ridiculous amounts of dedication on the part of myself and the others to the fragments of music Don called his compositions. These were days in which we spent most of our waking hours learning and memorizing a steady stream of these fragments and arranging them into songs.

A day like today seemed to happen after about five normal days. In fact, most of the days like this lasted two days, occasionally even three. They were comprised of the sleepless horror of either being the target or watching the target and knowing you soon would be next. Huge amounts of tea were consumed to keep us awake and alert.

A million questions swept through my mind at the speed of thought. " How was this man able to exert such power over us? How did he continue to manipulate us in such a fashion? Was a mind-control agent such as LSD being put into the tea? How was it that we allowed one man to control us all to this ridiculous extent?"

I had been standing out here, ducking this stick for what seemed like half an hour.
I glanced over to my left at the lighted window of the house. It looked like a book cover illustration, almost fake. Not real at all, just a cardboard cutout set up with yellow light streaming out. The walls were glossy red. I could see a part of my drum kit, a cymbal, through one of the windows and the piano in the background where I spent so much time. Other than the situation, it was a beautiful night, perfectly still, and just the right temperature.

"Talk man!" Van Vliet growled, and again another thrust of the broomstick. It had been hours since this had started as a mild interrogation session in the house. I think the basis for suspicion against me had been the fact that Don was convinced that I was "commercializing" one of his compositions. It was a song called *Fallin'Ditch* and anyone who heard it in the years afterward never once said "This is unusually commercial in comparison to the other compositions." It was an absurd accusation, as all of Don's accusations were.

I often suspected a touch of mental illness as the cause of Don's delusional state. We did nothing to alter his music. I was the guy in charge of transcribing his untrained meanderings on the keyboard into musical notation. I would then play them back so the others could learn them, and also had the daunting task of deciding who played what, how many times, and in what order. I'd never seen people work so hard on any project.

If a particular piece of music didn't sound right to Don - often this music was taught to the band many days after it had been created – then someone had to be blamed for this travesty. A drama would begin to unfold in which Van Vliet would ask a few casual questions. Tensions would begin to mount in anticipation. If he were not satisfied with the answers, as was often the case, this would soon escalate into a group meeting with one of us labeled as the conspirator.

Van Vliet was an expert interrogator. He was very relaxed and entertaining to all who were not "in the barrel." The suspected party would be isolated socially by being ignored a bit as Don would address the jury of peers and state his case. The defendant would become the brunt of all Don's sarcasm and humor. The goal seemed to be to completely strip the individual in question of all dignity, self-worth and pride. I was often called "nigger John." When I was given something to eat or drink, Don would say, "See, I'm so nice I'd even feed a nigger – Joohhhnnn" – drawing out my name sarcastically and speaking to me as though I was a rapist or murderer, or just some transient.

"Why?" I kept asking myself over and over again, " … is he doing this? What possible goal could he have in mind?" This album project was dragging on and on. Obviously, morale was extremely low. No one enjoyed living like this. I wanted to play onstage and meet girls. I had no social life. I wanted to make money and have some freedom to come and go, to visit friends and eat out in a restaurant or see a movie. None of us had a car of our own, and we hadn't played onstage in months. We were all nineteen and twenty-year-old kids and this guy, at twenty-eight, was our leader - the guy we were looking to for direction.

My intuition also told me that the music we were writing was not going to be received well by the public, and that all these months and months of 12-hour workdays were never going to be compensated for financially. This made my morale even lower. "How on earth," I kept wondering, "Could he not see that and keep saying that we were going to 'make it'?" How on earth could that wonderful blues band that played in my hometown three years back have turned into this horror story?"

After being haunted by these memories for forty years, and being asked about this experience repeatedly, I decided to write down everything I could recall. One cannot answer a simple question like "What was it like rehearsing for *Trout Mask Replica*?" with a simple soundbite. It's a long story, and one I would rather tell once than repeat over and over again. Maybe if I write it down, it will stop re-playing itself in my head.

The members of the various Magic Bands span several eras and age groups. The older members were born in the early to middle 1940s. Their early musical experience would be more connected with the big band era. The period of their adolescence spanned the early years of Rhythm & Blues and Rock 'n'Roll.

This group includes:

Don Van Vliet: Singer, composer, harmonica player, sax player and leader.
Alex "St. Claire" Snouffer: Guitarist/drummer and founder of The Magic Band
Doug Moon: Guitarist
Rich Hepner: Guitarist
Denny "Feeler's Rebo" Walley: Guitarist (contemporary, but not a member until 1975)
Gerald (Jerry) Handley: Bassist
Roy "Orejon" Estrada: Bassist (contemporary, but not a member until 1972)
P.G. Blakely: Drummer
Vic Mortensen: Drummer

The middle or *Trout Mask/Decals* era members were generally born in the late 1940s to early 1950s. (For the uninitiated, *Trout Mask Replica* is a landmark Beefheart album recorded in 1969 and

Lick My Decals Off, Baby was recorded in 1970.) Their early recollections would be of the end of the big band era, and the beginnings of R&B and R&R. The British Invasion occurred during their adolescence. The band members all had pseudonyms given them by Don Van Vliet.

This group includes:

Bill "Zoot Horn Rollo" Harkleroad: Guitarist
Jeff "Antennae Jimmy Semens" Cotton: Guitarist
Arthur "Ed Marimba" Tripp III: Drummer, percussionist, marimba
Mark "Rockette Morton" Boston: Bassist
John "Drumbo" French: Drummer

The last generation of Magic Band members (I'm only guessing here, not having interviews) were probably born in the 1950s. Their youth would have coincided with the heyday of the Beatles specifically and the British Invasion in general, and their adolescence would have exposed them to the end of the psychedelic era and, among other things, Captain Beefheart And His Magic Band. Most of these players were fans before becoming members of the band.

This group generally includes:

Jeff "Moris" Tepper: Guitarist
Richard Redus: Guitarist
Gary "Mantis" Lucas: Guitarist
Eric "Kitabu" Drew Feldman: Keyboardist, bassist
Bruce "Fossil" Fowler: Trombone
Gary Jaye: Drummer
Robert "Wait for Me" Williams: Drummer

Influences and styles in the Magic Band can be traced back to the same sources: names like Robert Johnson, Sonny Boy Williamson, Son House, Howlin' Wolf, John Lee Hooker, Elmore James, Muddy Waters, and BB King.

Early Magic Band members are more apt to remember the likes of Little Richard, Jimmy Reed, or John Lee Hooker. The later band members are probably more likely to recall the British Invasion of the '60s. This indirectly introduced them to some of the same influences - Muddy Waters, Howlin' Wolf, and so on - along with Chuck Berry, but all through the interpretations of such groups as The Yardbirds, The Rolling Stones, or The Animals.

The members of the early band were more likely to wear "Greaser" (a nickname derived from the fact that the boys used hair oil or pomade to achieve the desired style) or "Pachuco" style haircuts, and to wear khaki pants. Their successors were more prone to have bridged the gap between the surfer and hippy eras.

The *Trout Mask/Decals* band, my contemporaries, grew up around tie-dye shirts, love beads, and flared jeans. We were around during the "Love Generation" – the hippy era, and it influenced our look to an extent, yet we were not really part of that. We were an encapsulated counter-culture unto ourselves, trapped in a house in Woodland Hills on a quest to finish an album that would later land the position of 33rd in the top albums ever recorded – at least according to *Rolling Stone* magazine.

One thing all the members had in common was a fascination with drums, bass, guitar, and the various nontraditional rock instruments that came to be featured in later versions of the Magic Band, such as marimba and trombone.

By taking these same influences and adding a few new ingredients, the results can be extremely unique. Add a sparse desert setting, the Antelope Valley, near Los Angeles that was isolated enough by mountain ranges to remain an enclave partially detached from the cultural influence of L.A.'s urban growth, the high desert area became a creative center for adolescents with an abundance of time on their hands and little in the way of diversion.

John French: What do you think about the environment of the desert and the way it affected the way you thought about music?

Jim Sherwood: I think it drew me to music, because it was so boring up there. It was nothing. There was nothing to do. All you did was walk out through the desert. Nothing! What I did was just spend my time walking out to the bowling alley, which was about five miles away, and then walking back. Or [you could] walk downtown and go to the restaurant and get a malt or something. They had a great little hamburger stand called Bubi Burgers.

JF: Oh yeah, that was on the corner of Sierra and J?

JS: Yeah. You could go over there and pick up a hamburger and a Coke and fries for like 75 cents. Then, they had Foster's Freeze, which was only two doors up, which later on became a hangout for a lot of the guys.

JF: Right, which is also where the Bongo Fury *cover was (later) shot.*

Jerry Handley had a similar take:

Jerry Handley: I got interested in music when I was about 13 because there wasn't much else going on. I wasn't involved in anything else, and there wasn't that much activity to do. You were out stealing hubcaps or you were out playing music.

Fresh ideas and new approaches were more likely in a remote area, where the urban cultural influences did not have such an immediate presence. Add young adults from different parts of the country brought together by an (aircraft) industry closely attached to the Military Industrial Complex. Suddenly, a new cultural mixture emerges, ideas collide and re-form, and creativity takes a slightly different route.

Radio was a very influential link and common bond throughout the U.S. in the 1950s. Adolescents used it as a catalyst to start conversations and form friendships. Young bands developed and started imitating their heroes of the airwaves to celebrate cultural independence from their parents. A new sound began to be heard in the girls gymnasium on Friday nights after the game.

Such was the mixture of events that took place in the Antelope Valley and other areas of Southern California in the early fifties. America was the leader of the world, and a hero to many nations. We had "fought the good fight" both on the side of the Allied forces in Europe and Africa and against a formidable foe in the Pacific theatre in WWII. The U.S. had come out victorious and prosperous, recovering from a great financial recession. Americans had the spilled blood of their relatives to once again remind them of the cost of freedom. Many had lost loved ones, and patriotism was revitalized. Everyone was once again seeking the "American Dream," and enjoying the good times they felt they had earned after a long world war and the preceding depression.

Mortensen's Early Childhood

Vic Mortensen was the Magic Band's first official drummer, although unofficially preceded for a very short period by Paul (P.G.) Blakely. In his interview, Vic recalls his childhood back in the late forties and early fifties.

John French: Well, I think it might be good to trace back from your beginnings. Briefly describe how you got started as a drummer, where you grew up, where you were born and that kind of thing.
Vic Mortensen: Well, that's kind of funny because it's like growing up at your mother's knee. I was born in Ann Arbor, Michigan March 10th, 1942. We lived on a ten-acre piece of land out in the middle of nowhere. It was on a place called Hogback Road … my mother had a piano and my father had bought me a little parade drum. My mother would play the piano and I would play the drum. She would play marches, like Hail to the Victors, the University of Michigan fight song.
JF: How old were you?
VM: Started as a drummer (laughs) about the age of three.

During World War II, plans for relocating anywhere were impossible. All of the adults were engaged in the war effort. Individual dreams were temporarily suspended in lieu of patriotism. The Mortensen's, however, had probably already begun to form a dream of one day moving to warm and sunny California, "where the streets were paved with gold," to seek the American dream and escape the cold Michigan winters. Mr. Mortensen, a native of Denmark, worked in a place called Willow Run, working in a factory assembling bombers.

When peacetime ensued, the "American Dream" was again possible, and the Mortensens sold off some property and bought a new car and a nice travel trailer. Sometime in 1948, they settled in Claremont, California. Mr. Mortensen, who had always been a cook, sometimes spent as much as 16 hours a day making candy in his newly acquired candy store. Mrs. Mortensen was working in a hospital, and then would work several more hours helping in the store.

Denny Walley, Accordion And Guitar - 1950

At about the same time, five-year-old Denny Walley was living on the East Coast and beginning to study accordion. Born February 4th 1943 at Abbington Hospital in Willow Grove, Pennsylvania. Denny not only became a featured guitarist in the Frank Zappa band during the *Bongo Fury* tour (1975–1976), but also played on the 1976 recording sessions for the original version of the Captain Beefheart album entitled *Bat Chain Puller* (still unreleased at the time of this writing). In addition to the amazing slide guitar tracks on that album, Denny was responsible for the accordion part on the accompanying track *Harry Irene*.

The Walley family moved to Flatbush, New York, soon after Denny's birth. By the time Denny was seven, they had moved to the New York suburbs on Long Island. One evening, Denny's parents had taken him along to a cocktail party at the home of a family friend, where the children were soon relegated to the basement.

Denny Walley: Well, I found this box down there. I opened it up and found [a] twelve base accordion.
John French: What does that (term) mean?
DW: Well, the left hand had twelve buttons.
JF: OK, so that's small?
DW: Yeah, it's very small; it's like a child's size. I think it (the right hand keyboard) had about 2$^1/_2$ octaves. It was white with red keys and it smelled so good. The whole thing, it was like when I opened it up, it was like "Whoa – this is a VERY IMPORTANT THING!". I picked it up, strapped it on, and I was playing (with) both hands before the end of the evening.

Upon his parents' and host's simultaneous discovery and recovery from the initial shock that Denny had violated the non-snooping oath, they noticed that he was actually playing the instrument. His affinity for the accordion eventually prompted his parents to invest in lessons.

John French: How long did you continue to take those lessons?
Denny Walley: I took those for about five years.
JF: Until about the age of twelve.
DW: Yeah, then we moved to Lancaster...

Although Denny would play no role in the discography of either Zappa or Beefheart until 1975, this move initiates his connection with the residents of Lancaster earlier in the 1950s.

My Birth; 1948

I suppose 1948 may be a good year for me to interject a little of my own early memories, as it was the year I was born, on September 29th to be exact. My parents and my three older brothers had moved from Springfield, Ohio, to San Diego just prior to the beginning of World War II (my mother, Pearl, came out with my brothers, and my father joined her soon afterwards). She may have been the original "Rosie the Riveter" the first of the female aircraft workers. She recalls having her picture taken as the first woman (non-clerical, I suppose) to enter the gates of Consolidated Aircraft as an aircraft worker. The family eventually moved to San Bernardino, California, arriving the day the war was over in 1945, and I was conceived three years later after the 1948 New Year's Eve celebration, or so I've been told. My father continued to work in the aircraft industry from mid-wartime until his retirement in the late 1960s. My mother, like Vic Mortensen's, was also a nurse.

All of the members of the *Trout Mask* band were born around 1948 to 1950 and were baby-boomers. So, we all had our beginnings around the time Vic Mortensen's family moved to Claremont, and perhaps a year or two prior to Denny's first accordion lessons on Long Island.

Mortensen's Formal Training / Claremont 1954–55

Vic Mortensen began formal music training when he was 12 or 13, in the early to mid-1950s, on an instrument not of his choice: the piano, which he dutifully practiced "while my friends were out playing football in the street."

Vic Mortensen: After years of pestering, they gave me drum lessons. I wish I could remember the gentleman's name, but I literally went to his house and started learning to play the drums. He had been a drummer for Les Brown and his Band of Renown. So, the guy had some "chops." They didn't send me there to learn parade drumming. They sent me to a guy who had played, in those days, big band drumming. So I fiddled around and then started driving my parents crazy. They bought me a practice set. I have a photograph of me somewhere playing that. The bass drum is as big as your living room. It still had the palm tree on it because we got it used someplace and it probably said, Caruso And The Palm Knockers, or something, on the drumheads.

Like many drummers, however, Mortensen didn't truly learn how to sight-read drum music. Although able to study charts and grasp all the concepts, Mortensen would study what he was seeing until he grasped the concept.

Vic Mortensen: When you say "read," when I think of the cats that read music, I think of the guys in the "Johnny Carson Show" band, OK? They would pay someone else to go to their rehearsals, make notes on the charts, and then [they would] come in themselves and sight-read the stuff. Now, that's what I call "reading music" ... no, I would never deem to say I could read music ... fluently. One day, he let me sit down at the drum set, right? He started "hipping" me to the fact that, "all right, these are called hi-hats. And now that you know how to go dah, dat-de-dah with the drumsticks, let me show you what these are all about." Then, learning the bass pedal, where the bass pedal goes. When to use the hi-hat - boom, chick, boom, chick. We went through that for quite some time until I was able, in those days, to turn on a Benny Goodman record and try to "cook along with the boys." Always behind Mr. Krupa, if you will.

Because playing the drumset is more a matter of feel than of technicality, most drummers learn by playing along with other drummers. One learns to distinguish each drum from another, and certain roles are determined for each limb. Soon, Mortensen was playing well enough to land his first semi-professional gig.

Vic Mortensen: I played my first professional gig at the age of thirteen. There was a group of college kids in town. They had put together a little thing. It was called The Lamplighters if that will give you a clue. (Sings "Doo - wah") They called the drum teacher to see if he had a student that could cut it. They were in a jam, you know. So here I was, thirteen, man, and I show up - my parents bring me to the gig. (Laughs) John French: ... so, you must have been doing pretty well for the teacher to start recommending you for gigs when you were thirteen. VM: But, I could have been his only student. (Laughs) Who knows?

Actually, Vic had no way of knowing this because of the manner in which he received lessons.

Vic Mortensen: ... Those were different times. I went to this old boy's house... he had an old two-story house in Claremont. You know, really crotchety, and I'm sure he was associated in some way with the colleges there. Claremont was entirely a college town. No, this was like going to this weird, haunted house to have drum lessons.
John French: OK. You were probably going to high school by that time. Did you join in any of the music stuff in the high school?
VM: OK, let me lay this on you. In those days, there was no middle school, as it is today. You went to grade school from the first through the sixth grade. Then you went to high school, from the seventh through the twelfth grade. Because it was a small town and that was it. So, when we were in the seventh grade, you couldn't be on the football team, but you could be in the band. (Heh!)
JF: I see, so you were probably already in the band by then.
VM: Yeah, I was in the marching band in the seventh grade.
JF: Did they have a dance band?
VM: No, are you kidding? There were only like five hundred kids in the high school. I was also playing in the classical orchestra. I played "snare drum" (faux sophisticated voice) in the classical concert band. We did the music from Victory at Sea. I played snare drum and stood right next to the cat playing the bass drum. We'd go "bop-a-te-baaa," and there would be like a hundred and twenty-four bar rest, and so all we did was sit there and count. I'd wake him up and say, "Hey, wake up, we're coming to the part where you go "boom bah boom," and lay back for another thirty-two bars.
JF: OK. Claremont, where is that located?
VM: Claremont, California, is about thirty miles east of L.A. It's the home of the Associated Colleges of Claremont California. At least, that's what they used to be called - probably still are.

1954 - French Moves To Antelope Valley

It was around this time that I was introduced to the Antelope Valley, just before the age of six. In the spring of 1954, my family moved there from San Bernardino, about 90 miles to the south. The reason for our relocation was simple. My father had been working for a company called Northrup Aircraft in Ontario, California, not far from our home. Now, they were transferring him to their Palmdale location, Plant 42.

Coincidentally, at about the same time, Denny Walley's family moved to Lancaster. Although he and I didn't know one another during this period, we shared a common environment for a few years. He also made acquaintance with some of the main characters in the story.

Denny Walley Moves To The Valley

The "push/pull" factor (I learned that from a sociology class I took just before dropping out) that moved the Walleys (including Denny, his parents, and his sister Ellen) to the Valley was the same one that brought a lot of other families to the high desert in the 1950s. Denny's father worked for Republic Aircraft. He had worked for the company in Farmingdale, Long Island, and was transferred to Edwards Air Force Base, located at Muroc Dry Lake. Muroc was the reverse spelling of Corum, the surname of the family who had originally settled on the dry lake years earlier. Denny lived in the Antelope Valley from 1954 to 1958, and during that time made connections that would become valuable later.

John French: So, you loved it here, what were your impressions of the Valley, what were your first thoughts - the things you remember vividly?
Denny Walley: We arrived in the evening, by the time we drove from the airport to [our] home, the one thing that really impressed me was ... remember they used to have the garbage disposals outside, where you could burn your trash?
JF: Oh yeah, incinerators. We have one of those in our yard here.
DW: I thought that was the coolest thing in the world. Also, I could see foothills from the house, and I said, "Mom, pack me a lunch, I'm gonna walk over there." How did I know it was like 80 miles away? That was in the time when there was no smog. It was like you could reach out and touch it. "Yeah, I'll take this sandwich, go over there, and I'll sit on the hill and wave to you."
JF: Three weeks later.
DW: Yeah, right.

Although always claiming to despise the desert because of the heat, Don Van Vliet at one point admitted to a certain subtle beauty that existed in the desert. There was loneliness and the ever-present battle with boredom, but also there was a freedom that came with the isolation. Perhaps it was that very freedom that allowed him to break rules in music that hadn't been broken before, and to take a group of musicians on a search, exploring in unknown territories of sound.

Background On The Valley

The section of the Mojave Desert where we lived, called the Antelope Valley, is an arid region, but one that is attractive in its own special way. Primarily and initially settled by alfalfa farmers and cattle ranchers, the valley had a distinct agricultural inclination. Eventually, the United States Air Force discovered the open sky there, and a whole different breed of "valley-ites" began to augment the local population ("coots and codgers," as Zappa referred to them). Muroc Dry Lake was transformed into a giant runaway for experimental test aircraft, and soon became known as Edwards Air Force Base.

The alfalfa farmers would eventually begin to die out as the lowered water table from the larger population forced water prices up. The outskirts of town illustrate this fact, with such common sights as dried up reservoirs and collapsed windmill remains. Most of the farms are mere remnants, monuments to a different era, a simpler – perhaps more human - time. In the 1950s, many of the alfalfa fields had not yet been replaced by housing tracts.

Denny Walley: It used to be alfalfa, maize, and turkeys. We know that. I used to buck hay on some of the farms in the summer to make some money. Pick some corn and do all that.
John French: Yeah, this was quite an agricultural area then.
DW: It was fabulous then. Especially [coming there] from New York.
JF: From a city environment into that, yeah!
DW: After seeing that, I thought I was Davy Crockett, and they [the locals] thought I was from Mars.

French's First Impression Of The Mojave Desert
Several months before our move, my father had decided to buy a U-Finish house in an area called Quartz Hill, a small town a few miles northwest of Palmdale. This house had a purchase price of under $5,000 and was basically a wrapped or covered frame with no interior finishing. All the walls were open studs. No wiring or plumbing had been hooked up.

The desert had a quality that cannot easily be described. On the good days, when the wind wasn't blowing and it was not too hot outside, it had a subtle, surreal quality, a deafening silence, occasionally punctuated by a sonic boom - the result of the latest fighter jet being tested in the surrounding skies. I am sure the "coots and codgers" didn't appreciate this assault on their senses. This resulted in resentment growing between the established valley-ites and the newcomers.

Our home had not been hooked to electricity, and therefore we had no access to either television or radio. The walls were all open except for the bathroom. My mother hung blankets up to afford some measure of privacy. My father worked slowly on the house with hand tools.

I remember the metallic taste that the water had after being transported through the new galvanized pipe my father had laid by hand in the backyard. It was hard water, with a strong mineral content. The precious fluid even sounded different coming out of the tap: not such a high hiss, but more of a "hushing" sound, as though there was lots of air in the water, which had a cloudy look in the glass.

The house was without cooling or air-conditioning, but in the evening a cooling breeze would usually come. The screen-less windows were opened routinely in a hopeful attempt to cool the house for evening. Moths and other insects would collect near the coal oil lamps and lanterns that were our only source of light. However, those first summer evenings were long and cozy. My father worked "swing" shift, which was about 3:00 p.m. to 11:00 p.m. My mother, older brother, and I would sit outside and stare at the stars and talk. Sometimes my mother would read Bible stories to me by lantern light.

The weather was warm, often unbearably hot. Our food was kept in an old-time icebox, which actually held large blocks of ice. In order to replenish the supply, we would frequently visit ice machines. These were white, trailer-sized refrigerated vending machines. We had a camp stove, which was hooked to a large propane tank in the back yard. Our heater was a non-vented, floor-standing model in the living room, next to the hall door. My brother Phil laid asphalt floor tile over the bare concrete floors throughout the entire house, which involved dealing with thousands of one-foot squares of ugly brown stuff – the tile that came with the house.

The night air had a crystal clarity, making one feel more on board a starship than on a planet. There were no streetlights in our area. This caused the night sky to reveal much more of its personality, and the stars took on more of a three-dimensional depth, some seeming farther away than others. Because the summer nights were so warm and still, many people would turn off the TV sets (thus evading pouring mounds of stupidity into their otherwise healthy minds) and sit outside, conversing about simple things. I found these moments to be among the most magic.

Electricity came and soon we had our own two inch black and white television. This was a big deal for us. I remember watching *Alfred Hitchcock Presents, Gunsmoke, The People's Choice*, and a terrible version of *Robin Hood* with Richard Greene. Loretta Young had her own show, and Walt Disney featured *Davy Crockett, King of the Wild Frontier*. I had my own Davy Crockett outfit - a coon-skin cap, a buckskin jacket with fringe, a plastic musket and flintlock pistol, and a plastic powder horn.

Our U-Finish house was never finished while we lived there. My father eventually resolved to coexist with unpainted sheetrock and gypsum board (more commonly called drywall), which still showed the compound at the seams. An older couple, the Eastmans, had moved a house trailer onto the lot next to us and built an entire home, completely finished and landscaped, while our house still stood unfinished. We finally traded them; our unfinished house (which they eventually finished and sold) for their smaller but finished one. Our new home had wooden floors and wainscoting in the kitchen. Although a smaller house - two bedrooms to the others three - it had a built-on garage, and a big redwood enclosed patio. There were mulberry trees in the front yard, and a thick, green lawn.

Most of the indigenous vegetation in the Mojave Desert is short, dry weeds interspersed with an occasional Joshua tree. Some areas with a higher altitude or a higher water table have greater concentrations of juniper trees, an evergreen that appears more like a large bush and produces a small round berry that can be used for medicinal purposes. There were once antelope in the Antelope Valley, but they are long gone. The native wildlife consists largely of coyotes, jackrabbits, cottontails, field mice, and ground squirrels. There are reptiles, as well, such as lizards, horned toads, and snakes, including the infamous and deadly Mojave Green Rattlesnake, to name a few.

Man has changed the landscape of the valley more and more, depleting its water table for the sake of watering lawns, trees, and other plants that could never have survived there naturally. Once a landmark, the Joshua tree is now almost entirely removed from developed areas.

Palmdale

Thirty-five miles south of the town of Mojave lies Palmdale, named after the mistakenly identified Joshua tree, which the first settlers thought was a palm tree. It later became the home of Northrup Aircraft's Plant 42, which consists of several aircraft factories joined by a common runway. Mostly government contract work was done there: building bombers, fighters, and the like. In later years, Lockheed's L1011 commercial transport and all the Space Shuttles would be built at this site. Here lay the economic base of the "new" Antelope Valley. The painful transition occurred slowly.

Edwards/Air Force Base

I mentioned Edwards Air Force Base earlier, which is a flight test center for new designs in aircraft, mostly experimental prototypes. Edwards has a rocket engine test site also, the huge dry lakebed was excellent for emergency landings. Anyone who saw the film *The Right Stuff* knows that one important aerospace location was Edwards AFB in the Mojave Desert. The astronauts received some of their early testing and training there. Chuck Yeager, among others, broke the sound barrier in the open skies above the flight test center.

Twenty-five miles or so northwest of Edwards lies the small town of Mojave. The bulk of Mojave is situated to the east of the main road, Sierra Highway, and the train tracks lie to the west. It is a bleak, desolate area, whose high winds animate dead tumbleweeds and transmit huge amounts of dust everywhere. Mojave began basically as a large truck stop, which later became home to many of the civilian employees of nearby Edwards AFB. According to Don Van Vliet's memories, there was also a Marine base nearby, although this does not appear to be accurate and he may have been referring to the Air Force Base.

Glen And Sue Move Donny To Mojave

Somewhere about this time — the early to middle 1950s — was when the young Don Van Vliet, then known as Don Glen Vliet, was moved to Mojave. After living in a beautiful home in Glendale, CA, it is almost certain that he was disappointed and traumatized by the move. It obviously was the cause of a great deal of pain, as Don mentioned this particular snapshot of his youth quite often in personal conversation and interviews, and the story always seemed mixed with a good portion of bitterness.

According to Van Vliet, the reason for this move was an artist named Augustino Rodriguez. This artist's first name has sometimes been listed as Augustonio, Augustonino, or Antonio (on various Beefheart websites). Additionally, Rodriguez has often been referred to by journalists over the years as a "famed Portuguese sculptor," but I have yet to see a trace of his work. Anyway, after meeting young Donny at the L.A. Zoo, Rodriguez purportedly had recognized and nurtured Van Vliet's rudimentary sculpting skills until they had grown to the level where the word "prodigy" was applicable. Most of this information is derived from Don himself, however, and should be taken with a grain of salt. It is important to realize that those who were close to him have long considered Don to be a "teller of tall tales." Nevertheless, throughout the years, this background information on sculpting has been reported by several journalists as fact, though I can find not one shred of information on this "famed sculptor" under any of several spellings of the name.

Doug Moon: Alex and I come from the same place concerning Don. We both knew him in high school. We knew what a liar he was. He made up all these stories about his sexual conquests and all these things; you know ... we would go along with it just because it was good entertainment. He was entertaining and was fun to be around. But that's where the difference comes in, because a lot of people believed every word and hung on every word that he said. Frank, Alex, and I, and other people who knew him in the early years — we knew the "real" guy.

Alex Snouffer: He was entertaining. Just mark it right up to that. You never knew what you were going to be confronted with when you saw Don. "You shoulda seen ..." whatever. Here we go again.

Don Aldridge: When he told me that he was a child prodigy, I'm sorry, I didn't believe him. I'm not sure I do now. No one can really ...

Gary Marker: I got fourteen different stories and you know how it is with him. He would explain stuff, he would tell you what was happening, and every time the story would change.

Dennis Ling: I don't know that Don doesn't have some ... (laughs) fantasies. I have no idea. I knew that a lot of times when he talked to me about certain things in his life, I took it tongue-in-cheek, thinking that he was just ... blowing smoke.

Whether Augustino Rodriguez was indeed a "famed sculptor" will remain unanswered in this book though I made a valiant attempt to settle this question. It is almost certain that the man at least existed, as Van Vliet often described moments from his relationship with Rodriguez. Once, when we visited the L.A. County Museum of Art, while strolling past the La Brea Tar pits, Don recalled a story about Augustino (spelled the way Van Vliet pronounced it). He pointed to the sculptures of dinosaurs in the water and said, "I could *do* that stuff, man!"

This triggered his memory to tell me the following: at some point, Rodriguez had apparently taught Don the basics of sculpting, and eventually had him work with a nude female model. Van Vliet described being instructed by Rodriguez in employing the use of a set of calipers to make measurements of the woman's body. When asked his reaction, he stated simply, "I was really scared and nervous; I was just a kid and she was *nude*, man!"

At another point in time, when I was experiencing great anxiety concerning my career and future, Don tried to offer me encouragement. He told me that he recalled Augustino going through very rough times financially, and when Don had asked him what he was going to do for security, Rodriguez had supposedly replied by saying something like, "There is no security; security does not exist, it is an illusion."

"He just kept working - kept busy all the time," Don recalled. Laurie Stone, Don's girlfriend, seemed to recall this visit also.

The Vliet family, who were living in Glendale, California, at the time when Rodriguez is said to have been fostering young Donny's talents, apparently grew fearful and concerned about their only child's involvement with this sculptor. They were at the same time, however, proud enough to save a newspaper-clipping showing a young Don Vliet giving a demonstration of his sculpting skills on a local television station. Sue Vliet showed photographs of his early sculptures to gallery owner Michael Werner, probably sometime in the early eighties, according to a 1993 article in the British music magazine, *Mojo*.

"He was indeed a child prodigy with an early devotion to art. He sculpted in clay (a fact confirmed by Werner, who'd seen photographs of the pieces)." [1]

In describing his preoccupation with sculpting, Van Vliet demonstrated the same sense of hyperbole that became characteristic in all his later interviews. He claimed that he had locked himself in his room for months at a time, and that during this period he had sculpted "all the known dinosaurs," surviving only by having his food passed under the door.

The actual interpretation of this story may differ in some greater or lesser degree when the element of hyperbole is removed. Perhaps young Van Vliet actually stayed in his room for merely a few days and refused to eat with the family at the dinner table, preferring instead to eat in his own room. (After all, how many bedroom doors are high enough to slide a plate of food beneath?) Perhaps a ten-year-olds perception of sculpting a few dinosaurs from a child's book featuring pictures of the extinct creatures equaled reproducing "all the dinosaurs" in his world. Perhaps Rodriguez was a "famed sculptor" only to Don because of this same limited perception, in much the same way as a child might say, "My daddy is the strongest man in the world." Rodriguez may have been a local art teacher in the Glendale area. Perhaps it was Van Vliet's own imagination that created the illusion that Rodriguez was a famed sculptor.

Whatever Don's relationship with Rodriguez was in reality, it obviously concerned his parents enough for them to pack up and move ninety miles away after Don purportedly received an art scholarship to go to Europe at age thirteen (probably around 1954). Don has often indicated how devastated he was by this decision. However, the Vliet's relocation merely for the sake of their child's welfare could also be viewed on their part as quite sacrificial in the sense that they left behind a beautiful home and probably many friends. Then again, perhaps that house on Waverly Drive in Glendale was actually the home of Don's grandparents, which they may have been sharing with their offspring on an "extended family" basis.

---

[1] Mojo, Issue 2, December 1993, "Heart & Soul: Captain Beefheart," David DiMartino, p.82.

Why Mojave?

The "push/pull" factor of this move also leaves much to speculation. According to Van Vliet, his parents moved him to Mojave because they believed, as he would often quote (in true backwoods characterization), that "all artists are queers." The truth may never be known, since there have never been any interviews with either of Don's parents. This is due in part to Don's insistence of censure in his mother's case, and also to the fact that his father died before Don achieved any fame. Speculation insists that all possibilities be considered. Perhaps Rodriguez exhibited enough homosexual traits to convince the elder Vliets that their son should be separated from this man. Perhaps the Vliets feared indoctrination of their impressionable young son would lead to his acceptance of the homosexual lifestyle at an age when he was emotionally incapable of discerning whether or not this would be a wise choice. Perhaps they simply decided that he needed a few more years to just "be a kid."

However, attempting to prevent their son from becoming an artist might be considered prone to attempting to prevent a bubble from rising to the surface. Like water, Van Vliet would eventually "seek his own level," gaining worldwide acclaim in two unpredictable areas: rock music (for lack of a better term) and later, oil painting. His parents'efforts to separate him from undesirable elements at an early age, however painful to Don at the time, may have been more of a blessing than a curse.

Perhaps his parents decided that it would be best for Don if he could finish his education with no distractions, and have a chance to mature and establish more conventional values. This decision may have been based more strongly on father Glen Vliet's thought processes than on those of his wife. The passive and undisciplined Sue Vliet I met does not seem a likely candidate to have pushed for this kind of decisive action. She would later become the woman that Don would scream at for a Pepsi.

Years later, Don often joked that it seemed most of his friends came over not so much to visit him as to visit with his lovable mother. Sue always was a warm and friendly person. Her conversations were surprisingly revealing and showed a level of observation far above that for which son gave her credit. At times, he would passionately describe her as being "sooooooooo stupid," but this was probably more of a reaction to the fact that she disagreed with him than an evaluation of her level of intelligence. The dominance and lack of parental respect displayed by Don may have been a behavior he learned from his father and carried on after becoming the bread-winner of the family. Or it may have been a manifestation of his frustration for not being allowed to pursue his sculpting career.

So, the true story of the young Vliet's Glendale days may never really be revealed or understood, as the only living person who could probably accurately portray the story cannot be reached for an interview. Don has told the story himself, and as this book will show, he has often romantically and artistically stretched the truth. Were Jan, his wife, to write a book, she would only be able to draw her interpretations from his descriptions of earlier events. Even this would still be based partly upon (1) the bias of her loyalty and devotion to Van Vliet himself, and (2) the influence of his telling and re-telling various stories of his life. This elusiveness in itself may have a great deal to do with the interest focused upon this subject by many of the fans.

Life In Mojave

As an adult, Don recounted how he had sometimes roamed during his boyhood to the west side of the highway, the proverbial "wrong side of the tracks," to visit the hobos camped there. He recalled that they would occasionally offer him a tin can containing Mulligan stew to fill his stomach while they filled his head with stories of their adventures jumping freight trains. It is difficult to discern whether Don really had these experiences, or if they were fantasies that eventually became real for him. However, several of his later songs, including *Hobo Chang Ba* and *Hoboism,* had lyrics that showed strong insight into the lifestyle of the hobo.

The young artist had experienced what he recalled as a shocking transplant from his home in Glendale. One view of the environment in Glendale compared to that of Mojave shows such sharp contrast that it is not surprising that bitterness developed over his parents'decision. The Glendale of the 1950s was an upper middle class neighborhood filled with well-manicured yards. The Mt. Wilson Observatory was not that far away. (Actually, a film that depicts the setting and mood of this era quite well is *Rebel Without A Cause,* featuring icon James Dean playing the role of a troubled youth.) There were signs of culture and completeness everywhere. Crime was low, and decent people treated each other, for the most part, with respect.

In contrast, Mojave was dusty and dry. Culture was defined in primitive terms. The Military Industrial Complex had just begun to strongly dominate what had predominately been an agricultural area. Mojave was a bleak truck stop filled with cheap motels and small diners. It was a haven where weary truck drivers could grab a meal and some sleep before heading on. Heading north would lead up the east side of the Sierra Nevada range to small towns such as Lone Pine and Bishop, or ski resort villages such as Mammoth. East led towards Barstow, and eventually Las Vegas. West took one towards Tehachapi and Bakersfield, and finally to Highway 5, the dreary "main artery" of northbound or southbound vehicular transportation.

Van Vliet claims that, when young, he encountered violence in the form of men he described as Marines, but who more likely were airmen, nicknamed "wingnuts," from nearby Edwards Air Force Base, then called Muroc Air Force Base.

Van Vliet would describe being violently attacked by these military men and losing most his of molars as a direct result of their assault. As if to reinforce this fact, he would push in both cheeks with his index fingers, illustrating with the hollows that there were no teeth inside to impede this action. Whether the loss of his teeth was due to violence from the military men in the area or just bad dental hygiene is unclear. However, some later reports do lend credence to Van Vliet's assertion that he was indeed the victim of violent and brutal attacks. He claimed on several occasions that he was chased home by these "Marines," and once described swinging on a bar and kicking an assailant in the head with both feet.

Recounting these claims of violence and searching for the sources of Don's anger brings to mind a story that he related, presumably in reference to his early childhood in Glendale. He once described walking down a sidewalk as a youngster, and having a man toss a fifty-cent piece into his path. As Don bent over to retrieve it, the man kicked him in the mouth, sending him sprawling. A tearful young Vliet was then told by his assailant that this was a "lesson in life," or words to that effect.

As to the source of his genius, Van Vliet once related that he was involved in some childhood accident, which caused a severe but not critical trauma to his head. He said that "everything was different" when he awoke from this blow. Perhaps some neurotransmitter was released in larger quantities than before; some physiological phenomenon that could, if investigated, account for his amazing mental prowess.

Whatever the source, however, most people who knew Van Vliet would agree that he was no ordinary individual. Regardless of how uncomfortable or painful his relationships with others may have been, there seems to be, for the most part, a common respect for his uniqueness, his constant creative talents, his sense of humor, and his influence - on individuals, as well as on the worlds of music and art.

East Coast/Art Tripp

In a different part of the country during this period, the young Art Tripp was forming the basis for his later relationships with both Frank Zappa and Don Van Vliet.

Although Arthur Dyer Tripp III was born in Athens, Ohio, the home of Ohio University, he really considers Pittsburgh his home because his family moved there when he was about a year old. He started playing the drums in grade school. His father took him over to a meeting with the band director, who asked young Arthur what he wanted to play. After demonstrating the clarinet, trumpet, and a few other instruments, the band director played a snare drum, which young Tripp found interesting. He quickly made the decision to study drums and was given a practice pad (a little rubber square glued on a piece of wood) on which to practice stick control. Junior high school brought a real snare drum and the chance to play in the school band.

Mortensen In Claremont

Meanwhile, in Claremont, California, Vic Mortensen was having his first encounter with a person who would later form a particularly significant relationship with young Vliet: Frank Zappa.

Mortensen Meets Zappa – 1955

Vic Mortensen: I went to Claremont High, and that's when I (first) met Frank Zappa, when I was in the marching band in seventh or eighth grade, I don't know which. We had to go out and play (at) a football game, and in those days, the (drum) skins were literally skins. You would get out and it would start to "mist up" a little bit, and you'd keep tightening your heads,otherwise, you'd play the national anthem and it would sound like a funeral dirge, because everybody's playing a tom-tom. So you kept tightening them up and tightening them up and tightening them up. OK, then you get back on the bus and you kept loosening up and loosening up and loosening up. I've heard drums explode. So, I had gone up to the band room, to make sure that the drumheads were still loose enough. There was this crazy guy in there who had taken all of the band drums and lined them all up and had tuned them down to tom toms. He was going "bump bump a diggy bump bump a diggy bump bump" (Note: sounded like a Bo Diddley beat to me). *I said, "What the...are you doing?" He said, "Wow, man, I don't have a drumset and I just wanted to try out some different sounds." I asked, "How'd you get in here?" and he said, "Well, I know the guy (probably referring to the janitor). I was fascinated. He was doing some pretty good things. Didn't see him again until I was a freshman in high school. Never forgot him - that's how we got together years later.*
John French: So, how old were you and he and that time?
VM: How old are you when you are in the seventh or eigth grade? ... He was about a year older than I was. He couldn't have been much older. I had never seen him around the school. I said there were five hundred kids and there was "a dude in the band room that I had never seen at school."

So Vic seems to have been the first to encounter Frank Zappa, who would later become high school friends with Don Vliet, who would later become "Captain Beefheart" and form a "magic band." Although Frank does not mention living in Ontario (near Claremont) or a surrounding area in *The Real Frank Zappa Book* until a later date, he describes a lot of moving during this period when the family first came to California from Maryland. Two places mentioned are Monterey and San Diego.

Vic Mortensen: ... the next time I saw Frank Zappa, I was a freshman in high school (1958-9 perhaps) and he was jamming at a high school in Upland. They had a big cafeteria there, and there was a glass wall that separated the cafeteria from the big band room, at Upland High School. I was in there having lunch and the band room was empty, but by this time they were doing some big band stuff, and there was actually a drum set. You couldn't hear anything because of the glass. Normally, the room would be empty during lunch. I was getting my lunch, I looked in, there was a cat sitting up playing on that drum set and I knew it was Frank. But, I didn't even talk with him.

Jim Sherwood

Kansas-born Jim Sherwood lived most of his youth in San Bernardino California. San Bernardino is about 90 miles south southeast of Lancaster. It is lower in elevation and higher in humidity than the Antelope Valley. The Sherwoods and their four children Chuck (known as "Bone" because of his massive jawbone), Jim (known as "Bone 2" and later as "Motorhead"), Ivan, and sister Toni moved to Lancaster in the mid-fifties. This was due to a family incident that made it impossible for them to stay in San Bernardino. Jim was about 12 at the time and didn't think much of his new home.

John French: What was your impression of the Antelope Valley, of the desert in those days?
Jim Sherwood: (Big laugh) Well, there basically wasn't anything there. There was one housing tract that they had just built and that was where my dad bought the house. It was on Carolside.
JF: What year was that.
JS: It's either late '53 or early '54.
JF: So, it was pretty bleak to you, right?
JS: Yeah, it was just desert. There wasn't anything around. We had the little shopping center on the corner, and then they built the housing tract and that was it. Ours was the first street built.
JF: Carolside - that's where Don later lived.
JS: Yeah, Don Vliet lived up the block.
JF: At the time?
JS: I think he moved in a little later.

Denny Recalling Jim And "Bone" Sherwood

Denny Walley: I knew him and his (younger) brother Ivan and "Bone" his older brother. This guy would kick your ass as soon as look at you.
John French: Was Jim Sherwood musically inclined at that time?
DW: I couldn't say, because I wasn't actively playing anything. He wasn't involved in playing. He was one of the ones who had a real free spirit and was open to everything.
JF: What was he doing at the time? How do you remember him?
DW: Getting pussy.
JF: He was the good-looking guy?
DW: Oh yeah, real cool haircut. He was a great dancer, and his mother and dad had a big patio. They would have sock hops and all these parties out at the house and his mom would make tacos for like fifty people. She would make hundreds of tacos. They would play music all night – jukebox or record player – and his family was very gregarious in that sense. She really took in all the kids. She was a very wonderful woman.
JF: That's a pretty nice thing to do.
DW: Really. She took in everybody. Didn't care where they came from or what they did. If they had a problem or anything, (she'd) take them in. She would feed everybody. Kids dancing, and playing music, eating tacos and drinking Cokes.
JF: They lived in Lancaster also?
DW: Yes, they did.

Mojave didn't seem to hold irresistible charm for the Vliets, because they eventually moved to Lancaster. It was a much larger town than Mojave, and home of the Antelope Valley Joint Union High School, which at that time was the only High School in the entire Valley. The pull factor may have that young Don would not have to endure a long bus ride each day in order to attend class. Glen Vliet became a Helms Bakery man.

The Helms Bakery truck was an interesting affair. It consisted of a brightly painted yellow panel truck with large doors on the back. Opening these doors displayed a series of highly finished drawers, which extended from the rear of the driver's seat to the back of the truck. When these lower drawers were opened, a whole series of cakes, pies, doughnuts and other precious pastries were displayed. The need for this type of business was due to the fact that many families only had one car, which the man (the breadwinner of the fifties) would take to work. This left many a wife (the housekeeper, homemaker, and housewife of the fifties) stranded at home. So, the bakery was brought to her doorstep via Helms. There was also the milkman, who came early in the morning and left milk on your doorstep in glass bottles. As you emptied the glass bottles, they were placed in a metal rack, and he would take them in exchange. They would be taken to the milk factory, sterilized, and re-used over and over again. It was called "recycling."

Now, in America, when we really need to conserve petroleum products and help the environment by driving as little as possible, and when we need to recycle more than ever, it's a completely different scenario. Wives and husbands both work, both drive separate cars, and we buy our milk in plastic containers, which need much more energy to recycle than the old glass bottles.

Glen, Sue and Donny moved into a cozy little home on Carolside Street in Lancaster. The house was within a mile of the high school. The Sherwoods lived just down the street and Jim would eventually become friends with "Donny."

Jim Meets Don

John French: I'd like to get into talking about Frank and Don a little bit and who you met first.
Jim Sherwood: I met... that's a good one. Let me think. It would have probably been Don. Since Don lived on the block and we actually hung out with some kids that actually lived a couple of houses away.
JF: So, you remember him as what – a young teenager?
JS: Yeah.
JF: Like, fourteen? Fifteen?
JS: No, I think he was older than that.
JF: Was he driving yet?
JS: No, he wasn't driving yet, but it was only within a couple of years that he started driving.
JF: So, maybe fifteen years old, do you think?
JS: Probably, I never did ask his age. One of the kids that I worked with and hung out with actually lived across the street from him.

CHAPTER TWO:
PLATTERS AND PACHUCOS

Don leaving Grannie Annie's house in 1965. Courtesy of Doug Moon.

In *The Real Frank Zappa Book* Frank mentioned he used to have a job at a record shop:

"My part-time job in high school was working in a record store for a nice lady named Elsie (sorry, I can't remember her last name) who liked R&B."[2]

Jim Sherwood recalled that this was called Lee's Record Shop.

Jim Sherwood: That's how Frank and I got in touch with each other, because I collected blues records at the time. Frank was working at ... it was the record store in town.
John French: Lee's Record Shop?
JS: Lee's Records! Yeah! Frank was working there. Bobby (Frank's brother) took me over to the house to meet Frank and look at his record collection. Frank and I just hit it off. We were comparing blues records and songs and all that kind of stuff.
JF: Did you ever see Frank and Don (Vliet) hanging out together? Did you know much about their relationship?
JS: Not at all. Don was completely separate from Frank. I didn't know they knew each other until later on. Don was a friend of mine that lived up the block. Every once in a while, I would run across him, I believe he was actually the same year Frank was in school, or a year ahead of me. I didn't really know him that well, but every once in a while, we'd do stuff together.

I can find no information from anyone on whether or not there was actually Lee's Record Shop, but there most certainly was a Ling's Music Box. Thanks to Pete Lovio, I was able to track down Dennis Ling, the son of the owner.

John French: From what I understand and what I've been told, your father owned a music store called Ling's Music Box?
Dennis Ling: That is correct. It was originally on Cedar Street on the corner of Cedar and Lancaster Boulevard on the opposite side of the street from the Post Office. My dad moved it to Beech Street, south of Lancaster Boulevard across from ... Shopping Bag. I think my dad sold it in '59.
JF: OK, so I guess I must have just missed this detail. Frank Zappa mentioned in his book, The Real Frank Zappa Book that he worked in a record store. Was that Ling's Music Box?
DL: Not that I recall
JF: Yeah, I figured you probably worked in there for your dad.
DL: Yeah.

So, this settles the fact that Ling's Music Box was the record store Denny Walley soon will refer to as the place behind the Arcade Building, which was one block over, on Sierra Highway. Denny also mentioned Terminal Records, another shop, and others have mentioned Lee's Record Shop, but no one seems to know much about either of them.

Dennis Ling Recalls Frank

Dennis Ling: Yeah, I knew Frank. We had an art class together as a matter of fact.
John French: How was he as an art student?
DL: I don't really remember. Frank was always pretty much kind of a sit-in-the-back ...kind of a quiet guy. He wasn't like the rest of us - outspoken and carrying on, and giving the teacher a hard time.

---

[2] The Real Frank Zappa Book, Frank Zappa, Simon and Schuster, 1989 pp46.

JF: *So, he was a loner?*
DL: *Yeah, he pretty much was.*
JF: *And he wasn't outgoing or gregarious.*
DL: *No he wasn't gregarious. He may have been gregarious around his friends, but even in interviews and things, when you see interviews, he didn't get excited.*

Don and Frank: Buddies or Not?

John French: *So, Frank and Don didn't hang out that much?*
Pete Lovio: *No, no not that much, they did hang out but ...*
Wally Salazar: *I think it might have been afterwards, but not during the time of high school and The Blackouts. Because the thing is that Don ... (to Lovio) what grade was it that finally he started going back to high school, remember? ... I think Frank was already gone by the time he started back to school.*
Franklin: *Frank graduated about '58.*
WS: *'58 yeah.*
JF: *Isn't that when Don graduated too?*
PL: *No, he quit school didn't he?*
WS: *Yeah, he quit school – (then) he went back – he was in our grade.*

WS: *Yeah, the thing is, is that Frank was two years ahead of him ... right? OK, so when Frank graduated, what'd he do? He moved. He left the valley. So, in defense, Frank and him never really made that much contact.*
PL: *He did have contact, but not as much as people made it out to be, like they were buddy-buddies.*
Franklin: *I did see them together a few times.*
JF: *Frank says in his own book that he and Don used to hang out at Don's (parents') house and listen to blues records.*

An excerpt from Frank's book indicates there was a friendship and seems to contradict the above statements:

"I spent more time with Don (Captain Beefheart) Van Vliet when I was in high school than after he got into 'show business'." [3]

Wally Salazar: *No, but I think that that was mostly because ... when Captain Beefheart first started ... Frank took him under his wing. I don't truly believe that he really knew him like it said. I don't know why it was said like that, but when I read that, I said, "Nah." Ridin' down the Boulevard in the Oldsmobile and all that. He had an Oldsmobile, I remember that. I used to ride in it. I remember that. With the spinners on it, stuff like that.*
Pete Lovio: *Well, we don't really know.*
WS: *I used to hang out with Frank. My folks used to go and visit with them. My folks knew his folks.*

Dennis Ling recalls Frank and Don being acquainted.

Dennis Ling: *... (Don) was off in a different world than I was. He was hanging out with Frank and they were probably on the cusp of starting the Magic Band. I think that whole thing with the Magic Band started from a movie that Frank was doing.*

[3] The Real Frank Zappa Book, Frank Zappa, Simon and Schuster, 1989 pp36.

Frank's recollections seem to establish a close friendship:

"There were piles of sweet rolls in the kitchen, like pineapple buns that didn't sell that day – the place was crawling with starch – and we'd eat mounds of them while the records were playing. Every once in a while Don would scream at his mother (always in a blue chenille bathrobe), "Sue, get me a Pepsi!" There was nothing else to do in Lancaster." [4]

"Our major form of recreation, other than listening to records, was to go for coffee in the middle of the night to the Denny's on the highway." [5]

"If Don was short on cash (this was before he took over the bread truck route), he'd open the back door of the truck, pull out one of the long drawers with the dead buns on it and make Laurie crawl through the slot, into the locked cab, where she would sneak a few bucks out of his Dad's change-maker." [6]

"After coffee, we'd ride around in his light-blue Oldsmobile with the homemade werewolf-head sculpture in the steering wheel, and talk about people who had large ears." [7]

A Strange Quote from Don
In an attempt to show all sides of the story, one cannot ignore this quote, which says:
"Well, I never really knew him (referring to Zappa). *I ran around with mostly colored people there. I didn't really have that many acquaintances" - Captain Beefheart* [8]

According to all the early band members and Frank Zappa, he and Don knew each other quite well.

Vic Mortensen: … he (Zappa) said, "Here's my friend, Don … (referring to the first meeting at the roadhouse).

Denny meets Bobby Zappa
Denny Walley first attended Park View School, which is across the street from Jane Reynolds Park. After Junior High graduation, he then went to Antelope Valley Joint Union High School (AVJUHS). There, he eventually wound up meeting Frank Zappa through his affiliation with Bobby, Frank's younger brother. The first step was discovering Ling's Record Shop (on Beech Street), the nearby Arcade Building that contained a mutually appreciated burger joint, and the jukebox found within that burger joint, which contained mutually appreciated R&B recordings.

John French: OK, at this point, you had started going to a place called Lee's Record Shop [9] *that was behind The Terminal?*
Denny Walley: Yeah, Lee's Record Shop used to be right in back of a big grocery store (called Shopping Bag) Lee's was right in back of that. Then there was Terminal Records which was right inside the bus terminal.
JF: So, the bus terminal, was it like a tunnel place on Sierra Highway?
DW: It was on Sierra Highway, and there was a little alley that went through that accessed about four or five shops. (Note: this was an enclosed hallway with doors at either end, called The Arcade Building if I recall correctly.) *There was a place in there that had a fabulous jukebox and I used to go in there and get a Chilli Size for lunch.*
(Note: for the uninitiated, a Chilli Size is an open-faced cheeseburger on a bun with hot chilli

[4, 5, 6, 7] The Real Frank Zappa Book, Frank Zappa, Simon and Schuster, 1989 pp37.
[8] No Commercial Potential; The Saga of Frank Zappa, 1972, 1980, David Walley pp.111
[9] Note: Denny Walley remembers"Ling's" as Lee's" as does Jim Sherwood. The name could have been changed later, but for the sake of keeping the quotes accurate, I am leaving "Lee's" in.

poured over it – not exactly health food). *That jukebox had the original Richard Berry's Louie Louie, and stuff like that.*
JF: Frank mentioned a place where he used to go and eat lunch and he used to love the jukebox because it had Johnny "Guitar" Watson. Would that be the same place?
DW: Same place.
JF: So, you guys went there for lunch sometimes?
DW: Yes.
JF: So, there's the connection. What was your daily life like at that time? You were in High School, right?
DW: Right.
JF: Probably a freshman?
DW: Yeah, a "scrub."
JF: So, you guys would go down there for lunch from the school.
DW: Yeah, Frank was three years advanced from me. My connection to him at that time was his brother Bobby. That's how I met Frank. Bobby was in the same grade as I, along with Randy DuWeiss, whose father owned the Bowling Alley out on Sierra Highway?
JF: The Sands Bowl?
DW: Yeah. Also Bobby Atler, we used to call him "Wetback." We used to hang together and we were all really serious about our khakis.

The Relative Importance Of Khakis

In the early band, all the original members used to joke to me about the "Pachuco" era, wearing khakis, and such. Although I could understand that this was the trend of the late fifties, I didn't know much about it, having been in grade school when all this was going on. There were traces of the old ways left in High School, because certain people would dress the way their older brothers and sisters had dressed, but they mostly stood out as "different" or "not with it."

Finally, after all these years, I had a chance to interview Jim Sherwood, who clued me in. I was not only able to discover about the fashion trends of the fifties but also able to find that their source was none other than the Sherwood family itself, who had brought these styles and trends with them and had introduced them into the Antelope Valley.

"Pachuco" Culture Development '53 -'54

John French: What I'm trying to get is a feel for the mid-fifties Antelope Valley. Even though I lived here, I was just a wee lad. I just sort of remember the end of the "pachuco" era and the whole fifties thing. So, I'm kind of interested in what the teenage cultural mindset was like?
Jim Sherwood: With us coming from San Bernardino, it was a little bit different, because, that's a bigger town. We were raised in "Mexican Town" or close to it. In San Bernardino all our friends were Mexican. There was a whole gang environment. In junior high, there was about half a dozen white kids in the school. When my brother went to junior high, there were only two whites, he and one other. Eventually, there was a battle between the two. Either he had to lose his friend and become part of a club or get the hell beat out of him all the time. It was a totally different environment and probably one of the reasons we moved to Lancaster. The main reason was because my brother was getting involved in some criminal activities. The court said, "Get out of the County ...
JF: ... before sundown."
JS: Yeah, that's exactly right, too. So, anyhow, we bought the property and left. Then the house was built, so dad actually put a down payment on the house before they even

constructed it. It was a new housing tract.
JF: So, tell me about the "Pachuco" era.
JS: Actually, the "Pachuco" era was a carryover from when we moved (to Lancaster.)
JF: You're saying you brought it with you?
JS: We brought it with us.
JF: You're kidding me.
JS: No. Chuck being in a gang and all that, when we came up, all the San Bernardino kids had been into better clothes and things like that. When we went up there, they were all farmers with T-Shirts and Levis. So, when we went to school, we were wearing the khakis, black spit-shined shoes, and short sleeved checkered shirts (with big checks, two inch square). The trend later on became wearing the over-sized baggy shirt. I got my hand-me-down from Chuck that I had to buy from him. In my group with Alex and the band The Omens that was the style that we had for quite a while.
JF: It was baggier.
JS: Yeah, the "one-size-over" where it hung a little bit better on you, it wasn't real tight. It was a little bit baggier. Then we had khakis and we had the Italian hand-sewn shoes. The ones I loved came up to a little square in the front, not a point. We did have some that came to a point, but also ones that were squared. Those were the two styles that we wore most of the time. That was actually the band uniform at one time.
JF: I heard when Denny was talking on the tape, he was saying expressions like … Vato?
JS: That was Mexican slang … Esay Vato means "what a cool guy." Pince Vato is REAL BITCHIN'GUY, really cool.
JF: Pincy?
JS: Pince. It means "bitch" in Mexican.
JF: I heard Don, Alex and Doug talking about stuff like this, but I never really understood it.
JS: Well, they didn't either. They were the locals that we educated when we got up there.
JF: Well, then I'm getting it from the true source here.
JS: Pretty much, my oldest brother being in the gangs and going through that stuff, he brought it into his group and then when he started the Topos, his own gang up there, which became a car club later on, that was what we brought up.
JF: What does the word "Topo" mean?
JS: Topo means gopher or groundhog.
JF: Groundhog. So, it was sort of an underground cool thing?
JS: Well, it was actually a carryover from the club in San Bernardino because Chuck was in the Topos in San Bernardino. It was more of a gang that he started with the guys he hung out with. Then, it became a car club later on, when everyone could afford cars.

Alex doesn't recall Jim Sherwood bringing the vato style to the valley.

John French: Do you remember the "Pachuco" era being introduced in the Antelope Valley by Jim Sherwood?
Alex Snouffer: No, I just fell into it.
JF: So, he didn't redeem you from the farmer image?
AS: Well, I don't remember Jim Sherwood being my savior, let's put it that way.

Culture Shock For Lovio

John French: Talk to me about wearing khakis and the whole style thing. That was really important back then.

Pete Lovio: *There weren't many guys wearing that. It was just only the "Pachuco" guys wearing the khakis and French toes. I came from just south of Ventura County. eighty percent are Hispanic and the other 20 percent are American Indian. So, that was the dress of the day where I came from. When I came up here, I came up here looking for Mexican guys – Hispanics, and the only ones I could find were this guy (points to Wally Salazar) and his brother (Fred) and they were the only ones wearing khaki pants – khaki pants and French toes – that's what I was used to. So when I came up here, there was only a handful of Hispanics. I don't know how many Hispanics were in high school, not many. Most were Anglo. How many blacks were there? Not many. There weren't that many ethnic groups in high school at that time. They were all Caucasian. I came up here. I couldn't believe it. I was lost, man.*

Wally Salazar: *I remember him carrying his books across campus. He would just make a beeline. He wouldn't talk to anybody, look at anybody.*

PL: *I hated it here, man.*

WS: *Yeah, I know. You wanted to go back. (To me) I remember him saying it. From that period on, we always became friends.*

PL: *I had never been around so many white people in my life.*

WS: *Yeah (laughs). You wanted to go back because there were too many white people here.*

PL: *But you know what? Because of these guys here, Johnny, and the black guys, I became friends with the Mexicans and the black guys and that's where Frank (came in)… those were his friends. He didn't socialize with the white kids, other than Jim Sherwood and Don Ferize and a couple of other guys. We stood out. We liked R&B. We liked Oldies but Goodies. We were really unique at that time.*

Denny's View of "Pachuco"-ism

Denny Walley: *… We were all really serious about our khakis.*

John French: *This was the "Pachuco" thing you were talking about?*

DW: *Yeah, way down low with a little cuff about maybe a half inch. The shoes were really spit-shined with double soles. Your shoes were on a rake.*

JF: *What color?*

DW: *Black. French Toes, "Esay."*

JF: *Tell me more about the "Pachuco" look. Where did this come from?*

DW: *There was a legendary "Pachuco", Ernie Ponce. He was like the legendary "Bad Guy" from San Diego with all the Spider Dollies. Spider Dollies were the legendary "Pachuco" girlfriends who would light a cigarette and blow the match out with one nostril. Really sharp.*

JF: *A strrrrooooonggg nostril.*

DW: *That was kind of the look, but when I think back of how pathetic we were … you know, white guys.*

JF: *What was the mentality, what was the meaning of this, was it the "tough guy" image?*

DW: *The whole look was kind of "clean." You wanted to really look "clean." You'd go to Herman's – a place on Lancaster Boulevard – and Sierra Highway, which was a clothing shop.*

JF: *Oh, yeah, Herman's men's wear.*

DW: *You could get the most fantastic shirts. I mean things (affects Hispanic "Pachuco" voice) "probably from LA."*

JF: *What was the styling? What kind of shirt was the fantastic shirt?*

DW: *There were things like "see-through" stuff, and there was brocade black with silver lamé*

on it, three-quarter sleeves. Real big, loose fitting, collar buttoned to the top, much like the guys now. But the khakis had to have a crease that could cut your mother's throat. Spit-shined shoes - Cordovan was a big thing.
JF: Yeah, Cordovan Boot Polish.
DW: And if you could get some Echoes from Florsheim, that was it. That was it!
JF: Echoes?
DW: E-C-H-O - that was a brand.
JF: I was pretty serious about Florsheims once, yeah.
DW: They cost about forty bucks. (The average price of shoes was under $10 back then)
JF: That was a lot of money then. Now, you can't buy tennis shoes for forty bucks.
DW: You can't buy socks. That was the look; styling. Really dressing clean, expensive. Not like a suit and tie, casual wear, but only the finest, playing it "down."

Vliet's "Sharp Short"
   Don Vliet was the proud owner of a light blue 1949 Oldsmobile. It was his cool "short" (slang for car). It was actually less of a car in some memories. More often it was remembered as a rolling museum for not one, but two of Don's sculptures.

John French: You mentioned you went cruising with Don once?
Jim Sherwood: Oh, yeah. Couple of times. When he had his Oldsmobile.
JF: '49 Light Blue Olds with the werewolf in the steering wheel.
JS: Right – and in the clock.
JF: Oh, he had two.
JS: He had a werewolf in the steering wheel, and he took the clock out and put a werewolf in the glass there.
JF: And they were both clay sculptures?
JS: Right. Really well done too. Don was good at that.
JF: I saw only a couple of things that he did. One was a wolf's head and it was absolutely perfect. It was beautiful.
JS: That was probably the one he had in his steering wheel.
JF: Oh, really?
JS: All done with a toothpick. He put all the lines in it and everything. It was cool. He just flattened it out and started forming it with a toothpick.
JF: Did you watch him make it?
JS: I watched him do part of the one he put in his clock. The one he had in the steering wheel had already been put in.

   One thing that was almost guaranteed for all clocks in cars in the fifties: they never worked. It was a strange anomaly that for some reason beyond anyone's understanding that the clock that was mounted on the dashboard in any American car built in the forties or fifties never worked.

JS: I thought that was the greatest thing I had ever seen was taking that stupid clock out and putting something in that was actually cool.

   The teen mentality has always dictated one other important fact: in order to be accepted by one's peers, one must always live on the edge of the law. Many of the fifties teens found it popular to exploit this theorem in the manifestation of car height, in this case, as low as possible.

JF: So, did he have his car lowered (in the back)?
JS: Yeah, it was lowered, but legal.

The officer in charge using state-of-the-art equipment officially determined the legal height of a lowered car.

JS: What happened, if you couldn't slide a cigarette pack under the body of the car, then it was too low.
JS: Was that a flat side, or on edge?
JS: No, a box, a Marlboro box of cigarettes. That's the way they would test them.

Let the records indicate that the official equipment used to determine proper height is a Marlboro box, commercially and popularly known as the "flip top" box.

Pete Lovio: The only thing I remember a lot about is, Don had his car - remember?
Wally Salazar: That Oldsmobile?
PL: That Oldsmobile. He had like a baby-blue color. It looked like a '49 coupe. I remember riding with him, but jeez, that guy just couldn't drive worth a damn.
JF: Really? Van Vliet?
PL: Yeah! He was scary man.

The Blues

Vic Mortensen: Frank Zappa once told me, "Vic, you'll never be a blues player." I asked why. He said, "Because you've never drunk Thunderbird wine, warm, out a glove compartment."

Whatever indefinable element Van Vliet's music evolved into, it certainly seems relatively clear that one influence on not only Van Vliet and Zappa, but many of the early band members, was the blues. To be more specific, the Mississippi Delta Blues, but actually much of the early Chicago blues also plus the more recent R&B.

Ling's Music Box
Assembling the somewhat blatant contradictions in various interviews has been a chore, but the following small detail is still somewhat baffling to me. Three guys (Lovio, Salazar, and Franklin) all recall Ling's Music Box as being on the corner of Yucca and Lancaster Boulevard.

Pete Lovio: Remember where that record store was – Dennis Ling's dad's record store?
Wally Salazar: Yeah, that was back of the Railroad tracks. It was on Yucca and Lancaster Boulevard.
PL: On the east side of Sierra Highway?
JF: Someone (Denny Walley) told me that there was a record shop on Beech Street across from the old Shopping Bag (grocery mart).
WS: That was a different one, because after school we used to go over there (to Ling's). The store was on the corner.
JF: Which corner?
WS: The southwest corner.
JF: It's a glass company now.
PL: Exactly.
WS: Yes.

JF: So that was where Ling's Record Shop was located?
PL: You know, I talked to (Dennis Ling). He lives in Thousand Oaks. He's in production. He has an art show in Thousand Oaks. His dad owned the store. He says, "Yeah, I remember when you guys would come in there, and Jim Sherwood would come over and steal records. You guys would steal my dad's records and then play it for a while and then come back and steal some more and bring the old ones back." He was our age.
JF: So that's how you learned the songs, right? You'd steal the records?
PL: Yeah, Jim Sherwood and whoever else would go in and steal records.

There was some confusion caused by the mention of 'Lee's Record Shop' and 'Ling's Music Box.' No one can really clear this up for me. Ling himself declares the two locations to be different than Lovio and Salazar describe.

Cornet And The Blues
After hearing the blues on the jukebox at the Terminal, Denny was hooked. His mother bought two albums for his birthday: *I'm Jimmy Reed*, and *The Best of Muddy Waters*. Denny, Frank Zappa, and his younger brother Bobby all collected 45s they would find at the local Cornet 5 and 10 cents store, which was originally located on Lancaster Boulevard.

Denny Walley: I had singles that I had bought at the Cornet. They used to have a bin – about a five by four bin – filled with 45s that were "cutouts" - old juke box records from here and there and hither and yon. That's where I would find stuff. I have about 30 to 35 of those still in my collection with their little stamp on it – fifteen cents, thirty-five cents.
John French: Those are probably worth a fortune.
DW: You couldn't pay me to give them up. We used to go there and put them in a bag, because we never had enough money to pay for all of that stuff at once. I'd pick out about eight to ten records, put them in a bag and put them on "hold." They'd put my initials on it. Frank would do the same thing. There was probably only about three or four of us that collected like that. I am certain more than once one of us got into the other guy's bag and switched some stuff. Because all of a sudden I'd be looking in there for this thing and it wasn't in there and Bobby would be saying, "Hey, listen to this." "Hey, that was just like that record that I wanted!" That didn't happen much, but if the record was serious enough, you had to do what you had to do.
JF: Was it from listening to the jukebox that you got into blues?
DW: Well, the juke box, and then in Lancaster at that time you could pick up some other stuff, there was stuff coming out of Sun Village, and there was stuff coming from LA. Johnny Otis from San Diego. Some stuff was being played on the radio you could hear.
JF: Sun Village had a radio station?
DW: I just recall vaguely. I can't really say for sure. Maybe it was just the influence from there.
JF: That was in the days of segregation, so Sun Village was where the black people lived. They were called "Negroes" in that day.
DW: They were.
JF: Yeah and they didn't mind that. That was respectful.

Salazar Recalls Cornet

Wally Salazar: I remember a 5 and 10 cent store that they had on Lancaster Boulevard.
John French: Cornet?
WS / Pete Lovio: Yeah.

WS: *I remember my brother and I would go in there. We used to stop in there and they used to have these boxes on these wrought-iron type legs, it was real flimsy. They had all these 45s OK? What we did is we would look at the name of the record company, you know – certain companies. That's the ones we'd buy. We'd buy the song by labels. Go play 'em, if they turned out to be good, we'd keep 'em, if they didn't, we'd throw 'em away. I still have those records; I could show them to you. They had stamps on them – 35 cents. That's what they were selling at, that price. There was Bo Diddley, Magic Sam, Big Walter, Little Walter, Libby and La Fayette. Lot of those 45s we'd go ahead and copy … you know, learn off the records. My brother was the one that had the collection, but I have the records now in my house.*
JF: *Denny Walley mentioned something about going in there. He said that they were old jukebox records. They'd take 'em out of the jukebox and put them in the racks.*
WS: *That's right.*

Handley's Blues Roots/1958

Jerry Handley: *My first albums, when I was 13, were I'm John Lee Hooker and I'm Jimmy Reed. Those were the albums I got as a kid that knocked me out. That's kind of what changed me from listening to pop music to listening to blues.*
John French: *How did you first get introduced to it?*
JH: *Well, my older brother Norm, he's about four or five years older than I am had a buddy he hung around with that had these albums and brought them over. I was just getting interested in guitar at the time, so I hadn't really any direction, I was just learning how to play pop music or whatever, some chords and that. Then, I heard these (blues) albums, and that was it for me, I started buying all the blues albums. I didn't want to play anything else.*
JF: *This was during an era where there was a lot of surf music, right, and Connie Stevens and Rick Nelson, you know, the early Rick Nelson, before the Garden Party.*
JH: *Yeah, there was a lot of surf music in the early sixties.*

Snouffer's blues roots reach back a little further.

Alex Snouffer: *I wasn't allowed to listen to "nigger music."*
John French: *Where? By whom?*
AS: *By my dad. (Quoting) "I don't want you listening to no nigger music." Well, let me tell you something, this "nigger music" as he put it, was blues. Man that just fucking grabbed me by the stomach and I was just out of this room. Hunter Hancock used to play that stuff every afternoon and I'd just "dial him in there" you know. I started listening to that and 'hoo boy', it set me off.*
JF: *You're talking when? High School?*
AS: *Oh, fuck no. I was still in grade school. We're talking 1950 maybe. Fifty, fifty-one. We had one of those old radios that would squawk when you dialed it in.*

Hunter Hancock was a DJ who began his LA career in 1944 after leaving from Laredo, Texas. He was given a weekend job to play a one-hour show called "Harlem Holiday" which was aimed at appealing to the black community. This got him involved with jazz and R&B.

Zappa/Vliet Blues Roots
The young Don was a "blues fiend" according to Frank Zappa.

"Don was also an R&B fiend, so I'd bring my 45s over and we'd listen for hours on end to obscure hits by The Howlin' Wolf, Muddy Waters, Sonny Boy Williamson, Guitar Slim, Johnny "Guitar" Watson, Clarence "Gatemouth" Brown, Don and Dewey, the Spaniels, the Nutmegs, the Paragons, the Orchids, the etc., etc., etc." [10]

Frank On Guitar And Other Instruments

Johnny Franklin: My cousin, Sonny - whose name was Freddy Louis, we called him Sonny – he had bought a guitar, and this is before Frank had even messed with a guitar – he had this guitar – I think it was called a Gibson Les Paul Junior. It was a solid body as heavy as all get-out. Somehow, he brought that to the rehearsal and we all messed around with it, you know. Kids got a new instrument, you know. We were out in Frank's garage. I started messin' with it, Sonny messed with it, I don't know who all messed with it, but somehow I hit a coupla'notes on it accidentally, and he (Frank) said "Hey, lemme try that." So I handed it to him, and he started messin' with it and, I think he liked it." Then he started switching off – guitar, drummer ...

Wally Salazar: Xylophone?

JF: Yeah, he had vibes (Note: the xylophone and vibraphone or "vibes" are both tonal mallet instruments that are sometimes mistaken for each other).

Pete Lovio: I don't remember him playing that ...

Wally Salazar: He kinda started giving that up, you know. He stayed mostly with drums but he had the vibes and then of course he picked up the guitar. And once he picked guitar up, that was what he mainly stayed with ... was guitar.

PL: Who got him into the guitar? You (to Salazar) were playing guitar, right.

WS: Yes, that's when I was in the band. But then he wanted to play guitar, and I go "OK," so he played the guitar.

PL: I remember he told his brother's friend, he said he liked the sound of a sax, but he didn't like playing it because it gave him a headache.

WS: I believe that he was so talented he could probably play almost any instrument.

PL: Oh, yeah, the guy was a genius man.

Zappa/Snouffer / 1956 -7

Zappa was part of the high school band. One of the trumpet players in the band was Alex Snouffer:

Alex Snouffer: It started when I first met Frank. We were in the High School senior band together. He was playing drums and I played trumpet. He was a drummer. He wasn't always a guitarist. Anyway, we met, got to know each other a little bit. I suppose that it was probably within two weeks of each other we both got a guitar and started learning how to play the motherfucker. It was back in those days when if you could play Honky Tonk in ALL THREE CHANGES, hey, you were probably the best guitar man in the valley. We both were basically self-taught as far as that was concerned.

One of the things I shared in common with both Frank Zappa and Alex Snouffer was the fact that we all were in Mr. Ballard's band in high school. Mr. Ballard was a strict disciplinarian, and his motto was on a sign hanging in the window to his office. The sign was a piece of black wood with silver glitter letters and said, "Results Not Excuses." Ballard had a strange paralysis due to nerve damage, which I heard he received as a result of pulling somebody from a burning car after his own back had been broken in an auto accident. It was a believable story

[10] The Real Frank Zappa Book, Frank Zappa, Simon and Schuster, 1989 pp36.

because he seemed like the kind of person who would risk his neck for another. It actually gave him a touch of a "Frankenstein" ambience, because his speaking voice was a bit guttural and strained. In plain words, he scared the living crap out of me.

Zappa was eventually kicked out of the marching band for smoking in uniform. He forever thanked Mr. Ballard for relieving him of the duty of freezing his butt off playing at football games, for which Frank and I also shared a common hatred.

According to Doug Moon, Alex had a real tough-guy image in High School.

John French: So, did you know Alex before you joined the band? Do you remember him from High School?
Doug Moon: Oh, yeah.
JF: As "Butch" right? Butch Snouffer.
DM: Oh, he was a legend in high school as being a tough-guy.
JF: Oh really?
DM: Yeah, if he was walking down the street, if you wanted to live, you would cross the street and walk on the other side rather than to confront him - that's his legend.

Denny Meets Zappa

John French: When you met Frank, had you already started playing guitar?
Denny Walley: No, I hadn't. Bobby was playing acoustic guitar and Bobby and Frank shared the same bedroom. Frank had all of his stuff there. Actually, Frank was very much into art. Like, doing, caricatures of all these really "vato" guys from San Diego. Using transparencies and stuff and doing very cool almost "cartoony" type of scenarios.
JF: So, he was more of a visual artist at that time?
DW: He was a musician also. He was a drummer and he also played the guitar and was writing stuff.
JF: Already.
DW: Oh yeah, he had funny songs. He had this cowboy song called I Wanna Lay You, and it was a yodeling thing. He was mainly a drummer at that time. He was interested in everything and could do anything. Even in school, he stuck out. He might as well have been fluorescent.

Denny Walley On Don And The Gang Scene

Denny recalls Don Vliet as having something of the reputation of a notorious "badass" which meant mean, tough, independent and a good fighter. He was a loner who drove around in his light blue Oldsmobile with the werewolf head sculpture in the steering wheel. He never recalls seeing Don attending a class, but remembers him "cruising around" town in his "Olds." Denny didn't hang out with Don because, in his own words …

Denny Walley: I was a pussy compared to him (Don). There was another guy named Joe Casamas, who was also one of the "outlaw" guys in town. He had a big Packard twelve-cylinder car, and this guy was about five foot two. He used to drive this big thing around. He had to sit on telephone books to reach the pedals. There was another guy – Ernie Narajo, who was - these were the guys that if you saw them coming down the street, your heart would start pumping and you would cross to the other side. You would get the hell out of the way. Who knew what could happen? It was a small town, but their reputations preceded them.

Surprisingly, when asked about "Donny's" image of being a tough guy, Sherwood was amazed that anyone would have thought of Vliet cast in such an image.

Jim Sherwood: Donny was the kind of guy you could just slap around and tell him exactly what you wanted to do with him. I don't know, maybe somewhere along the line, he figured if he would yell at somebody it scares them off, I don't know.

Johnny Franklin had an idea as to why two people would view the same person in different ways.

John Franklin: People have different levels of understanding other people – different levels of relationships. This guy may get along with you good, do anything. Next guy may register different, you know.

Don A Badass?

John French: So, was Don an intimidating guy back then?
Wally Salazar: What do you mean by "intimidating?"
JF: Was he the kind of person who manipulated people, control-type of person, intimidate you into trying to do something his way?
WS: Yeah, in a way, because he wanted things his way, and his way wasn't always the right way. Just like with the sax in the band (saying) "Oh, this sounds pretty good," – he kind of wanted to do that type of thing. He was more a person that like hung out by himself.
JF: A non-team-player.
WS: There was time to mess around and there was time to be serious.
Pete Lovio: I heard stuff later on (that) when (he was) with you guys he was very intimidating, Jerry and Doug and you guys.
WS: I think that was probably later, though. He probably got a little bit of fame -power in his hands then he used it to intimidate. It was like "my way" – you know?
PL: Well he tried to do that a little with us but Alex wouldn't allow it.
WS: Well, nobody would stand for it.
PL: Not at that time, he was intimidating but not like with you guys. I read a statement about you guys when you were living up in Laurel Canyon I think. Something about Doug. Vliet got really pissed off at Doug for playing the bass wrong or something – not doing it right, and told him he couldn't play worth a shit, or something like that and to get the hell out of there. He was showing everybody how to do their parts. I don't know how true that was.
JF: Yeah, it was very true.
PL: But he was very intimidating in your time, but in our time, we didn't allow him to do that I guess.
WS: Well, yeah but he wasn't really involved with the band so maybe he would have tried to do something like that. He didn't really have that "power"… the band was firmly established, so … he couldn't penetrate and put his ways into our ways. Him trying to do things his way got him out of the band.

Alex remembers Don as later changing from the guy he knew in the early days. He spoke to me in one phone conversation as the young Vliet being a nice guy, the kind of guy who would give you the shirt off his back, the kind of guy who would be willing to loan his friends money when they needed it. In an interview, he touches upon this early Vliet.

Alex Snouffer: We were young, we were cruising buddies and all that. We just made the most out of everything.
John French: Did you get along pretty well?
AS: Most definitely.
JF: And he seemed like a pretty nice guy?
AS: I had known Don for quite some time. We hadn't run together, but I had known him for quite some time. So when we started running together it was just before I went to Tahoe. And, of course, when I came back is when we started the Beefheart band. Nah, he was a totally different person.
JF: In terms of ...
AS: Decency, not stealing from you – does that say enough?
JF: He was more honest?
AS: Sure. Anybody that steals from you ain't honest.

Beating Up "Wingnuts"

John French to Denny Walley: You said something before about Don having this notorious reputation for going up to Edwards and picking on guys called "wingnuts."
Denny Walley: Actually, "wingnuts" are Air Force guys. This is not something that I had personally experienced. The scuttlebutt was ... he didn't deny it at the time ... they'd go to Mojave, cause that was the closest town (to Edwards) where they (Wingnuts) would go drinking and stuff and he'd kick some "Wingnuts" asses. I don't know if that was true, but that was part of the reputation that followed him. Everyone thought that was valid so when they saw him ... (Snaps fingers).
JF: I know that he mentioned to me – he used to call them "Marines" but there is no Marine base near this area, so it had to be Air Force guys. I know that when he was a kid, he got beat up by them. He talked about that, as a thirteen or fourteen year old kid, they'd chase him home and beat him up. He said he had lost some teeth that way. He may have been just going back to get even, if that is a true story.
DW: If it is. I don't have anyone who can validate it, offhand.

Denny summed up Don's tough guy image as more of a front, a show.

Denny Walley: Don kinda fell into that (tough guy) category, because no one ever talked to him. No one knew him, but – you know him ... He's a tough guy and he could intimidate the shit out of you.
John French: This must have been around the time that he had to leave High School and take over his dad's Helms Bread truck. I think that was around 1957 or 58. Does that sound right to you?
DW: That is, exactly.

What I'm referring to here is a tragic page in Don's early history. During Don's High School tenure, his father Glen had a heart attack. Don himself said the doctor said this was caused by his father constantly bumping his calf muscle on the running board as he climbed in and out of the Helms truck over, which caused a blood clot. Don had to drop out of High School and take over the Helms Bakery route. This is probably why Denny never saw him in high school.

Frank recalls:

"*He dropped out during his senior year, because his Dad, who was a Helms Bread truck driver, had a heart attack and 'Vliet'(as he was known then) took over his route for a while – but most of the time he just stayed home from school."*

According to Mortensen, Zappa was intrigued by Don's dysfunctional home life :

Vic Mortensen: Zappa was fascinated by the relationship Don had with his parents. I mean, you had parents; did you call your parents by their first names? Did you walk into the house and go, "Sue, get me some tea." That ought to give you a little bit of a clue.

John French: (Frank) mentions Don's dad having the Helms Bread truck. He took over the route.
Pete Lovio: I think he did help his dad.
JF: Yeah, when his dad had the heart attack. That's pretty well documented.

Dennis Ling, in contradiction, didn't notice anything unusual about Don's relationship with his parents.

Dennis Ling: Yeah, I went to (Don's) house.
John French: What was your impression of his relationship with his parents?
DL: It must not have been anything out of the ordinary, because I don't remember anything extraordinary about it.

Jim Sherwood also recalls Don's relationship with his parents:

John French: It was because of Frank's fascination with Don's relationship with his mother. You know, how he was always saying, "Sue, shut up and get me a Pepsi!"
Jim Sherwood: Exactly. That was his famous line that we teased him about all the time.
JF: Did you know Don's parents?
JS: Oh, sure.
JF: So, you were at the house and you met them and saw that?
JS: A lot of the times, we didn't get to spend time with Don or we didn't see him a lot because his father was sick. He was dying, and Don was running the bread route. His father had a Helms Bread truck, and Don was running the route for his father. Every once in a while I'd go up to the house there and the bread truck was parked in the driveway and Don would give me a doughnut or something. He'd open it up and show me all the stuff that was in there.
JF: Stale pineapple rolls were usually the ones left over according to Frank. He said they'd sit and eat stale pineapple rolls and listen to rhythm & blues records.
JS: I believe that. I do believe that.
JF: Did you ever listen to Rhythm & blues with Don at his house?
JS: No, only on the radio when we went driving.
JF: But you were in the house and saw the relationship between him and his mom – which was (typified by that quote) "Sue, shut up and get me a Pepsi"?
JS: He had the same problem with his dad.
JF: He talked to his father that way?
JS: It was like he was really disgusted with the whole thing. He used to joke about –(how) he was really embarrassed about driving his dad's bread truck "cause he had to open his drawers in front of all these women." He had a really good sense of humor. Every once in a while he would say some really funny stuff.

So, apparently Don exhibited the same disrespectful, bullying dominance with his father as with his mother. As suggested by Jim, this may have been built upon the resentment he felt at having to drop out of high school to help support the family. The stress of dealing with an ailing parent combined with becoming the literal "breadwinner" of the factory perhaps made Don feel cheated out of a normal childhood. This could have resulted in several insecurities, one being the inability to finish high school in the same class and the stigma of being labeled a "dropout." There is a song on the album *Safe As Milk* called *Dropout Boogie*, which could have been inspired by this.

Mr Cool

Pete Lovio: I remember (Don) walking down Sierra Highway in a trench coat in 90 degree weather. Every so often someone would give him a ride.
John French: Oh, he didn't have a car?
PL: No – I don't know, he may have ran out of gas.
Johnny Franklin: The most I can remember about him is just dark sunglasses.
JF: Yeah, he always tried to be "cool" (Don said this to me himself about his younger years.)
PL: Trenchcoat in 90 degree weather?
JF: I don't know how cool that is.

The Blackouts

Alex Snouffer: Then, (Zappa) started his band, The Blackouts and he had guys like Junior Madeo playing with him.

Junior Madeo was a familiar name to me, because at Zappa's suggestion, he later auditioned to become a member of the *Trout Mask* band just after Snouffer left and prior to Bill Harkleroad joining.

Frank describes The Blackouts in his book:

"When I was in high school, in Lancaster, I formed my first band, The Blackouts. The name derives from when a few of the guys, after drinking peppermint schnapps, purchased illicitly by somebody's older brother, blacked out." [11]

John French: Was it Frank's group?
Johnny Franklin: It was Frank's group, yeah.
JF: So he contacted everybody, how'd he meet you?
Franklin: I was getting ready to catch a bus to go home, at Antelope Valley High, and one of my classmates, Wayne Riles, came up and said, "Hey man, this guy's startin'a band, are you interested in getting in?" Wayne knew that I had this old saxophone that I'd been playing around with for a couple years. He said, "The guy's name is Frank Zappa." I said, "Frank who?" - I'd never heard a name like that before back at that time. So he invited me to come to a rehearsal in the old Boy's Gym. So, that's my first time ever seeing Frank. Frank was a thin – kind of at that time, if I was to use politically incorrect terms - kind of a skinny, weird-looking guy. (Laughter) Well, I love him, Frank's great people, but that was my first impression without ever speaking to him. He had his drums set up there and I brought my little horn in. I don't know who else was there. Wayne Riles at that time was our vocalist, and he played bongos. Sometimes he would serve as alternate percussionist. Apparently, me

[11] The Real Frank Zappa Book, Frank Zappa, Simon and Schuster, 1989 pp45.

knowing nothing about music, I happened to make a few riffs and Frank said, "Man, I like that." He claimed there was something about my style that he can't describe but there was something about it that he was fascinated with. So anyway - I don't know if I can put chronology to this or not – but others started joining the group. Ernie Thomas, aah, Walley, Fred. Wally Salazar: The guy that played baritone ...

Franklin: Jerry Reuter!

WS: Right.

JF: How many people?

Franklin: Well – the total that it escalated to at one time? It fluctuated depending on what kind of gig we had and who was available. Sometimes we'd do it with five or six. I can recall one time it was like seven, eight.

Apparently, this was the first and only R&B band in the entire Mojave Desert at that time. Three of the guys (Johnny Franklin, Carter Franklin, and Wayne Lyles - Frank's description of the original lineup) were black, the Salazar brothers were Mexicans and Terry Wimberly represented, according to Frank, **"the other oppressed peoples of the earth."**[12] This was an integrated band in a time when segregation, although not enforced in California, was implied and assumed as the norm. I never experienced any rampant racism in my years growing up in Lancaster, but that doesn't mean that it didn't exist.

Wally Salazar: The thing is, when The Blackouts were first here, that was the only band in the Valley.

Johnny Franklin: We were the first Rhythm & blues band to originate within the desert here. Also the first band, I've been told, that had the cultural and ethnic diversity, that we were proud to have.

WS: That's Frank. Frank did not look at that, he was looking at the music. He didn't think, "Well, we're going to be diverse." That didn't even come up. It was "Oh, you play this?" That's it!

JF: To mention Sun Village the people out there accepted our group fondly – just young kids out there doing their thing. I think Frank really appreciated the way he was accepted out there in that community and always had a fondness for it.

Pete Lovio: I agree

JF: People out there stood behind him, like "Don't mess with Frank," and "Bring it on, Frank." We were doing jobs, we worked Palmdale, Lancaster, Edwards Air Force Base - we did a lot of local stuff. They sponsored us on a lot of local gigs, stuff like this. People that he'd (later) sing about in Village Of The Sun. He remembered me, he remembered Teddy. Teddy was an old gentleman. He was a string man, blew some heavy jazz. He used to play with Duke Ellington. That's what I was told. Look it up on the internet – Teddy Budd. I think he passed away in '87.

Driving Zappa To Black Out Rehearsals

Denny, as he mentioned earlier, used to buck hay in the summer for extra money, and apparently at this time, one could get a special agricultural driver's license at the tender age of $14^{1}/_{2}$. Frank, being an enterprising individual even at this early age, somehow managed to commission Denny to drive him to rehearsals.

Denny would drive him/them; sometimes to Sun Village, possibly to Johnny Franklin's house, and sometimes to Mojave, where Frank's Mexican girlfriend lived. It was a shotgun shack "across the tracks." A shotgun shack could be described as one of those little houses that have all the rooms in a row so that if you opened the front door and the back door, you could literally "fire a shotgun all the way through the house and never hit a thing." As the band

---

[12] The Real Frank Zappa Book, Frank Zappa, Simon and Schuster, 1989 pp45.

rehearsed, Frank's girlfriend would cook for everyone and they would take breaks and feast on tacos, refried beans, and rice.

Johnny Franklin: I never saw Frank drive. I don't think Frank learned to drive until he was about twenty-three. I remember his first car he bought, '61 to '63 Chevy Station Wagon. That was after he was living in Ontario. Frank was not driving (in the early Black-Out days) as far as I know.

John French: Were you actually part of the band at that time?
Denny Walley: In The Blackouts? No, I was just the guy who got them from point A to point B. I was not in the band at all. I didn't play anything. I was transport. I remember Wally Salazar ...
JF: Guitar
DW: Terry Wimberly ...
JF: Keyboards
DW: Frank, drums. Who knows bass? I don't even know if there was one. (Note: Bass players seemed to be a rare commodity in the Antelope Valley, but outtakes of interviews indicate that both Terry Wimberly and Johnny Franklin played bass at various times). Chuck Spencer, Henry (Strawberry) and those guys that sang ... you know, background singers.

I had met a woman who claimed to be a guitarist in The Blackouts and asked Denny about this ...

Denny Walley: I can't even imagine – in those years – a female guitarist – period — and Frank would be the first one to hire one.
John French: I think that's cool, because this lady claimed she did play in his band for a while, but she barely remembered anything about it. During this driving time you were living in Tamarack Fair, right?
DW: Yes
JF: Which is near the fairgrounds over there.

The Blackouts First Job

Johnny Franklin: I can remember the first professional job I had with The Blackouts. We played in Lancaster – we were little kids. It was '57, I believe it was. Did it at a place called Lancaster Women's Club or something like that.
Pete Lovio: Corner of J and 10th.
Franklin: I can remember, being kids, we all made $8 a piece (proudly). When you really figured out the time we put into it, we played four sets at forty-five minutes each. We really worked a total of three hours, not even that much. This was when construction labor were making $1.80 an hour. So I figured, "Man, that's not too bad. I'm up here having fun, and I'm making as much as the guys out there digging the ditches."
John French: (continuing train of thought) "Now, if I could do that eight hours a day, five days a week ..."

Doug Hears The Blackouts/1958

Doug Moon: I got connected in all this when I was a freshman in High School and Frank was a senior. I was on my way in, he was on his way out. So we crossed paths for the first time ...

This was probably around 1958. According to Doug, The Blackouts had a sax player named Steve Wolfe in their band whose brother was friends with young Doug Moon. Doug had met his brother through his studies in electronics:

Doug Moon: That's how I got connected up with this whole business. I was studying radio and electronics, and stuff. It was my nature. I met this guy — Steve Wolfe's brother. He was kind of a nerd, an electronics geek. I went over to his house one time and his brother Steve was a sax player in The Blackouts.
John French: Right, Zappa's band.
DM: Yeah, Frank was the drummer. I guess Terry Wimberly was in there and Johnny Franklin and you know all the others. I had always been interested in music and playing an instrument but I never had gotten close enough to get my hands on an instrument, or close enough to where I could get into it. Get started ... like when you grow up in a musical family ... I never knew anybody who played an instrument. Anyway, I went over there and (The Blackouts) were having a band practice at Steve's house - so I got to meet the band. Steve Wolfe, the sax player and I struck up a friendship. I used to hang out, and every time there was a practice, I'd go to their practice, and I'd go to their gigs and stuff. I even cut school a couple of times to go to their gigs. I remember getting in trouble for it.

Johnny Remembers Joe Adams

Johnny Franklin: I recall photographs, one in particular, that's out there on the Internet somewhere, I don't know where, but I've seen it. Some of the names are incorrect on the people that are shown. I don't know what to do about that. We did a show at the Shrine Exposition Hall years ago, Louis Armstrong was there. Dorothy Dandridge's mother had a band called The Titans, I believe. It was a calypso group. One of the LA DJs – I think his name was Joe Adams, was there. He went on to be pretty big in the radio world.

Joe Adams, according to internet research, was quite a figure indeed. An African-American, he was a member of the famed Tuskegee Airmen and then went on to become the first black DJ to host a radio show in LA – which eventually became the number one show. The musical theme for his radio show was composed by none other than Duke Ellington and Billy Strayhorn. He also hosted two short-lived television shows in the early days of television and starred in the movie *Carmen Jones* along with Dorothy Dandridge and Harry Belafonte. He appeared in 25 motion pictures altogether, including the original *The Manchurian Candidate* with Frank Sinatra. After a two-year run on Broadway with Lena Horne and Ricardo Montalban in the musical *Jamaica*, he was asked by the legendary late Ray Charles to become his personal manager – a position he has held for 48 years at the time of this writing.

Johnny Franklin: There's a group picture that they took there. I know everybody in there, 'cept there's one or two faces I just can't – one face I just can't place. But some of them have different names on them. Even Sonny my cousin – he's in there, Carter my brother. I could almost name 'em all, there was Wayne Rawls, there was Charles Reeves, there was Junior Madeo.
John French: Junior Madeo – I met him, he was a ...
Pete Lovio: Guitarist.
Franklin: Ernie Thomas, he graduated a year before you (pointing to Wally and Pete) I believe. Ernie Thomas, he was a trumpet player. Hmm, I think I just about named them all. Of course, there was Frank. Frank was our drummer.

Frank At AV College

Frank tried a semester of college, probably about 1959. According to Don, he attended for a semester, and this may have been the basis on which their first recording *Lost In A Whirlpool* came into being. Done on a small Webcor (Could this have inspired Van Vliet's *Webcor Webcor* from *Those Little Golden Birdies?*) tape recorder in one of the classrooms.

The piece sounds like a couple of guys basically goofing off. Frank's playing was fairly primitive at the time, as he had only been playing a guitar a short while. Of course, he was still primarily a drummer at this time. Vliet sings in a semi-falsetto voice, which occasionally slips into a more "pinched trachea - Howlin' Wolf" type of voice.

The song is typical of adolescent bathroom humor but still hints at the double-entendre that would so dominate his later writings by comparing love spurned to flushing waste down a toilet. I can almost see Frank suppressing laughter on the tape as Don improvises these lines. I had never heard this material until recent years and it helped me to better understand the formation of the relationship that I observed ten years later as *Trout Mask* was being created and recorded. The whole "anthropological field recording" concept and some of the theatrical things that Frank tried to initiate at the Woodland Hills house seems to be nothing more than an extension of this early concept of their collaboration.

Formation Of The Omens - Alex

Alex later formed a band with former Blackouts keyboardist, Terry Wimberly, called The Omens.

Alex Snouffer: Then, I teamed up with (Terry) Wimberly (keyboardist), by this time I could actually do a "sola" (tongue-in-cheek pronunciation). We formed The Omens, essentially.
John French: Terry Wimberly?
AS: Yeah, if he's still alive.
JF: So, you formed The Omens with Terry Wimberly?
AS: Well, actually he formed them, yeah. I was on guitar, I was LEAD (tongue in cheek) guitar, right? Then of course, the Salazar Brothers, Fred played horn and Wally, his brother played guitar, so me and Wally were an act. Then, pretty soon, we got Pete Lovio and Stan Mitchell and David Griego.

Moon said that The Omens were a band that formed out of the ashes of The Blackouts, and this seems to make sense as Alex mentions Terry Wimberly and the Salazar brothers, who Frank describes as members of The Blackouts, as being in The Omens.

Alex Snouffer: We had Stan Mitchell, and Fred Salazar and Pete Lovio, on tenor, Gary Burkey on alto, Jim Sherwood on Baritone, David Griego on trumpet, and Frank Lynch on trombone. So, we had a pretty good power section there.
John French: Pretty good memory, by the way.

Jim Sherwood was approached by Terry Wimberly to play in the band.

Jim Sherwood: Terry Wimberly asked me later on if I wanted to play horn in a band and I said, "Sure, but I can't play anything! I can't play shit." He's says, "Well, get a saxophone and we'll teach you how to play it." I went out and got a tenor sax.(Note: this may have been a baritone sax, because that's what Jim was eventually known for playing and also what Alex targets him as playing.)

Jim had played trumpet in grade school when his family lived in San Bernardino, so he had been at one time associated with the actual playing of music. This had not been formal experience. He and his friend Carlos Ocho, a friend who collected trains (miniatures I assume) and played trumpet had shown Jim a few riffs. At 13 years old, they would sneak off to smoke cigarettes and play the trumpet.

The Omens' rhythm section consisted of two guitars, keyboards, bass and drums. One guitarist was Alex and the other was probably Johnny Franklin. Terry Wimberly, who started as keyboardist, almost immediately switched to bass. The late Pat Prue was on drums. The band didn't use charts, but played by ear along to the rhythm & blues records, learning by association. Their repertoire consisted of stuff like, *Ain't Got No Home, Rockin'At the Drive In, Pachuco Hop*, and *Night Owl*. This was during Little Richard's heyday and the era proceeding:

Alex Snouffer: Not what they call Rhythm & Blues today, which is totally different than what it was then. Back then, that was top 40 shit, though ... we're talking '59, '60, that was all top 40 stuff on the radio. Of course, we got a lot of ideas from Hunter Hancock, who used to be a DJ in LA, and at night Wolfman Jack played all the stuff that we used to do, while he was still in Mexico, just across the border.
John French: Oh, is that where he was? And then he switched to someplace in Texas?
AS: (Resentfully) Yeah, then he came to LA and got all "commercial."

Alex remembers the first Omens performance:

Alex Snouffer: Down on Cedar Street, they had this place – I don't know what it is now, but it's still there, but at that time it used to be the community hall. It was right around the fire station and the cop shop and all that, you know. It held like fifty people or something. Well, the Topos – remember that old gang? - they decided to throw a gig and since (The Omens) were the only band in town and we only knew maybe a dozen songs (laughing), we played those all night. That was the very beginnings of The Omens, a scratch band. They gave us twenty-five dollars and a case of beer - for the whole band. We thought that was some pretty sharp shit.

East Coast Art Tripp
Art Tripp was having his own more conventional experience playing in the High School marching band. In his freshmen year he played the cymbals, eventually working his way up to Drum Captain, a position of some esteem, I suppose. In California we had First Chair Drummer, Second Chair Drummer etc. Like my own experience, Artie marched in the Rose Parade. Unlike my experience, he traveled from the East Coast by train:

Art Tripp: Yeah, it was brutal and it was warm. What we had was this guy from the University of Pittsburgh who was a band coordinator, and he came out and a year before we went out there he had us doing a physical fitness thing to where we worked out every day for a whole year. So, when we were in the parade, we were in peak shape. Nobody dropped out or anything. I'll never forget the band in front of us was a band from somewhere in Jersey. They had like fifty people, and they lost twenty two people – I don't know why I remember that – twenty-two people passed out or just got overcome with fatigue and they had to drop out and it completely decimated their band. The poor guys had to come out from Jersey – they didn't have the proper funding – so they came out on a day coach. We had come out on a Pullman you know, with several stops, Grand Canyon and all that. We'd get out and rehearse. We had one whole car, like a freight car on a train, that we used for rehearsing and we'd actually continue on our workouts all the way through there, so we were really in great shape. The following year we went to the Orange Bowl Parade in Miami. So it was the back-to-back Big Bowl deals. It was pretty heavy stuff for a young kid.

Handley Hears Snouffer: 1960

Jerry Handley: I first saw Alex, before I met him was when he was playing with a band called The Omens. They were a takeoff from The Blackouts that Frank Zappa had. I think that Zappa's band was in the late fifties. Alex, I believe played with The Blackouts with Zappa, you'd have to check with him on that. (Note: According to Alex, his first band was The Omens, and he never played in Zappa's Blackouts. However, there is a picture on page 45 of the *Real Frank Zappa Book* The Blackouts and the guitarist on the far right looks suspiciously like "Butch" Snouffer.)
Jerry Handley: They had horns, and R&B thing like an Art Laboe type of thing.
John French: You're like three or four years younger than Alex, right? So there's this span in age there?
JH: Right, I was in High School, like in my freshmen year, 13, 14. I went to their dances. The Omens put on dances in Lancaster, shortly after The Blackouts did.
JF: There wasn't much else to do in Lancaster in those days.
JH: That's about it, right.
JF: What was life like for you?
JH: I got interested in music when I was about 13 because there wasn't much else going on. I wasn't involved in anything else and there wasn't that much activity to do. You were out stealing hubcaps or you were out playing music. I took up the guitar, and when I saw Alex playing at The Omens dances, they had a hell of a band.
JF: How big was the group?
JH: The Omens had two tenors, a trombone; they had Terry Wimberley playing piano who I later played in a group with, and Alex on guitar. (Note: This could be why Doug had the concept that Jerry later played lead guitar with The Omens during the period Alex moved to Lake Tahoe).
(Also they had) a drummer, named Pat Prue, a white-haired albino kinda guy who was phenomenal. Pat (later) died of cancer. They had a phenomenal band, it was fantastic. They had this thing called "The Bug" that they did. They jumped all over the stage pretending they had this bug in their hand.
JF: I remember that. That was a pretty popular thing back then.
JH: Yeah
JF: I think I was in the 8th grade when I saw "The Bug" for the first time and I thought "what is that guy doing?"
JH: Yeah, well a lot of bands spun off from that. That's where I'd seen Alex, in fact he was called "Butch" at that time - "Butch" Snouffer.

"Butch" as he was known in those days was with The Omens for three to four years, as he recalls, 1958 (or 1959) to 1962. There seems to be an inconsistency in the interviews at to the time The Omens existed: Alex seems to remember the band starting about the same time as The Blackouts, whereas Doug and Jerry both recall The Omens "forming from the ashes of The Blackouts." This could account for why Doug recalls Terry Wimberly in The Blackouts and Alex recalls him as starting The Omens. Almost all interviews suggest the date for the origin of The Omens as being late 1958 or early 1959 agreed upon as the time of the origin of The Omens, except for Jim Sherwood who says this:

Jim Sherwood: The Blackouts broke up in '55. I joined them (The Omens) in '56, when they started.

Jim's version has Frank leaving town due to the fact that his dad was a teacher and they moved to Ontario, which is near Cucamonga, which makes perfect sense, since Mortensen recalls seeing him play with the High School dance band about this same time. The Blackouts, according to Sherwood, broke up in late '55 or early '56 because of this. Yet Frank did come up later while operating Studio Z and play dances with the "regrouped" Blackouts. One of the spots was the Village Inn in Sun Village, which allegedly burned down in the '70s. Frank graduated from AV High School in 1958.

Jim Sherwood: When The Omens were playing Frank would get some of the guys together and they would come back up as, The Blackouts. The black guys that were in the band were still living out in the village. Frank would just come to town and we would do a Battle of the Bands. Basically, the band was disbanded (in '55-'56) because when Frank left, they closed it up. You didn't see a lot of "The Blacks" after that.

Zappa basically says that he got a gig at the Village Inn and made $14 a week playing, which, although going much farther than it would today, did little to support the studio.

John French: So you're listening to The Blackouts at this time. What year was that?
Doug Moon: Late 1958 I think. So ... that's how I got connected up with these guys, then from there, after The Blackouts dissolved, The Omens were born, out of what was left of that - and that was the big band. I started to hang out with those guys. Pat Prue was the drummer in The Omens. Johnny Franklin was in that band too.

Sherwood Goes To Tahoe/1961
Anxious to leave Lancaster, Jim Sherwood moved to Lake Tahoe with a friend named Bill Hunter. Their plans had first included Las Vegas where Bill's father lived. The young Hunter apparently "flipped out one night" according to Jim, and had a disagreement with his father which motivated them to make a quick exit to Lake Tahoe.
All things must come to an end, as the inevitable demise of The Omens came in about 1962.

End Of The Omens/1962

Alex Snouffer: One thing led to another, after about four years with The Omens ... we all went our separate ways, and consequently, everything busted up and I just kicked around. I went and worked in Tahoe for a couple years and then came back into town and that's when I started Beefheart.
John French: ... How long were The Omens together, and what years?
AS: Hah! '58 or 9 through '62.
JF: That's when you were in them, but didn't they keep going after you left?
AS: Nah. Things just sort of went as things do, guys were getting married and all that, they had other responsibilities besides partying, know what I mean? It was basically a party-gang-band.

John Meets Doug/1962
Somewhere around this period, Doug took a job at North American Aircraft where my father worked. Their common interest in music spanned the generation gap and they became friends.

They soon discovered that they had other interests in common such as electronics and recording. My father mentioned to Doug that his son played drums.

John French: Do you remember coming to my house when I was just a kid?
Doug Moon: Yeah, you had your room in the back there.
JF: At the time, I didn't have a snare drum, I had three toms, a bass drum, and a high hat and that was it. You wanted me to go to some rehearsal with you because you didn't have a drummer. You came to my house and were standing in my dad's bedroom door talking to him, because he had all those tape recorders and stuff in there and he liked you a lot because he was into electronics and you guys worked together I think, at North American. I just remember you coming over and asking me to go to this jam session, and I was scared, I wouldn't do it. I didn't have a snare drum (a very important piece of equipment) and I thought everybody would think I was a jerk.

Solid Senders/1963
Jerry recalls Snouffer and he playing in smaller groups before Alex left for Tahoe.

Jerry Handley: Later on, I met and as I got older, (Alex and I) played in several bands together ... he and I had some groups that played around the Valley.
John French: Do you remember their names?
JH: Well, The Solid Senders is one that I remember. I can't remember any other ones. He might be able to remember some. We would play out in the Antelope Valley.
JF: Were these smaller bands?
JH: Yeah, there were two guitars, bass, and drums.

Alex recalls this band as being more of a surf band, as surf music was popular at the time.

John French: Didn't you have a band with Jerry before you went to Tahoe called The Solid Senders for a while, and that's kind of where you and Jerry got to know each other?
Alex Snouffer: Oh yeah, that was sort of our "blues/surf band" (laughs) I'm not kidding you.
JF: OK, Yeah! Well, you just about had to play surf music back then to make any money.
AS: Well that was about early '63 or something.
JF: I hope you had a reverb. Cause ya had ta have a reverb to do surf music.
AS: I forget if I did or not, I don't think so.
JF: So, you just played those big empty halls so if you stand in the back of the room, it will sound like Dick Dale.
AS: Yeah, oh yeah, Dick Dale, if you're going to do surf music, then you better "get into it."
JF: So that was back about '63?
AS: It only lasted about six months, then I took off.

Doug Moon recalls the band Solid Senders also:

Doug Moon: Yeah, that was another thing that Jerry and Alex I had going. There was an old R&B tune and it had a line in it "she was a real solid sender" I think it was a Little Richard tune. So they took that little catch phrase. I don't know what happened with the name The Omens, I think they had to retire that name. For lack of another name, they came up with that.
JF: So, was that an offshoot of The Omens? I believe some of the horn players were in that band.

DM: It may be that The Omens and The Solid Senders existed at the same time, and that's why they needed another name.

The Solid Senders probably existed after the demise of The Omens, since Alex remembers breaking up in 1962, and The Solid Senders starting in 1963. Handley recalls more of the Solid Senders and playing in Sun Village, a place Zappa would later immortalize in the song *Village Of The Sun*.

Jerry Handley: We had some horns too then. There was tenor and trombone. Some of the old guys from The Omens would come in and out. In fact, we'd go out to Sun Village. We played out there. Zappa had been out there and played a few times also.
John French: Now Sun Village was a predominately black area near Littlerock, right?
JH: Right. If you wanted to play blues, you could go out there. If you had a few black guys in your group, they'd let you in, you know.
JF: Ever any trouble out there, was it scary?
JH: No, we weren't worried about it at the time. They would have scuffles in the bar but they would take care of them right away, and it didn't really interfere with the band. ... They were just little nightclubs out there. Frank used to play out there quite a bit. I went out and recorded him one time. Wish I had THAT recording. Had it on a Norelco reel-to-reel tape.
JF: That was before they decided to make electric razors — which resemble small reel to reels.

Growing Interests: Art Tripp
Art Tripp, separated by several thousand miles is having a quite different musical experience.

Art Tripp: In any rate I got much more interested in drumming, and I started getting interested in percussion. To make a long story short, I started studying with Stanley Leonard, who was a timpanist with the Pittsburgh Symphony. That's when I started getting interested in the various percussion instruments. I started playing xylophone and all the little oddball instruments. So in my fourth year in high school, I asked Stanley if he thought – if it would be worth my while to go to music school and try to pursue it as a career. He said he thought I should, with some work and some luck I could make it. So I auditioned for a few schools and I ended up at – I got turned down at Eastman and also at Oberland because I didn't know anything about harmony and theory all these other people were way ahead of me, so ... the Cincinnati College Conservatory of Music accepted me and so I started out there in '62. About my second year, I started playing "extra" with the Cincinnati Symphony. Then the year after that, I started playing a lot. I wasn't a contract player, I was just a hired extra, but I played just about every week.

Snouffer In Tahoe
Alex joined Bill Hunter and Jim Sherwood in Lake Tahoe, in a cabin they were sharing with a Native American described only as "an Indian kid." Jim and Bill quickly hired on with a highway construction crew but Bill was almost immediately fired for involuntary supervisory outbursts.

Jim Sherwood: But I think within the first week he was telling some guys how to blow up rocks or something and they fired him. (Laughs).

On their way home from bowling one evening, Jim spied Bill's crumpled car in front of the emergency room at the local hospital. There had been a party at the house and Jim suspected trouble. He returned to the cabin to find the front door kicked wide open and no-one in sight. Going back to the emergency center, he found a trail of blood leading to Bill's car, in which was a huge pool of blood. After an inquiry at the police station, it was learned that in an attempt to persuade some dedicated partygoers that the party was over a fight had ensued. They had at first left peacefully, later changing their minds and kicking the door in. Bill, being more than a bit impulsive, grabbed a butcher knife, eventually stabbing one of the intruders in the chest. The police released Bill, but because of the incident they strongly persuaded Alex, Bill and Jim to all leave town.

Jim Sherwood: The cops had Bill and Alex down at the station. They explained what happened and they let 'em go, but they told us to get our ass off the mountain or we wouldn't see daylight for a long time. We took off. That's kind of when I got away from everybody.
John French: Do you remember what Alex was doing when he was up there? He said he was working as a key man for slots.
JS: That was later on. I don't know if he was in Tahoe or Vegas. I think he went to Vegas. That's where he met his wife. Her dad was the slot manager there and he was working slots. I saw Alex later on and that's the story he told me.

Snouffer and Sherwood also had a disagreement over a mutual lady friend, which ended in them parting company on less than tranquil terms. According to Sherwood, this was in 1962 – another conflicting date. The composite of information indicates that this was probably closer to late 1963 or early 1964.

Jim then went to visit Frank who was now living in Ontario, near a little town named Cucamonga.

CHAPTER THREE:
THE ROAD TO CUCAMONGA

Don blowing harmonica in Grannie Annie's house 1965. Courtesy of Doug Moon.

Moon In San Jose/Snouffer In Tahoe

Doug Moon and Alex Snouffer both temporarily left Lancaster. When Moon was a senior in High School, he had started experimenting on guitar in spite of the fact that he didn't own an instrument. Although discouraged at not being able to practice, he continued to get pointers from guitar players he met. Immediately upon him graduating from High School, the family entered into a transitional period when his recently unemployed father took a job in Texas. This left Doug with two major options: join the Navy with his best friend, or move to Texas with the family. The senior Moon's new job was the reconstruction of a historical site in Poledos, Texas. The family lived in nearby Temple, Texas - which Doug found less than inspiring. In order to escape the stark environment, he first visited relatives in New York and Chicago, finally winding up in San Jose, California, where he attended college to pursue his electronics career. In his apartment compound lived an acoustic guitarist who befriended him and here is where the figurative hook was set and Moon's musical interest began to develop.

Doug Moon: He did a bunch of Johnny Cash stuff and I got turned on to Cash. I am a big fan of his to this day. I remember learning a couple of his tunes, like Folsom Prison Blues and I Walk The Line. It was easy to play and he showed me some chords. I didn't have a guitar so I borrowed one.

It is probable that Doug left town with his family in 1961. Soon hereafter Alex left town along with the younger Handley. Snouffer doesn't really recall any real reason for going.

Alex Snouffer: Nah, it was just ... I don't know, I just wanted to go, so Jerry and I went up there. He was just up there for a couple of days and then he took the bus home. He just wanted to get away for a few days, you know get out from beneath his "mommy's thumb." We ran into an old friend of mine and raised hell for a couple of days. Then we put Jerry on a bus.

Although Handley had gone up to Tahoe with Alex, he came back shortly after a couple of weeks to take care of some business in Lancaster. It was an outstanding traffic ticket. It seems that the justice system in Los Angeles County takes parking tickets rather seriously, so anything that falls under the label "outstanding", becomes an offense just shy of warranting capital punishment. If caught, the person is usually handcuffed and immediately taken to jail.

I once had a musician friend who, as he was handcuffed and being taken to jail for outstanding parking tickets, managed to talk the Sheriff's deputies into swinging past my house. He asked me to pick up his musical equipment – worth a couple thousand dollars – that he was forced by the deputies to leave *unlocked* in his car in a bad neighborhood. Come to think of it, it was *my neighborhood*.

Back to Snouffer, who decided to stay in Tahoe for a time and found work in a casino.

Alex Snouffer: I was a key man for the slot department. In other words, I was a "goodwill ambassador". If they had trouble with the machines, with payoffs, or anything like that, I'd be present when the chick paid off their jackpots.

Moon Returns To The Desert

After one semester in San Jose, times were getting a little lean and Doug's parents had moved back to Lancaster in late '61 or early '62. Doug eventually went back to live with them. Upon returning, he began meeting friends who played guitar. It wasn't long after this that Moon bought his own inexpensive guitar, a Harmony or Kay.

Zappa Still Connected

Doug Moon: Frank was coming up once in a while and doing his crazy stuff and making his home movies. You know the kind of stuff that I'm talking about.
John French: I think I do, yeah.
DM: Pretty weird stuff, the kind of stuff that he eventually went to jail for. So, he was doing his thing and Don was around, but he hadn't really gotten connected yet.

After reading Frank's account of his alleged pornography offense, which was after this interview was taped, I was surprised at the contrast between the reality and the rumors I heard upon entering the band. When I first joined the Magic Band, Don especially seemed quite willing to expound upon his complete disgust with Frank concerning the alleged porno film production. Of course *The Real Frank Zappa Book* makes it clear that all Frank made was a little audio tape (sound only, non-techs) of himself and a girl bouncing up and down on a bed making suggestive sounds. This he sold to a man for one hundred well-needed dollars who turned out to be a sleazy undercover cop in Cucamonga, California who had requested such a tape. It was entrapment, pure and simple. The girl, by the way, was homeless, and Frank was trying to help her.

During *Trout Mask* rehearsals, probably early 1969, while visiting Zappa's basement/studio, he pulled out a 3x5 card and showed it to the guitarists, Bill and Jeff. Zappa explained he had worked these out while he was in jail. It was a series of alternate slack-key guitar tunings. Frank was always busy and had even made the best and most positive use of his jail time.

Back to the timeframe, it was during this period that Frank was described as "coming up" to the desert to do the Blackouts shows. The fact that Frank was still "coming up" suggests that he had moved. This was probably during the period when he was either living in Alta Loma or Rancho Cucamonga – the second is coincidentally the home of the oldest winery in California. The two locations are within a few miles of each other.

Frank Tries College

Frank had tried a semester of Junior College in Lancaster, and another in Alta Loma for the express purpose, according to him, of meeting girls. He eventually met and married his first wife, Kay Sherman, during this period. His attempts at conventional employment included working as a silk-screen artist, encyclopedia salesman, and finally at Tommy Sand's Club Sahara in San Bernardino, as a lounge musician.

Soon, he was connected with Pal Recording Studio in Rancho Cucamonga at 8040 Archibald Avenue. Paul Buff, an ex-marine, had built his own studio.

"He didn't have a mixing console, so he built one – out of an old 1940s vanity. He removed the mirror and, right in the middle, where the cosmetics would have gone, installed a metal plate with Boris Karloff knobs on it." [13]

It is always funny to note Frank's seemingly boyish explanations of events – especially when using old monster movie images like this. I enjoyed his humor.

Frank apparently worked with Paul for a time, even collaborating from time to time. He eventually made a bit of money from a film score and assumed the lease on the studio when Buff moved to Hollywood to design and build the Original Sound studio on Sunset. The very same studio where a demo tape would someday be produced by Gary Marker for an album eventually entitled *Safe As Milk*.

[13] The Real Frank Zappa Book, Frank Zappa, Simon and Schuster, 1989 pp42.

A little later as Frank's marriage was breaking up, he moved into the aforementioned studio and officially renamed it Studio Z. He told me in 1969 during the "anthropological field recordings" for *Trout Mask Replica* that the double-entendre name was not only his last initial, but it inferred "the last real studio." He supported himself by gigging at the Village Inn, in Sun Village, 80 miles away in the Antelope Valley.

Jim Sherwood: I lived with Frank and his wife; I stayed there in their house for a while. Then he had the studio, so Frank and I were going over and playing around at the studio. Then they went through the divorce, so Frank and I actually moved INTO the studio, which was really cool.

About this time comes the story of the third meeting between Mortensen and Zappa, and the first meeting between Don and Vic. Twenty miles or so northwest of Rancho Cucamonga was located Claremont. The main drag was the old Route 66, which had several stone roadhouses built by the road crews with stones found while clearing the fields for the highway.

Vic Mortensen entered one of these roadhouses and, while consuming an order of beer and pizza, became acquainted with the owner. The place had a couple of pool tables and a small stage, which caught Mortensen's attention. He inquired of "old Chet," the owner, and eventually struck a deal to bring in musicians to jam on weekends in return for free beer and pizza. It seemed like a win/win situation, and eventually Mortensen became a regular on weekends, bringing with him various musicians who would mostly play surf music for a biker clientele, who "weren't too choosy about repertoire."

Vic had formerly played music with a surf band called Frank Anthony and the Stingrays whose only hit, *Surf Bunny*, featured sparse lyrics about the measurements of the "bunny" herself.

Vic Mortensen: When I first started playing drums, I had no interest in playing vocals. In other words, when I wanted to play, even when I was "woodshedding," as a kid, I would buy instrumental records. You know - all of the old Dixieland stuff, all of the Benny Goodman stuff - and play along to the MUSIC, I always considered vocalists to be "frivolous." (ha) but, then again, that's just a drummer's perspective on things.

Meanwhile, Vic Mortensen was about to see Frank Zappa for the third time. Vic had heard that Frank was getting involved with a studio and had a few connections. He had wanted to contact Frank. One weekend, during Vic's normal roadhouse gig, Frank walked in with his friend Don Vliet:

Mortensen At The Roadhouse 1963-4

Vic Mortensen: The next time I saw Frank Zappa after having seen him on those couple of occasions ... he walked in (to the roadhouse) and he had Don with him. I had been trying to get a hold of Frank because I had heard he was starting to do some stuff, but I had never heard him play the guitar. By this time I would have been maybe a Junior in college - twenty one-ish, twenty-two-ish. (Note: this seems to set the year at 1963 or '64)

Vic didn't seem too impressed with leather-jacketed long-haired Van Vliet, who described his activities as "film-making."

Vic Mortensen: ... and Don was still doing that thing about how he had been working on a movie and all that business.

In truth, he was only considering being a part of Frank's *Captain Beefheart vs. the Grunt People*, which was still being written. Vliet was probably selling shoes at Kinney's for a living or perhaps working at the local aircraft factory, North American Aviation. In analogy, the impression was akin to a Hollywood waitress describing herself as "an actress."

Frank And Don At The Roadhouse

Vic Mortensen: I still recognized Frank; He was always different. I don't remember him as being a freak. I just remember Frank, because he was FRANK! He didn't look like anybody else.

Frank and Don had both started growing their hair long, although Frank's was longer than Don's. Don was wearing a black leather coat.

Vic Mortensen: I recognized Frank I said, "Are you Frank?" and we shook hands. He said, "Here's my friend Don." The only thing about that night that is really of any interest is that we packed up my drums, got on (Route) 66, headed east, and went on out to Studio Z. That night, we set up my drums in Studio Z, in Cucamonga, which was just a wide spot on the road in those days.
John French: So, what did you do?
VM: We boogied around, he showed me the studio and that kind of thing, and then we started ... I don't think we ... we may have played that night. He could have played me some of his stuff; he had all kinds of stuff in there.

Vic found a temporary niche for himself, as Frank was learning overdubbing and mastering the art of multi-track recording. Don was still living with his parents in the Antelope Valley during this period. Don recalled once that Frank used to play through a cheap tape recorder pre-amplifier in order to obtain a distorted guitar effect, which was later accomplished through the use of "fuzztones." Van Vliet stated often during my early tenure that Frank was "years ahead of his time."

The First Fuzztone?

Johnny Franklin: He was so far ahead of most people that I know. Some of the things that he was trying to do at that time I thought was kinda crazy, you know, but then I found years later that some of the sounds and some of the riffs and things that he was doing back then ... they all started doing. Now I can remember - shows how weird things happen, history probably does not record this anywhere, but I think it was in ... (whistles) '64 I believe it was. We were doing a gig in The Village Inn – matter of fact that's one of the places he talks about in Village Of The Sun – through his amplifier. I mean, the speaker went out on the job. I kept on playing, like "We gonna MAKE this gig." He said, "Johnny, I like that sound!" Well, me being in the electrical and electronic world – I was kinda like the McGyver-type on the side if there was an electrical problem at a gig I was in, well, that was my thing. I said, "Well, you do, huh?" To me, it just sounded like ... broken speakers ... OK? But there was something about it that he liked. He said, "Do you think there's something you can do to emulate this sound?" I started thinking ... yeah I think so." Well, I figured it out. It was to over-modulate the input signal with a pre-amp that would over-modulate it and it would get it to distort like that. Now, this was a very crude first attempt at something like that. I took some scrap parts from an old phono player. Got the amplifier section out of it and stuff like this. I had this aluminum box I got at Radio Shack. It had knobs and buttons and doodads 'n'stuff all over

it. It tended to work, but at that time, it had an AC hum in it. I didn't know how to get that AC hum out. But, to my knowledge, that's the first time that I'd ever heard of anybody purposely using what we call a fuzz box.
Pete Lovio: I heard about that, Fender or somebody got hold of it to figure out how he got this sound. Johnny's the one that really invented it, I would think - because of a blown-out speaker - to get that tone.
John French: Too bad he didn't get a patent on that.
PL: That's what I was telling him.
Wally Salazar: You don't think of that.
JF: Yeah, all you're thinking about is "I wanna get this sound."
PL: It was a way of life.

Moon's Progress
     Back in the Antelope Valley, Doug Moon was now starting to seriously study guitar. After meeting up with Jerry Handley, his interest had increased and he had begun playing a little in jams and with groups. His interest in the blues was sparking and he was playing guitar and harmonica together more and more.

Doug Moon: So by the time the band started up, I had a couple of years of guitar experience.

     Doug took lessons from a local guitar instructor named Bill Stewart. Stewart had formed his own band years earlier and played lounge acts in Las Vegas. After retiring from the lounge circuit, he had co-founded a retail business, Lancaster Music with former big band drummer Ronny Gaye. They both instructed at the store. Bill's small instruction room had one wall filled with photographs of his students, and Doug Moon's picture was, for a time, displayed on the white acoustic-tiled wall.

Doug Moon: I took lessons from Bill Stewart and just started hanging out with everybody that was a musician, going to clubs and listening to people like Johnny Trombatore and just trying to pick up licks here and there. I learned a lot more from watching other guitar players and picking their brain. "How'd you do that?" and "Show me those chords." I used to go over to Alex's house and say, "Hey Alex, would you show me how to play such-and-such a lick?" I just started picking everybody's brain, you know. Just robbing everybody for everything they knew, putting it all together to form my own guitar style - (laughs) which I'm still working on.

     Aside from Stewart's instruction and influence, which fit more into theory and learning standards, most of the guitarists Doug was influenced by were R&B and blues players. Johnny Trombatore was one such guitarist who Doug heard in a local club, which often featured musical entertainment imported from the Los Angeles area. Trombatore was in a group called The Mystics - a spinoff band from the Champs (famous for the instrumental hit *Tequila*.) The Mystics consisted of Trombatore, along with drummer Dash Crofts and sax player Jimmy Seals who later formed the group Seals and Crofts.

Doug Moon: My first recollection of him (Trombatore) was playing in a club. He was just around town. I just remember him playing here locally, doing club gigs. I can only remember one place called the Cuckoo Club. It was over there on Yucca. I wasn't even 21 so I had to sneak in. I was so impressed with (Trombatore's) guitar playing.

Since The Mystics consisted of guitar, bass, drums and sax, much of the harmonic burden pertaining to chordal structure was placed upon Johnny's shoulders. I once sat in a club for several hours and listened to a performance of the band. Johnny's solos consisted of chords and solo improvisations, interspersed in such a seemless manner that it was almost as if two guitarists were playing. The band also had great four part vocal harmony and played mostly covers of other artists, but also had quite a repertoire of their own original material. Their sound was similar to a group called The Knickerbockers, who were a club band in Hollywood who had one hit in the mid-sixties entitled *Lies*. Probably the only reason the song got airplay was because the band sounded eerily like the Beatles.

The performance of original material by a club band in those days was discouraged, however. The meat market mentality that existed (and still does today in a more devolved form) states: "people won't dance to a song unless they've heard it on the radio." So club groups were almost always strictly confined to performing covers of Top 40 radio hits, otherwise they didn't play at all.

Sherwood On Studio Z

John French: So, you were living in the studio.
Jim Sherwood: Yeah. That's when we did a lot of the music and Frank would invite the Harley (biker) group over. We would invite the Harley groups over and Frank would show a lot of the videos that we were doing. It was actually 16 mm movies. And we were playing the soundtracks that Frank made. We were trying to get their reaction. Frank was actually writing a whole bunch of material that he was going to take to the psych department at the College there.
JF: What was the context of the films?
JS: It was just weird stuff that Frank actually used in Uncle Meat. (He'd film us) driving up the highway and you'd see all the telephone poles going by and there was an overlay of a fair in the background with a Ferris wheel going around and lights flashing. It was just a lot of overlay stuff that Frank was playing around with.

Don Visits 'Z'

Don Vliet began to come down to Studio Z and experiment with Frank, the result of which was the formation of a musical group christened The Soots, which probably never performed. A few recordings that exist from that time include *Metal Man Has Won His Wings, Cheryl's Canon*, and a Howlin' Wolf-esque version of *Slippin' And Slidin'*. Zappa was hopeful that some of these could be released. He was told emphatically that it would be impossible because, amusingly enough, "the guitar was distorted."

There were other projects, one on which I believe I recognized Mortensen's drumming called *Teenage Maltshop*. Zappa's compositional style was already beginning to be recognizable in the piano-dominated introductory section before Captain Beefheart introduces himself as a "magic man" in a carnival hawker/WC Fields' style, with no musical accompaniment.

In *Metal Man Has Won His Wings* the music immediately bursts forth, a music surprisingly reminiscent of the early Magic Band. Zappa was obviously making headway in his production attempts. The young Vliet's repetitive Wolf-esque ramblings are buried in the mix. The song is brought to a halt with a typical blues kick - something Zappa may have learned while playing at Tommy Sands' club.

Ned The Mumbler almost seems autobiographical Zappa, with its subject of a guy feeling like an outcast in the high school with "*no teenage girl to call my name.*" Ned's daddy worked for the government, and so he had to change schools. In a voice reminiscent of *The Old Fart* recitation from *Trout Mask Replica*, Don's vocal, announcer-style knifes through a musical pause, *"Boldly, he steps through the door."* Frank makes a couple of comments about teenage girls going for football players, and Don (who claims to have played football) interjects, *"Ned's marvelous. He's not nearly as marvelous as I am, of course, but he's kind of a teenage Lone Ranger."*

Since this is my first hearing of this piece I am struck that possibly herein seems to lie the true basis of the Zappa/Beefheart relationship/rivalry as later on witnessed by myself and others who knew Don.

Don mentioned quite often that he played football in high school. It is also apparent that Frank had quite a dislike of football players in general, often amusingly referring to High School lettermen as "The White Horror."

John French: Don said he played football in high school.
Wally Salazar: No!
Pete Lovio: What?
WS: No!
JF: He said he was on the football team.
PL: Oh, you gotta be kiddin'. That guy was so... as far as I know...
WS: If he didn't want to get his shoes messed up, or was afraid of getting dirt on his clothes and all, he was not a football player.
PL: I don't think he was coordinated enough to play sports. He hated P.E. when he had to go.

Dennis Ling reinforced the squeaky-clean high school image Don projected:

Dennis Ling: In high school, his uncle (The Colonel) used to leave him his sport coats. Don was dressed meticulously in high school in sport coats with neatly-coiffed hair.

Tiger Roach starts off as a surf tune until the second section recalls an evolved sense of the same adolescent bathroom humor displayed in Lost In A Whirlpool. Resplendent with flatulance (noises a rather resentful Mortensen claims to have created though never receiving credit) and hawking-loogie effects, it is in keeping with the kind of gross humor Zappa used to contrast and frame his more serious moments. Don uses the same kind of disconnected image portrayal and vocal phrasing as in *Metal Man*. He suddenly emits a similar vocal texture as is later utilized in *Big Joan* during his scatting sessions. It is interesting to speculate on what would have happened had these two continued to collaborate.

Frank had also began writing a screenplay called *Captain Beefheart vs. the Grunt People* seemingly based in part upon Don's relationship with his parents. This line of thinking seems to be confirmed by the following statement by Mortensen who claims the original title was different.

Vic Mortensen: See, he (Zappa) told me he was working on a screenplay called Captain Beefheart and His Girlfriend Sue. Sue was Don's mother. Then there was something about "grunt people." But the first thing he told me about was Captain Beefheart and his Girlfriend Sue. Now this is before I had even met Sue.

One night in the Desert, Doug Moon and Don Vliet crossed paths.

Doug Connects With Don ...

Doug Moon: I remember I ran into Don. This was my first recollection of getting together with Don. Of course, I knew him from High School and a few times that we had just gotten together and BS'd and stuff. It was in one of the drive-ins, it was over on Avenue I ... Foster's Freeze or Tasti Delite. Something like that. You know Cokes and hamburgers, things like that.

This is not the "famed" drive-in that appeared on the cover of *Bongo Fury*. That was Foster's Freeze on Sierra Highway (right next to Bubi Burgers). This drive-in was about two miles away. It had a big tall beam on the roof lined with lightbulbs that went on sequentially from bottom to top, eventually ending in a stupendous finale: the lighting of a giant ice cream cone sitting on the very top end of the erect beam. Its symbolism probably stirred hope in the pubescent males who frequented the drive-in with their angora-sweatered dates.

John French: So it was a hangout.
Doug Moon: Yeah, it was a drive-in carhop thing. Real popular place, and the car clubs hung out there. At that time I was in a car club too. I had a '55 Chevy and I was into that whole thing. I was like Richie in Happy Days.

It was in this atmosphere that Don and Doug rekindled their friendship.

Doug Moon: So anyway, I ran into Don - I'm not sure if he had Laurie with him - and we started to talk. The conversation ended up on music. I was telling him about what I was into and what I was doing and he was very interested. He liked the blues and he knew about Jimmy Reed, and really liked that style of music.
John French: Did he play harmonica?
Doug Moon: No, at the time, I don't think he played harmonica. If he did, he didn't play very well yet. So, as a result of this meeting, we got together. I jammed around a little bit and he said, "Hey, I want you to go down to Frank's with me." He started telling me about Frank's studio (Studio Z). We went down to Frank's and I jammed on the guitar and did my guitar and harmonica thing, and Don sang. I remember Don was singing along with this stuff and Frank was doing whatever, maybe recording or playing along too. Don and I started to go down to Frank's on a regular basis ... w sat in on some of Frank's club gigs and played a few tunes.
John French: So, now you were playing in front of people. You are a participant instead of an observer.
Doug Moon: Yeah, that was it basically, although I had sat in a few other times with Jerry in a couple clubs.

Death March At Studio Z

Jerry Handley: Yeah I'd been down there. We did a recording in (Frank's) studio of the Death March, rock'n'roll style. I'd recorded down there; I don't remember who all was in the band as a matter of fact. It was with horns, I think it was with Alex. One of our bands with all of the horns in it did the Death March down in Frank's studio.
John French: That's funny, a rock version.
JH: A rock version of the Death March, everyone should have one. It was my first experience recording.

Wally Salazar: Right (after Frank) was out of high school, he moved down (to Cucamonga), and that's when he had that record company ...
Pete Lovio: Z Studio
WS: Yeah. I remember we went down there one time.

PL: We went down there and recorded.

JF: Jerry Handley said you did a version of the Death March. He said The Omens did a version of the Death March.

WS: Yes, we did, he's right (laughter). You know, sometimes someone would just do something and somebody else would pick it up and then we'd all get involved. That's the way it was.

Johnny Franklin: What I'm trying to figure out, now, I've never obtained the Zappa Mystery Disc. I heard a little bit of it on the internet, but I think he was recording things when we were just in there clowning around and practicing basically. That's when I met that lady, her name was Lana Cantrell. She was from, Sydney (Australia), I think it was. She was a big-time vocalist.

JF: She was a nice-looking lady, too.

Franklin: As I can recall, she was nice-looking (laughter).

JF: What did Frank have down there, was it elaborate, or was it just sort of thrown together.

Jerry Handley: Basically like an old store type of thing.

Doug Moon: It was crude, but it was comfortable. I remember that. It was just the kind of place where you could party all night long, and make a recording session out of it. So that's what happened ... just before Alex got back, Frank started to get together with Don.

JF: You'd been hanging out at the studio, and Don was coming down there. What was going on?

Vic Mortensen: What was happening is that Zappa and I would stay there. I didn't stay there every night of the week, but sometimes I would stay there two or three nights of the week.

JF: What kind of equipment did he have?

VM: At that time, in terms of what, musical equipment?

JF: Recording equipment.

VM: He had a five track Ampex – which everybody says "five track? What's a five-track?" This was the one that was built by Paul Buff. I'm sure there's already enough stuff in print about their relationship, but at this time, Paul was never around, and Frank was running the studio. He had the five-track Ampex with multiple recording heads and the whole business. He actually is the first guy I ever saw "play a studio." Even by this time, I had recorded with various puker surf groups. We'd go out to this guy's studio in Pasadena and it would be a converted garage, right? And the guy would have maybe a four-track, if that. Maybe even a two-track. Here was Frank working with this stuff. Usually what would happen is he might lay down a guitar track and I'd lay down a rhythm track. Sometimes we had a bass man, sometimes we didn't. Sometimes he (Frank) would pick the bass, whatever. I would go to sleep on the old day-bed out there and he would go back into the studio, plug directly into the board, and lay down maybe "eighteen" (in an exaggerated voice) more guitar tracks. He would just go on and on and then he would come out and wake me and say, "Hey, listen to this, I want you to add something here." He had a grand piano in there, and I actually remember him sitting at the piano, fingering the chords, while I played on the strings with timpani mallets.

JF: So Zappa had a lot of energy. He was one of these guys that would stay up all night.

VM: He lived on coffee.

JF: That's what I saw when I was down working with him in the studio. (Years later ... 1975-6)

VM: We had a twenty-four cup coffee maker down there.

So, let the scribes record that Studio Z's equipment included a twenty-four cup coffee maker.

John French: I'm curious about one thing. Maybe you can set me straight on this. Zappa had all this equipment in the studio, you know, a five track Ampex a was pretty good-sized machine for those days.

Vic Mortensen: *Well, it was still only about the size ... well, go ahead, I think I know what you're saying.*

JF: *Well, I'm saying, where did he get the money to buy this if he didn't have money for food?*

VM: *I don't know where he got his money. There is something ... I remember reading about his dealings with Paul Buff. Apparently, Paul Buff - in one thing I've read on Frank and I don't know this to be true because it happened before I got there - apparently, Buff went on to build that ten-track for Art Laboe, leaving Frank with the studio. As a matter of fact, it was said that Frank was in the studio before he even started having to pay rent on it, because Paul was taken elsewhere and would rather have had somebody in there. I think Frank got in there about 18 months before his regular lease was to start; my understanding was that Paul just sort of let him hang out there. He was changing the whole deal. By the time I got into that studio he'd already built the stage sets inside it. Bizarre sets.*

JF: *For what movie?*

VM: *I don't know whether it was going to be for one of the Beefheart things. He was just building really bizarre stuff, and then I think he wanted to do some kind of space movie. I mean, there was a room built within a room.*

JF: *Let me ask then, let's go on to the formation of Captain Beefheart And His Magic Band.*

VM: *OK. Now I met the guys ... these were the guys from Lancaster, like I say, Frank and I would stay there most of the week. And then the guys would come down on the weekend. He and Doug and Alex would come down from Lancaster and we would jam. Sometimes, Don would come alone, sometimes the guys would come, maybe one would come. I don't know I don't remember the schedule.*

JF: *You didn't mention Jerry, was Jerry not in the picture at this time?*

VM: *Ahh ... I don't think I remember Jerry.*

JF: *Jerry mentioned something about recording at Zappa's studio and doing a rock version of the funeral dirge.*

VM: *Then, he may have been there. I don't explicitly remember Doug, Jerry, or Alex, although I am sure they were all there. See, there were a lot of people coming in and out of there on some occasions - all kinds of people playing. Like I mentioned that drum set, if I could remember that guy's name, he also played the drum set we were talking about. I think he went on to become the original drummer for Linda Ronstadt. I can't remember his name. Cats like that were coming in and out all the time. Remember that I told you I had a drum set that been played by me, by Frank, by Jimmy Carl Black, and by you.*

JF: *YOUR original drum set?*

VM: *My original drumset and we've already accounted for all those people plus ...*

JF: *It's a Ludwig?*

VM: *LUDVIG!! (German pronunciation) Cocktail set.*

JF: *The toms are 12 and 14 right?*

VM: *Right.*

JF: *And the bass drum's 20.*

VM: *Right. And then I have a chrome snare.*

JF: *Yeah, OK, that's the set I remember you having.*

VM: *Right, OK.*

JF: *And it was marine pearl.*

VM: *Right, boy, you have a good memory.*

JF: *Yeah, well I played them.*

VM: *Well I don't remember every drumset I've played on. That's for damned sure.*

JF: *Well, I haven't seen them since I was sixteen, but I took a shot at it.* (Note: I was requested to get information on equipment by some of the fans via email, so I left this little detail just for you who asked. Also, I think it important to establish that though I may be an old fart, my memory is fairly intact. Here's proof I'm not making all this stuff up – just some of it.)

And again:

Doug Moon: So, as a result of this meeting, we (Don and he) got together, I jammed around a little bit and he said, "Hey, I want you to go down to Frank's with me."

Zappa spoke of intimate details of their teen years spent together. In lieu of the facts, it doesn't seem probable that Don had a "memory lapse," due to the fact that he had an amazingly acute memory, especially for people he met, as reinforced by this later Mojo article quote:

"And then (it might have been the drinks) mentioned the nickname of a close friend of mine whom he'd encountered for a brief moment backstage in Miami three years earlier and couldn't possibly have remembered." [14]

My personal recollection is that on numerous occasions, Van Vliet seemed able to remember people he'd briefly met months or even years earlier, and recall details of the meeting. So, it seems that the Beefheart quote above was an inarticulate attempt to disassociate himself from Zappa at a later point in time (early seventies), when their relationship was anything but cordial. This is the context in which early band members found themselves dealing with "the boy who cried wolf" syndrome. It seemed that much of what the early Vliet and later Van Vliet said needed to be taken with a grain of salt. The later Van Vliet would also claim among other things that he was never influenced vocally by Howlin' Wolf.

Snouffer In Tahoe

Summertime in Lake Tahoe is a very busy time. In such a beautiful setting, adding legalized gambling and great entertainment results in a triple hit which draws huge crowds of tourists and vacationers every summer. In the early sixties, Alex knew of a man (name unknown) who had a band up in the area. His specialty was to rent the American Legion Hall in Tahoe and have dances five nights a week. His dances were always packed.

Alex was beginning to tire of life as a key man in Lake Tahoe and was again desiring to play music. Snouffer had noted that the guitarist for the above-mentioned band was leaving. He had suggested that the bandleader give him a chance to audition, but the man, not taking Alex seriously, had just laughed. The leader had made a low-budget album of his group, which basically did cover tunes, to sell at the door after the dances. Alex had a copy of the album and had learned all the songs from beginning to end. One afternoon as the band was rehearsing, he requested a chance to sit in.

Alex Snouffer: So when I started playing, he said, "Whoa, who be this?" His other guitar man left, and I knew that was happening, so I just stepped in one night, no rehearsal or nothing, and went for it. So after he closed up (in Tahoe) that summer, we went over to Redwood City and played there for a month and then, I just went one way and he went the other.

All the while, Doug, Don, Jerry, Frank, and Vic were getting acquainted in southern California by experimenting, jamming, and recording ideas. Doug says that they spent months experimenting. Depending on the definition of "they." Does this mean Jerry, Don, PG, and Doug, prior to Alex's

[14] Mojo, Issue 2, December, 1993, Heart & Soul; Captain Beefheart, David DiMartino, pp90.

return? Alex indicates in the above section of interview that he was in Lake Tahoe for a "couple of years", which could have been from the beginning of one summer to the end of the following summer – two summers. According to the statement above, after the bandleader closed for the summer, they played one month and Alex left for Lancaster. It seems likely that he returned in approximately late September or early October of 1964. Being a natural-born leader, and just having finished two months of steady performance, he probably recognized the potential in Jerry, Doug, and Don's jamming.

John French: And so that is when you came back down here - to figure out the next move in your life?
Alex Snouffer: Basically,
JF: Then you got in touch with Jerry (Handley)?
AS: Well, yeah, because I hadn't seen him for a couple of years. When I first got back from the Lake (Tahoe) up there, Don was one of the first people I went to see. 'Cause he and I had been pal-ing around together before I left, so I didn't really go over there for any musical thing. Jerry had mentioned to me that he played harp. I thought, "OK," (doubtfully) - you know. (Laughs) I'd heard him play sax a few years before, and I thought, "This oughta be good," you know.

Apparently, Vliet (as he was known then) was not considered to be much of a saxophone player and had been purportedly kicked out of The Omens after a single rehearsal – according to Snouffer. Although Don is credited with having played saxophone in The Omens and The Blackouts, according to various articles, he actually never played sax in The Black-Outs at all, and only a few times in The Omens – after which he was immediately fired. According to all interviewed, Don had no ability to play any thing more than once on the saxophone. This put quite a damper on playing horn lines in unison or harmony with other players. Don would later say that he was kicked out because his playing was "too hip for those Okies."

John French: So, you're saying that Don sang with The Omens for a while and he played sax a little bit?
Pete Lovio: Well, he tried and he came along with us. A couple of times he got on stage with us.
JF: With a sax?
PL: I saw him with an alto sax. He would come in there with an alto sax. Of course, he always had the harmonica.
JF: Could he play? (Referring to the sax).
Wally Salazar/Pete Lovio: (in unison) Aaah, no. (Laughter)
PL: That's why Alex Snouffer would chase him away, cause all he would do was honk while we were practicing.
WS: He was putting out "beep beep" – just making noises with it.
PL: He tried. He wanted to get into the group so bad that he would try anything.
JF: When he came to rehearsals, he was sort of… you were saying… that he would disrupt things?
PL: He wanted to really be in a band so bad; he was (always) there.
WS: It was almost like – I don't want to say, "clown," but he always disrupted, he wouldn't really listen, he was like, on his own little tangent like that. He wouldn't really listen to what we wanted to do. We wanted to have the sounds down good when we were together. But with all his noises going on, the thing is if he going to participate, he's not listening to what was going or what we were saying.
JF: So, he wasn't a team player and you would say that he didn't really much know how to

play and he'd probably never had a lesson.
WS: Right. He made noises and all kinds of squeaky things and (he would) think that was really
nice. "Oh man, hear this, Jimmy?" – and make these weird sounds, you know, and that was it.
JF: He made a whole career out of playing like that. (Laughter)

Snouffer, comparing his former experience with Don on saxophone to that of his rumored harp expertise felt it didn't seem believable, but was pleasantly surprised.

Alex Snouffer: Sure enough, he was (good) ... I would say, far as I am concerned, he's the best
white harp man that I've heard, and probably takes out half the blacks with him. Know what
I mean? Know what I'm saying? I mean, that dude was flat good, man!

Don and Blues Harp

Pete Lovio: I remember Don was trying to play some Sonny Boy Williamson parts and stuff cause
this guy had a record of Sonny Boy Williamson. The guy had a little amplifier and a microphone
and Don started to try to play it. He was getting into the harp, you know, blues harp, back then.
John French: What year was that?
PL: That was at the time he was trying to get in with us - early sixties. He was listening to
Sonny Boy Williamson and Jimmy Reed.
Wally Salazar: Late '59 I think.
PL: Who was the guy that had the little shack room ... north of Lancaster Boulevard and west
of Sierra Highway? This guy liked harmonica. Older guy. I remember listening to this guy. Don
would go in there and practice. This was like the beginning of electric blues. The guy listened
to Sonny Boy Williamson, Jimmy Reed. Don was always trying to play harp to him like that.
JF: Now, was this a house or a store, or what?
PL: No, it was just a little old beat-up shack. I don't know if he was a bum or whatever, but
he was always drinking, but he loved the blues. He would put it on the record player and Don
would practice. I went over there a few times with my horn.

That Don impressed Alex with his harp (harmonica) playing also supports the theory that the guys had been getting together for a good deal of time – perhaps several months - before Alex returned from Tahoe. Jerry said that Don didn't play harp until later. Alex says that Don already was playing harp on his return from Lake Tahoe. Mortensen claims to have been Don's initial harmonica tutor, showing him various "cross-harp" techniques and explaining the basics of bending notes etc.

Doug Moon: The beginning of this whole Captain Beefheart thing was getting together with
Frank. So Frank and Don and I were getting together. Then Alex came back into town and
we got connected up with Alex and Jerry and we started talking about doing some things
musically and we got together and partied and jammed. The next thing you know we were
talking about putting a band together.

So, perhaps as an extension of the same experimentation that produced the earlier Soots project, Frank, Doug and Don were occasionally jamming and experimenting together before Alex came back into town. Due to the fact that Alex claims (and this without argument from anyone else), that he actually formed the Magic Band, it seems likely that he was the actual catalyst for its formation in spite of all the pre-Alex activity. Alex was the initiator, seasoned from playing in a band for several months, of taking the group to the next step.

Doug Moon: I think we were in the formative stages - trying to put this whole thing together. We spent like six months of jamming, experimenting, we didn't even have a name for the band, I don't know maybe we could have used the name Solid Senders for all I know. Whatever, if we used a name at all. We would get together and play for any occasion, mostly parties and jams, things like that, trying to put something together.

Everyone seems to agree that it was Alex who started the band, so it is possible that the other four were getting together on a completely unofficial basis for a time before Alex came on the scene. His presence and natural-born leadership may have been what catalyzed the actual formation of the group.

According to Alex, the timeline was (approximately):

> The Omens break up – 1962
> The Solid Senders break up – Early '63
> Tahoe - Spring '63 to late summer or fall of '64

Jerry Handley: So (Alex) came back and we had to find something to do so we decided to put a group together again.

This casual statement gives the impression that if there were any musical experimenting going on, it wasn't enough to warrant commitment as of the Fall of 1964. Jerry was playing guitar with the re-formed Omens according to Doug. Moon may have been taking the jam sessions more seriously, as it was his first real experience with a group and his first real acceptance as a guitarist.

John French: The next phase would be that Alex came back from Lake Tahoe and obviously he had been back for a while because you were hanging out with him.
Doug Moon: Yeah, we were all partying and having a good time, and Jerry (had) kept The Omens going … he was the guitar player in The Omens, in their last days.

So there appears to be a period of time in which Alex was described as one of a group ("we were *all*") that was "partying and having a good time."

P.G. Blakely

Jerry Handley: We were putting a new band together, (me and) Doug, who had been playing for a while. I had been hanging out with (him) for a while. He was interested in the blues. We'd get together and just jam a little bit. Doug and I … and Alex and then there was this fellow I went to school with since I was in sixth or seventh grade, P.G. Blakely.
John French: He was a drummer in the Pep band when I was in High School. He was a senior when I was a freshman. So, I remember P.G. really well. He was one of my (first) inspirations to get started playing drums.
JH: I can see that. Yeah - a few years older than you. He'd been playing drums a long time, all through school. He was one of the best drummers in the Valley.

P.G. was indeed an inspiration to me. He was actually the second person I saw (the first being a classmate named John Parr) actually playing on a set in person. P.G. actually reminded me of Jimmy Olson, from *Superman* comics. He had a fifties more than a sixties look and feel about him.

Don used to say he was "the kind of guy you expected to see with a pencil behind his ear," saying "Yes Sir! Gee whiz!" emphatically with a big grin on his face.

I considered him to be a great drummer at the time but I had no perspective at all, because I had only seen one other drummer in person. Needless to say that after watching P.G. play for the Pep band in high school assemblies, I was determined that someday I would play drums also. Listening to P.G. without watching the methodology, I found his playing to have a lot of feel. The overall effect and the sound he achieved was great, and he was a heavy hitter.

Don's Background/Singing Experience/Harp Playing

John French: Alex claims that by the time he came back to town he went and heard Don play harp and discovered that Don was a pretty good harp player. So at that point, Don had learned to play harp.

Doug Moon: Yeah, I think within a few months time he learned to play a few licks on the harmonica and of course at that time, you didn't have to be very good, because the proficiency among the white harmonica players hadn't gotten very high yet. It was the black musicians who we tried to emulate who were really good.

JF: Vic Mortensen also claims that he taught Don the harmonica. You remember ever hearing Vic play the harmonica?

DM: Actually, I think I do, but I don't remember him being very good.

JF: Maybe that's why Don wasn't very good (at first)?

DM: Of course, when you don't know anything, anyone who knows something is better. He may have triggered Don into getting into it.

Jerry Handley: He (Don) could whistle, that's all he could do at first. We'd be playing guitars and he'd come by, and he could whistle the blues, and he was damned good at it.

John French: Jerry mentions that Don used to whistle, that he used to whistle solos before he used to play harp.

Doug Moon: That doesn't sound unusual. I could see him doing that. I can't recall exactly any instance where he did that. He would try to communicate whatever ideas he had whether he could whistle it or hum it or squawk it out on a harmonica.

Now, this whistle of Don's was an unusual talent. This was no lip-pursing whistle. He created the sound with the back of his tongue and his soft palate, in his throat. He would whistle while smiling with a cigarette being held between his lips. He had excellent range and could whistle soft and pretty or loud and shrill. He could blow smoke rings while whistling. This was developed through the years into a private little sideshow for the band members. When the musical parts he was creating were high slide guitar parts, they were most often whistled, at first directly to the player, depending solely upon the player's memory and later, indirectly through a tape recorder, so the part could be referred to at a later date.

Sometimes Don would do bird calls which he could actually do quite well. Because of the nature of the way the sound was produced, he could change the quality and the harmonics of the sound by altering the shape of his cheeks, and closing or opening his lips. Sometimes he would blow air through his lips so they would rapidly flap open and shut while emitting an ear-piercing whistle, which would resemble a coach's pea-whistle.

CHAPTER FOUR:
DESERT CONVERGENCES

Don taking his hoover for a walk! Courtesy of Doug Moon.

Moon Meets Mortensen

John French: Did you meet Vic Mortensen at Studio Z?
Doug Moon: Somewhere along the line, because he was a friend of Frank's. I guess what happened was that when we originally decided, "Yeah, let's put a band together and let's do something." The drummer that was available at the time was P.G. Blakely, and so the first incarnation was P.G., Don, Alex, Jerry, and I.
JF: Jerry says that he and Alex actually were the first two and P.G. Blakely was the original drummer and then Doug came in, and Vic replaced P.G. So, I'm trying to get all the …
Don Aldridge: But that was all pre-Don.
JF: Yeah?

Don Up From Studio Z

Jerry Handley: Anyway, Don came up from the Cucamonga studio into Lancaster I don't know for whatever reason. To join a band or not, but he got together with all of us.

The impression that I later had when I joined was that Don had been spending most of his free time at Studio Z until the point in time when Frank was arrested. It was then that he decided to start (or join) the band. This does not take into consideration the fact that the band was indeed rehearsing with P.G. at the same time Zappa and Mortensen were still living and working at Studio Z.

Jerry Handley: So we had two guitars, bass, drums and then we didn't have a singer. That's when Don came up to Lancaster having played with or recorded (with Zappa), I guess, I don't know what. They were experimenting with movies and music down in Frank Zappa's studio in Cucamonga.

The whole idea of Don "coming up" from Cucamonga seems to suggest that he was living there for a time; however, according to Mortensen, Don would just show up on weekends sometimes alone, sometimes with others. More than likely Don was living at his parent's house and working somewhere, perhaps still as a shoe salesman at Kinney's. The reason he wasn't seen around town much was possibly because he was earning a living during the week and going to Studio Z on weekends, sometimes with Doug, and sometimes alone.

Alex Snouffer: Yeah. So I came back (from Tahoe) and … (Jerry and I) just started talking, and then he tells me about "Vliet can really play harp" so I started thinking "band" you know. So I thought, "Who else can we get in this mother?" and Doug Moon's name popped up, and we got a hold of Doug. Doug was considered at the time - well I don't know what he was considered. So there we had our two guitars and bass and I got a hold of Vliet and of course Vliet got a hold of Vic (Mortensen) and that's where he fit in.
John French: One of the comments I remember Don saying is, "Alex was the dictator of the group - from his Prussian background, he came to me and told me, gave me an order, more or less, that I was going to sing in his band."
AS: (Laughter)
JF: That was like, right after I got into the band, sort of in a half-joking way. So, is that kind of the way it happened?
AS: Yeah.
JF: So really, you started the band.

AS: Yes, I started the band, I hand picked everybody, except for Vic. We were hurting for a drummer, so, it worked out. Of course, personnel changes evolved over the years.

Doug Moon: That was the first incarnation of Captain Beefheart And The Magic Band even before there was a name for it yet. P.G. on drums, Jerry on bass, it was a weird bass, Supro, or something like that and then I went on guitar and Alex came back from Tahoe and he got into all of this stuff.

Although Alex takes claim for starting the group, it appears as though the members had already been considering this very move even without Alex. Alex described picking the members not so much based on musicality, as based on personality. The blues seemed to be the standard theme and catalyst that pulled these musicians together. He also describes that shortly after the band started, Don began to "change" as soon as he got a small taste of fame.

Don's Life: High School To Beefheart

It's difficult to speculate on Don's life at the time and impossible to interview him. He was still living with his parents, because the early band sometimes practiced at Granny Annie's. He was about 24 at the time, and may or may not have been the principal breadwinner for the family, as Glen, Don's father, could no longer work because of his heart condition.

I heard from Don himself that he had worked on the Helms route for a while, and also (in no particular order) as a hydraulics technician in one of the aircraft factories, probably North American. Jerry and Doug had both worked in this field for a time also, even after the band had started playing locally.

Alex Snouffer: He used to sell vacuum cleaners and he dug pools, he worked for a swimming pool company.
John French: Did he use a backhoe or just his back?
AS: Nah, ya gotta get down there with a shovel for some of that. He was a box boy at Safeway. That's where I met him.
JF: He said he was a hydraulics tech at an aircraft company. Did he ever do that?
AS: (Laughs) He wishes.

Van Vliet at a later point told me that he had conned his way into a job at one of the aircraft factories and worked as a hydraulics technician for a time. He said that he used to put a product called Chap-Ans (made by the same company who manufactured Chapstick) on his hands before his shift and then at the end of the day, when everyone else's hands were greasy, he would walk in and wash all the grease off his hands leaving no telltale sign of his profession. This could have been during the period when Alex was in Lake Tahoe, which would explain why Snouffer couldn't remember this phase of his life.

Don had also mentioned working for a short time for the *Ledger Gazette*, a Lancaster-based local newspaper, in the art department. Laurie, his girlfriend, once showed me a newspaper clipping showing a small ink drawing of a carriage drawn by several horses, and told me that Don had drafted it.

John French: He also said that he did graphic art at the Ledger Gazette for a while.
Alex Snouffer: He did. I don't know how far he got, but he worked for the Ledger, I know that, because I was working there at the time.
JF: Do you remember Kinney Shoes?
AS: Oh yeah, I forgot about that.

Pete Lovio: Don was a shoe salesman at Kinney's shoes.

Kinney's was a giant chain of shoe stores in the sixties. In light of this fact, I found the following quote that was printed in the May 14th issue of Rolling Stone magazine, 1970, more than slightly amusing, but typical of Don's hyperbolic mentality.

"For a brief while he was employed as a commercial artist and as a manager of a chain of shoe stores. "I built that chain into a thriving, growing concern," he recalls."Then as a kind of art statement I quit right in the middle of the Christmas rush leaving the whole thing in chaos." [15]

John French: In one interview, he says, "I built that store into a thriving chain".
Alex Snouffer: (Deep laughter) Whattaya expect?

Kinney's managed, however, to survive the chaos in which Don had left that thriving chain, and Don managed to survive Kinney's. He was driving a Corvette, dressing well, and seemed to often be able afford to drive to Hollywood to hear jazz and hang out with celebrities, who mostly remained nameless. One he did mention by name quite often was Steve McQueen, with whom he seemed to have struck up some kind of relationship, according, at least to his stories.

One story in particular related to me by Van Vliet involved Steve taking Don for a ride in one of his cars (a Porsche, I believe). They drove through one of the typically curvy L.A. Canyons (Laurel, Beverly, Topanga etc.). McQueen, known to be something of a daredevil and famous for his love of speed, was driving like a demon, revving the engine, and squealing the tires - barely avoiding skidding down several embankments. Don, trying to maintain his "cool", said that McQueen had a little grin on his face and kept glancing questioningly at Don out of the corner of his eye, as if to say "Can you take it, Donny?"

Another story Don told me was that he met Shirley Maclaine one night. I heard from someone that she had gone into Scotts (where Don's mother worked) and caused a problem because of a particular blouse she insisted be taken off the window mannequin in order for her to try it on. She later went skinny-dipping in one of the local hotel's swimming pools. Don claimed that she stripped right in front of him and he was with her the whole evening.

Timeline For The Formation Of The Band
My reasoning on the timeline is the following:

Spring/Summer 1964
Jerry, Doug, P.G. and Don unofficially jamming but not a group.
Mortensen teaches harp to Don at Studio Z during same period.
Doug and Don take trips to see Zappa.

Fall Or Late Summer 1964
Alex returns to Lancaster.
Nov/Dec 1964
Alex hears Don play harmonica and sing.

Late 1964 Or Early '65
Band official when P.G. is replaced by Mortensen.

[15] Rolling Stone Magazine; May 14th, 1970; No. 58; The Odyssey of Captain Beefheart by Langdon Winner. pp36.

Jerry Switches To Bass

Jerry Handley: He joined on, and lets see - Alex and Doug on guitar and I had not played bass in my entire lifetime and we needed a bass player, so I played bass.

Alex Snouffer: Jerry was still playing guitar at that time. I noticed, just to reflect a little on that, that Jerry's guitar was always out of tune on the high notes, you know. I would watch him tune it, and he would say, "that's it!" and I would say, "No, it's not, man!" He would hit a chord and, sure enough he was out. So I watched that for a while and finally I talked to him because we needed a bass man anyway, cause his bass strings were always on, always right there, it was the highs he couldn't hear real well.
John French: So, maybe he had a hearing deficiency in the high register?
AS: Yeah, he couldn't hear it. So I talked to him and I asked, "would you be willing to switch over to bass?"
JF: So you didn't just make this up because you needed a bass player, right?
AS: No maaaann ... that was the way it was.
JF: I heard about you paying off this guy who gave him the ear test and everything.
AS: Yeah, I forget his name though (laughter) but anyway, he started playing bass.

Doug Moon: I guess what happened was when we were getting together in the early days, Jerry had a problem. Somehow his hearing ...
John French: He couldn't hear high frequencies?
DM: Well, he could, but his pitch was off. And what triggered that (idea) was the fact that he couldn't tune his own guitar.
JF: Right, Alex said he couldn't tune the upper two strings.
DM: He could play the thing but when he would solo, some of his playing ability was good, chords and all, but the notes were just off. They were just flat or sharp. He'd go, "Jerry, just bend that a little bit more, it's just a little flat. We started to pick up on the fact that he had a poor sense of pitch at the higher frequencies.
JF: Was this early Magic Band days or was this just jamming around?
DM: Just as the band was forming. Now, I don't remember anyone else playing (bass). I'm trying to picture in my mind a bass player. I'm really at a loss for who was playing bass during this time when Jerry was still on guitar. And I was basically playing backup and trying to fit into this whole thing. I was kind of on the outskirts of this whole thing. I wasn't really part of what was happening yet. When it really took form was when we realized that Jerry had a very good sense of timing, rhythm and feel. He really felt those bass notes. Then it clicked, "Hey, maybe you should be a bass player. When we put him on bass, he was right into it. He just took to bass like a duck to water. Alex is sharp, really really sharp. He picked up on this right away. I think he is the one who really influenced Jerry, because Jerry wasn't easily going to give up, he had these dreams of becoming a jazz guitar player. That was never meant to be.

Origin Of The Name
Frank Zappa remembers the origin of the name:

"The way Don got his 'stage name'was, Uncle Alan had a habit of exposing himself to Laurie. He'd piss with the bathroom door open and, if she was walking by, mumble about his appendage – something along the lines of: 'Ahh, what a beauty! It looks just like a big, fine beef heart'." [16]

---

[16]The Real Frank Zappa Book, Frank Zappa, Simon and Schuster, 1989 pp37.

Doug Moon: *Even talking on the phone to Vic (Mortensesn) the other day, he had one point of view, I had another, we didn't completely agree on the origin of (the name) Captain Beefheart. Now I have a copy, somewhere, of that play* (referring to *Captain Beefheart vs. the Grunt People*). *See, that's where this later argument came to be over the name Captain Beefheart. Zappa claimed he had rights to it, so they had a battle over that. I don't even remember how they settled all that, or if they ever did settle it.*

Vic Mortensen: *Doug seems to remember this story differently, but I'll tell you my version of how Captain Beefheart And His Magic Band was named.*
John French: *OK*
VM: *Frank and I would sit around the studio – like I said, he never slept, OK – and we would sit sometimes and bullshit for hours about band names and one thing or another and sometimes we'd tape the stuff, just tape the conversations just because he always wanted to have a tape machine running. But anyway, we got to talking about clever little band names like everyone does. We got to playing on the character of Captain Beefheart, and I had already met Don, and I knew who he was, although he didn't call himself that, he was only going to be cast into that character if the screenplay ever got done. Anyway, Captain Beefheart was supposed to be a magical character. His thing is what he could do if a (container) of Pepsi were opened, he would drink the Pepsi Cola and he could make magic things ... he could appear or disappear. I told Frank, I said, hey wouldn't it be cool if Captain Beefheart had a Magic Band, and wherever he went, if he wanted the band to appear, he would drink a glug of Pepsi, and "BINGO" there's the band right behind him, 'jukin.' We had a laugh about it and he thought it was pretty clever and blah blah. Now, Don wasn't there at the time, but about three days later, a few days later I was down in Montclair - I was living in Montclair at the time - I got a call from Don. He said, "I'm starting a band. Would you like to play in it?" and I said, "I think that's cool" – because we had all played together and we knew we could work together. And I said, "What are you gonna'call the band." and he said, "Captain Beefheart And His Magic Band" and I said, "Far out!" I didn't even discuss it... I am sure he had heard it – the only place he could have heard it – was from Frank. But now Doug remembers them sitting around drunk out in the desert some night and coming up with the name of the band. But I think if Frank were alive, God rest his soul, we could resolve that problem immediately.*

John French: *Do you know anything about Zappa's movie (script), Captain Beefheart and his Girlfriend Sue? And then Captain Beefheart vs. the Grunt People?*
Jerry Handley: *The only thing I've heard is Captain Beefheart vs. the Grunt People.*
JF: *Vic says that Don used to come in (to his parents'home) and he'd say, "Sue, get me a cup of tea!" and his mother would scurry off to the kitchen like Edith Bunker. She would just do whatever he wanted, so Zappa made up this joke script called Captain Beefheart and his Girlfriend Sue.*
JH: *That's his mother you're talkin about? Yeah, he'd snap his fingers and she'd ... yeah.*
JF: *According to Vic Mortensen, since Captain Beefheart was this magic guy who could appear and disappear, that he ought to have this Magic Band that he could make appear and disappear. So that's the concept where Captain Beefheart And His Magic Band originally came from. And then Don decided to use the idea when he got together with you guys.*
JH: *Well, that very well could be, because that's the time frame, when Don was down in Cucamonga and that Vic was probably around at that time and they were working on that Captain Beefheart concept with Frank Zappa in the early sixties. And then he kinda brought the idea up to Lancaster. At the time we were starting this blues band, Don came*

up from Cucamonga. I was on the phone with Alex or Don, one of the two, and they said, "Well, we've got a name for the band, Captain Beefheart And His Magic Band … I just cracked up laughing man.
JF: That was my first reaction to the name. Doug Moon walked up to me and told me the name. He says, "I'm in this band" you know, and I'd already heard the name and I thought, "What a ridiculous name." and then he came up and told me that was the name of his new band, and I didn't laugh at Doug, because I didn't want to make him feel bad, but I was laughing inside.
JH: That's right, well, you had all the "cool" names at the time, you know. Like that Solid Senders which was one of our "cool" names that we had. And that was the thing, "cool" names. So who would name … I mean, it was so outrageous. I thought, "That's great, let's do it!" No-one will ever hear us anyway, right. Ha!
So, we went with it and it turned out that a lot of people heard about it. My kids (who) range in age from 22 to 31 years old said that their friends and friends'parents have heard of the band. You know, it surprised me.

Don once mentioned to me that the band name was one of the first names that fit in the with the new San Francisco band names, like Big Brother and the Holding Company and Country Joe And The Fish.

Vic Replaces P.G.

Since Paul "P.G." Blakely was replaced by Vic Mortensen, I was always wondering exactly why this change took place. According to Handley, P.G. had a time problem. He was always rushing, or speeding up the songs, or trying to play them too fast. Actually, Blakely didn't seem to fit into the band at all, he had a "nice guy" image and the rest of the band seemed to have a "bad boy" image. Whatever the reason Paul eventually was out, and Vic Mortensen was in.

John French: Just to skip back for a minute, when did Vic Mortensen come onto the scene.
Jerry Handley: He replaced P.G.
JF: Why did P.G. leave?
JH: He had a hard time keeping time. He was always rushing it. You know how drummers either lag or rush? He had a hard time just fitting in with the style of music we were playing and when we started getting into recording and things more seriously we had to get guys who could keep time.
JF: So Zappa knew Vic.
JH: Zappa knew Vic, yeah. He was from the Cucamonga recording days down there with Zappa and he was going to (Pomona) College down there.
JF: So who actually introduced him or suggested he be part of the band?
JH: It had to be Don because Don had the connection with Frank down there. Of course, Frank and Don and Alex all went to Antelope Valley High School together. They grew up together. Vic was from near the Cucamonga studio down there.

Vic's Drive

John French: So Don actually said " he" was starting a band.
Vic Mortensen: He said, "I'm starting a band," OK? But Don always starts everything (laughs). So when I went up to Lancaster, I got my drums in the VW bus and off I go, and on the way up I was going through Cajon Pass. I passed an old school bus type bus that said,

"Ike and Tina Turner Review." They were the only thing struggling up the hill more slowly than I was. That would have been in probably late '63, early '64, somewhere in there. The dates start to get muddy, you know. Anyway, I got up to Lancaster and that is when we started rehearsing at Jerry's house.

JF: You kind of took that as a little omen? (Referring to the Turner bus)

VM: I did, I thought that was cool. Yeah I did take it as an omen.

JF: You must be in the right place?

VM: Well, I thought, I must be going in the right direction. Who knows? You know, but I did take it as kind of an omen, it was kind of mystical. When I first got up to Lancaster, I crashed at Don's house. Funny little vignette about that: I was crashed on the couch, we'd come in the middle of the night, you know how it is. By that time, my hair had already gotten quite long. Oh, it was below my shoulders anyway. It was shortly after that that you saw me, so you know. Anyway, I was sleeping on the couch, and I guess Don's father got up in the middle of the night. Walked out there and freaked. He said he thought some huge broad was sleeping on the couch.

About Laurie Stone

Vic Mortensen: Seems to me I met her about the same time. I can't remember if she was part of the thing then or what. I think she was. I don't get the impression that they were a thing that started after the group started. I think they were a thing before the group. When I say "start the group" that means the day I walked in the door at Jerry Handley's house.

Don once told us that he had met Laurie at a mountain resort, either Big Bear or Lake Arrowhead. He was sitting in the lobby of the lodge or hotel that they were staying at. While looking out the window and enjoying the view, a girl walked up and crushed her cigarette out on the window directly in his line of vision. He claimed at the time he thought, "How hip, that's the girl for me" After that, they were together.

She lived out of Lancaster in an area known as Leona Valley, and her parents were not the nurturing types. Don mentioned that her father did his best to constantly lower her self-esteem. One of his favorite tricks was to constantly make fun of her feet, claiming that they were too large. According to Don, the environment of the house wasn't conducive to growing and so Don got her out of there and moved her in with either his family, or perhaps across the street to the Granny Annie's house.

Although I found Laurie to be pleasant for the most part, she did have a dark side and could be verbally cruel and physically violent. Don once mentioned her throwing an ashtray at Granny Annie. Her role seemed to be to get dressed and spend the rest of her day catering to Don's every whim. A very challenging role, as it turned out. However, not necessarily a role that was conducive to growth as it later turned out.

Laurie once showed me a wedding/engagement ring set and said that Don and her were going to get married someday. I asked Don about this later, and he explained that his mother had given that set to Laurie. It was a family heirloom, and being as how Sue and Granny were concerned about appearances, they were trying to encourage the two to get married.

Early Repertoire Of Captain Beefheart And His Magic Band

The early set list was comprised of a hodge-podge of whatever songs everyone knew from earlier bands coupled with Rolling Stones material, and blues songs. I recall seeing one tape with the label *Lonely Lonely Nights*.

Jerry recalls one song that didn't last long in the repertoire:

Jerry Handley: I was thinking the other morning about our first songs that we played in the band, with P.G. Blakely, and I remember playing "Oo Pooh Pah Doo". I can't remember who did that originally. To do all vocals was different up there because a lot of bands I played with were (playing) strictly instrumentals. We'd go play gigs and it would be instrumentals, basically. The Beefheart band was all vocals, so that was kind of different.

Snouffer had a lot of pride in the early band and rightfully so. The band had a great look and sound and was totally different than anything else going on.

Alex Snouffer: Then we started the Beefheart thing and we were playing good blues for a long time. In fact, that's how we got noticed to begin with, you know, down in "Hollywoody" (sarcastically) - because nobody else could do it as well - period.

It is certain that in no small part, Van Vliet's vocal talents and ability to mimic famous blues singers added a lot of attraction to the package.

The Concept Of The Band

Handley explains that the whole concept of the band was a big experiment. The guys that had gotten together were more blues lovers than musicians. He found himself surprised that the public seemed so entranced by the band. He remembers Doug being an inexperienced and average player who loved the blues, and worked hard to emulate his favorites on guitar and harmonica. At one point, he claimed that Doug could "play guitar as good as Lightning Hopkins could." However, he also claims that Doug took everything verbatim off the records, so he wasn't so much creating his own style of playing as he was "copping licks." Handley described Doug as loving the old country blues and getting into "bottleneck and things that hadn't been done locally."

Jerry Handley: He was a big fan of Sonny Boy Williamson. He could play the harp like Sonny Boy Williamson.

Not too many people have heard Doug play the harmonica, but he is quite accomplished and was a great player back in the early days of the band. His sense of phrasing was ideal and he was dead-on hitting the notes.

Jerry Handley: So, we got together basically out of a love of the blues.

"Vliet" as Snouffer often refers to Don had a comfortable and non-commital entry into the music scene as a singer. Snouffer recalls Don's early vocal attempts as just "fartin'around at parties" while "boozing it up." The musicians would take their instruments to parties and just sit around, a little drunk, and "jam" – making stuff up as they went along, and not serious at all at the outcome. In fact, often trying to be humorous by emulating famous artists through parody. The attitude was: "Think we can get through this?" Don's southern background helped, and of course, Alex said Don had learned a lot about blues from "the half million records he had." He was knowledgeable about the blues and knew how to emulate many of the more popular blues artists.

Yet Don was quoted as saying the following: *"I haven't listened to that much blues"* (Don Van Vliet, 1983)

John French: He had listened to the blues growing up, right?
Doug Moon: Yeah, he had listened to a lot of records when he was in high school and stuff. They used to get together, oh him, and Frank, and Alex ... those guys used to listen to R&B records by the stackfulls.
JF: What about guys like Jim Sherwood and Terry Wimberly?
DM: Oh yeah, Terry, they were all like part of the gang. Man those guys were really into R&B and stuff. That's where I got turned on to all that stuff. When I started liking blues.

Alex Snouffer: I heard him play harp, and then he started to do this Howlin' Wolf imitation and I thought, "Yo, buddy! This isn't bad at all." So anyhow, we just put it together.

Handley remembers that Don's grandfather had owned a plantation (presumably Granny Annie's husband who had a very strong southern drawl) and because of this Don had strong ties to the South. Vliet was described as having a lot of southern blood in him. Because of the fact that his family grew up listening to a lot of what Jerry refers to as "southern soul," the southern Negro music had become a significant part of Don's cultural heritage.

I had always marveled at Don's later inability to memorize lyrics for a one-hour show, when a few years before, he had been singing five sets a night. However, the songs he sang in the early band were songs he had listened to probably hundreds of times during his teen years, so the lyrics were ingrained in his mind.

Jerry Handley: Then he'd learn the words to these songs and he was a natural guy for a bluesman and we thought, "Well, let's give it a shot." Alex and I talked about it, here's a guy who has no background of singing in a band. So we weren't out to set the world on fire, we just wanted to play up in Lancaster and get some jobs, if we could get that good.
John French: Yeah, and little did you know where it was all going.
JH: Right! Well the uniqueness of Don's voice, being able to sing the blues and sound like it was for real. We weren't really imitating. He could "sound like" Muddy Waters and that but we still sounded like our own band.
JF: And it was a very powerful group.
JH: Yeah, very strong, very strong band.

Surpassing the British equivalents of blues bands (Stones, Animals, Yardbirds) if not in instrumental at least in vocal power, the band was indeed a unique musical group. These were men onstage playing together in a simple, primitive, yet extremely powerful style. The blues recordings were indeed not imitations but incredible re-interpretations of a music that was not familiar to the sixties surf audience, and only introduced indirectly by the British groups, but mostly on a much tamer scale. Captain Beefheart And His Magic Band seemed totally genuine, completely unique, and uncompromisingly convicted.

Rehearsals

Jerry Handley: We started rehearsing in my mother's living room. Most of our rehearsals for the band initially were at my folks house. We did our setup in the living room.
John French: And that was on...?
JH: J-10

JF: J-10, and the corner of J-10 and ... Twelfth St.
JH: Twelfth street, yes ... the initial band rehearsals were there for a long time.

Snouffer was the undisputed leader of the original band. He was described by Doug as "militant" but not manipulative, as Don would later become. He was a determined taskmaster and set attainable but challenging goals. He stood for no nonsense or wasted time at rehearsals, and had enough experience to shortly turn the Magic Band into a well-oiled machine, bringing out the best in each player and using them to maximum potential. He was considered by Doug to be a "pretty sharp guy" with above-average intelligence and good leadership instincts.

John French: So did (Alex) spearhead a lot of the decision-making early in the band?
Doug Moon: Yeah, he was a strong figure in the band. It wasn't until the later days that he just kind of gave up.

Pete Lovio: The one guy, though that just didn't get enough credit for all that was Alex. Alex was another Frank Zappa. He was the one that kept us together. Man, if you made a mistake, he'd get pissed off. He would make sure that you had your rhythm licks on and you were doing it right. Alex knew what he was doing. He was good. He had a great ear. He was the one that kept us together more than Terry (Wimberly). I thought Alex was more the leader than Terry.
Johnny Franklin: We were doing a gig at a place in Palmdale called the Royal Palms at that time on Sierra Highway. We were doing jazz there. I was playing bass and Butch was on guitar and we were doing a piece and I was playing and he turned and looked at me and said, "What was that? Do it again!" I did a kind of little variation on the bass lines, and he picked it up right there. We were doing Summertime.

Alex also initiated discussions – meetings in which all members would discuss their ideas for the band, which helped to keep the unit pulling in a common direction. Don seemed to go along with this and cooperated. Moon describes him as "collaborating" with Alex and the others. He also remembers that Don was not too interested in showing up for rehearsals when the band was working out new material. He would disappear and come back when it was time for vocals to be added.

Mortensen had stronger words when asked about Don's rehearsal habits:

Vic Mortensen: We'd be there; everybody showed up, we made it a point to get there on time for rehearsal. Don would come in and say, "Where's my harmonica?" Just screwing around, you know, "I could be out on the beach getting laid right now." Don, let's get with the program. And he'd say, "Where's my Bb harmonica?"
John French: He wouldn't have his act together.
VM: It was all part of his megalomaniac personality. Like, everybody has to wait for Don.
JF: Special attention.
VM: Well, but he has to keep telling himself he "deserves" it. Somebody at certain points would have to constantly say, "Let's get on with it." We'd play along. I would try to keep a flow. We all knew it was bullshit.

This paints more a picture of a prima-donna, one who has found that they are basically irreplaceable and has decided to take as much advantage of the situation as possible and exhibiting a certain air of abandon. It fits right in with the impression I first received one and a half years later.

John French: So, where was your first rehearsal with the magic band?
Vic Mortensen: As far as I know, it would have been at Jerry's parents'house.
JF: Jerry's parent's house at the corner of J-10 and Twelfth St. That's where I heard you guys first.
VM: Exactly.
JF: So how soon after you started to rehearse did you actually decide that you were going to start playing and get gigs?
VM: Oh, I think we didn't intend to put it together for any other purpose than to get gigs. It was the deal like as soon as we got together and woodshedded for a couple of days or even that long. Bear in mind that all of these guys, at least had some experience in the studio and were pretty serious musicians.
JF: Except for Doug, because Doug was sort of a beginner according to (his interview). He'd only been playing two or three years and he just started playing in front of people maybe a year before that.
VM: Well, yeah, he may not have been in it that long, yeah, that makes a lot of sense. He hadn't been playing that long.
JF: But he played well.
VM: He played well and we seemed to be going in a blues direction and he loved the blues. A funny story, a little vignette. We always accused him of playing thirteen bar changes. "Doug, you're playing thirteen bar changes!" Finally, we dragged out an old Muddy Waters record, or something like that. There it was, the old boy was playing thirteen bar changes. (Laughs) In other words, he was playing it correctly.

This could have been Muddy Waters' *Louisiana Blues*, which seems to have an extra measure added on to the end of the regular twelve bar blues.

Since Mortensen had never played the blues before, he was faced with the challenge of using his acquired skills, but crossing over to a new style of playing.

Vic Mortensen: So I was just trying to catch up. Blues was an entirely new thing. See, I could do surf. I could do big band, I could do dixieland, I could do all of the traditional things. But, see, there wasn't that much blues going on ...
John French: Did you feel like you were having a hard time understanding the blues?
VM: Not really.
JF: Did you consider it simple? Difficult?
VM: It was relatively simple, but I started discovering little things you can do; little subtleties.
JF: Like breaking footpedals.
VM: Yeah ... (Laughs)
JF: That's another story, I'll get to that.
Choice Of Repertoire

John French: So the band ... everybody sort of had a repertoire in their heads and started throwing stuff together and jamming and putting things together quickly? Or did you actually sit down and work out a set and say, "We're going to play all blues?"
Vic Mortensen: OK, first of all an economic reality at that time was if you want to get a gig of

any kind, you better play some (Rolling) Stones stuff. So we started laying down a Stones package, and you know, pop covers and that sort of thing. But basically Stones covers that we also started picking up like Hi Heeled Sneakers. Stuff like that. If we were at a gig, I usually called the playlist and I would call something like, "Red Dress!" We had little trick phrases for every song. Lots of times, there were classic blues songs that we were playing that I didn't know who the hell it was. I didn't consider it necessary for me to become a musicologist to play the drums on blues tunes. Because, once you get into it you find there are enough similarities to get you by.

JF: So, how did you feel about the blues? Did you start enjoying playing the blues?

VM: I enjoyed playing with the group. I enjoyed the music part of it. There were enough lively tunes to keep my interest up. You can chug right along doing a shout. (Sings) "got my mojo working". Keeps you awake, keeps you interested. I can see that regardless of what we had, what we were doing, if it had been garbage, I would not have been happy.

The "Captain Beefheart" Sound

The original band had a very simple stage setup. They used two Fender Bassman piggyback amps. The guitars both shared one, and the bass, turned up quite loud, was through the other. Alex and Doug both played Fender Stratocasters, though Alex sometimes used Jerry's red Gibson 335.

John French: When I heard you guys play, you had two Bassman amps, that you used for basically everything except PA. It was such a big sound. People were studying, saying, "How does this sound so big?" One of the things that my friends observed and that I noticed when I came later was that the bass was always turned up really loud. Very simple, but really strong. All the bass players all of a sudden wanted to play really loud. You commanded a lot of respect in the Valley, because you were in a band that was really going somewhere so everyone liked your bass playing a lot and emulated it.

Jerry Handley: Yeah, I really enjoyed it, that got me hooked on bass. I hadn't played bass before, I was a guitar player.

JF: Just for the record, what kind of bass did you play?

JH At that time, I had an old Rickenbacker.

JF: And what did you switch to eventually?

JH: I switched to a Guild double cutaway hollow body.

JF: Wasn't the Rickenbacker a hollow body also.

JH: Yeah, it was, actually. It sort of looked like an old Telecaster, but it was a Rickenbacker. Funky old thing. I hung …. (Laughs) my big deal was that I played with a bath robe strap for a guitar strap. I had an old cotton bathrobe with a long tail on it that I used for a bass strap. I did many jobs up there in Lancaster with this stupid bathrobe strap.

Mortensen Recalls The First Gig/March 1965

John French: So, what was your first gig with the band?

Vic Mortensen: It would have been a teeny bopper kind of thing. I think it would have been a battle of the bands. I remember doing a battle of the bands in Lancaster someplace.

JF: Exposition hall at the Fairgrounds.

VM: Probably. What knocked them out – we won the thing, of course – Don had been searching for something to do with his hands, he was playing the maracas and stuff. He had found some finger cymbals. We worked out a version of St. James'Infirmary Blues Don goes up to the microphone and puts the finger cymbals right next to the microphone and starts scraping them together with his one hand. With his other fingers raised very delicately. And he (makes sound of cymbals). I'm doing like a funeral roll on my snare that is tuned down to a tom tom. Now, dig it, everybody else at the contest that night had been playing surf, Rolling Stones, rock'n'roll of some kind ...

JF: Yeah, I was in one of the bands.

VM: By the time Don would finish that tune, there were tears in his eyes, just running down his cheeks. Everybody just stopped dancing and they were standing there looking up at us agape. It was incredible, an incredible experience.

JF: I think that probably by that time I had gone outside because I knew my band was gonna lose.

Second Gig

Vic Mortensen: Well, we played other battles of the bands ... That's the only one I remember in Lancaster. Then we gigged around ... we got this gig, we called it the "Fat Farm," there was a some kind of place where the fat people go and stay for a couple of weeks.

John French: Oh, yeah, that was the Bermuda Inn.

VM: We went out and played the "Fat Farm" one time. That was a trip.

JF: Sally Struthers was known to have gone there a few times.

First Manager

In the following excerpt from Mortensen's interview, he describes Don having had a car insurance problem of some kind. Van Vliet had described to me later that he had originally had a white Corvette and was driving north down Sierra Highway and during a left turn onto Lancaster Boulevard, he had been struck by a speeding vehicle. He said that his forehead had been lacerated and he had applied Vaseline to it every day and so there were never any scars.

Vic Mortensen: We had – going back to before we had Leonard Grant – we had an agent, he was Don's insurance agent. Don used to drive that Corvette, and somehow he'd gotten into some kind of situation, made an application to the insurance agency, but Don wrote everything in – do you know what "bubble writing" is?

John French: No.

VM: Like, Pachuco bubble-writing? The bubble writing they used to do as graffiti?

JF: Oh, OK.

VM: He filled out the entire insurance form in bubble writing. And he said something like, "Well, I was just driving down the street in my "short" (Pachuco for "car"), and somebody came and ..." and he sent this in to the insurance company. The insurance agent was a young guy, older than we were, but a relatively young guy, probably in his thirties. He sought Don out just to see what kind of a weird guy would do this. When he saw Don, he went, "Wow!" and found out we had a band. He said, "I wanna manage you guys."

John French: Jerry mentioned that there were some people kind of hoping of managing you guys, a young couple just out of college, a husband/wife team or something?

Alex Snouffer: Oh, I remember. Now I know who you are talking about, yeah I can't remember, well I can remember his wife's name was Julie. She was a knockout. (Laughs)

JF: That tends to bring the memory back around a little quicker.

AS: Yeah!

JF: So, Julie and unknown companion - what were they doing? Just a sort of an amateurish thing?

AS: Yeah, their hearts were in it to do it right, but they had no experience, didn't know anybody.

JF: Were they fans?
AS: Yeah.
JF: So, they liked the band. Did they take a commission on anything? Or were they just doing it as a ...
AS: Well, we never got that far (Laughs).

April '65/Pomona College

This outdoor event, one of the first Beefheart performances was performed at the field house building on an external platform/stage and was a battle of the bands. Vic's father, quite ill at the time, actually heard Vic play, but Mortensen didn't know this until years later, after his father's death.

The Bats

Another amusing story is about an offer from Hanna-Barbera.

Vic Mortensen: Now, one of the things this guy (first manager) got us was an audition with Hanna-Barbera. Hanna-Barbera Productions in Hollywood. We packed up our stuff and went to Hanna-Barbera. We're humping it down the hall and all the little chicks working in there are going, "That's right," and they take us back to this studio. We set up and start knocking out a few of our tunes, which in those days would have preceded Call on Me. We didn't even have Call on Me. We didn't have any original stuff then. I mean, we had the stuff we were doing. So, we played two or three tunes for these guys, and they said, "That's enough, boys, come with us. We go back into their office, and they pull out a little old record machine and play a 45 "OK, can you boys play that." We said, "Yeah, we could play that in our sleep!" He says, "Here's the deal boys: this music was done by a bunch of our engineers in the studio. We have the music, and it's already moving on the charts. We don't have a band." The deal was, the group was called The Bats. Now, being Hanna-Barbera, they wanted to have a group called The Bats doing live, like Monkees shit, right and also spin that into an animated deal. I mean, we looked in our agent's face, like I say, he was a young guy. His face just started flushing, like he was counting the money already, right? Then we said, "NO! We're not The Bats, we're Captain Beefheart And His Magic Band." You change the name of the group, and we'll do your thing, but if it's The Bats, we're outta here." I thought this guy – it was like you could see the veins getting larger in his neck - I thought the guy was gonna die right there on the spot.

This was probably a record called *Nothing at All* with the flip side being *Big Bright Eyes*. It was a studio creation by Danny Hutton. Hutton was a one-time Disney employee who eventually became an in-house artist at Hanna-Barbera. He actually had a cameo in a *Flintstones* episode.

It was evident that the band had developed its own personality and image and would not sell out to any commercial offers. There was more in store for the music world from Van Vliet and company than The Bats.

CHAPTER FIVE:
SURF'S UP, SURF'S DOWN

The Whisky in 1965. Courtesy of Doug Moon.

The "Second Generation" Players, Summer 1962-Fall 1966

What has mostly been covered up to this point is the focus on the late fifties and early sixties music scene in the Antelope Valley. The focus has been mainly on the original Magic Band members and other contemporary valley musicians involved in the music scene at that time including Frank Zappa. Coexistent with this scenario and at some points in the same timeline, there was a whole younger subculture of players out of which eventually evolved the *Trout Mask/Decals* band, for lack of a better phrase. In order to avoid confusion, I separated the stories of the original band from the stories that contain my personal perspective and that of my fellow musicians; including Jeff Cotton, Mark Boston, Bill Harkleroad, Merrel Fankhauser, Don Giesen, Randy Wirner and others.

This chapter covers some of the early development of these players and how they were influenced by The Blackouts, The Omens, and the original Beefheart band, starting with Mark Boston:

Boston's Musical Roots

John French: Let me ask you, you were born in Carbondale Illinois?
Mark Boston: Salem, it's not far from Carbondale.
JF: Well, it seemed like when we played Carbondale that there were some people there to see you - in the 1971 tour.
MB: Yeah, it seemed like there was – I remember talking to my old buddy I grew up with when I was a kid. I talked to him over the phone. I don't remember talking to anybody in Carbondale.
JF: I'd like to know how you first got started in music.
MB: Well, my dad was a musician. I just kinda got into hanging around with him.
JF: He played steel guitar didn't he?
MB: Yeah, steel guitar, bass, acoustic guitar. He taught me to play. The first instrument I played was "tub bass."
JF: Oh yeah, washtub?
MB: Yeah, with a stick and string attached to it. I heard an old black guy playing blues on one up Eureka - one of them "Love-In" parties back in the seventies?" That guy was good on that thing. He did things I didn't know you could do.
JF: They have a pretty good tone, do they use a regular bass string?
MB: They use whatever they can get their hands on. Sometimes it's a rope.
JF: We were talking about you learning instruments. Now, is bass the only instrument you learned from your dad, or did you learn something else or some other instrument first?
MB: Bass – and then standard guitar chords, you know, country& western. That's what I grew up playing: country& western.
JF: Did you ever play with your folks on stage?
MB Yeah. I grew up playing, and jamming with neighbors that came by and friends and my dad.
JF: Would you guys have jam sessions or rehearsals at your house?
MB: Yeah, and then we played this gig - he got me a bass fiddle – and I was really too short to even reach it but I tried. (My parents) decided to play a festival – and we went to it – I'd never seen that many people in my life, and I got stage fright and hid in a cornfield. My brother came and found me. He talked me into coming back

Needless to say, Mark got over his stage fright and came back over and over again.

Don Giesen: Mid to late '50s

I was musically closely associated with Don Giesen for the two years I played while in high school. He played rhythm guitar, drums and sang. Since he personally knew and worked with Jeff

Cotton during these early times, his comments are relevant especially in lieu of the fact that Cotton has declined to do an interview.

John French: What first drew you into music?
Don Giesen: Mostly in the early days, when (the television show) American Bandstand and one called Lloyd Thaxton's Let's Dance some of those kinds of shows were on. I always enjoyed watching those shows and seeing whoever the latest rock 'n'roll act was. When I was in the seventh grade while looking through a Sears catalog I saw the famous "single lipstick pickup" Sears Silvertone guitar which was probably made by DanElectro. So, I saved my money.

I had coincidentally taken over his route as a substitute after he had broken his wrist. My arrangements were made through the newspaper office, so I never actually had met Don. We went to different Junior High Schools, so we didn't know each other. After he had healed, he was bicycling around and found me one day delivering papers. He was a little upset because his route originally had over forty customers and in the short time I had it, it had dwindled down into the mid-twenties. This is one of the aforementioned paper routes I ran into the red. I guess I wasn't a paper-route kind of guy. He gave me a couple of sarcastic comments through his high-riser handlebars and rode away disgusted. When music brought us together a few years down the line, we kept looking at each other, trying to make the connection. Then it came up in conversation and we had a good laugh. Since my drumming was a lot better than my paper delivering, things turned out OK. Now, back to the interview.

Don Giesen: I saved up the $39.95 and ordered this guitar. Once I got it, there was a book with it – I think it was a Mel Bay book, but I'm not sure – and I thought, "Gee, this is hard," and put it in the closet.

Don's family soon moved into a neighborhood where he met up with the Beaver family and befriended Ron and Steve, brothers whose father had at one time played guitar as a young man back in Tennessee. He had played country music and knew the basic chord patterns. Don's interest in guitar was rekindled and he began taking his guitar to the Beaver's house where Mr. Beaver would teach Don and Ron the guitar basics. Don readily admits that Ron had much more of an affinity for the instrument. Ron's father eventually also bought his son a Silvertone guitar. The next step was that they started learning surf tunes, practicing either in the Beaver's garage, or in Don's bedroom.

Don Giesen: (There was a guy) in the same age group as Doug and Alex and all those guys. He was in a surf band (possibly the Solid Senders, who knows?) and had the famous Airline guitar that was from Montgomery Wards. My folks asked him if he was willing to give me lessons. So he would come over once a week and show me surf songs. I can't remember his name. He was in one of those surf bands that was around during that time, which would have been during the Blackouts/Omens period. I learned some stuff from him and I would go over and show it to Ron Beaver.

John French's Drum Inspiration
So, here's the story of how I started playing drums. I had a platonic girl friend by the name of Cindy Anderson. Cindy's mom was a single parent. I hung out at their house a lot during the summer before I was a freshman in High School. One night, Mrs. Anderson invited me to go to the

drive-in movie with them. We went to see *Kid Galahad*, an Elvis Presley movie. In the beginning of the movie, Elvis was sitting on the back of a big 18-wheeler cruising down the road. He was singing, "I'm the King - of the whole wide world," and he was keeping time by patting his open hands on his legs. This seemed to really impress Cindy Anderson who thought it was "boss" (a contemporary colloquialism like "awesome," or "rad" or "cool"), and since I *also* wished to impress her, I started doing this, hoping that girls would instantly be at my command. (Jay Leno once mentioned that he thought a Playboy swizzle stick would do the same for him). Although it didn't quite work for me as well as it had for Elvis, it did get me in the habit of keeping time to music that I listened to. I started listening to the different drums and what role each played in timekeeping. A few weeks later, Mike McGill, a teen friend talked me into reluctantly entering a "twist" contest (anybody remember the "twist?" – if the answer is yes, then you have my condolences). My partner was a girl named Cheral Dee King. She and I won second place in the twist contest. I had never danced before with the exception of school folk dancing. Of course, it doesn't take a brain surgeon to do the twist.

I became more interested when I discovered the music at the contest was to be supplied by a live surf band comprised of local musicians and I became really interested when I noticed that the drummer was my childhood friend, John Parr. He was one of my best childhood friends until Junior High where we drifted apart. I had been told by the aforementioned Cindy Anderson that he had started playing the drums, but I hadn't seen him for a while, and here he was - already in a band. I closely scrutinized his playing and learned a great deal about drumming from this observation. Remember this was a *small* small town. Main Street was seven blocks long. When they had a parade, you saw everyone you knew. Having a live band play was a *really big deal* for a kid my age (12) at that time.

Then, a few weeks later, I was at my friend, Gene Watson's house. I would ride my 10-speed bike over to his place nearly every day. Part (over half, in fact) of the attraction was Linda Nelson. She lived next door to Gene and was "real bitchin'lookin'" (the term "bitchin'was actually the bolder derivative of the word "twitchin'which meant the same as "boss", which has already been explained). Gene's friend, Karl Pearcy lived across the street from Gene and we often went over to listen to records, because, of the three of us, he had the best record collection.

Karl had a room off the back of his garage also, and the first time I tried alcohol was by consuming orange screwdrivers in that room. That night was especially memorable due to the fact that I was able to crawl outside and vomit several times, which gave me something really cool to talk about when school started next Fall and to write about in this book, evidently. It was one of those "rite of passage" moments. Why do males do these stupid things?

The next morning, I awoke with my head leaning at a 45-degree angle against a solid block wall, further enhancing my experiential definition of the word "hangover." Someone offered me orange juice for breakfast - an even further enhancement. It was Saturday, and I rushed on my bicycle, wind whistling past my ears at a deafening volume, to my pool-cleaning job at my wealthy neighbor's home. As I carried out this responsibility, I fell into the pool. This succeeded not only in stirring up all the dirt in the water (which was to be avoided at all costs during pool-cleaning operations), but also cleared my head. It also allowed me to discover first hand that swimming with a hangover while completely dressed requires much more physical exertion than participating in the same activity while relatively sober and clad only in a swimsuit.

Back to Karl. He had a drum record (33 1/3 LP), which Gene requested to be played because it was so "groovy" (which meant the same thing as "twitchin", "bitchin" which means the same thing as "boss," which has already been explained). It turned out to be by Sandy Nelson. I had never heard drums played in such a melodic manner and I decided right then and there that I was going to be a drummer.

It was a good summer for me. Cheral and I wound up swapping gum at the Antelope Theatre while watching yet another Elvis movie. I guess the leg slapping worked after all. She was the first girl I ever kissed. Does anyone ever forget that experience? Of course, when your friends (loosely defined) found out you were getting ready to kiss a girl at the "walk-in," (our name for a movie theatre that wasn't a "drive-in,") they all sat about two rows behind you making sure you stuck to your agenda. If you seemed a bit hesitant, they would say things like, "What are ya waitin'for, chicken-shit?" or "Smooth move, Ex lax!", which of course greatly added to the romantic ambience and spontaneity of the moment.

Cheral and I soon parted company. Social values dictated that, when in High School, "thou shalt not date Junior High girls." I did learn the secret of the bouffant hairdo during our lengthy phone conversations, however. Interesting thing is that girls wore their hair in bouffant hairstyles in those days. They would use tons of hair spray and "rat" their hair and smooth the top layer so that it eventually looked as though they were wearing a football helmet made entirely of highly-compressed hair with the added bonus of bangs. The ways you could tell them apart from football players were (1) They wore their eye shadow *above* their eyes, and (2) Their pads were not on their shoulders, but in a much more interesting location. I was told that girls would go for weeks without washing their hair just to achieve the desired affect.

Pubescent Legends

There was even a legend that a girl (usually described as Hispanic, but depending on the source) died after a black widow had secretly made a nest in her ratted hair. The eggs hatched and the young poisonous creatures ultimately bit her simultaneously in a moment of well-orchestrated, militant, homicidal, arachnoidal brutality. It is well-known that young Black Widows possess little self-control.

There were other little urban (or in our case, suburban) legends floating around. My favorite was the story of the boy and girl who parked their car on Gody Pass, a local "lover's lane", which had several areas where adolescents could park, take in the view of the city, and conceive an unplanned child all at the same time – for free. The story goes that a couple were in hot embrace when a pecking sound at the window drew their attention.

There, through the steamed-up genuine safety glass car window, appeared a hideous half-human creature growling and foaming at the mouth while desperately attempting to open the door of the car. The important part of the story is that he (why are these half -humans always *male*?) had a *hook* instead of a hand. This is important for two reasons: (1) It shows howprosthetics and people who wear them were often demonized, and (2) How did a half-human disguise himself as *completely* human so that he could obtain a prosthetic device (as in: "Yes, I would be able to recognize Bigfoot if I saw him again because he was wearing a *chrome leg brace!*").

The boy, terrified, was able to force his car to start (after the monster-movie tradition of several moments of nearly-dead-battery attempts, the girl screaming hysterically, the pecking on the window intensifying, until suddenly the engine fires up) and drive away, the hideous creature running alongside the car, eventually unable to keep up any longer and finally fading into the darkness behind. Pulling up to the girl's house, the shaken couple sits for a moment discussing their experience and chalking it up to hallucination and imagination. However, as the boy gets out of the car, he discovers a hook hanging from the outside door handle (fade-in to loud, dissonant music).

Being a father, I now have the perspective to be absolutely certain this story was made up by the father of a beautiful girl to scare the living daylights out of her dates.

Have you noticed yet that I tend to digress?

Drumsticks/Fall, 1962

Back to the drumsticks. Best of all, or worst of all, depending entirely upon your perspective, this was the summer when I found in a drawer a pair of drumsticks that my older brother Phil had left behind. Phil, my big brother, never approved of my becoming a drummer. I find it ironic that had the numbskull (a mere term of endearment, brother) not left his drumsticks behind, I would probably never have progressed further than slapping my thighs in time to 45 rpm records and would have eventually become a rocket scientist like Steve, my childhood friend who mom wouldn't allow me to hang out with because he seemed a little *effeminate.*

So, it is here that I officially blame my older brother Phil for my choice to walk the degenerative path to degradation, despair, financial ruin, and occasional critical acclaim as "Beefheart's weird drummer." At the same time, it is probably this very fact that slowed our progress in the space race to a mere crawl. Obviously, Steve desperately needed my help to speed things up.

The first few days with drumsticks were very discouraging. I found myself dropping sticks more than holding them. But I had been listening to drum rhythms and I was able to figure out how things were supposed to be. I already had some coordination between my hands and feet. Soon, I was pounding out rhythms on everything in sight. We had a yellow plastic wastebasket that, when turned upside-down had a surprisingly good sound that I used constantly. It was when the bottom fell out of that wastebasket that my parents began to consider that I could be serious. I also wore all the covers off my schoolbooks, which I laid out in drum-kit fashion on the desk each day after school. My Geometry book was the snare, English book was suspended tom, and Geography book was floor tom. I practiced all the beats this way until I had mastered the basics, and, of course, never did my homework. My instructors, however, were impressed that all my books looked well-used.

Ed And Mart's Fix-It Shop/Late Fall 1962

I found a used drum-kit in a little shop called Ed and Mary's Fix-It Shop, which was, coincidentally in the same building that formerly housed Lee's Music Box. My mother was a page (a person who puts books back on the shelf) at the library. She worked in the evenings with Mary, Ed's wife. I had gone down to the shop to pick up some repair item, probably a toaster, and there before my eyes was a drum set. It was an old used drum set but it was a *drum set*! There was a 24" bass drum, a pedal with a tennis ball for a beater, three tom toms of various sizes, and a hi-hat with some really cheesy cymbals. There was also a cowbell, a wood block and holder, and a bunch of sticks and accessories.   All the drums had calfskin heads, were hand-painted white, and bore the brand name WFL Drums, which I found out later stood for "William F. Ludwig."

I used to go in this shop every day after school and look at these drums. They were $75. It seemed like more money than I could ever hope to save. I wasn't good at business. I was the only kid I knew who successfully ran two thriving paper routes into the red. Then, one day, I went to the shop and the drums were gone. My heart sank, of course. I moped home and moped through the next week or two.

One morning, my mother said she was keeping me out of school that day. After breakfast she said, " Follow me" and took me into her room. Opening the closet, she displayed the drumset. "We were going to wait until your birthday," she explained jokingly,"but I doubt you would have survived that long." Now, my parents were definitely on the lower end of middle class. This gift probably represented the better portion of a week's salary for my father in 1962.

Practice Makes Perfect

The drums were cleaned and set up in no time. I was pounding away Sandy Nelson rhythms right away. My parents could not believe that I already knew how to play (trash cans and school-books, remember?). The only disappointment was that I had no snare or ride cymbal.

Tope Minter 1962

Tope Minter, our exterminator, was a drummer also. One day as I was playing (may have been the first day I had the drums), he asked to come in. He had been playing Sundays on a TV show out of Bakersfield CA, a decidedly country & western influenced area. There was a show on television called *Cals Country Corral* or perhaps *Kals Kountry Korral*.

There was a man named Cal Worthington who owned a car dealership called Worthington (surprise) Dodge. His commercials ran continuously through this country & western music show. Tope played on this show occasionally. Mr. Minter requested a chance to play my drums. I was more than willing (after all, this guy was on TV!). He played all the drums in a very unique way and used a lot of foot pedal syncopation. "Don't just play some of the drums," he offered, " Play 'em all!"

He talked to me about how most drummers seldom develop their bass drum foot and that he had been complimented quite often on his bass drum syncopation. I had never thought about this before. From then on, I tried in earnest to make up patterns that utilized the bass drum. I don't know whatever happened to Tope, but if you're reading this, "Thank you!" By the way, he's the only Tope Minter I've ever known.

Cal Worthington moved to LA and began to dominate the airways with extremely annoying car commercials. His interruptions of movies must have set new records in obnoxiousness. His use of animals in commercials was disgusting and degrading -exactly the kind of thing that makes you extremely rich in LA. Before this, Ralph Williams Ford (in the city of Encino) had been the dominant new and used car salesman. Ralph Williams had a salesman who perched his German Shepherd atop the hoods (bonnets) of cars he was selling.

Since Worthington had no class, as a parody, he started having every animal imaginable on his commercials, which he always called "My dog Spot." Worst of all, he wore flamboyant cowboy outfits, and promised if he couldn't make you a deal, he'd "eat a bug," and "stand on his head 'til his ears were turning red." His main thing was to have commercial interruptions about every five to six minutes punctuated by an extremely annoying commercial jingle, which featured adept banjo picking which became redundant after 60 playings on a daily basis. Cal probably made far more money than he needed and certainly did his share (along with Ted Turner) to ruin the presentation of film noire. This was when I quit watching old B&W movies ... which has nothing at all to do with the book I'm trying to write, except that I always wanted to vent my frustration with Cal in a very public way. Thank you, though this section will probably be removed by the editor.

Boston Family To California

Around this time, the Boston family had come out to visit friends who had moved to California. They had settled in an unheard-of small town called Lancaster. The cold dampness of Illinois proved to be the "push" factor, and the warm Mojave Desert and wide-open spaces was the "pull" factor which motivated the family to pull up stakes and move in 1963, when Mark was a freshman in High School. The family moved to Quartz Hill, which didn't have its own High School yet, so Mark was going to Palmdale High, and then to a temporary Quartz Hill campus, and finally to the permanent campus. He was in the first graduating class at the newly built Quartz Hill High School.

Jennifer

During my freshmen and sophomore years, most of my spare time was devoted to playing the drums and dating my steady girlfriend, who I will call "Jennifer" (because I'm a nice guy and want to protect her privacy – actually an idea I stole from Frank Zappa's book). Jennifer was the most beautiful girl I had ever seen. A slim brunette with pixie eyes, high cheekbones, and the most gorgeous tanned skin in the universe. She walked into my freshman year Geometry class wearing a mint-green boatneck blouse and matching full skirt and enchanted me so completely that I couldn't think about anything but her for most of my waking hours. She was the first to steal my heart.

Ludwig and Parr

I persisted in my dream to become a drummer. I would call my drummer friend John Parr and ride my ten-speed bicycle two to three miles to his house at night to pick his brain about the art of drumming. Although his father had recently died, prior to this his parents had given him professional lessons, and he was quite adept for his age. His Ludwig set was the Black Oyster finish like Ringo used (though this was slightly pre-British Invasion), but he had an extra floor tom in the style of the big band drummers. John taught me a lot about foot pedal syncopation. I would sometimes just sit and watch him play for hours.

I can't easily describe the intensity of this fascination and how it affected every aspect of my life. I would sit and actually smell the drums. They had a special smell from the varnish inside the drum when the heads were taken off. I still love that smell. I would sit and study every little detail of Parr's set and inquire as to his reasons for his setup. I remember somehow getting my hands on a Slingerland catalog and dreaming of the day I would be able to get a five-piece, red sparkle set.

Jeff Cotton/1962

Don Giesen: Somehow we (he and the Beaver brothers) *met Jeff Cotton. He lived by Piute school over by that housing tract, Tamarack Fair. He also had a guitar and he would come over on his three-speed bike with his guitar and we would show him stuff and he would show us stuff.*

At this point, Merrel Fankhauser came onto the scene. His father owned a company called Charter Air Service, which he ran in affiliation with an aircraft company. In 1962, it became necessary for him to move his operation to Fox Field, which was a small private airport slightly northwest of Lancaster.

Jeff Cotton's father worked at Fox Field and became friends with the senior Fankhauser. The two guitarists'fathers compared notes and decided to get their sons together. Merrel found Jeff Cotton to be a quick study.

Merrel Fankhauser: When I met Jeff he was fourteen and I taught him a lot of chords and things that he didn't know because I had already been playing for years and he was a beginner ... Jeff kind of got his own thing going and he really did progress and he got really good.

The Exiles

Don Giesen recalls the beginnings of a band Fankhauser started called Merrel And The Exiles.

Don Giesen: The two of them (Cotton and Fankhauser) got together and that's how The Exiles were formed - by him making Jeff his protégé - making him the second guitar player.
John French: Merrel was pretty young then, maybe about 18?
DG: Yeah, I think he was just fresh out of high school. I would have to guess (the year as)'62.

The first time I saw Jeff with The Exiles on stage was at a High School dance while I was still going with Jennifer. He had long, thick, straight blond hair, parted in the middle. It was longer than any boy's hair I had ever seen, although short by later standards. This was even before The Beatles had made it acceptable. Claiming it was part of his "professional stage appearance," Jeff had been so determined to keep his long hair that he had obtained special permission from the school to wear his hair long even though it violated the strict school dress-codes. The Exiles drummer, Greg Hampton, was a fellow that I went to high school with, so we eventually met and played in marching band together. Jim Fergueson was on bass guitar, and Danny Stevens played saxophone.

The Chevelles
At an assembly in high school, before I had re-acquainted myself with Don Giesen and when I was probably a sophomore, I heard his band, The Chevelles, play. The band was a trio which consisted of Don Giesen on rhythm guitar, Ron Beaver on lead, and a drummer whose name I cannot recall, but I will say he was quite good.

John French: And you were playing instrumental surf music?
Don Giesen: Yeah, the eighth grade dances and that kind of stuff. We had no bass player, just the two of us plugging into one amplifier. Our "idols" of course, were The Exiles, cause they did all the big dances at Jane Reynold's Park. They had all the suits with the rainbow stripes on them and the preacher-type black collars. They had green suede boots with the zipper up the side with the ring on it (all said in mock excitement.)

After I saw The Chevelles play in that high school assembly in early 1964 I began getting more and more of the urge to play in a band. However, I still had one little problem. My drums were not cool-looking. I had no snare drum, and I had no ride cymbal. However, that problem would soon be solved.

New Slingerlands/Spring 1964
In the spring of 1964 (which was the end of my sophomore year in High School), my father mysteriously asked me to go with him somewhere on a Friday night. I wasn't too happy about the idea, but I did it. I thought maybe we were going out to dinner, but it turned out instead to be Lancaster Music, which was owned by Ronnie Gaye. Ronnie was a drummer who had played during the big band era. My father pointed up to a high shelf at a brand new set of Slingerland drums with the black diamond finish. "I want to buy that drum set," he said.
I was in heaven. A new set! A BRAND NEW SET OF DRUMS! They cost $456. I never thought in a million years that my father would spend that much money on me. He was a factory worker; I think it took him two years to pay them off. We set them up in the living room that night. I brought Jennifer over to the house that night to show her my new set. I played and played and played for hours. Can you imagine this poor girl having to sit there and do nothing for hours?

The Continuing Jennifer Saga
Jennifer and I were mostly inseparable from the time we met in our freshmen year until she broke up with me during the summer between sophomore and junior years in high school. We had been through the Bay of Pigs invasion, the Cuban missile crisis and the fear of the Cold War and nuclear holocaust together. I was sitting behind her in English class when we first heard of the Kennedy assassination November 23, 1963. We witnessed the British Invasion and shared memories of the early Vietnam War.
Her reason (or so she said) for the breakup is because she wanted me to be a business executive and I wanted to be a jazz drummer. She started going with a lifeguard who owned what she described as an "adorable little baby blue Datsun sports car."(Note: further proof that chicks always go for the car).

I was heartbroken. Even worse, she had been going out with him for months while she was still seeing me! Girls are weird! Anyway, this was the beginning of some rather anti-social behavior on my part. It was my official entry into the world of "the walking wounded."

That summer, while I was still ignorant of Jennifer's two-timing; I had played drums all day every day, for hour after obsessive hour. In the mornings, I would swim, and during the heat of the day, all day, I pounded away to Dave Brubeck (whose drummer was Joe Morello), Pete Fountain (whose drummer was Jack Sperling), and other drummers I respected. I mastered much of the basics of what I heard and emulated the rest. I also listened and played along to all the popular Top 40 records I could get my hands on. In the afternoon and evening, I was back at Gene Watson's hanging out with Linda Nelson and Karl Pearcy and listening to more and more Sandy Nelson records. Musically, this was a time of extreme musical growth for me – at the cost of my relationship with Jennifer.

Mark Boston Early Bands – Influences

John French: Do you remember the names of the bands you played in after you moved here to the valley, what the names of them were and who was in them?
Mark Boston: The first band I was in was called The Naturals, probably about '64. That was the first Rock 'n'Roll or whatever – Top 40 (band). It had Ernie (Zane) Wood, and some guy named Bruce (possibly Brent Brac) on drums. I played the bass fiddle.

Like many of the bands from that era, the young high school bands had to learn a mixture of "grown-up" music along with the Top 40 music they really desired to play. A favorite "grown-up" piece was *Girl From Ipanema*, which would be played once every set when performing for older folks, hoping they wouldn't notice we were repeating our limited "adult repertoire." Ernie Wood, a local guitarist, fronted the band. Wood went on later to play in the Mike Curb Organization for a time. When I spoke with him a few years back, he owned a small postal service and was heavily involved in the Dutch Reformed Church. Now, he teaches guitar and gigs with some of my friends in local cover bands.

MB: Then I got really influenced by Paul McCartney and The Beatles. They were "the end of music" I thought they were "it."

Like many of the Valley musicians, Mark had found himself strongly influenced by the British Invasion. Unlike many, however, he had started playing before the British Invasion and so had a few years of experience over many of the young kids who heard the Beatles and decided to start up a band. He was breaking free of his parent's musical influence and finding his own direction.

Mark Boston: Then I went through a stage where I hated country & western and didn't want anything to do with it. I played rock'n'roll.

Michael Melchione

My first band experience came as a chance meeting with a gymnast by the name of Mike Melchione. I had admired his abilities in high school gymnastics the year before and had been encouraged by my coach, John Murnane, to sign up for gymnastics because of my physical strength. I took his advice in my sophomore year.

I had viewed Melchione from afar and never considered approaching him, as I was so terrible in gymnastics that I thought he would laugh me away. For instance, I spent several weeks landing on my tailbone while trying to perfect a front somersault. I worked up a round-off back handspring and while working on the back flip (the next step in the routine), I landed on my head, which made me re-think gymnastics as a way to impress girls. I now have a large bone spur in my neck as a result of those endeavors.

It was also at this point that I chose music instead of gymnastics as a main interest. It is hard to paralyze yourself playing drums …

Melchione was literally as strong as an ape - an all-around gymnast who could do a double back flip in tumbling. He also excelled in the parallel bars, rings, side horse, and free X.

In the fall of 1964, the beginning of my junior year, I was emotionally devastated by my recent separation from Jennifer. As I sat, melancholy, in Gymnastics class, I overheard gymnast Melchione tell a friend of his that he was looking for a drummer for his band. My ears perked up. I didn't know Mike played guitar. Having a new drumset, I could now play in a band without being embarrassed by my old drums, so why not give it a chance?

I approached Mike and the next thing I knew, he was picking me up for a practice with his band in his parents'car. The rehearsal was at guitarist Mark Thompson's parents'house. I had never met Mark before. It turned out that Mike was now dating Mike's former girlfriend, Claudia. That is how Mike and Mark met. Claudia was also Mark's neighbor. So, into this tangled web I walked. There was another guitarist named Carl Meyerholtz.

We set up in Mark's living room and started to play. They were playing guitars through Mark's tiny practice amplifiers. We played instrumental surf songs. It was mostly stuff I already knew. Our repertoire consisted of songs like *Pipeline, Wipe Out, Walk, Don't Run* and *Miserlou* (Melchione was a Dick Dale freak and did a fairly impressive impersonation of his hero).

After the rehearsal Mike helped me to carry my drums to his parents'beige Plymouth Valiant convertible. "You're a great drummer!" he exclaimed. I was elated. I had passed my first test. I joined the band. Mike was the leader, and he soon added Harold Fields on bass (a folk singer/guitarist with a good voice who didn't play bass or own one), and Chuck (?) on saxophone. We started rehearsing in our parents'living rooms, taking turns so as not to drive any one family completely nuts but each just a little insane.

Don Aldridge: They (Beefheart) were on the edge of it. But there were other people, like John French, who was playing with a band called The Maltesemen in high school and working with a guy called Mike Melchione who later on I worked with for a short period of time. Mike eventually went into the Navy and went into Seals training.

Besides being a reasonably good band leader, and a great gymnast, Mike had another very important talent which I feel must be recognized:

John French: He used to open beer bottles with his teeth.
Don Aldridge: Yeah that was his thing, he could open a quart of Coors with his teeth.

The Maltesemen
Harold Fields had the most charming personality of anyone in the band. He came up with the name Maltesemen because we played surf music. Surfers thought Maltese crosses were "boss." The Maltesemen played several local gigs. Our first earnings went to buy uniforms; gray preacher suits with the high collars similar to the first uniforms The Beatles wore in early pictures. They cost $18 a suit. We would all wear them to high school anytime we were having a gig that night.

Roehr's Music Box/Fall of 1964

Don Giesen: Cliff Roehr had the store called The Music Box, which used to be owned by a mom and pop and they were called the Lings.

Don Giesen's father was a square dance caller.

Don Giesen: My father knew the Lings because of his square dancing thing. He used to be able to get records from them to use for square dancing. When Cliff Roehr bought them out, he was a security guard out at Mira Loma prison. I guess he didn't like his job (and wanted to) get into something else as an entrepreneur.

Roehr's Music Box was conveniently located three blocks down the street from my parents' home. I went in one day soon after it opened just to see what it was like. Expecting only a record store, I was surprised to find that he had a few musical instruments. Cliff was very friendly and related well to teenagers. He had the franchise for Rogers Drums, of which I had never heard. He gave me a detailed description of why these drums were better than any other set on the market.

I wound up spending a lot of time at Roehr's. A few of my friends would eventually work here. A lot of the contacts I made were through this store.

Meanwhile another friend, Don Aldridge, was beginning to take an interest in musical performance. He was also a bit interested in writing, which later turned out to be his doorway into the music world. I had known Don since starting High School through a mutual friend, Dan Moore. Don also lived across the street from my (now ex) girlfriend. He always wore shades and had the perfect James Dean hairstyle. Not one hair was ever out of place on this boy's head. It must have taken an hour a day to style this hair.

Although we never played music together, we had parallel experiences in the local music scene and knew many of the same people, including a guy named Don Vliet.

Don Aldridge: Musically, I had a church background, I sang solos in church as a boy and then when I got into my middle teens, I began to go into secular (music). I began playing guitar when I was about 15. Bob Dylan made a big impression on me.

On the Mid-Sixties Music Scene

Jerry Handley: The music industry was really in the doldrums. That's why The Beatles hit so big; there wasn't anybody else really hot at the time. The Beatles hit in '63 and everybody was waiting for somebody, you know. We weren't really interested in doing something "commercial" - music and being POP stars - we were just a blues band in Lancaster who wanted to do some jobs. Do something different, bring back that old blues stuff, electrifiy it, and play a lot of Chicago blues. We loved Muddy Waters and Howlin' Wolf. If we could play that stuff, we were happy.

Jerry here portrays a feeling of playing for fun, without the sometimes overbearing ambition that turns groups into clones of one another, motivated more by commercial success than by art.

Up until the British Invasion, there had been The Beach Boys, the first true vocal surf group of which I knew, and a lot of instrumental surf bands, like the Surfaris *(Wipe Out)*. Then there was the "industrialized product": music like Connie Stevens, Rick Nelson, Neil Sedaka, and a more sedate post-Army Presley who was actually parodying himself in movies.

Doug Moon: All these bands were around. Merrel and Jeff - a bunch of new bands were starting up. Up until the early sixties, there were only a few guys good enough to really put a band together. You had The Blackouts, and then The Omens, and not much else. But all of a sudden, in the sixties all these young musicians were just coming out of the woodwork. You had Merrel and his band who were basically Beatle clones. So, you had several new bands starting to form and do things. So we had several local bands that were kind of doing the local gigs and maybe a dance or a car show thing. We used to have car clubs that sponsored concerts. They'd hire a band just as a fundraiser. There weren't a lot of gigs. A lot of these bands were too young to play in nightclubs. A lot of the nightclub bands were bands that they would import from LA. Back then, believe it or not, most of the clubs up here were union. So they would have most of the bands, who played at the clubs, like the DI (Desert Inn) and places like that were union, so they would have bands that came up from LA.

Some of my first musical experiences came from hearing bands in a local club called The Nile Room, which was attached to the Sands Bowl.

Doug Moon: So these up-and-coming young bands were just struggling to be heard. You had the garage bands. But nobody was really making a big name for themselves. So while all this was going on, Jerry Handley and the rest of what was left over from The Omens were just kind of jamming around trying to figure out what to do next. About that time, Alex came back to town. All this stuff started to come together.

Don Aldridge: In 1964, this valley was like a melting pot of bands. Eventually the whole thing culminated in what they called "Teen Town:" at the Antelope Valley Fair where all of the local bands would play. I always thought that if the kids around would have known what they were really about, this place would have exploded like Liverpool. We had some real talent. There was so much happening.

There was indeed a lot happening in this sparse remote region. The population density was low, but the electricity became stronger and stronger after the British Invasion.

The British Invasion had revitalized and radically changed the course of the music industry. Unlike the original Magic Band members and their contemporaries, kids in America were re-discovering blues through groups like The Yardbirds (my personal favorite and eventually a popular one with almost all the local groups). There were also The Animals, The Kinks and The Rolling Stones.

Some brilliant promotion scheme created Paul Revere And The Raiders, which, I suppose, was America's answer to the British Invasion. This manufactured band featured singer Mark Lindsey and they appeared on television often, I think even hosting their own show for a while. They wore revolutionary war costumes and had a cutesy bubblegum image. There was one thing I liked about them in retrospect; they had an anti-drug agenda when it was most needed. One of their anti-drug songs, *Kicks, had the line "Kicks just keep getting harder to find."* When they did a reunion band in the eighties, I believe they changed the lyrics to *"Chicks just keep getting harder to find."*

Robert Axelrod

Robert Axelrod was one of my small circle of friends, along with Harold Rudnick. Through these two, I was introduced into the Jewish community. I loved the Jewish kids because they had class and manners. They seemed more civilized than most. I remember Harold Rudnick, Bob Axelrod, Joey Pincus, Debby Reckon (who looked great in a lime-green bikini), and many others. I was invited to their parties and it was always a great time. This was an area of my life when I feel I developed a bit socially.

Axelrod was working for the Employment Department the summer between our sophomore and junior years and found a job for me at the Salvation Army Thrift Store. My boss's name was Miss (not Mrs.) Juhnke (pronounced "junky" which of course made her the butt of a series of running jokes between Axlerod and me). I kept this job for the next two years. While working, I spied what I thought was an extremely tall woman. This tall woman turned out to be a man with long hair. I was totally shocked. Please keep in mind this was 1964 or 65 and I was from a small town. I was to see this guy again, soon.

I Meet Jeff Cotton at Roehr's/1964

Roehr's became a hangout for musicians after school. It was right on my way home, and I stopped by almost every day. One day Jeff Cotton was there. He picked up a guitar and started improvising a blues solo, and I could see immediately that his playing was miles ahead of anyone in the Maltesemen band.

I talked to him for a few minutes. He remembered seeing me at a rehearsal at Harold Field's mother's house. He and fellow musician Don Giesen had hopped the fence just as I was doing a drum solo to see who was playing. It was a Bo Diddley-type piece called *Surf Drums* Jeff and Don told me they were very impressed with my playing, but thought I was wasting my time with those guys. I suppose this would be viewed as stroking the egos, but we definitely had a mutual respect for each other's musical abilities. I felt more in tune with these two and I was frustrated within the confines of the other band.

Jeff and Don were guitar instructors at Roehr's Music Box.

Don Giesen: Cliff wanted to get beyond records because he saw the potential that there were local bands around. It seemed he was thinking "If I can associate those bands with my store, maybe I can start to sell instruments, or maybe I can grow my business or get all the kids to come in because I'm the 'in guy'."
John French: Which he temporarily succeeded in doing.
DG: Yeah, so he coerced me and Jeff Cotton into (teaching) - "Hey, why don't you come over here and give guitar lessons?" He wasn't able get the Fender franchise because Lancaster Music had it, so he started selling Guild guitars. We started teaching there. Then Cliff started pressuring us "You need to persuade these people to buy my instruments. It upsets me that you play Fender guitars because the kids see you playing Fenders and that dissuades them from wanting to buy my Guilds up on the wall" That's kind of when we started saying, "Well ... we don't want to do that."

Jeff eventually quit working with Merrel. Rumour had it he and Ferguson felt that Merrel had a timing problem.

Don Giesen: But then, as time progressed they started thinking, "Well, Merrel has bad timing. We kind of want to get away from him."
John French: You're talking Jeff for example.
DG: That's why Jeff and Jim Fergueson wanted to get away from Merrel because of the timing and all that and now they knew all the songs. They wanted to take that next step forward.

Jeff and Don Giesen had teamed up by the time they heard me playing drums at a Maltesemen rehearsal, so they asked me if I would be interested in teaming up with them. I said I would practice with them and see how it went.

Don Giesen and bassist Jim Fergueson came over to pick me up for a rehearsal, but I was torn because of my friendship with Mike, who had been a great friend, so I waffled a bit and stayed with the Maltesemen for a while, although I actually felt I had outgrown them. Fergueson later confided that he was upset with me for my decision and, as he put it, "I wanted to beat the shit out of you." We laughed about it, but I thought secretly "He probably could have done it as he's huge."

Jim Fergueson

Bassist Jim Fergueson who was eighteen or nineteen at the time, lived right down the street from the Giesen's with his wife's family. He had made friends with Ron Beaver and Don Giesen and they would have jam sessions and exchange ideas on guitar. When The Exiles were forming, Jeff and Merrel needed a bassist, so they talked Jim into playing bass. Jim was large-framed and had the size and strength to handle the much larger fretboard of a full-sized bass guitar. Jim's mother bought him his first equipment, a Fender Jazz bass and a Rickenbacker amplifier.

The Maltesemen 2

In the meantime, The Maltesemen quickly became a quartet instead of a sextet. Chuck was the first to leave. He didn't seem to fit in and had very little rock experience. It was too bad, because his parents had the best garage of all in which to practice - an important asset in those days.

Then Carl Meyerholtz was fired. He resented this and kept our microphones at his parents' house. We went to his house to get them. No one was home, and the front door was open, so I walked in and opened the drawer he kept them in and left. The parents'threatened us with "breaking and entering." Carl wanted me to be arrested. I thought Carl was being a bad sport, told him so, and then I punched him in the fist with my nose. Turned out I was a lousy fighter. For some reason, I found this highly humorous and wound up back at rehearsal with tissue stuffed up my bleeding nose laughing hysterically at the utter pointlessness of violence. This led Melchione to begin seriously coaching me in self-defense. Lesson number one: never hit someone's fist with your nose.

The band was now a four-piece group and we played a private party at someone's home. A middle-aged lady who was a bit under the influence, decided she liked me. It turned out that her son-in-law who had recently moved from Hollywood had some musical connections and might be willing to manage us.

Rod Devon

Jim Taylor (the son-in-law) met with us at our next rehearsal. He drove a brand new Thunderbird. He was 24 or so and kept talking to us about songs that he liked, demonstrating the songs by singing them. They were mostly out of date rock 'n'roll do-wop stuff like *Oh Donna*. I could see it coming a mile away. This guy wanted to be our lead singer. I thought he was too old – and dated. Unfortunately, I was outvoted, and Jim Taylor joined our band under the stage name of Rod Devon.

Doug Moon/Captain Beefheart And His Magic Band

During this time, Mark Thompson and I formed the "walking wounded" society. We thought it was a unique situation to have broken relationships and therefore we were its only two official members. The usual arrangement was to get his older sister to illicitly buy us a case of beer. We would ride in his parents''59 Ford, wearing the weirdest clothes imaginable in order to attract attention, all the while becoming more intoxicated and lamenting our lot in life. We kept the leftover beer in my room and would have a couple of warm ones in the morning before school.

One night, as we sat in the parking lot of Orange Julius, the most recent local hangout, Doug Moon approached me. After the usual small talk, I found that he had just joined this band called

Captain Beefheart And His Magic Band. I thought it was a stupid name but was able to suppress my laughter because I had already heard the name, thus taking the punch from the punchline. "So he was a member?" I thought, "Well, they would never amount to anything with a name like that. "

The Maltesemen, Featuring Rod Devon

We started working with "Rod" and the more we worked with him the less I liked it. He was verbally abusive to his beautiful wife. He also bullied us and changed his whole singing style to one of hoarse screaming in a matter of weeks. The band plodded on and soon, we auditioned for the Teenage Fair in Hollywood.

Teenage Fair Audition/1965

We auditioned at the Ivar Theatre, which I believe was on Melrose Avenue in Hollywood. The same day we auditioned, another desert band auditioned: Captain Beefheart And His Magic Band. I didn't actually get to hear them, as we had to leave quickly afterwards because of the number of competing bands in the crowded theatre. It was like a cattle call. I did catch a glimpse of them setting up.

Beefheart's The Rage

Don Aldridge: So Captain Beefheart was all the rage. He was pretty new they were just breaking out around here playing the Elks club, playing various ...
John French: The animal houses..

Aldridge had spied an ad on Roehr's bulletin board, which read: "1956 Dodge, straight eight, real ginchy, call ... and it gave the number.

Don Aldridge: I said, "What's 'ginchy'Cliff, what is it?" "Oh," he said, "you know who put that there, Captain Beefheart - Don Vliet."

As they were speaking about this, Vliet drove up in the little Dodge. His father had just died and he was selling his car. Vliet and Aldridge were introduced by Roehr, who hoisted Aldridge up on the counter and insisted he sing a song for Vliet. The slightly intimidated Aldridge sang a Dylan song: *The Ballad of Hollis Brown.*

Don Aldridge: Anyhow, I did that song and Don said, "Geez, man, that's heavy! Heavy man!" - you remember him saying that all the time? I thought, "Wow, he likes me!" We became friends from that moment.

The two Dons left the shop together and Aldridge was driven by his new friend in the ginchy car to Doug Moon's house, who was listening to a Jimmy Reed album. Vliet's description of Jimmy Reed was, "Man, that guy's really" – and then pantomined shooting a hypodermic into his arm.

John French: That's kind of a shame because it seemed like Don would think that a drug was the inspiration for an artist's doing whatever he did.
DA: Well, even on an entry level, it may often be true.
JF: But, I mean, that it was brought up in such an endearing way, like "That's a good thing."
DA: Of course, we know, and I especially know, that it wasn't such a good thing. Anyhow, from that moment on, Don and I became almost inseparable. This is, like I say, '65.

CHAPTER SIX:
PRECOGNITION

Don in Lancaster 1965. Courtesy of Doug Moon.

Broken Pedal, Winter 1965

Doug Moon called me one night to ask if I would loan the Beefheart drummer, Vic Mortenson, my foot pedal. It seemed he had broken his and they had a rehearsal scheduled for that night. I was offered a chance to actually go to a Captain Beefheart And His Magic Band rehearsal. This was a big deal at this point. I had not heard the band play, but they were definitely getting all the local work, so I needed to see what was going on.

Doug picked me up and off we went. The rehearsal was held in Jerry Handley's parents' living room. As I walked in, Don was sitting across the room and immediately recognized me from the teen fair audition. "You're in that band with the jerk who does the jerk." he said, referring to the illustrious Jim Taylor aka Rod Devon. I was a little taken aback. After all, even though I totally agreed with him, wasn't he being a bit outspoken?

Later, he developed the phrase "Everybody's doing the jerk, and it's the jerk's fault for letting them do it."

Jerry Handley: The jerk that does the jerk?
John French: Yeah, and he was talking about this singer in this band I was in and I didn't like the singer either, so I laughed. (Mainly because I thought he was a jerk myself). Anyway, it was sort of funny when he said that, because he used to use that phrase in interviews. He would say "Somebody's doin'the jerk and it's the jerk's fault for letting them do it."
JH: I remember when you came to my folks'house ...
JF: Don was standing over by that sort of little divider between the kitchen and the living room with his Chloraseptic throat spray.
JH: Yeah, to keep it numb, ha.

Vic Mortenson

The drummer walked out and my mouth dropped open. It was the tall guy from the Salvation Army Store. His name was Vic Mortenson. He looked to be 6'4"or more. His hair was even longer than I remembered it. Although I'd seen the band briefly setting up at the Ivar Theatre in Hollywood, I still hadn't connected Vic with the guy I had seen.

As the band set up, Don spoke to Alex about future plans and I could overhear. "After we win the Teenage Fair," was his first line. That's all I remember hearing for sure. I was impressed at this kind of confidence that would actually allow someone to make such a positive statement about the future. He went on discussing their recording plans.

The band soon struck up with their first song of the evening, The Rolling Stones' *Heart of Stone*. Within seconds, Mortenson also broke a part on my pedal. It was only the leather strap, however, and it was quickly repaired with an old belt. I was completely overwhelmed by the brutal force with which he hit the drums as he played.

Alex Snouffer

Alex, who never said a word to me, seemed in control at the rehearsal. He was the one who would stop the songs, make suggestions and issue the orders, so to speak. Alex ran the rehearsal efficiently. In the course of the evening, they went through between fifteen and twenty songs. Everyone was very professional. I was surprised just a bit by how loudly Vic played. I felt that it was unnecessary to play this loud.

Drum Solo After Rehearsal

After rehearsal, they asked me to play. I was hesitant at first. These guys were a lot older than me and aside from Doug, I didn't really know any of them. Doug persuaded me to play. Don picked up some maracas and Jerry had a tambourine. They made me feel completely relaxed and assured me it would just be fun. I played as hard as I could and played all my solo licks that I had spent hours working out over the last two years.

I didn't look at anyone until I was done, and I probably played ten minutes. When I did finish and look up, perspiring, Vic was out of the room, and so was Alex. Don had a big smile on his face. "You scared the shit out of Vic, man," he said grinning. Although I doubted this was true I welled up with pride. Maybe all that practice was paying off.

Jerry Handley: Yeah, I remember when I met you, because they were starting to "romance" you a little bit cause they heard about your drumming. Alex and Don I think were ... Don always had his fingers out, you know, looking for things.

After a while, Vic came back in and sat with me for a time talking about drums and drummers. He turned out to be a really nice guy. He was influenced by Joe Morello, who drummed for the Dave Brubeck Quartet, as was I. Morello stood out back then because of his odd time-signature work. I recall Vic talking with the other guys. He was talking about ROTC training in college. He seemed like a very dominant personality-type, almost overbearing at times and definitely an alpha male.

However, the whole band seemed pretty nice. I especially liked Jerry, who was closer to my age, probably nineteen or twenty to my sixteen.

The Teenage Fair
The fair was held in and on the grounds of the Hollywood Palladium, which was basically a dance hall with a big parking lot down on Hollywood Boulevard. There were bands playing inside and bands playing outside in booths and tents that had been set up. There was a competition for bands who were not yet signed to labels.

The Fender tent (electronic instruments and amplifier company) and the Martin tent (great acoustic guitar manufacturer) were right next to each other on the west balcony. The Teen Fair concept was to focus on the demographics of teenagers and find out what kind of merchandising would best appeal to these post-British Invasion adolescents. Obviously, everyone knew who Fender was, but not too many kids had heard of Martin acoustic guitars - probably some of the finest made. I knew about them because my family included several guitarists.

We were assigned an inside booth and whoever did the scheduling must have been nuts because they assigned another band to the booth right next to us in the same time slot.

There was a black guy singing and playing guitar, everyone else was white. Two were sitting and two were standing. The drummer was playing this weird rhythm that accented the 3rd, 6th, and 8th beat on the hi-hat and snare. The kick was 1st, 4th, 5th, and 7th. It was a completely foreign thing to me. The black guy played rhythm guitar and a harmonica, which was held on a holder around his neck, Bob Dylan-style. I had never heard music like this and didn't really pay much attention.

I was excited and scared about playing "in Hollywood" and wasn't really concerned with anything except the fact that these guys were next to us and both of us were trying to play loud music. It was a difficult situation.

We had a little discussion with them and diplomatically agreed to take turns playing for the people. I later discovered that this black guy was Taj Mahal, the band was The Rising Sons and the lead guitarist was a young guy named Ry Cooder. What a contrast it was to be exchanging songs with them in this performance situation - surf music and Delta blues. Us in our shiny blue matching suits with toreador jackets and they, dressed more like the early Rolling Stones.

This particular Teenage Fair was probably held during the Spring break of 1965. Almost every band featured played their own version of *Gloria* by Them at least once. The place was packed and there was every conceivable type of group. The Standels (who were the Standel amplifier company's namesake group) played outside on – you guessed it – Standel amplifiers. We knew some girls whose parents had rented them a room in a hotel right next to the Palladium, so we went there to rest.

An interesting quote from Mike Barnes referring to the Teenage Fair at the Hollywood Palladium: "Van Vliet was keen to keep on top of what was going on in the local scene - spotting a sixteen-year-old drummer, John French, playing in a booth with The Maltesemen, he went over and made contact."[17]

Obviously, this is a small error, but as I mentioned before, I had already previously made contact with Don on several occasions, and jammed at a Magic Band rehearsal. I don't recall even *seeing* Don at the Teenage Fair although he was obviously there.

And The Winner Is ...

We heard that just as Vliet had predicted, Captain Beefheart And His Magic Band won the competition at the Teenage Fair at the Hollywood Palladium. I have been told since then by some band members that there actually was no competition. Who knows?

Alex Snouffer: Oh yeah, that was great. When you're in a situation like that, you know damn well, what you wanna do more than anything else on stage is to wipe out the other bands. I guess you could say we won it, if you look at it from that viewpoint.
John French: Do you remember getting any kind of an endorsement from Rickenbacker?
AS: No, Fender. They gave Ry and I new guitars. All we had to do was drive to Santa Ana to the plant and pick them up. Ry wasn't in the band at that time, he still had The Rising Sons going on. We included him in because we had gotten to know him. I told Ry, "Hey, man, do you want some equipment? Let's go down to Fender and get it." He said, "Well I'm not even in the band." I said, "They don't know that, come on."

Wild Days With Melchione

Around this time, Melchione's parents had bought him a VW bug. We went out driving through the desert the first night he had the car. Our favorite thing was to drive over the corner of irrigation reservoirs, which were basically large levees of dirt bulldozed into 10 to 12 foot high walls to hold irrigation water pumped from a well. The wall was about a 45 degree angle up, followed by a short plateau of five or six feet, and then plunged down again at 45 degrees into the interior.

We would go relatively fast onto the plateau and be raised completely off the seats (no seat belts in those days) and it was a rush to do this. We soon decided this wasn't rush enough, however, and decided that it would be much more exciting to *lay on the roof of the car on our stomachs* with our arms outstretched and hands gripping the door tops where the partially-opened windows formed a hand grip. We each in turn decided to do this and of course at the plateau of the levee would be holding on for our lives to the car, our bodies suspended, floating a few inches above the roof from the G force. Of course, to add to the excitement (and stupidity) of the situation, we did this while completely intoxicated.

Before Mike got his VW, we would often hot-wire his mother's little MG sport coupe when the parents were out of town and after carefully disconnecting the odometer, cruise around town - three people in a two-seater car. We always carefully marked the gas gauge, and filled it back to the mark after each episode.

Delta Blues

After the Teenage Fair, Mike Melchione was completely in awe of Captain Beefheart and also The Rising Sons. There was a connection, because they both found their roots in Delta blues, a kind

---

[17]Captain Beefheart, Mike Barnes, Quartet Books Ltd., 2000, pp19.

of music originating from the Mississippi Delta region, hence the name. These people often played bottleneck guitar and used open tuning to get that glassy effect.

There was a lot of harmonica playing in Delta blues, so Mike bought a harmonica, and a book on harmonica, and started becoming a Delta blues fanatic. Going to the library, he borrowed books on Delta blues. I remember seeing Blind Lemon Jefferson and Sonny Boy Williamson in one of the books.

It seemed to me that Melchione wanted to turn The Maltesemen into a Beefheart clone band. I didn't like the idea and resisted. "Rod" was trying to sound "bluesy." It wasn't working for me.

Sally's Birthday

To make things worse, two ladies, mother and daughter, approached us at the Teenage Fair and asked us to record a song they had written. They sent us the sheet music and Mark Thompson,having had some music training, played a bit of the melody on guitar for us. Jim sang the words:

"It's Sally's birthday today, but I won't be at her party to see her turn seventeen."

I didn't like this song much, but the studio time was booked and we drove ourselves and our equipment to a studio somewhere in Los Angeles. The guys seemed starstruck, (as in "We're RECORDING in HOLLYWOOD!"). I felt skeptical. It wasn't like we were doing anything that fit our rather fuzzy image. In my opinion, this was a stupid song and a lost cause.

The two ladies met us there and we laid down the instrumental track, as the voice would be overdubbed later. When Jim started singing, the ladies shook their heads in disapproval, puzzled frowns upon their faces. They went into Jim. "No, that's not it!" they exclaimed in the tracking room. "It goes like this - whereupon the elder burst into full operatic soprano singing the song as one might sing a very tragic tango (if I remember correctly, she even rolled her "r's").

It was obvious that the song had completely different chord changes and was in the wrong key for "Rod's" voice. It was one of those classic tragic-comic moments. Everything we had played that day was a waste of time and this woman was attempting to teach Jim to sing to a track that had completely wrong chord changes for the melody she was singing.

Between the Delta blues stuff and this, I was extremely motivated to leave the group. Actually, I liked the Delta blues, but I couldn't see trying to transform a surf band into something we weren't to begin with. I left the band shortly after this and as far as I remember, the band fell apart. After this, Don Aldridge teamed up with Melchione which he explains in the following section:

The Chosen Few

John French: So, when you worked with (Melchione), what did you do? This was after I worked with him?

Don Aldridge: Yes, this was 1965, we started a little band and Cliff Roehr ...

JF: Oh, you're talking about The Chosen Few.

DA: How on earth did you remember that? Melchione was playing harp and was (also) playing lead guitar for us. We practiced late nights at Roehr's Music Box. Cliff just handed me the keys and said, "You'll take care of me." Try doing that somewhere today. Cliff did it and unfortunately one of the guys breached his trust, and, I don't wanna get sued, but I will say that person stole a number of records and harmonicas, I think that was established. That was all unbeknownst to us, none of us even knew. I was very heartbroken over it because Cliff had always trusted me.

Intruders/Allusions

Jeff Cotton, Don Giesen and I then formed a band. We called ourselves The Intruders. Jeff and Don had their own commercial building where they gave guitar lessons and made good money. We rehearsed in the back of DJ's Guitar Lesson Shop.

Jeff's parents, while having some barbeque at a small place next door, had decided to rent the empty commercial building as a place that Jeff and Don could give lessons. It was thought that they had hoped to compete with Roehr. This lasted for about six months.

The Antelope Valley Inn Coffee Shop

One of the favorite hangouts of all my musician friends was the Antelope Valley Inn Coffee Shop. We would get paid in cash for our gigs, then we'd pack up our gear, unload the equipment in my folks'basement and go to the AV Inn to hang out in a big corner booth at 3 a.m. We'd either have small dinner salads with Roquefort dressing, or large chocolate sundaes with whipped cream – or both. It was our payoff for the hard work. We were usually in there about the same time all the drunks from the bar came in to sober up, so it was a madhouse, which added to the fun.

Jim Fergueson, our bass player, had a job there as a busboy. Tall and dark, he was the kind of guy who liked to make prank calls, like the one: "Could you page Mr. Meoff please? Mr. Jack Meoff?" I think things like this is where Matt Groening got his Bart Simpson prank phone calls, such as " I need Amanda Hugenkiss." Fergueson was married to a thin wispy woman called Donna and, as I mentioned before, lived in her parents'house a few houses down from the Giesen's. It was a strange relationship, but I didn't ask questions because they let us rehearse there occasionally.

A lady named Darline Bergh worked as a waitress at the coffee shop with Jim. She approached him about how she could go about giving her three daughters music lessons. Jim contacted us and we went to their house. The girl who wanted to play drums was Donna. She was twelve years old, and I thought she was the most beautiful little girl I had ever seen.

Their mother was going through a divorce. She later changed their name back to her maiden name: Blair. Since the girls were pretty serious, we made a deal with them. They didn't have equipment so we would leave our equipment there, locked in the garage, for them to practice on. In return, we were able to practice several times a week for shorter periods, because we didn't have the constant setting up and tearing down. It was a mutually agreeable situation and also gave the girls the advantage of observing us as we rehearsed.

Darline remembers that the Sheriff deputies would come in for coffee on their breaks and often tell stories about Captain Beefheart. They would describe their meetings as: "Well, we picked him up again, wandering around in the desert, high out of his mind on something. We just took him home."

Spring And Summer Of Fun/1965

After I left The Maltesemen, the new band consisted of Jeff Cotton, Don Giesen, Jim Fergueson, and myself. For a while, a guy named John Day played keyboards. We didn't try to be Beefheart clones. We just played Top 40 stuff. There was a lot of harmony, as everyone in the band could sing. I wasn't singing much then, mostly a song or two just as a novelty.

We eventually called ourselves The Allusions. A lot of our jobs were at Edwards Air Force Base, where we played the NCO club, the Officer's Club, and the Teen Club. We had enough schmaltzy stuff in our repertoire that we could please the older folks, but of course the Teen Club was the most fun. We even had a "manager" who was really just a friend who had connections at the air base. His name was Jeff Foster and we would give him a cut of the proceeds for booking gigs at the base.

Darline occasionally let all three daughters, Barbara, Sharon and Donna, come with us to the Teen Club to watch us play. Jim's wife went along as a chaperone. We had great fun playing during this period.

Jeff Cotton lived in a trailer park with his parents and little sister. During this period, he and I spent a great deal of time together at this park. We knew several of the girls who lived there and spent our days swimming, socializing and trying to impress the girls. We used to go for walks in the bright moonlit desert out behind the park. There was nothing but desert carved up with old dirt roads strewn with litter. We had great adventurous fun and spoke of our dreams of musical stardom.

Our imaginations also led us into wild conversations that contained subject matter fairly common to the adolescent male who wasn't interested in sports. We talked about music and the opposite sex, of course. We shared common views on UFOs and extraterrestrial beings, which it turned out were one of Jeff's passions. But most of all we shared a common dream of becoming great musicians, garnished with all the usual shallow thoughts that only adolescent minds can conjure. We were dreamers and it was a magical time. We bonded and had mutual respect for each other as musicians.

Some of the girls would occasionally join us in our little excursions, and we would sneak around and try to scare each other in the dark. Jeff and I and several of our other friends had jokingly started making a guttural falsetto sound with our voice as a way of mocking *The Day of the Triffids* - some "B" science fiction thriller only I seemed to have missed. We all seemed to outgrow this, with the exception of Jeff, and this later would develop into Jeff's "flesh horn" voice that was used on *Trout Mask Replica*.

Jeff's parents would often loan him their little Datsun and we would ride around town looking for something to do on weekends when we weren't playing. Many times, we would wind up going to a dance of a competing band to check out our competition. We took this competition very seriously, as each band in town strove to be the best. After all, the Alfalfa Festival each year held a battle of the bands and there was good prize money involved.

Recording At Glenn Studio

Merrel Fankhauser had recorded the early Exiles band at Glenn Studio in Palmdale. The studio was basically a converted garage with an Ampex three-track machine. It had two or three fiberglass jet plane cockpits standing on end with microphones inside the half shell. Everything was usually recorded at the same time, so background vocals were added by the guitarists while they played, standing behind these fiberglass cockpits which provided sound separation.

One night someone drove up and announced Glenn needed a band to record background tracks for a singer. We drove over and set up within the hour and I thus did my first decent recording session. It went well. The guy who sang was probably in his mid-thirties, and came in dressed in a bathing suit, thongs (these are *shoes*, folks) and a Hawaiian shirt. I still remember the first two lines of the ballad,

> *My love has gone out of my life, it's true,*
> *The days grow longer, what am I to do?*

The session went quite well, as the guy could actually sing, at least in the '50s balladeer/crooner style. Everybody seemed pleased and soon we were invited back to do another session by a different artist. This writer/singer played acoustic guitar and wrote a song in the "giddyup" rhythm of Buddy Holly. I remember the first two lines of his song also.

> *Come on baby, now don't be shy*
> *True love was meant for you and I.*

I played tom-toms on this song rather than doing a giddyup beat (William Tell Overture type rhythm) on the drums. The singer loved the idea. I had a 45 of this song until the mid-eighties.

Beefheart Wins Again

We played a battle of the bands at the Fairgrounds in Exposition Hall. The other bands that played were of no consequence, but this was the first time I had actually seen Beefheart – as all the locals called the band – perform live

Local Battle Of The Bands/Spring 1966

Don Aldridge: Now, there came a day when there was a battle of bands at the High School and we were still in High School. The winner of that was going to battle Captain Beefheart at the Exposition hall. I think we would have beaten you if it hadn't have been for me (laughs.)
John French: What happened to you?
DA: I had a band with John Parr, Jim Fergueson, and Mike Marler. (Note: Mike Marler was one of Jeff Cotton's students and was a reasonably adept player even then.) *None of us were as accomplished as you guys were other than John Parr certainly was on drums.*
JF: Jim and John were both accomplished.
DA: I was about to say that. They laid a foundation for us that was really good. We decided to do John Lee Hooker's "Boom Boom." I got lost on the lyrics and completely made a left turn. The band didn't know where I was. We totally blew the set. We went out, laid on the ground and were totally roaring laughing. What happened is you guys took it and went over and battled Captain Beefheart at the Exposition Hall.

There were two stages so that one band could set up while the other band played. To start their set, the Magic Band just hit a giant fanfare of chords with Don playing maniacal harp solos and Vic hitting lots of cymbal fills. It was quite impressive and very dramatic. They also had brought their own lights, which set a totally different atmosphere. The line up was: Don Van Vliet, vocals and harmonica; Alex Snouffer, guitar; Doug Moon, guitar; Jerry Handley, bass; and Vic Mortenson, drums – the original band. No one had ever seen anyone that looked like any of these guys before. They made the Stones look like little girls. I had only seen them at rehearsal, but their stage presence was a whole new experience.

After their fanfare, they broke into what Don announced as a Hooker tune but actually sounded to me more like Elmore James. Alex started with an amazing slide solo. His hair was all combed back, greaser style, but in a moment, the frenzy of his playing flung his hair down in his face. Everyone went nuts - probably more over the hair than the great playing. The band played through two Fender Bassman piggyback amps. They had a small four piece drum-set, but they cooked. I recall really focusing when Don sang *Evil*, Howlin' Wolf style. What happened to the atmosphere was mystical. The stage presence of these guys was magnificent. Even shy Doug Moon looked like the coolest dude on the planet. They played hard and tight. Don was very self-controlled and didn't move around a lot. Just stood there looking quite relaxed and cool until his turn, and then produced growls and howls like I'd never heard.

I was starting to be more and more impressed by what these guys had going. After the show I went and talked to this Beefheart character, although he kept telling me that Alex was actually Captain Beefheart. He talked a bit about my drumming and how I should keep going because I was really good. I liked this guy, but there was something about him that made me feel uncomfortable. There was definitely an air about him.

I remember him talking about how we should write our own stuff. He told me he had just written a line, which he quoted: *Children hock n' pepsis* - that was all he said. He scrutinized me closely to see what my reaction would be. I thought about it for a minute and surmised two things. Number one, he was a little beyond normal, and number two, he liked things with double-meanings.

"I get it. That's nice," was all I could think of to say - for me at seventeen, that was a lot.

I asked him that night where he got his voice idea with the pinched trachea sound. He told me I should listen to Howlin' Wolf, who I had never heard of at that point. Although I had already met the band and heard a rehearsal, they had played Stones covers the night I heard them, and this stuff was way more guttural and raw.

Vocal And Musical Influences

My own vocal influences started with The Righteous Brothers, especially Bill Medley, who I thought had a terrific voice. I soon realized, after listening to his version of *Georgia* and one day hearing Ray Charles' version on an album at the Cotton's house that Medley was copying Charles almost verbatim. I started listening to Ray Charles, and this opened the door to me. Soon I discovered James Brown, Jr. Walker and the All Stars, Sam and Dave, Wilson Pickett, The Isley Brothers, The Drifters, and many others, who had these great vocal styles I wanted to emulate.

This, of course, started influencing my musical tastes as well. I started listening to styles of black drummers and also trying to capture their feel. One of my favorite albums was an instrumental album of the James Brown band in which Brown himself played organ. One tune in particular caught my ear. It was *Song For My Father* done with that great horn section. Whew!

Back to Merrel

Then Jeff Cotton went back into Merrel and the Exiles, dropping out of High School in his senior year and studying by correspondence course. The Exiles had a local radio hit called *Can't We Get Along*, which was basically in the same style as *You've Lost That Lovin' Feelin'* by the Righteous Brothers. Some local bands would play clubs in LA using fake ID's if they were under age. Merrel had Larry Willey on bass and Greg Hampton on drums.

The Allusions

After Jeff left in the early winter of 1965, Don Giesen and I quickly re-formed The Allusions with guitarist Ron Beaver. It was during this time that I started playing harmonica a little bit now and then. Sometimes, Don Giesen would play the drums and I would stand and sing Van Morrison's *Mystic Eyes* from an early Them album. I also started dating Jeff's ex-girlfriend, Mary.

In those days, good bands had uniforms, and we were no exception. Our uniforms were white dickeys (which were fake turtlenecks with a bib front worn inside another shirt. The Blair girls used to jokingly tease us by saying how much they liked our "little white dickeys"), green velour shirts, and dark pants. Yes, we had even graduated to green suede Beatle boots with a ringed zipper on the side. Best of all, we had our own business cards printed on flourescent orange stock (complete with the original phone number crossed out and another written in). In summation, we had reached the pinnacle of adolescent rock-hood in the Antelope Valley.

Merrel Deserts The Exiles

Because of some contractual dispute, Merrel left The Exiles.

Don Giesen: They were playing up in Portland Oregon and during the second week, something happened where Merrel got in a super tizzy. Merrel just up and quit on the spot and left. The (club) got a replacement band and (they came) back down to Hollywood.

Giesen was the band's unanimous choice to replace Merrel, and was next to join The Exiles, also dropping out of High School and our band, The Allusions (which meant we now had to cross out the *written-in* phone number).

John French: That's when you dropped out of school and joined them, right?
Don Giesen: Yeah, so the three of them and Gino (the band's gay Italian manager) came over to the house and rapped on the door. We had this big super-long discussion with my parents in the living room that went on for hours and hours. (Mrs. Giesen must have thought this discussion extremely important, because she never allowed *anyone* in the living room and had a plastic runner from the door to the hall that you *better not step off of in* fear of incurring her dreadful and terrifying wrath.)

So it was that in 1965, a gay small-time manager named Gino talked the Giesens into allowing young Don to drop out of high school, take correspondence courses, and play clubs in LA using false IDs. What a salesman, this Gino.

Don Giesen: ... my mother wasn't really hot on the idea at all.

Soon the younger members were playing clubs without Merrel as The Exiles.

It was shortly after this that Merrel Fankhauser approached me about forming a band with him called, not surprisingly, Merrel And The Exiles. Is this getting confusing yet? So I joined Merrel And The Exiles, with Mark Thompson (rhythm guitar from The Maltesemen) on guitar and organ and Jim Fergueson on bass.

Most important in my musical development is that I was introduced, through Merrel, to Ike and Tina Turner because we covered *I Think It's Gonna Work Out Fine*. Oh yeah, Tina - now there's a singer.

False IDs

One of the most important pieces of technology for bands during this time was the advent of the copy machine, which had just become popular. In California during this period, the driver's license was still black and white on photo paper. This presented a wonderful opportunity for the young aspiring musician to alter his driver's license so that he appeared to be 21, thus allowing him the privilege of playing in bars and opening up to him a whole new world of drunken decadence and cultural ruination.

With the help of my fellow bandmates, I secured a typewriter that had the same style type as my driver's license. We then typed on plain paper the information needed to transform me into an adult. This information was then cut out with an exacto knife and placed over the corresponding spaces on the license. The altered license was then photocopied at the local county library's copy machine, producing an exact copy, picture and all, of the original, but with the altered dates. The copy was usually a little too good, and if you looked closely, you could always see the edge of the paper that had been inserted over the license. Nonetheless, the copy was then glued on to another piece of paper with rubber cement and laminated with plastic for that "glossy" look.

A year or so earlier, I had used my brother Phil's (the guy who left the drumsticks) birth certificate for my identification. It said I was 27 years old when I was actually sixteen. Back to the license, I only had to use my phony license once. It was inspected quite closely by a Sheriff who seemed satisfied, thus my phony ID passed the test. Interestingly enough, I never used it to buy alcoholic beverages.

Mark Thompson

Mark and Merrel were both working at Roehr's Music Box now as sales clerks and guitar teachers. Mark would come over nearly every day that spring of '65 and take me to AW Root Beer Stand, the new local hangout, and buy lunch. He would talk constantly about what stars we were going to be. "We're going to be rich!" he would say. I wasn't so sure, but the advantage of not totally disagreeing with this vision is that I was getting a free burger and fries pending our future riches. We did some original recordings during this period that later wound up being used on an album called *Fapardokly*.

Good-bye Mary

Mark Thompson started dating my girlfriend, Mary. Chicks always go for the guy with the car. When I found out, I was amazingly calm. I still missed Jennifer more than Mary. I told Mark that I held no hard feelings. Unfortunately, she was at all the gigs as Mark's date, and I soon felt pretty uncomfortable being in the band as it was like a little teenage soap opera. It definitely put a lot of tension in the air around Merrel and The Exiles, and so I soon bid the band a fond farewell. Happily, however, Mark and I remained friends through the years and still occasionally see each other. He's now a local attorney specializing in probate and divorce proceedings.

Oh No, Not The Exiles Again!

So it was for a few months, I was in The Exiles (Note: a different band) with Jeff Cotton, Don Giesen, and Larry Willey. Have patience! This musical merry-go-round is just about to end. The guys had come back into town, having had enough of living in Hollywood and starving. It was rumoured that Don was so hungry on one occasion, he ate an entire jar of mayonnaise. Gino Bellini turned out not to live up to his promises and it seemed like he was more interested in *doing* the band than *booking* the band. I was in my senior year in High School, and happily playing with my best friends. Larry and I had known each other since grade school, though I never quite forgave him for pulling the fringe off my Davy Crockett suede jacket. The newly formed Exiles played in the High School cafeteria during lunch. This band was strong, we had great harmonies and great power in our playing. Larry was the only true tenor in the band and could sing all those high McCartney harmonies and had a tremendous voice. Of course, we were only a copy band doing a mixed repertoire of Yardbirds, Stones, and Beatles, but at the time, we thought we were pretty hot stuff.

Winds Of Change

The Antelope Valley boasted several fairly good bands at this point and the music scene seemed to be gathering momentum. It was at this time that I began to be aware of the changes taking place in the industry. Before, the whole music scene had been club bands, playing Top 40 in bars. Now, there were places in Hollywood where younger bands could play. The whole scene was changing. Don Aldridge had a great insight into this. He seemed to be one of the guys who got around a lot. He was almost like the "scout" that went out to search for the best trails and came back loaded with information. He always seemed to be just getting back from Hollywood, where he had been checking out the scene. This combined with the stories I'd heard from the guys after their stay in Hollywood began to change my image of what a music career was about. We would all consult on these matters at our usual meeting place: Roehr's Music Box.

Don Aldridge: The whole world here was a microcosm of what was about to happen in the larger picture of rock 'n'roll. Just these little bands like Melchione and I and then Cotton was over there doing stuff with Merrel. Merrel And The Exiles, you were doing stuff later on… Long about that time The Chosen Few went to Los Angeles to cut a record with Johnny Otis. When we broke for the evening, we went down to the Sunset Strip and it was the very first time that the Grassroots were playing at the Sea Witch. Up the strip was The Trip and then the Whisky A Go Go.
John French: The Trip – where the Byrds played?

DA: *Yeah, the Byrds played at the Trip a lot. They were just breaking too. I think they had been out about a year. The Mob hadn't quite left and it was like the Mickey Cohen crowd wasn't quite cleared out of there but a lot of the clubs were in transition. Ciro's was still there, which is now the Roxy. After Ciro's it became It's Boss, and then it became the Roxy, and the Moulin Rouge became the Hullabaloo (which later became the Aquarius Theatre). It was like a carnival on the Strip. People hadn't left their fifties roots yet. The girls were still running around in ponytails but yet you could tell that something was really happening that was quite different. There were a lot of bands on the Strip at the time that hadn't broken into the mainstream nationally or internationally, like The Seeds with Sky Saxon and the Grassroots, who hadn't had a hit yet. They had a string of middle-of-the-road type hits there about '67 and '68 but this is '65 and they hadn't broken through. The Doors weren't even happening yet. They were playing down at Gazarri's as a house band, Ray Manzarek and Morrison and those guys. So, I mean the strip was like a carnival and you could feel the electricity in the air. I don't know how to describe it. Perhaps part of it was the fact that I was a very "rural" boy from Lancaster. I am quite certain that if I had gone in there a few years before it would not have been anything like that. It went from the 40s and 50s mob tradition of the supper clubs you know, where the movie moguls along with the east coast gangsters, who had moved in, like Mickey Cohen, Bugsy Siegel, all of that in the 40s and 50s - that supper club "Brown Derby" tradition with the big bands and everything. It was almost like they didn't know what to do next, because all of a sudden you had this upsurge of real rock'n'roll. You had the "Elvis" rock 'n'roll, which was really under the leadership of guys like Mitch Miller. All of these (new) bands and individuals like Dylan and Joan Baez, were breaking - and they were breaking all the rules. That's really what went on on the Strip during that time. And the Strip was just one microcosm of what was going on on the East Coast in Greenwich Village where Dylan got his start. And then up in San Francisco, was the Haight-Ashbury District. Of course anywhere where people began to congregate, industry followed. A lot of small record companies were popping up and you had a lot of these guys from the fifties like Johnny Otis who knew how to do it. Guys like Frank Zappa were coming along and didn't know exactly how to do it. He just went to Cucamonga and put a studio together. Johnny Otis even influenced him. If you read the liner notes to the very first Mothers' album, which is Freak Out, he credits Johnny Otis on the back of that album. So it was all a mixture of young really fresh young people coming in and doing new things.*

I Barely Graduate

High School graduation came. As it is for a lot of kids from dysfunctional families, it wasn't easy for me to muster up the effort to graduate. My father had deserted the family, and home life was tense, to say the least. I was spending most of my spare time in our basement listening to my favorite albums, repairing guitar cords and making speaker cabinets for our PA.

At one point, my grades became so bad and my attendance so poor that I was called into the Vice Principal's office. His name was Ernest Tosi. He had a prior dealing with me over a large Playboy Bunny, which I had painted on the girls'gym as a joke. He knew that I had artistic tendencies. My records showed that I was a drummer. He began to talk to me about another student he had encountered. He said I reminded him of this former student. He told me the guy had actually taken blank film and hand-painted each frame. It had been something like he had never seen before. He said the guy's name was Frank Zappa. The name sounded vaguely familiar, as I had probably heard Doug Moon mention him.

Tosi talked me into finishing school. He said that no matter what I started in life, I was going to have to finish it, one way or the other. I might as well do a good job so that I would look back with no regrets. I had a lot of respect for him, not only then but later on. I took his advice and finished what I had started. I found out that Frank had admired him and been inspired by him also. Ernie died in the early nineties.

My mother bought a roll of film for the graduation, which was about all she could afford. I remember my best friend from High School, Dan Moore, coming over and taking shots of me for her as she had requested. I felt so empty. The pictures look like a guy waiting for his execution. Dan was going on to junior college in town for two years, and then Northridge, in the San Fernando Valley for two years. I envied him. There was a plan to his life. His parents were giving him transportation and tuition.

I went to the graduation party and sort of wandered around with my date. I think her name was Susan or Sharon. She was a nice girl, but I think she and I were both thinking about other people that night. We danced. We played bingo. We went home. There was no graduation gift, no family celebration; just the hardship of dealing with a mother whose husband had deserted the home at a critical time.

Other Influences

I had begun listening to music that had eastern religious influences in it. Although I had been raised Christian by my mother, I was fascinated by eastern philosophies. I had read several books on the subject. Lamaism was my favorite. The Tibetans really had it together, or so I thought. I started looking around in thrift shops (I worked in one) for oriental clothes. I started burning incense. I read books on astral projection and psychic powers, and looked into Rosicrucianism.

A lot of what I was hearing in the music I was listening to was changing the way I looked at the world, as it was for a lot of kids my age all over the US. I felt as though I had been disconnected from my former life. No longer could I bask in that security I had felt when my parents were together. I had this whole new set of discoveries and a million questions no-one could answer. My friends were moving away, joining the service or getting drafted, going to college, and I was sitting here in this small town with a lot of big questions. My mother and uncle would sometimes fight, and I was protective of my mother, but I never really said anything, I just looked mean and hoped I could be seen as enough of a physical menace to keep the peace.

My brothers were all married and raising their families and I saw mostly the bad side of that type of situation. I didn't want kids and a family, which I felt was a waste of time for people in their twenties. Music was the only thing that meant anything to me. So I found myself conforming more and more to the image and the philosophy that was thriving in the sixties. The drug culture was something I absolutely did not accept at this time. I couldn't picture myself *ever* taking drugs. I was, nonetheless, interested in having these "religious" experiences (visions and out-of-body experiences) I had read about in the eastern religion books, so basically everything I was drawn to was drawing me closer to drug experimentation.

Hello Daddy/1966

My father had moved back into town and was living in Quartz Hill. I would go stay with him every now and then. Our band rehearsed in his little bachelor pad occasionally. It was a little house next to the Grange Hall. When I think back, he was pretty patient with us. He'd sit in the tiny dining area and watch TV with the aid of a small earphone in his ear. Although lots of kids go through parental separations, it seemed weird to have my mother and father living in the same town in separate houses. I never really considered myself as coming from a broken home. I suppose this was because my parents never actually divorced.

My father had temporarily deserted the family several times through the years, but only once after I was born. My youngest brother, 11 years my senior, had witnessed the previous time. He still has a lot of pain from those times, and their situation was a lot worse than mine. My dad would often pick me up on a Friday night and we'd drive out to Sarge's Restaurant in Quartz Hill where he would buy me a Spencer Steak. We didn't have much to say to each other but was nice seeing him again.

My Last Summer Vacation/1966

Nostalgia started creeping in. I was out of High School. Don, Jeff and Larry all still had one year to go, because they had dropped out to play in The Exiles. So, I was looking forward with dread to decisions and questions about my future – especially the draft and the war in Vietnam. I half-heartedly decided to go stay with my brother Phil and his family in Wyoming and work on the cattle ranch. I got all my hair cut off and announced that I was leaving the band.

Everybody in the group was bummed. I finally told them that I had a secret desire to be an up-front lead singer/harmonica player like Don, but more in a contemporary style of R&B. The band members all liked my singing and they talked me into staying as lead singer. Don Giesen would go permanently to drums. We were also getting more into the weird stuff. Jeff and I especially liked The Yardbirds, and the experimental sounds of Jeff Beck.

Unfortunately, Larry Willey seemed uninterested in our new direction. He wouldn't show up for rehearsal, and when he did, he didn't want to learn any of the songs we wanted to do. Working for his father who was a concrete contractor, his biggest ambition in music was to be "in the most popular band in Lancaster." There was a real division. Jeff, Don and I decided to get radical. We unanimously voted to replace Larry.

Now we decided to approach Mark Boston to play bass. Mark had been in a band called B.C. And The Cavemen with Bill Harkleroad. We had seen him play and thought that he was not only good, but had a certain appeal to girls, which was probably even more important to us then. We also approached Jeff Parker, another local who had been lead guitarist in The Jungle Jive Five (gotta admit, it's a funny name), to play guitar. Jeff Parker was the son of an English teacher at the Junior College. He was tall and had blond curly hair. Both these guys were nearly my age or perhaps a year younger.

Jeff Parker and Jeff Cotton on guitar was a winning combination. I think Parker had been one of Cotton's students back at DJ Guitar Shop and not only had great respect for his mentor, but had developed into quite a player himself. The girls loved these two guys. Mark Boston was a great bass player and fit right in.

Ironic Premonition

During this period of time, Jeff, Don G. and I used to have discussions. One of the things that kept coming up in a "Wouldn't it be great if" discussion was an isolation experiment. We all had become more interested in the more "outside" music of the time, such as The Yardbirds' *I'm a Man, Over Under Sideways Down*, and the Stones' *Paint It Black*.

We talked often of renting a place out in the middle of the desert, just an isolated shack we could set our equipment up in and experiment for a year. This would be a year of complete isolation from the music industry in which we would create our own outlandish music and then "re-appear" and blow everyone away. (More importantly in our minds – our hair would have grown for an entire year.)

Jeff Cotton and I talked of this quite often, and were actually trying to figure some feasible way to make our dream happen. It's ironic to think that we actually, in a sense, did have our vision come to fruition in the later *Trout Mask* band. Unfortunately, it would turn out to be much less fun than we had anticipated, but the good part was that our hair really did grow long.

Blues In A Bottle

Blues In A Bottle was the last of the garage bands my friends and I formed. It was also the best. We had our first rehearsal at Mark's parents'house. This was a pretty interesting lineup. The weak spot was Don Giesen, who, of course, was really a rhythm guitarist trying to play drums and doing an adequate, but limited, job. Don Giesen later was shipped off to Vietnam, where he served without mishap and came home in one piece - thank God. We are friends to this day. He was one of the lucky ones. One of my next-door neighbors Johnny Tivis, wasn't so lucky. I saw his picture in the paper – the obituary. He looked much the same as he had the last time I saw him, a young boy in Junior High School, only wearing an army hat. He was a casualty of a war that I still don't understand.

The band started sounding great at the first rehearsal. One of the first songs we learned was Wilson Pickett's *Ninety-Nine And One Half (Won't Do)*. During this time, we were getting copies of demo tapes of new Beefheart material indirectly through their drummer P.G., whose brother Bob would bring them over for us to hear. It was their newer, original stuff. Occasionally, we would do one of their songs, not to copy them, but more to pay respect. The most popular was *Obeah Man*. There was also *Here I Am, Here I Always Am* (both of which can be heard on the Revenant set, *Grow Fins*) There was one local band that even named themselves *Obeah Band*.

I was also strongly influenced by rhythm & blues people like James Brown and Wilson Pickett, and performed their material as well. My voice was kind of in the Ray Charles/Stevie Winwood category. I loved a lot of the contemporary black rhythm & blues and preferred it to the white "pop" groups. Through Beefheart (which is what we locals called the band), I had found out about their predecessors: Howlin' Wolf, Muddy Waters, Lightnin' Hopkins, John Lee Hooker, Buddy Guy, and others too numerous to mention. Our band performed songs by all of the above, plus new releases by The Animals, The Rolling Stones, and The Yardbirds. Our versions of the old blues songs were more contemporary sounding than the Beefheart bands.

One of my favorites covers that we did was *CC Rider* by Eric Burdon and The Animals. The instrumental riff was actually taken from Chester Burnett's (Howlin' Wolf's) version of *Smokestack Lightning*.

All in all, we were pretty excited. We had our own dance booked at Fair Center Hall, the biggest hall in town. This was the first time we would actually perform as the only attraction. It was rather intimidating and we were apprehensive about the turnout.

We played a couple of warm-up gigs and by the time we played our big dance, our confidence was up. The Blair girls – our ex-students – even came to hear us. I remember trying to light a small cigar I had with me, and I couldn't get the match to light. Suddenly, quiet little Donna, my drum student, all of 13 and more beautiful than ever, was standing in front of me with a lit match. There was something about this 13-year-old girl. But, yeah, and I was almost eighteen. She was "jail bait" - as we used to refer to minor females.

Our dance was a big success, and the turnout was exceptional, which surprised us, since we hadn't really been together that long. The car club was happy, the crowd was happy, and we were happy.

Patch Of Blue

There were a few other bands in town, but our main competition was Patch Of Blue (who I always thought had a cooler name), which included Bill Harkleroad (alternately playing bass or singing and harmonica), Ron Beaver (on lead guitar) and singer Paul West (who also doubled on bass when Bill sang) in its lineup. Patch of Blue was very much like the Beefheart band in its look and style. A lot of the younger bands that imitated Beefheart's look and style were also influenced heavily by The Yardbirds and most importantly by Jeff Beck and his electronic wall of sound approach. The combination proved to be very powerful in terms of sound.

Don Giesen and I were into the technical end of this sound. We went around investigating how certain sounds were achieved. Especially intriguing was the fuzz sustain that was so popular - that overdriven and compressed sound that made a guitar sound unreal. We found that by changing a few resisters in a fuzz tone we could almost duplicate this sound. We consulted an electronics nerd I knew and obtained this information. I rode in his car to my house, and in the back seat, he had a huge reel-to-reel tape recorder hooked to an AC converter plugged into his cigarette ligher outlet. On it was a tape of his favorite music (which was The Association, a very clean cut band made up of college boys with matching suits, degrees in music, and carefully styled Beatle haircuts). Every time he would slow to a stop, the tape recorder would slow down, and every time he would speed up, the music would follow suit. This guy probably thought he had the coolest car stereo in the world. This was before eight-tracks were cool. He also had a pocket protector for his pens. He later became manager for the local Radio Shack.

Anyway, this guy came down into the steps of my parents' dusty basement and sat at the crude bench illuminated by a pair of bare buzzing fluorescent bulbs which were in a fixture suspended by bailing wire from the ceiling (which was actually the kitchen floor.) There, surrounded by soldering utensils, wire cutters and duct tape, was our most hallowed possession: a FuzzFace. It was a type of fuzz tone (which is a simple guitar pre-amplifier run by a battery) which makes a guitar sound distorted. However, we didn't want small amounts of distortion. We wanted massive, destructive distortion that defied description in human terms. We didn't want a "wall of sound," we wanted a "terrifying tsunami" of sound.

Don and I looked lovingly at the electronic device that had the potential to make this dream come true and motioned our would-be expert to sit and inspect, warning him that if anything should happen to our beloved FuzzFace, we would bury him beneath the basement floor and he and his cool car stereo would never be heard from again. He glanced at it quickly and said, "Oh, this resistor needs to be changed from a "insert unintelligable electronic technical garbage talk here" to a "insert more of same here". We were prepared, having a whole box of resistors at his disposal. He looked at the little color bands (which told him the ohm rating of the resistor) and quickly picked one out of the box.

Plugging in the soldering iron, he removed the original resistor and replaced it with the more appropriate tidal-wave resistor. Don and I looked at each other apprehensively, hardly able to contain our anxiety, but wishing to remain cool in front of the geek. "That should do it," he announced lethargically, "See ya," and with that, our electronics consultant was gone and all our pent-up anxiety exploded into action. Don's tomato-soup-red Stratocaster guitar and black Fender Bassman piggy-back amplifier (already on standby) were ready for the test, even a double set of guitar cords lay on the floor just waiting to plug themselves into the new and improved FuzzFace.

It worked! This distortion was beyond comprehension. Finally, Jeff would be able to replace the tubes in his Magnavox guitar amp and have distortion whenever he desired.

These were really exciting times. We all were starting to let our hair grow by now, much to the dismay of our parents. I remember hearing the phrase "my hair is starting to get good in the back" said often right around that time - especially by Jeff Cotton. We would be sitting in a restaurant (usually the AV Inn Coffee Shop) and Jeff would tilt his head back to feel his hair brush his neck. He would emit sighs like one in the midst of sexual fulfillment and breathlessly say, "My hair is getting soooooo good in the back!" After a while, this got to be a running joke between Giesen and I, who used to drive around with our heads tilted back saying, "My hair's getting soooooooo GOOD in the back! Ooooooooohhh!"

Long hair, as petty as it seems today, caused quite a conflict in my home, and I was less rebellious and daring than some of my friends. Also, my mother was stricter and had more traditional values. It made it difficult for me. At seventeen, no matter how cool you could appear, there was nothing like a parent to make you feel like a total dweeb (similar, I suppose to "nerd" or "geek").

Battle Of The Bands/Late Summer 1966

One of the first things we played of any major consequence was yet another battle of the bands at the local Fair's "Teen Town" which usually happened around Labor Day – late August and early September. The main contenders for the prize were Patch Of Blue and Blues In A Bottle. We went to check out the competition, and I have to admit, they were very good instrumentally, though the vocals were not strong. It was a beautiful evening, and a good crowd. Ron Beaver's father had altered his fuzztone so that Ron could imitate Jeff Beck's wall of sound. It was a little better than Jeff's. We were depressed. It was a very impressive showing. I was a little worried. We sounded just as good, I thought I sang a little better, and we had altered Jeff's fuzztone. Unfortunately, the most important element was missing: my hair was shorter than Paul West's - or Bill Harkleroad's.

As it turned out, we were billed during the afternoon, the wind was blowing fiercely, and my PA (we had to furnish our own) consisted of a borrowed tape recorder microphone (which I dropped and broke) and a small stereo through two homemade cabinets. There was almost no audience. We lost. It was a humiliation that Jeff Cotton in the weeks to come would always blame on my hair length, whereas I was, and still am, absolutely convinced that it really had to do with the fact the resistor we used to alter his fuzztone was the incorrect ohm rating. "Kill the nerd" became my motto.

We Warm Up For Beefheart

We played a couple of High School dances and a show at Edwards and the band improved greatly during this time. The Beefheart band hadn't been heard from in a while locally, so suddenly, we found ourselves being asked to open for them at yet another dance at the Fair Center Hall. This was probably early Fall, 1966. We were a little nervous about opening for them, as we were now becoming a little more competition. However, we decided it would be a good chance to see how we measured up against the local benchmark.

For this dance, they moved a big flatbed truck trailer into the hall for the stage. Portable stairs were used to access the stage and a huge PA with monitor speakers was supplied. We had never been able to hear ourselves before, so this would be very interesting.

There was even special lighting brought in. This was to be a special event. By now, the Magic Band lineup had Alex back on guitar with P.G. Blakely playing drums. I had heard them once shortly after this change, and I was a bit disappointed, some of the magic seemed to be gone.

By now, Blues In A Bottle were playing really well. My harmonica playing had improved quite a bit. I was able to sing for four hours without going hoarse and losing my voice. Mark was very powerful sounding, and Don's drumming had come a long way - although I still hadn't convinced him that floor toms don't make good ashtray stands. Jeff and Jeff, the matching blonde guitarists, looked and sounded great on stage. And, most importantly, the right resistor for the FuzzFace had been found. We were starting to gain some momentum.

We played our set and I felt a real power in the band and in myself. This was the best setting we had ever played in. The PA was great, the stage and lighting were dramatic and the place was packed. We played with a conviction I had never felt before. I guess it was the heavy competition. Everybody sounded good, as we had been practicing almost every day.

The audience seemed really pleased and gave us better than average applause. We even threw in a band arrangement of an original that Mark had written called *The Clock On The Wall*. I felt like I had endless energy and danced and moved around like I never had before. Our band was happy and confident that night and we were in our prime.

When the Magic Band approached the stage, it got very quiet. They walked on stage and seemed to take a long time setting up. They were extremely casual. As I look back now, it seemed as if they were overly confident. Don was carrying a bunch of paper with him, and he looked almost bored. He was wearing a large black woven-straw hat that folded around his head like a witches hat. He was strutting around, staring defiantly at the audience. When they kicked off their set, I was surprised. They had a very thin sound. There was no excitement in what they were doing. Don was reading the lyrics off the sheets of paper. The only tune I liked at all was Yellow Brick Road. Everything else seemed watered-down and stale.

Was it just my imagination, or had our band just played better and gotten a better reception than the Beefheart band? I asked at the dance and around town the next day. People were happier with what we did the night before. I had the feeling we were on our way to something good. It just seemed that if we could start getting serious about our writing, that something really exciting was on the horizon. Unfortunately, we were also all facing the draft and that dreaded thing called the Vietnam War.

I recall recently having a conversation with Randy Wimer (friend and drummer for MU) who said he was at that show. He said that we "blew Beefheart off the stage" that night and Don Van Vliet was standing watching us with this peculiar conniving look on his face. Little did we know that two years later, three of the members of that band would be Magic Band members. Could this have been his vision and plan from that night?

John French: We opened for the Beefheart band. That was the first time they played their original material in town. It wasn't really well received, because they were sort of stumbling through it.
Mark Boston: Were they playing the Safe As Milk stuff?
JF: Yeah, they were doing Electricity, Yellow Brick Road ...
MB: That's the stuff I wanted to play. That's what I thought that I'd probably be getting into when I joined Beefheart. We never did get to play it. Well, I got to play Abba Zaba a couple of times. I still remember that bass part.
JF: Don made some pretty giant leaps (musically), but I think what happened with the Beefheart band at that time is that they were splitting off from Leonard Grant and I remember P.G. Blakely approaching Jeff Cotton and trying to get Cotton to spin off into some group that he was going to form. At the same time, Don called me. So, that's how I got in the band and then I was gone so I don't know what happened after I left town. But, it seemed like I came up one time and you and Jeff were still playing with Blues in a Bottle at a party somewhere. Do you remember that at all? It seemed like Bill was playing guitar in the band.
MB: Oh, we played a bunch of parties. I can't remember, that was a long time ago.
JF: I have a picture of us that was taken at the High School. It was for some dance. It was for that dance we were going to play at Fair Center Hall. That was our first "Big Gig" where we made – I think we made a thousand bucks for playing, which was a lot of money back in those days.
JF: I left town, and I don't know what happened to you after that. Do you remember anything about what was going on?
MB: I was still floating around. I got involved with that girl that I almost married because I thought she was ... impregnated. Her name was Sharon.
JF: Yeah, actually both of us dated the same girl (quickly thinking of the implications) er, I mean, at different times ...
MB: It happened a lot in the desert.

JF: Well, anyway, you weren't in any other major valley groups besides the Blues In A Bottle group?

MB: For a while I played with this old fellow – Leo and his wife. They just played that old fox trot/two beats to the bar kind of stuff. We used to play at that old folks place up there in Quartz Hill.

JF: Mayflower Gardens?

MB: Yeah, I played several gigs there with them. Then I joined this weird band called Captain Beefheart.

CHAPTER SEVEN:
PM TO A&M

Don with (L to R) Doug Moon, Jerry Handley, Vic Mortensen and Alex Snouffer early '65. Photo courtesy of Jerry Handley.

The Roots Of The Mothers Of Invention

I'm sure there are many conflicting stories about how the Mothers actually came into being, but here's the story according to Roy Estrada:

Roy Estrada: I met Frank in '64, through Ray Collins. I had a group (The Soul Giants) – I mean I was the one who took care of the management and booking and stuff. It wasn't "my group". (Roy joked that the reason he was managing the group was that he was "the only guy who had a phone.") We needed a drummer, so I put up an ad here at a local music store in Santa Ana (California) and Jim Black answered the ad and he joined. Then we got a gig through his wife ... at a place called Broadside in Pomona – it was a brand-new place that was opening up. When we started performing there ... evidently Ray Collins was working there as a carpenter. So before we started playing the (owner) asked us to take on Ray Collins as a singer and that's how we would get the gig. We said, "Of course we'll take him on." He started singing with us. (Later) we were going to lose our guitar player Roger ... a local guy here from Orange County - he was going to get drafted.
John French: Who else was in the band at the time?
RE: A guy called Dave Coronado - he would play two saxophones. He was ... a Las Vegas-type of player. Then we had the drummer, which was Jim Black, and myself. Ray said "I know of a guitar player." So, (on) a Wednesday evening, ... Frank came over and sat in at the audition and we said, "Yeah, of course," and the rest was history.

Frank recalls:

"During the early days, when Paul Buff still owned the studio, I met Ray Collins."[18]

John French: What did (Frank) look like then?
Roy Estrada: He had short hair. He was young and thin and ready to go. He had just gotten out of jail. That's what Ray said.
JF: OK, that was right after that entrapment thing that happened to him.
RE: Yeah, he had made that party tape with that girlfriend of his – a friend of his, not really his girlfriend. So, we were playing Top 10 music at that time – Gloria and all that kind of shit. He said that he had music that he had written. He wanted to know if we were interested in learning it and looking through it, so we said, "yeah." About that time, the sax player left, he quit – he wanted to go back to the Vegas circuit, so it was only the four of us then – Ray, Frank, Jim Black, and myself. We start rehearsing some of the music at the studio in Cucamonga - that was in '64.
JF: That was at Studio Z then?
RE: Yeah – the same place he had made the tape I guess (laughs). The stuff that we learned was that stuff that's on Freak Out. I mean, that's the stuff that we first started learning. We rehearsed the music for months.

Mortensen mentioned Zappa getting evicted from Studio Z because of the entrapment case.

Post jail, Frank recalls that after he got out of jail:

"It was so sad. I had to get the wire cutters and yank all my equipment out of there and evacuate "Studio Z.""[19]

The studio possibly remained in Frank's possession for a time, as the Mothers (or Soul Giants as

[18] The Real Frank Zappa Book, Frank Zappa, Simon and Schuster, 1989 pp65.
[19] The Real Frank Zappa Book, Frank Zappa, Simon and Schuster, 1989 pp60.

they were called at the time) rehearsed "for months" at Studio Z according to Estrada. However, Frank mentions evacuating the studio *before* he mentions the Soul Giants and the beginning of the Mothers.

John French: Did you play any of that music in the club?
Roy Estrada: Of course! Not at first, and maybe not at the Broadside, but we got another gig in Torrance, I think it was called the Top Cat (according to FZ it was the Tomcat-a-Go-Go[20]) *or something like that. In that place, whenever we would finish playing, we'd take a break and they'd let these girls come up and dance. They were wearing these Playboy Bunny kinda outfits (laughs). We would start playing the songs that we had learned - which (are) the ones that are on Freak Out - to see what kind of response we would get – you know. I mean, that place – nobody was there for us – they were there for the fuckin' chicks you know (laughs). So, we just started playin'them all you know, we thought "What the Hell, let's play 'em all."*

The Mothers Christened
Also interesting to note is the following blurb from an internet article on Zappa:

"After a brief period spent as Captain Glasspack and his Magic Mufflers, the band changed their name to The Mothers on Mothers'Day, 1965."[21]

The Real Frank Zappa Book has the following statement:

"On Mothers'Day, 1964, the name of the band was officially changed to the Mothers."[22]

My thought on this is that perhaps Frank is mistaken as to the year in which the christening took place. 1965 seems to make more sense. *Freak Out!* came out in 1966.

Roy Estrada: From then on, I think Frank started hanging out in Hollywood and that area. He met this other guy – I forget his name (probably Mark Cheka who Zappa hired for a short time as a manager) he was actually an artist – he was the guy who turned us on to this part we had in the movie called Mondo Hollywood. What it was, we were a band playing at a party in the movie. We were at a discotheque playing at a party. That is where we met Carl Franzoni and all these freaks. There was free-dancing. That was also where we met Herb Cohen. I don't know why he was there. His eyes opened up and that's where he snatched us, right there.

(Robert Carl Cohen was the director of the film, and apparently no relation to Herb, describes Herb Cohen as a New York neo-hoodlum type whose competitors received stones through their windows, with whom I'd been somewhat acquainted since 1960, and who ran up thousands of dollars in debts while running Cosmo's Alley prior to fleeing the USA and his creditors for several years, took The Mothers from Cheka and commercialized them with the help of people at Capitol Records - which pitched them as every good conservative middle class American's worst nightmare[23]).

As "advertised" in the artwork of *Freak Out* under the header *"Freak Out! Hot Spots"*... Cosmo's Alley eventually became Bido Lido's. It was a small club on Cosmo Street LA. started in 1957 by Herb Cohen and Victor Maymudes. (They had previously run the Unicorn folk club.) Cosmo's Alley was popular with young actors and musicians. Lenny Bruce and Lord Buckley would often perform there. By the early 1960s the club was in financial trouble and Cohen fled the US for a few years.

[20]The Real Frank Zappa Book, Frank Zappa, Simon and Schuster, 1989 pp65.
[21]http://www.nndb.com/people/737/000024665/
[22]The Real Frank Zappa Book, Frank Zappa, Simon and Schuster, pp68.
[23]http://globalia.net/donlope/fz/videography/Mondo_Hollywood.html

John French: So, that was Carl Franzoni, Vido (the artist) and, were any of the GTOs there?
Roy Estrada: I can't remember, they may have been. The party scene was shot at a large mansion somewhere in Hollywood.

May '65/Teenage Fair/Magic Band

In the last chapter, I wrote about the Valley Music scene from a different perspective - that of my contemporaries and I, covering that timeline up until just prior to my joining the Beefheart band. Now, I'd like to again backtrack to the time of the Teenage Fair, which I have already described from my point of view as a kid of 16, but would now like to show from the perspective of the original band and their contemporaries.

John French: So, you were getting ready to play the Teenage Fair, and that is when things turned around a bit.
Alex Snouffer: Well, that was the beginning of ... that was the "foot in the door" thing.

There is disagreement among the band members as to whether the performances entailed competition in a Battle Of The Bands, or it was just for exposure. There was, however, no actual compensation to any of the groups that played in the booths. Most of the groups played for the exposure and the experience.

Alex Snouffer: It wasn't a battle, per se, just a lot of bands played. They had a lot of turnover in bands. But I think we were one of the few that actually played there twice.

Mortensen recalls it as leading to a time of more actual financial security.

Vic Mortensen: Now, see, we were "discovered" if you will, at the Teenage Fair. Leonard or the gal (Dorothy Heard) that worked for Leonard Grant that was assigned to our group, if you will, found us and then talked Leonard into signing us. The first real paying gigs we got of any consequence at all were after got involved with Leonard Grant.

Jerry remembers the Teenage Fair as I did, as some kind of competition or Battle Of The Bands. I not only recall Don discussing in advance with someone – Alex I believe – saying, "After we win the competition," but also recall some kind of competition from my own experience of playing there with The Maltesemen. I remember also that we played on the main stage after playing in a booth, and the only way that could be attained was by having already gained a certain amount of recognition - winding up in the finals. I recall DJ Sam Riddle introducing us and piped applause, even though there was a crowd there.

John French: Where did you meet (Leonard Grant and Dorothy Heard)? Was that during the Teenage Fair?
Jerry Handley: Yeah, after the Beefheart band had been going for a while, we did the Battle Of The Bands at the Teenage Fair in the Palladium. I don't know if we came in first or second.

In my own recollection, the Beefheart band came in first in the Battle of the Bands at the Teenage Fair. This was mostly word of mouth from musician friends who had been there, but I heard also that first prize included a small amount of money, some music equipment, and a recording contract. As I mentioned earlier, The Rising Sons including Gary Marker, Taj Mahal, and Ry Cooder, were playing in a booth next to The Maltesemen. We took turns of about 20 minutes, them playing first, then us for the two hours or so we were both scheduled to play.

The Rising Sons/Gary Marker

John French: So, tell me, do you remember playing the Teenage Fair in 1965?
Gary Marker: Well, that's when I met Don.
JF: That's what I (thought). Let's talk about The Rising Sons.
GM: OK. (There was) Ry Cooder, Taj Mahal, Ed Cassidy, then there was Jesse Lee Kincaid, the songwriter who wrote (sings unintelligible lyric).
JF: OK, who played drums?
GM: Well, Ed Cassidy did for a little bit, but he was really a guitar player. He played drums until we got a drummer. What happened is we had Ed Cassidy, who later went on and started Spirit. He broke his arm, wrist, or something in the middle of Stateborough Blues. Then we got Chris Hillman's cousin Kevin Kelley (Hillman recommended him.) (He was a) pretty good rock drummer, but had a real personality problem. I forever have been suspicious of people named Kevin. It was the first gig The Rising Sons ever had. We were sitting there playing Traveling Riverside Blues, and here's this weird guy with long hair, big bright baby blue eyes, you know, he (Van Vliet) had that "moon face" then. Looking very strange. I mean, he looked like your friendly neighborhood dope dealer - "The first one's free kid, after that, it's a buck a stick." He's standing there and he's looking at Cooder mainly, and, of course, Taj Mahal, and it's like this absolute look of wonderment. It's like he can't believe what he's seeing and hearing. Doug Moon was standing right next to him. He (also) had (that) guy, Vic Mortensen with him.
JF: Of course.
GM: Big guy ... I looked and it's Don looking with these wild blue eyes and wearing a big leather coat.
JF: Oh yeah, he always wore leather.
GM: They were playing on the main stage that was the thing, so he had this big mid-calf length leather coat. (He was) looking absolutely staggered, because we were playing some pretty raggedy shit and just faking it all the way.

Birth Of The Cooder Obsession

Gary Marker: On one of the breaks, I heard him lean over and grab Doug by the arm and he got this really angry look on his face. He pointed at Cooder and he said, "There! That's the shit I'm talkin'about! That's what I want you to play!" Doug had this absolutely terrified look on his face, you know, because Cooder is all of what? Seventeen? And playing like "Cooder," you know? And Doug was looking like "Oh, you mean he wants me to do this? Oh shit!" So, (Don) hung around, he kept coming back and eventually Cooder and I started talking to him. He was listening because we were doing all the blues stuff. It was real raggedy Delta kinda stuff. We were doing it as funky as we possibly could.
John French: Did you only play there once or more often?
GM: There was a Martin Guitar booth and McCabe's Music booth. We played there every night. It was about a week.
GM: I remember that we were inside. What had happened was that it ended up so many people clogged around, because you know, we were pretty unusual, an integrated group playing this funky crap in there, instead of surf stuff, that finally the Fire Department came in and said, "You gotta get all these people out of the aisle." The guys in the booth said, "We

can't, that's what they're here for!" So they moved us outside. They gave us a bigger booth on the midway. So, outside we went, where there was more room for people to wander around. You know, we still kept getting crowds. (We were just a) bunch of guys just sitting around jamming. We thought, "Hmm, if we can attract people here, maybe we can do it better." They seemed to like this music. It was a lot of Jimmy Reed stuff, you know, and then we'd throw in Howlin' Wolf stuff. So, that's how I met Don for the first time.

Ry Cooder - Background

Marker had known Ry for years. Cooder was apparently a child prodigy who had been playing since he was three or four years old. When he was 11 or 12 years old, he wound up at Marker's parents'house. This was during Gary's high school years, when he had formed a band with keyboardist Darryl Dragon, who became better known in later years as "The Captain" of The Captain and Tennille. Marker describes Dragon as a "helluva boogie woogie piano player." On the day of the first meeting with Cooder, Marker, playing acoustic bass was practicing with Dragon and a couple of other players. Their band would occasionally back such groups as Dante and the Evergreens and Dick and Dee Dee, who had a hit in the early sixties with the tune *The Mountain's High.*

Gary Marker: My parents lived on a hillside and the house had a basement. We were in the basement, which had a piano. All of a sudden, between songs I heard this John Lee Hooker style guitar coming from upstairs. My brother had brought his friend Ryland home from school. Ryland spotted my dad's guitar, which was this classic 1927 Jumbo Gibson. He asked, "Can I play that a little bit?" So, he went in the hallway and closed all the doors so it would echo and he started playing all this blues stuff. I said, "Darryl, do you hear that?" and he said, "Whoa!" I don't think we had started playing yet. I said, "What the hell is that?" I went upstairs and here's this kid sitting here playing all this gutbucket blues, Hooker and stuff. I looked at my brother and I asked, "Where'd you get him?" (He said), "I go to school with him, he sits next to me!"
John French: Did you know what blues was at that point?
GM: Oh, yeah, sure! I already had a pile of seventy-eight Howlin' Wolf records and stuff but I was (mostly) a jazz fan, (and) wanted to be a jazz musician. So, I said, "Boy, you play guitar pretty good, kid!" He came downstairs and (Darryl and I) started playing, Darryl started playing and before I knew it "thump thump thump"– down the stairs (comes) Ryland yelling, "My God, it sounds like another Jimmy Yancey, or Pinetop Smith!" he couldn't believe the way Darryl played. So he went up, got my dad's guitar, came down and he and Darryl played and they did all these boogie woogie things. We all sat around goofing on those things for a while. This is High School stuff, but you know, I wish I had some recordings of it. Half that stuff was not bad, for a bunch of kids imitating old black guys.

So, that's how I met Ryland and off and on through the years we worked together. We used to do a lot of jingle recordings - like for Wonder Bread or Yeagel Oldsmobile. But he was still some local folk hero, he always was, because he could pick like crazy. He was an amazing guitar player.

According to Marker, Ryland was raised by "raving liberal parents" (his words) and was an only child. One day, he was sitting on the kitchen floor playing with a knife, unbeknownst to his parents. There was an accident, and somehow the knife wound up stuck in his eye, and so he lost sight in that eye. Whether or not the eye has been replaced with a prosthetic or not is unknown. Ry always gave a different story depending who he was talking to. In later years, he developed monocular depth perception, which enabled him to drive a car. But in those early years, his parents kept guarded watch on him, fearing that there may be infection, or that he may lose his other eye. Since this was pre-school, and he didn't have anywhere to go, nor could he watch television (his parents were against television), he was given a guitar as a gift. He developed a life-long affinity for the guitar.

Gary Marker: He obviously had some penchant for guitar playing, some ability, and it went from there. But he had a very early start. I used to joke. We'd be on the road, I'd tell Taj, "You know what? I bet you I could wake up Ryland in the middle of the night not even wake him up, just go over and put a guitar in his hands and he would start playing! It would be perfect". This guy just lives, breathes and eats guitar, that's all. You put any stringed instrument into his hands and he plays it.

Ry Recalling The Teenage Fair

Ry remembered the band next to his booth (which was The Maltesemen as mentioned earlier) as a Pachuco/Mexican Band playing all sizes and shapes of Fender guitars. He remembered us as having sequined suits and thought we were the Midnighters or Cannibal and the Headhunters or something. After the playing was over, Don introduced himself and Doug to Ry. Vliet introduced himself as Captain Beefheart, which made Ry laugh (maybe he'd heard the joke to which Mortensen earlier had referred, or perhaps he knew Uncle Alan). He told Ry something to the effect of "Doug thinks he's a guitar player, but he's really terrible" – a statement that was sure to instill confidence in any struggling young guitarist.

Don asked Ry to explain bottleneck to Doug, explaining that he had been trying to get "these guys" to understand what he was talking about for months. Ry described bottleneck as "no big thing" or something to that effect. Don would later mention to me that when he first suggested that Alex and Doug used bottlenecks, they laughed at him. He told me this at an early rehearsal, in their presence, and no one disputed the story.

Eventually, Ry was contacted by phone and invited up to rehearsal in the desert by someone, probably the original manager of the band, who had somehow acquired Ry's telephone number.

Jerry Handley: Frank (Zappa) used to come up and jam - and Ry Cooder. We'd met him at that time when he was playing with The Rising Sons – he and Taj Mahal.

Eventually, Ry, Gary, and Taj from The Rising Sons band wound up going to a rehearsal at Jerry's parents' house. Cooder's impression of the high desert was the same as most people: the wind blows sand in your face and you are surrounded by cheap real estate. Later, during a 1971 Warner Brothers tour with his own band opening for Captain Beefheart And His Magic Band, Cooder told journalist Chuck Powers:

"He had this house up in the desert near Lancaster, and all of his hard-riding motorcycle friends would sit around and drink beer and fall into the pool - real rowdy, hard-living guys with lowered Buicks, you know, chasing off across the desert. It was too weird. I wasn't making any money, and Don was crazier than hell. He was good, you know, real good. But crazy." [24]

Since Ry complained of the wildness of the group, I mentioned this to Alex Snouffer and read the quote. Alex laughed. Upon questioning, it was determined that Ry was just as likely to be "one of the guys falling into the pool" as anyone else.

---

[24] Los Angeles Times WEST Magazine, Charles T. Powers, May 30, 1971, pp21.

Van Vliet Performance Problems

Bear in mind that throughout all of this, Van Vliet had actually had no previous experience working with a band. Therefore, there were certain things about musical structure and chord changes, cues that needed to be known by everyone that Don had a difficult time recognizing. This limited the band's spontaneity in performance.

Gary Marker: Whenever Jerry Handley would get in trouble – it was usually a draft board thing - we forget about that stuff now, we used to always have some problem going with the draft board - I would fill in and I would have to play everything exactly (the same). It couldn't change (meaning there could be no flexibility in the arrangement, which severely limited the spontaneity)*, and Alex would be out there directing (Don) with the guitar neck as though it were a conductor's wand, because Don had no sense of time. (Alex) would cue him when to come in, because he would always miss the cues. He would know the songs, (but) he learned them by rote. It was weird, because his intonation was fine, but the timing ...*

Van Vliet himself had mentioned, shortly after I joined the band, that he had previously had problems with timing and understanding musical cues. He said that he had gone to Alex with a determination to learn and rigorously demanded, "Teach me this stuff you say I'm not understanding." He was illustrating this by grabbing an imaginary Alex's arm and moving him over to a particular place in the room as he described the incident, stomping his foot on the floor and simultaneously pointing down in a defiant and determined posture, emphatically saying, "OK, now SHOW me!"

Through the years, I saw evidence surface of Van Vliet's problem, which turned out to be less a "timing" problem (which could have been cured before I became a member) and more getting lost in the structure and missing cues. Marker here is the earliest to mention this particular anomaly. Most of the times, singers who perform in this manner are considered by the musicians backing them to be performers and *not* musicians.

Marker/Van Vliet Relationship

John French: So, you and Don became good friends after the Teenage Fair?
Gary Marker: Yeah - off and on. He would roll into town in what seemed to me to be an endless series of very high-end Jaguars – it was probably two or three of them. He would just call up and say, "Hey, are you doing anything? Can I sleep on your couch?" "Sure, fine Don, drop by." So, he'd roll into town and he'd have some agenda and he'd come in with a toothbrush, you know, like holding a toothbrush out in the open, no ditty bag or nothing! It was like the weirdest thing. He'd walk in. He'd wear pajamas. He would bring his pajamas all neatly folded on his arm, and his toothbrush.
JF: That's the only child bit I think.
GM: Maybe so. "Okay, Don." We'd hang out, we'd get loaded and we'd go out and listen to bands. I'd drag him around town to jazz clubs and stuff. It was kind of funny because he was kind of like aware of jazz stuff and even some avant-garde jazz stuff. It wasn't like a full-spectrum thing. He would know who Ornette Coleman was or something like that.

Perhaps partially because of his association with Ry Cooder, Van Vliet befriended Marker. I determine that it was at this point in time that Van Vliet began to be truly exposed to jazz, especially some of the more avant-garde. A culmination of several events happened within the same period of time, which led Don to look outside of his blues roots and seek for a kind of liberation from the confines that had been imposed upon him. One of the confines was a logical conditioning that began more and more to equate performing blues with cheap bars, low pay, and sleazy "meat market" dancing, done for the sole purpose of sexual conquest. Up until now, his tenure had been in a group that was still "paying dues." He and Doug, being the least experienced, were the most likely to benefit from the experience. Doug saw it as an opportunity to reach an end goal, whereas Van Vliet seemed to view it more as the end itself – or rather, a dead end. Since this was his first experience, perhaps his naïve only-child world didn't readily accept the idea that in order to achieve something of worth, one must get one's hands dirty. Don's strongest talent may lay not in his musical abilities as most would think, but in his theatrical abilities, which he had developed at an early age. First, with the bullying of his parents, which is well-enough documented to consider valid. Also, Don was considered the "teller of tall tales," and as Doug Moon so aptly stated, "Everyone knew he was a bullshitter." However, the friends that he made were made because of his ability to entertain by verbalizing what in most other's opinion was a fantasy world.

Van Vliet's theatrical abilities were able to convince others that he was a genuine blues singer, when in fact; he was merely playing a composite role of the heroes of his adolescence. Recall Handley's statement describing the early formation of the group:

Jerry Handley: *Well the uniqueness of Don's voice, being able to sing the blues and sound like it was for real, we weren't really imitating. He could "sound like" Muddy Waters" and that, but we still sounded like our own band.*

In this statement lies a bit of an oxymoron, a bit of irony. The phrases "sound like it was for real," and " we weren't really imitating," are highly contradictory statements. On the one hand, all the band members were fond of the blues, and had been strongly influenced by the blues. However, since they were actually covering tunes by earlier artists, they were, in effect, *imitating* their heroes, the idols of their youth. The more experienced musicians at this point were actually expanding upon the original arrangements to create a sound of their own, although Van Vliet was basically still at the first stage: imitating those artists he had listened to for years.

Frank Zappa had remarked that Don was a "blues fiend" and Alex, Doug and Jim Sherwood all seemed to agree that Rhythm & Blues played a large role in his teen years. Because of the fact that Don never "paid the dues," so to speak, learning the basics of song structure and understanding cues, he surprised Marker and others in the band by not being able to put the lyrics where they needed to be, having for years to be cued in by one or other member of the band. Bootlegs of live recordings indicate that in later years, Don was often lost in his own songs.

In later years, one undisclosed source related to me a story in which a famous blues artist opened for Van Vliet, who had been standing in the wings listening to the show with an increasingly apparent anxiety. At the end of the blues set, he was asked why the anxiety. "I can't follow *him*, man! *The thing is, that guy's the real thing!*" There is a certain admirable quality to be found in this rare moment of humility, but there is something else revealed in this statement. Van Vliet may never have considered himself real for the simple reason that Captain Beefheart *wasn't* real. The Captain wasn't the genuine article, but was simply playing the role of a fictitious character originally created by Frank Zappa. Although the character is definitely interesting, and Don is truly a pioneer, perhaps like "the old fart" about which he later wrote, he was gazing through a mask at the public: The "Captain Beefheart" mask.

Dorothy Heard/Lake Arrowhead
Now that the band had done well at the Teenage Fair, suddenly there was wider recognition,

and one of the first people to realize the band's potential and contact them was standing in the audience listening to a Magic Band performance on the main stage. There were actually at least three people in the audience that day who would later play a role in the band's story, Bill Harkleroad, Mark Boston (who Don later claimed to have remembered seeing and described as "the one with the eyes"), and a lady with some musical business connections named Dorothy Heard.

Alex Snouffer: I don't remember the first time I met her, but I remember meeting her. That's when she entered the picture. Then we went on from (the Teenage Fair) to (Lake Arrowhead). We did a lot of gigs up there. College places - shit like that.

Jerry Handley: I think Dorothy Heard had (seen) us (at the Teenage Fair) and then we did a job up in Lake Arrowhead and that was probably our first break. Dorothy knew we were playing up there. She came up to Lake Arrowhead. We were doing a three-day gig up there. She heard the band and that's where she got her interest in the band. We were with another manager at the time. Though I can't even tell you their names.

Smell Of Success - Summer 1965

Some of the band members were surprised after the Teenage Fair when they began to receive more recognition than they had originally expected. Jerry had originally thought that maybe the band "could get some jobs in Lancaster, if they ever got that good." Now, suddenly, things were taking several steps forward. The band could actually make a modest living by playing music full time. It began to change everyone's perspective as to the potential of the group. Also, people nowadays may feel that this had more to do with Van Vliet's voice and presence, but at the time, the conversations were more centered on the entire group as a unit, rather than focusing on Van Vliet.

Leonard Grant

Jerry Handley: That was probably the (first) breakthrough really. (Dorothy) got us "over the mountain" and signed up with Leonard Grant. He (had) a great management company, he had Frank Gorshin and probably still does. Dorothy was our connection with him.
John French: In what capacity did she actually serve?
JH: She was our hookup with the professional business world at that time. Because we didn't have a place, she had us rehearsing at her house ... a house in the Hollywood Hills. She was dedicated to the band.
JF: What else did she do? What was her background?
JH: She had (something) to do with Wolper productions ... with documentaries (working with) David Wolper (award-winning television and film producer). I don't know where that went. She had some good connections. A very professional lady, I think she kind of fell in love with the band. She saw the uniqueness of the Beefheart band like a lot of people did.

Snouffer Skeptical Of Grant

John French: So, enter Leonard Grant, and he gets you some gigs etc. and you didn't have a very good impression of him. He was Frank Gorshin's manager?
Alex Snouffer: Yeah, he was.
JF: So was he managing any other bands?
AS: No, I think we were the first band he had ever handled, you know? It's a whole different

part of the entertainment industry than he was used to dealing with.
JF: So, he wasn't specialized?
AS: Probably with actors and people like that. It's the same thing as if you need a lawyer, you get an entertainment lawyer, not just some joker down the street dealing with divorces. He's not going to be able to help you one iota. So, you need people in the business to help you in the business.

Zappa Comes A'Calling/Summer '65

No-one had heard from Zappa for a time, because this was basically when he had gone through a series of legal proceedings due to the efforts of one scumbag, Detective Willis. Obviously, the attention that was being focused on the Magic Band was enough to catch Zappa's attention, because he showed up at a rehearsal.

Vic Mortensen: I still remember the day - Frank Zappa came up to Lancaster. We had started to make some noise, we had done the Teenage Fair and it was getting obvious that we were going to start kicking some ass. We were rehearsing at Jerry's house and (Frank) sat on the couch and he was pissed, big time. Because he had yet to start the Mothers and he had been evicted from the studio because of that bullshit entrapment situation. He saw it was obvious that Beefheart was going someplace and he wanted a piece of the action. We said, "No, your part of the action was the Beefheart (name). The Magic Band situation was (my) part of the deal, and besides, what are you gonna do about it?"
JF: OK, let me go back and grab a few thoughts, because I wasn't there, just to clarify. You say, "he was the Beefheart deal," what do you mean?
VM: OK, in other words, Zappa had written a screenplay originally, called Captain Beefheart and his Girlfriend Sue, based on this character of Don. This irrepressible character of Beefheart, … you know what I'm saying. "And his girlfriend Sue," was, Don's mother.

Origin Of The Name

Apparently, Zappa at that time felt he was due some compensation for the name Captain Beefheart, which most likely originated with him. This had to do with his screenplay Captain Beefheart vs. the Grunt People (The name on the actual script) and the fact that Don had taken the character's name as his stage name :

Zappa recalls:
"The way Don got his 'stage name'was, Uncle Alan had a habit of exposing himself to (Don's girlfriend) Laurie. He'd piss with the bathroom door open and, if she was walking by, mumble about his appendage – something along the lines of: 'Ahh, what a beauty! It looks just like a big, fine beef heart'."[25]

I personally thought that Don's Uncle Alan was an extremely arrogant and outspoken individual, but I only met him once. However, Don seemed to greatly admire him and always spoke of him in glowing terms. Unfortunately, I always felt like Uncle Alan was a poor role model whom the young Vliet modeled himself after a bit too closely.

My brother, Tom French, who was a television repairman for many years in Lancaster, recalled meeting Alan in the late sixties or early seventies when on a service call. He said that everyone called him "The Colonel" and that he dressed in white suits and wore a hat befitting an old plantation owner. Apparently, Alan was a bit too outspoken with my brother during a service call, prompting my brother to immediately inform him where "The Colonel" could put his television set.

[25]The Real Frank Zappa Book, Frank Zappa, Simon and Schuster, 1989 pp37.

Zappa, in his book makes no mention of claiming any credit for the name. However, members of the band do consistently attribute the creation of the name to Frank, and Gail Zappa even once said to me that "Frank named him" when referring to Don. I recall various stories concerning this.

Vic Mortensen: (It) came from Zappa. Now, of the origin, I'm at a loss for words here, if you were a lexicographer - in other words, the history of words – the whole Beefheart deal came from an old black phrase. It says, "Wow, that boy's got one the size of a beef heart. In other words, a cock the size of a Beefheart.

The tongue-in-cheek name of the band was obviously a play on the idea of the concept of penis size, male sexuality, and the rock n'roll superstud image. Mortensen mentioned earlier that Frank was writing a script called *Captain Beefheart And His Girlfriend Sue*, which was most likely, the title that evolved into *Captain Beefheart vs. the Grunt People*. After being around Don for a while, I could also understand where the title "Captain" came into play, because Don certainly had a composite character partly composed of one extremely large portion of oppressive military leader. It could also partly be a parody of the superhero Captain Midnight who was a popular superhero character on fifties' black and white television. In fact, the early Captain Beefheart sketches had a definite superhero look.

Beefheart Name Not Challenged

Apparently, no real battle ensued over the rights of the name, probably because Zappa may have had his fill of legal proceedings for the time being. One of the things that actually drew Zappa's attention, though, according to Mortensen, was the fact that the band was beginning to gain a little notoriety. The band members didn't really notice it right away, thinking perhaps the new management people were merely blowing smoke. But suddenly a new level of performance opportunities were appearing, and the band was playing more in the San Fernando Valley and eventually, Hollywood itself at the Whisky A Go Go. Before, in Lancaster, the band was playing in bars and lodges (another name for private bars for the more seriously *dedicated* drinkers who became members for the express benefit of obtaining low-cost alcoholic beverages). Now performances were booked in colleges and large auditoriums, billed more as concerts, less as dances. Even when the band played in the Antelope Valley, people usually did more listening at the dances than actual dancing, creating a concert atmosphere. I was surprised to see half the dance floor filled with people sitting down, cross-legged, listening intently.

Vic Mortensen: I just know that once we got with Leonard Grant, I didn't worry about the money at all. I don't know if this will make sense to anybody, but I didn't want to worry about the money. John French: Well, you were happy with what you were doing and so the money was secondary.
VM: Exactly.
JF: Which is exactly the way art should be done, anyway.
VM: If I had enough money left over to go get a bottle of bourbon after the show or something. You know what I am saying.

A Father Dies/A Song Is Born

The band was rehearsing on Carolside at Grannie Annie's (Don's grandmother's) house. This house was directly across the street from Don's parents' home. It was an empty house at the time, because Grannie had either gone to stay with relatives or, more likely, had moved in with Sue. Vic received a telephone call. It was his mother telling him that his father had died. The rehearsal ended, and each band member in turn expressed their condolences to Mortensen. Vic was not shocked with the news. It was expected his father would soon die, but the natural grieving process began. Vic decided to wait until the next morning to drive to Claremont and help with arrangements. Sitting in the house at Grannie's Vic picked up a 12-string guitar that was lying around and began unconsciously strumming a tune. Don said, "I think I can put some words to that." The creation of the tune was started that night and finished later, but it became *Call On Me*, a more up-tempo version of which later appeared on the first album, *Safe As Milk*.

Vic Mortensen: But that was Call On Me, *and I wrote the music and Don wrote the words. And then when I was in Vietnam, my mother sent me both the* Freak Out *album that Frank had done, and the first Beefheart album,* Safe As Milk.
JF: Right.
VM: She sent me both of those albums with a little letter saying, "Thought you'd like to see what the boys were doing." When I looked on the liners it said, Call On Me *and I went, "Wow, they did* Call On Me!" *and I looked on the liner notes and it says, "Words and Music by Don Van Vliet." I thought Don had recorded the song, hoping I would hear it in Vietnam and it would cheer me up. Hah! (Laughter) All I did was think to myself: "I'm 10,000 miles away and the guy is screwing me here."*

Denver Whisky

Vic Mortensen: (Dorothy) got us in there and that's when we got the gigs at the Whisky A Go Go in Denver, and then we went to Hawaii. You know, the real honest-to-God, big-time playing gigs.

The Whisky A Go Go in Denver was the first of the high-paying (or at least higher-paying) bookings that were to come with the new management. The booking agency had gotten the band an audition with Shelly Davis, who owned all the "Whiskys" in the country. Impressed with the band, Davis wished to book the group at several non-LA Whiskys to give them seasoned experience, and then have them show up "triumphantly" to play at the Hollywood site (probably due to the fact, as Zappa described earlier, that Johnny Rivers was out of town or on vacation).

Confrontations With Van Vliet
Because of his reputation of being a teller of tall tales I started questioning later boasting by Van Vliet about violent confrontations in which he always claimed himself the victor. Thinking perhaps these stories to be nothing more than hot air, I probed the early members recollections. In Denver, Doug remembered times when the locals challenged the band because of their hair length.

Doug Moon: I remember confrontations. I remember Don standing his ground.
John French: He said he played football in high school. I was really surprised because ... there was one side of him - the artistic sensitive side and then there was this other side that played football? It was always hard for me to equate those two inside the same person, you know what I mean? Because they just don't go together at all.
DM: I remember him standing his ground on a number of occasions. In the band we had confrontations, like up in Denver, we were in redneck country back there. We were being confronted every time we went out some place. You know, back then, long hair was more of a Hollywood thing.
JF: Oh yeah, so you would run into this, (affects a southern twang) "Hey hippy, you look like a girl."

DM: So we had several confrontations back then. I remember Don being in the middle of at least one of them, and he was willing to kick butt if it came down to it. I settled the whole thing by pulling out my derringer and pointing it between this guy's eyes and him seeing me nervous with this derringer. The guy just turned white as a sheet. He looked at me and thought, "This guy is just scared enough to pull that trigger." (So he said) "That's OK, we didn't mean anything, we were just kidding."

Mortensen recalls an earlier confrontation with Van Vliet.

Vic Mortensen: Let me put it to you this way. I wasn't physically intimidated by him. I knew - if you ever played football - on the first play of the game, you get down and what you wanna do is give your opponent a whack. I don't care where the game is going. First play of the game, you give that guy a whack. "Here I am, you sonofabitch, and I'm going to whack you like that every time I come out!" You get him thinking about the whack. With Don, I knew that he was big enough and crazy enough to hurt somebody, and being – again getting back to this thing about not wanting to fail? We got up to a point where I pushed him up against a garage door one time and I thought we were going to go for it right in front of the Handley's. I told him, "Don, goddammit, if we do this thing, man, we're both going to get hurt! I'm not going to give up and you're not going to give up. And somebody's going to get hurt! And you're not going to be able to sing tomorrow and I'm not going to be able to play the drums." You know what I'm saying? But there were these little confrontations, but boy I'll tell you what, I would NOT have wanted to go down in a back alley with Beefheart. Because the worst thing you can do is get into a fight with a guy that refuses to quit.
John French: So you think he would have gone to whatever limits he needed to win.
VM: He might have gone to whatever limits he thought he could get away with. All I'm saying is: I wasn't physically intimidated by him where I just cowered. It was like, "Don, if you mess with me, we're gonna go for it!" He never saw it going as far as to fuck with me and I never saw it going as far as to fuck with him, but I was always in a position to say, "Don, godammit, that's bullshit. You come here to work or jerk off?" (referring to Don's bad rehearsal habits).

Moon's Derringer

John French: I remember you and I were in a liquor store. Somebody was giving us a hard time in the store and the next thing I know, I'm sitting in the car (next to) you and you have that derringer in your hand ready to ...
Doug Moon: That was my equalizer...
JF: Yeah, well, you had to have something. It was kind of wild back then. Alex, of course, tells the story about the time you were in Stockton, in a country bar, and these guys kept giving you a hard time and finally at the end of the thing, you pulled your derringer out and ...
VM: Stockton, I don't remember Stockton, I remember Denver.
JF: Well, something about, "will the real Okie please stand up?" (Note: This was an armed and light-hearted takeoff on a popular televison show called *What's My Line?* where panelists tried to discern which of three contestants had the actual profession all three were claiming to be.)

Holes in the Ceiling

John French: Of course, you never used that gun did you?
Doug Moon: Well, I fired it a few times when I got drunk and blew holes in the ceiling.

JF: *Of people's houses or in clubs or what?*
DM: *Of one of the hotels we were staying in. I blew the light fixture out.*
JF: *On purpose? Or it suddenly discharged in your hand. Or what?*
DM: *I was drunk - poor boys on a Saturday night - getting wild.*

Vic Mortensen: *Well, when we went to Denver, all of these bullet holes turned up in the ceiling of Doug's hotel room.*
John French: *Yeah, he said that one night, he felt like shooting the light out.*
VM: *Yeah, we reported it like, "Yeah, I think somebody broke into this room last night and shot the ceiling." We covered for each other.*

Rich Hepner

It was here that the band first came in contact with Rich Hepner, who would later play a small but important role in the band's development and, more importantly, was a strong influence on the guitar players in the Antelope Valley. When not playing at the Whisky, some of the members of the Magic Band had decided to visit a club that featured local entertainment. The featured entertainment for the evening was The Jags, a typical Top 40 club band with the added gimmick of having outrageous hairdos.

John French: *But they had these big pompadours. But we're talking about blow-dried hair, gelled, hairdos, we're talkin "MAJOR 'do's."*
Alex Snouffer: *Bouffant shit.*
JF: *Yeah, this was like a gimmick of that band that they had these 6 or 8″high pompadours, like greaser haircuts, but they had real long hair but it was done in the old fifties style.*
AS: *Yeah, they had a chick that used to do 'em.*
JF: *OK.*
AS: *They had their own hairdresser.*
JF: *It was a very exaggerated Elvis pompadour, from what I remember.*
AS: *Well, yeah, I guess you could say that.*

Mortensen Recalls Hepner

Vic Mortensen: *I wouldn't remember him unless ... Did he come out of a group we met in Denver?*
John French: *Yes, he did. Named The Jags.*
VM: *The Jags, or whatever, they were kind of slick. They wore suits on stage - that kinda shit. Drove snappy cars.*

Apparently Mortensen's fond memory of this meeting was the chick that did their hair, which accounted for yet another of Vic's sexual conquests.

Vic Mortensen: *Exactly. I remember doing the chick that did their hair. They had a full- time chick and she did their hair. They spent hours with this huge bouffant thing.*

Snouffer, however, seemed very impressed with the band's musical abilities.

Alex Snouffer: *They were a good band. They really were.*
John French: *What did they do?*
AS: *Club shit. Top 40 stuff. Of course BB King was Hepner's idol.*

JF: BB King all the way. Yeah, so this is what caught you the band's 'ear?
AS: Oh yeah, because he had it down, man.
JF: So, he was playing some other club in Denver while you were at the (Denver) Whisky A Go Go.
AS: Right.

Sacred 'Go Go' Tradition

The format of the Denver club was similar to that of all the Go Go joints. The band would play a live set. Then, while the band was on break, go go dancers climbed ladders into what looked like giant bird cages to dance to pre-recorded music, hopefully enticing the audience to follow suit on the dance floor below. Go go girls were attractive girls sporting bouffant hairdos, and dressed in outlandish costumes, sometimes very short "shimmy" dresses comprised of rows and rows of fringe that "shimmied" while they danced. Sometimes they wore bras and hot pants festooned with rows of spangles interspersed with rhinestones. The live bands usually didn't want the girls dancing as they played, because *they* were supposed to be the focus of the attention, *not the go go girls*.

Into the second week of the Denver performances, everything had been going well. Captain Beefheart And His Magic Band was packing the joint. This was a bit surprising to everyone, because this was typically "redneck" country, and the Beefheart band looked like a bunch of hippies and girls what with all that long hair n' stuff. The liquor was flowing, and the owners seemed pleased. However, a new owner appeared on the scene, one who was not experienced in club management, nor did he apparently have much in the way of people skills.

The new owner was sitting at a table with a young lady described by Mortensen as "some bimbo." Apparently, the enterprising and obviously randy young entrepreneur envisioned himself as being rewarded with immense sexual favors by the aforementioned bimbo if only he would allow her the permission to fulfill a fantasy that apparently had become one of this ambitious female's prime goals: to climb into the birdcage and shake her back-end to the seductive live music of the Beefheart group.

Cueing the band, Mortensen, a great believer in preserving the sanctity of go go tradition, led the band in walking off the stage in single-minded protest, leaving the imbibed bimbo in humiliating unaccompanied go go frenzy. The exasperated new owner immediately saw his dreams of sexual fulfillment dissolve simultaneously with the young girl's fragile ego, physically manifested as the depletion of her frenzied dance transformed into a questioning shrug. Anger stirred in his alcohol-filled veins.

Vic Mortensen: And this old guy comes sweating over ... "What the...?" I explained that "this is what we do." I bitched the guy out. He and I had a big argument, I told him "We're not here to provide music while you put one of your whores in the booth. We're the act here, man." The broad came down before we went back onstage. Bear in mind that we were packing them in the joint. There were lines outside. They had to move tables in from the restaurant to get enough people in (the lounge). This apparently had not happened there before.
John French: Doug described this place as being a red-neck kind of place.
VM: Denver Colorado - that's what you would expect. Denver is a redneck town. No, this is why it was so amazing. We packed the joint. I might not have had enough balls to do this if there had been four people in the room. Understand what I'm saying. If there hadn't been a line out the door and every night packed ...

The new owner had appeared to reach an understanding with the Magic Band and they finished the evening's performance and perhaps played another night. However, shortly after this, the band came in to rehearse during the day. According to Vic, they were "always working on new stuff."

Vic Mortensen: *We show up at the club, the club's dark* (meaning closed) *and there's a cowboy band onstage – one guy playing steel guitar and another on guitar – you know what I'm saying - a redneck group. And I went to the club owner and said "What is going on?" He said, "I'm gonna hire these guys, and I'm just gonna reduce the cost of my beer." Of course, we had a contract. We were all members of the Musicians Union. So we got the local Union guy in there and he sold out to the club owner.*

Right here, just let me inject that *I have never once been helped by the Musicians Union, anywhere, at any time.* These guys basically "help themselves" to a cut of the band's proceeds through legal mandate, but when time comes for them to assist a musician in distress, the above statement usually prevails.

Enter Gino - Or, "I Get By With A Little Help From The Mob"

John French: You said something one time about the club owner not paying you and you got some kind of "heavy", some interesting character to collect your money for you.
Alex Snouffer: Yes, his name was Gino Smaldone. And it's (probably) exactly what you think it is. Gino and his girlfriend used to come to the club and watch us play a couple of times a week you know and then all of a sudden, we're on break, and this is after the club owner started giving us shit about the money. And he owed us money, and we still had another week to go there and he wasn't going to pay us because of this and that … so, anyway, I was laying this on Gino and he (asked), "This guy's not going to pay you?" I said, "Well, probably eventually, but we'll have to go through all kinds of changes." He thought about it for a minute, he said, "I'll tell you what, you come to my office, tomorrow afternoon at 3:00, and I'll give you your money."

Mortensen seems to recall this story, thought not realizing that Gino had "arranged" payment-in-full for the band.

Vic Mortensen: I seem to remember meeting (him) … I remember that little vignette.
John French: Yeah, he was armed. Alex noticed this.
VM: It seemed to me we met the dude in the club, it wasn't somebody that Alex had known for life. It was some dude we met in there. He liked the band and we told him what was going on. As I remember it was one of these things like the guy says, "let me go make a phone call."

The reason Vic wasn't aware of the actual results of the situation:

Vic Mortensen: I always considered Alex to be the "nominal" head of the group in terms of all of that. Like, if you want to talk business, talk to Alex.

Alex Snouffer: I went there at 3:00, I didn't see Gino, I just saw his secretary. She looked up and said, "You must be Alex" - you know, cause I had the hair and shit - and I said, "Yeah." She reached in the drawer and gave me a check, signed by the club owner.
John French: Nervously signed, perhaps. Now this Gino guy, he had a gun - right?
AS: Yeah. I saw something on him (on the news) just before I left Denver (Note: this was years later in the early eighties when Alex lived in Denver and was working as a chef.) *'Cause we were about the same age, you know, and they got him; they busted him and sent him up for a few years for tax evasion and shit like that. The Smaldones were (allegedly) the local crime family there in Denver.*

JF: Perhaps an enterprising subsidiary of a much larger organization. (I might add, probably the tenders of the Local Musician's Union).
AS: Yes.
JF: So the band got paid and (were able to return) home. Thanks, Gino, wherever you are.

Mother's Progress

Roy Estrada: That was our first step into the Hollywood scene. That's when Herb latched onto us and from then on, he booked us into some clubs. We wound up doing the Whisky A Go Go. They were all mafia clubs; there was one off the strip on Santa Monica Boulevard (probably The Action). *We saw a lot of (celebrities). The Yardbirds would come into the club. Sonny and Cher would come in. One time, John Wayne came in, he was all drunk.*
John French: Frank mentioned something about John Wayne giving him a hard time.
RE: John Wayne was drunk and had a bodyguard. You know how Frank would always start riding on somebody, so we did it on stage, we started doing that and the bodyguard came up and said, "Hey, cut that out!"

The story, in *The Real Frank Zappa Book* is that John Wayne showed up with a couple of bodyguards, a male friend and two ladies. Wayne picked up Frank, slapped him on the back, and shouted, "I saw you in Egypt and you were great, and then you blew me." Frank, taking a dislike to "The Duke" got up onstage and announced:

"Ladies and gentleman, as you know, it's Halloween. We were going to have some important guests here tonight – we were expecting George Lincoln Rockwell, head of the American Nazi Party – unfortunately, he couldn't make it, but here's John Wayne."

The Duke staggered onto the dance floor, Frank gave him a mike, and he began to say, ... and if elected, I promise to..." A bodyguard interrupted and made him sit down, then threatened Frank with "big trouble" if he didn't "cool it."[26]

[26]The Real Frank Zappa Book, Frank Zappa, Simon and Schuster, 1991, pp73.

CHAPTER EIGHT:
BEEFHEART ART RISING

1966 shot of Don in John Stewart's Art Studio. Photo courtesy of John Stewart.

Goodbye Denver/Hello Hawaii
   So the band unexpectedly left Denver perhaps a week earlier than anticipated.
This was probably around August or September of 1965.

*Vic Mortensen: We did go back home, we went back to Lancaster, for a week or two,
something like that. Then we got the word that we were to go to Hawaii.*
*John French: Probably why you had a couple of weeks off is because the (Denver) booking
was cut short.*

   The Hemenway Lounge clipping from the local newspaper in Hawaii has the date of October
15, 1965.
   Going back two weeks would be the end of September, and the Denver booking cancelled early,
so it is reasonable to assume that the band had started their month-long booking in Denver either
the last week in August, 1965, or the first week in September.

*Vic Mortensen: I remember the trip (from Denver). For some reason, we couldn't get an air
flight. We had flown into Denver but we couldn't get a flight out because of some problem
with the equipment or some damned thing, at least that's what I was told. So we had to take
the train, OK? Now remember, I told you I was running around barefoot all the time. I was
barefoot in the train station. It wasn't because I didn't have shoes, it was part of my schtick.
"Look at that crazy son of a bitch." In fact, that photo of us playing in Hawaii has me
playing barefoot. We were cut short in Hawaii too. But I can't remember who pissed off who
there. Or whom, as it were. But I remember coming home (from Denver) on the train, it was
kind of a gas. Jerry and I would sit up in the observation car.*
*John French: I came back from Wyoming on a train in 1969, and I spent most of the trip in
the observation car.*
*VM: Jerry and I would sit up and do our little … we'd sit up there and pretend like we just met
each other on the train. "Will you send me cards?" Jerry and I had a thing that we would do
that went on for hours called "You hip?" He'd ask,"Are ya hip?"and I'd say,"Yeah, I'm hip."
etc. ad infinitum.*
JF: You remember a lot of fun in the band.
*VM: Oh God, it was always fun. Getting on the train in Denver, I remember people looking at
us like we were strange. Old military guys and … not so old. We were already beginning to
feel the hatred - the long-haired thing. I remember this other train pulling in and there were
these two little old ladies sitting on the train, and I was barefoot with my gallon of shampoo,
which looked for all intents and purposes like a gallon of urine, right? I jumped onto this
train car and ran down the isle to these two little old ladies who had been looking at us out
of the corner of their eyes, smiling and giggling, and gave them both a big smooch and ranoff
the car. I remember we did something in the Denver Train Station that involved Don,
another one of these things. We used to pretend like he was retarded and I was the only guy
who really could control him. He would go over and sit with some people and start going (in
excitable retarded voice) "I love you, I love you!" They'd start to freak, and I would run over
and grab him, "Now, Don, that's enough!" We'd go into this store and there would be one of
those carousels with postcards on it. Up near the front. Don would just sort of mumble
in and I'd walk around and all of a sudden he'd just start spinning this thing shouting, "I
wan' it, I wan' it!" The shop owner would freak. Here's this big guy in a black leather
jacket, spinning his thing, and I would come up and grab Don. I'd say, (in stern voice) "Don,
you just can't have everything you see." I'd pull him out of the store. We used to have fun*

doing mind-fuck on people. It was a ball. I had fun from the day we started until the day it ended. Maybe that was the only blessing in having it cut so short.

Early Band Dynamics

John French: There were some pretty wild times with that first band. I know Vic Mortensen said that Alex came ... Vic was done with rehearsal and "getting laid" as he put it. Alex came bustin' in the room and wanted him to party and jam, and Vic got in a big scuffle with him and picked him up. He actually said there were footprints; scuffmarks of Alex's shoes on the walls and on the ceiling. Vic was a pretty big guy, and Alex is more my size maybe a little shorter, but he is a about my size and weight, so I imagine that he could have thrown him around like that.
VM: He did, he tossed him around like that - like a rag doll. Pitched his butt out...
JF: Threw him through the screen door, that's what he claimed.
VM: I remember he pitched his butt out. I remember Alex threatened to come back with a knife or a gun or something.
JF: Was that in a hotel?
M: No, that was in Granny Annie's house across the street from ...(Sue Vliet's house).

Wealthy Heiress

After Denver, the band played the Hemenway Lounge in Hawaii. This was around the tenth of October, in 1965. While in Hawaii, the band was allowed some recreation time, and so Vic, who loved to surf, would go to the beach. He caught the eye of a young lady on the beach one day, and they began seeing one another, becoming romantically involved. This lady turned out to be a wealthy lumber heiress. As the story goes, Don claims to have talked to her about the band and convinced her to set up a corporation in which she and the band could mutually benefit from the entitlements.

Mortensen's ROTC

Meanwhile, other complications were forming in Mortensen's life which started before his father's death ...

VM: I was already involved with Frank and the guys and I could see myself wanting to be a rock'n'roll musician and having some success at it. I wasn't just, you know, we were getting beyond the garage band stage at this point. And I opted not to do the thing. But, later, my father was found to have cancer of the liver. Which is considered to be a terminal disease, which is in those days more terminal than it is now. Knowing that, he came to me and said, before he died, he wanted to see me take my commission, OK? So, we went, and I did that thing for him. I got a special commissioning ceremony. My grades had been good enough in ROTC that we were able to call the department and they had a commissioning ceremony and put the old bar on me. And there is a photograph somewhere of my mother holding my old man up, you know, wearing his one suit. And she's holding him up. After that, he went home and died. But, nonetheless, they (the military) had me by the balls.

Goodbye Mr. Mortensen

Vic's father's terminal condition allowed him to be exempt from military duty.

Vic Mortensen: Then, (my father) having died, since I was considered to be on reserve status. To make a long story short, when I got back from Hawaii, I got home and there was a letter waiting for me saying that I had thirty days to report for active duty. Bingo, I was gone.

Alex; Drums; Rich; Guitar/November 1965

The band considered their options. Alex immediately started considering who was the best replacement, and the name Rich Hepner came to mind. But Hepner wasn't a drummer, he was the great guitarist that Alex had heard in the group The Jags, in the club band in Denver. Alex envisioned himself switching to drums. Rich had fairly long hair already, which was being styled into a giant bouffant as part of The Jags onstage gimmick. So, Rich changed his look from a slick club band musician to sandal-wearing, bearded hippy.

Rich Hepner/Late 1965 to mid-1966

After Hepner joined the band, there was little time for conflict or power struggles:

Alex Snouffer: We were still playing blues then. It was pretty well established. So it wasn't like - the only thing there was to talk about was which gigs we wanted to play next so that we could make as much money as possible - how to further advance. There wasn't a lot of internal fighting then because we were too busy fighting off all the bad guys in corporate record-dom.
John French: Well that was a hell of a strong band. During that period I heard that band play one time, and I had heard the Vic Mortensen version play about two times previously. I got together with John Parr (my drummer friend) *afterwards. He was saying, "Man, did you hear Alex playing drums? The guy can really play!" The parts are simple, but they're really different, and his time is great. So, I just wanted you to know that there was a lot of admiration for your drumming as well as your guitar playing.*
AS: Well, cool!
JF: You had a Ludwig set? If I remember, white pearl?
AS: Yeah! I still got the bass drum.

Exposition Hall, The Return of Captain Beefheart And His Magic Band/November 12th, 1965

I had taken a date to the Exposition hall, a medium sized building at the Lancaster fairgrounds that held about 500 people. The new band lineup was playing for the first time. Unlike Doug and Alex, Rich was a BB King fan and emulated his style, giving the band a Chicago blues flavor that mixed quite well with the Delta blues style they had originally developed.

My date and I stood to the side of the stage and watched the band for four solid hours. That's how long those dances were, usually 8-12 hours. They were usually sponsored by a business, or by one of the local car clubs. It was a place for the kids to go in this little town. I was amazed not only at the sound of the band, but the image. By now, everyone in the group had really long hair. Hepner looked like a religious figure, a prophet of some kind, complete with beard and sandals. Don was wearing a faded pattern tie and a blue chambray work shirt under a leather vest. They were a very tight blues band. I still find it a shame that no one in the business had the vision, the presence of mind, the foresight to adequately record the band at this point. I truly believe it would have been one of the greatest white blues recordings in existence. The only recordings that exist of this band were released on the Revenant set, but they are basic studio demos, not live recordings.

It was an interesting combination to hear the Delta blues with these screaming guitar solos of Rich's. Alex was a competent enough drummer and had great time and meter. Jerry played simple, full lines. The sound was amazingly rich. I could almost envision myself in a swamp. It was as if the walls were gone and we were surrounded by trees, vines and murky swamp water. The stage was like an old boat dock. Don had a separate harmonica microphone through a Fender

Super reverb amp. Jerry Handley used a Fender Bassman, the old piggyback blond amp. I didn't really notice what Doug and Rich used.

I stood at all different parts of the stage, trying to soak in what these guys were up to. It seemed like all the lines were really simple so it wasn't the result of flashy playing. It was the blend and the conviction of the band that made the difference musically. The audience seemed spellbound. A lot of the people here were not locals. There were many "freaks" as they would later come to be known - longhairs and early stages of the psychedelic look.

Hepner truly added a great deal to the band. His solos were stunningly fluid. He seemed completely relaxed, almost nonchalant in his approach. The notes and the rhythms were dead on, and I had never heard blues notes played in quite this way, not having yet heard BB King; I had nothing to compare this guy with. His dynamics were amazing, and he seemed to be the essence of what really propelled the band into a much higher level of intensity.

Diddy Wah Diddy

Diddy Wah Diddy, an old Bo Diddley original, became the group's first official single. During this era, groups would record a "single" 45-rpm record with a "flip" side (unlike CDs, vinyl records have two sides), which was like a "B" movie. Usually the hit was on one side and the other song was a weaker song. In this case, a Van Vliet original entitled *Who Do You Think You're Foolin'*.

Jerry Handley: We were talking to our original managers (before Leonard Grant), they brought up a stack of old 45s and they had a lot of Fats Domino, they wanted us to bring back some old Fats Domino music. So we were listening to all these old records, (but) we really didn't want to do any of them. I don't think we ever played any Fats Domino. But we found Bo Diddley's Diddy Wah Diddy *and we liked that and somehow came up with our version of it. Bo Diddley probably rolled over, you know.*

The original (nameless) managers of the band, in a somewhat ill-defined attempt to expand the band's repertoire (Fats Domino?) had inadvertently included a few other R&B singles in a listening session. One song stood out to the band - *Diddy Wah Diddy*. Here was a song that fit in with their blues/Rolling Stones image and had the kind of riffs that could be easily adapted to their instrumentation.

Studio - Sunset Sound

One of the most popular Studios in Hollywood at the time was Sunset Sound on Sunset Boulevard.

Gary Marker: It was eight track then. One of my ex-wives was the traffic manager for that place. She booked all the acts in there. I was really familiar, because I had recorded in that studio a lot and with other bands as well. That was in the studio where the Doors cut everything, you see. It's like a little magic studio, "A" is or whatever they called the little one up front. Buffalo Springfield and all those people also cut in there. So, a lot of really good stuff came out of there. It was a really good sound, an intimate room. No matter what they did in the control booth – because later on they started putting in the digital stuff you know, and it was still a good room. It didn't make any difference, it was just something about the room.

John French: So the lineup of musicians on the Diddy Wah Diddy *session was Doug Moon, Jerry Handley, Alex Snouffer, Rich Hepner and Don Van Vliet, right?*
Alex Snouffer: Let's see, yeah.
JF: Somebody played harpsichord on the end?

AS: Yeah, played harpsichord and I think on the other side we did some hand-clapping crap, all that kind of shit.
JF: All that early sixties/late fifties overdub stuff, to give the song enhanced power and punch. Was Bruce Botnick the engineer by chance?
AS: Oh, yes, we can't forget Brucie!!
JF: Yeah, he was always there at Sunset Sound, I think he was their in-house engineer or something.
AS: Well, he ended up that way, yeah, at that time he wasn't, though. He was alright, he was just … he was an engineer/wannabe A&R man. He was kind of getting ahead of himself a little bit. That's why a lot of people kind of looked at him with a jaundiced eye. But Bruce was OK. He was trying to get ahead, but hadn't put in his dues yet. That was all.

Arrangement/Sound

Shortly after joining the band, the subject of the sound on *Diddy Wah Diddy* came up in conversation between Don and I. I was commenting on the power of the song, which was mostly due to the bass sound that had been achieved in the studio. Van Vliet took credit for that sound, saying something to the effect: (paraphrased) "I told Gates to do that to the bass, they argued with me, but I made him do it. Snouffer, however, disagrees with this:

John French: So should credit go to David Gates for the overall big sound of Diddy Wah Diddy?
Alex Snouffer: Let's just put it this way, it was Dave's baby. You know what I mean? All the way through. I mean, he was telling Don, "I want high notes on the harp here," 'cause there's this one little section in the song where he just stays way up there in the upper registers. I don't care how much Don wanted to take credit for it, Gates told him to play it that way. No, it was Gates'baby, one through ten. It worked.

John French: (It's) a very powerful record. It still stands up even today and it's because of the bass sound.
Jerry Handley: Right, right! You know whos really gets the credit on that strong a sound on the recording end of it was David Gates.
JF: David Gates, OK of David Gates and Bread.
JH: He came up with the idea of plugging the bass directly through the board (studio mixing console) and he could control it better I guess.
JF: Did he use a fuzztone?
JH: I think he had a … yes, he put a little fuzztone on it.
JF: So, it sounds to me like has a split signal where it has the regular bass sound and the fuzztone too.
JH: Right, it does. It went right through the board and it about blew the studio out, you know. And not out in the recording end of it, but in the booth, I could see the glass in the booth shaking.
JF: Well it was definitely a big sound and it was kind of a letdown when Frying Pan *came out which was the next single, right?*
JH: Yes
JF: Because it didn't have that big sound.

(Note: *Frying Pan* was actually the flip side of *Moonchild*, a song that was written by Gates for the Magic Band. Evidently, since *Frying Pan* was originally supposed to be a B-side, it neither received the attention, nor the production value of *Diddy Wah Diddy*. My mistakenly thinking it the single during the interview was because on the local station, the band had requested that *Frying Pan* be played, rather than *Moonchild*.)

Jerry Handley: I know, I wish we could have kept that sound somehow.
John French: Yeah, because that was sort of a trademark sound.
JH: I loved it, you know me, I was the BASS PLAYER, you know.
JF: Sure of course.
JH: "Crank me up man, let me go." We were able to do it live, cause I put a fuzztone on the bass when we played the Whisky and we were able to come up with that sound live too. And I only played it on that one song. I thought it was pretty strong.
JF: Yeah, very strong, and of course, Don's vocal on that … It was the first time I had really heard Don's voice because you couldn't really tell over those squeaky little PAs that they had at the dances and performances I had attended. I mean, you could hear him but it wasn't the same.
Gary Marker: Diddy Wah Diddy was a fabulous record; there was no question about it. I still love that record. I listen to it and think, "This thing was a monster!" It was a great sound with all that compression and that great voice.

I was completely taken by the great sound of the recording. By this time, I had been working on my blues singing a little. I was starting to understand the nuances and could appreciate just how well this Don Vliet could sing. I had never heard a voice like this man had. I had been to a couple of the band's performances, but the PA never really did Don justice. But hearing this, I suddenly began to realize how really good a singer he was. Also, the distortion and reverb on the bass gave the band a certain sound that was more powerful than anything I had heard.Wow!

East Battles West

John French: Diddy Wah Diddy did well with the DJs but it didn't make a lot of money. Why?
Alex Snouffer: Because there was another band on the east coast that released the same song. It was a good arrangement, though. I liked it, yeah. I liked ours better, of course, other than being biased; I liked the arrangement from an objective point of view. I liked ours better, but I did like what they did with it. (Of course,) I didn't dare say anything. (Laughs).

(Note: *Diddy Wah Diddy* was a minor local hit, partially thanks to (then stateside radio DJ) John Peel pushing it. But at the same time another group, The Remains, released a version of the same song, which impacted on the success of both recordings.[27])

John French: That kinda screwed up the promoting of the records.
Alex Snouffer: It messed both bands up. They pretty much had the east coast sewed up and we had the west coast sewed up. Either one of us could have taken over both coasts as far as play was concerned. But that was not to be, and of course, how many times does THAT happen? That's a one in a million shot there, boy.

JF: An obscure blues song that hadn't been recorded in many years being released simultaneously by two separate groups.
AS: On two separate coasts. That's a record company's, personal manager's - even a band's - nightmare.
John French: There was another recording of Diddy Wah Diddy that came out on the east coast, do you recall that?
Jerry Handley: Yeah, it came out at the same time, I can't tell you the name of the group.
JF: I think that's an ironic twist because it's like neither song really got the interest because

[27]http://diddywah.blogspot.com/2005/06/too-many-diddy-wahs.html"

both songs were out at the same time. Or maybe there was some confusion. I always wondered if that's why that song didn't go farther, because that was one of the most powerful songs I had ever heard at the time.

JH: I know that. I think our version of it should have gone much bigger than it did. The best description of it that I heard was when Wolfman Jack was coming out of Del Rio, Texas and we were out in the Antelope Valley. I think we were driving out to drink some beer or some damned thing, and here, it's on the radio. He says, "OK everybody on the highway, you'd better pull over, cause here comes Captain Beefheart and Diddy Wah Diddy." And you almost did have to pull off because it was so strong.

JF: So, what I understand is that it became a DJ it but it didn't make money because it wasn't distributed properly.

JH: They called it a turntable hit. DJs loved it, they just loved it. It wasn't a big commercial sounding record (though). Kids weren't ready for it, you know.

JF: Well, it wasn't exactly like, (sings) "Sunshine, lollipops and rainbows …

JH: (Laughter) It hit the market at a - that seems to always hold true that Beefheart was way ahead of their time, you know. I think Yellow Brick Road was probably the most commercial sounding song we did.

JF: Probably, on that album. But, right around that time, you have the Stones coming out doing a lot of the same (kind of) stuff.

JH: Yeah, and The Yardbirds were doing that kind of thing.

JF: That's right.

JH: They were more pop sounding, we sounded more like we were down in the gutter somewhere. Whose voice did you ever hear that sounded like Don's?

JF: That's true, it's what made the difference.

JH: We probably sounded too nasty for everybody, now that I look back at it, he didn't sound too sweet.

Recording Moonchild/Frying Pan

After the public's reaction and the relative turntable success of *Diddy Wah Diddy*, David Gates attempted to write a follow-up hit, using the same ingredients. It was a common practice during this period to follow up a hit record with another similar song in order to ride in the wake of the first. James Brown's *I Feel Good* followed in the wake of *Papa's Got A Brand New Bag*. *Soul And Inspiration* was the Righteous Brothers' answer to *You've Lost That Lovin' Feeling*. I talked to one engineer who told me that several bands would actually use the same basic track, re-edited with different overdubs for two or three different songs.

Moonchild

John French: So, then you went back and cut Frying Pan, right, that was probably the next thing?

Alex Snouffer: Well, I think Gates wrote that thing called:

French/Snouffer: (simultaneously) Moonchild.

AS: I have yet to figure out which one of them was supposed to be the A side. I think Moonchild, but then we just threw that Delta thing on the other side, Frying Pan.

John French: So, Moonchild was, in your opinion.

AS: (chuckles) Well, let's put it this way, it never was our cup of tea. When Dave sat down - just him and the guitar and sang it - it had a nice little lilt about it. I mean, it wasn't for us, let's put it that way, but it was an OK song. But by the time WE got through with it in the studio, us interpreting what he (wrote)? Even Gates said, "Boy, wasn't supposed to happen

like this!" (Laughs) But he said, "I'm gonna go with it anyway."
JF: So, he wasn't really happy with the arrangement?
AS: The interpretation. We followed the arrangement just exactly the way he had written it - whatever that was.
JF: Yeah, I heard his original demo. It was a demo with just him singing and accompanying himself on acoustic guitar.
AS: Oh, did you? Well then you know what I am talking about. By the time we got through with it, Moonchild *was entirely different, man.*
JF: One thing I noticed about that recording is that it seemed like it was in the wrong key for Don's voice.
AS: I'd have to listen to it again. I haven't heard it since we cut it.

Jerry Handley: And after that, we did Moonchild, *another 45.*
John French: Yeah, which was a very powerful thing, but not at all Beefheart.
JH: Right, David Gates wrote Moonchild. *He was trying to put another* Diddy Wah Diddy *thing out. And it just didn't happen. So, it fell out, I think after the* Moonchild *thing didn't hit A&M thought, "Oh, we don't know about these guys."*

Moonchild *does indeed seem too low in pitch for Don's voice. David Gates'demo had him singing the piece an octave higher in the same key. Van Vliet would have probably sounded a little more powerful had it been two steps or so higher in key. It was basically the same linear arrangement, but the band did add riffs that weren't on the original demo. Van Vliet's vocal seems half-hearted, as though he's been forced to do something out of character, and the song probably was just that – out of character for the band. Regarding David Gates' writing, it seemed to me to be a white man's attempt to write a down-home blues tune.

The failure of the song was the second punch that would destroy the band's credibility with A&M and their relationship with David Gates. It was also just the kind of situation to send Van Vliet and the band back to the drawing board to come up with their own material - something they wouldn't be embarrassed to be associated with.

Doug Moon's thoughts here seem to convey the opinion that not only he, but Van Vliet formed after the *Moonchild* disaster.

Doug Moon: THAT was the side that should have been promoted. (Referring to Frying Pan*)*
John French: Frying Pan
DM: Instead of that garbage. That's GARBAGE! (Referring to Moonchild*).*
JF: But what...
DM: Frying Pan *was a hot song.*
*JF: But it was never released (*Moonchild*) Was it ever released?*
DM: Yeah, but it bombed. Because the side that they tried to push was this Moonchild *garbage. That was that manager that we fired that tried to get us to do all this garbage. (Shouting) He tried to make a pop (strongly emphasizing the p's) band out of us.*
JF: Is it David Gates who you're talking about?
DM: Yeah, (reading) "supervised by Leonard Grant," - and he tried to make a pop band out of us. Well, you can see where he's coming from. This is the kind of people he's used to dealing with, (looking for photo, finds it) he's used to dealing with people like this ... (holding up a promo photo of Frank Gorshin).
JF: Right, Frank Gorshin (Grant managed Gorshin).
DM: Not an avant-garde blues band. He didn't know what to do with us. How we got hooked

up with him… that was one of our biggest mistakes.
JF: Dorothy Heard I believe.
DM: Anybody with a brain would have pushed that side (points to B side, Frying Pan), if they would've pushed that side on the radio, I think the record would have made it.
JF: But the trouble with Frying Pan was, in comparison - production-wise, it wasn't as strong as Diddy Wah Diddy. I think that is why they were pushing Moonchild, because it was a stronger production, it was a bigger sound; you know what I'm saying? It wasn't the band, it wasn't the sound of the band, it wasn't the personality of the band, but it was a stronger production and they put all their effort into that … Frying Pan was just a B side they stuck on there.
DM: If they would have put the effort into Frying Pan that would have been dynamite.

However, Snouffer disagrees with the pop band theory.

John French: Doug Moon on the biography thing (BBC documentary The Artist known as Captain Beefheart) says that David Gates was trying to turn the band into a pop band. Did you feel that way? Or was that just his impression?
Alex Snouffer: Well, let's put it this way, I don't know if he was trying to turn it into a pop band, per se, I mean, between Doug and Vliet that's all you heard … "Ah, man … blah blah … Top 40 band" - I never got that impression from him. He was trying to get a commercial sound that he could sell.
JF: And something that would follow up Diddy Wah Diddy, right?
AS: Yeah, I think so.
JF: It was produced pretty well.
AS: Oh, yeah, Gates' productions are great stuff. I mean, look what he did with Bread for crying out loud. He wasn't trying to do what they (claimed), but I wasn't going to argue with them. No, Gates wanted to turn it into a money-maker and he had to get a more commercial sound - rather than deep, whole-mouth blues. Even though maybe once we were accepted, then go back to do that, you know what I'm saying?
JF: Yeah, kinda integrate that into the show.
AS: Right, and then pretty soon just take over. But then we went the other direction and Canned Heat got all the glory. And they weren't even a good blues band. They were nothin', a little faggoty high-pitched, stump-scratchin' little ball-pinching okie, man!
JF: What was his name, Bob Hite or something?
AS: I don't know. He's dead now.
JF: I remember hearing one cut by the Canned Heat, little high squeaky voice and I thought, "That's the band that they're comparing the Magic Band to?" 'Cause I heard, "Oh, you guys are a lot like Canned Heat!" and I heard Canned Heat and just thought FORGET IT! So, at this point, Moonchild, what did it do, when it came out?
AS: (sardonically) Nuthin!!!
JF: Whose fault was that?
AS: Hell if I know.
JF: Just the wrong sound for the band? I felt like Don wasn't singing very well on it.
AS: I mean to use that as a follow-up to Diddy Wah Diddy, you needed something a lot stronger than that. Because that wasn't even a blues song and Diddy Wah Diddy was. Actually, we were more into it. NO, it didn't go anywhere.
JF: Do you think it was anything at all to do with A&M's promotion? Or did they promote it?
AS: I don't think they promoted it.

JF: Nobody really knows for sure.
AS: The thing just died a natural death and that was it.
JF: I've got a copy of the A&M sessions here somewhere. It's got one of the publicity photos, I think it's the one with (you holding) the trumpet. Don's holding a saxophone.
AS: Oh, I remember something about that, yeah.
JF: And P.G.'s in the picture.
AS: We took that down on Sunset or Hollywood Boulevard or someplace.
JF: Who Do You Think You're Fooling? Was one song of the four … What about the music, was that basically a band arrangement - head arrangement working from a jam session the way a lot of songs were written in those days?
AS: I don't recall. I think it was one of those things you stumble on and think you might be able to make-work. We actually started working with it. It wasn't like someone came running through the door with a piece of paper and said, "Whoa, here's our next hit."
JF: So, that was the flip side of Diddy Wah Diddy?
AS: I think so. I wouldn't swear to it. (Laughs)

Having known Alex for years, I would describe him as very level-headed in the business sense. He had a good perspective on the art/business relationship and was aware that sometimes compromise was necessary in order to achieve monetary reward. This was a main area of contention between he and Don, who always seemed to be indignantly insistent on artistic freedom (his own, no one else's) and never seemed capable of compromise, accusing the others of wanting to sell out.

Alex's main faults seemed to be his lack of confidence in his own business instincts, low self-esteem, and alcoholism. This left him less able to deal with the tenacious, yet sometimes blundering Van Vliet, who could always seem to get his way, even if he didn't know what his way was at the moment.

Yet Alex was still open-minded enough to go along with much of the innovative songwriting that went into *Safe As Milk* during the final weeks of rehearsal prior to recording. Snouffer's frustration with Don's lack of teamwork was alleviated by a few drinks now and then.

This alleviation would turn out to be Snouffer's Achilles'heel in the future, as he faced a lifetime struggle with alcohol. Van Vliet would later use this fact to discredit Alex whenever Snouffer attempted to alter the course Don had set. This would tend to embarrass Snouffer and he would become silent and passive.

For a while during this period, the band seemed to go into hiding. There were rumors through P.G.'s brother Bobby that the band was working on new material. They were practicing every day and putting together a demo tape. Perhaps the bad experience with Gates' *Moonchild* had persuaded them that they MUST write their own material. Nothing was heard from the band for several months locally.

Mixed Feelings

John French: All I heard (from Don) were terrible things about Leonard Grant. What was your view of him?
Jerry Handley: Oh, no, no. I don't have anything bad to say about him. The guy was a businessman. He got us jobs at the Whisky A Go Go down there.
JF: Well, a lot of people (Note: especially from that era) would say just calling him a businessman is something bad to say about him.
JH: He got business taken care of, and he was a very professional guy. He didn't really have

much to do (with us personally), he wasn't a real hands-on manager.
JF: So, what was Don's opinion of Dorothy and Leonard, because he always told me that they were terrible people.
JH: Well, it's all great at first, and then after he doesn't get his way, they're terrible. That's basically what happens to everybody that he (dealt) with.

As will be seen, there seems to be a pattern with Don in terms of the band's various business relationships with individuals or organizations. Many examples of this pattern come up throughout the story. However, Snouffer seemed to hold similar views concerning Leonard Grant.

Alex Snouffer: Yeah. I got no comment about "Lenny"
John French: You didn't like him, huh?
AS: No
JF: What about Dorothy Heard?
AS: She was OK. Her heart was in the right place. It's just … she couldn't do it by herself - managing anything or us - so she needed Leonard Grant. So she had to stay with him. Which made her and Grant (partners) … and I didn't like Grant.
JF: What didn't you like about him?
AS: Ah, he was attempting to pull some moves, man - you know, financially - that just weren't cutting it. And of course, that's the name of the game. You gotta watch your back at all times. Too many little things started to happen and not happen. So we just eventually went broke from him.
JF: But he did get you some gigs, right? Didn't he book you in the Whisky A Go Go?
AS: Well, he got us hooked up with A&M, Grant was still our manager when we did Diddy Wah Diddy*, so … after that period of* Diddy Wah Diddy *and all that, then we "took a powder".*

Van Vliet was beginning to distrust Leonard Grant and David Gates, who had envisioned the whole concept of introducing the band to the public. Van Vliet also complained of the audacity of Grant who interrupted the recording session so that everyone could sit and watch the campy and then in-vogue weekly series Batman. Perhaps this was because Frank Gorshin, one of Grant's most famous clients, occasionally appeared on the show.

Muddy Waters/Early 1966
A couple of friends of the band, Steve and Fran, lived in Hollywood.

John French:This is probably off the track, going backwards. Tell me about the time you guys jammed with Muddy Waters. Wasn't that at Fran's house?
Alex Snouffer: Yeah, we had been down at Fran's I guess we were rehearsing down there. Muddy Waters was playing at the Troubadour. Don got the bright idea, he said, "let's go down and get him and his band and bring them back here." And we thought about this, and we thought, "Well, will they come?" because the race thing was still pretty solid back in those days. Especially with those guys since they come from the South and all that. They were older than we were, of course. We went to the liquor store and stocked up on wine and beer and shit like that in hopes that they would. Then we went to the Troubadour and we talked them into it, the whole fuckin'band Muddy, James Cotton, Luther King, the whole gang.
JF: Who was the drummer then?
AS: I think it was Francis something. I can't remember his last name.
JF: So, you guys had your instruments set up and they jammed on your stuff kinda?

AS: Yeah, I was still drumming at that time. That's why I still have my bass drum, because the drumhead's all autographed by Muddy Waters and all.
JF: So, those were happier days?
AS: Oh, yeah, because we were still in the blues. This was before the bad times., Things were a kick.

The Return Of The Lumber Heiress /1966

John French: But I do want to bring up one thing. When I got in the band, Don claimed that he set up a corporation with (a lumber heiress who shall remain nameless).
Alex Snouffer: There was something like that that was supposed to happen, right? Because we had met her in Hawaii. Course, she had bucks obviously, and Richard (Hepner) was a courting' her.

Snouffer is probably confused here, as it appears that Mortensen was still in the band when they played in Hawaii. Mortensen claims that he is the one who had a relationship with the heiress.

Don's "Corporation"/Early 1966

John French: Then (Don) said, "I had a corporation set up with (lumber heiress) and it would have made us all rich but Jerry, Doug, P.G., and Alex sold their shares to Leonard Grant for beer money."
Jerry Handley: Oh no.
JF: So, I never knew what happened any of that, and of course, being a kid I believed everything I heard, so you know in the back of my head, I'm going, "I gotta watch out for these guys" you know what I mean?
JH: The band was just falling apart, and so we had sort of just dissolved the partnership with Leonard Grant. We dissolved the corporation and I think Leonard Grant, in my opinion, wanted to get away from the band, because he could see this band was not organized. (There were) too many problems going on internally with the band.

I find Jerry's description here that the band was falling apart a bit surprising in as this was just before I joined the group and they were talking about doing an album. Now that I look back, the difficulties with Van Vliet had come to a head and were almost unbearable at this point for the rest of the band. They tried to talk me into leaving Don and becoming the singer on more than one occasion, and I kept trying to mediate some kind of communication.

Alex Snouffer: Anyhow, Don got on his, "Oh you really oughta invest in this band" kinda trip and she was going to, I think. She did a few financial favors for us, but then Hepner got on whatever trip he was on and he split. When he split he left her high and dry and then she was hurt about the whole thing. So, that corporation never came together.

The truth may be that the lumber heiress had a fling with Mortensen in Hawaii, followed later by a relationship with Rich Hepner.

John French: Well, OK. Here's Don's story. Don's story is that he set up a corporation with the lumber heiress, and – I heard him tell this story dozens of times, so I know it. He told it to me when I first got in the band. "And P.J. (he always called him P.J. instead of P.G.), Alex,

Jerry and Doug sold their shares in it to Leonard Grant for beer money.
Alex Snouffer: (Laughter)
JF: That was his way of putting it.
AS: (More laughter)
JF: So it never actually really came together?
AS: (Laughing) NO! ... "Sold our shares for beer money?"
JF: Yeah, that would have been a lotta beer.
AS: Leave it to Vliet to come up with something like that.

Van Vliet's story may have been at least partially hogwash, but it succeeded in completely giving me the wrong impression of the rest of the band right in the beginning, and discredited them in my young inexperienced mind eyes enough that I became suspicious and questioning of anything they did or said. Whatever corporation that could have existed was dissolved by the time I was in the group. It's also difficult for me to understand how Don could have ever set up a corporation, which takes an immense amount of paperwork and planning, with his lack of organizational skills.

Jerry and Alex actually seem in agreement that Leonard may have been anxious to dump the band due to their internal problems.

Jerry Handley: We dissolved the corporation, and in my opinion Leonard Grant wanted to get out from the band, because he could see this band was not organized. Too many problems going on internally with the band.

It makes perfect sense that the corporation never came together. The heiress may have later become involved with Rich Hepner. Perhaps she did a few financial favors for the band. Hepner left her and the band, causing her to withdraw her support and never sign an agreement. Perhaps Don stating that he had set up a corporation becomes, in reality, Don talking her into considering it, perhaps starting the preliminary paperwork. Later, he blamed it on the band when she backed out.

John French: So then things took a dive after that. Was Leonard Grant still involved with the band at all at that point?
Alex Snouffer: Yeah, but we were on our way out with him. Or he was on his way out with us, however you want to phrase it.

Re-forming The Band/Mid 1966

John French: You were (back) on guitar, right?
Alex Snouffer: Yeah.
JF: So the change between Rich Hepner leaving, did that happen during your San Francisco gigs at the Avalon or before?
AS: Rich never played in San Francisco with us.

Snouffer did not seem to recall why Hepner left the group. Handley didn't fare much better on this question.

John French: So then, under what kind of circumstances did Rich Hepner leave the band?
Jerry Handley: That's confusing for me ...

During my early tenure in the group, Don would often talk about Rich Hepner as a BB King solo freak. The condescending tone was surprising to me, because Rich had been such an influence and highly-revered by so many of the local guitarists. He was highly respected as a player by all the members of the Magic Band and the group seemed to sound great with him. Nobody in the band spoke poorly of Hepner except Don. My speculation is that it may have had something to do with the emotional involvement with the heiress and Don trying to manipulate her financially. Perhaps Hepner felt that Don should butt out. Since Don thought of Hepner as a solo freak it could be that Van Vliet was envious of the attention Hepner was attracting on stage with his playing. I found myself watching him more than Don during the one performance I witnessed while he was in the group.

P.G.; Drums, Alex; Guitar/May – June 1966

John French: Handley mentioned that P.G. had a timing problem.
Alex Snouffer: Well P.G. did have a timing problem, but he straightened it out. At least he could stay in meter, but other than that, nothing fantastic about him as a drummer. Well, you didn't need to be fantastic for the stuff we were playing, you know what I mean?
JF: Alright. So Hepner's out of the band, you're back on guitar, P.G. comes in. You're playing gigs?
AS: Around that time was when we started doing a lotta gigs up in Frisco. During that bullshit. The Avalon ballroom, the Fillmore, Winterland, you know, places like that.

The San Francisco sound was just emerging with groups like Jefferson Airplane, Big Brother and the Holding Company, and the Grateful Dead. Suddenly, there was a new arena on which the Magic Band could emerge. Beefheart quickly became a popular favorite of the San Francisco set. Inspired by the atmosphere of creative openness, Don wrote a song entitled *'Frisco's So Free'* which title's alliteration revealed a certain naivete in that outsiders deplore San Francisco being referred to as Frisco.

Jerry Handley: The band was still going in the same direction basically, we were still doing the bluesy kind of stuff and playing the Avalon ballroom.

Further Decline Of Leonard And Dorothy
Again, the story of the strained relationship between management and band seems to be two stories, the one told to me by Don, and the one told to me by the rest of the band.

John French: The story goes with Don that you guys were all kind of taking sides with Leonard Grant and he was fighting you because he knew that Leonard was no good for the band, was holding you back etc. and all you guys were being romanced by Leonard Grant.
Alex Snouffer: Well, if we were, I sure missed it. (Laughs)

Later concerning Grant:

Alex Snouffer: But then he started pulling some little quick scams and I saw that happen and that's when I say, "Hey, we're outta here." I mean, Don saw it, too.
John French: I know he had a very low opinion of Grant.

Of course, from my perspective (based on observations made a few months down the road), Don seemed to have a low opinion of everyone with whom he was associated. Alex was "that damned drunk." Doug was "incompetent" and "a terrible player", Jerry was "screwing around with that chick," which means, he was forming a marital relationship with his wife, who was about to give birth to his child, and this sometimes took priority over rehearsal time.

John French: I know that P.G. was in the band for a short time, then there was a fallout with Leonard and Dorothy.
Jerry Handley: Yeah, the band went nuts at that time.
JF: See, now Don's description of this to me when I first got in the band is he said, first all he told me that everyone in the band was a bunch of lazy assholes. That was the first thing he told me, says "They're all lazy, they don't want to do anything."

Old Dead Black Guys

Van Vliet at this time began pushing for abandoning the blues covers and doing original tunes.

Gary Marker: Or, as Don used to say, "Why do you wanna play those old dead black guy's music all the time? Why don't you do something new? Instead of that old dead black guy's music?"
JF: Well, he did a pretty good job on it himself.
GM: Yeah, he did, (but) he felt like, "No, I'm beyond that, man! I've gone beyond that. I don't do that anymore. I do my own stuff."

Roland Kirk

This was obviously the point where Don began to tire of emulating the heroes of his youth. In his visits to Gary Marker, he was introduced to many new influences on the direction his creativity would begin to flow.

Gary Marker: (speaking of Roland Kirk) But he was – you'd sit in the audience and he was electric, I mean, that's all there was to it! He'd hit that fucking whistle and stomp on the stage and start banging on the drums and shit. Well, I took Don up to see him, the first time he saw Roland I thought he was gonna go berserk! He almost went nuts. He couldn't believe it! Here was this jazz musician doing all of this crazy stuff, and that was it, it was the beginning. I took him up and introduced him later. It was like the only time I've ever seen Don with his jaw slacked! It was like, "Man, it's a real pleasure to meet you!" Because, I thought Don was going to have one of his famous "heart attacks," because he'd say, "Did you see what he did? Did you hear that?" I'd say, "Well yeah, Don, that's why I brought you up here! So you could hear him!"

P.G. Leaves

So it was the fall of 1966 when P.G. Blakely left the Magic Band. There were many stories as to why this happened. The main thrust of the story seemed to center around the fact that P.G. had developed a rapport with Leonard Grant and Dorothy Heard and chose to side in with them against the band. This was when the corporation - an entity whose very existence seems vague and unclear - was supposedly dissolved "for beer money" according to Don. The band had been working on original material and was making little money. Its relationship with A&M was also in a state of flux, although the band was still contractually bound to the label.

As Jerry claimed earlier, the band was "falling apart." Everything was questionable, and the business dealings were at a standoff. Since the bad relationships had developed between the band and management, the band had been focusing more on original material. It was at this point that a major power-shift within the band took place. Alex began to lose his leadership to Don, who on a continual daily basis was slowly chipping away at the foundation of the band, undermining Alex's ability, and usurping authority.

Partially, how this happened was summed up by Doug Moon.

Doug Moon: It's like being a stockholder and he had 51%.
John French: OK. So how did he obtain that position? Because of the fact that…
DM: Because he was bigger and he could beat up any of us.
JF: Was that it?
DM: In a way, in a way.
JF: So he was into bullying you around if you disagreed with him.
DM: If it came down to that you would ultimately be confronted with a fistfight.

Obviously, physical intimidation played a role in the process, but Moon's words "in a way" suggest that there was more to it than that. Handley, although speaking a bit later, after mine and the other younger players entrance into the band observed the following:

Jerry Handley: Alex couldn't handle it all by himself, unfortunately. The more control Don had, the more out of reality the band went. That's probably the demise of that band, you could say … or you could say there wouldn't have been all the albums they did unless Don had all that control. I am not so sure that I agree with the direction the band went, because I think there was … they made the albums, I'll say that. But I don't know that it helped anybody greatly financially.
John French: It certainly didn't.
JH: I don't think it was a commercial success by any means, and it made a lot of unhappy people.

This reveals Handley's version of the goal of the original band: commercial success. They, like almost everyone who gets into the music business, wanted to make some money.

P.G. Blakely, the latest drummer for the Beefheart band, soon approached some of the players in my band, Blues In A Bottle. He had just left the Beefheart band and was planning on doing something with their former management, Leonard Grant and Associates, which included a lady named Dorothy Heard.

Jeff Cotton, Blues In A Bottle's guitarist, had expressed interest in working with P.G. if there was some chance of recording. There was even talk of a chance of getting on the television show, *The Dating Game*. I was disappointed.

Fall had arrived. Lots of friends were gone. It was the first time in 12 years that I hadn't gone to school. No friends to hang out with. There was no social life to speak of. I stayed at home and read comic books in an attempt to escape the dreaded reality of dealing with the draft. In the mornings, I worked for the Salvation Army thrift shop. I found myself wondering what to do. Blues In A Bottle was going to break up according to everything Jeff Cotton had said. P.G. Blakely, Beefheart's drummer after Rich Hepner left, had offered Jeff and the other guys some kind of chance to do something. I thought this let me out, never realizing they might have wanted me to continue singing. So, I was ready for a change.

CHAPTER NINE: CHOOSING MY WAR

Group shot of the Safe As Milk band. Photo courtesy of Guy Webster

Vietnam

In the fall of 1966, every male high school graduate who wasn't planning on being enrolled in College was inevitably forced to face the possibility of dying in a war many of us did not believe in, because it wasn't clear to us why we were there. Graduating the previous spring, all my fellow musician friends and I were trapped in what we saw as the statistical and moral outrage labeled The Vietnam War. In the years since, I have learned to understand this war and why we were there, but at the time, I had not the depth of understanding hence my perspective.

I believe that we felt this way largely because we were the generation that witnessed the assassination of a U.S, President on television. Then we were disappointed in the ensuing Warren Report – which chose to offer to the public an encyclopedic amount of seemingly non-relevant information and fiction. This report ignored dozens of contradictory eyewitness testimonies and is still being disputed.

My feeling is that due to this government blundering, my generation became inherently suspicious of anything the government had to say about anything. Add to this the confusion of anti-war demonstrators (many of whom were later found to be funded by leftist organizations), "eye-witness" accounts of war crimes we were supposedly committing, and the popularity of psychedelic drugs, a whole generation became "lost" at a time when we really needed to be focused and attentive.

During all this "make love, not war" hysteria - which may have saved a few lives of Vietnam but certainly did it's share to increase unplanned pregnancies here at home – I found myself in a state of limbo concerning it all. My parents were not keen on discussing politics; in fact, I don't think I ever heard a political discussion in our home. In this void, I developed indifference to the whole conflict, and wrote the whole thing off as "stupid."

I had three older brothers who were in the Navy, Army, and Air Force (from oldest to youngest) and my mother used to say "if you went into the Marines, I'd have a son in every branch of the military." I used to counter by saying, "If I went into the Marines, you'd probably have one dead son and three live ones." I had been attentive enough to look at the statistics and they seemed to indicate that the majority of those sent into the infantry either died or were permanently maimed.

My thoughts went back to my older brother, Tom, who had been in the Korean war in the early 1950s. I had talked to him of the reality of war. He had told me of he and his buddy being on adjacent telegraph poles, and his buddy being cut in half with machine gun fire. Tom was left with the job of climbing the pole - still freshly coated with his buddy's entrails - to finish the job.

He once described having orders to drive a munitions truck at a specific speed and stopping for nothing and no-one. It was night and the trucks had to drive a pre-designated number of yards apart so that if one was hit and exploded, the others could continue. In the headlights appeared the image of a young Korean boy, seven or eight years old, flagging him to stop. Tom continued driving as ordered and ran the boy down. The private riding shotgun vomited out the passenger door as Tom drove on. As it turned out, the boy was a plant for an ambush that would have killed my brother and the rider had he stopped, and may have threatened the entire motorcade.

He spoke of another private in his detachment having his leg blown off by a land mine and my brother having to watch and listen to him bleed to death as he slowly and desperately attempted to clear a path to him using a mine detector. These stories haunted me (as I am sure they did my brother) as I considered my seemingly imminent future.

I knew how the Korean conflict had ended. I had a good idea how Vietnam would end. In my opinion, this conflict had nothing to do with national security and everything to do with the momentum of ignorance. Yet I could be forced to pick up a gun and shoot at people I didn't know for a reason not clear to me.

The prospects of my going to College were slim. My father had deserted the family a few months before. My mother and I were now working for the local Salvation Army thrift store. I provided janitorial services and she did sales. My maternal Uncle John and his wife, Virginia (aka Virgie), were living with us. It wasn't a happy household. They shared a room off the garage in our Spanish-style stucco corner house in Lancaster.

So, here I was in total denial, lying on the couch in front of the French doors reading a comic book in some attempt to escape my thoughts. This silly little book seemed like a little doorway through which I could crawl back into childhood, where answers were simpler. It was quiet in the house, my Aunt Virgie was sitting in a rocker, my mother and my uncle were at work. I only worked half-days, so my afternoons were free.

It was typically warm Autumn afternoon weather: clear skies, low eighties. I gazed thoughtfully through the cheesecloth drapes and the vines on the adjacent porch. Looking at nothing in particular, I was lost in thought, desperately seeking an answer for my dilemma and finding none.

I was sure that Blues In A Bottle was coming to an end. Jeff Cotton had mentioned being approached by P.G. Blakely, seeking recruits for a musical project to be managed by Leonard Grant and Associates. Jeff seemed interested, and hinted at this in a conversation during a band rehearsal the night before. I was discouraged, disappointed, devastated. The combination of events in my family, the Vietnam War, the headlines warning about a new drug called LSD, school ending, and the band breaking up had converged to create a dismal picture of the future. I was shattered and felt isolated from all my friends, who had gone back to finish their senior year at high school, and so wouldn't be facing my dilemma for at least another year.

Physically it felt as though someone had taken a large tube and sucked all the life from me. I had been 18 for a week or two, which meant I had arrived at draft age and was facing the imminent Selective Service beckoning call. I could see no way to go to College, the only redemption from the draft besides being married. My father had betrayed the family and my value system had been turned upside down and dumped on the floor. To me, this October of 1966, I felt I had been cast adrift, and the world was looking ugly.

I suppose the comic book was a last shot at trying to hang on to my youth. I lay there a living monument to denial. Youth was almost gone. For about three years, like a lot of kids my age I'm sure, I had been thoroughly convinced that I would not live to see 19.

Even the family pet seemed to manifest this hopelessness. My dog, Terry, was crippled and could barely walk. It wasn't a time of hope or vision. All of us who lived in this household seemed very unhappy.

Van Vliet Calls

So, on that bleak Fall day, the phone rang, and the man on the phone said in a deep rather hoarse voice "This is Captain Beefheart - do you know who this is?" I replied, "Yes" chuckling to myself at the official sound of his voice. He stammered around for a minute ..."I was wondering, uh, I called to ... I was wondering if you would, want to blow drums with us." "Blow" was an old jazz term, as in "Man, that cat can blow." This gave me a clue as to Don's true musical tastes.

Looking back on this moment, I couldn't help but think that Don must have been a very insecure man to stammer around like this. Either that, or (as I later learned from experience) loaded out of his mind. Maybe he was distracted by something at that moment. It seems a man almost eight years my senior, who had a turntable hit and tremendous vocal capacity that I had witnessed with my own ears shouldn't be so insecure and stammering so much. Even at the time this thought crossed through my mind.

Honestly, my first thought was "I really don't want to be in this band." Everything in my consciousness said "No". His popularity had been waning recently. Although they'd had *Diddy Wah Diddy* on the charts with minor success, they didn't seem to have the magic anymore. I thought back to the night our band had opened for them at the local dance in town, and how many people had told me that the audience on the whole seemed to like us more than them. I felt it too. A couple of the guys in my band had been approached by P.G. and I was thinking that I was going to be put out of the picture and they were going to work with him. That was the scenario. I left a band that I figured was breaking up.

My answer was, "Uh, yeah, sure," disregarding all my thoughts. I had just made the decision to join the Magic Band. A lesson to be learned here is when confronted with major decisions, always say "I'll think about it."

Aldridge Recommends J.P. and J.F.

Don Aldridge, it turns out, was the person who actually recommended me to Van Vliet as the band began seriously looking for a drummer to replace P.G. He did so reluctantly as this interview segment shows.

Friendship Threatened

Don Aldridge: I felt very intimidated by your entrance into the scene. I didn't want you there, because I felt like you were going to take my place with Don...
John French: The friendship ...
DA: Yeah, I was not involved (musically) with the band. Now I felt at the time that you were the best drummer in the Valley.
JF: Well, actually John Parr was.
DA: Well, I first suggested John Parr.
JF: If he had kept playing, I would have had my hands full just keeping up with the guy.
DA: I was working nights in Burbank for an aerospace company. (The fact) that I was working with an aerospace company was a big bone of contention with Don (who would say) "God, you ought to quit that plastic job, that is lame."
JF: You were previously saying that Plastic Factory *may have been written about you.*
DA: (Nods in agreement) But, see, I was out buying all the dope ...

John Parr

During this period, according to Aldridge, Alex was again actually playing drums, I suppose with Doug and Jerry, as a temporary situation so the band could continue to rehearse. Don was inquiring of everyone he knew about a new drummer.

Don Aldridge: I said, "Well, you know, John Parr ..." now, I'm biting my cheeks to keep from suggesting you, because I knew that you could do it. I didn't think Parr would fit in.

Aldridge may have been right about this. Parr was definitely more of a jazzer than a rocker and when he played rock, he sounded jazzier. Parr at the time lived about half a block down the street from Van Vliet on Carolside. So Van Vliet and Aldridge went and checked on him only to find that he was working during the week in Van Nuys, some sixty miles away.

Aldridge states that the fact that Parr was working 60-odd miles away discouraged Don from pursuing a meeting with him. According to John Parr, however, Don *did* approach him and asked him to be in the band. John was already having some problems as a result of a surprise LSD experience. Apparently, while at a party in Van Nuys he was drinking a beer, which someone decided to spike with some LSD – apparently an extremely large dose. It had left Parr in a somewhat altered condition. He told Don he didn't think he could cut it. He then suggested that Van Vliet contact me.

Aldridge Recommends French

Don Aldridge: My whole thing was "don't get John (French) in this band, you know, cause that's going to blow your friendship here," but then again, I did. I said, "Well, you know there is another guy and he's probably as good as John (Parr) and I said, "He's a friend of mine and his name is John French," - and at that point, how you came in I don't know.

Aldridge's reluctance is certainly understandable. Van Vliet was, and probably still is, exceedingly good company and was even at that time considered a local celebrity. I remember him as being entertaining, charming, and having a great sense of humor. I have read many interviews in which the interviewer had a similar perspective regarding Don's company and conversation.

Van Vliet's unique perspective on life, his exceptional ability to coin phrases and create puns, euphemisms, and double entendres and his awareness of the world around him made him excellent and entertaining company. I often felt that when I was with him it was like being in a different world altogether. Cares and worries often seemed to be suspended in this magic land of escapism he called home. It was easy to see how difficult it was for him to work with others in the usual way. He wanted to play music, not work at it.

Unfortunately, it seemed that his lack of ability to comprehend the difficulty of the process of actually producing the results required rendered him suspicious of those attempting to do so. So, after the honeymoon period of entrusting his true self to a new player, he would often become disenchanted as they, like all the rest before them, attempted to seriously rehearse, thus taking away all the fun.

"Someone's had too much to think." Don Van Vliet

The impression was that he felt abandoned and often seemed later to suspect that conspiracies were taking place behind his back. Unfortunately, usually they were. Magic Band members were constantly confiding about this problem in order to find a practical approach to actually finish projects Don himself had initiated. His illusion of betrayal – which is how he interpreted any discovery of these confidential discussions - usually forced him to separate himself from those with whom he worked the closest. Unfortunately, most of those individuals he chose to eventually separate himself from were those who were the most devoted to his music, those who showed him the most support.

Don Aldridge: I'll tell you what he did say, "Well, he's that guy that's singing with that group over there." I don't (recall) whether he mentioned the name of the group or what. Well, actually I said, "John is a fine drummer." I suppose I felt a little guilty. Well, anyway, that was my role in getting you involved in Captain Beefheart, to the extent that I did.

Alex Picks Me Up

A rehearsal was set up for the evening after Van Vliet's call. Alex and Jerry came over in Alex's car to pick me up. Alex was driving a mid-fifties white Cadillac convertible, I believe. My drumset was pink-champagne sparkle and Alex looked at them with extreme disapproval, as though they were Barbie drums. They were Rogers drums, which I had purchased from Cliff Roehr. My tastes had changed in the year since I picked out the color. Actually my friend John Parr had suggested the color because they looked so good under lights. Nevertheless, we packed the drums and went over to rehearsal.

Carolside

It was probably late afternoon to early evening. We were at Don Van Vliet's mothers house on Carolside, which was on the west side of the street, as opposed to Granny Annie's which had been across the street on the east side.   I had already met Sue on a prior occasion.   As I was chatting with Doug Moon during a chance encounter on the corner of Beech Street and Lancaster Boulevard, she had walked up and I was introduced.

Sue worked at a local women's clothing store named Scotts and had just gotten out for lunch, I believe. She had a certain air of sophistication to her, and was quite a character. "Helllooooooooo!" she had said to me. I liked her, but also sensed a certain air about her which made me a little uncomfortable. A kind of "celebrity" mentality.

Don's grandmother, Granny Annie, lived at the Carolside house also. I believe I had previously met her on the same occasion as Sue, as I believe she was also employed at the same women's wear shop. Her name was Anne Warfield, but Van Vliet called her Granny Annie. He always called his mother Sue, which I found a little strange until I realized that most of what I would learn about Don was a little strange.

No-one was actually at the house this afternoon except Don and his attractive dark-haired girlfriend, Laurie Stone, who also lived there. Don did not introduce me to her. She was a really interesting person, had a very hospitable and friendly personality, and I liked her right away. She would always offer everyone tea, and had a special civilized way about her that struck me.

First Rehearsal

Since I was used to rehearsing with bands that worked really hard and made every rehearsal moment count, I couldn't believe the incredible amount of time that elapsed from the time I arrived and got set up until Don finally came in to do a song. We musicians were just jamming blues. Van Vliet seemed distanced, preoccupied and easily distracted.

My first impression of Don was after we set up for rehearsal that afternoon; he walked in after being outside stoned for 35-45 minutes. We were jamming without him, and waiting and waiting and waiting for him, and he walked in and said, "Wow, I got this great lyric, wait until you hear this, this is really heavy, Yeah," and he stares at the page for a while and then walks back outside. Never said another word. I'm thinking, "This guy is out there." Also, I had not a clue as to why Van Vliet might seem so disoriented, because I'd never been around people who were taking drugs.

Eventually, after the band warmed up and played for an hour and a half, Don finally joined in. He fumbled around for 20 minutes or so and finally got a microphone working for himself and started singing a few things along with us. At one point in the evening, things really opened up and I started locking-in with the band. I could see that Alex was happy with the way things were going. After the experience of playing with these guys, I realized that there was a chance I could enjoy the drummer's position. However, I still had misgivings about Don and my first impression was that he didn't seem to want to actually be in the band but wanted to call the shots, write the lyrics and use the band as a music writing tool.

In hindsight, and through the interviews for this book, I realize that the band's attitude about rehearsal was probably one bordering on despair. Business setbacks and all the disappointments in the business combined with Don's seeming lack of interest in actually performing and generating income had probably made them all feel a bit hopeless about the project. Although Don had a vision, creatively, of what he wanted to do, he had no vision of how to carry out that vision. Since he was apparently the one in charge at this point, everyone was looking to him for leadership, and he was supplying little insight on how to achieve what he was suggesting.

Indoctrination of John

At some point in the evening, I was finally confronted with the question as to whether I would be interested in joining the band and I decided that I would. On the one hand, I was very impressed with the way everyone played together, making the parts work together. Although we didn't touch on anything but blues, I hadn't been aware of what great players they actually were until that evening. On the other hand, Don's behavior complicated my decision.

Soon everyone left. It was probably somewhere between 10 and 11 o'clock, and Don suggested to Alex that he would drive me home. So, after everyone was gone, Don began to talk to me.

John French: I came in, strongly influenced by Don, and half-believing everything he told me. I was a bit intimidated by everybody, and, being pretty naïve, really didn't know what was going on. I was immediately strongly influenced by Don in negative ways. The first thing he said to me, after rehearsal, and everybody left, was, "I gotta tell you one thing about these guys - they're a bunch of (emphatically) lazy assholes." That was his introduction (of) the band. That was my first impression of the band, from an opinionated, singular point of view. So, I am half-believing this and thinking, "I have to keep this in mind," not knowing you guys at all - the only person I knew in the band was Doug Moon because he had worked with my father at North American (Aviation) in electronics. And at the same time, what I am seeing from Don is a guy who doesn't want to rehearse but you guys all want to rehearse and he keeps walking out and getting stoned and writing more lyrics. (In the meantime) we're not getting anything done.
Alex Snouffer: Yeah. And then when he (finally) wants to rehearse, hey, we're fed-up with it.
JF: Yeah, because you had been there for five hours.
AS: (Mimicking Don) "Whoa, no, we gotta rehearse!" – "No, YOU gotta rehearse!"

Doug Moon's reaction to Van Vliet's "lazy assholes" remark was merely a strong belly laugh. The situation in the band at the time was strained, not only due to the management problems and the record company problems, but also because two of the members, were facing fatherhood in a few months.

As far as the interpersonal relationship, (being 18) I didn't grasp what it meant to be facing parenthood. Alex and Jerry were facing parenthood at that time. Then there was the whole thing with Don with his fiancée Laurie Stone, living in a separate bedroom in his mother's house, along with his grandmother.

I had grown up in a more-or-less conventional family setting, so my perspective on this was although I was trying to keep an open mind, it seemed as though Don, a 25 year-old man, was being supported by his mother and grandmother, and not treating them very well besides. It appeared as though they were in a kind of bondage or fear of Don. When they arrived later that first rehearsal day (about six o'clock), they basically went back to their rooms and we rehearsed loudly in the living room.

If I were to use a singular word to describe Don's relationship with both his mother and grandmother and also the band, it would be bully. The word selfish also comes to mind, along with irresponsible.

Misgivings

Jerry Handley mentioned earlier that Leonard Grant had probably wanted to get away from the band because it was disorganized. I observed that the one person who was most disorganized was Don. To recap, he was often disoriented, most likely from ingesting large amounts of hallucinogens, and seemed totally self-absorbed with his writing. When confronted about any of this, he would go on the defensive and become verbally abusive, displaying anger and threatening violence towards anyone who opposed him. This for the most part caused all normal rational business discussions to cease, effectively cutting off any productive decision-making.

Looking back, I suppose the positive side of this was that had Don not insisted on doing things his own way, the music probably would never have grown and evolved into what it became. Of course, one could argue that although this later greatly benefited Van Vliet, it did little to improve the lives of his band members.

It was immediately evident to me that Don refused to listen to *anything* anyone suggested. Though Don was gifted with amazing creativity, it was evident from the beginning that he had neither the patience nor the discipline needed to formulate a process of actually bringing the raw musical ideas to fruition.

Rather than selectively disregard suggestions or comments, which were not immediately relevant to his creative process, he became self-absorbed with that process alone, making it the whole of his existence, from waking until sleeping. He began to evade all discussion on methodology, business, or financial needs. Because he put up this wall of defense around himself, and defended it with often vicious verbal assaults, the Magic Band members began to form resentment at this type of behavior.

John French: So, my first impression of Don was that he wasn't very responsible and that he didn't rehearse with the band much. You guys would sit around waiting for him to rehearse and (after hours of waiting) when he was finally ready to rehearse, you guys were ready to go home. Alex Snouffer: (mimicking Don) "Oh, (no) we gotta get this!!!!" (His reply) "Yeah, Don." That was just an ongoing thing as you soon found out. Cause he didn't know what he was going to do. That's why he'd always climb on the band, "You guys do this," "No, that's not right!" you know - all that? He had no idea what he was going to do. So to cover it up, that's why he started all that bullshit.
JF: And there was a lot of that.
AS: It was just ongoing.

One of the things that I noticed about Don right away was the fact that he simply seemed completely ignorant of the learning curve required to play a specific part. Either that or he was simply too impatient to go through the process involved in the learning of a new song or musical passage. My feeling is that this was due in part to the fact that up to this point, the Magic Band's repertoire had consisted largely of covering other people's simpler material, and probably each person had worked at home individually and developed their parts.

With the process of creating original material, players were confronted with new and often foreign passages of music. The process of learning was thus brought to the rehearsal floor, and, not being used to the time required, Don hadn't developed the knowledge needed to understand this process.

Something that I learned in later years was to always respect my first instincts about people, but still give people a chance and not judge them too soon. My big mistake here seems to be believing what Don told me about the band and himself, which was in almost direct opposition to what I was actually experiencing first hand.

I observed a group of men, the Magic Band, who would show up faithfully every day at the prescribed time, give or take ten minutes. Often they would find their illustrious leader still in bed, sleeping off a long night of "creating." He would often have something to show for it, a few lines of relatively deep and often philosophic poetry, which seldom could be used in any kind of song form. Stuff such as "Everything is a circle, the whole world is a circle."

The guys always seemed somewhat supportive of his "quest" or whatever Don considered himself to be going through at the time. At the same time, they would try to face the realities of the real world. One of which was the situation with poor Sue and Granny. We all must have looked like a bunch of stray dogs who played deafeningly loud music, so it was obvious to me from the beginning that Sue and Granny both had open minds and incredible patience. Not only that, but they seemed to be really generous; they were most obviously supporting Don financially, or at least *partially* supporting him. Plus, they were supplying a place in which we could rehearse.

Getting back to the band, they seemed more than willing to try new and different musical ideas. There were lots on tape. Many songs, which were never recorded or released, that had come out of a torrential creative session that happened just prior to my entrance lie dormant on acetate. Much of this, to my ear (affirmed by the band) seemed collaborative in origin. The band seemed more than willing to work hard to achieve some success and they seemed to all recognize that Van Vliet had a great but undeveloped talent for creating lyrics and music.

Doug one day jokingly commented that it was "too bad we didn't all read music, because we could just put charts up and refer to them and we wouldn't get lost so easily." Don immediately took offense at this saying something to the effect of, "Oh, so you're saying I'm not able to create music just because I don't *write* music? That's the *lamest* thing I ever heard, man. You're a union man all the way aren't you?"

Actually Doug's idea was quite good. If we had started using music to write down sketches of what we were doing, it would have been much easier to piece everything together without outside help. Also, individuals could have practiced their ideas outside of rehearsal, generally saving everyone hours of waiting on the next guy to learn his part. Ironically, this is what would later successfully take place during the *Trout Mask* rehearsals.

Righteous Brothers

One interesting comment that Don made privately to me soon after I joined the band was that at one point that he had heard me sing and really liked my singing. He said the possibility had passed through his mind that he and I could sing harmony that would put the Righteous Brothers to shame. He often told the guys in the band that I could sing "like Buddy Guy." I suppose this was because he thought of my voice as higher than his. Actually, my normal vocal range is actually a little lower than Don's, but I sang with a high, clear, "trumpety" (Bill Harkleroad's description) kind of tone, and I suppose this created that illusion of a "Buddy Guy" type of voice.

Whether Don was actually serious or not, I don't know. My instincts told me that Van Vliet was merely stroking my ego in order to gain my trust and boost my confidence.

Brushing The Pounding Clouds

It couldn't have been more than a day or two after I joined that Don introduced me to marijuana. He called it grass - saying it wasn't really a drug at all but really a spiritual experience. He assured me that it wasn't addictive and nothing like the way those high school films depicted it. He talked me into going with him and his friend, Gary Lambert, out into the desert and smoking some grass.

Don actually came to the door of my mother's house and met my mother, uncle John, and Aunt Virgie. He had been driven over by Gary in his silver and black 1960 Jaguar Mark IX. Gary was a teacher for the local Catholic High School, Paraclete. He taught art, and was actually a fairly proficient commercial artist. I wonder what the priests and nuns would have done had they known that he was a pothead. Incidentally, the last time I saw Gary, in the mid-eighties - he was 45 years old, and still living with his mother. He seems incapable of any responsibility, was on allowance, and was allowed to drink two quarts of beer a week. I think he experimented with a lot of psychedelics.

We drove out into an open desert area that was *next to* Paraclete High School. It was probably Lambert's favorite spot to park for a lunchtime doobie. To tell the truth, aside from making me cough a lot, it seemed like nothing happened at all. I do recall standing outside in the chill night air and looking up to see searchlights in town, advertising car lots. As they brushed past the clouds, I said something like "I can feel them" imagining it like running your fingers through thick soapsuds. Immediately Don had his scratchpad out, writing something down. "Listen to this, man! He read dramatically:

'I can feel the searchlights brush the pounding clouds.'

It seemed kind of Bette Davis/film noire-like to me.

Another time he said to Gary, "Feel my hands", and Gary grabbed his hands and they stood there under a full moon, holding hands and staring into each other's eyes, grinning. I burst out laughing and said something like; "You guys want to be alone for a while?"

Although I certainly don't advocate the use of drugs, I did sense a feeling of freedom and inspiration. I think it came from the fact that after years of sitting in a room-watching people watching television, I was actually living my own life instead of observing others acting out an artificial life. It had little to do with herbal remedies and more to do with independence.

I think one of the basic things that appeals to young people and gets them started on drugs is that it is a *deviation* from an otherwise dull and humdrum existence. Van Vliet seemed genuinely *alive* compared to almost everyone I knew. It was such a change from the painfully predictable existence (not *life*, but *existence*) that I had been rebelling against for years. I'm talking here about the daily rituals and habits that we seem to fall into religiously, fooling ourselves into thinking it's a *discipline* when in actuality, it is pure escapism – just in a different form.

Get up, brush your teeth, be miserable for eight or nine hours doing something you absolutely *hate*, suppress it all and never confront problems because you may *stir up trouble*, then go home and take it out on your family by ignoring them, yelling at them, etc. Eat dinner, and then fall into near catatonia staring at an electron tube that brings you hopelessly unrealistic drama acted out by unrealistically attractive people. Tell yourself that they're the lucky ones and you're just another number, convince yourself that there's *no hope for you to ever break out of the mold*. Above all, *never ever take a risk, face your fears, or step out of your role, no matter how confining it may be.*

One thing that appealed to me about Van Vliet was that he seldom seemed to be involved in any passive activity. He was constantly, if often rudely, taking charge of his life. He never, for any extended period, lost sight of his dream, his vision, and he stubbornly refused to allow apathy to entangle him in its confining chains. Of course, sometimes it made it almost unbearable to be near him, because his vision, his hope, and his creative imagination were untempered, and therefore practical application of processing his art into some viable presentation (without which it would have been positively *meaningless* simply because no one would have ever seen/heard it) required a process he seemed neither willing to undergo nor launch. This was partially what separated him from the Magic Band members, and later from business associates in general.

The Magic Band of that era were more prone to put in a certain amount of time each day hoping to accomplish a certain amount of work. Then, telling themselves they had accomplished something, they would go find a means of escape and relaxation. Don daily seemed at war with apathy, not only the force that tried to capture and quench his own spirit, but also anything resembling a manifestation of apathy in anyone around him. Unfortunately, he would often mistake deep thought or the normal processing of information, the learning curve required to master a particular passage of music as apathy when indeed it was quite the opposite.

Also, he seemed unaware that because of his lack of discipline, his own creative process had probably become just as much of an escape mechanism as watching TV – just slightly more productive. I say this because for every 10 to 15 song ideas Don jotted down, barely one was even introduced to the band. Therefore much of Don's creative time was wasted or hit-and-miss, and, in my opinion, was merely his method of relaxing and escaping. Unfortunately, he didn't often give himself time to be productive, so was almost entirely in creative mode. I often feel that his lack of concern regarding productivity almost certainly inhibited, and perhaps prevented, the other band members from developing their own creative instincts, thus condemning to be portrayed as mere sidemen by the critics.

From experience, I saw that everyone in the band had their own fair share of musical creativity, though no-one showed any propensity at all for writing lyrics. Much of the music on *Safe As Milk* is a result of collaboration. The critics looked at the songwriting credits, however, and immediately attributed everything to Don, referring to him as the band's "guiding genius."

Don suggested to me that Gary Lambert should paint a full-sized replica of the Gerber Baby's head on my bass drum head. This, I allowed, and Gary started work on it. I didn't see my drum head for months.

Herb Bermann

Almost immediately, perhaps as part of my indoctrination, I was taken to meet with Don's collaborator, Herb Bermann. Although Herb is credited with playing bass on some albums tracks, this is nonsense. To my knowledge he played no musical instrument, and certainly never on any Beefheart albums. Herb was a writer/poet, probably of the Ferlinghetti/Ginsberg mindset, who superimposed the physical hippy look on a decidedly beatnik mentality.

Don Aldridge: Yeah, he was more of a beatnik type. He was definitely more of the Jack Kerouac set. Herb Bermann was his real name, but Herb Masters was the name he was using.
John French: Oh, he always had Bermann on the recordings.
DA: Yeah but he didn't want to be - I think he had a problem with his Jewish-ness at the time.
JF: I didn't know he was Jewish until now.
DA: I don't think he wanted it known for some reason.

How they met seems unclear to everyone. Aldridge had been doing some writing with Don in the early days and suddenly Don was no longer interested in working with Aldridge because he had met Herb. This was probably sometime around the Spring of 1966.

Don Aldridge: Well it was very early days, because I was there when he came. Don began to haul a bunch of lyrics out of the shoebox, and he and Herb were working together. I felt like it was a little slap in the face there. (Suddenly it was) he and Herb, "This is the poet man, he's heavier than us." When Don found somebody that he thought was going to produce something, all of a sudden, that guy was like, "The center of the world."

Actually, I enjoyed Herb's company, for the most part. The first time we met was during the daytime, probably two o'clock or so. Don and I drove out Avenue. M. to just east of Quartz Hill – in fact, less than two miles from my childhood home. Sitting before us, isolated and surrounded by a big chain-link fence was a little frame house with almost no landscaping that I remembered from childhood hikes. It was a little spooky, with a haunted, Bates Motel kind of atmosphere. Don honked the horn and waited for several minutes. Eventually, a squinty-eyed, dark-haired, bearded man looked out the door suspiciously. He went back in and then came out with a key chain. It was then that I noticed the huge chain securing the gate (the word paranoid comes to mind). It had a couple of oversized padlocks and was wound in a serpentine manner around the posts. After a seemingly endless unlocking ritual, the gate was finally opened and we drove in. I was a bit apprehensive after we drove in as he locked the gate behind us.

All the introductions Don gave me during this period seemed to go like this: "This is John French, our new drummer – he's heavy man." Immediately following each of these introductions, I always felt deeply scrutinized and became grossly self-conscious for a few moments. Herb's appearance on a quick glance would probably place him in the same category as King Neptune. Upon closer scrutiny, he was probably in his mid-30s to early 40s, though beards always seem to blur the age a bit. He had a squinty-eyed half-smile on his face most of the time which forced its way through tensely-drawn, thin and slightly protruding lips. His voice was high and for the most part he was soft-spoken.

He had that kind of – how can you explain those eyes? That squinty look … "I'm looking through these eyes, they don't look open, but I can see through them." It was a too-hip-for-the-room look.

After my introduction, Herb looked me over, seemed to nod in approval, and ushered us in. I was then introduced to his wife Cathleen, who has been described by others as gorgeous. She was probably in her mid-20s to early 30s, and that seemed ancient to me at 18, so I didn't view her as a sexual creature, but more like I would view my mother.

Don Aldridge: … he had a really fine looking woman. She was rather amply endowed. I know Alex and I were impressed (laughs).

We sat down in the living room, me on a couch, the others on chairs, except for Cathleen, who walked through a mysterious beaded doorway into the kitchen. She wore a Madras-type dress and made us tea, I believe. I have no idea what Herb and Don talked about. It had to do with A&M, and a lot of positive affirmation stuff i.e., "We're going to be really big," "This music is the heaviest!" Etc.

Soon, two men showed up in a dark car, and if these guys weren't typical-looking underworld characters, then I wasn't a drummer. They came in, "Vinny and Tony," or whoever they were, and brought a very large amount of marijuana with them. I was introduced, and they looked at me as they might view a dead dog on the side of the road. The marijuana was wrapped in dark green shiny paper, if I remember correctly. After the contents were sampled to everyone's (including the men-in-black's) satisfaction, Herb left the room for a while, and then these guys were gone. I was still new to this smoking grass thing, and so I suddenly found myself with a stupendous migraine headache and wound up lying on the couch for hours. I remember fixating on a single bead in the beaded doorway and having tunnel vision for several hours.

Van Vliet would later say that Herb Bermann wrote the lyrics to *Electricity* after one of their first meetings. Don claimed that he should actually be given the credit, because all the lyrical concepts were his, and Herb merely stole them from him. Don soon talked about Herb as though their relationship was finished and he no longer needed Herb. According to Don, Herb was only trying to exploit Beefheart for his own devices. However, he was wise to Bermann, and he was merely playing along long enough to pick Bermann's brain about writing lyrics and poetry, thus using him and simultaneously turning the tables on him. These are not the exact words Don used; however he gave me this impression. My opinion here is constructed from little bits and pieces of information that came up during various discussions over several weeks. Since Van Vliet had no formal education in writing he was probably truly gathering some information on writing from Herb. My thought here was that Herb was being straightforward with Don and the reverse was not true.

Aldridge Recalls Discovering/My Inclusion Fall 1966

I had been in the band for approximately two weeks when Don Aldridge showed up one night, I suppose partly wondering how his relationship with Don was going to change.

Don Aldridge: Then anyhow, I came back again I came a week or two later, or whenever it was, and of course, after 33 years you don't remember the time, it all seems a lot closer together. But I came home from my job one night – I usually dropped in at Don's around one (a.m.). I got off about 12 and usually by one I was back in Lancaster. I dropped into Don's and you met me at the door. And I said (to myself), "Uh oh, here goes." And you and I and Don hung out that night, and we talked, - I don't know what we did exactly.

The conversation in part seemed to be some kind of introduction to the world of magic. It was interesting, because Aldridge seemed really serious and Don was watching me closely as my high school friend explained to me the fact that there are two types of magic, black and white. Black was considered "bad" and white "good."
Says Aldridge now: **I found out later there isn't any difference.**
I suppose it had a lot to do with the drugs, but it seemed apparent that there was definitely a strong occult emphasis in Van Vliet's life. I was drawn to this already, and so was a prime candidate to be sucked in more deeply to this mindset. It was the beginning of an unpleasant voyage. As I look back, however, I remember how seductively attractive it all seemed.

Don Aldridge: So we hung out together and then I drove you home in my little Rambler car and you and I sat out in front of your placed and smoked a joint and talked.

Neither of us remembers what we talked about. Our conversation probably consisted of things like saying (referring to the pot) "This is really some *good shit*, man." Of course, stylistically speaking, in order for you to really emphasize your words, you had to be holding your breath, so that the words came out of an extremely strained voice. Then, more smoky breath holding, and shaking our heads in approval, snorting to keep from coughing out the sacred smoke of the hemp.

Beware The Magic Bands
Shortly after I joined the Magic Band, Don said he needed to go somewhere and asked me to go with him. We were still living in Lancaster at the time. Surprisingly enough he drove over to the church I had gone to as a young teenager. It was a First Baptist Church. There was a marquee out front, which was changed each week to announce the title of the Sunday sermon. The latest installment was entitled Beware of Magic Bands! I suppose it did strike me as a bit eerie, like an oracle, or a sign.
However, Don was very up in arms about this. He thought that the church was personally attacking him. The church was on Lancaster Boulevard, two blocks away from the High School. I knew the church well, because I had sung in the choir, so I directed Don to the office. The pastor was a different guy than I recall and was just getting ready to leave, and may have had the door locked already, but I guess when he saw us he figured here were two people who definitely needed to get salvation.
Don was polite but firm, explaining that he was Captain Beefheart of the Magic Band and wanting to know what the meaning of the sign was. The pastor calmly explained that he was referring to the magic bands of the Middle East in the bible. Apparently they were marauding bands of nomads who practiced magic and plundered anyone unlucky enough to cross their paths. He didn't even realize there was a band called the Magic Band and was sincerely sorry if he had offended anyone.
I started thinking how much of a coincidence this was. I join the band, and within a few days of joining this title appears on the marquee of the last church I attended. I can't say that I didn't consider at later times that possibly my life would have turned out quite differently and for the better had I not joined the band.

Playing Shuffles

One thing I had always hated playing was shuffles. Shuffles are a kind of swing rhythm in 6/8 time. They're based on three beats. You play the first and third beat and skip the middle one. They're usually snappy and fast. It seemed like for the first two weeks I was in the band, all we did was play shuffles. At first I wondered why we were doing so many shuffles. Don finally told me. He said I had a time problem, he said I couldn't play a shuffle very well. So, we jammed a bunch of shuffles. I got so tired of playing shuffles I could have screamed! But I did develop a better shuffle from doing that.

Stewart's Studio

John French: And we would go over and see John Stewart in his studio, remember, that was above Stubbings Studio
Jerry Handley: He was a painter.

John Stewart was a mutual friend of Don's and Gary Lambert's. He also was a co-worker of Gary's – as an art teacher at Paraclete Catholic High School. He was a bit older and definitely appeared wiser than Gary, and so I'm sure he probably was a mentor to Lambert – probably taking him under his wing and showing him the ropes. He seemed much more stable than Gary, had his own studio, and was very productive, as I could see from his work.

John French: Yes, I heard that (presently) he (manufactures), little artsy boxes for collectors items that some product goes in. I can't recall the details. I'll have to find out. But (apparently) he's very successful.
Jerry Handley: I hope so.
JF: He was a nice guy, too. And of course, Gary Lambert used to come to rehearsals with his dog Flowers. Remember that. He would bring his dog Flowers?
JH: Oh, I remember him just vaguely. He used to play an instrument, didn't he?

(Note: At the time I didn't realize that Handley was probably referring to Gary's later study of congas and percussion in general.)

John French: No, he was just a friend of Don's. A friend of John Stewart's actually. And so he would show up with this huge German shepherd that would just crawl all over you.
Jerry Handley: Yeah, those were some wild times.

Back to John Stewart – it was mentioned above that he was renting the old space above Stubbings (photography) Studio. Frank Stubbings was a local commercial photographer who did family portraits, etc. He also had the oldest archive collection of pictures of the Antelope Valley area plus thousands of photos used in news stories. Until his death few years back, he specialized in aerial photography for the county and played a lot of golf. Stubbings Studio was an old two-storey framed business building that was unusual in two respects. One is that hardly any buildings in Lancaster were more than one storey, and another is that it was built in the tradition of the family business mentality of living upstairs from the shop. The upstairs contained a rather nice sized apartment, which Frank never used except for storage, and earlier on was rented to John Stewart.

John's studio seemed like the perfect artist's studio. It had an enclosed stairway going up the side from the street. It was one of those mysterious upstairs apartment doors I used to wonder about as a child. A flight of dark wooden stairs took you to the top of a small side room and the bathroom area. The main room was to the left. It was a fairly large room with plain wood floors and almost no furniture. There were many paintings sitting everywhere. There were four large windows in the front of the building. In the back corner was a doorway, which led to a small room with pads, pillows and mattresses on the floor, and a large hookah. It was John's bedroom/living room/kitchen.

John Stewart had done some picture-framing work and possibly hooked up with Frank through this channel. Normally, the visits to Stewart's studio were all in the evenings. My first impression is that it was a studio first, bachelor quarters second, and that Stewart was happily pursuing his dream of becoming a famous artist. He also owned one of the largest water pipes - or hookahs - I had ever seen. For this reason alone, he became an invaluable friend of Don's. We went through the usual "He's heavy" introduction (I being "he") and the usual scrutiny followed. John, however, seemed more intent on socializing with Don, whilst passing the hose to the hookah around the room. I spent many hours sitting in this room half out of my mind from smoking so much marijuana while listening to jazz.

I always enjoyed visiting Stewart as he seemed to always have his head on straight and maintained a perspective of life in the midst of all this chaos that was generally reassuring to me, and he legitimized Don a bit in my eyes, being an artist, high school teacher and "pillar of the community" so to speak. We went there quite often in the early days. I heard all the great avant-garde jazz artists; John Coltrane, John Handy, Ornette Coleman, Archie Shepp, Roland Kirk, and many others being played on Stewart's stereo. Oftentimes Don would bring these albums, but Stewart had his own collection.

The first time I heard John Coltrane, I felt I had to look no further. That was it for me. You could get no better. I didn't like where Coltrane went in his last few albums, but during a certain period I thought he had found musically whatever you could possibly find on this earth. It sounded as if the man had for a time somehow made a connection between his spirit and his sax and you could tell he had worked hard to get there.

The contrasts between John Stewart and Gary Lambert were amazing. John was taller and dark, Lambert shorter and blond. John Stewart was grounded and sincere, a self-made man. He had lived in his car while going to art school and struggled terrifically to get where he was. Gary Lambert had lived at home while attending College and was still living with his parents. Stewart seemed to always be involved in some project and had dozens of finished canvases arranged in groups, leaning against all the walls. Lambert seemed more interested in driving around in his big Jaguar trying to impress teenage girls. I would have trusted Stewart to teach art to my teenager. Lambert would have never had a chance.

Victor Hayden

I first met Don's cousin, Victor Hayden, at a rehearsal. He drove a white Volvo - the old kind with the rounded trunk. He had taken a felt pen and drawn rivets all over the car in perfect alignment with all the seams. Because of his rather full moustache and short hair, parted on one side, he reminded me of an old time photo of a conservative fellow who might be British and drive an MG sports coupe. In the back window of his car, on the horizontal space between the seat and the car body, he had put a doily, a little doll, and, if I remember correctly, an artificial plant complete with planter. It looked like some old lady's bed stand. Don called my attention to it. He said, "Do you know how *hip* that is, man? Can you imagine what people must think when they walk *past* that when it's parked on the street?" It did give a strange impression. I liked the idea myself. It was harmless and inoffensive, just strange.

Victor would occasionally visit and observe our rehearsals. Usually he would stay a few days, sleeping in Granny Annie's room. She would share Sue's room while he was there, to give him privacy. He seemed also to be yet another dope supplier for Don. I recall walking into Laurie's room one night, and there was quite an assortment of powders and pot lying on her dresser top. The connection to Gary Lambert, and ultimately to John Stewart, seemed to be that Victor and Gary had met at Chouinard Art Institute (at that time located at 743 S. Grand View St., L.A.). Chouinard, as I was later told, moved in collaboration with Disney funds to become the California Institute of the Arts in Valencia C.A. . Gary had actually graduated, but apparently Victor had only gone for a semester or so.

Stoned Desert Nights

Concerning these drug experiences, I recall one trip to the desert in Gary's Jaguar with Gary, Don and Victor. After smoking, I got out of the car, and all I could see all around me were giant hands made of smoke. They were grabbing me and trying to pull me into the ground and I could feel them. I got back in the car and pulled the hood of my coat tight over my head in terror. Victor Hayden thought that I was being ridiculous. However, I was genuinely afraid, even though part of my mind knew that it must be a hallucination. It seemed too real, and I couldn't control my imagination.

My Brain Is On Fire

One other night, at the end of rehearsal, Jerry was putting on his raincoat, because it was raining. Don had given me a joint earlier that night and told me to smoke it by myself. I obliged. (He told me later that he had been dipping the end of these joints in LSD – whether this is true or not, I have no idea, but the contraband on Laurie's dresser seem to include such items). As Jerry was putting on his coat, the rustling sounds were reminiscent of fire, and the next thing I knew (I know, this sounds ridiculous) I actually believed my brain was on fire. I could see smoke and flames coming out my eyes, and I could feel the unbearable heat. I was moaning and grasping my head in my hands. (Note: Reading this should give one pause to realize that we all should keep a reliable industrial-strength fire extinguisher on hand at all times ...)

Don implied that I was being ridiculous, and started telling me I was OK, but that I ought to stay over that night rather than going home. I had to lie down for several hours and actually wound up spending the night, falling asleep in his bed in the room next to the kitchen. Hotcha, Don's goldfish, was my only companion.

Flying Wolfshead

Don slept with Laurie in her room that night. I remember him saying that he would sleep with Laurie and made some comment about not caring what they, meaning Sue and Granny, would think. Apparently, there was some type of restrictions imposed upon him in this strange house.

The next day when I awoke, he was in the kitchen talking on the phone having a rather heated business argument with someone. As I sat on the edge of the bed putting on my shoes, I could see him. I don't know what the conversation was about, but as he said something to the effect of, "Oh damn, I didn't mean to do that, stop that," a little clay wolf's head he had sculptured literally popped out of the pantry, which was directly opposite him. I quickly ran around the corner to see if anyone in the pantry or living room had thrown it. But no one was in sight. There was no way Don could have tossed it, as it was going toward him from the opposite side of the room when I saw it. I had seen it in the pantry a few days before, and had picked it up and examined it, so I knew exactly where it was stored. The quality of the work was quite good, with a lot of detail and great proportion.

I asked him how this had happened. He reluctantly explained it - as though he had been found out - as telekinesis: moving objects with the mind. He told me he had trained his mind years before to move things, but didn't like to do it any more. I never knew whether to believe him or not. I saw no other explanation with my own eyes, yet anyone can be deceived. One thing that may enter in is that the night before I had been in a drug-induced state. However, on this particular morning, I can honestly say I didn't feel any effects at all of drugs and aside from this incident, in every other way it was a normal day.

A&M Send Notice

One sunny morning, as Jerry, Alex and I drove up to the Carolside house for rehearsal as usual, Don was standing in the driveway (instead of in bed in his pajamas) and showed everyone a legal notice he had received, I was led to believe, by courier. It was some kind of legal paper demanding that they (I wasn't under contract to A&M) make an appearance at a certain recording studio, showing the address of the studio, the date, and I believe the titles of the songs they wanted recorded. It was some of Don and Herb Bermann's original material, the stuff from the demo tape, some of which eventually wound up on *Safe As Milk*, I believe. I seem to recall *Electricity* and *Yellow Brick Road* being on this list – ironic as this was the very material Jerry Moss of A&M had labeled as negative months earlier.

I was excited and thought we were going to record. Don was angry and wanted to get a lawyer. A&M Records had judged his material as negative and he wanted no more to do with them. Everyone else seemed to be in agreement. I was a little disappointed. After all, this was a *recording* contract with a major label that was very popular at the time. I had never been in a band that had a *recording contract*. I also couldn't seem to understand why the problem with A&M and why the band didn't wish to record.

Later, it made more sense to me. It used to be the tradition that record companies would pay minimum recording costs to just *barely* meet their contractual agreement, *thus effectively legally binding the group AND the material* and often preventing it from being released. It was the worst form of control, and had more to do with power than anything else. The record company would then write off the group as a loss on tax statements. Van Vliet and company didn't want the band and the material to wind up as a "write off."

Mrs. Lambert

At Gary Lambert's suggestion we tried borrowing money for a lawyer from his mother. She lived in a fairly nice, upper-middle-class home. However, I had never been inside, and on walking through the door, I found the decor was horrifying. Everything was faux-leopard skin. The dust covers, the lampshades, her outfit, the curtains. It was too strange. Don explained his predicament to her in great detail and took pains to haltingly (business was never Don's strong point) describe why it would be a good investment.

It turned out she had already decided not to do it after consulting her astrologer and finding out her whatsit was in the umpteenth house of wherever. Don just sat there for a moment with a blank look on his face, got up, said thank you and left. Gary acted as though nothing had happened.

John French in Spring 1967. Photo courtesy of Guy Webster.

Mirror Man

During rehearsals Victor Hayden would sometimes walk around as the band jammed (these were daytime rehearsals) with a pipe full of marijuana and stick it in our mouths while we played. This would go on for an incredibly long time. I always had the feeling that Victor and Don perceived of the musicians as incredibly un-hip and was hoping this would open our eyes to the real possibilities.

I was still more or less under the concept that marijuana was devil weed and the next step to heroin. After all, that's what that film they showed in High School showed marijuana to be. Snouffer, who often referred to Victor as "that little punk," felt that much of this was wasted time.

John French: What were your recollections of what we were doing at that time?
Alex Snouffer: Not much. I mean, to be real candid with you, I didn't think much of the whole thing. I mean if we're just gonna sit around and get loaded, then let's do it and man, I'll go and get some beer and we can REALLY crank - kick this up a notch, you know? But I mean as far as some of those, "rehearsals" (they were) just dope parties.
JF: But we did get some stuff done, like Autumn's Child.
AS: Well, that's obvious, we got some stuff done, but it took a lot longer than it should have.
JF: Yeah, well, everything with Don took a lot longer than it should have.

Thus it went for a time. We would rehearse, often during the day, and sometimes at night. I would get really stoned sometimes, and sometimes have nothing. One particular day, after a rather long session of musical pipefuls we had the tape recorder running. Don was playing one of those big deep Hohner Marine Band harmonicas in the key of C (cross harp put the band in key of G) - one like Sonny Boy Williamson used to play.

We were actually loosely improvising on the theme to *Electricity*, developing various permutations thereof, and generally just experimenting with different rhythm patterns. I was playing P.G.'s concept of the part, sixteenth notes on the hi-hat cymbals with mallets. Both Alex and Doug were playing bottleneck guitar, and I believe only Doug was in open tuning. I was seated facing into the living room from the kitchen archway, Jerry to my right. Don was standing in the hallway entry. Doug was seated on a loveseat at the opposite end of the living room, and Alex was standing in the middle of the room.

Don actually started working off of a riff that Doug came up with, and between that low harmonica sound and Doug's great archtop bottleneck guitar was a very powerful combination of sounds. The jam went on for quite a while and only part of it was actually recorded and then the tape ran out. I felt as though I was under the influence of something stronger than marijuana. Probably because of the following experience: I remember looking up at the ceiling at one point and it appeared as if the roof had come off the house, and giant bees were swarming overhead. At the end of the song, Doug uncharacteristically went totally berserk on the guitar and started making strange out-of-time sounds with the bottleneck. I had never heard nor experienced anything like this in a jam. Alex was the most stable person (at least for me) and I looked over to see his reaction, he was just amused and laughing a bit. The song later became *Mirror Man*.

John French: Do you remember doing Mirror Man *in the desert? The very first time?*
Jerry Handley: I think we recorded that over at Don's (mother's) house.
JF: Right, and do you remember Doug just going crazy?
JH: Yeah, that was when the house went upside down, I think.
JF: Mirror Man was actually ...most of that was Doug's influence. The house did go upside down, well for me, the roof came off and there were giant bees up above us.

JH:(Laughter) I just flipped the house over, I was sane.
JF:(Actually) that was to keep the bees out, I guess. (Laughter) Anyway, those were days when, if I may go back to that time for a minute, when Victor Hayden, Don's cousin, used to come up, with his pipeful of marijuana and stuff it in our mouth as we were playing. Yes, and so the music did get a little bit more creative around that time.
JH: Yeah, I guess that's (where) Mirror Man *came from.*

At the time, I didn't really care for what we had played. My tastes ran to stranger music, but I felt like we were getting so weird that no one would give us a recording contract. My idea was to make money and at the same time do something valid. Remember, this is when most of the far out bands of the San Francisco sound were only a step or two away from the norm. We had just played something that was miles off the chart.

Don was, on the other hand, ecstatic. I think, in his mind, he had finally succeeded in breaking down the band's concept of that tedious norm of 4/4 time, three chord changes, and predictability, that had everyone's mind shackled and prevented the band from having any kind of unique vision. He felt it was a breakthrough and was raving about how good *Mirror Man* was, and I objected. My thought was that we would never be taken seriously if we put out something like that – that is, if we could even possibly re-create the chaos in which we had all just participated.

Victor immediately told Don that he should get rid of me, that I should be fired from the band, and that I was nothing but trouble. This discussion went on in my presence and that of the rest of the group for a long while after the tape had been played back and I had expressed my opinion. The discussion was very candid, brutally honest and completely insensitive to the fact that I was present and a relative newcomer to the group. It was as though I was eavesdropping on a conversation in which these two were privately expressing their most unflattering impressions of me. There seemed to be no regard whatsoever for what I was feeling: alienated, isolated and betrayed.

First Lid

I decided to buy my first "lid" of grass. A "lid" was so and so number of ounces of marijuana. Victor was one of the Magic Bands' suppliers. He reluctantly sold me my first and last lid of grass. I remember him pacing in Granny Annie's bedroom (where he stayed when he came up – she would share Sue's room). He was very undecided and anxious about selling me pot. I think he felt that I was too immature to handle it. Actually, I don't think anyone CAN handle pot, nor any other drug. It actually handles them. I never bought any more after this because it seemed dangerous, a complete waste of time and money, and it was far too risky to deal with any future legal repercussions. I wound up giving it to Jerry after I had smoked one joint.

Jerry had moved into a small house near the A.V. High School with Sue, his wife. I felt better leaving it with him. Jerry wound up rolling it all up and putting the joints in a little holder on his dining room table, on a little tray next to the salt and pepper. I found this a little amusing - as in pass the joints, please?

Uncomfortable and Alienated

Even in more relatively comfortable times I always felt uncomfortable and paranoid – probably partially as a direct result of things I was ingesting, knowingly and even perhaps unknowingly. The intensity was such that I felt I may get murdered any minute, or that some group of men in dark suits and sunglasses would just walk in with machine guns and take us all to an underground laboratory. I had experienced hallucinations and I was just confused enough not to know whether or not they were real. Suddenly I seemed to live in a new dimension of fear, which I had never experienced before.

The only thing I remember about those dope parties was that *Mirror Man* was done during a jam and we recorded it. It is about the only real thing that happened of any consequence. Actually, *Autumn's Child* and most of the rest of the album was worked on at evening rehearsals that included no chemical aids. We were all straight and sober. I worked on the bass part for *Autumn's Child* with Jerry for a while, because I had some ideas of how to finish up the part. He was very open and we co-wrote the bass part together. As Doug Moon has previously stated, many of the songs on *Safe As Milk* were collaborations and were put together in just this way. Don did have overall concepts, but much of the detail was worked out by the band during this period and even before I was in the group.

Perhaps Van Vliet's purpose during this period was to nudge the band out of its comfort zone and to force everyone to explore new areas: different blends of instruments, alternative rhythms, and richer harmonic structures. It may have also been his idea to form more of a group sound concept merely by encouraging the more interesting elements and discarding the mundane, hoping to elevate the group as a whole to a higher level of collaborative pursuit. The songs on *Safe As Milk* for the most part are interesting, but they seldom stray far from tried and true combinations that other recording artists had already achieved.

Van Vliet's concept may have been to build a band that could play at this higher level at any time. He used to talk to me about "telepathic" music, in which certain jazz bands he would watch seemed to know exactly how to move from one section to the next. I had little knowledge of the actual structure of jazz at that time. I came to find out later that the way that they were able to create the illusion of this telepathy as Don referred to it, was through mastering musical theory and form so completely that they no longer had to think about it in a conscious way.

This is a far cry from some guy buying a saxophone, taking LSD and blowing through it, and suddenly christening himself an avant-garde saxophonist.

Don's biggest mistake here may have been his disorganized approach, which didn't communicate to the players what he was attempting to achieve more than in the vaguest abstract sense. If his plan or vision had been communicated more clearly, perhaps rehearsal time could have been divided up into: creative sessions (like the jam described above in which *Mirror Man* was conceptualized by the group) and "formation" or "arrangement" sessions, in which already written material was arranged in preparation for studio, so that we actually knew where the beginning and the end were and where the finishing touches were added and the framework for the arrangement established.

Again, however, because of the fact that Don had almost no discipline whatsoever when it came to tedious tasks like finishing what he started, and seldom if ever did he want to do any of the detail or arrangement work, his focus was almost always on creation. This left the band with the thankless task of taking raw material and basically filling in the gaps (of which there were plenty) only to later find reviews of the albums giving all the credit to Van Vliet, and none whatsoever to the band.

Don himself could have clarified this and given credit where credit was due – especially with the press. Instead, he fed and watered this misconception until it grew into mythological proportions. The band members seldom, if ever, received any publishing credit, and so no royalties were awarded to Magic Band members except on rare occasions, such as *Plastic Factory*, in which Handley was given credit, and on the material co-written by Bermann. This alone caused there to be an even further lack of incentive to create.

When confronted with these issues, Van Vliet's response was usually to go into a tirade about how lazy we were, or - another more effective ploy to plead ignorance about it and say, "Is that right? I didn't realize that. Why didn't you tell me? I'll take care of it." Then later, after he had again received all the writing credit, the excuse would be, "Man, _____ (insert word of any producers, managers, business associates etc., throughout the years) - didn't do what I *told* them to do.

Even with our efforts, there were still gaps in arrangements. This was mostly due to the fact that although we had a list of unfinished songs, Van Vliet's thrust on creativity kept us from ever actually nailing down an arrangement and totally completing it. That subject will be dealt with more later.

Spiders Spinning Nines

Don always had a writing pad and was writing lyrics constantly. He would write down things that people would say, thoughts that came to his head, slips of the tongue, anything vaguely interesting. I remember one night he was writing or drawing something and there were about six people in Stewart's little room at his studio. Somebody called attention to what Don was drawing or writing and everyone began to focus on Don in an intense and slightly critical manner. Suddenly, a large black spider (probably a black widow) appeared on the floor, and everyone except Don and I became engrossed in the act of ridding the room of this unwanted visitor. The temporary arachnophobia acted as a smoke screen, distracting the group from Don to the spider.

With a vivid stare, Don fixed his eyes on me in a way as if to communicate something to me telepathically. I sensed that he was claiming or suggesting somehow to have summoned this spider in order to get people to leave him alone. I remember him wearing all black and sporting a large floppy black hat. A later inquiry vaguely confirmed what I suspected. "Did you see what I did back there with the spider?" suggesting in the following conversation that he had somehow summoned the spider.

Don't Rain On My Hookah

There was a hole in the ceiling of John's little room where we usually gathered. A large Christmas tree, much too tall for the room, was bought by John and placed in the room, with the top humorously sticking up through this hole. After the almost religious passing of the hookah tube we all sat there in a stupor, somehow, I suppose, feeling we were accomplishing something. Suddenly it began to rain, and as the rain trickled its way down through the branches of the tree, it brought a beauty to the room that I can't explain. The thousands of droplets each seemed to have a special role of reflecting a bit of tinsel or a colored light, or dripping off the bottom of a glass ball. It was a unique image, one that reminded me of happier times and was indelibly imprinted upon my memory.

Of course, it's probably important to note that had it continued to rain, the floor would have gotten quite wet, and we all would have been electrocuted by the Christmas tree lights. *That* would have been a Christmas to remember.

Sister Sheila Marie

On the occasion of one visit to the Stewart Studio apartment, there were a few people there taking art lessons from John Stewart, and one happened to be a nun, who was introduced as Sister Sheila Marie. She was most likely affiliated with Paraclete – the Catholic High School where John taught. She was wearing a pure white habit, and was a beautiful woman. Don seemed immediately taken by her. He studied her very closely, and she seemed friendly enough, so he struck up a conversation with her. He looked at me and said something like, "Man, it's so *weird* to see a nun here, in this place." It seemed to me that he was hitting on her.

More Doctrines, More Compartments

Don continued during this time to take me under his wing and indoctrinate me into his way of thinking. At the same time, the band was getting completely tired of making no money and coming to rehearsal to find Don still in bed after a long evening of creating.

One day, Alex took me to Doug Moon's mother's house. Alex's drumset was in the living room set up, and the amplifiers and other instruments were there also. They started talking to me about leaving Don and striking out with me doing a lot of the singing.

Basically, I found myself caught in the middle. On the one hand, I didn't really feel that the band was strong enough without Don to actually make a complete entity. On the other hand, Don didn't seem involved enough with reality to allow the band a chance to actually function on a business level. The guys were saying, "Let's dump him" and yet they seemed to have only a vision of playing a few bar jobs and sinking into oblivion. The resentment of Don seemed to be building and I was starting to house a few of my own issues. Yet I couldn't help but think that we needed him as badly as he needed us, and that sticking together was the only choice we had.

Don's influence on me, I must say, was productive in several areas. He had introduced me to new and unique musical and lyrical concepts. My head was swimming with possibilities and I was so strongly inspired to accomplish something new that it was easy to ignore the fact that there was little practical progress being made on any particular day. I would cringe at his descriptions of the band members as "fucking okies" or "ignorant savages", because I found them all to be nice people who merely lacked a certain depth of understanding concerning his vision. Our influence, holding him in check at this point in time, is what allowed the future *Safe As Milk* to be as widely accepted as it was. The album would not have been recognizable nor possibly even come into existence had not there been some restraint and resistance from the group to hold Don back and make him focus on finishing 12 songs.

John French: So he was sort of indoctrinating me into this more artistic view and sort of moving everybody back from me and training me in the way he wanted me to be. Saying, "This is what we're going to be doing, this is where the real stuff is." Of course, at the same time, I'm on all these drugs and he later privately admitted to putting acid (LSD) on joints that he had given me. This would explain the "burning brain" experience I had. So I was actually tripping and didn't know it. I didn't know whether to trust you guys or not, because Don had told me all these things about (the corporate) you. Yet, at the same time, I thought Don was very unreasonable and impractical on certain issues. So I would go back and listen to you and you would tell me not to listen to him, because he's ... (makes "crazy" gesture) ... you know? So I was caught in the middle, not knowing what to do or which direction to go in and being young, I was pretty indecisive about the whole thing. I should have sense in, my head to figure this out, but I had just been introduced to that wonderful drug marijuana.

Doug Moon: Uh oh!

JF: And that's what got me going.

DM: Hey John, I gotta apologise for that.

JF: Well, Don was the one who introduced me.

DM: I think I was ... maybe things wouldn't have gotten so bad at the end if I hadn't been such a pothead and druggie myself. That was probably my weakness. That was probably one of my major faults. I loved drugs (laughs) - not drugs, I loved psychedelic drugs - anything that was far-out. I didn't like things that made me stupid. I didn't like pills and things that blotted you out. I liked things that made me "see God" and "took me to a higher level" and "made me have out-of-body experiences." (He says these phrases with much sarcastic amusement) *and I was into all that kind of stuff. Unfortunately, I spread the stuff around the band every chance I got. I think that was a major contribution to the reason things got so out of control at the end. I mean things got so far out.*

The General Consensus

Although Moon was probably the first person to really decimate the established rules in terms of musical experimentation (on *Mirror Man*), he ironically had a different vision.

Doug Moon: I think if we had kept our heads straight, we could have stayed on a more reasonable sensible path and maintained a style that was a little more accessible. Maybe Don wouldn't have thrown caution to the wind and gone totally avant-garde ten years before the world was ready for it.
John French: Fifty years.
DM: We could have been down to earth enough to compete on the same level as The Doors and Paul Butterfield.
JF: I think the (magic) band (could have been) somewhere in between there.
DM: Like Creedence Clearwater Revival and all these bands that were making it and actually made some money, and had records and actually made a name for themselves so they could go on with their own lives.
JF: Pay the dues to have artistic freedom.
DM: Yeah!
JF: That was my point in the band, and I think that was everybody's point in the band is "why are we going so far-out right now? Why don't we do something simple that people will buy?
DM: What good is artistic freedom when nobody's going to even hire you to play?

Perhaps not more exciting for the diehard Beefheart fans but certainly more exciting for us as a band. If we had been able to become a financially viable group, it would have been much better for all of us concerned. Don could have eventually gone off and hired people to do exactly the kind of music he wanted and we would have all the freedom to pursue music of our own liking. But, I'm getting ahead of myself.

John Parr

John Parr, my drumming friend from school days, lived right down the street from Don as I mentioned earlier. He paid a visit to a rehearsal at Don's mother's house one day. It wasn't until after this that Don actually told me that he had asked Parr into the group prior to asking me. John had recommended me to Don. (Note: I believe both stories, Aldridge and Parr's show no conflict. Don probably contacted Parr without Aldridge being present.) John later confided in me that he didn't think I would fit in until he came to that rehearsal. He told me he had changed his mind; he thought I had really made the band sound even better. Because of the fact that I had so much respect for Parr's opinion and abilities as a drummer, this was a big boost for my confidence and encouragement to stay in the group.

Musical Struggles

We were starting to struggle through changing some of the songs which would wind up on *Safe As Milk, Call On Me, Autumn's Child, Electricity, Yellow Brick Road* etc. As I wrote earlier, Jerry and I sat for two evenings writing a bass part to *Autumn's Child*. It's not a very imaginative part, but there was nothing written for the bass in most of the song.

Don changed a lot of the arrangements. Some of the ideas were hard to understand, some vague in detail and we would usually wind up putting them together ourselves after he left the room, because he never showed anyone how it came together.

This began to be a routine for me. Although it was a painful process in a sense, I was enjoying doing something creative. Up until now, almost all the materials I rehearsed with bands were cover tunes of other artists. This was completely new territory for me. It was a bit rough at first. I hadn't been used to someone telling me what to play. Sometimes I had a hard time taking the criticism or just the dictatorial "Play this, man," approach Don would use when creating. But we kept plowing away and slowly getting things a little more established. Don was still the most disorganized. His lyrics were all on little bits of matchbook covers, coffee shop placemats and napkins. This was all carefully filed into a giant cardboard box or paper bag by throwing one part of a song on top of another part of an entirely different song. That is how the arrangements were in our heads also. Little bits and pieces, but not the complete vision of the whole.

Farewell John Parr

Within a few weeks of joining the band, I got up one morning to some terrible news. I had gone down to Roehr's Music Box. Merrel Fankhauser was employed there at the time. He was working in the store at the time as a counter person and music instructor. When I walked in, the first thing that he said was, "Did you hear what happened to John Parr?"

My good friend since the 5th grade had taken a final ride with a sawed-off shotgun. He never came home. They found his body in his car out by Quartz Hill High school. When Alex picked me up later for rehearsal, he drove me to the Parr house on Carolside at my request, and John's brother confirmed that it was true. There were no details, and I stayed only a second.

He was at a party months before, and someone had purposely dropped a lot of LSD in his beer without his knowledge. He had never been the same afterward. I had noticed the change in him. However, I just thought it was because I hadn't seen him for a while and he was smoking pot. My mother later told me he had been to the house to see me that same night just before he killed himself. I was out in the desert getting stoned with Don and Gary Lambert. For many years, I felt a tremendous sense of guilt. "What if I would have been home?" I used to think, "Things might have turned out differently." However, we don't live in the land of what-if. He was gone and I had to face it.

Don Aldridge: I drove by the school that night. Of all the times for me to be driving on 60th St. West, but I was. I went up to Gody's Pass by myself and I was doing a number up there. I came back and I believe it was on a Sunday night when he killed himself. If I'm not mistaken, it was Sunday night, and they found him Monday morning. When school (opened).

My wife's sisters were going to High School and were some of the first people to see his body in the car. One of them told me that she walked up to the car, because she saw blood, and the entire back of the head of the driver of the car was gone. She was probably 15 years old. She didn't know him well, so that probably made it a little easier. It must have been pretty traumatic for her.

I found out years later that John had left a note explaining that the reason he decided to kill himself in front of the school was as a reminder of how terrible drugs really were. A lot of thoughts went through my head. I was taking acid without my own knowledge, and found out about it later. I was acting strange to everyone who had known me. Was I about to follow in my friend's footsteps? Maybe this premonition I had had about my own death was true. I was scared. I really felt alone. John was one of the last people left who I was really close to. Now, he was gone. I had never known anyone who had taken his life. A few months later when the Beatles' *Sergeant Pepper's Lonely Hearts Club Band* came out, it seemed eerie to listen to the line:

"He blew his mind out in a car, he didn't notice that the lights had changed."

Don kept trying to control my emotion in a most dramatic way. He would get right in my face and say things like, "You can't let this do you in." I felt that it was perfectly natural to be grieving over my good friend's death, but I was made to feel like a freak. I also didn't feel that Van Vliet was showing any empathy for my grief. It was more as if he were concerned that I might become dysfunctional as a drummer, like he was trying to fix his broken radio.

He kept saying, "Don't go to the funeral, whatever you do DON'T GO, man. I went to my father's funeral, and it was terrible." I complied. I didn't go, but I wish I had. The reason I didn't is because Don was so insistent that I knew it would offend him if I went. Don was still pretty traumatized by his own father's death. I speculate that this was the reason for his symptoms of anxiety, which later escalated into a real problem.

The whole world seemed to change for a long time after that. I remember one night sitting at Don's dining room table sub-consciously drawing a picture of a tombstone, which seemed to again concern everybody in an almost soap-opera fashion. Eventually, the shock wore off and I accepted John's death as best an 18-year-old can. I never remember real grief, or crying, it was just depression.

Years later, I saw a movie in 1998 that dealt with the teen suicide. It focused on one of the friends left behind (played by Keanu Reeves) and how he dealt with it. Ironically, it was about musicians in a band. As I sat and watched the movie, I suddenly found myself crying and weeping like a small child, gasping for breath and didn't know why. I realized suddenly that I had never cried when my friend John Parr took his life, and now, it came out - 32 years later. It would have been better had I just been left to deal with this at the time, but I felt I had to suppress it or risk offending Don.

Mother Called

A few days later, my mother woke me to tell me that Don had called her at 3 a.m. and was yelling at her over the phone and calling her Sue his mother's name. He was telling her not to worry, that I wasn't on drugs. My mother was worried sick. She started asking me all kinds of questions about everything I was doing – was I on drugs? Was Don on drugs? I faced this on waking up in the morning and still groggy, still depressed over my friend's death.

The next day, in an adjacent room at his mother's house, I privately asked Don why he had called her. He denied the whole thing and made a big issue and scene out of it in front of the entire band, his mother, grandmother and his girlfriend. Not only did he deny it, he launched into a very public tirade that lasted for 10 or 15 minutes, telling me "You've *got* to get away from that mother of yours. She's *really* fucking you up, man."

From that day forward, my mother seemed to be one of Don's favorite themes of conversation when any dispute rose between he and I. He would say, "You've gotta get away from that mother of yours … etc."

In retrospect, I think that Don was very disoriented at this time due to his large consumption of LSD I saw him take it a few times. Other times, he told me, boastingly, about taking huge amounts of L.S.D, 2,000-5,000 micrograms at a time. These were quite large doses (most people took 500 to begin with) He may have felt a slight bit guilty for getting me involved with drugs. As I mentioned, he later had told me that he gave me a joint ("Here, you smoke this one yourself") that was laced with LSD. I'm sure that's what caused me to think that Jerry's raincoat sound was my brain on fire. (Funny thing, 18 years and my brain had NEVER once before caught on fire - I think I would have remembered.)

Having come on to the drug unexpectedly, with no prior knowledge was not a pleasant experience. Perhaps Vliet was concerned that I was going to follow in John Parr's footsteps and they would trace all this back to him. Had I been wise and a bit more confident, I would have probably walked out of the band right then. However, I was still facing the illusion that there were absolutely no other opportunities for me in Lancaster, and this was probably my best shot. It was either this or sitting around waiting to be drafted. After a lot of thought, I chose to stay.

Last Gig With Blues In A Bottle

I had one last gig to sing with the band I was leaving. Blues In A Bottle was playing a High School dance at my old alma mater, A.V. High School. Don had taken me under his wing for this period of time. After all, I was the youngest member of the Magic Band, and newest addition, and I think he was inspired because I seem to be open to his ideas. Also, it was important for him to form my vision of the music and the future of the group so that it wouldn't be in opposition to his plan. He asked to drive me to the school and I was honored and said yes. He had one of those old black Jaguars, a small sedan.

We first drove out Avenue J on the east side of town. After a couple of miles, there was nothing but alfalfa fields. We smoked a joint and drove along talking about life and the future and how marijuana heightened the senses and made one more aware. Suddenly a rabbit ran in front of the car and froze, blinded by the headlights. Don calmly and controlledly swerved the car to the other side of the road, and back again, without missing a beat, or becoming alarmed. He said, "See? If I hadn't been high, I might have hit that rabbit." It was an interesting and convincing moment for me, as it never seemed that people were intoxicated after smoking pot as they were when drinking alcohol, so I considered that there was a glimmer of truth in his statement. There was no slurring of words, staggering, loss of motor response - at least as far as I could tell. Only calling my mother at three in the morning and calling her "Sue", no big deal, right?

We finally arrived at the dance. I was late. I found later that if Van Vliet were giving you a ride to any activity that he was not directly involved in, he would ultimately find some clever and creative way to make you late. I hadn't worn a jacket, and it was a little cold that night, and I shivered walking to the auditorium. "Think warm," Don said to me, "your mind will make you warm." I tried it, and for the rest of the walk, I actually did feel warm.

The band was a little nervous about me being late. I came in feeling like some vain egomaniac Hollywood star. Everything was set up, and I had always helped set up the drums and the P.A. It made me feel like I had let down my friends. I imagine that I appeared somewhat arrogant to them. It was strange seeing them and being with them: it seemed like such a different world. In the short time I had been in The Magic Band, I had been exposed to a different world. Blues In A Bottle seemed young and immature to me now, a lifetime removed.

Gary Lambert met us at the auditorium. He and Don sat together over to the right of the stage against the wall (waiting, apparently, for someone to ask them to dance). Several people recognized Don and went over to talk. I think he signed a few autographs. *Diddy Wah Diddy* had just been out six months or so before. Interestingly enough, they would be thrown out of the building now, because of new security measures in schools.

I sang through a homemade PA with no monitors and blew my voice out pretty badly - mostly due to dehydration from smoking pot, I would imagine. It was rather intimidating to have a man who was considered one of the best white blues singers in America sitting there listening to me do the blues - we covered a few of his songs. That night was significant in my mind because musically it marked the end of my youth. I never did music on stage with a band after that and had that same freedom nor had as much fun. I played better music, but there was always tension and conflict and never the freedom I felt with this band. I said goodbye to my High-School friends and fellow musicians and walked out the door - little knowing that Mark and Jeff would play a big part in the future of The Magic Band.

Money From Handley's Aunt

The A&M contractual dispute had been a problem and the band needed a lawyer. We were finally able to borrow money from Jerry Handley's aunt.

John French: So then, I don't know what happened with A&M but I think we borrowed money from you Aunt. Do you remember that?
Jerry Handley: Oh yeah, yeah.
JF: And it never got paid back, I'm sure.
JH: That's right. She just passed away about a year and a half ago - never did get paid back.
JF: Yeah, that was one of the sad things that I regret.
JH: Me too, it got lost in the shuffle there. Nobody really got well enough (off) to take care of her. (It was $1000 if I remember correctly, maybe more.)
JF: Yeah, and your aunt lived over there on Cedar or Date - one of those little streets over there. I remember going to her house with you (and Don) and talking about this with her.
JH: The money she put up kept us going for a while there - for the Buddah recording.
JF: Well, I think part of it went to the lawyer, and part of it went to the house rent (on Amor Rd.).

With part of the borrowed money, Don eventually secured the services of a Beverly Hills attorney. Jay Cooper was his name as Jerry recalls.

Don's Creative Diversions

Now that the legal proceedings were underway, it seemed time to really get serious about the music. Don kept saying that we had to be ready, because it would all happen fast once the paperwork was done. That was good thinking; however, it seemed like the only one who was hindering the progress of the album was Don himself. He was still very disoriented and seemed to only half-finish anything he started. Also, he was quite prolific and 90% of his time still seemed to be devoted to creating new songs, especially lyrics. Since I had never been around him save the last three or four months, I thought perhaps it was just a phase he was going through and expected it to end once he regained his orientation. I'm still waiting.

Van Vliet continued to stay up all night creating and sleep half the day away. I remember more than once coming over for rehearsal and finding Don still in bed with his mother trying to awaken him. (This was, by the way, during the same time Van Vliet was claiming to have stayed awake for six months, a legendary time span that later grew to a year and a half according to some very gullible journalists.) Don was a really heavy sleeper. Sue would light cigarettes for him and wind up smoking them herself. "Don!" she would say in her pleasant way, "John's here waiting for you. You're going to turn me into a smoker if I have to keep doing this to wake you up." "Shut up Sue, get me a Pepsi!" he would half grumble back. Even after he got up, it was a long time before he would even be ready to get dressed. It was annoying and frustrating to everyone else, but anytime anyone confronted him, he would become quite hostile and the mood would be even worse than it was before.

He seemed to be having almost spiritual experiences during his late-night creative sessions. Some of them were quite interesting. Once as I arrived for rehearsal, I discovered that Don had been up all night. I was pretty disappointed but he began speaking excitedly about his latest realization.

"Everything's a circle, man!" He told me. He then went on to recite a couple of pages of lyrics, which seemed to consist of things like:

The earth's a circle; the moon's a circle
Your eye's a circle...

I don't remember anything specifically, but he referred to all the circles he could think of found in nature, the world, the solar system, life and death, the eyeball, snowflakes etc. He had connected them all in a fairly logical order. It was an enlightening moment and an interesting topic.

However, it never evolved into a song, and we missed a whole day of rehearsing because of the time taken the night before to write this one piece. Alex seemed really impatient and disgusted by this behavior. Everyone seemed afraid to say anything.

Usually, when he recited this new poetry "hot off the press," he was sitting in his pajamas on the bed, smoking a cigarette. There was a red bell pepper suspended by a thread from the ceiling over his bed, about arm's length high directly over where his neck would be if he were lying down. It had been hanging for some time and was slowly de-composing. He explained to me that he was studying its decomposition. He described it as beautiful. I could see what he meant; there was a certain beauty in all the colors. He observed that most people consider older people to be unattractive, because of the wrinkles and loss of flesh tone, but he felt that older people were much more interesting to observe than young ones. I imagine that now he must think the Keith Richards is really gorgeous.

He fed his pet goldfish, Hotcha, as I sat there in his room waiting for him to get dressed. That was a huge fish for the size of the bowl. He told me that goldfish would grow to accommodate whatever size their environment would allow. I said I thought it was too bad that humans didn't have that characteristic. He seemed really attached to Hotcha. He also had a dog, a small black poodle named Cindy. Laurie once showed me a picture of him sitting back in a chair in the living room, holding Cindy up over his head and looking up at her, a big smile on his face. Cindy was Laurie's responsibility, however. She fed her, washed her, walked her, and held her in the car when they drove somewhere together. Laurie seemed to almost fixate on the dog sometimes, almost as though the dog were an escape, or a way to avoid the intensity. Her life must have been pretty boring at the time because she seldom went anywhere with Don.

Black Jag Meets Bus Bench

However, on one particular evening I definitely recall Laurie being with us. Don was driving his small black Jaguar sedan west on Lancaster Boulevard, the main street in this small town. Laurie was in the passenger seat and I was sitting in the back. Suddenly, Don became visibly shaken and drove up over the curb, hitting a bus stop bench and sending it careening along the sidewalk barely missing several people. One man had to jump out of the way to avoid being struck.

Don explained that the brakes had gone completely out and the only way he could think to avoid a collision with the vehicles in front and stop the car was to rub the tires against the curb. Unfortunately, the momentum had carried us completely over the curb and almost struck pedestrians. Don quickly told Laurie to explain that she had been driving the car. I wasn't sure why he did this. When the police came, they asked who the driver was, and Laurie took full responsibility for the accident. There were a few spectators who remained until the sheriff began to question Laurie. I am sure this was due to the fact that we all looked a bit strange with our long hair and non-conformist clothes. It was evident that some of them were as puzzled as I when Laurie told the officer she was driving the car. However no one spoke up to challenge her story.

Don later explained to me that the reason he had instructed Laurie to say she was driving was that the cops were out to get him. I didn't think much about this at the time. Darline Blair, the waitress at the local coffee shop was familiar with all the Sheriffs who worked night shift. She later told me that the Sheriffs who stopped in for coffee said that they had often found "Captain Beefheart" wandering around in the desert, stoned out of his mind and delusional. They had merely taken him home.

After the car was towed to a mechanic's shop, it was discovered that the brake line had been purposely cut. Apparently, Don had an enemy in town. I thought perhaps the boyfriend of one of his sexual conquests, or a neighbor angered by the volume of the rehearsals, or maybe someone who just didn't like long-haired men.

J.F. Back On Track

I was getting more involved with the drums again, and starting to feel inspired about creating new beats. I had somewhat recuperated from the loss of John Parr and decided to use his death as a motivation. I thought to myself that all that I did I would dedicate to his memory. It's hard to explain, but it succeeded in getting me more involved with music and through the grieving process. I think it was a healthy way to heal the grief. I thought that somehow his life would continue to have meaning if I worked hard and became a successful drummer because of all the basics he had shown me in the beginning.

New Local Dances, Drumset

We played a couple of local dances during this period. I used the money to pay off the new set of Ludwigs I had been requested by the band to buy. Pink Champagne was not a color for the Magic Band. I went back to my friend Cliff Roehr, and traded my Rogers kit in on a smaller Ludwig four piece set. They were the right color, a manly black oyster the same color as Parr's set. Now my drums could be seen in public with the Magic Band. The dances were interesting, because we played stuff on stage I had never rehearsed. They would just start a riff and do the old blues stuff they had performed when Vic Mortensen first joined the band (minus the Stones tunes). It was great. Don was so spellbinding when singing and performing the blues.

The band played really well. It felt pretty good to be back on the drums in front of people after almost a year of singing. The first dance we played, Don's mother showed up and brought my mother along. That bothered me a little. She looked so strange standing down there with all those hippies and High School kids. It was a bit inhibiting. The audience seemed to like the performance. I had a whole different feeling about the band after playing with them. Even though we were doing this old blues, it was quite inspiring. I could hear the way the music worked together. It was less of a puzzle to me. I had been listening to a lot of old blues records, but many of them had the drums mixed so low in the track, it was hard to really make head or tail out of it. Plus, a lot of it needed to be modernized to fit a standard kit played at a higher volume.

The band had played these songs so much that they just flowed. They had done a lot of club performing under the management of Leonard Grant and Dorothy Heard. Since I had never met those two I had reached the conclusion from what had been said that they were just typical low-level agents out to make a few bucks but without the foggiest notion about what to do with a great group. Incapable of thinking big, they had lost a great group. Then, there were the unanswered questions as to what the band had done to discourage them.

The highlight of the first public performance with the magic band was *Tupelo*, which featured a brilliant performance from Snouffer and Van Vliet. It was a simple riff, but was dynamically punctuated by guitar, harp and vocals. I was so enchanted I could barely concentrate on my playing. The band went over quite well.

We played a second time in a bigger auditorium, the Fair Center Hall. Don seemed playful this night. He brought a cake mixer on stage. It was one of the old white porcelain types on a stand, with the big white bowl. I had no idea what he was doing, neither did anyone else, except Victor, who was there saying things like, "That is *sooooo* hip!" and "Just DIG it!"

Van Vliet also made fun of himself and singing the blues which he seemed not to be able to take too seriously. During the vocal breaks in Howlin' Wolf's *Evil*, he would say "Boogie wid de Wolfman", which was DJ Wolfman Jack's line. The audience seemed to enjoy these little humorous injections, however. The band just stuck to the blues at these two dances. We may have done *Call On Me*, and one or two other things from *Safe As Milk*, but mostly we stuck to the old repertoire.

Gary Marker

Sometime during all of this, Don went down to Los Angeles, probably Venice. He asked me to go with him, and we stayed at Gary Marker's house. I later found out through Gary that Don had been a visitor to this house quite often. As I mentioned earlier, Gary had been the bass player for the Rising Sons. While we were there, Don was asking Gary about Ry, I think to get in touch with him. Don told me he didn't think that Doug could cut the music. I thought Doug was perfectly capable of copping the licks, but he needed a little more time to digest them than Alex and Jerry. But it was apparent that Doug seemed to be retreating into a shell. He didn't respond quickly to anything said to him, and seemed to be preoccupied with something else. I think he may have been worried about the future of all of this. He was living with his mother, and he may have wanted to help her out a little more than he was able.

While we were at Marker's, Don also tried to call Jack Nietzche, whose name I somehow at that time connected with the Rolling Stones. Jack had apparently expressed some interest in the Beefheart sound. Don never got through to him, and we came home without accomplishing much more than me meeting Gary. As we drove home, Don told me stories about supernatural things that had happened to him. I remember one instance where he described an encounter while driving alone. He claimed he looked over and saw an open scroll floating above the passenger seat, but he couldn't read the writing. He claimed it was real - not a hallucination, and that he wasn't on drugs at the time.

Another instance involved an occurrence a few weeks earlier. He described being parked out in a place called Green Valley with a girl he had planned a rendezvous with. As I recall, they were engaged in sexual activity while sitting in the passenger seat of his car. His words were something like "I was ballin' this chick." Anyway, he convincingly told a story of spotting a UFO. He said that it really scared him and the girl because it hovered over the car for several minutes. He thought that it had done something to him, but he wasn't sure what. He felt something. Shortly after this, he seemed to start having slight loss of hair, which he attributed to this encounter. I suspected he was pulling his out in his sleep, as he seemed to do the same thing with his beard for years; he was not often able to grow a proper beard due to his obsessive behavior and a profound fascination for the action of tweezers. The results of all this were that he would almost always shave off the pathetic remains of his beard after it became apparent that most of it had been pulled or plucked out.

Evenings At Sue's

I spent a lot of time with Don and Laurie at his mother's house. He mentioned often during these visits that he had checked up on me before inviting me to join the group. I always wondered exactly what he meant by this statement, and felt that perhaps a bit too much of my privacy had been violated. In order to understand my reactions, you must realize that I was a fairly passive person who was also quite naive. I had been raised in a small town. I had never been in any sophisticated circles.

He claimed that he used to spend a lot of time in Hollywood and had rubbed elbows with a few movie stars. He claimed he had met Lenny Bruce on a couple of occasions and briefly spoken with him. Steve McQueen is another of the people he talked about meeting. He said McQueen was nuts and had a death wish - driving the canyons of LA with Don as a passenger at incredibly dangerous speeds and scaring the bejabbers out of him.

Gary Lambert would often come to Sue's house in the evenings, and quite often, we would go buy a chocolate cake mix and Laurie would bake it. One evening Lambert seemingly inspired by some invisible chocolate demon - smeared chocolate cake and icing all over his face and beard. He gazed at me for a long moment with a ridiculous grin and intense stare of liberation, as though he had just recently been freed from the shackles of sanity and was awaiting my approval of his recent accomplishment. At the time, he had a full beard and so spent the remainder of the evening enduring the quite noble and selfless task of picking out bits of cake residue. I kept thinking to myself, "I wonder if any of my High School teachers ever exhibited this kind of behavior in their private lives?" It seemed utterly absurd, time-wasting, and, come to think of it, that's one more piece of cake I could have eaten.

Manipulatory Confidences

In retrospect, I feel that Don was attempting to gain my confidence as much as possible during this time. I didn't realize this until years later. However, a lot of things later added up. He was allegedly giving me LSD without my knowledge, which he admitted to me at a later date. He also knew I had a religious background, and talked to me a lot about eastern religions. He also had a copy of the Tibetan Book of the Dead or some other book by Paramahansa Yogananda in which it showed pictures of his body lying in state after his death. Laurie once told me that Yogananda's body was kept on display for several weeks and never began to decompose or give off any odors. I kept thinking to myself that after I die, I don't care whether my body smells good or bad, what's the big deal? Bury the damned thing and get on with it.

I was, however, intrigued by the combination of things we seemed to have in common. A strong interest in art, music and religion. When I was alone with him, he was always confiding in me. Many things he said to me had a theme of "You understand me, but those other guys never will." I happily donned this seal of approval as a member of the buddy of Don's club as any young lost soul would. I thought that perhaps I understood him better and he felt comfortable with me. Perhaps I was more open-minded, or maybe he was just schmoozing me.

In retrospect it seems more likely that it was some kind of manipulative tactic as I watched him behave quite similarly with Jeff Cotton, Bill Harkleroad, and Mark Boston as each of them joined the group.

New Rehearsal House

Don's mother, Sue, owned a rental house down the street and around the corner from where she lived. It was vacant at the time. So we switched our gear and began to rehearse there. It seems like it was getting close to Christmas 1966 and I am just guessing that perhaps Sue wanted to decorate the house for the holidays and felt that having four guitars amps and a drum set in her living room could have been detrimental to the overall effect.

Don managed to get a hold of a flute around this time. He started playing it all the time. However he failed to really get a tone out of it, because he blew far too hard. This merely caused him to hyperventilate. The resulting sensations of dizziness and rapid pulse combined with the mixed variety of psychedelics he was consuming were then conflated with an acute case of hypochondria, manifested in terms such as "I'm having a heart attack." I am sure that this reaction had a lot to do with his father's death, which seemed to haunt him for years.

One night he sat looking at the flute, he said to me, "One of these days, I'm going to have a soprano sax. One night with the soprano and a hit of acid and I'll have it down, man." I thought this was a strange approach to sax playing. It was quite a revelation that all those wasted years of drum practice could have been replaced with one single magical night with the drums and a good healthy dose of LSD. The things your parents don't tell you …

Hypochondria

As I mentioned before, Don's father had died a couple of years before. Right around Christmas, I believe. I recall Don having sunglasses on one night when I came by the house. There was a Christmas tree up, and Van Vliet took me over privately and said, "Sorry about the sunglasses, man, but the Christmas tree and all, it reminds me of my Father." I think he may have been crying a bit. One day during the holidays I showed up for rehearsal only to have Don announce to me through the screen door that he was seeing angels around him beckoning to him. This seemed to be yet another drug-related incident. Obviously, the red flags with the words "Get out of this band NOW!" were popping up all around. However, they must have been written in a foreign language, as I seemed oblivious to all warnings.

On a previous evening, I had mentioned that his diet seemed a little inadequate. He used to eat a hamburger and a piece of cheese and that was it - no vegetables, no fruit, no salads and no grains. I knew a little about balanced diets, because my mother was a nurse and therefore dinner always tasted just like hospital food, but actually was a pretty balanced meal. Balanced I say, according to what was known in the sixties about nutrition.

When I mentioned the idea of a balanced diet to him, he became extremely upset with me, and fearful at the same time. For months afterwards he would bring up the fact that "I was fine until *John* (italics indicate sneering tones) said that I wasn't *eating properly*." Of course, all I had actually done was make him aware of the consequences of continuing to eat nothing but a fried hamburger patty and piece of cheese for dinner night after night. His own drug-induced fears had greatly exaggerated my warning out of the bounds of normal perception. Pure concentrated hypochondria, caused by visions of death, began to haunt him.

His attacks were getting more and more frequent. He would take me aside, and have me feel his heart. There was seemingly no end to the questions he would ask me about health and diet, like I was really an expert. It was exasperating, but I felt a lot of compassion for him, because his father had died of a heart attack. Laurie started fixing other things for him to eat. She would say, " Eat it, Donald, it's *good* for you." This became kind of a joke with the rest of us. Anytime we were somewhere eating we would always tell each other it's "good for you" in a faux-Laurie tone. Alex seemed to especially enjoy this.

Fantastic Voyage

Don eventually confided in me that he had taken a large dose of LSD (evidently supplied by Cousin Victor) and had gone to see a movie called Fantastic Voyage. The movie was about some little miniaturized craft, shrunk by a laser beam (or perhaps your average household shrinker picked up at any convenience store) that made a trip through a human body. Somehow, this movie (which I recently viewed on Sci-Fi Network and noticed had incredibly bad special effects and a set that looked like the early Star Trek episodes) traumatized Don. I guess the special effects were enough in 1966 when combined with large quantities of pure Sandoz LSD to send Don's already vivid imagination into "Super-Psychosomatic Land with Streaks of New Neurosis," for an extended vacation.

It became increasingly difficult over the next few months, to deal with Don's anxiety and fears concerning his own mortality. This, compounded with his lack of ability to communicate musically, organize his lyrics, rehearse with the band and finish anything he started exponentially expanded the band's problems. He was afraid to perform or rehearse (nothing new there) for fear of a heart attack. I have never seen a person in such fear, and in my mind, at that time, he was behaving so irrationally that if he had been under psychiatric care, I believe he could have been temporarily institutionalized.

I looked up LSD on the internet and came up with the following information:

LSD may produce thick chronic visual "tracers" which interfere with vision. This is very rare, and is not "damage" per se since it is reversible with drug therapy (probably neuroleptics, but I'm not positive). Most users if they report anything report the benign type.

LSD may produce a syndrome resembling Post Traumatic Stress Disorder. This is due to a massively bad trip ... Here is where you get your honest-to-god flashbacks from. It's also not very common.

LSD may produce a schizophrenic break in someone already susceptible to schizophrenia, again due to the psychological trauma of an extraordinarily bad trip. This, however, is a case of "if it didn't happen on LSD, it would've happened at some point".

The frequency of the above three chronic effects is less than 2:1000 which is about the same as the "normal" frequency of schizophrenia in the population.
Conclusion: normal people that drop LSD remain normal people, people with schizophrenic tendencies or other psychological disorders get more fucked up.[28]

With a diagnosis like that, it makes me feel much more secure to know this information is out there, readily available on the Internet to help our teens in their decision-making concerning drugs.

Friendship With Alex

Alex and I began to get a little better acquainted. He seemed the kind of person who studied you from a distance for a while before deciding whether or not he liked you. He was always a man of few words. I guess I must have gained his trust, because he started talking to me a little about Don. Not much, but enough to let me know that he was a little fed up with "Vliet" (pronounced "Vleet") as he called him. Financially, we were all in need. Don's mother had some money laid away, probably from his father's life insurance or something. He didn't seem to be lacking anything. Anytime he needed some money, he would say, "Sue, godammit, gimme some MONEY!" and she would. The rest of us were broke. I was still working for the Salvation Army thrift store, but I was trying to help out at home with my paltry earnings.

Alex seemed very levelheaded. However, his weakness was alcohol, and his sights were far lower. The height of his ambition seemed to be to just start a good club band, play six nights a week, and get a paycheck and a free drink at every break. I'd already played enough clubs to know that it was a sleazy way to make a living and a dead-end road.

Struggling in the Desert

At some point during these early rehearsals, Alex and Jerry became more impatient and financially under duress. They had both moved in with their wives, Mary Jane and Sue, in little rental properties and were attempting to set up some kind of housekeeping. Both women were pregnant, so Alex and Jerry were facing imminent parenthood. Alex decided that we should play without Don (since he refused to play locally) in a little bar and make some money.

Don was outraged, because he said we were ruining the image of the band. I was living with my mother at the time, working about three hours a day, and helping with bills at home, so I had a little sense of responsibility. I felt that there was nothing wrong with playing locally to make a bit of extra money to help make ends meet until the legal problems were resolved.

Van Vliet's feelings towards Alex and Jerry's wives were described in terms such as (paraphrasing, but close) "I saw them coming miles away and tried to warn those guys. I knew those women would fuck things up. They both got knocked-up the same night". This led me to believe that the situation that Jerry and Alex found themselves in was the result of a dual one-night stand. For years, this was my image of their marriages. Jerry is still married today to the same woman, has a stable income, and enjoys his grandchildren. He's still one of the nicest people I've ever met, and the stability of his marriage proves to me that all this negativity was just Don being upset that things weren't going his way. Alex's marriage to Mary Jane ended in a divorce in the seventies.

---

[28]http://www.erowid.org/chemicals/lsd/lsd_info7.shtml, Date: 31 Aug 1992, Lamont Granquist

Mr. D's

Alex booked a gig for the Magic Band without Don at a local club called Mr. D's. The Beefheart band had often played there in between other bookings as a fill-in job. We practiced at Doug Moon's mother's house, and Alex informed me that everyone was fed up with Don. Again, they wanted to break off from him and go it alone. I didn't think it would work and that we would just wind up being a club band. The band personnel all seemed to share, and be satisfied with a fairly low expectation of the band's future. I was convinced that Don was striving for a much higher goal.

If I was going to play clubs, I would have rather gone back to working with my buddies andhad some fun. I had joined this band hoping it would be a good business move, besides being enjoyable.

We played the club gig, performing a lot of old blues junk and just basically winging it through a weekend or two. Alex and I did all of the singing and even harmonized a few tunes. It was a refreshing change just to get onstage and perform. Don was very upset with the whole situation. I didn't see him for a while. I can't remember how things were resolved.

John French: Do you remember playing a gig as The Magic Band at Mr. D's. (A small bar in Lancaster where the early Beefheart band sometimes appeared when not on tour)
Alex Snouffer: Yeah.
JF: We just went in because we needed money, and Don wouldn't go do it with us, and the manager said they'd hire the band without Don and we could just play. So, we just got a bunch of material together and just played. I think we got $40 bucks apiece per night for playing.
AS: Don was upset.
JF: Oh, he was VERY VERY, upset by that.
AS: Because we didn't do WHAT HE WANTED!
JF: Right, and he was living off mama and living at home. You had a little apartment over on 10th St. West with Mary Jane, and Jerry had a little house over by the High School with his wife Sue. You guys needed to make some money to pay your bills. I think your wife was working, and I know that Sue was. It was a mess for everybody. There were a lot of personal problems involved. Don (appeared) to think that the only thing important was total loyalty to whatever he thought was the right thing to do and if you went against that, he would go on a tirade.
AS: That's it in a nutshell.

Gas Pedal Sticks

For New Year's Eve 1966, Don decided to visit his cousin Terry, who lived in a small apartment in Hollywood. Laurie Stone came, as did Victor and Gary Lambert. We took Gary Lambert's Mark IX, a 1960 silver and black Jaguar Sedan with an XKE engine. As we neared the halfway point of the trip down to Hollywood - about an hour and fifteen-minute drive - the car started speeding up and Don became frantic, because the accelerator had stuck in full position. This full-sized car with five people in it was moving along at quite a pace and Don was turning in between cars to avoid a collision. He finally had to resort to shutting off the engine and steering onto the dirt divider in the center of the road, barely keeping control of the car.

This was the second such mishap in a car with Don in three months. I had never experienced this once in my 18 years, and I was becoming a little worried about riding with him. Although he did appear to be a good driver, it seemed more than coincidence that strange things were always happening to the cars he drove.

Terry Vliet

Terry welcomed us to his home, a small but nicely decorated apartment in Hollywood. I stepped into the door and realized that we weren't his only guests for the evening. Now, as I was saying earlier, I had started smoking marijuana, and what better night to smoke than New Year's Eve? So, I was a little taken aback to find the front door open to reveal six to eight people inside sitting in a brightly-lit living room, waiting to be introduced. The room was immaculately decorated. However unnerving this may have been to me, they were quite accommodating and I soon perceived the atmosphere as quite congenial. Soon after we arrived, I realized that Terry was homosexual, and had a live-in male partner (whose name escapes me).

This really didn't bother me on a personal level. Although I was taught as a child that homosexuality was immoral, I also maintain the perspective that what I *believe* is one thing, and what is *fact* could be quite another. I had high school art teachers who were gay and it really didn't bother me. They were nice people, at least to me, and they didn't seem to have anypolitical or personal agenda. I figured what they did in their private lives was their own personal business.

There was no hovering around to try to coerce me to join their club. (Bear in mind, this was my first real social encounter with gays, so I was treading lightly, not knowing if there were some special unspoken rules I may unknowingly break). They were listening to an opera on the stereo, which was playing at a suitable level for conversation. Unfortunately, there weren't enough seats for all of us, and Don went off into the kitchen with Terry almost immediately for a private conversation. I occasionally glanced in and they seemed to be having an intense discussion about decisions Don needed to make. This left Gary, Victor, Laurie and I on folding chairs or left standing between the kitchen door and the living room that made us feel a bit like we were on display.

The marijuana tended to intensify any paranoia and it seemed like the only person capable of answering an inquiry was me. The people there (there was one woman, a very elegant lady, as a matter of fact) started asking us questions as a group, and I began answering. Gary and Victor repeatedly looked at each other and giggled like schoolboys each time a question came our way, and Laurie was usually quiet around strangers. So, I told them about the band, where we were from, etc. Victor and Gary seemed amazed that I could function. I think we were served hors d'oeuvres and champagne.

I found Terry and his life partner to be reasonably nice people. There seemed to be no special watching of the clock for the New Year, and we left, driving home without mishap.

Hollywood Motel

Don took some band's funds and went to Hollywood staying in a motel with the aim of finding a record deal. When Doug and I went down to see how he was doing, he seemed a bit upset because we didn't have any money to give him. He claimed he had spent all of his trying to see agents etc. I felt bad that I had no money to give him, but I had used all the money I made to pay off the recently procured drumset that was the right color for the band. The tone of the conversation seemed to be that Van Vliet had spent his money trying to help us, while we were selfishly spending ours on ourselves. A few months later, forgetting this conversation Don told me that he had spent all his/our money on a hooker, describing the whole situation in detail.

No record deal came about as a result of this particular expedition into Hollywood. The band seemed to be going nowhere and I seemed to be going there with them. After being in this band for three months, I wasn't very impressed with what I saw.

To reiterate: Don was always busy doing exactly what he wanted, and seldom what needed to be done. We seldom if ever finished a song. He never rehearsed with us except to jam a blues now and then. I was using drugs, something I swore I'd never do. One of my best friends was dead as a direct result of drugs. The leader of the band I was in was constantly having some kind of paranoid delusions that he was dying; nonetheless, he was constantly telling me that I was the one who was confused.

At this point in time, I wanted to leave the whole thing behind me. I figured that nothing could be worse than staying. Then I thought of the Vietnam War, and my dead-end life in Lancaster, working for the Salvation Army Thrift store making $23 a week and playing with my former band, a band whose members seemed to jump at any alternative that came along. I didn't feel that I could go back, but I didn't feel we were going forward either.

CHAPTER ELEVEN

FEARING FAME

...ion in Spring '67, a fabulous shot courtesy of Guy Webster.

Moving To Laurel Canyon

In January of 1967, it seemed there was hope the contractual problems with A&M were getting resolved. It was during this period that Don tried strongly to persuade everyone that a move to Hollywood was in order. He kept saying we had to get "out of here", meaning the desert, specifically Lancaster. I couldn't have agreed with him more on this point. The others did not seem so thrilled with the idea. I was ready to flee the nest and have a taste of freedom. Unfortunately, I later realized my wings weren't quite as well developed as I had thought. This was to be the first of many moves I would make while in the Magic Band.

We did one more car club dance, and made enough to rent a place in Laurel Canyon. Renting a big truck, we drove it to Sue's Carolside house and opening, the garage door, we found the garage was filled with furniture - presumably from the rental that Sue had sold or possibly from Granny Annie's house. Sue was present, trying to supervise what was taken and what was left. Don and she quarreled over certain items, while we all stood waiting for decisions to be made. Eventually, certain items were agreed upon and the process began. I noticed that Don hardly lifted a finger to help move anything. He seemed to always be preoccupied with something or disappear whenever there was any real work to be done.

Then Alex, Jerry and I came to my house and loaded up my stuff. I had never moved away from home before, and thinking this to be more of a permanent thing, I just indiscriminately packed everything I had stored away. As we were loading the boxes, the bottom fell out of a big one, and on the ground spilled, among other things, my childhood crayons. Inadvertently, I had packed some of my childhood things that were in a small box I had thrown in the larger one. I didn't realize what was in it.

Alex took one look and began laughing. I don't blame him. It was pretty amusing. Potential rock-star caught with crayons! What would the fans think? I was quite embarrassed, and took the box back in to repack, making sure to leave the crayons behind this time (although I did have second thoughts about including my Viewmaster 3-D viewer and the Lady and the Tramp slides). I mention this story just to show how young and naïve I was at the time.

Alex and Jerry left with the truck. I was to ride down later that evening with Doug. As the truck drove away, one of the neighbor ladies noticed that I was moving. She approached the house and began chastising me for moving away from my mother, "just when she needed me most." She went on and on. I was told I wasn't being a good son, my father had deserted and it was up to me to be the man of the house and I had no business going off with these "long-haired scalawags" (her words) and nothing good would come of it. They would probably wind up getting me on drugs and my life would be ruined.

Actually, most of what she said came true. No good came of the band, I was already on drugs, and my mother went through some really tough times. Along with the crayon incident, this did nothing to brighten the day.

Amor Road

I rode with Doug later that night in his Corvette to the house we had rented. A little over an hour and we were there. He kept saying things like, "We're getting close!" - like a father talking to his kids about Disneyland - "It's just around the next curve." We crossed Mulholland Drive and started down toward Hollywood, the road curved right and then back left. We finally arrived at a nice looking house on the corner of Amor Road and Laurel Canyon Boulevard. The truck was being unloaded as we pulled up by Alex and Jerry.

So, I stepped out of the car and looked at my first home away from home, so to speak. This is the first time I had actually been on my own and I felt intensely queasy and homesick about all that was happening. All these great memories from my childhood flickered by in little strobe-like images. Fortunately, teenagers have a built-in insensitivity to such things and the nostalgia left within the hour and never returned.

We finally got things together enough to go to bed. I awoke in the morning with Alex standing at the foot of my bed going, "John, man are you OK?" I opened my eyes and he was standing with a really concerned look on his face. "Man, you looked so still laying there with your mouth open, I thought you had croaked or something," he said. I laid in bed laughing for about five minutes. I had the reputation at home of being a heavy sleeper, but Alex was not yet used to the catatonic depths to which slumber took me. Once as a child, a bed collapsed while I was asleep. It made a horrible noise that woke up the entire household, who then gathered in my room and tried to put the bed back together to no avail – dropping it several more times in the process. I slept soundly through the entire incident, waking up to find the bed in shambles but myself unharmed and thoroughly rested.

The next few days were taken up with setting up the equipment and getting organized. Our new headquarters was a fairly nice three-bedroom house. I shared a room with Jerry that had its own half-bath. Alex and Doug bunked together. Don and Laurie took the small bedroom which was also the only house entrance to the music room.

The music room was a wedge-shaped room between the house and the garage. It could have been built as an addition. Because of the shape of the room, and its design, it was partially surrounded by other rooms - the garage, the living room, and Don's bedroom - with the exception of the short five-foot wall that made up the smallest portion of the wedge and part of the wall, which it didn't share with the living room. It had an entry door into the garage, and across from that another door that was the entrance to Don's room. It was an ideal rehearsal room, because all we had to do was cover the windows on the one outside wall, and it was fairly soundproof.

Alex Snouffer: *Well, that was during the* **Safe As Milk** *recording bullshit, you know. I had a lot of things on my mind around that time. Jane (wife) was due any day. (Regarding) the move down there - I missed a lot of stuff. Some of it I missed on purpose, other things just went by me or I wasn't there or whatever the hell. I was along for the ride about that time.*

This apathy went completely unrecognized by me at the time. Alex was there for every rehearsal and learned all his parts with no problem. Yet, for anyone who has faced parenthood for the first time, it's easy to realize that he must have been not only under a lot of stress, but having a hard time keeping his patience through the days that were to come.

We actually didn't have a record contract then. This was basically a leap of faith move, in that we had almost no resources but were just hoping for the best. The reality of this hit home very soon, as I looked in an empty refrigerator for breakfast – a view which would become quite familiar in the days to come. Many days were spent with little or no food and we were all under the stress of trying to learn how to get along with each other while living in the same house. For me, it was doubly difficult to adjust, having never been on the road at all and only knowing my fellow band members for about three months. I also had never really had to share a room as the youngest of my three older brothers had moved out when I was six.

Meanwhile, wheels were turning. Attorney Jay Cooper was across town in Beverly Hills negotiating with A&M for a release from the contract. Unbeknownst to us, a guy named Bob Krasnow, a veteran promotion man who was now working for Kama Sutra Records, was seeking to find one Captain Beefheart after hearing *Diddy Wah Diddy* and deciding this singer was the next Mick Jagger. A counterculture was developing, changing the whole face of the Sunset Strip and the music business in general.

Early Amor Road Efforts

But we were all in a little house on Amor Road busy setting up our instruments, tuning drums and guitars. The band was basically aware of one really important fact: the music was not finished. If someone just came to the house and said, "Play," we would have been clueless on all but one or two songs as to how to begin and end the songs. The arrangements were still a shambles. We tried in different ways to explain this to Don.

One impromptu meeting I recall happened in the late morning as we were standing in the kitchen. Don was saying that we needed to get a recording contract. I interjected that *our first step should be to finish the songs, so that we had a product.* Van Vliet's response was to turn to me and say something to the effect of: "Don't ever talk to me that way again, man, you understand?"

This was done with a certain body language that suggested violence would be the result of my not understanding. It was dead silent. No one came to my defense, and it was obvious that Don was behaving as a typical alpha male as this type of macho crap is now called. I swallowed my pride and said I understood, but what I was actually understanding was that one could not express a view that countered Don's in any kind of group setting. I had seen traces of this before, but that morning a whole new level of this was revealed to me.

Cantor's

Don asked me to take a ride with him one evening soon after our move. As we were driving, he started telling me about his sex life with his girlfriend, Laurie. I really liked Laurie and I thought it was quite disrespectful to talk about one's girlfriend in such a manner. I told him I didn't want to hear any more. It was one of the few times in these early days that I stood up to him. He was actually quite understanding, and apologized. He seemed puzzled at my reaction, however, so I explained. I didn't want to think about *his girlfriend* this way, because we were all living in the same house together. This seemed to satisfy his curiosity and we drove on.

We were driving south on Laurel Canyon into Hollywood, and he didn't seem to know where he was going. We passed the old Tom Mix cabin on the right, and the little Laurel Canyon store on the left. Once we actually turned onto Crescent Heights and arrived at Sunset Boulevard, he would turn one way and then another. It seemed like whatever our original motive had been in coming to town was lost.

Suddenly, he stopped at a place called Cantor's. I had never been there before. Cantor's is the Jewish deli in Hollywood. I don't know if it was my first visit there or not. I just remember that we went to the pastry counter and were ordering some goodies and all of a sudden a deep voice said, "Captain Beefheart". These two guys came walking up. They definitely recognized Don. They began by introducing themselves. Bob Krasnow was one fellow and I was sure for years that the other was Richard Perry from Kama Sutra Records. However, recent articles I've read have convinced me that I may have been mistaken about Perry, because he supposedly didn't come to California until later. I was positive that it was Perry who was with Krasnow. They said they had been sitting together one recent evening listening to *Diddy Wah Diddy* over and over, and had decided that they must have this man on their label because of his incredible vocal style. Don introduced me as the drummer, but they barely acknowledged my existence (which caused me to immediately start identifying with the chopped liver).

They had come out to California looking for Don with the express idea of signing him to a contract. However, no one seemed to know how to get in touch with him. At this, Don turned to me with that cosmic look of one who has been spiritually inspired - the same look he had given me in John Stewart's studio when the spider appeared.

Later, as he announced this news to the band, he focused quite strongly on the theory that he had been led there by forces unknown. I was very impressed with anything dealing with psychic phenomena in those days. Even in the song *Electricity* there was a theme of telepathy and oneness of mankind based on a flow of thought or spirit that could flow through enlightened people. I was still pretty much convinced at this point that Don was somehow enlightened. This had a great deal to do with how I reacted to him and why I appeared to be under his power.

However, Jerry had a slightly different perspective on this occurrence ...

John French: So, maybe that's true, maybe some antennae was picking up that he was supposed to be somewhere and that some little meeting of his future destiny was going to take place and it somehow subconsciously led him there.
Jerry Handley: Either that or fuckin' luck.

Whether or not the mountain came to Muhammad or Muhammad went to the mountain, the band was pretty relieved that some connection had been made so soon after our move. There was an attitude of "maybe things would work out after all."

Criticism and Self Esteem
Handley expressed the view that reflected the general consensus of the band during this period.

Jerry Handley: We weren't in a position to be negotiating, we didn't have a hit record. Our fame was like the old saying, "I'm a legend in my own mind," so that's where we were.

This lack of esteem was partially brought on by the usual things musicians have to struggle against: poverty, the image of being social outcasts, the two-year struggle with no breakthrough, the feeling of being adrift - no real home life, and the personal differences and struggles within the group. I also feel that a primary source of low self-esteem for the group was the lack of respect, which Don displayed when speaking to or about anyone in the band. He seemed to address us all as silly children, irresponsible childish good-for-nothings who couldn't even *play*. The latter part of that image was generously bestowed upon Doug for the most part, with Jerry coming in a moderate second. Alex was still musically respected. I suppose that because I was the *new guy*, my drumming was praised, but my opinions for the most part were brushed aside and I was constantly being reprimanded (quite publicly) for doing *lame* things, probably due to my age.

This word *lame*, I use in the vernacular of the time. It meant *unhip*, or *naïve* - inappropriate behavior.

This is not to say that there weren't certain behavior patterns in the band that reinforced this criticism. Doug was probably the most susceptible to drugs and the least able to handle them and this often made him the target of Don's wrath. I always felt that Doug had struggled with some deep emotional conflict that left him slightly scarred. His reaction to any hostile environment was to withdraw and escape by smoking a joint, thus distorting his perspective. From almost the day we moved into the Amor Road house, Doug began to withdraw, but not without reason. Van Vliet seemed to make it his daily task to somehow take the offensive position with Doug on any number of topics. Mostly, his playing was attacked.

Gary Marker: I remember being there one night where Don was doing his thing where he was bouncing around on his chair and he was getting on in one of those meetings? You know? I think this was the house in Laurel Canyon. "This is the goddamned guy right over here! It's all his fault," pointing at Doug.

It is interesting to me to have seen the contrast between this guy, who I will probably refer to more and more as The Captain, exhibiting this kind of ferocious and intimidating anger, and Don, the rather soft-spoken, polite, sensitive guy who wore pajamas and carried a toothbrush with him everywhere. It was very confusing to me to equate these two contradictory behavior patterns as coming from the same person.

I couldn't help but wonder at how Jerry had spent his time while we were living in Laurel Canyon. He went out and bought model cars - those little plastic kits - and built them. The guy was 23 years old with a pregnant wife, and he was building model cars. I couldn't figure it. To make things worse, he decided that the best place to lay out all the little pieces and the big piece of paper that told how all the little pieces went together was on my bed. If I wanted to go relax, I couldn't. Don came to me one day and said, "What the fuck is he doing that for?" I couldn't help but share his wonder (although I probably privately kicked myself again for not bringing my 3-D Viewmaster).

This probably is one of the reasons Jerry was later attacked by the Captain as "that goddammed guy over there" who "can't remember his bass parts." Jerry did seem to allow himself to get distracted a bit, but not nearly as much as Doug. During the recordings, Jerry only had problems with two songs in the studio, and the rest of the session he played quite well.

In retrospect it seems to me that Jerry was probably doing the same thing with the cars as I had earlier been doing with the comic books: trying to escape. I know Jerry was under a lot of pressure, facing parenthood, dealing with arrangements that Don seem to be changing every day. The spare time could be maddening, so perhaps he did this to turn his mind off for a while.

Although Alex seemed balanced enough, he had certain weaknesses, which I mostly heard about from Don. Don always said that Alex was an alcoholic, which was probably true. The stigma attached to this in 1967 was quite a bit more severe than it is now. I had a certain amount of fear of this side of Alex, probably due to my father getting drunk and starting fights with me when I was a teen. (He once tried to break my fingers and I slammed him down in a chair and ran out.) However, I can never remember Alex ever showing up for anything in an intoxicated state. Whatever drinking he did was on his own time. He was totally dependable. Also, I really don't recall ever seeing him drunk, although I knew he liked to drink.

Ry Cooder once mentioned how he had observed during an early visit to the desert that Beefheart seemed to have everyone scared to death. He couldn't decide whether it was a true fear being manifested, or an act the band did to please him. He speculated that it may be that Don would become this authoritarian shouting figure just to get everybody up, like a football coach with his team. He later decided that the whole thing was an act. Whether or not it was an act on his part, I did not know at this time, but I knew I wasn't acting. I knew that there was something about him that scared me, and it kept me a bit on guard all the time when he was around.

Kama Sutra

The Kama Sutra/Buddha Records office was on Sunset Boulevard. The old Original Sound recording studio was upstairs and the sign still stood. This is probably where Sandy Nelson, my original drum inspiration, had done all his recordings. I was a little excited by this. Ironically, I later discovered that it had purportedly been designed by Paul Buff - the same man who had built Studio Z (called PAL studios during his reign) in Cucamonga and later left to Frank's care.

Buff had recorded the Surfaris' hit *Wipe Out*, along with *Pipeline* by the Chantays – two big surf hits in Southern California. When he moved, he worked with Art Laboe at Original Sound, recording such groups as the Strawberry Alarm Clock and Sugarloaf.

We went in the office to find ourselves facing a long hallway lined with doors. The blonde receptionist, Linda, sat at the end of the hall, her hair in double braids. Apparently the office had not been there very long, as they had no intercom.

Linda's job was to answer the phone, make inquiries, put the person on hold and scream "BOB, IT'S JAY! ARE YOU IN?" and similar things, at the top of her lungs. She had to project her voice into all the offices, with doors ajar. This she did endlessly all day long. I wouldn't have wanted to get into any kind of verbal confrontation with this girl, because she seemed like the blonde from hell. Her picture appears on the original *Safe As Milk* dust cover. Anyway we walked up and Don said he was there to see Krasnow. "Name?" she inquired, loud enough to be heard in Long Beach. "Captain Beefheart," Don answered. "CA..." (hesitation and a quick look back at Don and slight questioning frown) - "CAPTAIN BEEFHEART FOR BOB KRASNOW !"

"Captaaaaaaiiiiiiiiiiiinnnnnn," Krasnow purred as he raced out of his office, smiling with hand extended, to greet Don. Here was a man who had the appearance of a mobster love-child. He was dark-complexioned and slightly balding with curly hair cut close to his head. He wore a bright paisley shirt and love beads and was dripping with the kind of affected schmoozy charm one had to develop when working with people who had high opinions of themselves. He invited us into his office, and immediately we spent an hour being constantly interrupted by phone calls he "just had to take." This man could change personalities and voice tonalities with each call and was obviously good at working a phone. His energy level was quite high.

He must have talked to 15 people while we were there. In between each call, and during breaks in the calls themselves, little pieces of conversation would ensue. This mostly consisted of him making rapid-fire inquiries such as "So, how much material do you guys have together?" and then, as Don would answer it would become evident that he didn't hear a word of the reply because he was listening to the person on the phone. The subtle clue that gave this away was when in the middle of Don's answer Bob would say something like "Heavy, baby!" to the guy on the phone. This was all punctuated by the soothing sound of Linda screaming "BOB - LARRY, LINE THREE!"

Alex Snouffer: Krasnow was just Krasnow, you know what I mean? He was a hustler.

After an hour of pleasant non-communication, it was determined that the next step would be for us to submit a demo tape so that they could hear what we were up to. We walked out the door after bidding farewell and burst into spontaneous laughter at the whole scene. All the people in the office were East Coast people and obviously felt very comfortable with each other. It was very laid back, chaotic, and informal, unlike what any of us were expecting. The usual West Coast type of office setting was very conservative and quiet. Like going to the library. This was much more interesting.

Demo Tape

We made a demo tape in our little improvised studio. I was put in charge of setting up the recording equipment so we could make the tape. Our equipment consisted of a couple of reel-to-reel tape decks my father had given me, a few beat-up microphones, and a bunch of broken down cables and adapters. I was really exhausted after attempting to piece something together. I had gotten so tired that I had fallen asleep on the couch in the living room. Doug came and awakened me. He handed me a red pill that looked like an M&M. I recognized it as a diet pill (prescription methadrine) a girl had given me. I gave it to Doug for safekeeping. He said, "Remember you told me to give you this when I thought you needed it? Well, I think you need it now." Laughing, he walked off.

I took this pill and within an hour, my pupils were the size of the moon and stayed that way all night. I looked like an owl. Van Vliet was worried about me. I put together a homemade recording studio out of old mattresses, lamps, and anything else I could throw together. I think that is why even today, I still hate *talking* about the technical end of music. When somebody starts rattling off to me about automated mixers and digital tape, I start yawning. We were supposed to have some kind of demo tape done before we went out shopping for a deal (remember my earlier suggestion about *finishing* the material before trying to sell it?). These were the good old days when you didn't have to go into a studio and finish your album out of your own pocket. Record companies heard the potential in these little home tapes, gave you a deal, and poof! There were some songs that had already been demo-ed, so basically I just edited everything we had on to one tape. We wound up using previously recorded tapes.

Unfortunately, nobody had bothered to give me any new tape. We had no money to buy one. I wound up using some old tape my father had given me. My father had this hobby of recording stuff off the radio and also made recordings of my family playing and singing. The tape I was using was of my Uncle John playing the violin. I was erasing it as we recorded.

At the end of one of our songs, I forgot to turn off the machine after a playback, and suddenly, there was my Uncle John playing violin. Kid that I was, I said, "That's my Uncle, man!" This threw Alex into hysterical laughter (similar to the crayon incident). Anything that had to do with family or closeness seemed to be very un-hip to Alex. I didn't understand in my naivete that it wasn't hip to have enjoyed being close to your family and how much of a kid I must have seemed to the rest of the band. As I look back now, I realize that I may have had a much happier childhood than he. Of course, at the time, I just felt lame.

Don was so unfocused that rather than just record a few things we already had at least basically arranged and rehearsed, he started working on a completely new song called *Chasin' Neva Will*. The lyrics were basically written before I joined the band and I recall a few lines;

> House o'six sittin'way up on a hill
> Moon in its kitchen, sunset neva will
> Be out on Tuesday if I pay my bill,
> Chasin' neva will
> Chasin' neva will

There was also another song worked out during this session that was never used. The music later became recycled for *Smithsonian Institute Blues* (from *Lick My Decals Off, Baby*) with a different bass part. Originally, the music was to a song called *Sugar Honey Sugar*, and seemed to be based on the lyrical theme of blues bassist Willie Dixon's *Spoonful:*

> Honey you want some sugar in yours?
> Yeah sugar honey sugar,
> (repeat first two lines)
> Face in my coffee, hands in my tea
> Lotta funny-looking people standin''round watchin'me.

So he just started working with Alex on new parts for these songs. I remember some of the riffs even now. We spent hours on these songs, and I believed we did get a take of *Chasin' Neva Will*. Yet I felt our little home demo session was somewhat a waste of time, since neither of these songs wound up on *Safe As Milk* – or any other Beefheart album. Don also kept joking around with Alex about the little "studio" I had devised, using mattresses and blankets to help soundproof the room and keep the instruments somewhat isolated. He said that the mood of the room just made him want to sing the blues, and he did just that for about an hour and a half. We just did all those old blues tunes for which the band had previously become so well known.

I was angry, because I had been up all night putting together this stuff so that we could submit somewhat of a demo tape. Don, the leader, instead of having a list together, just seemed to want to party and laugh about the mood of the room. I was really serious about getting something done that we could take to Krasnow. At the end of the night, it turned out we only had the one or two new things. Everything else was basically a blues jam.

Because I was so tired, I was very irritable. Later that day, in the late afternoon, I was trying to get the only song we had actually recorded spliced onto a demo of stuff previously done. The tape recorder went nuts and all the tape wound up on the floor. I cursed really loud just as Don walked in with a cute teenage girl about sixteen from down the street.

He verbally admonished me for my terrible language (though I'd heard him use the same many times with far more intensity in front of whoever he pleased) and demanded that I apologize to the young lady, whose name was Judy Whaley. This was when I first began to sense a contrast between the public and the private side of Don's personality. He could be extremely charming and thoughtful, and usually appeared this way on the private, social level. I'm talking about situations in which he needed to be on his best behavior in order to give a particularly good impression of himself. Privately however, in the context of business, he could be a complete tyrant, verbally abusive not only to the band, but to his own girlfriend. I apologized to the girl, barely noticing her at the moment as I was fascinated by this observation of the two Dons, and pre-occupied with the demo tape.

I found myself continually resenting situations like this, in which I was struggling to do something that needed to be done, while Don was off socializing with the neighborhood babes, or hanging out with the Kama Sutra crowd. Alex and Jerry were gone. Doug was in his room. This was the beginning of a long pattern of such situations in which I would find myself in the future.

Second Appointment

An appointment was made, and our demo tape was taken in to the Kama Sutra office. Don and Alex went, I believe, to the office on Sunset Boulevard. I recall Alex and Don coming back and having a few laughs about some of the cultural differences between these East Coast Guys and us "normal people." I inquired about the demo tape on which I had worked so furiously. It turned out that it wouldn't play on their machine, which was a two-track - a different kind of format from the four-track stereo I had used to record on. All that work had been for nothing.

John French: What was your impression of Bob Krasnow, Richard Perry and Artie Ripp and the whole Kama Sutra bunch?
Alex Snouffer: Artie Ripp was a joke. I don't care what his position was as president or how much money he had, he was a joke. Richard Perry was obviously the only one that had his act together and ...
JF: And went on to prove it.
AS: Yeah.

In terms of the actual production of *Safe As Milk*, there is a general agreement that it wasn't produced well and sounded thin. This may seem in contradiction to what is being said here but in actuality is not. Perry, inexperienced at this time, and though producing a disappointing overall sound, held things together and contributed an integrity that Ripp and Krasnow did not. It was this very consistency that later helped him develop into a recognized and respected producer. These traits are what Alex and I both viewed at the time and were referring to in the above exchange.

Anxiety Attacks

During this period, Van Vliet seemed to start having more problems with the anxiety attacks.

John French: Do you recall Don's anxiety attacks? Where he'd think he was having a heart attack?
Jerry Handley: Well, he'd say he was, yeah.
JF: He thought he was having a heart attack, and then he would drive himself to the

hospital because he didn't want anyone else driving his car.
JH: Right (laughter) Laurie had him eating too many vegetables. That was why he was having anxiety attacks.
JF: He started having these attacks and he would say, "Feel my heart, John,"
JH: Yeah, I remember that!

Jerry and I made light of this because as a band we had to in order to keep our sanity. This kind of activity from Van Vliet was unending and would have driven us crazy had we not developed a sense of humor about it. Yet, everyone did make an attempt to really listen to Van Vliet and understand whether this was just in his head or something serious that we ought to be concerned about. Don did seem very convincing one evening and was clutching his heart. We walked out to his car and Alex said, "Give me your keys," and Don said, "Uh, no, I can drive." Alex and I sort of looked at each other incredulously and got in the car. He drove to UCLA medical center and had tests done. I waited in the car in the parking lot for what seemed like a VERY long time.

Don finally returned. The doctor determined that he was having anxiety attacks. I surmise it was probably due to the stress of all the behind-the-scenes things that were happening at the time. It seemed ludicrous to me at the time, because Don actually had more support and help than anyone else. He was able to get money from his mother just about any time he wanted. He also had his girlfriend cooking, washing his clothes, and basically being his servant. I was filling-in and doing a lot of errands for Don that Laurie couldn't handle, like running tape recorders, setting up mikes and remembering guitar parts that he would write when the guitar players weren't around. Alex and Jerry were both dealing with new families and all the pressures that entailed. They were doing much more commuting than the rest of us because their wives both still lived in the desert.

But he did actually go to UCLA medical center, complaining of chest pains and not being able to breathe and that stuff. They gave him Librium and said he was having anxiety attacks. He would freak out. It started out in the desert. When he was taking acid. He would grab me and say, "John, I'm seeing angels! I think I'm dying! They're all around me." I thought, "That's an interesting pathway." Anyway, I was trying to be open with him, you had to be really open minded, but he was having freak-out attacks and he did go to the hospital and did get tranquilizers, which triggered what happened next.

I can understand his anxiety more in light of my recent discoveries. I was unaware at the time of many of the facts concerning the actual clandestine business negotiations. In light of these facts, Van Vliet probably had a great deal about which to be anxious.

Moon's impression, which may be partially valid, was that the anxiety had to do with Don's inability to communicate musical ideas:

John French: Remember when he'd have these anxiety attacks and he thought he was having a heart attack? You recall much of that?
Doug Moon: Oh, yeah! "You guys, look what you're doing to me!"
JF: Right, he'd blame us. All we were doing is trying to figure out what the heck he was talking about. "What do you want to do here, Don?"
DM: He was so frustrated, because he couldn't explain, he couldn't play an instrument well enough to convey the musical thought he was trying to get across, so he was inhibited by that and he would get anxiety attacks.

This may partially explain Don's anxiety. He was quite limited in his ability to communicate musically, and was trying to get his creative ideas across by whistling and humming. Of course, this limited him to a single note at a time, so he couldn't explain chords or harmonies.

Another Fake Heart Attack

We had several band talks or meetings during these early days on Amor Road. Most of them were un-planned band meetings. There was no television, so we would group together in the evenings and sometimes conversations would ensue. One particular evening, shortly after moving to Amor Road and before Ry began as musical director, the discussion became a bit heated. Don was constantly talking about his health, and the problems with his heart. This usually would wind up being blamed on somebody, often Doug, who was the convenient scapegoat for Van Vliet.

In an unusual moment of clarity, not to mention courage, Laurie submitted her thoughts. She suggested to Don, in front of the entire band, that perhaps he was just afraid of success. Behind closed doors, we had all considered this, but no one had actually had the nerve to talk to Don about it due to fear of the expected response. There was a moment of silence, in which the musicians sat carefully pretending not to be scrutinizing Don to see his reaction.

His reaction was absolutely predictable. Instead of considering the suggestion at all, Don began to rant at Laurie. The bulk of the monologue seemed to contain ideas such as: Laurie was NOT a part of the band, therefore had no right to speak; that was an absurd notion, why on earth would he be afraid of success? What gave her the right to feel she could speak this way to Don?

Needless to say, the meeting ended, and everyone who had a car disappeared. Although Snouffer recalls the evening slightly differently, I believe it was at this time that Don had another anxiety attack and he and Alex left and supposedly went to the hospital.

John French: Do you remember anything about Don's anxiety attacks?
Alex Snouffer: Oh yeah.
JF: He thought he was having heart attacks. What do you remember about that?
AS: Funniest one I remember was one night Don and I were around the house, not doing anything and Don, all of a sudden, "Oh God, I think I'm having a heart attack," you know, and he didn't let me in on any of this yet. He says, "Alex, come on! I'm gonna go to the hospital." So we'd walk out of the house, and I'd think, well, he's not having a heart attack, but something's going on. I say, "Give me the keys and I'll drive." And he'd say, "Oh no, I'll drive." (Laughter) And I thought, "Busted, you motherfucker."
JF: Exactly.
AS: Yeah, we went cruising for chicks. That was it.
JF: Really?
AS: Yeah, that was just an excuse to get out of the house to get away from Laurie
JF: To get away from Laurie?
AS: Yeah, cause he and I had gone to the zoo one day, and we met these two sisters who were from up here (Lancaster) and we hadn't seen them in years, and they were both foxes. So we walked around the zoo with them and set up a date for that night. So then, I had Fran's pickup truck at that time, and Don made some lame excuse up to Laurie, you know, so Don and I took off up to Woodland Hills and spent the night with the chicks.
JF: Oh, OK. So what was the prognosis of that evening?
AS: Pretty decent night out on the town.

Well, it may have been a decent night out on the town for Don and Alex, but it may never have occurred to either of them that we were in suspense until the next day, late morning, when both of them showed up. Jerry and his visiting wife went to bed, Doug finally crashed out, but Laurie and I were up all night. Her boyfriend had left the evening before thinking he was dying. He had made a big deal out of it, clutching his chest, feeling his heart, and generally staggering around. They had been gone for over 12 hours. We didn't have a phone at the house, and no transportation was available. I wound up trying to keep Laurie from being worried all night. A lot of stuff was going through my head also. What if Don was actually hospitalized and something happened? What if he couldn't sing any more? What would become of the group and the contract?

When they returned, Don was exhausted and made up some unbelievable half-hearted story. I never realized until hearing Alex's story that he had lied about the whole thing and that it was a ruse so that he and Alex could go party with babes. The funny thing is, they kept making jokes about a girl saying "lookit'the cute little water otter," which was obviously something one of the sisters said at the zoo.

Psychosomatic

One night, Van Vliet got up in a complete frenzy and insisted that he again be taken to UCLA medical center. The people at UCLA had ascertained that he was having anxiety attacks and that his chest pains were psychosomatic.

I had never heard of this last term, so it opened up a whole world of new dilemmas as I learned about psychosomatic illness. Don was very anxious, however, and so that much made sense. He thought he was months away from superstardom. We all did at this time because that was what Bob Krasnow was telling us, that we would be "bigger than the Rolling Stones." It was a stressful time. My biggest stress, however, was dealing with Don's stress. On the one hand I often had to treat him like a mother would treat a child – speaking soothing and encouraging words and trying to convince him that his health was OK. On other occasions, he acted like he was my dysfunctional father. I was still a kid, so he probably felt like he had to keep me in line when I lost my temper or did something foolish. Then he would turn around and do something really ridiculous, like stay up all night before an important rehearsal or recording session. Don seldom apologized for any thoughtless act or assumed any accountability for his irresponsibility. He seemed to have had an image of himself as being beyond the drudgery of anything resembling work.

Alex Snouffer: That whole thing was bordered around ... we'd have a song or songs down and now we needed to rehearse with Don. Even though we weren't going to be doing it in the studio with him, HE needed the rehearsal, so he could go in the studio and do it. But he kept coming up with all these excuses. And then when he finally ran out of excuses, you notice, and all of a sudden it's time to shit or get off the pot, all of a sudden, he'd have a "heart attack." My God, I've never seen a person have so many heart attacks and still survive. (Laughter)

John French: Yeah, he was doing a lot of acid when I first got in the band. I came to rehearsal – you know, I'm like eighteen years old – I came to rehearsal and he goes, "John! John man! I think I'm gonna die, man, I'm seeing angels! They are all around!" I'd say, "No, you're probably OK. You look pretty healthy!"
Gary Marker: Yeah, well that was the whole thing. You see, he would pull this shit all the time. He'd keep – everyone around him was always slightly off-kilter. He couldn't let things proceed in a normal orderly manner.
JF: Yeah, well then everybody would see how screwed up he was!
GM: They'd see how screwed up he was, but then he was ingenious enough that everybody would worry about him. He'd get everybody worrying about him. "Everything's going to be OK. You're not going to die, don't worry about it, Don." That kinda stuff. It would just never stop. It got really exhausting. He's exhausting to be around. He's like one of these emotional black holes. He sucks everything into himself.
JF: Yeah, I would get just worn out working with him, and I'd leave. I was in and out of that band a lot of times.

Topanga Corral

The band finally got so broke and hungry that Gary Marker talked us into doing what Don considered the unthinkable. We played a gig at the Topanga Corral. This was basically a biker bar that I think must have been the Canned Heat's home away from home. The Topanga Corral performance represented a couple of week's groceries in return for merely entertaining people who looked more like upright de-horned oxen in cutoff Levi jackets.

As I carried the bass drum in, a few of these castoffs from the Island of Dr. Moreau looked at what I was carrying as if asking themselves "Is that edible?" I myself was reciting that prayer that says "Yea, though I walk through the valley of death." After about 30 seconds, I had already resigned myself to the fact that I was going to die. I bravely faced this truth, adjusting my hi-hat and quietly tuning my snare drum – most likely for the very last time ...

Doug Moon seemed to be fairly at home, as did the rest of the guys. "You shoulda seen some of the places we played in Bakersfield," Alex reassuringly said. "This is Romper Room, man." The band was well-received, and I was, well, relieved. During the first break, I didn't leave the stage. I just sat on the drums and leaned against the wall, hoping to become invisible. By the end of the second set, I finally summoned the courage, or was forced by nature, to visit the men's room. As I walked across the open floor, I heard a loud warlike scream and turned in horror to see one of the denim-clad upright bullocks running toward me, arms outstretched.

He enveloped me in a bear hug, lifted me off the floor and swung me around in a circle, my feet sweeping nearby tables clean of glasses, ashtrays, beer bottles, and the heads of the unconscious. Suddenly I was freed, my head spinning, and dizzily I walked to the men's room thinking, "So, this is what death is like." Don saw my dilemma and walked over, "Hey, man, he's trying to show you he LIKES you. That's all." "How nice," I thought, "maybe I can invite him over for tea and crumpets."

Band Equipment

Doug was an electronics-minded person, a geek as he described himself. He had obtained a ham radio license. I think he had built some of his own equipment. He had worked with my father on the electrical systems of jet aircraft in the aerospace factory. He was able to read schematics and do all kinds of advanced technical work. He also played a pretty mean harp, and still does. A few years back I was subbing for a drummer in a club, and Doug came and sat in and played harmonica. It was dead-on. Doug had the best equipment in my estimation. I helped him rewind his Stratocaster Pickups, which made them much more powerful. Sitting for hours, I held the large roll of hair-thin copper wire as he wound the pickups with hundreds of winds (which he had to count, as I recall). His guitar body was sanded to plain wood and varnished. He used that for his straight guitar, and had another small hollow body Gibson for bottleneck. He had in/out phase switches and could get incredible sounds. I don't remember the model of his amp. It was small, but he had one big 15" speaker in it. It seemed large for the amp. His equipment always sounded great.

Alex played a Stratocaster, as I recall, through a Bassman amp. Jerry Handley had a Gibson hollow body bass through a Vox Bass amp.

Marker's Ideas

Since many of the songs, including Electricity, were written before I joined, I was often interested in how they came about. I asked Marker about this.

Gary Marker: When I heard the original version of it I said, "Make it a little jump tune, let's put a few riffs in here." I think Alex came up with the (sings beginning of song). I said, "Well, it's kinda jazzy," but it's really, really a blue-grass riff.
John French: Yeah, it's kind of a square dance type of thing.

GM: Yes, it's a psychedelic square dance. I said, "Let's break it up, let's – you were there, because it was in that extra bedroom or den or whatever it was.
JF: In Laurel Canyon.
GM: Yeah, and we worked on this kind of ... I picked up the bass and I played along. (Sings root, minor third, fourth, root) Boy, Alex whipped that together and it was in there in, like, two seconds flat. So, 'twas ever thus. So I wrote the musical bridge on that. He said, "Well, what am I supposed to sing?" I said, "You sing the same shit you're singing, it's all around the tonic" - no big deal.

On *Safe As Milk*, as Doug has stated earlier, there were many little moments of collaborative effort. This is just one example of probably dozens where a musician, usually a band member but in this case Gary Marker, would suggest an idea for a section of a song. *Electricity* up until then was just a drone in G, and suddenly it had a whole new section added just by a simple suggestion by Marker. The drum part for the main section of the song is basically the rhythm of the intro played on drums. The bridge has the drums following the vocal phrasing for the most part. It's actually a "one-two-three la-conga" beat.

Once a basic song concept was developed, the form would kind of "lie in state" waiting for whoever to come along and add some little bit here or there. This is the way I would imagine a lot of bands worked at the time. For instance, the intro to *Plastic Factory* seemed to be a puzzle and no one could quite feel comfortable with it. After I joined, one of the first suggestions I made was to do a "cut triplet" feel for the first three notes. (Cut triplets is like putting three half notes in the space of two.) Everybody seemed to like this little idea and kept it in. It was a small suggestion, but each song had a few of these personal embellishments from individual players.

Krasnow At Rehearsal

John French: So when Bob Krasnow and Richard Perry came to our rehearsal, Don called all these songs for us to play that we hadn't rehearsed. That were just like one riff things like ... I don't know if you remember one called **Mark IX.**
Jerry Handley: I do remember that name. Yes, I remember doing that over and over.

If Don had been wise, he would have allowed Alex to continue leading the rehearsals and handling the music end of things. Don was good at fronting the band, doing interviews, impressing people and attracting attention. Alex was a quiet, unassuming guy with a great deal of natural talent and drive. He didn't want the spotlight, he just wanted to play in a band and have the music together. When Krasnow and (I think) Perry came to the little rehearsal room, they wanted to hear the band play something, and Don, rather than picking something we knew - like *Yellow Brick Road* or *Call On Me* – picked *Mark IX*. This was a song idea that we had jammed one time in the desert. (It later was watered down and became *Love Lies* with different lyrics). We wound up jamming this thing for what seemed like an endless amount of time. Bob and company didn't seem to have much of an opinion - it was more indifference. They probably had a completely different taste in music anyway.

However, it was another of the moments when the obvious weak point was Don's lack of ability to do the right thing at the right time. He seemed to have absolutely no comprehension of what was an appropriate presentation. It certainly wasn't calling a jam we had only played once four months ago.

Behind The Scenes Negotiations
One of the most interesting things that I discovered about *Safe As Milk* was revealed to me by Gary Marker during our interviews in 1998.

Gary Marker: What you don't know, and what nobody knows, is that Don and I had this kind of arrangement and I had a semi-arrangement with Krasnow. I was supposed to produce Safe As Milk.
John French: You're kidding me!
GM: Nope! I had produced a few other things. They listened to it and said it was OK.

This brought back a series of memories. Marker and another fellow named Tom seemed to be at Krasnow's office quite often when Don and I would go to pay a visit. At one point, they spoke of labeling Don's music "Psyche-Delta" as a play on the word psychedelic mixed with Delta blues (as if I had to explain *that!*) They actually had posters (in the style of the Avalon and Fillmore concert posters) designed with the name of the band and this newly coined term. Even at my age, (perhaps *because* of my age) I considered this a cheap promotion trick that would quickly become outdated, leaving the band with a really stupid image in the eyes of the public. Then again, that was just my opinion.

Psyche-Delta
Also near this time, Gary Marker and the same other guy, whose name was Tom, decided that they were also the perfect guys to be the band's co-managers. Marker and friend persisted in coming to the house that day to propose their managership of the band. No one really said anything, and Don even seemed like he thought this might be OK – at least to them. Actually, he was again playing both sides against the middle by secretly giving us the impression that he wasn't so sure that it would work. The feeling in the room seemed to be that no one was really hot on the idea, but no one wanted to say 'no'to Marker because he was a friend, a great musician, and a nice guy. I finally asked them something – I don't recall exactly what - what their plans were on marketing the group perhaps, something along this line. At 18, I guess I wasn't supposed to know about this, because they seemed rather surprised. So surprised, in fact, that it seemed that they had absolutely no real specific answer to the question and just sort of changed the subject. Alex, who seemed secretly in line with Don's view that these weren't the right guys, looked at me with a kind of sideways grin and congratulated me later on my question. That was basically the end of the presentation and the meeting.

Gary Marker: I know that I spent a lot of time like up there at Buddah with Krasnow, hanging out with him saying, "You gotta do this, this has to be done, this is the way you market it, etc."

Bearing this in mind, and to be fair to Marker, he and Tom probably did have some really valid ideas for marketing the band, some of which may have actually been later used by Krasnow when Marker was no longer in the loop. My impression, being 18, and not knowing much but absolutely convinced I knew everything, was that they were the wrong guys for the job. In my recent interviews with Marker, I'm sure that my original opinion of him was wrong.

Marker "Greases Up" Cooder
Even back at the Carolside rehearsals, Don had talked of getting Ry Cooder in the band. One of his points beside the fact that Ry was obviously a great player, was the fact that he and Alex both had these "eyes" that worked well together "image wise", of course. I would just surmise that Don thought his best bet to get Cooder was to make Marker a promise based upon his ability to persuade Ry to join the project.

Gary Marker: (Krasnow asked) "Well, can you get Cooder in the band?" Of course, Krasnow didn't know who Cooder was, so as I said, I worked on Cooder. This is my old chum – here I am "doing a number" on him in order to get this gig because I really believed in it. I thought I could do a righteous job with them. So, I "greased up" Cooder and finally I called up Krasnow one day and said, "OK, he's softened up, you nail him." So, Krasnow called him up, said, "This is bigger than the Rolling Stones," and all that crap and Cooder said, "Oh well, what the ... ? I give up." You know how it is, you can only stand so much of this stuff. This constant assault. So he (eventually) went right along with it. It was all set, and I was going to produce that album.

Marker's statement here shows an underlying guilt. In the line "this is my old chum - here I am doing a number on him," is typical of what I've observed in myself and others who have been involved in the entertainment industry. When a promise of fame and success is hanging it the balance, it's really easy to somehow convince oneself that it's OK to temporarily override one's deepest values, deceive one's closest friends, or just plain lie outright in order to reach the goal. Situational ethics seem to reign strong over the next several years of my life. The one I seemed to deceive the most was myself, but I also betrayed my friends, and they me.

Ry Cooder – One of the Privileged Few

Ry Cooder: I knew him (Don Van Vliet) because I kept bumping into him, without really knowing anything about him. He was just a guy who kept popping up at the places I went to, and he'd start to talk. One thing led to another, and he said: 'I've got a band, I'm called so-and-so and we do this, that, and the other.'He was getting ready to record an album, and asked me if I would play with him, and I said OK. It lasted a couple of weeks, we didn't have much reason to play together. Our musical goals were totally different. In other words, he was only interested in what he was doing, and it smacked a little of self-conceit. He'd teach people to play what he wanted them to play. That doesn't mean he taught them to play, if you see what I mean. He'd take a guy and tell him to do this or that - regardless of whether they could play or not. He only told me to play a few notes. He was a note man, just like the Japanese. What I mean is that out of a certain assortment of notes he wanted precisely this one and that one. How you got them out of your instrument didn't matter, it was a question of his wanting a certain sound, (...) of his having a clear idea of something. He saw music in this complicated way of his own."[29]

Van Vliet seldom showed respect for long to any member of the Magic Band. The norm was to blame them individually and collectively for the band's lack of financial success and anything else that managed to go wrong. There were certain varying degrees of exception to this rule through the years, where certain people fell into a different category because of the value Don placed upon them. One of these was actually Cooder. He was allowed certain privileges and perks that other band members never enjoyed. Probably in part because Don realized how good he was, but also because Ry was quite non-committal about *joining* the group and remained aloof during the entire process of rehearsing/recording *Safe As Milk*.

It is interesting to note here that Ry reinforced basic concepts of rehearsal that all of us in the band had been attempting to employ, and which Don would constantly fight against. One big element was tying up all the loose ends, song by song.

John French: Yeah, but before that Ry really came in and tied the music together, cleaned up all the songs, remember that?
Jerry Handley: Yeah, right.

---

[29]Ry Cooder interviewed by John Tobler. ZigZag#69-70, 1977.

Ry As Musical Director

Ry Cooder: I said, "Look, I'm just here, you know, let's just see what you're doing." (Paraphrasing Van Vliet) "Well, I'll tell ya what we're doing. What we're not doing! First goddamn thing is this goddamn guy here" points at Doug Moon again "Get outta here, Doug you're just no use to us no, you can't" I can't tell you what language he used, but it was something like, you know, "Go away and let us do this." Quoting Don again ... "Another damn thing is I'll sure tell you, you know, the bass player here, Jerry, he just can't, you know, he can't remember the parts half the time, and I taught him, I taught him the music!" I'm going "Whoa, alright! One thing at a time." [30]

We really respected Ry as a musician and director. He was taking songs and putting them together so quickly I finally felt like we were starting to be like a band. In the five months or so I had been in the group, I don't think we ever had finished anything. Don was a great starter, but he was always too undisciplined to finish songs, yet he always wanted all the credit for everything. Ry was causing the music to come together quite well.

One thing I really liked about Ry was his ability to ignore Don's absurdities and just get to work. He always put his money where his mouth was.

John French: So, the album came together because of Ry. Basically, Ry saying "Come on Don, what do you want to do?" "Don, what's the next thing?" Don "Gotta get outta here ... GOT STUFF TO DO". Sometimes he would only come in for two hours flat, and if nothing got done, he would leave. So Don would finally wind up getting out of bed at four o'clock in the afternoon, and actually starting to participate and the music started coming together. It would never have come together without Ry.
Alex Snouffer: Yep.

Ry Cooder: But just to make those tunes work was a heck of a job of work, you know, it was not easy. Certainly none of it was written out, and certainly none of it was too well understood, but that's part of the appeal.[31]

Don would give Cooder brandy and cigars in some attempt to patronize, but Ry didn't need patronizing. Don would say later that he had to do this in order to keep Ry around, suggesting that Ry had to be spoiled and pampered. This is not so. Ry only demanded one thing: that we all knew the songs from beginning to end. There is a good possibility that *Safe As Milk* would never have become a reality without him. There are quite a few of Ry's own musical ideas scattered here and there throughout the album, although credit is given to Van Vliet for everything.

Don's bedroom, as I said before, was right next to the rehearsal room. Don would sometimes sing his musical ideas from the bedroom, and Ry would interpret them and teach them to the intended player. Often during Don's excessive absences (while he was off having a "heart attack," having a meal, showering, or one of the other numerous events that "just had to be done" in the middle of rehearsal), Cooder would write parts for the players, especially bass parts. He also had a great way of teaching drum parts. He was never vague about anything (like "play a strawberry," or "it's like a figure eight"). He would tell you exactly the rhythm he wanted on each drum. He was very patient, and didn't expect everything to be perfect the first time through. He had a logical order about rehearsal, and kept a list in his head of everything.

Probably the biggest difference between Ry and Don was again the fact that Ry had dedicated himself to mastering an instrument and understood the entire process of being able to play with

---

[30] The Artist Formally Known as Captain Beefheart, BBC Documentary, interview with Ry Cooder.
[31] The Artist Formally Known as Captain Beefheart, BBC Documentary, interview with Ry Cooder.

feeling. This caused him to teach others in the same way he had learned himself. He recognized everyone's strengths and weaknesses and knew that the finished product was not of immediate concern, and that the priority at the moment was showing everyone where to put their fingers. Our first rehearsals with Ry were filled with mistakes and false starts. Ry understood, being a player himself, that this was part of the process, and that things would improve with each rehearsal.

Driving To The Drum Shop

One story I recall is really revealing about Ry's state of mind in those days. First of all, he did not take any drugs that I knew about, save a cigar and occasional brandy, which he may have done only to please Don. He was a very disciplined man, punctual, honest, hard working and independent. He was kind of a boy scout of the blues. I remember one day I needed a part for my drums, a new hi-hat stand. He had come for rehearsal. I had no car at the time, and we couldn't rehearse without this stand. No other car was available, so he took me to Professional Drum Shop down in Hollywood. He had a little Datsun sedan. I have never seen anyone tailgate like this guy. All the way down and all the way back. There seemed to be a time is money theme behind all of this. Got things to do seemed to be his favorite phrase. Laurel Canyon Boulevard was a windy road. My stomach was in knots, thinking we were going to rear-end someone at any moment. His tail-gating may have been due partially to his monocular vision. That gave me little comfort during the drive.

The other side of the coin was that I don't think I have ever been around an older young man in my life. As much as I liked him, this guy was all work and no play. However, if I had a choice between working with him and Don, I would have chosen him, because things got done, people were paid and I could have found other people with whom to have fun. That was the one thing about this band that bothered me. No one seemed to have any fun, at least in my adolescent perception of the word. Don seemed so preoccupied about how hip everything was. Don't say the wrong thing. Don't wear the wrong clothes. Don't goof off. Don't do anything lame. I was 18, and I wanted to have a good time while I could. I missed my old friends.

First Rehearsal With Ry

At our first rehearsal with Ry, I had no idea what tune he was starting with, as he didn't really announce anything, just sat up and started playing the beginning licks to what became *Sure Nuff*. This was Ry's arrangement but it sounded like Muddy Waters to me. I hadn't listened to blues for years, but I recognized it as very similar to *Rollin' 'n' Tumblin'*. Since I had no idea what song he was doing, I thought he was just starting out a "blues jam" to get us acquainted. Ry, however, knew exactly what he was doing at all times, and what everyone should be playing. He could verbally describe in musical terms exactly what he wanted. It was he who inserted that interesting little half time boogaloo drum beat on the root chord that made it so unique and contemporary. Ry had an ear for what was in and knew how to create more accessible arrangements.

The Crossbow Incident

In the BBC Documentary *The Artist Formerly Known as Captain Beefheart*, Ry describes an incident when he first came to the Laurel Canyon Residence in which Doug walked in the room with a loaded machine crossbow.

Ry Cooder: Next thing, Doug comes out with a loaded crossbow in his hand: "Don't nobody move!" Got this loaded machine crossbow. I'm down behind the amplifier, man, I don't want to see no, you know, machine crossbow arrows coming at me. (paraphrasing Don) "Oh, get that fucking thing outta here! Get outta here! Go back in your room!" (Doug, softly) "OK."[32]

[32] The Artist Formally Known as Captain Beefheart, BBC Documentary, interview with Ry Cooder.

Although it seemed like I remembered something about this, the mind is tricky, so I asked Doug in his interview about this statement.

John French: I gotta ask you about this: Did you have a crossbow?
Doug Moon: I don't remember that. Alex was the crazy guy. He was the one that had weapons. I never had anything but the derringer.
JF: I remember you having the derringer. I don't remember the crossbow …
DM: It must have been something of Alex's.
JF: … but it seems like I remember something, was there a crossbow hanging in the bedroom, or anything?
DM: I have no idea.
JF: I recall you coming in and some kind of thing going down, and you were sorta laughing about it. Maybe you had your gun, I don't know … (Moon shakes his head) No? You were kinda laughing about the whole thing. It was an early rehearsal with Ry Cooder and it just sort of freaked him out. Maybe he remembers it as a full – what did he call it? Full machine crossbow? (Paraphrasing Ry) "Man, I didn't want to get hit with no full machine crossbow." I recall something like that happening, but I didn't remember what it was. You didn't own a crossbow, right? Where the hell did that come from?
DM: Alex had stuff like that. Knives and guns. He had that Luger, looked like a Luger but it was a Ruger, a .22. I remember we used to go down in the early days to Jack First's gun range and shoot that thing. He had that for years. He had some other stuff too. He had knives and stuff, he was into the weapons thing. I had the derringer. That was more self-preservation. It was a lot quicker and more effective than spending thousands of hours and all that money learning karate or something. Why do all that, just go out and get a derringer and stick it in my boot. That way, if I ever have a confrontation, there's a simple solution to a simple question. The only downfall being that I might have to shoot somebody someday. That would be a bad thing. As it was, it turned out to be an effective deterrent. (Laughs)

Marker's slant (although I don't remember him being there).

Gary Marker: Ry was good because he was telling these stories, he told this story about Doug coming in with a compound bow.
John French: I don't remember that.
GM: Me neither. Doug went into his room and he came out and my recollection was … that he came out with an ordinary crossbow and he went out in the backyard, there was a big rodent problem with squirrels out there. He used to just go out and shoot squirrels. I don't remember him aiming a crossbow at anybody and certainly not some high-tech thing. But that Ryland, he always exaggerates everything. He makes up these stories and they get more elaborate every time he tells them. The thing is that he can't tell the same story the same way twice.
JF: Well, it seems like I remember Alex having a crossbow hanging on the wall or something. And Doug grabbing it or something and just coming through the room saying "Don't nobody move!" as a joke.
GM: He was joking as he walked through the room. He never pointed the fucking crossbow, that was all cocked and loaded (and a) big graphite high tech thing at anybody. They didn't even make them then.
JF: It's kind of a funny story though.
GM: I heard that and I thought, "What is this?" You know this guy … God, Ryland, he just never stops!

However, just to clarify, Ry recalled a later incident in 1995 with almost the same clarity as I recalled and our memories were so much in sync on the incident that BBC editors were able to cut and paste between us in a very quick exchange. There is nothing the matter with Ry's memory, as far as that future event will show.

OK, enough about the crossbow already.

CHAPTER TWELVE:
NO NEST FROM WEST TO EAST

ry Handley, Don, John French and Alex Snouffer early '67
mo shot. Photo courtesy of Guy Webster.

Alex at Fran's

John French: You were living at Fran's, because you got disgusted about being there (The Amor Road residence), *well I don't know if you were living there, but you were going over there a lot to get out of the place.*
Alex Snouffer: Yeah, I ended up actually living at the place - that whole era there was a mish-mash of shit.

Alex had started hanging out at a friend's house. Steve and Fran (last name unknown) were a married couple who had befriended the band in the pre-A&M days, when they were a struggling blues group. The band had rehearsed in their home, located at the base of the Hollywood Hills east of Highland Avenue. Several of the early promotional photographs were taken on the porch of the house. Earlier, before I joined the band, there had been a jam session (mentioned earlier) at this residence with Muddy Waters and his band. Steve eventually was drafted, being sent, of course to Vietnam, leaving Fran behind who went through all kinds of legal maneuvers to get him out. She was seeing a psychiatrist, I believe, and writing numerous letters to various organizations. The doctor was giving her sleeping pills.

As I recall, the house was a little two-bedroom place with a detached garage. It was a small frame house with a porch, a hammock, nice shade trees and a decent-sized back yard. Alex went over there to escape from the confusion that was constantly going on with Don – what Gary Marker described as "keeping everyone slightly off-kilter."

Many times during the stay on Amor Road, Alex would come by the house in Fran's blue pickup truck (his Cadillac had died near the Hollywood Bowl) and we would go cruising around Hollywood. He always brown-bagged a little bottle of wine and sipped on it slowly as we drove around. (What was it Zappa told Mortensen – "You couldn't play blues unless you drank warm Thunderbird wine that was stuffed in the glove compartment of your car"?). Much of the time, we would discuss the music. I felt that the music on *Safe As Milk* was farther out than it needed to be.

For example, we would talk about the center sections of some of the songs, like *Dropout Boogie*. I felt that when the song went into waltz-time ballet, it was the end of its chances for radio air-play. It was too radical a shift for the average person to understand. Alex disagreed to an extent. He was actually more supportive of Don's musical ideas and felt that people hearing our music would be drawn to listen to it again long after *White Rabbit* and *Light My Fire* were just looked upon as sixties hippy garbage. I think he had a point here. How many times have you heard a Beefheart tune played in an elevator? In this area, I think Alex's perception was vastly underplayed. He recognized the music as something new and unique and was supportive of it's development. I was still dreaming about being famous and doing stuff like The Yardbirds during this time.

Yet, when it came to the subject of Don's behavior and his lack of ability to organize himself, his irresponsible behavior in the studio, his lack of ability to compromise with the group, Alex was fairly adamant about his feelings during this period. He felt the group had just as much of a stake in the financial health of the band as did Don and that our concerns should be considered. Alex felt that Don needed people to stand up to him, to hold him in check, because he didn't always make the wise choices that the band's collective mind would have made.

Alex later stated that at this point in time, he was just along for the ride, but it seems to me he was experimenting, observing, and quite active in the process. Don had been demanding his way for over two years. I believe that Alex felt the best way for Don to learn that his way wasn't always the best, was to let him have his way. Eventually, either Don would prove himself a worthy and successful businessman, or things would get worse, and he would eventually go back to having group business meetings and listening to others' ideas.

Alex's approach to me was to probe my mind and see what my thoughts were on the matter. "When you first got in the band, I watched you to see what your reaction to Vliet would be," he told me. Snouffer has always seemed a fair person, one who is willing to weigh everyone's opinion equally on the scale. He had given me time to think for myself, to form my own opinions. Once, at a later point, Snouffer told me that he always wished that I had been a little more willing to take a chance, a little more spontaneous. I couldn't agree with him more.

Another characteristic of Snouffer's was diplomacy. Alex was always careful about what he said. I can never really recall him saying anything I would consider spiteful or hurtful to me. He never humiliated me in front of others or put me down. He was very considerate of the feelings of those around him. In a sense, he brought out the best in people because he freed them up to be their selves.

I liked Alex a lot, and some of his views on life were very perceptive. One always knew where one stood with him. He didn't talk a lot, but when he did, it usually counted for something. I sensed he was suspended in indecision about dealing with Don's ego and felt a bit lost.

Safe As Milk demos

The recording of *Safe As Milk* was done at three studios. The first session was at Original Sound, upstairs from the Kama Sutra offices. Nothing from this session was actually used on the album. It could be labeled as a glorified demo session, and according to Gary Marker, that was exactly the purpose. We did *Sure 'Nuff* and *Yellow Brick Road* along with several other pieces, including *Abba Zaba*. Several points about the session are worth noting. Doug Moon and Ry Cooder both played on this session. Doug did fairly well with the songs, as I remember. Ry was constantly up in arms because he didn't feel Don was singing the blues. Don defended himself with the fact that he wasn't trying to copy anyone, but just be himself.

Near the end of the session, the bigshots arrived. I can't remember who was there, but it was probably Bob Krasnow, and possibly Artie Ripp, president of Kama Sutra. As the bigwigs listened, they seemed to approve. Don almost ran them out by showing them lyrics to dozens of songs written by Herb Bermann. It was too much: overkill, they waved him off. Even I could see that they were a bit irritated with him. He was like a used-car salesman.

Electricity

The drum parts to *Electricity* were taught to me in the studio, ten minutes before we did the song. Don came over and started talking to me about these new parts he had. I was a little nervous about learning something new. However, I liked them a lot better than the floating sixteenth-note ride that originally was done on the hi-hat. They were simple enough, because Don only had a rudimentary knowledge of drums, so he basically sang the ideas to me. However, it really made the song come together. When I say rudimentary knowledge, again, I am referring to being specific about what to play on what drum. He could vocalize drum sounds, like saying, "ka-chomp boom" and I would interpret what he sang into a beat.

Demo Session/Original Sound

I had forgotten that Gary Marker produced these sessions.

John French: You probably weren't there, but you may have been... we did a demo session for Buddah Records.
Gary Marker: I produced that. See, everybody forgets that.
JF: You produced it?
GM: I produced it!

JF: And it was where?
GM: It was upstairs, above Buddah Records at Art Laboe's Original Sound.
JF: Original Sound, OK
GM: That fucking mutant 10-track recorder that the guy had built up there.
JF: The same guy that built Studio Z!
GM: I wouldn't know, because I got out of the business around '70 or so.
JF: Yeah, but the same guy, Paul Buff built Studio Z then left there and built Original Sound.

It's funny how the memory works. After this moment in the interview with Marker, I could actually recall him being there along with a fellow named Gordon Shyrock. Everything fell into place. Also, I believe that Gordon Shyrock may have been the person with Krasnow when I first met him at Cantor's.

John French: You were in the studio, and produced that demo that we did – it was considered a demo, they were testing us out, right?
Gary Marker: Well, they wanted to see – the whole idea was that was all this stuff was going on behind the backs of everybody in the band. Krasnow was saying, "I gotta get something on tape. I gotta send it to Artie and Neil and" - I don't know all the guys who were involved – "So that they can hear what the band sounds like. Can you do that?" I said, "Let me take them in the studio, give me a studio to go in. Just tell them it's a demo, it's all live shit, whatever. And I'll get something." I tried to get a real clean sound without a lot of noise. I think I threw some echo on Don's voice a couple of places. Especially when he was doing Yellow Brick Road *– and of course, somebody kicked it off at this furious tempo and he couldn't keep up with it.*
JF: Oh yeah, it was way too fast.
GM: Way too fast, and I said, "Whoa, slow it down." He said, "No no, I want it bright like that, real bright tempo." I said, "Bright hell, you can't sing that fast! You can't think that fast, Don." (Laughs) We'd have these little arguments in the hallway, you know. He said, "Don't fuck with me man, I know what I am doing." I said, "OK!" So, he got out there and he couldn't hack it, so I threw some effects on it."
JF: So, the idea behind that is that, they needed something for Krasnow, plus they were kind of giving you a testing ground as a producer?
GM: It was a testing ground and even then they sent along a guy – you remember Gordon Shyrock?
JF: The big guy from Oklahoma who stuttered?
GM: He was from Oklahoma, yeah! He stuttered all the time, but he was a brilliant kind of musical historian. He was out of that whole Tulsa mafia, that whole bunch of them - Leon Russell and that whole bunch. (Maybe) Gerry McGee, too.
JF: I don't know about that stuff, man I just play drums.
GM: Anyway, they sent him along as a sort of watchdog, man, to make sure I wouldn't fuck things up.
JF: Who sent him along? Krasnow?
GM: Yeah, Krasnow sent him along, because he was afraid to let me handle you guys all alone in the studio.
JF: So, all this stuff was going on and the band didn't know anything about it.
GM: (Yes) I had this deal going on if I could get Ryland in the band and get him committed to working on the album … The whole thing with Krasnow was really kind of tentative.

Ry Upset At Demo Session
There was some commitment to hold the music to the blues, because there was a big urban blues revival with the white kids happening at the time. I remember hearing kids talking about

Muddy, the Wolf, and we actually played on the same bill with Buddy Guy in San Francisco. It had probably been brought about by the same influences that I had experienced. The Rolling Stones, The Yardbirds, and The Animals were all doing blues. Kids were listening to this and thinking, "What's this?" and reading the author's names. Just like my teen guitarist friend Melchione, looking up Delta blues in the local library. It was going on all over.

John French: Ry was very upset, because it wasn't bluesy enough, he wanted it to be a blues band, it wasn't bluesy. He'd say, "That's not blues." He seemed visibly upset by the whole session.

I could see that Ry was upset. He was talking to Don and Marker in the hallway and in the conversation that I overheard; there was the overriding theme of this music not being blues. Perhaps at this point, inexperienced as he was as an actual member of a band, Ry was holding onto his impression of the earlier blues band he'd met in the desert. That coupled with the fact that The Rising Sons had been a blues band. I was disappointed, because I felt that what we were doing was blues-based, and certainly as valid, but also original and contemporary.

I felt even then that this was a weak point in Ry's vision. Instead of wanting to do something fresh and new, which was certainly a definition of what we were creating here, he wanted to hold on to the past. Rather than create his own persona, he seemed more inclined to copy, to imitate. This was certainly a strong factor that set him apart from Don, and a point that would become clearly evident at a future time.

Doug Not On *Safe As Milk*
Snouffer does not recall a thing about this demo session. It was a quick one-night thing early in the relationship with Buddah. It is vivid in my mind perhaps in part due to the fact that it was my first official session with the band, and so has a special priority of for me.

John French: I forgot about it too, totally, until the other night, because I was talking to Doug, and he said, "I played on some of the cuts on Safe As Milk.*" I said " the only cut that you played on that I can think of is* Sure 'Nuff 'N Yes I Do *and then all of a sudden it dawned on me. I asked, "Where was this studio?" and he said, "Upstairs" and I knew that we didn't go upstairs to RCA when we recorded* Safe As Milk. *It was the ground floor.*
Alex Snouffer: Right.

I include this part of the interview because it clarifies that Alex and I agree that Doug did not play at RCA studios on any of the *Safe As Milk* sessions.

John French: It solved a problem, because Doug kept saying he played on all this stuff on Safe As Milk and I finally figured out why he kept saying it. I know he did not play on the RCA sessions.
Alex Snouffer: No, not in the studio.

Drugs And Craziness

Doug Moon: We smoked opium right in that (demo session) ... things got so crazy in the recording sessions, one of the last ones I was involved in, with Don's craziness that an engineer said, "Look, lets just take a break for a while and he passed the opium pipe. He thought we'd all get it together.
John French: Wasn't that one of the qualifications for being an engineer in those days was to have your own opium pipe?

***Doug Moon: They passed the opium pipe right around in the recording studio during* Safe As Milk.** (Note: demo session at Original Sound)
JF: And every producer had to be at least a drug dealer...
DM: That's the last thing I remember doing in Captain Beefheart and the Magic Band - smoking opium.

Moon's recollections in reference to "things got so crazy" and "Don's craziness" may have to do with the several problems already addressed. First was the extreme tempo to *Yellow Brick Road*, for which I may have actually been to blame. I believe that it was the first song in the session and I probably was nervous. It probably seemed just the right tempo at the time, until the three quarts of adrenaline that were running through my veins wore off.

Second was the conflict between Don and Ry concerning the "it's not blues" theme. This was a minor problem, but I saw it as a major conflict this evening. Since the group's plan was to have Cooder as part of the lineup, this was a crucial moment in diplomatic relations and it seemed inconceivable to me that the issue was going to be resolved.

Third was probably the fact that Don was changing parts right in the studio as we were beginning to record. Me playing a different drum part certainly affected the other players. I remember seeing a surprised look on their faces as we started playing. If I remember correctly, the little climbing section in *Electricity* was only added a day or two before, the song was almost completely different to before.

Fourth was the Captain's over-emphasis on how many songs he had written while talking to the Buddah business people. This was during the session before he overdubbed vocals and was quite time-consuming. It was apparent that everyone was getting anxious to have a finished product. This seemed to everyone to be an opportunistic moment of self-promotion that had nothing to do with the task at hand.

Fifth was probably the fact that since Van Vliet had never rehearsed any of these songs with us, we were still trying to figure out how many times to play certain sections of the songs (for example, *Electricity*). As I recall, when asked about things like this, Don would get very quiet and just a glint of paranoia would shine from his eyes. He was originally cueing us into the sections, which didn't work, because he would lose attention and hesitate, throwing off the band.

Finally, we did this all in about four hours, if I recollect, and there were five or six songs recorded. That's quite an accomplishment in itself. It's a lot of information to be stuffed into such a short space of time.

Forty Acres ... And A Mule

One of the times I didn't go to the Kama Sutra office, I recall that a deal was finally struck and an offer was made. The heads of the company had heard the demo tape which made them feel that the band could indeed give them a product. I clearly remember Don standing in the kitchen and saying, "They're giving us a $1,000 advance" I couldn't help but think to myself, "All the bands I hear about get minimum $10k advances up to $50k advances, and *we're only getting $1,000?*" This seemed like a rather paltry amount of money.

For years, I always believed that our advance was for $1,000. $200 each. For the album cover, we bought suits that cost almost this much, so there was no money left at all. Alex's car had been impounded, because it broke down by the Hollywood Bowl and he couldn't afford to get it fixed. Jerry and Alex were both fathers, and the expenses and pressures of parenthood were always knocking at their door. We never had food in the refrigerator; sometimes I only ate at the sessions or when we would go down to the office.

During the interviews for this book Gary Marker alleged that Don had misled the band. Marker had been in on the negotiations and he said it was *at least* $10,000.

With the way the economy was in those days, had we each received ($2,000-$4,000) we could have lived modestly but comfortably for six to eight months. I believe that three-bedroom, two-bath house we were renting in Laurel Canyon was about $185 a month at the most.

With this new information, new realizations poured into my head. Van Vliet was in a band of guys he had known for years and had worked with and bonded with over the last two. Yet, he somehow felt justified to mislead some of his closest affiliates concerning this. The whole band was signed to Buddah Records, not just Don.

All we had to do to receive our big $200 advance was sign the contract.

John French: We had this attorney and I can't remember his name ... it was Jay something.
Jerry Handley: Oh, Jay Cooper.
JF: Jay Cooper, right. So he was the attorney who supposedly gave us this contract, said it was a great contract.

I'm using the wrong terminology here. Cooper apparently had successfully negotiated the break from A&M Records and so oversaw the signing of the new agreement with Buddah. We were told in glowing terms how great this contract was. It was a one-year contract with four one-year options. I signed, knowing that being under twenty-one and therefore a minor, I could probably withdraw if a long-term relationship turned ugly. And it turned out later, we found out from another attorney (named Schlesinger, I believe) that it was the most standard contract and nobody in their right mind signed a contract like that because it's all in favor of the record company. Nothing had been marked out or changed at all.

Usually, there is a lot of negotiation that goes on before a recording contract is signed (or so I am told). The thing is pages and pages of legalese, so for a musician, it's a very intimidating situation. We don't know what to ask, because we can't understand the terminology, which is exactly why it's written that way. The contract first presented is usually a standard recording contract which is their way of telling you, we want everything, and you get nothing. It's the attorney's job to sort through this and negotiate a deal, whittling down the demands to as few as possible and getting the band a deal that will actually prove to be financially viable.

As I said to Jerry, nothing had been marked out or changed. I don't know whether Jay Cooper was just the wrong guy for the job, or whether he just didn't know any better. There were rumors that Buddah padded his wallet with a hefty sum to stamp his approval on the contract as it stood. Whatever the case, it was definitely not in our favor to sign this contract. I recently watched a television biography of Billy Joel. Artie Ripp apparently persuaded Joel to sign a contract that actually gave Artie a huge share of his earnings, even after he was no longer with the company. So, about now, I'm wondering who were those unseen forces that led Don to Cantor's that night.

Suits

We seemed to go to several stores looking for suits, and wound up at a place in Hollywood, which I seemed to remember being called Zeidler and Zeidler. Don had commented that I looked good in white, because I was wearing a white shirt and pants one day. So, he suggested that I get a white suit. At that time, double-breasted stuff was in fashion because of the mod look that had been popularized by the British Invasion. I found an Italian suit and tried it on. It was an instant hit and everybody said get it, so I did. I saw a pair of beautiful Italian shoes that I liked but couldn't afford. I kept looking at the shoes, but the suit had taken all my money.

Don found a suit at this same store, the pinstriped Brioni, if I remember correctly. We both had to be fitted and then left the store. Krasnow had a shirt and tie that he felt would go perfect with the suit, so he sent them to the cleaners and had everything delivered to the house. There was a box that came with the suit, shirt and tie that contained those shoes I had loved. Krasnow had bought me those shoes out of his own pocket. I have never seen shoes like these since. They were a great Italian design where parts of the sole came up around the sides. The heel was cut in angles to give it a really strange look, more like leather wooden shoes. I loved them. Thanks, Bob.

Jerry and Alex wound up getting their clothes somewhere else. It wasn't a place on the strip, but it may have been affiliated with the other store.

Lambert as Percussionist

So, enter Gary Lambert again. Don, on one of his trips to the Desert had met up with Gary Lambert. The last time I remembered hearing about him was Don was calling him a fag and running him off from his mother's apartment. Suddenly, Don announced to the band that Gary was going to be our percussionist. I'm thinking "What?" Gary had never played a drum in his life. The closest he had gotten to a drum is when he painted the Gerber's Baby on the front of my bass drum. Now, he was suddenly going to be the percussionist? And why did we need a percussionist? Gary showed up a few days later and stayed with us for a while. He started taking conga lessons and rented a conga drum. Actually, as he was playing, I started asking him about the technique, and he taught me quite a few things he had learned at the lesson.

Sister Sheila

A lady showed up at the door one night. I didn't recognize her for a minute, because she was wearing normal clothes. It was Sister Sheila Marie, apparently stepping out for a little fun. She came in with a friend, another nun I suppose. They stayed for a while, visiting and having tea and then left with Don. He was gone all night, and when he came home next day, he wrote a song called *Sister Sheila*.

Laurie seemed oblivious to all of this, but I'm sure that she was actually deeply hurt by it all. She kept saying, "Sister Sheila, she's *really great*."

Kama Sutra Office

We seemed to make several trips as a group during one period down to the Kama Sutra office. I mentioned earlier that Bob Krasnow had about a 300-line phone, and a different personality for each line. Each new line evoked a different voice tone, new mood, and various levels of aggressive/passive behavior. He, in my opinion, was an absolute genius at what he did. I think that at the time he was a promoter. Alex referred to him as a con-man, a hustler. Same thing, isn't it? Anyway, I had a great respect for Bob's phone skills and his ability to understand people and instantly relate to them.

We visited the office for several meetings. One time was just a quick meeting to discuss contract options. Another time to discuss photos, or the group sound.

There was a gentleman who used to make an appearance while we were there. He always seemed to have some sort of goods to sell and he was constantly dropping off something. Bob mentioned one day that he was the local "Jewish Mafia" representative. Apparently, almost everyone who worked for Kama Sutra was Jewish - Bob and Artie for sure. I found this out one day when the Six-Day War had just been won by Israel. "We won!" Bob was saying. Everyone was cheering.

There had been one meeting at which I was not present. It involved the behind-the-scenes negotiating between Marker and Krasnow for the production of *Safe As Milk*.

Gary Marker: We had a meeting. We went in for this meeting and sat around the big table up

there (at Kama Sutra's Hollywood office). ***The next thing I know, Krasnow (tells me), "There's been a change, here ... Gee, I'm sorry ... etc." The whole deal's off.***

Krasnow had brought Richard Perry in to produce Safe As Milk, dumping Marker, and he had found out at this meeting.

*Gary Marker: **Don sat there and didn't say a fuckin' word. Not a word in my defense. Not word one. Not anything ... like, "Well, I'd really like to have Gary along on this because he really knows about this kind of music." Not word one. I'm looking at him, I'm looking at Krasnow, I'm looking at Perry, and I'm (thinking), "OK, this is going to be a fucking disaster."***

It's obvious that Gary was quite upset with the decision and even more so that Don did not lift a finger to back his "friend." There could be a number of reasons for Don's behavior. One is that he could have been intimidated enough by the environment of the board meeting that he was afraid to speak. Although Don seemed rather outspoken with the band members, he had been known on more than one occasion to clam up to the powers that be.

Another possibility (and one that I believe is closer to the truth) is that he had absolutely no plans of ever using Marker as a producer and only made the promise in order to have Marker influence Ry enough to make him a member of the Magic Band. Another possibility is that after hearing the demo sessions, Krasnow and other Kama Sutra decision makers decided that Marker wasn't satisfactory. Another possibility is merely favoritism. Perry and Krasnow were friends. Krasnow once related a story about how he once sat up all night with Perry in New York talking him into producing *Safe As Milk*. It was Perry's first album – sort of like a doctor's first operation – *and we were the patients.*

However it happened, Gary Marker was suddenly and inexplicably booted out of the picture.

Richard Perry

And so it was that we found ourselves in Sunset Sound Studios to record the first track on the album. It was time to have a session with Richard Perry in charge. Richard, although inexperienced, was definitely a perfectionist. It was my thought that the idea of this session was to produce a single, a 45-rpm record with an A and a B-side. Bruce Botnick was the engineer. Krasnow was also there. He had started wearing a cowboy hat. The only reason Don could figure was the words to *Electricity* said "Bearded cowboy stains in black" Well, the hat was black, that's all I knew.

Sure 'Nuff 'N Yes I Do – **Sunset Sound**

Marker still had a certain sense of wanting to help Don in spite of the apparent double-cross.

Gary Marker: So the next thing I did is because it was Don's desire to have everything done at Sunset Sound, I thought the next best thing I could do was battle to get it done there.
John French: Which was a better studio (than RCA, where it actually wound up being done).
GM: It was a better studio. Don felt comfortable there, because he had worked there anyway. ...One of my ex-wives was the traffic manager for (Sunset Sound). She booked all the acts in there. I was really familiar (with the studio), because I had recorded in that studio (quite often) with other bands as well. In fact (the studio) where you guys cut Sure 'Nuff, *and coincidentally* Veterans' Day Poppy, *and the other things (*Moonlight on Vermont *and unreleased* Kandy Korn *plus the entire* Strictly Personal *album) was in the studio where the Doors cut everything, you see. Studio "A" - or whatever they called the little one up front*

- is like a little magic studio. Buffalo Springfield and all those people also (recorded) in there. A lot of really good stuff came out of there. It (had) a really good sound, (and) was an intimate room. No matter what they did in the control booth, (even) later when they started putting in digital (equipment) it didn't make any difference, it was just something about the room.

We only did one session and one song at Sunset Sound. Doug Moon was also in this session. It was *Sure 'Nuff 'N Yes I Do*. You can hear him playing a little slide on the fadeout. He wasn't even credited, but I don't really think any of us actually were.

Alex Snouffer: Yeah, wasn't that Sunset Sound?
John French: That was Sunset Sound. (With our) old buddy at the control board.
AS: Yeah, Bruce.
JF: Bruce Botnick, and Richard Perry, and I think Bob Krasnow was there (but) he was in and out.

This was an evening session and we took our time setting up. After doing take one, Richard listened to it and determined that there was a problem with the bass sound.

Gary Marker: Lot of bass problems, there were a lot of (problems).
John French: They made Jerry use a pick and he wasn't used to the pick, and he became uncomfortable.
GM: I can dig that. I have the same problem. I'm not really comfortable with a pick, never was. Being an upright bass player, (I didn't) tend to play upright bass with a pick. (Laughs)
JF: This is true.
GM: I'd be more comfortable playing an electric bass with a bow, which I did.

I don't recall a single session back in those days when the bass sound wasn't a problem. Hours and hours seem to go by, until Richard said "OK, let's just do one more." We did 78 takes of a three-minute song if I remember correctly. They wound up using take forty-something and editing part of another take into it. I couldn't tell the difference. My hands were bleeding by the end of the session. The feeling in my hands was gone after take twenty-five.
Marker repudiates my claim:

Gary Marker: Well, there were a lot of false starts.
John French: I thought we did 78 full takes.
GM: Oh no, it wasn't that (many).
JF: Well, (I am sure) we did that many (takes) I don't know if they were full takes.
GM: No, I think there were a lot of false starts, because there were a number of technical problems.

John French: I remember us doing 78 takes.
Alex Sn0uffer: Was it 78? And then they had to splice two of 'em together so they could get one good one.
JF: Yeah, I think they decided upon one in the thirties and then they put something else with it, because they changed the end or something. That was a terrible, terrible night. Like four or five hours of just straight playing.

Recording in a studio is like having sex under a microscope. It's as intimate as dining in the boy's gym. They put headphones on everyone. The technicians sit in a room observing you through glass.

They talk about you without you being able to know what they are saying, so you find yourself watching their lips. They separate you from all your friends with electronic gadgets and giant baffles. They take hours having each of you play individually while they get your sound. After you are thoroughly psychologically drained and haven't an ounce of feeling in your entire being they say, "OK, rolling, let's make a record!"

You count off the song and they stop you. They tell you that you must count it a different way because of the edits etc. They stop you in the middle of perfect takes because someone forgot a button, or they want to try a different technique. Then they order pizza at three in the morning, which you watch them (including the singer who will overdub later) eat while you do take 74. At take 80, they tell you to come in for a listen. They say, "Help yourself to the pizza" which now consists of empty cardboard boxes with dry cold cheese strings connecting an infinite number of oil spots. The leftover pepperoni looks like the angry red planet, and you hate the music business forever.

Gary Marker: Somewhere (along the way) when I went in, I noticed that – it was very obvious to me that Perry didn't know what he was doing. I kept saying to Perry, "Can you hear that hum out of that amplifier over there?" By that point, Krasnow was drifting. He had really good (production) credentials from way back. He had produced everything from Hank Ballard and the Midnighters to all this classic R&B stuff for King Records and for Federal." (However), he wasn't really "on it." Perry was in control of everything.
John French: My impression of Krasnow was that I would never have believed that he had produced anything before in his life.
GM: You would think so. I think he was the kind of producer who wound up in situations where he had great engineers.
JF: Maybe so, because all I can remember is him standing back there in the booth saying, "Heavy baby!" at the end of each take.
GM: Yeah, he was kind of into that scene by then. But what had happened was, I was thinking, "This is ridiculous, I'm outta here. I'm not gonna snort around here and be a "fan" anymore."

I learned a lot about the recording business in this session. We came back in the next night to do the vocal overdub. I recall that not all of the band members were there. Don was freaking out in the studio. He kept calling me out and asking me if his heart was all right. I think he was just bored and was making up for all the wasted time by doing something creative. Botnick had been turning up the signal in Don's headphones at Van Vliet's request. Don always seemed to have a hard time hearing his voice. Zappa later theorized that Don sang so loud that he actually imploded his ears.

Near the end of the night, Bruce Botnick pressed a talkback button as Don simultaneously moved one earpiece away from his head and inadvertently sent a dangerously loud amount of high-frequency feedback through Beefheart's headphones. He grabbed them, throwing them off his head and screaming, "Jesus Christ, man!" Everybody in the control booth groaned. That was the end of *that* night and also the beginning of a lifelong fear of headphones. For years, Van Vliet also repeated the story: "Botnick ruined my ears man, I think he did that on purpose." Sorry Bruce, I could tell it was an accident.

Replacing Doug
A few days before our next studio date, Don spoke privately to the band about replacing Doug Moon. Even I could see that Doug seemed to be living in a world of his own. I have read about Doug supposedly having a nervous breakdown during this and that this was the reason for his removal from the band.

My own observation was that he was withdrawing because he didn't like the direction the music was taking. He was smoking a lot of pot and was disoriented. He was possibly having difficulty with the arrangements, as he'd been playing less time than the rest. At rehearsals, he would, when asked to play any new section in a piece, argue with Don asking "Why is it necessary to change this?" He seemed frustrated that the band was no longer a blues band. He seemed to me to be hanging on to the past. However, he did seem to have dreams about making it big and what he was going to do with his share of the money. As the recording dates got closer, it was more and more uncomfortable to spend time with Doug, because he didn't know about the secret plans. I felt like a traitor, as I liked Doug and had enjoyed spending time with him. This was part of the situational ethics predicament I mentioned earlier.

I feel Moon and Van Vliet had a personality clash. Doug felt that Don was taking the band on the wrong road. I have to agree in terms of finances and profit. If Don would have sang more straight-ahead songs and let the band write their own arrangements, we probably all could have retired in about three years and had the money to afford to explore the new musical territories Don wanted to conquer. Van Vliet would still have had plenty of time and resources to do his art, and not at the expense of his band. I don't see anything ethically or artistically wrong with that stance. It makes more sense to me than what happened.

The patience and loyalty that Alex had for Doug shows through in this passage.

John French: It was during this time that it became apparent that Doug Moon was not going to be a member of the band for very much longer. So, what are your feelings about that? Doug was treated unfairly? Do you feel like he was losing it as a player?
Alex Snouffer: Well you say "losing it as a player." In order to get it as a player, Doug has got to try so hard - you hear what I'm saying? In other words, a lot of that stuff just didn't come natural to him.

John French: We moved down to Laurel Canyon - that was a pretty tough time for you.
*Doug Moon: Mmmmmm ... it wasn't until the end when I got the boot, when I got fired from the band. Well, it was getting pretty tough because, before ... yeah everything bad started happening once we moved down. When we were still up here, we were collaborating on **Safe As Milk**. I still felt really good about what was happening. It wasn't until we started going into the studio with the stuff that the shit hit the fan. It just ... the whole ... the songs radically changed right there in the studio. I remember because we had spent all of this time getting these songs down, you know.*

Actually, as I recall, many of the changes were added at the Laurel Canyon house, but Doug was increasingly absent from these rehearsals. This may have been due in part to the appearance of Ry Cooder.

Doug Moon: I was dogged determined to do my guitar parts the way I had learned them, and I had the songs in my head. I knew how they should sound. We had them down. We went in the studio, Don started to trash everything, change everything around, re-invent everything.

Part of the conflict may have been that Doug didn't want to change the arrangements and therefore refused to play the new sections. This created an environment in which he actually was in direct conflict with Don, who wanted to change *everything*. Doug's perception may have been, "This is the way we've been doing these songs for a year, and I'm not changing now." Part of the handicap of being a new player is that many times, one learns by rote - playing something over and over until it becomes second nature. This makes it more difficult to change or be flexible in new sections. Alex, a more seasoned player, was able to be more flexible and adapt to the new ideas, as was Jerry. As for me, it was *all new*.

Handley seems to remember Doug having a timing problem:

John French: We had done a session of Sure 'Nuff 'N Yes I Do,
Jerry Handley: Yeah, that's where we had the timing problem with him.

This was less of a timing problem than a problem of hesitancy from low self-esteem from Don's constant verbal attacks, and a lack of rehearsal with the new sections. Although Doug did seem to have a little more trouble than the rest understanding an odd time signature, he was technically much more qualified to play and remember a valid part than was Don. Van Vliet, though able to create endlessly seemed to put it all behind him. He used to equate his creative process with rehearsal - and they are two entirely different things.

Jerry Handley: I remember having talks with Alex and Don, you know, "how we going to get him to keep time? We gotta record".
John French: So eventually what wound up happening is that the consensus was – and Don was pretty much the spearhead of this as I recall - "Let's get Ry Cooder and get rid of Doug." So the decision was, we shouldn't tell him (yet), we'll tell him at a later date, it wasn't the right time to tell him.

The ironic thing about Doug's situation is that it was so similar to Don. I've often heard it said that people who remind you of yourself are usually the ones who irritate you the most. In a sense, some of Don's problems were similar to Doug's. Don and Doug both had a difficult time with last-minute changes. Don and Doug could both get lost in arrangements (recalling Marker's comments concerning Van Vliet needing to be "conducted" by Snouffer), especially when in the studio and under pressure.

The similarities were also offset by huge differences. Don always expressed and manifested a strong confidence, even when he didn't have a clue what he was doing. Doug would always admit when he was lost and this would set Don off, especially if he was in the middle of a creative moment. Doug was shy and and quiet. Conversely, Don was (when with the band and in his Captain persona) loud, gregarious, opinionated, and forceful.

My impression of Doug in the few months that I had played with him was that he was basically a good person who tried to treat people fair. He was inexperienced on guitar and so was under the tutelage of Alex most of the time, but also was quite a master of blues phrasing. He definitely had a creative side and was constantly experimenting with new ideas and different rhythms. He was the main influence on the original *Mirror Man* jam, and also an unreleased unfinished piece called *Maybe That'll Teach Ya*, which Don always thought was quite good but never did anything with. It was a combination of an Afro-Cuban type beat I made up combined with Doug's open G guitar playing. Don added harmonica and a couple of lines of vocal. He listened to the music over and over the following day. It was definitely and most firmly a collaborative effort, which may have been partially why it was never developed.

There is another motive Don may have had in getting rid of Doug. It may have been part of a longer term plan that he had already set in motion. In this comment from Gary Marker, a slight glimmering of this shows.

Gary Marker: I know (Don) was in an inferior position with Alex and Doug and Jerry and all that. So naturally his best defense was an offense. So he would set out after them one at a time and pick them off.

This could have been the beginning of a power play in which he eventually wound up replacing the entire original band. This could possibly have been Don's plan all along. Perhaps this plan was formulated the night that Don stood watching Blues In A Bottle warm up for his band. As my friend Randy Wimer had said, "I looked at him while he was watching you guys play, and he had this look in his eye, like he was planning something."

Marker Gone

John French: So, you left after ...
Gary Marker: I just, you know, you guys had just gotten into it and even Ryland was calling me up saying, "This thing is ..." and I would say, "Don't talk to me man, I don't have a thing to do with it. I'm sorry I got you into it." He said, well, I'm going to go with it. The music is really good and it could be a good thing." I said, "I think so too, I just hope it sounds OK!"

Moon's Perception

John French: And how did you feel, during that time. When we were rehearsing with Ry, during that time. I saw this happening to you. I remember you withdrawing, and you would stay in your room all the time near the end there. You'd play blues (for hours). You would come out for rehearsals, but you were in that room a lot. I remember, if I wanted to see Doug Moon, I had to go in the room, because you didn't come out much. This was after we had been there for a month or two. I really don't recall how long we were there, but it seemed like about four or five months. I recall viewing from the outside, and that's what I saw.
Doug Moon: That makes sense, because things were deteriorating for me. I felt like I was losing my say, I had a share in things - you know like, "Hey! I thought up this guitar lick." I had felt (like I had played) an important part in these songs we were doing, in this creative effort. I felt like I was being left out of the creative effort, and things were starting to change our objective. It got to be where all these professionals and producers started to take control of things and they were collaborating with Don and things just kept changing. There was no stability. There was no point of reference any more. Things were getting out of control. I felt that I wasn't important to the point of, " We had something good, if it's not broke, don't fix it." Now, this is a good song, everybody agreed on it, and we had a finished product. I thought that you can't improve on perfection and I thought these things were great. And then all of a sudden they're trashing everything in the studio. Basically when we moved down there, all of this started to happen. We started going into the studio with all this stuff. Everything started changing, all these people started to get involved, and put in their two cents. Started taking this thing that we had spent several years to create. This Safe As Milk thing was like the culmination of all the suffering and pain and deprivation and many hours that we had spent sacrificially to come up with this creation of which I felt a part. I had a say in it. I felt this was being ripped away from me and in fact it was ... and the ultimate insult was when I was wiped out like I had never had anything to do with it.

This last quote has to do with the fact that Doug had always been under the impression that the demo session we had done at Original Sound Studios actually resulted in tracks that were used on

Safe As Milk. This makes perfect sense, as he didn't hear the finished product for several months and by that time probably just assumed that the session we had done in that upstairs room had resulted in takes that had been used on the album.

Haircuts

At one point in time, Don had been badgering me to let my hair grow and make it look wild. Suddenly, as though it were a corporate decision, we were all strongly persuaded to get haircuts. I mentioned that upon first going to Don's house, he had spoken of a hair-stylist who was a real artist. He was called and came to the house. I don't remember his name, but for the sake of convenience, I'll call him Bill. Bill came to the Laurel Canyon house and cut our hair one evening, just before the *Safe As Milk* photo shoot. Doug had *still* not been told he was out of the group and I was getting a bit apprehensive about how this was going to go down. We all sat in the dining room and talked with Bill as he cut our hair.

One of the topics of conversation that came up was procreation. Bill was strongly opinionated on this point, and stated firmly that having children was just an ego trip and had to do with the importance of placing a "miniature me" on the planet. Of course, Jerry and his wife Sue did not find this particular section of the conversation appealing in the least. Jerry became upset with Bill and argued this point with him. Bill, who I strongly suspect was gay, apologized civilly to Jerry. This did little to clear the air, and Sue and Jerry soon left the room.

The next morning was photo day, and so we all dressed in our new suits. I was seriously annoyed with my new hair trying to brush it and getting nowhere. Don came in and said, "Don't use a brush, *sculpt* your hair, and with that, he moistened his fingers and demonstrated on his own hair. I tried it and was able to achieve something of a natural look. I felt like I looked like some kid at his Bar Mitzvah.

Photo Session/Webster and Wilkes

So, there we were at the Kama Sutra offices, all dressed up and ready to take pictures Doug was led away and we were told to drive to a house in Beverly Hills.

Guy Webster was the photographer chosen for the session. He was the art director at A&M Studios, along with Tom Wilkes. Since the Kama Sutra office in Hollywood was a branch office of the main office in New York, A&M's graphics department was probably a convenient place to have any Los Angeles area work done.

Webster had been highly-praised by Krasnow for his work and had obviously made a name for himself in order to achieve this respect.

An aspiring actor, he had begun his career as a fluke while serving in the Army as a conscientious objector. At first, not knowing what to do with Guy, they had him decorating Christmas trees and other menial tasks. Seeing Webster's patience wearing thin, they eventually had an opening in the photo department and asked him if he would be interested in tutoring some students.

Guy Webster: I said "Yeah, I know a lot about photography, and would be happy to do it." I knew nothing. I rented a couple of books out of the library there at Fort Ord and read them that night. I came in (the next morning) and started teaching the new recruits how to make prints and develop film. I had not taken any pictures of my own and a famous film producer, Jerry Wald, lent me his camera when I was in the Army and asked, "Could you take some pictures?" So, I took some pictures. I got out (of the Army) after six months, and instead of going to Yale I went to Art Center School of Design, they wanted me to go there. They saw this roll of film that I did when I was in the Army. It was all art photography. Well, they said, you gotta come here and go to school - and I did - not knowing anything about photography.

Within a year, I was taking pictures commercially of actors and actresses because I'd been an actor and I had lots of friends that were young actors who were pretty well on their way - like Jack Nicholson – people like that.

So, that started it. Then I was playing basketball with Lou Adler who was starting Dunhill Records, and he loved my photographs. He said, "Look, I don't have any money, we're just getting started, but maybe you could do the album covers for practice. Well, I was still in school, but I thought "This could be fun." We did the first cover, which was Barry McGuire's Eve of Destruction *and it went to number one in the country.*

That was it, I was a full-flight rock'n'roll photographer, having never planned that in my life at all, but I liked it. I gave up Yale, and my parents basically disinherited me. They couldn't believe that I could do such a thing. I got married very early – I was still in school – so I had to work hard. I just took every job I could get, and worked seven days a week. I shot for the LA Times - for the magazine section (doing) fashion shootings – along with rock'n'roll. That's what I was doing at the time.

For the session, the four of us drove to the location in Beverly Hills as instructed and Guy came out from behind the house and invited us to follow him back.

John French: When we did the Safe As Milk *session, we went to a house in Beverly Hills.*
Guy Webster: That was my father's house. He won a lot of academy awards and was quite an accomplished songwriter. He wrote The Shadow of Your Smile, Love is a Many Splendored Thing, Secret Love, *- on and on - the theme from* Dr. Zhivago. *I was working at that house. By the time you met me (1967), I had this big estate up in Benedict Canyon. It wasn't ready to use ... I didn't have a studio there. We shot in the back of my parent's house - behind the guest house.*

Guy was very upbeat, and this helped to take me out of the doldrums and thinking about Doug, but it kept coming to mind, "He should be here", all day long.

John French: There's a little background story. One of the guitarists was fired that very day. So there was just the three of us, and Don instead of the full band. I felt that it was very incomplete without Doug Moon being there.
Guy Webster: I remember that, yes.
JF: It was a very strange feeling for me. Did you notice that kind of a mood on the band?
GW: Yeah, I did. Whereas, on the second cover (referring to the Strictly Personal *shoot.), I didn't feel that at all.*

Webster wanted to try something with a fisheye lens and shoot us through the slats in a small greenhouse that was in the back yard. It wasn't a greenhouse really, just a little trellis-like affair that was barely big enough for all to stand inside. I was positioned in the back. Guy gave me a pair of those little round sunglasses to wear. The photo that appears on the front of the original *Safe As Milk* came from this series.

John French: What was it like – compared to some of the bands that you shot – how would you compare The Magic Band - as far as working with Don and the rest of us.
Guy Webster: When you guys walked in that day, Don was saying, "I want this to be sort of Abba Zabba." Very interesting, I didn't know what he meant, except I knew he was speaking metaphorically. I kind of got what he was talking about. I thought, "When I do this

graphic, I'll use an Abba Zabba *candy bar wrapper." That's what that was with the yellow and black squares - I built it on that image. I used the fish-eye also, because it had a kind of* Abba Zabba *feel to it. That's the only cover (on which) I ever used a fish-eye.*

As usual in any photo shoot, they tried to get us to look natural, but at the same time we were made to stand in exact locations so that we would line up in the lens. We spent some time behind his father's house and then took off up through one of the canyons and found an empty house.

Guy Webster: I think we shot in Franklin Canyon - right in that area.
John French: I remember going to a vacant house, walking in the back yard, and that's where the shot on the rear cover was taken.
GW: I did so many shootings in those years that they all sort of blend together you know?

Walking behind the property, Guy said something like "This is it," and started getting out equipment. I thought Wilkes was with him until the interview.

John French: Right, Tom Wilkes, now wasn't he your assistant on that first shoot that we did?
Guy Webster: No. That could have been Jim McQuarry, I'm not sure, or my brother Roger, who worked for me at that time.

It was a partly cloudy day and I remember Don commenting on the assistant being aware of every little change in light. He was constantly pulling out the light meter and checking it to make sure of proper exposure. This back yard in the canyon is where the picture that appeared on the back of the album was taken.

Don picked up a couple of acorns off the ground. It looked in the picture as though he was rolling a joint. I was sure later that this was intentional. There were several shots taken this day. I didn't realize, having never been on a shoot before, just how many pictures were taken so that there would be a good possibility of getting just the right shot.

The underlying theme in my head about this shoot is that I thought Ry Cooder would be included in the new band lineup, yet he wasn't there. It became clear pretty quickly that Ry was still undecided about whether to be a member and was still considering the whole thing a trial run. These personnel problems were to turn out to be a consistent theme throughout the history of the band.

Moon Fired

As we were shooting the album cover, Doug was fired by Krasnow.

John French: So the day came (Safe As Milk photo shoot day) and Doug was led into Krasnow's office. Krasnow said, "I want to talk to you, Doug. And we (left) and he found out. Maybe you don't remember that day, but I do, because I spent the following evening with Doug, consoling him. I think you were gone back up to be with your family, with Sue.
Jerry Handley: In moments of crisis I'd skip out, "Gotta go see the family." (Laughs)

Doug's Feelings

John French: And Bob Krasnow was the person who gave you the axe.
Doug Moon: Yeah.
JF: What was the reason? Do you remember any reasons?

225

DM: *Yeah, I remember exactly the reason.*

JF: *What'd he say?*

DM: *"Well, Don says you won't do anything the way he ... he can't get you to do anything anymore. You can't do any of the guitar parts right." Yeah, well, on the spur of the moment in the studio when I'm playing something it took me I-don't-know-how many-hours to learn. He expects me to redo it in an instant? I wasn't that kind of a guitar player. Maybe some studio musician could do that. So that's exactly what they did. They got somebody who could do it exactly the way Don wanted - automatically, like that. (Snaps fingers).*

JF: *Well, there was Ry Cooder and then his friend, Russ Titleman.*

DM: *Yeah. Ry Cooder was a studio musician. I wasn't a studio musician; I was just a blues guitarist from the desert that learned his craft from hours and hours of practicing my guitar parts. I memorized things. I wasn't an improvisational guitarist that could hear a melody line and do it. I had to practice.*

JF: *Did you feel betrayed?*

DM: *Yeah.*

JF: *There was no loyalty?*

DM: *I felt that my ... the part that I created in these songs was being trashed and Don was reinventing the whole thing on a whim, on a drug-crazed whim. That's why he was losing control, because of the acid. See, what really happened - pot was bad enough, but when we started taking acid, that's what really did it.*

Alex Snouffer: *Now, as far as ace-ing him out of the band, I thought that was pretty chicken-shit. Cause Doug had been there through thick and thin, you know, in putting these things together and all. Then, when it came down to the session, you know, enter Ry, which of course was fine with me, but we're talking a session here. We're not talking road band, even though he did go out with us that one time up to San Francisco. I don't know if Doug got any more compensation for it when they cut him loose or not, do you know anything about that?*

John French: *No, he didn't get a thing.*

AS: *Nothin', huh?*

Doug Moves Out

Doug came, got his stuff out of the house, and moved in with Fran. She had an extra room in her house, and I thought he was staying close hoping that something would break or that Don would change his mind. He later told me that he didn't want to go back and face his friends and relatives in the desert. I didn't have anything to do with the decision to fire Doug. Ry was in. Doug was out. It was very cut and dried.

The only trouble was that Ry was not really in. It was obvious that Ry's relationship with the band was strictly business. It was also obvious that he did not pose with the band for the album cover shots simply because he wasn't part of the band. I thought he had asked for and received extra money from Kama Sutra for being basically a music director/arranger. Later, I was to find that even this was not so and I believe the only compensation he received was a couple of guitars. It was pretty obvious that the band did need someone who could come in and cut through the crap, especially Don's diversions, and focus on accomplishing important goals. We didn't really see much of Ry after the album was done.

I was still thinking all the time about the draft and the war. I wasn't exempt just because I was working. College students and guys with kids were the only ones getting out. I was a prime candidate for induction. Some of my friends in Lancaster had already been drafted. My next door neighbor, John Tivis, died in combat. He was a year younger than me. Don Giesen went to Vietnam.

He actually enjoyed it over there - working in some kind of radio dispatch maintenance. He served two full terms and came home healthy in mind and body. He works today in Lake Tahoe as an upholsterer for himself and also a major casino. He is happily married and has two grown sons. About this same time, on the East Coast a future member of the band was studying music in New York.

Art Tripp/1967

About this same time in New York, Art Tripp, future percussionist and drummer of the Magic Band, was about to meet up with Don's friend, Frank Zappa, through a chance meeting with Dick Kunc, Zappa's studio engineer. I feel it's important to include this part of Tripp's interview here because of the time frame.

John French: Didn't you go to the Manhattan School of Music?
Art Tripp: Yeah, after that I was really kind of getting discouraged, because I always wanted to do new stuff, or even avant-garde stuff. There was very little happening anywhere really. In the symphony, they think new stuff was written in 1920, you know - or Stravinsky 1911 pieces or something. So there wasn't – I was getting involved locally in a lot of stuff, but that doesn't allow you to buy a loaf of bread. So, I thought, Screw this, and I got a scholarship to Manhattan School of Music and I went there. I was studying under Fred Hinger, who actually had been the tympanist with the Philadelphia Orchestra. In fact I had gone to Curtis to audition to get in, because if you get into Curtis, there's no tuition. I wanted to, I had been working on a Masters. I started working on a Masters in Cincinnati, but I could see I wasn't going to stay there. So anyway, Fred turned me down, and I was kind of both glad and sad at the same time. He said he wasn't going to accept me as a student, but he said the reason was because I was too far along. I was too accomplished as it were. So, I was flattered that he said that, but at the same time I really wanted to study with him. But as it turned out, when I got the Scholarship to Manhattan, Fred had decided to quit the Philadelphia after - I don't know how many years he played with them. I think he still is the greatest of all time as a tympanist. He had decided to go and play with the Metropolitan Opera in New York. So when he did that he accepted a teaching position at Manhattan School of Music. But, he didn't teach there, he taught at the Met. So when I'd go there, I'd do all my weekly studies at the School. But when I would take my private lessons from him, I'd go down to the Met. It was kind of interesting. It's a big deal when you go there. With all the rehearsal studios, it was really something. It was a state of the art building at that time and that was in '67.
JF: I recall you telling me a story about your scholarship not covering everything and when you got there you didn't have any other money and ...
AT: I was so stupid and so nuts that I just showed up and thought, "Well, they'll just have to wait for the money."
JF: How did that work out?
AT: Well, they didn't really want to wait for the money. They said, "Well, you owe us ..." I don't know what it was ... the rest of it. I said, "Well, I don't have any money and they said, "Well, here, sign up for this student loan." So I did. It was through the Federal Government. I wasn't there for – it wasn't very long at all, maybe six months or something. And then I met up with Zappa.

Art Tripp Meets Dick Kunc/Frank Zappa

John French: Anyway, back to Zappa, when you first got with Zappa, right?
Art Tripp: This gal I was living with at the time, got a job as a social worker up in Harlem, in order to support us while I was going to school. She had been a social worker in Cincinnati,

and they were screaming for workers up in Harlem or anywhere in New York. Since there was no problem getting a job, she went to work that very day. Unfortunately, they waited four weeks to pay you, because they were afraid you would just run off. So anyway, this girl who was an associate worker of hers was named Patricia Kunc and that, of course, was Dick Kunc's wife, who was the original recording engineer for Zappa at Apostolic studios in New York. Down in – I guess it was the village – way below tenth and Broadway, way downtown. She had heard about me through Adrian.

JF: Adrian - your girlfriend.

AT: Yeah. She had heard that I worked for six months with John Cage in Cincinnati, and I played with the symphony and I had done ballet and all this crap. So one thing led to another and Dick got interested, so they invited us over for dinner and drinks one night, over at their place. Maybe it was just drinks, I don't remember – I was really interested in drinks. So, we went over there and had a nice social evening. Dick got real interested and he was impressed with what I had done. He told me about this guy he was working with - Zappa, and I had just heard Zappa for the first time, it was like two weeks before then. We'd picked up some wayward kids in the village who were – this is before people were homeless. They were just kind of running away and we'd met them down there. We had them come up and stay at our place for a couple of nights because it was cold and they didn't have any place to stay. They were carrying Zappa's first two albums, Freak Out and Absolutely Free. So, I flipped it on. I heard Absolutely Free, and I thought, "Man! This stuff is too much!" I just couldn't believe it, because I hadn't heard anything like it before. My idea of rock'n'roll was either the Beatles, who were really getting popular about then, or the old stuff, Chuck Berry and that stuff. I wasn't interested in any of that crap, it was just boring. I was into much more complex music. When I heard that, I thought it was something else, and at the time, if anyone said, "Hey, who's your favorite rock'n'roll group?" I'd say, "Well, it's Frank Zappa and the Mothers of Invention." At that time, they were just called the Mothers of Invention. Frank hadn't started using his own name. It was funny the way it worked out. So I told Dick, "Look, I realize you're doing work down there, I could really use the money if you need to hire studio guys, if you need somebody to play bongos or xylophone or anything like that, because, I could really use the jack. So, he said, "Yeah, I'll let you know." I hadn't played a set of drums, where you sit down and play the trap kit, for several years. I was into other things, and it had been a long time since I had even done that. I wasn't even considering that kind of work. So, a few weeks later, he gave me a call and said, "Look could you come down Friday to the studio?" I said, "Yeah, absolutely." So I asked if they wanted me to bring anything, and he said, "No we have everything here." I said, "OK, great! So, I went down there and he took me into the studio and I met Frank and Herbie, you know, and Suzy Creamcheeze, you know Pamela Zarubica and all their hangers-on and all that shit. I was pretty impressed. I hadn't spent much time in a studio, I had done very little studio work, a little bit. But this was all different - it was very interesting, because it was real loose and exciting, you know. So finally Frank asked me a couple of questions, he asked, "Do you play regular drums?" I said, "Yeah, but it's been a long time!" He said, "Well, come on out here and play something, and we walked out in the studio, and there was a couple of sets of drums behind the baffles. One set, I found out later, was Billy Mundi's drums, and he just hadn't picked them up yet, because he had quit a couple of weeks or a month beforehand, right in the middle of these albums. They hadn't replaced him yet. I didn't know any of that. I sat down, and asked, "Well, what do you want me to play?" He said, "Play anything you want to play." So I just started playing. Just free-form stuff, which I always enjoyed doing. I played for quite a while, three or four minutes, and went all over the kit and played all these oddball things and different times and shit. I just kinda stopped and looked up and Frank was standing there with his mouth open. He said, "Man, you're a monster!" I said, "Really?" I didn't know what to expect, I didn't know what he had in mind. He said, "Can you play in five?" (5/4 time) I said, "In five?" I thought he was kidding you know. Of course I could play in five, there was nothing to it. He said, "Can you go (sings) cha boom cha boom boom etc.? I said (laughs) "I think I can do that." I did that and picked it up and improvised a little bit around it. He said, "Man, this is too much!" As it turned out, Roy Estrada and Ray and a few of them were sitting out in the waiting room, bullshitting. He brought Roy in and we played this little thing in five meter. He said, "This is too much, I'll tell you what, are you doing anything this weekend? Because we're going up to play a couple of gigs in north state New York." I said, "Yeah, I had a party." So, he said, "Well, why don't you come along with us?" And I said, "I don't know your music or anything about it." I had never played rock'n'roll or anything for years, since the late fifties. He said, "Don't worry about it, if you need to know, just watch Jim." He said, "Everytime I point to you, just start playing a drum solo." I said, "Yeah, I can do that!" (Laughs) he said, " By the way, it'll be about. $500" I said, "$500?" Adrian was making about $100 a week or something. I never saw $500.

JF: That was a lot of money then, too.

AT: Yeah, it was over thirty years ago. Absolutely! So, we went up and did those two gigs. I think it was the second gig we played. It was in this big indoor amphitheatre, and I think it was in Ithaca. At any rate, we were all sitting around backstage before the show and he said, "Why don't you just go ahead and start us off?" I said, "You mean, just go out and play by myself?" I said, "Alright, great!" So I just went out there and started wailing, you know? The guys started coming on the stage and we just played the show, every time a piece of music came up and I didn't know what it was, I just looked over at Jim and see what he was doing and I would just mimic that, that's how I started. Then we got into rehearsals – did some of the more complex stuff. Although the group really didn't play all the stuff that was on their albums, they couldn't get it together. That was kind of the situation through most of it.

JF: Did he give you a lot of written music in the early days?

AT: Yeah. Not so much for the straight-ahead rock stuff, but all the complicated stuff. He had never had a guy that could read, a conservatory-trained percussionist. In fact, very few conservatory-trained musicians. Well, he had Ian (Underwood) of course, who was his great musician. Don and Bunk both had legitimate training. But I was the first percussionist he ever had that could play all that stuff. He just went nuts. He started writing stuff, because Frank was very interested in percussion, he'd been a drummer himself at one time. I don't know how good he was, but he really could think in percussion. So, he just wrote all this stuff. More complex parts for the stuff he was doing, and I would just play it. So, when we got back, we were working on two or three albums simultaneously. The first thing he had me do was he had me redo all the drum tracks for Ruben And The Jets, because he didn't like what Billy Mundi had played. So, it was funny, because I hadn't had a lot of experience. It was funny to sit down with the phones and play to the track. The music was already done and they were just replacing his drum tracks.

JF: There wasn't a click or anything, so it was probably whatever Billy's time was...

AT: Exactly, it was kind of unusual, but it was simplicity itself. The parts were so ridiculously easy, it was real simple. He had little oddball parts, things that weren't real common in those days, but simplicity itself. It just couldn't have been any easier. It was a lot of fun. We sat there, and I think we did the whole goddamned album in a day. I mean I think it was a double record set, we finished that up. At the same time, we were working on Uncle Meat, which was far more interesting. I was playing a lot of vibraphone and marimba, miscellaneous percussion. *I really liked that stuff. To this day, it's my favorite album. I was really busy, and I was just working like 12 hours a day in the studio, some days I'd go for a few hours and some days we'd work around the clock, but I was putting in a lot of time. Meanwhile, he never told me that I was in the band.*

JF: *So, did you ever get studio rates for this?*

AT: *No. I didn't get anything. I wasn't smart enough at the time. I was just a young kid. I was just interested in playing.*

JF: *So you were doing this all for free?*

AT: *Well, as it turned out I did.*

JF: *OH wow.*

AT: *You know, I didn't even ask him. When we finally – I forget at one time – when they finally decided to pay us – I ended up getting like $300! (Laughs) For all that work. Christ, if I had been playing at studio rates, I would have made thousands - even at that time. But, I didn't care. I mean, it was the last thing in the world I was thinking about was money. Course, some of the older guys were much more interested in the money. (Laughs) Well some of them had families to feed and everything else.*

JF: *They had already done the free gigs.*

AT: *Yeah, I should have known, after that weekend we got back. We had a band meeting or something and what we were supposed to get paid, and Herbie only gave us three hundred, and we were supposed to get five hundred. I should've known right then. He said, "Something got screwed up and the promoter this and that" ... some bullshit. There were no records then, he did the accounting, but we never got to see any of that.*

JF: *So, did that happen a lot with Frank or was Frank more fair with his musicians?*

AT: *To be honest with you – 'cause Herbie always told me that he did the business and Frank did the music. I didn't believe that, but in those early days, that was probably the situation. I mean I think Frank was aware of what was going on ... but he didn't really ride herd on that much. I used to tell him, by the time I got to LA, or even at Apostolic, we'd go in the studio and just spend all day there. And I said (to Herbie), "Hey, why don't we rehearse somewhere else, rent a place for a couple hundred and week, and then, when we're ready, go into the studio at three hundred an hour, or whatever it is, then we won't have to spend so much time in there. All that money that we get from an advance, we could split that up, we'd all have more dough!" He (Herbie) said, "Well, I can't say anything about that, that's the way Frank does it, he's the music half of this thing and I'm the business half." At the time, I thought he was bullshitting me, but he may have been right, I don't know.*

CHAPTER THIRTEEN:
BUDDAH'S TAINTED MILK

...e only remaining shot from this late '67 session. Photo courtesy of Guy Webster.

231

RCA Studios

Remember Marker's little prophecy: "This is going to be a disaster"? Well, he was close.

Gary Marker: Cooder had called me up and said, "You know what they're doing? They're going down to RCA!" Now RCA was a four-track studio. I said, "RCA? RCA is the lamest place in town! What are they doing?"

The rest of the tracks of *Safe As Milk* were done at RCA Studios, just down the street on Sunset, a block or two from Vine. Hank Cicalo was the engineer. He was an amiable fellow with a sort of Mitch Miller look. Sporting short dark hair and a Van Dyke beard, he looked more like someone out of the beat era. But, he had a professional manner and everyone seemed to have a great amount of respect for him. The band didn't seem to have a problem with the fact that the studio had limited facilities, generally due to our limited lack of technical knowledge about recording techniques.

In the sixties, musicians only concerned themselves with playing and trusted the technicians to run the control room. Remember Doug's comment (an "electronics geek" according to his own words) when asked about Zappa's studio?

Doug Moon: I just remember stuff.

And Handley's reaction was pretty much the same.

Jerry Handley: It was just a small studio. He had the machines and all.

All we perceived when we walked into the control room were a lot of knobs and machines. I had a rudimentary knowledge of recording technique because not only was it my father's hobby, but my friend Don Giesen also had an interest. We had discussed various techniques, mixers, microphones etc. The studio to which we were assigned at RCA contained only a four-track Ampex machine. Sunset Sound was an eight-track studio, but we had paid little attention and weren't really aware of the differences.

Nowadays, musicians are much more aware of the technical aspects of a studio and many produce their own recordings, or have studios in their homes. One of the differences is in the fact that digital electronics has allowed everything to become much more accessible, in terms of price and also size. Studios were *very* expensive in those early days. This is probably due to the fact that tube electronics used immense amounts of electricity and also generated huge amounts of heat, not to mention the fact that everything was 50 times as big as it is now.

The room at RCA was actually quite a bit larger than Sunset Sound, and seemed more like the kind of room that would be used for an orchestra of moderate size. They had actually divided the room in half with large partitions and we all set up in a line facing the control room windows. To the left of that large window was a large door leading though the hall from which equipment could be brought in and out.

I knew that RCA was less expensive and assumed that the song *Sure 'Nuff 'N Yes I Do* had been chosen by the powers-that-be as the single. This was my logical reasoning as to why it was given special attention and a better studio whereas the rest of the material didn't deserve or need the same attention (referring to Buddah's mindset concerning the music.) In those days, artists would come up with a single well-produced song that was pre-judged as having hit potential and the rest of the album was often considered filler material. Even though I thought we had more interesting material than *Sure 'Nuff 'N Yes I Do*, I thought perhaps everything else was taking a back seat in the sense of budget.

I was a little less evolved in my thinking than I should have been. The Beatles' *Sergeant Pepper's* album had recently been released and was a concept album, possibly the *first* concept album (I'll leave that up to the experts at *Rolling Stone Magazine*). We may have all been a little less evolved in our thinking, or perhaps we were not thinking at all. One of the advantages of working in a *group* was the idea that there was a common pool of thought into which everyone's thoughts donated a certain amount of knowledge, which could then be taken advantage of by the whole. Unfortunately, the Beefheart band was far less a group effort and was already beginning to have more of the shades of a *dictatorship*. It's also apparent from what I have thus far written that Don Van Vliet was being less than honest with the group. There were a number of evasive maneuvers taken by Don during any band meeting. The real decisions, as I now see, were being made without our knowledge and Don was just creating a smoke screen to distract us from perceiving the facts.

The advantage of a dictatorship is that a certain powerful focus takes place. The disadvantage is that in the general scheme of *what was happening*, we were clueless from the perspective of the method of production. I recall no band discussion regarding the quality of studios, the efficiency of engineers, or the overall sound of the band. For instance, Jeff Beck had pioneered the heavy metal sound which Jimi Hendrix, a blues guitarist, combined with a psychedelic look in a winning combination. The group Cream did much the same thing, using guitar preamplifiers to achieve a giant sound.

As Van Vliet had mentioned many times, Zappa was the first person he had heard attain this heavy metal guitar distortion concept in the fifties by playing his guitar through a tape recorder amplifier. We were aware of Hendrix and Cream, as their albums they were displayed on Kama Sutra's office wall - something he probably placed there for inspiration. He recognized the sound when he heard it, he just didn't know how to achieve it. This is what made him less a producer and more a promoter. David Gates had come to the closest to recognizing that times were changing and used fuzz-bass with reverb and compression to attain the giant sound of *Diddy Wah Diddy*. In the pure concept of overall sound for the Magic Band I am inclined to believe that he was never topped.

As Marker was quoted earlier saying:

Gary Marker: Diddy Wah Diddy *was a fabulous record, there was no question about it. And I still love that record. I listen to it and think, "This thing was a monster!" It was a great sound with all that compression and stuff and that great voice.*

This was in the earliest days of stereo. A lot of albums (*Safe As Milk* included) were released both in monophonic and stereophonic sound. Stereo back in those days often consisted of putting a cluster of instruments on one speaker, and putting another cluster on the other. There was little panning of individual instruments. A panning control is like a balance knob on a stereo. If the knob is turned all the way to the right, everything comes out the right speaker and conversely with the left speaker. As the knob is turned from right to left, the sound gives the illusion of traveling from right to left. So, if each instrument has its own track and pan knob, you can pan them all slightly differently to give the illusion of placing the instruments in a lineup similar to the way a band sounds live on stage. This helps to define each instrument in the ears of the listener.

Of course, this is a completely simplified explanation, and I apologize to all the technicians in advance. The reason I am explaining this is so that the non-techs can understand that the big advantage to eight-track recording is that every instrument could basically be on its own track. Therefore everything could be panned to a precise location in the audio spectrum, giving it a bigger, more exciting sound.

In four-track recording, music was recorded on several tracks and then ping-ponged, or re-

recorded down to one track to make more room on the tape. For instance the engineer could record on three tracks, and mix all three tracks to the one left. Then, there would still be three open tracks. By the end of the session, the hope in the final mix was that all the volume balance (mixing) decisions had been correctly made in the tracks that were ping-ponged. If not, some vital part of the music could be buried underneath a tambourine overdub in a moment of hasty decision-making. It was crude and very limited. Often, mixing decisions were made a little too hastily in the ping-ponging sessions, thus altering the sound of the composition forever.

Another thing that was bad about this method is that anytime something was re-recorded in early analog (tape) technology, it added a generation of tape hiss and noise. This made the sound less clear and more unnatural, taking away even more power from the music. A good analogy would be making a photocopy of something, then making a photocopy of the photocopy, etc. Each resulting copy would have slightly less clarity than the one preceding it.

Gary Marker: I called up Krasnow for an explanation and he said, "Well, Dick (Richard Perry)" – he was calling him Dick by now – " is really confused by all those tracks. We took the stuff that we did on 8-track and reduced it down to four track." I said, "Are you kidding me? That beautiful state-of-the-art stuff?"

So, Marker's knowledge of recording technology coupled with his witnessing of Perry's lack of experience with the state of the art technology made him of the opinion that the album was headed for disaster. Though disaster was avoided and a product was produced which was well received critically (in limited markets), he foresaw many of the pitfalls that were to come, and the resulting diminished quality of the final mix.

Mike Nesmith

The Monkees, a product band that had been put together by producers who handpicked a group, manufactured an image, and created a television show and mass promotion, were also recording in RCA Studios at the same time Safe As Milk was being recorded.

Mike Nesmith befriended the band - especially Don. We used to go sit in his brand new black Buick Riviera in the underground parking facility. He was quite proud of the vehicle because he had commissioned extensive custom work and it had just been returned to him. Mike, it seemed, was not extremely happy in the Monkees and I think he considered Van Vliet and company true artists and felt a bit guilty for having reaped the financial rewards he had in such a manner. This is mostly speculation but also had to do with Don's opinions, which he would discuss with us privately. Nesmith never seemed very happy, but was rather serious and distant for the most part. From what I recall, the Monkees were actually playing all their own instruments on this album, whereas before the producers had merely hired studio musicians. The album was entitled *Headquarters*, and I believe it is the first album they recorded where they actually were allowed to play their own instruments.

Abba Zaba

For some reason, I couldn't bring my own drums to the session. Krasnow said that I would be supplied with rented drums. I spent several hours setting up and tuning the rented drums before I had a chance to get used to playing them. Once set up and miked, the sound was checked. Then, I had to sit and wait for hours without making any sound while everyone had his sound checked. Finally, after hours of waiting, it was time to play.

We started with *Abba Zaba*. We were all lined up parallel with the control booth out in the big tracking room. I was underneath a huge pole-less umbrella suspended from its center topside, which Hal Blaine, a great studio drummer, had left set up from his session. We were all wearing headphones at first if I recall. I was set up behind the bass amplifier. Alex was to the right of Jerry, and Ry stood to the right of Alex. I believe that they eventually did not wear headphones, because the amplified sound combined with the drums caused them to be able to hear quite well in the room.

This put me in a bit of an awkward position of responsibility, as I was the only one who could hear the talkback from the control room. They (the control room gremlins) would tell me when tape was rolling, and I had to be the announcer of any information given to the band. There were speakers in the room, which could be used, but I believe they were shut off for the most part because there was less of a chance of ruining a take with the tracking room speakers left off. I was pretty apprehensive, as this was much more intense than anything I had previously encountered, and a lot of people's time and money was being invested in the project. I have no idea what previous experience had prepared me for this, but for some reason, I was able to focus and just think about the project and the music for the most part. Perhaps it was abject terror of what might happen to me if I failed. After all, Don used to say, "A little paranoia is a good propeller."

So, I played the drum intro and the band came in right on cue. The band sounded fine, but every time we came to the bass solo, Handley would miss a note or two. Don had written it as an additional section to the song a few weeks prior to the session. I'm sure of this, because the version of *Abba Zaba* recorded in Original Sound for the demo produced by Gary Marker contains the solo. Each time Jerry blew the solo, I would get a little more apprehensive and impatient. We had been sitting for what seemed like all day, and now the first take was taking far longer than it should. We had a projected schedule and I intuitively felt that we needed to move along. I was getting deja vu of the *Sure'Nuff 'N Yes I Do* session. I had these terrible thoughts about being trapped in that studio forever, doing take after take in studio hell, my fingers bleeding again.

I think Jerry's problem was exactly the same as he had previously encountered in Sunset Sound: he was forced to use a pick. He was thus handicapped because he usually plucked the strings with his fingers. Most of the bassists I have worked with used their fingers rather than picks. However, to get the clarity in the studio, the engineers again insisted upon Jerry using a pick. This did not occur to me at the time.

This time it was my turn to throw a hissy fit. I finally stood and said in a rather forceful and childish manner that I needed a break. My hands were just healing up from the last marathon session. *Abba Zaba* was a much more difficult song to play correctly. I was thinking, "Why didn't they pick something that was less difficult for the first song? What's more, I had just been taught the drum solo fills that went with the bass part just recently and since the band hadn't been rehearsing, I wasn't used to them yet, and neither was Jerry. Alex had made a special trip over to the Laurel Canyon house, and we rehearsed the night before the demo session just to make sure everything was right, but we had been more involved in business than in music in the last two weeks.

Linda, the secretary from Kama Sutra, was in the booth, and she retrieved some paper towels for my hands and face. I remember her looking at me like I was some kind of madman, and for the moment I suppose I temporarily was. I was wet all over and extremely annoyed with Jerry, who really wasn't to blame. The real problem was the overall lack of preparation and Don's inability to understand the fact that the studio requires a much higher level of focus due to the many distractions and the sterile conditions. All the writing should have been finished before looking for a recording contract. Had that happened, everyone would have been better prepared.

Ryland Plays Bass

One of the producers – probably Perry or Krasnow at that point - decided to let Ry play bass on the basic track. He learned the part in ten minutes, and in a half an hour, we had the song wrapped.

He later went back and recorded one great guitar track. My favorite part on the entire album is underneath the lyrics, "mother say, son ..." He just looked like he was coasting. I loved this guy! What a player!

John French: Jerry couldn't play his bass solo. Ry had to learn to play it.
Gary Marker: I know he ended up playing it. I have a big argument about that. That's on that Ry Cooder list thing, you know, there's a whole Ry Cooder fansite. They know he's on that album. I said, "Well, he played the bass solo on Abba Zaba." They say, "NO, NO, NO!" I said, "Yes, that is clearly Ryland, because the attack is always a little ahead of the beat." You could always tell, because he always jumps on the beat. I said, "Believe me, that is not Jerry Handley."
JF: No, Jerry did a bunch of takes of it. I was getting worn out from beating the hell out of the drums. Of course, you can't tell on the recording.
GM: No, but it's just a classic drum part. I mean, it really slams away. It really is very African.

I mentioned on my drum solo CD *(O'Solo Drumbo)* that Don had asked me to come up with something African sounding for *Abba Zaba*. This was the beat that was the culmination of my search. A few years later, I heard the exact same beat on an African field recording, which surprised me a bit.

Last Minute Additions
Even with Cooder's methodical approach, there were still songs with parts left unfinished. Richard Perry came up with a couple of drum ideas. The main part to *Autumn's Child* was his. It has a slight reggae influence. Also on the song *Where There's Woman*, he established a drum pattern and added some echo to the snare. This prohibited me from playing any fills because the echo would not have worked with any busy parts.

During the recordings, I don't recall anyone staying at the Amor Road house except for Don, Laurie, and myself. Doug was out of the band. Alex was staying with his friend Fran. Jerry was commuting to the desert to be with his wife and baby a few hours a day. As we sat listening to the tapes of the previous night's work, I mentioned to Don that Jerry's part was improvised, because he wasn't actually around when the music was put together for *Where There's Woman*. As Don knew he wouldn't be around until the time of the session, he called Alex and asked him to come over a couple of hours before the session. Don sang the bass parts to Snouffer, who then overdubbed the bass part just as Jerry actually showed up at RCA.

Alex Snouffer: The only thing I recall is when I overdubbed that bass part on Where There's Woman.

Handley was rather puzzled by what he was hearing. Snouffer had overdubbed bass on the slow sections, but Handley's part was left on the fast tempo section. Jerry kept listening because he would hear himself, then he wouldn't. It was a bit of a puzzle.

The Three Stooges

John French: We had our three producers: Krasnow, Perry, and Art Ripp.
Alex Snouffer: (Quoting) "Heavy, heavy, heavy."

Artie Ripp came in to the session that evening. I remember that before we started that take, I wanted a Coke really bad. I walked up to him and not knowing who he was, I put a dollar (back

236

when they were worth something) in his hand and asked if he would go get some Cokes. There were always people running in and out, and most of them were just gofers, or sightseers, wanting to catch some exciting moment in recording history or some such nonsense. So I mistakenly asked the president of Kama Sutra/Buddah Records to go out for Cokes - in front of everyone. I look back on that moment as one of the most meaningful in my life. Just for a moment, the man actually looked like he was going. Then he delegated the errand to someone else. For what he later did to Billy Joel, he deserved the embarrassment.

The rest of the session went a little more smoothly. At least the instrumental tracks. The only one I had a hard time on was *Dropout Boogie*. I could not remember where we were in the song unless I heard the lyrics. Artie decided to coach me through *Dropout Boogie*. I was trying to look at the lyric sheet and remember where I was in the song. Voila, this bozo is standing there like a football coach waving his arms, conducting me as though somehow, brute force would inspire me to play with more enthusiasm. The problem was with the arrangement and all I needed was to be able to concentrate on the lyric sheet.

Grown So Ugly, Ry's pet project for the album, was finished in a very few takes and I believe it was done at the end of the same session as *Dropout Boogie*. We had spent so much time rehearsing it, I think it had no life left by the time we went to tape. Just like with *Sure 'Nuff 'N Yes I Do*, Ry wasn't happy with it. I can understand his sentiments from the perspective of the way it was regarded in the studio. We had a very short amount of time left in the session - maybe 45 minutes. We were all trying to quickly decide how best to use the time, and somebody suggested *Grown So Ugly* because it was well-rehearsed.

John French: And then we learned Grown So Ugly, *that song that was Ry's total arrangement from that Robert Pete Williams classic ...*
Jerry Handley: *He loved that style, I wish it had come out better on the album. It just didn't come across, but it was a great song.*
JF: *Yeah, I think it was like ... we've got an hour left, let's do that.*
JH: *I think so. It was kind of an afterthought.*
JF: *Yeah, we had rehearsed it, but he (Ry) was real unhappy with it.*
JH: *I don't blame him. We didn't do it justice.*

Ry seemed immediately displeased at the B-movie attitude the production team had regarding this song. This was a song Ry had nurtured into a full band arrangement, note by note, drum beat by drum beat. However, time was running out and it really was the logical choice because it was so well rehearsed. We did very few takes. Probably 5 with a couple of false starts, and it was done. Unfortunately, the tempo was a bit too fast which made it even more difficult for Don to sing.

Grown So Ugly was totally Ry's arrangement. He taught everyone note for note exactly how he wanted it played. He even sang it while he played, which wasn't easy. One of the reasons this song was almost second nature was because it is the only one we had rehearsed with a vocal. The song was in an odd time signature and had those tricky breaks. I was used to playing in odd time signatures, so I recall this as being easy. It's always much easier to learn a song when someone has taken the time to think out the entire arrangement and all you have to do is concentrate on your parts.

As an aside, Don, after listening to Ry's singing at rehearsals on the song *Grown So Ugly* told Ryland that he should be singing more. I think he took Don's advice.

Overdubs/Sweeteners
The basics were now done. It was time to add the sweeteners, which are overdubs specifically targeted to enhance the songs.

Sure 'Nuff 'N Yes I Do, as I recall had nothing added. It was a strong track on its own. *Zig Zag Wanderer* had gong (played by Alex), tambourine, and log drums (played by studio percussionist Milt Holland) overdubbed. Alex and I sing background vocals. That's me echoing Don after the bridge. It was Richard Perry's suggestion. After the take, Richard and Krasnow complimented my voice and said, "We should have you sing more on the next album." Surprisingly, this seemed to threaten Don, who I noticed at appropriate moments in the immediate future began to cast aspersions and make hypercritical remarks about my singing. The result was that, lacking self-confidence, I became extremely self-conscious about my voice, and hardly sang at all for years. It apparently did not take much to hold me down in those days.

Call On Me found the production crew getting a little carried away with clavichord played by a guy I remember only as Tommy and again had tambourine added by Holland. Horns were arranged and added by Richard Perry.

Dropout Boogie had harp overdubbed during the bridge waltz section by a lady harpist called in spontaneously during an impromptu evening session. She brought her date because she had been at a party. She was wearing an expensive white evening gown with subtle gold striping. I recall her sitting down at the harp and having to hike her dress up quite high to straddle the instrument. I amusingly recall Don later accusing Alex of trying to look up her dress. Although she was an attractive woman, I didn't really notice at the time, probably because she was ten years my senior. I did ask her many questions about the harp as she tuned it, and she was quite accommodating, explaining how to tell the strings apart (different colors) and how to play in different keys (pedals change the tuning). I still find harp to be an intriguing instrument.

I'm Glad had horns overdubbed in the same session as *Call On Me*. Vocal overdubs by Alex and John (on *I'm Glad*) were during the same session as *Zig Zag*.

Electricity had a theramin added, as did *Autumn's Child*. I have seen Vliet credited with playing the theramin, which is actually far from the truth. The man who actually played this obscure instrument was relatively well known, as he had played on the soundtrack for the film, *Spellbound*. He was Dr. Samuel J. Hoffman (called Doctor because he was also a podiatrist), and was the only theraminist in the Los Angeles Musicians Union. I recently found out that he died that same year, on December 6, 1967 having been born July 23, 1903. Other credits include soundtrack work on the classic *The Day The Earth Stood Still*. Though aged 63, he looked to be in his mid-forties, with dark hair and a pencil-thin mustache. His presence in the studio was an anachronism, as was the instrument itself. I was vaguely aware of the theramin, as years before, my mother had identified the sound in a television commercial and out of curiosity looked it up at the local library. Carefully concealed in a brown cloth cover, similar to piano covers, the theramin looked more like an old vintage 1920s style radio on 18-inch lathe-formed legs. It was probably mahogany with a dark brown stain. Two chromium antennae rods were taken out of a hidden compartment on its face and screwed into threaded holes, on the top right (player's view) pointing up, and the other on the left side, pointing out to the left. The speaker was mounted on the side opposite the player's position, and a microphone was strategically placed at its edge.

Hoffman had a professional air about him, and was quiet during his preparation. I am sure that he viewed us with a bit of fear and disdain, as our appearance was probably a bit unconventional to him, even at that time. Once he heard the music, and Don described to him in abstract terms an approximation of his role, he silently and accurately performed a perfect take after about three tries.

The theramin was played by moving the hands at varying distances from the antennae, the right of which controlled pitch, the left volume. This set up an oscillating frequency (sound wave) which was transformed into an audible sound by the amplified speaker. It was a very simple theory, but required a great deal of skill to master and control. It was evident that this man had a great sense of pitch, because everything had to be done by ear. Most of what he performed was of his own creation. Don was really excited to have this man in the studio, and treated him with a great amount of respect and honor.

Side Two (this was on vinyl, for those who haven't a clue as to what I'm talking about) begins with Richard Perry's announcement "The following tone … etc." I recall him taking several takes of recording his announcement and asking if it sounded acceptable, which seemed a little funny, in view of the fact that the whole thing was just a gag. The sound is actually an oscillator used to calibrate the recording equipment for more accurate recordings. It's supposed to be set at a particular frequency. The sound is then recorded, and played back with the original tone still running, and a meter then displays how accurately the recorded sound matches the original. The idea of having the oscillators go crazy like that was just a gag way of saying that the music was unusual.

Back to the tracks. *Yellow Brick Road* had celeste added by Tommy and features Taj Mahal on metal washboard played with thimbled fingers.

Abba Zaba is probably the piece that showed percussionist Milt Holland at his best. We who played were all carefully instructed in great detail as to what to play and where to play it. Ry Cooder played cowbell, Alex the wind chimes heard on the entrance to the bridge, and I played a large gourd with a handle called a cabasa, covered with a net of beads. It is the swishing sound heard on the downbeats. Milt himself skillfully played a little beat-up looking tambourine with hardly any jingles and a calfskin head. It is not only the underlying rhythmic stability of the entire body of the song, but also accounts for the tabla-like bent notes in the bridge sections. He would hold it up close to the microphone and barely tap the head with one hand while using the fingers of his other hand to tighten the head on the drum, thus altering the pitch tremendously. The result was a surprisingly powerful effect. Background vocals are Richard Perry, Don and myself.

Gordon Shyrock and Friend

Gordon Shyrock was a very likeable guy. He would talk to us after the sessions, just hanging out in the parking lot. I recall that he had a particular fondness for marijuana. One of his suggestions was that we should get together sometime on a social basis and just "get together and g-get f-f-fucked-up 'n'ss-shit." His slight stutter, combined with his charming Oklahoma dialect, made this phrase an amusing memory in our minds. For months afterward whenever anyone in the band decided to partake of the sacred weed, we would say, "What say we get together and g-get f-f-fucked-up 'n-s-s-shit?"

Alex Snouffer: Yeah, me and Fragmen (a friend of Alex's of dubious reputation who always wore white short-sleeved shirts and no tie. He was selling used cars when I met him) had just bought a key (Note: slang for "kilo") *of weed and we were selling it off and I sold that guy about three bags.*
John French: Incriminating evidence. So THAT'S where you were getting your gas money.

I had no money, and half the time I wasn't eating during those sessions. Don borrowed (I use the term "borrow" in the loosest sense, since not a dime was ever re-paid) any trace of money I could acquire. I finally became wise and said, "Nope, I ain't got no money." There was no food in the house. Occasionally I'd tell Krasnow, "Look, I don't have anything to eat, I'm so weak I can't hardly play and he'd give me money." I would keep it to myself, but of course, I was riding with Don, so I'd stop and buy something and he'd find out I had money, and he'd borrow it. And if I would say, "No, I don't have money, he would say, "The hell you don't." He'd take my money and I'd never see it again. So, I was pretty hungry. They'd always bring some food during the sessions, which was a lifesaver to me.

Alex Snouffer: I was doing a lot of speeding during that time, so food was not a real big issue with me.

Although I know little about the so-called Tulsa Mafia that Marker said Shyrock was part of I do remember Gordon and a friend, who was more of an East-Coast keyboardist, a little guy who seemed to always to be wearing one of the those John Lennon caps. He overdubbed some of the keyboards such as the clavinet on *Call On Me*, and the celeste on *Yellow Brick Road*. He was also responsible for the concept of doing background harmonies on *I'm Glad*.

Ry's Martin Scarred

Ry's vintage Martin guitar got scarred for life when Gordon Shyrock used it on an overdub. Ry allowed Gordon to use the guitar (for you non-musicians, this is one of the best acoustic guitars made) on one of the overdubs, just doing big chords to fatten up a track. After the track was finished, Ry went out, picked up his guitar in shock and cried, "my guitar!" in a noticeably dismayed tone. I approached along with a few others in the tracking room and noticed even from a distance a huge arc that had been scratched through the finish and into the wood by Shyrock's heavy-handed flat-pick style.

Gordon was genuinely apologetic, although his sincerity only seemed valid up to the very edge of actual financial compensation. When this line was crossed, there was suddenly a strong set of evasive measures, which came into play. Ry, not being strongly confrontational, resigned himself in disgust to the fact that Gordon's imprint would forever remain upon his vintage axe, and sadly quieted down, knowing reasonable accountability for repair was doubtful.

Alex In Wonderland

Alex Snouffer: God, I can remember we were doing **Autumn's Child** *and we're doing overdubs, right? And I had this jawbone, and they had me isolated out in this booth. And I was doing* **Autumn's Child** *(crack, imitates hitting jawbone). I was sooooo stoned, and I was listening to it and I was really into it and all of a sudden the tape would stop. "Hey, man, how come you didn't hit your note?" (Laughs) That happened two or three times before I finally got it right, you know. I mean, I would sit there and say to myself, "I'm really going to concentrate on this now, I'm gonna be ready for it," so I concentrated on it alright, with the jawbone hanging down here by my side.*

Russ Titleman

John French: Do you remember Ry bringing in a friend of his to play acoustic guitar on some of the stuff?
Alex Snouffer: Yeah, his cousin, what was his name? Titleman, Russ Titleman. (Note: Actually, Russ was not related to Ry at the time, but eventually became his brother-in-law when Ry married Susan Titleman, his sister).

I didn't get to know Russ very well. Ry seemed to take Russ under his wing and Titleman proved very adept and capable although very low-key. I think Ry's thought was to avoid overdubs at any cost, since with only four tracks to work with, it would be better to record as much of the sweetening (mostly acoustic guitar strumming) as possible on the basic tracks. In retrospect, it also seems that Ry may have had Russ there to help stabilize him through the insanity of the project. Unfortunately, I recall that Perry later did a lot of overdubbing and that, in retrospect, seemed to me to weaken the overall sound.

Ry's thought was to get some rhythm guitar happening, as most of the guitar parts were single and double-string lines, rather than chords. Cooder wanted to get some mid-range in there to beef up the sound. His impression of Artie Ripp was that the guy was more interested in looking good in his clothes than producing an album. Krasnow knew it was right when he heard it, but seemed to have no idea how the sound was created in the first place, and Perry was having his first solo flight on the controls - unfortunately at our expense. It was earn while you learn time at RCA Studios.

Cooder was new to the studio, but had more experience than any of us. I was on my trial run, so I had no perspective at all. I remember him looking in the booth at The Three Stooges - Krasnow, Perry, and Ripp - having these purple-faced raging quarrels about technique, sound, etc. Of course, through the window of a soundproof booth it all looked rather like a silly silent movie. This would actually have been quite amusing had we not had so much at stake. Ry would just turn with a half-grin on his face and groan.

Of course, we didn't know much, so the questions were running through our heads: was this par for the course? Ridiculous? Good business? Ry knew what we sensed, that there was trouble and conflict, and an unusual amount at that. Sometimes the arguments would spill over into the control room, and mostly Perry seemed on the defensive, Ripp would by hypercritical, and Krasnow was acting as the laid-back mediator. Most of the time, Krasnow was so laid back that crucial technical issues flew right over his head. However, his image was always the cool mellow fellow dripping with hipness. Of the three, Krasnow would probably be elected "Moe."

Disorganized Lyrics

The instrumental tracks were done. Now, it was time for the vocals. It was discovered at this point that aside from the Bermann collaborations, which Bermann always neatly typed, Don's big box with the napkins was the only representation of what he had done with the lyrics. He had never rehearsed with the band. Now, we found out that the arrangements didn't even fit any pattern of lyrics, because the lyrics for about half the songs were just little bits and pieces of things. Don presented me with the big box and I took on the task of sorting through all this mess and trying to come up with enough lyrics to do an album. I was sort of the band organizer sort of gofer, sort of peon - you know, "Let's get the kid to do it." He gave me this box with little tidbits of lyrics in it. Little scraps of paper with hints of what the lyric was. I had to hand-write all the lyrics out from those little scraps of paper. Or he would have never had lyrics from which to sing. I didn't have a typewriter. So I had to print them out by hand. I'd ask, "What is this?" "*Abba Zaba*" he would answer, so I'd put it in the *Abba Zaba* stack. I had the dining room table filled. Then as I would work on one song, I'd put them in order on the floor and then write them down by looking at the scraps on the floor. Richard Perry had to show him where to sing: "Don, I would suggest that this goes with this part" OK. So, you know, that's the way the vocals went together.

I persuaded Don to be seated at the dining room table. It was one of those Faux-Marble genuine Formica masterpieces with the chrome legs. I would pull out some scrap of matchbook or old napkin, or paper sack. He would usually be talking to someone, so I would have to get his attention each time. Then he would think about it and say, "Yeah, I'm sure it's *Abba Zaba*" etc. This went on for a couple of hours. I then had half a dozen or so stacks of weird little bits of lyrics on the table. This was the hard part. I then had to get Don, with his short attention span, to tell me what came next - to concentrate long enough to put all the lyrics to a single song in order. Then, I had to hand-write the lyrics on a sheet of paper with a ballpoint pen. If he made a mistake, I had to start all over, as he seemed easily confused if something wasn't written correctly.

Jerry Handley: Oh, yeah, I always felt sorry for you trying to keep him organized.
John French: Yeah, I was the kid that got stuck with the stupid details like that. He was very
trusting of me at the time. I was kind of naïve, so I believed and accepted everything he said
as absolute truth. So, he was really trusting of me and put me in charge of putting the lyrics
together. Also, he didn't know how to sing the words to the music that he had already
completely arranged, so Richard Perry helped him with that.
JH: If Richard was involved, then that's why it came out to be one of the most organized
albums he did.

I give Richard Perry most of the credit for the lyrical arrangement of *Abba Zaba*, which was the song that was giving Don the most trouble. When he found out about the dilemma, he took us to the office conference room, which contained a sound system. We played the tape endlessly. I manned the machine, and Richard coached Don step by step through the lyrical arrangement. I had tried to do this with Don, but he would not take any strong suggestions from me. Richard did a marvelous job of first comprehending, and second realizing and visualizing the completion of a lyrical arrangement that fit this rather unconventional music. This is not as easy as it sounds. Don knew some of what he wanted, and Richard took it from there.

Richard, however, decided also that his vocal talents were needed on this cut. He sang background on the words "Babit Baboon". Only he sang "ba-biddy baboon". "Babiddy baboon??" Don would later say, "Jesus, what was Perry *thinking*?"

The following is a definition from the online *Urban Dictionary* - Babit: A little man, also known as a midget, whose penis is as big as he is.[33]

Well, I guess this goes in keeping with the old Beefheart joke.

Vocal Overdub Babysitter

I was 18 to Don's 26 but I felt like I was Don's babysitter through the vocal recordings. He had to use earphones, and I perceive his trauma from his headphone experience with Botnick added an edge of stress and distraction. He didn't seem in good voice on some cuts, for instance *I'm Glad*, of which I'd heard a previous demo tape seemed comparatively flat and dry.

Don was still going through a great deal of anxiety. I stood out in the studio with him, occasionally feeling his pulse upon request, and telling him he was going to be all right. At times, he would snap out of it and act like I was in the way, and then he would revert right back to the old fake-heart-attack syndrome.

One time he definitely sprang to life was when he sang *Electricity*. I was in the control room during part of the vocal for that one, and Hank Cicalo gasped when the microphone distorted. He grabbed his head with both hands and said, "Oh no! My microphone" It was an amazing moment. I hate to pop the legend of Beefheart destroying the microphone, but we used the same mike for the remainder of the session. I was curious and went out with Hank as he inspected it. It was a Telefunken condenser mike, which had a small vacuum tube inside. The tube had temporarily distorted, but the mike was fine and was used for the rest of the vocals. Apparently, Don was standing farther back when he sang in normal voice, so when he used the pinched trachea voice combined with moving closer to the microphone, it merely distorted.

So it went for the four or five nights we went in to do vocals. Most of the time, I was standing either beside Don or in front of him. He would ask me to check his pulse and feel his heart to make sure he was all right. I would bring him water and keep his lyrics together. One particular strong and vivid memory I have is standing in front of him, with no headphones on in a completely soundproofed, darkened room while he sang *Autumn's Child*. Hearing the tinny leak from his headphones as my only reference, I wasn't expecting the kind of volume that came out of his

---

[33] http://www.urbandictionary.com/define.php?term=babit

mouth as he began to shout-sing "autumn's child got a loophole round her finger..." I could almost feel the concussion from his voice. It was very surreal, because he would wait for musical passages, and I could just barely hear a little leakage from his headphones, and then he would shout the next line and startle me with that volume again.

And so this became my world for those four or five nights: standing in a darkened room only illuminated by the light from the control room, and one small music stand bulb. Van Vliet seemed petrified by the pressure of having to perform. One of his big handicaps was being so unrehearsed. He didn't really know what he was doing in terms of the arrangements, so he had to learn everything in the studio as he was recording, plus he hadn't sung for months on any kind of steady basis. Of course, there were exceptions. *Sure 'Nuff 'N Yes I Do, Yellow Brick Road, Zig Zag Wanderer* and *Dropout Boogie* were some of the easier pieces. *Abba Zaba* was really tough, and he had to be "punched in" which means, doing little bits of the song at a time. The engineer would roll the tape 20 seconds or so before the last good line and punch the record button at the appropriate moment. Don is not a technical person, so this was not only tough for him to comprehend; it threw off his momentum and performance to an extent. It took take after take to get each section.

Grown So Ugly was another really difficult piece for Don. It had the odd time signature, which was difficult, plus the song was a piece he was unfamiliar with to begin with. It was an unnatural fit. Don would never count anything, so I wound up standing by him and mute singing each new passage so that he could feel where to come in. Of course, heaven help me if I cued him wrong.

Paying Dues

One night we rode around the Strip with Krasnow and Perry and this is when I got a small view into the private fears of Van Vliet.

Don was sitting in the back with me, on the passenger side. Krasnow was driving and Perry was riding in the front. Van Vliet kept going on and on about the fact that he didn't feel like he had paid his dues. This is an old musician's term meaning he felt like he lacked experience - hadn't suffered enough. This incredibly gifted man was so natural in his talent, and there was so much more he could have done. Unfortunately he was blind to the one thing that he needed: rehearsal. He just needed to rehearse with the band. I believe that this is what was on his mind. Some of his heart attack stuff may have been just an act of manipulation, but it was obvious to me that he was lost many times in the vocal overdubs and probably stressed-out as a result.

Unfortunately, because of the way Don thought about the creative process, it was difficult for him to go back over something that he had already created. In essence, his mentality perceived that he had done his job as soon as he finished writing the lyrics and had scattered his unfinished musical ideas out to the players.

He was absolutely right. He hadn't paid his dues nor did it seem likely he would ever attempt to do so. It wasn't in him to memorize lyrics, rehearse performances and work with the band. It was more his method to remain aloof and detached, creating more and more and rehearsing less and less.

I always felt that Van Vliet perceived this sort of activity as beneath him. Somehow, Don seemed to be of a mindset that looked upon rehearsal as menial labor meant for the proletariat. He often said that he hated musicians, and I often felt during our relationship that he hated me. Right from the beginning, it seemed that he would resort to any method possible to avoid rehearsing. Unfortunately, this is why many of the live shows that I have heard gave me the impression that he was partially, and sometimes totally, lost. His stage presence would, to an extent, make up for this. I would remember from rehearsal (when he was creating a new song) where he would say he was going to sing a certain lyric with a certain part of a song. Yet he would seldom sing it the same place twice nor in the same way.

Nevertheless, Perry and Krasnow convinced Don that he had indeed paid his dues rather than address the issues that must have been evident even to them at this point. Basically, they reassured him that he didn't have a thing to worry about; everything would be OK, etc. The usual garbage that automatically comes out of someone's mouth, truth or not, when someone's performance may be writing their check, was what I heard. They tickled his ears. I think he had a kind of anxiety, that he wasn't ready for this. I don't think he felt ready. Personally, what I gathered from it is that he was feeling kind of guilty for what he was taking credit for that wasn't really his, - and he was worried about how he was going to convince the world of who he was and was simultaneously afraid the world would find out.

Vocal Overdubs

John French: It's a wonder he made it that far. I don't know how much you were at the vocal overdubs, but I was there every night, holding his hand basically. I was the guy who just had to stand there. I stood there in the studio with no headphones on while he sang his tracks. Standing there, scared to death, he had to have me standing there next to him! He was absolutely petrified. And I was the kid he would trust, he'd taken me under his wing and kind of brought me up in the way he wanted me to go. So I was the guy that he trusted, so I wrote out all the lyrics so I was (saying)... "Here's the lyrics, here's some water ..." and that was my role, during the vocal overdubs. He really was having problems ...

Alex Snouffer: Of course he was, he didn't know what the fuck he was doing.

John French: He was lost on (some of) those takes.

AS: That's right.

JF: Don would say, "Come with me," and we would go with Richard or Krasnow and they would go and talk somewhere. I went to this meeting with them at Art Ripp's big apartment where he was trying to talk Don into dumping the band (real diplomatic, with me sitting there) and getting a big band with horns. I was sitting right there listening to this. (Mimics Art Ripp) "You know, we could do this thing and blah, blah. Don, you're a great singer and we could put a great band behind you like that James Brown would die for." - all this crap. Don's going, "I don't want to do that." The thing is, he COULDN'T have done that, because he needed people around him to hold his hand and to baby him through things and put up with (everything).

Mixing *Safe As Milk*

The mixing room was a separate room from the studio. It was out the door and to the right down the hall about three doors. The idea was that you didn't need a tracking room (the big room where the instruments go) for mixing, so it allowed mixing to be going on while other groups were recording.

Richard was the same in mixing as he was in the first session: One more mix, one more mix, one more mix. I couldn't tell the difference. I really wasn't happy with the sound although it sounded far better than the released album. It still sounded weak and tinny compared to the live group. The guitars sounded like toys, and there was no bottom to the drums.

He really was a perfectionist, in his own way. However, in retrospect, I think that he was absolutely the wrong person to produce the band. Because the album had three producers, Krasnow, Perry, and Ripp, we used to call it the battle of the producers because it seems like there were more cooks than soup.

This is not to say I don't respect Perry. His consistent behavior did a lot to stabilize what could have become a very volatile situation. I'm just stating that we should have had a seasoned producer with a track record instead of a guy doing his first solo flight.

Safe As Milk Finished

The album was done, and we now had a short period of time in which to relax. It had been reasonably stress-free to do this album, instrumentally, compared to other later albums. Being 18, and this being my first album, I definitely felt the pressure of the studio. However, the producers and engineers gave me a lot of compliments in regards to my drumming. Hank said I did some great kick drum stuff. These were guys that heard a lot of the greats, including Hal Blaine, an LA studio legend, and Jack Sperling, Pete Fountain's drummer, who specialized more in Dixieland and jazz, so it was very encouraging to me.

Instrumentally the album is the composite of a lot of ideas. Ry's influence, definitely. Doug, Alex, and Jerry's scattered guitar and bass ideas combined with Don's suggestions. A few of my own drum ideas were in there. Herb Bermann had written most of the lyrics (though he definitely did not play bass on anything we ever did - ever! He didn't even play bass at all to the best of my knowledge). I am sure that everyone would have a lot to say about the various influences that came together on that album. The first demo I had heard of *Sure 'Nuff 'N Yes I Do* that the band had made for A&M had a much different feel and was more uptempo. I actually preferred it to Ry's version.

The original *Electricity* hummed along and had more of a raga-drone to the music punctuated with volume pedal chords resulting in a slow tremelo effect. It had some great qualities. I wish that stuff could have been released so people could hear how the music evolved. *Call On Me* was originally a Byrds-type tune on which Don played finger cymbals. It was very slow, and Don's phrasing was very different. Most of the other pieces had a similar feel to the demos with more updated arrangements.

Redus Hears *Safe As Milk*

Years later, another guitarist Richard Redus, would play with the Magic Band. His first memories are of hearing the album *Safe As Milk*.

John French: When did you first hear Beefheart? Did you hear a record, or did you hear the band?
Richard Redus: Probably Safe As Milk. *See another facet here is that my parents owned The Third Eye, which was the first head shop in the (San Fernando) Valley. Do you remember it?*
JF: I think I do, yeah!
RR: It was on Ventura Boulevard.

Aftermilk

There was a lull in our schedule after the session was done. We did make Union Fees, which was a pretty good chunk of change for the time. So, we had a short period of time in May when we could actually relax a little and enjoy the fruits of our labor. We had a reel-to-reel copy of the instrumental tapes, which Alex and I sat down and listened to on several occasions. We were proud of our work and I must say that the instrumental tape we had was SO much more powerful than the finished album.

This was an interesting period of time, because there were visits to relatives in the desert. Don and Laurie went and stayed with Sue, and I stayed with my dad, who was now living about 10 miles from my mother in a small house in Palmdale. I spent the night there and he was telling me how much he wanted to get back together with my mother. He said, "I've got too much time to be without love."

When we returned to the Laurel Canyon residence, I mentioned seeing my father to Van Vliet. When I quoted his, "Too much time" line, Don immediately reacted strongly. "God, man, that's great! (sings) *"I got too much time to be without love."* From this one line, Don started writing, or should I say *dictating*, because his favorite thing was to get someone else to write it down for him. He came up with an almost epic song. Although the beginning starts out the same up until the passage *"every bird that flies by gets me high"* the rest of the song was quite different. Better, I thought. It was like an autobiography in a nutshell, and had a classic touch.

Alex came over and the two of them spent hours working this out and putting it on tape. When it was finished, I listened in amazement. Don had written (or co-written, since Alex was also suggesting ideas) a song from beginning to end in one sitting. Even more amazing to me was the fact that all the words were on the same piece of paper – hand-written by Don himself! It seemed that Don's attention span was improving.

There was at least one more major song that never was recorded. I think it deserves mention. It was called *Cobbler With Patent Leather Shoes.* I only remember the first two lines of the bridge.

> *She found her a cobbler with patent leather shoes*
> *No better man could be found with youth and luck to use.*

This song wound up being also recorded on tape with Alex playing worked out guitar parts. It was also an epic type of song, a long narrative style song. But, unlike *Too Much Time*, this song was sung more in the sea-shanty type style, with a voice similar to the one used on *The Dust Blows Forward* (probably with the influence of AL Lloyd in mind). Combine this with a song that was a little like Jefferson Airplane's *White Rabbit*, and you have a vague idea of the dramatic power. The music was more interesting, and the vocal more intense, but it was in that kind of vein.

Don said he had decided because of his experience in the studio to start carrying around pads of paper so as to keep his ideas organized. The pads that he chose were pads of plain paper that could be bought at a drug store and had about 200 sheets of 8 x 11 paper. He also bought half-sized pads and began drawing little funny cartoons. I recall him doing several one morning. They were all visual gags with no need for captions. One showed a mother about to breast-feed her child with a look of horror on her face because the child has huge shark-like teeth and an extremely mean face.

During this period, Krasnow would sometimes come up to the house and visit. He mentioned going to the Whisky and seeing the band Cream play. This was Eric Clapton, Jack Bruce, and Ginger Baker. He said that he had never heard so much sound out of three guys in his life. Clapton came out of that same Wall of Sound school of guitar I was mentioning earlier. Krasnow also brought a copy of *Sergeant Pepper's Lonely Hearts Club Band*, which he said was very heavy. Using the word very in conjunction with the term heavy was a serious commitment, which made me desire to listen to the album.

Don was very critical of all other bands. Rather than enjoying what was going on, he seemed to consider it a threat if anyone mentioned liking some other pop band. There was a lot of interesting stuff going on during this era, cultural exchanges were taking place, and people were becoming more aware of a lot of things. However Van Vliet judged almost all as lame.

One night we went down to the Hullabaloo, which originally was called the Moulin Rouge but was now a rock palace and saw a whole lineup of wannabe bands, none of which I remember. For the most part there wasn't too much to remember that night except that it was hard to think amid that volume level, and conversation was impossible. I never enjoyed being a spectator at rock concerts. I just wanted to play. Don spent the whole evening looking for girls.

There were a lot of colorful characters that came in and out of our lives. There was a very large hippy-looking fellow who used to come into the Buddah office. He had red curly hair in a sort of loose afro-type look and a full beard, medium length. This guy was the epitome of the hippy look, complete with sheepskin knee boots and matching leather vest, wide belt, and loose paisley shirt.

He always delivered copies of the New World Countdown from which I still have a page with our picture.

We occasionally invited girls up to the house. I remember one time two girls came and one was extremely tall, probably 6'2" or more. During this period, girls wore the shortest mini skirts in the world, and when this girl sat down on the couch, her knees were way higher than her hips, so she had to keep her knees together and be very careful as to not expose herself.

We were doing the typical joint (marijuana cigarette) smoking, where one person takes a hit, and passes it around the room. I never could understand this. Why couldn't we just smoke our own? It was always too difficult to pass these things around, especially when they became short and we became stoned. They were always being dropped, which is precisely what happened. I dropped the joint directly between this girl's tightly pressed legs and since her knees were higher than her hips, her legs made a perfect slope which the red hot ember slid quickly down underneath her skirt. This poor girl panicked, searching for the burning ember and thus exposing her pantied crotch to the entire room of fixated males. Yep, I sure know how to show a girl a good time.

I also made friends with the neighborhood girls, Nancy Whaley and another girl named Jan, whose last name I don't remember. Since I was the youngest guy in the band at 18, I was more interested in younger girls. Also, being eighteen, I realized that this could cause a lot of problems for me, so I just viewed it more as a social experience and tried to keep my emotions out of it. In order to hear the *Sergeant Pepper's* album, I had to sneak it over to Jan's parents'house, just across the Boulevard, and sit in her den listening. We would sit on the couch and kiss and then suddenly I would stop and go into a pose of being really intent on the music. Within a second or two, a parent would pop their head into the room to check on us. "How'd you know?" Jan would ask afterwards. I never did figure it out, but my parent sensor sure came in handy.

As we listened to *Sergeant Pepper's*, I was struck by the last song, *A Day In The Life* and especially these lyrics:

> *He blew his mind out in a car,*
> *He didn't notice that the lights had changed.*
> *A crowd of people stood and stared.*

It was if they were talking about John Parr. I couldn't help but be a bit astounded. As I listened, it got to the point where they were saying: *I'd love to turn you on...*

I thought about John being "turned on" by someone who put LSD in his beer. I thought about his behavior afterwards, how it seemed as if he had had a lobotomy. Somebody had taken the fire out of his eyes. It was quite an odd coincidence to me that this song would come out just after this.

Then I thought about the title: *Sergeant Pepper's Lonely Hearts Club Band* and our band's name: *Captain Beefheart And His Magic Band* and how similar the two names were. They both had a military title, the name of a food, the word "heart" and the word "band."

Cosmic, man...

This period was exceptionally fun after all the work. We weren't rehearsing as a band, although I practiced every day and played a lot of guitar in my spare time. We had a little money, and went out to dinner on occasion.

After watching me drum and work with Don in the studio, Krasnow seemed to notice me more and seemed to actually emit certain hints of what one who has a good imagination might have mistaken for respect. I went from chopped liver to meat knish perhaps, but there was a definite change in his attitude towards me, also I think toward the others. I think he realized that despite all Don's amazing creative talents, his strong stage personality, and incomparable vocal abilities that he was also incredibly co-dependent. There was a strange symbiosis in the band.

Krasnow found funds for me to buy an old vintage Slingerland kit for stage. This was a time when shiny and sparkly were *out* and old and vintage were *in*. People had started hanging old rusty tools on their walls as decoration, and driving Volkswagen vans with flowers painted on the side. Krasnow mentioned to me that he had seen a band in which the drummer played drums that were just *natural wood*. Ooh, what a concept. So, I *had* to have a set. I went to Professional Drum Shop, which was on Vine, just across from the Musicians' Union Local 47. They had just the set I wanted for a measly $125 bucks. I bought cases and stands at the same time.

Bob's Strategy

Bob had devised the perfect strategy to propel us to superstardom. In spite of the cynic that I was, I was about half-convinced that it was going to work. He wanted us to start rehearsing immediately for a concert performance at the Monterey Pop Festival. This was going to be *heavy, baby. Heavier than anything that has happened, baby*. All we had to do was play well and Bob would take care of the rest.

He rented us a rehearsal studio off Santa Monica Boulevard that was the strangest place I'd been to yet. It was like an old half-finished frame of a building in the front, and you had to walk down this dirt path along the side and suddenly you were in a little half-finished room. There was another spot at A&M (which was just around the corner from Kama Sutra). We rehearsed at these two places with Ry for about two or three weeks. Unfortunately, Don was going back into his old ways and wouldn't rehearse much, but the band sounded great. We polished off all the *Safe As Milk* tunes and things were shaping up. Don wouldn't sing, but he would spend most of his time saying the PA didn't work right, or "I gotta save my voice, man."

Part of Bob's strategy involved getting *Safe As Milk* out and distributed by the time of the Monterey Pop Festival, so that we could play, sweep the crowd off its feet, and have money in the bank within the week. Actually, it was a pretty good plan. Bob really believed that Don was the greatest white blues singer alive. He could see the potential and appeal of the band. He had managed James Brown when he was younger, and occasionally spoke endearingly about little special moments, like the day Brown turned around in the middle of a crowded hotel lobby and punched him in the chin, knocking him flat on his back. He would point to the scar and say proudly, "James Brown gave me this, man."

Anyway, Bob was tough, seasoned, and experienced. He had the mind for promotion and was doing everything he could for us. Don was interested in him managing us. I heard as they discussed this, that it would be a conflict of interests, so he would have to wait until the band was pulling in enough capital so that he could take a draw, quit Kama Sutra, and still be able to support his family. He and Don had already talked about forming Blue Thumb Records at this time. I had heard him bring the subject up on more than one occasion. The logo would be half an LSD capsule superimposed upon which would be a blue powdered thumbprint. "That's so hip man, the blue powder thumbprint of the guy who was holding the capsule." I never understood why this was so "hip."

CHAPTER FOURTEEN:
MONTEREY MELTDOWN

"stamp" outtake shot from late 1967. Photo courtesy of Guy Webster.

The week before the Monterey Pop Festival, Bob Krasnow arranged for us to do a practice concert at a love-in scheduled at Mt. Tamalpais, in the Bay Area (San Francisco). We were fairly well rehearsed, although the band mostly rehearsed without Don. I truthfully cannot remember much about the time just before the show. I do recall Krasnow telling me that there were drums there and I didn't need to bring my set. This is analogous to asking a tennis player to use someone else's racket at a tournament. There seemed to be no way to convince them that I needed my own drums.

As I recall, we flew up the night before, stayed at a hotel, and were driven up by Bob to the love-in. If you're not familiar with this phrase, it was a term used in the sixties during the hippie era. Everybody would go to a park and love. This meant (as far as I could tell) stumbling around mindlessly on hallucinogens eventually falling into the arms of a perfect stranger of the opposite sex preferably of another ethnic origin and language, the intertwining of two beautiful people eventually resulting in the birth of a love child.

Don Van Warlock?

Gary Lambert had flown up with us, I believe. I recall sharing a room with Gary the night before the concert. We were talking about Don's ability on stage to focus in on people and move a crowd in such a powerful way. At this point, Gary then said, "He really is a warlock, you know." I had never heard the word. I asked what it meant and he told me: a male witch.

I recalled the conversation with Don Aldridge when I first joined the band. My reaction to this was that if such a thing existed, then I didn't want to be a part of it. I have always felt that there was a supernatural world that we know little about. There are countless cases of strange events happening for unknown reasons. Suddenly, I felt as though I were involved in a situation about which I knew little. Even if there was no supernatural, the thought that this band was involved in witchcraft bothered me. What started going through my mind at this time was all the little experiences, the head popping off the shelf, the spider appearing and Don taking credit for it, the "Cantor's sighting." All the stuff I had wondered about started to bother me. Don considered himself a witch? I didn't know much about this but it bothered me.

Lambert described Don's power as "a power over other people." He talked about how Van Vliet could control an entire crowd with his power. I found it interesting but spooky.

I had not been completely unaware, of course, of the lyrics that hinted at occultism, and Don's seemingly 'psychic' powers. All of this I had previously considered, mostly with a sense of fascination up until this point. I felt as though the band would become very famous as a result of the events of the next two weeks, and we would suddenly be taken more seriously. I was excited about the financial aspect, yet the idea of promoting any true magic or witchcraft bothered me. The responsibility to be some kind of positive influence on the kids who would be listening to this music would now partially be mine. I wasn't sure that it was a good idea to be a part of something that seemed to dwell on the darker forces.

Even at 18, I felt a moral sense to set a good example, to the adolescents that made up such a large part of the audience. Music and musicians are a powerful influence on naïve kids and therefore there is a moral responsibility of the artist, in my boy-scout mentality, to be a decent role model.

Tamalpais Morning

The memory is a funny thing, because I remember riding in both a rented car and a bus to reach the festival. I think that what probably happened was that Krasnow drove the band to the edge of the festival grounds and then a bus took us inside the gates to the stage area. During the car ride, I was sitting in the middle in the back of the car. The radio was on, and suddenly, there was one of the songs from *Safe As Milk* - Abba Zaba I believe. This was the first time I had ever heard myself on the radio and it was a big thrill. My emotions and hopes were running high. I recall Bob looking back and saying, "Hey, is that heavy or what? Little surprise for you guys."

On the bus ride up, Don had conferred with me as to what song we should open with. I assumed we would just do the things we had rehearsed from the album. Don, however, was full of surprises, especially when it had to do with anything important. He was still occasionally going through his fake heart attacks and anxiety. I sincerely and naively felt at this time that he was going to be all right. I was expecting that after we did the Monterey Pop Festival the whole world was going to open up for us.

Van Vliet suggested that we open with the blues jam we had done once at his mother's house when I had first joined the group. It was called *Maybe That'll Teach Ya*. It was almost Afro-Cuban blues. I agreed. I don't know what on earth I could have been thinking of when I agreed to this, however, as the only other person in the jam was Doug Moon, who wasn't even here. It was a ridiculous idea to go on stage on a test-run for the most important concert of our lives and start with a song which neither guitarist nor the bassist had the vaguest idea how to play. It had mainly been Doug and I accompanying Don on harp. There were no set lyrics, just a couple of simple phrases and one chord.

This may have been another one of those occasions Gary Marker had mentioned in which Don would do something to set everything just a little off kilter in order to maintain control over others.

We were scheduled to play early in the morning, well, around 10:00 which seemed early enough to me. I have seldom been on the road where I actually knew much about the acts that were scheduled before and after. When one played these kinds of events, one mostly read about it afterwards. I did manage to get a hold of some kind of poster that showed a few of the bands featured that day. Country Joe and the Fish, The Seeds, and Every Mother's Son.

Lefty

We arrived in the mid-morning and walked to the outdoor amphitheatre area. It wasn't that big, but the stage was high, and the sound system looked and sounded impressive. Krasnow signaled us to get on the stage. We were wearing our suits from the *Safe As Milk* cover. The idea of that packaging concept (according to Don) was a Bonnie and Clyde-type gangster image to set us apart from the flower power crowd. I was the first on stage, so as to take a look at the drums. A horrible sight greeted me. The drums were set up for a left-handed player. This meant, to anyone who doesn't know, that I had to get a wrench and practically rebuild and retune the set onstage. I was furious with Krasnow, which accomplished absolutely nothing. The band had to wait for me backstage, and I had to make the audience wait for me onstage as I knelt in front of everyone and tackled this problem while trying to maintain some discipline over my temper. Many people just got up and left.

I was having a terrible time. This was worse than I could have imagined. In order to play this set, I had to turn the bass drum around. This meant that the legs of the bass drum, which generally angle forward to keep it from sliding away, were now angled towards me. There was no carpet to keep anything from sliding, which in itself is a horror story for a drummer. The hi-hat and bass drum slide even when the spurs point the right way. I was pretty frustrated by this. Bob kept coming on stage every two or three minutes and saying "hurry-up", to which I finally responded with four-letter expletives and some rather sincere death threats. To that, Bob decided the wisest thing to do was send the whole band onstage to motivate my struggle to yet higher stress levels.

Everybody got tuned up about three times and stalled around for five to seven minutes while I struggled to get this set even close to being playable. I finally sat down and just resolved to tough it out. I knew that a thousand things could go wrong with this set as soon as I started playing. With both hands and feet occupied keeping time, and only Krasnow on the sidelines, I expected the worst.

More Fake Heart Attacks

To make things even worse, Don was asking me to feel his heart because he thought he was having another heart attack. I wanted to tell him something like "I've got problems of my own, shut up." It was a very stressful situation and the others onstage seemed unaware of what was happening with Don. He seemed exceedingly troubled and I was beginning to wonder if the state of his mind might affect his performance, as if I didn't have enough to think about. I later found out that Don had been driven up to a place behind the stage (there goes my bus theory) and when he got out of the car, he fell on his face in the grass. He appeared not to be able to get up, Krasnow was telling him and the band (I was onstage in left-hand drum hell) to go up there anyway.

Don finally asked if I had told Cooder what song we were starting with and I answered no. When I told Ry that we were starting with a song we'd never rehearsed, his face took on the expression of one dealing with a terrorist. I hummed a little melody and told him the song was in "G" open tuning. He dealt with me like one negotiating for the release of hostages, but actually played a good facsimile of what I had explained with his amplifier turned down. "Yeah, that's it!" I said. Don bent down and asked, "What key harp did I play on this man?" I told him he needed a harmonica tuned in the key of C.

The only reason I can think of that makes any sense at all concerning why the Captain would choose this song was that it put him on an equal footing with the rest of the band. It's like a blind person turning out the lights on the intruder. Suddenly, no one on stage really knew what they were doing. The most interesting facet of Don's personality is that he seemed to shine in the midst of confusion. He started writing his best material when the problems with Leonard Grant and Dorothy Heard began. While we were stumbling along, seemingly going nowhere, it seemed Don was improvising great lyrics and playing powerful harmonica lines.

The band started hesitantly, sounding like a handful of tacks dropped on the floor. When Don came in, he had such a conviction in every harp note and vocal phrasing that it was like a powerful magnet that grabbed all the scattered tacks and pulled them into a giant cluster of sound. I was surprised by Ry's ability to fall right in to the groove on this piece. I wish we had a recording.

Surprisingly, We made it through the first number with little or no mishap. The kick drum was sliding around, but I would skip a beat, slide it back, and resume. Maybe *That'll Teach Ya* was a good theme for me. This morning's experience should have definitely taught me never to trust Krasnow's judgement concerning musical equipment, or at least drum equipment. I couldn't concentrate on anything musical so was almost impossible for me to put any feeling into the improvisation. One thing about Don was that he seldom cued an ending to an improvisation and so things seemed to go on dangerously long. The song seemed to go on forever and I finally just stopped playing out of frustration.

The next number was *Electricity*. I adjusted the drums the best I could. I looked down at my hand and discovered I had gashed my knuckles on a drum rim that had bounced out of position. The gash was dripping blood all over my white suit. I looked up, counted off the song, and off we went. Don sang the intro with his usual power. When he got to the end of his first "electricity", he just turned around, straightened his tie, and calmly walked off stage. When I say off, I mean "off." He walked off the back edge of the stage and fell on top of Krasnow, who was attempting to catch him. I wasn't surprised at all at Don walking off the stage. It just seemed right in step with the heart attack syndrome he was going through.

Alex Snouffer: Oh, I remember THAT!
John French: Mt. Tamalpais, San Franscisco?
AS: Uh huh! Do you know how much damage that did to our career?
JF: Well, that was the end of it right there, basically. From then on we were an avant-garde

band who was never going to make any money, basically. Remember, a cut from Safe As Milk was being played on the radio every half an hour? I remember that. I mean, they were pushing. They were pushing hard. And we were excited.
AS: Yeah! And that motherfucker froze in the middle of whatever song it was.
JF: Electricity.
AS: And walked off.

Anxiety's Grave Aftermath

So I turned around to catch the band's reaction. They were all to my right. The only person I saw was Ry. His good eye was following Don's movements off the stage. He had a puzzled bewildered look on his face, mixed with contained horror as his body did a half circle, following Don as he walked off the stage. It was actually quite amusing, but I didn't have time to laugh. Alex said something like, "Play, man!" and kicked it off with his guitar riff. We finished the song as an instrumental, playing it as written, ended, and left the stage in embarrassment and disgust.

I had to first cuss out Bob for the problem with the set. Bob told me that I shouldn't yell at him, because he had just recovered from catching Don as he fell off the back of the stage. "He landed *right on* me!" he said, "what the *hell's* he on anyway?" I had to go to the first aid station, a small tent, to have my hand bandaged. Don was there getting treatment for his anxiety. They gave him a librium, I believe. For the moment, I almost hated him, but at the same time was attempting to be sympathetic.

Trout Mask Replica?

John French: Don, started to sing, and turned around and walked off the stage. He said he looked down at a girl right after he sang Electricity and she turned into a fish and bubbles came out of her mouth. So he walked off the stage.
Alex Snouffer: That's HER problem, man.

It may have been the girl's problem, but it certainly manifested itself in Don's behavior and became the entire band's problem at that point. What Don was experiencing was apparently an LSD re-occurrence. A number of people who had experimented with this drug had spoken of similar experiences. They would be walking around in a perfectly normal state of mind, and suddenly, they would find themselves in the Emerald City or somewhere equally disorienting. Don seemed completely frazzled, but he had Krasnow to baby-sit him. He had just blown everything out the window and we knew it. I was gritting my teeth, trying to keep my patience and watching Ry walking in the distance. I interrupted Don's story about his condition, which I knew I would hear many times again, and ran to catch up with Ry.

John Pleads With Ry

Cooder was headed for the rental car. This young blues guitarist who I had come to respect so much in the last few weeks was not responding to any shouts or hails. I finally caught up with a very upset Ry, who had obviously already decided to leave the band. He had a wall around him already. Out of breath, I tried to explain that Don would be all right although I didn't believe it myself. Hindsight is twenty-twenty, or so they say. Had I known what I know now, or even what I knew a year later, I would have most definitely joined him and never looked back.

John French: I walked back to the car and tried to talk Ry into not quitting. I said, "Please, give it one more chance." And he said, "Nope, can't do it, got better things to do, can't work with that man."

Alex Snouffer: Oh, I knew he was gone. If we'd have finished that gig the way it was supposed to have been done, we'd have been in Monterey, because every other band that was there, Country Joe and the Fish, and the Airplane, and (all), went on to Monterey. They all went on to make some money, you know. We could have too.
JF: Yes.
AS: But, oh no, that was the end of that.

I'm not trying to imply that there is an oft-scheduled Magic Band pity party where we sit around reliving "how things could have been if only Van Vliet would have gotten his act together." As a matter of the fact, this is the only time we have ever discussed this since 1967. I was doing an interview with Alex for the Revenant *Grow Fins* box set, and when I mentioned this incident, the passions rose. This was a point in the lives of both Alex and myself where someone named Don Van Vliet let us and several other people down in a very big way. Huge amounts of energy had been invested in this project, which was to culminate in a successful concert just a week from that fateful day. It affected all of us then, and perhaps the course of our lives could have been different had we just been able to get our singer to rehearse with us.

John French: So, our lives would have been a lot different if we had played that day. We would have had tours, we would have had money. I mean, if Don could have ever stayed on the stage long enough for us to do a complete set. We would have had money and things would have been a lot better for us. You would have had some money for your wife and kid, Jerry the same, we could have, kept working together. As far as I saw, the band was pretty much supporting (the fact) that Don was the writer and had these song (concepts) Electricity - all these different things he was writing. It wasn't like the band was holding him back. They were trying to work something out, there was always some diplomacy there and there were all these things getting done where we would say "We can DO this. But, let's get it done, let's not take three weeks doing one song."
Alex Snouffer: The only thing that was holding Don back was Don. He can lay blame anywhere he wants but it's him, it was him, always was. Nobody, I didn't see one person ... and it didn't matter which personnel were in which band I never saw anyone holding him back.
JF: Except him.
AS: Except himself, yes. I mean, he can make all the excuses he wants, but that's all they are; excuses.

What I observed in the band at the time (excluding Ry) was a group of friends supporting a man for whose health they were sincerely concerned. No one said anything negative to Don, no one got upset with him. No one blamed him for losing Ry. No one said he didn't know how to handle drugs. Any of those points were valid points that could have been brought up. Don could have had several angry people in his face. Instead, everyone, though deeply disappointed, shrugged it off.

Ry Cooder: The guy seemed pretty weird to me at the time, like some kind of a circus character, a sideshow act, able to entertain you for just so long. Well, his act stopped to be entertaining, so I just decided to continue what I was doing without him. What I was doing then didn't amount to much, but I didn't see any future for us together; besides, his way of doing things was kind of militaristic, and everything about him pretty "Brown Shirt." But I think Safe As Milk *is a really nice album.*[34]

Everyone reacted in a slightly different manner. Ry quit the band. Alex was angry and went off to get drunk. Jerry, apparently, just blanked it out of his mind.

[34]Ry Cooder interviewed by John Tobler. ZigZag #69-70, 1977

John French: That was the day that Ry Cooder quit the band.
Jerry Handley: That's when he quit? No wonder I blanked it all out. That was when the bad stuff happened. I couldn't remember when Ry quit.

I watched as Ry closed the trunk containing his guitars. It was like a big page in my life turning. The trunk lid looked like a door closing to an opportunity in my life. I knew Ry was determined and independent and would not change his mind. The last six months of work had netted each band member about $200 a month. We had invested our lives in hopes of a better future and put everything we had into this project. Van Vliet's behavior and reckless drug abuse had just washed our hopes down the drain.

Gary Marker recalled Don's early drug abuse and was concerned about his friend's well being.

Gary Marker: You were over the top, man, this is beyond reality! What? Are you on another acid trip? He said, "No, No No, I've cut back on that! I've only had in the last month 17, 18, maybe 30 trips." I said, "Oh Jesus, Don."

Characteristically, Don would blame Ry for this setback in his career. Three years later, Langdon Winner would write of this incident, his only source of information being Van Vliet's spin on the story.

"The departure of the lead guitar destroyed Beefheart's chances in the San Francisco scene. The Monterey Pop Festival went on without him." [35]

Unfortunately, the whole situation was the culmination of Don's excessive self-absorption and use of hallucinogenics combined with a rich, vivid, and apparently somewhat dangerous imagination. Although I was young enough to sympathize with this man whose talents I greatly admired, I was also feeling much the same way as Mr. Cooder.

Alex Snouffer: After the gig, the band got scattered and everyone got back to the hotel as best they could, I guess. I ended up getting lost and riding back in the back of a Volkswagen fulla hippies.
John French: I have no idea how I got back, no idea at all.
AS: We were there for a couple of days, right. And you know, Ry, he had his Johnny Walker Red Label, you know. He'd always buy two fifths and we'd drink one fifth before a gig.
JF: Ry? I didn't know he was imbibing before the show.
AS: Oh shit yeah, he and I were birds of a feather, baby. Couldn't put two roomies together who had more of the same idea. Just really wailing all the way. I got in and Ry was already in, and he looked up at me like this (gives look of someone under the influence) says "You want some?" and I said, "you fuck an A buddy." I mean, he was really upset, I don't blame him.
JF: This was afterwards.
AS: Yeah, this was after we were through, well, we were through as soon as Don walked off.

I remember spending the day up at Mt. Tamalpais alone. I ran into Bob once, who took a picture of me. He thought I looked heavy. I watched the bands and enjoyed the day as best I could under the circumstances. I think I just blocked the whole incident out of my mind. Tomorrow was another day. Today, I was going to enjoy myself while I had the chance.

I remember little bits and pieces of the day. It did seem to have an air of love about it – at least through my young and naïve eyes. What I really sensed here is that there was no sense of fear. I didn't see any macho jerks walking around trying to start fights. I spoke with a lot of people I'd never

[35] Rolling Stone Magazine: May 14th, 1970; No. 58; The Odyssey of Captain Beefheart by Langdon Winner. pp37.

met for brief moments. It was an era of openness. A lot of people look back on this as corny. Perhaps it was, but I was young and optimistic. I was thinking that maybe there was a chance for this world to unite in a peaceful way. While a war devoured my friends'lives a continent away, people here were communicating on a very basic level and just spending time together. There weren't a lot of commercialized booths and moneymaking machines trying to scoop chump change out of the love in. There were just a lot of people having a good time together.

Back to Southern California

I have no recollection of the flight back. All I can recall is that somehow we wound up back in the desert for a few days of R&R. I stayed at my mother's house. She had been working at a part-time job for the Salvation Army Thrift Store, but now, the landlord, Charles Siebenthal, had offered her a job in his farm machinery business as bookkeeper, so she was doing a bit better.

Sue and Granny's Apartment

Sue and Granny Annie had moved from their house into a little apartment just down the street from my mother's house. One and a half blocks to be exact. It was about two blocks from where Sue worked. It may have been that Don's mother and grandmother had moved out just to get away from the rehearsals, and the responsibility of having Don and Laurie staying with them. Perhaps they sold the other house and used the money to get the apartment

I walked down to see if Don was there. He wasn't, so I had a talk with Sue and Granny. I explained what happened in San Francisco and Sue seemed concerned. Granny was very forthright in her opinion. She said that Don was irresponsible and hard-headed. He was also a fool, just like his mother. She said that he walked around like he owned the world when he didn't have a pot to piss in and treated all his friends like dirt. At this point, Sue and Granny got into a bit of an exchange over the fool statement, and I quickly made my departure.

Blues In A Bottle

I called around and contacted Jeff Cotton. He came by and picked me up. We went out to his parent's trailer because no one was home, and did some catching up. I found out that Jeff had been a little upset with me for leaving the band we had formed, because he wanted to keep working together. I was surprised to find this out, because our last talk had convinced me he was leaving. I told him about the difficulties with Don and what had been going on.

We heard a car pull up outside. It turned out to be Jeff Parker, the other guitarist from Blues In A Bottle. I thought I would be really happy to see him but he had changed. He was now rumored to be involved in some kind of drug trafficking and he had a really strange aura about him. He would stare, grinning, into people's eyes and try to intimidate them with his countenance. I looked at him in amusement, thinking, "If you only knew who I was dealing with right now."

Jeff Cotton and I went for a drive. He had a girlfriend. Someone else was driving his car and I was sitting in the back. Jeff was smoking pot and then blowing it in his girlfriend's mouth - mouth-to-mouth hallucination. He was playing an afternoon party, so I went with him. It was Blues In A Bottle, the band Jeff and I had formed. The band was set up in the back yard of someone's home. Randy Wimer was now the drummer, and Bill Harkleroad had taken Jeff Parker's place if I recall correctly.

The band played really well and Jeff never sounded better. Mark Boston was still on bass and they were doing more blues. Harkleroad would sing and play harp sometimes. I was sitting on the edge of a folding chair on a concrete slab and Mark's girlfriend, a girl named May whom I had dated about a year before, came over and sat down in my lap. It was an obvious stunt to make Mark feel jealous or uncomfortable in some way. She was sitting on my knees, so I quickly parted my legs which caused her to fall directly onto the slab on her tailbone. It's a good thing the band was loud, because she yelled in pain. I felt like it served her right. Mark was a friend, and I sure wasn't going to play any games with this dumb chick.

Everyone asked me how things were going. I sat in a bit with the band. It was old home week, and I didn't realize how much I had missed my friends up until now. It was such a good feeling to be back among my contemporaries. They had changed so much in these last eight or nine months. It amazed me. Jeff sounded better than ever.

I was later dropped off at Don's mothers and he was there. I came in and he was sitting on the couch with Laurie. Usually, Don was relatively cordial, but today, he seemed cold and distant. He wouldn't make eye contact, but kept staring at the television. I said, we needed to go see Krasnow and find out what was going on with the Monterey Pop Festival.

Goodbye Monterey

Reality hit on the return to LA. Our fears were confirmed bright and early Monday morning that Ry would not do the Monterey Pop Festival. I don't blame him. We all should have quit. I had this stupid loyalty streak in me, however. It seemed to me as though Don had turned down a lot of opportunities out of loyalty for us. Several weeks before, when I had overheard Artie Ripp trying to talk Don into getting professional musicians and singing the blues, I wasn't sure why he turned it down. He could've made a fortune doing that - if he would have been able to stay on stage.

However I was soon to realize that Don needed us more than we needed him. Inside this seemingly ominous and intimidating figure was hidden a frightened co-dependent child. A part of Don had never grown up and I was beginning to see this even then. I am not sure why I stayed. My dreams of being a famous drummer were gone if I stayed with this man, yet there was a curious bond forming between he and I that I couldn't seem to shake.

As our performance at the Monterey Pop Festival was cancelled that Monday morning, I stood there not realizing the full historical significance of this event - for us and the rest of the rock industry - until later. Krasnow had already been on the phone looking for a replacement for Ry. One thing about Krasnow, he could spring back into action immediately and quickly put disappointment behind him.

Monterey Retrospect

A man who views the world as differently as Mr. Beefheart has quite a difficult time communicating with that world. Although Don had a highly simplistic way of viewing some things, this view often ended where anything to do with communication or reality began. He seemed oftentimes caught up in a web of fabrications he seemed convinced were true in spite of all the contradictions. It seemed to me that he spun this web of deception to keep from facing himself. There was a phrase that was popular at the time, "Where are you at, man?"

Where somebody was at meant some sort of self-disclosure of opinion, platform or viewpoint. It was the culmination of who you were, unguarded and disarmed. Don was not one to let anyone know where he was at. In fact, he seemed absolutely terrified that someone may discover where he was, in fact at. Still, later on I would find him placing his question in several variations directly to many of the people around him, including me. It was as though he was facing us with his worst fear and studying our reactions in preparation for some future public confrontation with which he himself have to deal.

It also seemed Don was terrified of success. As I had written earlier, his girlfriend, Laurie, had suggested this to him one night at the house in Laurel Canyon during a meeting with the entire band. If you recall, Don was completely incensed that she would speak to him publicly in such a way and took her off to their room to give her a good tongue-lashing. However, there was a ring of truth in her words that the whole band, especially Snouffer, perceived. He turned around and said, "I think Laurie hit a little too close to home."

Don Paying Dues

Don, at some point during this period, actually did stop using any drugs at all for a time. This was probably a wise decision for him. The trouble was that for him to stop, *everyone* had to stop. Therefore it became a daily routine to castigate anyone who so much as took a hit off a joint. We would all have probably been better off had we heeded his advice, but instead, resentment crept in. The train of thought seemed to be, "*He's* the one who can't handle it, so why get on *our* case?" The way we fellow musicians dealt with this issue was to refrain in his presence from smoking pot. I was already beginning to see the negative effects in my own behavior, the paranoia, and a seeming inability to stand up for myself, always being undecided on whether I was right or wrong on any issue.

Don seemed fixated on the aforementioned paying dues question. He would talk about the old blues singers that he loved with respect. "Now, those guys really paid some dues, man. They know *where it's at*." Then, in the same breath he would talk about the jazz players and how they never got paid.

I recalled the times previously described during the vocal sessions for *Safe As Milk* in which Richard Perry would take us somewhere to eat, or we would go shopping just to relax. I remember Don mentioning that he had been told by various people that he had to pay his dues. He seemed to really think somehow that he did not deserve to be successful quite yet. In retrospect, it seems he may have been right. It may have killed him to become famous at that time. It may have killed us all. Perry would soothingly reassure Don that he was entitled to whatever level of success he could achieve right then. He had already paid his dues, and now was time for the payoff.

Of course Richard would say this. Kama Sutra was paying him well to make us sound as good as possible, so that they could promote us as well as possible and make us all wealthy. There was at one time a true possibility of the band becoming a gigantic success. In retrospect it is sobering to think of how many of the major stars of the Monterey Pop Festival went to extremely early graves directly due to the excesses of life that began streaming their way directly as a result of the springboard of notoriety the festival became. Perhaps they had felt the same way, that somehow they didn't deserve success.

In my ignorant bliss, I had no trouble feeling that I was ready for success. I thought it would be great to have some money. I wanted to assist my mother financially. I wanted to have some independence. I wanted a car and a girlfriend (the first seemed to be a pre-requisite of the second). I also wanted to prove to the world that I had made the right choice. Of course, I was 18, and didn't know what a "whole lotta nines were," as the saying goes.

All this time, Alex and Jerry had been strongly convinced that *Safe As Milk* was going to make quite a mark in the commercial music industry. They were betting their lives and their wives on it. In my youth, I was looking to them for direction. At that time, all three of us were angry to some extent with Don for ruining our big chance. We all respected Ry and his decision. We all respected Ry, period. He was and is a great player, and my only regret is that I didn't get more of a chance to work with him.

Cooder Leaves Town

Cooder went to Krasnow at the Kama Sutra office. Krasnow was lying on a couch when Ry came in. Bob told him that he had his work cut out for him, not aware yet that Cooder had already made up his mind to leave the band. When Ry told Bob he couldn't do it, Krasnow's reaction was first persuasion, saying things like, "Yeah, I know it's hard, it's rough and all, but you got it in you, and you're going to do it."

After it became evident that Ry's mind was made up, Krasnow began to make threats, using the age old "You'll never work in this town again," cliché, among other things. Bob continued threatening and haranguing Ry, telling him that "This is the end of it for you!" He even demanded that Ry give back the guitars he'd been given by Kama Sutra (apparently Ry was not compensated for his work on the album except with these two guitars).

Cooder had decided that the best thing to do was get outta town which is exactly what he did, by going to College for a year in Oregon, he was able to escape any consequences of his decision and get a fresh perspective on things.

Ry Cooder: The thing with Beefheart was just so horrendous that it just like, you know, it would kill you to be stuck in a thing like that. I figured if I didn't get out of town, it would kill me, you know.[36]

Gerry McGee

Krasnow informed us that a guitarist by the name of Gerry McGee was the man most likely and most qualified. Don and I went to a strip joint on La Cienega Boulevard to hear him play. I had never been in a place like this before, so it was hard for me to concentrate on his playing. There were nude women with tassels glued to their nipples, and they were twirling them in opposite directions. I still don't see how they did that, but since I've never had breasts, I never really had the chance to test the action under laboratory conditions.

Don asked me my opinion in the midst of this. "Oh yeah, the guitar player!" - I reorganized my thought patterns. He sat on a small stool on the back of the stage. He had light brown straight hair cut in a conservative Beatle cut. Although he didn't appear too happy with his gig, he was a great player. He seemed to be able to play any style, and I enjoyed the fact that he could finger pick. He was, however, a little more country-influenced than may be healthy for a blues band. We met him and he seemed cordial but distant. Nevertheless, Gerry gave me a good feeling, I voted in favor of trying him.

McGee First Rehearsal: *Flower Pot*

We rehearsed with Gerry at the house on Amor Road in Laurel Canyon. There is a song that was written around that time called *Flower Pot*. That title was my idea. I was walking with a girl down Sunset one night, and I was telling her that there were two lines of thought concerning on which side of a lady a gentleman was to walk. One school of thought said on the street side, to protect her from traffic and splashes. The other said the building side, in case a flowerpot fell out of a window. I mentioned this to Don. It seemed that *Flower Pot* would be a good name for a song since flower children smoked pot.

Gerry's guitar style was put to good use in this song as he played the first riff of the song in his warmup to check the amp. This is when I first realized that Don utilized everything somebody played to him, and changed his writing to fit the player. Later, I realized that he was strongly influenced by everyone around him. Don didn't really conceive of the complete song, he just said, "Play what you just played during this section". There were parts that Vliet then played on harmonica that Gerry copied on the guitar, all the while hammering a bass rhythm with his thumb. This fingerpicking style, which Ry also used, was suddenly found to be of interest. It would become a strong part of the style of Don's future music.

Packing Up Amor Road

We were running out of money and knew we were going to have to move. Everybody was gone except Don, Laurie, and myself. Oh yes, and Cindy, Don's black poodle. All the furniture that we

---

[36]The Artist Formally Known as Captain Beefheart, BBC Documentary, interview with Ry Cooder.

moved down was to be donated to the Salvation Army. The bed I had grown up sleeping on was included in this. I kept thinking about what a waste it all seemed. In the matter of a few months, I was losing most of the things I had used for years. It was a very insecure time for me. I spent these days practicing my drums. No one was around except Don and I. He would work with me on various rhythms. During this time, I learned a lot about the way he conceived of percussion, and listened to a lot of his influences.

There were a couple of girls in the neighborhood that I spent some time with. One was Nancy Whaley. I remember her telling me that she would always love me. She was 14 at the time. I was 18. I was a real pushover where girls were concerned. I used to go down and visit with her at her grandparent's house three or four houses down. Her parents were dead, I believe. Her father had been a director. I believe he had directed the original Dragnet series. Her sister, Judy, used to drive her around. She was 16, and pretty levelheaded. Nancy and I saw each other about six times over a period of several years. Whenever we saw each other, sparks would fly. I avoided getting involved with her because I felt like it would just complicate both our lives to no end and never work out, aside from the fact that we were both far too young. Besides that, Don had a way of saying very condescending things about and to my girlfriends. For instance Nancy was slightly knock-kneed. Don said that he told her to put an apple in her crotch and when it fell out, she'd be OK. What an insulting thing for a 26 year-old man to say to a 14-year-old girl. Ironically, Don was also slightly knock-kneed.

The Beatles album, *Sergeant Pepper's Lonely Hearts Club Band* had just come out. It was a big success, and I was very impressed with the sounds on the album and the supergroup Cream had just played the Whisky A Go Go. Krasnow had heard them and said that he had never heard more sound come out of three people in his life. *Safe As Milk* was getting some radio play, but with no live concert appearances to promote it, the momentum was already disintegrating. In Europe, a DJ by the name of John Peel was playing several of the pieces on a pirate radio station. Unknowingly, we were being well received across the waters.

It was now mid-to-late June of 1967. The album was being played on the radio. We could hear cuts from *Safe As Milk* on almost every LA Station. KFWB wasn't playing it, so Alex and I took a copy of it over to them and within a half an hour, we heard *Sure 'Nuff 'N Yes I Do* being played.

However, we were losing our house. Our record company did not recognize this reality. How could we rehearse without a house? How could we function as a group? So far, they had given us $1,000 (supposedly). I spent $185 of my money on a suit for the album shoot.

So we were broke. I hadn't eaten a decent meal in days. We went up to the desert for a few days, and I stayed at my mother's house. She was living in all alone in the home in which I had grown up. Working two jobs, her daily allotment of food consisted of half a can of Campbell's soup per meal. Times were rough.

"The truth has no patterns" - Don Van Vliet

Van Vliet was having weird hallucinations, thinking he was going to die, having "revelations." He kept telling me he didn't sleep for a year. He would tell people he didn't sleep during this period in his life, yet I saw him sleeping all the time. In groups of people he would ask me to confirm that he stayed awake for a whole year and, out of embarrassment and the desire to avoid conflict I would confirm this lie, thus reinforcing his story and helping him create his myth. I was confused. There seem to be a lot of half-truths and lies beginning to take root in my life. Each time I agreed with something Don said, the more I began to doubt my own perceptions of reality.

Yet I found myself fascinated with Captain Beefheart, and I could see nothing in Lancaster worth staying for. I seemed to be nothing but a burden on my mother, and she seemed distant and preoccupied with things in life that didn't seem to concern me. This man had befriended me at a time when I needed answers, and somehow, for some ridiculous reason, I thought he had them.

The Band Breaks Up

I can't remember exactly when it happened, but the original band definitely left Don at some point during this period. They had made up their minds. I had been accused of idolizing Van Vliet, which I didn't. It was almost more a sympathetic feeling that motivated me to talk the Magic Band into one meeting with their alleged leader at Sue's apartment. I acted as peacemaker, and somehow, they got back together and agreed to try it again. I don't even know if any of them remember this. It was such a brief period of time, yet it remains a very vivid memory to me.

John French: I actually got you guys to talk to him and we decided to give it one more go.
Jerry Handley: Yeah, cause the band was just about ready to split altogether.

I stayed in town during this period, and almost every day I would go down and visit Don and Laurie at Sue's apartment while she was away at work. He was always sitting with a paper pad. The television was on, but not actively being watched. He would have Laurie make us some tea and we would just sit and talk. Sometimes he talked about the zoo animals he sculpted as a child, other times he would mention Coltrane or another of his favorite musicians, and other times the subject would be the occult. He was constantly writing and his conversation was usually interrupted with a request of, "Wait, man ..." during which time he would scribble something on paper, looking at it approvingly and mumble, "Yeah," to himself.

The conversation would then be resumed, usually with the starting phrase, "The thing is ..." during which time he would attempt to remember what topic we had last been discussing. Often noticing a well-endowed woman on the tube, he would first check to see if Laurie was watching and if not, would look at me with a bemused exaggerated, and incredulous expression, making motions with his hands on his chest inferring "nice breasts." Then he would lip the word "Whew" and wipe the faux sweat from his forehead. His attention span seemed relatively short when viewed from this perspective, but all the while, lyrics were being written. Lyrics in this case which turned out to be *Y'Gotta Trust Us.*

As he read them to me, I first had the impression that it was his answer to the Stones' *We Love You*, which we had recently heard on the radio. Secondly, I started questioning the meaning of some of the lyrics. "What do you mean by 'to find us, ya gotta look within'?" was my most burning curiosity. I couldn't understand what us could possibly be within. Although seemingly irritated at the time, he later told me that he respected me for being concerned enough about the lyrics I was going to be supporting with my drumming.

I later spoke with Herb Bermann, after reading an interview in which he claimed authorship of these lyrics. I told him I saw Don writing this on a tablet at his mother's apartment. I asked him if it was possible that he merely typed the lyrics up for Don and forgot. "No way!" was his reply. He had turned over to Don about sixty lyric/poem sheets and this had been one of the songs on that sheet.

Evicted

John French to Jerry Handley: We lost the house in Laurel Canyon. You and I drove there, you were going to drop me off, somebody else had moved into the house, you drove me with all my belongings that I could fit into your black Ford over to Fran's house and left.

Meanwhile, back to reality. When we returned to Laurel Canyon, Jerry drove me to the residence. I walked in the front door and there stood a girl in her underwear. We both looked at each other for a moment like "Who in the heck are you?" and I walked back down the hallway like a madman. My drums were still here, and all my clothes. A guy met me about halfway down and began a frightened plea, so I must have looked determined to do bodily harm. He said, "Oh man, is this *your* stuff? Wow, we're sorry, we thought that someone just left it behind. We're using some of the furniture."

They were sleeping on the floor on our mattresses. There were frames, but these guys were too lazy to set them up. They were a bunch of Hollywood weekend hippies - people who had straight jobs during the week, then went out and played like flower children on the weekend - and this was now their crash pad.

I walked back and there was my drumset, halfway set up. I walked over and started tearing down the drums and putting them in cases. "I'm not mad at you, so just relax. The drumset is mine and I need it." As I think back, both of my sets were there, the Ludwig black oyster set and the natural wood set. Jerry was kind enough to help me pack everything we could and put it in the car. We had absolutely no trouble with the inhabitants of the dwelling while packing up my belongings. By the time we left, I had cooled down and made peace with the new tenants. It was such a strange feeling. I felt so violated.

I called Fran, Alex's friend, and asked if I could leave my stuff there for a time. She consented. Her house was a small frame structure. There was a day bed in the living room, and a hide-a-bed, which became my bed when I later stayed there. There was a bay window to the left of the living room, and a small bed was placed there in which Alex slept. There was a screened in room in which Doug stayed for a time. I suppose that Fran was becoming the refuge for the Magic Band victims.

I dropped off my stuff and said that I would go to the desert for a few days and try to find out what was going on. The ride up with Jerry was quiet for the most part. Both of us were trying desperately to figure out in our own minds what the next step was going to be. Jerry dropped me off at my mother's house. I had no money, and needed a little money to give Fran for groceries, and my mother loaned me $20 that someone had given her.

Sunset Towers

For a while, Krasnow arranged for Don and I to stay at the Sunset Towers, which I later found out was known for housing the rock artists during this era. I don't remember seeing any while I was there. I kept thinking "This place must cost a fortune, "Why didn't they just pay the rent on the house so that we could still rehearse etc.?" I basically watched Don sleep 10-14 hours a day and order room service. His girlfriend, Laurie, was staying with his mother and grandmother (parrrrty!). In the meantime, a couple of girls we had met came to visit and Don threw me his car keys. Now this was a sign from Don for me to get out of the room, but I wasn't supposed to actually *drive* the car. However, he had been rude to the girl's friend, a young Catholic girl whom he had been mocking because she wanted to save herself for when she got married.

So, I took the keys, went down and got in the car, and we had a nice drive all over Hollywood and wound up at Fran's house. We visited with Alex for a while and then I sat with this girl on the back step and talked to her. She was really young, I think about 16, and I was almost 19 by that time. I told her to forget what Don had said. I told her that she should do exactly what she felt compelled to do. Relating the story of my sexual involvement with a girl in High School, I was able to relay the trouble teen sex can cause.

Heaven knows why I did this. I certainly wasn't any angel myself for the most part, but there was something about this girl that was special. She was an attractive girl and I know she liked me a lot, but she had more going for her than the groupies that hung around the bands. Anyway, the girl gave me a hug and said thanks. We drove back over to the Towers and found Don and the girl visiting in the room, sort of in the smoking afterwards phase. I was worried that he'd be really upset. "Where'd you go man?" he asked, casually. This surprised me, and I told him and said that the car was OK. "Cool," he said.

Life At Fran's

Soon after it became impossible for Bob to charge Sunset Towers rooms to Kama Sutra's account any longer. So, I moved back to Fran's house for a short time. It was an interesting period, because I got to know Alex a bit better. We listened to Frank Zappa's albums and Alex educated me in the background of their rivalry a little more. Frank, in Alex's opinion, had a far greater knowledge of music than Don and also had the ability to market himself more efficiently. He also rehearsed, was a responsible band member, and allowed other people to occasionally have credit for things they contributed. Alex said that Don was totally jealous of Frank and in constant competition with him.

As we listened to the Mothers of Invention, I couldn't help but enjoy Zappa's humor and his way of editing little snippets together to make an intriguing and interesting product. I commented on this to Alex and he warned, "Yeah, I agree, but a word of caution: Don't ever mention to Don that you like Zappa or that we listened to him." I found this strange at the time. I knew that Frank and Don had been friends in the desert and all I could think was how much I would want to hang out with my friends if I had the chance. At this time, Frank was probably doing his tenure at the Garrick Theatre in New York, and so no one in the group had seen him for a while.

No Rehearsal

The band played at least two dates with Gerry McGee on guitar, the first of which I never had a chance to rehearse for, I hadn't played probably for a month or more.

We had a gig with Gerry at a club called The Peppermint Twist. It was a leftover from the earlier sixties days, when the Twist was popular. Even though the "Go Go" and "Twist" fad were long gone, the popularity of the places forced them into keeping their dated names. I don't remember what town it was in, except that one had to pass the place where they parked the Goodyear Blimp on the 405 Freeway to get to it. So, it was probably Long Beach or somewhere in that area. After we played, Gerry McGee complained to Don that my playing was lousy and out of time. If I would have been a little older, I would have gotten in his face and said, "How well could you play after not being able to touch your instrument for two months?" Living at Fran's, there was absolutely no place to practice.

Park Recreation Hall Rehearsal

Krasnow then arranged for us to rehearse at a park. I don't remember the name of the park or even what city it was in. I just remember that I had the old Slingerland drums with a plain wooden finish that I had bought at Krasnow's suggestion. I had been experimenting with tunings and trying to get a deeper sound from my drums. I would glue leather patches and use tape and use one head and two heads trying to find a sound I really liked. This set was what I took to rehearsal. I was really excited thinking that I had achieved a new sound. No one even noticed a difference. Ha!

Gerry McGee always showed up right on time. He was very business-like and each time that Krasnow would try to persuade him to commit to anything, he would ask, "Where's the money?" The kids at the park loved McGee. They would flock around him each day as we set up for rehearsal. He had a couple of kids himself and seemed to enjoy children in general.

At one of these rehearsals, Don was attempting to write a song. It was the wrong place and the wrong time to be doing this. We were supposed to be rehearsing for live concert appearances, and live concert appearances were Don's weakness in terms of not being prepared and throwing the band off, weakening the overall performance. Although Don himself was not a weak performer, he was full of anxiety each time we went on stage because of his neglect of rehearsal, and we were all hoping that there wouldn't be a repeat of Mt. Tamalpais.

As Don started to create this music, McGee emphatically stated, "I don't wanna play no Frank Zappa music." We all knew how this must have made Don feel, after all, he didn't consider his music anything like Frank's. Most people know that Frank's music is completely different. On top of that, Don was always speaking of how superior his music was to Zappa's, so to have someone listen to his music and call it "Frank Zappa music" was not going to set well. Although we knew what was going on in Van Vliet's mind, we had a little chuckle about it later. He wasn't exactly the most popular guy on the block after Tamalpais, and we were all paying incredibly for his mistake.

Interestingly enough, the musical suggestion that had caused Jerry to make his "Frank Zappa music" statement was that Don asked him to play *The Star Spangled Banner* on guitar. This was a full two years before Jimi did this very same thing at Woodstock. Hmmmmm ...

Yardbirds Santa Monica Civic Auditorium Sat. August 7th, 1967

We also played the Santa Monica Civic Auditorium on the same bill with The Yardbirds. We were the opening act. Krasnow's wife was backstage before the show. She gave Don some love beads to wear for the performance. She seemed to have a very calming effect upon him. I don't remember her name, but I remember her encouraging him almost like a mother would a child. Don responded in a very positive manner.

Gerry McGee walked onstage with his little tiny amp at the last minute - like he did this everyday. He was always cool and collected. We weren't loud on stage at all. But the sound man made us sound just as big as The Yardbirds. Jerry and Don did a great interplay during a version of *I'm Mad*, an old John Lee Hooker tune. The best audience reaction was to the blues. I think this was one of the best performances of the Magic Band in the context of public accessibility. We even had backup vocals worked out. Don was absolutely flawless, his showmanship and stage presence was incredible – probably a direct result of the lack of hallucinogens in his system.

Also, because I had been able to rehearse, I was playing a little better than at the previous performance. A glimmer of hope was apparent in Gerry's eyes. He seemed to enjoy this night. However, he was a businessman all the way and insisted on being paid each week by Krasnow. I think the going rate was about $250 a week. He had a family and needed to provide for them. I should have followed suit, but being young and naïve, considered that I wasn't worth it.

Custom Clothes Shop

Krasnow took us to some shop in Santa Monica where they custom-made clothes for rock stars. (I guess this was the old "clothes make the man" theory. We each got to choose whatever kind of look we wanted. I foolishly picked a "Southern Gentleman" look with a burgundy jacket with tails and riding pants. Gerry McGee went for suede and fringe. Jerry Handley chose an Africa dashika. Don chose some black and white cloth and had that famous umbrella shirt made that showed up on a promo photo, which appeared in the aforementioned freebie hippy newspaper called *New World Countdown*.

Stone Love

When we left the costume shop, I rode with Van Vliet. As was his usual practice, he made a stop at a supermarket to pick up a Pepsi and something to eat. He would listen to the radio, not so much because he enjoyed it, but to get a sense for the "pulse" of the hits, to study trends, etc. This, of course, he would have never mentioned publicly. A new Stones song came on the radio, which was entitled, *We Love You*. It was the Stones answer, I suppose, to the Beatles' *All You Need Is Love* that had been released a few months earlier.

Don was enthralled with this song. Parking in the market's parking lot, he turned the radio up and got out of the car. "Listen to that, man," he said, half engrossed in studying the song. It had a certain delta rhythm that he particularly liked and acoustic piano was playing the rhythm in low octaves. He stood, seemingly lost in thought, through the entire piece.

I always thought that *Trust Us* had been inspired by this song. He had heard it before, I believe.

Another Mutiny

While we were at Fran's, Alex and Fran both began to work on me about getting rid of Don and just being a four-piece group with Gerry McGee. A lot of animosity and resentment had been stirred up by Don's failure to perform at Mt. Tamalpais, and his basic instability as leader. One weekend afternoon, we invited him over for a jam session, and Jerry Handley drove down especially for the occasion. We played for about three hours, doing instrumental versions of every blues tune we could think of. Gerry was decidedly a country player and had that sound at times. However, he was such a great guy that the day was a real party and a real pleasure. This was actually the third time in less than a year that the band had asked me to take over as singer/drummer. The second was shortly after the Mt. Tamalpais incident and the first was when we played a club date in Lancaster without Don to make some money.

By now, I had been staying at Fran's for several weeks. Don would sometimes come down during this period, and we would go see a movie together. I remember seeing *The St. Valentine's Day Massacre*, *One Million Years B.C.* and *The Bible*.

When Don wasn't around, the main attitude of both Fran and Alex was that Don was an irresponsible fool who had ruined everything. I could see their point. There were a lot of jokes made about Don, Alex would walk up and say "Feel my pulse" etc. At the same time as understanding their point of view, I still liked Don and felt like he was needed because of his gifts.

Gerry McGee Quits The Band

Gerry was in the band but a short time, yet he had a profound influence on the musical direction the band would take in the future. Don had a great deal of respect for him, as did we all. He was prone to country playing more than anything else. Yet his adaptation of Don's ideas, along with Don's utilization of his playing styles, compounded to release whole areas of creativity that had never been tapped. Don has told me often that Gerry said to him "If you ever get something going, let me know." There was a mutual respect there, but Gerry was wise enough to realize that the band was a financial disaster.

As I have written Gerry was a finger picker. He used metal picks on his middle and third fingers and a flat pick between his thumb and first finger. This resulted in being able to play two parts at once, keyboard-like chords, and arpeggios. I had watched my brother Dave play this style for years, so I started studying it when I dabbled on guitar. I used my thumb and all my fingers, more like a folk player would. I read an interview with English guitarist Richard Thompson recently in which he stated that if he had to choose again, he would use a thumb pick to free up the index finger. This is more the style I preferred in my modest attempts to play guitar.

At this point, Alex began studying this technique in more detail also, although I believe he used some of it on *Safe As Milk* recordings. I showed him a couple of things I knew from watching my brother. Certain blues artists used this technique quite a bit. Leadbelly is the name that comes to mind. Son House was another. Most of those old country blues players used their fingers. I have heard that Ry uses his fingers with no picks. He did a little of both on *Safe As Milk*.

So, now we faced yet another dilemma: Who would be our guitarist now?

CHAPTER FIFTEEN:
PLAIN BROWN WRAPPER SHACK

Perry and Warners

Richard Perry had gone to work for Warner Brothers, probably as an in-house producer. He had a small private office with a desk. Don and I went over to visit him one late morning during the summer of 1967. This was after Mt. Tamalpais. Richard mentioned something about a female black singer he was somehow associated with, whose name slips my mind. After talking about her for a few minutes, he called her up and Don spoke with her for quite some time. After he hung up, he told us that she had told him that 1966 had been the Year of the Devil. I suppose somehow that came from the dreaded Mark of the Beast - 666, with one number turned upside down making a nine. Somebody had too much LSD and made a "discovery" and it soon became fact in hogwash heaven.

However, as I listened to Don relay this information, he seemed really seriously concerned with what this woman had told him. He seemed like he was searching for some hidden meaning to life and wanted to know what was going on. There was a certain naiveté to all of this, and yet he was so intelligent. He seemed really swayed by anyone who spoke convincingly on a subject, no matter how fantastic it may sound.

Jeff Cotton Joins

I felt that the best step Don could make at this point was to get Jeff Cotton in the band as a replacement for Gerry McGee. Jeff was an extremely talented musician, in my estimation. He had a lot of confidence on stage and a great blues repertoire. Besides, he was my friend, and I thought the rapport would help a lot. I felt that because he came from the desert and knew the background it would be a more compatible alliance than searching LA for the right guy.

I found him just leaving Roehr's Music Box. I was really surprised at how different he looked. His hair was a lot longer and he seemed really relaxed. I asked him if he was interested, and he said "Yeah, for sure." So, I set up a meeting between him and Don.

Jeff had a Fender Jaguar guitar. This was a guitar his folks probably bought for him when he had first started. Some of the first music he had learned to play was by an instrumental group called The Ventures. Ironically, Gerry McGee went on to play with The Ventures, who I believe played Fender Jaguars when they first started, then switched to Mosrite.

The Chicken Coop

John French: Then we finally got a house in that Reseda chicken coop place, and we started rehearsing.
Jerry Handley: I knew we were in trouble when we got that place.

Although the guitarist problem was solved, we still had to have a place to rehearse. Don still felt that it was best to live near LA. So it was in the late summer of 1967, Victor Hayden was put to the task of finding a house for us. Victor was always a great one for finding deals. He had recently found a beautiful Mark VII Jaguar which he was always driving over and showing off.

I enjoyed Victor. He was about my age, and we could relate better than Van Vliet and I (or, for that matter, Alex or Jerry, primarily because of the age difference). He was extremely different to talk with when Don was not around, which seemed to be the case with everyone. For instance, he liked The Beatles, but didn't mention this much to Don, because a conflict would usually erupt. He seemed to have an exuberant personality and would often talk in a mock Granny Annie voice as though she was there, disapproving. In a sense, I felt like part of the family, in that we all had gotten to know each other quite well. I knew Victor's parents Jack and Charlene Hayden, and we had visited with them on occasion. Jack was a very straight-laced salesman - insurance I think -

type with a strong voice and affected mannerisms that one develops in such a profession. Charlene was a stay-at-home mother, typical of those days. She was a very sweet and caring woman. Since Victor was an only child, like Don, he was a bit spoiled.

We stayed at Victor's parents' house for a few days, who I believe lived in Sherman Oaks, a small upper middle class town in the sprawl of the San Fernando Valley. Jack and Charlene were temporarily out of town, I presumed on vacation. I remember going into the garage for some reason oranother, and discovering a white 1960 Cadillac Coupe De Ville in mint condition. I always loved those old Cadillacs because they looked like space ships. I mentioned this to Don and he agreed.

It was a nice change to stay at the Hayden's. The yard was well-kept, and it was a nice neighborhood. I spent most of my time sitting in the back yard. There was a little pot smoking, but by this point, Don had come to the conclusion that he had to stop smoking this stuff because of the anxiety attacks.

Victor and I went to the beach one night, with a friend of Victor's whose name I cannot recall. We all were indulging more than usual in marijuana, and I started imagining seeing thousands of crabs crawling towards me in the near dark. It was all I could do to sit there and tell myself that what I was seeing was not real. It is such a shame that such a beautiful night at the beach could be spoiled by this kind of fear (so much for the harmless effects of marijuana). Victor could never understand this fear of mine that occasionally surfaced, perhaps because he never had the kind of experiences I did while under the influence. The trouble with hallucinogens is that they affect everyone differently, and I was not one who had pleasant marijuana experiences. I saw people fall asleep after smoking pot and couldn't imagine how they could, as I became completely hyper. It put me in a near-psychotic state of mind.

This is probably why I was able to have compassion for Van Vliet's behavior – especially the anxiety attacks and the hallucinations of seeing angels. Perhaps I had a similar type of imagination, especially with regard to fearful imaginings that became exaggerated beyond all logic. Someone who is capable of seeing a girl's head turn into a fish isn't likely to be able to handle every day life as easily as a person who is impervious to hallucinatory upheaval and perhaps just gets a little buzz. I often wondered what in the world my friend John Parr had seen or experienced that had been so severe as to motivate him to end his life.

Back to the house searching. Victor had some means by which he could locate the best deal on a rental in the entire LA area. I never found out his secret. He was extraordinarily talented at finding anything especially if it had to do with real estate. We looked at a couple of places with him, neither of which seemed to work. Finally we came to a property in Tarzana that, although run-down and in disrepair, seemed to fit the bill. We saw it at night, and it must have been a full moon, because we could see quite well. The yard was completely fenced in (except in the back at the alley) and had big chain-link gates at the driveway. There were many large mature trees in the front yard and the shaded ground beneath was almost completely covered with ivy. We later discovered that many of the trees were fruit trees, primarily fig.

An Italian family had owned the place back during the time when the San Fernando Valley was largely an agricultural area, and had grown as the family had grown. It had some very quaint features. The house was located on the right (west) side of the property, with almost no room between it and the property line. The house part of the structure was just a small one bedroom, one-bath dwelling. The living room was in the front, kitchen in the middle, and bedroom and bath in back. All the rooms were the same width. The kitchen had a brick floor and some kind of brick oven. The side door was a Dutch door, which entered into the kitchen. All the cabinets and shelves were fairly crude handmade devices, which gave it the ambience of an old European kitchen. The bedroom and living room were very plain and basic.

The chicken coop houses were both attached to the front house like a train, in single file. It seems like there was one that just was a couple of rooms. They were in worse shape than the front house. We used them for storage. The back house had a small kitchen, bathroom, and fairly good-sized living room, which contained a brick fireplace. All the walls were covered with a kind of wallboard called Firtex that looked a little like acoustical tile. It was all very cheap and crude. But there was definitely a possibility that this could be a rehearsal room. There was a large barn out back, some old machinery, and some vineyards. Behind the vineyard was an alley. Across the alley were apartment buildings. There was another small storage room adjacent to the front house on the east side of the property that had been set up as a laundry room. Tufts of grass grew up through large cracks in the asphalt driveway that went all the way back to the last house where the pavement ended. It appeared to me to be about two to two and a half acres of land.

So this dilapidated series of shacks became the new home of the Magic Band, or at least Don, Laurie, Jeff and I. Jerry and Alex never lived here. Don and Laurie took over the living room of the main house as their bedroom. Jeff and I shared the actual bedroom. I am sure that Don must have hated it here. There were spiders and dust. He was allergic to so many things. It probably seemed a big step down for him. Jeff and I had a great time. We loved it because of the old outbuildings etc. Unfortunately for Don, we were both still kids and liked to goof off in our spare moments.

We brought down some garden tools from the desert and spent a few days just clearing away all the weeds. The place had really been overtaken by vegetation. Don had nothing to do with any of that. He couldn't because of his allergies. Jeff and I had cleared paths to everywhere we needed to go within a few days and eventually had things pretty much under control. After unpacking the instruments, which Jerry had towed down in a rented trailer, we began to rehearse. I had an upbeat attitude about all of this. I felt good about Jeff being in the band. He was my friend, and I felt that I would better be able to deal with all the ups and downs.

Jeff immediately began commenting confidentially that Don seemed similar to Merrel Fankhauser in his dominating ways. These were little asides that were nervously spoken to me in moments of privacy. Cotton would naturally make this comparison at first as Merrel was the only other bandleader he had dealt with. It became very clear later on that Don was much more aggressively domineering than Merrel had ever been. Jeff also later rejoined Merrel to form MU, so it is evident that Jeff later changed his mind in regards to this comparison.

However, this early comparison made it uncomfortable for us. We were friends, but we couldn't really be ourselves in Don's presence, or there would be criticism and confrontation. Something that I began to realize was that Don had been closest to me in the band for some time because I was the most open-minded. Now he had a new young band member and he seemed to be intent on indoctrinating Jeff as much and as quickly as possible.

At the time, not understanding Van Vliet's tactics, I felt a bit jealous and alienated. I was no longer getting the attention to which I had grown accustomed. This is probably similar to the feelings Don Aldridge described when Van Vliet first partnered with Herb Bermann and later when I first joined the band. I found out quickly that Don was highly capable of a large degree of favoritism, and he seemed to always shed mounds of attention on newcomers while ignoring his more long-term associates.

I also felt disposed of in a sense. Condescending remarks quickly replaced the praise Don had formerly given me. This was done in front of Cotton quite often. I felt it was a conscious effort on Don's part to belittle me in Jeff's eyes and drive a wedge between us, severing some of our bonds. Similar to the way Don had belittled the other band members to me when I had joined. As time went on, I could see that Don was turning Jeff and I against each other. He would do this by pointing out little flaws in one's personality while the other was present. Usually this would result in either Jeff or I nervously chuckling at the one being criticized. Each time this happened, it was like a little knife wound that left a small but memorable scar and these little incidents became stones in a wall that was slowly built up between us. As time passed, these little wounds started grouping together so that a case history was built up in our minds, one against the other.

Our relationship began to deteriorate in that we no longer trusted each other. We confided in each other less and less, until eventually, we would only speak of music. Both of us began to develop the fear that anything said in confidence to one another might later be repeated to Don. To make things more complicated, Alex and Jerry seemed to be a whole separate subculture. We had little in common with them. Being 18, I didn't realize the problems they were dealing with themselves. Certainly I did not have the maturity to comprehend the stress either of them were under, facing marriage and parenthood.

Don seemed blissfully unaware of their circumstances and just seemed angry that they weren't available to rehearse more hours in the day. In their absence they were the constant targets of his criticism and their every fault was pointed out, analyzed, dissected, and magnified. The band soon consisted of the three of us (the good guys) and them (the bad guys). However, when they were present, he would seemingly turn tables at any opportunity and make Jeff and I feel like adolescent fools in front of Alex and Jerry - like a psychotic MC at a good ol'boy's meeting.

Handley's Growth

Jerry was practicing on his own during the day, and was growing in leaps and bounds. That was his period of growth. We were working on all that weirder stuff like *Kandy Korn* - all the *Mirror Man* album stuff. To his credit, Don often commented privately and at rehearsals about Jerry's improvement on the bass and his dedication to learning the new compositions. Alex was also deeply involved in developing fingerpicking and slide techniques. He was basically attempting to accomplish three things during this period. One was to musically assume the role of Ry in terms of learning his parts from *Safe As Milk* for live performances. Also, he was involved in getting Jeff up to speed on guitar techniques employed in the Magic Band. Alex was also learning the new material simultaneously and so his workload was heavy.

The new compositions I am referring to became the beginnings of the album which would first be recorded as *Mirror Man* and later re-recorded as *Strictly Personal*.

Avalon Ballroom/Chet Helm

We flew to San Francisco with a still-upbeat Krasnow for a performance at the Avalon Ballroom. It was our first performance, as I recall, since Jeff had been drafted into the group. It must have been my first performance at the Avalon. Although I don't remember the name of the hotel, it was right down the street from the Avalon, and across the street was a restaurant that served buffalo stew of all things. I shared a room with Alex, and Jeff shared with Jerry.

Blue Cheer

This time we played the Avalon, the main band was called Blue Cheer. This name was not only the name of a popular laundry detergent, but also the name of a certain form of LSD or acid. I jokingly asked the band which they were named after, and got a sullen look and no reply. Later, I heard them philosophically preaching to the sound man about the deep meaning of their name and how some drug-induced hallucination had revealed a sign from God that this was their destiny.

There were several popular forms of LSD on the black market at the time. I remember Orange Sunshine, Purple Owsley, Sandoz and Blue Cheer. Sandoz was supposedly the pure form that Timothy Leary took. There was also some stuff called STP. One rather dead-looking male individual who was a member of the audience came up to me staring deeply into my eyes with hyper-dilated pupils. He claimed he was on all of the above-mentioned drugs at once. It was looked upon as some religious experience, which he probably thought would qualify him for guru-hood any moment, if he could only live that long without mutating into some unrecognizable life form. He looked long and deep into my eyes, trying to psyche me out and I felt rather creepy. Then, I started thinking about the fact that somebody that stoned would probably be utterly useless in a fistfight, so I regained my composure and congratulated him on ruining his health and having no future before walking away.

There seems to be two ways to achieve enlightenment according to the hippy mindset: either years of meditation (following the eastern philosophies), or the short cut: lethal amounts of psychedelics. Of course, not bathing or shaving for about six months was an enhancement, which definitely gave one a certain ambience. Since California was not a practical place to find a mountain upon which to sit and meditate, most people chose the fast-food chemical alternative. We needed fast-food enlightenment on our highway to Nirvana. Now that God had been officially pronounced dead, we were searching for his remains.

Getting back to Blue Cheer, I heard them describing the deep meaning behind their music. Being named after this drug had made them feel as though they had some important message for mankind. Something about the power behind this drug and the incredible capacity to solve all of mankind's problems seemed to be the theme. It also seemed incredibly important to them to be as loud as possible; in fact, this seemed their main source of inspiration. They were a power trio (guitar, bass and drums) with a wall of amps each for guitar and bassist. The drummer nailed his drums to the stage with what appeared to me to be railroad spikes. He used the butt ends of large marching drum drumsticks with tape wrapped around the other end for better grip. He never hit any part of the cymbal but the edge, the loudest part, which you could barely hear underneath the thundering gross of guitar and bass amps turned to 10.

I found this all less than fascinating. I had grown up learning to appreciate near-acoustic level music played skillfully. These guys played anything but skillfully. This level of volume was enough to cause permanent ear and brain damage. I took bits of napkins and stuffed them in my ears while they played. I still marvel at the volume concept that so many rock musicians have. There is a level of playing that is comfortable for a band. The monitors can be heard, and no one is in danger of going deaf. If one man can take an acoustic guitar and play for five hundred thousand people and be heard by every one of them through a sound system, why do electric guitarists insist on such absurd stage volume levels?

Speaking of volume, I used to marvel at Don. He would stand on stage and complain because he couldn't hear himself through the monitors (if there even were any), then walk back and turn everybody's amp up to 10. I would literally be bleeding almost every night trying to keep up with the band's volume. It seemed ridiculous then, and even more so now. I remember being in such muscular pain on one occasion that I just went back to the hotel and sat under the shower for nearly an hour and a half trying to get everything loose again. And there's nothing like chronic tinnitis to soothe you into a deep and relaxing sleep in a sleazy, roach-infested hotel room.

Meanwhile, regarding the performance at the Avalon Ballroom in San Francisco, Chet Helm was the man in charge of that operation, which business I believe came under the name Family Dog Show. His picture was seen on the original *Safe As Milk* album sleeve as the man from whose open mouth the doll's head protruded. I remember meeting Chet during the recording of *Safe As Milk*. An icon of the era, he was a tall, bearded man who dressed outrageously with long coats and subtle psychedelic print clothes. He had a good rapport with Don and our bookings were based partially on reaction to *Safe As Milk* but also because of the rapport with Don. Ironically, we were already headed in another musical direction. The *Mirror Man* era had already dawned, during which we did long experimental jams with two slide guitars.

Two of the female followers of the group from the Antelope Valley (Mojave Desert) showed up and complimented the band on doing a great job. These two girls named Valerie Stopsky and Valerie Biggy had occasionally come to our rehearsals in the Desert at Sue's house. The latter had at one time (I believe) had an interest in Doug Moon. They thought the band had tremendously improved and were very enthusiastic. Instead of being encouraged by this, I thought they must be on drugs. In my mind, we seemed sloppy and unprofessional.

Of course, there were liquid projections on all the walls. For those of you lucky enough to have missed this, I will describe briefly. First, one must have an opaque projector, the kind they used to use in school to project transparencies on a screen. On the glass platform (where the transparency would traditionally go) were placed two smooth shallow glass bowls, one inside the other. Inside the bottom bowl was mixed oil and food coloring. The top bowl, which fits precisely inside the bottom bowl, was then placed on top and used to squish the oil/food coloring mixture around and said results were then projected onto screens (there were usually several people doing this on several screens). I didn't really see the big deal in this. One of my teachers in high school had spilled some coffee on her lecture outline with similar results. Maybe I enjoyed it more then because it upset her so much and sent the class into choking fits of giggling.

If one were lucky enough to be standing far enough away from the projector so as not to be subject to the immense heat created by the light bulb, the liquid projection could be quite entertaining – for about 11 seconds. Of course, if one's visual perception was enhanced by hallucinogenics; one could easily imagine discovering the meaning of life in these shows and become fascinated for hours. However, if one could go back in time and watch themselves watching this show, they would most likely view a drooling idiot dressed in an absurd costume with his/her mouth hanging open and pupils as large as Venus.

The Scene

Thrift store clothes were really in during this period and many kids bought their bizarre outfits at these stores. Many of the clothes they bought were really old-fashioned. Some of the kids seemed to want to achieve an effect of the Gay Nineties, or the Old West, and others were more content to look like Sonny and Cher on acid. I always felt that Sonny and Cher were frightening enough *without* drugs.

In between sets at the Avalon, a girl with enormous breasts walked up to me wearing nothing more than what appeared to be an old-time corset and long, translucent flowing skirt. She started telling me about her life, which consisted of living with eight other people and sleeping in a one-room flat. This was commonly referred to as a crash pad. This was what was happening a lot then. Someone who looked half-straight (a normal-appearing person, at least in this definition) would rent a crash pad and suddenly find dozens of his flower power friends sleeping on the floor, eating his food, using his bathroom, and borrowing his toothbrush – all in the name of love. This kind of activity was satirically personified in the movie, *I Love You Alice B. Toklas*, in which the Peter Sellers character finds himself in a similar situation. (Magic Band guitarist and composer Elliot Ingber makes a brief appearance in the film, referring to himself as a rent-a-freak). If you watch the film, he's sitting in the bathroom on the counter - in lotus position if I recall.

To crash meant to sleep. Of course, with some of the combinations of drugs and alcohol people took during this time, this common colloquialism could often be taken quite literally. I'm sure that more than once someone who had gone tripping (as in *acid trip*) the night before, woke up the next day in a whole new world of wonderment – with a broken nose or bruised head.

At the Avalon, people danced around with wild abandon, not looking at each other, but looking up with their hands flailing madly about. It was less dancing and more leaping and writhing. I could liken it more to some pagan tribal ceremonial to the rock music gods or something similar. I half-expected human sacrifice to occur at any moment, and persistently prayed I would not be the one chosen.

The liquid projections, combined with music played at a deafening volume resulted in sensory overload, which was supposed to create some kind of psychedelic Nirvana. Someone did scientific studies on sensory overload. I once watched a television special, which addressed this issue in which all hope for the younger generation was lost. Now, that lost generation is running the country.

Rich Hepner

While in San Francisco, we met former Magic Band guitarist Rich Hepner at the hotel. I believe he had heard or read somewhere that we were playing and decided to look us up out of curiosity. If I remember correctly, Jerry and I talked with him. He was not at all what I had expected. He had a razor cut, like you would see on a guy in Las Vegas nightclub act. His attitude befitted that of the really professional club musician. I couldn't really associate this comparatively neatly groomed man I was viewing to the bearded and sandal-clad guitarist I had seen onstage with the band a short time back.

Jerry and Rich shared "Don" stories. Apparently, everybody who worked with Van Vliet had found him quite exasperating. It was relatively clear that Hepner had left in a similar spirit as Cooder; deciding that it wasn't worth the struggle.

Don, in the meantime, was still having his anxiety attacks and asking me to feel his heart. One night, in a moment of complete impatience, I impishly told him it sounded to me like he was going to have a stroke. He became extremely frightened and I had to tell him I was just joking, but that I was sick of him doing this all the time. I was just a kid, and this was a heavy burden to carry around. It took all the excitement out of everything, and he'd already blown our chance at the Monterey Pop Festival.

Richard Perry and his wife were up for the concert and lightly reprimanded me for my insensitivity. He refrained from asking me about his health after that. Although I felt terrible about frightening him, it was really starting to play on everyone's nerves, and I couldn't handle it any more.

Haight/Ashbury

No weekend in San Francisco during this era was complete without a trip to Haight (pronounced Hate) Street. Ironically, this was where the love generation gathered. It was basically a ghetto filled with little stores that sold patchouli oil, incense, posters, and anything considered psychedelic in nature.

It had actually been sort of commercialized by this time to capitalize on the hippy movement. I saw a lot of love children there. I am referring to babies apparently produced as a result of the free love movement. I couldn't help but wonder what would become of these poor kids. Raised right in the middle of a drug culture. How could they ever establish any values? I remember thinking this even then, at 18 years old, "What were these people thinking?"

Haight Street was little more than a ghetto. The heavy drug users were starting to move in. The hippie movement had already officially ended in a parade of flowers, though its empty shell continued to influence fashion trends for several years. The genuine end had happened months before. The real hippies had staged their own funeral, with flowers and a parade, and gone back home. They were hoping to make a difference and probably did. Unfortunately, there was big money to be made from this whole concept and so it was capitalized upon. There developed, as is characteristic of anything in the U.S., a commercialized imitation of the real thing. Haight Street had become nothing more than a tourist trap trying to capture the image if not the essence of an era that had already ended.

Timothy Leary was irresponsibly and foolishly telling everyone to "turn on, tune in, and drop out." A whole subculture was developing out of the carcass of the hippie movement. People were jumping out of windows thinking that they could fly. The Beatles and other groups were writing songs about drugs and then publicly denying any inference in their lyrics as coincidental.

The music business spin-doctors were just beginning to see the flow of potential revenue from all the longhairs and were growing steadily more anxious for new ways to exploit the youth. It was a wide-open market, as everyone seemed to be breaking the rules, the bands, the record companies and the public. There were irresponsible people, driven by greed, making decisions that would directly influence the youth culture in self-destructive ways. But there was some good that came through all this, it did allow for new artists to be heard who would have been denied that opportunity had not the old guard been vanquished. However, there was a part of me that missed the stability and the order of the old ways while appreciating some of the freedoms of this new era.

I didn't want to perpetuate the problems I saw beginning to take shape. I felt like there was a big responsibility on me as an artist to somehow not sell-out to what I saw was going on. I was afraid of being caught in a lemming-run to the cliff. Yet another part of me was drawn into the psychedelic experience. It was seductively enticing and it was similar to what I had been reading about for years in those eastern religious books. I thought of it as a chance to read people's auras, to astral travel, to develop psychokinetic powers and telepathy. I wanted to understand the unknown. The world of the supernatural intrigued me and pulled me and many others into its occult mystique like a spiritual whirlpool.

I also felt like a lot of these people were misguided. There was something inside of me that said something was terribly wrong. Yet, for a few years to come, I would find myself hypocritically dabbling in this kind of lifestyle, which I seemed powerless to escape, because it was everywhere.

As I walked down Haight Street, I saw a spray-painted graffiti phrase: "Clap Is Love" paying homage to the god of gonorrhea. The free clinic had its hands full. These people and this lifestyle had no future and no honor, and not much responsibility. I felt like the children produced in this environment, would grow up with no sense of order. They would be blinded by a darkness caused by their environment and their parent's lack of depth. How could they possibly become responsible adults? What kind of world would they create?

As Bob led us around as if we were visiting a wonderful carnival of delights I sensed in him an air that had no concern for anyone. At the time, it may have seemed like a free and wonderful way to be. It allowed everyone to do their thing – one of the phrases of the time. Being managed by him was like being driven home by an alcoholic who - while thinking everything was fine - never saw the bus coming. Afterwards, he would blame everyone but himself for the disaster. A disaster he should have seen coming if nothing else by witnessing Don's erratic drug-induced behavior.

All of us seemed to have the same basic reaction: we were repelled by the commercial exploitation of the sixties movement. Don later referred to anything related to the love generation as that hippy crap. Alex used to say stuff like "Don't give me no flowers, hippy, or I'll smack you with an organic vegetable." Jeff and I were a little more influenced by the era, the fashions, and the fact that it was really our generation more than the others. I have to admit, I bought several bottles of patchouli oil and a little carved box from India in which to keep them. This impulse purchase was probably triggered by my fascination with the occult. The store had this dark, mysterious aura, and I found myself wanting to play the sitar for a moment.

Rehearsals for *Mirror Man*

Unfortunately, I didn't get much time to practice alone, because Don spent a lot of time in the rehearsal room (I'll call it the studio from now on) during non-rehearsal hours. Sometimes he would enter the studio, smoke a little weed (yes, he started again) and sit around jamming on guitar. Someone had given him a little portable tape recorder and he was always recording bits and pieces of ideas.

A few of the simpler guitar riffs from this era were created by him on the guitar while he was experimenting in this manner. We would sometimes jam together. The beginning of *On Tomorrow* was written like that. He would hammer the strings and get some really interesting sounds. He loved slide guitar, though sometimes I felt he overused it. We would be halfway through some piece and he would say "Can you play that on slide, man?" This often involved a process of re-tuning the guitar in a slack key tuning and re-learning the part. Occasionally I felt sections of songs had sounded better before the transposition to slide.

I decided to switch from traditional grip to matched grip at this time. For non-drummers, this meant holding both sticks the same way. I had originally started using matched grip, and the school system had demanded that I play the other way, so that all the drummers in marching band would appear "uniform." I discovered that with the volume levels we played at, it was impossible to be heard unless I used a great deal of physical force.

During one period of little band activity that lasted six or seven days, I made the switch. It was very awkward for me at first. The *Mirror Man* sessions have some really bad drumming on them in terms of technique. Part of that was due to this switch, only a few months before we recorded.

Part was also due to the extreme volume level at which I was trying to play. I used my arms for everything. There are three ways to hit a drum: arm, wrist, and fingers. The arm technique is the loudest and takes the most energy. I had to use this for everything, fast or slow. I started getting really bad aches in my hands, arms, and shoulders. I broke two foot-pedals and dozens of sticks. Krasnow had decided that we all needed to play through Dual Showman amps, which Fender had loaned to us on some kind of endorsement deal. These amps were the biggest they made at the time. They were large piggyback amplifiers (amp and speakers separate) with two 15 inch speakers in a huge cabinet. We had four of these things.

Don had everyone playing at 10 through the amplifiers, because it was the only way they sounded big. By big I mean with enough distortion. I kept saying that there were devices to preamp the signal to get this kind of sound. No one in the band was interested in any kind of effects or pre-amps to control distortion at lower levels. He also had decided that the only way to get a big sound was to use big strings on the guitar. This was going in almost the opposite direction of anyone else. The strings on these guys' guitars were huge.

Also, feedback became an interest. We had been to see Gabor Szabo at Shelly's Mannehole, a local jazz club in Hollywood, and Van Vliet strongly encouraged the use of acoustic feedback produced by hollow-body electric guitars to enhance the sound. The early version of *Dirty Blue Gene* is one of the best examples of this kind of feedback, employed skillfully by Mr. Jeff Cotton.

It was obvious that this album was going to be extremely different to *Safe As Milk*.

October 13-15, 1967 Avalon Ballroom; Big Red, The Biker Roadie From Hell

Krasnow was getting as many concerts booked as he could for us. He booked us again in San Francisco at the Avalon. He couldn't go himself, but thought that we should have someone to accompany us and so hired a roadie. Krasnow described this guy as being really hip and experienced. He assured us the roadie would take good care of us.

The day we were to leave, a 6'6" red-haired Neanderthal disguised as a biker appeared at our doorstep with a van. This was our roadie. He introduced himself as Big Red. I think he must have scared the hell out of Don, who suddenly went into his best behavior. I was too young and naive to realize what kind of trouble this guy could have caused. He seemed relatively benign to me. He lifted our amps around like they were feathers and gave us little chores to do, bellowing orders like some mountain-man commando in a loud whiskey voice. I think everyone was a little intimidated.

I don't remember much about this fellow except that he could barely drive, was totally uncouth, and always did the things the easiest way possible, even if it risked destroying us and everything we owned. How we managed to survive this encounter was probably due to the intercession of legions of guardian angels (as opposed to Hell's Angels). I seem to recall, being the youngest and simply outvoted, having to share a motel room in San Francisco with this guy. It was one of those things we all kept trying to worm out of - and I had the least seniority. So, I spent my stay in San Francisco tripping over beer cans and getting contact high on the endless number of joints this guy consumed.

Although Big Red didn't seem as experienced as other roadies we would be graced with later on, he made up for his lack of experience with brute force and total intimidation of others. Our drives to and from airports consisted of Don sitting up front with the rest of us in back desperately seeking something to hold onto to keep from being thrown into the bare and unforgiving metal walls of the panel van. While at the same time, ducking huge Dual Showman amps, which were bouncing and sliding around with each precarious twist of the wheel as Red performed yet another lane change at the speed of light.

At the airport, he settled into a loping gait and cleared a path for us, pushing the entire backline of the band in front of him on a cart. It was like the children of Israel following Moses through the parting of the Red Sea. Horrified onlookers would rush fearfully to the side of his pre-determined trail. "Gear coming through!" He would shout. However, we weren't allowed to fall behind without Red himself bellowing humiliating chastisement from the front of the line. So we scrambled like dachshunds on ice trying to keep up with a dromedary in this race through humanity.

Our arrival at the motel in San Francisco was officially called to order by Big Red entering the office, slamming his fist on the counter and bellowing, "Hey! We got reservations here!" Don was suspiciously quiet during all of this. I think he decided the best thing to do during all of this was go with the flow.

The concert (I believe) featured Buddy Guy, Captain Beefheart, and Blue Cheer. Buddy Guy was one of my favorite blues guitarists and singers. Unfortunately, this atmosphere did not allow me to enjoy him. The hall's acoustics were too poor to really hear anything correctly. The mindset of most sound men in those days was "if loud is good then louder is better" and finally onto "loudest is best." There wasn't much talk of EQ or effect sends, or balance. Just lots of big watt-hungry power amps.

One thing great about the Avalon was their posters. The artwork is available in books now. They had quite a collection on the walls of past posters advertising concerts. I studied them all and found the artwork to be quite high in quality and imagination. It reflected various symbols of psychedelia.

We Survive Big Red

I remember that after the performance as we were leaving the motel, Big Red didn't want to carry all our bags down to the van from the second floor of the motel, so he pulled the van up underneath the balcony and proceeded to drop all our bags on the roof of the van. They landed with a huge bang since this was a metal roof. Heads were poking out of doors as guests tried to figure out what the racket was about. Red was so tall that he could reach the luggage on the van roof while standing flat-footed on the ground, and loaded the van quickly. All of this weight on the roof of the rental van had delicately sculpted it into a concave shape. It was really more comical than scary. We did make it to the airport, and after yet another terrifying ride from LAX, we made it home. Afterward, we managed to convince Krasnow that Big Red was not our man.

The Cheetah - September 1967

The Cheetah was a large rock club next to the 405 freeway somewhere near LAX. It looked like a large industrial building of some kind. For this era, it was actually decorated quite nicely. There were the usual liquid projections, but this place had more of the hi-tech industrial look and was cleaner than most clubs. It had more than one stage, and was brighter than most of the clubs, which made the atmosphere a little more likable in some ways. I remember little about playing, except that I do believe we did some of the newer *Mirror Man* material here.

Van Vliet and Snouffer were not on good terms this evening. Alex was still living in Fran's house, sleeping in the living room, and remembering Mt. Tamalpais. He was probably having a lot of marital and financial difficulties and as he had already said, he was just along for the ride at that point. Van Vliet was calling Fran a witch and saying, "You gotta get out of there, man!" At one point, after being strongly persuaded by Van Vliet, I joined in and agreed about Fran. Alex looked at me with the most disgusted look. I really felt like I had betrayed him. He said nothing. I was being strongly influenced by Don once again and he knew it.

Herb and Cathleen Bermann Visit

The Bermanns were living in Topanga Canyon at this time, which was the home of artists, hippies and the like. Don's collaborator hadn't changed much though we hadn't seen him for a while. At the time, I wasn't really too convinced that Don needed Herb, and I always wondered why he was still in partnership with this poet/friend. I thought it was more of an attempt to show as much relationship between this album and the first one as possible - especially because of the changes in personnel.

One thing great about Herb was his organizational skills. Anytime he wrote something, it was typed and filed. This means all the words were actually in the right order on the same piece of paper! Don had a copy to work from and there were no boxes of napkins or matchbook covers. As mentioned before, Don had started buying cheap plain paper pads to write and draw on. That helped, because at least one knew that whatever he wrote was probably likely to be found on one of those pads – perhaps on several different pages in small remnants, but at least in a more approachable collection.

The Bermanns turned out to be rather warm, friendly people especially Cathleen. She, as I now was beginning to notice, was quite a beauty. She would relate some of their adventures together. They had lived in Alaska for a time, during which time they had a malamute that was in constant pain because Herb kept feeding it cheese. A visit to the vet revealed nothing more than chronic constipation. This was a big laugh for them this night.

Apparently, they had moved to this area from San Francisco. They were really Don's friends more than mine, so I wasn't invited into the conversations. Cathleen was doing some kind of work at the time. Herb was still writing. He called her his "old lady" in typical fashion. I saw him just as another of the many people in this society who fall though the tapestry of civilization and awaken one day to find that the world doesn't seem to have a space for them. I can relate to this.

I remember him one day being prompted by Don and giving a lecture to the band about how we had to work really hard and get this album sounding really good so he could make some money and his old lady wouldn't have to work anymore. This was during the days when we were putting in several hours of practice a day. It was also obvious that Don was blaming the band for the slow progress. If Don had been the type of writer who conceived and wrote his song totally separate from the band the songs could probably have been learned in several weeks rather than several months. As it was, the material was probably put together in months.

In light of recent facts, my feelings about Herb were tempered by what Don himself said about Herb. Van Vliet said that he was only using Herb to learn more about poetry, and Herb, in the meantime, was stealing all Don's ideas and calling them his own. I have recently read an interview with Herb Bermann and spoken with him on the phone for several hours. Herb claims to have written several songs of which Don claimed authorship including, *Trust Us, Safe As Milk* and several lyrics never put to music, including *Dirty Blue Gene, Flower Pot* and *Moody Liz.*

All of the above-mentioned lyrics were lyrics that Don claimed to have written. Sadly, and through my experience with Van Vliet, I tend to believe Herb, who really seems like a great guy. I thoroughly enjoyed speaking with him and it was wonderful to re-acquaint so many years later.

Don's writing techniques were limited by several factors. One was his inability to actually play a guitar and understand the nature of the instrument. His attempts at playing a guitar were severely limited, but when he would discover some new sound or phrase, he would become extremely excited. If no one was in the room, he would yell for help, seemingly trapped with his discovery until some method communicating it via tape or a guitarist learning and playing along with him could be achieved.

He almost always used some marijuana during these creative sessions, and this would add to the confusion of trying to get the essence of what he was doing. Sometimes, it would seem as though Jeff would be playing exactly what Don was playing and Van Vliet would be shouting, "That's not it, man, John, help me." I would then attempt to play guitar and do the same thing Jeff was playing (though not as well) and he would occasionally say, "That's it! Show Jeff." Jeff would then play exactly what he had been playing and Don would be satisfied.

Sometimes, the translator, whether it was Jeff, Alex, Jerry, or myself, would wind up actually playing something vastly improved and more musical than Don's attempt, and he would often claim it as his own, using the phrase, "You knew exactly what I meant." Many little bits and pieces of songs came together like this, but, though Van Vliet was always the one with the vision, credit for anyone's else's contribution was never considered.

Circumstances

We had first been rehearsing during the day, but this soon evolved to evening rehearsals to accommodate Jerry and Alex's lifestyles. Alex had moved out of Fran's house and into an apartment with his wife, Mary Jane.

John French: Right around the time that we got the chicken coop on Hatteras Boulevard in Tarzana CA., you and Alex were living (several miles) across town in an apartment. Well, you lived in the same apartment building, but he was living with his wife Mary, and you were living with Sue and Lisa, right?

Jerry Handley: Right.

JF: We were rehearsing in the evenings. (Also) you (two) were really (practicing) hard (on your own). They were long days because Sue was working and you were watching Lisa during the day, plus coming to rehearsal in the evenings.

JH: Yeah, that sounds right. I don't remember doing anything else at the time.

JF: Well, I know we rehearsed at night cause you guys had stuff going on during the day. I think Alex (may have been) driving a truck.

Pseudonyms

Around this time is when the idea of everyone having a pseudonym actually came into play. This was probably late-summer, early Fall of 1967. Alex and Jerry had come for a rehearsal but it was a particularly laid-back kind of day and Don was more intent on sitting in the kitchen with everyone and talking. I remember it being a nice, relaxed atmosphere. Somebody was joking around with Don, probably Alex, saying "Well, you've got a stage name, why don't we all have stage names?" This was how it started. Alex was writing down name ideas on a list and laughing at each one. The more ridiculous and flamboyant, the more popular the name was.

The only two names I can recall from this meeting are Antennae Jimmy Semens (Jeff Cotton's moniker), and Zoot Horn Rollo (which was originally my name, as I always wore old double-breasted thrift-store jackets). Don created the former name; the latter was Alex Snouffer's idea.

There was an entire list, and it seems to me that Rockette Morton was also on this list and was going to be Jerry's name.

Antennae Jimmy Semens came about as a result of a scalp condition Jeff Cotton had, doubled with the fact that he always wanted to be green and planned on having his skin permanently dyed that color as soon as the resources were made available. This was a result of his fascination with UFOs and little green men, I suppose. I think his favorite show was *My Favorite Martian*. He once confided in me that he had some kind of strange hole in his scalp under his hair that emitted "seeds" as he referred to them.

When Don found out, he told Jeff that it was nothing to be alarmed about and probably the way he was designed to reproduce. This, of course, brought huge waves of laughter from everyone in the room, much to Jeff's dismay, but he went along with the joke and took it quite well. The "semens" part of Jeff's name is inspired by this story. The fact that he wanted to have glass antennae permanently implanted in his scalp inspired the antennae part of the name. Jimmy? I dunno. Maybe he looked like a Jimmy to Don. Maybe it was because it was such a normal name tied to such an abnormal moniker that the contrast heightened the humor.

I used to imagine a doctor trying to keep a straight face as Jeff requested green skin and a glass antennae implantation. Also, I wonder, is this a service provided by plastic surgeons?

Later, in 1968, when Bill joined the group and Jerry left, Bill seemed more of the Zoot Horn Rollo type. Don walked out of his bedroom with a kick-drum head and a felt pen. He had come up with the name Drumbo as a play on the name Ringo and Dumbo and had scribbled it on the drumhead. He said to me in front of the others, "You know, Drumbo is a pretty hip name." I agreed and accepted the name, ceding Zoot Horn Rollo to Bill Harkleroad.

Later, he wrote a song named *Dr. Drumbo* in which the first line was: "Drumbo Ringo Jingo Mumbo Jumbo."

Upon Mark Boston's entrance into the group, the name Rockette Morton was given to him. Mark was very interested in flatulence and faithfully practiced his role on a daily basis. Don would carry matches around to light at needed moments, and it became a sacred ceremony. There was a section in the rear (no pun intended) of Salvador Dali's *Diary of a Genius* that was entitled *The Art Of Farting*. Since Dali was popular with the band at the time, this added to the sanctity of gaseous emissions being envisioned by the group as some kind of nebulous epiphany, a sign from beyond. Once, Don told Mark something to the extent of "You've got enough propulsion there to send you to the moon." So, Rockette, a name from the list, seemed to be the appropriate moniker for Mark Boston. Hence, on *Trout Mask Replica*, his flatulent noises followed by "Rockette Morton takes off into the wind."

Later band personnel received stage names. Ed Marimba, the obvious for Art Tripp as the marimba-ist of the group, was given to him probably in part because he liked to play pool and Ed seemed like the name of a guy who hung out in pool halls.

Winged Eel Fingerling is, in part, from "the winged eel slithers" line in *Beatle Bones 'n Smokin' Stones*. If you listen to Elliot Ingber's playing in *Booglerize* you can hear that he plays tasty little slithery lines that never really quite enter the realm of solo-ing. Isn't "fingerling" a wonderful word?

Greg "Ella Guru" Davidson was originally given the name Jewbo and, being Jewish, felt a bit uncomfortable with this moniker, though Jimmy Carl Black (Indian Ink) thought it was a great name and tried to convince him to take it.

Jeff Tepper drove a Morris Minor, hence the name "Moris." I understand he actually legally changed his name to Moris. I thought about changing my actual name to Drumbo, but ... somehow it just doesn't seem like it would look too good on a bank loan application. Of course, neither does the word musician when listed under occupation.

Eric Drew Feldman became Kitabu probably from the book Congo Kitabu by Jean-Pierre Hallet. Harkleroad mentions in Lunar Notes that Jean-Pierre Hallet actually contacted the band and visited them.

Denny became Feelers Rebo, though this name was originally given to the Jeff Bruschele, who later became a band road manager during the *Decals* era (70-71).

Bruce Fossil Fowler was obvious to anyone who knows Bruce. He is/was a fossil enthusiast, also a brilliant mathematician, as well as a great musician.

Gary Mantis Lucas - don't know, except that perhaps his physical appearance had a certain mantis-like quality.

I think I covered everyone I legally can here …

Jeff's Transformation
Don insisted on Cotton using heavy strings on his guitar. Jeff especially hated this because he was used to using super-slinky strings. It is really difficult to hold down a chord or do any kind of fast solo run with these huge telephone wires attached to the guitar. It seemed to me that in some ways the larger strings made the sound thinner and smaller. Jeff tried going back to smaller strings, and when Don found out, he was furious.

During most of this chicken coop period, however, Don was nice to Jeff. In fact, Jeff was the new young member that Don took under his wing. As mentioned before I went through a resentment at this point that might be compared to sibling rivalry. It was hard to see Jeff getting all the attention at first. For the first few weeks Jeff and I seemed to share this resentment of authority that Don forced on everyone. Don had a way of making one feel that their ideas were nothing compared with his.

As I had mentioned earlier, through the weeks, Jeff started gradually changing toward me. He would talk less about his feelings concerning Don. I felt as if Don was slowly turning him against me. Just like he had turned me against the rest of the band when I first joined - mostly by saying uncomplimentary things to me about the other players. He would react in a distant way to me. Sometimes he would just look at me and laugh with this strange grin on his face as if I was the lamest person he had ever met.

Yet, when it came to pot, we still found ourselves on common ground. We were just a couple of kids looking for a good time. We would inhale from a pipe and hold the smoke in our lungs with our hands over our mouths. Finally, when we couldn't stand it any more and our lungs were about to burst, we would exhale and cough and splutter until recovery. Then we would repeat the process several times until we could no longer remember what we were doing, or we lost the pipe.

This syndrome went on after rehearsals for a time. Then we would crash and wake up really late (10:00 a.m. or so) the next day, half-sick and groggy. Don finally became upset with this behavior (which was very similar to his behavior back when I first joined the band except for the fact that I always rehearsed with the band and knew my parts).

Although I resented his pointing it out to me, he was right. But it was difficult to be enthusiastic about rehearsal. During this period of time, Jeff and I had almost nothing in the way of material goods. Victor had brought over his old jeans for me to wear. I was washing my clothes out in the bathtub. We seldom went anywhere, barely ever saw any girls, had no social life, and were around someone who was constantly criticizing us. There was little or no money being made. Jerry and Alex would come over to rehearse and leave directly afterwards. They didn't have to deal with all the psychosis, or neurosis, or whatever term was used to describe Don's malady.

There was little self-expression in the music. Every rehearsal was tightly controlled by Don, which could be quite restrictive and prevented us from really developing our individual styles. I actually had a lot more freedom in this sense than the others, as Van Vliet seldom dictated note-for-note drum parts. Most of the drum parts were mine, so I had a bit of artistic input into the music. As before, Don never sang with the band, except an occasional phrase or two to show how the music went with the words. But the life was very unrewarding. I often dreaded starting the day, because it was predictable and seemed so restrained.

Don's Muse

During one of Herb Bermann's visits, Herb and Don began talking about a spiritual entity of inspiration called a muse. I had never heard this expression before. I gathered that it was apparently some spirit that followed a creative person around and gave them inspiration. Don was extremely excited by this. During one period, he was incessantly looking around the house and grounds to see if he could spot this creature lurking in some shadowy place. I wasn't too thrilled with this whole concept and remembered thinking that it sounded creepy

As the days went on, Don seemed to grow more and more interested in talking about his muse until it almost became an obsession. He was prone to obsessive behavior and this was definitely no exception. His hope seemed to be that if he found his muse he wouldn't have to rehearse at all and the muse would just play through him - like channeling. It now started making more sense why he was so motivated.

I had often wondered, if, like Alice Cooper, Don considered Captain Beefheart to be some spiritual entity that spoke through him. He would often speak about the music coming through him from out there and open his hands in an almost religious pose. I wondered often whether he was just saying this to patronize me because of my Christian background (partly because he only said it to me when no one else was present) or that he actually believed it. Of course, most creative people believe they are somehow inspired.

We had gone to see Ornette Coleman play at Shelly's Mannehole, a small jazz club in Hollywood. He was playing this little horn at one point that was very similar to a snake-charmer's horn in looks and sound. The reed was a double reed like an oboe, but much shorter and stiffer. It produced a very harsh sound, and Ornette had a lot of trouble playing it. The instrument was wooden, 16 to 18 inches long, and had a brass bell on the end. The good Captain did some investigating and found out that this horn was called a musette or simran horn. It was a snake charmer's horn.

This seemed to add fuel to what had become the fire of Don's preoccupation with his muse. His muse was female, he had ascertained. After a while, I started feeling like she was really around. Who knows? I do know that the musette eventually was found to work better with oboe and bassoon reeds than with the high-maintenance thick bamboo reeds that it came with.

Evolution of the Flesh Horn

Jeff did his "flesh horn" voice a lot. Don started getting Jeff to do this all the time. He would command Jeff to perform on cue. There was a kind of trained-monkey ambience behind Don's requests that made me uncomfortable. Jeff enjoyed the attention and thought it was funny, but to me, it just seemed like another way in which Don was able to manipulate someone. I really wasn't happy about seeing this happen to my friend. At the same time, I was berating myself and writing my feelings off as just jealousy because Jeff was getting so much attention. It seemed to me that Cotton would do almost anything for attention.

Merrel recalled Cotton having almost an obsession for attention in the early days of their relationship:

Merrel Fankhauser: (Cotton) got to a point where I felt, and so did my parents, that my dad once said "He would paint himself black in minstrel paint and stand naked on the street corner with his guitar if he thought it would give him attention." (Laughing) I went', "Hmmm ... that's interesting."
John French: So you feel that he did this to stand out?
MF: I feel that whatever Don told him to do ... he probably went, "Oh, all right! Great! That'll get me a lot of attention!" because Jeff would do lots of things to get attention.

At this point it wasn't the attention that Jeff was getting that was bothering me so much, it was the fact that Don seemed to be pulling his strings. I think that Jeff was and is a very intelligent guy, but I don't think he realized at the time how much he was being played like a puppet.

Rehearsals
Rehearse, rehearse, rehearse: that was about all we did when we returned from any performance. The neighbors complained of the sound levels and the police were always showing up. We hung blankets on the windows and rehearsed some more. My technique seemed to be getting worse. I was playing so hard, that I had become muscle-bound. It was slowing me down. My fingers felt like stubs and I could barely hold anything in my hands because of the pain. But I kept plugging away, thinking it would somehow change. Krasnow decided that he was going to use some new technique for recording the drums. He told me about two weeks before recording that I wouldn't be able to use any cymbals (!).

I think this shows just how little Bob knew about music. Using no cymbals was just out of the question. I had to use cymbals to get certain types of accents. Being as young as I was, I decided the best thing to do was to take my cymbals down for a few days and just try playing to the songs without them. I managed to come up with some unique ideas this way. I did keep my hi-hat, so I used it all the time. This is why the TTG sessions (known as *Mirror Man* originally when released in 1970) have so few cymbals in them, and the drum parts at times seem so redundant.

Safe As Milk Review
Safe As Milk had gotten a review, which I believe was in the Sunday issue of the *LA Times*. It could easily have been written by Pete Johnson, but I wasn't very aware of journalists at the time. I read the review with relish, in part hoping to see my name in print. The only thing the article seemed to really stress is that Don Van Vliet was the guiding genius of the group. This was the first time I had seen the word genius attached to Don's name. Because of the fact that *Safe As Milk* had no credits for individual players, the only thing the columnist had to go on was the songwriting credits, which were actually printed on the label of the vinyl itself.

Needless to say, I was pretty disappointed. I had been playing drums for several years and had come up with a great deal of the ideas on *Safe As Milk*. Everyone in the band had collaborated on various songs, and Ry Cooder had played a large role in bringing the music from a vision to a reality. Yet no-one's name was even mentioned. I felt cheated, and I also felt like Don had received more credit than he deserved. Lyrically, he probably was at a level one could consider brilliant, but to place him in the genius category and lay all the credit at his feet was a bit much. I had worked hard on that album, as had everyone else, and credit was an important thing, though I didn't realize it then.

At the time I read the article I felt a slight tinge of disappointment, laid the article down, and totally forgot about it. Life went on. I took the attitude of: "Who really cares who gets the credit as long as something get accomplished?" In later years, I would regret this decision, as it left me with no individual credibility.

Self-Promotion

One thing that I was often struck by during my tenure with Don was the amazing amount of self-promotion that flowed from his lips. I wasn't sure at the time whether this was a healthy attribute, or a nasty habit. During this period, it seemed like that particular trait grew to mammoth and unrealistic proportions. I would say that this was during times where The Captain seemed to be present, rather than Van Vliet.

CHAPTER SIXTEEN:
MIRROR MAN SHATTERED

John and Don shot in early 1968. Photo courtesy of Guy Webs

Collaborations Uncredited

Before I had even joined the band, I had bought an acoustic/electric guitar from Roehr's Music Box. I experimented on it just to have more of an idea of what everyone was doing. My family had four guitar players in it, the best of whom was my brother, Dave. He could finger-pick Chet Atkins style and had a repertoire of over 1,000 songs of which he could play and sing at least one verse. My father, uncle John, and cousin Fred all played guitar. I had never wanted to play guitar, but was more interested in piano. Although guitar lessons were offered to me constantly during my childhood, my father unfortunately would not support my interest in the piano.

During rehearsals, I came up with a few guitar ideas now and then. One idea I had recorded at Fran's house weeks earlier on guitar. I was using Don's tape machine. He heard the part and it later became part of the beginning of *Trust Us*. Another time, we were sitting around the dining room table at night after dinner. I was just playing first position blues on the guitar and came up with this riff that Don started singing to. It later evolved into *Kandy Korn*. The riff was the fast part of the song before it went into the wall of chords solo section. I also made up the drum beat for that section and the same with the little arpeggio in the introduction of the song.

I imagine all the members can attest to these little donations to songs. I also have to say that Don brought the ideas to fruition in a vision laced with fragments of his musical input and then we managed to finish what he started. Although still very difficult to understand at times because of his lack of musical knowledge, he would sing, whistle, play harmonica, or attempt to play guitar - often breaking strings - to get his vision across. Sometimes he would just verbally describe what he wanted, like the wall of chords in *Kandy Korn*. He kept pressing us into stranger and stranger music with more and more tempo change and less song form. There was always a vision of something in his mind. Whether it manifested itself as a poem, lyrics, a drawing, or music depended upon what tools happened to be available at the moment. It seemed to be screaming to come out of him, and it he could be very persuasive when inspiration struck.

Don seemed to occasionally have difficulty in getting started at rehearsals. This probably had more to do with the whole essence of artistic inspiration, which doesn't wear a watch and doesn't keep to schedules. A large part of the creative process has to do with spontaneity and obviously this could seldom be achieved at a scheduled rehearsal. However, a big mistake that Don continued to make was that rehearsal to him was always defined as a creative session, so basically there was never any review of what we already had done when he was present. When we just practiced - played something down that in our minds was already finished - Don's first thought seemed to be to add something more. He didn't seem to know when to stop at times.

Also, it seemed he was still very self-conscious about submitting his musical ideas to us for fear of some negative judgment, as Gary Marker would later confirm. Many times, this fear resulted in a lot of hem-hawing and beating around the bush. He would sometimes focus attention on some ridiculous thing, wasting several hours without actually accomplishing anything. Often, he would focus his attention upon some negative aspect of one of us, Jeff or I being the most likely targets, and after a lengthy castigation, he would seem satisfied that he was no longer under the gun and inspiration would arise. Unfortunately, this added to my dread of rehearsal, and I began to seek avenues of escape whenever possible.

Butch's Butch

Before Alex moved to an apartment, Fran once cut his hair. Don went into a tirade. We were ruined! Our image was shattered! What were we going to do about this? Alex sat there looking rather disgusted about the whole thing. This whole event escalated in Don's mind into the fact that Fran was actually plotting the demise of the band, this ridiculous hair trim being only the first step. It would lead onto greater and greater control as she gained her wicked stronghold through these devious yet subtle attacks. We should be on guard. Action needed to be taken. "Hey man, I'm not kidding about this! What kind of lame haircut is that! It looks like a girl's hair!"

My attempt to smooth things over at times like this was some pitiful mumble suggesting Alex might want someone else to cut his hair next time. Eventually, we would all sneak out of the room, one by one, and go practice. Don and Alex would be left alone, and with the audience gone the situation would de-escalate.

If we were playing when Don came in, and he was usually the last to show up, then he would sometimes pick up that energy which would cause his creative juices to flow. It was amazing the speed, which his mind could think up new ideas. We would have the tape recorder running, and he would be stopping the music and saying, "Get this! Get this! Oh man! We've GOTTA get this ..." often adding bits of self-promotion like: "This is so fucking HIP I don't believe it!" Then he would play something on harmonica, or whistle, or sing something. If it was a guitar part, he had to have a microphone through which to dictate. He would often play an imaginary air guitar and with that tremendous voice emulate what he wanted to hear, moving his fingers in pantomime. All of this was done by ear, and it had to be memorized. We would try to get each section down on tape as quickly as possible so that we could later assemble the parts.

Then we would try to play it all together. If anyone had trouble with their part for any reason, there was always the chance the naive impatience of Don would surface. He often took it personally, as though there was some underlying scheme between band members to sabotage the music. Unfortunately, we would have to rewind the tape to hear the part. Then, as we were listening, he would sometimes get the idea for the next section while we were listening back and want to record OVER what he had previously created. It was difficult to make him understand that he needed to discipline himself and retain his idea until we could again fast forward the tape to the proper location.

Beefheart was in and out of the room all the time. He was never a person to stand still unless he had a drawing pad in his hand. Although he often appeared lost in whatever he was doing, he would often interject something into the conversation just to let you know he was well aware of everything going on.

Don's attitude when present during these creative sessions was often like a doctor assigned to ER in that he would be mentally pushing and shoving all distractions and barriers out of his way often in a rude manner. He would tactlessly disregard everyone's feelings saying, "Shut up! We gotta get this, man!" Often, it was near the end of a long rehearsal from which he had basically been absent. Often, during rehearsals, he would be in another section of the house, talking with Laurie or his cousin Victor.

After several hours of band-rehearsal-minus-Don, he would suddenly come in from the other room with some "great new song," and was often greeted with a less-than-enthusiastic band, burned out, tired, hungry, and ready to leave. These situations would often turn into angry confrontations with either Alex or Jerry. Since Jeff and I lived with Don, we had little choice but to cooperate, no matter how tired or hungry we were. Don would accuse Alex and Jerry of not taking the band seriously enough, or being lazy.

Often, Don wanted Jeff and I to back him up, which put us in the uncomfortable position of between the rock and hard place. We were damned by Alex and Jerry for going along with Don, or we were damned by Don for NOT going along with his agenda, which we often did not agree with. Thankfully, Alex and Jerry understood our position and often we did something akin to psychodrama in which we acted out Don's wishes to shut him up, while maintaining an understanding with Alex and Jerry that this would occasionally happen. They had worked with Van Vliet enough to be used to this kind of outburst, which became more and more commonplace as time went on.

However, even with all the concerts we played and all the other distractions that came along, I estimate that the material for the *Mirror Man* sessions was probably written and learned by the band mostly during the four months between late July and late November of 1967. So, an amazing amount of work was actually accomplished.

Don Plays Guitar Onstage

One night before Richard Perry had completely given up on us, we were playing in some little club on the Strip. Krasnow hadn't bothered to provide something to sing through, so Monkees bassist Mike Nesmith was called. He brought his little rehearsal PA in and set it up for us. He stayed for the show. I think he didn't quite understand, but accepted and supported us. Don decided he would play guitar that night. He took my little acoustic-electric, plugged it in, turned it up to ten, and made squeaky squelching sounds, bereft of any musical sense. It was mostly feedback, but he was very serious about this. We all backed him in this experiment, although I had misgivings and wished I was playing in a normal band at that moment in time, feeling a little embarrassed. I watched the audience. Most of the hippies in the club left right away, clearing the room faster than a high school fire drill.

Back in the dressing room, Richard Perry walked in with his wife and said, "You guys are craaazzzy!" We all considered this a compliment at the time, so his comment was met with maddeningly joyous laughter, as though it were the ultimate comment. I think our reaction was a basic response to the combination of all the unfortunate occurrences that had taken place. We were just hungry, tired, and burned out. Dealing with Don had exhausted us of all normal reasoning, and this was at least some form of performance with which we could all identify. The club was a really sleazy place that paid almost nothing. Why not? We thought.

That club date was the point that I believe Richard Perry just gave up on us. Bob, on the other hand, was probably just as nuts as the rest of us at that point. He was trying somehow to juggle managing us unofficially, promoting us and still promoting for Kama Sutra. I have no idea what he thought about the band at that point. He just seemed to keep plugging away.

Beverly was at the performance (probably with Miss Pamela) and brought me a cape to wear onstage. It was an old magician's cape. I wore it that night for the second set. From then on, wherever I went, I wore that cape. I had it for about 15 years before I finally decided to leave the memorabilia behind.

Denver, Jim Morrison

About this time, we went to Denver and played for the Family Dog Show (same affiliation as Avalon in SF) there. There were three groups: Lothar and the Hand People, Captain Beefheart And His Magic Band, and the Doors. The Doors were just about the biggest thing in Southern California at the time. *Light My Fire* was their big hit and you could hear it constantly on the radio.

It was pretty exciting to me to be playing on the same ticket with these guys. This is one of the few times I got a little starstruck. I had heard their album at some girl's house one night. Don and Jeff and I had met these girls and had gone to their place to hang out for a while. They put on the first Doors album. Don immediately started putting it down. I didn't think much of the music, because I hated organ, and there were no interesting rhythmic riffs. However, *Crystal Ship* and *The End* grabbed me a bit. There was something hauntingly different about Morrison. At home, a few days later, *Crystal Ship* came on the radio and Don listened to it closely and said, "The guy's pretty good, man."

Now, we were at LAX all flying out together, and to be able to see these guys was fascinating. Jim Morrison walked around in a black leather suit with a white shirt. He was extremely thin and strikingly handsome, the perfect rock star look. His hair was medium length and he paced like a caged animal. Probably the drugs he was on had him convinced he WAS a caged animal, or it just happened to be part of his routine. It seemed a lot of people enjoyed this neurotic image. Sometimes it was hard to tell the affected mannerisms from the genuine. There was a feeling about being in the public eye that could make you crazy. Especially in those days. He appeared to me to be genuinely disturbed, but the whole thing could have been an act

I recall a conversation with Miss Pamela (Des Barres) and Beautiful Beverly as I called her. They were talking about being present at some social gathering where both Jim Morrison and Mick Jagger held forth. "It was like watching two giant egotistic peacocks strutting around," Beverly laughed as she described this event.

In the golden era of Hollywood, the studios sheltered their stars a bit. Even from my limited perspective of being in the public eye, I could see the point in this. Perhaps they tried to make their image a little too sterile at times, but there was a method to the madness. No one who is exposed to all that public adoration can escape the tremendous effect it has on the psyche. Even in the little taste of success I had experienced, there was a kind of paranoia coupled with fighting off the growth of your own ego. One could always wonder about saying the wrong thing at the wrong time and being publicly destroyed. Drugs were everywhere, and Ronald Reagan was governor of California. How much worse could things get? It was a feeling of being in the crosshairs and never knowing when the trigger would be pulled.

The rest of the Doors were fairly normal in behavior. The keyboard player, Ray Manzarek, was very conservative - almost to the point of snobbishness. Robbie seemed kind of stand-offish. The drummer, John Densmore was very friendly and approachable. He actually became quite good friends with Don. Later, he would come to see us at the Whisky A Go Go. He was studying tablas at the time, which are small drums used in ethnic East Indian music. Ravi Shankar had been made famous by his sitar (an instrument loosely related to the guitar) and for befriending George Harrison, he was to teach George how to play the sitar. Chatur Lal was the tabla player who accompanied him most of the time. I loved the sounds and rhythms of tablas. I never really studied the instrument itself, but I did try to emulate certain counter-rhythmic concepts on the drum set.

I was intrigued with The Doors because I thought that I may find myself in a similar position of fame in the future and wanted to learn anything I could to help me through. It was scary and intimidating at times to think that I was so unprepared for all of this. There was no one holding our hand and saying, "Here comes a bump, hang on." We only had Krasnow, who probably wouldn't have noticed if we fell off.

The flight to Denver was very relaxing. It was the first time I had felt any comfort in so long. I was very embarrassed by the fact that all my clothes were just filthy rags. I was still wearing the hand me down jeans Victor had given me. We were so poor. But there is nothing like a flight over the Rockies to put a different perspective on things. The cloud formations were unbelievable. It was a late morning/early afternoon flight. There was classical music playing in the headphones. I had been on other flights, but this I enjoyed more than any. It seemed like we were really close to something big, as though our break was about to come. Boy, was I wrong.

The Grateful Dead/Denver Love In, Friday September 29, 1967

Don was still going through a less-severe form of his anxiety attacks and immediately escalated the fact that we were at a high elevation into a major medical emergency. He was checking his heart every few minutes. Occasionally asking us to look at his eyes and skin color. He was afraid the lack of oxygen might hurt him somehow. We had been picked up by some hippie woman who was affiliated with the Family Dog Show in Denver. We had to go straight from the flight to the concert area at the park. Don had managed to have her stop at a drug store and get a small disposable canister of oxygen.

I noticed as we were walking from the parking lot that Don did not have his tape recorder, and I knew he had brought it in the car with him. I mentioned this to him. He immediately was infuriated at me for leaving the recorder behind. I couldn't seem to convince him that I had not touched it all day nor was I in any way responsible for its absence. I went back and looked for it, but it was gone, along with several song ideas.

There may be a Grateful Dead poster or other record of this, because they played either just before or just after us. Guru of LSD, Timothy Leary, was there.

We were to play a late afternoon spot at a Love-In at some big park in Denver. The Grateful Dead were playing some marathon jam session. It seemed like The Grateful Dead were always playing anywhere there were hippies and lots of drugs. I always put their music on the level of marijuana-soaked-birdbrain jam sessions. They seemed like the perfect generic hippy-generation rock band. Always ready to party, so what if the music wasn't that good? I never personally thought that they did much of anything except produce sheer quantity and ingest a lot of weed. (I think that I just made myself Public Enemy #1 with a million Deadheads, but bear in mind that I did hear some stuff in the late '70s that I thought was pretty good.) Redundancy seemed to be their theme. Growing up, I had heard people in the desert that were miles ahead of them musically, but they were to the hippies what Rolex watches and BMWs later became to the 'me'generation.

Timothy Leary came out and had everyone go "OM" for a while in a giant mantra-in. This was real sixties garbage. He gave a little speech about oneness and harmonious love. Finally, the chanting began. After about five minutes of "OM" meditation, Leary turned, winked at the band as though the whole thing were a big con, and strode back across the lawn to the parking lot, leaving his newly enlightened followers behind to spread the good vibes.

We played reasonably well, considering that it was outside, we had no time to warm up and there were no monitors. I only recall doing *Abba Zaba* that day, although we played for about 45 minutes. I had a great time there. I was really being swept up into the sixties scene in a sense. Although I had this one side that said we were all going nowhere, there was a side that wanted to take the ride. Besides, it was an escape from the grueling day-to-day existence at the chicken shack. Don started passing around his oxygen to everyone, we all were taking whiffs as we played, and it became a little theatrical stunt. It was funny, and Don suggested that this was the best way to get high over the microphone. Publicly, Don was being reasonably anti-drug at this time.

We were taken to our motel. It was a grungy little cabin off the old highway (like the Bates but more log-cabin-like) in which two adjoining rooms slept the five of us. I split a room with Don, and Jerry, Alex and Jeff were in the other. We had adjoining doors, which were open about half the time. We were playing two nights, probably Friday and Saturday and seemed to have time to set up and rehearse. I can't remember what tunes we went over. I think we were just doing some of the stuff from *Safe As Milk*. Don was always extremely concerned that someone was going to rip off his music, so we usually never performed anything before it was recorded and copyrighted. We did do a long version of *You're Gonna Need Somebody On Your Bond,* which eventually evolved into *Tarotplane*. This was probably unofficially the beginning of the *Mirror Man* session long-jam-tunes concept.

I always thought this was a shame. Playing in front of an audience, if they are enthusiastic at all, brings out something in music that can never be obtained in rehearsal or recording alone. I always felt that the best way for us to record would be *after* doing a month of concerts performing the material live. Better yet, doing a live album. It does make a difference. Unfortunately, Don was never capable of doing anything the same way twice. I don't mean exactly, like a robot. I mean in the sense of an arrangement. There was little cueing off of Don for anything because he was usually just experiencing the moment. This was fine when you were performing a simple format, like the blues, but these songs we were putting together were complex arrangements, which made them rather vulnerable to improvisation gone mad. Also, Don had not rehearsed with us on the new material, not even once.

In this sense, I would say that a singer also needs to be a *musician*, and I've worked with few who were. Most are singers who get lost on anything where you have to actually have some musical knowledge to find your way through the maze. Don always performed by winging it, which could have incredible results when all was well and he was in good form, but had devastating consequences when he wasn't so well or having an off day. I always considered this a characteristic of an amateur performer in others, but sometimes Don made this work quite well for him.

The Doors/Denver 29-30 September 1967

Our rehearsal went well. I loved the way Don sang *You're Gonna Need Somebody On Your Bond*. I didn't know who originally did the song, but this particular version was strongly influenced by Son House. It was powerful and reminded me of the early Beefheart blues band in the desert. I don't know why this song was chosen, but it was definitely a strong performance song.

We played a relatively good show that night. The Doors were kind enough to let us use their P.A. They were sponsored by an electronics firm called Jordan. Jordan only made small instrument amplifiers, no P.A.s. So the Doors P.A. consisted of a dozen of these small amps, two columns of three on each side of the stage. It seemed kind of precarious to me, but I guess they had some way of securing them so that they wouldn't fall over.

We went on and played hard and heavy. I think this was one of the best shows that particular band ever did. We had our little harmony parts down and all the songs were tight. The blues stuff sounded monstrous to me. Alex was playing some fine bottleneck, and Jeff did a lot of the double rhythmic picking so familiar in the Delta blues format. The audience there was really receptive and we had to do an encore.

When we finished, as was my custom, I looked for an exit outside to cool down. I found one upstairs in the back that led out to a small landing with half a dozen steps leading down to the ground. I walked up to the door and discovered all the Doors (confusing words, huh?) were standing out there talking. I heard someone say, "How we gonna follow that?" Jim, who seemed apprehensive, took a slug of beer and said, "We gotta do some blues, we'll do *Back Door Man*, that'll do it." Then they spied me standing there. Momentarily, pride welled up in me and I felt like a large balloon. It also helped me to realize that you never get so famous as to be immune from insecurity.

As they went towards the stage, I walked with Morrison. "Some crowd, eh?" was the only thing I could think of. "Ah, they're a buncha *squares*, man!" was his reply. Thus ended my significant though rather abbreviated conversation with the Lizard King. All I could think of was how could he use such an outdated fifties colloquialism like squares? Why didn't he say lame? I continued walking with him for a moment, just to experience the admiring looks of the crowd. I was still young enough to be really impressed with all this fame and notoriety.

The Doors were well rehearsed, and sounded just like their records except better. The music still seemed pretty limited in scope. Morrison, who was basically a big showoff, was all over the stage. He seemed to be having a growling contest with himself. He would snarl and curse at the audience. He seemed to know just how to milk the last drop from any moment of tension and make it work just right, a born showman.

Don always claimed that he blew out the speakers that night. He said he knew some way of holding a note just right and then grunting into the mike. This would cause weird ambience that the speakers wouldn't handle, according to his theory. Yet the Doors system seemed to be working fine. I never noticed anything blown out.

Don was probably at his best at this show. To anyone who had been paying more attention to the music than the hype, the Doors were blown off the stage. Morrison was good at cheap theatrics, like saying, "Mother, I wanna f___ you." - that kind of stuff was shock value back then. It's almost normal now. However, when it came to getting down to the nitty gritty, they came off like a bunch of college boys with a thin sounding band, a good press agent and a very commercial album. As I listen back to them now, I can appreciate them more than I did at the time, but that was my opinion at the time.

My First Trip To Psychedelic Land

After the Friday night show, everyone felt pretty up. It was my birthday, although I don't remember even being aware of it. I was 19 years old. So much had happened to me in the last year. I had only been in the band a little over 10 months. I have to remember as I read some of the stupid choices I made in this book that most of it happened before my 20th birthday. We went to Krasnow's hotel room to party and feast. It was a good feeling. I started feeling strange once we arrived at the hotel. Not physically, but mentally. There was a girl there from Lancaster, I believe. Her name may have been Stephanie, I'm not sure. She was on acid and having a bad time of it. Don was talking to her. Krasnow was just being his usual detached party-self.

Alex and Jeff and I decided to stay at Krasnow's that night. Someone had some LSD, and I wanted to take some. Don warned me not to do it. I wouldn't listen. In my mind, Don was only saying this because he was on an anti-drug kick for the moment, or perhaps because it wasn't his idea to begin with. Van Vliet was capable of mixed and confusing signals when it came to opinions on drugs. He would preach against drugs, but then abuse them himself.

Jeff had taken acid, and I felt like I had to have this experience to be on an equal plane with him. (Jimi Hendrix's *Are You Experienced?* wouldn't have had anything to do with this stupidity would it have?) He would relate his experiences with Don, and I always felt left out. If I did something naive in a public place, Don would often say, "Man, you need to take some acid and get hip." This wore on me, and I started foolishly believing that somehow I would understand so much more after this trip than I did before.

So Jeff and I dropped 500 micrograms of Purple Owsley LSD. Later, when I told Don how much I had taken, his reaction was,"Is that all you took, man? I took 1500 mics *my* first time." At this time in my life, I was very impressionable. This was like some kind of cosmic weightlifting. I was still the wimp with the dumbbells straining at 50lbs while Don was pumping 1,000. However, Don was the one who walked off the stage at Mt. Tamalpais and saw angelsduring rehearsals.

Krasnow Indoctrination

Alex stayed and observed us. He smoked some pot, had a couple of beers and eventually went to sleep. Jeff and I starting coming on to this acid.

Jeff and I were sort of in some kind of corny acid bond. We felt like we had really become of one mind or something. We were both very young and vulnerable. Krasnow just kept saying how Don was screwing up his career by trying to be so weird, and that he should concentrate on a really solid blues set. The train of thought seemed to be to simplify and live a better life. Then, in about three years, go ahead and do all the experimenting we wanted to after we had made it.

This made total sense to me and had basically been my plan since the beginning (sorry, I liked the idea of actually making money doing music, decadent though it may seem). I was sick and tired of living in a chicken coop and washing my clothes in a bathtub so that Don could use me like a painter used a paintbrush. It seemed really evident that we needed to follow Krasnow's advice. As I look back on this now, Krasnow's record speaks for itself in terms of success in the music business. Look him up some time on the Internet.

LSD is a very powerful substance, and not one that I would recommend to anyone. I didn't have any strange hallucinations. I just felt as though I had viewed the world through a completely different set of eyes. Even drinking water was a completely new experience. As I stood on the high balcony of the hotel overlooking the city, I grabbed the metal rail. I immediately felt like I was one with the whole infrastructure of Denver. We were up reasonably high, and it was a terribly impressive feeling, one that I cannot shake even today. I felt like I was feeling the hum of civilization through the metal pipes and also able to grasp the thoughts of the collective consciousness of the city. It was like a science fiction novel come to life. I felt like I was being introduced to a million new ideas all at once, and I was understanding them all. I felt like I was seeing a completely new and different perspective of the world.

As this realization of what we needed to do hit me stronger and stronger, I finally became so convinced that I woke Alex, who had gone to bed, and persuaded him to drive us back to the motel where we were staying so that I could immediately explain to Don the error of his ways. Alex agreed, exhibiting the pinnacle of patience. If I would have been Alex, I would have probably killed us, or at least wanted to. He showed an amazing amount of tolerance that night.

Don's Reaction

When we got back to the motel, we woke Don up and started talking about this stuff. He was furious with Krasnow for even suggesting such a thing. With us, he was very understanding. He talked Jeff and I through this experience, and we all laid down and got some sleep. I was buzzing for hours and thought about everything in the world at least 10 times. I kept smelling sulfur and Don said, "That's Hell you're smelling." It was as though he was telling me that I was sensing the presence of evil.

That night's performance at the Family Dog Show was a little weak, but we did fine. Our rehearsing had really paid off. One thing Don brought up to the band was that Jeff sometimes wasn't playing on stage. He would freeze and just stand there holding his guitar. It looked like he was playing from my position in the back, but both Don and Alex attested to the fact that he would just stop playing.

The following morning, we visited some local radio station for a live interview with some local DJ. It was very pretentious. I never would say a word at things like this.

Back To The Chicken Coop

The performance was over. I had a dread of returning. It was a little piece of heaven to get out of the chicken coop for a while. Not so much because of the poverty, but because of Van Vliet's control over the environment. Now we had to go back and try to finish all the stuff that was left undone. Putting together Don's music was like taking a dozen jigsaw puzzles and dumping them into the same box, then dividing the scrambled parts and putting several puzzles together at once. Everything was incomplete and disorganized. It made the whole effort seem intensely overwhelming.

It seemed like the band situation was either feast or famine, and mostly famine. Although Krasnow seemed to get us an occasional performance, the band never seemed to be steadily booked. Our constant back and forth shuffle between creating and performing was helping us to develop the kind of stage improvisation that led to the later *Mirror Man* and *Tarotplane* endeavors.

We needed better equipment and a way to keep more organized. We had the tape recorder that had been in Kama Sutra's offices. We also had several tapes on which wererecorded little bits and pieces of different songs; dating back from before I was in the band. Don would come up with ideas constantly, and immediately he would want them on tape. For a while, he used his little machine.

After losing that machine in Denver, Don began to depend on me to keep charge of all the parts on tape. He wanted to record a part on a split-second notice, and sometimes I could not find a blank spot on a tape. He would then start yelling about how I better not erase anything, which really added to the stress. Sometimes, he would forget the part and blame me, sometimes accusing me of sabotaging his music and holding back the band. In the event that I did erase something of importance, it was as though I were the devil and the CIA all rolled into one.

This kind of reasoning left me exasperated. I wanted very much to succeed. I had already realized that I was probably never going to be looked on as anything more than a sideman under Don's guiding genius, while other drummers who I felt were playing on a lower level but with more famous people were getting fame and money. We had all read various reviews of *Safe As Milk*. All the music was credited to Don. I had resolved to try and see this thing through. I had signed a contract that could last as long as five years, and I was determined to live with my decision and make the best of it.

Escalation Of Criticism

It was starting to become very clear that things were steadily escalating in terms of Don's criticism of Alex and Jerry. Also, I was becoming more and more inhibited and introverted because Don would criticize any manifestation that was basically me as though it were something to be ashamed of. Any goofing around or joking was considered lame. I felt as though I were under relentless attack. I had never been around this kind of intense criticism. Being young and unsure of myself, I fell prey to Don's acid tongue many times. I found myself also less and less keen to contribute anything at all to the music, knowing that it would just be swept under the heading "Words and Music, Don Van Vliet."

Victor's Visits

Victor Hayden would frequently visit the house during this period. Almost always, there were the open verbal critiques of the band and what a bunch of lazy assholes we were. Jeff and I would rehearse every day with the band, and we did our best, but the environment was anything but inspiring. Any time Don failed to communicate a part, it became our inability to play or lack of hipness that was at fault. Jeff and I got to the point where we would barely talk to each other. We would intermittently look at each other with knowing stares of exasperation.

Victor saw this as some flaw in our character. He would tell Don that perhaps he should replace us with professional musicians. Hayden knew nothing about playing an instrument as was evident to any musician who listened to his later bass clarinet solos. Don didn't understand much about music himself in the technical sense. Harmonica is not an instrument that requires years of practice and study. This is due to the fact that all of the notes on it are in one key (harmonic) so that one only has to be rhythmically gifted in order to make it work. It was difficult to make Don realize that a lot of the things he was asking us to do took great amounts of time to learn individually, and more time to put together as a group. However, I practiced as much as I could by myself and started developing the roots of my own style.

Musical Influences

We listened to various types of music during this period. I remember our turntable had to be plugged into a guitar amplifier with special adapters so we could listen to records. I recall one night when Don came in with John Coltrane's *Kulu Se Mama*. These moments were really special to me. I loved Coltrane from the moment I heard him and each new album was like a study in the growth of a giant. We occasionally had a chance to go hear some jazz at Shelly's Manne Hole. It was a little club in Hollywood where all the great jazz players appeared. Bill Evans was a steady player there.

We went there during this period and heard the Jazz Crusaders (who later became just the Crusaders). I loved their sound. Two horns always appealed to me. The drummer was great. I never was one for learning names of players, so I can't tell you who was in the lineup. I just remember enjoying the night immensely.

Beverly And Pamela

Pamela (later *I'm With The Band des Barres*) came over a few times with Beverly. Everyone called her "beautiful Beverly" and that is what she was to me. We were drawn to each other immediately. My esteem was so low that I could hardly fathom the idea that a girl this beautiful could possibly be interested in me. It took me a while to catch on. We eventually became romantically involved. Don warned me about this girl, like a father warning his adolescent son about the wiles of sowing his wild oats. He said she thought she was a witch so he had told her, "You ain't no fuckin'witch!" I thought perhaps he was just jealous or was trying to manipulate me in yet another way.

Back to the girls, Pamela was very pretty herself. She had a smile on her face all the time. I didn't know anything about her at the time other than she was a friend of Victor's. I remember little of the conversations because I didn't really personally talk to her much. Don never introduced me to her. She never wore bras and had a habit of rubbing her breasts in a slow rhythmic downward motion for the entire time she conversed. I found it a bit distracting myself. After one visit, Don remarked, "You know the way she's always rubbing her tits? That's so *hip*, man!"

Van Vliet was very friendly with outsiders and enjoyed talking *immensely*. He was never one to say, "Sorry, I gotta get back to work." He paid no attention to *time* in the sense of scheduling and in this way managed to quite often waste huge quantities of the commodity, especially if it belonged to someone else. It was quite exasperating trying to accomplish something within any sort of set framework.

Practice And Growth

Jerry and Alex were still living separately at this time with their wives in North Hollywood. I always envied the other players. They could practice anywhere and not disturb anyone merely by turning down or unplugging. Drummers were always limited by the time of day, and even when they did practice, they knew everyone could hear every little mistake they made as they attacked a new part.

I also envied Jerry and Alex for being able to get away from the constant madness that seem to be a part of everyday life with Don. He was inconsistent in everything. His only constant seemed to be criticism. Most of what could have been our private practice time was eaten up with whatever Don was in the mood to do at the moment. This was exciting at first, but became, monotonous then exasperating. If Don wanted to write a song, Jeff and I had to be there writing down lyrics and running tape recorders.

Because of Van Vliet's continued refusal to educate himself about the technical aspects of music and how people learned, we were constantly in conflict with him about how things should be done and in what order. Usually, it was his way or no way, so all efforts continued to remain in the usual jumbled state. Bits of songs would be put on a piece of blank tape and before I could take the time to catalog the tape so that I could find it again, he would be off to something else. Many times, he would write something instrumental and not title it. It was then up to me to give it some label or title by which I could remember it when he came to me three weeks later saying, "John, quick, get that thing we did, you know the one, the night the cat was acting weird. Whattaya mean you don't know where it is? You're taking too long, man! Good God, I'm going to lose this thing if you don't find it now! We've got to get this man, it's a hit. It means a lot of money for me, and a lot of money for you."

What I'm saying here is that Don continued to avoid taking responsibility for organizing his musical ideas. He took a bit more with lyrics, but still insisted on dictating while Jeff or I, or sometimes Laurie, wrote down his words. His knowledge of running a tape recorder was not limited, he knew the basics, but just refused to do it. I had seen him operate a tape recorder perfectly when he thought no one was watching. He always insisted upon deferring the task with the flattering request, "Can you do this? Man, I don't know how you *do* that, I could NEVER figure out one of those things! How do you do that, man? That's amazing." He had rehearsed these excuses so long that by now he could be writing a new set of lyrics while simultaneously saying his lines.

The Move To Woodland Hills

Eventually, after several months, and prior to Christmas, Van Vliet wanted to move to a better area. We were visited by the police on more than one occasion concerning complaints about our volume. I really couldn't blame anyone. It was ridiculously loud even for me at 19, when I liked loud music. This place was getting known as a musicians' hangout, and all of our equipment was protected by nothing more than rusted screen wire and old padlocks. Anybody could have broken in at any time and stolen the whole show during one of our visits to the desert.

This move was just before we went in to record what was originally called *It Comes To You In A Plain Brown Wrapper* (later released as *Mirror Man*.) It wasn't released until 1969 or 70, under the title Mirror Man, and was reported to have been recorded sometime in 1965 - prior *to our signing with Buddah.* Those folks at Buddah really had their heads on straight.

Woodland Hills

John French: We had moved from Tarzana, we were now living in Woodland Hills in that little cottage house. That really small house ...
Jerry Handley: Down the hill from the other one. (Note: referring here to the house where Trout Mask would eventually be birthed.)
JF: Yeah, on Golondrina.
JH: Boy, you have a good memory if you remember all that shit.
JF: Yeah (Laughs). Well, I've been writing all this stuff down for about three years.

The Cottage

Don found a little cottage in Woodland Hills, 10 miles or so west of Tarzana. It was in a beautiful old neighborhood up in the hills. It was just a small cottage. A one-bedroom with a den. Don took the den with Laurie, and Jeff and I got to share the bedroom. It was a knotty pine interior. The house was a great move upward from the chicken coop, though still modest and much smaller in size. There was a small garage with a dirt floor beneath the house and down the hill, half carved into the hill.

TTG Studios - The *Mirror Man* Sessions

John French: So, we went to TTG Studios and recorded the very first version of Strictly Personal *for Kama Sutra records ... what was later to become the album entitled* Mirror Man.
Jerry Handley: I think that's where the Doors were recording, too.
JF: According to the engineer they were. The guy who ran the studio, was an Israeli guy (Amy Andante). Do you remember much about the Mirror Man *sessions?*
JH: Just that they were disorganized. They were just jam sessions.

Krasnow finally booked time for the second album. It was to be a double album. I was recently reminded by Guy Webster of the original concept for the album. The album title was originally supposed to be called *It Comes To You In A Plain Brown Wrapper* with *Strictly Personal* stamped on the envelope. The double album was supposed to be split into two different groups. Disc One was the arranged music *(Trust Us, Kandy Korn, On Tomorrow, Beatle Bones, Moody Liz, Flower Pot, Dirty Blue Gene,* etc.*)* done by Captain Beefheart And His Magic Band. The other half *(Mirror Man, Tarotplane, Korn Ring and Finger, Gimme Dat Harp Boy, Twenty-Fifth Century Quaker,* etc.*)* was done as an improvised avant-garde blues album by Twenty-Fifth Century Quaker - a "different" group.

The idea here was that Captain Beefheart And His Magic Band would be us playing under our pseudonyms - which is why they were made up at the time. Whereas Twenty-Fifth Century Quaker would be the warmup act - us performing the more improvised stuff, using our own names, and dressed up in Quaker outfits. While looking at proof sheets in Webster's studio recently, he reminded me of this and it all came flooding back as I viewed the photos of us in the Quaker outfits.

The only bad thing about this, as I look back in retrospect, was how freaking HOT those Quaker outfits would have been onstage.

Kama Sutra seemed to be still quite interested in the group. Things were apparently looking up business-wise but I dreaded going into the studio. I had barely been able to play for the last 2-3 weeks. Feeling clumsy on the drumkit, I had low expectations of my abilities.

Krasnow was wearing the producer's hat this time around. Richard Perry had given up on us after Don's guitar solo in that club on Sunset Boulevard, and I believe that by this time he had moved to Warner Brothers. The studio Krasnow booked us into was called TTG Studios. Amy Andante was the owner/engineer. He was a member of the Israeli Army and had gone to fight during the six-day war. Geez, it would've taken me six days to pack. I was very impressed with this no-nonsense man. I felt like this was our last chance to break free of the losing streak we appeared to be on.

The studio seemed like a good, solid place and I liked the environment. In my recollection, the room was very large, almost as large as RCA. Don was set up in a vocal isolation booth to sing live on some of the takes. Needless to say, the band was apprehensive about this because of Don's unpredictability. It was extremely unlikely that Don's performance would be easy to follow, or that any of the live improvisational pieces would be of a reasonable length. Being out of shape and discouraged by our living conditions, especially the spectre of the legalities Don was facing, were two negative factors needing to be dealt with each day.

Krasnow had requested me to not use cymbals. I set them up anyway, hoping that somehow I could squeeze past this idea of his. He came out and insisted in his best salesman/promoter personality how I was going to be doing some really groundbreaking things by not using cymbals. They wanted to deeply compress the drums. I was familiar with the sound. It was exactly what they did to Ringo's drums on the *Sergeant Pepper* album. Yeah, real groundbreaking! I conceded, however, and the cymbals were removed, though I did get to keep the hi-hat.

I always felt that this album could have been much more effective had the Captain taken the time to realize he needed to cut the songs in length. There were no cues when to go to new sections. Half the songs didn't appear to have lyrics; Don was just improvising off a few words scrawled on a tablet. We hadn't even heard how most of the music and lyrics fit together. One of the things I find important in improvising is that you need to be used to playing with the musicians so you know what reactions they're expecting to an extent. We hadn't done any improvising with Don. Even when we did perform the songs, there was little discussion on length or cues, and none whatsoever on form.

In spite of the lack of rehearsal time prior to recording the band was fairly tight on most of the compositions (as opposed to the improvisations). I have listened to the instrumental tracks of these pieces many times, and felt that they were relatively solid. Don felt the instrumental tracks were quite good also.

However, any backup harmonies should have been done after Beefheart's original voice rather than before. It would have been easier for us to follow him. *Kandy Korn* was a mess. He did two vocals, both totally different for the most part. When the album was finally released, some brilliant fool brought both vocals up in the mix, thinking somehow they were both supposed to be there. Instead of realizing it was just "take one" and a drastically different "take two."

Laurie Would Like To "Turn You On"

If anybody tries to tell you that kids aren't deeply influenced by the music and bands they hear, don't listen. The last line on the Beatles album (Pepper) says, "I'd love to turn you on." One night before we left for the studio, Laurie decided to fix me some tea. I thanked her, as I usually had to fix my own. When we started recording, I realized that I was changing consciousness levels rapidly. I became hysterically happy and felt very energetic. It was during the *Mirror Man* recording. In my eyes, Krasnow as producer was very much the comic figure that evening. He kept hitting the talkback button after each take, saying, "HEEAAVVYY!".

When we went in to listen to the playback I thought this was some of the best music I had ever played. Wow! Why had I been so worried? My enthusiasm knew no bounds! I soon found out that Don thought this version of *Mirror Man* was terrible, and my enthusiasm had overshadowed his decision to do another take.

It wasn't until I got home and started really hallucinating that I began to realize that Laurie may have put some acid in my tea. She told me that it had been Don's suggestion, although he denied having anything to do with it. I couldn't sleep at all that night. The hallucinations were there. I remember being very aware of my brain and spinal cord, as though they actually comprised a parasitic creature which had somehow attached itself to my body against my will (probably as the result of watching too many bad science fiction movies in the fifties). In my mind, Don, Laurie, and Jeff were also infected with these. They made little buzzing sounds. We had to get rid of these things. Don kept talking to me. He convinced me I would be just fine. It was reassuring. I think he was actually concerned about me.

I walked in the bathroom and looked in the mirror. Convinced of what I was, I came out to announce it to Don. "I am a Studebaker", I said, quite seriously. "That's a great car to be," Don replied, equally as serious. Yeah, I was certainly in control.

I Decide To "Turn On" Alex and Jerry

Now, it was my turn to turn someone on. Don was constantly criticizing Jerry and Alex to Jeff and me. We went along with it because it was the only time he didn't seem to be criticizing us. He would say something to the effect of them needing something to hip them up to what was happening. I took this as my cue, in my psychedelic state of mind, to turn them on. One evening, when they came over for rehearsal, I repeated Laurie's recipe for tea. I handed a cup each to Jerry and Alex. The effects took a while. I was outside tripping away when a very vehement Jerry confronted me on how stupid I was. In my state of mind, I couldn't understand why he was so upset. Wasn't this the way to be? I look back on this incident now with much regret. Jerry really gave me a lecture on how dangerous it was to do such a thing.

Don couldn't have agreed more. He proceeded, right along with Jerry to tongue lash me to the limits about my endeavors. Alex was very cool about the whole thing, telling me I shouldn't have done it, but that he was going to enjoy the trip while it lasted.

What was completely strange to me was that when I had been turned on by Laurie, Don defended her actions, and acted liked I was a fool for being so upset at her. This was a confusing time for a 19-year-old. Which opinion was I to believe? There were many mixed signals like this. Stating one opinion at one time, another at another time. Whatever action one took, Don could always say that he was of the opposite opinion, depending upon who his audience was.

I took a good look at myself and determined to get out of this mental place by refraining from anymore experimenting with psychedelics. I did slip a few times, once in Germany and once in the Antelope Valley years later. Even as I look back today at some of those experiences, I cannot explain why they seemed so real or what they meant, if they indeed meant anything. Jerry and Alex were the deciding factors. I could have hurt either of them badly through my own irresponsibility. Fortunately everything turned out all right.

String Parts On *Beatle Bones*

As we finished up the sessions at TTG, Don talked Krasnow into putting strings on *Beatle Bones 'n' Smokin' Stones*. Don gave me the pleasant task one night of trying to write a score for the string players to play. He had sung something on a tape weeks before and wanted me to transcribe it. I could not find the tape and so I tried to remember the part. I finally found the part on a tape, but it was in a different key, and I had nothing with which to find even a relative pitch, so I wound up with nothing. This was a task beyond my abilities at that point.

Upon entering the studio the following morning, I tried to explain to the string players what I thought Don had wanted. After about five minutes of being stared at by totally confused string players, Van Vliet came into the tracking room and addressed the problem. He had Amy play the track and sang what he wanted the strings to play, which turned out to be nothing like he had sung on tape but much simpler. It was basically the descending Delta blues line that he had employed on several pieces, similar to the second section of *On Tomorrow*.

However, I was very impressed with the way Don communicated his ideas to these string players, although he did indeed completely change to a much simpler musical passage than he had sung on tape for my reference. I always wondered what this song would have sounded like with the original string part. The overdubs were completed in less than an hour. The lead string player compared the music to Stravinsky.

Artie Ripp Tells Me Of Our Impending Fame

Artie Ripp decided to make an appearance at the studio that morning. I shook hands with him as he was listening to a playback of *Beatle Bones 'n' Smokin' Stones*. He seemed to like what he was hearing. Meanwhile, I was starving and exhausted, having been up all night looking for string parts. We hadn't any food in the house. I went into a little break room replete with vending machines and purchased a chocolate candy bar, which I was ravenously devouring like the Cookie Monster. My mouth was crammed full of chocolate when Ripp entered and took this inopportune moment to give me a complete rundown of his future plans for the Magic Band.

We had suffered a big blow by losing Monterey, he was saying, but this European promotional tour was going to put the wind back in our sails. We and two other choice acts (which turned out to be Penny Nichols, a folk singer and Anders and Poncia, a folk duet) were scheduled to perform a few skillfully chosen spots which were to be blanketed by immense press coverage. All this time, I was trying to act as though I was interested in what he was saying and thought it was true, and my mouth wasn't stuffed with chocolate.

As he was speaking, I suddenly realized to my horror that I was drooling dark brown syrup down the front of my face. What can I say? It was a rough night. Artie noticed this as I reached for a paper towel to make myself presentable again. He looked away in a moment of tolerant disgust and then continued. The tour would catapult us to stardom, there would be mass press coverage in the States. We were already a big name in Europe. He told me that he hoped I was ready for the most "outasight" homecoming I had ever witnessed. Considering the source, I do not hesitate to say that I believed not a word of this.

The recording wasn't finished at this point, and was never completed, for reasons yet to be revealed. I didn't feel like this album was nearly as professionally performed as *Safe As Milk*. There was no Ry Cooder or Richard Perry in the studio to tie up all the loose ends, and make sure the lyrics fit the music. It was a hodge-podge. I didn't feel that Don's idea of creative freedom was working.

Things needed to be more organized and packaged better. Krasnow was not a producer, or I should say THE producer for this project. He was actually a hard worker and a real go-getter type. Unfortunately, his talents were not best suited to production of the Magic Band, or to the technical aspects of the studio in general.

When I listen to takes of this session, I hear several drawbacks. The vocals were not nailed to the track in a solid and logical manner. Spontaneity needed to be coupled with form and arrangement. The drums are weak in places due to my lack of individual practice time. There are overdubs that should have been re-recorded, like Alex's solo sections on *Kandy Korn*. Those are a few of the regrets I have for these sessions.

Alex Snouffer: There was a couple of songs. Like Kandy Korn *was a good one. I liked the whole idea of that song. It gave me some freedom too. I kinda lost it in the studio because my fingers wouldn't move because we took so many takes of this or that song. That's where, anytime you hear the foul- up, it was because my fingers wouldn't work. I like that song because it gave me a lot of room. I could go anywhere with it and it would all fit in.*

Handley recalled that during background vocal rehearsals, Don would come out and listen to us occasionally. His main reaction was usually to feign hopelessness in any possibility of us ever becoming singers. Then, he would give us some strange vocal coaching, in which we were told to pronounce words differently. At the chicken coop, he had coached Jeff and me on the original *Dirty Blue Gene* background vocals. His first step was similar: ridicule our pathetic attempts at harmony and then after completely destroying any confidence we may have had, and making us feel totally self-conscious, give us detailed word-by-word phrasing instructions.

In the earlier *Gene* session, I felt as though I had learned a lot in spite of the preliminary ridicule we were required to endure. Jeff and I began to sound really good together singing these parts. I am certain that I recorded us on several occasions singing along with instrumental tapes of the band. All those rehearsal tapes, which are in Don's possession, are probably never going to be heard.

Handley's comments regarding these sessions reflect a similar theme as the other band members'- critiques. I mentioned several of the other songs to Jerry, such as *Trust Us, On Tomorrow* and *Safe As Milk*.

John French: So we finished Mirror Man, *and we (did) all those half-assed overdubs on* Kandy Korn *for vocals that never came together. It was, (as usual) very unorganized.*
Jerry Handley: They needed to be refined, but the main thrust of the songs were good, they needed to be really refined and cleaned up, shortened.

I go into detail about this on the track notes for *Mirror Man*.

Album Finished: Mid-To-Late November 1967.

I thought Don had written some incredible music, perhaps some of his best. There was also still enough freedom within the arrangements to give us liberty to bring the music to life with our individual sparks of creativity. The drawback was that it wasn't really properly displayed, through a combination of Krasnow's lack of integrity, Don's inexperience as a composer, and our lack of practice time. Also I feel that our inability to confront Don on the finishing touches and vocal cues, and his lack of ability to focus on those finer detail points gave this recording an overall sloppy sound.

Don's Child Molesting Rap

John French: So then, I wasn't able to practice drums because; I don't know if you recall, but Don got busted on a trumped-up child molesting charge.
Jerry Handley: Yeah, that happened up in Lancaster.

It was around this point that we were all up in the desert for a few days. The version of this story is from Van Vliet. Don and Laurie were visiting with Gary Lambert at the house of Marilee Duncan, a lady who was a mutual friend. Don decided to take a walk. Gary wanted to join him, and Marilee's young daughter wanted to go along. There was a school a block or two away, and Gary and the little girl, of elementary school age, were playing on the playground equipment. Suddenly, the police pulled up. They arrested Don and Gary, I believe. The charge turned into a child-molesting rap. The attitude of the cops was, "Hey, we got Beefheart, ha ha."

A little background on the Antelope Valley is needed at this time. The area at that time was a training ground for Sheriff Deputies. There were almost more cops than there were people. I almost got arrested one night because I was running. I just wanted to run home for some exercise. I used to run everywhere. I asked if it was against the law to run at night. The police were ridiculous. Not really abusive, just green and dumb.

They thought they really had Don on something big here. There was a big suspicion of anyone with long hair, and Beefheart was the big fish that had caused all the problems of the sixties in the perception of these guys.

Don was really in a panic; not only of going to jail, but that something like this could really destroy his public image. I can attest to the fact that Don was totally innocent without any reservations whatsoever. Marilee was a good friend and had known Don and Laurie for a long time. This was simply a little girl going for a walk with Uncle Don while mommy washed the dishes.

Paranoia Equals No Practice

Although this was a lovely little house, it was very detrimental to rehearsing. There was really no room in the house for us to stay set up. Don was extremely worried about the law at this point and refused to allow me to practice. My only instrument wound up being an old snare drum with a bunch of my clothes stuffed inside. The band came over and every one would plug into one amp and just basically run through ideas at very low volume. I felt claustrophobic. I didn't want to be here at all. I set up for a while in the little garage beneath the house, but Don would send Laurie or Jeff down to stop me from playing because he was afraid the neighbors might call the police.

Painting On The Service Porch

Victor visited here quite often. It was closer to his home. We talked some about the band, but mostly he and Don visited. Don kept encouraging Victor to paint. He had been to Chouinard Art School, so I was led to believe, but there was no inspiration. Don finally talked Victor into setting up a small studio in the service porch. This was the only place in the house where I could occasionally unpack my gear and tune the drums. Now that was gone too.

Victor and Don both began to paint. I recently recognized a painting in book of Don's art that was done during this time, and I was a little surprised to see it. Victor's work was completely different to Don's. I liked it a great deal. One of Victor's better things appeared years later on the cover of *Bluejeans And Moonbeams*. While they were painting, I got a hold of some music paper and began writing rhythm patterns. There was not much else I could do. In the house, the television was on a lot, or Don was sleeping. So I escaped by learning to write some of the new rhythm patterns I was learning and creating. I had had about three or four months of drum instruction on the snare when I was in high school. Just school band type of stuff, no syncopated beats. I had never seen drum music written out for an entire set.

Writing Music On Golondrina

I began thinking in terms of the rhythmic stuff I had been playing. There was Delta blues influence, East Indian tabla, jazz (Elvin Jones, Jack DeJohnette mostly), and occasionally some ethnic music. It was during this time that I heard a compilation of field recordings of African rhythms, which contained a track with exactly the same beat that I had made up for *Abba Zaba*. Don played albums a lot. Mostly jazz and blues but some surprises. One night, I walked in to the sound of live circus music! Joe Henderson, Charles Lloyd, John Handy, Miles Davis (*Sketches Of Spain*), John Lee Hooker, Muddy Waters, Howlin' Wolf, Son House, Lightnin' Hopkins, Lightnin' Slim, Wes Montgomery, and Gabor Szabo were a few of the artists I remember him playing.

I would listen to all of these people and try to write down any unusual rhythms just to see if I could do it. Then, I started to practice reading these rhythms to myself, sort of singing them in my head. I would find any escape I could find to keep from getting involved in the head-trips that were going on around me. I really envied Jeff and the others, because they could still practice. I felt like my own ability was beginning to deteriorate.

It was during this period that *Moonlight On Vermont* and *Sugar And Spikes* were written. I recall sitting cross-legged on the floor with my little stuffed snare drum between my knees, keeping rhythm to these songs as they came together. I tried to imagine I was playing a set. I was very impressed with Don's abilities during these times. He was trying much harder to be organized and I don't recall really taping much of anything until it was finished. It was mostly taught and put together on the spot. My mind wandered a lot because most of this didn't involve me directly. I would just play when a section finally came together.

I think part of the reason Don was a bit more focused is because this was not so much a rehearsal room. There was more furniture than instruments, and so it was a less intimidating atmosphere for Don. Alex, Jerry, and Jeff would all plug into a small amp at low volume and Don would work on the parts with them and even sing along. He didn't need a PA to be heard, as his voice alone would be loud enough.

Sandoz In The Yard

Victor had once made a connection with someone who obtained some pure Sandoz LSD, supposedly from someone at UCLA. It was the same stuff with which Timothy Leary and his group had experimented. He brought a bottle of this over to the house and hid it in the yard. Unbeknownst to the others, I started going out and taking this. It was small amounts, 25-100 micrograms, but it was much stronger and more pure than any street stuff.

This was probably when I became the weirdest and the most unstable. Don was always trying to get us to dress strange, and I decided I was going to be the strangest. Laurie had an old red full-length coat that I started wearing. I was wearing a child's metal sand sifter on my head like a headband. I wore big red corduroy trousers. To top off this thrilling combination was my black magician's cape. I would go to the market in this getup.

I remember one night I walked outside while it was raining. I was standing out under the tree looking up, and the whole scene completely transformed before my eyes. Every little outline of every leaf seemed to phase out in two directions. I was suddenly underwater looking through seaweed and fish. I was in the ocean. It was completely realistic right down to the sounds. I felt the tail of a fish as it skimmed against my cheek. In the same way that it had formed, it dissolved back into the rain. I walked inside and Jeff asked me where I'd been. I told him out in the rain, but he didn't believe me. My coat was completely dry. Perhaps I had imagined even walking out in the yard. Later, I found out from Don that the whole area we lived in had been underwater several eons ago. So I preferred to believe that somehow I had walked through a time warp.

I suppose I was bored. Living with Don and Laurie was almost like living with mom and dad. There was nothing to do most days. Practicing seemed to irritate Don. I went further and further into my little world. I wasn't aware of this at the time. I thought that if I did enough psychedelics, I would somehow attain hipness or find myself. Don's criticism of me escalated even more during this period. I could do nothing right. If I walked in the kitchen for some breakfast cereal, I was "always eating." If I slept later than Don (very unusual, as he was a 10-12 hour a day sleeper), I was "always sleeping." Laurie was the same way. Jeff was distant. I still was trying to contend with the fact that the draft was staring me in the face, and the Vietnam War was just around the corner. Which world would be worse?

I would sit outside in the morning before Don arose, with a writing pad, just writing whatever came into my head. I also did a lot of drawing. I suppose I appeared like a little kid trying to imitate his big brother. However, I had been interested in art when I was younger and had drawn sketches most of my life until I got around Don. I kept taking acid and not telling anyone. I would look up at the clouds in the sky and they would move rapidly like time-lapse photography. All around on the ground were hundreds of children's playing blocks. Huge rectangular chunks of red gelatin floated through the air. Doors and windows, which I tried to climb through, appeared in blank walls. The knotty-pine walls had sap flowing through them like an enlarged view of a fish tail's arteries. Don, Jeff, and Laurie seemed so angry all the time.

Victor decided during this time that I should go see a psychiatrist friend of his. I think this was probably the same guy who had gotten him an exemption from the military. I didn't have any money, of course. The man had an office in Laurel Canyon, just across from the little country store halfway between Mulholland and Hollywood Boulevard. Somehow, a deal was struck and I was able to go see this guy for a couple of months. Basically, I just told him about Don, Laurie, Jeff, and how miserable I was living in that house with this situation. He listened intently for two or three sessions and told me that my problem seemed to be mostly that I was in the wrong environment. He asked me if there was any way I could talk Don into some therapy. In fact, his curiosity pulled him into visiting the house one evening.

Whenever anyone visited the house, Don went into his best behavior mode. Sort of like Wally Cleaver's friend Eddie Haskell on *Leave It To Beaver*. He could be very cordial, charming, and a brilliant conversationalist. Don was all these things, or could become all these things at the drop of a hat. It seemed more and more that there lurked within him a deep fear of being 'discovered.'

During these visits to the psychiatrist, I received a letter from my draft board. This doctor wrote a letter to the draft board, which I delivered in person. It was quite a while before I received a reply.

CHAPTER SEVENTEEN:
TIN CANNES

e 60s shot in Lancaster. Don's artist friend John Stewart rented the upper floor from Frank Stubbings. Courtesy of John Stewart.

The Whisky

The Hollywood Whisky A Go Go, on the Sunset Strip was sort of the Roxy of the sixties. This was at the time that clubs used to actually pay bands to play. Krasnow booked us for a weekend. The band at this point was not in good shape to play - especially me, because of the situation. I was in sorry shape to be playing on stage. I remember that I was still taking LSD.

Iron Butterfly

We were on the same ticket as Iron Butterfly. I believe they were opening for us. It seems like this was pre *In-A-Gadda-Da-Vida* days. I remember that they would end with this one particular piece where there was smoke and fog and I would look down from the balcony and see some kind of little ashtray thing with a flame in it sitting on the drummer's floor tom-tom. It seemed really corny. The band really believed in what they were doing and were fairly well rehearsed. At the time, I thought they were a real joke.

Beverly and Pamela were backstage in the dressing room with us. Beverly and I started wandering around and found the old go go girls'dressing room, complete with outfits. I picked up one of the spangled bras and fashioned it into a turban, which I was wearing around. My ego had really gotten big, and I was on LSD at the time. I went down to the very edge of the balcony where everyone could see me and started mock-conducting Iron Butterfly with one of my drumsticks.

Later, Don took me aside and said that he thought this was not very good thing to do. This was one time when Don gave a soft reprimand. It really made me feel ashamed of myself, which I rightly should have been I suppose. However, although I still think that Iron Butterfly is one of the worst bands that ever existed, I have never worn a spangled bra on my head (or any other part of my body) to this day. Probably as a direct result of all those Spangled-Bra Anonymous meetings I attended.

I think this was right at the end of my acid taking days. I sat down and had a long look at the image I had been portraying. The realization hit me that I needed to grow up. I guess I thought I was being really hip in doing things like this. I was showing off for the girl, Beverly, who thought it was funny. I had exalted myself and in reality was really just being a fool.

We played and it was at this performance that I first looked over and noticed that Jeff wasn't playing his guitar. Don and Alex had talked about it, but I had never seen him freeze up. I tossed a drumstick gently hitting him in the middle of the back. He was wearing a big yellow coat and hardhat, so I figured I was not going to hurt him. He turned around and I shouted, "PLAY!" as loud as I could over the music at him, and he started playing. During this time, he had a really interesting way of moving while he played. It had a kind of writhing, waving, snakelike quality. I had never noticed him move like that in all the times I had played with him before, and we had played together quite often. I have never known anyone who transformed themselves so completely. It was as if he was a different person.

Pete Johnson

A journalist named Pete Johnson came to hear us play and write a review for the LA Times. The night he came, we played rather poorly. Nothing seemed to be working for us. The sound was bad. We couldn't hear ourselves. This is before proper monitor systems had been developed. My microphone kept moving around and hitting me in the face. I couldn't concentrate. I was on drugs. Of course, some of it just had to do with the fact that we hadn't rehearsed in months.

I actually didn't meet Pete at the club, but later at TTG Studios beside the coffee machine. I remember Don introducing him to me as one of the few real human beings he had ever known. I studied Pete closely, trying to comprehend what a "real human being" was, as opposed to … one that wasn't real I suppose. Don talked Pete into going easy on us. We had moved and we hadn't had time to rehearse. It was difficult to just go on stage cold like that and make anything work.

John Densmore

John Densmore, the drummer for The Doors, had come to hear us one night. I remember him sitting in the dressing room talking with Don. Don's mother, Sue, suddenly appeared with her boyfriend Bob. She walked up to the dressing room door and said, "Hellooooo" in this funny and typical way she had of talking. She was a heavy lady with dark hair and lots of makeup. She had an air of sophistication about her and she dressed as one who had a few bucks. Sue was a wonderful lady. I think she had found some peace with the universe somehow or other. She always seemed happy and ready to help.

Helen

She said, "Oh John, I brought someone to see you!" With this, she reached outside the door and pulled a girl by the arm into the room. There was a little step up into the room, and the poor girl tripped and almost landed flat on her face. She ran about three steps and regained her balance.

It was Helen (name changed to protect her privacy). I had been in the same grade with her brother in school. She was two years my junior. I wasn't really too happy to see her. I hadn't expected anyone, and I was with Beverly that night as I recall. Anyway, I felt her embarrassment as she came tripping into the room and asked her to join me on the couch. She told me that she felt really stupid being there and that she maybe shouldn't have come. She must have been about 17 at the time. I felt bad for her and tried to put her at ease, telling her it was great to see her and asking how her brother Howard was.

After the show, we all went back to the cottage in Woodland Hills and had a visit. Helen and I barely spoke to each other. I really didn't know anything much about her. I wasn't sure why she was there. I did know that her father had worked with Sue for a time at Scott's - the department store I mentioned earlier. I suddenly liked having her there. She gave me some perspective. I felt protective of her because I knew her brother and respected him a great deal. I started thinking about the people with whom I was associating (especially Pamela and Beverly), and about my drug abuse, from a different perspective.

The girl I was with that night had been over at the chicken coop a few months earlier telling me how she and Pamela were going to take off all their clothes, cover themselves with chocolate syrup, and knock on some musician's door as a surprise for his birthday. This is the kind of empty-headed nonsense I was being influenced by. It had been maybe less than a year since I had joined the band, yet I suddenly realized that I was totally out of control.

Although she probably never knew this, Helen's presence made me make a little turn in my life that probably kept me from going over the edge. I started thinking a lot more seriously about the future and what I wanted out of life. I started setting some goals for myself. Unfortunately, it would be years before I would steer my way clear of this destructive pattern. Poor Helen and I became more involved at a later date and it was a shame for her to have to endure the awful situation of the band.

The Maharishi

Soon after this, while watching *The Johnny Carson Show*, Don saw an interview with the Maharishi, a Hindu guru the Beatles had brought to fame through their interest in meditation. He seemed like a happy little fellow. His big sell was that meditation would get you on a higher level than any drugs and would soothe the mind and body. What people were really looking for could be found through transcendental meditation, according to this fellow.

This was enough to convince Don that the whole band should be initiated. He was paranoid more than ever about drugs due to the impending court date for his charges. I was all for it - anything to get out around people. It all tied in with my quest for the unknown. It answered Don's need for a way to get drugs off the premises. Meditation would not work if one used any form of drugs, according to the smiling little man in the interview. This was obviously very appealing to a lot of parents whose children were losing their minds taking drugs. I'm sure the Maharishi took this into consideration, figuring it would be great for business.

Transcendental Meditation

So, off went the whole band in Don's Mark IX Jaguar to UCLA's Westwood Village in our search for enlightenment. The office staff met us with open arms when they realized that we were an up-and-coming rock group. Our initiation fee was waived. They told us that The Doors had been initiated. The experience had so inspired them that they immediately wrote *Light My Fire*. This is when I wanted out. I hated that lousy song. However, I went through the whole supposedly non-religious initiation. The big Bwana took me in this little room and lit some incense. He waved it around over some little religious fetishes and pictures of those blue women with eight arms and people with elephant's heads (I thought this was supposed to be non-religious?) There were flowers and the fancy tablecloth and all this other very impressive non-religious stuff.

Then he put his lips up to my ear and started whispering a single syllable, Ein, Ein, Ein, over and over again. This was my mantra. It was my cue to start repeating this along with him for a dozen or so times. Then I was to keep saying it silently to myself as he led me to a "meditation chamber" which was just a small dark room with a chair in the corner. I was to sit down in this chair and go under.

Something did happen. I did not go to sleep, but I lost consciousness of my surroundings for around 30 minutes. I opened my eyes to the darkness, wondering for a moment where I was. Almost immediately, the door opened, and some all-knowing, all seeing hippie chick with an all-knowing smile on her face came in and silently led me out of this meditation chamber. I had to admit; I did feel rested and calm. It was probably just from being away from the band environment and having privacy for 30 minutes.

So, suddenly our theme was "the band that meditates together stays together." I think Victor had gone also, because I remember several times when we would sit in the car together and try to meditate. Any noise could be very detrimental to meditation, so when I almost always fell asleep accompanied by loud obnoxious adenoidal snores, I became a very unpopular person to go under with. This really didn't bother me much because I liked going off to meditate. During those times, I almost always had good experiences, though I seldom meditated. I would just sit and appreciate the fact that I was alone. I recall just being so still one day that a squirrel came down and sat right next to me, staring into my eyes.

Don (according to himself) became an instant expert at going under. He could go under at the drop of a hat. That was fine. It was when he came out that the trouble started. Anything that anyone did (usually me) to disturb him after a meditation experience usually resulted in the wrath of one whose attainment has been spoiled.

Percussionist - Mike Rice

Where this guy came from I do not know and do not care. He was probably one of Victor's friends. Mike Rice was the "faggot from Hell." I actually didn't have anything against gays in those days and seldom use this term (at least since high school). The fact that Mike was gay had little to do with the fact that I labeled him this in my mind. I didn't even have the fact confirmed that he was gay until much later although it seemed obvious.

Don took a liking to this guy about the time that he decided Jeff Cotton was no better than me. The newness had worn off with Jeff: the honeymoon was over. I remember Don looking at us one day during rehearsal and saying, "What the fuck's the matter with you guys? All you ever do is eat and shit!" (I think they say this at self-help seminars, but maybe I'm wrong). This is the same man who would, in the presence of ladies, display open rebuke to anyone who used profanity.

Of course, now Jeff and I bonded again - by our overt and common uselessness. We began for a time speaking to each other again like human beings.

Mike Rice was going to become our percussionist, as Gary Lambert was at one time. I determined in my mind that no matter what, I would never play music with this jerk. He was loud, an excessive talker, and a pseudo-artiste type who had never paid any dues in his life. I hated the reception Don was giving this guy. What the hell was going on here? I had devoted everything I had, including hocking one of my drum sets to buy a guitar for Jeff, in order to play this guy's music. In this band, I couldn't make a living and he was acting like I was a piece of garbage. This Mike Rice guy had not lifted a finger to do any work, and I bet he couldn't even play. Nonetheless, here was Don spending hours with his new discovery.

The two of them seem to prattle on for hour after boring hour in the most pretentious tone. During this time, I took a lot of walks, read a few books, cleaned up my drums. I would have worked in a car wash rather than listen to these two converse.

Mike never really gained a position in the band, and this is when I began again to consider that there was indeed a God.

Bikers From Mojave

I used to know these guy's names, but I don't recall now. There were two or three bike types from Mojave (Don's home town in the desert) who came down to the Golondrina house on occasion. I think Don had known them since his childhood days, when he first moved there. All I recall about these guys is that they were some of the nicest people who ever came around. They were very down-to-earth and respectful.

The Sky Is Red

I remember overhearing a conversation between Don and Victor one evening. I was just hanging out with them as they talked. Victor was in his car, a little red Saab, ready to drive away. The theme seemed to be Victor having no idea what to do about his state of mind. "I mean the sky is actually blood red," Victor said, "It really is blood red!" "I know!" said Don, "but you can't go telling anybody that, they'll lock you up, man!" I thought at the time that this was some level of consciousness beyond the norm - something to really shoot for – a goal to set one's sights upon. Aren't we glad the sixties are gone?

European Confrontation

It was now time to get ready for the European promotional tour, which, according to Artie Ripp, was supposed to transform us all into international celebrities. My question: What was he smokin'?

We were going to Europe. Artie Ripp's big scheme for world domination was about to be underway. This was another time that Bob emphatically stated that I could not take my drums with me because they cost too much to ship. Drums and guitar amps would be provided at each performance. I was still living in this situation, which prevented me from practicing.

One night, when the band was over for a meeting, I mentioned that I didn't know how well I would be able to play. Don grasped this fear in me and immediately escalated it into a giant mountain of a problem. Rather than make arrangements for a practice hall, he quickly had the whole band convinced that I wasn't going to go. I suppose it was some fear of a repeat of Ry quitting the band at a strategic moment. My intention was never to refuse to go. I just was a little unsure of my abilities and was attempting to communicate this point to my fellow players. This tour had only three or four dates, but it had been blown up as a gigantic endeavor with mountains of press coverage. I had not been able to practice on a set with the band for months and no provision had been made to change that situation.

That night was the first time I experienced what in the future would become the norm. Don managed to have the whole band focused on me. I remember I was standing in the corner of the room next to the wall heater with four angry faces staring at me. Nothing I said seemed to convince them that I was on their side or willing to go. Don would turn everything I said around and make me sound and look like a complete fool. He had a great way with words, and could talk just about anyone under the table given the chance. He used just enough imagery, aphorisms, and double-entendre that nobody was ever exactly sure what he really meant.

This kept everyone, as Gary Marker had described, just a little off-kilter. I realize that I was pretty confused during this period so I may just have been misunderstood. In my mind, there was no way I was trying to back out of my commitment. I just needed a little reassuring. What I got was more like a Nazi interrogation session. It was a frightening feeling, which I never forgot. Yet it was a feeling, which I was to experience again and again and with much greater intensity.

The whole instance seemed to end when Alex started talking about his reasons for wanting to go. He mentioned that he did not want to wake up some day sitting in a bar half drunk, spilling some sad story to someone about how he had almost made it. He said that we were fortunate to have this chance that a lot of people didn't have. Being gifted and doing some job that you hated just to make a living was a lot worse than taking the chance and looking past your fears. I am not quoting him exactly, but he was very calm and talked as a friend. There was no threatening tone. I just told him I knew what he meant, and everyone seemed satisfied and went home.

Alex was always a peacemaker and he certainly diffused this situation. Although mostly silent, he knew how to talk to people and was a good leader. He was open-minded and stayed cool most all the time. There was a consistency about his behavior that made me really trust him. I often noticed him seeming annoyed with Don's eccentric and self-indulgent behavior. Yet he always seemed to make the most of rehearsal time. There was almost always some progress, and I think it had a lot to do with Snouffer's integrity.

Holidays

We spent the holidays of 1967 in Woodland Hills for the most part. Don bought rum and eggnog and we celebrated together. It was a peaceful time. Everyone was on their best behavior and there were good feelings in the house for the most part.

I do recall one disturbing incident in which a girlfriend of Jeff Cotton's drove down with friends to speak with him. She had just "accepted Jesus" and wanted to tell him of her experience. I was by this time so wrapped up in pleasing Don that I angrily ridiculed this poor girl in front of all her friends. Everyone in the car looked at me like they were afraid. It was an interesting feeling, because I was transferring the same treatment I was receiving from Van Vliet. I immediately discovered that this kind of power was very seductive. The ability to intimidate others is, once experienced, highly addictive. I wanted more of this. I am a Christian myself now, and even then had a pretty strong belief in this realm, but I allowed my image to get the better of me, and regret having done so.

The interesting thing that I discovered about Van Vliet's effect on me was that the public adoration of Captain Beefheart had somehow overshadowed what I believed to be correct behavior. I was beginning to emulate some of his worst traits, thinking somehow that I would be more successful if I could become more like him.

Scandinavian Airlines to Copenhagen

We were finally on our way to Europe. Our destination was Hannover, Germany. We had a scheduled stopover in Copenhagen. I was completely excited and in awe. Our airline, Scandinavian Airlines had really beautiful stewardesses. The passenger list was rather small. In their spare time, they would come and sit with us - asking us questions about the music business: who we had met, where we had played, what kind of music we played, etc. I had never talked to women this beautiful. I was absolutely intimidated at first and could barely mumble, but they were very kind and soon we were all conversing freely.

Our first stopover was in Copenhagen. We had taken off from LAX in the evening, and flown all night. We must have flown through to daylight. It was still light when we landed in Copenhagen, Denmark. Through what seemed like an endless wait, we sat in the airport with all of our luggage, catching little bits of sleep here and there. After several hours, and darkness engulfing the skies, we were told that takeoff was impossible due to weather conditions. Scandinavian Airlines provided hotel accommodation including transportation to and from the airport.

The memories are very vivid of my first view of Europe. The small bus on which we rode, the sound of the diesel engine, the beautiful clean streets, and smartly-dressed girls riding small mopeds about town. The hotel was a first-class establishment, and I felt like a hobo in my old clothes. We dined together with Bob Krasnow, who celebrated his birthday that evening with us. Each of us had our own room. I remember being the first to leave the dinner table because I wanted to savor every moment of privacy, having lived with almost none for an entire year.

I greeted a well-dressed elderly man on the elevator, who nodded his head, and walked down the hallway past rows of shoes waiting to be shined to my room. The door, instead of having a knob, had a handle, and I entered to savor the isolation. Looking out the window, I heard the distinct two-toned siren of an emergency vehicle and watched as the fresh snow reflected its spinning lights.

The next morning, I discovered a very sleepy Don, Alex and Jerry, who had discovered that Sonny Boy Williamson was playing locally in a club. They had gone out to catch the show and had gotten in quite late. They seemed to be in agreement that Williamson's performance had proved to be worth the effort.

Hannover, Germany

I remember little about our flight to Hannover. When we were transported back to the airport, Alex - dressed in his pilgrim clothes - was keeping to himself and taking a lot of pictures on his new 35mm camera. This seemed to irritate Don and he wanted to have a meeting in which it was stated that the band should try to stay grouped together. I believe that Alex at this time was already considering leaving the group, already having had strong misgivings about the band ever becoming a moneymaking enterprise. He had become strongly disillusioned after hearing the results of the *Mirror Man* album. At this point, Alex was truly "along for the ride."

When Don confronted Alex on this issue of remaining aloof in public, Snouffer seemed to take it as constructive criticism and was less detached for the rest of the tour. After a short flight, the band was checked in to a large hotel in Hannover. I remember standing in my room looking out the window in wonder at the architecture of the city. The phone rang, and it was Van Vliet calling; he asked that I come right over.

"It seems we have some visitors," he said. I inquired as to his meaning and he explained that there were some young girls who had taken a bus from some far away place for the express purpose of meeting us. Soon, there was a knock at the door, and I witnessed Don in his best public-relations behavior. These girls were 14 or 15 years old, and dressed in warm winter clothing: long coats, gloves and zippered boots. Don invited them in to our rather large room, took their coats, and had them sit at the table while he ordered tea. He was absolutely enchanting, as he asked them questions about their lives, their interests, hobbies, what school was like, their parents, etc.

Of course, the girls were equally as enchanting. I sat in awe listening to German girls speak better English than I did (maybe not *that* much of a feat). They were very proper and well mannered. Unfortunately, I don't remember a thing they said, I was too busy absorbing the picture and feeling of the moment, which I still see vividly in mind. They stayed for about one and a half hours, and then politely excused themselves, wishing us luck. We signed a copy of *Safe As Milk* they had brought with them, and they were gone.

Convention

We were to play at a European record company convention, which was being held that night in the banquet hall downstairs. Krasnow reminded us that this was a big event and we must play well. Of course, we hadn't played live for six weeks and hadn't even rehearsed as a group for just as long. We barely had a set list.

Equipment

So down we went, about 10 in the morning to the convention room. The equipment that greeted us was like a bad science fiction movie. Old tube amplifiers that looked like wooden radios greeted us. They had one tone: midrange. There was no volume to speak of ... I think they were accordion amplifiers.

Sitting in a heap on the stage were the most horrific drums I had yet witnessed. Probably about the same vintage as the amps, these old dance band drums still had calfskin heads and tom mounts that clipped to the kick drum rim. The snare drum stand (or should I say "non-stand?") was completely ruined and unable to hold the drum upright. The rusty pedals squeaked and moaned and needed oiling. Worst of all, to my horror, there were no sticks. I hadn't brought any sticks, and they hadn't supplied any.

That was the end of the excitement.

A fellow named Peter Meaden showed up and introduced himself. Apparently connected with the bookings, he had flown in from his home country, England, and just arrived in Hannover. Krasnow and Ripp were both gone, sightseeing presumably, and so I was in complete panic as to what to do about my predicament. Peter immediately hailed a cab and transported me to a music store, where the only sticks to be found were barely larger than chopsticks. They were so thin I could barely keep them in my hands.

Our Hi-Tech Equipment

Returning, I was greeted with a band who looked like they had just been given a two-hour dissertation on how stupid I was for not bringing sticks. I would have liked to give a small dissertation myself on how ridiculous it was to be managed by people who would arrange for us to be supplied with such inadequate equipment. Not only did the band have to wait for me to find sticks, now they had to wait for me to set up. It was a ridiculous set. I don't know who in their right mind thought anyone could possibly play these. I had seen better trashcans. I had to hold the snare drum between my legs balanced precariously on the faulty stand that wouldn't tighten.

Don didn't like the PA any better. It matched the speakers. We did a sound check. Had we ever sounded worse? I didn't think so. I could barely keep time, because both my knees were holding the snare in place, and everytime I started to get into it, the snare would started bouncing around in time to my feet. There was no way to contact anyone, because they were still out seeing the sights. We were stuck. This show had to go on.

Our Big Show: Mid-January, 1968, Hotel Conference Hall, Hannover Germany

I recall standing outside the doorway in stage clothes for what seemed like hours as one speaker and then another took his turn. Finally, we heard our name (the only thing in English up to this point) and walked in, like meat up for inspection. The tables encircled us as I recall, and everyone was facing in. It was all European businessmen. I must say that we gave it everything we possibly had. Don was really nervous and lost his place more than once. Guitar cords buzzed and popped, drums fell over, and cheesy cymbals creaked on precarious stands. I knew that this was at best a mediocre attempt. There was no way we could explain what was going on. The stage was right in the center of the room. We finished, and left to polite applause, feeling totally humiliated.

Wrath of Krasnow

Krasnow was absolutely merciless. Following us up to the floor, which contained our rooms, he started shouting in the hallway, and continued on a tirade that lasted for several minutes. The embarrassment and humiliation I had felt in that room, combined with the stress of the afternoon, and now Krasnow's yelling finally caused me to snap. I had had it with him and his ridiculous equipment arrangements. I loosed a barrage of words upon him - how ridiculously inadequate that equipment was - and asked how on earth he knew anything about equipment anyway since he couldn't play a note. It was the first time I actually stood up to one of these people, and it felt good to get it out. I think it caught him by surprise. He was embarrassed by our performance and was trying to take it out on us. We were humiliated, and it was his massive ignorance and bad planning that caused it.

Imaginary Nazis

Needless to say, the mood of the band couldn't have been worse. Poor Jeff Cotton had been stuck in a room with Krasnow. I decided to change rooms with Jeff. I would share a room with Krasnow for the last night so Jeff could have a rest. I was sitting alone in the room when Krasnow and some other business people came in and smoked some pot, immediately leaving afterwards. I must have inhaled some because I felt a little paranoid after they left. There was a knock at the door. I went to the door and a woman came in and walked over to the bed, pointing to it, and speaking to me in German. I couldn't imagine what on earth she could possibly be saying. Was she offering me sex? I finally called the desk and found a man who spoke English. He told me to put her on the phone. She spoke for a moment and handed the phone back to me. He explained that she wanted to know if I wanted my bed turned down.

I had never heard of such a thing. This seemed absolutely ridiculous to me. All one had to do was grasp some covers and pull back. I told him to tell her to go ahead. She then went through about a ten-minute ritual of very carefully pulling down the bedspread and folding back the covers at just the right angle on both beds. She then looked at me with a grin and picked up the ashtray, dusting it off. When she carefully placed it back on the table, she picked up two roaches (partially smoked marijuana cigarettes, for the unenlightened) and placed them carefully on the edge of the ashtray.

As she left the room, I stood gazing in horror at these roaches. I had gotten contact high and was paranoid to begin with. Now I was beginning to have visions of legions of Nazi stormtroopers marching into the room to take me off to the death camps. I could see myself in a few months, pale, debilitated, near the point of death, and too weak to play a decent Delta rhythm. Worst of all, they would cut my hair. Taking the joints, I flushed them down the toilet and then locked myself in the bathroom, somehow feeling as thought I might be safe in there.

Staying in there for hours, my fear of torturous death was quickly overcome by my curiosity as to why in the world there were two toilets in the bathroom. One was a bidet, of course, but I had never seen anything like this in my life. I spent the rest of the time combing and styling my hair, a reasonable occupation for someone awaiting the death sentence.

I contemplated the ridiculous effect that marijuana had on my mind the next day. Why did I ever think that stuff was good?

We stayed in Hannover one more night. Early in the evening, Don came to my door and asked if I wanted to go out sightseeing. I had no money, but he said he could pay for a cab. We wound up in the red-light district at Don's request. With such a fascination for hookers, this was sure to be part of the itinerary. We were taken by a cab driver who spoke no English, but a little French, so I asked him, "Ou est la jeune filles?" (which loosely interpreted means something like "please triple the cab fare, as we are ignorant, naïve American idiots).

The red-light district in Hannover was interesting, however, in the sense that the call-girls sat in windows like mannequins, like merchandise on display. If you saw one you liked, you would walk up a short flight of stairs, and proceed down the hallway searching for the room number to your night of dreams. Somehow, this never appealed to me, as I felt as though any woman who thought so little of herself wouldn't be very good company. It also seemed that sex in itself was nothing, and that it was something that could be enjoyed only with someone you truly loved - or at least looked really, really, really good naked.

At one point, Van Vliet opened the door and went to visit a lady. She looked like Hell to me, just used up. However, I could see him as he entered the room, and it was obvious that when he displayed his meager finances, he didn't have enough cash to successfully make a transaction. I was relieved, obviously. What was I supposed to do while he tested the merchandise? Stand on the street in the worst part of town without a dime to my name?

We then went to a club to listen to some blues. Of course, these blues were sung in German, and there certainly is more than a little something that got lost in this translation. I reacted with uncontrollable laughter, to the dismay of the band and everyone present. We had a beer and left quickly.

Being an international convention, the last night's performance could have been a big step for us. We had been told there were representatives from every country in Europe. Don was fast becoming disillusioned with Kama Sutra.

Don suggested that we should order the most expensive items on the menu in order to get back at the wonderful folks who had gotten us in that mess. I ordered lobster in some kind of sauce. We had champagne and some really wonderful dessert.

Later, Jeff and I got together. Someone had given Don, Jeff and I some LSD on – surprisingly enough - a postage stamp. I believe this is actually where Don got the idea for "licked the stamp saw a movie, dropped the stamp" in the song *Ah Feel Like Ahcid*.

Jeff kept suggesting that we take this LSD. I finally and stupidly agreed. What kind of idiots we were! We had a flight early the next morning and were scheduled to play a special unpaid engagement that evening at a popular club in London called The Speakeasy. Good planning, boys.

I can't believe I actually took this stuff, but I did. It could have been cyanide for all I knew. For once, something was in our favor: absolutely nothing happened. Jeff and I spent hours looking at each other and waiting. What a great way to spend an evening for a couple of young, naïve guys from the high desert in California. We actually got a good night's sleep.

London's Welcome

The next morning we boarded a prop flight to London. I was seated between two really fat men in seats that were made for the very slender. I felt I didn't need a seat belt because the overflow of their bellies into my seating space was like having my own air bag. Within five minutes of takeoff, I knew I was in trouble. This plane wasn't smooth like a jet, and I was becoming airsick. I have hardly ever been sick to my stomach in my entire life. This day was a definite exception. I barely made it to the bathroom, which I had to visit several times, and haven't eaten lobster since. It was really fun constantly parting the sea of fat to get to the restroom.

After landing, we entered the special area where we stood in lines and had our passports checked. As soon as Don handed them his passport, we could all see there was a problem. Krasnow showed up on the other side of the divider and told us in a loud whisper not to say anything about performing while we were there - like no one would notice his not-so-subtle attempts. There seemed to be some kind of paperwork that we were lacking. Obviously, the authorities were not buying in to the idea that we were on vacation. We were a band. While we were standing in line, an old man dressed in black came up behind me and kicked me hard right in the back end. Was it my imagination, or was I was beginning to sense some hostility in the air?

Alex disappeared for a while. While he was gone they had us all get out of line and go sit down on benches. Alex returned and whispered to me that he had flushed a lid of grass down the toilet. He had hidden it in his shoe, of all places. I had visions of us rotting away in some dungeon, our hands shackled to the walls of vermin-infested cells, a small bowl of gruel being shoved under the door each day, screams of agony from the adjoining chambers ... (and Don sculpting dinosaurs out of clay). Thank heaven for positive thinking.

I was quite surprised at Don's behavior. All the anxiety he had displayed at performances and just about every important event were seemingly non-existent today. He seemed a little concerned, but relaxed and seemed to be enjoying the experience. However, when someone asked Alex about his camera, it probably didn't help our position when Don explained that "it was a member of the group," giving the official a little grin. I'm sure they thought, "No, that fellow couldn't be on drugs."

A couple of official-looking men in uniform approached our bench. They led us one at a time, into a small room. I was third. We were trying to get our stories straight. My first thought was that Don was never going to stick to the truth, because he hadn't since I had known him. After all "the truth has no patterns." His "member of the group" statement had already convinced me that he was probably going to get us all in big trouble.

We were questioned individually. I was forced to take off my shoes and remove my trousers. Thank God Alex had the foresight to do what he did with the pot. They thoroughly searched me. One uniformed fellow even reached down and inspected my testicles - like yeah, what am I going to hide in there? The future? Or, perhaps he just liked boys - who knows? If I'd ever had any doubt about my sexual preference, I knew that day for sure that I would have preferred a semi-clad female guard fingering my testicles than this loathsome wanker.

I was questioned about a piece of paper in my passport case. I had written down a dream I had in Germany. They asked me if this was some kind of drug-induced vision. I told them no, and explained that I often wrote down my dreams because they were windows into the subconscious, which was precisely the truth. They seemed unconvinced. The grey area was, of course, the paperwork and the questions concerning what we were actually doing in the country. I told them we were a band on a promotional tour, and I believed that we were performing, but for no financial compensation. I said the tour was being financed by Buddah Records, a subsidiary of Kama Sutra Records, USA.

The Detention Room

We waited in the benched area for about four hours. Finally, some men came and led all six of us (the camera, remember?) through a side door and down a long hall. We were placed in a detention cell. Not surprisingly our stories had not coincided. They were sending us to Frankfurt, Germany the next morning. Why Frankfurt we never knew. No one was allowed to see us. Don seemed in high spirits and we all joked about being incarcerated. We exchanged experiences concerning the interrogation chamber and Alex took pictures of us in the room. "We'll get these in the British press" Don joked, "American Pop Band Receives Warm Welcome Abroad. It's evidence, man." I noticed that Don always seemed at his best when things were at their worst. When everything was in utter chaos and disarray, Don was content, and seemed right at home. I asked Alex if he remembered the detention facility.

Alex Snouffer: Oh, are you kidding? When we did jail time in London Heathrow? Yeah! We didn't have work permits.
John French: That was because of a guy named Peter Meaden. Do you remember him at all?
AS: Yeah, I do. I gave him my hat. The one I wore on Safe As Milk. I gave the little faggot my hat. When I was there in '73 I ran into Peter again. He was trying to get me to promote a band called The Iron Boys. He showed me a poster of them. "Iron" my ass. That was his big trip. I said, "Hey, I'm outta here."

After a fitful night's sleep in our charming little dungeon, we were cheerfully awakened by a morose uniformed individual who wheeled a stainless steel cart containing unspeakable delights into our tiny quarters while a guard stood watch at the door, in case the camera made a break for it. Actually, the cart contained typical jail food: powdered eggs, hash browns, white toast, and coffee. But since none of us had eaten in 36 hours, it seemed like a feast.

We were all hungry and weak and I was about to collapse, because I had been sick on the flight from Hannover. I looked ashen and pale. The thoughts were running through my head: Krasnow had first gotten us lousy equipment both at Mt. Tamalpais and now in Hannover and made us look like fools at the convention. Now he was screwing up the paperwork in England. I couldn't believe these people were actually in charge of a successful business - still can't, for that matter.

Frankfurt

Jerry Handley: Right, I remember that. And shipped us over to Frankfurt Germany.
John French: Yeah, and we didn't know what to do, we hardly had any money. Stayed in a hotel and you and Don went out and had some kind of fun that evening, and we saw a band play. I won't go into all of that.
JH: Lotta watches for sale in the street in Frankfurt.

We were escorted to a plane by uniformed guards. It was a really warm feeling getting on this plane and having everyone staring at us like we were common criminals. We were conspicuous enough already. I don't think another man on the flight had long hair. I was beginning to know I was right about Artie Ripp's big plans for the band. These guys didn't seem to know what the hell they were doing. Everything that was essential to our work was nothing more than an afterthought to them. We were all wondering if we would even get home by this point.

Don And Jerry Out On The Town

I slept on the flight. Frankfurt was a difficult place to be. We had no one to meet us or tell us what to do. I just shut up and let Don figure it all out. Whenever they went somewhere, I just followed. We wound up at some cheap hotel in what looked to be a bad section of town. I don't know where the money came from to pay for any of this. I didn't have a Mark on me.

The second order of the day was to get something to eat. What I recommend is this: do NOT have Chinese food in Frankfurt. It was the worst food I have ever tasted. It was supposed to be chicken chop suey, I believe; however, the intentions of the chef may have been the best, but he failed miserably in the actual methodology. I think they just had a big pot in which they threw whole live chickens. The chickens tore each other apart in the confusion and the result of their violence somehow wound up on my plate. I wound up spending most of my time fishing bones out of that glop.

Don decided to go out looking for hookers. This seemed to be Don's destiny in life. I think Jeff and Alex and I went to some club and watched a band for a while. We went back to the hotel and soon Jerry and Don came in, practically in hysterics. Don had found his hookers and persuaded a reluctant Jerry to go with him. These girls took them back to their place. I don't remember the details, but it was all done up in ropes and chains. They had whips and wore leather and all that ridiculous stuff that people do when they are too screwed-up to enjoy normal sex. Don and Jerry didn't know what to make of it, burst out laughing, and were expelled from the premises by the indignant ladies of the night.

We each had our own tiny room in a small hotel. My single bed had a thick white comforter on it. The room was cold, but I slept like a rock.

Back to London - A Hero's Welcome

The next day brought good news. Although English authorities had expelled us from the country, the press and public opinion had caused a turn of events. Apparently, Her Majesty was very concerned about someone coming into the homeland and making money which might actually leave the country. If we were there on business, we had to have work permits. A certain brain-dead promoter we knew had not arranged for these. Although we thought Krasnow was to blame, it was actually the fault of Peter Meaden.

Public protest had changed the official view of Her Majesty, however. Word of us being in a detention facility had apparently caused a small outrage and phones had been ringing. Actually, I think today that there is probably no better way to promote a group than to get arrested and spend a night or two in jail … it's probably the most attention we ever received.

While waiting on our plane at Frankfurt airport, Don began coaching us on how to behave; move quickly with confident motions, never focus on any one thing too long, keep looking around as though you're taking everything in. I thought it was a very interesting time to be giving us a crash course in public behavior. Don seemed excitedly convinced that something big was about to occur. Suddenly, it seemed as if he wanted us to act like other people, as though he were afraid for people to find out what we were really like. It was as if he were ashamed of us.

This time, we were given the executive treatment. We were taken to a decent hotel in a Daimler limousine. Our rooms were pleasant. The meals were great. Peter Meaden was there to greet us and show us the ropes. Of course, we wanted to show him a rope - in the form of a hangman's noose. London was fantastic. I wanted to stay there forever. All the things that I always associated with London were right before my eyes. The greatest relief for me was that these folks spoke English. There's nothing like trying to find a bathroom in Germany.

Middle Earth, Friday January 19 1968, London

We had a relaxing day. Our hotel was nice, though I wasn't used to these tiny elevators. Jerry and I were given a room together and we both slept soundly. He was the best person to stay with, and I had a great rapport with him. That night was our big concert. We were playing Middle Earth and I wanted to be rested and ready. That evening we were picked up by the same driver and car, and John Peel, the famous pirate radio station DJ, was inside the car awaiting us. As we were driven to the concert, we came across a huge line of people crowding the streets. The driver had quite a time manipulating the limousine through the crowd. Alex inquired of Peel what was going on and who were all these people. These people are here to see you, Peel replied. We all were a bit astonished.

A walk through a dark hallway and on to a precariously built wooden stage and we found ourselves facing a packed room. I have never felt so much electricity in the air. I checked the drums out for a few moments and with minor adjustments they were ready to play. These Brits knew about equipment. The set was decent, there were sticks, everything was fine. There was a smile permanently engraved on my face for the rest of the evening. I could barely see anyone, but it was obvious from the moment we walked onstage from the reaction that there was quite a crowd in this room.

Our introduction was made by John Peel himself, who seemed quite emotional. We may have been embarrassed in Hannover, Germany, but we were going to sound great tonight. From the first note until the last, I don't think anyone forgot anything. It was one of those spotless performances. You could barely hear the band for all the yelling and cheering.

I had discussed with Van Vliet how audiences seem to affect musicians. It's amazing how an unreceptive audience can just suck the life out of you like a giant psychic vacuum cleaner. This was part of the problem in Hannover. There's nothing like a roomful of record execs to send a musician's esteem to new lows. As we walked in that conference room, I could literally feel the energy drain from me. I had little left to give them by the time we were on stage.

In contrast, all I remember from this night was being filled with energy and feeling completely in control. I don't recall the entire set list, but it consisted mostly of songs from *Safe As Milk*, combined with some of the blues improvisations we were experimenting with, such as *Mirror Man* and *Tarotplane.*

After the show, we were taken to the dressing room where we sat for hours as a line of what seemed like hundreds of people walked in one by one to shake our hand or get an autograph. Many brought imports of *Safe As Milk* with them for us to autograph. I talked to these people just like I would talk to my neighbor. They talked to me like I was royalty. It was a great feeling. It seemed like we had finally gained some reward. We left feeling as though all that work had paid off. Suddenly all the criticizing and intimidation and eccentricities seemed very unimportant. It was a glorious moment, one of the very few I ever experienced, which is perhaps why I still love England and its people so much.

There was a feeling of awe in the entire band. Everywhere we went, people were taking pictures of us. We were constantly being interviewed. I had asked Don to please leave me out of any interviews. I just became the "tall mysterious drummer" (I'm only 5'11') as one journalist described me as I sat silently in Don's room during an interview, drumsticks in hand.

One of the reasons I desired to be left out of interviews was that it was impossible to keep track of the number of lies (harmless though they seemed) that Don fed to the press. It was fascinating to see him quote dozens of lines I had heard him rehearse hundreds of times and watch the press accept this as though it just came off the top of his head. "We got high in the high desert." "Everybody's colored or you wouldn't be able to see them." Interestingly enough, Don (as opposed to the Captain) was a slow thinker, who was easily confused and distracted. He was filled with fears and his biggest seemed to be the reality that someone could actually discover Don hiding behind the smokescreen of "the Captain."

After our performance, we were driven back to the hotel. There was a small party in Anders and Poncia's room. I went over after going down to the lobby to find out where everyone was. While in the lobby, I saw Jerry and Don walking up the front steps with a group of people that included two rather sleazy-looking young ladies. "He looks like bloody Jesus!" one of them exclaimed in a drunken stupor, attempting to point at me. Don later commented to me about the girl who made this comment saying, "Can you believe that chick? She kept saying she was 'pissed' and I didn't know what that meant, I thought she was angry. It means drunk – and she thought she needed to tell me?"

As I wrote earlier, Anders and Poncia were having a party in their room and we were all invited. I had not a clue as to who these guys were, but I will say that they seemed to have a lot more money than we did. Who was their manager? I thought to myself. There were about a dozen people having a few drinks in a small room. I was wearing my cape that Beverly had given me and staying to myself. Krasnow and Ripp were there, Anders and Poncia, of course, Penny Nichols, the Beefheart group, and a representative from the local booking agency that had booked the engagements, along with a couple of his secretaries. So, here was the entire entourage. I guess we had been the only ones to fly to Hannover, and the plan apparently had been to meet the others here.

Anne Buteras

There was a rather attractive young girl sitting on the edge of a bed which was next to the door. "Would you like a drink?" she asked me. I replied in the affirmative and we began to converse. She had the typical one-piece mini-dress that was very stylish at the time. Dark burgundy velvet, I think it was. She had straight dark hair, bangs, and the Mersey look, as I once heard it described, with heavy eye make-up. I was very taken with her accent. "Actually" seemed to be a favorite word of hers and just about every other young English person I met. All conversation had to have several interjections of "actually."

I was really a country dolt when it came to interaction with other people, and especially attractive women. I had nothing materially which didn't help. I was like a 12-year-old kid saying, "gee, shucks, golly." I had no confidence or self-esteem, but I covered it all with an air of egotism a mile thick.

I spied a full-length sheepskin coat lying across a chair. I had seen many coats similar but none like it exactly. It was tanned a rich chocolate brown. The wool was exposed around the cuffs, lapel, and edges. The thing that set it off was that it was embroidered with electric blue thread. I had seen many coats that were light brown with dark brown thread, but this one stood out. I told Krasnow I would love to have a coat like that.

The Speakeasy, Sunday, January 21st 1968, London

I believe this concert was canceled, although we did make an appearance and meet some folks. If I remember correctly, this was the performance, that caused us to get booted out of the country. Peter Meaden had something to do with it. I do recall hearing something about the club having damage from a recent fire.

John Peel Sessions, Wednesday, January 24th, 1968, Radio Studio at BBC London

John Peel, the man responsible for much of our popularity in England, arranged for a recording session at the BBC on a program, as I recall, called Top Gear.

It was an old radio station and it looked to me like something Bob Hope may have recorded in during the war. Instead of being filled with folding chairs for a studio audience, they had couches and overstuffed chairs sitting around the periphery and us set up in the middle. Again, we were supplied with decent equipment. The drumset was Premier and the amps were Marshalls. Everyone was happy with the equipment.

I think the engineers were having some sound problems. All the recording equipment looked really old. The mikes were vintage. We eventually played three or four tunes and that was it. We played well. Our small but intimate audience was great.

Back To A.B.

There was one person I was especially interested in seeing: Anne Buteras. We actually had a roadie, so I was able to go over and talked with this intriguing young lady who was there, sitting on one of the over-stuffed couches. She suggested we go outside. The limo was parked right by the front door. She and I got in and she instructed the driver to take us to all the great sights of London. It was night time. There was champagne in an ice bucket. I was in heaven.

I would have never believed a year before that I would be sitting in a limousine, in London, in the company of a beautiful girl, sipping champagne and being given a tour of the city. This was a little more than I had expected.

We wound up at Anne's and sent the limo back. She lived in a small flat. It was a one-room place with one bathroom down the hall shared with five other flats. We sat in front of a heater, which could only be turned on by depositing coins into a box on the side. It was cold at first, but she reached into a jar of coins and lit the stove. Her small, deft fingers fashioned us a hashish cigarette. This was a very ingenious and semi-complicated device made by extracting the tobacco from a cigarette. Cigarette papers were used, along with a rolled up matchbook cover for a filter/holder. Hashish was then crushed and mixed with the tobacco. The whole thing was smoked like a giant cigarette in a holder.

We drank wine and smoked this stuff and I became paranoid. I didn't want to be rude and turn down the hashish. However, hashish was derived from cannabis, and that made me paranoid. She was sitting on the floor with her arms wrapped around her knees off to one side. Her left hand was suggestively zipping the side zipper of her dress up and down, up and down up and down and she was staring into my eyes. When I noticed this, I found it extremely humorous, because in my head I started hearing really sleazy sax music like they play in strip joints. The kind they used in all the fifties movies whenever some gal was taking off her clothes. I started laughing and shaking uncontrollably.

I felt like a complete idiot. Somehow, this seemed to really turn her on. I was laughing like a maniac and this girl just got up and took off all her clothes. I suddenly became extremely quiet. I had hardly been around a girl at all for over a year. I was embarrassed. She walked over and crawled into bed. "You may get into bed with me," she said. I obliged.

After a few minutes she looked up into my eyes and calmly stated, "I should like it if you would hit me!" It was then that I realized that this girl to whom I was so attracted to was a masochist. I had heard the word, but I had no idea what to do, and I didn't want to inflict pain upon anyone anyway. "Just slap me on the face!" she instructed. Easy enough I thought. I wanted to appear a man of the world - that I had slapped my share of masochists with the best of them - with my technique down pat. I struck her on the cheek so softly that a sleeping fly would not have been awakened.

She looked at me, disappointed. I started realizing the attraction. I played drums hard from all the practice with the Dual Showmans. That probably really turned her on. Then the cape probably added intrigue. I was wearing the right uniform but I was from the wrong army.

In the morning, she made me tea on a little hotplate in the corner of the flat. There were curtains hung up around this area to conceal it from the rest of the room. She had to catch a bus to work, so I offered to take her by cab, I suppose to make up for not beating the crap out her the night before. I really was captivated by her. I was just a silly, naïve kid who fell in love at the drop of a hat. This is what continued isolation had done to me.

Apple Department Store

The coat that I had spied at the party the first night was purchased at a store called Apple and was affiliated with the Beatles' new corporation. Bob took us all there to look at clothes. Don suggested that I buy a pink shirt with yellow Tweety Birds all over it that he had found. It was very cartoonish and funny and I liked it, but I was disappointed that we could not find a coat like the one I had seen in Anders and Poncia's room.

Bob's Coat

That evening, when I returned to my room after dinner, there was a surprise awaiting me. Bob had talked the singer into selling him the coat I liked. Bob had his good moments. I think it was to make up for the screw-ups in Germany and with the work permits. Thanks again, Bob, wherever you are.

On to France

I knew I was going to miss England when we left. I had freedom to come and go as I pleased. It was great to play and be so well received. The privacy was nice. Even having to share a room with Jerry or Alex wasn't so bad. There was no tension to speak of and it seemed like this had been a very successful leg of this mini-tour. France was our next stop. We were going to the Midem convention. It sounded like Peter Meaden's last name, so I expected the worst. Since we hadn't been given an itinerary, I didn't know much about what the plans were. We were all basically uninformed.

Cannes - The Riviera

We arrived in France in the morning and were taken by taxi to a high-rise condominium. I was so excited about being on the Riviera. I had heard so much about this cosmopolitan center in my youth (wait a minute – I was still in my youth) and seen movies set in this location, and now I was actually here.

I don't remember why, but I do recall that we all immediately went to sleep. It seemed as though there were two or three beds in each of two rooms. I remember the language barrier as being very inhibiting – even worse than Germany. No one seemed to speak English, nor did they seem interested in helping.

When we arrived at the condo, Don asked me if I remembered from my High School French class how to ask the time. I spoke to the man in the office through a little reception window. "Quelle heure est-il?" (Translated loosely - "we are dumb bozos who forgot our watches') I asked. He answered in French, and Don asked me what he said. "How the hell should I know?" I replied.

Don's Dislike Of Watches

Don seemed to have a real dislike for watches. There was always this thing about anyone looking at a watch. It especially bothered him if he was talking. He communicated the point that we shouldn't need to watch time. I didn't wear a watch, because I lived with Don and knew that each time I looked at that watch, I would be letting myself in for it. Also, playing in this band had left me unable to *afford* a watch. Because of Van Vliet's hatred of watches, he was late much of the time and always had to be prodded and encouraged along.

Fortunately, Krasnow was an expert on keeping Don on time. He had dealt with other "great artists" and their eccentric temperaments I suppose.

We had slept most of the day. The flight left England late the night before. We had basically been up all night. I walked into a bedroom that had no windows and shut the door. When I got into bed and turned out the lights, it was pitch blackness, and the comfort of a deep sleep came quickly. The words "get up" nudged at my consciousness, and I opened my eyes to see Krasnow's silhouette illuminated by the living room lamplight in the open doorway. Bob urged us on, telling us to get dressed as we had a concert to do. It was like a drill sergeant routine. We were up and quickly out of there, hating every moment of this grueling task. Our scheduled performance was just down the street, just west of this condominium.

Pre-Beach Filming In Cannes/First Concert - Indoors In The Big Room

Handley remembered the beach performance we did, but I recalled this performance the night before.

Again, it was "go on cold with new equipment" time that evening. The band before us was a killer jazz group who did a version of a song we were all familiar with from an old John Handy album. It was a fast jazz waltz with an amazingly fast guitar solo. The band was really cooking. We had to follow this group and Don became insecure. He began to ride Alex about how good a guitarist we had just heard. "Why can't you do that?" he was asking him. "They're so hip sounding! Do you *hear* that? That's guy's *good*, man!"

Alex, with a disgusted but restrained expression, tried to explain to Don that we were a *blues-rock* group and they were a *jazz* group, but Don would not listen.

This was a small concert, maybe 500-600 people standing in a room. I think it may have been in one of the hotels, perhaps in a convention room or similar facility. Again we had almost no time to get ready. It seemed to me like the equipment was fine and was probably the same equipment we used later for the familiar beach setting. It was almost as good as the equipment in England, except I believe we were using Vox amplifiers. Things went together a lot better than I had expected. I had been able to secure some decent drumsticks in London, so that helped me immensely. Also, the equipment was already set up, which is psychologically a better position to be in than if one has to schlep one's own equipment around, especially in front of a crowd for whom you are about to perform.

I don't remember much about the performance, except that we seemed to get a good response from the crowd. The people were receptive. Someone was filming this for a television program. I tried to ignore the cameraman who at one point laid on the floor looking up between the hi-hat and tom tom. It was a bit distracting, but exciting at the same time. Don seemed scared at first, but as soon as he saw the reaction of the people, he relaxed. The jazz group had played great, yet they had received a relatively mild response. The crowd was more involved from the first note in what we were doing.

Our Condo From Hell

We were shuttled back to the condo. Don was taken with Bob and company to meet a French DJ who had promoted the band. It was then that we made an important discovery. There was no food, and we had no money and we had not a clue where Krasnow and Don were. Hoping they would come back, the evening was spent smoking and drinking lots of bad-tasting water. Everybody tried the best they could to talk about anything but food.

Press Conference

The next day, Krasnow and Don arrived. We were whisked down to a reception of some kind. It was within walking distance and so we strolled as a group down the sidewalk. There was a French businessman dressed in a suit walking with us (perhaps the DJ from the night before), he seemed to be the local representative. As we walked along, people kept asking us for our autographs. This is something I had barely ever experienced, and certainly not at this level. Rather than signing my name, I felt obliged to write little thank-you notes to everyone who asked for my autograph. As I stood signing yet another autograph on the steps, the Frenchman grabbed me gently by the arm and spoke in English with a strong accent, "Come on, come on, what are you doing, writing a letter to everyone?"

This Frenchman must have been the booking agent for the local events. Once inside we were taken to a banquet or conference area that was set up with champagne and hors d'oeuvres. Jeff and I looked at each other hopefully and with all the intensity of our teenage metabolism and rushed the tables. We finished off almost all the food except a few olives and crackers, as the reporters stared.

Remaining in the place for an hour, I found I was bored in ten minutes. No one seemed interested in talking to Jeff or me and there was nowhere to sit, so I eventually sat on the floor, back in a corner with my cape spread out around me. Don later reprimanded me for sitting on the floor and acting weird. (Wait, isn't this the whole mystique of being a rock star – to act weird? and besides, I wasn't acting.) It had been two days since we had eaten. Though not knowing it at the time, I had a slight case of hypoglycemia, a blood sugar problem that leaves one feeling easily fatigued and light-headed. That, combined with the weird schedule, had left me disoriented.

CHAPTER EIGHTEEN:
STRICTLY PUBLIC

Don and Alex with friend and supporter John Peel in 1968. Photo courtesy of Colin H

On The Beach, Saturday January 27, 1968, Cannes, France

After the press conference, we were driven by Bob in a rented car west for a short way. There was a stage set up on the beach with the ocean in the background. Krasnow explained this as a television thing that would give us great exposure in France. It was a bit windy, but for the most part beautiful. We were actually playing rather than lip-syncing, which was unusual for a filmed appearance. The sound was bad on the beach, but a crowd had gathered. This is the place where the well-known picture was taken which was later used for the French release of *Safe As Milk*. I remember playing *Sure 'Nuff 'N Yes I Do* and *Electricity*. It was a great time in spite of the hunger.

Again, we were dropped off at the condo, and Jeff and I asked about eating arrangements or being given some money. Bob just drove off. He came back a bit later a picked us up. He had rented a car and we were going to drive to Monte Carlo. The entire band and Krasnow were stuffed into a little compact car. There were slight clouds, which gave the hills and cliffs a certain surreal quality. A trip like this could only be appreciated after a good night's sleep and a hot meal. Unfortunately, we were broke and each of us probably wished, as I did, to be here with someone else or at least fewer people, OR perhaps a car that was bigger. There wasn't much talking. I do recall Don discussing starting a record company with Krasnow.

We drove for what seemed like half an hour or more, perhaps longer, on a windy road next to the ocean. I knew little about Monte Carlo or Monaco, except for the fact that Grace Kelly had married Prince Rainier. I knew there were casinos, and we drove by a few and took a couple of side roads up through magnificently styled homes. Snouffer took pictures from the window of the car. It was a completely different world to anything I had ever experienced. Bob stopped at a small café and bought us all a light lunch, which helped ease the hunger, then we drove back to Cannes.

Somehow, Jeff and I wound up alone at the condo that night. We were so weak from not having a good meal that we became giddy. It was the first time in a long time that Jeff had really opened up. We discussed how terrible this situation was. The tour had been only halfway planned. Germany had been a disaster, thanks to Bob and the lousy equipment. England had begun with an unfortunate mishap, thanks to Bob and Peter. Now, we were starving, thanks to Bob. We searched the place over and found nothing to eat.

The next morning, Bob popped in with a loaf of French bread and some jelly. He left, saying he would be back in a minute. We didn't see him until that evening. Jeff and I devoured this loaf of bread within moments. We walked around outside, studying the culture and trying to understand it. Girls rode by on bicycles powered by small motors – mopeds. People hustled here and there, not much different to Santa Monica, California in some respects, yet a world apart.

In The Hotel Nightclub

Although it wasn't originally planned, Krasnow had made arrangements for us to play in a hotel nightclub that Paul McCartney was scheduled to visit. We had heard rumors that the Beatles had bought a copy of the master tape of *Safe As Milk* and were very interested in our music, especially John Lennon. One of the promotional items Kama Sutra produced was a poster of John Lennon lying on a couch in his home reading, and on the wall above him was a *Safe As Milk* bumper sticker.

We were shuffled back into a makeshift dressing room to wait. A man with what I can only describe as makeup that looked like war paint began speaking with Don. His name was Arthur Brown. Apparently, he was a singer, although I had not heard of him, being so out of touch with mainstream music for the last year and a half. I have never heard any of his albums to this day. I just remember his makeup that looked absolutely savage.

We were escorted out to the stage area. The equipment we were supposed to use was the house band's equipment. It was a Latin jazz band if I remember correctly. All the drums were tuned really tight and high-pitched, exactly the opposite to the way I tuned drums. The PA was tiny, and so were the amps. This was definitely bossa-nova time, with a crowd to match. We all looked at each other, shrugged, and started performing the best we could under the circumstances. We were supposed to do two or three numbers, but Bob stopped us cold after about two minutes. It was obvious that we were not going over too well, and the equipment made us sound tinny. Bob made some kind of public apology, which, of course, very few of the French-speaking crowd understood.

We walked into the kitchen, just off the stage area, where Bob told us that McCartney was in the audience and wanted to meet us. That we should leave our equipment and go follow him. We walked back out across the dance floor. Arthur Brown was just starting his set as we walked across the dance floor in front of him to the tables. "Ladies and Gentleman, I give you dignity incarnate: Captain Beefheart And His Magic Band!" Alex took this as some kind of insult and went back to get a knife out of his guitar case so he could carve up Mr. Brown. Krasnow talked him out of it. It seemed to me that Brown was sincere, and Don seemed to think so also. I later heard that Brown was a great admirer of Don's music.

We sat and listened as Arthur Brown sang and danced around like a madman to the accompaniment of solo drums. The crowd was laughing, and I didn't understand why. A Frenchman (I think this was the same guy who had said, "What are you doing, writing letters to everyone) leaned over and said to me, "He's singing that DeGaulle (prime minister of France at the time) should go fuck himself."

Paul McCartney

We had spied Paul sitting behind us with a group of three or four others. He eventually stood and motioned to us to follow him. He was wearing a white suit with a pink shirt, no tie, and black shoes. We followed him outside and were immediately swamped with photographers and journalists. I had never realized what a bunch of pests these people could be until this moment. My hunger was probably putting me near the edge to begin with. McCartney, however, a veteran of these situations, took it all rather casually, making jokes and stopping for a mock pose, then suddenly changing his mind just in time to ruin everyone's shot.

Off To The Hotel

The photographers were all motioning at a statue and gesturing fanatically to us. "What? You want us to what?" laughed McCartney, "You want us to pee on the statue?" We all burst into laughter. "All right then, here!" He gathered us all around him and with his arms around us all, posed for about five minutes while everyone snapped away.

Jerry Handley: Well, they took pictures of us with McCartney, I wish I had pictures of that.

We started to walk again, and I was totally blinded by the flashes and kept stumbling over things like some clumsy oaf. We finally managed to make it to a hotel and get on the elevator. A few of the photographers were still there as the doors closed. "Go away, shoo!" said McCartney, swatting at them as one would swat at swarm of mosquitoes.

Penny Nichols and her manager, a bearded, serious man in his mid-thirties had followed relatively close behind. We assembled in Art Ripp's room. Originally, it was just Paul, the five of us and Penny and her manager. I noticed she had her guitar with her. Someone pulled a gigantic piece of hashish out of their pocket and placed it on the table. "Don't suppose anyone knows how to do this." they quipped. "Well, now, I think I may be able to handle it!" replied Alex, laughing. They smoked this together but unfortunately, everyone still seemed a bit tense. I just passed it by this time. No more Mr. Paranoia for me. I think I would have liked the sixties a lot better had they left the drugs out.

The door kept opening and opening until there were 12 or so people in the room. Anders and Poncia, our English booking agent, Artie Ripp, and finally Krasnow along with the Frenchman, whose name I don't recall. The manager was urging Penny to get out her guitar and play for Mr. McCartney. It was an obvious stab at opportunism, which everyone else, including Penny, immediately realised. I'm sure McCartney was constantly plagued with this type of behavior. Although it was supposed to be a clandestine and well thought-out scheme, we were all aware of it. Penny was very reluctant. She was a nice girl, and didn't want to exploit the moment. She sat down opposite Paul, on the floor with her guitar and began tuning, and tuning, and tuning, stalling for time.

Paul engaged in conversation, made jokes, laughed and had a great time. He was a charming person. Time passed, and occasionally I would catch a glimpse of Penny's manager motion to Penny, subtly but with conviction, to play a song. It was obvious that Ms. Nichols was employing a great deal of effort just to summon up her courage for the moment of truth. Paul was watching this from the corner of his eye. Just at the moment when Penny thought she could stall no longer, she took a deep breath and, like a parachutist on her maiden jump, formed a chord, raising her hand for the first strum. Paul reached his hand out and asked, "Say, may I borrow your guitar for a moment?" Like a hot-air balloon being deflated and packed away, she passed it to him. He began playing guitar right-handed, which I thought was odd. I knew he played bass left-handed. Later, he switched and played left-handed equally as well. Jeff was doing his "flesh horn" thing, and seemingly having a good time. I was completely silent the whole time. McCartney at this point, was one of the most famous people in the world. I wanted to take everything in. I was absolutely star-struck.

Don had been talking with McCartney, joking with him. I don't recall much of the conversation. Small talk mostly. Paul seemed to be a charming and thoughtful man, he listened intently, made appropriate replies, and seemed totally genuine and down-to-earth.

He started making up lyrics to the melody of *On A Clear Day* singing: "She's got cancer" and just joking around with all of us. Don would later say "McCartney and I wrote a song together," but the extent of their creative efforts was at best a couple of silly lines to this dreadful piece about a girl who had cancer, sung in black-humor style. The reaction of the majority of the people in the room was exaggerated and somewhat patronizing laughter. Although it was funny, it wasn't *that* funny. The fun was about to end, however. Slowly, the business people starting focusing more and more on Paul, like vultures assessing a carcass, until he finally had to get up and step out on to the balcony for a while.

Artie's Big Aspirations

There was a bay window seat, and Paul, Alex, Don and Artie Ripp wound up sitting together talking business a little later. Artie Ripp made an absolutely sincere (and insane) proposition that the Beatles should sign with Kama Sutra, because "he could make them bigger than they already were." Krasnow, Van Vliet, and Alex were all witness to this moment of madness. Snouffer found it simultaneously ridiculous and amusing, but it may have been the beginning of the idea that perhaps Kama Sutra, under Ripp's leadership, was not the best label for Captain Beefheart And His Magic Band.

Alex Snouffer: Well, listen, John, this is the same Artie Ripp that when we were in France wanted to sign Paul McCartney to a contract. Remember that? (Hilarious laughter)
John French: No. Did he?
AS: Remember that night, we met McCartney? It was me and Paul and Don up there and there's a little audience out there and there was this momentary slack or whatever the hell it

was and here comes Artie Ripp. He starts talking to McCartney and wants to (more laughter) re-sign him to Buddah! You know, the whole Beatles thing, he's going to make them even more famous! I'm sitting there and I look at Paul, and Paul got that little boyish grin on his face and then he went back and talked to Ripp and I just went back and lit another hash joint.

Meanwhile, the English booking agent took McCartney's seat and proceeded to get ridiculously drunk. He eventually wormed his way off the couch ending up lying on the floor singing old war tunes and shouting thick-tongued nonsense. I found this extremely amusing, as he was always so conservative when sober, and now he looked like a raving fool.

The party eventually died down and Paul escorted us back down to the lobby. He stayed on the elevator and I looked at him and said "Goodbye," - the only words I spoke to him all evening. He was an icon, and I was face to face with him. I had never met anyone that famous before, nor have I since.

Our Only Real Meal In France

Later that evening, the local French DJ (yeah, same guy) who had done so much to promote us took us out to dinner. At this point, I was practically comatose. I hadn't smoked in the room at the party, but my mind was a blur. This wonderful man was trying to communicate with the band but all I could think of was getting something into my stomach. I can't remember a thing that was said, just that it was pleasant. Aside from that, I would have much preferred the AV Inn Coffee Shop at the moment, so I could just order something from a menu written in English. Where's Darline Blair when you need her?

Bouillabaisse

The next morning, before we left, Bob said we had to have a bowl of a special soup he had been eating almost everyday because he liked it so much. He said it was "made from every type of fish all mixed together or something," as I recall. We walked to the café with Penny Nichols and her manager. I remember her manager stopping and looking at a man rummaging through a trashcan. "One of the richest places on earth," he observed, "and this man has to grovel in trash cans for food." I only wished I had thought of that ruse earlier myself.

We May Be Hungry

John French: I don't know where you stayed (in France), but Jeff and I stayed in this little condominium. And we had almost no food for three days.
Jerry Handley: In France?
JF: In France, on the Riviera, no food.
JH: Alex and I had a hotel room, (laughs).
JF: You guys stayed with those folk singer guys. There was a girl folk singer named Penny Nichols.
JH: Yeah, she was there at that party, yeah. I had some pictures, I don't know if I still have them or not. I was taking pictures off the balcony of the Riviera in Cannes. Out of our hotel room.

Back Home To Hell

Just as Artie Ripp predicted, the band was welcomed at the airport by swarming masses of beautiful teenage girls with raging hormones who nearly succeeded in ripping off our clothes. (Just kidding ...)

We came back to LAX to the reality of barely having enough cab fare to make it home from the airport. Customs took forever, especially for long-haired hippy types who may have dope on them. Don was suffering from some allergic reactions to the air-conditioning system on the plane. He was an absolute terror to be near when in this condition. We arrived home, slept, and on waking discovered that someone had turned the heater on and left it on all night. The house was a total oven. Don hated heaters worse than he hated corny jokes and lame people. Jeff and I were both interrogated to see who had committed this espionage.

We spent more time just sitting around. I couldn't practice, because Don was still paranoid of the police. The band was still disorganized. I felt useless, like I was just in the way. It seemed like two weeks went by and it was becoming apparent that something was wrong.

Back To The States/Strictly Personal/MGM

John French to Jerry Handley: So, we come back home, then we're here for a while and we record Mirror Man *again, right. I'm talking about the second recording of* Mirror Man, *right (which eventually came out as* Strictly Personal*). Bob Krasnow did a deal with Jay Cooper again. I guess he pulled some strings. I heard later that he paid somebody in the Kama Sutra office to lose our contract so they would forget to pick up our option. Then, he got us to sign a record contract with MGM Records, and we went in and re-recorded all the stuff that we had just done at Sunset Sound with Bruce Botnick at the controls. So, that was the one where he did the song* Ah Feel Like Ahcid *which was just sort of a studio jam.*

It was February of 1968, and I had been with the Magic Band for nearly a year and a half. Every step had been tedious, difficult and, for the most part, unrewarding. Don was writing more song lyrics and seemingly indifferent to the fact that nothing seemed to be happening. We had no income, no bookings, and there was an unbearable tension in the house. I could use the term verbal abuse to describe Van Vliet's treatment of both Jeff and me with no exaggeration. I felt at a loss as to what to do next.

To make things worse, Jeff had been "invited" to his local Selective Service Center, as the Vietnam war was raging on. We fed him amphetamines for a week, slept in shifts and stayed up with him to keep him awake. What we wanted to present to the Draft Board was a completely incompetent drug abuser whose mental capacities were nearly destroyed. I would think that just being in the band would have made him convincing enough, but noo … After a week of not sleeping, Jeff looked absolutely terrible. He could barely talk, and mumbled nonsense most of the time. "Ah, that's better," we thought.

To add fuel to the fire, Don borrowed some of Laurie's mascara and rubbed it around Jeff's eyes, making him look like more like a victim of the Holocaust than a musician. Jeff was taken to the Selective Service Center early one morning. He stood in lines all day, collapsing from exhaustion more than once, was awarded a classification that made him at least temporarily exempt from the draft. We picked him up later that day, stumbling around the streets of downtown LA.

Bob And The Big Deal

There seemed to be no news from Buddah or Krasnow for a time and I was aware that what seemed like private negotiations were going on. Don explained some of this to us, but the whole plan was not revealed. I had mentioned earlier that Krasnow and Van Vliet had talked about starting a label together. Don's idea was to call it Blue Thumb. This concept had been talked about more than once, and I had overheard them planning this for several months. Bob apparently thought it time to take the band on to bigger and better things.

I'm not sure who did what. I just remember sitting in that same Jay Cooper's Beverly Hills office waiting for a phone call. Apparently, someone in the New York office of Kama Sutra records had purposely slipped our contracts into the wrong time slot so that our options would not be picked up. This seemed about right. We had signed with them in early 1967 and now it was early '68. It was suggested by Don that Krasnow had paid someone off. If Buddah failed to pick up our option, by giving us written notice within the prescribed time, we were legally free to sign with a new company.

I personally thought this a bad move. It seemed as though the best thing might be to try to work things out with Kama Sutra. They had really put a reasonable amount of effort into promoting the group. Buddah had apparently had misgivings about the results the Mirror Man sessions. It was actually unfinished, but the vocals that had been added were erratic, and there was no hit song structure. All the pieces were long, and nothing was danceable so to speak.

"If only the vocals could be arranged to fit better with the music. If we had a place to rehearse," were the thoughts running through my head. It seemed better to me to try to work with the label, which might yield some measure of success that we could build upon. What was happening here was deception. It was inevitable that this would result in legal ramifications. Even I, at 19, was aware of that.

Sue Financing The Band

Don's mother had allegedly been paying a lot of the expenses for the house in which Don shared with Laurie, Jeff, and I. She took care of Don whenever he needed anything. I felt extremely uneasy about this. Anytime Don had a dispute with us, this fact was immediately thrown in my face. "What about my mother?" Don would ask. I felt indebted to Don because of her and thought I needed to repay her, as though donating my entire life to the projects Don cooked up did not earn me a right to have something to eat and a place to sleep.

Strictly Personal Photo Session With Webster

I'm not sure of the exact chronology here, but sometime during this period, we did a couple of photo shoots with Guy Webster. Both were shot at A&M Studios. The first involved a young female model in a negligee or some other suggestive apparel, and a bunch of female mannequins for props. I remember little about this session.

The second is clearer in memory. We first went to Western Costume Company and spent a few hours looking for Quaker outfits, among other things.

John French: Did you go up with us to Western Costume Company?
Guy Webster: Yeah, I remember going through the costumes.
JF: I know Krasnow was there, and we picked out all those things...

The idea, at the time, was to have the band dress as Quakers for one set of shots, and then as ourselves. The album cover would have the return name and address of one group (Twenty-Fifth Century Quaker) and the address of the receiver as the other (Captain Beefheart And His Magic Band).

Guy recalled the concept:

John French: With the **Strictly Personal** *shoot, what was your thought on that? Did Don give you the idea to go into those costumes, or was that totally spontaneous?*
Guy Webster: I think that was Don's idea, it wasn't mine. He had talked about the **Twenty-Fifth Century Quaker** *and all that.*
JF: Tell me more about the **Twenty-Fifth Century Quaker?**

GW: Well he used to sing blues as the **Twenty-Fifth Century Quaker,** *and afterwards you came out without the masks.*

I had forgotten this concept of Don's. The idea was that rather than having an opening act, we would come out in Quaker outfits as Twenty-Fifth Century Quaker, and do a blues set (our form of blues ... *Mirror Man, Tarotplane,* etc.) and then come back on as Captain Beefheart And His Magic Band and do the more "composed" pieces, such as *On Tomorrow* and *Trust Us.*

Guy Webster: So that's what gave me the idea to shoot that cover. I kept it very mysterious and unusual. I love that look. It's one of my favorite photographs I've ever done. I used it for a poster for a show. I had a big black and white exhibit in which I used that picture.
John French: We had a lot more fun with that shoot.
GW: Yeah, that's right. It was against this scrim that I had that I left out to be weathered. It was basically a blue scrim that turned magenta – with the exposure to the sun and the rain – which I wanted. We did it in black and white, but I had used that in color for something else once. Just a beautiful thing that I always loved. I still do stuff like that.
JF: I get so many compliments about that. People ask "Where did you guys come up with that?" One musician friend of mine told me that he opened up the cover and for about five minutes, he was shaking. When you can have that kind of effect with a piece of graphic work like that ...
GW: That's what upsets me. We don't have albums anymore. They're very impactful. People used the album (covers) to imagine the group performing or whatever. But, CDs don't have that impact, it's very minimal. You guys – along with Zappa and his band – were the cutting edge at the time. That intrigued me – that's where I always wanted to be. Through the years – because I became well known – anybody who had a band would want me to shoot them. I wasn't always attracted to their music. When I would do their covers, it would upset me. I was doing Andy Williams, Johnny Mathis, Liza Minnelli, and all these ... people. But, I never was excited about it like I was with avant-garde rock bands. I was making a lot more money, but I wasn't as happy ... that really intrigued me. People who were doing more avant-garde things – that's how I wanted to be – with my photography. But doing middle-of-the-road people, I had to be very safe.
JF: Didn't you have some kind of a name for the production company that you formed with Wilkes?
GW: For a few years, we used to be called "The Corporate Head."
JF: That's right... there was you and Tom Wilkes and ... who?
GW: Oh, we let anyone else who wanted to be in it be in it, but they didn't do anything. There was a drug dealer that we used to include in our corporate head – just as a joke. We had a toilet in our ad. Somebody sitting in an outhouse, and Tom and I were dressed in skivvies (long-johns) with toilet paper in our hand.
JF: Right, one of you had the seat, and one of you had the roll. That was a very funny shot.
GW: That was fun. We had a good laugh at that one. We thought the double-entendre was funny.

Practicing At The Park

The plan was to do another album as soon as possible with much of the same material we had already recorded. There was already a tour set up in Europe. We had to rush through a recording session, and leave directly for Europe. Bob and the engineer would mix the album and Bob would fly it over to us for our approval.

My only place to practice was an occasional hour or so in the dusty, spider-infested garage with a dirt floor. I had to close the door and the only light whatever was filtered through the cracks in the door. The drums got filthy and moved around a lot because I had nothing to put underneath them and the ground was not level. The hi-hat would sink into the dirt and all the hinges and everything moveable were corrupted. Still, I managed to loosen up a little this way for the sessions.

Krasnow rented another park recreation hall in which we could practice each evening. This was a similar situation as to when Gerry McGee was in the band. Bob may still have been doing promotional work for Kama Sutra at this time, to cover any fact that he was in on the failed options scheme but I'm not sure. We practiced here during the evening most of the time. We ran through the songs a few times. However, true to form, Don decided to write drum parts to a new tune we weren't going to even be recording, right in the midst of all this pressure. The drum parts to *Moonlight On Vermont* were written during this rehearsal time. I remember Don sitting at the drums and playing the basic drum part at the end of the song. As I mentioned earlier, *Sugar And Spikes* had also been written during this era, though at the house and probably a month or so before the tour.

Since most of this time was again frittered away on material that wasn't even going to be recorded, we couldn't quite get a few things back together, and all the changes we needed to make were just head arrangements. No notes were written down to remind us of what needed to be done. We were in chaos once again. There were many loose ends and much guesswork and improvisation in the coming session.

Strictly Personal At Sunset Sound

So it was that we found ourselves at Sunset Sound Studios again. The studio had a completely different feel to it without Richard Perry behind the console. It seemed more open and relaxed, in fact, it seemed as though the control room had been rearranged. I originally thought that Bruce Botnick was the engineer for this session, but after studying the album notes, I see credit goes to Gene Shiveley and Bill Lazerus. Some of our sessions were during the day and some at night.

There was a European tour lined up for us which started in early May. The studio had been booked for the week immediately preceding our departure, so we were involved in preparation for the tour along with dealing with a grueling studio session.

So, it was a marathon session with everything more condensed and chaos generally reigning. I was using a Premier set that Krasnow had bought with Kama Sutra funding and had shipped over from England direct from the factory. He mentioned that he thought I sounded great on Premier drums and bought a set while he was over on business – probably setting up the tour with the booking agent. He called me directly from the factory and I ordered exactly what I wanted from a catalog.

It was a double bass drum set. They were white with chrome accessories. Don said it looked like a kitchen sink. I loved the whole idea. The only trouble was that they sent really cheap hardware completely unassembled and I had no tools. I finally got them together enough to use in the studio.

Studio Instrument Rentals was supplying amplifiers for the band. It was a fairly new company just starting out. The band members ordered new amps from them to be delivered once we returned from Europe. Because of this, there was at least the illusion that things were on a more even keel.

Don relaxed a little in this session and it seemed like things were lightening up generally. *Ah Feel Like Ahcid* was written basically in the studio with Alex playing along with Don reading words he had just written and it reminded me of the LSD on the stamps that someone had given us in Hannover. It was obviously a Son House characterization based on *Death Letter* and was one of the first things recorded. I believe that Alex used both a D tuning and a G tuning on the two guitar tracks, so it had this disconnected feeling, which Alex described as two radios turned to different stations.

Months earlier, I had seen Yusef Lateef's drummer bowing cymbals (with a cello bow) at Shelly's

Mannehole. This had given me the idea to experiment with different percussion sounds. I had been experimenting a little with transducers (primitive pickups) while we had lived at the chicken coop house. I used one of these transducers on a maraca in *Beatle Bones 'n' Smokin' Stones*, which was recorded the first night right after Ahcid. It was recorded instrumentally with Don adding vocal later. I noticed that the drum sound seemed metallic and mid-rangy, which is exactly the sound I wasn't looking for. I mentioned that I liked the TTG drum sound much more. Of course, this time they were allowing me to use cymbals, yet the drum sound was not to my liking.

Kandy Korn was also recorded instrumentally and by this time I was cringing at the drum sound and kept complaining that the sound was metallic and crashy sounding. It turned out that in TTG, they were using compression on the drums to achieve the sound; here, they were merely using limiters to achieve the sound. A brief non-technical description is that compressors compress the sound by taking soft sounds and turning them up while at the same time taking loud sounds and turning them down. Everything on the set sounded a little more in balance that way. Limiting, in comparison, just pushed the loud things down a bit (loud things as relative to drums means cymbals and snare drum, the more metallic sounds), but didn't bring up the softer sounds (the more rounded tones of the toms and kick drum, a very important aspect of my playing). This was what was giving the drum sound that metallic edge I didn't like.

Safe As Milk and *Trust Us* were also recorded this first night. I can recall little else about the instrumental portion of the session. Don sat in the control room most of the time as the tracks were instrumental with vocals to be added later. He seemed happy with the progress and the session was surprisingly less tense than most and a lot more relaxed than the rehearsal atmosphere had been. Whenever outsiders were present, Don went into best behavior mode. The engineer, in this case, was like a buffer zone between Don and the band and allowed us to relax and enjoy things a bit more than usual.

I recall overdubbing group vocals in the afternoon, although the first instrumental session was done at night. The vocal overdubs were actually fun in this session. None of us had a clue as to what we were doing because Don never saw the need to rehearse vocals, so we just did sections at a time. When one part seemed satisfactory, we would go on to the next.

This was one time when Don seemed very reasonable in his approach. We were in a big rush to get this done, and he definitely rose to the occasion and communicated his ideas in a more professional manner. There were no tantrums and little strife. The lead vocals were recorded first and then the background vocals. This gave us the ability to follow what Don was doing. Don may have had a separate vocal session when the band was not present, I don't recall. I do recall that he worked with us, line-by-line, lyric-by-lyric. I recall the little pop-up toaster sound on the song *Safe As Milk* being the cellophane wrapper to a pack of cigarettes crunched in Don's fingers and he sang with us on the background vocals.

These vocal sessions were so much better performed than the TTG sessions. Don had obviously either done some homework or perhaps he just felt more confident about his ideas, or had at least thought about them ahead of time. Also, Krasnow showed a different side of himself and took control of the console. There were no "heavy baby" comments throughout this session like the earlier sessions. Things came together much better and sounded more arranged, especially vocally, in comparison with the chaos at TTG.

We must have done at least one all-night session and the last thing I recall tracking in the sequence was *Mirror Man* - really early in the morning. We were basically all in a catatonic state and had been up for probably 36 hours at least.

Mirror Man had a little more arrangement to it, and the amps we were using gave us a much stronger sound. We knew approximately what we were going to do this time and talked down an arrangement with cues, so that the song wouldn't go on endlessly. Everyone was listening. I recall

Don being in an isolation booth and we had no eye contact with him at all. It took him forever to get all his paraphernalia working correctly: harmonica mike, vocal mike, and electric flour sifter. This was all put through a Leslie speaker, which apparently had to be set up in another location. Everyone had to have headphones, and the mix was crucial to the interplay of the players. I still wasn't pleased with the drum sound on *Mirror Man* and so the engineer and Bob worked on this until it was probably one of the best drum sounds of any of the early recordings. I only wish they had found this sound sooner. We played an extended version of *Mirror Man*, one take, for nearly 20 minutes. It came together much better because we had actually played it on stage live and so had the crowd reinforcement of what worked and what didn't work.

Near the end of the session. Jeff and I had to borrow Don's car and go pick up guitar strings and drumsticks. Jeff always drove as Don always thought I was too crazy to drive. There was no way I was going to Europe again without drumsticks. I had already talked to Bob about making sure there was a decent set over there for me this time. Everything seemed to be falling in line. We were in a place called Wallich's Music City on the corner of Sunset and Vine. It no longer exists. It was a very famous spot to hang out and listen to records. They had booths inside in which one could listen to albums. These were like display windows on the street. You could always go by and see people listening to records. It was a great place to go and hear the latest jazz releases.

As we were picking up our stuff, I looked up and noticed a King soprano sax sitting way up high on a room divider type thing behind the counter and pointed it out to Jeff. After asking them to get it down for us and after looking it over, we found it appeared to be in operating order. I had played in high school band and knew a little about horns. I believe it was $180. Jeff and I looked at each other. We had barely $200 between us from the session monies, but we had to have this horn for Don.

Back at the studio, we called him outside and presented him with his sax. It was a used instrument, but he loved it. It was one of the few times I saw Don really genuinely thankful for something. He immediately took it out and started improvising. As soon as I heard him play, I wondered if we hadn't made a terrible mistake.

Back To Europe

We left straight from the studio and went to the airport. My drums were taken by Dolph (I suppose short for Randolph or Rudolph) who was the owner of Studio Instrument Rentals. This was the same guy the guitarists had ordered the guitar amplifiers from and they were, of course, going to pay him with monies (ha ha) from the upcoming tour. Soon, we were again on a flight bound for Europe. Almost all the dates were in England, and that is where we would be based. I was beginning to feel as though I had actually gotten over the hump. Things were beginning to look up. I had a new drum set (which I again was not allowed to take) and when I got home, I would hopefully have some money.

Middle Earth Revisited, Friday, March 5th, 1968, London

I well recall this particular night. It was our first night back in England. We were playing at the only place we had ever performed in the UK before, and so we felt at home. Don had just gotten his soprano saxophone, so the first thing he did was take it out of the case and, put the bell of the instrument over the microphone, and start blowing. We played for what seemed like forever. There was a lot of experimentation and I don't think we ever actually got around to playing much of a set. It was a reasonably strange night, and I wish that a tape of it existed, because it was one of the few times that the band seemed to improvise well.

I just remember vaguely being able to see the audience because of the lights, and that the drums felt really uncomfortable. I got off the kit for a while and just walked up to the microphone with a flour sifter, which we had used on *Mirror Man*. It had a pickup mounted on the side and was plugged into an amp, the microphone was just for effect, and gave me an excuse to stand up for a while. The only tune I really recall doing that night is *Kandy Korn*, which had just been recorded. We had been playing a lot previous to this performance and had just finished the new album, Strictly Personal, so we were probably in fine form that night.

Other songs in the repertoire were probably *Abba Zaba, Mirror Man* (which we did almost every show) and *You're Gonna Need Somebody On Your Bond* (which turned into *Tarotplane Blues* eventually). Even though our repertoire was limited at that time, we were more open to what could happen at the moment, and so there were some outrageous moments on stage.

Don told me later that someone had given him a glass of water with LSD in it. "Every time I play at this place, somebody gives me acid, man," he said. In retrospect, I believe that Don was probably just having reoccurrences because of all the LSD he had previously consumed. I think that this experience was not unlike that in Mt. Tamalpais, where he walked off the stage after a girl's head turned into a fish.

That fact probably heavily influenced our performance and set the tone for the tour. I know that we played very loud with a high amount of physical energy and were drained after each show. The drum kit I had was uncomfortable to play and I kept knocking the skin off the knuckle of my right index finger. Some nights I would have to alter my grip and hold the sticks like baseball bats, because my hands would ache so badly from the heavy pounding. And as if the band wasn't loud enough, Don would go back and turn up all the amps. We were using double-stacked Marshalls, similar to what Cream used, so I am told, so we were extremely loud even without being turned to full volume.

The Speakeasy

This tour did not have quite the romance of the first tour. We were taken by cab instead of limo to the hotel. It wasn't a great hotel, but was passable. There were a lot of Indians and Arabs in the lobby reading newspapers all the time. There was a place called The Speakeasy, which I mentioned from the first trip, in the basement. It had been relocated here perhaps temporarily because the original had burned. We ate, drank and hung out there a lot at night. There were local bands playing, mostly club cover groups. A lot of the places were just houses converted into clubs. We played a few of these on this tour.

I never recall playing at the Speakeasy during our first short tour in England, although someone wrote about the show and said that we weren't well received. I believe we missed the booking due to the fact that we were expelled from the country and sent to Frankfurt. We used to joke and say, "We weren't well-received? Well, you can say *that* again." I have also read rave reviews on other shows that I am absolutely certain we never played.

One good thing about this tour was that we always had some money, so everyone was well fed. Although I must say that I missed having a good hamburger now and then. The only place we could locate then that sold hamburgers was called Wimpy's, after the character in Popeye cartoons, who ate burgers all the time. They smelled and tasted like dog food on soggy buns. Occasionally, when we were desperate, we would send out for these terrible things.

The Zodiac

We had a roadie for this trip. He was a young Australian chap who seemed nice enough. He had been supplied a small white van by the booking agency, and always wore a wide brimmed bush hat. He was a tough guy and looked like he had been around the block once or twice. We also had a car with a driver to take us to all the performances. The Australian would go on ahead and set up our gear. The car was called a Zodiac. It was a little crowded for all six of us, but we managed to squeeze in. The guitars went into the trunk. We basically got out of the car, walked in with the guitars and played, got back in the car, and drove to the hotel, or back to London. The tour was low-budget all the way. Don used to call this English Rip.

Indian Journalist
There was an Indian journalist who came with another English female journalist to visit us at the hotel quite often. They were both university students and so the interviews were probably for a campus newsletter of some kind. The Indian was quite interested in our music and asked me many questions about my drumming. He wanted to know how much influence eastern music had upon my playing. These sessions turned into quite involved interviews in which I was describing the various types of beats that I had adapted. My style evolved from listening and combining the facets of several kinds of music.

Indian rhythms were definitely strong on the list. I had listened to a lot of tabla playing and was trying to capture the circle effect of infinity (as Don often referred to it) that I felt in the rhythms. I didn't try at all to grasp the time signatures, because it seemed absolutely beyond what anyone who listened to my playing would ever understand or recognize. Delta rhythms were the next big factor. There was really no drumming to speak of on most of the early Delta blues I had heard. Just vocal with guitar accompaniment. Alex had given me a lot of pointers from his experience playing drums with the band. I had taken this and adapted some really simple rhythms from some of Sandy Nelson's beats and stumbled onto a slightly different sound than I had heard before.

The other big influence had been Elvin Jones, the dynamo behind John Coltrane. His thrashing and bashing had a counter-rhythmic approach, which kept everything flying at a slight tilt. He always sounded just on the edge of falling, but always gracefully catching himself. He listened a lot to McCoy Tyner, the great piano man, and much of his accent depended on the direction of the piano chords.

In the early music, what we played on stage was mostly improvised around a few basic riffs. The whole substance was how much we listened to each other. There was a lot of risk-taking and searching which kept the music a little more fresh than just playing a standard set with everything exactly the same every night. It was definitely a lot more work, but I basically enjoyed this tour. The *Strictly Personal* and *Mirror Man* albums reflect the very roots of where we took the music on stage. It became more and more spontaneous as we played. After six weeks on the road, I think we could have made a much more interesting record than either recording mentioned so far. We knew how to read Don better, and he was following some patterns that made him a bit more predictable to us. Unfortunately, Van Vliet didn't enjoy practicing or performing with the band and seldom did we rehearse together. But for a short time, we were actually beginning to be like a real working band. This is what I had wanted to do in the beginning.

Jerry Handley: I didn't realize we were there that long, four or five weeks.
John French: Yeah, it was a long time, we also went to Rome.

Rome Pop Festival Saturday, April 5, 1968, Palazzo Della Sport, Rome
The highlight of the tour for me was a big rock festival at the new Colosseum in Rome. I had never been to Rome, but I had read much about the Mediterranean and was familiar with the history. Archaeology had been one of my interests as a child, and I was really excited about seeing some of the ruins first hand. I remember landing next to the Mediterranean, which looked turquoise in color. We were then shuttled by bus into Rome. As we entered the Eternal City, we passed right by the ancient Colosseum, I was absolutely in awe. I remember thinking, "I am

actually here!" Right in the middle of all this, Don looked over at me and started talking about how he couldn't understand how anyone could get all excited over a bunch of old buildings.

Knocked Off The Sidewalk

When we left the bus, we were on a very narrow sidewalk and as I was turning to look for the hotel entrance, a very tall male Italian dressed in a nice suit probably in his mid-thirties bumped into me very hard and knocked me into the street, where I was almost hit by a speeding vehicle. It reminded me very much of the stupid football players I had encountered in the High School corridors less than two years before. Welcome to Rome.

Don's Weight - Postage Stamp Towel

I shared a room with Don in Rome. Don was moody. He would warm up to one band member, and then after a few days, tire of him and move on to someone else. I could only guess it was my turn again. We had been up very late and so everyone decided to sleep that afternoon so that we could be completely rested for the festival that night. Don decided to take a shower and he came out with a towel wrapped around him, laughing. He had really put on a lot of weight. "Look at this bath towel!" He marveled, "I make it look like a postage stamp!" We both had a good laugh, but I felt bad for him. I realized his weight was probably really bothering him.

Don had a lot of physical problems. He had allergies that made it hard for him to sing under certain conditions. Gas heaters absolutely devastated him. He had dry skin which would flake off his face at the most inconvenient times, like right during a press interview. He was still occasionally dealing with psychosomatic symptoms, which left him puzzled and fearful. Now, he was quite overweight. No way around it. His hands would get swollen and burn if he used the wrong soap. Going on the road must have been absolute hell for him.

Wild Cab Ride

We were given the taxi fare after dinner by Bob to go to and return from the festival. I didn't know a thing about Italian money – lira as I recall. Riding in a taxi in Rome was something I was looking forward to. I remember reading that these drivers were totally wild. It was all I could do to keep my wits about me while we were whisked at unbelievable speeds through tiny streets filled with pedestrians, barely missing dozens of people by inches every minute. This was a way of life here, and everyone seemed really calm about the situation. Don and I could not communicate with this driver at all. We just sat and held on.

Julie Driscoll, Brian Auger Trinity

We were to go on after Julie Driscoll and the Brian Auger Trinity, and just before Donovan. I had time backstage to check out the drumkit and make it feel comfortable. All those little adjustments and the tuning could be a really stressful bother onstage in all the confusion. In those days, I used a four-piece set with a ride on the right, a crash on the left, and hi-hats, which was the average person's perception of what a drum set was all about.

There was a thin, dark-haired very attractive girl about to go on and so I went out in the audience area and sat to observe. Her name, I found out later, was Julie Driscoll, and the band was the Brian Auger Trinity. Brian played the Hammond B-3 organ, and as I recall there was a drummer and guitarist with him. It was the only performance I saw, but I was really impressed at how good they were. Julie had really short hair and moved around in a very fluid manner. She had a strong rhythm & blues influence and pulled it off quite well. Brian played right on the edge of jazz, butstill kept it pop enough to maintain the audience's attention. The song I recall them playing was, *Help Me.*

Our Performance

We played quite well that evening. I thought that the audience response was fairly good. There was a lot of energy, though I would say that only about 50 percent of the seats were filled. We seemed to be able to do no wrong. Don was in excellent form in spite of no stage monitors and trouble hearing himself. I saw a small snippet of this performance in the BBC documentary *The Artist Formerly Known as Captain Beefheart*. It was a bit misleading, because the music overdubbed was *Pachuco Cadaver* which had not as yet been written. I noted that Alex broke a string. I could see him taking off his guitar and switching to another.

Donovan

Don and I spoke to folk singer Donovan after we played. We were backstage and he was about to go on. There was a problem with the monitors and we warned him about it. We spoke with his father for quite a while who was quite proud of his son, you could see this.

Back To The Hotel

We were whisked back to the hotel. I was with Don again. When we arrived at the hotel, the cab driver tried to take more money for the cab fare than what the meter read. I didn't know anything about lira or exchange rates, but I could read the numbers. I got into an argument with him. Don kept saying, "Just give him the money, man, let's go!" but I persisted. A small crowd began to gather and I kept saying, "Give us the correct change," pointing to the meter.

Soon, a police officer walked up. I pointed to the meter and the money, and suddenly the driver, looking rather disgusted and sheepish after being reprimanded in Italian by the police officer conceded and gave me the correct change. I snatched it out of his hand, "No tip for you!" I thought, and turned and bowed to the crowd and we were on our way to the entrance of the hotel with some change, with which we had dessert. This small victory was good for my self-esteem. I was 19, half way around the world in a country whose language I didn't understand, and yet I had won an argument with an Italian about a cab fare. This made up in part for the guy knocking me into the street earlier.

Little Tour/Roman Ruins

The next day, we had to leave Rome. I wanted to see some of the sights. A man who I vaguely recall (it's been 30 years) showed up while we were having breakfast. I believe that he was a journalist. I recall him speaking English. He was very friendly and persuaded us to join him on a quick tour of a few of the ruins. We did, and I was able to walk through a few of the areas near the hotel and just soak up the feeling of ancient Rome on a very beautiful day. I would love to visit Rome again, the impressions that it left me with are still wonderfully strong.

Our driver was a wonderful man also. I remember being in a vehicle like a Jeep with no roof and sitting in the back. The driver took the long way to the airport, and we found ourselves viewing even more ruins and ancient carvings. We drove through streets lined with history. Ornate sculptures embellished the architecture at every turn. I was in awe. This, to me, was much more impressive than meeting Paul McCartney.

Drum Destruction

It may have been Manchester where I decided to destroy the drumkit on stage. Our performance was about halfway through. I believe we were facing east in the room we were playing in and it was a large stage, possibly at a university. About halfway through the performance, I was playing with my eyes closed, because beaded perspiration would run into my eyes and burn badly. Don had stopped playing and unbeknownst to me had walked over and put the simran horn directly up to my ear.

*John French: He had that simran horn too, remember that little east Indian snake charmer horn
and he was playing that and both those ... that thing had a double reed and it was just piercing.
Jerry Handley: Right, right, he was brutal.
JF: Yes he was.   So, there was one night when the drums fell apart on me.*

A sudden blast of this shrieking instrument cut through the din and nearly deafened me, startling
me so badly that I hit the ride cymbal with an incredible force and it completely broke all the way
around the bell and slipped over the stand to the floor. I hadn't noticed it missing, and when I went
to strike it again, I lost my balance and fell backward, drum throne and all, to the floor. On the way
down, my right toe had hooked the kick drum, sending it, and the suspended tom, toppling
forward, and my left foot did the same to the hi-hat stand. When I stood up, not one drum was
standing, save the ride cymbal stand with nothing but the jagged little bell part (the center four
inches) still mounted on it's top.

A spirit of theatrical anger overwhelmed me, probably from being embarrassed. Don's horn in
my ear was painful and I was pissed at him for doing such a stupid thing, as well as the fact that
this set was such a cheap piece of crap. I picked up a microphone stand used to mike the drums
and called the road manager over. I asked him to point the mike at the drumset and I used the
microphone stand like a sledgehammer and destroyed the entire set. I only remember Alex to my
left looking over and grinning at me. The roadie kept backing away, and I kept shouting "Hold the
mike closer dammit!" When the set was destroyed to my satisfaction, I calmly walked off the stage,
bloody yet triumphant, reveling in my rage, satisfied that I had given the audience their money's
worth. I think this was way better than Pete Townshend, and certainly more spontaneous.

Kicked Out Of The Hotel

John Peel brought a record player to the hotel so we could have something to listen to besides
BBC. Television was pretty bad in England compared to what I was used to in the States. We would
all gather in the room I shared with Jerry, I believe, and listen to jazz or whatever John had brought
by. One evening we had off, we were partying a bit, just listening to music and having a drink
or two. Probably smoking some hashish, and Don kept insisting on playing one cut over and
over again. Each time we would replay the cut, he would insist on increasing the volume. Finally,
someone complained, and the manager came up to ask us to please turn it down. He was
actually quite nice about it, but as soon as he left, Don turned the volume even louder.

The next day, we were told to leave. Our lack of cooperation had forced that decision on the
management. I was really angry with Don about this. It was such a foolish and childish thing to
turn the volume up after the guy had been so nice about it. His macho ego would force him into
behavior that seemed absolutely adolescent at times (and this coming from a guy who the night
before had smashed a drumset with a mike stand).

In this hotel, we were right above the Speakeasy, they had great food, and reasonable prices
with a good atmosphere. It was convenient. I had settled in and felt comfortable. My attitude about
this was "Now we had to move because the big baby leader wanted to show who's boss with the
volume control." The manager had been extremely reasonable with us, and there was no reason
why Don couldn't have cooperated except for his gigantic ego. I would never understand this facet
of Don's personality. But it was part of the same element that allowed him the freedom to sing with
such passion on stage, and control the people around him with such intensity.

Saturday, May 11, 1968, London School Of Economics

This show was in a large room with a high temporary stage in the center. I remember people being
all around, even in back of the stage. Most were in front, of course, because the visibility was better.

A representative from Premier came down for this show. I had previously trashed the first kit they had loaned me and now was in possession of a much nicer kit. The representative appeared, with his wife or girlfriend, out of curiosity. He introduced himself and his friend and then began to inquire as to how I had so thoroughly destroyed the kit. I told him it was a lousy kit and apologized for the destruction, but had found the drum set quite unusable and as it broke onstage, I felt I had no choice but to theatrically dispose of it.

John Peel

Though most of the time we were crowded into the Zodiac with our driver, we (Don and I) were at least once transported by John Peel and his lovely wife. He rented a tiny car in which we rode in the rear. I recall stopping somewhere for a bite and Don saying that John's wife was interested in hearing about my observations of Don's psychic abilities. So, I spent a time with her in the back speaking of this. At one point, Don asked Peel to pull over, as he wanted to hug a tree. I think Don probably had to pee and didn't want to say anything in front of Mrs. Peel.

It seems to me that the place we played that night was actually a house turned into a club. It sat on the corner of two streets. The walls had been opened up so that more people could see the stage. This was a very curious venue indeed.

John French to Jerry Handley: That's where we met John Mayall, and Eric Clapton was there, except I didn't know much about who Eric Clapton was, unfortunately, back in those days. It was in a little house and someone had cut windows in the walls and it was like a psychedelic clubhouse. That's where we played. He was in one of the rooms and we were in the other one.

Wednesday, May 14, 1968, The Toby Jug, Tolworth, England

This was a daytime performance, if I recall. It was a club that ran lengthwise north and south and had a parking lot on the west side. The building was divided in two parts, and we played in the south end against the east wall to the width of the room. After the show on the west side of the room next to the windows, I was helping myself to a drink from a little corner bar when I was approached by two fellows who were quite unhappy with the music and wanted their money back.

I recall the conversation escalating to where I eventually wondered if a fist fight were about to ensue, so I held a bottle in my hand by the neck. Alex walked up, and feeling more comfortable about having some back-up, I gently told the fellows that if they didn't care for our band, then they shouldn't have paid out their good money for the tickets, unless, of course, their only reason for coming was to bitch at the band and cause trouble, in which case they'd carried out their dream and should now leave. Or, if they'd never heard of us, then why come in the first place?

They left, and Alex complimented me with words I treasured by saying, "That was cool, the way you handled that situation!"

Thursday May 16th, 1968, Zodiac Club, Star Hotel, Croydon

I recall that we arrived here early in the day and the equipment was set up. Don, as usual, wanted to write something. We started trying to follow what he wanted. We had no tape recorder and so were trying to follow his usual frantic, "We gotta get this" creative instructions. Every idea Don ever had was described by him as "a hit," or "the best thing yet," or "this is the one that's going to make us a lot of money." None of us road-weary musicians could follow his vague musical instructions, and he became very upset and stormed out of the club. It put quite a damper on the show that night. In the car, there was a lot of verbal follow-up containing the usual put-downs and accusations that the band didn't really want to make it, and that we were all a bunch of lazy asshole... assholes. The truth is, it was an inappropriate time to be trying to create a new song. I don't think anyone gave a damn about Don's opinion of the situation.

Morris At The New Hotel

We had moved to a new hotel that was right down the street. It wasn't as nice as the hotel we had been staying at before. The front door was locked at 10:00 at night, and the only way to get in was for the elderly night desk clerk to wait up for you. We had a key to the front door, but only one. It was hidden out in front in the bushes, but I could never find the damned thing. The night clerk was an old man named Morris, who had probably dedicated the better years of his life to serving others. He must have been in his late sixties or early seventies. This poor old man would wait up for me every night. He was concerned that I might get locked out, so he would sit in the back in his little room and read or something. When I arrived, he would come to the door in his robe and let me in, as he did this first evening.

"Good evening, sir," he would say in a very proper English accent, "Would you care for some tea and biscuits before retiring, sir?" "Certainly" I replied, not knowing that he would have to make the tea from scratch. Here was this wonderful old man with white hair, looking a little like Carl Sandburg, making me tea in his robe and slippers. I sat for a good 20 minutes with him in the small kitchen in back of the hotel while he busied himself with the task at hand. I couldn't help but marvel at the fact that he treated me completely without any prejudice although my hair was past my shoulders, I had a beard, and was wearing a magician's cape. I wasn't exactly the norm, and I had been treated rather poorly by most of the older generation while I had been here. This old man didn't seem to notice or care. He even insisted on carrying the tea and biscuits up to my room. I was deeply touched by his kindness. Then, of course, totally humiliated by the fact that I had no money to give him as a gratuity. I left an envelope for him later.

Saturday, May 18, 1968, Southampton University, End Of Term Dance, Southampton

When one is on a tour like this, it is easy for one performance to run into the next. I remember very little about these individual performances. I know that Don had brought his musette with him. He also had the soprano sax, of course. One of the funniest nights was near the end. It was an end of term dance at Southampton University. We played at 5:00 a.m. for one hour. All these guys wanted to do was dance slow with their dates, and suddenly the band from Hell appeared on stage and did the weirdest music they had ever heard. Suffice to say we were not that well received. The majority of our audience cleared the room by the end of the first song.

Jerry Handley: We had to push our car to get it started up there.
John French: Yeah, that was in Southampton. That was in the south of England, we drove all night, do you remember what we were playing?
JH: What we played....music?
JF: No, do you remember what kind of situation that was? The performance was for a prom (U.S. for "end of term dance) at a university.
JH: Didn't we play some colleges?
JF: Yeah, and this was a college and it was for a dance, can you imagine? We were playing for a prom, it was an all-night party and we were playing at dawn, so here we are out there playing to these burned-out college kids that are dancing, and they are trying to dance to us playing Mirror Man. (Laughter) and Kandy Korn and Don had just gotten his soprano, so he was blowing that over the microphone.
JH: I pitied the poor person on the other side of that soprano sax when he played it.
JF: Yeah, cause it was (loud).

Sunday, May 19th, 1968, Frank Freeman's Dancing School, Kidderminster
We all seemed to be in excellent form for this particular night. Alex played particularly well and the way the stage was set up I could see him quite clearly. However Don did a version of *Rollin' And Tumblin'* that seemed to go on forever. It had a lot of power, but after the first seven minutes, it became quite monotonous and a really difficult pace to keep up. I wasn't quite sure why we didn't just do *Sure 'Nuff 'N Yes I Do*, as it's basically the same song, but an original. We managed to do it, but were exhausted after the show. A lot of what we played on this tour was more improvised and less arranged, which made each night different. The band was playing more like the original band had played; simply and with a lot of force, but with the added strength of the influence of our own material. All in all, many fans were there, the place was crowded, and there was a very enthusiastic response to each piece we played, so the audience really inspired us.

Middle Earth, London,
Road weary was the mood for this show. Why were we booked here twice, I'll never know. We showed up late (not our fault; the car had to be pushed again) and then found that some of the equipment was malfunctioning. I had to sit on the stage and fiddle with a broken drum pedal. Audience heckling was apparent for the first 15 minutes or so we were there. Don went up to the mike and said, "There seems to be a mixed reaction in the house tonight." He gave no explanation about what was going on and this seemed to be like pouring salt on the wound. The volume of heckling increased dramatically. Finally, we were able to get things together, but it was a tough show, as when you get off to a bad start with an audience, it's nearly impossible to turn it around. By the end, people were happy enough, but the enthusiasm just wasn't there.

Club A Go Go, Newcastle
We became lost trying to find this club, as we had driven up from London. It was late afternoon when we finally asked directions. I recall rolling down the window and asking some fellow on the street if he'd heard of the place. He didn't understand me. I said it again, and his face lit up: "Oooh, the cloob a goo goo." He went on and on about how to get there. The brogue to my untrained ear sounded Scottish. I didn't understand a word he said, but the driver got it all. I thanked him and we drove off to the club. It was a medium-sized club with a lot of thick dark tables with initials carved in them, and the smell of ale permeated the entire building. Our Australian roadie was there, sitting casually on the front of the stage, one foot slung out sideways fiddling with the hi-hat, which was giving him fits. Someone having a drink had been mouthing off to him and he finally told the guy to bugger off with quite a bit of determination. Alex looked over at me and grinned "This bloke don't take no shit from no one," he observed.

I wish we would have had some money to give this guy a bonus at the end of the tour. He set up for us, tore down and loaded the entire backline by himself every time we played and I can't remember one time that he was late setting up or tearing down. I never saw him drunk or out of line. I don't remember his name.

John French: And, do you remember playing in the Club A Go Go in ... Newcastle?
Jerry Handley: I remember Newcastle, that's where The Animals were from originally.
JF: They sounded Scottish, they had very strong accents. There were knife marks all over the booths, it was a rough looking place. They carved their initials in all the booths.

The performance that night was quite good. By this time, we were into our stride. I think that the main problem with the band was that Don didn't like to tour or perform. However, it was the best thing for us.

Krasnow Appears With Strictly Personal

Krasnow appeared in the middle of all this with the final mix of the album. In those days, they would cut an acetate just for listening purposes. It was made from the master tape, and looked exactly like a $33^1/_3$ long play record. The soft plastic, however, was only good for a dozen or so plays. Bob had brought one of these with him. It seemed as though our little problem with the record player being too loud had prompted John Peel to take his player back, so we had nothing on which to listen to the acetate.

The Stones' Office Building

Bob had arranged for us to go to the Rolling Stones business office one evening so that we could hear the album at a good volume through their system. We took a couple of those great black English taxis over to the office. As we listened, I was aware of all the phasing and other effects Bob had used to modernize the album and make it psychedelic, for lack of a better word. He had edited little bits and pieces here and there in order to package the album for the most commercial selling potential. Jeff and I were probably the most naive to this process, and were just enjoying the fact that it was done. I liked it, actually, and thought that it had more appeal to the teen market. Don and Alex were seething the whole time. I'm not sure how Jerry felt about all this.

As we left the offices, I noticed in the elevator that neither Don nor anyone else had the acetate. I mentioned this to Don and he immediately began to launch a tirade at me about how stupid I was to forget the album. Nobody but me seemed to notice that it was not my responsibility to bring it in the first place. Again, I was extremely humiliated by this in front of others. I rode with Don and Alex back to the hotel if I remember correctly. Don was discussing how Bob had ruined the album. There was talk of getting rid of him. There would soon be more.

Jumpin' Jack Flash on TV

I had heard from someone that The Rolling Stones were going to make some kind of special appearance on television. There was only one television in the hotel. It was in the lobby. There was a bunch of old men, some Arabs, watching some trivial stuff, so I asked if I could turn the channel for 10 minutes and they agreed. The Stones were performing *Jumpin' Jack Flash* on television. According to sources I checked, May 24 1968 was when the single was released, so it all coincides. I haven't been able to find a video of this on the net, but I do recall watching it in the lobby.

The interesting thing is that one of Van Vliet's claims is that he and Alex wrote *Jumpin' Jack Flash* while in the Stones' office building and that somehow the room was bugged or something, and they stole it from him. I recall nothing of the kind happening.

It would have been quite a feat for them to record the song and release it the same day...

Jerry Handley: I remember Don didn't want to do a job during that tour and I had to go to the hospital and pretend I was sick one time, remember that?
John French: Really? In England?
JH: Yeah,
JF: I don't remember that.
JH: Yeah, he just wouldn't go on stage, you know, he'd get on one of his things?
JF: So, you had to fake out and go to the hospital.
JH: I faked I got food poisoning and went to the hospital and the guy...cause I wanted a letter, so that we wouldn't get sued because we had a contract to play.

Krasnow And The Tour Money

John French: We found out, uh, I can't remember the guy who was the booking agent, but we found out that Bob Krasnow had gone in to him, retrieved all the concert money, and taken off. We were supposed to go to Belgium, which were the last dates of the tour.
Jerry Handley: Right. Holland.
JF: Maybe it was Holland. So, we skipped out. We had to skip out because we knew we weren't going to be able to pay our bills, and so we left.
JH: I knew we had left early, but I was thinking it was because Don didn't want to finish the tour or something. I didn't know what our reason was.

I only have a vague memory of this. I can't remember exactly how we found out, whether I was called in my room at the hotel and told, or whether we were getting ready to leave for Holland. It seems to me that we were in the lobby ready to leave and were checking out of the hotel. Suddenly the hotel wanted money and called the agency, who informed them there was no money available.

It was perhaps a quick thought on Don's part to cancel the Holland dates and leave for the States immediately, possibly with the idea of convincing the management of the hotel that we were off to Holland and would return with money. It was obviously not our responsibility to pay the hotel personally, and we had no funds now that the money was gone. I'm sure that it was Don's idea not to play Holland, but I am not sure why. We were already in Europe, the performances were booked, and the tickets were already in our hands. It could have been that we would have to fly home from Holland via London Heathrow and since we had already once had trouble in London, he was trying to avoid any legal entanglements for which we were not at fault.

I just have a vague memory of standing in the lobby mid-morning keeping, my mouth shut because I didn't know what was going to happen, and it always seemed like deception was the name of the game, rather than truth. I found that it was better to remain silent rather than open my mouth, either speaking a complete contradiction or becoming part of the deception. I couldn't understand, even then at 19, why Don in particular seemed to think it more appropriate to lie than to just tell the truth. However, I was the kid of the group and just watched, thinking I would learn something.

The group consensus at that time was that we should pretend to leave for the airport with the intention of going on to Holland, and instead fly back to the States immediately. We had no money to pay for any more expenses and the hotel bill itself might have been more than the Holland performances would have paid. We had no idea how we would get home unless we left immediately. We had our plane tickets and a few pounds between us, and the smartest move seemed to be to leave while we could.

That meant we had to cancel the performances on May 31st 1968 at Paradiso and Fantasio in Amsterdam, and on the 1st of June at the Canada Club for a TV show called "Rood-Wit-Blau" in Alkmaar, Holland, also the Lijn 3, Amsterdam on the same day.

I think I've actually read reviews on some of these shows that were never played. Interestingly enough, critics who are paid to go to concerts and write reviews sometimes get a little confused and temporarily become writers of fiction. It's too bad we couldn't have gone to Holland. I played Amsterdam in 1975 and again in 2004 and loved it.

Alex Snouffer: That's when we raced to the plane on the taxi way. We flew back.
John French: That's right, it was on the runaway.
AS: Yeah, we had to run for it. (Laughter).

I remember nothing at all about the flight and was dreading home. There had been freedom here. I loved London. I kept thinking, "What could the States offer but more of the same drudgery as before?" I didn't enjoy living with Don, and the situation at the house was looking even more grim now that we were completely devoid of any earnings.

An outtake shot from the Strictly Personal shoot early '68. Photo courtesy of Guy Webster.

CHAPTER NINETEEN:
TOM MIX HOUSE OF STICKS

Back In The USA

After our return, I assessed my situation: I was in a band where most of the guys were older than me and I had no common ground with them. I lived with the leader who at times seemed like a tyrant, constantly belittling and berating the band members. I had very little creative input into the music, which left me artistically frustrated. My best friend in the band had been alienated from me by Van Vliet through manipulation. Everything seemed beyond my control. I had no money, no car, and no freedom to go off for a few days by myself and just sort things out.

Since the move to the house in Woodland Hills, probably because the house and property was so much smaller, all the intensity had seemed to increase.

Jerry Handley: Don did not want to play near the end there (referring to the '68 May tour) Do you remember?
John French: Didn't he?
JH: He was sleeping, and I just remember you couldn't even wake him up over there.
JF: I think he was probably getting sick. Because when he came back, he was in terrible shape. I remember, just in awful shape. Yeah he didn't fare well on the road. I don't recall being conscious of that over there but now that you mention it, when we got back he was feeling pretty bad.
JH: I remember trying to wake him up in England. It was like he was dead. Totally out of it. Wouldn't wake up, took an hour or two.
JF: Yeah, I remember some of those times. In fact, I missed a trip to Stonehenge because I didn't want to leave, knowing he'd be angry if I went and he didn't. I was still intimidated by him.
JH: He had a terrible fright. A fright of the stage? I don't know.
JF: Yeah, he was very afraid of the stage. (Note: later I recalled that Don claimed someone had given him a glass of water with LSD in it when we had first appeared at Middle Earth. Perhaps this had an effect on him throughout the performances.) *He was still going through that anxiety stuff, you understand.*
JH: Yeah, right! It made it rough on everybody - too bad.
JF: And he'd get lost in songs on stage, didn't know where he was.

Indeed, Don had seemed not to fare well after the tour, and his skin problems had erupted with ferocity. Immediately upon arriving home, Jeff and I were sent out on a mission to get pharmaceutical relief in the form of an ointment only available by prescription - a special medication he had used - in order to overcome his allergic condition. Jeff and I were sent out with foreign currency to buy this product. There was no one who would accept the money. We tried several banks etc., most of which were closed and finally wound up going to the airport, an extremely long drive, which had a currency exchange window. It took forever, but we finally got it. Because of the time we took, Don was furious upon our return, even though we had the medication he so desperately needed. He asked sarcastically "What'd you guys do? Go back to the airport?"

Bob Shows Up With The English Booking Agent

Bob Krasnow called a while after we returned. The English booking agent had decided to fly over to collect the hotel and other expenses that were never paid. Bob, in all his wonder, decided that he would personally bring the guy over to see us, so that we could explain why we had skipped out and without paying.

John French: Soon after we got back, Krasnow had the nerve to bring the English booking agent over to our house. The booking agent then told us we owed him for the hotel bill.

Alex Snouffer: Oh, well, just a second, let me check my pockets ...

There was also some problem with the Dutch performances we had cancelled. There were some legal fees, etc. Because Krasnow was Jewish, Don decided to shave his mustache into a Hitler look for the occasion and brush his hair to one side to complete the illusion. It was quite funny actually. Bob hardly let it bother him.

MGM vs. Kama Sutra

John French: Let's see now, we came back, that was when we found out that the album wasn't going to come out because MGM didn't want to deal with us due to the fact that we were still under contract to Kama Sutra (Buddah). Some shenanigans had been pulled in the Kama Sutra office, but MGM wasn't buying it. They (Buddah) were saying that we were still under contract, even though they didn't pick up our option. We were into them for a lot of money at that point.
Jerry Handley: Yeah, they promoted Safe As Milk, *I guess.*

We're Only In It...

Suddenly, after two years of criticizing, Zappa, Don showed up one morning with Frank's latest album, *We're Only In It For The Money*. This was a shock to Jeff and me, as Don had basically convinced us that Frank was public enemy number one and had stolen all his main ideas from Don (the name *Suzy Creamcheese* and the title *Lumpy Gravy* are two I recall). I found the album to be hysterically funny. One of the things I enjoyed about Zappa from the earlier albums was his sense of humor. This was even better, and the Mothers dressed in drag was an hilarious concept. They were the ugliest drag queens I have ever seen. Frank definitely seemed to know how to market himself. Don listened to it a few times and then surprisingly decided to call Frank up and say hello. Frank had moved his band out to the West Coast at this time, which he mentioned in his book.

"We returned to California in 1968, we moved into a large log cabin, once owned by old time cowboy star Tom Mix, at the corner of Laurel Canyon Boulevard and Lookout Mountain Drive." – Frank Zappa [37]

I remember going with Don to the phone booth, as we had no phone at the house, to call Zappa. I stood outside one of those old glass enclosures. I watched Don's expression and laughter and it was easy to see that he had at one time been really close to Frank and they were recalling their friendship.

Don Becomes Frank's New Special Friend... Again

Frank Zappa had returned to LA after a long engagement at the Garrick Theatre. After all the negative things Don had said about Frank, it was mildly surrealistic to actually witness Don and Frank's relationship first hand. Not only was I intrigued with knowing this guy Frank Zappa, who I had first heard about through our mutual former High School Vice Prinicpal, Ernie Tosi, but I was also very curious about how this was going to work with the seemingly volatile relationship with FZ that Don had portrayed for the last year and half.

Jerry Handley: In Laurel Canyon, Frank Zappa had the old Tom Mix Cabin down the road a bit. I remember going to some jam sessions down there. You know, going down and just plunking around.

---

[37] The Real Frank Zappa Book, Frank Zappa, Simon and Schuster, 1989 pp101.

John French: I met Gail. She was pregnant, with Moon if I remember correctly. That's when we were supposed to get "creative freedom." Those were the buzzwords: "creative freedom."
JH: That's true.

Creative Freedom

Ever since Jerry Moss of A&M had labelled Don and the band's demo tape as "too negative," Don had been up in arms about having what he called "creative freedom." Even with Buddah, Van Vliet seemed to have a lot of frustration with *Safe As Milk* as a finished product. I recall Krasnow arguing against the use of a Theremin in *Autumn's Child*, and *Electricity*. Krasnow was saying, "I'll hire some broad to come and sing the part." I was in the studio overhearing this and had laughed at his suggestion, thinking *"and that's going to be less weird?"*

There were also some overdubs that Don was upset with - clavinets on *Call On Me*, the doo-wop vocal harmony on *I'm Glad*, and at least one vocal overdub sung by producer Richard Perry on *Abba Zaba* irritated Don ("what the Hell is he singing? 'Babiddy – Baboon'?" he comically mimed). The obvious inclusions at the last minute by Van Vliet of three-four sections in otherwise four-four (*Dropout Boogie, Plastic Factory*) were questioned.

Creative freedom was a term Don coined to describe his passion for getting his own way completely. There was no "creative freedom" for anyone else - therefore it was a bit of an ironic term. "My freedom is your slavery" may have been a better phrase.

Tom Mix's Cabin

The old Tom Mix cabin was just down the street from the house on Amor Rd. that the Magic Band had lived in when we recorded *Safe As Milk*. I had been there one time earlier, with some of the people from Buddah Records during Safe As Milk - Bob Krasnow and Richard Perry, if I remember. The only thing I remember is a lot of businessmen there with women who were not their wives, and that someone had "popped an amy". "Amy" was amyl-nitrate - later called poppers. Somebody popped one of these capsules and put it on a handkerchief and then we all breathed the fumes from the handkerchief. The result of this was a very powerful dizzying, numbing effect and a lot of giggling from the ladies. It only lasted moments, but I remember Alex saying he used to do this on roller coaster rides. Amy was a roller coaster ride in herself, and this was the first and the last time I ever tried it.

I also remember the cabin being occupied by a group of artists headed by someone called Vido, or possibly Vito. This is mentioned in Pamela Des Barres' book. I didn't know much about these people, and from what I saw at the time and read later, I'm probably better off that I didn't know more.

Are You Don's Brother?

Don introduced me to Frank who, as I recall, was sitting on the couch to the right listening to some music. There were other people there, but I didn't recognize anyone and wasn't introduced to anyone else.

Don said "This is John" and I said "Hi" and Frank immediately looked at me and said "So what … are you Don's brother?" - very sarcastically. And, puzzled I said, "No." I must have looked genuinely puzzled, as indeed I was. "Why would he ask me this when he knew completely well that Don was an only child?" I thought to myself. These guys have been friends since childhood, and Don is an only child. I guess it was because I unconsciously acted like Don, though I wasn't aware of this.

Jerry Handley: He took quite a shot at you.
John French: Yeah, and it was the first thing he said and there were (other) people in the room - really made me feel weird, and I didn't say anything the rest of the night because I was so uncomfortable.

It was only later that I understood - when I saw myself on some footage - that I had actually started taking on some of Don's mannerisms. I was told later that I have done this quite often with other people I am around for any period of time. However, at that particular moment in the log cabin all I knew to do was say, "Uh, no." When this subject was mentioned to Bill Harkleroad he suggested that Van Vliet was so insecure in himself that he tried to make us all into images of himself as a way of seeking approval.

Gail Zappa came in at one point. I don't believe we exchanged any words. She brought Frank some food. Don later mentioned that Frank ate every two hours.

It was pretty impressive to be in the room with this living icon of rock. I had a great deal of respect for Frank's work, and Alex had mentioned him quite often and always seemed to have something good to say about him. He also warned me never to speak to Don of our conversations concerning Frank. Simultaneously, I also felt like a real schmuck because of Zappa's comment to me.

Frank was very businesslike. He was smart. No free drum sets. No money out front. No hype. He wanted to see what Don had in mind before he put his money on the table. Frank was very conservative as a businessman. He had worked hard to get where he was and it didn't seem he was about to give Don a free ride. Because of the problems Don was having with drugs, anxiety, and staying on the stage during a show, I was wondering just how much Zappa was willing to actually invest in Don.

I noticed that Zappa called Van Vliet "Donny," which I first thought was a condescending term. However, I later realized that Donny was what Frank had always called Don. They were childhood friends, and the name had stuck. I perceived that Frank had a very warm feeling for his friend Donny.

Donny's Friend

The entire Magic Band went to Frank's within a day or two. Of course, when I say, "the entire band" I am not quite sure who was in the band at the time. I am absolutely sure that Jerry, Jeff and I were there, along with Don. However, this was almost certainly prior to Harkleroad's inclusion in the group, but I don't recall Snouffer's presence at this meeting. I remember Frank shaking hands with each of us in a very businesslike manner and wondering to myself if he was serious or just putting us on. It was hard for me at first to look at this guy with what I viewed as a Groucho Marx mustache and think that he could ever be serious about anything.

However, his conversation immediately revealed how intelligent and thoughtful he was. Unlike Don, Frank was very socially open. He surrounded himself with people and made his life an open book, whereas Don seemed very secretive and afraid to open up to people and seldom really seemed to be himself in group situations. He always seemed hesitant; wanting to re-think everything. His reactions were, more often than not, composed of things he had previously written down.

Zappa said that no one needed to go to college to get a musical education. All the education anyone could possibly need was available at the local record shop. He then played several records, the only one of which I remember was Procol Harum's *Whiter Shade of Pale*. He would play a contemporary piece of music and then sit and talk about his reaction to the piece and ask for our feedback. He seemed genuinely interested in what even I thought - which took me a bit by surprise. I basically said nothing during the meeting, or as little as possible, still being a little gun-shy over the "Don's brother" remark.

However the contrast between Zappa and Don was obvious to me right away. The feeling I got from Zappa was that he was a reasonable man, far more reasonable than Don. He seemed to possess a great command and yet he was not at all affected in his mannerisms, but seemed relaxed with who he was. Frank was a shrewd businessman who seemed to have learned the ropes and pitfalls, while Don was still quite naïve in this area. Zappa was not a bit ashamed to admit that he listened to all the popular groups, while Don, even while listening secretly, seemed more prone to admit only to listening to jazz. To sum it up: Don seemed to fear what others thought of him while Zappa seemed totally confident in being exactly who he was. This immediately gained my respect.

Frank talked with us for a while at this meeting, which wasn't business, but mostly just a "bring the boys over so I can meet them" session. One thing that resulted from this meeting for me is that I came to believe that this man was a no-nonsense type person and a hard-worker. Ever since the return from Europe, I had been considering leaving the band, because I felt that there was just too much nonsense - from Don certainly, with his ravings and drug problems - but also from the business people. The big difference I saw here was that Frank wasn't a con man, which made me feel I could trust him to do what he said he would do. The second thing was that I could see that he was not at all intimidated by Don, but at the same time held a unique and proper respect for him. It was a good balance that allowed Don freedom to express himself artistically, yet put reasonable parameters and expectations upon him.

Frank was also an accomplished musician and producer (at least to my knowledge) and would understand the needs of the musicians in the band and also recognize the difficulties we had dealing with Don's unorthodox approach to music and his often unreasonable manner of composing.

Motorhead

Jim "Motorhead" Sherwood used to frequent the clubs that Frank would play and was really impressed with the progress FZ had made as a guitarist. Years later, jazz keyboardist George Duke would state that Frank was highly underestimated as a guitarist. Motorhead heard Frank playing Wes Montgomery style. He remembers High School days of going to Frank's house and seeing him sitting out on the lawn playing for hours on a little Mexican guitar his uncle had given him. His dedication to music amazed Sherwood.

Motorhead spent a lot of time repairing the heater in the basement of the log cabin after Frank and Gail moved in. He found a gas shut-off valve with a swastika engraved on the handle. He traced it back and found that Germans had owned the factory that made many of the metal castings for heaters pre-World War II. This is where the piece originated. He wound up putting this piece on his Harley-Davidson motorcycle – swastikas and Nazi helmets being very popular with bikers.

The feeling I got that day, and still get to this day when I think about meeting Jim and possibly Jimmy Carl Black at the log cabin was that these guys were like high school buddies, and I felt immediately comfortable around them - at least as comfortable as I would allow myself to feel. I could be myself, though out of practice, and there was no sharp criticism of my actions. I thought maybe Frank's presence would ease some of the discomfort Jeff and I were feeling around Don.

So it was that I decided to stay and give it a try. I felt that of all the people I had met in the business, Zappa was probably the only one who had a reasonable perspective from which to deal with Van Vliet. Perhaps he could bring Don's vision to fruition with some expediency and without the inclusion of a major disaster.

Black Magic

Many times, Don had mentioned to me that he and Zappa were both deeply involved in Black Magic, so I asked Sherwood about this. He seemed to think that this is something Frank would not be interested in at all.

Jim Sherwood: He wasn't that type of person. Frank was strictly a businessman.

Don had mentioned in conversation several times that Frank and he had more than one strange experience during this time. One time they were driving somewhere a car could not possibly have gotten on travelling in the wrong direction and it nearly caused a head-on collision.

Jim Sherwood: I think that was Don's acid problem. I'll tell you exactly what that story was (about). Frank had a yellow station wagon he used to drive. He and a woman were driving back from somewhere one night. The woman was supposedly a witch. She told him that she was a witch. Frank didn't really care. He said they were driving back home and she reached up and was rubbing the back of his neck, and he didn't realize that he was driving in the wrong lane going down the highway and all of a sudden a car was coming right at him. He said somehow they just "got out of it." That's probably where Don's little fantasy came in.

Another story I heard at least twice was that Frank and Don turned onto a secluded street and saw a "witch" making twenty foot "hops" down the sidewalk. There was also the episode where a friend had seen a disembodied hand in his house, which terrorized the fellow by following him from room to room and attempting to strangle him. Being eighteen, I ate this stuff up, and being naïve, I believed some of it. Though the latter story was a bit hard even for me to believe.

Don Aldridge recalled a strange incident that occurred in 1966 while standing in front of Van Vliet's mother's house with Don:

Don Aldridge: ...a car was driving up the street. Don said something to the effect – "He's lost," or " he's cooked," or "he can't get out of this." I'm laughing, kind of snickering about it. Then, he says, "I'm going to turn him around again." And the guy turns around again at the end of the street - and then went on I guess ten, or eleven times. This guy just going from one end of the block to the other, driving slowly, turning around, coming back. And then he said, "Now, I'm going to let him go, and the guy drove away." Coincidence? I don't know.

John French: Part of the reason I stayed in the band as long as I did was because I was trying to figure out how he was able to get me and my friends to do the things that we did, and how he turned us so violently against each other, to where we almost hated each other when we were in that house. Something that I would say was "in the supernatural realm" that was causing the problems that were going on.

DA: Yeah, of course, they're all going to say we're nuts...

JF: So what?

DA: ...I began to take it so seriously that I just wanted away from it.

Peeping Don

Another story Don used to tell me was about the girl that lived next door to his family home undressing at her window so that he could watch her. He said she pretended that he wasn't watching, but "she knew I was watching, man." I also was led to believe that he dated her for a while. Don was always describing himself as a voyeur.

Jim Sherwood: ...he'd say, "Yeah, I got this neighbor girl next door and she's got great little nipples and great tits," and all this stuff. He'd peep through the window at her. That's basically what I know about it.

John French: One person said that he thought that Don was actually pretty much in love with this girl, that he actually did date her for a while and that her parents broke off the relationship.

JS: Yeah, as far as I know, I think he did date her for a while. Or, at least, had a girlfriend-boyfriend relationship with her. I don't know what happened.

Another slightly amusing story he would tell the band is that he had a girlfriend (perhaps the same one) whom he would take out into the middle of the desert at night in his Oldsmobile and she would take off all her clothes and run around in the dark naked. He said something to the effect of "after a while, I remembered to bring a flashlight." One night, she supposedly had a guy visiting her home who was interested in her. Apparently, he had dressed up in his best suit and tie. Don showed up, and, being familiar with the house, snatched up some scissors concealed in her mother's sewing kit. At the opportune moment he cut off the poor suitor's tie, sending him scurrying home due to a costume malfunction.

Re-Visiting The Origin Of The Name "Captain Beefheart"

Jim Sherwood shed a little more light on the subject of the relationship between Frank Zappa and Don Van Vliet. One of the things Frank immensely enjoyed about Don was his sense of humor. Magic Band guitarist and founder Alex Snouffer also spoke about Don's great sense of humor and I had seen glimpses of this many times myself, though sometimes as the brunt of the joke.

I recall some lady telling Don that he had "really great skin" and his reply to her was "my secret is that I don't use soap." He was completely straight-faced when he said this, and the woman completely accepted his answer though it was a line straight out of a television commercial for a soap called "Camay" - which claimed not to be soap at all. Often, if he had a television on, he would mute the volume and insert his own dialogue, having everyone in the room in hysterics because of his quick wit and twisted humor.

John French: That's probably why Frank enjoyed being around him too. Frank loved anybody who had a great sense of humor.
Jim Sherwood: He was really funny ...creative too. It was off-the-wall.

I had asked Jim Sherwood about his slant on the name "Captain Beefheart" and how it had come into being. He recalled Frank writing a screenplay called *"Captain Beefheart vs. the Grunt People"* being set in a place called "Happy Valley."

Jim Sherwood: Frank wanted Don to play the part of Captain Beefheart. He would talk to these imaginary kids in his room. Then, his mother would come in and say, "Don, this room smells terrible! It smells like a camel's been smoking peanut butter in here." He'd say, shut-up Sue and go get me a Pepsi!"
John French: ...I always had the idea that the Grunt People had something to do with Don's relationship with his parent's and how he treated them.
JS: I'm not really sure about that, because I never really got Frank's feelings about it. ...The Grunt People were just another race of people on a different planet.

Though I have never read the script, I think that the fact that Captain Beefheart's mother's name is "Sue" and the Captain yelled the same thing at her as Don yelled at his mother, Sue, it is either a miraculous coincidence or Frank gleaned this characteristic of Don's after a visit to la casa Vliet. As Vic Mortensen, the Magic Band's first official drummer had pointed out, Frank was fascinated with Don's relationship with his parents.

Lover Not A Fighter

Jim also seemed to have a different take on Don's "badass" image as portrayed by the younger Denny Walley, who mentioned Don beating up "wingnuts" (air force servicemen) in Mojave:

John French: Did you ever hear stories about Don beating up "Wingnuts" in Mojave – Air Force Guys?
Jim Sherwood: I'll tell you, I don't think Don could fight his way out of a bag.
JF: Really?
JS: He was not a fighter. Don was definitely not a fighter. That was the story that went around. Don was a totally different kind of guy than that. Don was really creative and that, but anytime something would happen that would stress Don out, he would get sick. He could actually make himself break out in a rash. He used to get mad at somebody - then, he would just break out in a rash. (He'd say) "I'm sick. I can't do "this" or I can't do "that." It was really weird. I was kind of amazed at what Don could do. As a fighter? I don't think so. I've never seen him do anything.

Don constantly portrayed himself as a fighter, who had to fight for his survival in Mojave while being chased by servicemen. I think this was probably used as an intimidation factor, and it worked quite well on me. No musician wants to damage his hands in a fight, so I steered clear when Don would threaten me and caved in more than once to his threats.

Drop Out Boogie
Jim confirmed that Don had dropped out of high school to take over the bread route for his father, who had a heart attack.

John French: Do you remember Don graduating from high school?
Jim Sherwood: I don't think so. I think Don - because his Dad died and all that - actually left school.

Ian Underwood
Back at the Cabin, Ian Underwood arrived late afternoon after we had spent a couple of really enjoyable hours with Frank. Ian appeared to be Frank's assistant/pianist (I actually didn't immediately recognize him from the drag photo on the album, nor was I one to read the names on album jackets).

Frank excused himself immediately and instructed Ian as to what to play by handing him a large ream of sheet music covered with Frank's very recognizable transcriptions. Frank was apparently unable to play piano, so Ian would play the ideas so Frank could hear if he had written what he had indeed meant to write. I watched this process for a few moments and was interested in the fact that Frank was responsible enough for his compositions to have learned theory and was able to write music fluently. Unlike Don, he didn't seem nearly as prone to delegating any phase of the music process to others. Unlike Don, Frank didn't seem to be afraid that anyone would steal his ideas, and openly worked on his music in front of all of us.

Another thing I appreciated about Frank is that he seemed to have a schedule for his day. He had time to meet and socialize with us, but after Ian arrived, it was clear that he was now scheduled for working on music with Ian.

I recall us staying around for a while and I wandered out to a garage or shop, which seemed to be on the northeast end of the house, which actually faced Laurel Canyon Boulevard.

Jim Sherwood was in this room working on something mechanical; I learned later that this was probably where he got the name Motorhead. We introduced ourselves. I forget who else was there, it could have been another of the Mothers, I can't recall. Motorhead was very friendly and spoke about how full of treasures this old log cabin was, and how he had found a complete set of lock-picking tools. He then pulled what looked a bit like a leather wallet out of his hip pocket and opened it up to display the entire set of tools, each in their own little sown pocket.

The Situation Continues

Jeff and I had been paid nearly nothing for months. We had recorded two albums, gone on two promotional tours, and we were still having to share a house with Don, who seem to begrudge us even this. I'm sure that neither Jerry nor Alex had been paid for anything more than the small amounts that trickled through from the Avalon Ballroom shows, though I don't recall even getting paid for these. I do believe I once received a check for $200 in the mail from the Cheetah engagement for which I was later penalized by the Musicians' Union for receiving.

Obviously, I was not a "where's mine" kind of person, and neither was Jeff. Both of us seemed to have bought into the image Don was painting for us of ourselves - that we were useless, worthless, and were lucky to even be in the group at all. I'm not sure if it was the drugs, the constant belittling statements, having nothing, or the combination of the three, but we both seemed to have lost all vision of self-worth.

I strongly believe that this is exactly the way Van Vliet wanted us to feel and respond. His power of control over us was based, as far as I can now discern, upon not so much his intimidation, though that was indeed a factor, but his ability to keep us centered on the illusion that we were worthless. I must admit, he did a really good job of it, and it was decades before I was able to shake off this image of myself, remnants of which remain to this day.

My behavior at that time was so controlled by this self-image that I allowed myself to be led into such a downward spiral that it kept me in a state of almost constant depression. Jeff and I, during this period of time, were both speaking to each other a little more honestly about our feelings, but at the same time there were certain boundaries, already strongly in place, which neither of us would cross. The mental power of our leader to control and manipulate us, even in his absence, was overwhelming.

Nonetheless, there was a small room in my mind where I could go. I did this often when meditating, which was mostly for me just 30 minutes of guaranteed peace, when I could sit in the yard in a chair and not be disturbed or interrupted. In this sanctuary in my mind, I was absolutely sure that I was being duped, that I deserved better, that this man I was working for was a liar, cheat, thief, and con-man. I was certain that he needed us - not the other way around. He would constantly tell Jeff and I that we were nothing without him, yet it was evident that he was more of a co-dependent than either Jeff or me, who had both made more money as High School students than we had playing with Captain Beefheart.

All the events, when laid out logically in my mind, led me to the same conclusion, but there was little outward reinforcement of this line of thought. Don's public behavior, in stark contract to his private behavior, had earned him critical acclaim as a guiding genius. His voice was exceptional, and this earned him even more accolades. His larger-than-life public persona and his natural charm reinforced publicly the exact opposite of what I had seen in private. He was hailed in the press as the guiding genius, and most of the attention seemed to center upon him.

Can a man both be publicly hailed as a genius and at the same time be evil? Perhaps...

After the meeting with Zappa, who I perceived as being a man completely different than the man portrayed in Don's ravings, I was convinced more than ever, in that little corner of my mind, that Don was a man not to be trusted and that his behavior had absolutely no basis in any ethical foundation.

But I was nearly as much drawn into the public persona of Captain Beefheart as the rest of the outside world. I was also struggling with my own values - my Christian faith, basic moral values and precepts that I had embraced, along with logical reasoning - that seemed constantly on a collision course with Don's decisions and behavior. There was a part of me saying, "If the world is embracing this man, then perhaps I need to be more like him, because my ways are getting me nowhere, and his seem to be bringing him profit."

So my mind was divided against itself, and as the old saying goes, a house divided against its self cannot stand. As long as there was a doubt in my mind about my own direction, and there were many doubts in my mind, then I could not possibly take any sort of decisive action. So it was that I remained, for some time to come, in this state of mental servitude to Captain Beefheart.

There was no doubt in my mind that Don was brilliant - perhaps a genius. But my observation was that this genius certainly seemed to need a great deal of assistance. His lyrics definitely were impressive (though many I actually later found out were actually Bermann's), and his musical ideas unique - fragmented though they were. I couldn't help but wonder at the fact that, had he given us - his band and assistants - the credit we deserved, he would still have stood out as a larger-than-life figure and would have simplified and solidified his relationship with band and businessmen alike in a way that would have been to his advantage.

Yet constantly he chose the low road - the route of deception, brute force, manipulation, and perhaps downright thievery - which created more difficulties and obstacles, caused more problems, took more time, wasted more money, and alienated those closest to him.

This situation in which Jeff and I, along with Laurie, found ourselves was increasingly falling into the definition of the word "cult." And, as I was about to find out, it would become more and more cult-like as time went on. Our wills were slowly being devoured, toyed with, and altered. We were slowly and methodically, whether consciously or unconsciously, being isolated more and more from true reality and indoctrinated more and more into The Captain's "reality."

The main force against us, in my mind, was the public adoration of Don. To complicate things even further, to whom could we turn for counselling? Our parents? Who could actually be open-minded enough to comprehend the total effect of our experiences and give us viable feedback?

My instincts told me that Don's problems with the music industry were not so much due to the industry's shortcomings as to Don himself. As Alex stated earlier:

Alex Snouffer: The only thing that was holding Don back was Don. He can lay blame anywhere he wants but it's him, it was him, always was. Nobody, I didn't see one person ... and it didn't matter which personnel were in which band, I never saw anyone holding him back. I mean, he can make all the excuses he wants, but that's all they are; excuses.

The House On The Hill

We had earlier noticed that just up at the end of Golondrina Drive was a house on Ensenada, the cross street. It was bigger than the cottage and had always had a certain mystique about it. Though it looked two-story from the front, it was actually a split-level house, with a balcony in the front, containing many rows of windows. Don came in very excited one day and said that the house was for rent and that we may be moving into it.

Jeff and I were also excited, because this was finally a place where we might be afforded a little privacy. There was an upstairs bedroom and a downstairs bedroom with two separate baths. All the other rooms were upstairs, and the living room was where we could rehearse.

Jeff and I walked out into the middle of Golondrina and gazed up at the house on Ensenada Drive. After all the disappointments we had faced in the past several months, and the lousy living conditions, we both had an unspoken vision of hope.

Little did we know, things were to get worse.

Much worse indeed ...

CHAPTER TWENTY:
SWIMMING UPSTREAM

*Alternate shot from the Strictly Personal session early 1968.
courtesy of Guy Webster.*

"...Years have gone by and memories tend to get altered in that amount of time. That's a normal thing, to have dates and times and things...you remember what you remember from your perspective. Although you may have the same basic picture, the details can vary. So what you do, you get everybody's story, and you come up with the compromise and now hopefully you will get something that is a little more accurate instead of just one person's point of view." – Doug Moon –

The "Trout House"

As Jeff Cotton and I looked up at the house on the hill, we had hoped that this was a sign of better things to come. Not so long ago, we had lived in the converted chicken coop in Tarzana. We then moved into the pleasant but cramped cottage on Golondrina Street in a sleepy neighborhood in Woodland Hills. Now, we were moving into a split-level house one block up the road. The house, though a bit run down, had a certain "air" to it. It was from an earlier simpler time and had probably been owned originally by people who left when the neighborhood became too crowded. Jeff and I joked with Don that the many windows on the upper story reminded us of the airship in *"Master Of The World"* - a movie starring Vincent Price that was based on the Jules Verne novel.

We never really saw anyone there at the house, though occasionally at night the upstairs windows would be lit up as though the house were peering down at us expectantly or perhaps calling to us. It seemed almost as though this framework contained a soul. Jeff and I had expectations of getting out of the tiny crowded cottage and having a bit more personal space had lifted our spirits.

Don soon signed a lease and moving day arrived. We carried most everything up the road. I remember that Don had a king-sized bed, and the floppy mattress was almost impossible to carry. Jeff and I not only had to carry this mattress up the street, but up a very steep driveway, down a narrow walkway and into the upstairs bedroom. Don's cousin Victor walked along beside us (I think everyone in the family had a severe allergic reaction to anything actually considered "physical labor") taunting us with phrases like "onward young lads," and "it's like watching a Laurel and Hardy movie" as we staggered with our serpentine load. I ended the day by shampooing all the carpeting in the empty cottage so that we could collect out deposit, and, exhausted, staggered up the hill in the early hours of the morning to collapse into deep sleep on my mattress on the floor, but not before reviewing my plight and wondering about the future.

Don had been a different person on the road. He was, for the most part, more enjoyable. The lack of a territory that he could easily claim forced him to open up a bit more and contain his ego. The public scrutiny forced him into his best behavior. I observed, however, that he didn't seem to fare well on the road physically. The lack of energy, though making him a bit more complacent and easy-going, drained him of his creative force and that took some getting used to.

Touring is not easy. It is a very difficult way of life. Living out of a suitcase, and not having those creature comforts we take for granted at home can make life far more complicated. Even the simplest things; losing a toothbrush, getting your laundry done, or having a decent cup of coffee, can be exhausting and time-consuming. For my part, the good outweighed the bad. I could walk out of my hotel room and walk to any of several cafes, sit alone or with a band mate and have a meal in peace. No one saying "is that all you do... eat?" I was in heaven. I felt independent; I was my own man. Well, as much of a man as a nineteen-year-old could be.

But all good things eventually come to an end. The tour had ended disastrously. We had been left in England with nothing but the money in our pockets. Bob Krasnow had allegedly confiscated all our tour earnings. We had cancelled two performances in Holland -- one at the famed Paradiso -- and flown home early and penniless, leaving behind a very large unpaid hotel bill. Don, ill from the road, was a terror to be around, and Jeff and I were again trapped in that tiny cottage with he and Laurie. His tolerance for us seemed even less in the wake of his maladies and the circumstances of the business, and so the contrast from the tour was an awakening for both of us.

Little did Jeff and I know how much our life was now going to again change. We were aware of the falling out with Krasnow, and the fact that Don was seeking a new outlet for his music. What we didn't realize was how drastic a change we were in for in just about every respect.

Jeff and I spoke a bit about Don's almost Jekyll/Hyde personality, in which he exhibited a very charming public personna, but privately could make life very difficult. It was as if Don Van Vliet and Captain Beefheart were both encased within one body but had completely different traits. I spoke to Doug Moon about this in his interview:

Don Van Vliet / Captain Beefheart

John French: Do you think he started believing that there was a Captain Beefheart, and that he was really two people?
Doug Moon: Oh yeah, definitely.
JF: It was more like he would put it in this file or that and say, "OK, this is Captain Beefheart?
DM: Yeah, ...at first it was like playing a role. Like being an actor and playing a role. It's like when you see William Shatner, who do you think of? Captain Kirk, "here's Captain Kirk!" It's like a famous actor that plays a role so long that they become that person. When they are seen in public, they're referred to as their character rather than their real name, and people think of them as being that character...

It started appearing to me, just vaguely at first, but more as time went by, that there did seem to be a definite change in personality – not just an "I'm on my best behavior" mentality – but an actual marked change in personality between Don Van Vliet, the guy I lived around, and Captain Beefheart, the guy in the public eye. Maybe I was making more out of this than was there, maybe it was, as I wrote earlier, just the scrutiny of the public putting Don on his best behavior.

Alex Leaves

Soon after the move, Alex left the band. I was really sad to see him go. He had been a buffer zone between Don and I and now I felt completely defenceless against Don - as though someone had confiscated the walls to the fort while I was asleep. There had always been conflict between Don and Alex. Alex could barely tolerate Don's complete lack of ability to schedule a rehearsal and stick with it. He would be late showing up, and then want to stay after to create new compositions.

Alex Snouffer: I got tired of the horseshit - Don's, the company's, and the whole music industry's. I had a wife and kid at the time. I had to do something about this. I couldn't even rely on these people to even put a goddamned meal in our mouths. I said, "Fuck you, I'm outta here." Don did something to me one day. I think I went over there and we were supposed to have rehearsal promptly at "whatever o'clock" and he was in bed. That was all it took. I just snapped. I left my equipment and everything. I went home and told Jane. She asked, "Where's your stuff?" I said, "I left it there." Her brother-in-law, Dave, who happened to be a cop, went over and got the stuff out. That was the end of that. They came around and asked, "Are you going to be in this band or not?" I said, "Not! We're through. Subject closed." I got fed up with being broke, so I went out and got a job as a truck driver. When I went and did that, my family life really started bubbling after a while. Unfortunately, it didn't last, but that's just the way things are.

I have a vague recollection of going to Alex's apartment one day, perhaps with Don and Jeff. That must be the scene he's describing here. It was the only time I ever saw the apartment where he lived with his wife Mary Jane. I didn't know her very well, but she was a beautiful woman with fairly simple needs. Having a baby does alter one's perspective on the "starving artist" lifestyle.

Sue Handley and Mary Jane Snouffer had been friends previous to meeting Jerry and Alex. Don always said that he "saw them coming" and "knew what their scheme was" - as though some devious plot had been formulated by these two to carry half his band into domestic slavery.

Jerry and Alex had been close for years, Alex having been Jerry's mentor in the early days. Handley had taken up guitar directly due to seeing Alex playing with the Omens in the late fifties.

Jerry Handley: Well, there was no organization. The key word was organization. That's why Alex left, before then. He saw it. And it wasn't going to get organized, that's what put me over the edge, you know. Alex had left because he gave up on Don ever getting organized and it going in a professional direction. He just gave up on him. We had a big brouhau over that, and Alex left. I think subconsciously when Alex left, I was done with it myself.

Jim Sherwood: Butch Snouffer - he changed it later on to Alex St. Clair. It's not Alex, it never has been Alex, it was always Butch. I used to go to his house all the time. We hung out. We were good buddies for a long time. We were tight pals.
John French: You remember him as a young musician learning how to play?
JS: He was already a guitarist with the Omens. Him and Wally Salazar were the guitar players, Terry (Wimberly) was keyboards...

Don Aldridge: I had a good time with him. If you wanted to party, Alex Snouffer was the guy to party with. They called him Butch. He was a lot of fun. ...One time we were in the desert in my rambler: Don, Doug, Al. We're industriously choking on some serious Mexican marijuana, when I saw a helicopter. I - pointing skyward and holding in a hit - said, "Chopper, man!" of course referring to a possible police surveillance. Alex, from the back seat, holding in his hit, said, "Ain't no [Hell's] Angeles out here man." He spent 20 minutes ribbing me about my paranoia.

Alex had been relatively cooperative with Don in terms of listening to his ideas and trying to formulate them into finished compositions. During the rehearsals at the Chicken Coop in Tarzana, both Alex and Jerry seemed to take a renewed interest in the material being put together for *"It Comes To You In A Plain Brown Wrapper"* and I saw a giant leap forward in both regarding musical growth. There was no need for a Ry Cooder, as everyone pulled his own weight. The music created during that period was the most involved Don ever became in the creative process. Usually, he delegated someone else - Ry Cooder, myself, Bill Harkleroad, etcetera to actually handle the details. During that period, however, Don had been totally immersed in the arrangements as well as creating the parts.

Don Aldridge: I believe, that Alex filled a hole that Don couldn't fill. Don could not control him the way he could a younger guy. He couldn't influence Alex that way, but then again Alex was game. He would say, "I'll do it." I know Alex liked to party. Alex was one of my heroes. If I could have looked like Al Snouffer, been like him, played like him, I would have put my eye out. The guy was like "The Fonz" - he was like the epitome of whatever it is that was happening. He never said, "Hey, I haven't got time for you man, or , "We're too busy being rock guys or being blues guys" or – never like that. I was your personified snot-nosed kid. I wasn't in that league at all, but he made me feel like I was.

So, Alex anachronistically carried with him some of the personae of the fifties, was well-liked, approachable, and had a biting wit of his own. He had accepted Van Vliet's creativity and helped to make it valid, but his tolerance was wearing thin and the pressures on his life were increasing. His history with Van Vliet had been one of conflict.

Doug Moon: I can remember Alex and Don coming real close to having an all-out brawl.

Obviously, there had been tensions with Don in the struggle for leadership. By the time I had arrived, this seemed to have developed into a mutual respect or perhaps a resignation on Alex's part – perhaps a little of both. Van Vliet was not one to go quietly into passivity. Now that Alex had formed the band and developed them into a solid team, Van Vliet was itching to take over the controls and fly the plane in a new direction. Snouffer was open enough to realize his own creative limitations and recognize Van Vliet as a visionary. *Safe As Milk* had been well-received in England, and Alex probably saw this as validation of Don's work. But, he also saw the abuse of power and irresponsible wasting of time, and time was something of short supply in Snouffer's life.

It was hard for me to imagine The Magic Band without its founder - the guy who had supplied the initial impetus and directed the early band. I knew that I would miss him terribly; both in terms of personality and also because of the restraint he imposed upon Don. I couldn't imagine how Don would change now that the restraint was removed.

Junior Madeo

Frank suggested a guy to Don that went way back to their days in the desert. He was known as Junior Madeo and he lived in the Bay Area. Frank flew him down for a few days. Junior stayed with us. It was a totally different atmosphere in the house having him there. Don was, of course, on his best behavior. There were no tantrums and none of the tension that usually existed in the house. Junior was a balding jazz player who sounded a lot like Joe Pass. He had a similar kind of guitar as I recall - a red Gibson 335 - actually very much like the guitar Jerry sold to Ry Cooder.

My impression was that he did not at all fit in to the style of music in looks, personality or style. He was technically really a good player, but it was all rapid-fire scales and flat pick strumming and soloing. He taught Jeff and Jerry a number of exercises and ways to improve their playing and I had the feeling that he probably made part of his living by giving private lessons. He was a very likeable guy, and the time he spent with us was inspiring in some ways and in others, it was just going through the motions of him being there for a few days. I knew he wasn't the guy. He left unceremoniously with a promise of "we'll be in touch."

Don Buys A Piano

Don decided to purchase a piano during this time. I can't remember really understanding any special reason at the time. The main change in his daily habits was that he was going over and seeing Zappa now and again. As I look back now, recalling our first visit to Zappa's, he seemed to be composing a lot of music on the piano. He would transcribe music for the piano on regular manuscript paper (the kind with five lines in a row - called a "staff") and then Ian Underwood would come over at a prescribed time and play it back for him. Perhaps Don was influenced by Frank's techniques and inspired to try his hand at composing on the piano.

The piano was one of those big upright numbers, which was probably made around the turn of the century. It had been "redecorated" during a period of time when American interior decorators seemed to be completely obsessed with mirrors. This piano had mirrors all over the front. Actually, it was convenient for the player, because rather than just staring at blank wood and a wall, one could look up and see the room in reverse behind you.

As I recall the piano movers had to remove the kitchen door from the hinges, bring the piano down the three steps and tilt in on it's side on a large packing blanket, slide it through the opening diagonally in order to miss a counter that was about three feet inside the door and then stand it back up. This was not an easy task at all and the piano cleared the door and counter by a fraction of an inch.

Tape Player Breaks Down

We had an old Ampex two track tape deck from Buddah's office and the same old box of tapes. Don's moments of inspiration would come unexpectedly and he was nearly frantic about getting some record of his inspiration on tape or it would be lost forever. The normal scenario was Don trying to get something recorded before he lost it and me attempting to find a blank spot on used tape. He seldom bought new tape and when he did, it usually was filled within a day. Ninety-percent of these unusable meanderings one would sift through in order to find 10 seconds of "that's it! Don't lose that part!"

If I failed to find a blank spot, or in a moment of thoughtlessness erased something already recorded on a tape, Don's usual response was to lose the part, blame me for ruining the moment, and say over and over for days "I can't believe you did that, man. Disgusted, I pulled the fuse.

John French to Bill Harkleroad: I don't know if you know this or not – but I just got tired of taping Don and him never buying any tape. So, I finally just said, "The tape recorder's broken." …That's how I started writing the stuff down. It contained him, because he couldn't just endlessly rattle off streams of stuff for everybody to do. He had to put a little discipline into it himself.
BH: Right, that's pretty smart.
JF: You know - that whole 8½ hours that he spent.
BH: (Jokingly) - And he knew every note, like Stravinsky knows his scores.

Describing Transcribing

Don really did not know how to play piano, but he was gifted enough to use his ear and come up with little riffs and such. He would never play anything twice, and most of what he did sounded like meandering, but occasionally he would discover something of interest and stay with it a while – at least within the theme. One day as Don sat down at the piano and started jamming, I picked up my music book (in which I had been writing drum patterns) and transcribed a little of what Don was playing. I had little formal training, but I knew from playing the French horn where the notes were – but only on treble clef.

I laid the book on top of the piano and went downstairs to the bathroom to shower. As I walked out with a towel around my waist, Don was standing at the base of the stairs with my music book. "Can you actually play this?" he asked, his eyes blazing with excitement. I told him "I think so, with a little practice." He asked me to demonstrate and I later did. He seemed amazed. "You mean you can write down anything I play?" he asked. I explained to him that anything capable of being played was theoretically capable of being written down. "However," I added, "it is a slow process, and you would have to play each thing several times for me to be able to write it down."

Post Krasnow – Pre TMR – Cooder Fixation

We still needed a guitarist. I had no way of knowing, but during this time, Van Vliet was still hung up on getting Ry Cooder back, and especially after Alex left. It was a dream of which Van Vliet could not rid himself. Don had already burned that bridge by walking off stage at the Mt. Tamalpais Love-In - the warm-up for the Monterey Pop Festival. In retrospect, that was probably the point of no return in terms of the group ever being a commercial success.

Gary Marker: Well, he would call every now and then. (He'd say to me) "Listen, would you like to get together? Would you like to work with this band?" But the whole thing with Don was - He still had this fixation on Ry Cooder. He wanted Ry back in the band again. He figured he could patch up whatever it was, get him back etc. One time, Ry was doing a little date in some small club in Hollywood. Don rolled into town. He said, "Why don't we go see Ry?" He was playing mostly instrumentals and was singing a few vocals - just with bass, drums and a piano player. I have this distant cousin named Randy Newman, and he came in and played a couple of tunes. We went to see Ry in the dressing room and (Don) started haranguing him about the old thing, "Hey man, why don't you let me write some stuff for you? You're playing all these old dead people's music." And Ryland's looking at me, with that one eye, going, "He's on a roll again, isn't he?" When we left, I said, "Can't you lighten up on him? What's the matter with you, are you nuts or something?" - Well, that's kind of a rhetorical question, you know.

If The Zoot Fits...

Jeff and I got together and talked after Madeo flew home, which was in June of 1968. Don was willing to give him a try, but Jeff and I felt that Junior was completely wrong for the band, although we all liked him. It was at this time, in the true tradition that "misery loves company," that Jeff and I cast our votes for Bill Harkleroad as Alex Snouffer's replacement.

Don seemed really open and for once actually listened to us as though we might know something. So it was that Don called Bill on a pay phone and asked him if he would be interested in joining The Magic Band. Apparently, Bill was ecstatic. He told his friends, "I got in Beefheart, man!" according to one friend who had know him at the time. All of nineteen years old, Bill had no idea what he was in for, and shame on us for not telling him.

His book states, "Finally, the call came to go down and audition for Don. I hadn't played the guitar for over six months – just too stoned! So once I got the call for the audition, I threw my guitar into its case and put 20 joints in my socks and a couple hits of acid in my pocket and got a ride with Jerry Handley, the group's bass player, who was also living in Lancaster. So he drove me down to Woodland Hills for the big try-out."[38]

Reading this now, I realize that I must have taken hits on marijuana cigarettes that had been stored in Bill's socks. This could explain a number of health issues I've had over the years, or at least why the burning herb seemed to emanate an exclusive and pungent aroma.

The attitude was completely different with Bill than it was with Junior. Instead of actually listening to Bill's ideas as he had with Junior, it was all image and con from the beginning. Don set an alarm clock which went off precisely as Bill arrived though I seem to recall Don re-setting it several times. This was supposed to impress Bill as to Don's "psychic abilities." The plan seemed to succeed. Bill, Jeff and I were younger, more open-minded (translated "naïve") musicians, and Don's plan was to use this as much to his advantage as possible.

We jammed with Bill and he played quite well, though seemed a little rusty. I had remembered his great abilities as a soloist from long ago, hearing him play with the local groups we all were in during High School. But I felt uneasy. Even though we all had big smiles on our faces at this reunion, all did not seem well.

---

[38] Lunar Notes, Bill Harkleroad, SAF Publishing Ltd., 1998

John French to Bill Harkleroad: You had joined the band that day, right? The first day you came down?

BH: I played in the jam session and everybody went, "Oh wow," he can play great. It was funny, because I hadn't been playing, so I was sort of freaked out, but I knew that you two guys were on my side.

JF: Don introduced you to Frank by taking you to the Log Cabin, right?

BH: Yes, I played the jam session, "OK, you're cool, you're in the band, let's get in the big Jaguar." Victor and Don and I went down to Frank's house, that's how I went down and officially met Frank.

Rock And Roll Circus

Bill was impressed with the log cabin. There were a lot of people at the house and it must have been pretty exciting.

Bill Harkleroad: Oh yeah, it was weird. I remember (Frank) coming down the big stairway that was in the center of everything - like a movie or something ...it was a big day for me because Jagger and the Who and all (were there) - because (Jagger) was putting that Rock And Roll Circus thing together.

The Rock And Roll Circus was a filmed event in which The Rolling Stones, The Who, and several other artists, including Jethro Tull, Taj Mahal, Marianne Faithful, Eric Clapton, Mitch Mitchell, and others performed in a circus-like setting. The event took place on December 11, 1968, but wasn't released for years because apparently The Who upstaged the Rolling Stones at their own event, having just come off the road and being more seasoned.

Frank's Entourage

I'm no expert on Frank Zappa music, but Bill once said to me *"every time I ever went to Frank's house there were thirty people there."* This triggered my early impressions of hearing *Freak Out* and *We're Only In It For The Money*. My impression was that he had a lot of people around and sometimes recorded them just being themselves, and then often wrote songs about the peculiar traits about these people. Sherwood confirmed this.

Jim Sherwood: Frank had the most amazing ability to put all that shit into music. It just amazed me. Like, I told him about living with Ronny and Kenny down in Cucamonga and all of a sudden, here comes, Let's Make The Water Turn Black. ...I'd go tell Frank all these stories and he'd just die laughing. Even after we got into the Mothers, Frank would have all the strange freaked-out people around his place. That's where the "Bizarre" came in, because they were just really bizarre - probably a matchstick shy of being in the loony bin.

Jeff Teaches Bill

Jeff Cotton spent a good deal of time teaching Bill the guitar parts on music that had already been written. I was not aware of this at the time – probably due to my involvement with the piano work Don was giving me. Jeff mentioned this to me in a phone call and I suddenly remembered Jeff and Bill going off alone and working on music that had already been written.

John French to Bill Harkleroad: Even though I was musical director on the keyboard parts on Trout Mask, I know that Jeff had a lot to do with filling you in on what was already written - such as songs like **Veterans Day Poppy, Moonlight On Vermont,** *and* **Sugar And Spikes.**

BH: *Veteran's Day Poppy was written with me (meaning after Bill joined the band). That was the first song that was written with me (in the band), and that's why it had a little more of a "bluesy feel" to it.*

Don used to say to me *"I always have to write those fucking blues parts for Bill."* I never quite understood this, nor did I see any real difference in what he would have Bill play than what he had Jeff play. Usually, he didn't really say who played what anyway, as that was later left up to me. But occasionally, when he wrote employing the old method of whistling, singing, and harp or horn notes combined with verbal instruction, it didn't seem like Bill's parts were more "bluesy" – at least to me.

Red Volvo

Don decided to buy a little red Volvo, but he couldn't talk Sue into giving him the money for it, so he did something very strange: he had me call her. He gave *me* a little sales pitch he had written down and had Jeff Cotton drive me to the Topanga Mall because they had really nice quiet phone booths. I called Sue and spoke to her about ten minutes, caught up on things, and sprung the sales pitch. She immediately sent the money and Don bought the car.

Rosemary's Baby

Don soon sold his Jaguar to Frank. The back seat was a little ripped, so he asked me one day if I could fix it. He had bought some upholsterer's thread and needles. I had mentioned that my father had been an upholsterer, so I guess he thought I had picked up this ability by osmosis. I said I'd try, and took the back seat out of the car. I brought it up to the patio and heard Don saying to the others *"Rosemary's Baby* is out... we've got to see that."

I went in the house a little later and the television was on. "Is this *Rosemary's Baby*" I asked – clueless to the fact that it was a new movie just out playing at the theatres. Suddenly, I found myself embroiled in a huge talk about how I was really selfish wanting to go see *Rosemary's Baby* when the seat needed to be fixed.

Don, Jeff, and Bill came out a little later, as I was stitching up the seat, and left in the Red Volvo to go into Westwood and see the movie. Interestingly enough, the movie I had spied on the TV was Fellini's "8½" - which was the exact amount of hours Don said it took him to write *Trout Mask Replica*. I wasn't sure why I wasn't invited to see the movie, but it certainly made me feel terrible to be left behind to finish up this chore.

Let's Re-Record Strictly Personal One More Time

I was either not aware of this, or I had forgotten:

Bill Harkleroad: *Basically (Jeff) showed me that entire album* (Strictly Personal). *I was learning the whole album, because we were going to re-record it. Jeff showed me the parts. He knew both parts (to* Kandy Korn*).*

If Bill joined in June 1968, then it was most likely four months or more between the time he joined and our first recording session with Frank, which probably happened in late October. Jeff impressed Bill with his knowledge of the music.

Bill Harkleroad: *He was a very sharp guy and he helped me a lot. He was very – I could tell something very paranoid and weird was already going on with him by the time I got in the*

band. But, he knew both parts to the three songs we're talking about, and Beatle Bones And Smokin' Stones.

The revealing statement here is "I could tell something very paranoid and weird was already going on with him…" Jeff, as Bill indicated, knew both parts. I think this goes to show not only the level at which Jeff had engaged himself in Don's music but also the abilities that Jeff already possessed as a player. For Bill, it must have been an unusual setting in which to walk. I remember Bill during this period of time as being very friendly and smiling a lot. He was happy and excited about being in this band, yet he was noticing signs and subtle things that made him a bit uncomfortable.

Jeff As Alex's Replacement
Back to Jeff teaching Bill the parts, Don Aldridge was under the opinion that Jeff Cotton was actually Alex's replacement in Don's mind.

Don Aldridge: I'm going to be ridiculed far and wide for this. I still say, the moment Don got a real good listen to Jeff Cotton, he said, "This guy's going to be in the band." I always felt that Jeff was Don's idea all along. …I don't think he had long term plans for Al Snouffer in that band. Doug was gone and he basically fired Doug, then Jerry came next and whether Jerry left or was fired I have no idea. It's my blatant statement that Jeff Cotton was Alex replacement in the magic band. I still say he was although I realize the chronology doesn't back that up. I saw the look on Don's face when Jeff popped on the scene. I'm telling you - he had it marked, he knew what he was doing, and eventually he put a band together that was the band that he wanted. It was the very best band he ever had too - if you want to talk about the avant-garde thing.

Aldridge does have a point here, and there are certain indications that it may be true. Don could have very well wanted Cotton to replace Alex, but at the same time he may have wanted both in the band for a time so that Jeff could absorb Alex's style and technique firsthand. This would explain the chronology. Jeff was an amazing guitarist, even when I first met him, and the fact that he knew both parts (his and Alex's) leads me to believe that Don may have been telling him privately to learn everything he could from Alex. This was probably also why recordings of each song were so important to Don, as they were the reference for new material that Bill listened to and practiced along with after Jeff would show him the parts.

I recall Bill speaking about *Moonlight On Vermont* that had a more down-home feel before Frank produced it. Bill used to speak of the way the guitars interacted as being like "ducks floating in a lake." This may be where, later on, the name Mallard became the obvious choice for a band name for the 1976 former Magic Band.

Lifestyle Of The Poor And Artistic
During this time, we had very little food in the house. I recall Don coming from the farmer's market with some raw vegetables. Laurie would cook this stuff to the best of her abilities, but nothing ever tasted good to me. Bill had been in a cult just before coming into the band. The owner of the cult had a head shop in Lancaster. I think his name was Fred.

Fred had talked Bill, who was roughly 6'4" and 120 lbs., to go on a diet called "The Mucous-Free Diet" or some similar wording. Poor Bill looked absolutely emaciated when he came into the band. He had been on this diet that required the members to work their way down to eating only one apple a day.

Unfortunately, the economics of this seemed to turn a light on in Don's head. Don had always kind of leaned toward the health food mentality. Now, here was a diet that perhaps would work for the band and save on the food budget besides. Not only would we be cheap to feed, but even less able to defend ourselves in our weakened state.

We had started eating these vegetables as phase one of the plan. Fortunately, somewhere along the line, this plan got lost in the shuffle, but not before we had all been weakened to an extent by the diet. It was during this time that I started realizing that this band was a cult itself. We were more and more cut off from the world. This reality was the only one we experienced daily. The ever-more-controlling Don was constantly talking in paranoid terms about "the establishment" and how we were not a part of it. He also started focusing more and more upon our individual weaknesses.

Jeff And John's "Different Vibe"

Bill hadn't been around Jeff and I for a long time. Actually, I hadn't known Bill that well before he came into the group. He always had played with different groups, and we had met on occasion. He had, however, gotten very close to Jeff when he and Cotton had worked in a band together after I had gone on to fame and fortune with "Beefheart." So, he knew Jeff's personality and was struck by the fact that both of us seemed quite different.

Bill Harkleroad: I was struck with the difference in yours and Jeff's vibe after I was around you for a while. There was a vibe going on that you guys had changed, and I was adjusting to that. I was more awestruck by being in 'the band that I wanted to be in more than anything on planet earth,' so I don't know that I ever perceived things like that. I know you did and you were a lot more level-headed about things like that. I was just in the band and whatever was happening was happening. Now was the time to learn how to play the parts.

Total Absorption

Bill Harkleroad: And that was the beginning of the idea of, "Oh, God, we're going to work this hard? Oh No!"
John French: Yeah, we did work exceedingly and excruciatingly hard.

Bill's observation here was shared by me as well, and I have no idea as to Jeff's thoughts on the matter, but I feel like we worked unusually hard and for very long hours each day. The music projects were totally absorbing all of our time, to the point we neglected bathing and eating regularly. It seemed sometimes I awakened already seated at the piano, pencil held loosely between my lips, and poised to prove to everyone that I was completely and insanely dedicated to this project.

Bill's Impression Of Jerry

John French: Since Jerry was the first bass player when you got in the group, what was your impression of his dedication to the music? Did he seem pretty serious?
Bill Harkleroad: Actually, yes. He seemed like a very nice guy. (emphatically) VERY nice guy.
JF: That's the impression I got even when I talked to him recently. Great guy.
BH: He was nice to me, supportive to me – this hippy kid coming out of this LSD cult – jumping in his car, going down there. He seemed like he wanted to work, like it was a serious business. I got the feeling that maybe he was a bit frustrated with things not happening. But you were in the band, so you would know about that. That's just the feeling I got from him.

365

JF: I asked him, "What was your real reason for leaving?" and he said, "Well, I was having a nervous breakdown. Do you remember him being really worried and tense and upset?
BH: He didn't show it. It was tough for me to know, John.

Jerry did seem quite determined to rehearse and although he'd lost his best buddy in the band and was living in adverse circumstances, he would still show up for rehearsal and go over material everyday.

"Maharishi Guys"

Bill Harkleroad: When I came in the band, you guys were "Maharishi Guys." I came down there with a pocketful of joints and some acid. He (Jerry) took acid, I don't know if you did...
John French: I don't think I did.
BH: Don did, Jerry did, and I did.
JF: Did you guys go up to some place called, "Fountain of the World?"
BH: Oh yeah. Went there two or three times. One day we went up there and laughed at their little talent show. I think Victor was part of that.
JF: I think I was dating that girl Beverly at the time. I was much more interested in hanging out with a girl.
BH: Yeah, I don't blame you. As a matter of fact, yeah, that was Beverly.
JF: It was a rare commodity in those days, you know, to actually have a date with a female who was interested...

In Remembrance Of Beverly

Since her name came up, it might be fair to mention Beverly and talk about her for a minute. Her full name was Beverly Eckert. She was a friend of Pamela Des Barres (author of that intriguing groupie dreambook: *I'm With the Band*) who has probably become more famous sleeping with musicians than I ever will become for working 14 hours a day as a musician. Beverly was known by everyone as "Beautiful Beverly" and she was just that: beautiful. Heaven knows what she saw in me, but she would occasionally come around and save me from the tedious monotony of Don's self-infatuation. We went to see a couple of movies together during the *Trout Mask* rehearsals.

Before that, she once invited me to a séance, having been intrigued by the occult. I was uncomfortable with the idea, and so turned her down, and believe me, it was hard to say "no" to such a beautiful woman.

I didn't know much about her personal life except that Don was constantly on my case to quit seeing her. He told me she was trouble and was a big methadrine freak. According to Don, she was shooting meth and I would wind up at some hospital, sobbing over her dead body.

Beverly, on the other hand, kept telling me that she wasn't doing that and offered to take off all her clothes and allow me to inspect her entire body for needle marks. I was so shy that I blushed when she said this and thus never made the inspection she offered - further proof that this band had made me completely insane.

Don Meets Manson

I didn't want to go to the The Fountain of the World mainly because of a gut instinct that something wasn't right at the place.

Bill Harkleroad: Well, it was a creepy place, that's where Manson was. Don met Manson, right?

John French: Oh, Don met him?
BH: Yeah! Charles Manson showed him his bus!

This probably pre-dates the Manson murders about one year. Maybe this is why I had a strong premonition not to go up there.
John French: So - did you meet Manson?
Bill Harkleroad: I was there but I didn't meet him, I saw him and Don and the bus thing happen. I was just kind of standing around. I wasn't sure who it was and didn't know anything about it until - obviously later when the big stories hit. Then I recognized that was the person.
JF: Wow, one person compared Don on a lesser level to Manson, one of the people I talked to recently.
BH: Well (laughs), I did in the book (Lunar Notes).
JF: When that thing happened, people were saying, "Boy, I can't believe that this could happen." And I'm sitting there thinking, "I can!"
BH: Me too.
JF: You know, where somebody can have that much power over you... But that's for a later question.

I remember distinctly not wanting to go to the Fountain of the World, which I sometimes confused with the Spahn Ranch because of the later association of Charles Manson with both locations. After doing some research, I find that the Fountain of the World was located in Simi Valley, whereas the Spahn Ranch (later home of those lovable Manson followers) was located nearby in Chatsworth, California, at the north end of the San Fernando Valley.

The Fountain of the World aka WKFL (surprisingly, not a radio station, but short for "Wisdom, Knowledge, Faith, Love) was founded in 1941 by Krishna Venta (real name Francis Herman Pencovic), who had formerly led a convoy of rocket ships to earth following the destruction of his home planet, Neophrates. I believe they landed on Mount Everest in 1932 - though Sir Edmund Hillary never mentioned seeing any of the rockets. Mr. Venta claimed to be 244,000 years old. Of course, I am highly suspicious of all octogenarians who round their age off to the nearest thousand, but then again I used to be so naïve that I thought octogenarians were people who ate nothing but octopus.[39]

Pencovic, after a messy divorce which included child support payments, founded the new religion presumably because he thought he would have a "religious exemption" from the support payments – or was it to seek universal wisdom? The exemption idea didn't work, in case any of you readers are considering a similar scheme. The court eventually ruled against him in 1955 2 apparently deciding that God probably would like people to take care of their offspring.

Considering a different approach to meet those support payments, and after sending a threatening note to President Roosevelt, he committed a series of crimes including burglary and larceny under the name Frank Jensen (who was only 5,000 years old) and for this spent some time in a mental institution. In 1948, Venta pronounced himself the Messiah with the words "I may as well say it, I'm the Christ. I am the new Messiah." All the followers wore robes and went barefoot, and the males had long hair and beards. All who joined this Messiah Complex had to donate all their worldly possessions to the group.

They then started an avant-garde rock group known as...wait, I'm getting my cults confused here. Pencovic, who claimed he would never die, did just that in a suicide bombing by two of his former followers on December 10, 1958. After failing to resurrect, his followers dwindled down to nearly nothing. I have to give credit where credit is due, however. The followers, during the height

---

[39] Pencovic vs Pencovic, 45 cal. 2d 97,287 P.2d 501

of their popularity, contributed to helping the homeless, fighting wildfires, and administering aid to victims of the crash of Standard Airline's Flight 897R which crashed into the Simi Hills back in their heyday. You have to remember though, that people who can be convinced by someone that he is 240,000 years old and led a convoy of rockets to earth can be talked into anything. But, I had a great deal of fun writing about them.

I can't explain it exactly, but there was a feeling inside me that The Fountain of the World was the worst place in the world - not realizing that perhaps I was living in the worst place in the world. I had arranged to go out with Beverly that evening. Don was really upset with me for not doing what he wanted, as it was supposed to be some kind of "band bonding party" but I stood up to him and refused to go.

I did stop seeing Beverly soon after this. She did, in fact, die not that long afterwards. Undisclosed sources tell me that she was not a meth freak, but a heroin addict who was obsessed with death, collected stuffed frogs, and painted the inside walls of her apartment a dark grey. I was both sad to hear the news and really angry that Don was right. I also wonder why a girl like that was attracted to me.

In retrospect, I suppose it would have been much better for me had I gone to meet Charles Manson at a place founded by a guy who claimed to be 240,000 years old. I would have probably felt right at home.

CHAPTER TWENTY ONE:
PURGING THE MAGIC

Jerry's Struggle With His Family

It comes as no surprise that Jerry Handley and his wife were having problems because of the financial woes. More than once, Sue came over to the house to confront Don with the problems Jerry was going through because of the band. Jerry was having a harder time relating to the situation in the band because the five of us were now living under one roof while he remained the outsider. For several months, he would show up each day to rehearse. We were rehearsing *Veterans Day Poppy* and *Moonlight On Vermont* plus the material we were re-recording from *Strictly Personal*. So we would go over a few of them each day. Don wanted us to be able to play any tune through without vocals, supposedly to help us improve our memories. Ironically, Don should have been more concerned with his own memory, as he was the guy who always forgot his lyrics on stage. Also, there was absolutely no discussion at all about performing anywhere.

Perhaps Sue was the only sane one among us. I recall Jerry beginning to have an extreme nervous condition and to be under a lot of stress. At the time, being nineteen and therefore clueless, I was a little disappointed with the fact that Jerry was married to begin with, feeling that he needed to be "free." I had done a lot of babysitting and diaper changing of nieces and nephews, and so had no interest in babies.

Don started criticizing Jerry more and more. He pointed to a string and fret on his bass one day and asked, "What note is that?" Although Don did not have a clue what note it was, he knew that Jerry didn't know off the top of his head and it would take him a moment to answer. "How in the fuck can you call yourself a bass-player when you don't even know where any of the fucking notes are?" he screamed at Jerry. I might point out that Don couldn't have found middle C on the piano had his life depended upon it.

So Jerry, taking this in stride, sat down and made a chart and learned where every note was on the bass. But this didn't seem enough for Don. For a while, everything Jerry did was turned around to make him look bad. This was obviously because Jerry's wife had stood up to Don and told him off and Don was now seeking revenge on Jerry. It was obvious after a time that he was purposely antagonizing Jerry so that Handley would leave the group.

Bill On "Beefheart Guitar"

John French: Had you done much fingerpicking before you got in the band
Bill Harkleroad: I had been fingerpicking before, playing slide guitar, and was learning Ry Cooder licks and I had learned all the parts that were on **Safe As Milk***. But, I was immediately shown the "Delta Rhythm." (Sings) – that six against four thing.* (Note: probably the best example of what Bill is referring to is the second section of *"On Tomorrow"* where the entire group goes into four / four time together and Don is singing "We won't have to talk" etc.). ***Then, the metal fingerpicks.***
JF: What was your technique before?
BH: Yeah, just plain fingers - with a pick.
JF: With a flat pick? So, you were using a flat pick between thumb and index and then the other three for..
BH: Other two.
JF: Other two, okay. So was it hard to get used to using the finger picks?
BH: Yeah, it was terrible.
JF: Yeah, I hated those metal finger picks. I tried using metal finger picks and I thought, "God, how do these guys do it?"
BH: I'd chew those things on there and they just made this bloody mess and finally after my fingers got callouses, they were almost like Snap-On tools, like a socket wrench? They'd go "click! - because of the callous."

Bill's method of learning made him the easiest to work with when it came to teaching parts. These songs that Don wrote were comprised of a series of riffs, often in different keys and time signatures, which were really not that difficult to play on piano for the most part. It did certainly take an open mind and a different approach. I didn't really sight-read piano music and could just barely read and play piano at all. Harkleroad's approach, knowing this, was to have me give him each note or chord in a "vertical" fashion, in a sequence without rhythm. This methodology allowed me the ability to teach him the notes and the rhythms as two distinct parts. I would first play the sequence of all the notes and / or chords, and then I would pound out the rhythm sometimes singing the notes simultaneously. He would then say "thanks," excuse himself and go master that part, not returning until he was ready for more.

Jeff was more of a feeling player and would expect me to play the part in a fairly concise manner, which took a few minutes. After I would play it to his satisfaction, he would often just try to figure it out by ear without asking for notes. Sometimes, the notes couldn't be played on guitar in the same octave. So often things were transposed. I also made more mistakes in reading working this way, and Jeff would then occasionally mention to Don that the notes were sometimes different. Don suspected I was "changing the parts," which made it difficult for me and caused more than one "talk." There is more on this later...

I think basically Jerry learned by ear, so I needed to play the parts for him also, but the bass parts were generally easier to play than the guitar parts (until Don discovered that the bass could play chords also). Jerry was not around long enough for me to recall his methods quite as easily. However, Jerry was always easy to work with and had a really good attitude.
I believe the whole song (minus drum parts which weren't written) was learned by the end of the day.

Jerry Handley: You were actually writing the music down at that time.
John French: Yeah, I started writing it down. It worked pretty well - for that album.
I didn't get to play drums much. That's the interesting thing, people say, "you've got such an interesting style of drumming. And when you get down to it, you find out that they think I was playing bad on purpose. (Laughs) They didn't know it was because I never got to rehearse. (note: this should be appended by the fact that I did rehearse for many of the TMR tunes near the end for 14 hours a day for a few weeks, but I still was not up to speed in my actual playing abilities because I spent most of my time on the piano, writing parts for Don.) On Trout Mask, *I got to rehearse for maybe two or three weeks (with the band) before the album.*

Handley's Last Days

Jerry Handley: It was just a different band and I wasn't enjoying it that much either.. It was like, wind us up and turn us loose ...like a wind-up band.
John French: Yeah, it lost a feeling during that period of time.
JH: We were all trying to play what Don was thinking in his mind.
JF: Do you remember a lot of paranoia about Don screaming at somebody if things didn't happen a certain way.
JH: Right, Don had everybody afraid of him - that he wouldn't like it if you didn't do it his way. It ruined the band - everybody lost their individuality.
JF: So that was the end of what I am going to classify as the first incarnation of the Band.
JH: Yeah, I was the last guy in the original band to leave.

Blues was the basis of the original Magic Band, and everyone played within certain parameters. Most blues songs had similar chord progressions, or none at all. Some were just a single chord with riffs. This allowed everyone to take some liberties with the music and express themselves individually within the group. Although Don's musical ideas did spring from the roots of blues, it was a much more complex music in the sense of memorization, and composition. When I refer to "composition" I refer especially to Strictly Personal era music, such as *Trust Us, Safe As Milk*, and *On Tomorrow*. These songs were probably the most "composed" songs that Don ever wrote, most of the music after this was processed through someone else, and so had their mark on it as well as his. Much of this music had to be played nearly exactly as written, or it would distract someone else and cause confusion.

I already mentioned Don really focusing on Jerry. At that point, he knew far more than Don did (about notes on the bass), but Don had a way of making other people feel as though they were inadequate for displaying exactly the same qualities that he could have found in himself had he bothered to look. Jerry also started receiving a lot of verbal abuse and criticism for his playing, his schedule, his priorities (children and wife) ad infinitum.

Being young and stupid, Jeff, Bill and I all started agreeing with Don that Jerry's "head wasn't into it like ours were." After all, we had no family, no cars, no outside restrictions. We lived together, ate together, and did music together. Unfortunately, we also began to talk about Jerry together - encouraged by Don, who seemed to be learning quickly that young musicians were much easier to manipulate. We began to alienate Jerry, who already felt like a square peg in a round hole with all us "kids." We were three to four years younger at an age when three years made a lot of difference. We were already friends with each other and still had a lot of the bonds of our younger pre-Beefheart days.

Jerry Handley: Alex left the band at that time, and that was pretty much it for me. In the starting of the band, and when he left, that was kind of like, well, I didn't have anybody that I felt that close to in the band. And the band was obviously going in the wrong direction. He left, because of that reason. Once he did it, I thought, "well, might as well give up on it."

John French: Well, Jerry put it this way, as long as things didn't go (Don's) way, he would fight to make them go his way

Don Aldridge: Yep, he did.

JF: And that's what I saw over and over.

DA: Well, you know women are usually smarter than we are. I thumbed my nose at Sue Handley. She didn't like Don much, and at first, I didn't like her. But you know, the more I thought about it – of course, I've had a lot of years to reflect now - but she knew. She loved (Jerry) and she saw that this wasn't going to work for him. So, she was motivating him towards getting into the main stream and getting himself work. I really think she was.

JF: Obviously, she did the right thing. He's got a good family, kids grown up, he's got grandkids.

DA: Jerry Handley, I might say, and I want this on the record, is one of the nicest guys I met in that whole thing. Jerry is a super nice guy and I just I never (heard) a bad word out of him. I really liked him a lot.

JF: He practically was my cab driver, I had no car and he would say, "Where do you need to go?" and he would take me anywhere. He was very patient.

DA: You could just sum it up with Jerry by saying "well-mannered." ...and friendly, very friendly. You know how you get, if you knew any other bands, the head trip that you would go through even being around them - but he wasn't like that. Neither was Alex like that, or PG. Now Don was ALWAYS a head trip.

Shoplifting

One of the stupidest things I ever did in my entire life was allow myself get caught up in stealing. I did it in phases. A friend of mine introduced me to it in Junior High school. He stole a peashooter from a five and dime store when we were kids and while I was with him. Later, I wanted to find out about girls, so I stole girlie mags from the corner store as a kid. In my early bands, I stole microphones and speakers for PA equipment. Then, there were phases of time when I would steal nothing.

I had gone quite a while without stealing, but present conditions in this band struck up my interest once more. There was nothing much of anything I could call my own. I had neither car, nor money, nor control over my life - even what I ate. Occasionally, I would go to the supermarket with Jeff Cotton when Don sent him out to shop. During these times, I would sometimes steal a candy bar because I was dying for chocolate - or anything else to put in my stomach for that sake. Sometimes, I would steal two or three chocolate bars and stow them away for later. This later turned out to be the cause of a big problem.

Bill's Guitars's

John French: So, what kind of guitar did you have when you first got in the band
Bill Harkleroad: I had a Fender Duo Sonic – a three quarter sized Fender. I had a couple of Mosrite Pickups in it.
JF: Why did you want Mosrite?
BH: I was trying to "soup up" my guitar, right!
JF: Yeah, it was sort of like putting riser handlebars on your bicycle.
BH: Exactly! Good analogy! But there were some guitars floating around in the band, and I think really quickly, I ended up with a Telecaster that we had bought at some shop right in Woodland Hills there. Later, Dick Kunc rewired it for me. But there were three or four funny guitars floating around in the band. An ES 125, that was almost like a 175 jazz-type guitar but it was a slightly smaller version. There was another one that I don't remember exactly, it was like a Les Paul, but it was a hollow body, arch-top guitar. Then, very quickly, I went to the old standby Telecaster.
JF: What color was it?
BH I'm color blind, but it was that "creamy color"...
JF: Ok, kind of a beige. I had forgotten that you were color blind..
BH: Yeah very!
JF: So... you didn't know I was black all these years?
BH: No, but when I heard you play, I knew it!

Trout Mask: A Day In The Life

Shortly after Bill became the other guitarist in the group, we settled into a kind of rigorous routine of processing Don's creative outflow. This would be a typical non-eventful day in terms of anything unusual happening.

Bill Harkleroad: OK. In the morning, you would be around the piano. Jeff and I, and later Mark - actually things started rolling before Mark (became a member of the band). You're on the piano over there with a cup of Joe, and Jeff and I are either in the little laundry hut which happened a lot at the very beginning – practicing parts. Then, one by one, we would come in and work on new parts with you on the piano. Then we would try to play them together without drum parts. Then, sometimes it would be, "let's all play them together." I still haven't seen Don yet. It's noon or one in the afternoon - 4 or 5 hours in to the day and we're doing this. Somewhere along the line, Don comes out, and creates some kind of distraction for whatever he's into for the day. Sometimes it was, "let's work on this song," or "we're going to do this song." Or, " no, play this part that way" or whatever. He wasn't too emotionally over the top about "you're fucking up everybody's life." Yet -That wasn't happening. Then...more of the same. Sometimes at that point, I think some of the lyric writing thing where Jeff became "paper monitor" started happening. Right? And that might break up things a bit. That was a very typical day. You just did it all day long.

John French: Right. What would you say our average workday was back then?

BH: I said between 10 and 12 hours was an average work day, and longer often. Does that jive with what you think?

JF: Yeah, exactly.

One of the most difficult challenges in writing about all this is the chronological development of the events and what order they fell in. The earliest days after Harkleroad's arrival seemed to consist of Jeff and Bill off somewhere as Jeff taught Bill parts. This was at night, or in the late afternoon. Jerry would show up relatively early (by musician's standards, as we are a bit more nocturnal, because we generally play in the evening) and the time was spent with as much rehearsal as possible during the daylight hours because there was less chance of neighbors complaining about the noise.

I recall us always rehearsing in the little laundry shed, the drums back in the corner opposite Sue Vliet's old automatic washer, which had been given to us when she moved from her house to an apartment. It was a crowded area, but we all managed to squeeze in and would go over the Strictly Personal material apparently, plus I recall distinctly rehearsing *Veteran's Day Poppy*, *Moonlight On Vermont*, and *Sugar 'n Spikes*.

Trout Mask Encounters

So then, I then asked Bill what he would consider to be an atypical day – to focus more on the traumatic times, the "talks," and the cult-like cloud that slowly encircled the house and choked out our individuality.

Bill Harkleroad: Just on the time basis, it would be anywhere from a short one of four hours to 24 hours straight, easy.

John French: Yeah, I remember some that were even two days.

BH: Longer, yeah, almost two days straight. The content would be anything from our total lack of understanding an artist's point of view and that our mother hated us and we should hate our mother, which was a big point that was brought up a lot. Not to get into content a lot. It's hard for me to separate it because I was always thinking, "What was this guy doing?" - you know? What was he consciously trying to do? He was trying to tell us we were rednecks and he was this great artist and he was going to mold us, right?

This touches upon what would become more and more the norm as time went on. When Jerry was in the band, this seldom happened in his presence, as he was not "in the ring" so to speak, but living with his wife and separated from the band physically, and therefore the cult-atmosphere whose tentacle-like grasp was even now beginning to enfold us into a web of what I like to call "en-darken-ment."

It was a kind of reverse realization – a "dumbing down" process in which our individual opinions were more or less subtly condemned, and our conformist views – basically what Don himself would present in the form of lecture, often in the midst of these "talks" as we often called them, were praised.

It was a bit of Pavlov, mixed with Synanon, interrogation procedures, sleep deprivation, and brainwashing techniques all rolled up into a bundle. It was actually brilliant work on Don's part. I think his most brilliant work ever - his total control and manipulation of four young men. This was group encounter in which negative reinforcement techniques transformed us into obedient minions. Synanon was later mentioned to me by some friends who had gone through the program as, perhaps rehab for alcohol abuse. Wikipedia is the source of the information below, which provides a bit of an introduction.

"Synanon, initially a drug rehabilitation program, was founded by Charles "Chuck" Dederich Sr. (1913–1997) in 1958 in Santa Monica, California. By the early 1960s it had also become an alternative community, attracting people with its emphasis on living a self-examined life, as aided by group truth-telling sessions known as the Synanon Game. Synanon ultimately became the cultish Church of Synanon in the 1970s and the group disbanded permanently in 1989 due to difficulties with the Internal Revenue Service."

Then later:

"Control over members occurred through the "Synanon Game." The "Game" could be considered a therapeutic tool, likened to group therapy; or a social control, in which members humiliated one another and encouraged the exposure of one's innermost weaknesses, or both." [40]

The "church" of Synanon, as it later became known, has many cultish similarities to what was happening at the Trout House. When I read "The "Game" could be considered a therapeutic tool, likened to group therapy; or a social control, in which members humiliated one another and encouraged the exposure of one's innermost weaknesses, or both" my blood chilled. Don would often say that he had studied at the library about our various assumed "mental illnesses" and I had the distinct impression that he was following some twisted and deranged psychological train of thought concerning what I would later hear called group therapy.

I'm not saying that group therapy cannot be helpful, I am saying that it can be treacherous, cruel, and traumatic when guided by an untrained obsessive paranoid with a secret agenda comprised of a complicated network of defense mechanisms fashioned to cloak his own insecurities. To top this off, it is my opinion that Van Vliet had actually convinced himself that he was "helping" us and I heard him more than once describe himself as a "philanthropist." Perhaps this is why we were so convinced that the destination of the path he was leading us on was worthy of the pain we would endure to "arrive."

The First Church Of Beefheart

People often ask me "why didn't you just leave?" Well, I tried, but it's harder to get out of a situation like that than mere physical removal of your body from the premises. When someone gets inside your head and causes you to doubt yourself so completely that there are fifty wars going on inside your own mind and you are divided, you cannot make a firm decision and stick to it quite as easily as "I think I'll quit this job and get another." This happened over a period of several months and snowballed into a victorious cult by the end of the year.

The first step in putting someone in this mental state is to find naïve people.

The second is to gain their trust and confidence, so that they eventually reveal their weaknesses to the "overseer."

The third is to establish yourself as a sort of "superhuman," by constantly proclaiming what you know that they don't, causing those people to look up to you as a kind of "guru" and establishing

[40] http://en.wikipedia.org/wiki/Synanon

yourself as a formidable physical foe helps.

Fourth, you begin to remove the trust and confidence that the people you are assuming control over have with each other by encouraging them to talk to you about the others.

Fifth, you have confrontational meetings in which one person is the "target" and the others are encouraged by the "overseer" to attack, criticize and humiliate. The overseer points out all the faults that each participant has stated about the target, thus unifying them against the target.

Sixth, encourage violence, beginning with a one-on-one controlled encounter, picking the person with the most violent temper and pitting him against the least likely to prevail. Eventually encourage group violence against the "target."

Seventh, this creates and generates even more mistrust between the individuals; dividing and eventually conquering them.

Eighth, the individuals cannot stand up to the "overseer" without support, having been verbally and physically abused in the group "talks" and lacking esteem. The group mentality thereby snowballs into a syndrome of turning each individual in the group against themselves whenever they do have a glimmer of revolutionary thought and quickly breaking their will, so they fall back into lockstep with the "overseer."

This is merely my observation of the steps involved in the process I witnessed with my own eyes over the period of about a year – the nine months of the rehearsal for *Trout Mask Replica* being the most intense and defined period.

Communion?

Though I didn't consider it at the time, I later considered the possibility that perhaps small amounts of LSD were being added to our tea, unknowingly, by Laurie at Don's request. I have no proof of this, but it is quite possible that this happened. Whenever the "talks" were going on, it seemed like there would be a point in time – usually about $1^{1}/_{2}$ hours in, when Don would say "Laurie, make us some tea, please." It wasn't a request, but a command. Laurie would be in the kitchen – usually by herself – but sometimes with Jeff - and make us all a huge mug of tea which we would then drink while chain-smoking cigarettes.

The bottle of LSD that had been hidden in the yard had disappeared when we moved. I often wonder if it wasn't taken to the new house and stowed away for use as a mind-control agent. Don used to say to me all the time "you need some acid, man." And yet, if I took it, he would be upset. I often wonder if he was upset by the fact that I took it of *my own free will* but still considered it necessary for our "enlightenment" if administered under his supervision.

Sandose was very mild compared to the street versions of LSD. This was the laboratory stuff used by Timothy Leary, and one capsule divided into four mugs could cause just enough confusion in the neurons to give Don slightly more of an edge in control. Don Aldridge actually triggered this possibility in my head. I kept thinking "how could we have all been so passive?" Then I read the following in his interview:

Don Aldridge: Well, you have to understand, I'm not saying that it is true, I am saying – you have to understand what we were hearing out here. We were hearing that "if you go up there to the house, don't drink anything, because they might put acid in the drinks.
John French: Yeah well, I did that a few times myself to band members (Jerry and Alex) which I am not proud of. Laurie did it to me. Right in the middle of a recording session while we were doing Mirror Man (at TTG Studios) I realized that I had just come on to acid while we were in the studio.
The Golden Hand Of God?

John French: Why do you suppose we allowed that kind of control over our lives?
Bill Harkleroad: I can speak for myself and you take it from there. Before I joined the band, I was coming out of an LSD cult.

Bill was already primed for indoctrination into the same thing Jeff and I were already being indoctrinated into – Don's own private cult. Bill was nearly the perfect fit. The transition would be simple. Bill's state of mind at the time was ecstasy, and his opinion of Don at the time is revealed in his following words:

Bill Harkleroad: So, I am at that point now to where I'm not getting out of the Army yet. I'm worried about losing my life in Viet Nam. I've been taking acid and have been pretty spaced-out here for a while, and my favorite bands on planet earth were Captain Beefheart and Frank Zappa - those two bands. What am I going to do with my life? How am I going to make a living? What the hell am I going to do? I'm going to die in Viet Nam. I'm pretty scared. I get the invitation to go join this band. I'm in Captain Beefheart? Are you fucking kidding – excuse me, but - are you kidding? I'm in Captain Beefheart? As I told Don one day in a conversation, "I feel like the golden hand of God picked me up and dropped me down in the most perfect situation. I'm so lucky I can't believe it." That's the state of mind I was in, and I told him. I said, "This is unbelievable! I love the music". I even liked Strictly Personal. I liked where that was evolving to. I hadn't been freaked-out by Trout Mask yet. I had known you and Jeff. Unbelievable. And here's my hero, and he really worked it, and I was the "special guy" the first month, right? Before I became one of the major culprits, so I was a very weakened person, and he was very good at doing that, as we all know. I was coming from a place where it saved my life. It not only saved my life meaning I could be a garbage man - or a Coca Cola truck driver. It meant that I was in a band that was going to be rich and famous, I was going to get babes, and man! Is this unbelievable.
John French: Babes! Yeah! How many babes did you get approached by when you were in that band?
BH: Well, does that fit?
JF: Sure does. Fits with me. The first thing is he disarmed you, by the honeymoon time, the "romancing time," in terms of, "you're a great player and you're a great guy etc."
BH: ...to keeping us up days without food - the brainwashing... At that point, I had nowhere else to go. Of course I thought of leaving many times. I think it showed a greater weakness in me than you had. I think the time Mark – we went down the street and pulled him out of some drug store – where he was hiding and he was going to go hitchhike home. I never did that.
JF: Jeff was going to do it too. Remember? He had his clothes packed. He left once!
BH: Did he?
JF: Yeah!
BH: I don't even remember it. I remember Mark and the thing is, it was just so abusive. I didn't (try to leave) I never did!
JF: I left three times.
BH: Yeah, you kept coming back for more.
JF: NO, I mean, I left three times during Trout Mask!
BH: Really?
JF: Yeah! I left once with Jeff. And then I came back. Then I left again...well – we'll get into that.
BH: So that explained how that happened. He was my hero. He even created it more, then he disarmed me and then just pushed me in the mud so fucking far I had no chance to see up.

Isolation

Though I am not expert on this, nor have I studied cults, it seems that a certain amount of isolation is necessary. It's sort of the "petri dish" that's necessary to develop whatever culture of cult one is trying to spawn. The Spahn ranch is a perfect example, as is "The Fountain of the World," or the tragic Jim Jones cult in Guyana. When someone sets up a synthetic alternate reality - which is in essence what a cult is – one cannot have free-thinkers interfering with the process and offering useful opinions that often counter the corporate mindset the cult-leader is attempting to create.

John French: Do you think that isolation had a lot to do with that? - You know, being in that house and being isolated from the outside world. We hardly saw anybody.
Bill Harkleroad: Absolutely, like I said, it's textbook brainwashing. Sleep deprivation, food deprivation, and no contact. I mean, that's what they do at Wings seminars now. They put you in this room without any light and you're stuck in this thing separated from the world.

EST seemed to me like the same kind of thing. When I first heard about this in the mid-seventies, I thought "here's another cultish mind-control event that will deceive many." It was more of a "hit 'em and run" philosophy, in which the people were isolated for a couple of weekends in a hotel, and mentally dissected. That was my opinion, of course. The leader of the cult was deeply interested in Zen Buddhism, so it was a religious experience in a sense.

Dali

John French: Do remember going to the museum and seeing Dali's stuff?
Bill Harkleroad: I wrote all about it big time, yes! The melting clocks and Dali's car.
JF: That car was great wasn't it?
BH: With the mannequins and the paint squirted inside the snails.
JF: And that warm smell and all those plants. Do you think that had a big effect on the way we played? Do you think that inspired us in the way we played?
BH: It did for me.
JF: It definitely did for me, yeah.

Since our little conversation went into such detail on the effect of Dali's work, I'd like to interject a few statements about the effect Salvador Dali's work had on me.

Prior to our visit to the museum, Don had called us in to his room in the evening and had his girlfriend, Laurie, read to us from Dali's book humbly entitled, *Diary Of A Genius.* This was an interesting slant on things and showed me more of this other side of Don once more; the only child, wanting to be read to each night. He would put on his pajamas and get in bed and Laurie would read to him.

It was one of the only periods of time when I found myself willing to drop everything I was doing (there was almost always more work than time) and sit spellbound, listening to this man's writing and drinking in photographs of his work with my eyes.

I was fascinated by the way he could form worlds together and have them share shapes and lines. The idea of his work struck me so strongly. I think, in part, due to earlier experiments with LSD, because I had "seen" some of the things he painted in a sense. Lines and worlds seem to separate and whole other parallel realities began to appear. There were crystal clear images of whole other dimensions. Actually, aside from that, my experiments with drugs were horrible experiences, because the after effects of these experiences would be total confusion and memory lapses. I would also be terribly paranoid and unsure of everything, but there was this one positive upside of actually having my mind opened up and shown things I would have never perceived any other way.

Back to Dali, after we finished the group reading of *Diary Of A Genius*, I borrowed the book and re-read it myself. I studied the paintings and perceived that this multi-dimensional approach could be set to music and specifically drums. Suddenly I had a vision and a purpose! As a group, we were actually doing a very similar thing. Instruments were playing in entirely different "dimensions" and sharing only pulse as their common denominator. I could use the drums in effect as the "common lines" of the painting and also suggest each of the dimensions at the same time. I was daring to accomplish this by using bits and suggestions of each rhythm and tying them together in such a way as to achieve a "whole" drum part.

I must say that at this point in time, I was so totally inspired and taken up with this vision of drumming, that it's probably the only thing that kept me from complete insanity during the worst of what would come. I could block out this immediate and terrible world for a few hours and actually dream of greatness on my instrument. This was my first giant spark of vision combined with ambition, and I was so excited at the prospects, I could barely contain myself.

When people ask me "why didn't I leave?" after hearing my description of the terrible things that were going on in the house, this vision, this inspiration is probably one reason why. There was no one in the world doing what we were doing. Where was I going to find a more "politically correct" version of this controlled deranged and utterly brilliant work going on? We were doing something that would be spoken about for years, and I knew it. As much as I hated being verbally abused, humiliated, and beaten up; the reason I stayed is because I absolutely HAD to see this project through to the end. Bill seemed to agree when recalling this period of time.

Bill Harkleroad: The thing I said that I got the most out of the Beefheart band and the changing times, on the positive side, is that I was shown that an artistic life was a real positive way to live your life, as opposed to, "You're supposed to go build airplanes, carry your lunch pail to the thing and that's what a real man does." So working at the post office was not the only way to come to life. It validated an artistic lifestyle.

It was such a moment of coincidental juxtaposition. As Bill and I (and the entire band) were at the height of our interest in Dali, his exhibit came to the Los Angeles County Art Museum, or perhaps was already there and Don had gone to see it on one of his many absences from the house.

Bill Harkleroad: Going and seeing the art excited me because it was opening doors, and I realized actually, that I really was an artist. That stuff was exciting to me. That's the best gift that Don gave me.

One of the other things this interest in Dali created in my mind was a little hiding place where I could go and dream. It was a spot that nurtured my creative instincts and kept them alive in the face of the most suppressive force I'd ever encountered.

LA County Art Museum

The whole band went to see the Dali exhibition at the LA County Museum of Modern Art. Victor Hayden also went with us, and he may have brought a friend. I recalled many of the paintings from the book and was amazed to see them in person. I loved his technical ability and the way he would paint two and three scenes cleverly intertwined. There were many sketches and a few very tiny "oil on plywood" pieces. I loved everything and just drank it in. I was extremely impressed by Dali's mastery and life-like images. He was a master, indeed. Seeing his work in person did even more to convince me that I could do great things on drums if I completely applied myself.

The highlight of the show was an old Model A Ford that was sitting in a huge metal tray. This was actually on the roof of the museum. There were female mannequins inside and sprinklers on the ceiling that rained water down on the artificial occupants. There was the warm smell of moss and plants of all kinds were growing inside the car. There were real snails, and then snail shells with oil paint squeezed into them and cut off with a razor - something that Victor loved. "That's so severe" Victor would say. It was one of his favorite things to say.

Nothing could have prepared me for the feeling I experienced when seeing Dali's flawless work in person. I studied closely each little brush stroke as carefully as I could and wished that perhaps someday I could paint like that. Each painting reinforced within me the desire to somehow accomplish on the drums what Dali had done in oils. To achieve that amount of greatness on my instrument became almost an obsession.

The reality of the situation was that I had precious little time to devote to my quest. Most of my day was either taken up with transcribing and teaching parts to the songs, or sitting through Don's ridiculous "talks" about our "things" as he referred to them condescendingly. However, whenever there was a lull in Don's creativity and the guys were caught up on all their parts, I would go into the sweatroom, (laundry room) and practice drum patterns that I had written out in my spare moments. Often, I had a drum pattern page hidden in between transcriptions of Don's work so that I could occasionally jot down an idea that came to mind, but I hid them from Don for the most part, because he was so threatened by someone else's creativity.

I can say without reservation that I tried to do on drums what Dali was doing on canvas. Whether I succeeded or not, I'm not sure. I think I fell far short. However, the music, and how I interpreted what Don wrote and conceived of it's arrangement was largely built around Dali's paintings, in which two or three worlds were present and interweaving with each other. The parts that Don wrote for several of the pieces on *Trout Mask* were disconnected and seemed utterly unrelated. The way I conceived of putting them together was much in the same way Dali would connect his unrelated images.

I tried writing my drum parts in much the same way. At times, there are two or three worlds that are interconnected in my drumming. My most ambitious attempt at this appears on my drum solo CD *O Solo Drumbo*, on which I attempted to play three parts in 3 different time signatures at the same time. It's weird what this does to the mind, which can only really concentrate on one thing at any one time. When you're playing something like this (and I had to learn it by rote), your mind continually wants to follow one or the other of the time signatures and ignore the rest. Or, to think of the whole thing as one long drum part, which is how I learned it. It's one of the most difficult things I ever learned. I wrote it during *Trout Mask* and never really succeeded in playing it (because of lack of patience) until about 1997. It became like a meditation at that time.

Dali's Car

That evening, after everyone else had gone to sleep on the living room floor, or perhaps in the downstairs bedroom, Don said, "Let's write something." I got my book, and because the rest of the band were sleeping, we left the lights off and used a candle. This makes me think that at least one band member was asleep in the living room. I sat to Don's right on the bench and wrote as he played each part. This was written by Don on piano, and it was entitled *Dali's Car*. He would make sure I'd transcribed one part and then he would play the next. We spent about 1 to 2 hours at this and then went to sleep.

I go back and forth as to which piano piece was written first and never can decide for sure. I am almost positive it was *Steal Softly Thru Snow*, yet at times I think it was *Dali's Car*. I know this, they were the first two.

The track notes give the explanation of the piece, but I remember a few other things, such as the fact that Don's usual method of composition was "hunt and peck." Most of the time, Don did not seem to have a vision of what he was shooting for, he just played until he found something he liked, and then I would write it down. At first, I just tried writing by watching his fingers, but I quickly found it more efficient just to play the part up higher on the keys and usually, once I achieved that, which was quick, I could write it down without having to make Don repeat it so often.

Van Vliet mostly used a "one position" technique of playing piano. He would put his fingers on the keyboard, and play only what his fingers would reach, not moving his hand position. This was not always the case, but most of the time, during the writing of this album, this was the general pattern.

The next morning, I taught the guitarists the Beefheart piano composition. It was only for two guitars, and I think this may have been because Jerry was busy and couldn't make rehearsal. However, it could also be that (since my memory can't seem to clarify) that this was written during the period after Jerry left and before Mark arrived.

Jeff and Bill were playing *Dali's Car* when Don awoke, and thus a system for the writing of the album to beat all albums was established. The interesting thing about *Dali's Car* is that there is no way to actually play it as written on the piano, so the guys must have left out some notes somewhere along the line. I wish I would have had the presence of mind to transcribe it "as played" for later reference.

Steal Softly Thru Snow

Soon after *Dali's Car* becoming a reality, Don and I were busy at work as he wrote his first piano composition that included bass - *Steal Softly Thru Snow*. This was written during the daytime, and the band members were in the room as I recall, at least for part of the time. They may have eventually wandered off to practice in other parts of the house or in the shed later on and eventually it was just Don and I sitting at the piano.

This was a rather interesting experience, because Don created in a different manner on the piano than he did when singing, whistling, playing harmonica, or playing guitar. Each part by itself was harmonically conventional, but he would often play the next part (for the other guitar, perhaps) in a completely different key. When these two parts are played at the same time, you get dissonance, which achieved a kind of "third part."

Dissonance is the effect of sound waves of close proximity in frequency "competing" for your attention – similar to the way adjoining red and green objects compete for your eyesight. Most people find it unappealing, and therefore, musical "rules" are set down purposely to avoid dissonance and achieve it's opposite, which is "harmony"

Interestingly enough Zappa talks about similar things in *The Real Frank Zappa Book*, in which he would take two things recorded at two different times in two different tempos and combine them. He called it "xenochricity". Here, though, there weren't different tempos so much as different length parts in different key signatures. The effect was similar, in that the two parts combined created a "third" part, which makes the music actually sound more complex than it actually is.

I mention this as Don's association with Zappa may have influenced him in this decision. However, my deepest instincts tell me that dissonance in Don's compositions was achieved most likely by him taking his hands off the keys to take a drag of a cigarette, and putting them back on the keyboard in a completely different position. Zappa, on the other hand, was more conventional and had educated himself in such things as key signatures, so any dissonance in his compositions was absolutely intentional.

There is evidence to suggest that Gary Marker may have had influence in this also. At this time, Don visited Gary, according to Marker. Marker was cutting up tapes and putting together ideas that were totally disconnected from each other. This was all done manually by splicing tape, according to Marker, and Don asked about it. Marker explained the theory, to which Don replied something to the effect of *"That's the stuff I wanna do!"*

Spawning Trout Mask

Though Jerry recalls learning a song that was written on the piano, he doesn't recall the name – It was *Steal Softly Thru Snow*. Don had a very strange aura of expectation the first day we started actually working with the written music. He came out with this child like excitement, like he'd just gotten a new toy and was anxious to try it out. He said something like, "Are we ready to teach them the song?"

I was caught a little off-guard, but replied to the affirmative and we began. I wasn't expecting to work on this so soon, and so was a little apprehensive about my abilities to go through the parts and recall the sound and feel of each section. However, after a few minutes of uncomfortable tension as I struggled to read and play piano parts for the first time in front of a roomful of people, things started to fall into line.

Don may have felt "legitimized" in a sense, because of his competitive spirit. He was composing material on the piano – just like Frank Zappa did. I could be wrong about this, but I'm sure there was something like this going on in Don's mind.

Don was extremely anxious to observe the process of me teaching the band this song firsthand. He was also strangely unguarded that day, and showed his excitement and enthusiasm in a way that put us all at ease. It was almost like normal people.

The first parts were learned fairly quickly – over a period of about two hours. I taught each band member one section at a time. They would then play that section together as I was working out the next section. Don got Bill partially isolated from the rest and focused on him for about 30-45 minutes on the very first section of the song. Bill knew all the notes and the rhythms, but Don worked with him on what he called "the shape" of the part. Also, as I recalled, Don changed the part drastically to lay better on the guitar, as some things didn't translate to guitar from piano very efficiently. It sounded way less mechanical afterward and Bill was really pulling the sound out of the guitar. It must have been some concept that worked for a lot of things, because Bill seldom sounded less than great.

It was actually the first time that I really felt like an integral part of the rehearsal, as drum parts were almost always an afterthought. Here I was - right in the middle of everything, interacting with every member of the band. It was invigorating.

After the first section, Don inserted a small section, which was the pause before the vocal comes in with "The black paper..." Once that was in, they played through those two sections with no drums a couple of times. The drums were in the laundry shed out back at the time.

After Don heard a couple of the parts played back on guitars and bass, he appeared satisfied that I knew what I was doing, and disappeared into his room. I knocked on the door to ask him who played what in the next section thinking - *"this is HIS composition"* – holding the manuscript paper and my primitive notation in my hand, and Don said, "you know what to do, John!" making a "pushing away" gesture with his hand, and shut the door.

Thus not only the delegation of transcribing and teaching the parts was laid in my lap, but also the complete responsibility of arranging the parts into some semblance of a "song." It was a giant leap of responsibility and stress for me to have all these decisions to make. Where was I going to find the time to practice drumming?

This was a bit of a slow process, as each section took about half an hour to teach – each guy about 10 minutes each. Since there was an average of 12 sections a song, and the players had to memorize all these riffs, it took about six hours to really get a song to a crudely "playable" state. Remember, we were breaking new ground, so to speak, and breaking a lot of musical rules along the way.

So it was that I began the painful process of trying to figure out how the pieces of the puzzle went together. Although the album credits Don as arranger, it was actually John French sitting at the piano with all those parts in front of him who was figuring the arrangements on the fly. I qualify that by saying "on the songs written on the piano." See the track notes for more information about this. There was no set system, and sometimes more notes were written on the piano that could be played. There were many problems where the parts had to be transposed to different octaves than originally played.

Also, a lot of the sections were in different key signatures - and different time signatures simultaneously. This wasn't going to be easy. But then it started coming together a little better. Using common denominators from math, I was able to determine how everyone could start and end together in each section.

At first, everybody was a little lost, because those "touchdown" points in the rhythm were not together very often in the same place. But soon, we all learned how to concentrate in such a way that we could hear every part, yet concentrate on our own and count so that we were seldom lost.

Thus, many of the decisions regarding the actual overall structure of the songs written on piano for the album *Trout Mask Replica* were set in motion by me on that day. I tried to keep the whole idea as simple as possible, so as to not only make the process efficient and quick, but also to not overwhelm the guitarists, who had the massive job of learning what turned out to be hundreds of short riffs, some very difficult to master, or at least unfamiliar to the normal flat-pick strumming guitarist – which these guys obviously weren't. They did have to stretch their limitations on a daily basis to keep up with the challenges.

The Musical Process

Of course, these weren't "songs" in the sense of the conventional components (intro, verse, chorus, bridge etc.). Songs generally were much simpler but more organizationally structured. "Songs" had a set of chord changes 12 to 16 bars long that were played through about 4 times (the basic framwork of the song). "Songs" usually had a "riff" or "hook" (usually played during the tonic, or root chord, the tonal center of the piece) that was played through in between verses and at the beginning and end.

These "compositions" of Don's were almost all riffs (short one and two measure phrases of music) and often there was no tonal center, or it randomly changed from section to section, or there were three tonal centers at the same time in a particular section. It was as though someone had taken a blank jigsaw puzzle, randomly picked up pieces and scribbled little pictures on each one, and said, "Put this together, I'll be out later to see the thing when it's done."

In this sense, one can say that Don did not fully "compose" the music on *Trout Mask Replica*. In order to actually "compose" a piece of music, one must actually conceive of it as a whole and place it within a framework (which I would liken to the edge of a jigsaw puzzle) presenting a completed piece to the musicians, which is how Zappa wrote much of the time. What Don basically did here is find a series of one or two bar riffs, or parts, that he liked, have me write them down, and then say, in essence, "make something out of this."

In a quote from Rolling Stone magazine, however, here is what Don decided to lead the public to believe:

"When Beefheart learned of the opportunity to make an album totally without restrictions, he sat down at the piano and in eight and a half hours wrote all twenty-eight songs included on Trout Mask. When I asked him jokingly why it took that long, he replied, 'Well, I'd never played the piano before and I had to figure out the fingering.' With a stack of cassettes going full time, Don banged out Frownland, Dachau Blues, Veteran's Day Poppy, and all of the others complete with words. When he is creating, this is exactly how Don works – fast and furious."

And later:

"The trouble is that once the compositions are down it takes him a long time to teach them to his musicians. In this case it took almost a year of rehearsal." [41]

As one can imagine, it was pretty frustrating for me to read this later on, as I had really toiled within my role and vision to make certain that everyone knew what they were supposed to do at any given moment.

Occasionally, as Don would write, he would say, "this is a bass part," or "this is Bill's part." He often complained that he had to "write those fucking *blues* parts" for Bill Harkleroad. Actually, I find little on *Trout Mask* that sounds like a "blues part." I find an overall abstract relationship to blues in much of the music, due to Don's influences in youth, but I also find bits of jazz influence, and even classical influences all thrown together.

Bamberger writes in his book, *Riding Some Kind of Unusual Skull Sleigh* that what Don actually wrote was "chamber music" for the group. I disagree. Chamber music is a much more disciplined form, for the most part, and follows much stricter rules. All the sections fit together to make a whole and the parts and sections are much more defined and complimentary to one another, following chord patterns which are repeated. If Van Vliet had written "chamber music" as Bamberger suggests, it would have taken us much less time to learn than trying to figure out how to put together the fragmented bits and pieces he actually did give us.

This music was more random, and if I may be so bold to suggest, the complexity of the music had as much to do with the fact that Van Vliet didn't know what he was doing as with anything else. When one simultaneously breaks two or three basic rules of composition in music (which most "rock" bands, even the ones who claim to be "far out" do not), then the outcome of the music is going to sound more "complex" to the human ear.

Like I said, I came up with a simple process of compiling and teaching this music to the other players, which I explain in more detail in the track notes for *Trout Mask*. Basically, I worked with common denominators to come up with equal lengths for each section. As a drummer, this kind of thing was mathematically simple and because of the fact that Don had mentioned we were doing a double album and the time it took to learn each piece seemed to be about six to eight hours, depending upon the piece, I figured we had a couple of solid months of work just to actually assimilate the material, but months of work lay ahead in memorizing the hundreds of riffs that make up the whole. This was going to be a daunting task.

Remember, since these guys didn't read music (well, at least they weren't reading the music I transcribed, though I think Bill and Jeff must have had a general knowledge of theory), they had to memorize everything, which was a process in itself. There was also the general human error of forgetting a section or two and mixing up the order, so, after a few days, I realized that my job was going to be even more complex. I had to transcribe, then arrange and teach simultaneously, and then I also had to keep meticulous track of all the parts in the exact order that I taught them to each player for later reference. To make matters worse, I had to come up with working titles for each piece, so that I would know where one song ended and the next began, as Don seldom gave a title to anything. I should have just numbered them, but I would usually put something on the paper to remind myself of something that happened that day, or something that was impressed on my mind so that I could recall the piece to mind more quickly.

All this started out of one half of a used manuscript book and a broken pencil and no eraser. I soon saw that the best method for doing this was to re-write everything from the rough draft once the arrangement was decided laid out.

Often, (and I started with *Steal Softly*) if a part didn't seem to fit with another part, I would search until I found something that would work. This often took a few minutes, and I always assumed that if Don didn't like what I heard, he would just tell me, "That doesn't go with

[41] Rolling Stone, May 14, 1970, The Odyssey of Captain Beefheart, Langdon Winner, pp 38.

that, I meant *this* to go with that" or something to this effect.   However, that never happened, even once, that I recall. This could have been for several reasons. One is that he just didn't know how things were supposed to go together. Another possibility is that he didn't care how things went together. Another is that he didn't remember enough about what he had written to know the difference.

Bear in mind, however, that Van Vliet would also listen to a player occasionally and give a critical assessment of how he was playing a particular part, but this often had more to do with nuance than the actual notes. If he didn't like the way the part sounded on guitar, he would work with the player, sometimes re-writing and/or simplifying the part, and then I would generally ask the player to show me the new part so I could write it down. Sometimes, Don would spend hours just working with someone on nuance and feel, just to get the part working correctly. Most of the time, the guitars weren't plugged in, so the sound he would "pull out of the players" would be strictly technique, never gimmicks or electronics. This was his area of strength: feel, nuance, dynamics, and instinctual characteristics, the same thing one hears in his extraordinary voice.

Influences / Raw Talent

John French: To be absolutely fair, I do remember him "pulling things out of all of us.
Bill Harkleroad: Oh, yeah!
JF: Saying, "Hey, that's not the way that should be played. It should be played like this." Getting us to move a different way or think about it a different way. All of a sudden it would start "sounding," coming to life.
BH: Oh, absolutely. He got us in motion and used us as the physical tools of his art to sculpt things after the fact. I don't think he had specific intentions in the beginning of playing those piano parts. I think he thought he had a rhythmic feel and didn't know enough melodically to create anything. This is just my hit - your were there - But that he had no specific intention, he was just an artist, banging out the fucking piano stuff, and after we got the parts together, we became the clay he molded into certain parts, and I really learned a lot about guitar playing in that process.
JF: And you were breaking new ground. We were all breaking new ground.
BH: Absolutely, and it really helped me. My right hand technique of (sings a rhythm), rhythm things that happened through the process – that was him. I give him all the credit in the world for that. He just didn't have specific intentions. He didn't know what the fuck he was writing.
JF: To be real fair again, a lot of that (guitar-related) stuff he learned from Alex. Alex was a killer rhythm player – of course, Ry too. Alex developed a lot of Ry's techniques and stuff. When Alex was first in the band and before he became completely disillusioned by what was going on, he had a very interesting (technique), and he would throw his guitar around while he was playing it and stuff. He was a very cool player.

Wasting Time

It's hard to say how much time we wasted during the so-called "talks" that Don would instigate and then preside over, but it was a lot. A lot of time getting mentally and physically abused when the time could have been put to much better use practicing and developing the compositions even more, fine-tuning them and putting more energy forward to make the finished product more focused than it was.

John French: Let me ask you this. How long do you think it would have taken to learn Trout Mask if we would have had a normal kind of band situation, without Don's paranoia?

Bill Harkleroad: You know the nooks and crannies of that so much more than I do, John, but – I would say if it took nine months for us to go through that process – I would say a month.
JF: Really? I would say three, just to be safe, because it was new stuff, I mean we were breaking totally new ground.
BH: I'm thinking percentage wise that everything was ten times longer and weirder. I think you're right, because actually we had gotten a third into a lot of those types of tunes and it changed the style of playing and I'm playing things and going, "What am I doing?" My fingers are all over the fingerboard and I'm memorizing these shapes and I don't relate it to a chord or anything, it's just characters that I'm reproducing. So, you're probably right. It probably would have taken longer - especially to memorize them all.

Mutual Respect

Bill and Jeff had a great deal of mutual respect for each other as guitarists, which solved the old problem "who was going to play lead guitar?" It was obvious that Don's music wouldn't have a place for a guitarist who played conventionally anyway, so this did put both Bill and Jeff on a completely different planet musically-speaking. I never sensed a rivalry between them.

Bill Harkleroad: I have to go back before the band. Jeff and I became buddies before the band. I turned him on to drugs. We started taking acid and stuff and I was kind of the bad influence there. Jeff and I never played together during that time. Early on, I mean, we did a little bit, but we weren't in a band, but we just kind of played a little bit. It was more about Jeff and me hanging out. I think it probably deflated the "gunslinger" image. I considered that Jeff Cotton, Ron Peters, and I were probably the three good guitar players in town. I thought that I was better than Alex and those guys even when I was seventeen. Because I didn't know anything about rhythm and it was, "I can play a bunch of notes." So, that was my mindset. I was wrong, but that was my mindset. I thought Jeff was one of those guys and he scared me a lot. Before the band, when I would hear him play something, I would go, "God!"
John French: Yeah, he was a killer player.
BH: Yeah! I think Jeff respected my playing too. It was a reciprocal thing and when we were in the band, being so beaten down, I think it was a mutual respect. He knew the parts, but he could show them to me and I learned them awfully fast. So, I had a great deal of respect for him, he could really play.
JF: From the outside looking in (to the guitar player domain) it was the most unusual combination of seeing two guitarists who were both killer players – in different areas; you were more like the tapestry guy with the real fine line get every detail and Jeff had this more "grab it and go for it and claw away and pull sound out, you know. Just seeing you guys, it was the most non-competitive situation I ever saw between two guitarists.
BH: It was just, "here we go again, let's learn these parts and practice our asses off. We just did that.

To elaborate, I have never seen two guitarists work together so well in my life - before or since. Jeff and Bill had completely different approaches to guitar in several aspects. Bill was much more interested in articulation and exactness, and Jeff was totally concerned with "feel" and a kind of "wild abandon." These poor guys worked so hard. They would break strings and there wasn't any money for strings, so they would take old broken strings and tie them together to keep practicing.

Now and again, Don would insist on playing something on guitar to show somebody something. He would almost always get far to clumsy and wild and break strings and throw guitars out of tune, move bridges around etc. I would get so disgusted with this and always vowed that if I ever played guitar in his band, he would never play my instrument. He'd look at me and say something like "Oh, I see I've upset Jooooohhhhhnnnn again..." dripping with sarcasm.

Theory And Training

John French: You guys of course, learned everything you knew from Don, according to the books. We know better, however, that you guys were great players before you got there. You played professionally in bands, that you were doing cover tunes of all kinds of stuff. You were probably doing original material I'm sure.
Bill Harkleroad: When I joined the band, I was starting to learn John Coltrane tunes.
JF: You had studied some music theory too.
BH: A little bit.
JF: You had played flute?
BH: Yeah.
JF: So, you knew some music theory. I'm just bringing that in.
BH: It's just hard for me to say that now, since I have really studied since then.

The fact is that at least Jeff and Bill had participated in some form of musical training so that they had at least a rudimentary knowledge of music notation. As I stated earlier, they never actually read and transcribed parts during the *Trout Mask* creation era, but that doesn't mean that their knowledge of theory was non-existent.

CHAPTER TWENTY TWO: CORNUCOPIA OF CHAOS

Arrested

One night, we needed to stock up on a few groceries. For some time now, Jeff and I had been going into the markets and stealing about half our food. We were hungry, and desperately foolish. Stealing is never an answer. However, people do stupid things when they're desperate. On this particular night, Jerry drove the rest of us, Bill, Jeff and I, to the supermarket. It was a different market than the one we usually went to.

I started getting nervous because this seemed to be getting out of hand. However, I was like a lemming, obediently jumping into the ocean like the rest. I don't know how much Jerry actually knew about the plan, if anything.

When we got to the market, Jeff and I stashed a few items and took a few items up to the register. We were all standing there when they rang us through and I recall being nervous and reading the TV guide at the counter to help remain calm. Jeff paid for the food we had actually bought and we walked outside.

"Hold it right there!" we heard a voice shout, and two plain clothes men started pushing us up to the front wall of the store. There is nothing more humiliating than being caught doing something you know is wrong. I was devastated and embarrassed. I couldn't see anyone else, but I felt worse for Jerry than anyone. How was he going to explain this to his wife? He hadn't taken a thing, and neither had Bill.

When you get spread-eagled against a wall, they basically want you totally off-balance, so you are actually leaning at about a 45 degree angle against the wall. I didn't know this, and I had food held under my arms that I actually still thought I could conceal. "Get your hands up there!" this guy screamed at me, "and get those legs back!" He pushed my hand up against the wall higher and started kicking my shins to slide my feet out about four feet from the wall. Being kicked in the shins is no pleasant experience, but I didn't feel any pain at all. I was totally numb.

We stood there for several minutes as they collected food. After they collected all the food, they led us through the store to the back storage areas and sat us on boxes. I remember distinctly this one cop or security guard shouting at me, "If you have any drugs in your pocket and you attempt to swallow them, you will be dead before they hit your stomach, do you understand?" I mumbled "yes" shamefully. "DO YOU UNDERSTAND?" he screamed even louder. I looked up, and he had his revolver pointed right between my eyes. I could see the bullets in the chamber, staring menacingly out at me.

It was a strange calm that had come over me. Being trapped like that, I just didn't care. I looked him right in the eyes as though I were completely bored and said, "I said yes, OK?" A look of puzzlement and shock came over his face caused by my lack of fear.

Interestingly, I didn't care if I lived or died. I was thinking to myself, "if only he'd pull that trigger, I'd never have to go back to that wretched house again." That was almost my exact thought at that moment. That's how unhappy I actually was at that point in time. I hated living with Don, being so broke, dependent and controlled. I was absolutely miserable – and this was only the *beginning* of the misery.

We were to wait back there until squad cars arrived at which time we were then marched through the store. Before they took us out, they handcuffed us together, but they "daisy-chained" us. That's the best way I can describe it. They made us cross our arms in front of us, and they cuffed our crossed arms to the person next to us. I suppose this was to make it more difficult for us to attempt to break away from them.

We were then marched out through those poor middle-class shoppers, who looked scared to death of us. I guess we were a scary looking group. Long disheveled hair, blank stares, and hungry and irritable. Inside, we were just scared to death. When we got outside, we were then re-cuffed individually with our hands behind us, and the security guards took back their cuffs. We were roughly pushed into the squad cars, Jeff and I in one, and Bill and Jerry in another.

Welcome To Our Jail

We arrived at the Van Nuys Jail and were made to empty our pockets. We were then fingerprinted and our mugshots were taken as we held a number under our chin: front and side view. We were led down a hallway to the cell, which was on our left. It contained eight double bunks, two of which were occupied by a couple of guys who had set fire to lawn furniture and thrown it into the pool at their apartment building - something to tell their buddies about Monday at work.

We actually made friends with these guys and had good conversation, joking around about our situation, which lightened the air a bit. The guys were interested in the band and when we mentioned Zappa, they basically seemed to want autographs.

We had a phone call coming, and I was elected to call - but who? Don didn't have a phone at that time - he always used pay phones. So, I called Victor Hayden's parents, Jack and Charlene, and was totally honest with them. It was late by this time, probably 11 or midnight. Charlene answered the phone. I was a little relieved; because I knew her a little better than Jack and felt more comfortable telling her what had happened. "Oh, John, I'm so sorry this happened to you." She said. She had gone through this with Victor a while back when he had been busted for dealing pot. "Tell Vic to get Don." I said, and hung up.

I don't know if I ever got to say "Thank You" Charlene. I never remember her ever throwing this situation in my face or saying anything snide or sarcastic to me in the months to come. She was totally understanding, and one of the sweetest people I'd ever known. Her voice reassured me, in my devastated condition, to remain calm.

I went back to the cell and told everyone what happened and they were relieved that I was able to reach Charlene.

"This is really going to mess up Don's plans," I said.

"What do you mean?" Jerry asked.

"Don is going to have to sign something with Zappa quick to get us out of here, and that will make the contract in Zappa's favor." I replied.

It seemed to me that at this time we were still sort of "in limbo" with Zappa and Krasnow. My instincts were telling me that Don would choose his friend over Krasnow. After the way Krasnow acted with us at his house, I doubt he would have helped us. I knew Frank would.

In the front of our cell was a concrete wall with full-width windows made of reinforced glass with what looked like chicken wire inside. Right in the very front, on the right, was a toilet. If one had to go to the bathroom, that was the only place to go. I'll never forget that night, how much I had to go to the bathroom and how I held back for hours until everyone was asleep before I went.

A short while after we arrived another cellmate arrived. This guy was apparently a drunk who knew his way around the place. The bunks were just a steel platform with a thin pad and no pillow, but this guy had his act together. He folded the end of the pad over to make himself a pillow, laid down with his feet hanging over the edge of the mat, shoes still on, and fell sound asleep in a matter of (literally) seconds. Didn't even say "Hi" to anyone.

I lay most of the night, wide awake, staring at the ceiling, on the top bunk, second from the left facing in. I was reflecting upon my short but disastrous life. I couldn't understand Don. He was so gifted and could be so charming, but he was impossible to live with. I had never had such a low opinion of myself. I swore to God that I would never be in jail again. Here I was, like a caged animal, unable to go anywhere save this eight by twenty-two foot smelly room. How long would it be before my life would change for the better? What could I do about it?

Zappa Bails Us Out

I think I must have eventually fallen asleep. I think I recall being awakened and given some really terrible breakfast (very similar to the breakfast given at the airport security room when we were detained in London less than a year before) and then lined up. We stood in this line for quite some time and were being led out to a bus. "We're going to LA County" some fellow inmate informed me. *"Oh no!"* I thought. I'd heard really awful things about LA County Jail.

Just then, some officers walked up and pulled the four of us out of line. We were marched up through where we came in, given our bags of belongings, signed out and released. We walked out and Don was sitting in his White Jaguar waiting for us.

"I can't believe how fucking stupid you fools are!" - was his welcoming statement. "I gave you money, how come you just didn't tell them you forgot to pay?" he asked.

"It's a little hard to explain when there's a gun pointing at your head, and the food under your arms is falling on the ground outside the store." I replied. "Shut up, John!" he snapped disgustedly.

Don went on to explain that Zappa had bailed us out, and he had to sign some agreement to get the money etc., just as I had anticipated. Well, this was a terrible situation alright, but the one good thing that came out of it was that whenever I found myself in a group of unruly violent malcontents, I always asked, "Hey, you guys know who Frank Zappa is?"

"Wuh, yeah," they would say, "what about it?"

"He bailed me outta jail once!" I'd say proudly.

"Far out!" they'd reply.

Immediate acceptance and total respect from any malcontent, hoodlum, drug dealer, or murderer was mine from this moment in time forward.

Don's Mounting Pressure On Jerry

Don began to pressure Jerry in various ways. It was obvious to me that he was trying to make things unreasonably difficult at a time when Jerry was already dealing with an unbearably difficult personal situation. Now that he'd been arrested (Jerry didn't steal anything), we had to go to court together every couple of weeks. He had to deal with his family knowing that he'd been arrested. It must have been really bad for him. I also felt bad for Bill Harkleroad who, as I remember, didn't steal anything either. Those two wound up in jail because of Jeff and I.

Jerry Handley Leaves

Jerry Handley: It was shortly after Alex left that I left. He and I basically started the band. I always thought that Alex and I were the two that wanted to play and have a blues band up in Lancaster, and got Doug and Don at that time, who wasn't "Mr. Beefheart" in those days. Alex and I went way back, as I said. He was my mentor. I don't know who you looked up to as drummers, but Alex was my mentor in the blues bands. He really personified the blues guitarist. That's what I was going to be. He was a helluva blues guitarist.

Jerry finally succumbed to Don's pressure and quit the band. I think it was a rather difficult decision for him to make. I really missed him when he left, as he had been my best friend in the early band, and was always willing to drive me somewhere I needed to go. He had paid a lot of dues to be in the band for the four years or so that he was a member. It had been a big dream of his to "make it" in the music business.

Reality had stolen his dream away. He was the last original member, and I felt a sense of history's loss in his leaving. I had felt a little more like someone was on my side just having him in the group. Although we had several differences of opinion and he had given me a tongue-lashing more than once (most that I deserved), I had respected him and I knew that things were going to be a lot different with him gone.

Handley's Last Straw

John French to Jerry Handley: What actually put you out of the band? What actually made you decide "That's it?"
JH: Well I was having a nervous breakdown, that might have been part of it.
JF: Oh, well I can see why. You had a wife, you had a kid, you had another on the way, right?
JH: Right, well I don't know, well probably Jennifer was on the way,
JF: Yeah. I think you had one on the way. And I know Sue was concerned about what was going to happen to you guys.
JH: She had some clarity, she wasn't in it, like we were.
JF: Right, she had an objective point of view.
JH: Exactly. We had anything but....so, I had that kind of clarity on one side and then going to rehearsals and being put under the pressure cooker there.

I know it was heart-wrenching for Jerry to leave. He was visibly quite disturbed by the whole decision. However, Don did not seem at all interested in Jerry's emotional state at the time, nor did he seem to show one ounce of sadness at Jerry's departure. It was as if Jerry were some bum on the street who was nothing more than a nuisance to him. There was none of the camaraderie that usually accompanies musicians that play together for years. No feeling of, "well, we had some good times together in Europe, but I understand why you have to go."

It was the same as with Doug and Alex. All Don seemed to care about was who he could get to replace them quickly, so as to continue with his plans. These were guys that he had worked with for approximately two and a half (in Doug's case) to four years (Alex and Jerry) and yet Don did not seem at all visibly upset by losing contact with his friends and parting company.

I found this a bit curious. I know that when I joined the band, I had to leave a band of friends to join a band of strangers. It was tough for me, and although Don befriended me in the very beginning (for motives I suspect in retrospect as being purely for "proper indoctrination of the new bandmember") I still had strong reservations and doubts about my decision, and probably for good reason. I felt very lonely and missed my friends, especially Don Giesen and Jeff Cotton.

Whose Bass?

It wasn't enough for Don that Jerry just left, however. For some reason, Don decided to keep Jerry's bass when he left the band. This erupted into a rather ugly scene. Don had somehow gotten the impression that when Jerry traded his bass in and bought a Framus (I believe that was the brand name) with money partially received from Buddah records, that meant that the bass belonged to Don and Jerry had no right to it if he was going to desert the band. Van Vliet was very adamant about this. I felt that it was a ludicrous position to take. When Jerry came to pick up his bass, he wasn't let into the house. His bass remained locked in Don's closet for some time.

John French: So, do you remember that when you left the band, Don didn't want to give your bass back to you.
Jerry Handley: Right, yeah, yeah.
JF: I couldn't believe that. I was there, I thought what can I do about this, it's in Don's closet, and your father came down I think, because you were working to talking to Don I mean, He stayed there all night one night.

Jerry came to the house on numerous occasions to retrieve his bass, and his father even came down once and stayed for what seemed like an entire day. Don just ignored him for the most part.

I was ashamed at this point to be associated with Don and could barely speak to Mr. Handley. I felt like this decision was completely one-sided and that Jerry had been through enough. I couldn't look his father in the eye.

He stayed at the house, if I recall for about 24 hours straight, sitting most of the time in a chair in the living room. Eventually, after the senior Handley had been worn down, Don had a "talk" with him outside somehow convincing him that the bass should be left behind. I remember Don giving me the impression that he had somehow "enlightened" the senior Handley in some way.

Jerry Handley: (He was) trying to talk sense to Don. But Don was in a state of mind ... whatever his problem was, he felt like I must have owed it to him or something.
John French: My God, what did you owe him? I mean, you had been there all that time, you started the band, it was your bass to begin with.
JH: Well, he showed his colors, you know. When it came right down to it, you were just whatever he could get out of you at that time - that's what he thought.
JF: So that must have been a pretty sad feeling for you, to walk out from this guy that you'd been friends with for years, and gone through and paid all these heavy dues and then he is doing this.
JH: Absolutely. It was. It hurt me a lot, but I wasn't as close to Don as I was to Alex. Alex and I went way back. We hung out together before we were ever playing in bands together, cruised around Lancaster.
JF: Well, that was like Jeff Cotton and I.
JH: Yeah, so when Don did that, I thought, "What an asshole," you know, cause he was. He was being a real asshole.

It was an embarrassing and unreasonable situation, not the first nor the last I encountered in working with Van Vliet.

How Weird Thou Art
Most people who knew Don for any period of time saw both sides of his personality. One on one, Van Vliet could be really enjoyable company as Don Aldridge recalls:

Don Aldridge: One of his favorite things to say was, "Man, you're weird. You're strange.
John French: He'd say that to me a lot.
DA: The thing about it that I didn't realize at the time was that was a mechanism he used for gaining control of people. On one hand he was telling you that you were so different, you're special, you are above this other crap around here, on the other hand, he was telling you, "I noticed that, no one else knows what I know about you."
JF: ...Like he was suddenly becoming your best friend.
DA: Before long, I began to believe that he DID know...
JF: What he liked to do was isolate people from other people.
DA: Very compartmentalized.
JF: You'd be in the same room with 5 other people, but you couldn't really communicate with them because he had done these manipulatory things. It just got really strange.

Bill had mentioned that Jeff and I seemed to have a different "vibe" about us when he first entered the group. Now he elaborates...

John French: Did you see changes in other band member's personalities that you would attribute to Don's influence?
Bill Harkleroad: When I joined the band, I didn't know you as well as I knew Jeff, but I knew you and Jeff both exhibited stuff that kind of freaked me out. You were different. You guys were already affected before I got in the band. All of us were affected as much as you can be without going to an insane asylum. Yeah, tremendously so, is the answer.
JF: What do you think caused that to happen to us?
BH: An intentional thing on his (Don's) part.
JF: Was it to suppress our creative abilities - to keep us from maybe drawing attention to ourselves?
BH: I think those are the outcroppings of the central thing of him being able to control a situation and own it all and have it be "Don's World." Those things come from that.
JF: So you're boiling it down to the main thing.
BH: The main thing is him totally controlling a situation. One by one getting members eight or nine years younger than him. One by one romancing them and then beating the shit out of them. ...I'm talking about emotionally "crushing" people.

Bill's reference is to a mental state, not physical abuse. Physical violence eventually came into play, but it was mostly encouraged as a "healthy" way to work out our differences. It was usually one band member against the other as the "overseer" looked on. I will go into this more later, but this was one of the steps I mentioned earlier that I observed in the process of the growth of the cult-like atmosphere that slowly strangled as much individuality as possible out of each of us. I mentioned to Bill that I recall Don being physically abusive to him at a later point.

Bill Harkleroad: Okay, well I don't even remember it.

I've noticed that a lot of things that were traumatic seemed to be blanked out by both Bill and Mark. There are things I remember clearly that they can't recall, or that when I mention a certain circumstance, they will suddenly dimly or clearly remember it.

I Can't Help Myself...

Doug Moon: (regarding a conversation with Gary Marker)
John French: (Gary Marker) said, that he was just a few units shy of a doctorate in psychology and he had this whole different explanation for Don's behavior. Don's behavior was completely out of his control and that he was suffering from a delusional thing that caused him to behave in ways that he couldn't handle ...erratic behavior, and it had nothing to do with his own will, or the fact that he was a bad person. What do you think about that angle? I am just curious.
DM: I definitely think he was out of control. I think he was controlled by forces – unseen forces.
JF: Supernatural?
DM: Yeah.
JF: Did you ever see any manifestations of supernatural occurrences – things you thought were out of the norm?
DM: With Don? Yeah!
JF: I'm not talking about hallucinations or anything, but I'm talking about actual things that happened that could have been the result of some supernatural thing that Don had tapped into.

DM: Oh yeah, definitely. I noticed behavior and things that he did and said that I believe were directly the influence of supernatural forces.

Sun Zoom Spark?

What if, as a lot of fans seem to think, Don's behavior was just a necessary counterpoint to our resistance? What if this behavior that Don exhibited in manipulating us was nothing more than what was necessary to break down the barriers that separated us from doing something really great? Could the work we accomplished have been achieved had he not employed the seemingly unethical methods he did? Could his goal have been accomplished any other way?

I think "yes" - that it could have been achieved in much less time and with a great deal more accomplished in a shorter period of time. Comparing cruelty and abuse with negative and positive magnetic poles or light and darkness seems like apples and oranges. I believe that great things can be accomplished peacefully through showing others love, gratitude and understanding as opposed to cruelty, condecension and manipulation.

Is the only reason I enjoy food that others are starving? Is the only reason I appreciate life because others have died? Is human suffering and war necessary for peace to exist? Can I only enjoy health because others have terrible diseases? Negative aspects may cause me to be more grateful, but are not necessary for my fulfillment.

My thought is that if I can visualize a world where people accomplish great things through love, maintain peace through harmony, maintain health through proper diet and nutrition and have enough food for everyone on planet earth then why is that not possible? If it is conceivable, then I believe it is possible.

Motorhead Sees The Dark Side

Jim Sherwood: I just remember going over there and Don was yelling at all these poor guys and I'm thinking, "Shit!" Alex was there. Another time, I went down to the Rainbow Room and they were playing down there. (It was) the first time I went and saw them working. God! Don was throwing the microphone on the floor and he'd say, "I can't hear myself!" and he's yelling at the guy up in the booth instead of playing. It was just a whole lotta weird shit. I thought "Jesus, Don! What happened to you man?" He was just a totally different guy to me. He was so ... it seemed like he was extremely paranoid and trying to control everything you know? I said, "What's your problem bud?" (laughs)
John French: Yeah, that's a pretty ongoing theme in the interviews.
JS: Yeah, so maybe he was that way, but not when I knew him, not when we were growing up as kids.
JF: That's interesting. That's a different side of him than most people he worked with have seen.
JS: Yeah, I'd never seen that side at all. The only things I saw were one time at that club and then out at the rehearsal thing. Before that, Donny was the kind of guy you could just slap around and tell him exactly what you wanted to do with him. I don't know, maybe somewhere along the line, he figured if he would yell at somebody it scares them off, I don't know.

In Contrast To Frank...

John French: But as far as when you were working with (Frank) in the room, you never felt the feeling that you felt with Don yelling at his band?

Jim Sherwood: No, never. Frank would give you a dirty look once in a while if you played something wrong or bad. It was a dirty look as much as it was a "Oh, come on now" kind of look. Like, "You can do better." Or, if I was making a joke and would say something really stupid, Frank would just kind of look at me, like " No, man, that's not the way it is." Other than that, I never had any trouble with Frank at all. In fact, Frank was never really a part of the band itself, it was just like the band was our family and Frank was our leader, that was the way he was treated, as the leader, and that was what he wanted it to be. There was a closeness from time to time, but there was no family kind of thing there, with Frank. He's got a business thing to get going and he's gotta do this. We just kind of do what he wants.

JF: But there weren't bad, ill feelings. There wasn't a tense-ness. He allowed "fun" in the band.

JS: Well, yeah, and that was what was great about it. And with him doing all the sound effects, and doing this and that, Ray Collins doing little puppet shows during the show – it was fun. It was a kick! It was great.

Favoritism

There seemed to be a kind of favoritism that was instilled in certain people. This kind of was a rotational thing, as otherwise, the control would get off-kilter and there would have been mutiny. I saw more of this with Jeff Cotton, as Don spent a lot of time with Jeff. Jeff had taken on the role of "scribe" and wrote down nearly everything Don committed to paper during this period, which was a surprisingly large amount of material. Compared to the music, I would say that Don probably wrote 10 times the amount of prose, poetry and lyrics as he did music. Most of his time was taken up with verbal creation rather than musical creation. So, the favoritism seemed to sway toward Jeff through most of the *Trout Mask* era.

Aldridge recalls earlier bouts of favoritism.

Don Aldridge: He did this with Gary Lambert, the teacher. Well, one day, all of a sudden, Gary was gone, and no one was talking about Gary any longer.

Of course, anyone Don needed to complete a goal (like needing a bass player for a session after Jerry left) was prone to receiving a ration of favoritism for a time.

Gary Marker: The thing was, he would cut me a lot of slack for some reason or other, I don't know - maybe because we were contemporaries or something.

John French: Well, it was the same with you, the same with Elliot Ingber. He did that with Art Tripp too.

GM: He would buddy up with somebody in particular to use that against other people in the band. Like, "Why's he hanging out with him all of a sudden?" It was kinda like favoritism kinda shit. So, he would run that number. But he would let some people get by with some stuff like, "Oh yeah, he can do whatever he wants but you, you ain't shit!" - THAT kind of attitude.

Enter Gary Marker

At the point that Jerry Handley left the band, the vacancy needed to be filled immediately. We were about to do a session with Frank and we needed a bassist for the session. Don contacted his old friend Gary Marker. I hadn't seen Gary in over a year and I was a little nervous about him showing up, especially with the intense environment that had developed.

John French: Did you consider (Gary Marker) a permanent member of the band when he came in?
Bill Harkleroad: To tell you the truth, I don't know if I even thought about things like that at that point. I was so struck with this. You guys had an intense environment already going. I didn't perceive things like that.

Marker Shows Up For Rehearsal

I recall at that time that I didn't even have a decent drum set and nothing was set up in the room, as I had been transcribing piano parts for Don for weeks and the drums were disassembled in the laundry shed. Everything of mine had been sold to help pay bills except an older Slingerland four-piece set. It was a natural wood set I had gotten through Krasnow. The bass drum head was broken, and we had no money to replace the head. There was an old 24-inch bass drum (relatively large) in the laundry shed, so I decided to try to incorporate it with the other drums. It took a lot of time, because I had to switch hardware and I wasn't quite finished when Don showed up with Gary.

Don's reaction upon seeing the drums lying on the floor with heads and hardware scattered about was to become furious with me for making such a bad impression on Gary. I think the worst impression made upon Gary this particular day was not by me, but by Don. As a nineteen year old, I withered and became extremely embarrassed by Don's unbridled verbal attack in front of Gary, who I hadn't seen for months, and Bill, who I barely knew. Jeff was used to this behavior by now, and so I knew he understood.

Marker kept saying something to the effect of, "It's fine Don, no harm done, he'll be done in a few minutes." Interestingly enough, it took longer for me to stand and listen to Don's accolade than it would have taken to just finish the job and be set up. These kinds of outbursts were an ongoing occurrence and something that I could just never get used to. Don's stinging words would bounce around in my head for days as I tried to understand just exactly what I had done to deserve this kind of treatment. Eventually, the resentment building up from these attacks took their toll on my respect for Van Vliet. I soon became very indifferent to his music or lyrics, because they came from a man who didn't practice what he preached.

> *My smile is stuck, I cannot go back to your Frownland*
> *My spirit's made up of the ocean and the sky,*
> *And the sun and the moon and all my eyes can see*
> *I cannot go back to your land of gloom*
> *Where black jagged shadows remind me of the coming of your doom*
> *I want my own land*
> *Where a man can stand by another man*
> *Without an ego flyin'*
> *And no one dyin' by an earthly hand* [42]

Marker First Poppy Rehearsal

John French: Do you remember the first day you came up to rehearse?
Gary Marker: No, I sure don't.
JF: I just wondered if you remembered. He just gave me one hell of a bad day that day.
GM: I do remember one thing. I remember that you seemed to be in a kind of constant state of abject terror.
JF: Yeah he scared the hell out of me. I didn't know what he was going to do.
GM: Well, you never knew because he was unpredictable. That's the whole thing. And once

---

[42] "Frownland" excerpt, 1969, Beefheart Music Co. BMI

again, it gets back to the whole control deal - to keep people around him constantly off-kilter. You never knew what he was going to do next, or what he was thinking, so you're always trying to second-guess him. It's the abused-spouse syndrome. It was very much the same kind of thing. You never know if you've done anything right, you know, if you're gonna get a compliment or you're gonna get smacked across the face.

Zoot On Marker

John French: As far as Marker, what was your impression of him as a player?
Bill Harkleroad: I knew that he came from a band that I was a fan of. Taj Mahal, so I thought "Oooh, he's a pro-guy!" Again, other than that, he seemed to be just another "Jerry." I mean, I didn't know enough, you know? He played fine, he played the parts fine. I was already starting to feel the difference in how I was being pushed to play with so much aggressive hand techniques and he was playing more like a standard bass player that didn't create a sweat. That's the feeling I got, was that you, me and Jeff were like over the top gritting our teeth and playing our asses off and he was more like, "I'm a bass player, and this is how we play!"

Gary rehearsed with us and we probably learned one song or maybe two. The only song I recall for sure playing was *Moonlight On Vermont*. Don touched up the drum parts a bit, adding a twist here or there, but basically it was the same thing I had been playing.

Frank Visits

After meeting Frank at the Log Cabin, I was a little apprehensive about seeing him again. My first encounter with him had been the "so, who are you? Don's brother?" evening. The second was our time with him at the Log Cabin listening to music and just hanging out. One was bad the other good, but he hadn't heard us play, and I was hoping that our impression on him would be favorable. I was also wondering if Don would blow up at me the same way he had in front of Gary Marker.

I could tell by Frank's conversation at the Log Cabin as we listened to music that he was exceedingly knowledgeable and I knew also that he was self-trained.

Jim Sherwood: I was amazed by the man. I think he's probably one of the best musicians I've ever heard. I've heard him play blues. I've heard him play jazz. I've heard him do the classical stuff. It's all self-taught. He taught himself on guitar, how to do that. He taught himself to read music. He was writing symphonies. It just blew me away. His musical ability, as far as his ear goes, it was incredible.

Don had Frank come up to the house one day. I can't recall how Frank arrived, but it seems to me that Don drove over and picked him up. This was one of two times Frank was actually at the house as far as I can remember. It was mid-day, or perhaps a little before. We had just learned *Moonlight On Vermont* with Bill Harkleroad. Don had worked out some drum ideas on this song the night before with me. This was one of the few songs on *Trout Mask* that Don was very specific about what he wanted. I already had a drum part to the song, and mostly what he added were embellishments in certain sections, but they were very specific.

Frank came in from the downstairs door. The house had a strange floor plan wherein the "front" door actually opened to the bedroom. Anyway, I recall having my drum kit set up facing the fireplace wall. Don asked us to play *Moonlight On Vermont* for Frank. I was a little nervous, as all the embellishments Don had added were fresh in my head from the night before, so I was still using left-brain thinking rather than the more intuitive, creative right-brain thinking.

We played the song down. Don never sang with us, but he may have actually sang that day to make an impression on Frank. It was like an "audition" in my mind. When we finished, Frank started raving on about my drumming, saying "I've always wanted a drummer who played like that!" – to Don. He really complimented me, which made me feel a little foolish, as the parts were Don's and the whole band was playing great. I felt self-conscious. However, I quickly recovered and basked in my moment of glory. Also, I was greatly relieved that everything had gone well.

Frank then asked me "what's that?" and pointed to an open manuscript book sitting on the piano. "Oh, that's some of Don's stuff that I write down for him." I'm not sure of the song, but the guys played their parts. He said, "play the other part with them on piano." I told him that I didn't actually sight-read piano parts, but just knew enough to write what Don was playing and teach it to the guys.

After this, he showed Bill a chord or chord progression on guitar, which wound up being used on the end of *Veteran's Day Poppy* in the last slow section.

Bill Harkleroad: **Veteran's Day Poppy *was just kind of the first thing we did and it was coming from I think kind of the first couple of open - ended jams that I had done when I tried out for the band and then played from there, and a couple of the "bluesy" things we were doing in the key of E ended up being the tune. The last half of the tune was actually a minor 9 chord that Frank Zappa showed me and I was dinking around with …Don wanted to use that.***
John French: Oh, so it was sort of collaborative.
BH: Well, I was just sitting there playing this chord that Frank said, "Hey, if you play this cool G maj 7 with an E bass note it's a cool chord. I didn't know what it was then.
JF: So was that (the first time) when he came up to the house one day.
BH: Yep! The first time I saw Frank at that house.

It was a short visit, perhaps an hour, and Frank needed to go, telling Don he needed a ride to Hollywood. "Hey Drumbo," he said, "Come with us, I'll buy you lunch."

So, I wound up walking down the stairs with Frank and Don and riding into Hollywood. We stopped at a Fried Chicken place called Chicken Delight, and Frank bought us all a box lunch thing, which we sat outside and ate. Unfortunately, I didn't enjoy this trip much. I was constantly on guard that I might say something which would later be used as evidence against me in "talk." This was part of the environment that was so ridiculous. I had actually gotten to the point where I was double-thinking everything I said and I'm sure everyone else was the same.

It seemed at the time that there was an art studio somewhere in Hollywood where Cal Schenkel had set up shop. I don't know if it was his shop, or part of Frank's rehearsal place, or what. I do recall that Frank was showing us some cover art ideas and said that Cal would probably be doing the artwork for Don's album.

Wild Man Fischer

One of the most puzzling things to me was why in the world someone with Frank Zappa's talents would actually spend valuable time working with the man who called himself Wild Man Fischer. It seemed to me upon first encounter that Wild Man Fischer was a man who was mentally disturbed and probably violent. He couldn't sing, and his music was something you may hear a wino in an alley raving about.

The band came to Sunset Sound one night with Don. I can't remember whether we were there to record or not, but it seems it was more of a social call – most likely before the one session later described at Sunset Sound with Frank at the controls. When we walked into the control booth, Wild Man was in the studio trying to sing a song acapella, I say "trying," because in my opinion, this man could not sing and certainly seemed more in need of intense therapy than a recording studio.

His song was probably entitled, *Merry Go-Round* and I could probably find this on some rare recording of alternate music were I prone to do a search. However, I didn't want to hear it then, and I certainly don't want to hear it now. This man was running wildly (Gee, hence the name I guess) around the studio attempting to sing in a voice that was half way between the most obnoxious cartoon character voice you ever heard and a demon-possessed lunatic.

There was nothing special or gifted about this man, in my opinion. His frantic, sobbing, vocal emissions (I can't think of a better word to describe them) were asking the musical (?) question, "*Why don't we Merry Go, Merry Go, Merry Go Round, Come on let's*...etc." Wild Man and Frank took a break after this and we all walked out in the drive for a smoke. I remember not having matches and I walked up to Mr. Fischer with my unlit cigarette in my lips and beckoned for light, lightly pulling his lit cigarette over to mine.

He turned jerking his hand away from mine (we had met and talked previously to this, so he knew me) and looked at me with the fiercest gaze in his eyes, "Hey, that's my cigarette, man!" "Relax, Wild Man, I just want a light, OK?" I replied in as soothing a voice as I could. "Well, get it somewhere else, man!" By this time, the urgent pitch and volume of his voice convinced me that here was not a reasonable man.

When we went back in the studio, Zappa went out into the tracking room, put on his guitar and spent several hours (probably more time than the entire *Trout Mask* instrumental session) overlaying Fischer's voice with accompaniment. He used an octavider (an instrument that makes an electric instrument sound lower or higher in pitch in octaves) to play the bass parts and overdubbed chords and lead guitar.

As I thought about Zappa's six hour limit on instrumental track time for *Trout Mask* later, I thought back to this extravagant session for a man who was obviously mentally unbalanced. I am sure that Zappa did several tracks with Wild Man, and I'm sure the expense tallied to a rather higher tab than *Trout Mask* ever achieved. Also, Sunset Sound was surely a more expensive studio than Whitney Studios in Glendale (where *Trout Mask* was recorded). "What on earth could have been going through Frank's mind?" I thought to myself. It surely seemed almost a slap in the face to Don.

If you are a fan of Wild Man Fischer, I apologize. I am merely trying to convey the feeling here that there was some physical evidence to warrant what was in Don's mind concerning Frank's packaging of him under the same category as Wild Man Fischer.

Drum Parts On Veteran's Day Poppy

Marker came to the house shortly after the Frank Zappa visit to work on two other songs – *Veteran's Day Poppy*, and *Kandy Korn*. I only remember the former. I had a date with Beverly that evening and Don decided – as soon as she showed up – to write the drum parts to *VDP*.

John French: Do you recall the night that Don taught me the parts to **Veteran's Day Poppy** *at the end, you know, where he wanted those funny drum breaks? There was a girl named Beverly that came up to see me that night and we were going out on a date. He decided to write the parts just as she got there. So, she had to sit there for two hours while he wrote all these parts*
Bill Harkleroad: (Laughter)
JF: I think in his head he figured, "Well, John will learn them fast cause he's in a hurry." You know what I mean?
BH: Boy, you think better of him than I do. Knowing the guy, I think he was fucking with you

man, and "Ah, he's got a girl here and I'm going to make him have to stay."
JF: Yeah, I think that was part of it.
BH: I think really that's where that guy was coming from a lot of the time.

Shuffle Section – Veteran's Day Poppy

Gary Marker: *I do remember lobbying heavily to put in a little shuffle section. Which we cross faded – right?*
John French: *Oh, so that was your idea.*
GM: *Yeah, I got it in there and Jeff was going, "I don't know. I don't think he's going to like this." I said, "Well, that's OK, just run it past him. Don?" He says. "Oh yeah, that's OK, man, sure, fine! That's nice. Can you make it work?." He finally he finally got me aside and he said, "Was that your idea?"*

On The Playing Of Soprano Sax

Gary Marker: *I think it was somewhere around* Trout Mask *or whatever it was. I went up there and he said, "I'm playing soprano sax now!" I said, "When did you learn how to play soprano sax?" He said, "No, really, I can do it, I can play soprano! You'll be surprised!" I said, "I sure as fuck will be surprised! I want to hear you play, …this is gonna be good!"*
John French: *Did he play for you?*
GM: *Yeah, he did, and I said, "Well, let's put it this way. Coltrane is not spinning at 300 cycles per minute in his grave!" He said, "Well, fuck you, man! This is important stuff!" …Well, it was noodle noodle noodle.*

Dexter And Ornette

Gary Marker: *I worked with everybody from Dexter Gordon to Ornette Coleman, you know. Ornette Coleman was generally considered to be pretty avant-garde then, you know.*
John French: *You played with Ornette* and *Dexter??*
GM: *Yeah, …how I learned to play bass was with Dexter Gordon. I was probably seventeen years old and I'd been playing bass for like maybe a year and ended up in some session somewhere and Dexter Gordon wanders in. I'm going, "Oh my God! It's Dexter Gordon! When he would walk through the door, it was like a McCormick reaper. I mean, he was huge, then. This is like early sixties. I was hiding in the corner and he looked around and said, "You, come here! You play that bass over there?" And I'm going, "Umm, ah, well…" "Get up on the stage!" he goes "Cherokee, one, two, one two three four…" People later asked me how I learned to play bass and I said, "Through the "horror method! It's like: Play or Die!"*

Motorhead On Don's Sax Playing

Jim Sherwood: *I thought it was really funny, because Don got out the soprano sax and was doing that shit with the soprano? I know he couldn't play it, because I couldn't play it. That's what Frank did with us at the Royal Albert Hall in London. He said I was supposed to sneak over to the band and pick up the soprano sax and just blow the shit out of it. Just blow tons of notes at random. That's what I did. So, later on when we came back, here's Don playing* soprano sax and he was doing the same shit I was, just blowing the hell out of it and didn't know what he was doing.

John French: *A lot of people feel that he was a musical genius.*

JS: *I don't think so. I think he was copying a lot of my shit, and maybe other people's, I don't know. You know what was really weird about that is that a lot of the jazz people – Frank would have me do a solo on baritone in the clubs, and I'd be playing some melody lines and that, and he would just say "go off on it," and I would just start blowing the shit out of everything. You know, as fast as I could possibly blow and move my fingers is what I was doing. That became avant-garde later on, because John Cage, and a whole bunch of jazz musicians grabbed a hold of that and thought it was the greatest thing in the world.*

John Thomas on sax:

JF: *What do you think about his horn playing?*

JT: *I thought it was another thing in that same world where conceptually, he knew everything in that world he needed to know, but technically he didn't have what it took to be consistent. He would play records by Rahsaan Roland Kirk. It wasn't like he was off in his own universe. But at the same time, if he thought he was John Coltrane or Roland Kirk, the thing is those things got there through work.*

Later: *His voice was incredible, but he didn't know when to come in. His horn playing could be divine, but he didn't know what he was doing and couldn't do it twice. I'm not faultinghim for that - I'm just saying, it was different. You can't really put him on the same classas musicians who might sound exactly like him but got there by a different approach, with self-discipline and a love of music. He got there simply from conceptual power with no self-discipline and no sense of how it all worked. (He would) just force his conceptual intellectual power out there, and something would happen and then one of them would be good and that would be "it." I'm not demeaning that approach, because obviously, it made some cool music and it is as valid as the other. But as a musician that you could admire and could grow from, well, I think those other guys have more to offer in that respect.*

Dyslexic Don?

Gary Marker: *He would do that really kind of angular (writing) – not even cursive. I remember asking him when you guys were down at Sunset Sound, I said, "Can I get the lyrics to Abba Zaba? I would like to do that with my band." Don wrote about 2 lines, then he handed the tablet to you and said, "Here. You write them out!" It took me a few seconds, but then I realized, Jesus, this guy is so lazy he makes everyone do his work and then I realized: the fucker's dyslexic. You would hand him something to read and he would have trouble reading it. You know, "Wait a minute, I think I must need glasses, what does this say?" You'd have to read it to him. You'd have to write stuff for him. You know he never read a contract, because he signed anything anybody put before him. ...I know he could read if it was big enough. I saw him - I think the last time I saw him performing was down at the Roxy - and he was using cue cards ... God. I thought, "this is fucking amazing, he's using cue cards because he can't even remember the lyrics to his own songs."*

French Attitude

Gary Marker: *I remember when we finally ended up at the recording session, you also seemed to be in major panic mode. Ryland used to say, "You know that guy John is a really good*

drummer." I said, "Yeah, he's good. He's better than Don deserves." He said, "But, you know, he's got this attitude, it's like Iyore in Winnie the Pooh. It's like 'Oh, we'll never get this done. It'll never happen, it's not going to work'." I said, "I haven't really noticed that." He says, "You haven't?" And I said, "No, I mean next to you, you're so fucking negative about everything, how would I notice that?" "That sounds like shit!" – you know, that's Ryland's whole approach. But you did have a little of that, you had this constant thing, like "Oh, this isn't going to sound right. They're going to hate us. They'll never sign us, we won't get a record out." You used to do that a lot.
John French: Yeah, well, I wasn't far from the truth was I?
GM: No! I mean, this is back in Safe As Milk standards and by today, that's pretty conservative stuff.

Zappa At Sunset Sound

Zappa finally set some time aside to record us. This was at Sunset Sound Studios in Hollywood – the same studio in which *Sure 'nuff 'n Yes I Do* was recorded with Richard Perry at the board. It was also the same room in which *Strictly Personal* was recorded.

Marker recalls Zappa being "befuddled" by the new studio equipment in Sunset Sound, which was all new solid-state as opposed to the older vacuum tube technology. It was either 16 or 32 track recorders that would play at 30ips – twice as fast as the older machines. The clarity on tape was astoundingly different.

Gary Marker: When he heard the first playback he was really pissed, because he couldn't understand why the EQ was all off. It was like, "Shit, there's really a big EQ difference, isn't there?" - at 30ips. I'm sort of always interested in the technical end of it, so I said, "Well, yeah, there's a big difference." You actually can catch more stuff – more overtones and things like that with more clarity and stuff. He got pissed at me. I said, "Well, the faster it goes, it makes sense. You have more room on the tape to catch things. He kind of like looked at me and then he turned to Don and said, "who is this guy?" I got in an argument with him in the booth. I said, "I've only worked in the studio maybe 10,000 times. So, I kinda know the way it works.

I was unaware of this at the time, probably because setting up drums is a gigantic nightmare. I only wish guitar players had to take their guitars apart and re-assemble them each time they go to a new spot so they would understand. Trying to maintain a creative state of mind when you're dealing with wing nuts, oily pedals, and adjusting the height and tilt of the cymbals while some clueless studio assistant is already trying to place the microphones on the drums before they're even set up is completely maddening to me. I always try to set up the night before, or several hours before I play, so I can go away, wash the grease off my hands, and get myself into the correct state of mind.

We did the takes fairly quickly, and I went in to listen to the playback. It was very shrill-sounding to my ears – especially Bill's guitar. I was thinking "Zappa's got a strange idea of how this song should sound." I thought that he was trying to produce us like a rock band. From Marker's interview, I'd say perhaps the sound had as much to do with Frank's unfamiliarity with the equipment as anything else.

It came time for Don to sing. I think I took a break and went outside for a smoke, as I didn't like to be in the studio when Don sang. Marker recalls Frank's instructions to Don during this session.

Gary Marker: Don would go out and do a vocal overdub, he would say, "Donny, do your bird whistles OK? Come on, you can do them." It was, "I wanna get it on tape, I wanna get your

bird whistles on tape." And Don was like, "Oh, come on, Shit, let's get this done with!   Let's be serious here."   So, he did his bird whistles. I had heard them before. But I had no idea – that's a real talent that he has. Well, Zappa was like, "Don't sing Donny, on this tune just do your bird whistles, OK? Zappa would have killed to have Don's voice.
John French: Oh yeah!
GM: Because Zappa couldn't sing.
JF: And Don couldn't function in a band without a lot of help.
GM: I walked back into the booth and something was happening and Zappa said something. He'd forgotten that I was with the Rising Sons and all that, because he used to come around a lot when we used to play. At some point, I think, Don reminded him and it didn't really mollify him that much because he was such an arrogant asshole. It's not good to speak of the dead that way, but he really was. Some of it was humorous and for effect and some of it was genuine arrogance. He made some remark about something I did on the bass part. I said, "Well you know, Frank, at least I don't have to watch my fingers while I play. And that was it! He didn't speak to me the rest of the night. He always watched his fingers when he played, he had to watch what he was doing, he didn't know what he was doing on guitar. You ever see any films of Zappa? He watches his fingers when he plays.
JF: Yeah, I noticed that.

Important Disclaimer: Gail Zappa, this is not my opinion. It is Gary Marker's opinion. Please don't sue me. I'm broke anyway. Frank fought against censorship. Gary's just exercising his first amendment right.

Marker's Equipment And Technique

Gary Marker: Funny because I have a CD – I have the vinyl somewhere – but I got a CD of Trout Mask, and you know those things that were cut at Sunset Sound do have an unusual sound to them. It's kind of an ominous sound to it - in my way of thinking. I've seen a couple of those songs that we did that night written up as being some of the scariest records people have ever heard. Veteran's Day Poppy as being a scary song? Well, OK!

Victor Shows Up With Strictly Personal

Victor Hayden came to the house one day with a copy of *Strictly Personal*, on Blue Thumb Records. Don was stunned and surprised. As he looked at the album cover, he said, "This is MY total concept! That fuckin' Krasnow even stole the label idea and my logo! Look at that, man, that's MY concept!" It was true, as I recall, Don had conceived of the cover design for *Strictly Personal* during the *Safe As Milk* sessions. I believe it was at a Guy Webster photo shoot that he told me about his idea which originally was to be titled, *It Comes To You In A Plain Brown Wrapper*. The idea was a joke based upon advertisements in magazines selling pornography and body-building books that read the same thing.

He also had spoken to me about the *25th Century Quaker* idea. Space-Age Quakers walking around in modern-looking versions of Quaker suits.

Don Aldridge: Yes, this started almost right at the very beginning (of him meeting Don), when he heard me and then began to listen to my material, my own stuff . He wanted to call me Sean De Gama and the Twenty-Fifth Century Quaker, or how bout Little Donny Aldridge?

When I reunited with Guy Webster at his studio in Venice, we were looking at photos of the band dressed in Quaker outfits and he reminded me that at that point in time, Don had perceived that we appear onstage as *The Twenty-Fifth Century Quaker* as a warm-up act, take a break and change, then come back up as *Captain Beefheart And His Magic Band.* I had forgotten this concept and it sprang into my mind clearly. Suddenly it dawned on me that the whole double-album concept had been to have an album of improvised blues (*Mirror Man, Tarotplane,* etc.) and another of arranged music (*On Tomorrow, Trust Us,* etc.) the first being the Quaker group and the second being the Beefheart group.

I recall Don telling of a conversation between Bob and himself in which they envisioned starting their own label Blue Thumb Records with the logo being a "capsule of LSD" with a blue thumbprint on it. The blue being powdered Sandose LSD on the thumb of the handler of the capsule. I had the feeling that there was a bit of admiration in Don along with the resentment for Bob's allocation and realization of their shared vision. It was as if Don thought that Krasnow was somehow "beckoning" to him, saying something like, "OK Don, I've shown you I can do it, I've shown you I can make it happen, now join me and we'll become millionaires together."

Rodeo Drive

The entire band soon went to visit Krasnow at the Blue Thumb offices on Rodeo Drive in Beverly Hills. I don't remember a great deal about the office. It seemed to me he had a very small office with no one working for him. Some rumor had spread that Bob had been deeply involved in black magic and could make "sparks jump from his fingers." I was always fascinated by the supernatural, and so I was really looking forward to a "display" of these remarkable powers. It was a small, dark office off a back parking lot area. I thought "dark, good, all the better to see the sparks clearly." I remember him wearing very non-standard clothing. No business suit and tie, or cowboy hat, which he had worn during *Safe As Milk* days. It seemed like it was an African Dashiki or something of the sort – like a robe. It was almost more like a "sorcerer's look," as much as I can remember.

Wasn't this shortly after the Rolling Stones released *Her Satanic Majesties Request?* Hollywood is all hype – smoke and mirrors. BK was pulling a good one this day. He was smiling and happy. He had the attitude of one who had not only pulled the wool over someone's eyes, but was enjoying the reaction of the one who owned the eyes.

The story as I recall went something like this and is a sort of review of the rumors and conjecture that was flying around: When we re-recorded *Strictly Personal* for MGM Records with Bob before the spring tour of Europe in 1968, Bob had mixed the album and brought it over to us in London for listen. Don was upset with the phasing, calling it " Electric Bromo Seltzer" or some such amusing coined phrase.

A Verbal Agreement With Blue Thumb

So, here was Don, who had already made a verbal agreement or even possibly signed with Frank Zappa his friend, suddenly deciding to go with Bob Krasnow. There was a verbal agreement reached that day between Bob and Don. I recall Don instructing me to write out lead sheets for everything we had recorded with Frank so that Krasnow could get them copyrighted. *Moonlight On Vermont* and *Veteran's Day Poppy* were the two songs I transcribed. I don't recall transcribing *Kandy Korn,* though Harkleroad and Marker both insist we performed it in a session with Frank.

I then took the charts over to Bob's home. He lived somewhere in the SF Valley at that time and I recall Jeff driving me over. (Don never allowed Mark or I to drive his car, but Jeff and Bill drove constantly. I think I didn't have a driver's license at the time.) On another occasion, the entire band had been to this house, which was a different house than he had lived in during *Safe As Milk* days. Bob on that visit had played us an album by an English group he felt were copying our look in some ways. The group was Jethro Tull.

When I knocked on the door this night to deliver the lead sheets, it was answered by one of his children. He came to the door angrily shouting at me, "I TOLD YOU GUY'S NEVER COME TO MY HOUSE!" I found this interesting, as I don't remember us ever having been told anything of the kind. I believe there was a problem with his wife not liking the band to be around her kids - perhaps because Don had used some racial epithets while at his other house. Our recent earlier visit, when Tull was played, had actually been during the daytime, and no one but Bob was home.

"I brought the charts you said you needed immediately, Bob, sorry. I'm not coming in or anything." "You sure as hell aren't." - was his warm reply as he snatched the charts from my hand and slammed the door. Jeff and I quickly left.

Alex Jams With Marker's Band "Fusion"

Gary Marker: You know, the funny thing was that maybe three years later when he (Krasnow) started up Blue Thumb? Krasnow was over at my house all the time, because I had this band called Fusion and he was a big jazz rock "head." He wanted to sign us up. Ahmet Ertegun signed us anyways, so it did us a lot of good, like zip. Finally, he came down and at one point Alex was coming over and playing with us. We were going to use him on rhythm guitar on some stuff. He's a good player. Cooder used to say, "Man, that fucking Alex? He's a fucking solid rock! I've never played with anybody who was more solid! It's just like he never dropped a beat in his life. He was just really an astonishing guy. If he would have been black, he would have been one of these workaday guitar players in the south who was always there and you could always depend upon."

Gary Marker: (writes) "Well, Krasnow's appearance was a surprise to me as well, but didn't have quite the effect that it apparently had on Alex. Back then, Krasnow was inclined to do stuff like, get blasted on acid and decide to drive over to Marker's house-because maybe they'll be playing some of that weird jazz stuff, and very often some local jazz heavies may be sittin' in and jamming. And usually there are a couple bitchin' babes hangin' out, too. They never went home with Krasnow, I don't know why he kept hitting on them."

Krasnow, aside from being a bit of a party animal and loving to hang with groups, was actually interested in Marker's group. He liked the music and was thinking about signing Fusion to Blue Thumb. Marker told Krasnow that they had some demo tapes he could hear, so he took him to the other part of the house and played the tapes for Krasnow, who, upon hearing them, asked to hear them again.

Gary Marker: He looked at me – I don't know how loaded he was – but he said, "You know, I really fucked up didn't I?" I said, "What do you mean?" He said, "You should have produced that Beefheart album! You should have done it! You knew about that music didn't you?" I said, "I still do!" I said, "You know what? Why don't we just kind of go on from here. I don't want to hear about it now. It's very nice of you to say that to me, but it doesn't pay the rent!"

Snouffer had been rehearsing with the band for a while and really enjoyed the group.

Alex Snouffer: ... I didn't know that those guys even remembered me. ... There was this keyboard player that did a lot of double time rhythm stuff, which saved me a lot of work on guitar. All I had to do was fill in the cracks.

John French: *Marker had a great respect for you as a player and so did Ry.*

AS: *Oh yeah?*

JF: *Ry and Marker would both comment that your rhythm was "like a rock." They called you a "motherfucker,"- which I understand is a good thing.*

AS: *(Laughter)*

JF: *So, how come you didn't stick with it?*

AS: *That's a good question. They were rehearsing over in Santa Monica and I lived in North Hollywood at the time, so it was kind of a trip. One rehearsal where we were cleaning up a song, who walks through the door but Krasnow. I just thought to myself, "oh fuck, not again." I had just gone THROUGH this hassle. Here he comes through the door. He and Gary went off and talked about whatever they talked about. I was just hanging out with the rest of the guys, saying, "OK, what can we do with this, but my heart wasn't in it. Soon as I saw Krasnow, everything that was up here just went down here (motions with hands to floor.) Now, as far as why I didn't go back for another rehearsal I don't remember. I just remember telling Gary, "If you're involved with that guy, I don't want anything to do with it."*

Thus ended Snouffer's tenure in Marker's band Fusion.

Frank in the log cabin circa '68. Photo courtesy of Art Tripp.

Mark Boston

Around October or November of 1968 Gary Marker had decided to withdraw from any further work with the group. This may have been partly as a result of his feelings for Frank, or conversely Frank's feelings for him. It could have been that he was a temporary sideman. He had his own group, Fusion, and also seemed to take Don far less seriously than Don had desired to be taken.

I had been practicing in the old laundry shed outside. Coming in at dusk through the kitchen door, I heard both guitarists talking with Don about who would play bass. There didn't seem to be much doubt about who was being strongly considered as a replacement for Jerry, at least in Don's mind. Mark Boston was on the top of the list. At that time, I personally didn't think that Mark would fit into the band because of his country roots. I thought that this would be a cause of friction and conflict with Don, who was always putting down country music and calling anyone who spoke with a southern accent an "okie."

Bill seemed to share a similar opinion. He was probably the most verbally opposed to the idea of Mark joining the band. I think we both liked Mark, but considered for similar reasons that it may not work. Part of it may have been we were trying to save him from the grief we were going through. I kept my mouth shut and offered no opinion other than "let's try him out." I recall Don referring to him earlier as "the guy with the eyes." He had seen him play with Blues in a Bottle and also spied him earlier in the audience at the Teenage Fair, while CB & HMB performed on the main stage at the Hollywood Palladium at the Teenage Fair years before.

Mark Recollects His Audition

Mark was summoned to appear. I believe he came down with his parents, "Dot and Dink," accompanied by his girlfriend the first time.

Mark Boston: Oh, I remember my audition, yeah. I remember I brought (Sharon) and she was hanging on my foot while I was trying to play. She was sitting there at my feet hanging onto my legs. I remember you guys wanted to know if I brought my bass, I said "yeah." I plugged it in and I didn't know what they were going to play, they said, "just jam along with this and see what you think." All of a sudden, somebody said, "And" (laughs). I just started. I had no idea what was going on. I just started making racket; you know - seemed like the thing to do.

Dot and Dink, Mark's parents, seemed very business-like and respectful about this whole situation, though a little uneasy. Sharon looked as though someone had just run over her puppy. Don spoke with Mark's parents in the kitchen for a time, having some tea. We hung out with Mark, catching up from the days when life was simpler. I recall the entourage leaving through the side living room door and walking down the never-ending steps to the street where their car was parked.

The future Rockette was accepted into the band and Don seemed pleased with him. He would go pick up his belongings and return. A million thoughts were passing through my mind. I had watched three of my friends be inducted into this band/cult. I'm not sure if I even knew what a cult was at that point in time, but I knew something was wrong. Of course, with the constant verbal criticism, I wouldn't say the phrasing "I knew" was exactly it. "I sensed" might be a better term. I was sure inside myself that this was not a good situation for myself or my friends to be in, and now, there was basically no one left to restrain Don. He had age, size, and experience all on his side, and that wouldn't be a bad thing if those advantages weren't being abused, but I sensed they were.

Mark turned out to be a natural, and caught on to the parts faster than Jerry had. He had a little problem with certain syncopations, so I worked with him on those. Bill was very good at explaining rhythms in a technical manner as was I. But Don would intervene and say that he didn't want his music ruined with "stupid theory ideas" - all that old "dead composer shit." And so for a time, Mark became Don's pet, his favorite, and for a time Mark enjoyed a certain exclusiveness from the rest of us - the "honeymoon period" if you will.

Unfortunately, the decision to not really work with Mark on rhythms at that time made it difficult later for Mark to catch on to some of the more complicated syncopations in the music. Syncopations are notes that come in-between the beats. Most of this music had sixteenth note syncopation constantly, as Don was especially keen on syncopated rhythms. Often, Mark would play the note in a slightly different place than was written, and often, I had to just resign myself to the fact that he would continue to play it that way.

I just recall that he was really quick to learn tunes and didn't have any problem with the odd time signatures at all. Every one (including me) was a bit astounded at the speed with which Mark learned his parts.

Boston had an interest in writing lyrics, and approached Don with some of his poetry. I knew this was not going to be received well, but at this point, I just allowed everyone to work out his own relationship with Don. Don, of course, discouraged any form of creativity or self-expression among the band members. I could understand lyrically why he would do this, because his poetry and lyrics were obviously brilliant to many. His lyrics seemed to be getting better and better. He was growing daily and spent a great deal of time writing, or rather dictating to someone, usually Jeff, almost daily. I really can't claim to understand Don's poetry. I know from a literary point of view that his writings must be fairly good, although I have never really sat and discussed his writings in detail with an expert on the matter. I do know that critics and writers seem to have a great deal of respect for his lyrics and poetry. There are some things he's written that I immediately liked, and some things that never appealed to me. I suppose that's true with anyone.

There are questions as to the origin of some of the lyrics. Herb Berman claims, and I have no reason to doubt him, that he wrote several of the lyrics to songs on *Strictly Personal* - including, *Safe As Milk, Trust Us*, and *Dirty Blue Gene*. Aldridge says he recognized "pieces" of his work in several of Don's lyrics years later...

Don Aldridge: For years I saw pieces of my lyrics end up on various projects. Things that I knew I did, but I couldn't prove it. Whether he knows it or not, they all went in his shoebox and, with Don, I don't think that he even thinks that way, it was more like, "Well, of course it's mine." I really think that's how the guy thinks. It's like, "Well I'm the inspiration to this, and I went and did this."

Mark shared some of his poetry with Don, and the initial response was something like, "Gee that's nice," however, within a few days, Don started accusing Mark of stealing all his ideas from poetry books etc. Mark quit writing - at least to my knowledge - and that was the end of that. Don worked hard to quickly establish with Mark, as he had with the rest of us, that he would be the sole creative force in the group.

In a sense, I think we all recognized and accepted that Don was the main creative force anyway. I had dedicated myself to transcribing his ideas and arranging them into compositions. Jeff had dedicated himself to taking dictation. Bill dedicated himself to getting caught up, and Mark just seemed to go with the flow.

My overall impression of Mark was that he was the most able to be himself and was more comfortable inside his own skin than the rest of us. He didn't seem to worry about his shortcomings, and concentrated on developing his strengths. We were often entertained by his amazing physical contortions. He was in the shape of a yoga master, could sit in lotus position for hours. I'm not talking a spiritual meditation master, he was just physically like a man of rubber. It wasn't unusual to watch Mark walk through a room in very believable slow-motion or at normal speed but bent over backwards 90 degrees at the waist.

Boston Impression Of Musical Direction

Mark had a similar impression as Bill upon entering. We would tour, have fun, make money, have babes, and it would be rewarding overall. I think he was less aware of the "different vibe" that Bill had sensed, or probably just decided to accept things as they were.

John French: So, you felt like you were going to be doing (music) like Safe As Milk and we were going to be touring and making money etc.
Mark Boston: Well that's what I thought!
JF: So, then, what is your impression of the early times back then? You know, as you realized that it was going to be a lot different than you thought.
MB: Well, it scared the hell out of me, but at that point, I really wanted to be in a band. I thought, "Sooner or later we might get around to playing some of that Safe As Milk stuff."

Mark's inclusion into the band was very similar to the experience with Bill and Jeff. I always liked Mark and spent some time with him the first few days he was in the group. Although not as close as I had been with Jeff, Mark and I had our share of youthful good times together. Mark invited me out one night to smoke some pot with him, which he had brought along. We sat in the yard and just talked. Mark had a real love of nature and I recall him commenting on making a song out of the sounds of the crickets. I told him I thought it was a great idea.

Unfortunately, in the back of my mind, I was already assessing what Mark's assimilation would probably involve. Don was able to glean fragments of our conversation from each of us over the next few days. As with Bill and Jeff, it seemed that Van Vliet's primary goal would be to drive a wedge between Mark and I and compartmentalize Mark so that he could better control the situation and discourage independent thought; an obvious threat to his leadership and control.

Mark On "Making It"

Mark Boston: I remember always wanting to just "make it." That's all we ever talked about was just "making it."
John French: Yeah, "making it" - being successful.
MB: Make it big -Yeah. That took a lot of practice and a lot of work. We practiced for months and months and I was getting really tired of it.

Handpicked And Investigated

I remember Don saying to me when I first joined that he had been "checking on me" - or something to this extent. He had asked a lot of people about me. I suppose that this is natural if you're thinking of working with someone, it's only natural that you'd want to know something about them. But I got the feeling when Don was saying this to me that it was more than simple curiosity or an informal background check. It was more as if he was telling me that he had something on me - some dirt, or some dirty little secret that he would pull out at the opportune moment.

Don Aldridge: I think he was looking into your background through me. Because he was always picking my brain about you.
John French: Well, the thing is, one thing I noticed that we all had in common is that we were all very passive people - he knew he could "whip us into shape."
DA: Exactly.

Trout Mask Replica - Member's Christening
So thus was formed the *Trout Mask Replica* band. We didn't have all our pseudonyms as of yet. We had actually toyed around with the idea of the alias names back during the days in Tarzana in the chicken coop house. I remember Alex writing down names and mine was originally Zoot Horn Rollo. Jeff's was Antennae Jimmy Semens and Jerry was Rockette Morton. Alex's was some German-sounding thing like Count Von Schlepp.

I remember Jeff being really self-conscious about some scalp condition he had and telling me "I've got holes in my scalp and *seeds come out sometimes*." Jeff would never allow anyone to look at his scalp and view this wormhole into another dimension, but it was apparent that he had some (whether imagined or real, I don't know) scalp anomaly. As he was speaking to Don about this one day, Don came up with the idea of these "seeds" having reproductive powers and that's where I believe the "Semens" part of Jeff's name came from.

Since Jeff wanted to have a glass antennae surgically mounted in his skull as soon as it was financially feasible, the "Antennae" part came into being, and Jimmy...? Well, maybe he just looked like a "Jimmy" to Don.

It was quickly decided that the name Zoot Horn Rollo was better associated with Bill. I'm not sure, but it seemed to me that Drumbo came about as an obvious joke on the name "Ringo" (the Beatle's drummer). In fact, Don later wrote a song for me called *Doctor Drumbo* and the first line was, "Drumbo Ringo Jingo Mumbo Jumbo."

Don had started calling Mark "Mort" shorly after he joined the group. It was a bit of a joke between them. "Hi Mort!" Don would say in this really low voice and Mark would laugh, speaking back in a low voice - usually saying something like "zip" or "zoom." Probably, he had already christened Mark and I wasn't aware of it yet, as the name was actually passed down from Jerry.

Phallic Symbols
There seemed to be a lot of emphasis placed on phallic symbols. (I was a little relieved to get christened Drumbo). Antennae Jimmy Semens always gave me the image of a giant walking penis with semen coming out his head, and Rockette Morton the rocket being (in Don's eyes) modern man's technological monument to the penis. Don had often talked about always wanting to see a rocket launch, because of the absurdity of man trying so desperately to "fuck the universe" or some such words. There was also the vacuum cleaner, which appears in several of the *Trout Mask* photos and outtakes. Also, the Blimp, and the phrase "fast and bulbous."

I think Don was laughing at the fact that no matter how interesting the band's music might be, or how hard we worked on it, the only thing the girls would be interested in were sexual connotations.
"This is the thing that's going to make Captain Beefheart fat, Frank, it's the Blimp, it's the Blimp... Daughter don't you dare, oh mama, who cares? It's the Blimp, it's the blimp."[43]

The Lighthouse - Roland Kirk
Occasionally, we'd get out of the house and do something fun. There was a band trip to "The Lighthouse" in Hermosa Beach to see Roland Kirk play. We sat right in front. I could see his eyes underneath his shades (he was blind), and as he stomped around, he sometimes stomped on my

[43] "The Blimp" Beefheart Music Company, BMI, 1969.

knees. What a moment for me - for all of us. Roland was overheard later, during a break, saying he was going to "suck the brains of the babies." I have no idea what he meant, as it was out of context.

Roland Drives A Car

Marker related an amusing story about the blind Roland Kirk insisting on driving a car down vine street at 3:30 in the morning near the Hollywood Ranch Market.

Gary Marker: This guy Cottontail kept reaching over to the steering wheel, "Hey!" he'd say. Roland was saying, "Motherfuck, motherfuck! If Ray Charles can fly a plane, I can drive a car! Don't fuck with me! Get your hands off this wheel godammit. Just tell me right or left!" Great moments in jazz history? I don't think so.

Trout Mask Replica

Don began writing more and more lyrical stories, such as the old fart. There was a whole series of these that included several characters and were to be included in some kind of book form. There was the "girl that smiled a lot", who Don later claimed was a precognition of his wife, Jan. Jan didn't appear on the scene until after *Trout Mask* was released, but it's a stretch to think of this as precognitive - it could have just as easily been Miss Pamela from the GTOs - who always was smiling.

There were the Drazy Hoops (mentioned in *The Blimp*), Big Joan, and Thread with the sort of drooped body. I always thought Thread was inspired by the 6'4" very thin Bill Harkleroad, who used to slump a lot to hide his height.

Don told me once privately that "The Old Fart" was actually inspired by me. I wasn't sure whether to be flattered or insulted. He said something about the sign of the fish and my Christianity being symbolic and some of my withdrawn behaviors being little things he used to inspire him with this particular character. This made sense I suppose.

Anyway, this character's mask, the old fart, is where the name *Trout Mask Replica* obviously came from. The old fart was some character that viewed the world from inside a mask of his own creation. He had a perfume-atomizer breathing device to supply air. It was as though inside this mask, he became invisible, unattached to the environment around him. It was very much like Don's relationship to the band, and I often felt that Beefheart himself was "The Old Fart."

Richard Redus

John French: Did you guys ever come up to the Trout Mask house?
Richard Redus: Yeah, we came up there probably either right before or right after **Trout Mask** *came out. Mike (Hamilton) had been invited up a few times to just hang out. So, I tagged along with him just one time. The band was rehearsing. I don't know what song it was. Don was going through some insanely elaborate metaphor about how to play this part, "As if you were jumping off a ski slope...etc." I was very fascinated by his very intense personality. The music was obviously like nothing anybody else was playing. As soon as I heard it, I dug it, because for one thing it was so different, and for another thing I was really grabbed by Don's lyrics and his picture of the world that was nightmarish and cartoonish at the same time. He'd mix up lightness and darkness and the spiritual and the mundane and put his own incredible creative twist on it. I quickly got into the music.*
JF: When did you first hear Beefheart? Did you hear a record, or did you hear the band?
RR: Probably **Safe As Milk**. *See another facet here is that my parents owned The Third Eye,*

which was the first head shop in the Valley. Do you remember it?
JF: I think I do, yeah!
RR: It was on Ventura Blvd. ...We had records playing all the time and they were all psychedelic records.
JF: Oh, OK.
RR: Safe As Milk was on the turntable when it came out.
JF: Did you consider that a psychedelic record?
RR: Yeah. Looking back, I still consider it a psychedelic record.

Shelly's Manne-Hole

Shelly's Manne-hole was a jazz club in Hollywood which Don frequented. I had gone with him there at least once during the *Safe As Milk* days. I believe it was to hear Gabor Szabo, a jazz guitarist who employed feedback techniques. On two or three occasions during the *Trout Mask* rehearsals, we made a group trip to the club to hear groups. Once, it was to hear the Jazz Crusaders, which was one of my favorite times. Another was to see Yusef Lateef. His drummer influenced my playing a bit, especially his hi-hat technique. Ornette Coleman was another we heard.

Disowned By Frenchy

As mentioned earlier, the entire band had been arrested for shoplifting. This was while Jerry was still in the group. Bill, Jeff and I had to go with Jerry to a couple of court dates and the judge said because of our exemplary behavior in court and our respect of the court system (we all dressed in suits - I wore my *Safe As Milk* suit - the only one I owned) he was going to be lenient.

We could have been charged with burglary because of the circumstances of us all having been in a group. However, we all got off with $65 fines. I didn't have any money, and although Don could have paid this off with the advance money he was getting from Zappa, he made a point of stressing that my *parents* should pay for this. At this point, my father and mother, who had been separated, had just gotten back together. When I called, my father viewed this whole thing as trouble and basically disowned me. He said not to ever call back and that I wasn't welcome at their house.

I was crushed. This was a tough thing to take, however, I couldn't really blame my father. They didn't realize the kind of trap I was in and that although I wanted out, I didn't really know how to make the break. I felt a bit indebted to Frank, who had bailed the entire band out of jail and had advanced an undisclosed amount of money to Don for our expenses. I also felt a debt to Sue, Don's mother, and Marge Harkleroad, Bill's mother, who had both invested thousands in the band, at a time when that was a substantial amount of money.

Tensions Mount

As weeks went by, tensions mounted in the house. There was little food and little money to speak of. We weren't playing anywhere and Don's only resource was Sue, his mother. I found it exceptionally odd that a man nearly 28 years old would still be dependent on his mother for his support. Don then talked Bill into getting money from his mother, Marge. This gave Bill a little more freedom than the rest of us, as Don would lend Bill his car to drive the 75 miles or so to the Antelope Valley to obtain money from his mother. Bill would also get to see his old friends in the desert occasionally. The rest of us barely had any contact with the outside world, so I envied Bill for his small vacations.

I must say it was extremely frustrating for me and I'm sure for the rest, to be stuck in this house with no outside resource and no way to make money. We were all making more money when we played gigs in Lancaster than we were making now. The stress of this situation on young horny men was obviously starting to show. It was a socially unhealthy condition and was about to get much worse.

The first sign of trouble I saw on the horizon was when Jeff would come to the piano to learn parts. He questioned everything I played, every note was closely scrutinized. I go into this in detail in the next chapter, however, for the sake of continuity, I should mention that Jeff would come back to the piano saying that he forgot a part and could I please play it again. I would oblige and he would snap out something like, "That's not what you played me the last time."

Now, at first, I regarded this as me, my human error, lack of training, absent-mindedness etc. But as it began to happen more and more - and only with Jeff - I realized that it wasn't me - something must be "cooking." I began to double-check everything I played. I had a system worked out between each player and myself. Bill was the easiest to teach parts to, and Jeff was the most difficult. Not because Jeff was "dense" or slow at all, in fact, he was brilliantly quick to grasp things. It was more in the manner in which he insisted the parts be introduced.

I always had the uncomfortable feeling that Jeff envied my position as "musical director" and felt me to be completely inept for the position. This was probably my own insecurity creeping out and pasted on him.

It was not as if Jeff didn't know how to do this on his own. He was by far more qualified to process this information than I. It was more as if Jeff didn't want to take responsibility for any decisions concerning Don's music because he was fearful of the negative consequences those decisions may cause if Don discovered his music was being altered in any way. Marker had mentioned this earlier in relationship to the shuffle section he had added to *Veteran's Day Poppy*.

I didn't feel like Don knew enough about music to recognize that something had even been transposed to a lower or higher octave and time seemed to prove this true, as he never asked me about any transpositions I did. I would occasionally consult with him on some matter, but usually he was sleeping (about 12 hours a day it seemed) or gone. So in order to expedite the process of learning, I made most of the arrangement and transposition decisions myself based on what I knew of Don's taste in music and what I think worked best.

For the musically-challenged, "transpose" means simply to make higher or lower. If you look at a piano keyboard, every eighth note is an "octave" higher - meaning it's the same pitch (like "C") but the vibrations are twice as fast, thereby making it in a different frequency. A piano has notes that go lower and higher than a guitar, so if Don would play something too low (usually the case, as he often played in the lower half of the piano during this period of time) it would need to be transposed up an entire octave at least to make it possible to be played on guitar.

Sometimes, the upper notes were high enough, but the lower notes weren't, so I would ask Jeff if I could borrow his guitar, and find a happy medium where the lower notes could be raised, but the upper notes would stay in the same octave. This sometimes gave a fuller sound. Occasionally, Laurie would walk through the room as this was happening tell Don, and later, I would be accused of "sabotaging the music." I kept doing it anyway, because somebody had to make the decision and I was the delegate upon whom this thankless job was cast.

The Writing Process

If my role were to keep the music straight, then Jeff's role was simultaneously cast as Don's transcriber and reader of poetry and prose. Each thing that was written became "the greatest thing ever written" and Jeff became Don's cheerleader more often than not as these lyrics, poems and prose were written. Don would then insist that we all stop whatever we were doing at the moment and listen to his latest inspiration. Anyone caught not paying undivided attention would be the target of an intense scrutiny, often resulting in another dreaded "talk."

The usual comments, "that's so 'heavy,'" and "that's great!" usually could get us by when we weren't in the mood for a spontaneous poetry recital. I personally found most of these readings a big pain in the ass, as it disrupted the flow of the work I was doing with the band. Jeff often got behind the others because of Don's constant need for someone to which to dictate to. However, there were times when we as a group were genuinely impressed with some piece of work. There were other times when we were all burned out and didn't want to hear a thing and just pretended. Then there were all the combinations of people not interested or enthusiastic while others were. All these group dynamics were held under closer and closer scrutiny until accusations of lack of interest and commitment began to surface. It was then when the monster began to arise and show it's ugly face more and more.

The "Talks"

The "talks" as Don referred to them, were cleverly started on a low scale by Don with a few seemingly reasonable questions. Then, they would usually slowly evolve into a more hostile interrogation-type atmosphere. Don, being a writer and a poet, was very good at manipulating words and conversation. In the beginning of these talks, he would ask a few questions, and as the person became more uncomfortable, knowing what would come next, he would include another member in the interrogation and get them to focus with him. Soon, everyone in the room would be pawns in Don's game. The "target" would be isolated and surrounded by the others, who stood by while Don as overseer verbally belittled the "band-member-of-the-day" into some conversational trap.

If a person became impatient as they would start to defend themselves, Don would react with some question regarding their personal condition. "Why are you so hostile, man? Why are you so fucking mean, man?" Or, in the case of a nervous twitch or movement, "What's this thing you're doing with your foot, man, are you masturbating?" Where in the fuck are you at?" (I noticed a strange pronunciation in the word "at" when used in this question, it was always pronounced "et" with a short "e" and I was always puzzled as to this pronunciation because he always used the regular pronunciation of "at" in any other context.) He would get right in our faces and stare us down intensely asking "do you know how smart I am? Do you know what I can do to you with my mind?

No matter what approach the target took in their own defense - a defense we should have never had to make - we found that Don's clever use of words could quickly paint us into a corner from which we seemingly had no escape. A lot of his statements made no sense - perhaps intentionally. Most were laced with suspicions of mutiny. At the time I supposed, in my confused state, that not being able to make a strong defense was a sure indication that I was wrong. This was Don's logic: if you didn't have the right answer, you were guilty as charged. I thought at first that if I didn't know the answer to these questions, then there must be something wrong with me. Don had already belittled me in front of the others to the point where I thought myself to be only one step above a brainless moron. So it wasn't hard for me to become outwardly convinced that perhaps he had a point.

However, on a deeper level, I felt like it was total BS and Don was the only one with the problem and he was not only wasting our time but being a total idiot. He was the one sleeping the most, and doing the least work. He was the one with the least technical music ability and was co-dependent on us to take his bits and pieces of music and put them together into a playable organized form. We were the ones nurturing his ill-conceived child (the music) and changing it's diapers daily as needed.

As we looked at each other, no matter who was the villain of the day, we all were just filled with enough doubt and insecurity that we wound up playing absurd roles. In my case, my confidence

...d of my Sophomore year, my father bought me ... Slingerland drums for $456 – a lot of money in ...s. My drum throne was a kitchen stepstool, and ...d surf drumming to a stereo set up directly ...y head. My room was adjacent to a separate ...which I was facing). This was the back yard of ...house I grew up in, with the grape arbor in the ...nd. I was so proud of this set and had to have a ...o I set them up on a carpet, combed my hair, put ...orite shirt, and had my mother take this photo.

All photos courtesy of John French.

...he only good snapshots ...ther and I. This was a ...ot and I was about ...old here. It was taken ...ernardino, California, ...place.

...y best friends, Dan Moore, and I. This shot was taken ... my rare visits to Lancaster. His father, Thomas ...ok this photo, a sort of of study in contrast, I suppose. ...r, Dan's daughter looked at this photo and asked, ...What happened to John?" Dan was the guy who ...wn and talked me into leaving the Trout house in ...d Hills. He had seen the changes in me and was very ...d about my state of mind.

This was the High School photo taken in my freshman year, just about the time I began playing drums. I divided my free time between brushing my hair and playing my drums.

L to R: Alex Snouffer, Paul (PG) Blakely (drums), Doug Moon, [...] Van Vliet, and Jerry Handley. T[...] was a pre Vic Mortensen shot. [...] PG did rehearse with the band, though no one recalls him actu[...] performing with them until mu[...] later. The hairstyles suggest la[...] 1963.

Photo courtesy of Doug Moon.

[P]ictured from L to R: Larry Willey (Bass/ Vocals), Don Giesen (Rhthm Guitar / [V]ocals), John French (Drums/ Vocals), and Jeff Cotton (Ld Guitar / vocals). This [b]and was just previous to "Blues in a Bottle" and probabl.y taken late Spring 1966. [It] evokes a lot of memories of fantastic days – the magic and joy of youth and was [r]eally our heyday. The shot was taken by a beautiful blonde girl named Pat [S]helton using my camera – an old 35mm De-Jur I bought from a guy named [B]ehnke, who had photos published in National Geographic. It was my idea to do [a] photo shot at Littlerock Dam, about 25 miles from Lancaster. Pat set this shot up [a]nd it's still one of my favorite photos, except, why was that geek wearing plaid?

Photo courtesy of John Frenc[h]

A Newspaper clipping from the Antelope Valley Press. This was about 2 weeks before I was invited to join the Magic Band. This was taken on the back steps of the music room at Antelope Valley High School. The photographer decided that this squinty shot, with all of us looking directly into the sun, was the most flattering. The paper added "The" to our real name "Blues in a Bottle."

ANTELOPE VALLEY PRESS SEC. 1
THURSDAY, OCTOBER 20, 1966

O PERFORM—"The Blues in a Bottle" will provide he music for the second of a seris of twice-monthly dances scheduled by the AV Fair. The musical group will appear Friday night in the Industrial Building at the fairgrounds, 8 'til midnight. Left to right, front, are Jeff Cotton, lead guitarist; and Mark Boston, bass guitarist. Left to right at rear are Don Giesen, drums; Jeff Parker, rhythm guitarist; and John French, vocalist.

I mentioned our gig at the Topanga Corral, which was around the time of Safe As Milk session, and booked by Gary Marker. How about that donation? This was basically a biker club and the guys were a little rough around the edges but definitely intimidated me at 18.

TOPANGA CORRAL
Presents
CAPTAIN BEEFHEART and HIS MAGIC BAND
Plus
PAUL POTASH, Folksinger
Thursday, March 16, 1967
9:00 p. m. to 2:00 a. m.
2034 Topanga Boulevard, Topanga

Donation $1.00 **№** 80 **455-9060**

Found in my mother's scrapbook was this Los Angeles Times clipping of a typo-ridden article by Pete Johnson (who later co-produced Shiny Beast). This was actually a terrible performance done around the time of the Mirror Man recordings. I had recalled Mirror Man sessions as November of 1967, and this article is 3 months later. I think I first met Pete at the sessions. Don had invited him down and introduced him as "a true human being."

Los Angeles Times ★
I—SAT., FEB. 3, 1968

eefheart Band t Whisky a Go-Go

BY PETE JOHNSON
Times Staff Writer

The renaissance of rock blues bands has produced few very good vocalists. To see a Janis Joplin (Big Brother and the Holding Company), you must sit through a dozen Bob Hites (Canned Heat) or worse.

One of the exceptions to this parade of mediocrity is Don Van Vliet, lead singer of Capt. Beefheart and his Magic Band, a quintet appearing at the Whisky a Go-Go through Sunday with the Iron Butterfly, a rock quartet.

Voice Knifes Through

Van Vliet's voice knifes through his lyrics in incredible swoops and dives, from hoarse shouts to clenched throat whines which could curdle vinegar. He augments his singing with adept work on harmonica and on a strange horn which resembles a candle holder.

Opening night they suffered from badly balanced sound which muddied their playing and caused some rather random musical passages, the result of group members being unable to hear themseives or each other.

However, the group has intriguing maferial, an individual sound and compeling stage presence. All are very good, though sometimes excessive, instrumentalists.

Van Vliet and his band —John French, drums; Jeff Cotton, bass; Alex St. Clair, lead guitar, and Jerry Handley, rhythm guitar—offered extended versions of "Sure 'Nuff 'n' Yes I Do," "Abba Zabba," "Down in the Bottom" and "Somebody on Your Mind" for their first set. All were strongly up-tempo, most

Not Conventional

It tinkers with struc-with traces of a Bo Diddley beat, and all mixed in bits of other standard blues.

This is not, however, a conventional blues group. It is as close to Frank Zappa of the Mothers of Invention as it is to Howling Wolf or Muddy Waters, whose singing styles have influenced Van Vliet's vocals.
tures and sounds within a loose blues framework. roaming from straight electric blues to psychedelia to anarchy, tossing in some jarring transitions and multiple endings.

Somehow it prevents all this from turning into an aimless snakepit of sound, though there are worrisome moments.

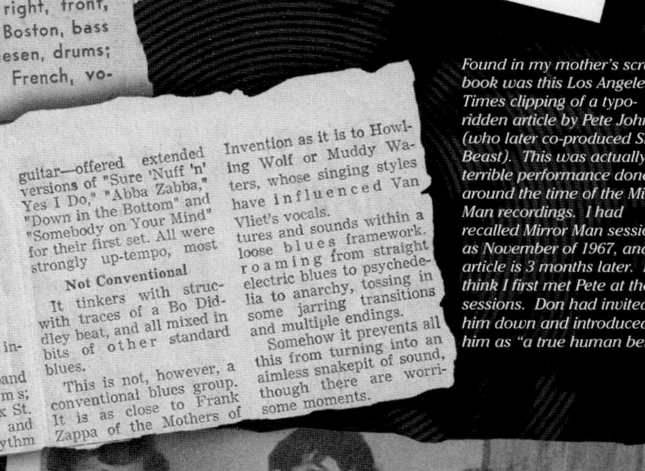

CAPT. BEEFHEART and his magic band can do more for a song than most new groups in sight. Their personalities are fab as well as their on stage performances.

An amusing photo of the band in a Tigerbeat Magazine. The caption certainly captures the bubble-gummer British Invasion slang of the time. This was probably an A&M promotional shot from 1966.

The "Whisk" a' Go Go around 1965. Fix that sign, guys. This was during Johnny Rivers' heyday, and I can almost hear the thud-like beat of "Memphis." The Magic Band may have been opening for "Them" but I also recall that earlier, Don mentioned that the band had opened for John Lee Hooker.

A posed shot in which Don's character, apparently taking his Hoover for a walk, is humiliated as the shameless vacuum takes a pee on the tree of fake house owners (Alex Snouffer and Laurie feigning disgust. Probably taken early 1964.

L to R: Doug Moon, Jerry Handley, Rich Hepner, Don Van Vliet, Alex Snouffer. This is the Diddy Wah Diddy era band and is a remake of an earlier picture taken on the same porch with Vic Mortensen in the background. Don was very happy with Jerry Handley's "Paramahansa" look in this photo.

This photo looks as though it was taken on the sidewalk in front of King's Photo shop on Lancaster Boulevard (which still exists, though all the buildings across the street are gone). Doug was studying photography, and may have been there to pick up supplies. I recognize the kids in the photo from High School, but cannot place their names. Don, apparently, was fed up with being the subject of Doug's photographs, or maybe he was just showing off for "the chicks."

Photos courtesy of Doug Moon.

Photo courtesy of Guy Webster.

Shot just prior to [...] shot, one of the im[...] portraits of me.

A photo of Grannie Annie's house. She was Don's grandmother, and lived directly across the street from Don's mother's house on Carolside Avenue in Lancaster, where I practiced with the band. This house had been sold by the time I joined the band, but is referenced in the book by Vic Mortensen as the house where he and Don wrote "Call on Me." In the background is Laurie Stone, Don's then-girlfriend. The Corvette pictured belonged to Don and was later sold to Doug Moon, when Don bought a black Jaguar Sedan.

Don used to stand in the doorway to avoid getting feedback and hear himself a bit better. Here, he's playing harp. His hair had just barely started to grow out. This was taken in Granny Annie's house. (Ann Warfield).

An early promo photo of The Magic Band while they were still managed Leonard Grant and Associates. L to R are: Don Van Vliet, Doug Moon, Mortensen, Alex "St. Clair" Snouffer, and Jerry Handley.

Lower three photos courtesy of Doug Moon.

From the Safe as Milk shoot, our first shoot with Guy. Neither of us could remember where this was shot, but it seemed to be some kind of a drainage canal. It was a strange day, cloudy, then clear. Guy's assistant kept a close eye on the light meter.

...er outtake from the Safe as Milk
... taken, I believe in a tunnel that
...rt of the same drainage system
...e photo.

...courtesy of Guy Webster.

Joshua Tree on Avenue K in Lancaster. This was originally about ½ mile from where I live presently. The area now totally developed, this reflects an earlier period in the sixties when the road crew actually 'SPLIT' the road to avoid bulldozing this beautiful specimen of local indigenous flora.

Photo courtesy of Doug Moon.

John Peel championed the group from day one whilst in the U.S. and when he started his Perfumed Garden show. L to R: John French, Jerry Handley, Don, John Peel, Alex Snouffer, and Jeff Cotton.

Photo courtesy of Colin Hill.

...s actually an outtake from the ...s Milk session. I believe we are ...drainage tunnel and Guy shot ...rilliant portrait using nothing but ...ble light.

...courtesy of Guy Webster.

Photos courtesy of
Guy Webster.

Alex Snouffer –"stamp" portrait
outtake. Also a shirt made
at the same boutique.

Don Van Vliet -- One of the "stamp"
portrait outtakes, one of which was
eventually used on the Blue Thumb
version of "Strictly Personal" The
shirt he was wearing was custom-
made by a shop on Santa Monica
Boulevard that specialized in
tailoring clothes for rock groups.
Guitarist Gerry McGee was in the
group at the time and had a rawhide
pullover shirt designed and made.
He was replaced by Jeff Cotton
before this shoot.

Jerry Handley – "stamp" portrait
outtake. The shirt was made at
same Santa Monica boutique.

John French – official
"stamp" portrait. Cape
was given me by friend of
Pamela Des Barres, who I
remember as "Beautiful
Beverly." My "custom"
outfit was too tight, and I
gave the jacket to Beverly
in trade.

ring the "Mirror Man" session, a
ing female model was brought
posed in a giant crib with a baby
ll outfit on, and we stood around
. It was a take off of the "Safe
Milk" baby bumper sticker as if
baby had grown up. We then
re either taken to a different
dio or a different part of the A&M
otography studio where Guy had
up several mannequins and
ught in dolls for a shoot. I
ieve that Don had most of the
otos destroyed, as several poses
him holding a young girl doll
the expression on his face
ade him appear as a pedophile.
is upset Don and he insisted that
ne of the photos be used. I tried
ind the rest of the shots from this
ssion, but they have all vanished
e this single shot.

other version of the centerfold
ot from the album "Strictly
rsonal). Guy mentioned that he
d left this backdrop outside for
veral months and allowed it to
come "weathered." He pulled it
for this shoot.

otos courtesy of Guy Webster.

Don Van Vliet – outtake of Strictly Personal shoot, the hat and feathers were rented from Western Costume Company in Hollywood, along with much of the wardrobe.

Photo courtesy of Guy Webster.

A closeup of Cotton. I originally thought this [could?] be one of the "stamp" portraits, but later rea[lized] it was an outtake of th[e] later "Strictly Personal" session.

Photo courtesy of Guy Webster.

Beatle bones up on what's happening circa '67.

Courtesy of Art [ ] who snapped [him?] and Jimmy Car[l Black?] en route with T[he] Mothers.

Don with the "Drumbo" chimney sweep's hat. I believe this hat was actually the same one used in the Laurel and Hardy film "Dirty Work." The fellow at Western Costume Company seemed convinced it was, and why would anyone in Hollywood lie?

Photo courtesy of Guy Webster.

A promo shot from 1970 with L to R: Art Tripp, Don, Mark Boston, Bill Harkleroad and John French.

Photo courtesy of Jim Marshall

John French and Don Giesen in 1971, in the background is Lancaster's Exposition Hall where the Magic Band played in their early days.

Photo courtesy of Don Giesen.

...nd Jan caught on
...era sometime in 1972.

...o courtesy of Art Tripp.

Caught by Jan Van Vliet at the Knebworth Festival,
England, 1975. The line-up here is Greg Davidson,
Bruce Fowler, Elliot Ingber, Jimmy Carl Black, Don
and John French.

Promo shot for the Ice Cream For Crow session 1982. L to R:
Richard Snyder, Gary Lucas, Cliff Martinez, Don, Jeff Moris Tepper.

John French in Proper's Specific Sound studio during
the recording of his 2008 release City Of Refuge. He
was joined on these recordings by Bill Harkleroad,
Mark Boston, Greg Davidson and John Thomas.

was so low that I barely believed I could exist outside this environment. Yet there was always a part of me that knew this was all wrong-that something was terribly amiss and my friends and I were in the presence of an evil person who was stealing away our individuality and independent thought, ripping our souls to shreds.

Limb Crashing Down

John French to John Thomas: Let me give you a couple of other examples. It was during Trout Mask rehearsals in the house, the whole band was there. One time he was very very angry with me. He was focused in on me the target of a "talk." At one point, he stopped in the conversation and just went (breathes heavily with angry look on face and finger pointing toward imaginary "John".) He was pointing at me with this awful look of intensity on his face. Just then, this branch came down from one of the trees and crashed on the roof of the house. He got right in my face and said, "Do you know what I could do to you?" He said it in his Howlin' Wolf voice, really intense and angry. I was just standing there with my eyes wide open going, "No, I don't!" Trying to think of how I could smooth this over so we could get on with this album and I could get the hell out of there. At that moment, an artist friend of his named John Stewart showed up, and when John showed up - I think God sent him to save my life - he had heard me talking, replying to Don's trumped up accusations. John Stewart walked in and Don instantly turned into "Mr. Charming," "Mr.Wonderful," "Oh, John, good to see you, how great that you're here."
John Thomas: You didn't hear me being an asshole did you?
JF: Well, he didn't hear him, only me copping this plea to try to get things smoothed over.

John Stewart looked at me, very puzzled, and said, "Was that you I just heard talking? Looking away, he just shook his head, baffled.

Brainwashing - Coercion - Abuse

There were days when I was completely puzzled by Don's behavior. He seemed to want to get this album done in a hurry, but then he would start questioning one of the band members about something. It usually had something to do with a very minor thing, like not being able to play a particular part quite right, or perhaps the person was just having a "bad day" as we all do sometimes. Marker mentioned that the idea seemed to be, in his view, that Don wanted to keep everything slightly off-kilter - just enough to keep everyone tense and uncomfortable.

All Night "Talks"

This questioning would begin to escalate into something bigger as Don would draw other players into it. We all knew that this was something minor that could be handled between the two of them, or best yet, completely left alone, because people are not perfect and should be allowed their faults. However, Don would persist and get each member involved until the whole group was actually sitting around talking about this supposed "problem" or "hang-up" so-and-so was having. It was probably late summer or early fall of 1968, when these "talks" as we would sometimes call them began to happen.

I found myself caught between total boredom and fear at these talks, unless I was in the "hot seat." Then it was like a kangaroo court, an absurd and judgmental counter-productive rap session that brought out nothing but bad feelings and amplified resentment.

As Harkleroad said in his book, I kept sitting around thinking, "What's Don trying to do here? What's his plan?" Most of the time, we couldn't talk our way out of these situations, because Don was so wonderfully brilliant with words, he would just have us tongue tied and confused.

Many times, Don actually had me totally convinced that I was a terrible, awful person who only thought of himself and his own selfish interests. Then, after the talk, I would go away and evaluate myself, and re-discover that I was working 14 - 16 hours a day for a man who wasn't paying me, and was only getting one meal a day - a tiny bowl of soybeans. I barely had time to bathe and most of my clothes were rags. I decided that by no stretch of the imagination could this possibly be described as selfish. Stupid? Yes! Selfish? No. I decided pretty early on in the talks that I wasn't the "bad guy," and neither were the other players, it was Don's paranoid delusions - *he was the bad guy, whether he knew it or not.*

The Center Of Attention

As I mentioned, Don would insist that everything center around his whim of the moment. If he was in the mood to write lyrics, many times he would dictate to Jeff, while the rest of us stood around attentively listening. If we weren't attentive enough, as I often seemed not to be, then an interrogation took place. Sometimes these little talks would last for days, wasting even more precious time. Many times, the reason I wasn't attentive is because I couldn't understand why in hell I was standing around wasting time listening to something I wasn't interested in when I could be teaching parts to Bill and Mark, or working on drum parts. I truly didn't find these dictation sessions interesting at all, and I knew that I would hear anything that Don considered truly "inspired" twenty or thirty times, read to the entire band at Don's request by Jeff, in his most obnoxious "Blimp" or "Pena" voice.

But Don considered it very important that we pay attention during these special creative times. He would dictate and sometimes he would be writing about someone he was about to interrogate or already had interrogated while they were still in the "hot seat." I believe *Human Gets Me Blues* was written during an interrogation of me. *Bills Corpse* was during a session with Bill. The tension would mount as we realized that Don's eye contact was becoming focused on one individual and there would be a sense of dread as we realized that soon we would be spending time in a far more uncomfortable manner.

A Spiritual Haunting

There was a spiritual side to this that kept haunting me. Having been raised a Christian as I mentioned earlier, I had turned aside into the occult at a fairly early age. I studied things like Astrology, Astral Traveling, Telepathy, and Psychic powers. I had a fascination with the spirit realm and unknowingly, I believed I opened a Pandora's Box of trouble into my life. There was a deep and dark emptiness inside, a bleak hopelessness and a sense of despair that haunted me all the time. The only way I could temporarily escape this was to either stay extremely busy, or be in Don's "good graces."

Captain's Pet O' The Day

There always seemed to be a favored person for periods of time. These periods of time could be hours or days. During this time, a certain individual would be "taken under Don's wing" and befriended. This could include being invited to go somewhere with him alone. It might be a talk alone in the "magic bathroom" (about the only place of privacy in this small house.) He would take someone into the large bathroom, turn the water on for background noise, and have a conversation and a smoke with someone. It might be an invitation into his "private quarters" where he would have his girlfriend Laurie make us tea. We might talk about any number of things. He might invite you for a walk outside and smoke a special cigarette (he liked Balkan Sobranies) or a joint, although there was almost no pot smoked during this period.

During these times, usually everyone else just worked hard and the "special" person would have certain freedoms. Like, they could take a break occasionally without being questioned as to their motives. They could make a cup of tea without being cussed out for being in the kitchen (which became more and more "off limits" as the cult atmosphere heightened).

I found myself during these times usually taking advantage of the situation to just get menial things done that I barely had time to do otherwise. Mostly, I would wash my clothes and organize my personal belongings. Perhaps dust off my drums and take a walk occasionally to get some well-needed exercise (we were all in terrible physical condition from smoking and lack of exercise.)

Party In An Empty House

I recall one time, I believe it could have been Thanksgiving 1968, when everyone was gone to be with family. The only ones in the house were Don, Laurie and I, and then Laurie left also to spend time with her family. It was the only time I recall being alone in the house with Don for any extended period of time. It was daytime, and I went down the hill, either to borrow something from a neighbor or to check the mail and when I came back, Don was in an extremely distressed mental state. He seemed absolutely frightened to death, the blood drained from his face.

I asked him what the matter was and he answered me saying that while I was gone, several people had appeared in the house having a party. He said they were walking around talking and having drinks and he could hear them and see them. I didn't get a lot of details because he was visibly upset. I didn't understand this much at the time, but I assumed the same role as during the *Safe As Milk* sessions when he had been having the anxiety attacks. I just kept him company. I looked around the house and told him all the people were apparently gone because I could find no one.

So we just hung out together, talking, laughing, and joking. He was not at all accusatory or demanding. There was no paranoia, at least of me. I wasn't suspected of any foul deed. It was quite a refreshing time. As I had stated before, one on one, Don could be charming and a real companion. He was funny, personable, and really more like "just one of the guys." Unfortunately, in a group situation, all that changed.

I remember Don saying "hey, why don't we have burritos?" This, interpreted meant, "John, would you make me a burrito? Then, you can make one for yourself." We ate the burritos and then stood, smoking, drinking tea, and talking in the kitchen, all the while standing up. Then, he gave me a kind of pep talk in the style of the "wise old sage to young upstart." He told me that he had worried about so many things when he was younger, but then one day he just got up and faced whatever was happening as though yesterday and tomorrow didn't count at all. He got right up in my face and said, "I'll give you a piece of advice, man." "I prepared for something profound, some life-changing bit of information."

He said, "Never think it's you, John. Never think it's you."

Initiation

After the holidays, we went back to work on the album. The tenseness returned and the talks continued. If Don had a favorite for the time, often, this "special" person would be the one Don would first include in his interrogation of another. This inclusion would usually begin with Don saying something demeaning about the target of the next talk, asking, "Do you know what I mean?" to the one basking in the present favoritism. The person almost always answered "Yes." To answer "No" was unthinkable, and risked being put in the hot seat yourself.

The "special" person and Don would sit facing the "accused" (usually for having an expression on their face that Don didn't particularly like at that particular moment or taking too long to learn a more difficult part). It was almost as if "Captain Beefheart" were taking over at this moment, because suddenly, Don would become very critical of every possible trait of the person under the gun. Sometimes, he would just ask annoying and degrading questions and make particularly unflattering statements that would, with his excellent vocabulary, cause the "target" to squirm in discomfort. This was all achieved in a calm, deliberate manner, - the distant rumblings of a coming storm.

During later years I was reminded of Don's behavior during these times while watching Anthony Hopkins' character in *Silence of the Lambs*. Although Hopkins' character was obviously more dangerous, he did seem to emanate a certain hypnotic, spellbinding aura in his monologues, stripping apart any defenses the person may have and reducing them to a useless lump that, to me, recalled some of the intensity of which Don was capable.

Don would just seem to relax and enjoy the person's uncomfortable position like a sadistic parent letting their child wait for the spanking in apprehension. At this point, the anticipation of a very uncomfortable immediate future would cause the person to become extremely uncomfortable and self-conscious. Don seemed to enjoy this at times and actually bask in it. The person would often try to escape the interrogation or brainwashing session (which Don always referred to as a *"talk"*) by saying that they wanted to learn the next part to a song, or to rehearse something.

Don would then accuse the person of something akin to diversionary tactics. "Why are you trying to change the subject, man?" He would ask and then, as others in the band became aware of what was going on, he would include them. "Hey, tell me what the fuck he's trying to say. Is it my imagination, or is he nuts?" or words to that effect.

At this point, it would begin to get more serious and intense. Those not directly involved were now seeing the dreaded clouds of "game time" approaching. Don would then usually officially slip into the "talk" mode. Don would generally make himself comfortable by having Laurie bring him his cigarettes and a cup of tea or a Royal Crown Cola or whatever else he may desire. He often sat in a chair at the end of a room divider at the west end of the living room. He would then sarcastically say something to the effect (to Laurie) that "so-and-so's having a 'thing' or going through a 'thing'." They would oftentimes have a short exchange on how much time "So and So" was wasting, including observances like, "He's so fucking selfish wasting our time like this while we're all sitting here starving."

Soon, the whole tone of the "talk" would be to blame every problem, shortage of money, contractual dispute and unpaid bill on the "target," making a case against this particular person that would burden even the strongest-willed individual into tinges of guilt. I seemed to remember that all these things were the other "so-and-so's" fault just last week and that when the other "so-and-so" came out of his "thing" (apparently some arbitrary spiritual state conjured in the rich imagination of the Captain) then the problem had been solved, though it apparently had miraculously returned - at least in Don's mind. So, a new scapegoat was periodically needed on which the blame for this catastrophic set of circumstances could be blamed.

During most of this time, we were all undernourished and in deplorable health. Our main intake during the day was Lipton's Tea with honey and milk and occasionally a stolen piece of toast accompanied by far too many cigarettes. I say stolen, because it was strongly disapproved of to go into the kitchen and actually eat something during the day. In the evening, when there was food, we would eat sparingly sometimes, other times relatively well especially after Frank started advancing a little money which only seemed to happen just a bit before we actually recorded.

I found myself escaping into the bathroom sometimes, just to stand and look in the mirror and ask myself this simple question, "How on earth do I get out of this terrible place?" None of us wanted to desert the rest and all of us wanted to see this project through because we were already committed to it strongly, yet it became a more miserable environment with each passing day.

In the beginning of *Trout Mask* composition and this era of time, things were a bit more relaxed. There was always resistance if one faced the day as though one deserved to live and have thoughts of his own. If I got up and went into the kitchen, it was sometimes met with some sharp reference to he fact that I was "a useless human whose only function seemed to be to eat and shit." This eventually evolved into the kitchen being "off-limits" and I remember days of tremendous hunger pangs.

I've read of other rock bands going through these periods of lacking. However, there was a comradeship between the members, more of an "all for one and one for all" attitude that kept their spirits up even when their circumstances were terrible. Here, it was a terrible physical circumstance, but an even worse mental and spiritual condition and no comradeship. Hope was a rare commodity, and I ceased living and began existing shortly after rehearsals began. Most of the time, I felt too weak physically to fight back against the ridiculous accusations made against me and had a lot of trouble concentrating. But even when I physically felt good, my spirits were already at such a low that I usually succumbed passively to the false guilt placed on my shoulders. I might add that I think this went for everyone in the Magic Band.

Lack Of Communication

We (the band members) eventually all quit communicating with each other unless it was directly related to the music learning process. I think this may have been the key to Don's control over us: divide and conquer. If you're in agreement with one other person, it makes it harder for you to succumb to ridiculous allegations. However, if you are alone, and no one dares come to your defense for fear of being labeled traitor, then it is much easier to be manipulated against your own will and better judgment.

Betrayal's Wicked Wreath

At some early point, it was only natural that we all became extremely untrusting of each other. Don would take us out during our "special" times and basically fill our heads with the things all the other people in the group were saying about us. "Jeff thinks you're really stupid," was Don's favorite line with me. Also, he would say, "You know, I *can't* be myself in there," as an explanation for his never becoming "one of the guys." He would never actually explain why he couldn't be himself. It was expected that you already were "hip" enough to know. The whole thing now seems like a massive verbal illusion, which resulted in manipulation and control. Fear was the outstanding theme of our lives. Fear of not being "hip" or of being selfish. Fear of being verbally humiliated or even physically attacked. Fear of being the "target."

Color Me Depressed

John French: Do you remember when he had us paint the living room red?
Bill Harkleroad: Oh, Chinese red, blue and yellow.
JF: I don't remember the blue, I just remember all the walls were red for a while.
BH: Well, we did three different colors. The kitchen was yellow, his room was blue, and the living room was red.
JF: Do you think those colors represented something? Because, he said he used to go out and study psychological texts at the library - you know when he'd leave the house - that's what he told me he'd do.
BH: Really? Wow!
JF: Yeah. So do you think those colors had some kind of play on...
BH: Could have.

JF: Let's see, his room was blue, so that maybe that represented some kind of serenity, so we'd always equate him with serenity, where as the living room was red and that was a color that would make you work more, and the kitchen was yellow, like warning, like don't go in here and eat food or you're gonna die!
BH: ...you lazy fuckers! (laughter from both) I wouldn't put it past him but I wasn't aware of any intention like that.

Don did mention to me during this period that there were certain psychological effects of different colors upon people. This is why street signs are certain colors. Yellow is a warning. Red is urgent. I recall him mentioning that red was an "energy" color. Maybe he thought 12-14 hours a day was just not enough...

John French: I wondered about that at the time he did the painting. See, I was aware - he had told me he was going to the library and I picked up on it because he kept saying, "Man, I've been studying about you, and I can't figure you out!" you know, in those talks that we would have. He would call me a catatonic, he'd call me this and that, because basically I would just sit there mute, because I thought, "No matter what I say, I am damned!" so I might as well just sit there and say nothing because it gives him less ammunition to use on me. You know, of course, we all turned against each other when that would happen because if you didn't turn against the other guy, they would turn against you, so we all wound up, I don't know, being traitors to each other sort of. Of course, that put walls up between us to where we couldn't communicate with each other any longer.
Bill Harkleroad: It kept us from banding together and saying, "What are we doing here?"
JF: Yeah, what are we doing with this jerk?
BH: I truly believe it was a conscious effort to keep us mesmerized and separate, yeah!

It seemed truly ludicrous, in the face of our situation, the amount of work we had to get done, the snail's pace at which songs were being finished, and the fact that Don was constantly deriding us about "wasting time" that suddenly all work careened to a stop in order to paint the interior of the house. Jeff and Don went to the stores and bought supplies. I recall moving everything into the middle of the room, storing the drums in the shed, and scattering a couple of drop cloths over the floor. Jeff and Don returned with supplies - brushes, paint, rollers, trays, and plenty of masking tape. The ceiling was masked-off by Jeff. I must have been the "bad guy" this week, because I remember painting the living room late into the night all by myself, while the rest of the band went somewhere with Don. We didn't have a ladder. I stood on a red vinyl and chrome kitchen chair, which also served as my drum throne. Laurie was in the other room sleeping, having helped paint the bedroom she and Don shared blue.

The following day, I took down a light fixture that was in the middle of the living room. We had never been able to use this light and so a couple of dim lamps were all we had for lighting. One sat on the piano, and the other, a much smaller one, sat on the lower part of the room divider. This light fixture was amusing to all of us, as it was a fake wagon wheel, with small glass enclosures on the top half, which concealed light bulbs. I took it down and rebuilt it so that it worked from a switch that was by the side door that went out onto the balcony and down the stairs.

The house was put back together within a couple of days and was much cleaner and less cluttered. The intensity of the red paint (it was enamel and shiny), really did change the mood of the room. It was starting to get cold, winter was creeping on. There was an oil heater in a small basement area (more of an access room than a basement, and the room divider concealed the heater, which had vents on each side. We checked it out, but Don insisted that it not be used. He was extremely sensitive to heat. I have heard rumors that Don now has multiple sclerosis. I have no idea if this is true, but a friend of mine with MS says that one of the first systems she developed was a sensitivity to heat that caused her to go into an extremely weakened state.

There was a fireplace in the living room, and Mark became my hero when he began foraging a few pieces of firewood and starting a small fire in the late evening after Don went to bed. Sometimes the four of us would gather around this flame, sitting on the floor and watching the flames lick the air and draw our cigarette smoke into the opening and up the chimney with blankets wrapped around us. Mark hadn't smoked before he joined the group, but certainly began afterwards. One thing we never seemed to have was a lack of cigarettes.

Ninja Loaf

For most of the "training" for *Trout Mask*, we all slept in the living room. The downstairs bedroom had several beds in it for a while, but a bunch of things got stored down there and it was so stuffed full that we wound up sleeping in the living room. I almost always slept in my clothes on a full-sized mattress that was folded up in the form of a couch against the south wall and located between the side door and the fireplace. It had a madras Indian type spread thrown over it and that was my only blanket at night.

I recall being so hungry one night that I crawled, commando-like, on the floor in slow motion and snuck a piece of bread out of the loaf, terrified the rattle of the wrapping would awaken someone. I crawled back holding the piece in my mouth until I could cover up, and I ate this piece of bread silently, hidden under the covers.

I would go off occasionally by myself and reflect on my situation and this is when I really went back to my Christian roots. I started praying for some kind of answer to this. There was almost no love or comradeship in this situation. We all became like trained automatons and what we did was seldom praised or rewarded or enjoyed. We were all working for the good of this project, and if we were sick, it was claimed to be just our psyches or subconscious making an excuse for us to be "lazy." Psycho-babble like this seemed to be constantly brought into the conversation by Don.

Those moments of praying by myself silently would clear my head, and I could go back into the situation and have some peace inside. It made me consistent and that's what this project needed.

My First Summons

One night, everyone was gone from the house except for Laurie and myself. I heard a knock at the bottom door, the front door, which actually opened into the downstairs bedroom. I proceeded to walk down the stairs and answer the door. Laurie stood on the stairway and cautioned me to ask who it was. The voice said a name I had never heard. I opened the door and this fellow said, "Are you John French". I replied in the affirmative and he handed me a paper. I asked what it was, and suddenly realised it was a legal document and that I was being sued for $200,000 by Buddah Records.

"Give it back to him!" Laurie suggested. This seemed like a good idea, so I handed the paper back to the man. "You have legally received a summons to appear in court." the man said and quickly left, the summons still in my hand. Now, I didn't know what a summons was, so I started inspecting this document and realized that it had to do with the little switcheroo done in the Kama Sutra office back when we signed with MGM. Someone else had apparently become wise to the trick, and now we were being sued for breach of contract.

Don arrived home, and I walked upstairs to explain what happened. Laurie got to him first. "John just took it, didn't even try to do anything." This infuriated Don. He grabbed me and slung me around into the wall and my head hit with a "thud" that knocked me semi-conscious. I was dazed and bewildered, and in shock. Had I just been violently accosted by a man who was always writing about peace? Quickly, his fist sunk into my unsuspecting stomach, knocking the wind out of me. I slid to the floor gasping for air completely unable to defend myself. "What the fuck do you think you are doing, you moron?" he bellowed at me.

This was a turning point for me. Don outweighed me by 40-50 lbs. I thought he was "streetwise" and had fought before, while I was not practiced in any form of violence besides hitting the drums. He was 8 years older than me. I was really scared. I was holding my hands over my face and had my feet drawn up to my chest and he was kicking me in the shins. I was still unable to breathe or speak and he was saying "Speak up, asshole, why did you fucking do this to me?"

Now, I knew that he would use violent force on me. I also knew that I was working for nothing more than food and shelter to help him realize his dream of a super album. After this incident, whenever I talked to somebody who "talked with their hands" I would wince or duck, thinking they were about to hit me. I started suspecting that everyone was like this underneath, and that I had to be on guard at every moment.

This wasn't the end of it though. When the rest of the band came back, Don alienated me further by insisting that I sit in a chair while the rest of the band stood around me. Don was the instigator of this, and I could read fear and confusion in all my fellow bandmate's eyes. "Where are you at?" Don would ask me suspiciously. "Just whose side are you on, theirs or ours?"

Betrayal

Mark, Bill and Jeff, scared, confused and bewildered would ask similar things. They were all afraid that if they didn't, they would wind up being the "target" of this hostility taking my place. I looked through the thick air in the room in the house on Ensenada Drive in Woodland Hills and sensed that nothing would ever be the same between my friends and I again. When this happened to me, I didn't even know what a summons was.

Development Of The Drum Style

Having been in the role of sitting for hours teaching everyone the parts of the songs, I was completely familiar not only with all the basic rhythms that Don used over and over and again, but also his favorite rhythms, and all the delta and jazz influences and how they were working together. So, I started taking delta, jazz, and Latin beats and try to combine them together - in the hope of playing two or three rhythms simultaneously. I would usually use snare and kick for one, toms for another, and cymbals for another. Sometimes I would divide the set other ways, like kick and toms, hi-hat and snare, then cymbals, always assigning a different rhythm to each.

Sometimes, I would make a part more homogenous, by just playing a rhythm with an accompaniment that suited that particular beat. The main thing was that my goal was to play at least two different rhythms at the same time. This, of course, took hours of practice. In order to understand, I should explain basic drum beats.

Conventional rock drumming involves learning a few familiar beats with many variations. That is the extent of our vocabulary, because it takes years just to make certain rhythms sound smooth and driving. Fills and slight variations are added and are generally simple to add, as the few basic beats become so much a part of our basic vocabulary that we can go in and out of them easily. Everything always revolves around some basic rhythm that's played until it's ingrained in our nature.

The reason I was excited about this stuff is that it was a completely different approach to drums than I had ever heard before at that point in time. Latin drumming had done bits and pieces of this, but usually with familiar and basic patterns in various combinations - just different than rock. This was miles away from that, because it was a mix of different styles and influences played at the same time.

I didn't get much time to practice. We had a lady who lived just across the street who was constantly calling the police and complaining that I was too loud. I would take my drums out in the shed and practice for hours during the daylight hours while this woman was gone to work. As always, the guitarists could practice all they wanted to un-amplified - day or night. Eventually, I started trying some of these parts with the song *Hair Pie*. Bill was the only one who really noticed. He said that what I was playing was completely different than anything he had heard, but that it fitted perfectly and kept everything together.

This was all the encouragement I needed to keep experimenting. I realized also that time was against me. The rest of the band knew most of the songs, and it seemed like I was just getting started. I had spent so much time transcribing, teaching, and arranging that I was quite a bit behind. The advantage was, I knew every note of every song by heart and could actually play to a "recording" of them in my head.

So down I sat with the music pad and a pencil. I had taken all the piano transcriptions and re-transcribed them on $8^1/2$ x 11 inch music paper and put them in neat little folders - like the ones kids used to turn in reports in grade school. It was the only way to keep track of so many parts and songs. After this seemingly endless task, if someone forgot a part, I could walk over to the briefcase I had them in, pull out the folder and find their part in a matter of seconds. Before this, they were all written in a wire bound book and completely out of order.

Benedictine But Not Monk-Like

The first act of real violence after Don's attack on me was me attacking Jeff Cotton. During this early period in rehearsals, shortly after Mark Boston joined the band, we still had a bedroom downstairs that we all shared. Everyone had gone to bed except Don and I, me being the present benefactor of Don's favoritism that particular night. He had bought a bottle of B&B - Brandy & Benedictine. "Have some," he said, "it's made by monks in France."

I was not one to indulge in alcohol and Don knew this. My father was an alcoholic, and this turned me off alcohol, even though I occasionally liked to get blitzed just for laughs. I had been under a lot of stress and working hard transcribing and arranging parts of *Trout Mask*. It had been extremely difficult the last few days because Jeff Cotton, as I mentioned earlier, had been coming back to the piano after I had played a particular part for him asking me to play it again.

When I would play the part for him again, he would often say, "That's not the same thing you played last time." I surmised rather quickly that Jeff and Don were perhaps discussing my level of competency regarding transcribing parts and accurately playing them back on the piano. I was admittedly not adept on piano, so it is not surprising that I would make some errors, but the majority of complaints were from Jeff - Bill and Mark had almost no complaints.

At the time, Jeff's duties as Don's personal scribe kept him quite busy, so his guitar practice time was quite limited. Some mornings, I would wake up to find that Jeff and Don would just be finishing up an all-nighter. Jeff would then sleep all day, causing him to get behind Bill and Mark. During this period of time, Jeff was almost completely transformed into a caricature of himself, talking less and less like Jeff and more and more like the voice on "The Blimp" and Pena. I found this particularly annoying, because I always disliked what I considered to be "phoniness" in people. Bill and I got along very well because we were both for the most part fairly down-to-earth, as was Mark. Mark was a performer, but he was always himself and for the most part, relaxed and comfortable with who he was.

Don was insisting more and more that Jeff read aloud in his "Pena" voice as we sat listening, preferably spellbound, to reams and reams of (what I considered) the nonsense poetry and prose that Don was daily dictating to him. Small sections of it were relatively amusing, but it was annoying to me because of the time-frame we were working in and how far behind we were in actually finishing the double album - most songs of which I had yet to learn on the drums. This became quite frustrating to me, and it probably became evident during the readings to the point where I now believe Don sensed a chance to drive a substantial wedge between Jeff and I.

So, this particular night, I was up with Don alone in the living room - the others asleep downstairs. I might add here that Don was almost always excessively charming on a one-to-one basis. This is the same kind of charm the public saw for the most part. I never once recall Don ever accusing me of anything one-to-one. It was always in a group situation, where he could immediately take control and pull strings, manipulating us into more and more treacherous acts against each other. Don was particularly charming this evening, offering me a drink, telling me what a great job I was doing. He would flatter on a personal level to no end, telling me what a great percussionist I was and that there was no one else "out there" who even compared. I knew this to be untrue, but it nonetheless tickled my ears.

So, I had a drink of this rather strong liqueur. We talked of many things and had a pleasant, disarming conversation for the first hour or so of the evening. I was relaxed, and eventually became a little drunk, getting drunker all along without really realizing it, as Don kept re-filling my glass. I was drinking and smoking, and taking in a moment of luxurious private time with the "main man." Jeff Cotton's name kept coming up more and more during the evening, at first in reference to the parts I was supposedly "playing wrong." I told Don I didn't understand this, because Mark and Bill seemed to be doing just fine.

Don then gradually revealed to me that Jeff Cotton thought I was stupid. He explained that Jeff was constantly berating me to him behind my back and had been doing this for some time. Young, gullible, and drunk, I accepted all he told me at face value and thus began a slow and seething anger within me. Soon, Don was explaining to me that I shouldn't take this crap, that I was working too hard and deserved more respect and that Jeff was out of line to speak of me this way.

Throughout the entire night, for several hours, Don chipped away at my better judgment and became increasingly bold with his "revelations" to me about Jeff. Then came the advice. "If I were you…" and started suggesting ways that I should confront this, that I had a right to know what was going on. I don't recall the words, but I do recall the outcome.

Jeff's Wakeup Call

Just before the break of dawn, a very intoxicated Drumbo descended the staircase, dragged Jeff out of bed, forced him outside under the patio area next to the laundry shed and started pushing him around. This was a guy who I had been friends with for two years prior to the Beefheart band. We had been inseparable at times and had never raised a finger towards each other in violence. We had never had an argument or even yelled at each other. We had been just about as close as any friends could be and suddenly, here I was violently confronting him.

Jeff was absolutely caught off guard and scared - obviously shaken from my drunkenness, unusual behavior, and the fog of sleepiness still hovering in his head. I was drunk and out of control. I slammed him into the wall several times. I don't recall ever striking him, but I did a lot of yelling, pushing and shoving. I felt completely justified in my actions.

Victor

Eventually, Jeff's nose was bleeding and I found myself standing there with Bill and Mark, who had been awakened by the ruckus, looking at me as though I had completely lost my mind. About this time, during a lull in the "recreational activities," for some odd reason which I still don't understand, Don asked me something to the extent of, "Don't you think Victor has had a lot to do with all this?" Desperate for a scapegoat, and feeling Benedictine and more guilt, I immediately said, "Yes," for absolutely no logical reason.

Victor was quickly summoned over to the house and in twenty minutes arrived. We were still out on the patio, mostly having a verbal spat, Jeff looking horrible, but not really physically hurt. He was bleeding a slight bit from his nose, sleepy and completely drained emotionally with dark circles under his eyes. I was just an out-of-control sleepy drunken mess and still shouting in anger. As soon as Victor viewed Jeff a look of terror arose in his eyes. He denied any involvement. All I can figure is that perhaps he and Jeff had talked about me and this is why Don had suggested he come over.

It gave me a quiet satisfaction to see Victor uncomfortable. Although I liked Victor for the most part, his freedom to come and go and his relationship with Don sometimes cut me to the quick. His usual attitude towards the group situation was quite condescending and his posturing seemed to indicate a mindset of, "Don, it must be terrible to deal with what these guys are putting you through" - all the while not having a clue as to what Don was putting us through. He'd never witnessed one of our "talks" - probably because Don knew that if he ever did and word leaked out to the family, his mother would have stopped sending him money.

Victor, like Don, was quite charming in a one-on-one situation. He could converse on a variety of subjects, and I often enjoyed our conversations. Yet these comments to the group really caused me to seethe at times. He was still living at home with his mother and father (Jack and Charlene, the l atter of which Don pronounced with a hard "Ch" like Charley) and came and went as he pleased. He was always wheeling and dealing and seemed to have cool cars and all the money he needed.

I knew that Don was grooming him to be in the band, a symbol of true nepotistic decadence. He was a useless, meaningless addition to the group. After this day, I felt that if nothing else, Victor would choose his words around us - or at least me - a bit more carefully.

After this, Jeff and I were at complete odds with each other for most of the time. In the band environment, whichever became the target, the other became the aggressive assistant prosecutor. We were at enmity for almost the entire remaining time of the *Trout Mask* rehearsals until I left. It was a large price I paid for my outburst. I don't know if either of us ever apologized for our actions toward each other. However, there are few things I have ever been more ashamed of in my life. It isn't the last time I would erupt in violence against a band mate.

This shame procreated and began to be shared by all as time went on and we foolishly became more deeply embroiled in Don's world of puppetry. It became an important tool for Don. Now, it was far less likely that we would ever talk about this to outsiders because we would make ourselves appear as cowards; betrayers of our friends. This allowed for even more control, as now, we were concealing our own shortcomings and our shame for becoming the people we were. Lies begat lies.

It also divided us as a group and in a sense, made us more "efficient" as worker-minions. Less time having fun, exchanging cordialities, and more time working toward "the common goal" or completing our master's work. As time went on, we had more violence toward each other. Don presented this to Zappa as just "healthy boys working out differences." I am sure that Zappa had no clue as to how intensely cult-like this situation had become. Zappa, we were told by Don, regarded it as a "healthy exchange." I was invited by Gail to the Zappa complex in 2004 and Gail, after hearing a bit about the atrocities, said "Frank and I had no idea this was going on."

Healthy it was not. It was devastating to our personal lives and our social development. We all became victims of our own fear and lack of confidence and prisoners of our shame. Don's manipulation of us became much easier as time went by, because we had become conditioned to respond in the manner he desired. On the surface, we seemed like a super-efficient well-paced band, ambitious and extraordinary. Even our middle-aged neighbors, the Catalanos, seemed to view us as long haired "Leave it to Beavers." the "nice young men who lived next door" is what I'm sure they thought for the most part. The disease that tore us apart as individuals remained a well-kept secret.

CHAPTER TWENTY FOUR:
SPACE IN SCARCITY

John, Jerry Handley and Don, England 1968. Photo courtesy of Colin F

Trips To Beach

There were some good times that I remember during this period of time - though more analogous to the hour walk in the prison yard. We sometimes loaded into Don's tiny red Volvo and drove out through Topanga Canyon to the Malibu beach and just walked in the beauty. Three of us used to squeeze in the back - usually Mark, Bill, and I. It was completely uncomfortable, but the trip was worth it. It was a pleasant release to just stand listening to the waves, empty my mind of all worry, and meditate. Though the atmosphere was still dominated by paranoia and second-guessing everything, the environment was like a pillow to my tortured mind, and an hour or two at the coast never hurt anyone.

There was a white bull terrier that used to follow us around at the beach. We called him the "pig dog" because of his pink nose and that oddly-shaped snout. Occasionally we would meet up with others at the beach. I noticed that whenever I talked to someone, Don seemed to be listening from a distance. I mentioned to some young girl that we had once been with a record company that seemed to have loose ties to the Jewish Mafia. Don later took me aside at the house and suggested that I should not talk about such things. I had no idea he was listening so intently, which added to the fishbowl environment even more.

No Thanks, Mr. Morris

At some point in time, Don discovered the book, *The Naked Ape*, which had just been published. There's a part of me even today who still hasn't forgiven the author of this book, Desmond Morris. Don would have his girlfriend read the book to us and as she would come across some point, Don would stop her and relate that to one of us. It was like being scrutinized by "The Brain Police." I heard that Zappa song once, listened to the line "who are the brain police?" - and thought, "I know who they are."

This added to the self-conscious attitude of fear we all had developed. Now we were dealing with "body language" and began to "read" each other's every move and become more superficial than ever. Specifically I recall Mark Boston being accused of having "latent dictator qualities" because he sometimes stroked his mustache. This was only one of many such absurd theories that became strongly embraced by Van Vliet.

Thanks to Mr. Morris' idiotic book, all postures, hand movements, placement in relationship to others, body language and simple characteristics and habits could at any moment fall under Don's scrutiny and become the subject of yet another "talk." It became increasingly difficult to simply be oneself.

Mysterious Hair Circles

At one point in time, Don's hair was falling out. This was not a normal hair loss where a few more hairs wind up in the brush because of male-pattern baldness, because Don had hair long after I went bald. This hair fell cleanly out in *clumps*. Needless to say, this was a strange phenomenon and one that I still find inexplicable to this day. If this weren't strange enough, the patches on his head, when examined, wound up being almost perfect circles approximately the size of a silver dollar.

With Don's twisted logic, he finally came up with the answer. Drums were in the shapes of circles, and I was the drummer, so somehow this was *my fault*. (I think now that it was the same alien life forms who are now creating *crop circles*).

This burst of brilliance came to him during yet another "talk" where I was in the role of "target." I was beginning to really tire of this nonsense. I had made up my mind that this was absolutely ridiculous and utterly insane. After examining myself closely, I concluded that I was doing *absolutely nothing* and *devoid of any covert thoughts* which would make me guilty of anything I was being charged with, much less these missing circles of hair.

I wanted out. Yet there were circumstances now that made it difficult for me to just pack up and go. I had no transportation, no money, and my family was upset with me. I really had nowhere *to* go. Also, I really liked Sue Vliet, Don's mother, and she had been pouring a lot of money into the band. Don constantly reminded us that she was partially supporting the band with shouted statements like "what about my *mother*, man?" Also, there was Bill's mother, who had also poured thousands into the band at this point. In Harkleroad's book, *Lunar Notes*, he mentions that this money was his college fund. My folks didn't have much money, although Don actually thought my mother had money and was "holding out." I told him that I was a "big boy" and my mother wasn't financially responsible for me. This made him angry, because I was insinuating that he wasn't a "big boy." It is true that I had little respect for a man almost thirty who was still living off "mommy." Interestingly enough, in the two years before I joined the Magic Band, I actually performed more often and made more money while in high school than I had made after being in the Magic Band.

Don's Illness

Don told me on several occasions that he had been diagnosed as "Paranoid Schizophrenic." I felt a common bond with my friends, Bill, Mark and Jeff and even Laurie, Don's girlfriend, whom I was quite fond of partially because I viewed her merely as a victim of circumstance. We were all victims of the symptoms of Don's illness, his paranoid delusions and the resulting social situation it created and trapped us all within. It was my opinion at this point that Don was mentally disturbed and that this could become dangerous. It was evident in part by his behavior the day he discovered the "party of strangers" in his house. It was also evident by the extreme paranoia and delusions that motivated him to such extremes of behavior. It was all based on Don's fear and his perverted sense of reality.

Early Drawings By Don

During the "talks," Don started constantly drawing. He had started buying cheap pads of plain paper and drawing quick hard-edged sketches. His most manic output would be during our talks, where he might draw 50 - 100 drawings. It wasn't the output that bothered me, but was the subject matter. All of these drawings depicted the same basic feeling. They were drawings of monsters devouring each other - terrible views of destruction and violence depicted in a simple cartoon-like form. It appeared comical to the casual observer, but I felt as though these drawings were a direct manifestation of Don's mental state, a state much more seriously close to being dangerous than any outsider would perceive. We were *living* these drawings.

Pearls Of Wisdom

My mother, Pearl French had a strong disdain for Don, sometimes calling him "laughing boy" and various other names. She was very concerned that I was in a bad situation and said, in agreement with Zoot, that I had "changed" drastically. I wrote most of this off as "un-cool parental-meddling," but a lot of what she said was an accurate assessment (although sometimes anachronistically naïve) of the true situation. She would write supportive letters to me that I abhorred, even dreaded, because they were "motherly." Don got wind of these letters and began sending Jeff down to the mailbox to retrieve them. The good Captain would then open them and have Jeff read them to the entire band to embarrass and humiliate me.

Pearl, (my mother) then got wind of the fact that these letters were being read. She lived a block from Sue Vliet, so they probably talked about this. She started writing the letters to Don instead of me, saying things like "I know you're reading this to the band, so I just wanted to say "hi." Unfortunately, in her naivete, she also had heard that Don was giving the band drugs in form of "shots" (she had been a nurse) and this gave Don further ammunition to mock me and raise the level of hilarity. This made me appear foolish even though I had nothing at all to do with these letters.

A Cymbal For Jeff

Each letter I dreaded because I knew that the reception of these documents (which Don still has as far as I know) was like an invitation to the next "talk" of which I would be the "guest of honor." I really began to resent Jeff, because it was he who would retrieve these letters and carefully read them to the band. One night, after such a talk, I was setting up my drums in the living room and I looked over at Jeff, who was recuperating from being the target of a "talk," and just impulsively threw my ride cymbal at him. I threw it flat, not "frisbee style" and it hit him in the shoulder and crashed to the floor.

He ran out the door and I chased him down the street. As soon as we were out of earshot of the house I shouted "Jeff, slow down, I want to get out of there too. Let's go together." But Jeff was too fast for me. I was a smoker and Jeff wasn't, so I quickly became winded. He ran like a rabbit down the road and disappeared from view. I walked, winded, back to the house. Don quickly got on the phone and summoned Alex, who actually came into the band for a short period of time to replace Jeff.

Helen

Helen, who was now of driving age and had been given her brother Harold's old car, came down to see me. The first time, she brought a friend - a girl named Becky, who was a sexy blond. After they left, Don asked me to talk with him. We went outside and he said, "Man, tell Helen the next time she comes down to bring Becky, and we'll all go out somewhere together." This was a little creepy. Don was almost twenty-nine, and Becky was probably sixteen. I told him she was "jail bait" and he should stay away from her. Helen was probably the same age and so I didn't touch her, which may have made her feel a bit odd, but the law was pretty strict on this, and I didn't need any more trouble with the law.

P-K-Ro-P

Occasionally, Don would play the drums. I was outside one day and heard him playing and calling me. "John!" he kept saying in an almost pleading tone. I came in and Don was sitting at my drum kit. He was wearing his favorite indoor clothing that consisted of a black faux-Oriental robe with red piping that reached halfway down his thighs over his pajamas. He was playing a really simple, but infectious drumbeat and didn't want to lose it.

"Write this down, quick!" He said, in rhythm with the beat. I quickly got the music book and jotted it down in about 30 seconds, as it was simple. "Did you get it yet?" he asked. I looked to check it over and an impish thought crept into my mind: *Don was completely in my control.* So, I looked at the book, puzzled, and said, "No, this is really hard to write." I walked around the drums for a good five minutes, staring at his feet, looking at the way he held the sticks, and appearing to be really deep in concentration, occasionally holding the book up and pretending to scribble.

I was having a good laugh. This was one of those priceless moments, seeing Don ensnared within his own creative process and actually having to completely concentrate and be totally vulnerable. I finally told him "I think I have it, so you can stop." He shouted over the drums "Are you sure? I don't want to lose this, man. I can't lose this. It's too good." I finally convinced him I had it and he stopped playing and stood up.

"Oh, man, I hope you got that - see if you can play it" he commanded. I sat down and played it exactly as he had. It was a very simple beat, but, as I said, very infectious. That was the beginning of a song called Ant-Man-Bee. He called it P-K-Ro-P because of the way the last four beats sounded.

Alex Returns And Disappears

The only song I remember learning during Alex's short return was *Ant-Man-Bee*, which employed the P-K-Ro-P beat. This was a song that Don wrote partially on the piano, but the beginning was actually written in the old style of Don humming parts and giving basic ideas. I recall Alex being there and us working on this song, and suddenly someone didn't understand a minor detail of the arrangement, either Bill, Mark or myself - Alex being the new "special friend."

Don's reaction to anyone who misunderstood his sometimes vague attempts at musical communication was basically just to lose his patience and throw a tantrum and so that's what happened. Basically, he just ripped Bill, Mark and I apart for screwing up his song.

Alex could see right away things had disintegrated even more than when he had previously left. He didn't stay long. Jeff's fantastic parts were written upon his return a little later. Don created the parts on piano and Jeff copped the licks, but they weren't written down until later. The interesting thing is that *Ant-Man-Bee*, minus Jeff's parts, is almost exactly what Don wrote that evening, we just worked it out post-tantrum. There were a couple of technical problems that needed to be solved to make the song work.

Unfortunately, Don would not allow this kind of theory exchange to be used by us in his presence. He would become completely upset, because this went against his "scales are for fishes" and "train yourself, strain yourself" philosophies, which fans have so strongly embraced. "Just PLAY IT, man!" he would shout.

When we started talking in musical terms in Don's presence, he was suddenly unable to understand us and rather than bother to learn some simple terminology to aid in communications, he became threatened and insecure - because his ignorance was suddenly exposed. He would attack the "instigator" who was in actuality, only trying to be of assistance. I can't remember anyone in the *Trout Mask* band who ever rubbed their musical knowledge in Don's face. This caused us to reach an unspoken mutual understanding that any talk of musical theory in front of Don was "taboo." We worked out musical problems only in his absence.

Jeff And Pearl Pay A Visit

Bill, Mark and I were working, chipping away at the puzzle-like mountain of parts Don had pounded out on the piano, trying to put things in some kind of order and make some sense of the pieces. One day, Jeff unexpectedly showed up driving my father's car with my mother as a passenger. It was the first visit from anyone in my family.

My mother in the same house with Don was a hilarious combination. I was still viewing her as a parent who "just didn't understand," and Don as mentally disturbed, so I didn't feel that loyal to either one. Pearl French always was a strong woman who spoke her mind, and when Don showed his drawings, which covered practically the entire south wall of the living room, her comment was, "If that's what was going on in my mind, I certainly wouldn't go around exhibiting it for others to see."

I had to really summon all my emotional control to keep from laughing hysterically. I have already mentioned that these drawings mostly were of cartoon-like demon-animals devouring and attacking one another. Don did this little phony nervous laugh that he sometimes employed when befuddled or stumped and she then called him "laughing boy." I had to summon even more control to keep from laughing and rolling on the floor. I admired her courage and at the same time felt like a total coward. However, I had reached this point of confusion through a long series of well-planned steps, where as she was walking in, taking a snapshot, and leaving. She was the shouting child in "the Emperor's new clothes."

My mother had come to inform me that my father and she had decided to pay the fine for my shoplifting offence. The one condition: that I come up a few days for a visit. It was an interesting situation. Don knew that Jeff had probably been talking to my parents about the situation in the Trout Mask house. He knew that as soon as we got in the car, we would be discussing my leaving the band. Don's dilemma was that any objection on his part would simply reaffirm whatever Jeff had said, and so he pretended to be the gracious host, put on his most charming act and said, "Of course, that's a great idea." I gathered a few things and as we walked to the car, Pearl said, " I don't buy that phony act of his for a minute." My reply was, "Shh, he'll hear you, and I have to live with him even if you don't."

As soon as we were in the car, Jeff and I became our old selves again. We were friends before the band, and as soon as the "brain police" were out of sight, we resumed our friendship. It was a strange feeling. I felt like Jeff and I had instantaneously taken up where we had left off two years prior - like a time warp.

Bob On Rodeo Drive

We decided to go straight over to Bob Krasnow's office on Rodeo Drive and tell him the situation. When we arrived, he saw us immediately, and then we told him the situation. At this point, Bob really stuck his foot in his mouth by saying, "Well, just remember I *own you guys*, because I have you under contract." I was shocked for a second, because I had never seen this greedy selfish side of Bob actually manifest itself so blatantly. Once I got over the initial shock I reminded Bob that we were (1) Under age and (2) Not under contract to him because we hadn't as yet signed anything.

Suddenly, Bob became our "friend." I am paraphrasing, but his reply was something to extent of "Hey, you guys, don't let a piece of paper stand between our friendship. After all, we go way back." A more appropriate phrase would be "taken aback" by his behavior. We had both thought that Krasnow was probably an OK guy. Dealing with Don, anyone would have a difficult time. Suddenly, the scales fell off our eyes. We saw Krasnow in a completely new light. Returning to the car, a little shaken, we began to laugh about the music business and what a joke these people were. I can only say that my future dealings with record labels for years afterward mostly affirmed this fact. Most of the major labels are filled with manipulative thieves culled from the bottom of the tank.

Summations

I am asking myself as I write: How on earth after leaving the house did I manage to find myself back in the band? I cannot remember exactly. I recall spending a couple of days with my parents. I recall my mother sitting in her rocking chair speaking to me about her concerns for my welfare (I was only nineteen or twenty) and having a surprising amount of insight into the reality of my situation, pretty much nailing the situation. I recall having a couple of talks with Jeff, and something about Bill and Mark coming up and persuading us to come back. It's very unclear why I went back but I can probably speculate the following.

I had been away from home for two years and had changed drastically in that time. I had been to Europe, taken drugs, met Paul McCartney, and lived in a cult-like environment that was so strange that most people couldn't even begin to imagine what it was like. In my perspective, my parents and friends now appeared to me like aliens from another dimension. I saw them as pathetically naïve, although sweet and well-meaning. I didn't disrespect them at all, but my perspective had been tremendously altered and I no longer could relate to my past life.

However, my mother recalls coming out to my little room in the garage as I was packing my things to go back. She tried to talk me out of going, but I said, "I've got my head screwed on straight, and I'm not going to let him scare me anymore. I'll be all right." I don't recall going back at all, how I got there, who I rode with or anything else. I just know that Jeff and I both wound up back down there.

Party At Zappa's
During the *Trout Mask* rehearsals Zappa had a party at his house. It appeared to be a birthday party for a rather tall leggy British secretary that worked in the Bizarre/Straight business office. I believe her name was Pauline Butcher. We drove up in the red Volvo, I believe to the new house just North of Hollywood in one of the Canyons. I recall distinctly Jim Sherwood showing up on his chopper and parking in front of the new Zappa house, which was quite an impressive place.

I think the birthday may have been the excuse, because it also seemed a bit of a housewarming, as this house was, I believe, the first house that Frank and Gail had actually owned. It wound up being the only home they ever owned, as they never moved again. The Mothers were there and all seemed in good spirits. It was a culture shock to actually mingle with people who liked to have fun. It took a while for me to remember what this was like. I didn't mingle much and barely spoke to anyone, obviously uncomfortable around happiness.

As we walked up to the house across the lawn I noticed that there was an attached garage and driveway to the right of the property. The house was a split-level place. Ironically, the layout was similar to where we lived except much bigger and fancier. Frank must have been doing quite well in order to afford a home like this, it was gorgeous, and in a nice neighborhood. I grinned to myself thinking what the neighbors must think this evening. The Mothers and the Beefheart group descending upon the neighborhood in the same night - we were a pretty wild-looking group for that era.

The house was on a slight incline that descended from front to back. Also, the "main" floor of the house was above, and one had to climb stairs to a porch in order to actually get to the front door. But we didn't go upstairs. There was a front entrance to the lower part of the house, which was actually a sort of half-basement - a fairly good-sized room. My memory is vague now, but it seemed to me it was divided into a main room, with a smaller room to the left where, I believe, Frank eventually had a film editor working, and that was enclosed and had a door. There was also a small partitioned area to the extreme right that was Frank's composition space. It was separated from the main room by a rather large open entry way with no doors. I could see his music scores on a drawing board. In the left rear corner was a dumb waiter that came from the kitchen.

Zappa entertained by showing old 8 and 16 mm silent home movies that he had taken in Lancaster years before. Some of these showed a very young Don Vliet and his mother Sue. One animated close-up of Don's face showed him moving his mouth at high speed and making a lot of silly faces, pointing to a Pepsi he was holding in his hand. Another showed a much-younger Sue Vliet, in the kitchen, baking something if I recall (or perhaps flattening lard with a red enamel rolling pin).

It was a defining moment for me, as I could actually see the evidence that Zappa and Van Vliet had indeed known each other. The black and white pictures and images etched themselves into my mind as strong impressions and feelings.

There were then some scenes from what appeared to be the Fair and Alfalfa festival in Lancaster with several guys with pompadours who I did not recognize walking around. I remember a ferris wheel lit up in the dark. Also, there was one fellow who had his shirt off and there were pimples all over his back. Jimmy Carl Black yelled out "Oh, pop those zits!" - and everyone broke into laughter including me.

Jim Sherwood later recalled to me that since there was nothing to do in Lancaster, you had to get creative. If you knew a guy, like Don, with a car, you could load it up with booze and friends and go park out in the desert - preferably on a hill overlooking town to view the lights. The entertainment would be supplied by the radio. Dr. Jazzmo was on until midnight then Wolfman Jack came on. Dr. Jazzmo played blues - Sonny Boy Williamson, Elmore James and Memphis Slim to name a few, then he would go to commercials and sell religious recordings. On other nights, Sherwood's mother would have "taco feeds" for the neighborhood kids, who would gather at their house:

Jim Sherwood: Oh, yes. She had taco feeds all the time. Then, all the kids would come over and they would call her "Mrs. Bone!"

Back to the party, it was obvious that these guys felt relaxed around their leader and the contrast to our situation was so apparent to all of us that it almost made me uncomfortable for Don. There was a real casual family kind of rapport between Frank and his band, and they were all closer to the same age as their leader. Perhaps this is the biggest difference between these two: Don was an only child, and Frank came from a large family.

Jim Sherwood: Our band, the original Mothers was the only band that was a true band. We played off the feelings of each other. It was a family group.
John French: And don't you feel that had something to do with Frank's first burst of popularity?
JS: Oh, absolutely. Because it was the individuality of everybody in the band that created that whole effect that Frank wanted. Frank loved it and he thrived on it, even though it wasn't exactly the music he wanted to hear.
JF: Yeah, technically. He wanted it more intense.
JS: Anyway, that was our family. Everyone respected Frank, we love him, and we did exactly what he said.
JF: Did he treat you well?
JS: Well, actually Frank was into business. He took care of music, he did the rehearsing, he wrote everything. He took care of the concert halls. He and Herbie ran everything. We didn't do anything but just go play.

Frank also showed a film spot of his wife Gail, nude, sitting in what appeared to be a hotel room. From Frank's (the camera) point of view he walks across the room to her. From the camera's perspective, you then see Frank's foot extended and touching her belly. Frank showing it to a room full of guests many of whom were emitting catcalls and war whoops similar to what one would hear in a strip club. It made me a little uncomfortable.

John French to Art Tripp: Then we watched films that Frank had taken, one of which consisted of Frank with his foot on Gail's naked body. I was kind of embarrassed, you know. I thought, "Geez, it's kind of weird to show films of your wife to all these people?"
AT: I remember that. I think those were taken over on their first European tour over in Germany.

After the films, a birthday cake was brought in. Don had said we were going to a party at Frank's, but this was my first clue that it was a birthday party. Perhaps it was just "in addition to" - as Pauline's birthday just happened to be on or near housewarming night. Pauline was Frank's secretary, and also lived at the Zappa house according to Art Tripp. As Pauline, being a rather tall lady and apparently the guest of honor, bent forward to blow out the candles, a strand of her hair caught on fire. Fortunately, it was quickly extinguished. She had her hair in a bob with bangs as I recall. The flame-up had a rather sobering effect on the small circle of friends, about 20 people who had come together. It was if someone pulled the fader quickly down on the laugh track. Everything became silent for a moment as everyone contemplated how badly this moment could have ended.

Art Tripp

I walked outside to escape the fragrance of burning hair. Zappa's house was split-level and the lower level was a semi-basement area and served as Zappa's workshop/studio. The front wall was partially exposed and as I recall a couple of steps led up to the front yard. The back wall of the basement was totally underground, as I recollect, and the front yard sloped down towards the street. It was out here that I met a rather stimulated Artie Tripp making-out with his then-girlfriend Joanne, who sounded British when introduced. Artie was sporting his trademark green mustache, and I knew little else about him save that he was a drummer.

Meeting Mothers

I also again touched lightly upon conversation with Jim Sherwood Bunk Gardner was also there as was Jimmy Carl Black, "The Indian of the group." Jimmy was a lighthearted fun kind of guy, not too serious about music, very serious about partying.

Jim Sherwood: A lot of the funny scenes that Frank used in the songs and that we did on stage was the funny stuff that we joked about when we were touring. A lot of that stuff Frank would write, and he'd put it into song, any of that funny shit we came up with. That was so amazing - that he could do that.

For me, it was a rare evening out and a taste of what it was like to be in a more "normal" rock band environment. In many ways, I really envied these guys.

John French: Where did you get your nickname Motorhead?
Jim Sherwood: That was at Studio Z with Frank. It was actually originated by Ray Collins. Ray would come in and we would sing. I used to design some when we were in high school. Then, a couple of local guys did some of my designs that actually wound up in Grease - an old Mercury. Some of the cars that I showed lowered and chopped and channeled. I was drawing them all the time. I was doing that and Ray came up one day and said, "Your head is like you got a little motor in it - Little Motorhead."

This triggered a memory of Van Vliet and Snouffer laughing one day and saying to or about someone "it's like he got a little motor in 'im." I think they were talking about Jeff Cotton, who was always wired. His brain was always going a million miles a second and he'd say things that were completely hysterical off the top of his head.

Cruisin' Flashbacks

Motorhead remembers cruisin' with Don in his '49 Oldsmobile on Lancaster Boulevard, which is about all there was to do in those days. Don was actually pulled over and given a ticket for driving too slow - in a twenty-five mile-per-hour zone. The whole point of cruising was not where you were going - because you really had no destination - but to see what was going on where you were. Of course, most of the time what was going on was other cruisers looking at you to see what you were doing. It became a kind of syndrome - a social way to pass time.

When the kids got hungry, they'd pull into a drive-in burger place - like Fosters Freeze (where the *Bongo Fury* album was shot) or Tasti-Freeze - both places were named after the soft-whipped ice cream that came out of a big stainless steel machine when the lever was pulled.

Cruising became a big thing everywhere. Van Nuys Boulevard in the San Fernando Valley was one of the really popular places to cruise. It also became a showcase for customized cars, and provided positive motivation for teenage boys to fix up their cars with chopped tops, custom paint with pin-striping, and chrome wheels. Later, tuck 'n roll black Naugahyde upholstery was the cool look.

Jim Sherwood: We'd sit down (low) in the seat, you could just barely look over the top of the window and you'd cruise up and down the street. When Donny and I would go cruising, he always wanted to take off down to LA. What we would do - two different times that we did it, we went in the Olds one time - we would go down at night and hang out at the clubs, until they closed up.

The Whiskey A' Go Go has been mentioned already and is located at 8901 Sunset Boulevard in Hollywood. It opened in 1964 with live music by Johnny Rivers (*Memphis / Secret Agent Man*) even though it was touted as a discotheque. They had a female DJ in a cage above the stage who played records during breaks, and one night, while she danced to the band, the image of "Go-Go" girls was born, as the audience thought it was part of the act.

The Rainbow Room is a bar and grill which is located at 9015 Sunset Boulevard, right next to the Roxy - a popular nightclub where Frank Zappa recorded *Roxy And Elsewhere* in the mid-seventies. The Rainbow was founded in 1966.

The Troubadour is a popular nightclub, located at 9081 Santa Monica Boulevard, which was opened in 1957 by Doug Weston. It became a popular place to showcase up and coming folk singers in the sixties. In 1970, Elton John made his premier performance at The Troubadour, being introduced to the audience by Neil Young.

Zappa Early Hollywood Days

Jim Sherwood: (Zappa) actually lived down the road from (the Tom Mix cabin) for a while. That's where he first met Gail. They had a house down there, him, Pam Zarubica and Gail. I'd go down and visit once in a while. That's when he first started working with the Indian, Ray Collins and Roy Estrada. That's when they first started the Mothers. '64 was when Frank got with the Mothers, they were actually trying to come up with a name, but they were working together. Once in a while I came down, I had a little Fender guitar, and Frank would have me sit in on some of the concerts down there in Whittier or Torrance or something. I would be playing the background to Gloria.
John French: Freak Out had already been recorded?
JS: Yeah, that was already done.
JF: Was that done at TTG studios?
JS: Yeah, TTG in Hollywood, and that's - all the people Frank knew at that time came in. They were all added to the music.

Buzz Gardner

Because of Don's reunion with Frank, we occasionally became a more social group, and one night descended upon the habitat of Bunk Gardner and his trumpet-playing brother, Buzz. I think the small house they lived in was in Glendale. The house sat sideways on the lot, back from the street, and was partially behind another residence. We all walked into the living room. Bunk was expecting us, but I think Buzz thought we had descended from the cosmos, and his eyes bugged out for a moment. He quickly got over it and became extremely friendly.

This was definitely a bachelor pad and these guys had probably lived together for years. There was a fairly high-end set of stereo speakers hanging from the ceiling by twine or wires and the whole thing was completely inundated with cobwebs, as was anything stuck back in the corner of the room.

Buzz had a set of trumpet mouthpieces stuck into a piece of hardwood that had several holes drilled in it to accommodate them. He explained to me a bit about how different mouthpieces affect the tonality of the instrument. I didn't catch much of it, because there was either hashish or pot being smoked in the room, and I became a little high from the smoke.

Not much of consequence came out of this particular night aside from the fact that I was starting to think that Frank Zappa was going to be a good influence on Don and perhaps make him a little more friendly with the outside world. Don told me later that he talked Frank into hiring Buzz to play with the Mothers.

Art Tripp: Well, I don't know if that is true or not, all I know is that Buzz got in the band because of Bunk. Frank may have hired him to play some trumpet on an album or on a studio cut or something, I don't know, but before I knew it, Buzz was in the band. I liked Buzz, he was a good guy, and he had a good sense of humor and he had been around a lot. On the stage he was kind of shy, and it was easy to get over on him.

Herbie Cohen

At one point, it became pretty apparent to Frank that we needed some equipment. I was still playing with broken drumsticks, the guitar players were recycling their strings. I remember watching Jeff and Bill tie old strings together from a broken one so that they could keep practicing. Don took us to Frank's business office. I have no idea where it was for sure but it seemed like it was near the Wilshire District in Los Angeles and quite an elevator ride up. We met Pauline Butcher, Frank's assistant, and saw a small picture of John and Yoko, nude, taped to a pillar in the main office. "He played with himself to make his cock bigger," Don said.

Herb Cohen was a guy we had heard stories about from Don. He was Frank's manager. We had heard stories that he had been a gun runner, a smuggler - and been involved in all kinds of nefarious activities. So, it was a little intimidating to meet the "legend."

After a short wait, we were invited into in his office. After a brief talk, he started writing down what we needed. The list was long and I was last. I was unprepared, and started rattling off a long list of stuff, rather than having the presence of mind to have had it all written down. Herbie looked at me disgusted, and said "write it down and send me the list."

Later, to simplify things, an allotment of money was given to Don to buy equipment. The guys all bought new guitars. Don wound up buying me a used Gretsch drumkit at Woodlowe's Music in Woodland Hills. I think he paid $150 for it. It was missing some vinyl and the bottom heads were gone. I knew that a sizeable allotment of money had exchanged hands to purchase equipment and I was sure that he probably saved himself a lot of money by buying these old beat-up things.

I was pissed, as I had sold my new Ludwig drumkit to buy Jeff a guitar the year before. The drums I was playing were falling apart, and Don had even asked me to give my old drums to Bobby - Frank's brother, to help him, as he was having a rough time. These new drums were the low-end Gretsch kit partially covered with sea-foam green satin vinyl. They were used, and the heads were worn. They sat in the house for a week. Don finally decided to have a "talk" to discuss my lack of appreciation for these old beat-up drums.

Mother's Business Meeting

I could tell just by talking to Frank, who was quite accessible, that he was much more logical and down-to-earth than Don, especially concerning finances. One could "reason" with Frank and he would consider the logic and respect the opinion. Another quality I noted on a different visit to the Zappa residence is that Frank would have business meetings with the Mothers in which they were freely allowed to express their honest opinions. I sat in a room adjoining and could easily hear every word spoken. Frank, unlike Don, was a patient listener and if he won a point, it wasn't through intimidation, but common sense. I almost laughed out loud as I listened to the complaints of the band. They had it so much better than us. The things they were complaining about seemed so minor in my perspective.

Don And Frank Comparisons

"The high point of our relationship (according to Rolling Stone - and aren't they some kind of authority on these matters?) was making the Trout Mask Replica album together in 1969. Don is not technically oriented, so, first I had to help him figure out what he wanted to do, and then, from a practical standpoint, how to execute his demands." - Frank Zappa."

One thing I really came to respect about Frank was his anti-drug policy. He was strictly against the use of illegal drugs in the band - at least during shows or rehearsals - and anybody caught   partaking was in serious consideration of being ejected from the band. From rumor and hearsay, I was led to believe that Frank never took drugs, or possibly tried marijuana once and didn't like it. I felt that this was certainly one very positive influence he had on the hippy generation. They saw this guy on stage who coined the term Freak Out, and was a "Freak" himself, and yet he didn't use drugs to "get there."

Don, on the other hand, was as conflicted about drugs as he was about anything else. For a time, he would be absolutely anti-drugs, and then he would go buy some hashish and coerce everyone to join him in partaking. After the age of twenty, I decided I didn't like drugs, although I would occasionally ingest a little hashish, which suited my physiology better. It would basically just relax me a little. When I smoked it, I developed a severe cough and became extremely paranoid, and this was not an ideal state of mind in which to be when living in a house that was already overflowing with paranoia.

I recall one time Don sent Jeff and I to Zappa's house to buy some hashish from the film editor (with advance money Frank had given us for the album). I think they were working on *200 Motels* at the time, and Frank had the editing room right in his house. He would have been appalled and probably fired the editor had he known. We walked in, bought the hash then walked into Frank's work area, I suppose in order to make this seem a "social call."

I recall this particular night, he seemed upset and I asked him what the matter was. He said something to the effect of not being able to get the musicians to do anything. I said, "I understand what you mean." This meant nothing to me, except that I was trying to show Frank some empathy in his situation.

However, it seemed Jeff perceived this as me identifying with Frank *because I couldn't get the Magic Band members to do anything*. Of course, this could not have been further from the truth. I have never seen anyone work harder than the Magic Band members, and to this day, I have never seen anyone work that hard or be that dedicated to anything. We were almost obsessed with this album - probably due to the cult-like trance in which we found ourselves. Unfortunately, because of this statement, Jeff repeated my words to Don is such a way that I became the target of yet another talk.

" The Real Frank Zappa Book, Frank Zappa, Simon and Schuster, 1989 pp 51

Transcriptions Redone

The days and weeks ran together. After visiting Frank's house and seeing his musical notations, I was inspired and also I saw something that needed to be done to organize my scrawlings of Don's riffs. I talked Don into buying some decent manuscript paper and a good ink pen so that I could copy all the *Trout Mask* parts for future reference. Don was suspicious of this at first, but I explained it in the context of this being an "important work that deserved better than rushed and disorganized pencil scrawls in a high school music theory booklet." I am sure I didn't use those words, but I did talk him into the supplies and some little notebooks too. One for each song, the kind you would use for a term paper or something.

Victor actually drove me to a stationary store. Now, stationary departments happened to have been my favorite places in a store. I found out later on that Bill was really attracted to stationary stores also. There's something about all those little papers and inks that is so fascinating. The really good stores were kind of … mysterious.

I took the transcribing of these parts quite seriously. I used one page for each guitar and one for bass. A lot of the songs did not have drum parts yet, so they were never written out, save the ones I had already transcribed when I had previously "quit" the band. I didn't write the drum parts, mainly because I figured Don would pull out the transcripts later and say "See, I DID write all the drum parts" which is not true.

To Become A Composer

During this period of time, while I was busy writing out these transcriptions, Don's paranoia found a new niche into which I seemingly fitted. It seems that, unbeknownst to anyone, even myself, I had formed a clandestine plan to become a "composer" and proof was that I was devoting all my time to music writing. I can't say that the idea of writing music didn't appeal to me. I loved going to Zappa's and seeing the little table where he sat and wrote his music. He had really good copy, and it was yet another facet of his work that I admired. I even enjoyed the smell of the ink and paper. There was something magical about it all.

However, my deadly secret only existed in Don's mind. I was really just trying to get everything organized for future band members. I knew that with the turmoil in this situation, there would most likely be changes in personnel. As it turned out, the charts were used for years by several incarnations of the band to faithfully reproduce the recordings live on stage. In spite of all the nearly unbearable paranoia and suspicions, Don was doing something different and I felt it was valid and was going to change the way people thought about music, sound and art.

I think part of the problem was that Don's mother, Sue, had bought a new TV, so she gave Don her old console color television. Van Vliet would have us all come in his room (where the TV was now located) lie on the floor, and watch TV together, laughingly saying "this is more important than music, John."

Another Visit To FZ's

The basement at Frank's new house became the meeting place for the band on a few occasions. One of the first ones was just to discuss the album, recording, progress and etc. We were all sitting in the little area to the far right where Frank had the dumb waiter and had his music board set up with transcriptions. On this occasion, Frank and Don, who Frank called "Donny," got into a serious discussion about music and musicians. Frank finally ended the conversation with a phrase which, as I recall, was "Donny, you've got such a selfish view of the universe."

John French to Don Aldridge: That's what Frank used to call him. Donny. I thought it was, for a short time, it was a put-down.

DA: It was an affection thing.
JF: A term of endearment.

I also noticed the name "Donny" being used by Sherwood in his interview. In the same way, some of my relatives still call me "Johnny" as that's what I was called when I was a kid growing up, by my parents. Since Frank and Motorhead both knew the young Van Vliet, this is probably where that term came from.

I think I had been so programmed by all the negative things I had heard about Frank to be on the defensive that I just naturally assumed this was a sarcastic put-down - a way of being condescending - and a way of belittling Don. However, Van Vliet never seemed to mind when FZ addressed him in the manner.

Don Aldridge: Well, he was intimidated by him. Zappa was a genius. I know that right now it's very "in vogue" to say that Don was the real thing, but Frank Zappa was a genius, and Frank Zappa wasn't only a musical genius, he was a marketing genius. He knew how to promote himself: Frank Zappa! You name anyone else during that period of time who could have done the kind of stuff he was doing and actually got accepted in the "mainstream." We were listening to Lumpy Gravy *in 1968. And that was the time when they were doing,* Yummy Yummy Yummy I've got Love in my Tummy. *Zappa was doing stuff like* Bow Tie Daddy *and* Hi Boys And Girls, I'm Jimmy Carl Black and I'm the Indian of the group. *That kind of stuff was happening and yet over here you had all this bubble gum music and everything yet Frank was penetrating the mainstream. To me, that took genius.*
John French: Well, he coined the term, "Freak Out" and that became a buzzword.
DA: Yeah, and laughing at us all the time he was doing it - and laughing at himself.
JF: Having a great time and still putting out these rather intelligent statements.

I noticed that when I was at Frank's he always had a huge amount of activity going on directly and indirectly. There was artwork hanging on a board for him to OK, he was editing a recording, he was writing orchestral scores, practicing guitar, or having a meeting. The man was constantly busy in direct correlation to Don, who was sleeping half the hours of the day, watching television for several, and occasionally taking a day to describe the nuance of one part of a song to one or more of the members. The two were total opposites.

Insanely Jealous?

Don Aldridge: And Don, in my opinion, and this is really coming from almost an outsider's observation - was almost - ..."insanely" jealous of Frank. I think "insanely" might be the most appropriate term I could use because I personally believe that Don became insane. I believe that he "lost his balance." Now, that's from a guy who did not live with him as you later did and you maybe know more about it. What they're calling "genius" now was BS in 1965. When I was there, he was just BS. I knew most of it as BS. I didn't believe him.

It was hard for me to penetrate the defense mechanisms enough to really discern anything like this at twenty years old. I was wrapped up in music and almost obsessive about getting it right. I had internalized a lot of things, put up a wall a mile thick to defend myself, and was wary of everything going on, thinking any moment I would get "nailed."

My impression, however, as I observed the two of them, was that Frank was relaxed and open, very approachable. Don seemed tense, on best behavior, sort of synthetic, and subdued. I think this was due to the fact that it was obvious, not only to him, but to us, that Frank was a much more successful recording artist and yet didn't seem to have any of the airs associated with a rock star. Yet, there was something also about Don that Frank didn't seem to have in that Don seemed more... soulful. Frank was business-like where Don was charming. Frank's music seemed a little stiff and conventional, Don's was bluesy and had grit.

John French to Don Aldridge: A lot of people, what they saw in Don's music and what I saw in Don that I didn't see in Frank as much, is that Don could write something like Dachau Blues (or) Steal Softly Thru Snow ... things that have incredible lyrics that were heartfelt and went right to the core of a situation and said something about it.
DA: What I have said in the past and what I will say is that he was extremely clever, there was a part of him that touched deeply. Anybody who was anti-Semitic - and this was very odd to me, because he seemed to be - by his very use of his language - seemed to pull a hard line on the black/white issue...
JF: That partly comes from his southern roots.
DA: But yet, when it got over into the area of the Jew - he could be touched with some things. He had this odd little compassion for certain issues.
JF: He used to say that his best fans were hung-up Jewish people.
DA: Is that right? Well, there's no doubt that I felt that Dachau Blues was a heck of a statement. I felt like it was really a powerful statement. He claimed later on that a good deal of his anger towards Zappa was due to the Jewish American Princess thing that Zappa did.

This song, of course, is referring to a much later time. I did even at this time detect a certain social awareness that seemed more - well perhaps I should say less sordid than Frank's work. There was more of a classic poetic ring to some of his work that I didn't sense much in Zappa's. Of course, I haven't heard the full Zappa repertoire, but I've heard enough to understand that it could have tacky lyrics - things that Don just wouldn't write.

John French: This something that I admired in Don, that he did have. He did try. It seemed like he was interested in the influence he had on the public. Whereas, on the other hand - the very people around him, the people who loved him, who were doing everything they could to help him get his music out - he didn't care about for the most part. It seemed like the more negative influence, and the more everybody was screwed-up around him, the more he was at peace, or the more he liked it.
Don Aldridge: You know, I probably took (Frank's music) a little more tongue-in-cheek than anybody as far as Frank goes and all that. I think that Frank just took a shot at everybody. I don't think that he was singling out a particular group and saying, "They're somehow less than us," or to be disdained. I think he just took a shot at everybody.

Aldridge makes a good point here. I do recall Frank saying somewhere that he was an "equal-opportunity offender." He also didn't seem to be attacking people so much as satirizing them and saying "learn to laugh at yourselves." I also felt sometimes that Don's criticisms of Frank were based partially on his jealousy.

John French: If you're close to somebody, you can say something about their particular quirk or background, like "whoa isn't that just like a Jewish person" - and its not taken by your Jewish person friend the same way as it's taken in a public arena. You would be called anti-Semitic, especially with the stupid media now.

Don Aldridge: Right, yeah, we're living in this "politically-correct" society where it's impossible to really say what you think, and what that does is limit discourse. When you do that, you have a "mind police" type situation going on. I think Frank resented that and I think he saw that in the fifties and sixties growing up around here and he said, "Hey, look at it! It's not that serious. Laugh at it a little bit. Look at yourself, you're an ass." He was trying to tell Ernie Tosi that at Antelope Valley High School. Everywhere he turned - now, there was bitterness and there was anger and resentment there, but the way it manifested in his music was very laughable to me - although I didn't say that to diminish Don's lyrical ability. Don was a lyricist, there wasn't any doubt. He was a "prankster with words" as John Peel said. He had "a genius" I don't necessarily think he is a genius. But he had an innate ability to put words together that often might never mean anything in and of themselves, but just came together and really made a statement. Now, I can't say he didn't do any of that.
JF: And he definitely triggered a lot of images.

Influence

Don Aldridge: Yes. If we can sing any praise to the avant-garde movement in music today, you have to consider Don Vliet. Groups like the B-52's, Talking Heads... I could just go on and on with some of these more modern, more contemporary people today are really looking at Don Van Vliet and he has inspired a lot of people. A lot of the stuff you guys put together
John French: A lot of people say he dropped the ball after that. A lot of the stuff that he did after that was actually taken from that era or shortly after that.

Sex, Drugs And The Environment

The contemporary alternatives to what Don was doing were things like Led Zeppelin, whose whole "sex, drugs, rock and roll" approach often mixed with a little Satanism and Occultism turned me off entirely, although I liked a lot of their music. Although this environment was terrible, and Don was a very unkind taskmaster, his art did have more redeeming value, at least in my mind. Whatever his personal demons were, his music and lyrics (some, at least) had a clarity that spoke volumes about the one-on-one guy that I personally knew, but who never showed up at rehearsals. In a sense, I felt that Don's music was more "pure" than Frank's music. It said things about the fragility of our environment and the state of the world. *Trout Mask Replica* was bigger than Don. I think part of the reason it's lyrics are so astounding is that Don would often write in front of a captive audience (us), so he would get instant feedback from our reactions to each line. *Dachau Blues* one of my favorites, was written in this manner. It was also written on an occasion when there was no turmoil in the room, and so I have happy memories of it as I do, *Well* and *Orange Claw Hammer*. I also like the things those compositions are saying, as well as others, but more on that later in the track notes.

Song Arrangements

I managed to eventually persuade Don that I wasn't planning to become an evil manic composer and undermine the band. During this time I experimented with a couple of different arrangement ideas. Most of the songs I arranged so that the whole band would start each section together and end together. The lyrics and imagery were so different and colorful to *Neon Meate Dream Of A Octafish* that I explained to Don that I was going to take a different approach to this piece. I decided it would be interesting to deviate. I figured out who would play what, and from the beginning to the end of the song, there were no "touch points" where sections end or begin together. It was just a free for all from beginning to end with only pulse holding us together, so there was a set tempo. Don was very concerned that it wasn't going to work, but then when the guys played it for him, he seemed really pleased. That was a very tricky one to do because everyone became completely responsible for where they were at each moment.

I remember the guys standing at the foot of the stairs in the downstairs bedroom rehearsing acoustically. The guitarist could hear a faint resonance of their notes, but Mark could not hear the bass tones as they are much lower, so he would push the neck of the bass up against the wall, and the wall would reverberate and help him hear the notes. I envied them because I didn't have the opportunity to practice with them very often. My instrument wasn't nearly so quiet nor so portable. They all worked so hard on this album to make it great. It was a shame that Don could not appreciate this effort. I have never seen musicians so dedicated to a single work.

Frownland was one of the last songs written on the piano and also has a different approach in arrangement. I decided to just give everyone their parts and not suggest to them at all how to put it together. The first section was obviously supposed to go together a certain way, but after that, they were on their own. The end project was a polyrhythmic association of melodies that groped and fought for your attention from beginning to end. It never sounded quite the same anytime we played it. The completely free drums in various parts made it stand out more in the wildness category and it became the opening song of the album.

I remember the guys would practice individually. Sometimes standing facing different corners of the same room in the wintertime when it was cold. I was so nuts I could hear all of them at once, and pick out mistakes and wrong notes.

I used to laugh when I would hear a Rolling Stones song. One riff - usually played by everyone, a chord change, some snappy lyrics, and they were done. Here we sat with 12 riffs each a song, memorizing until we were half-mad with repetition, and dealing with this time-wasting cult stuff to boot.

Van Vliet was probably capable of playing the same thing twice, but just like all of us, he would have had to practice to perfect his playing. He chose not to do this but rather to play "free" always. His theory was that there was no such thing as a wrong note. With three guys playing in three different keys and time signatures, who was to know whether his notes were wrong or not?

After a period of transcribing Don's parts, I became good enough that I could usually watch him play it once and write it down. I recall Bill once saying, "Hey, you're getting pretty good at writing that shit down." He was the only one who ever noticed this stuff. With Don, there were certain patterns that he used with his hands time and time again. Once I saw his position on the keys, I could usually play it after a couple of attempts. Please make note of the fact that in spite of all the hostility and conflict, I still considered it a privilege to be this integral a part of the project. Although I didn't feel it was ever going to make me wealthy, I did feel that we were doing something that would be conceived as artistically and historically important.

It was during this period that I overcame much of my fear of Don. I took my drums out to the little shed and began working on drum parts for the songs. I would bring in the drums in the evening and we would play down the songs for which I had drum parts. The parts usually worked the first time. I knew this stuff pretty well. I remember Bill positively commenting on the parts to *Hair Pie* and *Sweet Sweet Bulbs*.

Don started writing drum parts at this point, and most of the stuff was just playing time over the music. They were simple shuffles and patterns that he could play himself. He would sit at the kit and play something, then he would get up and I would just play what he played. Most of the stuff was really remedial, although some of the shapes and ideas were definitely innovative. Especially interesting to me was the P-K-Ro-P beat on *Ant-Man-Bee* (is this a pun on the name of Andy Griffith's aunt?) and the parts on *Neon Meate Dream Of A Octafish*.

There was a little peace in the house for a while. I was practicing drums every day, something I had never had time to do because of teaching all the other parts and being trapped at the piano all day. They came together really quickly and it was really a nice release to play. Of course, there was a somewhat neurotic woman down the street who constantly complained of the drum volume. She can be heard talking to Don on the home *Trout Mask* recordings heard on the *Grow Fins* set.

Jeff Bruschele

We started having a lot of visits from Jeff Bruschele. (The spelling has been done so many ways I have no idea which is correct.) Jeff would come over and listen to me playing the drums. At first, I really enjoyed his company, but after a short while I caught wind of what seemed to be an underlying theme. Jeff would compliment me on my playing and say, "Gee, I wish I could play drums like that," to which Don would reply, "I bet you could." This wasn't the first time I had seen this "romancing" as Jerry Handley referred to it. I became sure that Don was thinking of replacing me with Jeff. When the thought first occurred to me, I thought, "ridiculous, he doesn't even play!" Then I realized that Victor (who was integrated into the band as The Mascara Snake) wasn't exactly Eric Dolphy on the bass clarinet either and put two and two together.

Actually, I relaxed at that point. I had overcome my fear of Don for the most part and now that I wasn't a cowering, subservient minion, I no longer qualified as Magic Band personnel. I would like to qualify that statement with regards for my fellow band mates. We all were deceived and manipulated by this man. I had been in the band longer than the other three, so I feel I just saw through the façade after three years and became a little wiser. However, I was sure that I would be out of the band soon. So, since I no longer posed a "threat" to Don's control (since I would soon be gone) all I had to do was play out my hand and finish the album. That was my desire and my thoughts at the time.

China Pig

Doug Moon would occasionally come up to the house during this period. He found out where we were living. He told us he was living in Granada Hills and doing some kind of electronics work. During this period, Dick Kunc had been over to the house and had given - or loaned - Don a new piece of technology called a cassette tape recorder. I laugh as I write this now. However, it was quite an improvement in amateur recording, as one didn't have to fiddle with reels and tapes. The tape was contained within a little cartridge that was easy to load and remove, thus giving even Don no excuse for not being responsible for his own recordings.

The interesting thing is that this was just a much smaller version of something that was developed a few years earlier that my father had owned. They began making cassettes that contained $1/4$ inch tape. The whole concept is, the bigger the tape and the faster it ran, the better the sound fidelity. However, bigger meant more cumbersome, and the original cassettes I saw were four times the size of the standardized cassette used in this particular device, and for many years forward.

On one of Doug's visits, he brought his guitar and sat in the living room playing some folk music or something with finger-picking. Don came in with the cassette player and some lyrics he'd written and said "play one of those 'pa-chunk, pa-chunk' things…" and that was how the recording of *China Pig* came about.

Doug Moon: He made such a big "to-do" about giving me credit for it and making sure that my name was on the album and all that, because of how badly I was ripped off on the Safe As Milk *thing. My name was taken off all the credits for the musical songwriting.*

Safe As Milk had been more of a collaboration from what I gathered. Herb Bermann's interview give the idea that Don taught every piece note-for-note, and to an untrained musician that may have seemed like a thorough songwriting session, but the band was usually, at least when I was there, taking a singular impression of Don's or a couple of vague hummed riff ideas and developing that into a song. *Safe As Milk* was a collaboration, Don's ideas strongly influenced the music and some of the lyrics, but much credit needed to be given to the band and specifically to Ry, who finished off many of the compositions, even creating some parts himself.

CHAPTER TWENTY FIVE:
ANTI-LOGICAL FIELD RECORDING

...in 1968 contemplating the universe across the street
...the Trout House. Photo courtesy of John French.

Drumming To The Blimp

Finally, having the time to focus on drums, I was sweating away in the laundry shed, working on the parts to *Hair Pie*. In order to get away from it for a moment, I decided to try to play the drum part to *The Blimp* which was Jeff's recitation accompanied by Zappa's music. I stopped suddenly, because I realized that this was not a "Captain Beefheart Song" and therefore, if anyone heard me playing it, I may have to withstand yet another ridiculous interrogation. Sure enough, within a few minutes, Mark came out and in a somber tone stated "Don wants to talk to you."

I walked into the house. "There was a raven on top of the shed. Do you know what that means?" Don asked.

"No." I replied (However, I probably should have said "nevermore.")

"The thing is (a very overused Van Vliet phrase), it means you're not 'into it' man." ("into it" was a colloquial phrase used to denote that a player was not playing from his heart and soul as in "Wow man! Did you hear Hendrix at Monterey? He was really 'into it' dude!")

I couldn't believe my ears. A "sign from heaven (or perhaps more appropriately, that other place)," in the form of a stupid black bird with an IQ of three and a half had informed Don that I wasn't "into it." I think it had something to do with Don's twisted logic. A raven was like a sign of death, there was no "life" in my playing, therefore he came by to quote "Nevermore." Come to think about it, I was sweating like a pig and probably smelled like something dead. This is probably what attracted the little black guy. He probably thought he had stumbled upon a *feast*.

I have no idea how Don could get off making fun of my Christianity and then saying something completely ridiculous and superstitious like this. He used to ridicule me for being a Christian (which I never talked about), but it was perfectly sane for him to say "a raven on the roof means you're not 'into it'?"

"And what the fuck are you doing playing Zappa's music?" He asked. "Why were you so "into" that thing he did the other night?" I thought back to the night in question. We had all been invited to a jam in Zappa's basement. He used to have jam sessions at his house where he would just plug a couple of mikes straight into the machine and turn it on. I can't remember who all was there. I was playing an old set that I had given his brother. It was the Slingerland set originally bought for me by Buddah Records.

Frank had a little line that he taught everyone there. It was in three-four time and stayed in the same meter throughout the entire piece. It was simple and I played my brains out on it in a similar style to *Mirror Man* and *Strictly Personal* because I didn't have to think about odd time signatures or anything complicated. It was just a simple rolling melody designed for a jam session. Frank knew how to write a simple framework over which musicians could improvise. Don didn't seem to have a clue how important that was to a player and never allowed anyone a space to improvise or express himself musically in his music.

I came upon what I considered the perfect answer. "Frank's piece was so remedial that *anyone* could get "into it." It's so simple I didn't have to think. "Your music is much more complex." I added, " I thought maybe we might perform *The Blimp* someday on stage and I wanted to make sure I could play the drum part." He bought it. I really wasn't lying. Don's music was much more complex than that piece we had played at Frank's. I didn't mention that the main reason it was could be because when someone doesn't know a thing about music or playing an instrument, they often come up with things that are nearly impossible to play, not necessarily because of their musical genius, but because of their musical *ignorance*. However, I left that part out.

For instance, if I put a chimpanzee on a Synclavier (a fancy synthesiser/computer which I think is obsolete now) for an hour and then printed out the music the chimpanzee played, it would probably be extremely difficult to play. Also, if I put a couple of children at the Synclavier, their results would also be difficult to play. If I spoke for twenty minutes in total gibberish (breaking

448

all the rules of language) onto a tape for an hour, and asked you to duplicate my speech, could you? It would be difficult wouldn't it? Why? Because *you have no basis on which to build your performance*. What I mean here is that there is no common language to group the syllables into and no "familiar" groundwork (words, sentence structure.

Whataboutifijustbreakonesimpleruleanddon'tputspacesinbetweenmywords? Isitmoredifficulttoreadthis,orsimpler?

I am making absurd examples (except for the last one) in order to make a point: Music that is difficult to play is not in itself validation that the composer is a genius. Don's famous saying, "You train yourself, you strain yourself" may make for good copy in some journalist's article, but in the real world, that journalist couldn't even *write* the story had he not trained himself to develop his writing skills. The Magic Band could not have played Don's music had they not "trained" themselves and disciplined themselves. So this whole concept to me is an absurd hypocritical contradiction of what was actually going on within the Magic Band.

I was trained just enough in musical notation to transcribe *Trout Mask Replica* from Don's amateurish pounding at the piano. So, that training directly *aided* Don in his creation of *TMR*. I speculate "what if" Don would have been able to write music and understand at least basic music theory? (It wouldn't have taken him long to learn how - he was brilliant - right?). Well, Don would have wound up having to spend hours and hours of time at the piano transcribing parts - just like Frank Zappa did. What would this have accomplished? A better album, that's what! Why do I think this? Several reasons; I would have been able to practice drums everyday - *instead of sharing the composer's responsibilities* - for one thing. Another thing is that Don, rather than sleeping and watching TV half the day, and conducting forty-eight hour interrogations would have had something to keep him busy. Another is that Van Vliet would have realized the technical challenges his compositions created.

A large majority of Don's time during the *Trout* rehearsals was spent dictating skeins of poetry and prose which have to this day never been published, and according to Don's own words, never will be. This was mostly hand-written by Jeff Cotton, whose schedule was already filled with learning his guitar parts. This caused Jeff to be under a considerable amount of stress, sometimes losing a whole night's sleep and then staying up the next day to remain "in sync" with the band's progress - while Don slept the entire day away and woke up in the evening - all ready to go after everyone was completely exhausted from practicing since 9 or 10 in the morning. Bill and Mark didn't have this problem and so were under less stress. I felt it necessary to get 7-8 hours sleep a night to maintain my health in spite of any scheduling demands. My philosophy has always been to prioritize taking care of my body's needs and that is probably the most important key to any consistency I displayed during this period.

Don would give confusing instructions when writing a song. While Van Vliet was creating a new piece, everyone better pay close attention and get it the first time. It came like the birthing of a premature baby, causing stress and concern and when it was over, it was over. If the baby died, it was always someone's fault. Usually it was always Don's fault, for he lacked the communication skills to get his ideas across and never had an outline of what he was doing.

In his ignorance Don always thought that someone who couldn't immediately play what he asked was actually playing some kind of power game. Although we all attempted explanations, he never understood that it was his lack of skill as a communicator often causing the problem, coupled with the limits in the musician's ability to be able to instantly play "everything" Don conceived. Bill actually did some terrific things "on the fly" that I could never have done. He would figure out things in his head and be standing there for thirty seconds or so and Don would be all over him. "Just fucking PLAY IT, man!" he would say, or something similar. Bill would wave his hand in a way to say "I'm thinking about it, just a second!" Then, he would play it or come close to what Don wanted. I'm sure this procedure took its toll on Bill, but he actually could do it as often as not.

I wasn't so lucky at following these verbal commands at first. I needed to have a picture or reference of some kind and I found Don's instructions extremely confusing and also bothersome, because I'm not a verbal person and also because it could all have been avoided had he bothered to take the time to learn to *communicate* in musical terms.

This lack of musicianship also made it extremely difficult for him to put his lyrics to music especially on the farther-out *Trout Mask* and *Decals* sessions, because he didn't understand counting measures and so although his intuition was great, he was often lost. The reason I know this is because he would write sections of music, and sometimes sing to it once or twice. Yet, when it was time to record vocal tracks, he would sing the same words *in an entirely different section*. Almost everything recorded by him was intuitively performed, whereas we could seldom do anything intuitively, because it took a constant intellectual process just to keep from getting *lost in the complexity*, much less being able to play anything with spontaneity.

You never heard Don play a composed part on the saxophone. He is always soloing in a free improvisational style. In my opinion most of his saxophone soloing with the band was loud and musically meaningless, especially in live situations. It had a lot of energy and conviction, but often went nowhere and seldom had any relationship at all to the accompanying music, often causing the majority of the uninitiated to leave in droves. However, there are a few recorded exceptions that are wonderful snippets of his potential. *Dachau Blues* (here we go again) great bass clarinet parts and *Wild Life*, which has a brilliant saxophone solo. He could only play them once. He could not re-create what he had done, or even play in a similar nuance. His saying "scales are for *fishes*" may have sounded really clever to journalists. Unfortunately, it was a cover-up for what would become his biggest downfall, the ability to "re-create" his best moments from the studio on stage, regardless of his mood, state of mind, or initial audience reaction. He lost many in his audiences who may have stayed and become avid supporters had he been able or willing to reach out a bit more in his performances, rather than arrogantly demand that they surrender and completely enter his domain, which could change radically with each passing show.

Because I wasn't good at following Don's verbal abstract instructions, but could follow Zappa's simple *musical* instructions, Don felt that I was playing games with him. I could understand from his perspective how he could think this. It must have looked like that to him. However, I was quickly tiring of trying to live in a musical world that was totally controlled by someone whose perspective was devoid of the knowledge of important details like counting measures and establishing key signatures and modes.

How My Next Evil Plot Failed

In the following, I am going to try to describe in detail one particular "talk" in which I was the target. It's always easier to remember bad things that happen to one's self and the firsthand experience is still quite clear in my mind. I don't remember anyone else going through an experience quite as bad as this one, but I could easily have forgotten, because it wasn't my head on the chopping block.

Don had not written many drum parts for anything. Seldom were drum parts the focus of his attention. I had written a lot of parts myself for earlier stuff, and now the time was drawing near when we would be recording. I mentioned being in the shed practicing and Mark calling me into the house. Obviously, my days had been taken up with transcribing, playing piano parts, listening to Don recite poetry to Jeff, listening to Jeff recite it again and again etc. - not to mention all the time wasted on "talks." There hadn't been enough time for me to devote to drum parts.

My defense for not having drum parts was simple, and I explained it logically. I explained it would be easy for me to learn drum parts, because I knew all the songs from memory. I actually could sing everybody's parts to every song I had transcribed from beginning to end. One can accomplish great things when one doesn't watch TV, make contact with the outside world, drive a car, have a girlfriend ... or a *life*. My whole *existence* for almost a solid year had been these songs. My thoughts were shouting, "HOW ON EARTH COULD ANYONE IN THEIR RIGHT MIND POSSIBLY CONCEIVE THAT I WAS TRYING TO SABOTAGE THE MUSIC? "

After several hours, there was a lull in the talk, I could feel myself tense up and nothing had been really resolved. Everyone was angry with me and Don was storming about saying, "How in the fuck could he *do* this to me?" Feeling uncomfortable, I walked outside to have a smoke and think. It was about one in the morning. I was looking at the moon, a beautiful full moon, and I had some kind of revelation about how this project would get done and how things have seasons and everything was going to be fine.

How Bout A Nice Hawaiian Group Punchout?

I walked in with a really positive attitude, and facing the hostile looks, I stated my revelation, trying to assure everyone that the drum parts would be OK. Unaccustomed as I was to public speaking, I probably stammered a bit. For some reason, Don's face expressed not anger but rage. Suddenly, as we were standing there in the kitchen, Don shouted "Get him!" On that verbal cue, all four of them started hitting me at once, mostly in the face. I can only recall this kind of physical group attack happening to me and only this once, but it was absolutely terrifying. It seemed like a planned thing that Don had worked out with the guys while I was outside.

I had been scared, but this time I actually thought I was going to die and it was more real than anything before. I remember being cornered in the kitchen and hand after hand hitting and slapping me on the face and upper body and also being kicked (Mark was more of a kicker so that was probably him) and pushed into the stove and cabinets. This was the most frightened I had ever been and I shouted "stop" several times.

Beefheart And Broomsticks

After this was done, I was led/pushed out onto the patio by the laundry shed. I was pretty dazed and obviously scared out of my wits.

John French to Bill Harkleroad: I want to see if you remember (this). There was one time when I was the target of a talk. Don got a broken broomstick and had me up against the outside wall of the laundry room at the Trout house, and he was jabbing at my stomach while you guys were standing behind him. Sort of standing in a semi-circle. Do you remember that? BH: Wow! I see it very faintly, but as you say that, yes I do!

This went on for a while with Don shouting at me and stabbing at my stomach with the broomstick. The point of the stick went into the wall several times and I could see huge splinters sticking out of the wall. I seemed very confused and disoriented during many of these fights, almost as if I were on drugs. Again, I seemed incapable of defending myself, as though I wasn't really there, or in charge of my own body. Like I was viewing the situation through my eyes, but I wasn't really there completely. It was as though I was watching television. Don's shouting continued for 30 minutes or more as the broomstick end jabbed at me innumerable times before there was finally an end to this.

For a long time, I stood there with my back to the laundry shed wall being grilled about my alleged lack of responsibility regarding the drum parts. It was late and I was tired, but this went on for hours. Nothing that I said made any difference. The actual purpose of this was just to break me down, and I was pretty well broken down by this point. I felt like a marathon runner on their last mile, barely able to put one foot in front of the other.

I finally asked to please go to the bathroom and was allowed off the patio. I went into the downstairs bathroom and looked in the mirror. My face was swollen and bruised. I stared at this swollen mass and found myself incredulous. "How can this be happening?" I asked myself. I walked out of the downstairs bathroom and sat on the end of my bed, completely exhausted, and fell into a deep sleep. It was such a deep sleep that time passed by completely without my knowledge.

In what seemed like only seconds later to me, I woke up from a dreamless sleep to early sunlight streaming in the windows and the nightmarish vision of the whole band encircling me shoulder to shoulder and staring in dissatisfaction. Don had the look of a parent who had caught their child with its hand in the cookie jar.

"Wake up Man!" he shouted. I learned to hate those words. I had heard them at every "talk" we had. Don always claimed that we were all "asleep" and that we'd better all "Wake up." I still get angry to this day when someone says "Wake up!" to me.

I stood up and Jeff began to hit me in the face again, stating again and again that he didn't want to do this but "had to." It was like the old "this is going to hurt me more than it does you, son" speech. If he didn't, Don might turn on him. I had been asleep long enough for the numbness to leave and now my face was extremely tender and each blow Jeff dealt stung bitterly. Tears streamed from my eyes to add to my embarrassment.

Somehow, I wound up back upstairs. For a while, I sat on the piano bench as Don kept asking the same tedious unanswerable questions on and on. It was fairly light now, late morning, and I asked for a cigarette. Don threw one at my feet as one would toss a piece of meat to a mongrel dog. I picked it up, lit it, and moved over to the fireplace. I was backed up against the outside wall of the living room, next to where I slept. There was no ashtray, so I sat on the floor and flicked the ashes from the cigarette into the fireplace.

The next thing I knew, I was waking up to a burning pain in my right hand. I had fallen asleep in a matter of seconds after sitting down and as everybody stood watching, the cigarette had burned up to my fingers and seared the skin. I threw the butt in the fireplace and stood up. "That'll teach you to fall asleep on me," Don snarled.

Punched On Chin

At this point, Don shouted "When are you gonna wake up, man?" He then walked up and punched me square in the chin, hard enough that my head hit the wall quite hard. I felt the skin on my chin split and blood oozed down my beard.

Everybody in these talks had to have an obligatory shot at the target and when it was Bill's turn, he walked up and said something which we later made jokes about. The expression on his face told me he had no idea what in the world I had done wrong but he had to come up with something. He said, among other things, *"I thought YOU had the guts!"* and shoved me into the wall a couple of times. What this meant, nobody will probably ever know, including Bill, but it was at least something we could laugh about later. Like - "Did you bring the guts?" "No, I thought you had the guts." Don had the little cassette player at this point that had been given to him by Dick Kunc, and turning it to "Record" began reciting on the tape in a mocking theatrical tone (similar to the very end of *Old Fart At Play* - i.e. 'his excited eyes…') "As the soapy wood xylophone plays it soapy wood melody," in a sing-songy mocking tone while Laurie, his girlfriend laughed and said, "Yes, John certainly is a soap opera isn't he?" I remember this clearly and recall that Laurie had later joined in on the talks - probably out of sheer boredom.

Don kept raking the microphone across the dark rosewood Venetian blinds that Frank Zappa had removed from his newly purchased home and given to us. We had put them up after painting the living room. I guess they were the "soapy wood xylophone."

At this point, I moved to the piano bench as Don continued to mock me. Finally, he had an inspiration to write lyrics. Although he had a tape recorder, to flaunt his unquestioning control, he demanded Jeff write the lyrics down. He dictated the lyrics to *My Human Gets Me Blues* - which was directed at me in a sense. He like to belittle us by calling us "closet queens" and the line "I knew you under your dress" was a mocking line aimed at me. "Just keep coming, Jesus, You're the best-dressed" he said staring at me, as Jeff wrote. "You look dandy in the sky but you don't scare me, 'cause I got you here in my eye."

I sat, exhausted and drained, and seething with anger. To increase my humiliation, Don played back the tape he had recorded of the event. Everyone laughed and joked about the situation. I found out years later that Frank Zappa had a recording of this. He thought it was some kind of theatrical thing. Once, in July, 2004, I was invited to the Zappa compound along with a roomful of people, one of which was Matt Groening. After watching a documentary on Zappa's life, a technician, Joe, played a copy of this tape. I recognized it - 36 years later - and told Matt, "In a minute, Don's going to say, *'and the soapy wood xylophone plays it soapy wood melody'.*" Sure enough, in just seconds, you could hear Don saying that and then slapping sounds of me getting struck in the face. Matt shouted, "turn that thing off, man. That sound is John getting hit."

Standing In Front Of Windows/Death Threats

Eventually, Don somehow maneuvered me over to the front of the living room. I remember standing with my back against the windows that faced the street. There was a balcony out side the windows with a rickety rail and then a long drop to stairs below. "I'm going to throw you through this window," Don informed me. He looked at the band members standing behind him. "He attacked me, right?" He asked. Everyone nodded to the affirmative "It was self-defense, right?" Everyone nodded in agreement again.

I was tired, exhausted, drained, pissed off and incredulous. "What in the world is any of this accomplishing?" This had happened too many times. My back was to the window, but I could imagine my body hurling over the broken railing, accompanied by shards of broken glass. I could see my body lying on the ground below, cut and broken... as my fear caused my imagination to run wild.

"Wait a minute," I thought, "He's bluffing." I looked him in the eye and for a moment I sensed that he knew that I was onto his game. Don was too smart to do something like that. The only way he was capable of that kind of act was if he became enraged and out of control. He was neither. This was a bluff.

I remember clearly the thought going through my mind: "I wish I had a way to capture this on film. If someone could only see this, if our neighbors the Catalanos, could see this, they would tell me that I'm the sane one here. Don is the sick person here, not me."

I truly believe that the only thing that saved me and kept me sane through this was the fact that I had faith in God and believed in Jesus. That's why Don had been making fun of Jesus in the song lyrics.

"I'm not going to die, and I have nothing to fear," I silently assured myself. I put my hands on Don's shoulders and shoved him back from me. At this point, Don punched me in the stomach a couple of times. I grimaced in anticipation, but he was "pulling his punches" it didn't hurt at all. This was a theatrical performance. It was a tough guy game Don was playing. I was beginning to understand the tactics. He could see the realization in my eyes. This was probably about noon on the day after the slap-fest.

"Watch him!" Don instructed the band members, like some hoodlum chief to his cronies, and left the room for a moment.

As soon as Don left the room, I said, "I'm going to the bathroom," and casually walked out of the room, through the band members, and no one attempted to stop me. I stayed downstairs for a time. It was probably one or two in the afternoon, so nearly twenty-four hours had elapsed since I'd been called in the house. We had all been awake all this time. My face looked less swollen (how quickly we heal at nineteen), and I washed the blood out of my beard and took a shower. Don disappeared for several hours and I think everyone took the opportunity to sleep while they had the chance.

Re-assembly occurred after dark. We all had tea and I sat in my usual spot, on the piano bench, which was again the hotspot. I had decided upon a plan and was more relaxed. I was really angry at Don for the ordeal he had put me through, sick of him to the point of no longer caring about him or his wretched project. He asked me, "So, what's your story, man?" For a while, he spoke about how much he'd tried to "help" me. He suspected I was catatonic, etc. Basically, it was a bunch of time-wasting psychological hogwash. I said, "You're right Don," and tendered my resignation.

Don was really taken aback and a look of panic came upon his face. "Ah ha!" I thought to myself, "This man needs me more than I need him." So, then I really played it up. I decided to use everything against him that he had said about me. "I really have been holding you guys back and I realize that now." I stated. "You guys would really be a lot better off if I was out of the picture because I'm so selfish and lazy, I can see that now. The music would be so much better if I hadn't sabotaged it. And I'm sure just about anyone would be better on the drums parts than me."

Don was standing behind everyone else at this point and only I could see his face, which I only glanced at and pretended not to notice, but he was almost white as a sheet. "I think it would be best for everyone here if I just left," I continued. I realized that my words were absolutely ridiculous contradictions to everything I had actually done for the past several months, and so did everyone else, though nobody could acknowledge that fact, because for the past day and a half, I had been accused of *"Magic Band Treason."*

There was a bit of silence. After all, what could you say to this? I was the problem, they had reminded me of that all night, and now that I realized that point, and had "seen the light," I realized that the best thing to do was "sacrifice my musical career for the greater good of the band."

The lyrics to *Electricity* kept going through my head:

> Go into bright, find the light and know,
> That friends don't mind just how you grow.

I had done the noble thing. I was chuckling as I thought what must be going through Don's mind. A few *Trout Mask* songs were transcribed and lay on the piano, untaught, and I was the only one Don thought could efficiently translate them to the band without bringing in an outsider. Note: Though Bill later would become "musical director," he used tapes and used a different process. Although Bill had some music theory, he was far enough removed from it at this time that it would have been a severe setback to not only replace a drummer, but "relearn" how to read transcribed music. This is why I write "I was the only one who could *efficiently* translate them." The band was in such a state by this point that any outsider would have immediately recognized the madness of this situation and ran out the door in terror. I was holding a winning hand and I knew it.

Don composed himself and gave this order: "You're not leaving here until you write down all those drum parts to the songs you know." So, I was now being held hostage until my ransom was paid in full. This is proof, to me, that Don did not have as much to do with the *Trout Mask* drum parts as he later claimed. Why on earth would he need me to write down drum parts that he "composed"? I found myself becoming a little more sane as I sat there, exhausted, face swollen and stinging. I knew I had done the right thing.

I actually had every intention of leaving. Who wouldn't want to get out of this hell-hole? I actually wound up so rejuvenated by the thought of freedom from this madness that I stayed up all night and most of the next day writing down my drum parts from memory to several of the early *Trout Mask* songs.

Don's "Sincere" Appeal

The following evening, I suddenly became Don's "special friend" again. He asked me to come outside with him and in the darkness by the south side of the house, illuminated only by light escaping from the windows. As we had a smoke, he gave a very convincing speech on why I should stay and actually said he "needed" me. This was a very emotional and heartfelt moment, and I almost never saw Don appear this sincere in my whole experience with him. It was a great and convincing act that moved me, but I already knew by this time that the closeness of Don's relationships to others was in direct relationship to what service they could provide for him.

I was frustrated inside. I wanted to leave, and now he was taking away my chance. I couldn't go if asked to stay without becoming the "subversive guy who ruined the album," in the same ridiculous manner Ry was blamed for "ruining the band's chance at the Monterey Pop." Within twelve hours I had evolved from the role of "evil saboteur" to the role of "band's last hope" (neither of which accurate depictions). It was a clever ploy, no witnesses ever saw Don regard me in this manner. His cover of omnipotent leader was not blown, and I was now caught back between the proverbial "rock and the hard spot."

I do not believe that the *Trout Mask* album would exist as it does today, or even close to what is today if I would have left the band at that time. The process we had developed over the last few months would have changed so drastically that the album would have been quite different. Before you get the idea that I am saying this because of overblown pride, I also think that it would not have been nearly the same had *any other* member of the group left during this period. *Lick My Decals* is a far superior album musically in many ways, and Bill Harkleroad is 90% responsible for that, so I am not trying to draw accolades for my "brilliant" work as arranger, director. I am just stating that there was a delicate co-dependency, a "band ecology" if you will, that would have been destroyed and altered, because each individual's personal input (contrary to popular belief and endless poorly-researched articles) is such a strong and important piece of the whole.

Jeff Tepper, in the Mojo article mentions that Don used to refer to us as "okies," which is sort of an earlier form of the word, "redneck." This generally refers to a person who exhibits low-class traits, doesn't have much ambition or education, and comes from a low class background. In this particular timeframe, (*Trout Mask* times) Don hadn't really received any major recognition. He hadn't really spent time with musicians or done much networking in order to meet new players. All the musicians he had worked with on a professional level up to this point had come from the Antelope Valley, which basically was almost an enclave unto itself.

None of us came from wealthy or even upper middle class families. We were basically from financially challenged households. We had all gone into the Magic Band almost straight out of high school. This may have given Van Vliet quite a feeling of superiority. Not only was he older, and street smart, had rubbed shoulders with a few celebrities, and was a fairly successful blues singer who had attracted attention on his first single. He had probably been exposed to the "finer things of life," including perhaps a guided tour into the sophisticated world of art, as a young boy. His mentor, Augustino, if the stories are valid, had probably given him access to books and literature that gave him an insight into the world of art. He had most likely received a fairly high-level perspective of the art world at a relatively young age.

Also, his only-child-as-king-and-center-of-universe environment may have caused him to view himself as a "superior being." He was, in my best observation, and also in his own words, a spoiled brat. His mother catered to his every whim and was still supporting him even well into his late twenties. That coupled with his extraordinary gifts in sculpture, lyric writing, not to mention his great voice and harmonica playing, had probably nurtured a feeling of superiority that he had grown as accustomed to as an old pair of shoes.

Perhaps it was this perspective that caused him to view the *Trout Mask* band as "okies." We were relatively ignorant of art, having had no training or exposure other than perhaps an art class or two in high school, in which the highest form of achievement seem to be football and the proof was the letter on your lettermen's jacket. Van Vliet obviously had contempt for his parents. It had showed up many times in conversations. Once, while sharing a childhood photo with us, which was a picture of him and his kneeling father, he contemptuously said something to the effect, "Imagine someone like me being under the care of someone like that." Speaking often in terms of disdain for his mother, he would often cast aspersions upon those of us who made any reference to loving our parents. He had often sarcastically chastised me for referring to my mother as "mom," and any mention of "loving" my parents brought immediate criticism.

Yet, many of the great artists of the world come from poor families and much worse backgrounds than we Trout band members. Many of the great blues artists had very poor families. Don's own philosophy was if you want to be a different fish, you have to get out of the school.

I now knew that the talks were absolutely ridiculous and a total waste of time, energy, and words. *Trout Mask* would have been done months earlier if Don would have merely shut his mouth and let us work. This was portrayed to the world as Don benevolently and patiently teaching a bunch of sub-humans his music - philanthropist that he was - as in the following quote from Rolling Stone Magazine:

"The trouble is that once the compositions are down it takes him a long time to teach them to his musicians. In this case it took almost a year of rehearsal."

My experience which I described above was just one of dozens of "talks" in which each band member was put through a grueling ordeals. We all walked out of this situation with a lot of scars and unanswered questions.

Anthropological Field Recordings

"I wanted to do the album as if it were an anthropological field recording - in his house. The whole band was living in a small house in the San Fernando valley (we could use the word cult in here.)" - Frank Zappa[45]

Don and Frank had decided to record the album at the house, which I thought was ridiculous, plus I wanted to get the hell out of that house for at least a few days. I didn't know at the time and didn't read until much later that this was because it was intended to be an "anthropological field recording." One night a huge truck drove up and in it were all the amps (we didn't have guitar amps, save an old Sears Silvertone), microphones, and various paraphernalia needed to do this "field recording." We practiced with the amps and set the living room up for recording. Dick Kunc came over a few days later, probably mid-morning, and set up microphones and the mixers. I remember two little Shure 8 channel mixers stacked on top of each other on a card table in Don's bedroom, though Frank states it was all built into a briefcase.

"I was working with Dick Kunc, the recording engineer on Uncle Meat and Cruising With Ruben & the Jets. To make remote recordings in those days, Dick had a Shure eight-channel mixer remounted in a briefcase. He could sit in a corner at a live gig with earphones on and adjust the levels, and have the outputs of the briefcase mixer feeding a Uher portable tape recorder." - Frank Zappa[46]

Frank brought some of the GTOs up to the house. I thought that was a big mistake. They were

[45] The Real Frank Zappa Book, Frank Zappa, Simon and Schuster, 1989 pp 51
[46] The Real Frank Zappa Book, Frank Zappa, Simon and Schuster, 1989 pp 51-52

just in the way for the most part. We didn't get much recording done the first day, only I think a couple of sound checks and the talking stuff that you hear, like *I Run On Laser Beans*. Even most of the talking sections (*Fast n' Bulbous*, etc) were done later in Whitney Studio where we wound up actually recording *Trout Mask Replica*.

"I had been using that technique with the M.O.I. for road tapes. I thought it would be great to go to Don's house with this portable rig and put the drums in the bedroom, the bass clarinet in the kitchen and the vocals in the bathroom: complete isolation, just like in a studio - except that the band members probably would feel more at home, since they were at home." - Frank Zappa[47]

Microphones were set up inside and out. It was a little strange living there under these conditions. We felt like we were being "studied and observed." In a sense, we were. The interesting thing is, by moving in all this recording equipment and bringing over the GTOs, it was a completely different atmosphere, which somewhat defeated the whole "anthropological field recording" concept. Also, because it was a very basic recording system, the idea of sound isolation really didn't work - because we had no headphones with which to hear one another. We could only hear what was audible - in the case of Don and Victor on the patio, it was leakage through the window.

Victor Hayden

A microphone was set up outside on the shaded patio next to the laundry shed. This was where Don and Victor stood when they played horns on *Hair Pie Bake I*.

John French: So, what was your impression of Victor Hayden playing on Trout Mask?
Bill Harkleroad: It really pissed me off. Vic was a talented painter. I think the things he had to put up (with) to be around Don, (caused him to) adopt the snottiest little fucking attitude I'd ever been around. He might be a wonderful person now, but then, he was a snotty little attitude junkie. ... He's breathing with a horn in his mouth, moving his fingers, and he's in the band? - after the effort we put in on those parts? I wanted to fucking kill him! I should have wanted to kill Don, but I was in denial of that.
JF: Anyway, in the context of that, what do you think of this particular quotation of Frank Zappa's? Where he said, "That's the best horn interplay I've ever heard!" referring to the beginning of Hair Pie Bake 1 *- the one that was done at the house - with Don and Victor?*
Note: This is not an exact quote but a paraphrase of something I heard Frank say when we heard the master of *Trout Mask Replica* for the first time.

Bill Harkleroad: ... Let me just separate - does it need to be relevant to Frank's remark? My commenting on Frank?
John French: Well, you don't have to comment on Frank, but just the ...opinion of an outsider who heard that.
BH: ... I don't know that I would agree with that statement, but I wouldn't say it's terrible. I think actually it is kind of cool. Musically, I liked what happened. But it's hard for me to separate things like that. I liked what happened, but again, it was just a frozen moment. When you just throw a bunch of rocks over a cliff and you take a photograph of it - that's what it felt like. I remember hearing Victor not being able to get enough air through there to make a noise, and then Don really over-blowing. At moments, Don would find something that sounded good on the horn and he'd stay with it, because he could push a lot of air through

[47] The Real Frank Zappa Book, Frank Zappa, Simon and Schuster, 1989 pp 52

it, and he would get cool tones. Victor on the other hand, he just couldn't even push enough air through there to get much out of it. So, no, it's not the coolest interplay, but musically, I thought it ...worked.

I'd like to mention that Victor never rehearsed with us, so the idea of "feeling right at home" was even further defeated by the fact that Don decided to just include Victor - who knew basically nothing about bass clarinet - in the recording session at the last minute.

Sax Playing

John French to Doug Moon: Yeah, I was thinking about that the other day, because there was one point in time in 1975, there was a club up here and I was playing drums for a band. It was a group called Supergroup. Mark Boston was playing bass. Don showed up at the club and pulled out his sax. Mark Stegman, a local guy, came up to me afterwards and said, "I didn't buy that psychedelic sax bullshit for one instant." (Doug bursts out in laughter) I had to kind of laugh, because, what you were saying is that the genius seemed to be more in the convincing the public that this was actually something valid.
DM: That's a real good way to put it.
JF: That's the laymen's term that works the best. I was thinking about John Coltrane. Here's John Coltrane, who came up through jazz, played with Miles Davis, played with all these great jazz players. Studied scales, studied all the scales that fit on the scales and all the modes and everything and found out how everything inter-related and he was playing "out", but he always knew "where he was."
DM: He knew every note - he was in control.
JF: Well, he was improvising, you know, he was always looking for something new.
DM: That's what jazz is.
JF: But he had this foundation. He had a foundation that he could draw on.
DM: If you're playing in a structured scale, as far out as it sounds, I mean, they're all notes that are connected musically
JF: But Don's idea was "the only scales I'm interested in are the ones on fish." ...It was always related back to nature because, the hippies were natural, "oh wow, yeah, I know what he's saying." There also seemed to be this influence of saying, "well, if I throw all the rules aside, rather than going through all those rules, then I'm already where all these other guys are striving to be. I'm totally free." So that was the philosophy that seemed to go behind it.

Recording At The House

Frank, it seemed to me, had an idea of how he wanted to present Captain Beefheart and it seemed out-of-sync in a sense. He was already introducing foreign influences (GTO's) into the environment, thereby not really attempting to capture what was actually going on, but attempting to capture his image of what he *thought* was going on. *The zany antics* theme was a little too prevalent. He also was making suggestions for us to do things that we'd never do. Like, for instance, during a poetry reading in the bathroom - probably between Don and Jeff or Victor - he came up to me and whispered in my ear "blast into the bathroom and shout "It's the blimp, it's the blimp." I told him this was not going to be well-received by Don, but he kept nudging me to do this. To appease Frank, I finally did, and the resultant displeasure immediately registered on Don's face.

What I'm trying to say is that the mere introduction of all this paraphernalia, the extra people at the house, and the "directorship" of Frank, there was little that resembled what actually occurred at the house. Don was completely different, on "good behavior" mode, and there was this sort of "faux-happiness" that was actually a little uncomfortable, being the "cardboard cutout" version of the band. I think Frank's intentions were good but his concept was inaccurate and may have been based on Don's distorted descriptions of the environment.

Frank was really trying to record us the way he worked with the Mothers, and we were a totally different medium. He was not that familiar with our daily routine, having only visited the house once and had not a clue what it was like to live there, because Don had hidden the truth about the cult-like situation.

It also seemed to me that the big emphasis that first day was on "hysterical hijinks" and "the wonderful world of Beefheart" than on the music that we as a band had worked so tremendously hard to perfect these last several months. It was all hype and superficial. I remember us all poised at our instruments for what seemed like hours waiting for the stupidity to end so that we could actually *play*.

Another completely alien factor were the Acoustic solid-state amps we were playing through and our setup in the room. The amps had a cold "brittle" quality and with no preamps or effects devices, the sound was very sterile. I usually was set up with my back to windows, almost central in the room with the amps behind me. Now, I was over by the room divider facing the fireplace. The guitarists were across the room, their amps facing me, and it was a completely different acoustic environment and actually hard to "feel" the group playing.

When it finally did become time to play, Don and Victor were outside on the patio, horns in hand, playing and encircling the mikes. Finally, someone gave us a cue, I shouted "AND" and we played *Hair Pie*. When I listened back to it later, I realized that Dick hadn't yet set our band levels in the living room. So, though the horn mic was cued up, all you hear in the beginning is ambient leakage from the house of the band. Gradually, the instruments are cued-in - one at a time.

The music attracted the attention of two boys hanging out in the area. One of the boys was Bob Sobo, now a guitarist who is married to a wonderful singer, Sandy. They were worship leaders at a church in nearby Palmdale called "Harvest Church." They began talking to Don, who could talk for *days*. We in the band all groaned. We'd just gotten started, and now we were suspended in time while Don visited with the neighbor kids. We knew that this potentially could take hours. Frank went out and met them. The next thing I knew, Zappa was bringing them into the house, re-setting up a couple of my drumkit mikes, and interviewing them about politics. Argh! Bill and I especially were going out of our minds. This wasn't a recording session at all, it had nothing to do with anything going on at this house for the last six months. However, these boys were extremely precocious and it was quite impressive to hear their views on politics.

If I remember correctly, the lady came over to complain about the noise again sometime during the next days' recording. In the background on the Revenant set, you can hear typing. This sound, if I recall, is the sound of Don's unprepared lyrics being typed - far too late to actually perform any of them with the band during the house recordings.

Trapped In Our Environment

"We taped a few selections that way, and I thought they sounded terrific, but Don got paranoid, accused me of trying to do the album on the cheap, and demanded to go into a real studio. So we moved the whole operation to Glendale, into a place called Whitney, the studio I was using at that time - owned by the Mormon church." - Frank Zappa[a]

At one point Don walked in with Frank through the kitchen door. They stopped us from playing and Don went into a detailed analysis of how we were "trapped in our environment" and couldn't rise above all of this to play. My analysis of Don's analysis is that he was terrified of Frank asking him to actually sing live with the band - which was the whole point of this endeavor. Blowing

---

[a] The Real Frank Zappa Book, Frank Zappa, Simon and Schuster, 1989 pp 52

random horn parts over an entire song was one thing, actually performing a vocal with a band with which he had never rehearsed was another.

There may have been another point to this, like, since we'd busted our asses for nine months in severely-deprived circumstances using broken strings and sticks to perfect this material, maybe we should actually go into a studio, where:

We didn't have mountains of tape hiss.
There was EQ on the mixing board and processors to make the music sound right.
We would have proper monitoring to hear each other.
The amps could be separated, thereby having much more control over the finished sound and more clarity.
The room would have proper acoustics.
There would exist the ability to properly mix this music which neither Frank nor Dick were actually even familiar with - certainly not enough to mix "on the fly."
There wasn't a neurotic neighbor lady complaining about the noise.
Don would be able to overdub all the vocals he hadn't rehearsed.

I liked the idea of going into the studio, if nothing else, to get the hell out of this house for a few days. What I didn't like was the idea that Don had transferred the blame to us with this "trapped in our environment" story. I knew Don needed to overdub, and so did everyone else. We would soon prove how prepared we were as a band. I do, however, notice on the house recordings that I wasn't as prepared, so this must have been shortly after I learned all the rest of the drum parts.

Vocals Not Ready

In a discussion with Marker, I touched upon the fact that Don never prepared for a recording. He never rehearsed, didn't know where the words went, and was basically 'winging it' most of the time when he overdubbed his vocals. If he didn't like something, there was always "take two."

John French: Don was so disorganized. I was used to being in bands where we rehearsed. We knew our stuff before we went anywhere. Half the stuff we did in the studio, like **Dropout Boogie***, I never knew what the arrangement was on it because we never played it clear through.*

Gary Marker: Well, the whole thing is, that's what you do in a studio. You have to remember, when you got in there at the time that they started doing Safe As Milk, was that era when bands would get in there and just fiddle-fuck away hours and hours in the studio working on the arrangement and literally writing shit in the studio. So that was pretty commonplace stuff then. People would go in with half-strung ideas and they would develop them. They'd put it on tape and say, "Nah, that doesn't work, let's put a bridge in here!"

JF: Well, that session, the Safe As Milk session it was more like people watching their watches. I mean it wasn't like, "Oh, we're going to spend a month in the studio putting together an album." No, we were like, "OK, are you ready? Do you know this tune? Take One! Let's go!"

GM: Well that's the deal. I can't remember how many thousands of "X" dollars... Krasnow had a very specific budget. They told him, "You have to do this and get it out for this amount of money."

JF: So, see, we didn't have that time in the studio and I was worried about that because I knew that Don didn't know how to sing many of the songs yet.

GM: No, he had to constantly be coached.

So, here we were three albums down the road and working on number four and Don still hadn't developed any kind of rehearsal system and was still unprepared to perform his vocals.

There was a period of time that went by after all the portable recording gear was picked up and shipped out. I'm not sure if it was a few days or a few weeks. I moved my drums into the laundry shed and practiced for hours a day, because I wanted to be in the best form possible for the recording session.

Six Hours

Shortly thereafter, Van Vliet came back one evening after having met with Zappa regarding recording in a studio. In my head, I had envisioned that we would go into Sunset Sound for four or five days, get some decent sound checks, and record about four to six takes a night for four to five days. I was in for a shock. "Zappa will give you guys six hours in the studio to do the basic tracks." It was "pin-drop" time. Record all the basic tracks to a double-album in SIX HOURS? We quickly recovered, but I couldn't help but think about the hours I watched FZ piss away recording one track of Wild Man Fischer's album at Sunset Sound. After being in this house for nine months and being exposed to so much nonsense, the one thing we had going for us as a group was our insane dedication to this music. I think I was the first to speak up. "We can do it." We all agreed to give it a go.

Cover Art Shooting

I recall very little about the cover art shooting. I do recall that "The Mascara Snake" was not at the Trout House the day it took place. We did a few different locations, and Don was intent on having that vacuum cleaner in the photos. He also had Jeff reciting poetry, which can be seen in outtakes. I do recall distinctly that the bridge shots were near the end of the session, and the photographer suggested that someone get under the bridge. Everyone was afraid to go under the bridge but me. So, I went under the bridge, inspecting it for spiders and finding none. There was an old lamp in the yard with the shade rotted off from the weather. Don was holding it and the plug bumped me in the forehead. "I'm safe from spiders but not from Don," I said, jokingly, grabbing the plug to avoid getting bopped again. The cameraman said "Yeah, hold onto that, Drumbo!"

Later, Don would say that this particular photo was really "heavy" and I thought "yeah, it symbolizes him draining off my energy like a leach." I guess you might say by this time, I was pretty resentful of the cult situation and felt like I had a fairly objective view of how bad it really was.

Studio In Glendale

We didn't record in Sunset Sound as I had expected. Instead, we were taken to a place called Whitney Studio in Glendale, California. It was a bit more of a drive than going to Sunset Sound. This was an older studio and didn't have solid-state equipment. I have no idea how many tracks the multi-track machine was capable of recording but I believe it was an eight-track studio. The room had a big pipe organ in the back center. There were also large tall baffles concealing most of the rear wall. I went exploring. There was a door in the center of the rear wall and when I peeped in, the first thing I saw was a snare drum on a stand, with mechanical arms holding drumsticks - all controlled by the organ keyboard. The room also housed all the pipes for the organ and if I recall there were other percussion instruments in the room. Later, I thought to myself, "this was like the original synthesizer."

Four And A Half

The instruments arrived in a big truck similar to that which had delivered the other equipment to the house, and the same Acoustic amps were supplied for the guitarists. I sat up my drums in the far-right corner, my left side faced the control booth. Three baffles were set up to my left going toward the control room for the amplifiers. Mark was next to me, then Bill, then Jeff. An Acoustic amp was placed in each booth. The guitarists all stood out in the room, so they were able not only to hear me, but to hear themselves and each other. Bill stood directly in front of me. Mark to his right, and Jeff a ways off from Mark's right.

My drumkit was simple to set up and we were rushing against the clock to do this quickly. The mics were quickly placed and the sound check was done in probably 20 minutes. I was given headphones, but this quickly was nixed by me as they literally flew off my head when I played, because I played so hard and moved so stiffly. Also, often parts called for me standing quickly up to catch and mute a cymbal. So, they wound up putting a wedge monitor in my booth. This caused there to be severe leakage of the guitars and bass into the drum mics.

When we got to *Hair Pie* - Don requested that I put cardboard on the drums.

"Usually, when you record a drum set, the cymbals provide part of the 'air' at the top end of the mix. Without a certain amount of this frequency information, mixes tend to sound claustrophobic. Don demanded that the cymbals have pieces of corrugated cardboard mounted on them (like mutes), and that circular pieces of cardboard be laid over the drum heads, so Drumbo wound up flogging stuff that went "thump! Boomph! Doof!"- Frank Zappa[*]

Unfortunately, it took away all the natural bounce of the drums and caused me to have to play really stiffly. As I hadn't got too much of a chance to practice on a daily basis, it is one of the reasons why the drumming is so "stiff" sounding on the recordings.

In order to prepare the set, I had to take all the cymbals off, put the cardboard on and replace the cymbals. The disks on the drums themselves went quickly, as I just laid them on the heads. At the end of the take, I had to reverse the procedure.

Of course, anything that can go wrong will - especially when you are under the gun, the clock is ticking, and time is of the essence. We had some major setbacks. One was that my kick drumhead broke. Another was that Jeff decided to use the Silvertone amp because the Acoustic sounded too brittle - though I think he made use of the kick drum down time to exchange one for the other.

Another was Don's decision to play horn on *Big Joan*. There was no way around this, as he wanted breaks in the song where the horn played alone and the only way we could perform that was with him in the studio to achieve the interaction between him and the group. I would say this was the most time-consuming decision, as Don never does anything quickly or efficiently and it took a lot of preparation to set up the mic and get him located in the right place. If anyone asked Don to hurry, he would reply with something like, "I HATE watches, man." He wound up standing in front of me and next to Bill. It was the first time Don ever performed anything in the same room with us since we had started rehearsals for *Trout Mask Replica*.

Trout Mask Session
In spite of all of this, we actually finished the basic tracks - mostly in one take - in 4 hours and 37 minutes if I recall. Okay, I'm going to blow my own whistle here, I think I did a pretty good job organizing the music and learning my drum parts at the last minute. However, I was very proud of every one of my band mates for their perseverance in the face of such obstacles. There was a muffled cheer that went up in the control booth when we finished, and a look of complete amazement and respect on everyone's face when the four of us triumphantly walked into the control room.

[*] The Real Frank Zappa Book, Frank Zappa, Simon and Schuster, 1989 pp 52

Mark Boston: I think we were rushed through that session. I think that was a shame.
John French: That was a shame?
MB: All the work we put into that, they should have given us more time to get it down right in the studio. They rushed us through. We were all dead tired. I think it could have been done a lot better.

I recall hearing a playback of *My Human Gets Me Blues.* Now, please be aware that we'd never heard ourselves recorded until this moment as the playbacks at the house were through headphones. We stood shoulder to shoulder behind Frank and Dick, and looked at each other in amazement. So THAT'S what we sounded like. Big smiles came on our faces. We had just successfully conquered our Mount Everest.

Of course, there were tracks that had already been recorded. *Well, Orange Claw Hammer, The Dust Blows Forward,* and *China Pig* - had all been recorded at the house. There were also *Veteran's Day Poppy* and *Moonlight On Vermont,* from Sunset Sound, and *Hair Pie Bake I,* from the AFR.

Dick Kunc had a lot of interesting slates. One made it onto the album: "She's too much for my - or anyone else's - mirror." He made a little joke on every take and it kept the experience pleasant.

Frank "Sleeps" At Console

Later, when the Zappa/Beefheart feud again broke out, Van Vliet would say that Frank "slept at the console" during the recording of Trout Mask Replica.

John French to Don Aldridge: In the Beefheart Biography (BBC) when Zappa talks about working with Don and producing Don he states that if it would have been a straight normal producer, there would have been a number of suicides involved. Frank wasn't kidding, because it took strong people to deal with the kind of intensity that Don put out.
DA: I think he was being serious.
JF: Yeah, I think he was being serious, but I don't think people really realize that he was.

I do remember Frank nodding out for a moment one night during a playback of a mix, but I certainly recall him being active and lively during the instrumental tracking session. There was a spirit of teamwork where everyone was just really rushing around to make everything work because of the time constraint. Also, I do believe that Frank was recording every night at the same studio and actually pulling double-duty, so he had a right to be tired. Don had a way of capturing a single moment of time and exaggerating it for appearance sake. Frank was alive and well during the recording and mixing sessions.

Vocal And Horn Overdubs

"The basic tracks were cut - now it was time for Don's vocals. Ordinarily a singer goes in the studio, puts earphones on, listens to the track, tries to sing in time with it and away you go. Don couldn't tolerate the earphones. He wanted to stand in the studio and sing as loud as he could - singing along with the audio leakage coming through the three panes of glass which comprised the control-room window. The chances of him staying in sync were nil, - but that's the way the vocals were done." - Frank Zappa [50]

I'm not sure how many nights Don took doing overdubs. I know we came once or twice to the studio with Don while he overdubbed vocals, horn, sleigh bells and dialogue with "The Mascara

[50] The Real Frank Zappa Book, Frank Zappa, Simon and Schuster, 1989 pp 52

Snake." I also remember being there for some of the mixing sessions, and meeting John Mayall, or at least having a little talk with him one evening. I didn't know who he was. He asked me for change for a five-dollar bill. I hadn't seen a five-dollar bill for so long I had forgotten what they look like. He wanted to make a phone call and needed change for the pay phone in the lobby.

The sleigh bell overdub on *Hobo Chang Ba* was a little uncomfortable to me. Zappa was at the controls and said, "It's time to overdub the sleigh bells. Drumbo, go out in the tracking room." I went out and Dick followed, setting up two condenser mics about six feet apart. I stood there with a sleigh bell in each hand - they had handles - and Frank had me holding them up in the air toward the two mics to get me positioned when Don slammed through the door and angrily said, "John, get outta here." I walked back in the control room, a little embarrassed.

Don took a shipping quilt, picked up all the sleigh bells (there were many sets) in the quilt as though he were cradling an infant. "Play the track" he commanded, and in the section of the songs he wanted, he lightly hopped up and down, shaking all the bells at once. It was a very big sound. Don later told me "Frank was trying to put a Hoodu on you."

Okaaaay - but I did like Don's methodology. When the guys saw the number of sleigh bells he had ordered, they figured, with conventional playing, that between the band, the engineers, and Frank holding a set in each hand, that there were still some sets left over.

"How are we going to play all these at once?" Frank asked Don. "We'll overdub them" was his reply.

I do recall the most obvious case of Don being out-of-sync, as Frank mentioned above. It was on *Pachuco Cadaver*. Don wanted to overdub some horn on the end of the piece. So, he assembled his soprano and took it out into the studio. Not wearing earphones, he became totally out-of-sync with the track. He came back through the door and asked "how was that?" I was surprised at his asking. My thought was that it sounded like crap. However, two things were going on in my mind. Perhaps he intentionally *wanted* it out-of-sync.

It wasn't me playing, so *who cares?*

In the quaint tradition of "it's not worth going through the bullshit to find out what the bull ate" - the answer was a unanimous "sounds good" from everyone in the room. I figured that he could listen to the playback and decide for himself whether or not he wanted to replace it. If he didn't like it, there was always "take two" - a convenience which had hardly been given his band. In the time it had taken him to set up and overdub, we could have done 3-4 complete takes. So, I didn't care, and I certainly wasn't going to open myself to a later verbal assault for suggesting that he was out of time with his music. I think everyone felt the same on that one. Unfortunately, no one wants to tell the Emperor he has no clothes if they risk being beheaded.

CHAPTER TWENTY SIX

BEEFHEART TO BEEF

...very first piece of music for Trout Mask Replica, Steal Softly Thru Snow, ...scribed by John French. Photo courtesy of John French.

Easter Morning Master

"After it was mixed, I did the editing and assembly in my basement. I finished at approximately 6:00 a.m. on Easter Sunday, 1969. I called them up and said, "come on over; your album is done." They dressed up like they were going to Easter Church and came over. They listened to the record and said they loved it." - Frank Zappa[51]

March 31st, 1969 is the day on which Easter fell that year. What a year it had been. I hadn't reached the age of twenty-one yet, and I had just completed my fourth album as drummer for Captain Beefheart. Frank called us up, waking Don I'm sure. Don told us the master was finished. We went to Frank's basement / studio wearing our "cover photo" clothes to hear the final mixes of *TMR*. I distinctly remember Frank introducing a guy to us who was his new guitarist / singer. Lowell George was his name. I wasn't aware of the fact that Ray Collins had quit, nor did I even actually know the complete lineup of the group.

Art Tripp: See, what happened was, - we were in Chicago. Ray Collins dropped a bombshell on us. He just said he was leaving the group. In fact, Frank, and Ian and I were in a taxi going to the gig in Chicago, and just out of the clear blue Ray just says, "You know, I think I'm going to leave the group." There was just this dead, stunned silence - we were all at a complete loss for words.

More on this later - Lowell was just leaving as we arrived. I recall shaking hands with him. He was nervous and a little shy and I was a little puzzled why Frank had hired a guitarist, since he was one himself, and a singer, not knowing yet that Ray Collins had left.

Frank had a two-track tape deck in the basement - the same one he had recorded us on the night of the jam - the same jam that Don later inquired as to why I could get into Frank's music more than his ... anyway, I didn't realize this, but it was probably mainly there for editing and monitoring purposes. Frank did a lot of his own work. The editing of voices and music on *TMR* was all done by Frank. I doubt if Don had much input into this facet of the procedure.

He punched the button and we listened. It was amazing to hear it all at once, compacted together, mixed properly, with all the clever edits and introduction that Zappa had pieced together. Frank's abilities really were the finishing touch here, and for this he deserves great amounts of credit. I loved the way it came together.

There was still a little problem hovering in my mind: "What's next?"

Reaction To Trout Mask

John French: What did you thing when you heard **Trout Mask**, *when it first came out?*
Gary Marker: It was difficult at first, but I laughed most of the way through it. ... I found the humor in it. My wife is an English Literature grad who went into business school etcetera. She's somebody who knows James Joyce, chapter and verse. So, she asked, "Who is this Beefheart? What is this band?" So, I put on **Trout Mask Replica** *and she laughed all the way through it. She said, "That's brilliant, that's so funny!" I said, "So, you get it - that there is a lot of humor in it?" She said, "Yeah!" I said, "Well, there's a whole world of people out there who are deadly serious about this stuff. They try to reinterpret all of this." I see it the same way (as my wife) and I think this is where everybody misses the boat. One thing that Don had - that didn't always come out - he had a wicked sense of humor. On a lot of this stuff he was simultaneously poking fun at himself, the listener, (and) all these people who were into this*

[51] The Real Frank Zappa Book, Frank Zappa, Simon and Schuster, 1989 pp 52

mysterious horseshit. A lot of it was intended to be humorous. It was a deliberate thing and that is the sad thing about a lot of the real whackos. They don't see the humor in it. It's to their detriment. They're the losers really.
JF: Some of the later band members I worked with - they were really nice guys, I mean, really nice guys - but I thought they took Don a bit too seriously.

Don Aldridge: Trout Mask is probably one of the greatest albums of the Rock Era. Which I consider is over. I think Trout Mask Replica was probably one of the greatest albums ever cut. I honestly believe that. Although it wasn't my forte - it wasn't what I liked. I think that it influenced a great deal FAR beyond its generation. I almost think it was his swan song cause I don't think he ever quite came up to it again.

Ray Collins Quits
Ray Collins dropped quite a bombshell on the Mothers and Frank when he announced, in a Chicago cab on the way to a concert, that he was quitting.

Art Tripp: We just rode along for what seemed like an hour but it was probably just two minutes. Frank finally asked, "What do you mean?" He said, "Well, I'm leaving!" He didn't even offer any explanation. I had this crushing sickness in my stomach. I couldn't believe it. To me, Ray was the unofficial motivator of the whole band. He was just responsible for half of the humor, Ray didn't really play an instrument, but he was a great singer.

Everyone was puzzled by this sudden decision, but it eventually was revealed much later.

Art Tripp: Ray never liked the far-out stuff. He did it and he did it very well, but he never really liked it. Ray was more into, "Woo bop shu bop" - type stuff. Which he was very good at and he is to this day - a golden voice in my opinion. But Ray was a fuckin' riot, man. He was just so funny and he was so good on the stage. He was good at ad-libbing and he was just good at sight humor and gags. To me, he was just the real essence of the band. I just loved the guy, I didn't worship him, but damned near , I just thought he was the "cat's meow" and so when he said he was leaving, I was thunderstruck. In Ray's own inimitable vagabond way, he just left. He had nothing in mind. That's when (Frank) probably hired Lowell.
JF: So, maybe that was one of the reasons why you didn't like Lowell is because he didn't live up to the image of the guy that was there before.
AT: Yeah, I hadn't thought about that, there probably was some resentment there. I probably thought, "Well, who the fuck is this? - after Ray Collins, we get this schmuck? But, as it turned out, Lowell was a lot of fun. Of course, none of us were that deep into personal relationships at that time. We just lived together all the time. You know how that goes. Believe me, you know how that goes. But then I realized that Lowell was a good guitar player and he was a good singer, and he had a good sense of humor. He liked to drink, and so he was OK. We got along fine. But I just never really warmed up to Lowell that much.

John French to Jim Sherwood: A lot of people considered Ray Collins to be the sort of the spirit of the Early Mothers - the front man.
JS: I think he was. He was a hell of a singer. What an incredible voice he had. I supposed he was the leader of the group, because all Frank did (originally) was replace the guitarist. The guitarist had quit. Jim, Ray, and Roy were left without a guitarist and Ray knew Frank and said, "Hey, let's get Frank." At that time, Frank was playing jazz.

Marker Analyzes TMR

Gary Marker: A lot of Don's stuff, most of that stuff - Trout Mask Replica as well - is really very heavily riff -based. It's sort of a sequence of riffs. And they are strung together, sometimes in a jarring kind of way. When I read reviews - I don't know who that guy was - I read a review of it in Rolling Stone. This was thirty years ago, and he was saying, "Jesus Christ, these guys aren't even trying!" - something like that. Well, I'm thinking that this is all very logical to me, because it's a series of riffs strung together with kind of latter day-beatnik poetry sung over the top of it. I mean, really, it's not a big stretch.

John French: Well, it's a big stretch when you consider that it's being done as a rock album.

GM: What was purportedly a rock album.

JF: Well, it was done with rock instruments, how about that?

GM: Had it been say 1959 or '60 with primarily acoustic instruments or electronic instruments, it would have been avant-garde beat poetry. You know, or poetry and jazz - something like that. It's just that what he did is take this concept. Somewhere along the line he got this notion that, "We're going to take all these strange ideas and take all these images strung together and hype it up with an electronic kind of background and jarring rhythms." Once again, you see how rhythmically his personality aligns with his musical forte. You're always a little "off-kilter." The listener, the friend, the musician, he always keeps them slightly off balance. It's unpredictable. If there is any key word that describes what he does, in all phases of his life, it's unpredictability. You never know what to expect from moment to moment.

JF: That's an interesting way of putting it.

GM: Well, that is also the way he maintains control, because HE knows what is going to happen most of the time.

JF: Right. He knows what's going to happen because it's always going to be what isn't supposed to happen.

GM: Sometimes it is "off kilter," but there is a strong internal logic, so you think, "Of course! This is exactly what's supposed to happen. This is after you have been strung along through A,B,C,D, and E. By the time you get to F, you're ready for it, because you know that's going to happen. It seems like the right thing even though you didn't quite expect it. You know what I mean?

The Aquarius Theatre

A landmark of Hollywood for years was the Earl Carrol Theatre that was built in 1938 at 6230 Sunset Boulevard in Hollywood, California. One of my first trips to Hollywood in the daytime had been with friend Mark Thompson. I kept leaning out the window of the car, goofy 16-year-old that I was, and saying in a silly voice "Oooh, are you a star? Can I have your autograph?" Mark was laughing hysterically and nearly crashed into a pole at Mel's Drive-In on Sunset. I remember at one point, all my attention became focused on a fabulous building, with inscriptions on the side, and I was in awe, because I realized that I was looking at a real genuine monument to early Hollywood. I remember it being called (Franke Sennes') "Moulin Rouge."

I viewed what later I found was called "The Wall of Fame." It was the personal inscriptions of more than 150 of Hollywood's most glamorous stars of those wonderful early years of Hollywood. It was breathtaking to see all those autographs etched into the neatly arranged cement slabs that were so stunningly integrated into the front wall of the building.

The eighty-foot wide main stage contained a sixty-foot wide turntable, or revolving stage. The ceiling contained three giant swings, which could be lowered down mechanically. There was an elevator to bring things up from below to the stage, and a revolving staircase. It was pure Hollywood glitz and glamour in the best and most respectful perspective. It was also the site of the 1955 (hosted by Steve Allen) and 1959 (hosted by Raymond Burr) Emmy Award shows at a time when there was a bit of dignity in Hollywood.

Later, the stage lighting was upgraded and a complete movie theatre screen and sound system was installed. It was a very flexible venue, and an awe-inspiring sight to behold. It eventually became *The Hullaballoo*. It may have been called that in 1967, when Don and I attended one night to view several groups showcasing and met up with Bob Krasnow and Richard Perry. Later, it became the Aquarius Theatre - complete with psychedelic-painted exterior. It is hard to believe that this building had been completely constructed in only 75 days in 1938 and yet contained technologies that weren't matched for 30 years by any other venue.

Benefit Concert

John French to Bill Harkleroad: Do you recall us playing at the Aquarius Theatre?
BH: Oh yeah - Artie - with the women's underwear on his head and the green mustache. I met him the day I joined the band and that was the second time I saw him.

Denny Walley: When I came out I think I had gone to the Aquarius Theatre. The bill was The Mothers, Captain Beefheart and his Magic Band, and Jethro Tull.
JF: So, you were at the Aquarius Theatre in 1969?
DW: Yeah, it was like, after Hair *happened. Actually, I think the Tubes painted the theater.*
JF: Oh, so all that psychedelia on the outside...
DW: All that was done by The Tubes.

Ironically, the Trout Mask Band only played live one time... you might call in Van Vliet's "spruce goose." It was at a Cancer Benefit, I believe, and was held at the Aquarius Theatre in Hollywood. The Mothers were onstage sound-checking when we arrived, and while standing in the audience area, pre-show, Zappa asked me "What do you think of my new drummer?" I looked up and saw Artie Tripp playing these wonderful fast passages with a lot of double-stroke rolls - really smooth and seamless. I think Zoot used to refer to it as "pinstripe drumming" because of the incredible precision with which Artie played.

Buddy Miles was on the bill before us as I recall. This place had the revolving stage, so we were able to set up while Miles was on. We were also able to start playing before we actually appeared, so that it was a nice illusion. Rather than these dumb clubs where you have to walk out on stage in full view with no curtain and check your sound for five minutes. It's very anti-climactic and takes all the wind out of your sails to have to do this.

However, rather than making a grand entrance, Don handed me a broom. "I want you to go sweep the stage" he said. "You mean, as a theatrical thing... to catch people off-guard?" "That's right!"

So it was that the first five minutes of our only show consisted of me sweeping the stage of the well-known Aquarius Theatre.

The main flaw to the evening for me was the fact that we played the "simplest" material to accommodate Don's (and Victor's) non-rehearsed un-preparedness. *Big Joan* was our big opener - those repeating phrases with all the horn breaks. It went on for what seemed like forever. However, *Hair Pie* was a different story, as we just played it down and it showed how tight the group was.

Don may have spat some lyrics out on *My Human Gets Me Blues*. I have no idea how he did, as I was busy playing and we all just stuck to the arrangement.

There was no way to really focus on Don's vocal with all the distraction we had to face just by playing the music and keeping the arrangement straight. The band played flawlessly.

Art Tripp: I remember that exactly and that's the first time I ever heard the Magic Band, and Beefheart, and I went out and sat in the audience and I thought, "Jesus Christ, this is too much!" ...I just couldn't believe it. I immediately flipped for it. I remember coming backstage and met, or re-met everybody and thought, the way they were dressed and everything, "Shit, this is it!" It was absolutely amazing! After all the stuff that I had done, and then to hear something like that I thought, "Fuck an 'A'. This is something else." That's when I got to know everybody and I think Don had told me to come up to the house sometime.

Denny Walley: I remember it was the most unique-looking unit I ever saw. You guys were dressed in long deer-hunter-billed hats and Don with the shuttlecock on top of the hat. It was just incredible-sounding. I remember Frank in the wings down squatting on one leg in his Fred Segal stretch bell-bottoms, black and white with horizontal stripes.
John French: Was he studying it? (the music).
DW: He was like - you know the way he chortles? Like laughing or chuckling, with the one hand sort of holding his nose, almost like a pacifier type of thing. Looking at it lovingly as though it was just so wonderful. I got that impression from (my view in) the audience. He made a deliberate effort to come out and be visibly seen from the audience. He watched the whole show.
JF: Do you think that was like a stamp of approval from him?
DW: Oh, I'm sure - not that it needed it. I think Don was doing something that Frank would have loved to have been able to do, but he was so regimented. In his own way, he very much admired this free-form thing. ... But Frank looked as though he held a very high admiration for what you were doing. He was praising and adoring the whole effect. ... I thought it was fabulous that stuff like this could live and have an audience. I mean, at a theater that holds 2500 people and it's packed. ... I thought I must have been living on another planet. I didn't even know this stuff was going on. So, it was very exciting. ... I remember when Jethro Tull, got through with their set, ... Ian Anderson came out to the audience and he had a bucket of chicken or something and he was sharing it with everyone. He was sitting there watching Don.

Later, Artie wrote: *"One of the better shows was the first time I saw you guys perform. I'm sure you recall, because it was a "benefit" (probably Herbie's benefit) at the Aquarius Theatre in Hollywood. CBMB was on the bill along with the Mothers, Canned Heat, and I don't know who all. I'd heard Trout Mask, and flipped, so I was anxious to hear you all live. I wasn't disappointed. It was a great show. I believe we were on before you, so after your show I came back to talk with everyone.!"*
"I'd met Don up at Zappa's place- the old Tom Mix log home in Laurel Canyon- at about the same time that I either met Jagger, or said that I met Jagger so many times I believe it to be so. Anyway I thought Don was pretty hip, so that was another reason I was anxious to see the show. I believe we were on before you, so after your show I came back to talk with everyone. (Don) invited me up to Ensenada Dr., which I eventually did visit, usually after getting about half tuned up at the Corral, or down at the Tonga Lei in Malibu. Anyway, that's how the whole thing started in my case."

MOI - Aquarius

As I recall, The Mothers of Invention performed after us, as I recall. I had never seen them perform, and had only heard bits and pieces of albums with the exception of *Money* that I'd heard a year or so earlier two or three times. Frank was a great Master Of Ceremonies and gave a demonstration of how he could conduct the band in an improvisation. He showed a few hand signals and then had the band play what each one represented. Then, he did a series of hand signals and the band went crazy with textures and shapes that really spurred the imagination.

Jim Sherwood: Yeah, Frank loved that shit. He'd have all the guys do that. He'd have Roy do it on bass, or the drummer just go berzerk like that. Frank's idea of music was vocals, talking, any kind of sound or effect was part of the music. That's exactly the way we played it. We made the noises he wanted us to make. He had certain signs for them, specific noises. He had signs for random playing. High notes, low notes. Whatever he wanted. He directed the whole thing. Frank played to the mood of the audience. ... Frank would say, "What do you wanna hear? He'd let the audience choose.
John French: That's great.
JS: Then, at other times, we'd start playing, and we'd be playing some melody line like Burnt Weeny Sandwich *- you know, one of the instrumentals there ...* King Kong *or something like that. Then, Frank would just take off on a blues trip.*

There was a part of the Aquarius show that felt "fake" to me - because of Victor being up there. It wasn't like we actually played or rehearsed together, and so it felt "artificial" in that sense. Bill didn't have the same impression.

John French: Artie was in the audience and I asked him "What did you think of the band?" and he said, "Man, I thought that was 'it' man! I said, 'This is it'!" Those were his words, I believe.
BH: That's the way he would say it, yeah.
JF: Of course, once he got in the band and he saw the fake backdrop and the post holding up the set, and that it wasn't really that secure after all? Then he had a completely different view! Because it was a façade - a part of it was, right?
BH: A façade - I don't know if I would want to say that, because I think that would be a fake, there's something fake about that. I don't feel that it was fake in any way, because we were true to whatever we were doing. We were "doing" it. I don't think we had a "Okay, we can't play, so we're going to jump around and wear weird clothes."
JF: Well, we were valid musicians, I felt like the Magic Band, Mark, Jeff, you, myself, were valid musicians. We could play the same thing twice.
BH: Oh yeah!

The band played a consistent and recognizable framework in which Don allowed himself and Victor musical liberties he refused to offer anyone else. It was the consistency of the band that made the performances work and allowed the two cousins the freedom to be spontaneous.

John French: At that time, we could go and duplicate that album anywhere. If there would have been a group consisting of Don Van Vliets and Victor Haydens, the music would never had sounded the same way twice. It would have never have sounded close to the same.
Bill Harkleroad: It would have never have gotten done!

JF: Right! So, that philosophy, (reflected in) one of Don's favorite sayings was, "You train yourself, you strain yourself." The thing is that Don applied that philosophy only to himself (not to the group). So it was like, "You play it exactly - note for note - the same every time. There was no spontaneity in the music, there was no self-expression in what we did. Basically, we were (perceived as) just a bunch of robots up there doing the bidding. Not that we didn't do a pretty good job of it, but it (became) stale. We could go onstage in our sleep and do that!

What I was attempting to create a dialog on here is the music vs. theatrics. Most of Don's horn playing on stage was really theatrics. If you create a semblance of chaos with the musicians, by giving them disassociated fragments of riffs to play in different keys, you wind up with a perfect backdrop that allows complete freedom. Who's to know you're not playing a "part" when everyone else sounds that disconnected also? But the band was stuck playing the exact same thing every performance.

Bill Harkleroad: We did the painting, why are we doing the same painting again?
John French: Exactly, and yet that was the framework in which Don could do just about anything he wanted to and it would still seem musically valid.- because of the fact that it was dissonant, we were all playing in different keys and time signatures all the time.
BH: It was a pretty intelligent thing for him to do, because he could be complaining about the monitors or whatever, and that's even part of the show!
JF: Yeah. I remember it seemed like (almost) any show that we ever did with Don, the first thing he would do is totally alienate the soundman.
BH: Absolutely. "This is wrong, I can't hear!" It was his paranoia. He was so freaked out every time we went on the stage.

But, was he really freaked-out, or was he just acting? I've watched a lot of performances over the years, and he always seemed to be pre-occupied with the sorry state of the monitors. As a singer, that's supposed to be done at the sound check. But Don would always joke around saying, "I don't need my sound checked!" Funny as it may be now, it was frustrating to go on stage, trying to be perceived as a relatively valid group, and have Don putting lyrics in the wrong place and making the sound man's life miserable for an evening.

Artie Remembers John Cage

Artie had been introduced to the avant-garde pre-Zappa when in Cincinnati. He writes: *"Cage was hired as Artist In Residence by the Cincinnati College-Conservatory of Music at the University of Cincinnati (whew) for 6 months. That would have been 1965-66. Since I was such a far-out nut with talent, I sort of fell in with him. I got to play a lot of his music, and attend some of the functions which were typically thrown for him by the influential upper-class movers and shakers who liked to think they were intellectuals, and "with it". I was in heaven due to the exposure to his music and moreover his philosophy, but also because he was a heavy drinker despite being a naturalist, and I loved to drink too. The shows were always memorable and unique, but what sticks out in memory was a lecture given by Cage to a large group of psychiatrists and psychologists. Morton Feldman was in town just to be with Cage for awhile. Feldman was a modern composer of some note from New York City (Cage was from upstate). At any rate somehow Feldman and I were asked to accompany Cage to this lecture. My guess is that the large crowd of mental health care professionals were there to more or less psychoanalyze Cage, since he was a famous* oddball; but most of them sat there dumbfounded as Cage weaved through his rather mystic philosophy and musical notions (which were one in the same). There were few takers after at the Q & A period. Those who did ask questions seemed to be trying to challenge him, but they ended up sounding stupid. As a friend of Cage's asked one time, "If you don't know, why do you ask?" Well I was immensely impressed. As we left the hall Feldman was falling down laughing. He turned to Cage and said, "They just can't bust the artist!" Sound familiar?"

Jeff Bruschele

John French: Do you remember right after Trout Mask *was recorded when Jeff Bruschele ...*
Bill Harkleroad: ... When Jeff Brushcele broke Jeff's (Cotton) ribs, you mean?
JF: Well, no, this was earlier. Don was "romancing" Jeff to be the drummer. Do you remember him doing that before I left?
BH: No!
JF: Yeah, he was doing that. Jeff would say, "Man, I'd really like to play drums!" and Don was saying, "Yeah! You could probably do that man! He was saying that around me a lot.
BH: It sounds right, it would be typical - par for the course.

After the mixes to *Trout Mask Replica* were finished, we just spent some time at the house working on new stuff. Dick Kunc "fixed" the tape deck, and Don bought new tape and would just sit at the piano for hours playing. He would then present this tape to us as a "finished composition" and Jeff, Mark, and Bill would have to sort through all this meandering, pull out the gems, and learn them for a new composition called *Animal Gass.*

Since there was nothing new to play drums to yet, and I wasn't involved in the musical process so directly, I felt left out. I thought that the best thing to do at this point was to just live my life the way I wished. I cleaned out the bottom bedroom, made up a bed with clean sheets, washed and arranged all my clothes, showered daily, cleaned up the house and my workspace and spent time reading in the evening. Sometimes, Don would be upstairs dictating to Jeff and if I wasn't needed for something, I'd be downstairs reading or writing out drum patterns. I made myself break the habit of this "total absorption band-as-cult" pattern and became much more sane.

Don would give me an occasional abstract glimpse of what he wanted on the drums on *Animal Gass* but there was nothing really to play to yet. No distinct arrangement. So, I worked on my drums, taking them completely apart and putting them back together while fine-tuning certain things to make the set more playable. I cut out new cardboard circles on which to practice and basically just became my own person with independent thought. I put in about 8 hours a day thinking about the band, ate dinner, and then went off to my own life.

I set the drums up in the laundry shed and worked on all the *Trout Mask* parts daily to keep that stuff "dialed in." I noticed, during this time, that Jeff Bruschele was coming around a lot with Victor. I was becoming suspicious that something was up, but I wasn't quite sure what it was. One night, while practicing in the laundry shed, Bruschele came out and watched me. I remember being seated with my back facing the door and Jeff saying, "I really think I could do that, man." Don would reply by saying, "I'm sure you could."

Art Tripp Visits

John French: I remember you coming up to the house. In fact, I remember him playing something new for you and you went out in the kitchen and turned on the water. Because you

wanted to see if you could keep your attention on it with something distracting you.
Art Tripp: Exactly, yeah.
JF: Which kind of upset Don, I believe. (Laughter)
AT: He said he loved it - but, I don't know - he said he loved anything that was nuts. I remember that, I came out several times.

Final Conflict

The final conflict I had to face in the Trout Mask band was when Jeff Bruschele (The Faux Drumbo) came over with Victor one mid-morning shortly after the recording of *Trout Mask*.

We were set up to play in the living room, because we had been working on *Animal Gass* the night before. I had the cardboard circles on all my drums and cymbals because the lady down the street was again complaining and had called the police who finally said, "One more time and we'll have to take some action which will involve court and a fine."

There's nothing like playing on cardboard drums. Jeff and Victor came through the door and were standing in the kitchen as though awaiting something that had been announced. I knew this was the day, for some reason, that Jeff would replace me. Don came out with the soprano sax that Jeff and I had bought him years before, sat in his chair, turned to face the band straight on and his command was, "play a strawberry." This was totally out-of-character for Don. My thought was "play a strawberry? What is this hippy shit?"

John French to Bill Harkleroad: We were playing. We were set up, we were playing through an amp or something - that Silvertone that we used. Anyway, we were "playing a strawberry," or attempting to "play a strawberry," and Don all of a sudden jumped up and was glaring at me. I recall this very vividly, I don't know if you recall any of this at all.
BH: Oh, this is sounding really familiar, yeah.

I gritted my teeth and just sat there for a minute. I didn't feel like improvising. In fact, I felt like being a million miles away. I wanted a girlfriend and some normal friends. I wanted to tour - anything but more of the same. I needed a vacation from this madness.

I started playing half-heartedly on my cardboard drums along with the others. Suddenly Don stopped playing and fixed an angry gaze upon me. There was a deafening silence in the room. I looked at Don straight in his eyes, which were intense, intimidating and by this time, predictable. It was the same look that later Merrel Fankhauser would call Don's "demented pirate" look. The fact that Jeff Bruschele was there, after all the talk about how he wanted to play drums, made me think that this whole moment was a setup and Van Vliet was just pushing my buttons and baiting me. I stared back, in great apprehension but little fear.

He got up from the chair, put his horn quickly down and rapidly walked around my left side with great conviction until he was at the back of me. My first thought is that he was going to play something on the drum to demonstrate what he wanted me to play, so I started to get up. At this point, he grabbed me by the shirt collar and belt from behind, like a barroom bouncer, and propelled me to my right towards the staircase. I lost balance and fell about halfway down to the second landing, in a heap.

Bill Harkleroad: (in a whisper) Wow!
John French: And he said, "Take a walk, man!" Do you remember him doing that?
BH: I do.
JF: You do?
BH: I totally remember it.

Art Tripp: I guess I did hear that story, I had forgotten. That's unbelievable!
Gary Marker: This is certainly not what I would call the ideal "pink slip." Rather than getting bounced from the band, I would much rather get a phone call from an attorney. Not be tossed down a flight of stairs.

I stood up and walked down the remaining stairs. I wasn't hurt at all - at least physically - or was too numb to notice. I felt like a piece of trash that had just been wadded up and tossed out. I walked out the front door of the house down the stairs and out of sight as quickly as I could.

Par For The Course

John French: So, this was pretty much par for the course for the Trout Mask *era. We're just touching on little points, but there was stuff like this happening constantly, people getting beat up. You know, we turned on each other. I know that I beat up you, you beat up me, Jeff beat up me and I beat up Jeff - you know, it was just on and on.*
Bill Harkleroad: Yeah (Bill is agreeing with "yeahs" after almost every sentence above.)
JF: Don was suspiciously never the target of any of this, because he was the instigator of it, and it was very obvious to all of us. But we didn't know how to get out of it. We were like lemmings, in a big swarm of lemmings running off the edge of the cliff, and we're going, "I don't want to fall off this cliff!" (in desperate voice), *"but we're all going anyway!" You know?*
BH: Right! (Bill is again affirming everything I say.)
JF: I felt like I was swept up in a thing that I couldn't get out of.
BH: Absolutely!
JF: So, (back to the stairway) I took a walk!! I went to Wyoming and Jeff Cotton wound up leaving maybe three months later.

Escape

After being literally ejected from the band, I took a walk down Canoga Avenue feeling exhilarated and quite happy to be out of the house. It was probably about 11 a.m., and I was walking along feeling free, as though I'd just escaped a POW camp. Everything looked so beautiful (no, I wasn't on drugs) and fresh, like I was seeing it for the first time. Canoga Avenue is lined all the way down the hill with pepper trees on both sides of the road.

After a few minutes of enjoying my newfound freedom, I realized I didn't own anything except what I was wearing. Like Jerry's bass, Don would probably never allow me to retrieve my drums, my clothes, anything. It was all gone - not that I had a big net worth to begin with. I still felt good. However, in order to remain free, I knew that I was going to have to hide out for a while because the guys would be out looking for me. I knew the perfect spot and had thought about it many times. Near Ventura Blvd. (north of where we lived) was a small hill on the west side of the street. It was behind some homes, and I could sit up there and see everything. I walked up a dirt path behind some stores and found myself on a hillside with tall yellowish grass. After finding a good vantage point from which to view the road, I sat on a large rock.

I felt completely at ease and totally in control of my life for the first time in months, maybe years. No one could criticize me for the way I sat or the way I held a cigarette. No one could interrogate me or put me through any of those awful moments again. It was such a relief.

After a while, I saw Don's red Volvo riding down Canoga Avenue and then back up. Back and forth for what seemed like a couple of hours. I sat there watching. I was trying to imagine what they were saying, who was in the car, and what thoughts were going through their heads about now.

My mind was slowly dissolved into a meditative state into which crept a haze of ghostly thoughts slowly forming into images, then reality. I had been duped. What was it Don used to say? - "Somebody's doin' the jerk and it's the jerk's fault for letting him do it." - That was it. It seemed clear now what he had meant. My former friends were in that house where I had spent the last several months. We had all been force-fed more private information than anyone should know about anyone else - and very rapidly. The resulting shock had put up the framework of the walls between us that would eventually separate and confine us. The encouragement to hurl venomous darts during our talks nurtured the resentment to lath the mental walls and prepare them for plastering. Violence was the plaster, which sealed the walls. Our only door revealed Don, and the only window to the others was through his music.

Under the cloaking of music we hid, hoping our invisibility was complete, and would protect us from the dreaded "talks." Our personalities were suspended - cocooned in confusion and frozen in time - replaced by blind devotion to another's will.

Jeff buried himself inside the character of Antennae Jimmy Semens. His voice, his mannerisms, and his personality almost totally altered into a performance rather than a life. Bill buried himself in his guitar parts, and withdrew further and further into a brooding study of various rhythms and patterns. Mark became an animated character, zipping around the house to entertain a missing audience. I buried myself in transcriptions of hundreds of piano riffs and drum parts, supposing my dedication would protect me from the nightmarish encounters that increasingly focused their ugly eyes upon me.

Who would I have been had I been somewhere else? How would my friends have turned out in another environment? It was too late to tell and there was no way to re-enact the events in another setting and hope for a new outcome. It was what it was. I sat here, catching a glimpse of freedom, but struggling to free myself from the web-like cocoon that had been my home for the last $2^1/2$ years.

The red Volvo finally went back up the street for the last time and the world I was re-living dissolved in the same manner it had appeared: as smoke into the air. Now I had to decide what to do next, and mentally slapped my way out of the haze. I would have some time before they would be back and yet I didn't have a dime or know anyone whose phone I could use to call home. So, I prayed.

I heard a noise as I was praying, and a young boy, about ten years old, appeared on the path. He was walking a dog of medium size, mostly white with large brown patches. The boy saw me as I sat there unmoving. I was worried that his discovering me might frighten him. After all, I was a bit strange-looking. He didn't seem at all frightened, but stood off a distance.

We began to talk. I was really surprised to find how precocious this 10-year old man was. He was talking about science and space and had knowledge far beyond anything I had learned, or at least retained. He spoke about the relative gravitational pull of the various planets, the distances of the nearest and farthest stars, time travel, etc. It turned out that he had just written and published his first science-fiction book. I almost didn't believe him for a moment. The book was over a hundred pages, as I recall - obviously an ambitious work for a boy this young.

I smiled to myself. I wondered if Don had been anything like this as a child. I imagined the young Van Vliet sitting in his room sculpting all the dinosaurs at about this age, and telling his parents just to leave his food at the door. Don, however, by his own confession, was a spoiled brat. This child seemed very respectful, courteous and attentive.

The boy finally asked me what I was doing up there. I told him exactly what I had been through with this band situation. I was completely honest. "I made a few mistakes," I told him, "I just want to call my family and I don't have any money. I don't know anyone here." "You can use our phone," the boy said. I thought about this for a minute. How would I feel if my ten-year old child brought someone home who looked like me? I was a little amused and concerned at the same time. "Hey Mom, look what I found! - Can I keep him??"

It had been an unusual day. My deepest discomforts lay in my fear of imposition on the kindness of others. Desperate times calling for desperate measures, I said, "Thanks," and stood up to follow. He finished walking his dog, and then took me back up Canoga where we turned right into to a nice upper middle-class neighborhood. "We're Mormons," he told me. My concern level went up a notch or two. "Would these people have me arrested?" I thought. By this time, however, I was committed.

The boy handled this very well. "I'll go in first and explain," he said. "Smart!" I thought. Thank God this was in the days before every pervert and child molester known to man has been interviewed on national television to the point that if you even look at a child you're under suspicion.

I must have looked pretty ragged. I had a completely untrimmed beard, and my wavy ratty hair was 18 inches long. I was wearing bright red corduroy pants and a striped velour shirt - not your typical friend Junior brings home to meet the folks. But soon the door opened and a kind-looking gentleman in his late forties or early fifties came out. He looked at me for a moment, a little puzzled, but kept the kind face. "My son told me what happened," he said. "You're welcome to use our phone, come in." "It's long-distance, but I'll reverse the charges." I explained.

I walked in to this peaceful home. It was quaint and comfortable. The wife was sitting in a chair. It seemed like she was doing something with her hands. I hadn't had even a gulp of water in five hours and I must have looked it, because she immediately got up and fetched me some water. I used the phone, feeling a bit uncomfortable in front of strangers asking my parents if they could pick me up. My mother was on the line and wanted to know a few details. "I'm in some people's house who let me use their phone, but they need it back quick," I lied to end the interrogation.

I was asked where I could be picked up. The thought had not even occurred to me until now. I didn't want to wait at these people's home - that would have been presumptuous. "I'll be at the Holiday Inn near the corner of Canoga Ave. and Ventura Blvd." With that, I thanked them, and hung up the phone. There was a silence in the room. The boy was sitting with his parents in the living room, I was in a section of the room where the dining table was and so I came back in and they offered me a chair next to a lamp table.

They asked me for dinner, if I remember correctly, and I declined at first but then had something to eat with them. I wasn't really hungry at all. I felt fine. I was relaxed and confident that these people understood and wanted to help.

I told them a short version of the story, editing for purposes of the child, but describing the violence and the interrogations. I poured my heart out for over an hour to these total strangers, who I trusted more than my own fellow band-mates that I grew up with. They listened with sympathetic ears. There was such a peace in that house. The boy was talking to his parents not as a kid, but as a human being, as an equal member of the household. They seemed to really love each other. It was such a contrast to where I had been.

I finally decided it was time to go. It would be another half-hour or hour before I would get picked up. My brother Tom, who lived about 20 minutes drive from my parents, was going to drive down. My father was so insecure that in all the time he had lived in Southern California, he had never once driven to the Los Angeles area, because he had heard the traffic was bad. I would see familiar faces soon, with mixed feelings.

Holiday Inn

I went into the front doors of the Holiday Inn. My appearance was probably a bit shocking to the guests. This was during a time when this was absolutely frowned upon by most adults. I walked up to the desk and explained my situation and asked if I might sit in the lobby to wait. The desk clerk was very understanding and consented, as long as I didn't bother the customers.

As I sat waiting for my ride, my thoughts ran through the past three years. My parents and friends had warned me about all this and everything they said had come true. My best friends in the band were now alienated from me and from each other all because of the words and actions of one man. I thought about the power of words and how when they are used the wrong way, can bring about such bizarre results.

I thought back to the very beginnings of the band and wondered again at how in the world my life had become so twisted. My mind re-played the last three years of my life and kept me from feeling self-conscious sitting in the hotel lobby. It all seemed so surreal.

A white two-door Chevelle showed up in the parking lot. My brother was driving and there was my mother sitting in the passenger seat. A few months ago, I had gotten in this car with Jeff and my mother and driven to the desert. I sheepishly approached the car. My esteem was at a very low ebb. It wasn't fun having to go back and face the silent "I told you so's." My family was very understanding and loving, and there was seldom a critical word said to me while growing up. However, you could feel the thoughts and the unsaid words as we drove.

I remember little about the ride back to the desert. I had figured out my taxes for two or three years back, because I hadn't filed for that long. Thinking ahead, I had the refund mailed to my parent's house and it showed up in a very few days after my arrival. What perfect timing. It was probably mid spring of 1969. According to Zappa, the first time we heard the finished *Trout Mask Replica* master was on Easter Sunday, March 31st, 1969, so it had to be some time after this. This year stands out in my head so clearly. So much happened in such a short length of time.

I stayed with my folks for a couple of weeks and almost immediately shaved my beard. Dan Moore, my high school friend came by to see me and said that I looked like an "Italian Vampire." My folks immediately suggested that I get my hair cut, and since long hair always seemed like a big bother, I had no problem. I looked so different. I had gained some weight, and my face looked heavier.

I bought some oils and a small pad of paper with canvas texture and painted a couple of paintings. I remember distinctly painting a skull with a rose growing out of its head. Dali influence most likely. I worked several days on it and was really proud of the detail. Years later, I saw a Grateful Dead logo that looked surprisingly similar. I was removed from everyone I had been around and in a house with people I felt like I was getting to know all over again. Not to strangely, I missed the intensity of the music, I missed my drums. I missed my friends, even though we were so angry and the situation so glum.

A Second Look

Within days I somehow wound up back at the house on Ensenada Drive. I remember Don taking me to Zappa's. Because of my "new look," Don suggested that I wear a straw hat with a green visor - one like fishermen wear. I remember meeting guitarist Lowell George again. He remembered me years later and recalled my strange fashion look that night.

Victor Hayden's reaction was strange. Don explained that Victor had "never realized how sensitive I was." As I would talk to Don, he would give me special treatment, and I knew this was just a "honeymoon" period and soon everything would be a big mess again. He kept saying I had this "earphone posture." I asked him what he meant. He explained that I would listen to him with one ear cocked forward, as though I was hard of hearing. I think what I was really trying to do was believe what he was saying and I was concentrating a lot on every word. Everything seemed too perfect, but I had been so programmed for this environment.

Don told me that Laurie had cried when I left … I thought about all the terrible things she had said to me and about me during our "talks." Talks she often became involved in as the situation deteriorated more and more. I had always liked Laurie, and I felt like Don used her and someday he would toss her out.

Thinking about Laurie crying made me view the whole situation from a much more confident stance. I was acting like a different person and because I looked so different, everyone was reacting to me in a completely different manner. Although Laurie had said all those terrible things, she obviously liked me a great deal, or she wouldn't have cried. That same thing was true for all the rest. "The guys thought a great deal of me too," I thought, "just like I thought a great deal of them, but they can't show it because of this environment." We were being held emotionally hostage.

We were working on some new song, and Don was very interested, suddenly, in exactly what I was playing on the drums. He had an idea for a beat, and he wanted to see if I could play it. It was a simple rock beat, yet it was years before I heard anyone else do anything like this. He showed himself as the innovative creative force he truly was.

Dan Moore Talks Sense

I had fallen asleep on the couch and I must have been up late because it was mid-morning when I awoke to find my friend Dan Moore at the house. He had come down to see me. How strange, I thought. Dan wasn't very adventurous for the most part, yet here he was in an environment I had described as totally hostile. We had some small talk and he asked me to take a walk with him. "I am very angry with you for coming back here," he told me directly. "I came down to get you. You don't belong here."

I was shocked and surprised. Dan had never once since I had known him ever really been very confrontational or assertive. Yet, today, he was talking to me like a drill sergeant. I knew he was right. I wasn't happy staying with my parents, but I sure wouldn't be happy down here. His car was parked up the hill and behind the house. We sneaked up and pushed the car back out of the parking area into the steep driveway we shared with the Catalanos who lived next door. He coasted out of the driveway and into the street. It was all down hill for quite a ways, so we just kept coasting.

I started laughing. I had just left all the new clothes I bought with my tax money in the house. It only amounted to a few things, and I knew that I couldn't go back there and just talk my way out. We kept driving.

I didn't want to go home, and I had some money, so I rented a room at the Antelope Valley Inn. It was a fairly nice place. I just wanted to be alone for a couple of days.

I sat around writing. I had bought some pens and paper and I just wrote all my thoughts. I was trying to write free-flow, like Don, probably because I had been around him so much. I didn't know what else to do. I sat by the pool in the daytime and wrote. I sat in my room at night and wrote. Three days passed, I ran low on money and went back to my parent's house.

Will The Real Drumbo Please Stand Up?

My suspicion about Jeff Bruschele was correct. He became the drummer after I left, using my drums and even wearing my clothes. I saw a picture of him once with the band and thought for just a moment it was me! Don called him "Drumbo."

This actually was typical Van Vliet behavior - illogical and self-defeating. I could understand why Don wanted me out - he felt he was losing control over me. I seem to be standing up to him more and more. I wasn't really interested in living the cult lifestyle any longer. However, I kept asking myself, "Why would Don, intentionally destroy a group that was the most well-rehearsed band he ever had - a band that was so tight?

Cliff Martinez made a statement that I think fits here:

"Beefheart drummers don't grow on trees. After I got into that style, I realized that you can't just go out and pick some studio drummer to play like this."

John Goes To Wyoming

I had a plan. My brother Phil and his wife and 3 kids lived on a ranch in Wyoming that belonged to her parents. I had thought about going back for a summer when I first graduated from high school. Now would be a perfect time. I wanted to see what it would be like to drastically change my environment. I also felt that Don's pull on me and his strength over my will was so strong that I had to put physical distance between he and I quickly.

I suggested this to my parents. My brother Dave was living in the basement of their house. He was seventeen years my senior and had just gotten out of prison. He had served a year and I would rather not disclose why as it might be an embarrassment to the people involved. He paid his price, and that is what matters. Dave offered to drive me to Wyoming in my father's car.

Over the phone, Phil said that I could hire on as a ranch hand for the summer. I wanted to go as soon as possible to get away from Southern California. We made the plans, packed the car, and left within two days. We drove through Barstow, and the car immediately started heating up. We made it to Vegas, replaced a gasket, and everything seemed fine. I remember taking a nap while Dave drove and waking up in some gas station in Podunk, Nowhere with the hood open and Dave and the attendant talking. I got out to find out that the engine head gasket had blown between two cylinders, and so there were only four actually powering the car. However, we decided to continue.

The car ran surprisingly well. I recall going through the Rockies and how wonderful the scenery was. Then, when we finally hit the outskirts of Wyoming, it seemed dismal and plain. I began to have second thoughts. "I'm crazy," I thought "These ranchers will eat me alive." It must have been late May to mid-June of 1969, as I recall seeing fireworks stands preparing for the fourth of July celebration.

We finally arrived at the ranch in the early evening just before sunset. My brother was working out in a field and saw us. He was smiling as he ran toward the car. It seemed like old times. It was the first time I had felt good about seeing anyone in a long, long time.

I recall having bought a pair of Florsheim dress shoes which I was wearing. I was almost immediately asked to help herd a huge bull into a retaining pen. I jumped down in this pen and immediately discovered my right Florsheim buried in moist bull dung. "My initiation," I smiled as I thought, "but then again, who better to deal with bullshit than I?"

Dave worked on the car over the next few days while I became acquainted with the ranch and met the overseer Russel Finch. He had just taken over and was Phil's brother-in-law and the owner - Henry's son. He took me off over by one of the pens and we talked "business." "I can only pay you $8 a day," he said. I couldn't believe my ears, but I acted as though nothing were wrong. It was like out of a movie. They didn't pay by the hour, but by the day? These were 10 hour days, so I would be making $0.80 and hour. I choked down my thoughts, and accepted the wage.

Ranch Rehab

My early work on the ranch was mostly flood irrigation. There were canals carved in the hillsides of all the ranch land. These were fed from the river. In order to water a field, you had to dig little ditches in the canal ditch banks and allow water to flow onto the land. There were dams made of canvas stapled to a pine pole that were put in the canal to hold the water to a certain level.

There was more of an art to this than one could imagine. Too much water and the hay would turn yellow. A whole field could be destroyed through neglect, and the value of each field was high.

The hay fed the young steers and the cattle that produced them. The steers had to be fattened for market at the feedlot. Almost the entire ranch economy depended on how well things went at the annual market. The hard work was therapeutic. I quickly adapted to my new environment.

Encampment Wyoming is in a little Valley at the north edge of Grand Teton National Forest. It was actually beautiful country. Not like the yellow prairie we had crossed to arrive here. This was beautiful land. Trees, lakes, fish and wildlife were all in abundance. Unfortunately, the culture was as much in lack as nature was plentiful. I had just gotten a hair cut and they thought my hair was too long. I figured the best thing to do was just get a shorter haircut - which I did after about a month. Why let a little protein spoil such a great setting?

I remember a couple of the guy's names. One was called Verlyn. He was an older fellow who needed the work to supplement retirement. Another was named Levi Herring, whose birth had resulted from some alleged infidelity. Then, a cousin of the family, a nineteen year old named Bernie I believe, came to stay on the ranch. He had gotten into some trouble at home, I think he wrecked the family car after having a few beers. This was his "community service" so to speak - and a chance for him to get out of his environment and straighten out his life - much like me. He was interested in art, and so he and I talked about painters and art.

Bernie and I hung out together a lot. I talked to him about my experiences in the band and my belief in God. Mostly, I just answered questions, not trying to proselytize. I remember us going out one night and buying some beer. We parked on some side road of the ranch and just sat for hours talking. There's not a hell of a lot to do in Wyoming on Saturday night, but it was a bit easier having a friend.

The summer passed fairly quickly. My brother and his wife were very conservative Christians, and there was a wide chasm between us in terms of open-mindedness and acceptance. Communication could never really be anything more than surface small talk or me listening to their strong opinions. I didn't feel I could share much with them. I wasn't in the same mind-frame, but I respected their home and appreciated their taking me in for the summer. I also knew that they cared about me.

Haying Season

Haying season on a ranch is something I'm glad I experienced at least once in my life. When it's haying time, everything else stops and it becomes time to "mow grass." There were several machines for mowing. Some fields were mowed with a big clipper attachment that looked like hedge clippers that fastened to the tractors. Some were done with a "windrower" which not only cut the grass with similar clippers but gathered it into rows by conveyer belt to the center and left it in rows called (not surprisingly) "windrows."

The alfalfa or hay that was merely mown had to be raked into windrows with a giant rake about sixteen feet wide pulled by a tractor. It was retractable, and as the correct position was reached to leave the row, the rake was retracted and immediately set back down to rake from the other side of the row until the next row, until the tractor approached the next irrigation canal, then the tractor did a U turn, and repeated the process from the other side.

Then, homemade machines the locals called called "droobies" were used to scoop up the windrow into a small stack which was then picked up by a tractor fitted with a special shovel-like attachment that hydraulically lifted and stacked it on the hay stack. Sometimes a person would be needed to stand on top of the stack with a pitchfork and keep the edges from rounding so the hay would sit higher.

I spent many days driving everything but the main tractor. My favorite job was the rake, which I became fairly proficient at using. I would take off my shirt and stand on the main beam of the tractor and casually steer. It was hard, pleasant work and very fulfilling to see a field of hay stacked for winter storage.

Another pleasant experience was getting up on the back of a cutting horse that knew exactly how to cut a calf out from the herd. The first time I did this, I didn't realize the horse knew exactly what to do. It gave me an unexpected series of lurches which nearly sent me flying out of the saddle. I didn't get to do much horseback riding, but I loved the feeling. Once I got the feel of how the horse worked the calf, it became a simple matter of balance and anticipation.

Branding calves was quite an experience. One of my first days on the job, we rounded up all the calves of a certain age in a pen. My job was to walk up beside them, grab their opposite rear flank, and pull them down on the side, quickly reach down and grab their hind leg, hoping not to get kicked, and drag them over to the branding area. I always thought that a brand was kind of like a stamp: you know - quick. It turned out that they hold the iron on for several seconds - five to ten - if I remember correctly. The smell of burning hair and flesh was a little nauseating, and listening to this poor animal bawling from the pain was a real lesson for me. They also give each animal a shot, probably some antibiotic, and the males are castrated with no anesthetic. This all happens within 30 seconds to the poor animal, and then they get up and walk away, scared to death of people for the rest of their short lifespan, at which time they are sent to the slaughterhouse and turned into roasts, hamburgers and steaks.

Animal-rights activists and vegetarians would have been appalled at the scene. I just found it interesting. It was a way of life for generations of men, a culture that some would violently oppose, but I respected the hard-working men and women who lived in this area. Young children in this area made extra money by trapping animals and selling their skins. Teenagers socialized at church and at The Sugar Bowl, a little store / maltshop downtown. The town actually consisted of about 8 or ten stores. It was a tiny, tiny place.

Summer Grazing

Since the ranch was on the northern edge of a national forest, the government would grant grazing rights in the summer to areas basically inaccessible to the public. Phil and I got up early one clear, crisp morning and drove a huge tractor into this forest area. Our job for that day was to repair the barbed wire fence so that cattle could be herded up into the grasslands. This was some really beautiful country. I recall walking fences one day and coming upon a fawn lying perfectly still in the grass, it's only means of defense being it's camouflage coat.

In earlier times and before modern transportation, ranch hands would stay up in the hills the entire summer, so there was a cabin with all kinds of old-time canned goods. It was a real touch of Americana. I would have loved to have had some photos of this area.

I rode up the following day with Henry Finch, the owner. He had four-wheel drive pick-up and when we got up into the forest, on to the dirt road we'd been following, there was a place he wanted to go to, and he just turned into a growth of young saplings and started knocking them down with his truck - boom, boom, boom - we drove quite a ways up through this area until we reached a clearing. Well, *that* was different...

Small Town Life

All was not perfect in Smallville, though. Everyone knew dark secrets about everyone else, and it turned out it was a regular *Peyton Place*. If I would have lived here all my life, I supposed I would have been just as big a part of it. After all, besides pitching hay, there wasn't much else to do except gossip or do something to be gossiped about.

When I had a chance to do some exploring, I found that the ranch had several cabins on its several hundred acres. One was the original homestead cabin built by the ancestor of the present owners. I used to go over to these sites on my day off and just walk through them. I found old appliances and antiques that would have fetched quite a price anywhere else. They were just junk here. It was an amazing look at a fading way of life. From what I understand, all these ranches have been bought up by big corporations now, and the town is really in bad shape economically.

I Order TMR

A couple of time while in Wyoming I took a day and went into Rawlins, which was the nearest town of any great size. Anyway, I asked Joyce, my sister-in-law if there was a record store and she took me to one. I went in and ordered *Trout Mask Replica* from a guy who looked at me like I was from a different galaxy. He did have really nice snaps on his western shirt and his pointy-boots were shined to a proud glow. I had just had a wisdom tooth pulled, so I probably had a swollen jaw and I was still numb and could barely speak.

On our next trip to "the big city," I picked it up, paying, I think, $3.98 for the double album. As the cashier was ringing up the sale, I quickly ripped off the shrink wrap and opened it up. No picture of me was inside. Instead, The Mascara Snake was in there. I looked on the credits and found, not surprisingly, that I hadn't been credited with drumming on the project.

Years later, I received the following letter via beefheart.com

"I'm 41, a partner in a record shop in W. London, and my name is Bean for the obvious reason, almost. When I was a punk I did a fanzine called "Big Eyed Beans From Venus", but after 8 issues started changing the format and the name. It was "Electricity" for a while, ended up as "Suction Prints". People had started calling me Andy Bean by then anyway, and I eventually got it changed legally. I had the great pleasure of meeting Don on the first day of the Waddington gallery exhibition of '86, where he chatted with me and 3 or 4 other guys for about an hour and a quarter, despite Jan's efforts to get him to do more art-related things ("Not now, Jan, I'm talking to these guys!"). He was tolerant, considering we all wanted to talk about the music, and it was about 45 minutes before anyone got round to talking about his paintings! The highlight for me was when I asked why John French got no credit on Replica, to which he pointed to the "lurking under the bridge" shot on the back cover and said "That's SOME credit!" I have absolutely no idea what he meant by that."
Andy Bean

"Some credit" just means that he allowed my photo on the back cover. He didn't actually give me credit by name, but "allowed" my picture to be placed on the back cover. Needless to say, I was extremely disappointed. All that work - nearly a year of my life - and nothing at all to show for it. I took the album home and played it for my brother. I told him, "I arranged some of this music." To which he replied "this is arranged ?"

John French: What was your impression of the music on **Trout Mask Replica**?
Jim Sherwood: I loved it. I loved all of it. God, I mean, it was amazing. The time signatures were so different. When I saw him play, the drum signatures and the guitar signatures were completely different, but they went together. Frank told me that Don was actually playing piano at the time. He'd play the lines and show the guys and say, "This is how I want it played," and he'd sit on the drums and he'd play that, and sit on the keys and play this and say, "This is what I want played." I thought that was really great, because, his harmonica playing got really good.
JF: So, that's kind of the story that Don told Frank and Frank told you?

JS: *Yeah, Frank told me that Don would tell the guys exactly what he wanted played. Sometimes they'd demonstrate it on the instruments, or something like that.*

John Thomas: *Well, I also think that the music and the creativity came so much more easily to him and so it didn't seem so profound and earth shattering and convention- shaking as it did to someone like me who saw (the beauty) in his work. Like someone who didn't give a damn about what was on the radio and didn't give a damn about sweet lyrics in a song, but was writing something completely different. It was very off the wall and refreshing to me, but maybe it was natural and he couldn't see the profundity in it that I did. Because it was more (that) his everyday life was like that, and to me, it was delightful and refreshing. I could appreciate what he was giving away, and I say that for the whole band, because you guys all went through hell to produce something that I as a teenager listened to and laughed at. I said, "Listen to The Old Fart At Play, ha ha ha ha!"*

John French: *Someone asked me the other day if I could see the humor in what he was doing, and I couldn't see it* (Note: In the context of enjoying it). *I knew it was humorous, but it was a joke that I already knew the punch line to. I knew it was humorous, but the way it was conceived made me not like the way it was being presented. I didn't like the way I had been used and the way I felt. So, I couldn't laugh at it, and every time I heard it, I felt the way I did when it was recorded. Even five years later.*

JT: *You guys had more at stake than art. When I heard it, all I heard was the art. But you guys had your lives imbedded in it.*

JF: *Yeah.* (Mock announcer voice) *Try this! No security! Deplorable living conditions! Verbal and physical abuse!*

River Nearly Damns Me

One cold, windy and rainy morning, our pleasant task was to meet all the other ranchers in the area and dam the river up a bit higher. The river was dropping and the ranches weren't getting enough water.

I was up to my armpits in water, dragging branches and anything I could find up to the dam to divert a little more water to the side canal. I turned to face upstream again and was horrified to discover that 4 or five guys had managed to find a huge uprooted tree and it was coming sideways down the river straight at me. I did a slow-motion run in the water in an attempt to avoid a collision. When I realized I couldn't avoid it, I attempted to leap upon it . It merely turned, and the log rolled over me and pinned me to the bottom. I was helplessly trapped and couldn't move for some time. I felt somebody grip my arm and I was pulled free. I came up sputtering and gasping, "Thank you, thank you!" My rescuer was a huge obese gentleman with a kind face. He smiled and said, "It's OK."

It was a cold, windy rainy day, and I have never been much for being wet in the wind. My experience had left me shaking, because I actually thought I was going to die. I went back and sat in the pickup, shivering and feeling a little stupid. Everyone was very supportive, many came up to the window to make sure I was alright. I didn't meet many people in Encampment who had a macho chip on their shoulder. I was surprised to find that these people, unlike people in LA, were very concerned about each other. They accepted each other's strengths and weaknesses and tried their best to get along.

...o shot from 1970 with Don and Mark Boston.
...courtesy of Jim Marshall.

Back Home By Train

In the fall, I reluctantly said goodbye to this beautiful country and bought a train ticket home. We sat down for breakfast that morning for the last time, and Phil and Joyce looked at me and said, "We want you to stay."

"Thank you," I said, "But there's not much for me here." I knew that I had a different destiny to fulfill somewhere else.

I caught the train in Rawlins, the small town seventy miles or so to the North. My brother and his wife drove me to the station and saw me off. "Put most of your money in your sock," my brother advised, "That way, if they get your wallet, you still have most of your money."

The ride home was filled with expectations. I was in great physical condition. I had lost all my fat and was probably down to 155 or so. I had a lot of energy and a great desire to get on with my life. I would go to college, get a degree in something or other, and get on with my life. After all, I was still young.

I picked up a LIFE magazine at the LA Train Station. It had a huge mass of people on the cover. The article said "Woodstock." I hadn't heard a thing about it, so I bought the magazine. The only thing I knew about the music business was that the Stones guitarist Brian Jones had died.

Mothers Disband

In *The Real Frank Zappa Book*, FZ writes the following:

"I was paying everybody in the band a weekly salary of two hundred dollars - all year round, whether we were working or not, along with all hotel and travel expenses when we did get work. The guys in the band were pissed off - as if their welfare had been canceled - but at that point I was ten thousand dollars in the red." [52]

Frank decided to disband the Mothers Of Invention around this time. There were probably many reasons, and one was that Frank was a perfectionist, and wanted to play more challenging compositions. I had heard it said that his main thrust was to be a composer, and the Mothers was just a commercial enterprise to support his real ambition.

Jim Sherwood: One wrong note anywhere and the hair on the back of his neck stood up. The guy was just ... he wanted it played right. That was probably one of the main problems with the original Mothers, is because they'd get drunk and stoned and shit like this, fucking up his music, and he was getting tired of it.

There was apparently a party atmosphere in the band. A recent Don Preston interview explains in part that Frank broke up the group because he wasn't getting laid as much as the other guys and he also hired too many people to be able to afford.

John French: How did you feel about the disbanding of the original Mothers?
Jim Sherwood: I didn't think it was necessary. I think there could have been other ways around it. But I agreed with him. He said, "What we need to do is we're gonna break up for a while. What you need to do is go out, infiltrate other groups, get your music going that you wanna get going, and then we'll get back together later on, and we can put all that together." That's exactly what he told the band when it broke up. The Indian said, "Ah, man, we're making good fucking money now, why should we stop?" They didn't want to lose the money we were making. Frank says, "I'm sorry, I can't do it. If you guys can't go along with this, that's it. I've got to get out of it, I can't take it any more."

[52] The Real Frank Zappa Book, Frank Zappa, Simon and Schuster, 1989 pp 107

Blue Cross Drugstore

After coming back to Lancaster, I settled into my folk's garage room, the same one I had lived in when in high school. I went out looking for a job the day afterwards and found one that day. My first job was as a stock clerk in a small drug store. It paid minimum wage, but the district supervisor liked me. He wanted to make me the manager of the store. But, when it was found at the central office that I had been arrested for shoplifting, I was immediately fired. The supervisor told me to fill out another application and just leave off my arrest record. It didn't work - their bonding company wouldn't bond me. Later, I found the state would have bonded me and I could have continued with the job. At that time, I can't imagine how much harder it would have been for me had I been a black kid looking for work with a blemish on my record. I would have probably been ridden out of town on a rail.

Mission Linen Supply

My second job was at Mission Linen Supply as a janitor. It was a place that supplied uniforms, napkins towels and tablecloths to various restaurants and other places of business. They would collect all this stuff, launder it, and send it back. They had me walking around with a dust mop. I worked about three hours in the afternoon, and so I enrolled in Junior College, following a basic Liberal Arts program. I was going with a girl I will call Helen - the same girl who used to come visit me occasionally.

Mission Linen Supply fired me after about five weeks. In a conversation with one of the workers, I talked a little about my background. When my supervisor found out I had "once smoked marijuana" he started nitpicking my work. He found three spots back in corners where I had failed to use the dust mop one night, and fired me on the spot, no second chance. This was immediately after five weeks of not one complaint being spoken against me.

Lancaster Music

There were a couple of local old-time musicians who had opened a music store years before in Lancaster - the same place my father took me to buy my first set of new drums. Their names were Ronny Gaye and Bill Stewart. I went in and talked to Ronny, who was a former big band drummer. He said he'd hire me as a drum instructor. I said, "Great" and showed up the next day. It turned out it wasn't so great. He hired me for $1.25 an hour. I was teaching drums to about 25 kids a week. They each paid him $10 for a half an hour lesson. For each two lessons I gave, I got paid $1.25 while the store pulled in $20.

That wasn't the worst part. Ronny would pull me out of a lesson and have me doing sales during lessons, so the kid was essentially sitting in the little studio on his own two-thirds of the time while I was out helping customers and moving stock. Even worse, many of the kids had been taking lessons for a long time and couldn't even read the first page in the book! I always felt like I had treated people fairly, and I just could barely handle this kind of exploitation, but I did it for about three months or so. During Christmas time, and they had me delivering Spinet Pianos to people's homes *by myself!*

Rattlesnakes And Eggs

Helen, my girlfriend, got in a car accident one Friday evening while I was at work - the store stayed open until nine o'clock on Friday nights. I went to see her the next day and discovered her in a neck brace. I didn't find out until later that she was with some other guy when this happened. Her mother, who didn't really like me much, was actually upset with her for not telling me the truth. I found out later on by reading her journal. Oops. She should have put a lock on it.

She kept bugging me about not being "in music," as though that was the only thing that made me worth anything. I didn't want to be "in music" anymore, but she kept telling me I was a "real downer" and making me feel like a total nerd for wanting to just live a straight life and get an education. She liked "bad boys" and mistakenly thought I was one.

Finally, one night she persuaded me to go see some musicians who lived together up in Lake Hughes, a little resort area in a nearby valley. They were looking for a drummer. I think she had been talking to them about me. When we showed up, a guy named Marty Prue opened the door and said, "Hi John French, come in." We went in to this little house and there was a party going on. Marty had been in Viet Nam and was back from the war and going to school on the GI Bill. He was the brother of Pat Prue, the original drummer for The Omens.

The other members of the household were bassist Tim Meyer and his girlfriend Christina, her little boy Simon, and a trumpet player named Keith Kennedy. I hadn't been to a "normal" party like this for years. There was pot there, and like a fool, I smoked some. The stereo was playing an album by a group called Blood, Sweat, And Tears with their hit *Spinning Wheel*. I really liked horns (probably as a direct result of Alex Snouffer), so when I began listening to this music, I became really inspired to do some writing. I was no good with lyrics, but had some musical ideas. My friend, Dan Moore, was a writer of sorts, so I asked him to give me some of his poetry. I wrote some things to bits of words that I liked and he later revised the words to fit the music.

I played with these guys for a short time and recruited the services of a keyboardist named Jim Harper. Helen was ecstatic. I was now once again a "cool guy" and somebody worthy of her company. However, it was a bad road for me. Perhaps it was the marijuana, the combination of my bad experiences in the Magic Band, I don't know what, but I felt I was going back downhill a little bit at a time.

Jimmy's Surprise

Helen and I went to a night party up at the band's house. The band had adopted the name "Rattlesnakes and Eggs" a moniker thought up by Simon, the little boy who lived with the group. I used to look at him walking around and wonder what his future would be like. He was getting stoned on marijuana at four or five years old. This particular night, I had come not to play music, but to socialize. This was one of the popular hangouts for the local 'heads' (pot smokers) who needed some place to hang with the like-minded. There, sitting in the room, was Jeff Cotton. "John!" He said, "I was hoping I'd see you here." It was a really emotional moment for me and I asked him to come outside.

Jeff And Jeff, An Unstable Compound

I had not really heard any news of the band at all, but I was a bit curious as to what had transpired since my departure. Once I got past the initial emotional response of seeing my old high-school buddy and ex-cult-survivor I became curious and began asking Jeff questions. As I had surmised, Jeff Bruschele had joined the band to replace me. I knew that was in the works when I was there, so I was not surprised; it was totally predictable Don Van Vliet behavior to attempt a bone-headed stunt like that.

Unfortunately for Cotton, the "talks" continued to escalate in frequency and intensity, and one night, after Cotton was knocked to the floor, Bruschele walked up and kicked him in the ribs, breaking several and sending Jeff to the hospital.

Cotton's Ribs Kicked

Talking with Harkleroad, he couldn't remember if I left first, or Jeff. I told him I left first. Memories, as Doug Moon mentioned, have a way of playing tricks on us, but soon it started coming back to Bill.

John French: Yeah, it must have been three (or four) months later, because I saw (Jeff) in the fall after I came back from Wyoming, and he had his ribs broken ... he told me Jeff Bruschele had kicked him in the ribs.
Bill Harkleroad: That's right.
JF: And it was one of those "talks."
BH: Right, you got it.

Artie also confirms recalling this incident:

John French: So, Jeff Bruschele took my place as the drummer for a while and then, that didn't work out. I guess he had an altercation with Jeff Cotton, and kicked him and broke some of his ribs.
Art Tripp: Yeah, I remember about that, yeah.
JF: So, there was a lot of that kind of stuff going on in that house.
AT: I heard a lot about it, and it continued to a lesser degree for many years after that.

Seeing Jeff kind of shocked me and certainly took me out of the party mood. I asked Helen for the keys to her car, and Jeff and I sat in her yellow Mustang hardtop for quite some period of time talking about all the crap we had been through. It was like old times in a sense, to see Jeff again. We were able to speak freely and it was apparent that there were no hard feelings on either of our parts. We both knew that we weren't being ourselves in that group. This forgiveness on Jeff's part was a big relief to me.

Even though I had not partaken in any drugs that evening, the whole time I talked to Jeff, I kept seeing hallucinations of Navajo patterns rolling by - from top to bottom of my line of vision. I told Jeff about this and he said he saw them also.

I walked back in the house after a couple of hours and Helen was sitting next to some guy who had his arm around her. She got up quickly and came over to me, but she was upset with me for leaving her. I apologized, and told her that Jeff and I had a lot of catching up to do. I hadn't told her (nor anyone) much about the bad things that had happened in the Trout House.

Jeff came back into town with Helen and I and I drove Jeff home in my little Datsun I had just bought. We met the next day at his folk's mobile home, where he was staying, and talked more. Jeff wanted to start a group with me, but I told him I thought it was a bad idea. We had too much history together. I said I thought it would be better for us to go in different directions, which was too bad.

Art Joining Band
Art started spending more time up at the Trout House, mostly talking with Don. He used the same term Jerry Handley used and said Don was "romancing" him. Don probably realized Artie was a talented and trained musician who already had a name playing with the Mothers and so would be an asset to him. He probably figured that Artie's musical training would be a plus in terms of his ability to play more difficult passages. Plus, he was a little closer to Don's age.

Artie was fed-up with the Mothers by this time and Frank had pretty much broken up the band as Artie had known it. So, Tripp was looking around and definitely in "what next" mode. Don sensed this, and probably because of his own frustration/jealousy the two of them found a common bond in their dislike of Frank.

Art Tripp: I was looking around. I was sick of the Mothers, I was sick of the business part of it. ... I didn't see any future in it. Frank had pretty much broken up the band as I had known it, which I had really liked, and I didn't see any reason for it, and didn't agree with it, but he had the control. I was just disgusted with the whole thing.

Zubin Mehta / LA Philharmonic

Art Tripp: In fact, at that time, Frank and (The Mothers) and some other guys had started in rehearsal for this big concert he was going to do over at UCLA with Zubin Mehta.
John French: Right, 200 Motels.
AT: Yeah - a lot of the music that became that - he had been writing for years. At any rate, I didn't want any part of it, I thought, "Fuck it!" It was interesting to do that kind of show, but I thought, "Piss on it." As far as I was concerned, he owed me money and it wasn't happening.

It is obvious from Art's choice of words that he had become very disillusioned and jaded by his experience with The Mothers. When things began changing, first with Ray leaving, then later with the introduction of new members, it became an uncomfortable environment in which Tripp found himself dissatisfied.

Art Tripp: Then, as a sidebar, Frank had started what he called his little "power quartet." Which I don't know if you even remember, it was - Frank was going to play guitar and sing and all that shit. Ian played piano and horns. I was going to play drums. Instead of getting Roy, he got … I think his name was Jeff Simmons or something.
John French: Oh, I remember, yeah.
AT: Who was an accomplished rock singer and bass player. I couldn't stand this motherfucker. He made my skin crawl. He was one of these oodly-coo you know, feather boa type kitschy rock players at the time. Kind of a Jimi Hendrix imitator…
JF: A glamour rock kind of guy?
AT: Yeah, and I just couldn't stand this guy. He was obnoxious and he was stupid. So here's this guy playing bass, and I was playing drums and we started rehearsals. Frank and Herbie rented this rehearsal space down on La Brea somewhere and we started rehearsing and it was like pulling teeth. I couldn't stand it. Of course, Ian - nothing ever stuck on Ian - he just didn't let anything bother him. He was just playing the music. I kept calling him and I would say, "Ian, I hate this fucking guy. I can't stand this!" So about that time, I'd been hanging around out there at Ensenada there with Don and everybody. I thought, "Maybe there's something there." I kept expressing my opinion to Don on this. I said, "I'm fed up with Zappa and this whole thing." So Don really could see the advantage of that, I'm sure. He thought, "Well, hell, this guy used to play with the Mothers," and maybe he thought I would add some notoriety to the band and - I don't know what he was thinking, but I am sure it something along those lines. Plus, we got along real well together.
JF: Was Jeff playing in the band - Jeff Bruschele - was he playing in the band, or was he gone by this time.
AT: He might have been, originally, doing a little. Simmons was gone, or what was his name? Semens, Jeff uh….
JF: Antennae Jimmy Semens? - Jeff Cotton.
AT: Jeff Cotton, yeah. He had ridden off into the sunset, too, I think.

Note: Don later said to me of the choice Zappa had made in getting Jeff Simmons was that Frank was trying to copy him by getting a guy whose name sounded like Jeff "Antennae Jimmy Semens" Cotton.

Rosh Hoshanah / Yom Kippur

Meanwhile with me, it was during this time that Helen's (who was Jewish) parents were probably (and reluctantly) starting to think that it was time to initiate me into the first layer of traditional Judaism. Being as how I had a Christian background, I found this fascinating. My first experience was being invited to some kind of atonement service which I remember being called Rosh Hoshanah. This was a time of fasting (which nobody actually seemed to do) and prayer, a time of repentance and cleansing the soul of sin. The culmination of which was Yom Kippur, which, if memory serves, is the Jewish New Year. The Yom Kippur service, as I recall, was a feast at the end of the previous fasting, and a celebration of the cleansing and fresh start.

Traditional Americans do this differently. We stuff our selves with food and candy like pigs from Thanksgiving thru to New Year's Eve. Then, New Years Day, we make our resolutions (exercise, dieting, abstinence etc.) and start our "fast" and "repentance" - which usually lasts 3-5 days.

I found the Jewish experience enlightening to say the least. I was now looking at the tapestry from behind, in a sense, and viewing my own religious roots from the other side. It was interesting how compatible the various aspects of the celebrations and feasts fit together with what Christians later came to view as "symbols," and foundational principles of their own doctrines.

I look back and realize that I was probably being (reluctantly) groomed to enter the world of traditional Judaism by Helen's parents because of the strong possibility of marriage between Helen and myself. Of course, I'll never forget this wonderful girl, but we eventually wound up finding separate paths. Ironically, she eventually converted to Christianity.

Mike Glick

At this Yom Kippur service, during the big feast that they had, I met a saxophonist named Mike Glick - all of seventeen years old. He and his family had just moved from New York - Brooklyn I believe. We talked about music and made plans to jam together sometime.

Junior Woodstock

R&E had a little daytime outdoor party one relatively warm weekend. It was like a mini "festival" and about 200 hippies showed up to drink wine, smoke weed and listen to musicians jamming and local bands performing. Helen and I rode out about mid-morning with a drummer friend, Randy Wimer, and there were already a lot of hippies there. I hadn't expected to see so many "lodos" awake that early in the day. A guy named Tom Bryden came walking by Helen and I with a flute in his hand. He looked at us with a big grin and said, "Hi" really friendly. Helen immediately looked at me and said, very emphatically, "That guy's *crazy*!" Randy Wimer set up his drums - a brand new black set of Rogers, and we jammed all day. Randy was working with Merrel Fankhauser, the founder of MU.

Years later, I wound up buying Randy's drums from a third party and I played them for years.

Charts

I borrowed a Wurlitzer portable piano from my keyboardist friend Jim Harper and started writing charts for songs I was writing with Dan Moore. I was really unhappy with my rip-off job, and I absolutely hated school. Even though I studied *The History Of Western Civilization* with all my might, the best I could do on any test was a D. I fell asleep during lectures, once literally falling out of my chair, as the lecturer, Mr. Rogan, droned on. I was miserable. The charts I did were pretty primitive, but I was only writing for a 4-piece group; Guitar, Bass, Trumpet and drums. It was a challenge to see how much sound I could get out of four instruments.

These guys all sang pretty well, so we worked out harmonies to make the music work. It was pretty serious stuff, though, and almost sounded a little "jazzy" to my ear. We put together four songs of mine, *Reign Of Pain, Purple Hours, Father Of Lies,* and *Countin' The Rings* together, plus a song Keith Kennedy had written called *Hidden Faces.*

Somebody (I think Tim Meyer, the bassist) booked us at a little free college show featuring the Vicki Senseman dancers. Vicki's husband was Al Senseman and he was running sound. He looked so much older than Vicki that I asked "are you the dance teacher's father?" - which of course immediately made us best of friends. The girls quickly worked out routines to these songs and we played for a small audience. I was surprised that the music was actually fairly well-received.

The JC Blues

School was really boring. I hated it, and started cutting more and more classes. I quit my job out of disgust and because they wouldn't pay me for lessons. Most teachers who teach get most of the money for the lessons and pay the store a room rental fee. I was still staying in my folk's garage writing more music. During Christmas Holiday (this was before it became "Winter Break") I wound up with a pretty bad case of pneumonia from smoking a whole carton of cigarettes in three days while writing a piano song. It was more like soundtrack music.

On The Cover Of The Rolling Stone

I was sitting in the Junior College cafeteria one day in early 1970 and one of the band guys handed me a Rolling Stone magazine with Don's picture on the cover. I was impressed. I really didn't think *Trout Mask* would ever receive this much recognition. I was also furious. It was only Don's picture, and that band deserved just as much to be on the cover as Don did. I supposed I could be considered along the same lines as the character in the film Galaxy Quest who keeps saying to the Captain, "Oh yes, it's always all about YOU isn't it?"

However, I hope from what I've previously written you can see that *Trout Mask Replica* would never have existed had it not been for the group effort involved. All those guys worked so hard. I recall Zappa always allowing his band to be fairly high profile, and I really believe it helped them in post Zappa years to make other connections more quickly. Also, in my opinion, it made Zappa even more popular, because he gave his musicians more recognition and it made the shows stronger.

I opened the magazine and read the article. Then, I became livid. The article was comprised of an interview almost entirely with Don, and it contained serious fabrications and exaggerations, which not only exalted him to a position far higher than he deserved, but also belittled the players. I must remind the reader here that this was a serious investment of time for these people, not to mention the degrading and almost inhumane circumstances involved in the process. Also, the music business is just that - a business, and in order to survive in the industry, a player must seek to receive as much exposure as possible. These guys were getting zilch.

It was very interesting for me to see things so objectively. I had been away from Don's indoctrination process for almost a year, so I was thinking much more clearly now than ever before. The constant repetition of lies had faded out of my life. I no longer considered myself worthless and stupid. I knew I had creative abilities of my own. The separation had given me a much clearer vision of what Van Vliet was about, and how gigantic his ego actually was. Not only that, but the ruthlessness with which he established these fabrications was just unbelievable. What did the guys in the band think when they read this stuff?

Meanwhile Back At The Trout House

Since I was not in the band at the time, I can only go by the information I derived from interviews with Art, Bill, and Mark, and from my conversation many years ago with Jeff Cotton. I wasn't surprised to find that Jeff Bruschele had been my drum replacement. There isn't much information on this particular period, so some of it I will try to reconstruct just using timelines and such. I left the band back in May of 1969.

I went to Wyoming in June. Bruschele must have joined shortly after I left. Cotton was out of the band by that next fall. Amougies Festival in Belgium, in which Frank hosted and also jammed with TMB was in October, so Art Tripp hadn't entered the picture yet, at least as a band member. Bill Harkleroad unbelievingly enough, learned to play both guitar parts simultaneously on a few songs for Amougies (October 24-28th 1969), which must have taken him several weeks, and there's no telling how long Cotton was in the desert before I saw him at the party, but as I recall, it had just been recently, as he was still taped up with broken ribs.

So, Bruschele was probably in by mid to late May and Cotton was out by early fall - shortly after the Mothers disbanded. Usually, festivals like Amougies are booked months in advance, but I had never heard of it until after the fact. Since Amougies Festival was late October, Bill was probably working on dual-guitar parts September through late October 1969.

Artie Tripp And The Magic

Artie had been visiting the Trout House and had noted that Zoot had taken over my role as musical director by that point. For a time, Ian Underwood was considering playing guitar as a replacement for Jeff Cotton. Van Vliet's paranoia soon kicked in.

Art Tripp: The way Don tells it, Frank had sent Ian out to spy on him. But I think in actual fact, Ian was just interested. Ian is a great - he's interested in anything musically, and he certainly was at that time. He was just like an open book and he just wanted to learn everything. So, he came out and Bill was teaching him to play guitar and I guess the "plan B" anyway was to get him to play guitar good enough to play in the band, and then they'd have this good musician in the band etc.

Don later told me that Ian would have to stop practicing and go downstairs to lie down and rest because learning the music was giving him headaches. I imagine, however, that the truth was that Ian was picking up on the "cult" situation and it was probably affecting him. Frank, I doubt, needed to spy on Don, he was always busy creating his own music. So, the rivalry between Frank and Don was back - at least on Don's part.

Tom Grasso

Around the time Ian was learning guitar, a keyboardist named Tom Grasso also joined the group for a short time. Don later referred to the guy who owned the piano as an "existentialist who wore Lennon glasses."

Art Tripp: We had this band that consisted of Bill and Mark, and of course, Don (and) me. Ian was trying to learn guitar. ... We had Tom Grasso playing piano. I still wasn't doing much playing. I was doing about as much playing as Don was singing. He almost never sang, and that really came to a head in later years. But at that time, he was virtually doing nothing except bullshitting and working with Bill at night. It was just like "a scene." I mean, there was all this talent there, there was all this music there, but nothing ever got done. So, then we started in rehearsal with Grasso, and Grasso was a very strong personality. He was a very self-willed guy and of course, so was Don. So they got into a beef really quick.
JF: Right, there's an accident waiting to happen.
AT: Yeah, they got into a beef relatively early on and they had a big argument one day and Don kind of put the challenge to Tom, like, "If you don't like it, get out." and he said, "Well that's pretty easy, fuck you" and he left - that was it.

Thee Experience - 1969

Art Tripp kept telling Don that he would join the group and accept Don's invitation, but he wanted something really solid (like any thing in music is ever solid) and that he wanted to make some money (like anybody would ever make any money). He wanted to tour and record. Don assured him, as he always did everyone, that this was all going to happen.

Art Tripp: Oh, yeah, absolutely, I said, "Yeah, I'd like to do that," so eventually, I did. Actually, we had played a gig together. … This little quartet that Frank had put together were supposed to do a gig, I don't know what (the group) was called, Zappa or something. Beefheart and the Magic Band and (Zappa) were going to do this gig at Thee Experience on the east Sunset Strip there, Marshall Brevitz' place. … That was the one and only gig that the Zappa contingent played, and I was playing with him and with Beefheart. We both did, in fact that was the first time I ever really played with Beefheart.

"Thee Experience was a small nightclub located on the very east end of the Sunset Strip at 7551 Sunset Boulevard in Los Angeles, California. The nightclub opened and closed in 1969, and featured some of the best cult and legendary groups of the 1960's including Alice Cooper, Captain Beefheart, Big Mama Thornton, Frank Zappa, Delaney and Bonnie and many more. The shortlived club was briefly famous for its psychedelic façade featuring Jimi Hendrix." - *Jacob Grossi* [53]

Art sat in a month after Amougies Festival. Bruschele was no longer drumming. November 28th and 9th and December 4th, 5th, and 6th were the nights they played, according to Theo Tieman's website.

John French: Wasn't that sort of the beginning of when Rockette Morton started doing his stage stuff with the bass solos and such?
Art Tripp: Maybe, that's very possible.

I heard from Bill at the time that Mark had turned into a phenomenal performer and really won the crowd. Don had Mark play the parts from *Hair Pie* as a solo. I recall that occasionally at the Trout House, Don would have one person play his parts for everyone else, and Mark was always really good at this, moving around like a rubber man. He was extremely entertaining to watch. This was one of the really constructive things Don would do, as it forced everyone to perform in front of an audience and gave us more confidence.

Tripp, however, was just responding to the music and hadn't really learned my drum parts.

Art Tripp: But here they're playing music that they are familiar with and I had never played before. So, I was just playing anything that sounded right to me. I wasn't playing "the parts." I didn't even know what I was expected to do. … Anyway, so that gig ended and that was it. I didn't want anything more to do with Zappa. That's when I decided to join up with Don and the other guys.

In an email, Tripp elaborated on Thee Experience.
"Thee Experience as you know was a rock club on the East Sunset Strip which was owned by Marshall Brevitz (sp). Marshall had owned a club of the same name (although much larger) in Miami, which had been named after Jimi Hendrix's band. We played at the Miami club a couple of times when I was with the Mothers Of Invention, and had a ball. As you recall the Hollywood

---

[53] http://www.concertposterart.com/article/display/Thee-Experience-Los-Angeles-California

club didn't so much have major names booked there as it did have major names getting fucked-up there. It was usually crowded, but had a western openness about it, in contrast to some of the stuck-up rock joints in London like the Speakeasy. Fortunately for us in the biz, but unfortunately for Marshall, he let a lot of us run bar tabs, if he accounted for it at all." "I remember sitting with Hendrix one night trying to have a conversation with him, but he was in such a heroin/alcohol stupor he was totally unaware of what part of the world he was in. Well we were all pretty pathetic, but we were 'HIP.' I had a long conversation with Joe Cocker one night before he became a huge rock star. I was impressed with his intelligence and insights. I believe he was a big fan of both Zappa and Beefheart." "The house was packed one night for a show by the Bonzo Dog Doo Dah Band, and I'm surprised anyone survived to remember. It was the single most hilarious act I've ever seen - full of "in" jokes and riotously funny material. People (myself included) were literally falling to the floor laughing. Not too long afterward Neil Reschen (sp), who managed them - and also had reportedly bilked Herbie and Zappa's management company out of a million bucks - asked me if I would like to join the band. Maybe the drummer had left, or whatever. I seriously thought about it, but the band wasn't making much money, and I was reluctant to get involved with Neil. I think they eventually disbanded. Musically they weren't first rate, but man what shows they put on." "Thee Experience didn't last too long- a year or two at the outside, I think. In the meantime we all moved to Felton. I later heard that Marshall came to a sorry end. I think the partying, drugs, and shady business dealings caught up with him. It's funny how a lot of people from that era really believed that flower-power hippy horseshit. Many of them went down hard. The ones still alive are now screwing up society for the rest of us. They dominate Hollywood, the media, politics, and even the courts - the proud tradition of Woodstock. Oh well, the South shall rise again."

The timeline is just right. Jimi Hendrix had rented a house in Benedict Canyon in October to take a break from touring. In between recording sessions at TTG studios, evenings were spent at the Whiskey A Go Go. Thee Experience opened up, and Jimi, hearing that the Whiskey had blacklisted all musicians who played at Thee Experience, played an entire week at Thee Experience, and with radio coverage, helped to keep the club afloat for a time. Hendrix allowed Brevitz to keep all cover charges.

Return To Trout House

Back in Lancaster, Helen had gone to New York to see the sights and came back with a slightly snobbish view telling me that nothing I did was "inspirational." It was probably about this time (in actually a non-related thought process) that I decided I was going to go get my drums back. I had just recovered from pneumonia. I got up in the middle of the night and drove down to the Trout House in my little 1960 Datsun sedan (try to find one of those). I parked up in the driveway behind the house, knocked on the kitchen door. No reply. I knocked again, harder. Again, no response. I knocked harder with my fist, and Don answered the door in his pajamas.

He seemed happy to see me, and I told him right off that I was there to get my drums. He said, "OK" and quickly changed the subject. This was in January of 1970 - right after the New Year. Don said, "Wait a minute" and left the room. I looked around the dark house and was struck by the change. Perhaps because I hadn't seen the place for several months (seven, in my best estimation) I was looking more closely than before but, no, this place was a pigsty.

Everything had been written on or drawn on in felt pen by Don. There was a big painting hung over the window in the kitchen, which made it dark and dreary. When I first looked, it looked as though it was painted on an old twin-sized mattress, because the frame was so wide. On closer scrutiny, it was actually canvas very poorly stretched. The painting, I later found out, was entitled "Bub n' Gil" and was a hard-edged cartoon-like black and white.

On the refrigerator (or was it the shower stall?) was written the phrase "I'm going to leave this old piece of toast, the center ain't got no nutrition." The kitchen cabinet doors all had Van Vliet originals painted on them. The living room had the old upright piano, but in the corner where the stereo had been now sat a baby grand. This turned out to belong to Tom Grasso as Art Tripp recalled.

A drumset - mine - sat in almost the same place as I usually had put them. Jeff Bruschele or Victor Hayden had covered them with artist's canvas on which they had traced the cartoon landscape from a child's sand sifter. This was something I'd previously talked to Don about doing with the set.

There were also several guitar amps that left barely any foot room. The living room also seemed dark and dreary, the windows, stuffed with squares of foam rubber, almost had a "boarded-up" look, like these people were living in the *Night Of The Living Dead* or something. It was an eerie feeling walking back into this environment, and having it so radically changed. It was as though the dysfunctional housekeeper had become non-functional and all sense of even partial order had ceased,

All of a sudden this beautiful, exquisite creature walked out next to Don with a wonderful smile. "This is Jan," Don said, quite lovingly. "You don't have your shoes on Jan and it's cold," he said and ran off to the other room to get her shoes. "He must be in love," I thought, "I've never seen him do anything for anyone before." I actually have to say that I was a little self-conscious standing there with this beautiful girl who I had just met smiling at me. She was wearing a mid-thigh white nightgown or shift and was very quiet. Don returned. "Turn around for John," he said, and she obliged by elegantly striking a toreador-like model's pose with her arms and slowly turning, as though modeling the most elegant gown, all the time smiling. Don and I talked, had tea, and of course, he was very cordial to me, probably because his fiance was sitting right there with us. In fact, at a later point in time, he accused me of coming down to get my drums at this strategic point because I knew he couldn't do anything about it. It would have been hard to plan, since I knew nothing about his life.

Jan left the room for a few minutes and he walked up to me closely and in a very-audible but suppressed voice inquired, "What do you think, man?" I said, "She's beautiful, Don, congratulations."

In a very slow emphatic whisper, he announced, "She's nineteen years old!"

"No more than a baby-child," I added, completing the line from the popular Muddy Waters' song. He then asked me if I remembered in his writings about the Drazy Hoops and all the other non-published stuff he wrote if I recalled the character simply referred to as "the girl who smiled a lot?" I said, "Yeah."

"That's her, man! I foretold her arrival!" he told me excitedly. I never checked her ID, but I don't think it said "the girl who smiled a lot." That description could have as easily fit Pamela Des Barres, who had a beautiful smile and was always smiling.

However, the marriage did last. As far as I know, they are still married.

Don Aldridge: (on marriage to Jan) That one sure lasted didn't it?
John French: Yes, it's lasted a long time. I think that - it didn't stabilize him at first - but eventually did. I think that mended that love relationship that he had before, with this girl where the parents cut it off. I think Jan was the person who fulfilled that emptiness. He was much more of a human being with her than I had ever seen him be.

Jan And Laurie's Accident

I believe Don must have been close to his 29th birthday, since it was January of 1970. He told me a little story about Jan and Laurie going down to get some food at the market. They had taken the Volvo, and Don said that shortly after they left, he had a premonition of danger and prayed, "God, help them." He said they rear-ended a car that stopped abruptly in front of them, or perhaps had been rear-ended by another car. He claims he "saw" the accident in his mind as it happened and he saw them "go back" instead of forward in the seats. However, Jan had suffered a hip and lower back injury as a result which gave her trouble for years.

A Little Jam Session

Jan disappeared to the bedroom, and Don looked at me and gestured toward the drums. "Wanna play?" he asked. "Sure," I replied and took the drummers throne. The first thing that struck me was how big the sticks were. "Who uses these?" I inquired. "Oh, that's Art Tripp, he's the drummer now." I couldn't believe he would use such gigantic sticks. They were actually the biggest sticks you could buy, the size was 3S. The "S" stood for "Street" and they were parade-drum sticks, usually used outside on those drums you carry on the leg with a shoulder strap.
Don sat at the baby-grand and we played for about 20 minutes or so, just random free-playing, which is really the only thing Don could do on the piano. It felt good to be on my own drums again, but the music didn't really thrill me. I liked arranged things with substance, this was almost more like noise.

"Geez guys, it's a little early isn't it?" came a muffled, drowsy voice from the stairwell. I recognized the voice as Bill Harkleroad's.
"Hi Bill, how're you?" I greeted him.
"John, wow, what're you doin' here?" he asked
"I came down to get my drums." I said bluntly, determined.
Don quickly changed the subject, asking Bill to play a tape for me of some song he had written. Jan returned and they went into the kitchen and Bill and I talked a bit. I recall walking over to the upright, which I believe had the recorder and everything sitting on top, and picking up a script entitled *Alice In Blunderland*. "It's an opera, Don's writing a rock opera. He's going to play God." "Isn't this what he's been doing all along?" I sarcastically thought to myself. I read a couple lines of dialogue from the script, closed it and laid it back down.

Art Tripp: So, I was coming out during that (time). I really had never played. It was so easy for a rehearsal or a get-together to just turn into a "bullshit session." Which would go on - you know - for days. So, I never did any playing, really. ... They'd play a few things and just ... we'd kinda start working, you know, he was working on some new stuff for a new album.
John French: Wasn't he doing an opera? Or he was thinking about it? - and Alice In Blunderland was part of that?
AT: Yeah!
JF: And he was going to be in it, playing "God?"
AT: Yeah, It was called Alice In Blunderland, and then I think later he was going to change it to The Bread Eaters. In fact, at that time, I had a gig playing with The Smothers Brothers. They were doing a summer special, and I got hired to play percussion on it. I remember that because when we played the gig, I met Tom and Dick. I approached (Dick) about possibly financially sponsoring this project. It was an interesting concept, which, obviously the time was right for it because look what happened with Tommy! Of course, that was a much better-conceived-and-carried-out plan - and much better music as far as mass consumption. It seemed to me that I wrote down a lot of the music for it. Some of the music just turned out to be ideas. It really wasn't tunes - maybe a little sketch. There was no limit to the stage action. He could just do that having a cup of coffee. He could just lay out opera after opera after opera - with Don's fertile mind.

Bill turned on the machine, and I heard the song *Alice in Blunderland*. I was surprised. This was a normal instrumental song, like you might hear on the radio. It had sections that were a little non-commercial and one that came directly out of *Big Black Baby Shoes*, but at a faster tempo. I asked Bill who was playing besides he and Mark. *"That's Art Tripp* on drums and Elliot Ingber playing lead."

My memory kicked in: "Elliot Ingber, oh yeah, he was the guy Don first approached to replace Ry Cooder," I recalled. After Ry quit in Spring of 1967, we had gone to the old Tom Mix cabin (pre-Zappa) and in one of the bedrooms was Elliot with his band Fraternity Of Man, playing powerful lead guitar at extremely high volume. Elliot Ingber always looked like "King Neptune" to me. It was the curly hair and the long beard. He had appeared in the movie *I Love You Alice B. Toklas* as the "Rent-a-freak" as he put it. No dialogue, just sitting on the bathroom counter moving his head in faux LSD-meditation posture. Also, it seemed he had written that song that was used in the film *Easy Rider* - yeah, *Don't Bogart That Joint My Friend*. That's a funny line. It was a country-type tune.

"Gee, Bill, this song sounds dangerously similar to something that could actually make money." I said half-jokingly. "You wouldn't want that to happen now, would you? That would be copping out according to all those stupid music critics who get paid by the word." We laughed. Bill said something like, "Yeah, wouldn't want anything catastrophic like that to happen now, would we?"

After this slightly cynical exchange, Don called in from the other room, "Play it again, Bill. I'm writing words" We looked out into the kitchen. Jan was sitting on the counter facing the back door, and Don was standing in front of her, and they were hugging and kissing like a couple of kids at a make-out party. "OK lovebirds," Bill returned, "but this is the last time, I just got up ya know." I was surprised to hear this kind of exchange between Don and anyone. It was obvious that Don was deeply in love, and had lightened up quite a bit - at least for a time. I was happy for him. I was also happy for all those who had to be around him. What a relief it must be.

Don and Jan both left the room eventually. As Don left, he told me that he and Jan were going down to get their marriage license. "Here's our engagement ring," he said, and tossed me a sealed can of cake frosting. I caught the can and held it. Stuff like this didn't surprise me after having lived with Don for nearly three years.

Bill and I talked and caught up on things a bit, and in a little while Mark Boston came upstairs and I was a little surprised at his appearance. Bill had looked pretty much the same. Mark looked quite different. His hair was a lot longer and he actually looked more like I had looked before I left. His beard and hair were long and his demeanor and countenance even had changed. I thought about this for a minute. When I left the band, he had only been in the group maybe five or six months at the most. Now, it had been probably thirteen or fourteen months, and Don's "environment" had probably affected him more. He seemed a lot more mature and independent, but also darker, moodier.

We all talked for quite a while. Eventually, Don and Jan left. I started packing up the drums. Bill asked what I was doing and I said, "I'm taking my drums, Bill - you know they're mine, so don't argue with me." I already knew that Bill and Mark were probably going to catch hell for letting me walk out of here with my drums, but I was determined to get my property, even if I had to fight them both. Mark conceded pretty quickly, but Bill seemed pretty determined. I stopped what I was doing, walked up and looked him right in the eye. "Bill, you know these are my drums and that I have a perfect right to them." He looked at me and smiled, "You're right, John." I could tell he was torn between respect for his friend and what was right, and Don's inevitable unreasonable reaction - which he would have to deal with later.

Bill and I always had a special comradeship between us. Even in the band, it was as though we both knew what a joke a lot of the fighting was. Although we were caught in an absurd current of psychodrama and, mysteriously couldn't seem to make it to shore, we both seemed to have a perspective with each other whenever we made eye contact. I knew Bill was going to be under "The Wrath of Don" for allowing me to have my drums, but I knew he didn't care. A dark-haired beauty of a girl with Hispanic features came upstairs. Bill introduced her, but I don't remember her name. She was his girlfriend. I took the drums out and loaded them in the car, only to find out they wouldn't fit. Bill and Mark came out and talked to me while I was working on this problem. It was like we were friends again and we just talked about crazy stuff that twenty-year-old guys talk about; girls, music, cars, movies, etc. I finally figured out how to get the drums in the car. I had to take a wrench and remove the door from the car, put the bass drum case in, and then replace the door. We all laughed at the size of this car and the size of these drums. I had to move the seat all the way forward, which put my chest almost into the steering wheel. I bid the guys farewell, and left, with my drums; my nose almost touching the windshield.

Laurie's Special New Home

Mark Boston had started seeing Laurie shortly after Don booted her out to form a relationship with Jan. He felt sorry for her, as I imagined did we all. Laurie was like our sister. We all loved her and had bonds that last for me to this day. She was now temporarily living with Don's mother, Sue, and grandmother, Granny Annie in a tiny apartment a block from my parent's house.

I remember going down and seeing her a few times. We would sit outside and talk. She was still friendly to me, but I could tell she was deeply hurt and really unhappy about where she wound up. She had nothing, no resources, no job, and no direction. I think she just felt totally lost. One day, she was just sitting staring at the wall of the apartment with the hose running. She had flooded the lawn and all the earthworms were crawling up the wall, making for dry land. Sue Vliet came home from work and said, in a sweet tone, "You need to shut of the water, honey, you're making the worms come out." Laurie spat back, "I'm doing it on purpose because I like seeing them trying to escape and save their lives."

I think Laurie must have had a lot of anger brewing in her soul during this period. One day, Mark showed up and they embraced and he asked how she was, etc. Then, he gave her some money. I left shortly after this to give them some privacy. What a strange turn of events.

Artie's View Of What Happened

Artie was doing a few gigs here and there - like the Smothers Brothers Summer Special - had some savings, used a credit card, and hustled a bit of pool to keep afloat. He did almost no playing whatsoever at the Trout House during his tenure as drummer. They recorded the *Alice In Blunderland* piece that I remember hearing, and also it seems I recall hearing *Flash Gordon's Ape* with Artie playing a very conventional type of rock beat, but with his own wonderful touch.

He had taken his snare out to the house, as mine had been stolen in my absence, but other than that, he just used my old Gretsch Set. Though officially a member of the band, nothing seemed to be getting done. He sat while Bill and Mark learned parts from tapes and Don would "coach" them on nuance.

Art Tripp: I wasn't playing anything. I am sitting in on these rehearsals. And when asked I'm offering my comments, or sometimes when I wasn't asked. But I really hadn't played except for a real little bit.

Mark And Bill Live With Artie

Mark and Bill sometime between January and April or May of 1970 moved into Art Tripp's spare bedroom in Laurel Canyon. It was coincidentally a similar kind of floor plan as the Trout House;

split level, with the spare bedroom downstairs and the bulk of the house above. There was an entranceway and a big stairway to the upstairs, with a wall separating the stairwell from the downstairs spare bedroom. The upstairs was two bedrooms, a bath, a nice-sized living room, and kitchen.

This may have been after I took my drums. Artie had his drums set up downstairs and perhaps decided that rather than moving all his gear, why didn't Mark and Bill live there so they could keep rehearsing. This also gave the newly-married Don and Jan some privacy.

Tripp To Be "Drumbo #3 (Or Perhaps "Erasure?")

Tripp was a bit bewildered and befuddled by exactly what Don expected him to play to the music. The drum parts for the most part weren't written out.

Art Tripp: Everytime that we played something, I would just play whatever I thought sounded good, which was pretty weird shit. It was totally different than the parts you were playing which were fantastic - just unbelievably well-written. I mean just really great stuff - the drums parts - to this day, I think that.
John French: Thank you.

No one actually ever told Art that he was expected to learn my parts. They insinuated this, but it never really was forced. No one here seemed to be communicating. I think part of the problem was that Don didn't know how to relate to a musician who wasn't embedded with the cult-programming, so he was a little helpless.

Art Tripp: So, as a result. I did nothing. So, we would have these rehearsals and maybe everybody else would play and I wouldn't. So I thought, "this is going nowhere." I went on with my life. Don could just never come out and say, "I want you to play like this - in a tune already established in the band repertoire - I want you to play John French's drum part."

Don would send Mark over to Artie's with tapes. They were instrumental tapes of the *Trout Mask* sessions, and separated drum tapes and it was implied that Artie should learn the parts.

John French: What were these tapes?
Art Tripp: I don't know, they were probably Trout Mask!
JF: Were they just drums or were they the whole thing.
AT: The whole thing at that time. I think it was the whole band.

I did for years have a set of tapes of the separated parts of the drum parts to *TMR* that I had gotten from Don. They were run off for whatever drummer replaced me to learn the parts from.

Art Tripp: The kind of drumming I was interested in was along the lines of Japan In A Dishpan. *Incidentally, the cut that made it to the album was not my favorite. I loved the album, but I can still to this day shake my head when I recall that Decals was supposed to be a commercial attempt. Jesus!*

What Is The Other Story

Art Tripp: There became a separation, and Don wasn't out front enough to say, "Either do this or we can't use you." And nobody else said that...

This is a strange behavior pattern I had noticed early on in Don. He never summoned the courage to fire Doug Moon back in the *Safe As Milk* days, but instead had Krasnow do the dirty work. He didn't tell Gary Marker that Buddah had chosen another producer after promising Marker the job for getting Ry in the group. Neither did he summon the courage to defend Marker at the board meeting. Perhaps the reason for the "encounter group / cult" atmosphere was in order to achieve the kind of control that would not require the usual amount of courage to confront an awkward situation.

It takes far less courage to confront someone who has been broken down and humiliated. There's not nearly as much valor needed to order someone to do something when their ego is crushed on the floor and their esteem is shattered. The normal way to confront this situation as leader of the group would have been to take Artie aside, and explain that he needed to study and learn the drum parts written as best he could because the material had already been recorded.

Sayonara Bill And Mark

After a period of time had passed - I'm guessing a few months, as no one seemed to recall the actual dates - Bill and Mark moved out of Artie's spare room.

Art Tripp: So, I came home one evening, and everybody's moved out. Nobody said anything to me. So, I thought, "that's interesting," I didn't know what the hell was going on, and I was a little scared.

I found it a little odd that Artie had any fear whatsoever. All he really had to do was pound the sidewalks and register with the Musician's Local 47. With his credentials, skills and experience, he would have been working all the time. This was far before the age of drum machines. Drummers were still in high demand, and he was one of the best in all the ways it counted. He could read, had varied experiences, and was a great timekeeper.

Art Tripp: I didn't know what the fuck it meant. Except it seemed to me to say that I wasn't in the band anymore. I didn't know what to do. I just left it go for a couple of days.

CHAPTER TWENTY EIGHT:
STUPID SURRENDER

*Drumbo practicing circa 1971. Photo courtes
C. Michael French (no relation).*

Mark And Bill's Midnight Visit

Meanwhile my state of mind had rapidly deteriorated and I was basically in a state of depression. I had been through three jobs - fired from two and quit one because of the exploitation. I hated college and was falling asleep in classes. I had no money and was just sitting in my parent's garage room writing music and smoking far too many cigarettes. I was staying in a room that was built next to my parent's garage, which wasn't attached to the house. One night - probably in March or April, 1970, I awoke from sleeping to see a shadowy figure in the room. Sleepily, in a fog, I figured it was my girlfriend, who occasionally showed up late when she was feeling the urge. I could make out two silhouettes on the window from the streetlamp. Soon, I realized it was Mark and Bill.

I turned on a lamp. "Don wants to see you." Mark said. It was kind of funny to have Mark and Bill delivering a message from "da boss" like a couple of thugs. I was glad to see them, however. It had been several months, and they were my friends. We were "war buddies," in a sense. I got dressed and decided to go see "da boss." Bill had what I recall as a huge Dodge sedan, probably a '59 or '60. It was yellow and white. It was one of those big "yank tanks" with the double fins, a really ugly car. The one thing about those old beasts is that they were comfortable.

It was about an hour and ten minutes to the house. The sun had just begun to rise. As I recall Don and Jan's bed had been moved into the living room against the piano wall and there were chairs set up in what used to be the bedroom. I couldn't understand the logic of this. It gave them no privacy AND nowhere the band could rehearse. I was unaware that both Mark and Bill had probably been living with Artie for most of this time.

Don was very cordial and offered me some tea. Jan was no longer the adored creature he had introduced me, but was now more of a "fetch us some tea" or "Jan, write this down," status. She had begun to be, more in a sense, Don's "mother" in the best "shut-up-Sue-and-get-me-a-Pepsi" sense, and a replacement for Laurie. The honeymoon, it appeared, was over.

I don't recall as much of the meeting as I would like. I recall Don talking small talk for a while, just to loosen us up, I suppose.

"I'd like you to come back to the group, John," He said.

"Oh? I thought I was the guy who sabotaged your music," I shot back.

"Are you kiddin' man? I never thought that!" he replied with a little laugh. This was his stock answer to anything he said and later realized was pure hokum.

"Lying as usual," I thought to myself. However, truth be known, I missed the music more than I hated his lies and deceit. I missed my friends. This is the reality I had known and become accustomed to and it appealed to me more than old farts ripping kids off for lessons, or people who thought I was "on somethin'" because I forgot to mop under a couple of bins. I wanted to be talked back into the band, but I wanted to send out a few jabs for the idiotic accusations that had been leveled against me.

"The thing is (one of Don's most over-used phrases, along with "you know what I mean?") that none of that crap that used to happen goes on here anymore - does it?" he asked, making eye contact with Bill and Mark. I looked over and saw Mark hesitantly shaking his head "no," softly saying "No," and looking at the floor in shame for his lie. Bill was more resolute. "Nope," he said, as though better rehearsed. Neither of them looked me in the eye. I chose to ignore this obvious fact.

I was thinking to myself "It doesn't happen here because you don't want Jan to see it, but it probably happens somewhere else."

"Truthfully, John, I'm about to come into the big money and I'd like to see you get something for all that work you put in. The college kids are really into *Trout Mask Replica*. They like it because of the ecology themes. Artie's out. He can't play your stuff, man - too fucking lazy. YOU'RE the guy that made this happen, now it's time for you to collect your reward. Why should Artie step in and make the big money?"

I didn't know anything about Artie at the time. I knew that he had some schooling back east and could read well. Unfortunately for him, I had made sure that most of the drum parts were not written down. The beginning of this conversation was a big put down of Art Tripp, how he was a terrible person etc. Why in the world I didn't take all this with "a grain of salt," and give Artie more of the benefit of the doubt, I have no idea. I had just previously read the Rolling Stone interview and knew that Don's "truth" was tremendously distorted, and some was out and out fabrication. He used to always quote himself - like he was quoting the Bible - and one of his sayings was, "The truth has no patterns." Well, one thing I knew for sure; his truth certainly had no patterns.

The only thing I can figure is that Don kept stroking my ego about how great my drumming was and the flattery probably blinded me to the truth of what was happening here.

John French to Art Tripp: So he was saying … Artie doesn't understand your drum style or whatever. You could have read it if it would have been written down, for the most part. But it wasn't written down. I made sure of that. Most of the drum parts I made up myself. I'd say 50% I wrote myself or I interpreted them from something that Don said. I take a lot of credit for the drum parts.

AT: Oh, yeah, and they were great!

JF: Thank you. I didn't write them down because I thought: "The one thing I'm going to do is to prove to the band, at least, that Don did not write these parts."

We talked for a long time. I was the "honored guest" and after a year of being away, I had completely lost my sense of how shrewd and devious this man could be. I had lost my defenses and been sucked right back in

All the dialogue is, of course, the best that I can remember, and there was much more said, but this was the essence of the meeting that morning.

… It all came down to me foolishly saying "Yes."

John French to Art Tripp: I didn't really like the idea of going back and playing with him, but there wasn't much going on in the desert and that's a whole other story.

This was probably the most incredibly stupid thing I've done it my life. Truthfully, the situation I was in had worn me down. I missed the music horribly. I had played in a couple of cover groups and it was like a humiliating nightmare. The fact that I was traumatized by having experienced the *Trout Mask* year coupled with my lack of ability to cope with college life or find a decent job had taken me to a point of resignation - damned if I do, damned if I don't. I had thought that there were opportunities awaiting me. I had found out that basically I was looked upon as a low-life drug-using hippie by the desert community.

If there was an opportunity for me to turn things around, this was probably it. And this time, I wouldn't get pushed around and manipulated … little did I realize I already had been.

Mark and Bill at this point were told by Don to play the new material for me. I know they must have gotten as tired of this "trained monkey" act as I did. It was a little humiliating sometimes to be commanded (never asked) to play on cue at any time Don desired to hear his music. Nevertheless, they put on their instruments and proceeded to play *Peon* for me as an opener. I was totally overwhelmed by this piece. More on this in the track notes.

I believe they went on to play quite a few things from the album including, *One Red Rose That I Mean, Bellerin' Plain, Flash Gordon's Ape*, and many more. I was stunned by the growth of the music. It had the feel and even the outside-ness of *Trout Mask Replica*, but the phrases were longer (thanks to tape) and Bill and Mark, having rehearsed together without drums, were so locked-in it was amazing. I was really inspired by hearing this.

Artie Out, Artie In

My understanding is that Artie was out - that he'd been fired. Don was very adamant about making this point. The reality is that nothing at all had been communicated to Artie. According to his interview, he wound up going down to visit his girlfriend.

Art Tripp: Finally I went down to see Joanne, who was living down in Hollywood there. I went over to see her one day, and I said, "What do you think happened?" She said, "It sounds to me like you're out of the band." I went, "Hmmm ... I think you're right." She said, "That's probably good." I said, "Yeah, but I don't have anything else going on."
JF: In retrospect, she was probably right.
AT: How many times the women are ...

At this point, the only money Tripp had most likely made with Don was playing in a small club in Hollywood. From the timeline, perhaps five to six months had passed. Perhaps Artie was still in a bit of shock from the Mothers disbandment. He had moved from the East Coast and perhaps felt disconnected. He certainly had the resources to take care of himself, but apparently something had made him feel as though he couldn't make it without the group.

Art Tripp: So I said, "What do you think I oughta do?" She said, "Well, why don't you call them for Christ's sake?"
John French: Yeah, communicate.
AT: Well, that's a thought. (Laughter)

Is This The Party To Whom I Am Speaking?

Art Tripp: I think I called them from her house. I called out to Ensenada and YOU ANSWERED THE PHONE!
John French: I answered, oh great!
AT: I thought, "Uh oh!" I'm out.
JF: So, you didn't know anything about this?
AT: I knew nothing at all. You were in a bad spot, because you didn't know what was going on. You probably said something like, "Well, I don't know what's going on." And I think I told you or something...anyway, I said I'd be out. So I got in the car and I felt terrible, but I gotta go out there and face the music, and see what's going on. So, that's when I show up that day. You didn't know anything more about that than I did. As soon as I walked in, I saw you, I saw the drums and I thought, "I'm history."

For the record, I don't remember it this way at all. Actually what I remember is that Artie and Joanne were still living together in the same house in which Mark and Bill had shared the downstairs room. I don't remember a call but there certainly could have been one. I just remember being out under the shed patio of the Trout House working on my drum set and fine-tuning it. All of a sudden, I heard a "clomp, clomp" sound and there was Art Tripp, wearing a white shirt, black pants, and wooden clogs looking back at me. I remember the eye contact being like "What are you doing here" - on both our parts. I was totally puzzled as to why he was there, thinking he had been fired and was history.

John French to Art Tripp: I just kind of went (sucks in breath) because I thought "Oh, no, this guy's gonna hate my guts because they threw him out and got me in the band." (As it turned out) we all had this meeting and (your) main idea was "I would like to still work with you guys." You were pretty open and out front about it. It wasn't like a big deal, you know, and I'm going, "What's going on here?" I thought this was already settled and that you were long gone already. So then, I find out that you hadn't even been told yet. I think you just found out when you came out that day.
AT: Yeah!

We awkwardly spoke for a moment after the awkward silence, and I clumsily invited him into the house. Since I really didn't know that Artie had never been fired, I was trying to be silent, like a wise sage. Don, Bill, Mark, Artie, and myself sat in the living room for a time. Don was in his best form. As Marker had said, "He liked to keep everyone just a little bit off-kilter." Well, everyone was definitely primed for the next step.

John French to Art Tripp: So, I am sitting there in this meeting feeling like shit, because I thought you were a pretty nice guy. That's when it was decided that you would play marimba. I thought, "He's going to play marimba?" I didn't know you played marimba. I thought you were just going to learn from scratch, and I thought, "They're nuts. They're going to get this guy and he's just going to have to learn from scratch?" So, that was my first impression.

I only knew Art as a drummer, not a percussionist. I didn't know anything about all his training, as I had only met him briefly on one occasion and had only seen him play drums. So I naturally concluded that this was one of Don's hair-brained schemes similar to Jeff Bruschele, Mike Rice, Victor Hayden and Gary Lambert. I had come to the conclusion that ability was not an issue for inclusion in the Magic Band.

Ed Marimba Born Not Christened

Art Tripp: So then the wheels started turning and I thought, at that time there was just Bill playing guitar and Mark. I think it was Bill that came up with the idea.
John French: Don actually thought of it.
AT: Okay well, somebody decided that since I could play the marimba, why didn't I play the second guitar parts on the marimba? I thought, "Yeah!"
JF: Which turned out to be a fantastic sound, by the way.
AT: It was. I thought, "Yeah, I would much rather play marimba anyway. First of all, the parts were already there (meaning "written down"). *I didn't have to learn a new style. I didn't have to copy you or anything that had been done before, so it was just perfect. So there for a crazy while, it just seemed great.*
JF: And, we got to do the double drums stuff which was fun, too. And you got to do your drum style with Don, doing Spitball Scalped A Baby - *kind of free-improv things.*
AT: Exactly and you were just great and I thought, well shit, this is perfect and there for a while it was. And that's when I think you moved in to the Laurel Canyon house with me, and we had some more meaningful rehearsals.

I was coming down for rehearsals when I was still going to school and rehearsing a couple of nights a week. The very first thing Artie learned on the marimba was the beginning of *The Clouds*

Are Full Of Wine - the intro of which later was used on *Golden Birdies*. This is when I first discovered that Artie could actually play. So, now I was feeling a bit intimidated, because this guy could play marimba and drum kit. I suddenly thought of Artie as a "legitimate" musician.

I Move In With Artie

Tripp had a house on Laurel Canyon Blvd. It was only one block from the original house the band had moved into on Amor Road - pre-*Safe As Milk*. It was kind of a modern boxy split-level design. The "carport" underneath actually was the floor of the upstairs guest bedroom. It had forced-air heating and air conditioning. My bedroom was downstairs and the door was across a short hallway facing the entrance. It had it's own bathroom, and was a fairly large room - about the size of a garage.

Rehearsals

I began the very first day, within an hour of moving into Artie's, to work on the drum parts for the new album. Don had asked me to use as many parts from *Trout Mask* as I could, because people would be able to relate, and the albums would have a little more consistency. I agreed and thought it would be a good idea, however, I did write some new parts along with using the old, and I modified several a bit to fit the music better.

Bill and Mark came over for the first few weeks. We had great rehearsals together. This was fun. We loosened up a bit and joked around with each other. I go into detail in the track notes as to the methods and approaches Don and I used in creating the drum parts for *Lick My Decals Off, Baby*.

Grant Gibbs, Al Liefer, Mark Green

Don's "dream team" consisted of a personal manager, Grant Gibbs; an accountant, Al Liefer; and an attorney; Mark Green. Mark Green was not an "entertainment lawyer" so to speak. I remember that during one of our later business meetings, he came in late because he had been at a murder trial. Entertainment lawyers don't do murder trials, they specialize. I didn't know that back then - a lawyer was a lawyer etc. This is probably one of the reasons Don wound up with so many contractual problems.

Grant Gibbs, as I recall, worked in Zappa's business office for Straight Records, where Pauline, the secretary also worked.

Don And Jan At Trout House

Don and Jan were still at the Trout House, and I was actually commuting for a while to rehearsals before I actually moved down. My idea was to finish my semester of college and then move closer to the band location. One day, when I showed up for rehearsal, Don and Jan were the only one's at the house. Don was having Jan massage his scalp and he sat in a large wooden chair with its back to the kitchen entrance way.

"You realize, John, that I am a King," he told me matter-of-factly. "John, you know I am." I said nothing, but I realized that I had just walked back into the same mess I'd escaped from one and a half years before.

Mark And Laurie Together

Don Aldridge: Well, from the outside, a lot of what I know of the **Trout Mask** *era is from what I heard from others. I heard that he just "gave" Laurie to Mark Boston.*
John French: No that isn't the way that happened.

Eventually, Laurie moved into the Trout House with Don and Jan. Now, this was a situation I wouldn't wish on anyone. I suspect that Laurie was secretly still in love with Don, and Jan and Mark may have sensed this and were ill at ease. I recall showing up at the house one Saturday morning when Sue was down visiting. Mark had eaten one of Don's bananas and Don was raving on about it. "I can't believe you would do that…" etc. I remember Sue, always the peacemaker saying, "Oh now, Don, that's just human nature." "That's why I hate humans," he shot back, "because of their nature."

It's interesting to note, in lieu of this comment, that when I feed my dogs, I have to separate them, because one is blind, and the other will always try to steal it's food. Van Vliet always stressed how wonderful animals are and yet I see the same behavior prevalent in animals as he would denounce in humans. Actually, animals have helped me to understand man's worst behavioral traits in an honest and natural way. When my dogs try to steal each other's food, it's amusing and revealing at the same time. When some person tries to steal my food, it makes me a little angry. (Of course, when a person tries to steal my dog's food, I get a little confused.) Don's reaction was natural, but Mark's behavior wasn't that far out of the norm. It was, after all, only a banana.

Don And Jan At Kon Tiki

Don told me that while living with Mark and Laurie he had grabbed Grant by the lapels, lifted him up off the ground and said "GET ME OUT OF HERE, MAN!"

Obviously, the stress of everyone living together was getting to be a bit much. Eventually Don and Jan temporarily moved into a motel on Ventura Blvd. Called the Kon Tiki. It was one of those low-budget places with a Polynesian setting. I recall visiting them there and Jan had to sleep on the floor, if I recall, because of her back problems. She was going though some kind of therapy.

I had always thought that Grant Gibbs had come up with the funds for the move to Kon Tiki, and then Art Tripp revealed in his interview that it had been his credit card. It was a Gulf Oil Card that could be used at Best Western Hotel.

Art Tripp: Christ, he was taking the band out and eating dinners etc. and it was all going on the credit card. I didn't care, but I never got paid back.
John French: Of course, you didn't get it reimbursed, right?
AT: I ended up losing the card.

Drop Out Drop Out

At a band business meeting at Artie's, it was suggested that I quit school. Don kept saying, "We've got to get this stuff done, man." I kept saying, "But it's only six weeks and I'm already rehearsing with you guys." Eventually, as usual, Don's will won out over mine, and I agreed to drop out of college. I returned to Lancaster and filled out withdrawal slips for all of my classes and left them in the teacher's mailboxes, which were attached to their doors. I put them in envelopes with a little note explaining that my work was making it impossible for me to complete my classes.

John French to Art Tripp: I remember right after - they talked me into quitting school, because I was going to college. They said, "Man, we gotta have this album done quick, so you gotta quit school" and they kept bugging me about it for about two weeks. I finally quit school, I moved in with you.

Later, when I received my final grades, I had a series of withdrawals marked as "W's" on my report card with the exception of my English class. The teacher was a Black Muslim activist and she gave me an "F." I have tried to have this erased from my record several times, to no avail.

508

Old Ways

Although it happened very subtly, I soon noted that I was beginning to slip right back into my old subservient pattern with Don. Not as radical as before, but the power was still there, and I still didn't know how to fight it. I could feel myself being led by the nose. The school thing was the first step.

Joanne

Artie's live-in girlfriend - Joanne - was still living with him at the time. She was English, and as I got to know her, I discovered through conversing with her that she had formerly been the girlfriend of singer Graham Nash, of Crosby Stills and Nash - probably just before he moved in with Joni Mitchell. She was a reasonably attractive lady, and quite friendly. I liked her, although I tried to keep my distance, as this was Artie's girlfriend and I barely knew either of them.

I remember Artie calling me upstairs one night. He said, "You gotta try this man," and he and Joanne pointed to this plate with all kinds of crackers, olives, hot peppers and other various "deli" foods. They had me make this special "cracker sandwich" - like a mini-dagwood - and eat it. It was quite good, I have to admit. I think I wound up polishing off half the tray because I was so hungry. However, my point here is that Artie and Joanne really tried to make me feel welcome to their home. It must have been a bit strange for them having a boarder, although I later learned that Bill and Mark had lived downstairs for a time, and before that, Don Preston, keyboardist for the Mothers had stayed with them.

Crazy Jerry

Art Tripp writes: Ah, yes. "Crazy Jerry" Buchanan. I first met him after a show with the Mothers at the Shrine Auditorium in L.A. After the performance I hung around - I guess to have a few beers in the dressing room. As I was leaving I noticed this strange looking guy wandering around in the near-empty hall as the crew was cleaning up. He came up to me and told me in a speedy raspy whisper (his normal speaking voice) that he had listened to the whole show underneath the stage laying on his back with his feet jammed up underneath the stage floor. When I asked him why, he said, "So I could feel the vibes." That endeared me to the guy right away. He was a little intimidating looking as you remember. He sort of had those Ichabod Crane features-chiseled jaw, nose, etc.-and he wore a ratty-looking wig over his bald head. He had on old western boots wrapped with tape that had partially become unravelled, and the soles were real thin. Naturally, I invited him up to the Laurel Canyon pad, where it was still difficult to discern what he was saying. He asked if he could crash there that night. Joanne and I were a little reluctant, because he was so out there, but yet he had an integrity that seemed to shine through. We finally went to bed, and the next day we came out to the living room where he had left his blanket and pillow neatly folded on the couch along with a sweet note thanking us for our hospitality. We were surprised, relieved, and impressed in that order.

He became sort of a regular over at the pad. He usually brought along an ample supply of disoxin gradunet, which was a powerful amphetamine. Turns out he had a prescription for some sort of injectable speed along with his works, etc. He used to carry them around in his boot. It was all legal. He spent a lot of time in the concrete bunker formed by the intersection of the Hollywood and Ventura freeways. He said he'd get in there and play his tenor sax to the rhythms of the overhead traffic. He was nuts about high voltage electricity. He'd even try to stick a finger into a wall socket now and then. He and some pals used to climb the fence at a local electric generator plant just to experience the power, but he had just recently stopped

*doing that after a friend of his got too close to a generator and had a leg burned off.
I don't imagine Jerry was much of a sax player, but I think he didn't care. The stories Frank
used to tell about Jerry bending steel rebar across his chest were true. He showed me where
he'd broken his ribs in the process. He was "powerful strong", as a friend of mine used to say.
I think he scared Frank, which put the kibosh on any return visits to the log cabin. Frank liked
to collect oddballs simply to talk or write about them later. A guy showed up one night with
a .45 wanting to shoot Frank. "The Gnarler" (Dick Barber) evidently talked him out of it and
was able to subdue him. Soon after that Frank moved up near Mulholland Drive to a more
secluded environment (you know where it was).
Jerry had a fascinating background. He was well educated and extremely bright. He was in
prison once - presumably for drug offenses - where he literally wrote himself out. He wrote
an impressive thesis about why he should not have been incarcerated, and the prison board
released him. It's true - I read the thesis. It could have been a doctoral paper. I could be wrong,
but I believe his mother was on the board ...
I never saw Jerry again after we left Hollywood. I liked him a lot, and underneath all that
weirdness was a real sweet guy. I hope he's alive and well today.*

Bye Bye Joanne

Don decided to show up with Jan one evening and have a meeting with Artie. I already knew
what it was about, as he had been talking about it for weeks. He didn't like Joanne and made it
obvious in every way he could. Now, he had decided that Artie had to get rid of her. He was about
to insist that Joanne and Artie break up!

As he walked up the stairs, he looked at me and said, "Don't ever envy the position of band
leader, I get stuck with all the crummy jobs." I thought, "What business is it of his if Artie and
Joanne are together? Why does he feel he has any right to interfere?"

After the meeting, during which I stayed downstairs, I found that this was indeed true and that
Joanne was indeed going to leave. Actually, I couldn't believe it that Artie would put up with this.
Joanne spent a few days looking around and landed a job at Lawry's, a fancy restaurant on La
Cienega Blvd. She moved out shortly afterward, and Artie wound up spending more and more time
with her at her apartment.

The Midnight Creeps

I could feel the same spirit I had felt before coming back. That controlling environment that had
been a part of my life before and I craved so much to get away from was back to a minor degree.
However, the fact that I wasn't living in the same house with it caused me to disregard it. Already
committed, I was living in denial and holding all my anxiety about the situation inside. As I look
back now, I realize that Don had me cut all my ties to my former life (school and home) before
actually starting his encroachment, again, upon my will.

Living With Helen

Helen showed up one night for a visit. She spent the night and the next day, she asked me a
favor. She wanted to look for a job in LA to be close to me and get a place nearby and she
wanted to know if she could live with me until she got on her feet. I said yes, being completely
naïve about the fact that this was essentially Artie's house. Things like asking his permission never
seemed to dawn on me. I ignored my Christian beliefs about living with her, the risk of pregnancy,
and the unstable life I was living. The only thing I could think of was that I wouldn't be alone. It
was a totally selfish decision.

Artie The Pool Hustler

Artie began to disappear each night. He would leave the house at a fairly early hour and go play pool. Apparently, he was quite good, and he would win money quite often for his efforts. He still plays pool to this day and is even better from what I hear.

Gon Bops / Mariano Bobadilla

Grant Gibbs called me and told me to start looking for a drum set. He said to get exactly what I wanted. I went around and started looking at drums. I didn't like any of the sets in the stores. I wanted something really unique and primitive. One day, I was standing in the front of a music store on Vine in Hollywood and leaning on something staring out the window. I realized I was leaning on a conga drum. I struck it once and knew it was the sound I wanted.

The brand name was "Gon Bops" and their plant was down in East LA. I called him at the factory and asked, "Can you build me a conventional drum set?"

"I can build ANYTHING!" was his humble reply. Mariano Bobadilla was his name. Visiting his "factory," I found that it was just a small backyard setup, but what a setup. It was all in sheds in the back of a rather narrow lot. He had an eight or ten man crew and I didn't see one idle moment from anyone. I went into his office and saw that he made all kinds of percussion instruments and there were orders worldwide for his merchandise written up on a chalkboard on the wall.

He had pictures of custom work he had done for various clients.

I had drafted out plans for a kick drum (ordered two) and a floor tom. I would use two of his Tumbas and one African Drum for the "suspended" toms in front.

"I'm going to have to build special forms for these," he said, "that'll cost you more."

"Uh uh," I replied, "You already quoted me a price of $900 and that's what I have."

He looked at me with an expression of respect. "OK, but it's going to take a while."

I think it was about 2 months before I actually got the drums.

He showed me around. I found out how they formed the drums. He showed me the Philippine mahogany. Then he showed me the special patterns they used to form the wood. "I'm really just a glorified barrel-maker." He said, and laughed. "I took my design to an acoustics lab and they put a computer on it and told me exactly how long it needed to be to get the sound I wanted. That's why my drums sound so good." He continued to show me the factory. "We boil the wood here," he said, pointing to a steaming forty-gallon drum filled with water and mahogany staves "and then you can bend it like noodles."

We knock these steel hoops over the outside and put these discs on the inside to form the drum, with animal glue on all the joints. Then it goes on the lathe - I'm going to have to build two special jigs to hold your drums on the lathe. "Then, they get painted over here." It was all amazing to me. I really liked this guy.

Then his wife came out with some soft drinks. She was… well, gorgeous. I had a good feeling about this man - and you could get machaca burritos on the corner.

Rehearsals With Bill, Mark, And Artie

Artie started joining us for rehearsals. Occasionally, we would strike the set and rehearse at the Trout House, still maintained by Mark and Laurie. Most of the time, however, the rehearsals were at Artie's. For the most part, we seldom saw Don. He claimed that he was taking care of Jan because her hip was still giving her problems.

At Artie's House

Now and then, Artie and I would just play through the tunes by ourselves. Just xylophone (he didn't have a marimba yet, which I believe was at least an octave deeper in intonation). It was a strange combination. He just put a couple of microphones on the set and played through an amp. Art also showed me quite a bit on the drums. Just little tricky technical things about holding sticks and technique that turned my head around. I started practicing more and more. This, incidentally, was the first time I had ever had time to actually practice - without someone complaining about the noise - since *Safe As Milk*.

Often, Bill and Mark would join us. The songs were coming together nicely and sounding really good. Art had made some arrangement with Don as to what his parts were and they started coming together quite well. However, Art could do his stuff in a half and hour, and nail it, because it was written, and then he would leave and go play pool. So, Bill, Mark and I would practice on and on, even though we already knew most of the stuff. I think it was mostly out of habit. If you didn't spend your whole life practicing, you weren't "into it" - and there was danger of a raven landing on the roof.

Time was passing and I realized that I could have easily finished school and had a year of Liberal Arts courses behind me and still done this album just fine. It was summer and we still hadn't recorded.

Trout Mask Parts Revisited

Eventually, I got a hold of the separated drum tracks from *Trout Mask*. They had been run off onto 1/4 inch tape and were playable on a tape deck I was using. So, I was able to re-acquaint myself with all the old material.

The Underwoods

Ian and Ruth Underwood came by one evening for a visit with Artie. I told them Artie wasn't home, but invited them in, as it was an honor to have them at the house. I had never met Ruth before, and barely knew Ian except in passing at the log cabin. Ian had been a member of the Mothers until they were disbanded by Frank and still was working with him at present. Ruth played many percussion instruments, but I was only aware of her mallet work. Don had told me that I was her favorite percussionist, which was quite a compliment, as I heard that she was extremely good.

I was telling them that I wanted to start playing double bass drums and Ian told me that my old set was still up at Zappa's. This was the Slingerland drumset that I had loaned to Zappa's younger brother, Bobby at Don's request. They now were apparently just sitting around gathering dust in the basement.

Ian and Ruth went up to Zappa's (which was just around the corner) and managed to get all the drums for me. I was really happy to get them, as I didn't have the Gon Bops yet and I wanted to set up a set in a similar configuration so that I could begin to practice the double bass patterns I had been writing.

Double The Kicks

After a visit to the local hardware store where I bought stain, varnish and sandpaper, I worked for a week - practically asphyxiating myself and Helen in the process. The only place to work was in the room. There was no garage or workshop. Within a few days, however, I had refinished the set and bought the new Asba pedals I needed to complete the set. I immediately worked for days on double bass technique and made up a bunch of exercises for myself that I faithfully went through each day.

CHAPTER TWENTY NINE:
PUT MY DECEPTION ON, BABY

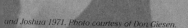

and Joshua 1971. Photo courtesy of Don Giesen.

Cadillacs

Don called one day and said that he thought I should get a safer car since I was going to be driving in LA. I was still driving my 1960 Datsun sedan. It was a tiny thing, but got forty-one miles per gallon. I could see his point about safety but didn't want to spend the money. He said "Don't worry about the money, just go to this address and check out this car." He also made arrangements for me to go to Al Liefer's office once a week and pick up a small check for expenses. Just to give you an idea of 1970 prices, I believe the house Artie was renting was $185 a month. Today, it would probably cost $2,000 or more for the same place. Anyway, we had our expenses (utilities, rent, musical equipment) paid by the accountant, plus we received $150 bi-weekly (if memory serves) for incidentals, groceries, gas.

I went to the address Don had given me for the car. The man looked like an east-coast mobster. His dining room table was littered with pink slips and registrations. Helen had driven me over, so that if I wanted the car, I could drive it home. The car was a pristine white 1960 Cadillac Coupe DeVille. It looked like a giant spaceship and of course today is a collector's item. The man had taken the car to a shop and had them do a valve job on it that cost $185, I saw the receipt. He sold me the car for $300 cash. It ran perfectly. I was in heaven. Here was a safe car that was big enough to put my drums in.

Bill and Mark also got Cadillacs. Bill's was a 1950 Dark Blue Limousine that was immaculate. Unfortunately, as soon as we moved, he wound up driving Don and Jan everywhere as their unofficial chauffeur. Mark's was a 1960 four-door, but it wasn't in as good a shape and cost half as much. It was a two-tone dark blue. I think because he was living in his own place, he needed to cut back on expenses.

The Only Person In This Band Anyone Is Interested In Is Me...

Soon after this, we had a meeting at Artie's house with Don one afternoon. It was upstairs in the living room, and Don sat at a chair opposite the stairwell. I recall sitting down on a stool knowing that he had something to tell us. He looked at me and said, "You know, John, my only problem is that I'm a human being."

Don then got down to the main purpose of the meeting and explained to us that the only person in the band that the public was interested in was him. He said that we were all expendable and should be glad that we were along for the ride. He went on to say that the business office was going to be drawing up contracts and that he wanted us to sign them soon.

He went on to say that since he was a singer, he didn't need to carry around tons of equipment on the road and that he wasn't about to pay for the shipping of our instruments when we went on tour.

After this meeting, I was totally depressed, but not too surprised. I could see Don had been working up to this for weeks. All the "meetings" so far had been designed to lower our self-esteem and destroy our confidence. It did a pretty good job, too. If you think you're worth nothing, you're more likely to sign your life away.

The "Contract" Board Meeting

As I said, we had started collecting a weekly salary from the office of Brown, Liefer, and Slatkin, CPA. Al Liefer, as I mentioned earlier, was Don's accountant.

Grant Gibbs had met with us on occasion, and was sporting a beard and the kind of clothes a retired sports hunter would wear. His favorite phrase was "I'm glad we have this resolved." Don told me once that Grant's observation of me was that I had that "evangelical glint" in my eye. In the context it was said, it was definitely meant to be condescending.

Elliot Ingber was now in the group, and I was his ride everywhere, as he didn't own a car - well, one that ran anyway. So, I picked him up and we drove down to Third Street near La Cienega, where the CPA's office was, and, after parking in the basement lot, were guided into a boardroom with a big long table and several chairs. In front of each of five chairs (representing the five suckers they expected) were glasses overturned on napkins, and a copy of the contract.

Elliot took one look at this, walked quickly out the door and disappeared. I went down and found him on the corner, thumb out, trying to hitch a ride home. I read through the contract, but decided not to sign that day. I believe that Mark and Bill signed, but Artie looked it over and said, "I don't think this really is enough "bread" (for money), so I gotta think about this. Don was giving his usual "it's more than you guys deserve" comments. Grant and Al both seemed really cold businessmen.

I was intimidated, as I think everyone else was. The meeting was set up in such a way to serve just that purpose. It was time to play "herd the hayseeds."

Art Tripp: I took the contracts and I went down and talked with the president of Local 47 (Musician's Union) of which I was still a member. He took me in the office and spent an hour with me. I showed him the contract and he just about passed out. He couldn't believe it. He said, "This is the worst piece of shit I have ever seen." What it means is: you guarantee them everything; they guarantee you absolutely nothing. You say, "I'm signed up for whatever you want to do for whatever cost or no cost, and you show up and you do this and give all this up, and they don't guarantee you anything. They don't even guarantee they're gonna pay you." I said, "Huh!" (Laughs)
John French: That was your next clue, right?
AT: We went through every page of that contract and that was the first time I ever sat down with somebody and went through a performance contract, and it really opened my eyes.
JF: Let me ask you something: Why do you think that all of us were so stupid as to allow ourselves to get caught in that?
AT: Well, we just didn't know any better, and we really wanted to play the music ...

Two Sides Of The Coin

As I have said, Don had a charming side that made him what I have referred to since as a "silver-tongued devil." He could talk anyone into anything. All of us liked the appeal of the music. All of us wanted to perform it on tour. I had an investment in this and falsely felt that the recognition would be a stepping stone to something better, but it was apparent right away that all that talk about "it's time for you to get your share of what you earned" that was so prevalent at my re-induction, was now replaced by "they're only interested in me and you guys are just along for the ride out of the goodness of my heart."

John French to Art Tripp: And on a personal level with Don ... I mean, didn't you like Don on a personal level? He was charming, he had a great sense of humor, but then there was this whole other side that nobody ever saw except us.
AT: Yeah!
JF: Which makes it difficult, even now, when you're getting interviewed by these guys who are Beefheart "fans" right?
AT: Yes.
JF: Who are saying, "Well, isn't that what artists do?" Bill was saying (in an interview) "He totally fucked me," you know, and the (interviewer) is saying, "Well, isn't that what artists do?" - like it was a perfectly valid question, like if it was a serial killer; "he killed my wife," - "Well, isn't that what serial killers do?"

AT: *The thing is it wasn't that uncommon I mean, it was certainly not in our experience, and none of us can believe we actually went through with that. The fact is, it's happened in other circumstances, especially the colored blues bands. They go through all that shit, then they put the whammy on them, and then they give up everything and get nothing. It's really typical.*
JF: *And years later, after they have (lived a difficult life and) died a miserable death, then, they're suddenly "recognized."* (laughs)

I was laughing to keep from crying. This decision I made to stick with it was not out of any encouragement regarding the contractual agreements. The agreement stunk. I could read enough legalese by this time myself to decipher some of it into plain English and see that it was "all for Don and none for the band."
Some of the terms were:
1. Accountant's, Managerial, and Lawyer fees came off the top
2. 50% of what was left went to Don
3. All equipment transport, transportations fees, hotels, came out of the remaining.
4. We split what was left 5 ways. (Elliot had joined the band)

Art Tripp: *The fact is that we were more interested in the "art" of it, and we knew somehow, we'd probably be provided for and nobody was thinking (about) that. None of us had that much personal responsibility. I'd done this good thing with Zappa, but I didn't make much money with him. The only brush I had with reality was when I did contract gigs - like, studio stuff. Then again, I was in the union, and I knew the union would take care of it. I didn't pay any attention to it. I got money and I thought, "Well then, let's just go on."*
John French: *I tell this to people who are thinking about going into music. I say, "Well if you want to be a musician, I would suggest this, go to college, Major in business and Minor in music - because you are going to get overwhelmed otherwise." That's my words to them.*
AT: *That's absolutely correct. A lot of what has happened in the history of music would never have happened.*
JF: *Yes.*
AT: *Because without that stuff where people are just willing to "throw themselves on the pyre" of art willingly a lot of that stuff never would have happened.*
JF: *That's what we did. We "threw ourselves on the pyre of Art" didn't we?*
AT: *And thought we were lucky to do it.*
JF: *Because we didn't know any better.*
AT: *It was unconscionable, but by God, we did it!* (laughing)

This brings up important philosophical aspects of the importance of "art." Is the sacrifice of many of the artists truly "worth it?" Do artists truly have any choice? Or, are they so driven in their quest, that their destiny demands undeniably that they suffer? How does the public play into this? Isn't there some illusory romantic aspect of viewing an artist as "great" only if he has lived some poor miserable existence? Van Gogh is mostly remembered for cutting off his ear and shooting himself. Is this in itself some important aspect in the credibility and the validity of art? I don't buy into any of this, but I certainly seemed to then.
When the pre-*Safe As Milk* Van Vliet struggled with his seeming "success," his major source of self-doubt seemed to spring from the concept that he hadn't "paid his dues." Was Van Vliet driven subconsciously to sabotage his own career in order to fling himself into the "wilderness of dues paying?" Was his abuse of band members just an extension of the concept that "those who succeed in art must suffer?" Did he somehow feel that only through creating this excruciating

environment would his band members "deserve" recognition? Most importantly, how would his music and art have differed in style, uniqueness, and power had he not believed he needed to pay dues?

If he indeed believed this concept, how much of this view influenced band members to adhere to similar beliefs? Could this, in part, be an explanation for the amount of control and abuse they were to endure? Is this why I myself came back, time and time again, to relive various versions of the same dysfunctional relationship?

The Ugliness Comes Back

Phase two in the John French re-indoctrination process began: Don called me up one night for a meeting. "Mark's fucking around, man," he said. "We need to talk." My heart literally felt like it sank. I wanted to leave right then, but I was committed. I had taken this car, and I was drawing money under salary. This was exactly the mindset that Don had wanted.

Nightmare Deja Vu

The first talk was at the Trout House, now Mark's house. On the way by, I stopped by the Kon Tiki. "I thought this wasn't going to happen, Don." I said. "So did I, man, but he's really messing around. I don't know what his story is." Don replied. "Well, I'll meet you up there." As I got in the car Don said something to the effect that if Mark started playing games to feel free to smack him. I drove to the house with mixed feelings. I swore to myself I wasn't going to cooperate in this folly. It was the start of the ugliness for which I had previously left the band.

The night was all talk, basically. I think I recall it being a problem between Bill and Mark, which never should have required a band meeting to begin with. It was their business and really didn't affect rehearsals. I felt that the only reason this happened was that Don felt that he was losing control. People were beginning to actually enjoy their lives, and Don didn't seem to like this.

Shortly thereafter, there was another meeting at Don's new house. He moved into a small house across the canyon from the Trout House. This time the subject of the meeting was Bill, who supposedly was doing some awful thing.

Let me describe a day in Bill's life back then. He was living in a little tiny house or rented room somewhere by himself. He ate sparingly and kept his expenses to the bare minimum, like some monk. All day long, his meditation was to concentrate on Don's piano ramblings coming out of a four-inch speaker. He interpreted this into something playable on guitar and weeded out the dross (of which there was plenty).

Don was in the habit of calling people at all hours of the day and night to give them ideas. "Bill, wake up man, you gotta get this!" he would say. Bill would obediently put a tape recorder up to the phone while Don whistled what often seemed like an endless part into the microphone. Sometimes, Don would insist Bill get up and come over. Bill had no girlfriend and no life outside the band. Once a month, he would drink a beer and consider it a party. That is my outside view of the dedication that Bill had to Don's art.

So, with that in mind, this meeting was a joke. It had to do with Bill's new subversive evil plot to overthrow the band. It was pure bullshit, and we all knew it underneath, yet somehow we allowed ourselves to deny the truth and mindlessly follow Don's lead. It would end up in an all night talk with everyone exhausted, disgusted and angry. A complete waste of a perfectly good night. I noticed that the target was always Bill or Mark. Artie and I remained suspiciously immune for this period of time.

Helen and I were starting to have a lot of fights ourselves, so it was spreading over into my private life. There had been and instance where, when I was still living in Lancaster at my parents and going to school, she and I had quarreled on the phone. I told her that I had homework to do and that I had to hang up. She wound up coming over. I opened the door and told her to go home.

As I shut the door, she began screaming at the top of her lungs. She had a very shrill scream. I opened the door and slapped her, saying "Get a hold of yourself." She kept screaming and I slapped her several times.

That happened once about eight to ten months before. I had apologized to her and her parents, and things went back to normal, but now, I was starting to slap her occasionally, and we argued constantly. I was taking my frustrations out on her. I tried to get her to leave, but she kept forgiving me and staying. It was "abused spouse syndrome" and this went on for about a year - escalating at times and going dormant some times for months. This lowered my own self-respect and made me even more vulnerable to the cult control, which again was growing vine-like into my life.

If You Drink Don't Think

I came home after one of those "talks' and had a couple of drinks of something, because I was shaking from frustration. I drove back over to Don's and confronted him on these issues. I asked him why he had said the "talks" had stopped when they apparently hadn't. I had caught him in several lies and I brought them all up. He admitted lying to me about one personal point (which I care not to share publicly as it's not relevant and would only hurt innocent people) but then backed off on the bigger lies.

He then began saying things like "You're drunk!" and "It's really difficult to reason with someone who is inebriated. I just can't look into the eyes of a drunk!" This was stated with a very snobbish air. I had had two standard sized drinks, and all it had done was relax me a bit. This was just Van Vliet going on the offensive and I didn't have understanding enough to see that at the time.

Don's Painting

Don began to paint with acrylics on matte paper after he moved to his little house. Mark Boston would come over and spend all day helping him by cleaning his brushes and mixing his paints. I remember Mark telling me that he would hold the paper up on a board because Don didn't have an easel, and Don would get so violent in his application of the paint that he would knock Mark flat on his back.

Mark seemed to enjoy this. He had grown up in a large family and to him this was just "playing." The interesting thing here is that the whole "urgency" of getting the album finished seemed to disappear as soon as I dropped out of school. Mark was obviously not working on the music. Neither was Don, not that he often did. I had learned all my drum parts within a few weeks with the exception of a couple of pieces and now spent a lot of time just taking Helen to movies or going to the beach. We even made one trip to Disneyland.

Don's First Rehearsal With Band ...Tragedy – Wind-wing

After all that had happened, I knew that it was only a matter of time before Don would include me in one of his "talks" again. The first time Van Vliet came to a rehearsal at Artie's, he walked in the door and looked at Bill, Mark and I and said something to the effect of "Jesus, I can't even get through the door, man, because of this giant wind-wing." I knew what he meant. A wind-wing was a triangular piece of glass in a car, and the three of us had "vibed' him out. It was the usual BS. Don went upstairs to use the bathroom.

Give Him A Chance

I was definitely angry about this. Bill, Mark and I had been working for weeks together. We had almost all the material learned, and the few things that were left I had requested help on because I didn't like what I was coming up with for drum parts, especially *Space Age Couple* and *The Clouds*

Are Full Of Wine. We had worked like crazy, except for an occasional day off, mostly because Don called rehearsal off so that Mark could help him paint or Bill could drive him somewhere.

I walked upstairs to get a drink of water. I had cottonmouth, I was so angry. "What's with Don?" I asked Jan. "I thought this stuff wasn't going to happen any more."
"Just give him a chance!" She replied. I stopped. No use talking to her. He had probably fed her so many fabrications about the rest of us that she was totally in the dark as to what the real situation had been.

I went back downstairs, and awaited the dark cloud I knew would descend. As it worked out, we only wasted about an hour meditating on the evil plot the three of us had formulated and Artie came in and unknowingly started asking about the music. Suddenly in "good behavior mode," Don immediately began listening to the music and writing drum parts. Most of the double drum parts (Artie's half) were written in a couple of five-hour sessions. He basically just responded to Don's suggestions and interpreted it to his style.

I could see that I was in for one Hell of a ride, once again.

The Bitter End West - Early September, 1970, Los Angeles, USA

I believe our first performance, several months after moving to Los Angeles and practicing endlessly, was at the Bitter End West a new club that had opened up as a West Coast version of the original Bitter End, in New York. Elliot was really up for this show and was excited about his solo in *Alice In Blunderland,* which hadn't been recorded yet.

I walked in to discover that the stage was very shallow and small. My drums just barely fit on the stage. I looked to discover that straight behind my head was a huge Acoustic amp - Elliot's. I groaned. Elliot played really loud and I was to be right in the path of the sound. These Acoustic amps were infamous for their brittle sound. Don mentioned to me before the show that Elliot was nervous about his solo because all of his close friends were coming to the show."

Art Tripp had a new girlfriend he had brought for the evening as a date. Maria was her name. He seemed distracted. Don, when introduced, sang "MA-RI-A" full-voice as an excerpt from West Side Story. He then offered her a cigarette. She said she didn't smoke. "WELL YOU BETTER START!" Don shouted. Artie said she actually took a cigarette and tried to smoke it. He was laughing about it later.

We played and after the first song, it was apparent that the audience didn't care for us at all. There was a very polite applause, to which Don commented something to the effect of, "That's hardly worth getting my heart beating this hard for." Elliot's solo, as anticipated, practically blew the top of my head off. I wasn't wearing ear protection, and I know that I actually physically felt woozy after this solo. He was playing through a solid state amplifier with two twelve inch-speakers and a preamplifier for distortion, and he was still piercing my entire body with his high notes. I was actually in pain. They say that keyboardists and drummers suffer the worst ear damage because they are sitting as opposed to guitarists and singers who are standing, therefore having the strongest part of the sound wave blowing under their heads.

During the break between shows, we were mingling with the crowd. Somebody walked up to Don with a paper, seemingly to get an autograph. "GRAB HIM!" he shouted as the guy ran by me through the crowd. Laurie tried to grab the guy. It was actually the only time I ever remember seeing Laurie at any show we did. The guy had just served Don a summons. It was one of the most cowardly underhanded things I have ever witnessed in person. I have no idea what the summons concerned. I could speculate that it was for a performance we cancelled at the Fillmore. It also could have been any one of the numerous papers Don had signed unknowingly binding him to someone he had long since forgotten.

Car Accident

We had driven Helen's yellow Mustang to the show that night. Afterwards, some of the guys were going to a restaurant, but before I could get the name, they took off. I was trying to follow Artie's Kaiser Manhattan down Wilshire, but shouldn't have been driving, because I was still reeling from the volume of Elliot's amplifier.

I saw them turn left, and as I was waiting in the left turn lane, the light turned green, I unconsciously thought "left turn arrow" and wound up crossing into the path of a car doing about thirty miles-per-hour. Helen yelled "stop" and I hit the brakes directly in front of the car, and looked over to see her crawling over the seat towards me, as the car was approaching her side of the Mustang - T-Bone style. Fortunately, neither Helen nor I were hurt, but her yellow Mustang was severely sideswiped. We were spun about ninety degrees around.

Orange County Club Gig - September 1970

I believe this was either right after or just before *Decals* was recorded. Grant Gibbs came on stage and read a rather corny introduction. It reminded me of the mayor in the movie *Giant* reading the speech about James Dean's character. He ended by saying something like, "Here stands the man who said, 'I'm not really here, I just stick around for my friends,' ladies and gentlemen, I give you Captain Beefheart!" The problem is, that these kids weren't really interested. They wanted to rock. Don had security people watching us after the show. He made up some story about the fact that there may be a riot. When we finished playing, the security people guarded us by making a blockade as we walked to our cars. Absolutely no one was even attempting to come near us, so it was a bit ludicrous. "Did you see how I made those guards line up for us?" Don later asked, laughing.

Pepperland
Fri. Sept. 18, 1970, San Rafael, CA

This was on the same show as a group called Hot Tuna. We wore tuxedos and also played the following night, staying in a Holiday Inn. Mark Green brought his wife and was amazed that the music sounded exactly the same as on the album. I was surprised he'd ever listened to the group at all. His wife had large breasts and displayed them like jewelry in a display case, which made it really difficult to not stare - especially when you're a testosterone-ridden twenty-one year old. Somebody in the audience shouted "Captain Beefheart for President" he said, "No thanks!" We again wore tuxedos. Grant brought us champagne and this whole image of us as refined eccentrics was a bit silly. Gibbs tripped and spilled the champagne on stage and the resulting puddle made us all a bit wary of the dangers of death by electrocution. Don gulped his drink and threw his glass on stage, we followed his lead to cover Grant's klutziness.

Sat. Sept. 19, 1970, San Rafael Ca.

I wore a robe and pajamas onstage at Don's request and took a nap during Bill's solo on *One Red Rose That I Mean*. Just before the show, one of the roadies (Bill Shumow and Jeff Bruschele) moved an amp that Mark had one of his basses leaning up against. The bass fell and the tuning head broke off. Thank goodness he had a spare. After the show, they found a fellow asleep in one of the giant white subwoofers next to the stage. No one could believe that this guy had withstood that volume.

The Shrine Auditorium - Sept. 26, 1970 Los Angeles

Don was late to this and I believe there was a problem with the law that made him late. I recall him leaving after the sound check, which seemed absolutely insane. Somehow, the police mistook them (Bill, Don, and Jan) for criminals and stopped them. The police had their guns drawn. Don was really frightened by this. They still had to go home and change and the delay made them 30-45 minutes late. I used my Gon Bops the first time at this gig. We wore tuxedos, and Elliot had joined for this show. He wore combat boots with his tux.

Lee Michaels was the main act and they had to cut his show short because we started late. The crowd mobbed the stage. My stuff was back stage and I was loading it into the car as SWAT team officers - in full body armor and carrying automatic weapons - ran by chasing raving kids in tie-dye shirts.

Another Interesting Evening

Helen and I drove home, and as I made a right turn to go up Crescent Heights (which turned into Laurel Canyon) off Sunset, a car pulled out of a parking lot and blocked the whole street in such a way that I was forced to back up to give the car access. I looked around behind and saw nothing, but the Gon Bops were blocking my view and unbeknownst to me, some moronic woman in a small blue sports convertible had tried to squeeze past me by going between my car and the curb. I backed up and doing so, my bumper sideswiped her car and crushed the fender and door in. I was starting to get concerned about my own driving.

Recording Lick My Decals Off, Baby

Finally, we went into the recording studio. The studio of choice was the Record Plant in Los Angeles. It seemed to be the "in" place to go. I thought it was a little decadent, myself and definitely over-priced at $180 bucks an hour. Who needs a studio with a Jacuzzi anyway? It was probably where "everybody who was anybody" recorded, and we were with a guy who'd had his picture on the cover of the Rolling Stone, so extravagance was embraced.

The studio was long and narrow, I didn't care for the shape of it at all. The control booth was in the back and just as wide as the room. It had a sliding glass partition just beyond the drum booth which was a little quarter-circle affair stuck back in the corner. It had permanent baffles, which made it really difficult to get the drums inside and was ridiculously cramped.

Problem With Bass Sound

As with almost every session I had ever been to, they had trouble getting a bass sound. It seemed to take a long time. Mark was using (if I remember correctly) two different basses, a Fender Precision, and a Gibson Thunderbird. His amp was a TNT amp and was huge. I believe they finally wound up taking a direct box - meaning his signal went directly into the mixing board.

Artie In Separate Booth

Artie's marimba had been delivered days before the session, and he was put in the glass isolation booth right next to the drum booth. We all used headphones as monitors. I had learned how to keep them on my head by this time.

Tripp On Decals

John French: *Maybe we could just brush on your reminiscing (s) of the* **Lick My Decals** *session. We kinda passed that by.*
Art Tripp: *That was a good example. Because, when we did that album, besides some of that little marimba stuff I did. I really had no parts.*
JF: *Right, you didn't have a lot of parts for that did you?*

AT: No, you played most of the drums and I played some drums but not too much. What I did was just basically free form. I thought that was what I supposed to do. I thought that was my "lot in life."
JF: Space Age Couple *I remember Don coming over one night and of course, after ripping into everybody for two hours...*

John French: *We finally got down to* Space Age Couple *and couple of other things where we actually worked out double drum parts. Basically, he was having you play "shapes" and I was playing more rhythmically.*
Art Tripp: *I remember - what was that tune? (sings)*
JF: *(recognizing)* Woe Is A Me Bop.
AT: Yeah, OK, I had an actual part on that I just played. That was just something that sounded fine for me to play and everybody liked it so... it became the "Part".
JF: *And you had that wonderful part in* Flash Gordon's Ape *... that interlude.*
AT: Yeah, but then again, it was free form. We only did it two or three times, in fact, I didn't like the take they used as much as the other ones. I just basically responded to what was going on. It wasn't a part that I repeated again and again. That was pretty much it.

I was surprised when Artie said this as I had always considered the interlude in *Flash Gordon's Ape* as something that Don played on the piano, recorded to cassette, and gave to Artie to transcribe. What seemed to reinforce this concept was that Tripp played exactly the same interlude night after night on stage on the tour - note for note.

Art Tripp: But the thing that never ceases to amaze me even to this day and I've told this a hundred times to other people, is I actually thought, and I think some of the others actually thought that this was a commercial effort. (laughter) I mean, Trout Mask *was just too far out and now we're going to do* Lick My Decals Off, Baby, *which we expected to hear on AM radio. That to me just shows how goofy we all were.*
John French: *Well, I am going to say this and you may not believe me, but I never believed that stuff was going to be on AM radio.*
AT: Yeah, well I didn't either, but going in to it...

Artie On Don's Voice

John French: *Well, we had the potential to do that, but with Don's voice and the power*
Art Tripp: *Oh, the voice, well that ruined every album we ever did.*
JF: *What's that?*
AT: His voice, but what I am saying is that the music itself, a lot of times when it started, we had a germ of an idea like a melody, God forbid. Or something that was repeatable, like a repeatable part, where you could tap your foot to it. And that was just the initial thing laid down and then we just piled things on top on top on top. Then went different directions and all over the map, until it was just an unrecognizable piece of ... ART. Almost all of those tunes were like that. Certainly Space Age Couple *and a lot of them were like that. That's not to say that on any given tune you could pull out one of those lines or one of those parts and make an entire piece out of it - on that one little four bar riff or something. I mean, it was there, it's just that he didn't know when to quit. And I sure didn't either.*
JF: *Well you couldn't tell him where to quit. No one could tell him where to quit.*

Tripp On Musical Direction

John French to Art Tripp: But, on the other hand, what was your impression of his lyrical approach and his singing and his horn playing, for instance.
AT: Well, it was all stupid. It was all ridiculous. I mean, it was a lot of fun, and I enjoyed it, but as far as having anything in mind... as far as trying to sell it, it was ridiculous. I loved it. I had a ball doing it, but sooner or later, whatever inkling you had of having to do something that might be appreciated by somebody else, in a commercial sense, was just immediately out the window. Don, I think, was a terrible singer. He had a very limited range as opposed to what everybody said he had a 12 octave range or whatever and he barely had three. Except for a little squeaky falsetto.
JF: There's one of the myths. The 5½ octave voice.
AT: Horseshit, but that was good press.

I was surprised, actually, to hear Tripp say this, as I actually always enjoyed Don's voice. I didn't always care for how he seemed to overdub in a random manner and not actually know where he was going to sing what. It often took away from the music and was confusing. But when he nailed something, it was impressive.

Tripp On Vocals And General Direction

John French: But as far as the blues singing, let's go back to blues, I know you don't...
Art Tripp: Well, that's a different story.
JF: What do you think of his blues singing?
AT: Great, great stuff, because Don was a great impersonator. Don had a great mind for that stuff. First of all, a great artistic mind - and he would get right to the essence of things like that. It was very loose-formed, and it didn't require that he was able to do the same thing twice in a row. That's why he didn't rehearse, because he could never remember - he couldn't think like that his vocal tracks were always done at the end and he would just go in there and squeak it out the best he could. He was under tremendous pressure, because he knew he was completely inept at doing that. So, in the blues, it was perfect. It was free-form, he'd listened to all those guys, whether he heard them live or listened to their tapes or recordings. It was easy for him to impersonate. He had a knack for the harmonica - he was very good at that - so it was a natural for him.
JF: You heard his early recordings like Diddy Wah Diddy and Safe As Milk?
AT: Yeah.
JF: So, you heard the stuff previous to Lick My Decals and Trout Mask.
AT: That was good, that was very good and in that idiom, he was good at it. But I think Don was almost always under a tremendous amount of pressure to produce, and to produce in a way that he knew he was utterly and completely incapable of doing.
JF: To perform.
AT: To perform for sure - absolutely to perform. But, also to produce something that he could only do it his way, and he was such a spoiled little tyrant that he would always get it around to his way, so anyone who could have helped him and make that into a better project, was immediately shouted down or intimidated away. So, he was both his best friend and his worst enemy in the same guy. And I think that put a tremendous amount of pressure on him. Then later on, when he had actual contracts that said, "You WILL produce this album, it WILL be this, it WILL be that", he was at a complete loss. It was a tremendous amount of pressure.

And he was a nervous fucking wreck. He was breaking out all the time, he was always running, he couldn't focus on anything more than thirty seconds at a time - just total escapism. Well, you can do that when you're by yourself and putting it on canvas. But when you're around other guys...

JF: It just doesn't work... yeah!

AT: Sooner or later you have to go with hat in hand to somebody who does know how to do that and go "help!"

JF: Exactly, and trust them.

AT: That's why he ended up with some pretty high-powered guys that he was able to bullshit into helping him, like Ted Templeman, and like three or four others that helped him. I might be going back to, I don't know who, Krasnow, Artie Ripp, all those guys all the way through the last thing he ever did. Because, sooner or later, you have to say this is what it is, it's going to go on that album, and you're gonna be responsible for the results. So, here he is at the helm at this confused mass of artists, that are kind of ballyhooed by the whole thing and don't know what to do. Or if they did know what to do, it's not going to get done because he's going to shout them down. And so the pressure in the end was all on him. It must have been a tremendous strain, you know. I think in the end that's what led him into getting out of it altogether. Plus he had this tremendous talent for painting, which (is what) he should have done all along. His foray in the music was a sidebar.

JF: That was the way he had total control. He could just do whatever he wanted.

AT: And nobody else to blame - nobody else to involve. He didn't have to ask any questions, he just did the best he could - whatever he thought was good, and that was good enough to where a lot of people did get interested. I think Don is probably one of the greatest painters. I saw some of his work five or six years ago and it was some of the best I had seen in the entire history of Art. I mean, it was just overwhelming stuff. He had all these years to season it and to develop his own style and an unlimited imagination - absolutely unlimited. So the music part of it to me was just a - I liked it and I wouldn't give it up for anything - it just was no more than an interesting foray into art that just happened in the history of music. It wasn't - I don't know. It was good stuff, but it certainly wasn't for mass consumption.

Gary Marker: I remember sitting off in a room one time with Cooder and Don and having Cooder - Cooder couldn't sing worth shit - going over Grown So Ugly *with Don. He must have gone over it a thousand times with Don. "No, no, no, listen to the accent, man!" sings "Grown so ugly, don't even know my self..." "No, it's four beats a bar, listen, listen!" you know. Don was really having trouble getting it. I was thinking, "Oh, man, he's got that voice, but he just can't put it in the slot."*

John French: You know, I remember him having trouble, I mean, Ry always sang it at rehearsal, because it was his arrangement, so he always sang it. Then Don did it in the studio and I though, "Gee, Ry's phrasing was actually better than Don's." That's interesting, never thought about that.

As I recall, Don was constantly saying this album was going to be "big." He had quite a sales-pitch and it made us all temporarily hyped-up and excited. I was probably the most skeptical Doubting Thomas. I had been through all this bad stuff with Don from the *Trout Mask* days and had heard much of the same talk even then. However I still had moments of wondering if perhaps I was wrong and would fall prey to Van Vliet's sales pitch. Although we were recording this far-out material, Warners did seem to be supporting the group 100%.

Don kept telling us to "get ready, this is it" etc. At that time, there certainly was quite a bit of interest in the band, at least from our perspective. The Rolling Stone and Creem articles, Warners interest, the upcoming tour all combined did cause us to speculate for a time that things would pick up. However, I can surely say that from what I was observing and experiencing, it still looked like Van Vliet was going right back into his old ways, and, unbelievably enough, we were following along.

Dick Kunc

Dick Kunc was flown in for the session. I know not where he lived at the time. He stayed with Artie and I in the guest room. We had a great time getting re-acquainted. Phil Schier was his assistant engineer. Dick recorded all the basic tracks. I think we took four or five days.

Invasion Of Suit Men

I remember that although things were going fairly well in the Studio, we hadn't rehearsed this maniacally and obsessively for a year and so there were a few trouble spots. Added to that was the fact that it took a lot longer to get a "good" sound on each instrument than, as in the *Trout Mask* session, just to set up a mike and turn it on. Also, different sounds were required on different songs that required varying amounts of time. Plus, some of the pieces had two drums kits, so they had to mic those up out in front of the drum booth.

The third or fourth night in the studio, Don brought the business people in their suits so that they could first lecture us on the cost of this project and then stand and stare at their watches. I can tell you, there's no bigger turn-off to creativity than a bunch of suits standing around staring at their watches. I guess they expected it to be finished in $4^1/2$ hours - like *Trout Mask*.

The Vocal Overdubs

Van Vliet and Kunc seemed to have a bit of tension between them. Dick was a guy who spoke his mind and joked around a lot. He was practical, and he was used to working with Frank Zappa, who was a guy who understood technical studio problems and limitations. Van Vliet was totally ignorant of the mixing board and it's limitations. For $180 an hour, I think he must have thought he was in an environment where there should be no limitations.

Feelings Getting Worse And Worse

When it came time for Don's vocal overdubs, Dick Kunc took every type of conceivable microphone and set it up in the studio in a big cluster. Don had been saying he wanted his voice recorded correctly "for a change." When Don asked what this was all about, Dick replied, " Since I have no idea what kind of vocal sound you actually want, I am going to have you sing and I will give you samples of every conceivable sound you can achieve." Then, you can decide which you like. I thought it was a great plan. Don did not seem to understand, and thought it was some kind of joke on him.

Dick appeared to be oblivious to this, but I could sense that Don was building more and more of a case against him. Finally, Kunc was fired, but in typical Don fashion. If I remember correctly, Artie and I were the ones who actually had to tell him. We both apologized and said that we had no idea what it was about. Dick was obviously hurt and shaken by the decision. I enjoyed having him at the house, and so did Helen. She said it was nice to be around someone like Dick, who got up whistling and read the paper in the morning.

I Come To Visit With Helen

I went to the Record Plant the next day to watch as Don overdubbed his voice. Unfortunately, he was never easy to work with in the studio. Phil Schier, however, was a more non-threatening type of guy and Don trusted him. However, it was apparent that Don was not prepared again and was winging it on several pieces. It wasn't a comfortable experience, and we left after a very short time.

Elliot Ingber Brought On Board

After the Sessions were over, Elliot Ingber began to rehearse with us. Don loved Elliot. Unfortunately, Elliot really didn't have the type of mind that could understand the strange music, so it was tough for him to learn the material. He doubled a lot of Artie's parts.

During this time, we rehearsed more often over at the Trout House. Elliot and Don also had brain-storming sessions in which basically Elliot gave Don ideas that he used almost verbatim. The most vivid memory I have is of Elliot describing in detail the promotional b&w film for *Lick My Decals Off, Baby.* This happened at Don's house while I was there.

I remember him describing in detail the plain doormat as the announcer's voice said the names i.e. "In Bel Air, it's Drumbo, in Santa Anita, it's Ed Marimba..." etcetera. Then, the "In Plainview it's Captain Beefheart" joke and Don appearing and doing "the hand and toe investment." Then Elliot described Don's sock-less foot clad in the strange strapped-shoe knocking over the container of pancake batter, the dark-hooded Mark carrying the sifter and the one string, - all of it. Of course, he was never given any credit for this concept, which was almost totally his. Instead, Don was hailed as a genius for making an avant-garde film noire commercial.

Ingber's ideas, in my estimation, were key influences in the way the band was presented and also musical influences in several pieces that were recorded in the future on *The Spotlight Kid.* There was a bass riff from *Hair Pie* that, when Mark played it as a solo piece, always got a reaction. It had always been a favorite of mine also.

Elliot pointed out that the riff was obviously striking a nerve and why not use it in a song? Thus was birthed *When It Blows It's Stacks.* Elliot was neither intimidated by Don, nor did Don ever try to control him. They were basically the same age, and Ingber would give input into the lyrics and had the beatnik hip-ness to shape the lyrics into attractive pieces. I made up a drum pattern for this song and purposely incorporated a strong backbeat on the snare to give it a dance-able rhythm.

Ice Rose was another piece that was worked on at the Trout House, but it never developed the way *Stacks* had. Ingber had a lot to do with the lyrics on both pieces mentioned and should have received credit.

TV Ad

Larry Sechrest and John Fizzdale were hired to shoot the promotion film. Mark, Bill, Don and Jan went to the Studio. I only heard a little bit about this shoot at the time. I recall going by to visit as they were editing, but I didn't stay long as I didn't want to distract from the production. It was in a small video studio which I recall being in Burbank somewhere. The announcer who had done the "Ginsu knife" commercial (along with many others) was hired for the voice-over.

Warners Plans A Tour

Although we had been doing local "warm-up gigs," quite successfully, the idea for a tour became reality. Don began planning the tour right after we finished the album and announced that Warners was going to actually sponsor a tour. I thought this was a good plan, as they had every motivation to make it a success. From what I understand, this isn't usually the case. I am extremely naïve about the music business, so I can't really tell you exactly how it usually works. To the best of my knowledge, tours are synchronized by independent booking agents to coincide with recent releases from their clients. The idea is although they work independently, the release and the tour obviously compliment each other and so agents try to work this cooperatively to the utmost advantage.

Warner Bros Sound Lot (Bonanza)

Since we were with Warner Brothers Records, they made special arrangement for us to use the sound stages at Warner Brothers studios in the evenings for rehearsals. It was a really great idea and was a little more centrally located. It also gave us the chance to work in a large room. It's hard to explain unless you've done it, but the sound in a large area has completely different characteristics and it can be a little overwhelming to walk onto a concert stage after rehearsing in a small space for months. There is no presence to the sound, it all goes out except for a faint reverberation. It gives you the illusion that your volume in insufficient for the hall and results in overplaying.

It was really an exciting experience for me to drive up to the gate and actually be allowed to drive on the lot and park right next to the sound stage, walk through this little door into a huge room. Whenever I wasn't needed at rehearsal, I would climb the stairs and go up in the overhead rafters and walk the ramps. It was really high, and gave a great perspective of the room. Often, other band members would show up late. I usually arrived on time or early with Winged Eel Fingerling, who depended on me for a ride, since his sports car had been disabled for quite some time, and was semi-permanently nestled under a bush in his yard, and covered with a tarp.

Little Feat

The band Little Feat, which featured Lowell George on guitar, rehearsed in the same area as us but earlier in the day. I remember very little about them. I do recall them hanging out as we rehearsed one day and something broke on my set as we were rehearsing, but their road manager came over and remedied the situation, which I thought was extremely thoughtful.

Mostly Don And Elliot Blues

Many times at these early rehearsals, Don would show up and sing blues while Elliot played guitar. One side of this was frustration for me. I always thought that if Don could sing the blues at rehearsals, why couldn't he have done them on stage and recordings and made some money so that we weren't always in such bad financial straits? The other reason for my frustration lie in the fact that we had a lot of work to do to get the band in order and Don still never rehearsed with the band. There was even a PA supplied, so he had no excuse.

We couldn't rehearse until Don and Elliot were done jamming blues. I can't say that I didn't enjoy hearing this, but it's such a shame that Don just couldn't share his blues singing with the world.

Elliot's Plan

Elliot had a plan for our stage show. He wanted to put together a set list of material that was sequenced so well and so tightly, that there was barely room to take a breath. He had been listening to Beefheart material and compiling this list for quite some time, and it was apparent that he had put quite a bit of thought into it. It was actually quite short, as I understand, compared to what rock performers generally did. It was about 45-50 minutes, if I recall correctly, with nary a moment of silence in the entire set. It was designed to just pelt the audience into submission and also to clearly release the power of the well-rehearsed band.

Little Golden Birdies ..Elliot's Idea .. Don Doesn't Like

Although Elliot came off as a rather passive hippy who would probably have been an ideal roommate for Gandhi, he was actually quite insistent that we do things his way. "Just TRY it!" he would say. His self-assertive attitude took us all a bit by surprise, but his ideas seemed to be very valid, and so even Don seemed cooperative up until the evening that Elliot edited bits and pieces of two of Don's compositions and came up with *"Those Little Golden Birdies, Look At Them."*

Don's reaction was something like, "Elliot, I'm not sure that I like my composition cut up like this." "Just do it, man, you can throw it out later if you really don't like it, just try it," Elliot would say, and Don conceded. It wound up going over quite well at concerts eventually being recorded, of course, on *Clear Spot* years later. After it's release, at the end of the recitation, Don would point the mike to the audience and they would recite the last line, "Webcor, Webcor."

Overcoats
The tour was getting close. I was packed. We had Bill Shumow and Jeff Bruschele as roadies and they were painting our names on equipment and making sure we had cases for everything. Artie came in a couple of nights before our departure and said, "Look what I found, man!" He displayed a camel's hair overcoat to me. Now, being from the West Coast, I didn't know much about overcoats and nothing about camel's hair. He explained that we were going to be traveling through a lot of very cold country and I should have an overcoat.

So I went out the next day, walked in a thrift shop in Hollywood and for $18 I bought a hand-stitched pristine camel's hair overcoat. I found a little trick to packing for a trip. For a week before leaving, I would "live" out of my luggage, to simulate what the road would be like. That way, anything I had forgotten would become evident to me within a few days. When you're gone for six or seven weeks on the road, you want to make sure and bring everything you need, or it can get expensive.

Reunion With Ry Cooder
We found out that an old bandmate, Ry Cooder, would be joining us on the tour as the opening act. I thought this was really great, as I loved Ry. I hadn't heard his material yet, and actually didn't hear his album until the end of the tour, though I did hear most of the material live. What irony, such a twist of fate that Ry would be joining us. I was looking forward to seeing him again.

Party At Warners
Just before the tour began, Warners decided to throw us all a little party. We went to one of the sound stages and found they had set up this little reception. The area was a partitioned area, probably part of a set. There were the usual deli-trays, plastic cups, and a dozen business guys running around in suits.

Meet Ry's Wife Susan
I was standing with Helen by the celery when Ry walked up with a lady. I had seen Ry at a couple of rehearsals, him leaving, us arriving. It was always good to see this man. I respected him a great deal and still do to this day. Ry said, "My wife wanted to meet you, she's intrigued by your clothes." I realized I must look pretty strange. I was wearing a pink laboratory duster with turquoise pants and girl watcher sunglasses. I had shiny galoshes on over my shoes, although it wasn't raining and was wearing a chimney sweep's cap.

It turned out that Susan was quite a charming and beautiful lady. She had been involved in some kind of conceptual art. I later remember a conversation in which she led a large group of people to allow themselves to be placed inside some kind of large bag. She filmed it from the outside, as I recall, because she found the random shapes interesting. I believe she may have been an art instructor. I later found out she was the sister of Russ Titleman, who Ry had brought in to play guitar on *Safe As Milk*.

Bus To Airport
Warner Brothers was even thoughtful enough to provide transportation to the airport. We Showed up at the Warners lot and boarded a bus. It was an exciting day. Even though it was decent

weather, I decided to wear my overcoat as it was bulky to pack. I noticed that everyone had on an overcoat. I think Bill was wearing his old standby leather overcoat that looked like it had been through a couple of wars. Artie and I were both wearing Camel's hair and Don and Mark Boston were both wearing dark blue "raincoat type" overcoats.

Don stopped and stared at all of us. "What is this?" he demanded. "Mark and me, you and Artie." He actually seemed angry about the fact that our pairs of coats matched. I said nothing and boarded the bus. I wasn't going to allow anyone to spoil such a great day. Helen had dropped Elliot and I off in my Cadillac, and as I sat on the bus, Ry and Susan drove up in a classic 1940's "woodie" station wagon. It was pristine and completely restored. "What a great looking car!" I thought. I felt as though this was going to be fun. I always enjoyed being out of the private, controlled and suffocating environment that Don so efficiently created. This environment was much healthier. Here were 10 musicians, 2 wives, 2 roadies, and a manager (Grant Gibbs) going on tour. The mindset would open up and there would be a much healthier daily life. Perhaps this would spill over into our private controlled environment and things would improve.

Warner Brothers had guaranteed our group $1,000 a night plus expenses for the tour. I don't know how much this was in comparison to other groups of the time. There were thirty-three dates total. I figured that I was getting $100 a show plus expenses according to our agreement - so I would finish with about $3,300. Don would finish with 5 times that amount, $16,500.

CHAPTER THIRTY:
TOURS 'N QUAKES 'N BIG MISTAKES

Don in 1972. Photo courtesy of Art Trip

Cities On Tour

With the help of a gig list from Theo Tieman's Website, Electricity, I obtained this information and thought it might help spur my memory. So, I give special thanks to Tieman for his tireless research. Memory will only allow me to comment on a few, but I will try to remember as many events as possible.

Temporary Carnivoric Vegetarians

As an example of how strong a hold Don had on the band, a few weeks before the tour, Van Vliet had thoroughly convinced everyone in the band that we should be vegetarians. Well, at least me. I had been eating only vegetables. This was something I always wanted to do anyway, as I know the bad effects ingesting meat can have on the human body. Jan seemed to be pushing Don in this direction. I think this also might have had something to do with Elliot's influence, because he was feeding himself mandarin oranges exclusively - which I believe he had decided was the only actual complete food. They were good, as I recall Helen stuffing sections of one in my mouth as I drove Elliot, Helen, and myself to the Warners soundstage to catch the bus.

That first night (we arrived the night before our first performance) we all met in the dining room for dinner and Don announced, much to the dismay of Jan and Elliot, "I don't know about you, but I'm having a steak." So after weeks of eating nothing but vegetables, we all suddenly became instant carnivores and devoured meat. Actually, I had been feeling pretty queasy as I hadn't really studied in detail exactly how to balance the proteins and carbs in a vegetarian diet. It had left me a little weak and made it difficult to concentrate. After that first meal on the road, I felt better.

Diamonds

We were staying at a Holiday Inn, in fact, most of the hotels on this tour were Holiday Inns. As I was walking to my room after dinner, Van Vliet shouted to me. "Look!" He opened up the icemaker and reaching in with both hands, grabbed huge amounts of ice." "Diamonds!" he shouted maniacally in his best mad scientist voice at the top of his voice, "thousands of diamonds." He scattered them all over the floor. This was a prankster-ish side of Don I seldom saw. I had heard he could be quite the clown from the early band, but this was something I hadn't seen in a long time. It was a good laugh and lightened the mood a bit.

Sound Check

The next day, before the sound-check, Don called to tell me he was a little ill and would appreciate if I would check the sound system for him. "What do you mean?" I asked. "Just sing through it and make sure I can hear something, OK?" he replied. He used to often say "Sound check? - I don't need my 'sound checked'!" - as a joke, and outsiders would laugh, while the band groaned. The shows often had big glitches in them due to Don's "not needing his sound checked" attitude. It wasn't funny to those of us in the band who had to perform live with a guy who understood so little about technical issues. On several occasions, I watched him completely alienate the soundman in the first five minutes of a sound check. The soundman is "the guy" who has complete control over what the group sounds like out front, and can manipulate the dials, if properly motivated for revenge to make the band sound tinny, muddy, unbalanced and weak.

Don had a thorough disdain of the road and I believe he also had an extremely hard time sleeping. When he was out of his own controlled environment, I sensed he became a bit more fearful than most. It's much easier to project a certain larger-than-life type of image when all you are doing is staying at home and doing interviews. However, the road opened the door to a much closer scrutiny. Since Don, by his own words, was a "diagnosed paranoid schizophrenic," I am sure there was a certain elevation in paranoia associated with this scrutiny.

For the most part, my second tenure in the band had been witness to far less of the cult-like environment and it's effects upon the members of the entourage. I knew it was there, awaiting the moment to rear it's ugly head, but the fact that we weren't all gathered together on the same property greatly raised the control threshold, while we remained safely below, only occasionally poking up through into the dreaded cult stratosphere when we wandered too far up a hill. However, I always sensed strongly that under the surface, Van Vliet was quite uncomfortable with his lack of immediate control over the group's environment. It seemed to me that he would actually have preferred the former *Trout Mask* type of environment - us all living together in the same compound once again.

It also seemed to me that there was always lingering the fear that someone might actually interview a Magic Band member and, in a moment of weakness, they might actually become honest and speak openly of some of the less attractive aspects of being led by the Captain. There was the added fact that we were touring with another group and associating with people who worked under more fair leadership (although I have heard that Cooder can be quite negative), start comparing notes, and eventually jump ship for fairer seas.

One of the main things I noticed during this tour, was that Don seemed to isolate himself to a large extent. This could have been my interpretation, but it seemed like every time I saw Don, he was always with Jan, going somewhere or busy doing something and couldn't be bothered with social exchange when it came to band members.

I was nothing more than a sideman. I didn't realize it at the time, but that's really all I was at this point - at least in the business sense. I was no longer ever approached by any journalist - even for a short statement. It was apparent that we were viewed as nothing more than as we had been portrayed as in the Rolling Stone article; young naïve musicians hand-picked, individually and completely trained by Don Van Vliet. We were treated as trivial and dispensable.

At the time, this didn't bother me much. I wanted to go onstage, enjoy the experience, and be out of the focus of the limelight. I was shy and didn't care much for focused attention, except when I was playing. I would have been uncomfortable talking to reporters, because I would have been torn between telling the truth, or fabricating a story that would remain consistent with Van Vliet's already accepted image. I wouldn't realize until later what a devastating effect this had on my own personal chances for success.

I was a drummer with a unique style and above average abilities. Given any small amount of recognition at this point in time, I might have been able to make the connection that would have allowed me to carve out enough of a niche for myself to have remained active in the music business and made a decent living and have had a more productive life. Instead, I became a name (pseudonym actually) only known by a few obscure critics and never received anything but minimal recognition until such a point in time that it no longer mattered. It is too late now for me to pursue the musical ambitions I had nearly 40 years ago. I have different priorities, conflicting responsibilities, and a daughter who needs my support - not an "absentee Dad on the road." I have seen enough of the devastating effects absentee fatherhood has had on families.

I believe this holds strongly for the rest of the band. We had three strikes against us.
1. Van Vliet's chosen musical direction made us obscure enough as it was.
2. His "copywritten pseudonyms" made us somewhat anonymous.
3. The final nail in our career coffins was his policy in regards to interviews and exposure to the press.

Many people have suggested that we were jealous of the amount of attention Don received. I think this is an untrue and unfair statement. I never recall hearing one band member ever complain about the fact they weren't being interviewed, or that Don was receiving too much focus. All of us were rather relieved at the time that we didn't have to deal with that aspect of the music world. On the same hand, we were all giving full support to a man who already had publicly gone on the record making statements about us that were absolute falsehoods. In order to not cause him harm publicly, we remained mute.

As time went by it certainly became more and more apparent to me that the image Don portrayed of Captain Beefheart was unsettlingly out of touch with the true workings of the group. Not only this, but it became uncomfortably clear that the inertia being generated by this image was making it almost certain that the truth was less likely to ever be revealed, and was being rapidly diminished at a geometrically expanding rate. Thus the band, engulfed in a pit of mythology and legend, would never be given their fair share of credibility.

Even now, were it not for the fact that Van Vliet has become almost completely inaccessible, former Magic Band members (I'm referring mainly to pre *Shiny Beast*) would not be receiving the small amount of attention and recognition they now are enjoying. Unfortunately, they are also faced with the fact that a major portion of the attention is from fans and critics completely saturated with and indoctrinated by the legend and the mythology created by the Captain himself. So, this belated attention is not only for the most part misguided, but also seems more like a search for a replacement or substitution: a "little Don," so to speak.

Band members obviously have a choice here to either try to be the one who "takes up the cloak" and becomes somehow an artificial fulfillment of the former glory. So then, it becomes yet another illusion, and so the one creating the illusion must face the fact that the original is still being perpetuated. Lie begats lie in this scenario. I do not compare this with the Zappa tribute groups - like "Banned from Utopia" or "The Grande Mothers," in which Zappa compositions are faithfully and accurately performed by some of the former members, thus perpetuating a tradition of music for the large and still-thriving fanbase.

The other choice is to actually be oneself. I actually attempted this with a CD called *Waiting On The Flame*, which has some compositions I wrote from my own heart, ignoring the labels pasted on me by the Beefheart fans. Unfortunately, since my name is only known by Beefheart fans, my music was met by critics portraying me as "trying too hard to prove that I'm not like Van Vliet." Also, according to this critic, it was too "clean;" there weren't enough "flaws."

However, the people that I mainly associate with and enjoy friendships with were my main testing ground. They all seemed to enjoy the music, the general consensus being "It's nice to hear something that you've recorded that isn't weird and that I can actually enjoy." I am sure there is a large audience out there that feels the same way. However, I was NEVER able to reach them, because of the category in which I was placed merely because of my association with Van Vliet. This pigeon-holing has affected all of us who were associated with Captain Beefheart.

The later members, however, benefited. They were drawn to the music from *Trout Mask Replica* and *Lick My Decals Off, Baby*. We, who did those albums, were more drawn to the band because of *Diddy Wah Diddy, Safe As Milk,* and *Strictly Personal*. We also grew up in the same town with Don (with the exception of Arthur Tripp III) and so saw the early blues band and their powerful interpretation of the old blues classics laced with spellbinding Delta rhythms.

The very music we associated with the worst times of our lives was, by the younger generation of players, associated with some of their best times.

Eastown Theatre Fri Jan. 15, 1971 Detroit, Michigan

We had to wait for The Amboy Dukes to finish their sound check. I spent the time exploring the venue. After thirty years, it's hard to recall, but I'm picturing it as an old movie theatre. Once the drums were set up and properly miked, I walked over and grabbed the vocal mike and had the band play a little of "Mirror Man" and I bellowed the lyrics as loudly as I could into the PA. As soon as I could adequately hear myself, I gave an OK to the soundman.

I had never had the opportunity of singing on stage with a decent monitor and this system was really good. I remember Bill looking at me, grinning, with a look of nostalgia. Although Bill and I never played in pre-Beefheart group, he was probably thinking about how different our present situation might have been had we younger musicians joined forces and put our own group together. I'm sure it would have been more fun.

Elliot had purchased some electronic device that would allow his guitar to have a Leslie effect. I think it was called a Univibe. With today's technology, one can have in a small box what would have amounted to a huge, expensive, heavy and impractical rack of gear. Elliot was very happy because his unit worked great, and he was really relieved to be able to try it out on *Mirror Man* before the show. Art had done something really clever with his drums. He had purchased a small canvas tarp, set his drums upon it, and drawn the outlines of where all the stands went. This made it easy for roadies Bill Shumow and Jeff Bruschele to set up his drumkit night after night.

That night, I went on stage first and it was a little intimidating. It was a rough looking crowd and someone forcibly threw a handful of peanuts in the shell that hit me directly in the face. It stung like small pebbles and the expression on my face caused laughter. This was a tough group. My instincts cut in, and I sat down on the stage, picked up the peanuts, shelled and deliberately ate them, one by one. The crowd responded with applause and cheers. When I finished, I went over and did a short solo on the drums, initiating our performance as planned.

Artie came out and we played a double drum solo for a short period of time. We then would stand and, keeping time, walk to the middle of the stage facing each other, eventually playing "pattycake." Then, I would put my right hand on his right shoulder and he likewise, and then left hands on left shoulder and we would pat each other on the shoulders. This usually got a laugh from the crowd. Then, both would walk back to our instruments and I would temporarily become an observer. Art would then aim and shoot a raygun at the audience, eventually saying "Ronnie Raygun" as a pun on then Governor of California Ronald Reagan. He then played his marimba interlude from *Flash Gordon's Ape*.

This was followed by Rockette Morton's appearance. He would generally perform the bass parts from *Hair Pie*, having plugged-in during Art's Marimba solo. As he was performing, the guitarists would come out and prepare, and on his last note, giving a moment for applause, I would shout "and" and we would go into *Big Joan*. There were several variations in the show until it was smoothly dialed-in. Eventually, Elliot, satisfied that it was the best it could be, quit "tweaking" the set list. As we left the club, there was quite a group of people standing outside watching us board the bus, and I never saw a group of tougher-looking folks in my life. We waved "hello" and they responded very openly, the scowls replaced by smiles.

Who Do You Trust Now?

When we arrived back at the Holiday Inn, we were invited to Don's room and there was a large birthday cake. Written on the cake were the words "Happy 30th Birthday Captain Beefheart - Don't Trust Anyone Over Thirty." This cake was apparently compliments of Warner Brothers. I believe Hal Haverstadt was there representing Warners, and perhaps Mo Austin, but I couldn't be sure. Of course Grant Gibbs, plus the guys from Ry's band and the Magic Band also attended.

Don, quite devoid of foresight, had been adamantly telling everyone in the *Trout Mask* band for years "don't trust anyone over thirty." This was an "anti-establishment" phrase he clung to from the sixties. This night was a rather amusing moment - for everyone except Don - who remained suspiciously quiet. We all had a piece of cake, and the conversation picked up soon enough. I think we actually sang

"Happy Birthday" to this guy whom we apparently could no longer trust - at least according to him ?.

Everyone was fairly excited about the tour beginning, and so we had little thought about the birthday after about 5 minutes. After the party broke up, I went downstairs for a while, and when I returned, I found that Don had placed the cake on the hallway floor beside his room entrance. In what was left of the cake were Don's footprints. He had trampled the cake into a pulp.

If I haven't mentioned it before - Don loves shoes and used to say he had a "shoe fetish." In fact, he could be have been christened the "Imelda Marcos of avant-garde rock." I am sure that he had dozens of pairs of shoes even then and they were all in pristine condition, as he was quite careful with them. Now he had a pair with sticky icing all over them. It must have taken a great deal of anger to overcome his obsession with immaculate shoes.

I stood in the hallway laughing at the image. I realized the joke message had obviously upset him a great deal. I also thought about how many dozens of times Don had made me the brunt of his jokes - on a much less benign level much to my displeasure. If something like kharma truly exists, no more accurate manifestation could have been made than this. "Lighten-up Don" was all I could think. After all, I had learned not to trust him well before he was thirty.

It was a rather amusing moment for me, and I went to my room laughing, only to find Elliot (we were sharing a room) nearly naked on his bed in full lotus position. I think he talked me into doing a bunch of breathing exercises because I seemed "uptight." I guess you could say he thought I was "prana-challenged." It was actually quite an education. I had to breathe in through one nostril, hold the breath for a specific length of time, and breathe VERY SLOWLY out the other nostril. My nostrils had never before had such a workout. Even now, I get compliments on my well-sculpted nostrils.

I did wonder, even at the time, why Warners had signed Don. He later would say, "I'm like the hood-ornament on a Rolls Royce." I often felt as though it was Warners way of portraying their selves in a philanthropic light as "the friend of the artist." Companies of this size can write off a non-commercial product like this - especially one in which the leader has made the cover of Rolling Stone - and yet portray that they are doing so "in support of art." The photo-ops and the politics are all a part of the schmoozing of the public and I found it no different than politicians kissing babies.

In today's market, Don could have never gotten a deal. Warners did treat him well, but now all the major companies are run by accountant's figures. Then, there was more of a "free-spirit" mentality. An openness - partially brought about by the hippy movement - which, for a time, allowed something other than "product" to be released.

UNKNOWN CLUB Jan (Sat. Or Sun) 16 Or 17, Cincinnati, Ohio, USA

Both my mother and father were raised in Springfield, Ohio, and many of my relatives were still living in the area at the time. My cousin, Pamela Latimer, a very attractive blonde, came down with a few friends to see the show. The club's name has escaped me (as most names do) but it again appeared to be a revamped movie theatre. I recall it being narrow, not more than twice as wide as the stage. It had a dance floor in front, which basically was taken up with standing spectators, it had tables in the rear, and a large balcony above, with seats in the front and tables in the back. I remember a lot of glass. I sat with my cousin and her friends and watched Ry's show, which had a cool response, but I really loved his stuff.

It was the first time I actually had the opportunity to hear his show. I loved Ry's musical ideas and guitar playing, but I found his singing to be more of a novelty, as though he were playing a role, rather than being himself. Don had actually encouraged him to sing after hearing him sing *Grown So Ugly* while rehearsing *Safe As Milk*. His band was loose, and so many of the "grooves" that he was trying to achieve wound up lost in the debris of reverb and bad musicianship. Often, during this tour, I imagined how good his music would have sounded had the Magic Band played it. Not that we were necessarily better musicians, but that we were dedicated, while his band was composed of sidemen along for the ride.

Usually, I didn't like sitting out front before doing a show. It gave me a terrible feeling of anticipation and I'd wind up with a bad case of stage fright. I can literally picture myself from the audience while I am onstage and suddenly I'm not focusing on performance, but on image. Fortunately, by this time, I felt like I could have played the set in my sleep (I think I did once). The place was really well decorated and had a nice open feeling with its high ceiling. The sound system was really good, and if I remember right, the sound man was in the balcony.

After we played, there was a really good response and people were trying to get into the dressing room. They had to secure the doorway. I remember someone from our crew walking in later, and while the door was open, a girl saw me and shouted, "Drumboooooooooooo!" quite enthusiastically. The club manager laughed lovingly, "Oh, that's cute!" He said. "You really know you've reached them when they start saying your name like that." I wanted to go out and talk to her, but for some reason, we had to stay inside because of some corny security precaution. I think that's the only time an American female fan showed any enthusiasm at all for the percussionist in the Magic Band.

Ludlow's Garage January (Sun. Or Mon.) 17th Or 18th, 1971, Cleveland, Ohio

Jim Tarbow was the owner or manager's name. I recall him as having red or auburn hair and beard and sort of a modern day "Robin Hood" look about him. We had to walk down a ramp to get into the dressing room, which was under the floor of the actual performance room. The performance area was a big room and everyone sat on the floor or danced. It was an old garage, and so they left the original sign and didn't change the name.

It seemed from the stage perspective that the room was wider than it was deep. Somebody had built some giant chairs - two or three - big wooden chairs with arms that some of the "elite" would sit in. At one point in the show, Don had suggested that I bring a floor tom (drum) out from the set and play at the edge of the stage. I complied and it felt so good that I grabbed the drum and ran through the crowd pounding on the drum and screaming at the top of my lungs. (Important Disclaimer: I was not using any mind-altering substances by this point in my life) I recall that at the end, Artie and Don went out to do a version of *Spitball Scalped A Baby* and I joined in later and for my final note of the song, I spilled my entire case of drumsticks (probably 25 or 30 pairs) onto the drumset just to see what it would sound like. When I came back out to collect the sticks, I found that audience members had taken them as souvenirs; thus, my first big expenditure of the tour - about $100 in drumsticks - took my entire earnings for the night.

Upon arriving at the dressing room, I found a livid Don in a frenzy over the fact that Sechrist and Fizzdale, the film guys, had missed the last piece (spitball) because they ran out of film. They were, however, busy filming Don's frenzy. After the camera was turned off, he turned to Artie and said, "I should get an Academy Award for that performance."

University Of Pittsburgh Tues., January 19th 1971, Pittsburg, Pa

I remember a large room with no seats at a college. The stage seemed to be a platform made of plywood. There was a pool table in our dressing area and Artie's mother was there. Art was giving a demonstration of pool techniques and the filmmakers filmed him. Art Tripp recalls the following:

Art Tripp: That was at the University of Pittsburgh. I don't remember the name of the large hall. Yes, they took pictures of me playing pool - I suppose with monocle and all. Also an accomplished bassoonist entertained the band and hangers-on with the opening bassoon solo from Stravinsky's Le Sacre Du Printemps (The Rite of Spring). *We should have gotten him in the band, but of course he'd have been ruined for life...*

The door from the dressing room to the stage was in the far left (onstage perspective) corner of the room. We had to walk out through the scattered groups of people to get to the stage. It was very haphazard and unprofessional. The sound was not that great, as the acoustics of this room left a lot to be desired and I believe they had students running the sound. By this point, I seldom recall having a sound check. I think Don had nixed them by this point.

There was a long plastic tube (thin, like laundry bag material) probably 3 ft. in diameter, which somebody to the left of the stage began to fill with air and feed snakelike out over the audience. Everyone seemed to grab the moment and put their hands up to support this silvery snake as it meandered out over the audience. At the end of the show, some rather tall fellow gathered up the plastic into a big ball and carried it around like a duffel bag and was hitting people over the head with it. Don told me later that he came up behind and hit Don over the head and Don angrily turned around and ripped the ball to shreds. It had smashed up his hat a bit.

Plane Flights

There were so many plane flights on this leg of the tour and I learned to actually sleep on these short flights. I really didn't like flying, and every time we took off I was listening for strange vibrations in the engine. Jeff Bruschele was a bit of a prankster. I recall one time they served us spaghetti on a flight and it came with a little paper cup full of Parmesan cheese. He took the cup of cheese and dumped it on the guy's head sitting in front of him. The guy was stunned, and really didn't do much. I think he thought the stewardess (they were still called that) had spilled it accidentally. Bruschele and Bill Harkleroad were laughing about this. I noticed that they seemed to get on quite well. I didn't really find humor in the degradation of another person - even on this pranksterish level - so it didn't strike me as amusing. I was embarrassed and felt sorry for the poor guy.

Another instance that Bill told me about (probably during a *Clear Spot* tour) was that he fell asleep on a flight and his mouth was hanging open. Jeff tore up a napkin and made little paper balls, which he very carefully dropped in Bill's mouth one at a time and continued the procedure until Bill's mouth was full. Bill said he awoke spitting paper out of his mouth to the horror of his fellow passengers.

Carnegie-Mellon Institute Tues. - Wed. January 19th - 20th, 1971, Pittsburg PA

Warners had supplied us with a Kustom PA system for use when there was no house system available. This was a tacky PA to say the least. It was upholstered in black naugahyde tuck 'n' roll (like those cars I talked about earlier and probably by the same people) and had a primitive mixer/amplifier combination, and a few mics, maybe six or eight altogether. The high-impedance mics had cables which were only 20 ft long, which put the roadies mixing the sound right in front of the band. It was ridiculous.

This PA was meant for a club band that didn't have sound-men. The idea was, someone put the mixer/amp next to them and adjusted the controls from stage. I suggested that they make a "snake" which is basically a set of extension cords for the mike cables. They had one made up, but it turned out that the mikes were high impedance and would not work at all on a cable over 20 ft. I think this was the night when we first discovered this whole situation.

I recall this auditorium as being fairly new or refurbished and painted. The carpeting was nice and the acoustics were good. It was fairly small - 350 to 500 seats. Bill usually stood directly to my left onstage and as we were waiting to begin a sound check. Bill was standing next to me with his guitar around his neck waiting to start and we'd been out just long enough that everyone was punch-drunk from the combination of traveling, lack of sleep, and unusual diet - not to mention the stress of touring and performing. The stage area was crowded and he was quite close to me.

Someone, I think Don, called to Bill from behind and to my right. As he turned in a clockwork direction to respond to the call, the tuning head of his Stratocaster whacked me right in the forehead. I was tuning my snare, therefore looking down, and didn't see it coming. To add to the comic effect, the guitar was turned up quite loud and of course amplified sympathetically (in this case double-meaning) in response to the collision. "oh, sorry John, are you alright" was Bill's reaction. He was genuinely concerned. Actually, it didn't leave a mark as I had my chimney sweep cap on and it had actually just missed actual flesh. I started laughing, as much out of fatigue as the situation. This is what happens when you play one-nighters and don't get enough sleep for a few days.

I remember that evening as we sat in the dressing room that there were some toys in a closet and Mark and I, giddy from lack of sleep and tired of the film crew filming our every action, began playing with these toys just to be off the wall. Actually, I think they were probably stage props for a play - a rubber knife and some helmets and masks. Mark had the rubber knife he was shaking into the lens of the camera with a ridiculously ominous face that actually appeared as a very comical image in the film. I thought it was hilarious and was on the floor laughing.

Don, however, disapproved immensely of our shenanigans and gave us quite a tongue-lashing after the show. "Man, how could you do that? That was lame, man!" he kept saying, "do you want people to think that's where you're at?"

"So, what if they do?" I asked. This did not go over well. The show seemed to go OK. It was often hard for me to judge from the stage just how the audience was reacting. What sometimes seemed like a good show to me sometimes later was reported as a total bust.

Elliot Ingber, Portrait Of Rent-A-Freak As Roommate

There was hardly any interaction between Don and I apart from when he was criticizing me for something or asking me to do him a favor. He spent a lot of time with Jan of course (who was traveling, I assume, at the expense of the band). However, aside from his little joke about "diamonds" in Detroit, I barely saw him except at the performances.

My roommate, Elliot Ingber, had some amazingly strange habits, having been a bachelor and a "hippy freak" most of his life. He was fairly quiet most of the time actually, and for the most part, I tried to ignore his eccentricities, figuring he probably thought me just as strange. He could be hilariously funny at moments. For instance, one evening, he was particularly enthralled with some really cheap B movie about a married woman having sex with various men. Of course, it never actually showed the sex; they would kiss, the woman would then assume a look of ravenous desire and they would dissolve to black as the music increased in intensity.

Elliot was explaining to me that this "chick" had a real problem because she was addicted to (and in his best cowboy voice, a total change of character for Elliot) "haaard loooove." He went into vivid detail as to all the various social implications, never cracking a smile, but keeping me in total stitches for 20 minutes or so as he explained this woman's behavior in pseudo-psychiatric language, interspersed with plenty of cowboy colloquialisms.

Most of the time, I stayed in the room, because we had absolutely NO money. We kept asking Grant for some pocket change at least, to fritter away on non-essentials like TOOTHPASTE etc. Grant kept saying, "when we get to New York City, you'll get some money and we'll have some time off."

I came into the room one night, really uptight (I suppose I embraced the "angry young man" image a little too seriously). I'm not sure why I was angry, but Elliot could see this. "Take your shoes off, man," he said to me. I took my shoes off and he had me sit cross-legged on my bed and do the yoga breathing exercises that he had taught me earlier. He spent a lot of time really explaining the whole idea that this cleansing exercise would calm me. Actually, it worked. I used it a lot after that.

My favorite thing was to soak in a hot tub. Being a drummer, and playing as hard as I played, my muscles were hard as rocks and I was stiff all the time. When we finished playing a set, I could actually take off my clothes and wring them out. I would be so dehydrated that one night I drank (for lack of being able to find any water) seventeen 12 oz. Cokes in a row! (not recommended, I had a sugar high that nearly exploded my brain, but I didn't know sugar would do that back then). That was at Ludlow's Garage. It was this physical exertion that caused a lot of my snappy attitude, which I really tried my best to hide. I felt exhausted all the time, and lying in a hot tub seemed to calm me.

Unknown Rock Club Thurs. January 23, 1971, Ithaca, NY

Although I can't find any record of this, I am absolutely sure that we played a club in inland New York State prior to playing Ungano's in Manhattan. It seems to me that we actually drove from Pittsburgh by bus and were not able to have a sound check or anything. This particular night, I became Don's "bad guy" for some reason, and the whole time we were in the dressing room prior to the performance, he was ragging on me about something in front of the entire band, Jan, the road managers, and Grant Gibbs.

If you've never been through this kind of experience, you can't realize how having the "star of the show" on your case can affect your morale. Don was never specific about what he was holding against you, so I would resort to just saying things like, "I don't care what you think, I'm just here to play drums." I resisted the attempt to "cop out" and say "you're right Don, about whatever you're upset about," because I felt that was just being phony and going along with something that wasn't real.

Because of my former experiences with Don (ejected down stairs comes to mind among other things) I had quite an aloof attitude towards him and probably a pretty complicated defense mechanism. He had not really been friendly at all during this entire tour and I would, overall, describe his attitude toward us as "snobbish." I felt as though I was doing my job to the best of my ability. I didn't drink nor did I take drugs. I was always on time and played the set down without mistakes. Don was a whole different story onstage. He was completely different each night, his lyrics were in different places, and one never knew what he wanted or what to expect.

I was always a little tense on stage because of this, second-guessing if I was cueing the breaks correctly in *Big Joan*, wondering if he wanted me to join Artie and he in *Spitball Scalped A Baby*, and basically filled with anticipation as to whether or not I was reacting in the way Don would approve of that particular night (and what he approved of varied greatly from night to night). I wasn't looking for Don's approval for my own acknowledgement, but rather for the wish that the tension would dissipate and we could actually ENJOY this tour.

The actual club had a dressing room more towards the back of the room. It's entrance faced east and the bandstand was at the back of the club. We had to walk down the right side of the audience to get to the stage. It was a standing room dance type atmosphere. It seems like we went over quite well in this club. Because of that, Don seemed to be more amiable after the show, to my great relief.

The Difficulties Of Touring

I know that it sounds like I'm just criticizing Don, but these are the actual things that I remember. It was not that pleasant touring with him. I know he actually hated going on the road. There were probably numerous reasons. I think he had problems with sugar and drank too many cokes on the road. He was also drinking a green liqueur called Chartreuse quite a bit. He would bring the bottle on stage with him. It's also very difficult for a singer on the road because every weather change affects the voice, and so the vocal cords respond differently each night. He also had terrible allergies and I think sleeping in a different bed every night with different types of pillows and bedclothes washed in various detergents didn't help either.

My Own Attitude

There's always two sides to every story. I'm not sure how I came off back then. I know what I was feeling inside. I felt as though I was barely tapping my potential as a person. I was getting typecast as a drummer who dressed weird and played even weirder music. We were playing for audiences half of which would get up and run for the exits 3 songs into the set - sometimes right after Don started playing Soprano on *Big Joan*.

There seemed to be no "band rapport." This is what I missed the most. I always had envisioned being in a band with friends - equals - who shared the glory and disappointments and lifted each other up. I know that is mostly a fairy tale and that few bands ever have true "equals." I unfortunately felt mostly like an extra in a bad movie.

After working on *Trout Mask*, I had realized what a few more hours a day of dedication could add up to after a length of time. Even with the terrible conditions of *Trout Mask* rehearsals, I still say that I learned a lot about my potential there, and Don had a lot to do with that. He would goad me on and challenge me into doing things I never dreamed I could do.

My biggest regret, as I experienced this tour, was that these people I was with really didn't seem to have a rapport or social life with each other, and that was also something I had to give Don credit for. I also knew that I was probably never going to get interviewed and that any ideas I had musically would likely not surface and even if they did, I had already been "pigeonholed" into a category that I would have never chosen for myself.

New York City

We drove by bus from Ithaca to New York City. Our bus driver was a new guy and I think this is where he showed up. Don walked up to him in the morning and said, "Hello, I'm Captain Beefheart!" and the driver, a little feisty guy with a rather high voice and strong Eastern accent said, "Yeah, and I'm Captain Kangaroo!" There was laughter all about, and we started getting on the bus. As I mentioned we had this funny "salute" that Don had made up called "The Hand and Toe Investment."

Each morning, as we would get on the bus, the Magic Band members, (at least Mark and I) would greet the already-seated passengers (Ry's touring group usually) with the "hand and toe investment."

I explained all that to say this: I remember this as being an important day and a kind of turning-point in the tour. It was at this point that Ry began to groan and complain each time the beloved "hand and toe investment" was executed. It was a little disappointing that Ry couldn't appreciate the lighter moments and silly times that were like a pressure valve that released frustration in a healthy manner.

The bus ride very long. Or, it seemed that way. According to a map, it's less than 150 miles and probably took about 3 hours. Since I was completely unfamiliar with the area, I only remember that we seemed to come in to Manhattan on a bridge that was south of the Holiday Inn where we stayed. I believe it must have been the Lincoln Bridge.

Don's Aloofness

As I previously mentioned, Don seemed to be really aloof during this tour and it seemed even more so after we arrived in New York. There seemed to be a real lack of communication between him and the band. I was concerned that this was going to affect our performances on stage, but it didn't seem so, although Don remained unpredictable and often was lost in the arrangements.

Ornette Coleman

It was during this time that Ornette and Don first met. According to Bill, they spent a lot of time together. I did meet Ornette briefly in the hotel elevator as he, Don, and Jan rode up to their room. It was one of the few times I saw Don in New York, other than on stage. If this would have been John Coltrane (who had already died by this point in time) I would have been star-struck, but Ornette's music was not really my cup of tea.

Don later told this story:

" 'You know', Ornette said to me, 'you're nothing but a chicken shit white hunter'."

"And I said to him, 'listen man, you can say that, but I know this bar in Texas I'll take you to, and I won't even go in there, man, but you can go in there'!"

Suffice to say that I was happy to find that the two of them got along so well.

I remember Don saying, "Ornette seemed to really like Jan." I wanted to add - "along with every guy in the universe" - as she was gorgeous and sweet. Don went on..."I think the reason he liked her so much is because when they smile, both of them expose a lot of their upper gumline."

I always thought that was a curious observation, and it seemed to make Jan a bit uncomfortable.

Bill And I See The City

I had mentioned earlier that we were not allowed to draw any money up until this point and that Grant Gibbs said we were going to get some money and have time off when we arrived in New York City. Grant, true to his word, came up to me in the Lobby, the second day we were there and handed me a fat envelope with my name on it. "Here's some money, John. He quickly walked off. I opened the envelope. It contained twenty one-dollar bills. I couldn't believe my eyes. These guys should have joined cheapskates anonymous.

Fortunately, for Bill and I, we met a couple of girls, one of whom was a friend of Artie's, and they took us around town in a Mustang and showed us some of the sites of the city. I remember that it was extremely windy that day. The wind chill factor was 70 below. I have never felt so cold in my life. Whenever we parked and walked, we would have to step inside stores just to warm up, and then walk back out. I spent my $20 on a pair of gloves, and some toothpaste.

We did get to go up in the observation tower of the Empire State Building. I was awe-struck, mostly with the architecture of the Chrysler Building, but also with the overall somewhat antiquated vision of what the "future" would be. I imagined myself as a visitor from another planet, viewing Earth for the first time and seeing this. It's hard to describe, but it made me feel as though it transformed my entire view of the world in one instant.

Theft

The night we played, Don and Jan were visiting with Ornette at his apartment. Langdon Winner and Bill Harkleroad had hailed a cab and the plan was to swing by and pick up Don and Jan at Ornette's place. Obviously, Bill was the baby-sitter of the group - why couldn't they get their own cab? At this point, Bill had accumulated a wonderful collection of guitars - including a beautiful vintage Stratocaster, his old standby Telecaster, and a Gibson hollow-body used for slide. Don had bought himself a beautiful new Selmer Soprano Saxophone and a Tenor. He played the soprano every night - often to see hoards of music fans rushing for the exits.

Don apparently had called Bill and instructed him to pick up his horn, collect Langdon, and head over in a cab to Ornette's. When they arrived, Bill went up to Coleman's apartment to meet him and collect Don and Jan. Apparently, several minutes went by and Langdon, also wanting to meet Ornette, finally gave in to his impatience - apparently forgetting a trunk-full of instruments with which he had been entrusted.

The cab driver seizing the opportunity drove quickly away. It was a "Gypsy" cab, as I heard they were called. It wasn't affiliated with an actual cab company, and therefore no trace of the instruments was ever found. I had gone to Ungano's as I recall, with Mark, Art and Elliot. All our instruments, as I recall, were left in the hands of the roadies, so our equipment was intact. We were completely unaware of the fact that the theft had occurred until they showed up.

Ry and I were having a little talk about the tour thus far. He seemed to be a little disappointed with his group. Ry was such a perfectionist that I could see that it would be tough for him to have a pickup group. He needed a really dedicated group. The Magic Band was, if nothing else, dedicated. Because of this, the band could basically play a great set every night. Tonight, however, there would be a few bumps in the road.

Ungano's Club Thur. 1-21-71, New York

The club was playing some background music. It was Rod Stewart with The Faces as I recall. Don came up to the mic and shouted something to the effect of, "Turn That Shit Off!" The rest of us nodded in agreement that this was an excellent way to set the mood of the room for our performance. It did go well, however, in spite of the incredible misfortune.

Someone loaned Bill a guitar for the night. As I recall, it was an inexpensive hollow-body with really light strings - completely different than the feel of his guitar. I barely noticed any difference in the output, but it must have been devastatingly difficult for Zoot that evening to play - especially pieces like *Peon* and *One Red Rose That I Mean*.

I recall Gary Lucas saying he was at this show and heard Bill play *One Red Rose That I Mean*, and thinking it was the hippest way to play guitar he'd ever seen or heard.

Obviously, Don and Bill were both in pretty low moods that night. I was now aware of Bill's guitars, because he told me about them, but I didn't actually know about Don's horns until later. In spite of having to use a borrowed guitar, about which he describes "ripping the strings off the bridge," I recall his performance. It was flawless. He was such a pro that he rose above his feelings and the situation and played so well that it inspired a very young Gary Lucas to follow in his footsteps.

The Heartbreak Of Percussion

I was just thinking this may be a good time to speak of what a royal pain transporting drums can be. I have already talked about the burden of the limited amount of practice time to be had when your instrument puts out 120db of sound acoustically. They're extremely bulky and usually all the stands weigh a ton. In the seventies, the stands were smaller. Now, they're gigantic. Multiply that times all the drums and cymbals and you have one hellacious pile of heavy metal. One of the reason I haven't played more in recent years is that I would actually lose money transporting my drums. I have rented drums occasionally, but this is really just a different kind of inconvenience.

Besides being expensive to rent, each set has to be adjusted to meet my specifications so that they "feel right.' Then, each drum has to have a certain type drumhead, top and bottom. Then, they all have to be tuned. For a while, my drum solos required 8 tom toms, plus snare and bass, for a total of ten drums, plus all cymbals and stands. I don't even like to dust my drums much less move them around that much. It was really wonderful to have a roadie set up my kit for the show. Jeff did a great job, as he had played drums for a time, and so knew what he was doing.

Washington. D.C. Television Show WDCA

We traveled from New York to Washington D.C. I recall being there in either late morning or early afternoon. We went directly to a television studio to tape a performance for broadcast. I believe it was a public TV or a subscriber TV station. We set up our equipment while the guy did a preliminary interview with Don to get the "feel" of the group. When he finally rolled tape and began announcing the show, Don stood up and tickled him, blowing his whole image. These public images of Don seeming "playful" were in such contrast to actually working with him. The show went well. We had an abbreviated set that Don had worked out with Elliot, who would then brief everyone individually. Elliot was a real team player, and he had a great perspective on how to present the material.

Smithsonian Stranded

After checking in to the Holiday Inn, we went off to see the Smithsonian in a Limousine. It was really interesting to me, I checked out dinosaur bones and moon rocks and a thousand other things. I didn't realize up until then how many of the dinosaurs were smaller creatures. Mark Boston and I got separated from the entourage and came out of the institute doors just as the band limo was pulling away on a drive from which we were separated by a vast lawn. Mark and I ran across the lawn and Mark being less of a smoker than me beat me by about fifty feet.

As soon as he got in, the door closed, and I saw Don signal the driver and the limo took off without me. I know that everyone saw me, and even if they didn't, Mark knew I was there, yet they took off and left me miles from the hotel with no money. My mind is blank as to how I made it back.

Boston University
Sergeant Gym, January (between 21stand 28th) 1971, Boston, Massachusetts

It was actually fairly decent weather in Boston. It's one of the few times I went outside. I had walked several miles through the snow in Cincinnati to check on the snake we had built for the microphones. I remember walking with some of the guys in the band out for lunch somewhere and there was a great feeling in the fresh air.

I only remember one evening concert although two have been mentioned. It was a very good show for us. There was a couple making love in the front of the room. I didn't see them but was told about it later. At least they weren't making war...

I recall being completely sopping wet with perspiration after the performance - more than usual. We went over quite well that particular evening. The sound system was quite good and it was one of the few times I could actually hear the drums. I was playing the Gon Bops, which had heavy skins and were really hand drums that had been slightly modified. They were half the volume of a normal kit. I played extremely hard in order to hear myself above the din of the group. That night, they were properly miked and I could actually hear them.

Large Theatre
Thursday, January 28th, 1971 Wilkes Barre, Pn

Let me just say that I would never live in Wilkes Barre. It's the coldest place I've ever been. I believe it is a coal-mining town. We arrived on the bus late the night before the performance and I remember trudging through a parking lot filled with deep frozen snow. Not soft snow. You walked on top of this snow. This snow wasn't for skiing; it was for forming into weapons of war.

I clearly remember Carl Scott backstage at this performance. He had a headset and microphone on and was giving light and sound cues from backstage like a pro. More about Carl later, but suffice to say somewhere along the way, Grant Gibbs had jumped overboard and Warners had sent Carl Scott to replace him. Apparently, Carl was a "strictly business" kind of guy. We were in what appeared to be a college or university theatre.

We were given a beautiful large dressing room with catering. One thing about this show was very much like the movie *Spinal Tap*. We became lost meandering around the labyrinth of hallways, exits, and entrances trying to find our way to the stage, eventually succeeding, of course. It would have been nice to have a guide familiar with this place, to lead us to the stage. I think the dressing room was a couple of levels below the stage

This was a legitimate theatre environment, with curtains, lighting, a great sound system, and tier-seating. I remember that Ry's performance was really well received, but when we came out, it was as though someone yelled "fire!" and everyone ran out. Perhaps it was the regional tastes that killed us. I personally think that having Ry and Beefheart on the same bill probably did more harm than good. It was like putting spaghetti sauce over maraschino cherries, we just weren't that compatible.

I distinctly recall Don playing sax at this show, which was odd, as his sax had been stolen. There may be an answer to this in the fact that perhaps Carl Scott had brought Don's old King (the gift from Jeff Cotton and I) or, perhaps he rented one, OR perhaps a new one was bought for him with the tour money. I have not a clue, but I do recall him playing sax, because that was at the beginning of *Big Joan* when Don hit the audience with saxophone, played directly over a mic that had been EQ'd for vocal. This was the most noticeable negative response I had seen to Don's saxophone playing and I started getting concerned that perhaps he shouldn't hit them with the sax until later in the show. I told him this but it just culminated in another talk...

Carl Scott

Carl Scott had a bit of history with the band. He was one of the first guys Bob Krasnow seriously talked us into considering for a manager around the *Safe As Milk* days. I remember going to his house in Laurel Canyon. He lived in an "A" frame house with a balcony loft upstairs. I remember we had to wait for him for a bit and Krasnow explained that Carl was managing a group called Harper's Bizarre at the time. When he came down, I first was impressed that Mr. Scott was a rather large man in the weight department. He had a very no-nonsense get-the-job-done confidence and remained a bit distant in order to assume that role and keep things moving.

Art Tripp writes: I liked Carl Scott at first. When he went on that tour with us, he eventually was giving me a little too much attention. I hadn't realized he was homosexual, but when he bought me an expensive gift, I figured it out. I refused the gift and told him I liked him, but not in that way. It was pretty strange. I can't recall that sequence of shows you mentioned ending with either Pasadena Civic or Albuquerque. Frankly I'm just proud to be associated with anyone who can spell Albuquerque.

Grant Leaves

For a time, Grant Gibbs had been on the road with us. He seemed to constantly be worried about this or that and I felt he was extremely weak as a leader. We needed a strong manager, someone who could confront Don on his eccentricities and help keep him centered and moving along. Don was as difficult to deal with on the road as elsewhere. He didn't know how to handle a microphone. He was incorrigible when it came to meeting a schedule. His sleep cycle was constantly changing as he would sometimes stay up all night talking to someone, and then wish to sleep in the next day when we needed to be dressed fed and on the bus at 8:00.

Grant's favorite line was, "I thought we had this matter resolved" - which he loved to use when problems would repeatedly surface after they had once been addressed. Unfortunately with Don, certain issues were never resolved. They continued to be problems as long as he was in the music business. It had to do with his methods of doing things and his philosophies, some of which have previously been addressed in this book. Things like the proper use of a microphone - something you would think any singer would take the time to learn - were never learned by Don.

Don would hold the microphone incorrectly; thereby modifying it's impedance so that the soundman could not possibly get a decent volume level or pleasing tone. Don would scream at the soundman. "That's not the way my voice sounds! What the fuck is wrong with you, man?"

Obviously, there needed to be a "heavy," someone not connected to the band, who could walk up to Don, confront him, and tell him to quit acting like a rude, spoiled brat. Also, we needed someone who knew that twenty one-dollar bills in an envelope was not sufficient per diem for three weeks on the road.

Exit Gibbs Enter Scott

Grant Gibbs was certainly not the man to confront Don on these types of issues. As nice as Grant was - and I assure you he was a wonderful hardworking, honest, sincere businessman - he couldn't handle Don Van Vliet when "the monster came out" as it often did on tours. So, at some point in time before this moment and after New York, Grant Gibbs left the tour and Carl Scott, who now worked in some capacity for Warners, took his place.

Bye Bye To The "Winged E"

This is when Elliot also left the band and went home. I am positive it was after this show. I recall being really upset with him for indulging in drugs because I was sharing a room with him. I believe he was getting the drugs from Jeff, Ry's bass player. I became pretty angry, because we had gone through a search in one of the airports. I thought we were drug-free. I had already been through this once in London, and I didn't like being this vulnerable on the road just because someone couldn't curtail their drug use. Although I don't think Winged-Eel brought any drugs into our room, I was still pretty upset that the touring party had drugs at all. Some states were VERY strict in their enforcement of drug laws. I didn't want to get arrested - ever again.

I recall in a quick band meeting we had earlier, (this could have been back around Pittsburgh or D.C.) that after all the business had been taken care of it was asked if anyone had any questions. Elliot raised his hand and said, "I want my own room." Everyone immediately looked at me like, "what'd you do John?" I always blamed myself a little for Elliot's departure. He and I had bumped heads a couple of times over issues like this. I just felt that if I was sharing a room with someone, they shouldn't bring something illegal into that room, because that involved me, and that made it my business.

Cocoa Beach

My first impression of Florida when I got off the plane in my rubbers and overcoat was, "Oh God, thank you, it's warm!" We had just come from the coldest location on the tour, to the warmest. From Wilkes Barre, PA, to Cocoa Beach, FL. I was in heaven. We were met at the airport by Charles (Chuck) T. Powers from the Los Angeles Times. He was a journalist, probably a staff writer from the LA Times and had been assigned to do an article on the band for WEST magazine, a Sunday addition to the paper.

I didn't spend much time around "Chuck" as he liked to be called. However, he spent quite a bit of time with us and covered several dates on the tour, all the way through to Albuquerque, NM, one of the last tour dates.

Thanks to my habit of not throwing much of anything away, I have this article, although I have been charged with hanging onto the past because I have kept a small box of Beefheart memorabilia around. This article is definitely going to come in handy in the following pages.

Our hotel was right on the beach. I took off my shoes at 10:00 at night, and strolled with a beer (a special occasion as I seldom drank) out to the beach. We - Artie Tripp, Jeff Bruschele, Bill Shumow, and Bill Harkleroad - brought a couple of my Gon Bops down to the beach and sat in the sand. We just let loose. "Finally," I thought, " a place to relax and be outside without freezing to death." This was like heaven. To me, this was what all the work was about, hanging out with friends and spending time together. Jeff, Artie, and I exchanged rhythms and drank beer. We clanged around on cowbells, laughed and fell in the sand for half the night.

Broken-Down Club

All that Powers describes is a run-down club. There are no dates included in the article, and the timeline that I have so far seen gets off around New York City and stays off, so I am just guessing at dates but remembering the order from the article. I remember a room that looked like a Country Club dining room with the tables removed. They had a portable bar in the corner, the kind that are used at wedding receptions in hotel banquet rooms. The crowd seemed totally disinterested. I don't even remember a stage. We just sat up on the floor. It was completely the wrong venue and crowd for the band. It almost seemed as though the booking agent just had to fill a spot and put this in to pay the hotel cost for the night. I also remember playing during the daytime, in the afternoon about 2:00. It was completely disheartening. That is my image and it is firmly imbedded in my mind.

Yet Chuck Powers describes a totally different picture here:

"For Beefheart, Cocoa Beach hadn't been so great. The audience, young and nearly catatonic on drugs, got up and staggered out. When he had finished his set, perhaps 75 were left out of an audience of 300. Beefheart suggested that those who left had been 'joggled out of the nest.' 'Maybe people like music that is more ordered, comforting,' someone suggested. 'You mean you want to order something from room service," Beefheart said, 'as opposed to walking down and getting an orange off the tree?'
The answer was flippant, but he meant every word. Beefheart believes art surrounds us naturally and that the sound of geese honking overhead in the night is among the 'heaviest music' in the universe." [54]

Van Vliet Gives Scott A Gift

We had a little time to kill in the morning. As usual, the bus was announced to arrive at a particular hour and didn't arrive until much late. I was walking around in the gift shop, which carried all those stupid joke greeting cards and glass shelves with gag gifts, such as "whoopee cushions" and "joy buzzers." I noticed a box marked, "The Perfect Diet Utensils." I opened it to find a fork with no tines, and a spoon with a big hole in the bottom.

I entered the bus before Don, who often was the last to arrive, and often had to be pried, struggling and fuming from bed. He walked on the bus with a strange prank smile and I knew something was up. He walked over and handed highly overweight Carl Scott the "gag" diet kit. Everybody on the bus sort of gathered around as Carl opened it up and discovered the tine-less fork and bottomless spoon. He didn't laugh, nor smile, nor even look up. He just closed the box, threw it in a bag, and continued reading. I thought it was a rather childish prank on Don's part.

I'd like to point out that after Carl began managing the details of the tour, things did go much smoother. He was a seasoned businessman and knew exactly what he was doing and never showed a sign of weakness. He also made sure we had cash for essentials - like cigarettes and toothpaste. Also, he was basically alone. He ate his meals alone and had no friends really on the entire tour. I have to say that I was quite grateful for his arrival, as almost immediately Don seemed to cheer up and the performances began to go much better. Even when the audience did not enjoy the show, we had a good time for the most part.

[54] WEST Magazine, 'Beefheart in Blunderland,' May 30, 1971, Charles T. Powers pp18.

Orlando

We drove by bus the next day to Orlando. It seemed like a couple of hours. On the map, it only appears to be about 40-50 miles. I remember being really struck by the vegetation. I had been raised in a Desert environment. I had seen a lot of Southern California landscapes and many in Europe, but I had never witnessed the kind of vegetation I was seeing here. It was completely foreign to me. We stopped at some souvenir place that sold stuffed baby alligators among other things. Most in the entourage were upset by this - it seemed a bit barbaric.

The Orlando Concert

It was raining but warm that evening. I will quote Power's article here again:

"It was a strange place to play. Moonlight and ragged clouds glowed through the tattered patches of canvas stretched over a high metal framework. The hall looked like an airplane hangar with no walls. Puddles lay on the floor, and the audience, mostly high-school age, sat on the damp concrete passing joints back and forth." [55]

We were driven in the bus to the site of the concert and everyone felt quite good about this night. Don was more friendly and seemed really "up" about the show. I think he was also happy about having Chuck to talk to. Chuck had actually come this night with Ry to cover his show, and we met him backstage before our show. Cooder had not gone over too well, which seemed to always indicate that we would be well-received. It had been that way for almost the whole tour.

I think also that Don loved the rain and humidity. It really agreed with him, and he seemed in top form. I remember the main problem I had that evening was that the Gon Bops had cowhide heads, and they were all completely loose from the moisture. I would have to tune them, and they were painfully slow to tune. So, I went on stage early and told everyone they might as well relax for a few minutes. I tuned the drums, which were on a riser behind the rest of the band. Usually, I was on the same level as the other players. I think Artie's set was placed lower, because there wasn't enough room for both on the riser, and I was actually the main drummer.

After getting the Gon Bops tuned, the band came out. I believe that I was still starting the show at that time and then Artie joined me, and then Mark came out. Then Bill, Elliot and Don and the show took off. It was a great show that evening. I believe it was the best set we played the entire tour. Everyone seemed very pleased. No mistakes, no glitches, just a lot of well-played, high powered music.

Afterward, Bill Shumow and Jeff Bruschele came over and told me that because of the humidity, when I played steam was actually coming off my body. As the drum riser was backlit, it made for an amazing visual effect where it looked as though I were giving off energy fields to the audience. I guess high-school kids smoking dope would truly enjoy this if nothing else. It was like my evaporating bodily fluids were giving them a light show.

The Cooder/Beefheart Connection Revisited

Powers decided to explore the reasons why Cooder quit the band just before Monterey and quotes Cooder thusly:

"Beefheart, Cooder remembers, had a habit of walking off-stage in the middle of a performance or of issuing orders from a darkened bedroom during rehearsals. 'He had this house up in the desert near Lancaster,' Cooder recalls. 'And all of his hard-riding motorcycle friends would sit around and drink beer and fall into the pool - real rowdy, hard-living guys with lowered Buicks, you know, chasing off across the desert. It was too weird. I wasn't making any money, and Don was crazier than hell. He was good, you know, real good. But crazy.'" [56]

[55] WEST Magazine, 'Beefheart in Blunderland,' May 30, 1971, Charles T. Powers pp 20.
[56] WEST Magazine, 'Beefheart in Blunderland' May 30, 1971, pp 21 Charles T. Powers.

Amusingly enough, I read this quote to Alex Snouffer over the phone and his reaction was that he remembers Cooder as being one of the guys drinking beer and falling into the pool. "He should talk," was his amused reply.

New Orleans

New Orleans was the next stop on the tour. We played in a converted Warehouse. The path to the dressing room was on a strange ascending catwalk up to a small corner room that you imagined would contain and old desk, safe, and ledger. There was a large wooden-bladed floor fan sitting in the room.

I decided on a whim to bring the fan down to the stage. I turned the fan on during a point in the drum solo performance and "played" it with my sticks, lightly pushing them into the blades. At one point, a blade was chipped, which set the whole thing just enough out of balance to bounce a bit, and as if on cue, Bill Shumow walked up, grabbed the power cord like a leash, and walked it off the stage like a dog. This brought a big round of applause.

To quote Chuck again:
"When Beefheart and the Magic Band began playing, the contrast to Cooder's music was marked. This group gave the impression of being absolutely together - natural and powerful, like stormy weather." [57]

I was happy to read this. It gave me outside proof that the band was good. Something I seldom heard or felt from Don.

Atlanta

We flew to Atlanta the next evening, landing in the dark, and being driven to a hotel near the airport. We played a large auditorium, which could have been a sports arena of some kind. Ry's set was not well received. He had technical problems, and the group was not together.

The Beefheart set was magical. It was a perfect night. The soundman was great, the stage monitors gave Don just the foldback he needed to hear himself well. We looked and sounded great. Ry commented that we might well be the best band in the business, which I took as quite a compliment. Ry was quoted as saying, "They're certainly running away with the tour." The audience asked for "more" at the end of the night, and as a joke, Don walked up to the microphone and whistled "More," the standard tune by the same title. This brought laughter and cheers from the audience. We actually did play an encore here, though we were slightly hampered by the absence of Mr. Winged Eel Fingerling.

Carbondale, Illinois

Carbondale looks to be about 120 miles or so from Salem, which is where Mark Boston was raised. We heard on the bus ride that some of his old friends were coming down to see him, but when I recently interviewed Mark, he only remembered talking to a friend on the phone, who called the hotel.

The concert was in a fine hall with good acoustics and Cooder's set went over well, which was a sure sign that we would not be well-received. Sure, enough, people began to leave in droves. "It's not music," said one young woman. Another complained: "The band's not bad, but I wish Beefheart would leave his clarinet stuck on the microphone without himself attached."

Don seemed to take the stance that it was great to have this kind of reaction, and acted as though he was glad they left. I used to wonder at this kind of logic, being as how I would have liked to have made enough money out of this large investment of time to make it worth the effort. However, we

---

[57] WEST Magazine, 'Beefheart in Blunderland' May 30, 1971, pp 21 Charles T. Powers.

seemed to all be having a good time at this point. The set was really together, and we played with conviction.

The Sylmar Quake

Landing in Minneapolis we glided across the tarmac, as the muzak on the plane switched to local radio reception and I suddenly heard that there had been an earthquake that had caused quite a bit of destruction in the Los Angeles area. It was centered in Sylmar, a small town just off the 405 Freeway and the last stop before actually crossing the San Gabriels. This concerned me a bit, as it wasn't far from either Lancaster or our homes in Woodland Hills and Laurel Canyon.

The Guthrie Theatre Minneapolis, Minn.

I do remember one thing about Minneapolis, it was much colder than I wanted it to be. The bus driver was telling us that the wheels of the bus were often frozen to the ground, and they had to use welding torches to free the wheels so they could drive. Where was Florida when you needed her?

The Guthrie Theatre was pretty much the same reception as Carbondale had been. It was a theatre in the round. In fact, a few years later I happened to be in Santa Maria Junior College's theatre and found that it was an exact copy of the Guthrie Theatre. It was really deja-vu. I walked in while the place was empty and stood thinking "this reminds me off someplace..." Sharon Brady, a friend I was visiting, explained that it was a copy of the Guthrie. The stage was a pentagon-shaped thrust-stage and so we were surrounded by audience. I thought we would be well-received, because as we started out, Artie and I got a great reaction from the crowd. Unfortunately, it was evident as the show continued that the crowd was not interested.

One fellow actually came back and asked us for his money back. Artie asked, "How much was the ticket?" The guy told him and Artie said "Sure," and pulling his wallet, gave some money to him and turned casually to finish his conversation backstage.

More Accessible Music?

Don's reaction to all of this was to remain aloof and pretend not to care. I knew it must have bothered him that his creation was being figuratively "spat upon" at about 50% of the performances. I wondered if, in secret conversations with Jan, he was formulating his next move.

Earthquake Aftermath

We had a small break in the tour and flew home. I had been following the news and discovered that none of my friends had been injured and there was little quake activity in the Mojave Desert, where Helen and my family lived. The area hardest hit was, in fact far from any of our homes. I remember calling Helen from the hotel in Des Moines. She told me she had signed up for college and was moving out. I was a little surprised and emotionally torn about her decision. It caught me completely off-guard. Now, as I look back, I would have said, "Smart move, you get your life going, I'll see where mine takes me."

Ice Rink, Des Moines, Iowa

We stayed in a motel in the middle of nowhere, were driven somewhere, played, were driven back, and flew home. I know for a fact that there are several performances for which I cannot account (we did 33 in total) and I know more than one happened in ice hockey arenas. I recall the limo pulling up on the ice next to a plywood path that had been laid out to the stage. John Sebastian opened for us at one such show, just him on guitar - strumming and singing. It could have been here that this took place.

Fly Home

My car somehow wound up parked in front of Don's house in Woodland Hills. We were transported, perhaps by a bus, to the car. Mark asked me for a lift across the canyon to his house. When we got in the car, the windows were rolled up, and it was really hot. There was a big crack in the vinyl dashboard.

"I don't recall that being there when I saw the car last." I said.

"Probably earthquake damage." Mark replied.

I drove up to the desert to visit Helen and visit my parents. She had decided to sign up for Junior College and get some more of her liberal arts units completed. I told her I would miss her, but understood. The earthquake had been pretty scary, she said. Aftershocks had been happening ever since, and, as we spoke, a gentle but ominous rocking came, the house creaked like a fine old ship, and a vase on the mantle made a tinkling sound.

She asked how the tour went and noticed quickly that my arms had really developed from playing every night. Well, playing drums that are half as loud as conventional drums made me work twice as hard. I hadn't noticed, but I was pretty toned up. I was exhausted, and the time off was a welcome relief.

Helen came down and saw me off for the next leg of the tour. We were playing a few dates in the Southwest.

CHAPTER THIRTY ONE:
NO FUN, NO FUNDS

being interviewed sometime in 1972.
o courtesy of Art Tripp.

Albuquerque

We flew to Albuquerque to play at the University. Now we were playing in a desert town, which was more my type of environment. I liked the dry heat, and the cloudless skies and took a long walk in the morning after the show. I was told that a large nuclear arsenal was buried deep within the hills surrounding the city.

As soon as we got to the University and went backstage, I sensed a bad feeling about this night. The place was filled with 60's radicals and we had one completely defiant moron who somehow got backstage. He was drilling me with questions about the environment. He made about as much sense as Al Gore. "Well, if you guys are so worried about the environment, why did you fly here? Was it just a good excuse to continue dumping thousands of tons of pollution into the atmosphere?"

I tried to explain to him that I felt any problems that we had, we needed to gradually change, giving ourselves a chance to modify our behavior and adapt. He clearly did not even want to consider such a thought. I could understand his ideals, but like a lot of radicals in those days, he wanted all the change now, without considering the impact - the usual sign of impatient youth.

I tried to explain that I felt our message was important, and that us flying on a jet that was already flying here whether we were on it or not had the advantage of getting us here a lot sooner so that we could spread the environmental message. But this meant nothing to this guy, and I imagined that most of the crowd may have an equal slant on things.

Sure enough, they didn't like us at all.

One thing I do recall about this performance was that Don played the bass clarinet, and I believe it was the only time on this entire tour that he actually played it. Usually, he played the soprano and occasionally the tenor, before it was stolen. I had thought before that he played the bass clarinet (which was actually Victor's as I recall) because his sax had been stolen. But writing leads me to believe that somewhere along the line, he bought another sax, or brought his old sax from home, possibly via Carl Scott.

Armadillo Headquarters - Feb. 1971, Austin, Texas

According to the West article, Albuquerque was our last tour date, and that could be true, however, I remember distinctly playing Austin and Houston Texas.

We were well received at this performance so I recall. I think it was more of a counter-culture center similar to Berkeley and a few years behind the (California) times in a sense. There was a freedom not unlike the Middle Earth in London in the late sixties. I don't recall a thing about the concert arena itself, I basically remember someone associated with the club transporting us to the Airport for a flight to Houston. It was a lady as I recall and she was instructing us in the finer aspects of the characteristics of armadillos for most of the ride. She was also the one who told us how well received we were the night before, as I can't remember a thing.

Unknown Club - Feb. 1971, Houston, Texas

I remember several things about Houston, but the primary impression I had was that it was very, very, very humid. The humidity was at 100% according to someone at the club. It was a fairly small place, and the audience seemed indifferent in a sense. They were just interested mostly in partying, save a few dedicated fans who remained after the show to talk. I recall the heat and moisture from the people's bodies actually seemed to form clouds in the room, as if we were in a giant steam bath. They had to open the doors and turn on fans to remove the moisture. After the show, it seemed like about half the audience went out the door to a big party at the beach, and there was talk of surfing. It looked like they all were anticipating a good time and seemed that it was a fairly standard activity.

I was not at a very good point emotionally, because it looked as though financial problems were still on the horizon, and I had a life outside of the band. I was pretty deeply in love with Helen and wanted to make some money and get married. Unfortunately, the band seemed to be right in the middle of my relationship and personal life. I felt as if I was back in the goldfish bowl and there was no privacy.

I remember sharing a room with Bill and speaking with Helen on the phone about all this. We soon after had a meeting in our room and Don was interrogating me about my mood. Bill started sharing intimate details of my "private" conversation with Helen to the rest of the band at the meeting. I think the mentality was and continued to be for a long time that we had no right to a private life, no right to pursue happiness.

The cult mentality had not left - it had merely changed costumes. I think Bill thought he was doing the right thing by bringing up this issue, but had he been away from this environment like I had for a year, he would have realized that he and I both had rights to a private life - and an income.

Another Turning Point

Although I would remain in the group for several months, this day was definitely a day that impressed on my mind the simple fact that I had to get out of here and never come back, if for no other reason than my own sanity. I could not stand this insistence that membership in the Magic Band carried the understanding that I become a sycophant (or should I say psychophant??). I did not desire to be reduced to the level of minion again. I had a right to pursue my own creativity, seek my own fulfillment, have a private life, and be paid for my time.

Tripp On Tour

Art Tripp writes:
"All the gigs were pretty much the same, with a few exceptions. The audience always loved them, and I'm sure they'd be surprised at some of the scream fests we had following many of the shows. Every time Don screwed up he blamed somebody else. I do recall that show in Cocoa Beach when all the kids were so wasted, that there was near silence - and that happened to be a great performance as I remember. The promoter told us later that most of the kids' parents had worked at the Space Center, and since so many of them had been laid off they used their connections to import and sell hard drugs, which their kids ended up buying on the street. Doesn't seem so shocking by today's standards.
Did you play that show (Massachusetts?) when we played only 35 minutes and walked off? The audience was pissed, but afterwards we convinced ourselves that if we couldn't do it in 35 minutes, then what the hell. Most of the audience took a different view. Some started yelling, "Beefheart's a rip off!" The dressing rooms were on a floor above the hall, so Don went out on the balcony and started yelling back, "Beefheart's a rip off!" I thought it was hilarious at the time, but then I hadn't paid the big bucks to see us, so to speak."

Homecoming

We were home for a few days, and then while we were gone, our beloved accountant Al Liefer had decided that Artie and I did not deserve a place to live. In the 7 or so months I had been in the band, all the bills had been paid through the accounting office. Now, suddenly, while we were on tour, they had ceased. Zon Murray, the landlord, a former bit-part actor, was in the process of evicting us.

Evicted

I went back to the Laurel Canyon house to discover Zon had already rented it out to someone else even though my clothes and all Artie's belongings were still in it. The people answered the door and told me the news themselves. It was ironic, I was standing within site of the house on Amor Rd. in which this very same thing had happened to me 4 years earlier. Fortunately, these people were very understanding, and allowed me to grab my clothes and personal belongings. They had moved everything of Artie's into the downstairs bedroom (my room) and told me that if Artie and I could get some way to pick it up, they would help us get it out of there. Zon was trying to rent the house as "furnished" with Artie's furniture, claiming (rightfully so) that we owed him back rent, and so the furnishings essentially, in his mind, were his.

I eventually had to stay with my folks in the desert. I recall not even having enough money to buy gasoline for the Cadillac. Chuck Powers had Artie staying at his house.

To make matters worse, my Union Dues, which were very minimal, had not been paid, and so for the second time, I had been kicked out of the union, which meant I wouldn't get paid until I re-instated my membership, which would cost a small fortune. Little did I know yet that there was no pay to receive.

Warners Explanation / No Money

Don, Jan and Bill had gone out of town to go fishing. Apparently, someone had some money. I went to Warners to pick up some tour money. Although I can't remember all of the dates now I recall clearly having kept track of 33 performances over the last six or seven weeks. Our original contractual agreement which we signed with Don through God's Golf Ball Productions, stated that Warners would guarantee to pay the band $1,000 a performance plus expenses. Since Don was taking 50%, it left us to split the other 50% between the four (five before Elliot left) of us. I figure Warners owed me between $2,700 and $3,300. Artie and I split about $700 a month between us - including rent, utilities, and groceries. In 1970, we could have lived comfortably for several months on $3,000 apiece. I wanted to get some rent money to Zon - out of principle. I also needed drumheads and sticks for the final performance we did at Pasadena Civic Auditorium.

I went to the Warners office and asked to see Carl Scott. They directed me to go down a hallway to the right and I went in a little area that seemed divided up between 3 or 4 people with industrial metal shelves. I found Carl after a moment in a semi-isolated space surrounded by these shelves. "John," he said, "hand me one of those KimWipes behind you, please." I handed him a box of tissue, while thinking what a strange way he had of greeting people. He quickly took one, cleaned his dark glasses and quickly put them on. I couldn't see his eyes at all. "How can I help you?" he asked me coldly.

"Well, I need to get some money, I'm being evicted and I don't even have gas in my car. I have no food, nothing."

"I'm sorry to tell you this, John, but the tour money all went for expenses, there's nothing left." Carl quickly and flatly replied.

I was in shock and wishing I'd studied yoga so I could kick my own ass for coming back into this band. I felt I knew where the money had gone - Don had spent it. If there was no money, how could Don afford to take a fishing trip? Carl tried to blame it on Mark's extensive telephone calls to Laurie. "Oh, yeah," I said, "Mark spent $15,000 on telephone calls?"

As I left the office, I ran into various people who recognized me from my previous visits. Hal Haverstadt was one of them, and I think Mo Austin may have been with him. "Hey, John," he said in that typical schmoozy businessman's voice, "Really sorry about what happened. Gotta run."

I watched him walk out the door and mentally calculated how many Mercedes payments he'd be able to make with my share of the tour proceeds." A few other people walked by and expressed their "condolences." I felt terrible and I had this deep gnawing fear in my gut, along with a great deal of anger specifically aimed at Don, and generally at Warners Brothers Records, God's Golfball Productions and all the lying bastards associated with it, and every Beefheart fan who treated Don like he was God.

I went to Al Liefer's office only to sit for several hours. Al came in after an extended lunch, smoking a cigar and laughing with his friends. I asked to speak with him and he looked at me as though I were some fly he was going to have to take the trouble to swat. He basically told me that no funds were available, Don and the "board" had put everything "on hold .... etc."

Pasadena Civic Auditorium

We had one last performance to wind up the tour. It was at the Pasadena Civic Auditorium, and Little Feat were opening for us. I figured the best way to get a few bucks was to say that my drums needed repair. Somehow, I talked to Don on the phone, probably he called me at my folk's house. I told him that my drums needed repair work and that I needed money for that or I couldn't play. Magically, funds were released. This gave me a bit of money to buy essentials. After the performance, some people came back stage and someone handed me a paper cup and walked away quickly. It was a baby chick. Why would someone do that? I looked at it closely and surmised that it was probably being picked on, as it was missing some of the fluff from the top of its head.

The little guy loved my beard and thought I was its mommy. I'd put it on the floor and lay down several feet away and it would run to me. Helen knew someone with a chicken ranch, so we took it there. It was a huge amount of trouble for a baby chick, but at least it had a home for a while.

After The U.S. Tour

At this point, I had been in the band nine months. I was "in the red" several thousand dollars. I had discovered shortly before the tour that I wasn't being paid, I was "drawing an advance against earnings." I keep forgetting, musicians don't get paid - especially if they're in the Magic Band.

John French: But then, if I may go back to before Felton when we came back from the tour and what did we discover - besides the fact that Charles T. Powers shouldn't drive after drinking airline drinks?

Art Tripp: We weren't getting shit.

JF: We didn't get anything. Basically we came and we were penniless and our bills hadn't even been paid. I was ejected from the musicians union for the second time for not paying my dues. Our manager, Grant Gibbs, was supposed to take care of the bills, but nothing was taken care of.

AT: That's right.

JF: And so, you and I, who had been living in Laurel Canyon, all of a sudden come back. There's people living in our house, with your furniture in there. And my stuff, my clothes, everything, and we don't have a place to live. Do your recall us staying with Charles T. Powers (a L.A Times journalist who covered us on the road.)

AT: I remember very well. I stayed on with him for several weeks after that. Maybe even a couple of months. I can't remember how long I stayed there.

JF: Yeah, you were there the longest, I was there briefly there. I think maybe a week, 2 weeks. Trying to figure out what to do. We played the Pasadena Civic Auditorium as part of the tour. The last leg of the tour, and then that was that.

Then, all of a sudden, Don is up fishing in Santa Cruz, and the band moves up there.

AT: I didn't want to leave LA.

JF: Yeah, I didn't either. I knew it was going to be bad going up there. But anyway, before we made the album that we were working on in Felton (Spotlight Kid), we did another move. (to Trinidad, but I'm getting ahead of myself.)

Staying With Chuck Powers, Journalist

With my gas tank scraping empty, I remembered that I had started a little savings account in a bank nearby and went over to draw out some money for gas. After filling up the tank, I went to Chuck's house and met with Artie. We sat and consoled each other about this terrible situation. We were trying to figure out how to get Artie's furniture, and our clothes and belongings out of the house that Zon had already rented. Then Artie left for a while to visit Joanne. Charles wasn't home, so I checked out his record collection.

Ry's Album

I found Ry's album on the shelf and put it on to listen to it. It seemed over-produced, layered too heavily with overdubs and stiff. However, what really stood out to me was his great slide work and his rather tongue-in-cheek vocal delivery. *Alimony* was my favorite song. I had heard all this material on the tour, but wanted to hear the "studio" version of the repertoire.

Chuck's Opinion Of Don ...

Chuck finally came in from work and we sat and had a beer together and talked. I told him of the predicament, which he had already had some knowledge of through Art. He invited me to stay for dinner and sleep in the spare guest room. I accepted. He then proceeded to tell me his impression of Don after spending several intense weeks with him on the road.

He started out by saying that Don wanted his own way about everything and didn't seem to care whether it hurt anyone else or not. In order to get his own way, he surrounded himself with a group of "yes men," (pausing to apologize to me for calling me that but nonetheless sticking to his description) in order to feed his own ego and maintain a position of authority for all the wrong reasons. He couldn't play the sax very well, but no one would notice, because the music that he wrote was so bizarre that the sax playing seemed to be intentionally non-musical.

He then said that Don had a big front and scripted himself to make himself to appear more clever than he actually was but that he was actually quite insecure about the public finding out who he really was. Although he gave much credit to Don's lyrics and compositions, he felt that although Don would have really liked to have been better accepted, he didn't have the technical ability or the organizational skills to actually bring it off himself, but his pride caused him to refuse any help.

I marveled at this man's insight, and have always deeply respected the fact that he took the risk and told me his true thoughts. I had to admit that I agreed with him and didn't really know what to do. I said that I was in such a turmoil all the time I was in the band, that I never had enough energy or focus to really confront the problems Don had brought upon himself and eventually, us.

Artie Disagrees

Artie came in at the end of our discussion, as if on cue, and I asked Chuck to share with Artie what he had told me. He did, but Artie disagreed. "No, man, you've got it all wrong. Don isn't like that at all." All I could think to myself was that I had been around Don longer than Artie, Bill, or Mark. I had discussed in detail various aspects of Van Vliet's problems with the original band members, including the founder of the group, Alex Snouffer. I had to find the strength within myself to believe that I was right, because no one else would agree with me. I also knew I was under contract until fall, at which time my option would either be picked up or not.

My feelings were that Artie was a very loyal person. Though he had been really jaded by his experience with Zappa, his guard wasn't really up that something even worse could happen to him by not paying attention to the warning signals that were already coming through to me loud and clear. Also, another facet is that Artie was never truly the "target" of any talk. Because of his age and experience, and also perhaps because of his probable lack of tolerance at any such attempt, he was basically freed of that monstrous weight. He did, however, experience and take part in talks where Mark, Bill, or I became the "target." At first, I think he reacted like we all did, that this was somehow necessary. As time went on, it became more apparent that something was amiss.

Artie Recalls C Powers

Artie writes: "I liked Chuck Powers immensely. I think he ended up with my old bass drum with the South Sea Islands scene painted on the front head, which was internally illuminated. Of course he and I became serious drinking buddies. His sister-in-law came to visit for a few days, and she & I fell in love for a night. The last I heard, Chuck was transferred to New York at the L.A. Times bureau there. I'd love to know what happened to him. Several years later he wrote a lengthy article in which he discussed the best Mexican food in L.A. He wrote some nice things about me, but he also mentioned that I had introduced him to the homemade fast food delights from the Burrito King in Echo Park, which was incomparably good. When I moved back to L.A. in 1978 I went to that same Burrito King, and sure enough there was a framed blow-up of Chuck's article on the wall, complete with my picture. I figured that would certainly be worth a meal on the house, but the gal who waited on me couldn't speak English, and I think she had the intelligence of a half a glass of water. The owner wasn't there, so no free burrito. I had a two-day resentment over that one."

Move To Santa Cruz

I think I contacted Don, who was still out "fishing" somewhere while Artie and I watched our life fall apart at the seams. He told me that we were all moving to Santa Cruz. My first thought was that I didn't want to go. Here, in LA, I had friends and contacts. What the hell was in Santa Cruz? However, since I was still under contract, I felt that I needed to fulfill at least one year of the agreement. I had about six months left.

Mark and Laurie were still at the Trout House. A lot of Don's stuff was still there, and the rent had been maintained, meaning there were funds available, but someone was selectively prioritizing certain bills while ignoring others. My lightning-fast mind didn't grasp this at the time. I remember going up to the Trout Mask house one evening, and there was a U-Haul truck (huge one) backed up to the front steps and blocking the whole street. Why these guys didn't drive up the driveway instead of walking all that stuff down the stairs is beyond me.

Don was standing in the street, drawing, when I drove up. He had a dog on a leash. It had been a stray or something. I think Don found it on his excursion up the coast. He named it Ivley Beebler, which I always thought was the coolest name. It was an English Sheepdog, and the name fit it perfectly. Van Vliet began to tell me that he had just come back from the desert and had met my brother Tom. Tom was my favorite "big brother" and his opinion was the most important thing in the world at that time.

Don proceeded to tell me that Tom had said some really condescending things about me to him - that I didn't have my head on straight and I was a "flake" etc. If anything could have made me feel worse than coming back from the road and having no money, it was this.

Mark came down carrying a cupboard door that he had removed from the kitchen. It had one of Don's paintings on it. I believe every door actually had been graced with a Don Van Vliet original. The landlord showed up, discovered this fact, and demanded that the doors be replaced.

This is one of the few times I saw Don cave in. He gave the doors back. The people who moved in had a lease option and eventually bought the house. They still had one of the original door paintings a few years ago when Elaine Shepherd shot the BBC Beefheart Biography. The door/painting was given to Bruce Fowler, who agreed to return it to Don. Bruce had done his interview in front of the Trout House.

Oh Calcutta!

Art Tripp: I remember what it was (switching to after the 1971 tour in which we did not get paid) *and right at that time this guy down at the Union* (Musicians Union), *who became a good friend of mine, offered me the job to play percussion with* Oh, Calcutta, *and I really thought about it. But at that time, that was when Beefheart and everyone was moving up to Felton. I thought, I've got two choices: I can stay in LA and play the show, or I can leave and go up to ... I thought, well hell, the show - the guy told me I would have to play every night and I'd only be allowed to sub a guy once every two weeks and I thought, oh shit.*
John French: That was a real risque theatrical musical.
AT: Yeah, it was a big thing at that time. It had a tremendously long run in New York and it was expected to do the same in LA. As it happened, the show only lasted about two months and then it folded. I didn't even know much about the show, I was just interested in doing it for the money and for the experience. But, anyway, I didn't do it. I have often thought, I wonder what would have happened if I had stayed in LA. I could have been doing like Ian was doing; making a lot of money in the studios.

Bye

Helen somehow talked me into letting her come up and live with me. I think that I was so desperate for someone on my side that even though I knew it was going to be a disaster for her, I said "Yes." I should have told her to stay in school. It was strange, because she invited me to her parent's house for a "goodbye dinner" which she had prepared for just the two of us. Then, we went into the living room, where she asked me, in front of her parents, if she could come live with me. I felt that if I said "No," that I would be insulting her in front of her parents, and I think that was just enough balance in her favor to say "Yes."

Ben Lomond

The actual location of the new band residence was halfway between two villages; Felton, and Ben Lomond. I drove up in the white Cadillac and arrived after an all-night harrowing drive on Highway 99. It was a compound of several cabins built as additions to a main house. It was situated on a river and behind a small isolated shop that sold Redwood Burl furniture, mostly tables and clocks. Jan and Don were temporarily sleeping on their bed in the living room of the main house and when I came in, they were awake, and Jan was reading to Don about the American Indians, and how they fought and struggled for independence from the white man. Don grabbed the book and pointed to photographs of various tribal chiefs. "Look at that guy, man, he's so hip." He would say.

Arnie Rubenstein

Mr. Arnie Rubenstein was our landlord. He seemed like a nice enough guy. He was young and ambitious and doing OK for himself. He had a backwoods look with his trimmed beard, plaid shirt, and longish hair, but faintly hidden was a shrewd businessman. I liked him, and when he looked at me, it was as though he was looking at someone he knew, as though I reminded him of someone.

"He thinks you're his rabbi" Don later said, smiling. With my long dark hair and beard, I had been told by one of my mother's older Jewish friends that all I needed was a braid and a hat.

The Cabins

There were five cabins in this compound. Two were upstairs and shared a common redwood deck, which had just been built. Three were downstairs. Everything had been picked out already except one upstairs spot. That's where I would live. The place had the feel of an old resort area, and I'm sure that it had once been a small resort facility for weekenders and vacationers, the main house being the owner's quarters and office. Artie lived in the big house. I took an upstairs cabin, Don and Jan took the other. Mark and Laurie took a downstairs cabin next to the main house, and Bill slept in the bedroom of the cabin in which we rehearsed.

Bad Times In Felton

Art Tripp: So, anyway, that's when I finally went up to Felton and joined up with Don and the rest ... you're pretty well familiar with that.
John French: So what were your impressions of what happened to the Magic Band in Felton? I mean, that experience up there and basically what went on. What are basically your observations.   You were sort of - Mark and Bill and I seemed to be the ones that Don was pulling the strings with more than you. He kind of left you alone. Just as an outside observer, what did you see, what were your impressions?
AT: I just stayed away from it. I didn't want to get involved in that shit and I knew it had been going on for a while and everybody was used to that stuff, but it was all new to me. All of a sudden, now I was "in it." I was in the middle of it.
JF: Still, you weren't really as deeply into it as ...
AT: No, I wasn't getting the same treatment.
JF: You hadn't been pulled into that "circle of torture."
AT: Exactly, I was just an unhappy witness. I didn't like it, but I didn't know what to do about it. Now, I'm stuck. Now, I'm up in the middle of nowhere,
JF: Yeah, no money.
AT: I'm in this band, and I don't know what we're going to be doing all I knew is we weren't getting any money and we weren't eating right.
JF: All you had was this little grey Kaiser sitting out there to drive away.
AT: Exactly, and every night I would escape down to Santa Cruz and hustle this guy that owned a pool room out of a few bucks. I'd get drunk and come back and start the whole thing over the next day.
JF: Yeah, or get good cooking from Marilee Duncan.
(Note: Marilee Duncan was the lady whose daughter took a walk with Don and Gary Lambert back in Lancaster, causing the arrest and child-molesting charges. Connecting the dots, she could have been part of the push-pull factor that made Don decide to move to Santa Cruz.)
AT: Absolutely, she saved my life. I really liked her.
JF: Yeah, she was a nice lady.
AT: Yeah, she really was. So, I don't know, it felt peculiar, but we did manage to get some stuff done.

The Musical Process

Many songs were written during our stay in Santa Cruz. I cover this in the track notes section of *Spotlight Kid*. Some of the songs not recorded, unfinished or unreleased were:

Semi Multi-Colored Caucasian
Clear Spot (different arrangement, in 5/4 time)
Suzy Murderwrist
Pompadour Swamp
Little Scratch
No Flower Shall Grow
We Got Love's What We Got
Witch Doctor Life
Circumstances
Ubenso Cinco
Flaming Autograph
Dual at Abdul's
Navy - O

Jan would sit in the upstairs cabin and type lyrics out and Don would call up stairs and say, "Jan, toss me such-and-such" and she would drop down the lyrics to whatever song he had asked for off the balcony. So Jan, at this point, became the paper monitor. I thought to myself, "One less burden on the band members and also she never recited lyrics in a screechy, parrot-like voice." She did occasionally reluctantly read something to us at Don's request, but for the most part stayed to herself. I liked Jan more and more. She was like a "buffer zone" between Don and the band at times, and it made the relationship slightly more bearable. At the same time, I really think that Don had her convinced that we were all scumbags, because rather than friendship she projected an air of tolerance.

I often thought, "If Don considers us all to be such slime, why doesn't he just fire us so that he can get people he respects, thereby setting us free to pursue other more lucrative musical quests?"

Much of this material was written by the "whistle and sing" method of composition, where Don would stand in the room and make stuff up as we all sat there waiting. It was laborious and tedious work. We couldn't lose our attention span or Don would have a tantrum and that would be the end of rehearsal and often the beginning of a "talk." We had to keep these all as "head arrangements" which meant that if anyone forgot a section before we recorded a rough version, it was gone for good. I speak mostly about these particular details in the track notes. I for one, never have worked well this way. It was like being in a classroom with no books. You're lectured, and you're expected to retain everything. It was boring as hell.

As you can see from the list above, Don (partially) wrote an amazing number of songs during this 3-5 months in Santa Cruz - besides the actual *Spotlight Kid* material. I say partially, because many of them were really nothing more than sketches - rough drafts that were never finished. One of the things that made rehearsal difficult was that we were rehearsing all these songs, not knowing which ones would actually be used. It was, as usual, disorganized, disorienting, disenchanting and just this side of unbearable. A little "off kilter" perhaps, and maybe that was the goal. Much of the material was simple and didn't require a lot of rehearsal, so we were highly over-rehearsed.

Life In Hell / The Third Level

Unfortunately, here was to begin the acceleration into the cult-like environment. Over the next few weeks, Helen arrived to take up quarters. This resulted in Don immediately beginning to indoctrinate her against me whenever I was rehearsing. Many times the band would rehearse without Don, and I would discover later that Don had spent several hours talking to Helen. This troubled me, because I felt that it is inappropriate for him to be spending so much time with my girlfriend. I was relieved that Helen and I were getting along better - with the absence of any domestic violence.

I can truly say that this period of time was when I probably really learned the meaning of the word "despise," because I must confess, I actually began to despise Don around this time. Perhaps from all the attention that had been focused on him (at least compared to the rest of us,) Van Vliet had truly allowed the "Captain Beefheart" image to "go to his head." He was belligerent and egotistical for the most part. He also would constantly probe into private matters that were truly none of his concern.

It was a very difficult time for me, as I was not involved in the initial music process for the most part and so would come in and just be expected to put my part immediately to the music, with no familiarization process allowed. I almost dreaded rehearsals. There weren't many happy times and Mark, Bill and I mostly had again started to distrust and fight each other. So, there was tension and paranoia present all the time.

The Felton Cult Experience

John French: Well, before we go into all that, I know this is uncomfortable, but just as an outsider, what was your impression about what was going on there as far as Don's control over and manipulation between Bill and Mark and - the human dynamics that were happening there.

Art Tripp: Well, I hated it. I mean, I didn't like it at all. It was unattractive to me and it made me feel extremely uncomfortable. But, at the same time, I was in it, in a way, and I was stuck and didn't know what else to do. It was kind of like a "guru" situation. The guy had the "whammy" on everybody and we ... all seem to alternate elation with intimidation and it was just really weird.

JF: Do you recall Don rehearsing with the band up there much?

AT: No, not really, I mean, he was present at some rehearsals. I was always sorry to see that happen because I knew once he walked in the music was going to stop and the conversation would start and the shouting and all that shit and it would just go on and on for hours. It did seem to level off a little and it did seem like we got a lot of shit done. However, Bill took the ass-end of that. He really took it hard. He really got the shaft in that deal there.

JF: Yeah, and I hate to admit that I doled some of that out to him.

AT: Oh, I did too. I remember coming home drunk one night and everybody was beating up on Bill, and they kinda bugged me until I got involved in it. I had to do some serious amends to Bill later. He took it, and I just couldn't believe how gracious he was. Saying he knew it was just stupid and crazy at the time, he accepted my apology.

JF: Do you think - what do you think Bill's motivation was for hanging around? What do you remember coming out of his mouth during the times? I'm going, "How does this guy take this?" Do you remember?

AT: I don't remember what he was thinking at the time, except that he was just trapped. He let himself get trapped and he was in it. I think he really liked the music and I think he was really learning the guitar.

JF: Well, I remember something about Bill from that time that he kept saying. "I don't wanna leave because I don't want to do that to you guys. I don't want to put you guys on the spot." I thought that was kind of a cool thing because he had a loyalty not only to Don in particular but the to band in general.

AT: I can believe that.

JF: He was a very strong person in that sense.

AT: I think you just get trapped.

JF: Yeah, we were all trapped up there weren't we?

Why Are We Here?

I kept asking myself, "why are we here (referring to Ben Lomond/Felton). How in the world could this possibly have been a clever, strategic move business-wise?" The only real answer I could come up with - and I'm not sure when this came to me, perhaps much later - was that the isolation, deprivation, and condescending circumstances aided Van Vliet in gaining back a near-total control of our minds, similar to the Trout house.

Why Didn't We Go?

Art Tripp: Guys have a way of putting themselves into a situation. All they have to do is say, see ya, and take off down the road, and we don't. We linger and we stay and we put up with this shit, but basically, I think all of us were really enthused about the music that we were doing. I do think that all of us liked it. Maybe didn't understand it all the time, but we liked it and we kept - at least for my part - I tried to keep focused on the long objective, which was getting out there and doing shows and making records.
John French: Yeah, right.
AT: And there was always that in the background. You just get used to that style, you know, putting up with all that bullshit and that crap, you know.
JF: Let me ask you this: If Don had not lived there or have been present, if the tapes would have been sent to us and we'd have been living there, how much different would circumstances have been.
AT: Well, it would have been a lot more livable. A lot more enjoyable living because in my experience in living with groups of musicians, you get a distinct affection for each other and a kind of a camaraderie that you do for, well for anything, I mean guys hanging around a pool room will develop the same kind camaraderie, you know each other and you develop your own humor and your own in jokes and all that shit.
JF: That was always missing from that band.
AT: Yeah, except when we went on the road. Then on the road, it was a lot different; the pressure was off, there were a lot fewer "sessions,"
JF: The brainwashing sessions, or the "talks," as we referred to them? Also, there was a lot more public exposure so there was a lot less of that that could happen, because we weren't as isolated.
AT: Yeah, and putting it another way, you got a little of the fruits of your fucking labor.
JF: Not much though.
AT: Well, you got some. At least you got the adulation, and you got to appreciate people that were appreciating what you had done. There was some gratification there.

Jeff Bruschele

Bruschele actually wound up following us up to the compound and staying in a spare bedroom in Artie's house. He eventually brought his girlfriend with him. She was a beautiful quiet girl, and rather tall as I recall. I recall his little Volkswagen bug breaking down and he and the girl hitchhiking constantly. Or, he would be under the car working, while his girlfriend sat on an old chair and read the manual to him.

My Angry Outburst...Helen

One night during the more stressful times, Helen and I got into a shouting match over something. I was yelling something like, "You dare to judge me?" - a couple of times. It was, as most domestic squabbles, pretty silly and petty. Of course it was heard by the entire entourage, as there was little privacy. Don immediately called a meeting of the other members to discuss my inappropriate behavior. Although a minor squabble of molehill proportions, Van Vliet miraculously transformed it into a mountain of concern. This resulted in another "talk." In which I was the "target."

In a group meeting with all the women present, Helen was officially turned against me and so I was thus isolated from even my girlfriend. That was truly the end of our relationship, though we stayed together for several months - trying to make it work.

The "talks" kept escalating until they reached nearly the level they had during *Trout Mask*. Bill often became the target of these talks. Ironically, Bill was working harder and longer than anyone to bring the album together. He was usually the first one up for rehearsal, and he stayed longer than anyone. He also was working on a solo project, *Big Sur Suite*, for which I believe the piece *Odd Jobs* may have been originally written, which later wound up on the original *Bat Chain Puller*.

Zoot Horn Rollo - Target Of The Year

I recall terrible talks up here, Bill getting thrown in a large dumpster (probably with me as part of the throwing team), and not only that, but Laurie actually threw some burning paper inside with him and almost started a fire. I recall earlier that Van Vliet was lightly jabbing Harkleroad in the abdomen with a butcher knife during a "talk" in the rehearsal studio, while screaming at him at the top of his lungs. I recall Mark and Bill fighting outside and Don looking at me during this and saying, "Man, I wish it was like it was 500 years ago when things like this could be settled man-to-man! You know what I mean?" raising his fist as a visual example.

I can't imagine why any of us stayed.

Once, Don staged a "funeral" for Bill, forcing him to lie on the floor while we were expected to stand around and make comments about the "deceased." Most of this cultism seemed based on Don's obviously demented version of "therapy", which was absurdly akin to "therapy" in about the same way alchemy relates to chemistry. It was superstitious, ignorant, self-indulgent, manipulative and just plain sadistic. Artie was not involved in the majority of this, except when he occasionally would have a few drinks while out playing pool and come back in the middle of a "talk."

Again, since we turned against each other, there was again no communication among the musicians. As a contrast, it was interesting for me to go downstairs to Artie's in the evenings and watch, in Don's absence, Bill, Artie and Jeff joking and clowning around, playing games etc. It seemed such a contrast to viewing the same group when Don was around. These were nice, normal people. "How does Don affect this powerful influence over people's behavior?" I kept asking myself. "How am I going to get out of here?"

When we could, we rehearsed every day and the rehearsals were laborious and boring affairs. All the songs were slow, for the most part, and the one I hated to play most of all was the title track, *The Spotlight Kid*. It seemed to me to be a cutesy self-portrayal of an ego-ridden man who ruined his and his band's chances of becoming solvent through blatant self-indulgence. I had lived it, and I found nothing "cute" about eating government food and being stranded in these various locations, living in fear and dread each day. Had Don buckled down years before and worked and listened to his original band a little more objectively, he probably could have had some money by this point so that he could experiment musically, instead of with people's lives.

No Money, Welfare, Food

There was no money to speak of, so we eventually all had to apply for government surplus food. This involved driving to some place down the road, filling out tons of paperwork, and then driving back to pick up a couple of boxes of processed cheese, spam, and various grains in brown paper bags. I remember Don saying as I walked up the stairs, "Maybe this'll teach you guys to work a little harder" as I ground my teeth together. Sue was still sending her son money. There's a photo of us taken during this time, showing four skinny band members and a very plump leader. The expressions on our faces tell the story better than words ever could.

Dentist

Arnie Rubenstein had come by one day to fix something, and he noticed I was holding my mouth. I had a really bad toothache as one of my lower eyeteeth had crumbled to pieces. Arnie immediately gave me a card and said, "Call this man, he's my dentist. Tell him to put it on my tab." Here's another time in my life when a Jewish person was very kind to me.

Riding to the dentist in Bill's limo with Don and Jan - who had taken to having Bill chauffeur them everywhere - I was holding my jaw in agony. Don said, "For God's sake man, why don't you just put the pain out of your head? That's what I do!" This reminded me of a story I had once read about a Tibetan Monk who was tortured by the Chinese by being hung upside down over red hot coals. He was lowered closer and closer to the flames and his only recourse was to "leave his body" and go into the "astral" world to escape the pain, in a state similar to meditation.

However, I went to the dentist. Screw the mystics, this worked.

Arnie Get Your Gun

Helen and I were awakened to a thumping on the roof early one morning. We were hoping for Santa, but no luck. Mr. Rubenstein's voice was recognizable and I went out to see what was going on. Suddenly, the electricity went off. Arnie and an unidentified associate got down off the roof with a big pair of rubber gloves and a pair of insulated shears. They had cut the main cables to the house, leaving us with no electricity.

As we began to draw nearer to him in an effort to find out what was going on, he casually pulled out a small handgun and checked to see if it was loaded - immediately convincing me that it was just fine for him to shut off the electricity. As it turned out, the rent had not been paid for some time and Mr. Rubenstein was now in the pleasant process of evicting us. Don was angry with Rubenstein - after the fact. However, he said nothing to him at the time, as he had no defense. This whole insane move had been his decision.

I was angry with Don. Obviously, someone was pulling strings. We had done a major tour and I figured with the money that he originally held in the account, plus the tour money the production company surely should have been able to pay rent. Ironically, Don decided at this time to move even further north to Eureka. Apparently, Victor Hayden had been up there for some time and had been searching for a property to house us.

Poker

The final days in the drab drizzling rain of Felton were spent playing poker in Mark and Laurie's cabin. We took a bunch of extension cords and fed a cable from an unscrewed light bulb on the shop in front to Mark's living room. Don kept insisting that we play poker. I lost continually because I have no interest in games. "Man, you better get with it, John, you owe me over $400," Don said to me one day. "Just take it out of what you owe me, Don," I shot back.

Don left for Eureka with Jan to choose the property. We camped outside and made hot dogs the last night in Santa Cruz. Mark, Laurie, Jeff B., Helen and myself had a great time. It was fun to spend time together, minus the instigator of the "talks."

"Why, if there was no money to pay the rent here, do we have money to move to Eureka?" I was asking myself. I had to leave my car behind and then return later to pick it up. However, there was a giant U-Haul truck parked in the yard, and there was obviously funding for that.

Move To Eureka

Helen and I drove in her car. It was a long drive, up past San Francisco, through all the small picturesque coastal towns. We enjoyed the trip as best we could, but there was a dread in my mind about what this was turning into. I had two or three months on my contract and I wanted out of this situation.

Eureka was grey and overcast, and the whole area looked as though someone had painted everything with smoke. We had to drive through Eureka to Trinidad, a little further up the coast. There were some beautiful views along this drive and the last view before the turn inland was almost breathtaking. It was a large bay, and as you came around the corner, you could see it from an elevated position.

The wood-frame property on which we would be living was another compound. We drove up a gravel driveway to the right of a row of buildings that faced to the right. There were three or four houses connected together, the main house was where Bill, Artie, and I would live. The middle house was Mark and Laurie's and at the end was an upstairs apartment that Don and Jan would occupy.

The compound was owned by a woman named Della Mallory, who was a professional horse trainer. She was in Europe, and I was under the impression that the property was being leased temporarily until her return. The first evening there, we stood in the gravel driveway and I was throwing stones at a can resting on a fencepost.

John French to Art Tripp: It was almost like he had a Zen thing happening. I remember one time he was standing with his back to a fencepost upon which I had placed a tin can. I was throwing stones at this can as we spoke. It was 25 or 30 ft away. I was coming very close, but no hits yet. Don was speaking with us for about 20 minutes. He picked up a rock, as he was leaving, and without even looking, turned, threw and hits it dead center first time.

It was cold and damp in Trinidad and this house had huge rats. We were hundreds of miles farther from the music industry, and we were still penniless. What was the plan?

Helen Forced To Leave

Don had a short meeting with me in which he told me as though it was an official directive that Helen must leave. I was partially relieved, as I felt this was a terrible situation and that she deserved better. I told her that Don had decided this and explained that I didn't feel I would be here much longer either. She was upset with me, however I could see no point in fighting the situation. I was still bound under legal contract to Don, and I had about 2-3 months before that first year would be over.

I drove back with Helen to Santa Cruz, picked up my unregistered car, and prepared for the drive back to Eureka. We had a very emotional parting. I think under different circumstances things might have worked out between us. I had and still to this day hold a deep respect for Helen.

Rehearsals

Basically, we were tying up the loose ends for the album. Mostly, we just went over what we had rehearsed, and what we should have recorded months ago rather than prolonging this agony.

P-K-RO-Pete

Although it was never recorded, Don wrote a song during an evening rehearsal called *P-K-Ro-Pete*. It was based on the *Ant-Man-Bee* drumbeat, which was called the *P-K-Ro-P* beat. I always thought it was a rather fun piece and wondered why Don never recorded it. Another song written here that did get recorded was *White Jam.* I helped a bit with the piano transcriptions. The old piano from the Trout House had made it up here.

Final Rehearsals For The Spotlight Kid

The final rehearsals were wrought with the same kind of fighting and tension as there had been during my whole tenure with Beefheart. I remember one instance in which Bill was slapping Mark around. Mark's mouth was all bloody and I was concerned about him, and indignant as I was, I intervened on Mark's behalf and starting punching Bill around. Actually Mark looked pretty well shot that night, and it was the most vividly scary moment for me seeing him like that.

Now, all the fighting since I had returned to the band had been slaps and pushes and shoves for most part (between band members) - nothing serious. However, I was more brutal with Bill this particular night. I think all my anger at the band situation came to a head. This is the only time in my life I have actually hit anyone in the face with my fists.

I grabbed Bill and hit him in the mouth. He ran backwards and fell into the drums. Artie and Don were watching this. I went over and grabbed him by the lapels and turned him around, hitting him again. I punched and punched at him, until he staggered outside and then I punched some more and walked him backwards in circles around the small lawn. "How does it feel?" I screamed, "getting bashed around like that? Are you enjoying receiving it as much as dishing it out?" I had completely lost it.

Finally I walked into the house, into my room and burst into tears. I was totally ashamed of myself. "What in the world is the matter with me?" Bill was as much my friend as Mark was. How could I have done that to him?" As I sit here writing, tears come to my eyes and I have to write, "I'm sorry, Bill." As I analyzed the situation, I knew that I never had in my life behaved this way until I was around Don.

Bill walked around for days with blood matted to his lips and teeth. Every time I looked at him I cringed, but I had a really strange response. I laughed and said, "Bill, man, I'm sorry." I... laughed. The only thing I can think is that I somehow had to disconnect my feelings of guilt from what I had done. I couldn't handle it. However, Mark wasn't in much better shape, and neither were my knuckles. Violence is so terribly stupid, senseless and wasteful.

Spotlight Kid

Finally, it was time to record. As I mentioned in the track notes, the sessions were done at Warner's (the "artist's friend") Amigo Studios, Burbank California. With the exception of *Alice In Blunderland* and *Booglerize*, which were recorded at our old digs, Sunset Sound, in Hollywood CA.

Amigo Studios

Amigo was a beautiful, high-end studio. The speakers in the control room were built-in to wood paneled walls. The console and machines were all state-of-the-art. *Decals* engineer Phil Schier sat at the controls.

Grant Gibbs had found us a hotel in Hollywood as I recall. We had flown down and were being taxied back and forth to the studio. I shared a room with Mark on the second floor and Bill and Jeff Bruschele shared a room across on the opposite balcony. Art stayed alone and Don and Jan, of course had their own room.

I thought the sessions went fairly well except I was unhappy with the take they used of *Blabber And Smoke.* Also, I was perturbed with the whole idea of hiring an outside drummer to redo *Glider* (one of my all-time favorites). All Don would have had to do is tell me he wanted "rock" drums with a backbeat, and I could have easily done that in the first place at less cost to the band. Either that, or Artie could have done it.

I remember one moment that clearly defines this era for me. I had gone to the studio after we had finished the basic tracks. I actually seemed to recall this being at the Record Plant, but I could be wrong. I know it wasn't the same room we recorded the basics in at Amigo. Bill was there with Don, setting up to do harmonica overdubs on *Glider* and other tracks. I came in to say, "Hi," and Don basically ignored me and had an attitude as though I were some street bum. He actually asked me to get out of the control room because "he was busy."

Bill walked out of the tracking room with me and said there were going to be some journalists coming over to cover the recording of the Beefheart album. He said Don had told him that he was going to "do us a favor" and not tell the press about "how the band had held him back," and "what we had done to him."

I looked at Bill, totally puzzled and asked, "What exactly have we done to him, Bill?" I felt really sad for Bill, and completely angry with Don. At this point, Bill was still convinced that somehow we had held Don back from the success he deserved. I thought about the hours Bill and I had both spent listening to tapes and ideas and carefully getting everything "just the way Don wanted it." A whirlwind of thoughts raced through my head about the hours I spent transcribing *TMR* songs and then re-doing them all in ink, only to be pitched headlong down half a flight of steps and given no credit at all on the album. He had given Jeff Bruschele, an amateur drummer, not only my drum set, but even my stage name, and actually tried to erase all possible evidence of my existence and participation in the project. I thought about Cotton's broken ribs. I thought about the fact that after all that suffering and humiliation, all I had to show for it was a double vinyl album I had to buy myself in Wyoming - only to find out I hadn't even been credited for playing drums, much less arranging much of the material. I thought about the fact that for a year the band did almost nothing in the way of performance while I was gone save the Amougies Festival with the "fake Drumbo" and Thee Experience with Artie Tripp. I was looking at Bill, and thinking, "How could he possibly think that we could have done anything more for Don? How could he possibly feel that we haven't gone excessively above and beyond the call of duty? What kind of power can Don hold over people that can cause them to think so little of themselves?"

This became a moment of clarity.

I went back to the hotel we were staying at and contemplated the whole lousy mess. I examined every facet of my personality to see what in the world could have allowed me to ever submit to such foolish and absurd accusations. How could I possibly have ever felt this man would change and allowed myself to be trapped twice in this same situation? However, I had signed a contract about a year ago, and I felt obligated legally to see it through. I had about a month left.

Unfortunately, this is what goes through my mind when I hear *The Spotlight Kid*. It's probably a lot different than what you hear…right? Now, maybe you'll understand if I don't play it too often on my CD player.

Pacific Northwest Performances 1971 Late Summer, Early Fall

As I recall, we left LA and flew directly to Vancouver B.C. for a performance. We were opening for Quicksilver Messenger Service and it was in some huge arena. This should have been a moment to be excited about, yet even on the cab ride to the airport, Don, who was sitting in the front of the cab or hired car with Jan, was all over my case about something.

I only recall him saying something really hateful to me, to which I replied, "Why do you hate me so much, Don?" He replied that he was "incapable of hatred" and then said, "Just fuck you, John." To this day, I have no idea what in the world I could have done to bring this on.

That night when we arrived at the hotel in Vancouver, we had to have a "talk" about my "thing" which, again, wasted huge amounts of time, made me miserable, made no sense to anyone, and accomplished absolutely nothing. It was relentless and my head was spinning. I was nearly out of my mind from dealing with this and it was showing in my curtness and sarcasm. There was never any specific wrong that anyone committed, it just seemed to be that when anyone was themselves, relaxed a little, or showed any signs of that dangerous thing called independent thought, there had to be major discussion.

I made up my mind that I wasn't about to cop to anything. I had done nothing wrong. I knew it, and to hell with Don. That was the attitude I decided to keep. After the performance, I went back to the room to sleep. I was rooming with the roadies now - Jeff Bruschele and Bill Shumow - everyone else had their own room. Bruschele and Shumow had to get up early to drive the equipment truck to the next city. I got up later and was assembling all my stuff and packing for the plane ride, when I realized that my plane ticket was missing.

I announced this immediately. Don was absolutely insufferable about this and I was right at the end of my tolerance of his verbal abuse. As we walked through the airport, Van Vliet's diatribe towards me was relentless. He threw every demeaning comment he could my way in front of the entire group and Jan. "I can't believe you're so fucking stupid as to actually lose your ticket. What kind of moron are you?" - I was called everything from moron to imbecile to my all-time favorite, which I still find amusing even when aimed at me - "dunce-bud."

I remember the band getting on the flight and leaving me at the airport. I am totally blank as to how I ever got to the next city - perhaps a later flight. I did eventually manage getting there and showed up for the concert. As I walked in, the whole band was there, including Don and Jan and the roadies. Jeff Bruschele came running up to me. "John, I am so, so sorry." I got up early in the morning and in my morning stupor and the rush, I grabbed your ticket by mistake" - this was heard by the entire entourage. I looked at Don and summoned my dirtiest look of disgust possible and said in as loud a voice as I could project, "That's all right Jeff, anyone can make a mistake" - never taking my eyes off Don.

Mr. Beefheart didn't really speak to me for the rest of the tour, and I didn't miss the company. I felt liberated.

Shipped Back To Eureka

After the tour, we were shipped back to Eureka without being given a dime. There was no food at all in the house except for a small bag of Bulgur, which is a grain I had never heard of before. My car was parked in the yard with a broken drive shaft, and the weather was cold, damp and cloudy. My only memory of this time is reading a recipe on the back of the bag of Bulgur that called only for ingredients we had in the house, baking soda, water, etc. I would bake these little biscuits and everyone would come out and grab a couple, and I would bake some more. It was the only food we had for days.

Don Calls

After a few days, we received a call from Don, who was at the studio doing the final mixing. He would appoint a time, and someone would stand next to the phone until it rang. I was standing in a pay phone across the street from the house in the rain at night. "What I want you to do, John, is start your own group." Don said. "Artie's going to play drums for me now." He went on to say that I would be happier in my own group and that I had to leave the Gon Bops behind, because Artie was going to play them.

I hung up the phone and made an assessment of the last year and a half. I had made no money, but actually owed God's Golf Ball Productions, according to the books, somewhere in the vicinity of $6k. The only thing I had to show for my efforts was a $300 broken down automobile with no gas that needed a driveshaft, which was actually purchased as part of the production tab, so I still owed for it. In return, I had recorded two albums of material, done a major US tour and played several minor engagements - including the three recent Canadian gigs.

Car Stranded

Now I was stranded in this god-awful rat-infested place 700 miles from the only place I knew as home. The only thing I could think to do is call my Father and ask him for a loan. I hated to even consider doing that. Not because I was so "proud," but because my parents were so broke. I called and he wired me $100 (which went a lot farther in 1971 than it does today). Jeff Bruschele was a big help to me during this time. He was sympathetic about my situation and drove me around as much as he could in his little Volkswagen. I recall him opening the bonnet of the VW to check the gas level with a stick because the gas gauge was broken. We drove to junkyards and I found a used driveshaft for $20, which I installed myself with tools I had in my trunk. I charged up the battery and took the car for a test drive - it drove beautifully.

Mark and Laurie, who had no car at all, gladly rode with me, and we spent about an hour down by the beach on that site I mentioned earlier as being such a great view from the road. I felt so close to Mark and Laurie, we had been through so much together, yet I couldn't just honestly talk with them about how I felt about the situation. I couldn't hug them goodbye even though I loved them and would miss them terribly. It was as if there were boundaries between us we couldn't break down.

Back Home Again

I had to take all the drum heads off my drums and pack my clothes and other belongings inside in order to make everything fit in the car. The drive was fourteen hours and I did it the following day, stopping only for gas and food. I arrived in the evening at my parent's house, feeling like a fool for having to come back to Lancaster again. I called Helen and we visited. My last dollar was spent on a pack of cigarettes.

Don Wants Me To Start My Own Group...

As I mentioned, Don had wanted me to start my own group. He had written one song, *Dr Drumbo*. I still have the lyric sheet somewhere. He told me I could be the "next Dr. John" doing stuff like this (which I suppose was a step or two up from his other comparison of me - to Tom Jones!). Basically, Don wanted to produce me as drummer/singer of a power trio. I didn't want to do anything musical related to Don. My thought was: physician, heal thyself. I just wanted as far away from him as I could get.

I unpacked my stuff and took out my little file folder in which I kept tax-records, etc. I found the contract I had signed with God's Golf Ball Productions and looked at the option date. Ironically, it was dated as the same day I looked at it! In plain words, I had signed this contract exactly one year prior to this day. My option had to be picked up by written notice and they had failed to do that. I was free from any contractual obligations to God's Golfball Productions. I breathed a sigh of relief.

Al Liefer

A few days later, I had a meeting with Al Liefer to discuss my "future dealings" with the company. I drove down and walked in the waiting room, barely able to contain myself for what I had to say. Al called me in the office. I'd never been in the back part, only the waiting room. He was quite cordial, but controlling. We talked about the band, and the idea of me having a solo act. Al said that Don had a lot of confidence that I could sing and lead my own group.

He also explained to me that I owed a lot of money and so probably a lot of the early royalties and concert earnings I made would go into paying off what I owed to the company. This was quite a setup, and I was enjoying every minute of his guilt-ridden lecture to me about how I would have to unfortunately "work really hard" to get myself out of debt.

"Yes," I said, "but there's one small problem." "What's that?" Mr. Liefer asked curiously. "My contract has expired. You didn't pick up the option, which expired yesterday. According to the contract, you have to give me written notice previous to the expiration of the contract."

Al looked completely shaken and lost all composure for a moment and then assumed a completely different line of reasoning. Whereas a moment ago, he had been lecturing me on how much money I owed, now it was more along the lines of; "Yes, well, John, I always felt that we had a good understanding and we certainly shouldn't let a piece of paper come in between us." I ignored him. I had heard this speech before - from Bob Krasnow - almost word for word.

"And if you or anyone else thinks that after recording two albums, doing a major US Tour, plus various other gigs and donating a year and a half of my life to all this isn't worth more than $6000 or whatever you say I supposedly owe you, then you're as crazy as Don, and I happen to know you're not." I got up and left.

Don was waiting in the basement parking lot with Jan and their "chauffeur," Bill. "How'd the meeting go?" he asked. I gave him a big grin. "Great!" I replied. "Hey, my tank is completely empty, man, can you loan me some money so I can get home?" "Yeah, here," and handed me two dollars. "Thanks," I said, and grabbing the money, I got in my car. "See ya round!" I said, waving and screeching out of the underground parking lot. Two dollars: my total earnings for the last year and a half.

CHAPTER THIRTY TWO:
TWO SPOTS.
CHEAP SHOTS

with Art Tripp photographed by Art's mother on
Clear Spot tour 1972. Photo courtesy of Art Tripp.

The Spotlight Kid Tour

After I left, Artie became my replacement, and Elliot (hello again) came in to cover the marimba parts. My first thought when I heard Elliot was back in the band was that he had originally left because of me, just as I had earlier suspected. Various opinions seem to reinforce the idea that the first performances on the *Spotlight Kid* tour were nothing to write home about. In one phase, the opening act for Beefheart was a trained chimpanzee act. The band was loose, and uncertain about endings. Elliot at times appeared as though he were not part of the group. The audience seemed dissatisfied and left in droves.

One person who was in the audience confided to me that it was "like circus act." Not only was the band un-prepared, with uncertain endings, but they were playing in Woolsey Hall - in a really terrible acoustic environment, so the sound was not up to par.

Little by little, however, the show tightened up and the band began to regain some credibility. Mark was becoming more and more of a stage presence, and Bill was beginning to feel more relaxed in front of an audience. Artie's drumming improved nightly as he re-acquainted himself with the role of timekeeper. His physical endurance improved as time went on, and he began to enjoy the role he had been given.

By the end of the tour, the band's sound was improving. During one show at the Academy of Music on Fourteenth Street in New York, the group not only sounded much better, but had endings worked out rather than just grinding to a halt. Even the physical appearance of the band had improved. Don was wearing a elaborate, flowing cape, which had embroidered depictions of "wind gods" on the back. Things were going better, the band was coming into it's own sonically, and Don's performance had improved.

But there was still the underlying trend in some people who had come expecting the "Magic" of the earlier music to be somewhat disappointed with the more accessible direction Don had taken. It was a mixed-signal to the audience in the opinion of some. Was Beefheart trying to go commercial or not? What was this boogie-rock in comparison to the brilliantly disconnected compositions from *Trout Mask Replica* and *Lick My Decals off, Baby?* What happened to quench the fire that fueled his staunch stand against conformity? Was he "selling out?" What had happened to the uncompromising genius-creator of Dada-rock who thumbed his nose in the face of the "mama heart-beat" rhythms that had dulled our senses?

Don was working on his next album already, which he had tentatively named *Brown Star* - purportedly his visual description of an anus. It later became re-named *Clear Spot* - after a revised version of the song of the same name.

Into The Unknown

Since I was out of the picture from 1971 until 1974, this would be a good time to read Bill's book, *Lunar Notes*. I still have a lot of questions from that era: When did Roy Estrada join and when did he leave? When did Alex come back into the picture? What was the exact timeline?

It is also a time when I just wandered around with no particular direction for years like some shell-shocked Viet Nam War casualty. All I had was an old beat-up drum set and no self-esteem. Of course, self-esteem is often highly overrated. I suppose we need a certain amount to survive, especially in the businesses where you are more exposed to the public. Actually, I have had some of my more lucid moments during times when I didn't think too highly of myself.

In fact, I find one of the most beautiful traits and strong virtues in a human to be true humility. It is also one of the more rare of human traits. When I talk to somebody who exhibits this remarkable trait, I find myself in awe, wanting to be more like her or him. It's also an elusive quality, because once you notice the slightest trace of true humility in yourself, it runs like a mouse for a hole as your ego says "wow! I so humble..." As soon as other people praise you for your humility, it's gone, and pride raises it's ugly head.

I had been totally jaded by the music business and really wanted nothing more to do with playing in a band during this period. In fact, I nearly hated Don. I had to keep telling myself that I only hated what he had done, and not him in particular. I desperately tried to be objective about the band in general and Van Vliet in particular. At the same time, I was relieved to be away from that pressure cooker environment in which every nuance of one's behavior was carefully scrutinized for flaws. If it wasn't the public scrutinizing you, it was Don, who was a much harsher judge than any critic ever dreamed of being. It was refreshing to laugh and joke with friends again, and shrug off the weight of all that nonsense.

Don Giesen, my guitarist friend from High School, had actually just gotten back from Viet Nam. I believe he had been drafted into the army shortly after I left town with the Magic Band in 1967. He suggested I get a job working in a furniture store as a deliverer. I was hired to replace a fellow who had punched out the guy I was assigned to assist. As it turned out, this punched-out soul was a young, unstable and hateful individual who outweighed me by about 30 pounds and looked like he worked out constantly. He was a thief, and was extorting not only money but also stock from the store. He would constantly "Jekyll-Hyde," being a marvelous guy to the management, and throwing dining room tables and lamps at me when we were alone. He drove so recklessly that one day on a dirt road he nearly rolled the delivery truck. I couldn't seem to convince the management that they had Jack the Ripper working for them.

Why No Music

People ask me a lot why I didn't go audition for groups back then. Basically, I didn't like the whole drug scene that was going on. There seemed to be no escaping pot no matter where you went. One look at the hippy residue, the drug culture, and the low level of the music convinced me to flee for my life. In my head, by 1971 the hippy culture was dead and gone, but the remnants and negative effect on society would be around for years.

Don Giesen wanted to build a small studio, but he didn't have the funds. He decided to become an upholsterer to make money so that he could buy the studio gear. He wanted me to work with him building furniture. I was still torn between wanting to do music and be a "normal" person. Musically, there didn't seem to be any place I fit in. I wasn't a rock artist, and I wasn't a jazz artist. One guy whose band I used to occasionally set in with during this period told me, "Frankly, I used to think you were a horrible player. You were always playing stuff that distracted from the music." I was constantly over-playing and adding odd beats that I had created. There weren't any other bands doing what Beefheart did. However, although I found the music challenging and rewarding to perform, I certainly didn't like the cult atmosphere and financial situation.

Piano

While working for the furniture store, I bought a piano. In those days, you couldn't buy a little digital piano. You either had to get a Fender Rhodes, a Wurlitzer, or an old upright, which was cheapest. I found an old upright for $150. It was a beautiful looking instrument, with hand carved wood on the front panels depicting birds flying to or sitting upon branches. I came home and played for hours to escape from the effects of coping with my co-worker's daily issues.

Recording Ideas

My father gave me an old reel-to-reel deck he had and I started experimenting with ideas in my old garage room. Unfortunately, most of my early writing was really "sing songy" James Taylor type of songs, and my lyrics just weren't that good. Every now and then, I'd get close, but for the most part I didn't like my own creations. I didn't realize that you had to write all the time and maybe one out of fifty things would actually be good. I would get hung up on one song trying to make it better, instead of just going from one idea to the next until something clicked.

I had to practice every one for several days before I could put it on tape, and then I would overdub guitar on the other channel. I wrote *South Of The Valley* during this time, which wound up on the Mallard album.

I quit the furniture store after a few months. My co-worker (whose name was also John) had a permanent frown on his face at all times and seemed completely angry with everyone. He would make me walk backward when carrying furniture and walk too fast in an attempt to make me fall.

One day, he set a bunch of lamps on the back of a delivery truck ("lorry" to you Brits). With the door open he commanded me to "watch those lamps" hopped in the truck, and drove off at breakneck speed. I had jumped in the back seconds before and thrown a packing blanket over all the lamps, which were mostly glass or ceramic table lamps, and secured the blanket while hanging on with my life to the side railings with the other hand. The back roll-up door of the truck remained open and it was obvious that he was attempting with his driving to cause the lamps to shatter on the road below and get me fired for negligence.

When we arrived at the store, I quickly folded the blanket and grabbed two lamps, which I carried nonchalantly inside the building as though nothing strange had happened. The look of puzzlement on his face was worth the trouble momentarily, but this daily idiocy was taking its toll on me. The final straw was when we were carrying a dining room table into a display room that was in the very back of the store. John kept pushing and walking too fast and I asked twice for him to stop pushing as I had almost fallen down. I finally braced myself and with all my weight shoved the edge of the table into his mid section and commanded him to "stop it." His reaction was to throw his end of the table up in the air, tilting it towards me, with the express purpose of the whole thing landing on top of me.

I merely walked to the side and watched it crash down on a display of lamps (ironically the same ones I'd already rescued once) and end tables. "I would suggest you clean that up," I said, and strode past him to the office, where I explained that I could no longer work with this maniac. I told them of the dining table incident, and said that I had nothing to do with the damage.

There must be some kind of curse on my life, however, as they fired me and kept him. Interestingly enough, he was not only an unlicensed driver, having lost his license because of reckless driving - making me the only legally-qualified driver of the pair - but he was also going to be drafted within the next 90 days into the armed services. I had done a great job for the company, and worked well with everyone else to whom I had been assigned. No one had any complaints, but I was still fired.

The owners of the store thought he was great (even though I was the third person who had difficulty working with him.) I was politely given two week's notice. To add to my frustration, I had been an "on-call" worker and though I had worked every day since being hired, the management "coincidentally" found no work for me during those last two weeks.

I reviewed my "real job" record. It was discouraging.

1. Fired from drug store because of previous shoplifting record, even though the superintendent liked my work and wanted to make me the manager.
2. Fired from the linen supply store after it was found out that I "had once smoked marijuana."
3. Quit the music store because I felt they were practicing unfair business methods and cheating the drum students I was attempting to teach.
4. And now, laid off because the management took the side of a violent hypocritical thief over me because he was a "friend of the family."

I was a bit discouraged to say the least. After my experience in the band, I was beginning to wonder if the only people who became successful in the world were those who were the most evil. I felt like I had done my best in all the jobs and in the band. I found myself doing deep introspection. I kept asking "what in hell is wrong with me?"

Dance

I was seeing Helen again. The domestic violence that had happened in '69 and '70 had stopped shortly after I left the Magic Band. I remember the last incident, though not serious, really scared me. I didn't know what to do about my behavior and so I actually sat and wrote, "I will not hit Helen again" one thousand times. It may sound silly, but it cured me. I still think that a lot of this abuse was just a symptom of the cult situation, as I've never really had symptoms of this since.

Helen had been taking dance classes, so I took an adult exercise class with her once a week. The theatre and dancing classes really complimented each other. One thing that I quickly found out was that my muscles were exceptionally tense and I needed a lot of stretching. I worked hard at the exercises, and I found that much of my stress levels decreased in direct proportion to the increase in muscular flexibility.

To Sew Or Not To Sew

Don Giesen was getting the material together for his first upholstering shop and wanted me to join him. After discussing it with Helen, I turned him down. He is now the head upholster at Harrah's in Lake Tahoe. I sometimes wonder what would have happened had I become his partner. I've always enjoyed working with my hands, and even today Don and I are great friends.

MU

Don and I often visited Jeff Cotton, who had joined the band MU. The leader was Merrel Fankhauser - the same guy he used to work with in Lancaster, along with Larry Willy (Exiles) on bass, and Randy Wimer (Jungle Jive Five) on drums.

Don Aldridge: I only know what I like I'm not at all sure I know what's good, but Jeff Cotton's slide in MU was just superb in my opinion. I believe that band could've crossed over had they not made the monumentally stupid mistake of moving to Hawaii. Merrell's writing was never better. Although I don't think he ever really belonged in that band, it was a great group.

Comment: Musically speaking, perhaps, but the monumentally stupid mistake may have been because of the deeply entrenched occultism in the band. They actually seemed to believe they were reincarnated Lemurians. When we would visit, there were lots of fantastic stories about witches throwing powders into fireplaces and people waking up two miles from their home and not knowing how they got there. Don Giesen and I would discuss this on the drives home after visiting them. MU seemed like a cult situation itself, but Merrel was much more amiable and the band actually made money playing hotel parties.

Rattlesnakes And Eggs

Even though I didn't consider the guys very serious, I rejoined the band Rattlesnakes And Eggs after guitarist Marty Prue (younger brother of drummer Pat Prue - the drummer for the Omens) called me and said they needed a drummer. I liked the guys and it was music. They made a bit of a living and there was potential for something, although they were a bit too much on the "zany" side for me. Tim Meyer still played bass and Keith Kennedy was still on trumpet. They had a new keyboard player, a seventeen-year-old kid name John Thomas.

John Thomas

Marty was of the Mormon faith, and spied young John Thomas playing in a band called We're Only In It For The Money who were obviously Zappa fans. They often dressed in fifties garb and did "Ruben and the Jets" stuff because their earliest gigs were at Mormon dances and the parents preferred the old fifties stuff to the stranger stuff, like *Brown Shoes Don't Make It*. John described their set list as a "goofy little repertoire."

He had heard Rattlesnakes And Eggs play and was a big fan. I had seen one of their shows after the US tour. It was at the local community college. They performed a lot of original material including one of my songs, *Reign Of Pain* and had really developed in their sound and musicianship. They were still going in ten directions at once, but were excellent performers and entertainers.

I'm not sure what had happened, but the band became divided. After I left in 1970, Tom Bryden had joined as flautist, guitarist, and vocalist, and a Pete had joined on drums. The wives had all gotten involved in some theatrical aspects. The entire group was taking tap dancing lessons, and this appealed to me as I was studying tap myself, but at the same time, it also seemed like the band was a bit "cultish" and definitely had a communal lifestyle that didn't appeal to me at all.

Seeing a rock and roll band come out and tap dance together was a bit of a stretch for most folks. Then, to see the same band come out in fifties garb and do a complete set "in character" was even more of the same. Eventually, the theatrics (which had strong support from Pete's wife Marianne) became a little bit of an overbearing issue, and the band split into two factions. Tom and his wife Karen paired up with Pete and his wife Marianne against Keith Kennedy, Tim Meyer and Marty Prue.

The band had become a bit too much of a "co-op" in terms of living together in a run-down hotel in Pearblossom, about 25 miles or so southeast of Lancaster. They had moved to this location from Green Valley, where I had last visited them. They cooperated in everything and perhaps the biggest flaw in this was exactly the opposite of the Beefheart cult experience - lack of any strong leadership or centralized vision. There was a lot of talent in the group, but there was a hodge-podge of original ideas that had been thrown together in such a way that the group had no real distinct musical identity. They did have a great deal of local popularity and I thought that perhaps I could focus their direction a little more.

In order to keep everything "fair" - every decision the band made was made from the politically correct standpoint of not hurting anyone's feelings or tromping on toes. It was more like a controlled anarchy musically. It was a hippy commune domestically. When Marty Prue decided to marry his present wife, Sue, and the announcement was made in the newspaper, it caused the band to lose their food stamps and welfare checks. The modest financial assistance had brought them a bit of stability, which was now swept away.

Marty and Sue had gotten their own place, and this had caused an even further rift to occur. Now, Marty's newly established Mormon values were coming into conflict with the pot smoking / free love atmosphere of the band. Resentments were beginning to brood, and the band was thrown off-balance.

When I first was actually introduced to John Thomas, he looked at me and said, "John French of Captain Beefheart and Autry Sam's fame." So, I discovered that he'd had some knowledge of the band. Autry Sams was actually a local black blues singer of no particular fame. He had hired me to sing and play drums on a demo several months prior to this meeting.

John Thomas was ecstatic. He was in "the best band in the Antelope Valley," and he was only seventeen! I met him at a combination jam-session/tryout where we played for about an hour. I was really impressed with John's playing and went over to tell him so. He told me "I like you're playing too. So, now, we're even."

John Thomas: *That's says more than anything about what kind of smart-aleck I was.*
John French: *Well, I didn't it that way at all. I took it more like you were returning the*

compliment and a little socially uncomfortable with the whole situation.
JT: Socially crippled might be a better phrase.
JF: Well, you were 17, I was 23.

I was particularly impressed by JT's ability to improvise. He had a well-developed ear, as opposed to most keyboardists who were classically trained and thus restricted to playing what was written rendering them stiff and predictable. I asked JT about his background and lessons in order to gain insight into this particular outstanding trait.

JT's first experiences on piano started at age five, when he began picking out by ear what his older sister, who was taking lessons at the time, was playing on the piano. Eventually the teacher, impressed with his determination and consistency, began giving him lessons. This only lasted six months or so, until the family moved. No more piano lessons meant that classical training, which develops techniques crucial to great pianists, was lost, but in its place, JT found himself developing his hearing and ability to form chords based on sound rather than looking at music. Because of this foundation, he was able, unlike many, to improvise early on, rather than be dependent on written music and became more intuitive as a result. It was obvious to me that he was unusually adept at improvisation for someone seventeen years old.

John Thomas: So, I've always been thankful that I've learned that way, because I think it has helped me to be a better musician now instead of being the kind of pianist that if you take the music away, they don't know what to play.
John French: What I noticed about your playing when I first heard you play is that, "this guy uses his ear," where as so many keyboardists I have met have that classical background and it's very limiting.
JT: I never regret the training my imagination got by having to think in terms of the sound instead of in terms of some intellectual statement.
JF: Your control of dynamics and time show that that - you have a lot of intuitive abilities that most keyboardists don't have.
JT: Right. It took me a lot of years to realize that was something that was working for me. Because, like most people, I was much more aware of what I didn't know and what I couldn't do. I wasn't able to appreciate what I was able to do and took it for granted.
JF: Right, and that's what the schooling tells you! You don't have the education, therefore you are NOT VALID!
JT: Right. I mean, I was lucky in a way that I "skipped" the schooling. With the way I think and my tendency to be analytical and intellectual, it probably would have dampened my love for music and would have turned it into something else early on when I was impressionable. It doesn't "hem me in" like I think it would have if I had gone to Berklee in my teens or early twenties, or done something like that. I wouldn't have had a sense of myself enough to keep that (special) "part" of me.

JT played hymns in the Mormon Church from the time he was 11, and attributes his reading ability to some of the pressure this experience put him under, as he was reading four part voice leadings. He would often approximate these, as they were a bit over his head, and often, he would transpose them to a simpler key as he read.

Not Serious

I could tell pretty quickly that the Rattlesnakes And Eggs band really didn't have what it took to actually do something serious. Marty was married and was constantly torn between his marriage and the band. Everyone else was single, but we were held in check by Marty's altered lifestyle. For me, however, it was a complete escape from the music business, and a time to do all the things I hadn't gotten to do when I was 18. We were just a bunch of crazy guys in the middle of nowhere playing some slightly tilted original music. A surprising by-product was that girls actually associated with the band and liked us - something totally new to me.

The old hotel (that was supposedly haunted - more on that later) we lived in was definitely falling apart. It was basically a "compound" - a bit like Felton only single-story. It was more of a house that had rooms added to it for renting out. There was a restaurant and a bar in a separate building. The restaurant was absolutely a perfect rehearsal room. The bar was great for having parties. It was a semi-deserted place on Highway 138 just west of the little town of Pearblossom that had been immortalized in Aldous Huxley's book *The Crows Of Pearblossom*. I decided that it was probably just what I needed to get past the Beefheart experience and it did help. It was a healing time for me.

At first, I was a little out-of-control. Once, while drunk on tequila, I decided to paint my room with a broom. I think what happened is, I had skipped the normal growing phase of an 18 year old, and so a part of me was still that age, and needed to catch up with the rest. I was nearly 23, but I dated underage girls, smoked a little dope with the guys, and generally became less responsible.

Also, my ego was out of control for a time. I was a big fish in a little pond. One thing that kept me in check was JT - this seventeen year-old kid. He was living here with these older guys, and I felt the pressure to attempt being a bit of a "role model" in terms of cleaning up my act. So, the "wild oats" days quickly were over, and I focused on the group more after a time.

Ghost Town

The hotel became a kind of haven for party-seekers, and people would just show up to jam or have a few beers and listen to us rehearse. When we didn't have a gig, we threw parties and would buy a keg or two of beer and sell people tickets redeemable for beer. It was a little chaotic, but most of the time people behaved themselves, and since no one in the Antelope Valley seemed to care one iota about creating any kind of activities for teenagers, this was a welcome outlet, for going a little wild but still having parameters.

Friends would volunteer to be "bouncers" and we never let anyone have more than two drinks. We kept a pretty careful eye on anyone who seemed out of control and made sure that "designated drivers" were with each group. I never heard of a single incident occurring from these parties. One time, we decided to use wine instead of beer. We got a great deal on a case of wine, so we served punch and everybody passed out at 11 o'clock - it put everybody to sleep. I remember thinking, "Where did everybody go?" We were actually playing in the bar section that night though we rehearsed in the restaurant, which was the best room. During a break, I walked into the restaurant part, and they were all passed out on the floor, sound asleep. We all laughed. Our slogan became "serve wine, play less."

It was a free-spirit atmosphere, in a sense. We were having fun, and pretty serious about rehearsing together everyday for five to six hours a day and separately we individually practiced to hone our skills.

It soon became apparent that it was just a party band. For me, it was time well spent, as these guys were all nice people who treated me well, and I was able, in a sense, to re-acquaint myself with social reality and become a bit better balanced.

When I first moved there, there was a fellow named Benny Page who was sort of the band "roadie." Though he lived at the compound, he was basically a free-spirit party guy who sold a little dope to make a living. I had procured a room right off the main part of the hotel, which was really more of a large house. I painted the room, carpeted the floor, and installed a king-sized waterbed a friend - Mike French - had given me. I had a little closet for my clothes, and a small wood burning stove for heat. I scavenged around and found an old headboard and a swinging door both of which I refinished and put a stereo in the adjoining main room, where there was a couch and fireplace.

I had broken off the relationship with Helen shortly before joining R&E and was seeing a girl I'd met in theatre, who I will call Sharon Brady, who I had almost immediately fallen in love with when I saw her in a play as she was a beautiful girl with an outgoing personality. She and I had a great summer together. I noticed, however, after a while that she seemed to have a roving eye for the guys. I also knew that she was going away to school, sent by her parents, to San Luis Obispo. It was a Junior College, but they had a great theatre department. They had the theatre that I mentioned was the replica of the Guthrie Theatre in Minneapolis.

I broke off the relationship for two reasons. I loved her, but saw that her personality was still forming and that she would probably go in a different direction than I. I also felt like it wasn't fair to her parents for her to be driving secretly twice a month to see me. That was a very difficult decision for me.

Young John Thomas Was A Zappa / Beefheart Fan

John Thomas, or "JT" (as he is affectionately known by his friends) had developed a taste for the music of Frank Zappa, and indirectly thereafter, for Captain Beefheart. FZ was "The Hometown Boy that Done Good" in the eyes of many of the local musicians. Three of JT's slightly older friends - David Eisenberg, Tim Little, and Richard Hill - took young nerdy John under their wings and introduced him to Zappa.

John Thomas: I realized that this was the guy that was using the same tools as all the other pop music I'd been listening to, but was using them for a whole different purpose. It was challenging musically and it was social commentary. He was saying something that seemed important and intelligent, instead of "I love you, baby." The music had elements of - I didn't know it at the time - but it had elements of Stravinsky and 7/4 bars and just stuff that appealed to me intellectually. I thought, "Wow, I've never heard anything like this before."- also his sarcasm and his wit and his attitude was something that to me, as a young smartass, totally caught my admiration.

JT found himself almost exclusively listening to Zappa for a spell because it was the only music reaching the depths that appealed to him. Rick Morris, another contemporary of John's introduced him to *Trout Mask Replica*.

John Thomas: I listened to that and it was just like the weirdest, strangest, excuse for music that I have ever heard. I even memorized (and) can still recite Old Fart At Play word for word from memory. ...We listened to it had a great laugh, (saying) "Aren't these guys freaks, isn't this weird? Isn't this the weirdest stuff?" We listened to the music mostly, simply (because) it was affiliated with Zappa and it was weird. I didn't get it.
John French: Matt Groening's first intro was (also) through Zappa. Don (was) lucky to have had that connection.
JT: In a way, because that might have given him an avenue. Let's say Zappa might have wedged the door open a little bit so that when Beefheart came busting through it was already accepted.

JT considered Beefheart a lot more non-traditional than Zappa. He heard more of the influence of Varese and Stravinsky in Zappa's music and didn't really "get it" when it came to Beefheart. Zappa, though using contemporary instrumentation, connected with John in the way that it made "more musical sense."

John Thomas: Don's thing was ...another universe of music that I'd never heard. Of course, at first it sounded chaotic, like cacophony - the poetry sounded like nonsense, like pure goofiness. John French: (jokingly) But after analyzing it, you found out that's exactly what it was.

R&E: A Year In The Life

We played all the local clubs, threw parties to pay the rent and were always nearly broke, but I seldom missed a meal (except when JT annoyingly ate my food), and there was the refreshing idea of working with people who actually attempted to work together. Unfortunately, the band had five leaders, or depending on your perspective, five followers with no leader. We were trying to go five places at once, and this made it tough.

Theatre

Before joining this band, I had taken a theatre class with my girlfriend Helen. This was around the same time I took the dance class. The instructor's name was Sam Anderson. I enjoyed his viewpoint of actors and the kind of discipline/fun kind of philosophy he had about work. I had also enjoyed the improvisational work in the class and my work seemed to impress Anderson.

Look Back In Anger

Sam was holding readings for an "angry young man" play entitled *Look Back In Anger* and I felt I fit the bill perfectly. I asked the band if they would allow me to do this play and work their schedule around it. They knew I really wanted to do it, so we made up a schedule of available hours. I made a copy and turned it in when I read for the play. I read for and got the part of Jimmy Porter, the lead character. It was only a college production, but it gave me experience in front of an audience saying lines rather than hiding behind drums. I doubt if I was a very good actor, but I worked hard to understand the craft and felt as though it helped me to overcome my fears of public speaking at least a bit.

Sam was a great director/teacher. He never used fear, intimidation, or anger to get his point across, so I trusted him completely and just following his direction. He knew how to bring out the best in people and was a very gentle and kind man. He left after a few years to follow his own dream. I saw him in many television bit parts in the seventies and years later, he played the principal of the school in the film *Forrest Gump* in which he says the line, "your mother is a very persuasive woman."

JT Early Piano Experience

I have noticed that JT has seldom written much music over the course of his lifetime, and I was interested as to why a guy who does such interesting melodic solos and has so much music inside would not pursue writing music to a larger extent. His answer came in the form of a childhood story. I think this story relays a lot of what's wrong with music education. It also reinforces some of Van Vliet's anti-education views to a point. However, JT had a structural knowledge of music even at an early age.

Somewhere between the ages of seven and ten, John's mother entered him into a piano competition. JT had been writing his own little compositions for years, and his mother thought it would give him a chance to play them in front of an audience. At the audition, the judges of which he describes as "a bunch of stodgy, old hag piano teachers" he was not accepted into the competition simply because he wasn't allowed to play his own music.

John Thomas: They didn't say it in a nice way it was sort of THE way - it felt to me like, "Who do you think you are coming in here and trying to bend the rules - don't you know?" I felt so ashamed and so embarrassed. ...It really had kind of a devastating effect on me and I think that it (caused) me to be overly sensitive to what I did.

A Zoot Visit

I was playing at some club in Lancaster when lo and behold who came in but Mr. Bill Harkleroad. I hadn't seen him since the split, probably close to two years. He had brought *Clear Spot* with him and wanted me to hear it. The only stereo available was in my elderly parent's living room. So, at two in the morning, we sat for an hour listening to *Clear Spot* at low volume and catching up on old times. I always had a close bond with Bill and it was great to see him. I noted that each time I tried to approach the dreaded subject of Don's relationship to the band, Bill would veer the subject off to a different direction. My instincts told me that things were still not well.

Bill mentioned that he wasn't too happy with some of the cuts, like *My Head Is My Only House Unless It Rains,* mainly because of the rather syrupy content. Bill wasn't much of a romanticist, and this was one of the main areas in which we differed. I occasionally like to reminisce, and Bill hates to reminisce, at least he used to. I am much more an emotional person, and Bill is more cerebral and logical.

One of his favorites, that night at least, seemed to be *Hit A Man.* He pointed out the modified *Blabber n' Smoke* drum beat. Also, *Big Eyed Beans,* which I think was our unanimous favorite.

Bill said that Ted Templeman had really made a difference on this album. Although Bill states in his book that Don had "the final say" on everything, I do recall him telling me that he (Bill) and Ted did a lot of the decision-making as far as logistical arranging and overdubbing, which made the songs more accessible. I can personally believe this quite easily, as Don, who was constantly creating, never seemed to know when to stop on a song. Unlike some of the previous albums, the songs on *Clear Spot* had a consistency from beginning to end and I found nary a digression into an alternate time signature or alternate themes. The songs worked very well, were strong, valid, and yet danceable. I felt like the band may finally make some money. This made me angry in a sense. I wasn't going to be there for probably the most commercially successful period of the band. When I see videotapes of the performances, I see guys that actually seem to be having a good time on stage.

Clear Spot

Clear Spot, in my estimation, was the best attempt at grabbing the Top 40 gold ring that Don ever created. It was because of several reasons.

Art Tripp's drumming on this album was a great mix of conventional drum technique, mixed with just enough of the style I had developed under Don's influence to tie it in to previous works. The mix created a clean timekeeping pace, while still being interesting and unique enough to not disappoint the fans of *TMR* and *Decals.*

Roy Estrada was a more conventional bass player, and as much as I missed Mark's chordal fingerpicking technique personally, the public would never be able to accept it. Roy and Art, who had already played together with Frank, laid down a strong foundation for the gliding and sliding guitars.

Bill Harkleroad had really come into his own by this time. His playing was just fantastic on the entire album. Not only that, but his arranging skills had developed to the point that he understood enough to keep the boundaries clear and not steer clear of avant-garde detours.

Ted Templeman, a seasoned producer, knew just how to capture the unique quality of the band and not be intimidated by Don. He gave the album some life and used effects - especially reverb - to give the album a bit of "spark" that appealed to the more average listener. Most band members I have spoken with agree that the sound achieved on this album was the best overall they ever heard on any Beefheart album. Part of the reason for the great mixes is that, according to several people, Templeman kicked Don out of the studio during the mixing.

Unfortunately, the one song that received the most airplay seemed to be *Too Much Time* - with the Blackberries singing backup, and a full horn section. To me, this misrepresented Don as more of a soul-singer, in the best tradition of Otis Redding. Though this was a facet of Don's style - in the *I'm Glad*, and *Call On Me* sense, it wasn't a complete picture and forsook the delta-blues/jazz roots and took him over into the soul or R&B area.... exactly where the rest of the album didn't fit.

Williams Auditions

When Robert Williams was going to boarding school in Philadelphia, he first met Van Vliet after a show. Later on, in 1972 after he was out of boarding school, and back in Boston, he heard CB&TMB was playing in Boston. He saw the show and thought that Don's yelling at the band was part of the "act" - like the good Captain shouting to "row harder." Unfortunately, it was a human drama that went on constantly.

Robert Williams: I was thinking, it's like "Mutiny on the Bounty" its Captain Bligh - Captain Beefheart - you know. He was "taking care of the mutineers."
John French: Well maybe that was his plan, but instead of making it an act, he just decided he enjoyed "the real thing" more.

Williams had heard that Dr. John was looking for a drummer and got a job as a stagehand so that he could audition. Dr. John didn't really feel Williams was the right guy for the job, but Williams' drumming caught the ear of Van Vliet.

Robert Williams: I guess Don's guitar player said, "That's the best drum solo I've ever heard in my entire life." Beefheart puts him arm around me and says, "Man, if I ever need a drummer, then you're the one."

Don Comes Calling

The members of R&E had gone to see CB&TMB play at the Troubadour, or the Roxy, or somewhere in LA. John Thomas, who was now a big Beefheart and Zappa fan was playing Clear Spot everyday. I wasn't too thrilled about hearing it although I thought CS was a great album. Unfortunately, at this point in time, I just wanted to erase Don from my memories. I felt like my experience with Don was too complicated to explain to the guys - it would take a book to explain it.

One night, I got a call from Don. He was still living in Northern California and claimed the band was doing all right. He still wanted me to start a group that he would write songs for. He was very friendly and talked to me for a long time. I refused his offer and eventually gave the phone to John Thomas. "Your hero wants to talk with you." I said. Thomas was pretty excited. "Is this Don Vlee-et?" He asked. Don was quite nice to the young JT, and spoke with him for quite some time.

I was impressed with *Clear Spot's* more accessible appeal and started thinking more about the band. I went out and bought a copy of OUI Magazine[58] because it had a Don Van Vliet interview. It always bothered me that they never interviewed the band members.

I was impressed with the article. I felt like Jan's influence had probably convinced Don that if he ever wanted to make money in music, he needed to back off the "art statement quest" and play some good accessible music. I know fans think that *TMR* and *Decals* were actually Don's major accomplishments. Artistically speaking, I suppose that is true. Speaking from the human realm, I always felt that *Clear Spot* was his crowning achievement - at least in terms of teamwork. Unfortunately it was too late, as the public already had him pigeon-holed in the weirdo slot.

The reason I believe this is simple: it was an album in which Don Van Vliet was not trying to make an outrageous art statement in order to outdo Frank Zappa. Instead, it was an album that captured

---

[58] Oui Magazine 1972 Elliott Wald pP104

the feeling and pulse of the original Magic Band - capturing elements of Delta Blues and Jazz, yet was innovative and completely original. It was a marketable product that had the potential of allowing Magic Band members to actually make some money and receive some recompense for their unusually hard work. It symbolized to me that Don may be "seeing the light" in terms of his responsibility to his devoted musicians, and thinking of someone's welfare instead of his own fame. I started to soften in my view towards Don. Maybe he had "seen the light" and realized that being in a band was about more than "how weird we can be," or "how can I make the most outrageous musical art statement ever." It was about a group of people trying to survive. When I read the following excerpt, I felt as though the possibility existed that Don had actually changed.

Beefheart: I guess I had some kind of an ax to grind due to having quit art when I was 13. I'm telling you the truth. I guess today I feel better than I ever have. I have this group together no, but I don't have it together; they're really together. I'm just out there playing the harmonica and singing. I'm in the group rather than being Captain Beefheart with the group hiding behind the cape of the mystery man. Now it's called "Captain Beefheart and THE Magic Band," instead of "HIS Magic Band" - that was never my idea, anyway - and I'm glad of it. I don't want to lead the damn group, I just want to blow.

In this case, I felt like Don was at least trying to do what all the Magic Band members had wanted to do all along: play accessible music and make a living. I don't think anyone in their right mind could call *Clear Spot* a "cop-out" or "sell-out." It was solid and original, but it was also danceable and accessible. It seemed like things could be better for the Captain and the Band.

I missed a lot of the major touring of the band during this period, 1971-1974. It's interesting that at the same time I was missing my friends and wishing I was on the road. I was a bit envious, and probably was the most so when I found out the band was opening for Jethro Tull.

First of all, I thought Anderson had a great group and was thoroughly professional. I would have loved to have had the opportunity to meet Anderson and his group personally. Bill said that Anderson actually reminded him of me, which I found curious, as we don't seem to look a thing alike. I was mostly impressed by Anderson's showmanship and ability to portray the "renaissance street musician" image and make it work so well. He is, today, one of the wealthiest of the Rock Artists, and deserves every penny (or should I say "pence").

Boston On Opening For Tull

Mark Boston: When we in front of a crowd, the bigger it was the better I liked it, because I just felt like I could fill that void out there. You know how when you first walk out in front of a big crowd there it's just like a big void - like a vacuum - and you've got to fill it. I started off the whole shebang with a bass solo. ...That scared me to death, especially when (we were) playing with Tull. I remember walking out onstage and there's twenty thousand people yelling, "We want Tull." I remember lighting my cigar and putting it in my little case, I would go out there by myself and do that wild bass solo. During the bass solo I'd stop right in the middle of it and pull that little case out, pull out the cigar (which was still lit. I (would) just put it in my mouth smoking and walk around staring at the people, (laughs) they didn't know what was going on, and I'd just flick the cigar and go right back into the bass solo. Then Artie would come out, and by the time the band's out there, we had everybody in the palm of our hand.

I Leave R&E

After a while, it became apparent that the conflict between Marty's lifestyle and the rest of the band was becoming more of a tug of war and restricting the band's freedom to leave the area. I felt that it was only a matter of time until the band either dissolved, or just settled into being a local club band.

John Thomas: One more thing I would say for the record. The impressions I got from you, and your intensity and the way you sang and played and wrote, would lead the band artistically because - even though there was a lot of enthusiasm in the other members - I don't think anyone had the kind of vision that you had. The best songs were always the ones that you wrote. Of all the musicians who I've ever worked with that influenced me the most to want to be the best musician I can and to believe in myself it would be John French.

Thanks JT. OK, it's in here, for the record. It just goes to show how easy it is to pull the wool over a seventeen-year-old's eyes...

I do recall that part of my reason for leaving is that I felt responsible for John Thomas. His parents had consented to let him live with us, and I really worried about him being around guys five to seven years older and how this might affect his life. He was busted for pot with his friends, and I felt terrible about this and it embarrassed me a bit when I'd see his parents.

One amusing incident I recall is that I had loaned the band my '60 Cadillac one night as they wanted to stay in town and party and I wanted to go home. I believe that my date drove me home, and I awoke to the phone ringing the next morning about 8:00 a.m. It was JT's mother, asking if she could speak to him because he had a dentist's appointment. I said I didn't know where he was as he wasn't in his room and sat down the phone to look around. I finally looked out the window and saw his head leaning up against the back window of my car. The guys had taken him to a party, gotten him drunk on plum brandy, and driven him home, leaving him in the back seat, rather than helping him into his room. It was cold outside, he was hypothermic and had been sick to his stomach. So, he could barely think and had no idea where he was when I awakened him.

John French: I went out to the car, and there you were, passed out, sitting up in the car, and some of the former contents of your stomach displayed predominantly on your shirt on the seat. I remember going back in and saying to your mother, "I can't find him." (laughs) then proceeded to ...
John Thomas: Wake me up, pull me out, clean me up.

I was pretty upset with the other guys for not helping him into the house. The desert, not having a nearby body of water, drops sharply in temperature at night and so there are big extremes in temperature between night and day. I told his Mom that he was sick and cancelled the appointment.

Another reason I left the group is that there was the constant presence of drugs at the house. Mostly, it was just a little pot, but the compound was gaining a reputation as a party house, and people would show up looking for Benny - who had been evicted shortly after I joined - so they could "score some dope."

We had some strange visitors as a result of this reputation. There was a place called the Delta Lady Saloon that held a yearly "Rattlesnake Roundup." Apparently, they gave a prize to the person who caught the largest rattlesnake. I can't imagine a more dangerous and irresponsible contest. One night, some of the group were just jamming in the restaurant room and two guys walked in wearing cowboy hats. They were really drunk redneck hippies. They mumbled something about the rattlesnake roundup in between guzzles of beer, which they seemed to consume by the bucketful.

Eventually, I walked with them out to their pickup as they were leaving. On the seat were three large glass jars, and each contained a Mojave Green Rattlesnake. It doesn't take much imagination to envision what a quick jab on the brakes could have done on these jars, which were sitting on the seat, unsecured, and the resulting tragic chaos.

Another interesting pair of visitors was Jano Zahoric and Karel Skakal - two Czechoslovakians who had fled the country while it was still a Soviet satellite country. Jano was a hunchback, and Karel was quite tall, and the pair of them made quite a contrast. They had come to the US via Canada and had seen me play with the Magic Band in Vancouver, as I recall, just after *The Spotlight Kid* recordings. Karel and I became good friends for a time. He eventually wanted to play drums and bought a set. He also was kind enough to build me a practice pad set out of mahogany and plywood, so that I could practice without disturbing anyone.

Bye To JT

John French: So that was our meeting ground. I think I worked with that band for maybe 8 or nine months and you stayed with it a little longer.
John Thomas: Maybe eighteen months total.

After I left, a drummer friend I had known from college, Phil Tynan, became the drummer for a short time.

I also heard that John Thomas had been in a horrible car accident. One night, while driving on the freeway at night, he felt something on his hand and looked to see a scorpion, which had probably been attracted to the car by the smell of the leftover fast food wrappers. He reached to flick it off his hand and, not noticing a parked truck, plowed into it at 65 miles per hour, eating the steering wheel and breaking his jaw.

I visited him in the hospital the day after. He came out of the accident relatively unscathed, but had to have his jaw wired shut for quite a period of time. I went to an R&E concert at the large Fair Center Hall and was shocked at how thin John had become from the liquid diet. The band sounded great, and one of the pieces was called *Gross Abnormalities* - a piece John had written to convey the auto accident experience. Phil Tynan was a great drummer and did a very smooth and flowing drum solo during the show.

Post Snakes JT

R&E continued on for a time. Drummer Russ Foutch replaced Phil Tynan, who after the Berklee School of Music and R&E, hit the road with Ice Shows for a couple of years. Eventually, right at the moment the band had a chance to go play out of town and make some decent money, Marty's wife, Sue, lost their first child in a miscarriage. He, of course, could not leave town, and R&E lost their chance to step up in the world. They explained to Marty that he should go. However, Marty was a strong part of the "spirit of the band" and without him, it just never quite recovered, eventually dissolving.

John Thomas: After I realized that dream was evaporated, I thought, well, "What I should do is go back to school. I'll go back to college," so I enrolled at Antelope Valley College started taking some music classes. Played sax in the jazz band. I played oboe in the concert band.

John continued to live at the old hotel for a time after the band broke up. Keith Kennedy became a husband and father and stayed at the compound the longest. The place has long-since burned down - with the exception of the restaurant portion of the building, which is now called "The Trading Post."

Karen

Former R&E member Tom Bryden was married to a woman I will call Karen. She was also interested in dancing. We occasionally worked together doing mostly tap and Tom encouraged me to dance with her, as we were a good team. It was fun for both of us. She was teaching part-time at Courson Park in Palmdale. I would observe classes and dance with her afterwards, working on new routines. I knew a few steps, started making up my own, and began developing a style.

1973 - Denny Auditions For Zappa

Denny Walley, as I mentioned, had moved from New York to Hollywood to audition for Canned Heat - an audition that never happened. Denny, not wanting to put Frank on the spot after moving to the LA basin didn't approach Zappa about playing with him. He decided to do studio work for a time. Eventually, he wound up playing with Jimmy Carl Black in his group "Geronimo Black." He had also been subbing in another band for the guitarist now and then, playing slide guitar, and it was during this period that Jim Sherwood heard him play. Motorhead had been in touch with Frank and knew that he was looking for a slide player and told him about Denny. Frank responded:

Denny Walley: "What? Denny Walley? He plays slide guitar?" He had no clue. Motor came by the house and said, "Look, Frank wants you to come by and audition tomorrow." "Get outta here! You gotta be kidding!" "Nope!" Next day, I drove my amp and that Danelectro Belzouki - you know the black one with the weird shape? Took it down to Discreet Records - the place that Herbie used to have. I went down there with George Duke, Nappy (Napoleon Murphy Brock), Terry Bozzio, Tom Fowler, and Frank. I started doing Advanced Romance and he asked me to play and man, I was ready.

Trouble In Beefheartland

Don and Jan were living in Trinidad California at this time in a beautiful house overlooking the beach. He was driving a new Corvette. In the interview with Alex, I found out that the same situation, with slight variations, was happening regarding finances during this period. I had heard a story about Mark's welfare money so I asked Alex.

Alex Snouffer: Well, Mark had just finally gotten his welfare check and had cashed it. DiMartino was up there, we were having a rehearsal, or just hanging it up for the day. So Don wanted to take Andy to lunch, so he goes over and he conned Mark into giving him his money. You know, "I'll pay you back" and blah blah... So, he and DiMartino went off and spent Mark's money. Of course, he never got repaid, and here's Mark; still hungry - you know what I mean? John French: So these guys that worked their butt off never got paid for what they did. After all that time devoted to the music. AS: Well, Mark's applying for welfare. What do you think? You know what I mean? Does that give you a clue? JF: And this was after you had gotten paid and the rest of the band hadn't and Mark was on welfare? AS: Right. The only reason I DID get paid was because I came down here (meaning Los Angeles area). I told them I'd blow their whole operation up, if I didn't get my money, and I got my money and I still blew it up. Fuck 'em.

Theatre

Back in Lancaster, I was drawn back to theatre class, although I had broken up with Helen and Sharon after that. Theatre struck a chord in me. I took another more advanced acting class from

Sam Anderson. I was again living in my parent's garage, and didn't have a stitch of pride or ambition. I just wanted to explore every artistic channel and wasn't yet interested in getting married and settling down.

There was a symbiosis involved here. My parents had a caretaker for their rather large yard. I had a little room in which to sleep, that was all I needed. I made a little money here and there by playing gigs and chipped in on food. As I look back, I think of myself as a dysfunctional bum with a "failure to launch" issue. However, I couldn't see that at the time. I was actually a little younger than Van Vliet had been when I first joined the band. He was still living with his mother, grandmother, and girlfriend at the time.

A Company Of Wayward Saints

Readings were held for another play, called *A Company of Wayward Saints*. It was a satirical look at a commedia del arte group, which was a type of traveling entertainment group popular in Italy during the Renaissance. I landed the lead part and played Harlequin, - the leader of the group - a kind of acrobat, actor, and sexual tease. I made my own costume and because of all my dance and theatre experience, I was able to fake my way through enough gymnastics to make it appear as though I was (shudder) athletic.

It was quite an experience. Sam Anderson was a really great director and teacher, so I learned a great deal and my self-confidence was building, finally, a bit.

Visits With JT

By now, John Thomas was working part time, going to college, and playing in a band with some of his friends. Not a serious endeavor or a moneymaking experience for sure.

John Thomas: I was pretty involved in the college. I found some identity being in the music department there. Then I was just filling in with little local gigs and whatever things that came up. It was just four friends playing to have fun. We would play Miles Davis' So What, Frank Zappa's I Am The Slime, and Tom Bryden's (one of the members) original songs. It wasn't any kind of focus in a commercial sense; it was about us being musicians. I think I stayed on the Antelope Valley music scene in a certain capacity. Through you, I was available ...and I think as Mallard started to become a reality, once whatever reality transpired, that made (the) guys all mutiny from Don, I was there as a keyboard player.

During these times, I would go over and visit John Thomas. He had developed a great relationship with Tom Bryden. Tom's father-in-law was an aircraft worker but also quite the handyman and so did a lot of work on houses. He finally bought a very small house on the outskirts of town, with the plan of adding on to it eventually and selling the property for a profit. In order to keep the property safe, Tom arranged for John Thomas to live in it. It was perfect for John, who was going to the Junior College, as it was less than a two-mile drive. JT was also working as a fry cook at night and playing organ for the church on Sunday. During this time, he experienced and epiphany of sorts.

John Thomas: But there was one time, I remember the moment clearly, I was living alone. I used to do this thing where I would put a record on the first thing in the morning and listen to it. I would listen to Kind Of Blue and Sketches Of Spain by Miles Davis and another record that I would do that with at that time was The Spotlight Kid. I would listen to it, but it never hit me as "good music." This one day, after I had been listening to the record for maybe a week, ...I had gotten over my objections to Don's rough and gravelly voice. I had overcome the foreign-ness of the weird rhythms and the funny guitar sounds and the odd hi hat - all that stuff that was so out of mainstream with normal 4/4 rock grooves, and "Led Zeppelin" guitars. Then one day, suddenly, it just "dawned on me." I thought, "this guy is the only person in music doing this. This guy's vision is singular. Nobody is even close. There's no predecessor. There's no antecessor. This is the most special and unique use of music that I have ever heard. Lyrically, melodically, and rhythmically, all of it." Suddenly it all came into focus like that in that one morning, that one listening. I realized that if I ever wanted to be associated with something that was truly on the leading edge, I couldn't do much better that to understand this music and how it all came together. From that point on, everything else sounded different to me, too.

John French: Because your perspective was now altered.

JT: ...or expanded, or even completely obliterated... my previous perspective. This is the same sort of experience that goes along maybe with that first time you take LSD and you realize that everything that you thought was solid really isn't? Or everything you thought was dead, really is alive? ... One of those kinds of moments that changes your whole idea about everything you believed. That's what this experience with the music was like. Every proceeding song just started to go deeper and I think I just sat down on the bed and was just going, "Wow! How could I have missed this before?" Then I remember that I thought, "I'm so glad that I did the repetitive thing," because actually, I learned, I got something that I never thought of before. It was a really important experience for me. When I got the message of Grow Fins, I was floored. When I realized about Click Clack and the rhythmic thing and the two different trains, I was floored, that's all. Even if that record was only ten percent of what it could have been, the ten percent that it was: I got, because I had no idea about the missing ninety percent. Rather than it being some freaky thing that no one else could dig, I was going to embrace it, you know? It was suddenly a real living, breathing piece of ART.

Total Eclipse

In theatre class, I was given the opportunity to perform a bizarre excerpt from the play *Total Eclipse*, which is based on the lives of two homosexual poets in 18th Century France. In the scene, my lover stabs me in both hands with a knife. We worked out special effects with a retractable knife and stage blood and actually had a couple of people believing that I had accidentally been stabbed in the hands. I was reading some books about theatre and starting to really become inspired.

Model

The girl I was seeing at the time was quite the game player. She pitted me against the theatre instructor, who was in love with her. It was a silly soap opera situation. The girl was beautiful and I couldn't seem to get her out of my head. Eventually, she made a big scene and chose me over the class instructor to be her companion at a theatre party, thus nearly ruining my friendship with Sam as apparently she had never told him she was seeing me.

During this time, I was helping Tom Bryden with a roofing job on a custom home. It was heavy, hot work, and I was in very good shape physically as a result. Karal Skakal, the Czech I mentioned earlier, now shared the small house with JT.

Karal had his drums there, and sometimes in the morning before work, I would go by to pick up Karal, and play his drums as he got ready. JT would be sleeping in the same room and he didn't seem to mind me clubbing away at all. It was the only practicing I did during this period.

Summer Stock With Sam

Sam had encouraged me to try summer stock in Wisconsin. He had me try out for a musical, and my loud theatrical singing combined with Sam's influence at his former alma mater, and some rather creative bio information landed me a small but important role as the bully in *The Roar Of The Greasepaint - The Smell Of The Crowd.*

At this point, I was beginning to really coming to peace with myself concerning my former Magic Band days. I felt a new confidence emerging, and I certainly didn't miss the deplorable living conditions, and cult situation of The Magic Band. A lot of people still called me "Drumbo" and asked why I wasn't pursuing music, and why I had left the band. I couldn't explain it to anyone in a short-attention-span sound byte, so I didn't try. It was far too complicated and I had pushed the whole terrible memory of that experience deep down and buried it. I did not want to think about Don Van Vliet ever again.

I was making some decent money now doing handyman work with Tom Bryden for his father, and because it wasn't a nine-to-five kind of job, and gave me the availability to leave myself open for opportunity. Acting and dancing had replaced music as an outlet.

Trinidad Trouble

Tripp (writing) continues with the Beefheart breakup in Humboldt County:

After the mind-numbing result of Unconditionally Guaranteed, *the die was cast. When Andy DiMartino "came on board" several months prior to that album, everyone saw some real hope for producing a good album. He was small physically, but he had a very open, no-bull-shit demeanor. I believe he was an ex-marine, which was a welcome contrast to all the artsy, PC, California weirdo menu we had been treated to in the past.*

He intuitively saw right to the heart of the problems we had getting the music composed, rehearsed, and ready to rip. Accordingly he pretty much extracted Don, and isolated him from the group. Don seemed delighted with the situation - after all he didn't know a thing about production, and I think he was weary of acting as though he did. Andy pulled the best out of all of us musically. First Alex and then I started meeting with Andy to use him as a combination sounding board and confessor. He was well aware of the situation, and he didn't understand how it could have gone on so long. Honestly I couldn't either.

At any rate we all went down to Hollywood and recorded the basic instrumental tracks. The music was much simpler, and had better content than Clear Spot. The tracks were at least as good, probably better, than anything we had ever done. Then most of the guys went home. I stuck around a little while, but as I recall I didn't enjoy witnessing Don putting the vocals on; so I headed back up to Trinidad.

When we finally heard the finished product, it was dumbfounding and embarrassing. As I recall, you could barely hear the tracks that were apparently mastered way down in order to hear Don's low voice (sound familiar?). I ended up apologizing to the guys that owned the record store in Arcata who had stood behind us for so long. I think they were embarrassed too, but had the class not to show it. If I'm not mistaken, they had even given Mark and Bill some free rent until we got paid (could be wrong on that one).

The offshoot was that Alex and I had a long meeting, and we decided that we had to have a heart-to-heart with Bill, Mark, and Marc Marcellino (sp) - who had been a friend of Andy's and musician for some of Andy's projects - to tell them what we thought about dumping Don. We knew this album had to bomb, and continuing on under the circumstances was just about unthinkable. We didn't know how they'd take it, but it turned out that they had been fed up too, but were afraid to express it. All of us got together and spent a day or two discussing the possibilities.

A tour was coming up and I felt we had to play our cards prior to the tour in order to have some clout. We finally called Andy and made certain demands: We wanted $500 a week for the *tour, and we wanted to have round-trip airline tickets in hand before we left Humboldt County - beyond that was up to negotiations. $500 a week sounds like pretty small taters now, but you recall that was good money then. We thought there was a chance they'd agree to it, but not much of one. We new they were stuck with the commitments, but we also believed they could afford the dough providing they'd cut their own take a little! I'll never know if they could have worked it - it never got that far.*

Andy went ballistic, even though we all in turn got on the phone and expressed unanimity. He flew up from L.A. during the next day or so, and with Don/Jan in tow we had a big meeting over at Bill and Mark's apartment. The meeting was pretty pathetic- they kept trying to isolate us in an attempt to sign us on either as a group, or individually. None of us acquiesced. In a last ditch effort they secretly tried to hire Bill for big bucks to be music director/player, and to teach new musicians the music - at least for the tour - which was only about two weeks off. Bill declined.

They refused to up the ante, so that was pretty much it. Whether they couldn't meet our financial demands, or whether pride prevented it, I don't know. I heard that the tour was predictably awful. People would yell, "That's not Rockette Morton, where's Mark?" and the like. I must tell you that whatever the outcome happened to be, I'll always admire Andy for telling Alex and I the truth as he saw it prior to the split.

The line here that is most telling to me is "in a last ditch effort they secretly tried to hire Bill for big bucks to be music director/player, and to teach new musicians the music." Don needed a musical director. He didn't have the ability to teach musicians his music as he had long ago delegated that to Bill, and before Bill, to me.

The fact that his dedicated Magic Band had become such an important aspect of his compositional process should have been rewarded with publishing credits, which instead went to Andy DiMartino - an outsider who had nothing to do with the musical process. The fact that his band was treated with less respect than sidemen was indicative of the illusion Don had created of himself as the sole proprietor of his work - and was reinforced by outsiders who had not a clue and accepted the articles and interviews as truth.

Smotherman, one of the players in the pickup band, describes the musical process Don used to "teach" the Magic Band: "he was just singing them to us and we played what we thought went along. And after we learned them in our own fashion, years later I heard the albums they were off and we weren't playing them anywhere near what the other guys were doing."[59]

Why didn't Don notice this? Simple, he didn't know the difference.

Stepping back in time to the confrontation:

Alex Snouffer: I'm going way ahead now, the big showdown up in Arcata. I mean when (the) Di Martino brothers were involved in it. I had talked to Andy on the sly and he had told me a couple of things ...that Don had told him - and this was after we had come back from England. Artie was drumming then, and these guys never got paid for that tour. I did, because I came down from there and got on the accountant's ass. He kept giving me stories at first and I said, "Look, I know better, man."
John French: Those guys never got paid for that last tour?
AS: Never did. What they had in their pockets when they got home was all they got. Don scammed their money. Finally the accountant got so pissed off at having to put up with me - because I was merciless, man - so he gave me my money, ...I got $8,000 which was what I was due. Don pocketed their money and gave them this big cock and bull story - backed by the accountant - I found this out later.

[59] Captain Beefheart, Mike Barnes, Quartet Books Ltd., 2000, pp 201.

JF: *How'd you find out?*

AS: *I forget. I think it was DiMartino, but there was another go between there, I forget his name.*

JF: *By the way, the accountant was Al Liefer? - Brown Liefer, and Slatkin?*

AS: *Right, some shit, yeah. So, anyway, what had happened is Don and the accountant kept telling them, "Well, the money's still hung-up in England." Through some technical thing, and they fell for it. Oh, I think maybe they got a couple of hundred bucks that Don said "he got for them"- you know - from the accountant. I finally blew. I finally said, "that's it brother." These guys go over there and put out for you and you turn around and stab 'em in the fucking back when they're starving to death and everything else, and you're sitting in "fat city" - getting fatter.*

JF: *Well, he had a pretty nice house on the beach. He was driving a new corvette. He was doing OK.*

AS: *Well, of course, you'd do OK too if you had $90,000 in your pocket for thirty days work. Anyhow, I just blew up, and that is when I got the guys together one morning, man. I'm sitting there, it's nine o'clock in the morning, and I'm sitting there with a pint of tequila man, just getting primed. And DiMartino is up there, and we just got them altogether - and I busted him so fucking bad. I mean, told him everything that I had found out. I didn't tell him who I found it out through - I just told him that I knew. And I told these other guys exactly when it had happened, how it had happened and why it had happened. And, they didn't believe me at first. I was a rebel with a clue.*

JF: *Well, you had originated the band, you knew Don from high school, you knew him, longer than anybody, so you could see through that stuff. What was Don's reaction to all this?*

AS: *Don's reaction to it? I don't think he could believe what he was hearing, that he was getting kicked out - or we were quitting - however you wanted to look at it.*

Alex, from everything I could see, was a guy who hated confrontation. He didn't like to cause "scenes." He was a very low-key kind of person - and surprisingly sensitive. His major fault lie in this fact, because in order to cope with what he didn't confront, he drank to numb himself to the effect it was having on his psyche. This behavior led to alcoholism, which eventually led to his death; about ten years after this interview transpired.

A recent statement from Michael Smotherman[6] cites that Don fired the band. However, he and the rest of the replacement group, from everything I can gather having not been there, were in LA when this scene was taking place. They were not witness to the actual events. Also, I'm sure that the fact that Andy and Don chose not to accept the MB's demands for the next tour would, in Don's mind, be enough for him to state that he "fired" the band. From the band's point of view, having refused to stand down from their demands, they quit. I suppose both are valid statements, depending entirely upon your perspective - and what Mr.Van Vliet told you.

CHAPTER THIRTY THREE:
YOU FOLLOW ME, I'LL FOLLOW YOU

John circa '74 shot by Bill Cody, a relation of Buffalo Bill. Photo courtesy of Bill Cod

"I mean, if they were concerned about being puppets, they should have spoken up about it instead of leading me on to believe otherwise. But then again, who the hell's a better puppeteer than me? Huh?" - Don Van Vliet [60]

The reason we never spoke up is because … Don failed to make us. Puppets, after all, have no free will of their own.

Art Tripp writes: "I believe Alex did relate to me at some point that he got paid from the accountant, but I didn't remember the amount. I'm glad he got something. He deserved it - as we all did. That must have been the tour with Alex, Roy, Elliot, Mark, Bill, Don and I; which probably was the final tour with that band. Bill Shumow (sp) was road managing then, and he was at least as fed up with Don as the rest of us. He later did some wheeling and dealing with the Mallard band, but that's another story. To be honest, during the last days of that tour I received a nice little chunk of money from Shumow on the QT. I don't recall the amount, but I was grateful. It wasn't $8000. Whether or not he paid anyone else, I couldn't say.
As you know those kinds of shenanigans are so commonplace in the entertainment business, that it can be considered normal operating practice. There was a degree of that going on in the Mothers, and I know from talking with other popular musicians of the day that it occurred in most bands. Putting aside the obvious misconception (all rock musicians make great money), the real irony is that it's such small taters. Fighting and clawing over table scraps is not something I volunteered for. I think it's hilarious that Don always complained that the business people stayed up all night huddled under a bare light bulb scheming how to screw us, when what he really wanted was to screw the business people and us as well! I really think that's funny! Of course one can see why the smart ones, like Zappa and others set up their own labels, distribution, booking, and all the rest. That way they have near complete control of their product.
In regards the Magic Band, I don't think any of us were in it for the money; and I'm including Alex in that. No musician honestly interested in financial gain would ever have had any dealings with Don whatsoever. The closest commercial product with Beefheart that I had anything to do with was Unconditionally Guaranteed - and you know what happened there. It would have been impossible to make any worthwhile money with a band fronted by an irresponsible nut who couldn't count to four. In contrast using the same personnel, sans Don, the Mallard band could have made it if it weren't for the deep seeded distrust or animosity between Bill and Mark."

I don't know if I would call the Bill/Mark conflict a deep-seeded distrust or animosity. It seemed to me more that they simply wanted different things. It was more a clash of values. Mark, I believe, was willing to settle for less musically and didn't really desire to delve as deeply into the technicalities of music as did Bill. It caused a rift, but I recall the mutual respect they had for each other and a lot more comradeship than Art may have sensed. Also, I think that Don probably encouraged the conflict in the best "let's you and him fight" tradition, and fed it as much as possible to keep up the same walls of separation that were described earlier.

The Magic Band / Mallard

Though I was first excited about Summer Stock, I was now getting worried and feeling uncomfortable. Sam Anderson had offered to let me stay with him during Summer Stock. He was going to rent a house, and could afford to as an instructor. I could stay with him rent-free and do some house-work for room and board. Good plan, until suddenly the girl we both were interested in planned

[60] Captain Beefheart, Mike Barnes, Quartet Books Ltd., 2000, pp 200

coming for a visit. It didn't look like the kind of situation with which I wanted to get involved.

Bill and Mark called me one morning. They told me of the breakup with Don and how he had been ripping them off so badly. They called to see if I wanted to sing with them. They were saying to me, in essence, that I had been right about him all along. This was after five years of loyal duty to Van Vliet. I never have known anyone to work harder or remain more loyal to their employer than Bill and Mark to Don - and I am generous when I used the term "employer." I wasn't really that interested in getting back into music, but my theatre situation called for an alternate plan. I said I'd come up for a few days and get a feel for the group.

Up To Eureka
I wasn't really crazy about going to Eureka again though it was good to see my old friends. They took me to a friend's living room where they had been rehearsing. Bill apparently lived behind this house in a literal shack with no insulation - just a bare-frame shack like you would see in the old south - like a sharecropper would live in. Artie was there, and so was Alex. It was old-home week. Alex seemed kicked back - about the same. Artie seemed withdrawn and unhappy. Mark and Bill seemed determined.

Mark Marcellino
I also met their keyboardist, Mark Marcellino, who was now part of the entourage. He seemed like a nice enough guy. After a time, I didn't really feel that he "fit in" with the rest of the group.

Jamming
They played a few of the songs for me, and I liked the then-untitled *One Day Once* immediately and went outside to write lyrics for it. In about a half an hour, I came back in with the finished lyrics and sang it to the music, which was actually in the wrong key for me.

Singing Again
Now I hadn't really sang with a band for 8 years, so my voice was very undeveloped. I did the best I could but I certainly was no pro at this point. It was like starting all over and it was very intimidating to step into the vocal spot in the Magic Band. They seemed happy however, and asked me to join. I was ripped right in half. I really had gotten deeply involved in theatre and was still considering going to Summer Stock in spite of the obviously uncomfortable circumstances. On the other hand, I had bonds going back for years with all these men. It was a chance to fulfill a dream I had long since left behind.

Theatre Out / Band In
I decided to join the band and made this announcement to Sam. He was a little upset, but I knew that they had other people who were interested in doing Summer Stock, who had already auditioned for the role. It would be a very simple matter to replace me, and would probably open up an opportunity for someone who was younger and had dreamed of theatre roles all their life.

I went down and picked up my stuff, then hitched a ride back with a friend of the band's named Bill Cody, who had been in LA visiting friends. He was a descendant of "Buffalo Bill" Cody. We drove his little pickup and listened to music. Cody was from the East Coast and really serious about baseball. We had very little in common besides music, and his taste was similar to mine, so that was about the full extent of our conversation.

Artie Leaves
When I arrived, I discovered that Artie had already left. He went back to Pittsburgh to sell

insurance or something. Isn't it funny how life pulls these tricks on someone? You make a decision based on one set of conditions and immediately, the conditions change.

Art Tripp writes: "We started into rehearsals which produced much of the good stuff used on Mallard. *After several months, I didn't see much future in it, so I blasted off to Pittsburgh, PA."*

Audition For Drummer

We auditioned a drummer whose name slips my mind after all these years. He was a Beefheart fan, but really didn't seem to have a lot going in the way of experience. Although he was a nice person, his playing was weak and held the entire group back. It was decided that I would play drums and sing, which is not an easy task. We actually should have kept this guy, but I had neither the patience nor depth of character to see that at the time.

Return To Poverty

Mark Marcellino and I shared an apartment together. I was really shaken when I realized the depth of poverty with which The Magic Band guys were dealing. It was worse than I remembered when I was in the band. Here I was again in a musical group, living in Northern California and eating government food. This time, I used food stamps. As I lived with Marcellino for a while, I didn't feel he was right for the group. He was more of a "pop" singer/player and wrote pretty ballads etc. I think it's ironic now that those were my thoughts then - because I was basically the same kind of writer. I had written very few things that could be placed in the category where I felt this band fit.

John Thomas

My old buddy from Rattlesnakes And Eggs, John Thomas, was the keyboardist I best thought could fill the position. He had the background and the tastes that coincided more with what the group needed to do, and what would obviously be expected. My main thought was: could I find a singing style that would work?

Playing Clubs

Alex Snouffer: Well, anyhow, a week or two after that was when you came up and John Thomas came up and Marcellino cut back to LA and we just started club - gigging you know. Going up to Crescent City and out to Duck (Blue) Lake or (laughs) whatever that lake was.
John French: Geez. That was fun, though.
AS: We had a good band - a good club band - I'm serious.

To interject something here, this statement probably is one of the most telling concerning Alex's vision. He seemed to constantly set his sights a bit low, aiming for the club circuit rather than the concert circuit. I'm not sure if this is because he preferred playing clubs, or thought it made more sense in the long run. This seemed to be a bone of contention between he and Don on more than one occasion. Don, in the early days of my tenure, would say, "I don't want to play those Okie beer bars the rest of my life." Van Vliet was very adamant about this, whereas Alex seemed to migrate to this vision of the club band whenever the opportunity presented itself.

John French: We were doing a lot of cover tunes up there and trying to figure out a direction. We put together a demo tape - and they decided that the vocals were weak.

Alex Snouffer: Well, there was a lot of other shit going on there.
JF: Well, there was loyalty to Don (referring to Warners), and "We don't want to upset Don."
I thought we had some kind of interesting material there. I thought we were getting a good start.
AS: Yeah, there was a couple of things there I enjoyed.
JF: There was just no money, we were up there starving.
AS: Yeah
JF: We needed to be down here (LA) if we were going to do that. We were too far away, too isolated.

Humboldt County appeared to me to be an economically depressed area. There was a lumber trade, but there were more and more restrictions being placed on the lumber industry out of concerns for the environment. Arcata, where we lived, was a college town, so there was not a lot that went on in the area that wasn't related to the college. There were a few clubs, but they were mostly attended by the locals, and a lot of the college entertainment was booked-in from elsewhere.

We decided as a group to play clubs to bring in some money for paying rent and bills. To me, this was a big mistake - the first of many group mistakes. My first individual big mistake was to actually move to Eureka, in the middle of boony-land. These people were wonderful folks, but they were still living in the sixties - at least in my opinion. It was all organic food, smoking weed, and sort of a restructured flower-power mentality. It was a cultural enclave, and everyone in the group was far too dug-in and comfortable. Alex went on numerous fishing trips, Bill had a girlfriend and was cutting wood preparing for winter. I should have said, "Yeah, I'll join the group on one condition: we get the hell out of here."

Instead, we wound up spending huge amounts of time putting together a hodge-podge set of cover tunes and playing in the local bars. We didn't sound as good as the local bands, because we had just learned the material. I found out quickly that the weather in Northern California wasn't conducive to developing my voice. I was sick all the time and felt like I couldn't shake it. I would force myself to get up in the morning and run everyday. I'd run a mile or two, and come back and have to lay down for a while. Many people told me that I had The Eureka Grunge or some such name - which was not at all encouraging.

It didn't help that where we lived, we seldom saw the sun. I was depressed a lot because of this (I found out years later that lack of sunlight can actually cause depression) and I missed all the theatre friends I had made. I worked every day on writing lyrics, but with me, the song usually came first, and I had devote much of my time to memorizing lyrics of the copy songs we were doing.

Because I shared an apartment with John Thomas, I had little time to think about creating music. I require a lot of silence in order to create music. Unfortunately, John had an acoustic piano in the living room against the wall that was common to my bedroom. I heard Hanon scales and other piano practice exercises everyday we lived together. It drove me crazy and completely wiped the slate clean of any musical creativity. However, I knew it was important to John, so I didn't say anything. While he practiced I would go out and jog each morning.

Internal Conflicts

The predominant factor that I was unaware of at the time, was that ghost of Don lingering in the background. There was an underlying fear of getting into that kind of ugliness about music again that we'd experienced with Don and the fact that we were secretly looking at each other thinking, "Well, who's going to lead this thing?" - because we always had Don leading it. We were trying to be democratic but at the same time realizing that we weren't going to get a lot done. I don't think it was ever really a power struggle. It felt more like an identity struggle. The Magic Band had been spearheaded by Don's vision and the visionary had been excluded. Like a chicken with its head cut off, we were flip-flopping around with no real sense of direction. Did we continue to follow the old Magic Band vision, or create a new one?

Blue Lake Rehearsals

We were first rehearsing at a place called "Portuguese Hall" which we shared with another band. We paid them rent, they paid the proprietor. Unfortunately, we didn't realize that they had not asked permission to have a band in there during the day in their absence. A caretaker soon discovered us and both groups were quickly kicked out. I felt bad for the other guys, but they should have asked permission. I don't recall the name of the group, but they were the best local band, had played together for years, and were kind of a boogie-blues group that did mostly cover tunes.

We rented some space at a studio in Blue Lake during the day so that we could rehearse. I worried that Bill and John's tastes were leading the band into too much of a "jazz fusion" image for the band, which I thought was a big mistake business-wise, but when I brought this up at a rehearsal, I was told bluntly to "keep my mouth shut" by Bill - which was devastating to me. Alex gave a little snicker when Harkleroad said it, which didn't help either. I was both upset and puzzled as to why, in this early stage of reformation, there couldn't be more of an open dialogue about our direction.

John Thomas: I remember we were rehearsing up at Blue Lake. We would go there every day to take songs like Dancin' In The Streets *and do them without a female vocalist, without a horn section and still turn it into a vibrant and vital experience. It was one thing for me to be in R &E and learn from Tim and those guys. But, to go into to the Magic Band and see, and this was a band that had a record deal just waiting - waiting for it to be ready, and guys who had been making records for the last eight years - really intense. This was like the real deal. I just remember feeling the electricity and it being really educational. So this is how a band works. This is where the limits are. This is where the limits aren't. This is what they'll do. Cause if you would have said to me, "Hey how bout doing* Dancin' In The Streets," *I would have said, "Are you kidding, that's some girl in Motown with a horn section." But you actually said, "Hey, this is what we're going to do!" and I tried it, it was so exciting. So my limits and horizons were expanding everyday that we rehearsed.*

Surprisingly, one of the songs that we seemed to get the best reaction to - not only in the band, but from the audience, was a cover of Joni Mitchell's *Free Man In Paris* from the album *Court And Spark*. Mitchell was an artist I'd always wanted to meet and I still admire her work immensely.

We were struggling to find an identity but were already swallowed up by a former identity. We had the stamps all over us - "Beefheart's weirdos" and it was apparent that the majority of the people we played for really weren't that interested or intrigued by Don's vision - they wanted to hear *ours* - and we were struggling blindly to find it. The pressure was on and we had precious few resources:

John Thomas: Look, we only have such and such an amount of time, we gotta get tight, we were waiting to hear what we are. I'd never experienced that - it was really very educational for me.

Leadership

John French: I felt like Bill was kind of the unofficial leader, but that our votes were behind him. He had amazing musical ideas and was a phenomenal player.
John Thomas: Energy too. Even as much pot as he smoked, his energy level was (high) huge. I could remember trying to imagine: "What would this guy be like if he didn't smoke pot?"

Bill was the guy who seemed to be in charge. There were some things very good about that, as he knew how to make the music have a "sound" that worked. My problem was that I was still trying to re-develop a vocal sound and he seemed to be urging me to copy Don, which I didn't think was a good idea. He wanted the raw edge, but the music seemed to need a different sound vocally. The fact that our best reaction was to *Free Man In Paris* suggested to me that I sing in a more natural voice. Of course, half the time, I didn't seem to have a voice at all.

Club Dates

The Magic Band, as I mentioned was just performing in the local area. Anywhere else, it might have been a good idea, because it gave us a chance to get re-acquainted, kept us in shape physically and made us some money. Unfortunately, in Northern California we made almost no money, didn't hang out together at all, and because of the climate, I was constantly ill.

I tried bringing this up a few times and finally wound up outside a club in Crescent City shouting at Bill and John about giving me some help with the gear (PA and drums, which I was setting up alone). We would sleep on people's floors, couches, even propped up on chairs in the kitchen in freezing weather. It was horrible circumstances in which to perform.

One night I stayed at a lady's house with her and her boyfriend. It was an old farmhouse and my bed was a four-foot loveseat. At about six, after 3 hours of sleep, the lady got up and went outside. She began calling poultry towards her with this high shrill gobbling, honking sound and the poultry would answer by honking. "So, I'm staying with Mother Goose" I thought. I fantasized visions in which appeared vague images of shotguns, flying feathers, and shredded aprons …

This woman then proceeded to bring in a huge load of wood, and drop it, piece by piece, into a wood stove in the kitchen, which was right next to me - CLANK, CLANK, CLANK. By this time I had managed to realign my $4^1/_2$ - foot couch-formed body into a semblance of something that resembled a life-form and hobble into the kitchen.

As I quelled my impatience with good behavior, I have to say that I admired this woman. She cooked an entire breakfast the likes of which I have never eaten in my life, complete with eggs, ham, biscuits and gravy, and even a pie and lots (and lots) of coffee on that wood-burning stove. I told her I liked her kitchen and she said, oh, this isn't the kitchen, the kitchen's through there and pointed to a doorway in the corner. I went and looked, and there was the original kitchen of the house. It must have been 80 years old. It was filled with antiques and sported a hardwood counter and a hand pump at the sink. It hadn't been used in years, as the foundation had failed and the counter looked like a ski slope.

Van Vliet Pays A Visit

One of our gigs was a local high school dance in a gymnasium. We set up in the afternoon, and a friend of Mark's helped me with some stage monitors so that I could, for once, hear myself sing. There was a temporary stage set up - probably the same one the pep band played on for assemblies - in the middle of the retracted bleachers on one side of the room. Across the room they had the bleachers opened out about halfway, so people would have a place to sit. As we were playing our first set, a small crowd of people were clustered over in the left corner of the open bleacher. Looking closer, I saw Don and Jan Van Vliet sitting on the bleachers.

I didn't go over to them at the break, but many people came up to me and asked "Is Captain Beefheart going to sing?" - with expectant looks on their faces. It became obvious that soon people would be chanting "Beefheart" at the top of their lungs. So, I finally went over and said "Hello." I hadn't seen them since 1971 - three years earlier - in the underground garage after my enlightening meeting with Al Liefer. There wasn't much point in talking as the din of piped music resounding in the gym made it impossible to say much. I did ask him if he would mind singing a couple of songs and that I would find out if it was OK with the guys. He said "Sure," and as time approached to begin playing again, I asked the guys, starting with Bill and everyone agreed except Alex, who was missing. I guessed he was out back having a drink, a smoke, or both.

Eventually, he wandered back, but we started right off. Fifteen minutes or so into the set, I called "Don" - rather softly and everyone started applauding as Don stood up and walked to the stage. Alex looked over at me like an assassin at his mark. Alex had recently seen, firsthand, the things that Don had done to the band and was still upset with him. Theirs was a war with a much longer history.

Alex Snouffer: But either way, he wasn't singing with me on stage. Then Bill, when he'd come to our gigs, would let him come up on stage.
John French: I invited him up on stage one time. We were playing a school, and he showed up.
AS: Yeah, heh, that's the one.
JF: And he did a couple of blues numbers and left.
AS: I remember climbing on Bill, because Bill was kind of ram-rodding that band. I was furious as soon as I saw what was happening. I asked, "What are you letting him up here for, man?" I was damned near ready to walk off.

I had no idea Alex would be so angry, but then I hadn't actually experienced the break up of the band or had the inside information. It had all been pretty vague and no one had discussed the details with me. When I actually found out during the Snouffer interview how things had actually transpired, I was able to understand better his anger.

I figured that it was a public "goodwill gesture" to bring Don up onstage and send out a message that things were OK between us. These kids didn't know all the ins-and-outs of the situation, they just wanted "to hear Beefheart sing." I think it was their homecoming dance, so it was a big deal to them. We did *Rollin 'n' Tumblin'* as I recall, and *Down In The Bottom*. Simple blues, no harmonica, Don was a good showman, and the kids loved it. Why he wouldn't have explored the possibility of doing a blues album instead of going "pop" always puzzled me. The reaction to Don singing the blues was always the best reactions he received overall.

UNCONDITIONALLY SCARRED

I had read a bad review in Rolling Stone of *Unconditionally Guaranteed*. The critic had said something to the effect that Don should "quit making an ass out of himself in public." I thought the critic was a little tough on Don personally but also felt that he deserved some criticism and, I have to admit, it was a bit satisfying to read this. But then again, I have never heard the album. I heard one track, and I thought it was completely foreign to anything that should have ever been on a Beefheart album.

We had a meeting at the Arcata apartment one morning before riding to rehearsal together. Bill told us that Don had met with him the night before and asked him to come back as his musical director. Bill was having second thoughts about this, and it was obvious, although he said he turned down the offer. but it did seem in my estimation that used it as a bit of leverage; as in an implied "I could have done that, but I turned it down for you guys …"

One of Don's comments to Bill was about me. He said "John is too much of a Playboy to ever be taken seriously as a singer." I found this hilarious. Thank God, the rock group The Faces chose the overtly-moral Rod Stewart as their singer … and Led Zeppelin - why if Robert Plant hadn't been their singer, I'm certain he would have joined a monastery and taken an oath of celibacy. "Too much of a Playboy??" - and this from the guy who used to borrow my money to help pay for hookers? I was laughing so hard, I nearly dropped the contents of my pipe onto my favorite smoking jacket …

A few years earlier, Don seemed to think that me fronting and singing in my own group would be a good idea - and discharged me from The Magic Band on that premise.

A second point from this exchange is another slam of the hammer to drive the point home: Why did the guy who taught his band "teaspoon by teaspoon" need a musical director?

Anyway, one night The Magic Band was playing in a club called the Mad River Run. Who should come through the door, again, but the Captain. He was wearing one of those navy-blue long-sleeved wool shirts, no hat that I recall. He had one of his drawing books with him, naturally. He had that sort of "pop" image he had cultivated for the Mercury attempt at commercialism. It was more of a "Three Dog Night" look, and it actually fit him well. He looked to be in great health, the best I'd seen him in a long time. The climate definitely agreed with him.

At the end of the night, Alex's girlfriend Sandy, who was at the club, caused a scene with Don. A little intoxicated, she was yelling, "How could you do this to these people?" I was a little embarrassed for her, but she had lived through this event with Alex, and was probably very sincere in her passion. She was out of line, and Don was being fairly quiet, but when she grabbed his arm, he finally sternly shouted something like, "Cool it, woman!" jerked his arm free, and walked away.

We were playing the next night at the same club, as I recall, so there was no equipment to load etc. I walked over to tell the guys that I was going with Don for a while and didn't need a ride. Alex's girlfriend walked up and French-kissed me like a schoolgirl. I was a little stunned. "What brought this on?" I thought. Now, I look back and think: she was trying to reinforce the Playboy image! No one had noticed, they were putting their guitars in the trunk. I never mentioned this to Alex.

As we were walking to his car Don looked at me in amazement. "Wow, man, you've really loosened up," he observed. I explained to him that I had studied dance and music and that all the exercise had really stretched out my muscles. I had to admit that it was really good to see Don. Especially not being in the group, because he was always so cordial and charming to outsiders, and I was an outsider. We got in his car, a late-model Volvo sedan. "I thought you owned a Corvette," I said.

"Jan made me get rid of it." He replied, "You know those things are totally unsafe," he said, in a half-statement / half-question. Then the seatbelt buzzer went off and he amusingly reacted with: "God, and now I have to listen to that noise thanks to Ralph-fucking-Nader." I couldn't help but laugh.

We wound up at his house, talking all night, not an unusual practice when hanging out with the Captain. He played *Bluejeans And Moonbeams*, which had just been recorded. The only thing I really liked was *Same Old Blues*. He said, "The only thing good about this album is the cover, and the line 'the camel wore a nightie' from *The Party Of Special Things To Do*. The line didn't do much for me. However, I did like the painting done by Don's cousin, Victor Hayden. "I got them to do this cover - Victor's art - really heavy, man!" he grunted. I hadn't heard him say that for a long time, and grinned inwardly.

"Look at this!" he said. He pointed to a song title, *Captain's Holiday*, "I didn't even play on this, man!" He said, in his best 'astounded' voice. "They just did it. I missed the session."

I might mention here that I was totally struck by the contrast of the standard of living between Don and his former band members. He and Jan lived in what appeared to be a three or four bedroom, two-bath home with an attached two-car garage. The home was fairly new, well insulated, and very comfortable. It's front windows opened to the ocean. In contrast to Bill's 12x12 foot shed with the homemade loft and wood stove, and Mark's mobile home, there was obviously a big contrast in prosperity levels.

We wound up staying up all night, joking, listening to old blues albums and laughing about everything. He even danced this old Pachuco scarf dance, and looked pretty nimble doing it. We drove into Arcata, a small college town to the south of Trinidad. As the sun came out, we spied a friend of Mark's who I only know as "Sam." He was sitting in his car, drinking Southern Comfort.

We all had a drink together and walked around the town, which was just waking up. "My God!" Don exclaimed, pointing to a well-endowed black woman strutting across the street, "She looks like a pair of tweezers I had once in a nightmare!"

Don drove me just down the road to my apartment, and I was relating my side of the story about how in 1967 in England, I had destroyed a Premier drum kit on stage during a performance at one of the Universities. He had always thought I was angry with him, and that's why I did it. He had come up to me onstage and blown the Simran Horn in my ear. Now this little horn was a loud as a bagpipe drone and twice as piercing. I had my eyes closed and when he did this, it not only hurt my ear like hell but scared me.

As a result, I had wound up hitting the cheap and sadly thrashed Zen cymbal a bit too hard breaking it completely around the bell so that it fell over the cymbal stand. When I went to strike it again, it wasn't there and I lost my balance on the drum throne and fell backwards, hooking the drums with my feet and knocking them forward. When I stood, there was not one drum left standing. I took a mike stand and pulverized the set in rhythm to the music and had the road manager hold a microphone to catch the sound.

We were laughing hysterically at this story as we walked up the stairs to my apartment. He stopped me halfway up the stairs, on the landing. (If you recall the way I left Trout House, you can understand, I was a little shy of the combination of Don and landings by this time.) "Listen, I just talked to Frank, he's going to help me, man, and you should be in on this." So, now I knew why he had showed up. It wasn't friendship; it was business. He needed a musical director.

John Thomas: *That's the first time I ever met him personally. I don't know why he came by the apartment that time.*
John French: *He came with me.*
JT: *Yeah, he was coming to sort of woo you in some way. I don't know why.*
JF: *He and I had stayed up all night one night talking. I came back with him and we were laughing about some incident that happened.*
JF: *We came in and you were trying out this new sleeping bag of yours. Her name was Joy and she had (just) given you some ... joy.*

Don and I actually sat on the couch. My cat, Planet, started attacking my ankles with his needle-sharp canines. JT and Joy were encased on the floor in a giant sleeping bag. We talked for a while and suddenly Joy, wanting to use the lady's room climbed out of the bed, nude, and walked into the other room. No one said anything, but what man cannot marvel at the wonders of nature?

John Thomas: *She was actually a great comfort and she was the first person to introduce me to the Grateful Dead. Who I didn't like and didn't "get." But one time, we had taken acid together and we were listening to the Grateful Dead and suddenly, I "got it."*
John French: *Thank God, I never had that experience.*

Joy had a friend named Jean, who became my special friend when I was living in Arcata. But Jean wasn't there that particular morning, in fact, I had only met her at the high school dance we had played. We later started seeing each other and she eventually began to stay at the apartment more and more.

JT remembers Joy being a nurse, but if I remember correctly, she was actually a midwife. Perhaps she was a nurse first and a midwife later. She once told me that they used to make placenta soup after a birth. Shortly after this, Joy came over to make us dinner one night. I was a little apprehensive about what she was making, but it turned out to be vegetarian, thank God.

Demo Tape

The Magic Band made a demo tape of what we thought was our strongest material after a few months of rehearsal. It included *Reign of Pain*, which I had co-written a few years before with Dan Moore, my friend from the desert. It also included *One Day Once* and a slow blues ballad, *Let That Child Live*, a sort of ecological anti-abortion song (I know, a strange combination). We recorded it in Bill's shed with a borrowed Teac 4-track machine, which was actually quite a nice piece of technology at the time.

Return O' The Cap

During this period, Van Vliet would often show up at the apartment John and I shared and just hang out. I could feel a bit of that closet control-freak, prying at the lock. He complained about my cat, like I was supposed to remove it. I left the cat in the room, to express my lack of interest in his manipulative tactics. At one point, John Thomas asked him about the controversial era of the *Trout Mask* band, and Don brushed it off with a story that had something to do with not really understanding why "those other guys" had to fight so much. I was instantly seething with anger. He knew exactly what was going on in that house, and he had caused most of it and set the rest in motion. Now, he was taking no responsibility for his actions.

I said, "I need to talk to you," and we walked outside. As soon as I was far enough away from earshot of anyone else, I stopped and turned, facing him directly. "Look," I said, "if you ever lie to anyone in my presence again about what went on in the Trout House, I solemnly promise I will do my best to kick your ass." I meant this with all my heart and I said it with total conviction. I did it privately because I felt that it was really between he and I and I wasn't doing it to be "macho," but to let him know I wasn't going to go along with any lies concerning that subject.

I personally deplore confrontational situations like this, but I certainly wasn't going to allow him to speak of the *Trout Mask* experience in front of me in such a manner and get away with it. I had lived through that *Trout Mask* era with Don as a young naïve kid, but now I was a man, and I had to confront him on the damage he did. "Hold on, man!" He said, raising his arms, "Ok, calm down." I didn't want to calm down and I told him so. I told him that he treated us like shit and though I didn't care whether he admitted it publicly or not, he wasn't going to lie about it to my friends in my presence - especially a young kid like John.

We were distracted by a snake, which slithered by, stopped and look at us curiously, and then slithered away. "I can't imagine what that snake's ancestor did to wind up cursed with no legs like that," Don said, I supposed to appeal to my religious beliefs.

Didn't Like Singing

The band decided at this point to pack up the demo tape, take the long pilgrimage to that Mecca of Music, Los Angeles and see what the "verdict" would be. Bill wanted to talk to some people at Warners - connections he had made during the *Clear Spot* days. Whoever he talked to said that the singing was weak. Actually, I couldn't have agreed more. I had only started singing four months previous to this - after an eight-year hiatus. The songs were mostly in the wrong keys, and I was sick most of the time.

On top of this, I could feel that Bill was really looking for another "Don" in a sense. He actually suggested one day that I sing with a small object in my mouth to mess up my enunciation and make me sound like an old blues guy. I couldn't really blame him for missing Don's voice. I felt totally inadequate to even begin to fill his shoes. I also felt like the best way to be the singer in this group was not to attempt a sound-alike vocal style, but to sing in my natural voice and develop the style around that concept.

Besides, I always considered myself to be too much of a playboy.

Band Breaks Up

Bill Harkleroad disbanded the group after this verdict on my singing. I was relieved. I wanted to get out of Eureka in the worst way and he seemed more or less settled. Mark was the most upset. This band had been his whole life, and he was a team player. Alex decided to go on the road, playing clubs with an old friend, Denny King. John Thomas, well he was young enough not to be that concerned.

John Thomas: I didn't really understand and wasn't even really a party to it. I was sort of "me too", whatever happens. I don't think I was included because I didn't have the sense to understand the forces that were at play.

Drive Home

In November of 1974, we set off for home. I had brought little with me, save my drums and a couple of old tape recorders and worn-out clothes. John had a small trailer that fastened on his car, so we loaded everything we owned in the trailer and with almost no money at all, started driving. It's a long drive - 14 hours - and I wasn't looking forward to making the drive again so soon after having gone down in Alex's Chevy II. However, JT and I became absorbed in a conversation that was so deep that we arrived in San Francisco - the approximate halfway point - after what seemed like an hour. We were both stunned. It was as though we had gone through a time warp.

Later we were forced by an empty tank to stop for fuel and were completely penniless. It was less than a hundred miles at this point. I had an idea; we actually unpacked the car and pulled the back seat out. Finding enough spare change under the seats to get a few more gallons of gas we drove on. I still laugh about our good fortune, or dumb luck, to make it home.

We arrived in Lancaster (here I go again) on November 21, 1974. The reason I recall that date is because it was my mother's birthday and she came out to greet us when we pulled up and said, "I can't believe it, you showed up on my birthday." I had left in late spring, so the whole adventure had taken five or six months at the very most.

John French: We came back down here to Southern California. I don't know what you were doing during that period of time.
John Thomas: I started living in a house with Mark Brandt and Joe Davies (drummer and guitarist friend) and we started playing with the LaGarde twins - a pair of twin brothers from Australia who played fairs and Elks lodges. But they played enough that they could actually hire us for $50 a show to go on the road with them and drive their motor home.

Don Contacts Me

Don called me soon after I arrived in town. I agreed to help him move back to the Desert. He and Jan had to move in with his mother (I think this is a musician thing) and had a lot of stuff to move. Sue, at this point, owned a mobile home on the east side of town. I told him I needed some time to get well (I was really run-down at this point) and that I would let him know.

Karen Leaves Tom

Karen, my dance instructor friend had left her husband. I had seen it coming for a long time. They were drifting apart for a long time, basically because she wanted nothing to do with pot, and he still liked smoking with guys. She also recently had become a Christian. Everyone expected that Karen and I would get together - even her parents, but that was not to be.

Back In Lancaster

Needless to say, I had lost all my aspirations about theatre, and received a relatively cold reception when I visited the theatre department a few days later. Sam was obviously not too thrilled with the fact that I had deserted him after he had pulled a lot of strings to get me into Summer Stock. Most of the friends I had in the class had either gone off to a four-year school or were working at some other career.

After a brief reunion and birthday celebration, I had some serious decisions to make. Don wanted to move just after Christmas. I had a month to sort things out. How many times would I have to start over?

Don had to leave Trinidad. I was originally supposed to ride up to Northern California with Joy - John's girlfriend from Arcata who was visiting friends in San Diego. However, I wanted to spend Christmas with my family, so I opted instead for a 24 hour-bus ride. Looking back, perhaps I should have taken the Joy ride.

Don And Jan's Move

There is nothing like a 24-hour Greyhound bus ride to enlighten you to a whole different value system. All the nightmares of a bus trip occurred. The shrieking kid running down the isle, the vomiting drunk, and the guy who had seen Bigfoot were all riding that bus, which stopped about every 20 minutes.

Don and Jan both arrived to pick me up at the bus station. Jan had really blossomed and was a beautiful woman. She was always a private person, so I am not going to say much about her. However, there was one moment that I found amusing. I don't think she'll mind me relating this.

We hardly said two words to each other the whole time I was there, but at some point, when Don was off getting the car, she looked at me and said - in an attempt to make conversation and out of the clear blue - "Did you know that the spines on the cactus help keep them cool?" I think one of the reasons I kept trying to give Don another chance is because this exquisite, intelligent and charming woman, who was such a lady, believed in Don and supported him so completely.

It also gave pause to reflect that Don could be so charming and so cordial to people who weren't working with him. His lyrics cried out with phrases regarding social disorder and impending ecological disaster. I saw so much good in him, and yet he always seemed to treat his band and co-workers in the cause so unjustly - while criticizing the same behavior in others. It was confusing to say the least.

I slept on the floor in the living room of the Van Vliet residence. My partition was a stacked wall of boxes, which afforded me enough privacy to get dressed. Each day for dinner, we had grilled cheese sandwiches and Campbell's Soup prepared by Jan. It was the only time I had ever shared a meal with them. We rented a U-Haul truck and Don said, "Jan and I want to give you something for your help, we'd like to give you the Hudson." - this was the car that Don had purchased in 1970 when we all had gotten cars.

"Great!" I said, "Thank you, I need a car." So Jan came out of the back of the house with the paperwork and we walked out front to look at the car. Unfortunately, being this close to the ocean had really taken its toll on the paint. The car had a large plastic cover over it and we took it off to reveal spotty rust all over the body. I opened the door and sat in the driver's seat, and Jan stood by the door explaining how to register the car. Don kept humorously interrupting her and making jokes. "Stop it!" She said playfully, "You're like a giant gnat or something!" They seemed to really have a good time together, and there was a pleasant feeling about the whole experience.

Jeff (Pre-Moris) Tepper

That evening, we walked to the neighbor's house. Again, I was able to appreciate a spectacular view of the ocean. It was up on a cliff overlooking the Pacific and you could hear the waves all day and night. "There's someone I want you to meet. He's this college kid who plays my music, man!" We knocked on his door and a really pretty blond girl answered. "Hi Tina, this is John - is Jeff here?" Tina nodded and beckoned us inside. We entered this tiny cabin-like house and Jeff and I shook hands as we were introduced. He was obviously a Beefheart fan. "Will you play some stuff for John?" Don asked. Jeff walked to the stereo, put on his guitar and sat in a chair, as I recall. We stood behind and watched as he played through some of the *Trout Mask* stuff along with the album.

Moris Tepper: "I had this four-track and - I think just for the hell of it - started figuring out the guitar parts to Trout Mask Replica. *One day he came over and I played him* Dali's Car, *both guitar tracks, and his jaw dropped. A couple of days later I played him* Fallin' Ditch *and* When Big Joan Sets Up *and pretty soon I had 15-16 of the tunes fully down, both guitar parts. He couldn't believe it. He said, 'Man, I'm going back to LA, and you'll be my guitar player and we're gonna go back into the business.' It was really romantic and fun. It was very cool."* [61]

My impression was that although he was an amateur, he had a real intuitive gift of understanding odd time signatures and dissonance. He played the parts with a flat pick and though he was "roughly correct" most of the parts were in need of tweaking. He had no finger technique, but it was still pretty impressive that he could follow along with the music.

John French to John Thomas: I went back up on a bus, packed all his stuff in a van - he had tons of stuff - boxes and boxes, and all his paintings (and) moved Don here. Jeff Tepper was his neighbor. So, that's where I met Jeff, who was listening to Trout Mask *and learning it by ear. It was pretty crude, but he was doing a pretty good job for trying to listen through all that music. It was pretty amazing.*

As we were walking back, Don said, "What do you think?" I told him my view. Don was under the impression that Jeff was playing things correctly, and I explained that he needed a lot of work. In essence, I told him that Bill and Jeff (Cotton) were both better guitar players at sixteen than this guy was at 20 - or how ever old he was, and that playing that stuff correctly meant he was going to first have to "unlearn" what he already knew and "re-learn" it correctly. Also, I mentioned that I didn't think he tuned his guitar very well.

What I didn't tell Don was that it was obvious that Jeff was a "fan" of Don's and totally spellbound by his presence - exactly what Don did not need at this point in time was another young, naïve, impressionable member in his group to feed his ego. He needed a healthy dose of reality and an appreciation and respect for his players so that he wouldn't migrate back to his cultish and career-destructive comfort zone.

Apesma / Totem Pole

I suppose my favorite moment during my short tenure as a Van Viet houseguest was later that evening. Don and Jan invited me into their bedroom - actually because there was no place else to sit. We sat informally talking and laughing - they half-lying on the bed propped up with pillows and me sitting on an adjacent chair. Don had Jan pull out a couple of poems that she eloquently read to me (notice I can't say enough nice things about Jan - no one can.) Anyway, the poems were *Apes-Ma* and *The Thousandth And Tenth Day Of The Human Totem Pole*. I have to admit that those are two of my favorite things Don has ever created. They're both brilliant in my mind and have both pathos and humor which juggle your emotions between both extremes.

[61] Captain Beefheart, Mike Barnes, Quartet Books Ltd., 2000, pp 217

Loading And Loading

Since Jan was impeccable about organizing, all the belongings of the Van Vliet's had been neatly boxed and labeled. There were paintings in the garage. Victor Hayden showed up, and I was surprised to see him. Many of the paintings were his. He looked a little more "hippy-like" and had been living in his car as I recall. He had several paintings in storage that were to be moved with Jan and Don's stuff. In fact, they were the same large canvases that he had done in 1968, when he was living in Chatsworth, CA. He offered to pay me to help store the paintings, but I refused money and said I'd take care of it. A big fault of mine seemed to be that I never felt my services were worth anything.

Jeff Tepper came down that evening, and as I was loading Don's and Vic's paintings into the truck, the three of them stood ogling the art while I struggled to load it on the truck.

At this point, I realized even more so that Tepper, at this point was what my close friends and I like to jokingly describe as a "drooling fan" (as opposed to a "non-drooling fan.") I kept hearing, "Jesus, man, that's heavy!" and "Oh, man, that's so hip!" They actually wanted me to stop and hold each piece while they viewed it. I finally became angry and told them to "Stop it! and grab something - lend a hand." This, of course, made me the "bad guy" in the eyes of everyone. I could tell already that Tepper had me labeled as a guy who was rough around the edges and didn't appreciate art, but I was on a mission and had a deadline. The evening took on a dull glaze, but the truck was barely loaded in time for the takeoff time.

The circumstances were such that it was a necessary "adult decision." There was limited room and I was pre-occupied with concern that not everything of Don and Jan's would fit in this huge truck - which was the biggest we could rent. I still had to finish loading the 18-foot truck (with an extra cab over storage area), hook the Hudson up to a tow bar, and rig the lights. It was already dark and we were supposed to be on the road the next morning. Don hardly helped at all. Anytime there was work to be done, Don was doing something else - visiting with Tepper and/or Victor, in the house with Jan. I finally forced him to hold a flashlight for me as I hooked up the brake lights between the truck and the Hudson.

Victor was less than useless. He was my age and kept whining about how he had some "back problem." I wanted to give him an adjustment in the back end with my boots. Things hadn't really changed in that department - they were the "elite" and I was the "help."

Departure / Farewell

Don and Jan walked out of the house the next morning with strong emotional feelings about what they were about to do. They both stood out in front, holding hands first looking at the ocean and then at the house. This had been their wonderful home. It was obvious they loved it here. They were now about to lose it. Someone asked, "Did Don ever cry?" I think that this day, he did. In spite of everything, I couldn't help feeling a little sad for him this day.

I had given them some space to say "goodbye" and after ten minutes or so, I walked up and said, "I'm sorry you have to leave here, Don." He choked out the words, "Thank you, John," and patted me on the shoulder. This was another unusual behavior. I can't remember Don ever patting me on the back or shoulder or showing any affection to me at all. "Maybe losing the Magic Band was the best thing that ever happened to him," I thought.

Catskinners Or Angels?

We started the long drive back down but only made it about a block. The Hudson (which was being towed behind the truck), kept violently turning left and right. There was no way to get on the freeway with this happening. I pulled over and we stood scratching our heads.

I prayed a lot in those days, so I just prayed, because I didn't know what to do. All of a sudden two guys walked out of the woods. Now, this wasn't really a woods, it was just a little thicket between us and the freeway embankment. There was nothing else there. They came around and looked at the car. One guy walked over to Jan and asked, "you got any pantyhose?" Now, Jan's a conservative person, and to be asked this by a total stranger completely baffled and embarrassed her at the same time. The expression of puzzlement that immediately came to her face just about sent me into hysterics.

She went and found some in a piece of luggage in the Volvo. The guy came to me and said, "Put these on" (just kidding - I saw "Deliverance" and all kinds of stuff was going through my mind) - actually he said "Wrap these around the steering wheel and then slam it in the door. It'll give the car stability but it has enough give to allow you to turn." The guys disappeared after a couple of minutes, back into the woods.

"Man," Don said, "I think those guys were angels or something! Did you see that? Two guys with the perfect solution to our problem walk out of nowhere? I mean, there's nothing through there but the freeway. That's too weird."

The Drive

I didn't want to tell Don and Jan, but I'd never driven a truck this big in my life, much less towed anything behind it, so I was a little apprehensive. I got in and started driving and the Hudson now followed obediently and smoothly behind. What a relief. We had to do a 180 degree turn to get on the ramp to the freeway, and suddenly, after a bit of skidding of the Hudson's front tires, we were on the road. 24 hours later, after picking up Grannie Annie in Santa Rosa and hitting some really severe fog banks, we arrived in the desert.

The Van Vliets rented a small storage facility and we managed to get everything of theirs in it. I remember Don coming up to me and saying, "Well, John, one thing you can never say is that I'm a materialist." I found this amusing simply because I had loaded box after box of Don's shoes. I'm not talking about shoeboxes, but boxes that could contain 10 pairs of shoes each. Don loved shoes, and he had certainly stocked up on them.

Don Keeps Calling Me

Don kept calling me over the next few days, but he had nothing happening and hadn't really decided on his next move. I told him that I wasn't going to do all the work for him and I would only be available if he actually got something going on his own. He called one day really upset saying that he was going to "go to Alaska and become a lumberjack." I shot back, "This, coming from the guy who couldn't even load his own furniture?"

I didn't see him for a while after that. He ran into his old pal Don Aldridge.

Don Aldridge: I saw him in '75 ... I was a drinker and I didn't realize that I had a problem drinking at that time but I did. Actually, my first wife and I were there for dinner, and we got drunk there at the Sand Sailor. We spent the whole evening together. He bought me a bottle of Cabernet. We finished that off and then went and got more. He had a couple of albums with him. One was Strictly Personal *and it had the* Twenty-Fifth Century Quaker *and I said, "Hey, that's me! I'm on there." I don't know what we talked about. I got very drunk that night. He called me the next to day to see how I was doing and if I was OK I was hung-over pretty good. I had already told Don, "I'm not going to work with you," because months had dragged on and nothing was happening. He kept trying to establish his co-dependency where I was going to do all the work, and I said, "No, that's not my job, you're the leader." He didn't initiate anything for a long time, and didn't know what to do. I didn't realize that he was contractually bound and really couldn't work at all.*

Royal Academy Of Dance And Music

During this period, I resumed dancing with Karen in the desert and supported myself meagerly by painting signs. Karen and a friend, Angela Termeer, decided to form a partnership and open a dance school that they humbly named The Royal Academy of Dance and Music. They were eventually threatened with a lawsuit by the true British Royal Academy if they didn't change their name. However, they ignored it, and I suppose that the real Royal Academy decided that they were no threat.

The girls start picking up a lot of work as the Royal Entertainers, so I did a few shows with them. We danced to records, mostly and mimed the lyrics occasionally. One thing about dancers is that they always have a lot of energy because they're always involved in aerobic activity. Between that and my stretching exercises, I had never felt better.

Blunders In Wonderland

They decided to do as their recital a dance interpretation of *Alice in Wonderland*, so I painted eight 11 x 22 foot backdrops in three weeks (or was it 8½ hours??). I hardly slept at all and sometimes worked for two and three days straight. I was also dancing in the show and had to rehearse. After the opening night, the girls gave me a trophy, and the whole audience stood up and gave me a standing ovation. However, I never got paid - Deja-vu. This was the end of my relationship with the school, which eventually closed down.

Mark Boston And Ian

Mark, meanwhile, had gotten in touch with Ian Anderson.

Mark Boston: See - I started Mallard. I wrote to Jethro - (Ian) Anderson, told him the Beefheart band split up and I was wanting to do something. He called me back in Eureka within a week up after I sent that letter. He told me to meet him in LA in a month. I had no money and no way to get down there. A friend of mine gave me a truck. I had to rebuild the engine in it - in the rain. I did it. I was determined. I went down and met up with Ian and basically Ian said, "Well, I'd like to do something with you but you gotta get Bill and Art Tripp."

Mallard - May 1975

Bill Shumow got in touch with me. This was probably early 1975. Bill, Mark, and Artie were going to do an album in England - funded by Ian Anderson. It seemed they weren't going to be able to use the name Magic Band, because of legal complications with Don. He apparently owned the rights to the name, and also apparently owned the rights to all our pseudonyms. Shumow asked me to come on board as singer and I said I would give it a try. I wasn't expecting much.

Since I was working at the dance studio with Karen, I arranged for us to rehearse in the back during the mornings. Mark, Bill and I had a rehearsal at the dance studio and I could see right away that there were things about this situation that made me uncomfortable. First of all, Bill was ram-rodding the effort, which was fine, as we needed a leader. However, I really felt that for the band to work (they hadn't adopted the name Mallard yet) we needed time to sort out an identity.

As it was, Bill had written *Road To Morocco* and we went through that, as well as *Reign Of Pain* and *One Day Once*. No one was talking about a direction, a band concept, a group sound, a group image. I think it would have been better to take six or eight months, hole up somewhere and work our asses off writing about 50 songs and come up with the best ten or twelve, and by that time, we would actually reach an understanding. I saw this as nothing more than a half-cocked attempt.

My regret is that I didn't know then how to express in words what I was feeling. I knew Artie was going to play on the album and I was just drumming for the rehearsals, to kind of get everyone together. So, what was going to happen? Suddenly, after rehearsing these tunes that had been thrown together and them getting used to my feel, Artie was going to step in and everything would go smoothly? I was very unsure. I should have stepped out and done the project. But I wasn't prepared, and my singing would have been only slightly better than before.

The biggest negative influence was I wasn't really happy about the idea of singing lyrics written by Bill's friends, Albee and Wagstaff. I have a real problem with singing words that don't appeal to me. So many people's philosophies clash when it comes to this. Given six to eight months, I think we could have come up with a killer album. As it was, the Mallard album was pretty good, but the story behind it makes me know that the whole thing was a rushed procedure.

I often regret this choice. Perhaps it was a bad call on my part, because I think I could have struck a balance between Mark and Bill that would have led to more compromise, and perhaps a more successful attempt. It was another in a series of bad decisions I made when I was younger. I can truthfully say that my main reason was lack of confidence in myself: I just didn't think I could do it.

If I recall correctly, Bill contacted Art Tripp in Pittsburgh. Art met them in England. I didn't recall hearing that they had gotten together with Art beforehand. Bill's book, *Lunar Notes*, confirms this. I do recall that Mark was pretty upset and disappointed with me when I told him my decision. We didn't really communicate much after this until 1977.

As I look at the band dynamics, it later seemed clear to me that Mallard was doomed from the beginning, due to negative programming from Don. Don had told all of us for years in various ways how we were nothing without him. Not only had he led the group into obscurity and financial disaster, he had also kept everyone in poverty conditions from 1967-1974. We were all programmed for defeat. It would have taken some time with us sitting down in a house andtalking things out, realizing that it wasn't us, that we weren't the "bad guys."

It would have taken some time to develop that kind of trust in each other. Then, we could probably have developed a sound and gone into the studio. Once everyone realized that we were all on the same side, it would have been different. Bill's reaction was to take over the project and push it in the direction of his own personal tastes, rather than what would be the best for the group. I don't think that he considered it any less than a necessity - and in a sense, with the short timeline, he was right.

The first album was more of a group effort, but it still lacked the kind of continuity that a band needed to rise above the norm. Mark had worked with Bill in control for so long that it seemed natural to him. I had been away long enough to realize that things needed to be talked out, in a healthy, honest manner. I didn't think that could have possibly happened.

Art Tripp writes: "I have a hunch if I had signed on after the first Mallard album, that the band might have been successful. Sam Galpin was a musician as well as a good singer, and he was manageable. Without me, I don't think Bill had enough juice to shoulder the whole musical operation. Not that I'm so great, it's just that Bill and I worked well together, and we had a more or less tacit understanding of each other. Who knows? It's a rotten business, and that's why I got out."

CHAPTER THIRTY FOUR:
THE SECOND-CHANCE KID

Promotional shot at the Winterland Auditorium in
Photographer Donald Setaro

Record Plant With Zappa

Don had gotten himself locked up into so many contracts that he was, in a sense "legally gridlocked. When he approached Frank Zappa, the only thing FZ could see to do was hire him as a band member. Before I quit hanging out with Don for a time, I went down with Don and Jan to the Record Plant in Hollywood, where FZ booked blocks of time in the middle of the night.

The night I was there, George Duke came in with a small synth, sat it up in the control room and plugged into the mixing board. He played from the control booth with Frank issuing orders about what he wanted played. "Duplicate my guitar line, one octave higher" he would say. Duke was so quick at learning that he was done within a few minutes. "Now, put a harmony to that." Again, Duke finished within minutes.

"Get your harmonica, Don," Frank said. Don got his harmonica and went out into the studio. Frank asked him to duplicate some riff on tape. Try as he might, Don could not. "Forget it," Frank said. Don came sullenly through the door. " I failed!" he said. I thought this was probably a good moment for Don. It reminded me of the many times he would castigate someone for hours simply because they couldn't quite grasp a part.

Don and I decided to have a beer from the vending machine. "Do you want a beer, Jan?" Don asked. "No, thanks," she replied. "Beer makes her fart," Zappa said. It was really crude, but funny all at the same time. I suppressed my laughter so as not to embarrass Jan.

Early *1975 Bongo Fury* Rehearsals

Denny Walley was guitarist on the *Bongo Fury* tour and so soon met Don.

John French: What was it like working on that Bongo Fury *tour with Don? All of a sudden, the first time you'd seen Don for years, right?*

Denny Walley: Yeah, I met him in two rehearsals. He really tried to be intimidating. He used to try to threaten me because I had this black leather vest with a button on it that had me and Jimmy Carl Black hugging and making these weird faces. He'd say, "Hey man, you know Frank don't like seeing that, he don't like that guy!" I said, "That's too fuckin' bad, because I'm wearing it." So, I squared off with Don right away, because I'm basically a hardass if you try to push me. I'm really a nice guy, but I don't like to be intimidated. I don't do well with that kind of treatment.

JF: So, the first thing he did is try to intimidate you

DW: Yeah, but I shut him down immediately because I kept wearing the thing and he saw that wouldn't work and then he would try something else. He was a general nuisance for a while until I got to like him. Then I just tolerated it because he was going to keep doing that but he was genuine, he was just testing to see how big the cell is, you know?

Early 1975 Don And Frank - *Bongo Fury*

Jimmy Carl Black: Him and Zappa never did get along. Never. In fact, when they came to El Paso, Frank wasn't even talking to him any more ... would not even acknowledge that he was around. Beefheart was drawing pictures of Frank as the devil with horns and a tail ... Frank really didn't like it." [62]

I'm going to speculate on what I think happened during the *Bongo Fury* tour, based on my experience and observation of Van Vliet. Don, in his characteristic ungratefulness, showed his appreciation for Frank by drawing belittling pictures of him onstage - sometimes showing them to him while he was playing. As I hear about this stuff, all I can do is laugh and think about how many

[62] Captain Beefheart, Mike Barnes, Quartet Books Ltd., 2000, pp 224

times I tried to help Don and it backfired on me. It's a huge responsibility to take a band on the road, be the musical director, and try to keep the music together on stage. I imagine it must have been difficult for Don to move from his seaside home and to take a job as Frank's singer. It must have been difficult for him to move into his mother's mobile home with his wife and live with his grandmother and Sue, his mother. But my thought was that Frank was trying to help him, and that Don was playing the impish prankster. But, after all, isn't that what fan's love about Don? I found it childish.

How does Don treat people who try to help him? Well, with me, look at the example as I tried to load his paintings on a truck and him asking me to hold each of them for viewing - even though we were on a time limit and had to leave in the morning. He made me feel guilty for finally refusing to present an art exhibit when I said "Show's over." How did he treat Frank? By making fun of him in front of his band and being irresponsible with his gear, and generally making it more difficult for Frank to perform.

People in a group like Frank's probably have a certain amount of resentment for their boss because that's human nature. As a child, you hate your parent's authority, you hate your teacher's authority, and then you grow up and hate your boss's authority. Zappa's band was playing his music, rehearsing on his schedule, and probably getting paid as sidemen - but it's his show. In this situation the easiest thing in the world is to subtly stir up that natural resentment the sidemen are bound to have, chip away at his image and win over the trod-upon peasants by belittling Frank in front of his band, bit by bit, encouraging just a slight taste of mutiny.

My gut feeling and the impression I received from the guys in the Zappa band, from the Jimmy Carl Black interview, and from Don himself, was that Van Vliet basically bit the hand that fed him - just as he had done many times before. It was the kind of typical behavior I had seen in Don and it was still thriving. From Denny's point of view (one of the Zappa band), he loved it, because of the unpredictable behavior, but he also saw the difficulties.

Denny Walley: Oh, no problem, I loved it, it was different every night. He'd be drawing pictures. I just loved it. He was always flying by the seat of his pants. Everybody else had to worry about it, but I loved it. I had no problem whatsoever. I thought it was great. You never knew what was going to happen. With Frank you knew: this is going to happen now, or this is going to happen that way. With Don, Frank had no control; you never knew where the hell he was going to go, which I looked at as a breath of fresh air.

John French: I'm sure Frank didn't look at it that way.

DW: No, he didn't. He hated it.

JF: He said it was pretty tough. In the BBC Interview.

DW: Well, you know there were a lot of other problems other than on the bandstand. In the hotel, trying to get to the airport on time, everybody trying to meet in one place. You know, he kind of had his own schedule and needed constant attention and adult supervision. The knarler was elected the man.

JF: Who's "The Knarler?"

DW: Dick Barber. They called him "The Knarler." That's what the old Mothers used to call him.

JF: So, Dick Barber was on the Bongo Fury tour?

DW: Oh yeah, he was Don's babysitter.

JF: Don used to call him "Plaidfinger" (a play on "Goldfinger" and the fact Dick always wore plaid).

I was about to apply for the job of babysitter once again myself...

Greg Davidson

Greg writes: "I met Don going backstage after a concert in Chicago where he was with Frank on the Bongo Fury tour. I asked him if he was going to have another band after the tour. He replied yes and I told him I could play the guitar parts and wanted to play in his band. I auditioned for him at a hotel (I have part of that on tape) and after a short while he told me I was in the band! I didn't believe him. Three weeks later Don called me up and said we had a gig in England in 3 weeks and to be in L.A. on Monday to rehearse."

From what I understand, Gary Lucas also met up with Don on the tour and also auditioned for him in a hotel room. I recall him telling me this story during our Magic Band reunion experience. I also read online that Ken Duvall auditioned for him in Boston. Don chose Greg Davidson who later Don dubbed as Greg "Ella Guru" Davidson - probably because of Greg's love of the song.

Greg discovered Beefheart through a Warner/Reprise sampler album his brother had bought. It contained the song *Ella Guru*, which he loved. This prompted him to buy the double album *Trout Mask Replica*. He describes himself, amusingly, as being "horrified" when he heard the album as he only liked a few songs and had just spent five bucks.

Greg Davidson writes: "Being cheap I was determined to listen to it every day until I felt I got my money's worth. As time went on I started liking more and more of the music. It was scrubbing my brain of the predictable music that predominated the radio waves. I then looked forward to listening and playing along with a lot of the tracks.
Then I discovered Strictly Personal *and I went to a new place. Now I could get my Blues (although mutated) fix along with the odd rock that I liked. To this day, your drum solo after* Trust Us *still scares me! I feel ghostly entities trying to force there way into our realm with that pounding on the tom toms. Though some, like Don, claim to hate the phasing effects that were put in, to me that adds to the eeriness of the album. It was like a journey into a Vincent Price basement."*

Karen's Proposal - June 1975

My old dance buddy had me out to her house for dinner. She wanted to become a night-club singer/entertainer in the worst way. Her proposal was that we start a band. Now, I had already worked on other projects with Karen, and although she worked hard for the most part, I always seemed to work harder and got nothing out of it. So, I told her, "no" I wasn't interested in being a night-club drummer. She said, "What are you going to do? Just sit in Lancaster and rot?" I told her "If God wants me back on the concert stage, he could put me there in a month." She scoffed shook her head.

Herb Cohen Calls - June 1975

I was out trimming my parent's lawn (they were retired, so I did this for them as often as possible) when my father came out and said, "Someone named Herb Cohen is on the phone." I walked in and Herbie, Zappa manager, was indeed on the phone and offered me some money to do a couple weeks rehearsal and two performances with Beefheart in July. I said, "Yes," and hung up." I liked Herbie. He was a crook - according to a lot of people - but I always got a straight answer from him and he always did what he said he would do financially.

That night, sleeping in my parent's garage-room, I awoke to see Don standing in front of me, drawing book in hand, like some fedora-laden vampire. "You should do it, man." He said. I replied, "I will, but only if you never wake me up like this again." Don had a nasty habit of calling on people at all hours of the day and night and waking them from an otherwise pleasant sleep. Don left, and I went back to sleep.

I showed up at Discreet Records on the prescribed date to start rehearsal with the Beefheart band. There was a big warehouse like room in back of the offices. That was Zappa's rehearsal studio. Attached to the back of the main office was a small rehearsal room completely covered with black acoustic foam rubber. Denny later nicknamed this "The Rubber Room." The band, as I saw it that day, consisted of Jimmy Carl Black on other drums (presumably in case Drumbo deserted), Greg Davidson, Elliot Ingber on guitar (remember the Winged "E"?) and a bass player who I believe was Tom Leavey - Denny's brother-in-law.

Greg Davidson writes: Jimmy was very friendly. Whatever you taught him to play he seemed to do it without any major problems, though you may have toned it down the drum parts for him, I don't know. But he was fun to hang out with for sure. One night he and I went to visit some girl he knew who managed an apartment building owned by Chuck Berry. Another girl was there too, a friend of Jimmy's friend. We were all talking and Jimmy says, "I've got to go do a radio interview, I'll be back". We turn on the radio, Jimmy is talking and they play a few songs of his band and then he comes back as if nothing had happened. We stayed the night. Thanks Jimmy!

I Become Musical Director

Elliot, in my opinion, was going to be a challenge. I loved the "Winged Eel," and so did everyone else, but he was always in the group more as a soloist rather than a person relied upon to play the intricate parts. Even in his own estimation, he often said, "I had a hard time copping the licks," and I had no reason to think that anything had changed. Robert Williams gave his impression of Ingber in his interview.

Robert Williams: Now Elliot, he played with us, I think he came over and jammed with us once. I met him. He jammed with me and Feldman, but, he seemed so uncontrolled. I thought it hard to imagine that he could play a song.
John French: He had a really hard time, as he put it, "copping the licks." Playing anything that was arranged - especially an odd time-signature - was really tough for him. But, he would work really hard at it. He'd have me stay after rehearsal and say, "What is this?" I'd go over stuff with him.
RW: Oh, to try to help him understand it.
JF: Yeah, so I'd play the drum parts and I got to the point where I could play a drum part in one time signature and sing his part. I mean, it was like my brain started splitting. The whole time we were touring, I was constantly singing stuff to him. I was screaming at him on stage. I said, "Don, I hope the audience doesn't think I'm pissed off at Elliot because I'm always screaming. I'm singing to him, that's all I'm doing." I had to sing at really high volumes so it looked like I was screaming. He said, "That's cool that they think you're screaming at him. That's fine." It goes along with what you were saying about Don screaming at the band. "I thought it was an act." No, he just had too much sugar, that's all.

Greg Davidson writes: Elliot. Yeah, I stayed at his place for a few days - quite a character. He used to listen to his guitar on the records with headphones trying to duplicate what he had recorded. He sometimes asked me for help! He slept in a sleeping bag on the floor. I could just see his head poking out at one end with his beard lying out too. That was a lot of hair coming out the top of that bag! (Laughs) He is a very serious guy.

Don showed up and I greeted him outside in the alley next to the parking lot. Predictably, he was completely unprepared and no one had charts or even records from which to work. It was exactly what I would expect from him. I knew why I was there and so I went to work. Don had given me a set list of material he wanted to do, and after discussing the practicality of the set list and making a few substitutions due to the time constraints, I made up a tape from that.

Greg Davidson writes: I guess you could say Don was "in charge" but you handled all the music arrangements. You had a lot of it written out. I also already knew some of it. If someone wasn't playing their guitar part correctly you picked up a guitar and played it. We usually divided the band in two sections. So Jimmy and Elliot would play their parts and then you and I would play ours. They sounded like two different songs. And then we would play together and a 3rd song emerged. I guess you say Don was in charge of lighting. One day he stopped practice because he couldn't stand the color of the flood light in the room and had to have it replaced! We also did some great jams after rehearsal, some of which I recorded.

I had been writing songs on guitar for years at this point and actually had developed enough proficiency to play decently, as long as I didn't have to use picks. I hated picks, and still do. We got together that day, and learned *Abba Zaba* from the tape. I gave Jimmy Carl percussion parts, and I played the tom parts. I liked Jimmy right off.

Greg was kind of irritating at first. He was so energetic and an obvious fan, and his energy just kept distracting me and causing digressions, generally wasting time. He was like a big puppy in the room nipping at my ankles. I was figuring out the guitar parts from the tape. I had watched the original guys play the tune enough that I felt I could aid them in learning Greg caught on quickly, which was reassuring, and Elliot had played what we were working on (*Abba Zaba*) before. Sure enough, it came together - that is, except the bass parts.

I told Don we had to get a different bassist. He beat around the bush all of the next day and wouldn't dismiss the guy. He just couldn't fire him.

Greg Davidson writes: If you remember we had a bass player during our first rehearsals. Zappa came by and said "How's it going?" Don looked reluctant to say "Ok." so Zappa said, "What's the matter?" Don said we really didn't like the bass player's performance. So Zappa said "Why don't you fire him?" and Don hemmed and hawed. Zappa said, "Do you want me to fire him for you? Don said "Gee, Frank, would you?" So Frank walked in to the rehearsal room, summoned the bass player and said "This may sound funny, but you're fired." and walked out.

Frank could have been a little nicer, but perhaps this was his way of telling Don that if he was concerned at all for this guy's feelings, he would have just tactfully taken him aside and told him that he wasn't working out. Rather than that, he had some one else do his dirty work for him. Memories of Doug Moon came to mind as this happened.

The next step was who to get? Elliot Ingber suggested Buell Neidlinger, I had never heard of him, because I didn't know anything about the LA music scene. If I had known who he was, I would have probably been greatly intimidated by his presence. However, about an hour later, this unassuming hippy-ish looking guy wearing all white east-Indian looking clothes came in. We had been working on *My Human Gets Me Blues* and it was just at the point where everyone could play their parts.

I had requested Don bring the charts to the *Trout Mask* songs so that I wouldn't have to figure them out all over again from the record. These are the ones that I got in trouble for writing because, according to Don, I had a secret evil ambition to become a "composer" back during *TMR* days.

I handed Buell the bass chart, which really wasn't a chart, because it only had each different section written in musical notation. It didn't specify how many times anyone did anything. So, I took a few minutes explaining to him what to do. He could read, supposedly, so I thought, "Well, here's your chance." Little did I know!

I counted the song off and we played it down from beginning to end. Buell never faltered, even on the middle section where everyone plays in a different time signature. He read down a *Trout Mask Replica* song cold! It was then that I realized this guy was not some marijuana-soaked birdbrain, but an actual real live professional player. Buell actually had me believing that Rockette Morton had walked in the room for a minute.

Well, we voted Buell in spontaneously and unanimously, but things are never that simple in the world of music. Upon hearing that Buell was in the band, Herbie Cohen walked in looked at Neidlinger and said, "You - get the fuck out of here - NOW!" Buell, picked up his gear and was out in one minute. I went to Herb and asked him what the hell that was about. It turned out that Buell had at one time felt that Cohen owed him some dough (which he probably did), and Buell filed a report with the Musicians's Union and it caused some problem that resulted in the obvious ill will that still existed. Because of this, unfortunately, we still didn't have a bassist, and I had a bit of ill will towards Herbie.

Finally, Don walked in, "Don't worry, we have the bass covered." He explained that Bruce Fowler, trombonist on the *Bongo Fury* tour was going to play the bass parts through an octavider. "Air-Bass" - I didn't pick up on the double-entendre at first. Bruce could read, so that lightened my load. All I had to do now was work with Greg and Elliot.

Greg Davidson writes: Bruce was very cool. He's such a great player, friendly, low key and very intelligent. I think he was the one who got me backstage in Chicago. We visited his brother Tom, Zappa's bass player and Bruce had a nice girlfriend who I believe was a dancer. In England I hung out with Bruce one night at the Speakeasy where I met Ginger Baker. Bruce had this really funny way of dancing! And of course, he really did talk about fossils wherever we went.

Davidson Meets Hollywood

Greg Davidson writes: I loved it right away. One of the original Mousketeers was the receptionist at Zappa's rehearsal space, which was Herb's offices too. Ray Collins was there, he was really friendly. Of course meeting "Drumbo" for the first time was like "Wow, it is THE Drumbo." And, of course, I bothered you about all the details of how you got your drums to sound a certain way and why did you reverse the beat on this, that, etc. - all the fan type questions. Jimmy Carl Black and some others took me with them to McDonald's - radical, huh? But considering who I was with it was still cool. Herb was never really a friendly guy. One day Don wanted me to get a Fender guitar. I had brought my Gibson SG from Chicago and he said the sound was too muddy since Elliot was playing a Gibson too. Herb asked why I was going to buy a new guitar. I explained and he said "What the fuck's the difference of how it sounds? The audience can't tell the difference." Can you imagine?

Brown Derby Coffee Shop

The first day, I think we all took off to the Brown Derby Coffee Shop on Vine Street, just North of Hollywood Boulevard. I rode with Don and Gregory, whose energy I wasn't used to as yet. When we got out of the car, he kept poking at me while talking. I can't remember if he was teasing me, or just gesturing, but after about four of these I growled "STOP IT!" in the meanest voice I could conjure. Don looked at me and said, "Wow, I've never seen you react like that to anyone." I supposed I was just marking my personal space. I grew to like Gregory, but my first impressions were that he was high-strung and distracting, and I was already thinking that I had a serious challenge before me to get this group into shape.

Greg Davidson writes: It was at the Brown Derby that I saw Don take a few markers out of his plastic container of art materials that he always carried with him and quickly drew a woman that walked by our table. It was then I discovered how art could capture the essence or energy of a subject. He drew a quick lined sketch of her and put color down but not all contained within the lines. It wasn't a "realistic" drawing but Don captured the motion of her and her chaotic energy because of the way the color was catching up to the lines.

The St. Moritz Hotel
Next to the Discreet office was a sleazy Hollywood hotel called the St. Moritz. "Saint Moritz" was probably the patron Saint of junkies, because this hotel was full of Hollywood hoodlums who looked like they'd slit your throat for a dime, much less a nice Gibson or Fender guitar. Being the thoughtful character he is, Herbie arranged lodgings for Greg Davidson at the dive.

Don, playing on my sympathies, said I should stay with Gregory at this hellhole. "Why don't you?" I asked. "Jan would kill me" (his stock reply for anything he wanted to squirm out of) was his reply. So it was that I stayed with Greg Davidson, and worked with him on some of the *Trout Mask* stuff. We went through the repertoire and decided for the challenge, to try to learn *Dali's Car*. I wound up playing this with Greg and later with Denny Walley on tour.

Greg Davidson writes: Yeah, ok, the St. Moritz Hotel! You stayed there with me, it was $35/week for 2. It was there that I saw my first avocado. You sliced it open and exclaimed it was rotten. Ray Collins lived in that hotel down the hallway. I think he was painting sets for movies at the time. Not a great hotel but just fine for us, eh? We were never in it very long. We were always out rehearsing and going out at night. I can't even recall sleeping there. I remember being in the elevator with Don. It was an old elevator and it made this loud hum as we descended. Don started humming along with it and broke into 'Singing through you to meee'...

In order to avoid staying at the St. Moritz one night, I took Greg up to my parent's house. He slept in my garage room, and I slept on the couch. I remember that he really loved my parents and hugged them both "goodbye" with much thanks when he left. The guy was starting to grow on me. We drove the 1950 Hudson back to Hollywood, and just south of Palmdale, I received a ticket for doing seventy-five miles per hour - uphill. The Highway Patrolman could not believe it was a straight-six engine, so I showed it to him. The speed limit at that time was 55 - to help save gas during the energy crisis as I recall.

Staying With Don
Gregory stayed with Don on another occasion to escape the St. Moritz.

Greg Davidson writes: In the desert you and Don and I went for ice cream. Do you remember Don was eating an ice cream cone and some of it dripped on his wrist and he FREAKED out. He was really self-conscious of it for some reason. We had to get him napkins to wipe off the ice cream. Don took me to a Denny's in Lancaster and we sat there until the sun went down and then the sun came up. He wasn't tired at all. I won't even go into what happened there. What was funny was Don would often say to someone "Do you know who Captain Beefheart is?" and a lot of the time the response was "No" and without missing a beat he would say "Well, I'm Captain Beefheart!" as if they had said "Yes."

Of course, it was occasions like this that I seriously thought Don was absolutely trying his best to sabotage his own project. What bandleader stays up all night and keeps one of his musicians up also? I was at home, working on parts to songs, and I think we took the weekend off. Greg stayed with me one night, and Don one night. Greg was so burned-out from this all-nighter he could barely focus the following day.

House Of Pancakes

Greg Davidson writes: One night we all went to a pancake restaurant.

One evening after rehearsal, we all went to a pancake house as Greg and Don were in the mood for pancakes. I was not a sugar person, so I had a traditional breakfast. As we sat there, Don raved on and on about the manners of some guy, who, at one point, blew his nose on his napkin. "Did you hear that?" He ranted. "That's disgusting!" he exclaimed, with a special emphasis on the last word.
A few minutes later, our order came. Don put butter and syrup over his stack of pancakes and...

Greg Davidson writes: Don did something wrong as he was eating and pancakes were coming out of his nose! It was pretty disturbing.

It was a pretty disturbing thing all right. Don choked on his food and bent over and a thick milky liquid ran out of his nose all over his shoes and socks to the dismay of the surrounding clientele. I ran into the men's room and grabbed some paper towels and asked the waitress for a damp towel and cleaned off his shoes. He was very embarrassed, and I think that he probably outdid the nose-blower in the gross-out department that evening. Once the panic dissipated, I thought it was a bit amusing, as it was almost like a kharm-ic moment after his angry protests about the guy blowing his nose.

Supernatch?
Gregory had a similar supernatural occurrence to the one Don Aldridge described earlier with a car late at night in front of Sue Vliet's house years earlier:

Greg Davidson: One evening Don and I were leaving his trailer standing on a small paved lot. There was a road that extended for miles in front of us. A little dark Triumph whizzed past us going down the highway off into the distance. I looked at Don and he smiled and wiggled his eyebrows. All of a sudden the same car came in from the same direction it had the first time, pulled into the parking lot drove around in a circle and sped back out down the same road again. I didn't press Don too much on the incident!

This street that Gregory referred to was 10th Street East in Lancaster. It was later re-named "Challenger Way" after the Shuttle explosion. This was the street used to transport the finished shuttle from where it was built - Plant 42 in Palmdale, to Edwards Air Force Base, where it was then flown, via the back of a Boeing 747, to Florida. The street was fairly barren at the time, the only thing out there being the mobile home park where Don lived.

Pinks

John French: Any particular instances, anecdotes etc. Going to "Pinks," "Canters," "The Brown Derby Coffee Shop on Vine?"
Greg Davidson: Oh Gawd, yes. I had the misfortune of asking where I could get a hot dog (Chicago has great ones everywhere). *No one could think of anywhere. Then I think it was Ray Collins who said "Pink's on LaBrea." So Don, the vegetarian, takes me there. They only had foot longs so I ordered one for myself. Then Don buys one! He's eating the damn thing and he looks at me and says he's only eating this so I don't feel homesick. Later on that night he said he was feeling ill and blamed ME because he ate that hot dog.*

I went to Pink's with Don and Gregory - because I didn't have much choice, as Don was my ride home. It was a step down from Arby's - another place Gregory wanted to go - which was several steps down from anywhere I wanted to go. I remember Don and Greg doing a lot of talking and I just listened in. I could tell that Greg was a fan, and was enjoying this chance to get to know his idol, but it was a little crazy for me, as I just kept thinking about the ticking clock and the truckload of work that still needed to be done.

We were sitting it what appeared to be an enclosed aluminum patio with picnic benches. It was illuminated with fluorescent lights. Don kept complaining about the "flickering." "Can you see that, man?" he kept saying "It's driving me nuts."

Designer Jeans

As I said, another time we went to Arby's. Gregory loved all this meat, and I was not a fan of it at all. Anyway, this was during the era of Designer Jeans - like Jordache and Sergio Valenti. Davidson had a great sense of humor. A young couple came in wearing matching Sergio Valenti jeans and stood in front of us at the counter as we were waiting for their order. Greg turned around, and in a semi-secretive spy-type voice, complete with shifty eyes, whispered "Is it just me, or does the guy have a better ass than the chick?"

Don, occasionally would shriek in a high-pitched falsetto laugh when he found something particularly humorous and I have a high-pitched giggle that sometimes erupts - usually at the exact wrong moment. This was one of those moments, we both exploded with laughter, and everyone in the place viewed us with disdain.
"He's right!" Don wheezed, "the guy does have a better ass."

Canter's

We had lunch one day at Canter's delicatessen on Fairfax Avenue. I hadn't been there since the *Safe As Milk* rehearsals. We sat at a booth in the middle of the room. Greg and I on one side, and Don and his artwork on the other.

Greg Davidson: We had a great time at Canter's. It was you, Don and me. It was a LOUD place as the plates in the kitchen were clattering. I recorded Don saying some really funny stuff there like he loathed hot ice and a routine about scissors and water.

What Don was saying was "Bring me my scissors and those hot waters." In his best Vincent Price / Beefheart voice with a touch of a British accent for added theatrical flair. It was Gregory's turn to laugh hysterically, but at least he had a loud place to help camouflage his outburst.

Chicago TV Show - July 1974

Our two performances consisted of a Chicago TV taped appearance before a live audience, and Knebworth Music Festival in England. We flew to Chicago and were driven to the television studio where the audience was waiting to get in. We did a quick setup, - no roadies - and got ready to play. There were two rented kits for Jimmy and I. At the sound check, Don was having his usual trouble remembering lyrics, and so everything had to be stopped while Jan quickly scrawled out cue cards for Don. The audience came in, and we were told by the announcer to wait until we were announced and the applause began before we played.

The other person on the bill was Tom Waits. There was also some guy who did about 10 minutes in-between tapings. He had a guy and a girl mannequin torso strapped to his back and he would dance on his hands and feet, like a monkey walking around, his upper torso concealed by the female mannequin's flowing skirt and his tuxedo covered legs exposed as the male mannequin's legs. This gave the impression of two mannequins dancing together, which was indeed a surreal image. When I first saw it, I hadn't seen the gimmick yet and it definitely caught me by surprise. You've got to remember, that this guy couldn't see where he was going, which made for a couple of amusing moments as people jumped back to avoid collisions and stage technicians ran to grab boom stands and move cables - and this was just the rehearsal.

But the real clown act was after Tom Waits played a flawless set to warm applause, and the dancer-duo did his number, we were cordially introduced by the host and the applause began. I went into *Abba Zaba*, the band did a great intro - and Don completely blew the lines and stopped the band. This was a little embarrassing the first time, but after 8 or 10 false starts, we had to walk off the stage in total humiliation.

Greg Davidson writes: How could I not remember? Soundstage back then was a small room with a few tables in it with fake drinks for the audience. I had my parents and even my grandmother there (poor grannie). *We played and they video-taped. As you remember, we would start a song and then Don would stop the song. This happened over and over. Don would complain that the levels in the monitor were changing. The stage tech would say "I just talked to the audio engineer and he said he isn't changing the levels" And Don replied, "Well this artist says he IS!" We never did get a decent recording done. I don't think we ever finished one song. Years later I tried to get a tape of it but they had erased it. I suspect Don may have stopped the songs for having a problem with remembering the lyrics.*

"What the hell was that all about, Don?" I asked backstage.
"I had to do that, man! That fucking Herbie is trying to let Tom Waits (said in the most disgusting tone possible) ride on my coattails, and I'm not going to let him do it." Don said.
Okay. Yeah, after Don's cunning ploy, who would ever hear of that disgusting "Tom Waits guy" again?

Greg Davidson writes: When we did our ill-fated video taping of Sound Stage in Chicago I talked to Tom Waits a lot (Herb was managing him too). He is really smart and very cool. Years later I would go see him and he would always welcome me backstage with great descriptions of Don. He has great observational skills.

Returning To His Vomit

I often have read that Don hated performing his own stuff and likened it to a dog returning to its vomit - I paraphrase, but it was something like that. Yeah, better to find a bunch of other naïve dogs and train them to return to the vomit instead? Jan was writing cue cards for Don, and I was pulling

Don aside and drilling him on his lyrics. Of course, all Don wanted to do was draw, enjoy the sights, talk endlessly for hours on unrelated topics, and just appear to the public as "one of rock's true innocents." My frustration was growing. I'd just drilled his band on the music, now I have to drill him on his own lyrics and where to come in? Was this the way Don was going to recover from his shameful commercial cop-out and the bad press he got from the tour with the pickup band?

Knebworth In July

Of course, knowing Don to be quite a teller of tall tales, I wasn't sure if he actually had purposely sabotaged the TV taping, or he actually didn't know his own lyrics. Knowing Don, either was a strong possibility, and Jan was right there looking like she was totally concerned also. This rather spoiled the little vacation we were about to have. I thought Knebworth would be a great experience, but maybe not. After leaving Chicago we flew straight to London. I love the UK. I'll say it again. I LOVE THE UK! We were picked up at Heathrow and driven by limousine to a hotel in London, where Jimmy Carl Black taught me how Texans party.

First you have a beer. Then ... you have another beer. Then, you call some friends, and you ALL have a beer. There's a common theme here somewhere, but I just couldn't put my finger on it ... It was obvious that Jimmy is one of the warmest people I have ever known. It was like I had all my family member's best most loving traits rolled up into one person and put in the body of a redskin. If you're reading this Jimmy, I hope you laugh. I love ya Jimmy.

He somehow got us into a party in London at the late Madeline Kahn's apartment. She was over from the states filming *Sherlock Holmes' Smarter Brother*. She was sweet and warm and friendly. "You're an American aren't you?" were the first words out of her mouth. We had about a five-minute conversation. I wasn't sure who she was and all of a sudden I remembered her role as Miss Trixie in *Paper Moon*. "Miss Trixie has to go "winky tinky!" I said. "That was me!" she replied. I hadn't seen *Young Frankenstein* yet, but later appreciated her great talent for comedic-parody. We lost a great one there when she tragically died before her time.

The next morning I did what everyone does when they go to Europe: I bought an over-priced leather jacket. After this, we were driven, by limousine, to Knebworth and checked into a quaint little inn that seemed to be at the intersection of two roadways. It had two huge wooden tables in the dining room. Jimmy had met a beautiful girl the night before, and she came with us. I couldn't help but like this girl, whose name I now cannot recall. She was very friendly, a great conversationalist, and had a very pleasing voice and personality, besides being extremely beautiful. I think she was only nineteen years old.

That evening, we had a magnificent meal in the quaint dining room all seated around the huge table. Everyone was in great spirits and excited about the performance the next day. Everyone except me, of course. I was always thinking about details and how to make the performance better. I knew the band was loose, but would probably hold it together. My main concern was Don and the lyrics. I didn't want a repeat of the Chicago performance.

Knebworth England, as I recall, was a beautiful place. The concert was staged in a large field to the west of us. The night before the concert, rather than having a good time, I was coaching a very non-serious Don on his lyrics and of course, it was like trying to get a five year old to drink his milk. He was incorrigible. I think the whole thing was a set-up for attention.

Monty Python (the comedy group) were doing bits in between each act. I knew little of them and wasn't a big fan, and so I wasn't that interested.
My drums had been rented and were delivered to the stage, so I had to go up and "tune n' tweak" them before we played.

Although I wasn't nervous for myself, I was nervous for the group, especially Elliot, who had major problems with odd time signatures and was basically a "feel" player. Jimmy Carl also seemed a little on the inebriated side. During *Abba Zaba*, he came up with a beer can and a drum stick, playing the cowbell part on the can, a huge grin on his face. Don later commented negatively on this to me. "Did you see Jimmy with the beer can?" he asked me later, not at all amused.

Greg Davidson writes: Jan had solved this problem of the lyrics by the time we got to Knebworth. She wrote out all the lyrics on white cardboard and placed them on the monitors so Don could read them while we played (in front of 225,000 people). Well, that part worked out well except that he sang the right words but not always in the right section of the song! By the way, you tap danced very well at that concert.

Besides that, the set went well, and we all got in the limo to leave. Herbie was there in the limo, and some fan, a guy (weren't they all?) came up, opened the door, and tried to get in the car Herbie kicked him back and slammed the door, exclaiming "Fuckin' parasites!" This guy was tough, however he had dealt with a Frank Zappa who hadn't that long ago been knocked into an orchestra pit by some weirdo. A Frank Zappa who was seriously injured and spent a lot of time in a wheelchair and had chronic back pain for the rest of his life. Perhaps Herbie had a good reason for this attitude.

Mysterious Hug

We were booked into a beautiful hotel for our final night in London before our flight back, and as I was standing at the desk filling out the registration card a strange thing happened. Someone walked up behind me and gave me a very affectionate hug - like I was a big teddy bear or favorite pet. My blood sort of ran cold for a minute, because I thought it was Jan, and I was embarrassed. When the person let go, and I turned around, I discovered that it was Don. He looked a little emotional. "Thank you, John," he said softly, and walked off. He did have his magic moments ...

Roxy

After the flight home, we were going to play the Roxy. I had arrived home rather zonked from the jet lag and all, and slept almost all the first afternoon, into the evening, and woke up the next day, feeling great. I came into my folk's dining room and there, sitting at the dining room table, was Karen with a big smile on her face. I already had it figured out, just from her expression and mood. I was now "in the big time" and she was going to latch on to me, as a relationship with me would be advantageous. Do women really think men are that stupid?

I liked Karen a great deal, and she had used me a great deal for her own gain, but I still enjoyed her company. Her personality was really fun loving, spontaneous, and she always lifted my spirits. She was also a "toucher" when she spoke. In conversation, she would unconsciously reach out and touch your arm or hand when she made a point. I loved this, it was a kind of warmth that was very reassuring in a sense.

I was playing the Roxy that night. Herb liked to keep things moving along. Karen wanted to go with me that night, but I thought it best she go on Saturday instead. All the gear was moved to the club and so we arrived in the afternoon to set up and sound check. Everyone was there with the exception of Jimmy Carl Black. Don was furious, Jimmy was still in Texas. Rumor had it that his wife thought he was cheating on her - which he was, actually. He was in trouble.

John French: Well you have to - when I worked with Don I went into a mood and it was sort of a dark mood. When I played in that mood, that's when he was the happiest (with me at least). It was a weird thing but I got to where I didn't like it. I started remaining in that mood more. It was like a spirit that would come on me almost. I'd go in somewhere, someone

would say something to me, and I would "acid tongue" them to death.
Robert Williams: I know what you mean, it was like Don used to say, "Man, we gotta have that tension" you know. Personally, I can't picture myself sitting behind a drum set with this big goofy grin on my face like I'm the happy-go-lucky guy back here. I just can't picture myself rocking my head from right to left and smiling at the kids.
JF: (Laughing) It's Ringo!

I noticed first at the Roxy that I sort of went "into character" when we played. It bothered me a bit. I started getting meaner and more intimidating with people.

John French to Alex Snouffer: Then out of that we played the Roxy. Then after the Roxy , Herb came up and said, "OK we're setting you up for a European tour." And I was thinking I was out of there at that point. But I decided to go ahead and do it, there was nothing else going on for me.

Herbie was really on the ball. He knew how to get a ball rolling and how to keep it rolling. We returned to LA and I went home. I had rented a little place next door to my folks house for $50 a month. It was a perfect place for a trashed-out bachelor artist. Everything was funky and old and I loved it. It had been built by the now-deceased neighbor for his daughter to live in while she was in college.

I showed up at the Roxy later that afternoon to do a sound check and rehearsal. I was able to use my own drums these two nights. Jimmy Carl Black had said he couldn't show, but Don got on the horn and insisted he come. It was a good show both nights. I remember at one point that Bruce was playing a little solo and some clown in the audience was heckling him. Don said, "Come here, man" over the microphone and the guy came around to the side of the stage. At this point, although I didn't see what happened, Don claims he kicked him in the jaw, just hard enough to shut his mouth, not to hurt him and said "Now, keep it shut?"

Greg Davidson writes: It was a blast. A lot of ex Mothers of Invention were there. So was Frank Z and his family. People actually talked to me because I was in the band. We did two shows for two nights. As usual it was all guys who approached the band after a show asking all kinds of technical questions. I was on stage when lo and behold a blonde longhaired woman was standing up in the audience shouting "Greg! Greg!" "Finally!" I thought ... After the show she came up and I discovered I had gone to high school with her back home.

Herb Says Tour

The shows at the Roxy were fairly powerful. I felt like the band had done a great job musically and also been quite entertaining. Herb Cohen went to the Saturday night show, and apparently, he thought so also. As I was walking outside, Herb walked up next to me and asked if we could talk. He told me that there were plans underway for a major European tour, which would begin sometime in October. I had been surprised a little by the Roxy bookings, but this really excited me. I hadn't been to Europe (with the exception of Knebworth) since 1968 - six years previous. I felt like the band was still rough, but had the potential to do a great tour. Don was in fine form and seemed to have lost his lyric amnesia.

I had no hesitancy in saying yes as long as the money was right. Herb said that my services would be needed as musical director and that I would report to him on the progress of the band etc. Then, he announced that upon returning, there would be an album recorded. Don already knew about this and was gathering material. My head was swimming for a minute, but I agreed to do the album project also.

I would like to point out at this time that I believe all this was Zappa's doing. He wished his friend well and was obviously pulling many strings to make everything work. Herbie must have had the preliminary bookings for the Roxy and the tour well in advance of his calling me in June - and had probably started working and planning out this timeline during the *Bongo Fury* tour at Frank's request.

Tim Meyer

The bass player in Rattlesnakes And Eggs was a guy named Tim Meyer. He was always a technically oriented person and a skilled craftsman besides. After finding out that I was playing guitar, he approached me about building a guitar for me out of Redwood Burl. He said that mine would be a prototype and he would take pictures of it for a business he wanted to start, but would only charge me for materials.

I needed a guitar, as I was borrowing Tim's actually, then Don Giesen's for a time. I wanted a Stratocaster. We spent a couple of days in Hollywood going from store to store and picking up all the best parts we could. I bought the best tuners of the time - Schallers. I found a set of vintage Stratocaster pickups, a nice maple neck, all the switches, pots, bridges and other paraphernalia.

I noticed that I had developed this air of intimidation. I insisted in a rather assertive manner that I wanted a discount price and, I managed to get one in every place I went. There was one place where I didn't ask, and that was Red Rhodes Guitar repair shop. He had a great little shop that had been in Hollywood for years. I asked him about Strat pickups and he had a set that he claimed came out of a '58 Strat. I paid $35 apiece for them with no argument. I think Denny had recommended this place to me.

Tim spent several weeks and built me an extraordinarily beautiful guitar. When I saw it, I was totally shocked at how beautiful it was. He had even cut little frames that went around each pickup, out of the same wood. There was no pick-guard. Instead, he sprayed several extra coats of Varathane on the front to protect the wood.

I immediately ordered a red Anvil road case for the guitar.

Indian Ink And Ella Split

Jimmy Carl Black wouldn't be returning for the tour. I had heard tell that his wife was suspicious of his philandering on the road and was keeping a tight leash on him. I didn't see any problem there as I could handle all the drum parts more easily myself, and it made the band a more manageable unit. Greg Davidson, who was from Chicago, had gone home and would not return. I heard that his father had offered to purchase a Jack-In-The-Box franchise for him. We talked on the phone, and Don tried his best to talk him into it, but Greg refused. I actually had grown to really like the guy, and I still think he could have developed into one of the better guitarists that the Magic Band ever had. So, I was sad to see him go.

Greg Davidson writes: Don was almost always nice to me. I have memories of spending countless hours driving around with him in Jan's Volvo and going various places. One day after an all-nighter at the Denny's he THEN took me to the Antelope Valley Dog Show. It was an all day event, it was stiflingly hot, and I was exhausted, but in spite of all that, we had a great time of it. Occasionally Don would rag on me, like complaining about what guitar tuning I was using or he would say "Stop it man!" I would say "What?" And he would answer "That thinking you're doing, I can feel it." But all in all, he was pretty decent to me.

All in all, Greg spent approximately 5 weeks as a member of The Magic Band. This would still be what I consider the "honeymoon" period. Don was on his best behavior during most of that time and there were no "cultish" moments to speak of, though I was frustrated with Don's lack of responsibility to learn his own lyrics and where they go in the songs, he seemed changed in the sense that there was a bit more respect for the musicians. Part of this was that he had mostly adults in the band and not so much the young, naïve fan-types. Greg was probably more in the latter category in terms of being a fan, but he was also an exceptional guitarist who, in three weeks was able to grasp the strange concepts of the music and turned out to be a very strong player. It was obvious that he was quite familiar with the music.

Greg Davidson writes: After we played the Roxy I came home to Chicago because we didn't have any other gigs lined up. While I was home I was just sitting around playing guitar. My Dad suggested I get a job. I received a few phone calls from Don, you and Herb. One time Herb said he had booked a 7-week tour of Europe and some other countries. I asked him how much money we were going to get paid. He said "What the fuck's the difference how much you get paid? Because after those 7 weeks you'll have the next 7 weeks of your life to worry about." Thinking back, I would have to say that was the main reason I left, the coldness of Herb and the uncertainty of the future. I got a job doing special effects on movie film. Years later I became a "Dr. of Naprapathy" fixing people's back and neck pain. I'm currently playing in local blues bands in the Chicago area.

I was unaware of Herb's rudeness with Greg. I don't know exactly why, but he was always respectful with me and when I was in his office, there was always a cordial and businesslike approach to everything we discussed. He seemed realistic, though he couldn't understand why it took us so long for the band to learn the music. He had not a clue as to the fact that Don's music was more complex than Frank's - mainly because it broke so many rules. Also, I wasn't working with musicians who were readers.

Denny Walley
Denny Walley is a GREAT slide guitarist. I loved his playing immediately. I have to say that when I found that Denny Walley was going to be the guitarist for the tour, I had only vaguely heard him play for a moment in Zappa's rehearsal studio while the band rehearsed. When he showed up for the first rehearsal and I listened to his fantastic sound I was really happy. Denny could pull more sounds out of a guitar with a slide than anyone I had ever heard. He had the advantage over others of developing his style apart from Don. This caused him to use smaller strings, and different tones, which was a big advantage. His sound was established before he became a Magic Band guitarist. He was well-read in the blues idiom and had a musical vocabulary that wouldn't quit. I knew that working with Zappa had probably familiarized him with odd time signatures, so that would probably not be a problem.

Previously I have written about his roots with Frank in the Lancaster area. Just to review a bit of history seems in order. The Walley's moved to Lancaster from the East Coast before Denny went to High School. Denny was friends with Bobby Zappa, Frank's brother, back in their high school days. He used to drive Zappa to Black Outs rehearsals when he was $14^1/2$ because he had a special "farm" license. He didn't know Jim Sherwood much as a kid in High School, because they associated with different groups. They occasionally bought records together at Cornet, which was a five and ten-cent store on Lancaster Boulevard. Denny had moved with his family back to the East Coast. In late 1974 or early 1975, Motorhead found out Denny Walley was in Hollywood and had been for some time

John French: Denny Walley claims you recommended him to Frank.
Jim Sherwood: I recommended Denny, because Denny was a monster slide guitarist

JF: You don't have to tell me.
JS: We knew each other in high school I think he was in a couple of my classes or something like that, but I don't really remember that much about him. He never played music or anything around me. I tied up with Denny (later) and his brother-in-Law, Tom. We started talking about this and that (and came) to realize we went to school together.

The inclusion into Frank's group - no longer officially called "The Mothers" - was a godsend to Denny in terms of financial security.

Jim Sherwood: Denny really thanked me a lot. He said he was kind of struggling and all that, and Frank was paying him really good money.

Another point in which I find the comparison between Frank and Don fall strongly in Frank's favor. He may have not been, in terms of some, "the real thing" in terms of what some considered to be the most soulful or genuine non-compromised composer, but he definitely treated his musicians in a way that worked in the real world. Also, musicians who played with Frank were able to transfer their learned and developed skills to other groups. Frank transcribed a lot of music for his group to play - another totally different approach from Don.

Denny Walley: At one point when Frank handed me a whole pile of music, I said, "Hey, Frank, how bout if I play it and then you write it? This shit is overwhelming, I can't read that."
John French: Flyshit on paper, I think was your reference.
DW: When we went on the road, I was the only guy that didn't need a music stand. They were still reading, I knew it because I practiced it like ten hours a day. Since I'm an ear musician, once I learned it, I didn't need the paper. I was the only one up there who knew my shit and knew theirs too, and they were reading it.

Denny's first tour with Frank was the *Bongo Fury* tour, where he met Don. He recalls touring again with Frank before Frank suggested he play in The Magic Band. The idea was that when Frank was not touring, or doing more orchestrated music where he needed strong sight-reading skills, Denny could play with Don. When Don wasn't touring, Walley would work with Frank.

Denny's Slide Technique
A lot of people asked me questions about various player's techniques, and I thought the following interview material would be of definite interest to slide-guitar enthusiasts.

John French: Let me ask you. Do you prefer metal slide or bottleneck better?
Denny Walley: I use metal, but I just got a neck from the bottle of - I guess it's Vodka - from Finland, that has a frosted outside to the neck. It has some granularity to it. It fits my pinkie perfectly. The finger of choice now is little finger.
JF: Didn't you used to use...
DW: I used to use the finger next to it. I would use my little finger to play sevenths if I was doing little chord things.
JF: So, you like a little bit of a rough surface?
DW: Yeah!
JF: Why is that?
DW: Well because when you rub that against the string I mean it just keeps the note going and going. I can make it louder without doing a thing. You can control the volume.

JF: Really? So that's the reason huh?
DW: Oh yes, you just move that thing around, cross string, cause you know how it's wrapped, and you do little circles. Then the faster you do the circles and the more pressure you put on the string, the louder it's going to get. You can get feedback things that you will just not believe.
JF: So, that's how you got those tones to sustain so well. I always wondered about that. I found a rehearsal tape of before we went on the 1975 tour. I could hear you on the background, dead on, on everything. Those notes, those slide notes, I was thinking, "God, how is he doing that?" You were pulling them out of the guitar. And with everybody else they'd die and just fall in the water, you know?
DW: That's it! That's what used to happen, because they would just play (the note) ... then they would put pressure and that would just kill it because they're not movin' it. But I always kind of snuck up on the pitch just a little bit, just enough to get tension, you know.
JF: So, you played slightly flat and then pulled in?
DW: Yeah, but going towards it, you could feel it getting louder - and stronger, so you're not worried that it's going to be flat.

Transcribing

During late July and most of August, I went to Don's mother's mobile home on a daily basis to transcribe material for the new album which would be recorded after the tour. I wanted to get a head start on this material and be familiarizing myself with it during the tour. I spent hours and hours a day for a couple of weeks, transcribing pieces that Don had pulled out of his cassette archives. He was pulling out all the stops with this material. Three pieces were really long non-repetitive linear pieces: *The Thousandth And Tenth Day Of The Human Totem Pole, Seam-Crooked Sam,* and *Odd Jobs* (a piece I believe was pulled from the *Big Sur Suite* material).

I made a copy of the original piano pieces, which I kept with me and immediately began interpreting these charts on guitar. Perhaps one of my true gifts was the ability to sit down and patiently listen to these piano tapes and interpret them in a fairly accurate manner. I received no compensation for this work. It was tedious work, but I enjoyed this sort of challenge. This particular stage of the process was not that tantalizing, in fact it was downright boring. It was the end product, actually hearing a finished recording of something transcribed, arranged, taught and rehearsed and knowing intimately every step of the process that was somehow rewarding to me in spite of the sparse financial rewards.

Denny Walley: What points do you think that I could give some sort of finite (clarity) to?
John French: Well, I would say, that one thing that really would be of deep concern to me is the musical process. That is the thing that has been portrayed by Don as him teaching everybody every note, getting players and training them, basically extolling his own virtues while belittling the efforts and the abilities of the players that worked with him.
DW: Well, John. As far as that goes, there's a lot of myth behind a lot of people. I happen to be in possession of tapes and I've been at your home in Lancaster when you were deciphering stuff from him playing on the piano, you would interpret it, you know. Give out parts and say this was what goes where etc. But that was before me. I was privy to that like two years after I was in the band. Then, after that, when the creative process came to, "OK you played all those songs, here's a new record deal you need new songs." I can say a third of the stuff, like on Bat Chain Puller *and some other stuff, I came up with the lines on it - Ode t' Alex and a few other things - Don actually whistled the solo to Ode to Alex, so I give him that, but I took it a little bit further.*

My interpretation of this statement and from being there is that Denny was learning parts more directly from Don. Example of this would be Don giving Denny the original demo of *Electricity* and having him learn the harmonica part note-for-note. Or - as Denny said, Don whistling something to him - like on *Ode t' Alex*. There was a lot more of this method of composition used on *Bat Chain Puller* than during *Trout Mask Replica* - where a few things - like *Ant-Man-Bee* or *Sugar 'n Spikes* was whistled and hummed to the players. One thing for sure is that Denny certainly did "take it a little farther." His solo work - especially on *Bat Chain Puller* and *Ode t' Alex*, was exceptional.

In a discussion I'd had with Tripp in his interview, we were talking about the interpreter of Don's work being the composer, and I was playing devil's advocate in this instance. I said that I had transcribed later compositions from piano in which there were long streams of passages, albeit played in the same chordal mode all the way through from beginning to end with no "culling" of parts. On a smaller scale, it was familiar to Tripp's experience with transcribing and playing *White Jam* on the *Spotlight Kid*.

Art Tripp: Well, I am sure he could, in a lot of instances, and I'm not trying to denigrate his ear by any means. He had a great way of hearing things.

CHAPTER THIRTY FIVE:
PRE-PULLER BEST-OF TOUR

...any Carl Black, Don and John at the Knebworth ...tival, July 1975, shot by Jan Van Vliet.

September 17-18, 1975, Royce Hall, University of California, Los Angeles

Don had mentioned that he was playing at one of Frank's concerts at Royce Hall. He would be a guest, playing soprano during a segment of the concert. I was put on the guest list. I sat in a seat right on the aisle and after about three minutes of sitting, someone clutched the back of my neck with their fingers and sent chills down my spine. It was non-violent, more of a friendly touch, but it startled me. I turned around to see Jan Van Vliet sitting behind me with a big smile on her face, apparently quite pleased at herself for sneaking up like that.

Zappa's show was impressive to me. I was particularly enthralled with a piece called *Duke Of Prunes*. He had a guest conductor for most of the show, but then came up himself and conducted a number or two on his own. I remember him taking off his shirt, which I thought was unnecessary, which resulted in a number of war whoops from the party animals. Frank's method of conducting was strange to me. I had a hard time following how things were actually divided into measures, and found this distracting for a while.

I finally closed my eyes and concentrated on Terry Bozzio's drumming. I was very impressed with him as a player because of his excellent reading skills. He performed impeccably. I don't remember much about Don's solo, probably because I had heard so many in my life, another sax solo wasn't really something of which I savored each moment. Besides not being that audibly appealing to me in the first place, these solos symbolized empty concert halls and empty pockets - all in the guise of "self-expression." I always felt that I understood what he was saying - or at least what he was trying to say - as I had heard many of his influences. The heart was there, but the foundation was not.

Rehearsals

I believe our actual rehearsals for the tour started in September and lasted about 5 weeks. I just basically remember that I worked a lot with Denny initially, to get him briefed on every song as quickly as possible. He was very open with me and even changed the finger on which he placed the slide at my suggestion. Because of the fingering of the Beefheart material, it made it much easier to play with the slide on the pinkie finger as opposed the third finger.

Denny was a quick studier, so then I focused on dialing-in Elliot to the material. One of the rules I had to make was "no pot at rehearsal." This was something that Frank had enforced and so Denny and Bruce cooperated easily. It was a little tougher for Elliot, but he did it, and as soon as he did, the parts fell into place faster and faster. Bruce was reading most of the stuff down and had it completely memorized in no time, so he was so low-maintenance that I barely spent any time with him.

The last week or two of rehearsal, Frank moved us into the big room, as he was doing final rehearsals with his new lighting setup, and so had rented an even larger place in which to rehearse. This was great for us, as we could set up on a full-sized stage with a complete PA. We were able to find the best setup for ourselves. Elliot was on my right, Bruce on my left, and Denny stood on the other side of Bruce. This way, I could sing parts to Elliot if he was lost.

Lies Begat Lies

There was a pay phone right outside the doorway of the rehearsal room and Don angrily called me out to the phone. "Hey man, Harkleroad's saying now that HE wrote *Trout Mask Replica*! It's in this article, man. Look at that picture. He's even wearing a shirt I bought for him!" I was preoccupied, in the middle of a rehearsal, and didn't have a chance to glance at the article. Don handed me the phone, "TELL him, man," he angrily commanded. I have no recollection of what I said. I do recall Denny coming out and asking if the guys could take lunch while I was on the phone. I said "OK" and they took off. Here's the quote:

Attributed to John French in Melody Maker October, 1975 - to Steve Lake.
"He professed himself very surprised at reading some of Harkleroad's assertions. His own view was that the musicians had not been in control, at least around the time of Trout Mask, which was the only album he said he was qualified to talk about (which is odd considering he appeared on all of them prior to Clear Spot). He concluded, 'Whatever Harkleroad might claim about his guitar virtuosity at the time - I was there. I would watch Don going over all Harkleroad's parts with him with incredible patience, Don's very musical. It's true that Don can't play guitar, but that never stopped him getting his ideas across'." [63]

The truth is, with the "boss" standing right over my shoulder, I may have exaggerated here. I don't ever recall saying "I would watch Don going over all Harkleroad's parts -- as that never happened - but I may have said that. I did see Van Vliet going over an occasional section of some random part that needed work - mostly on nuance. This was rare - 5% or less of the material. I also had just had a brief, exaggerated summary of the article delivered to me by Don, which sounded like Bill had said a pack of lies. When I actually read the article much later, it was too late for me to change what I had already said, and I couldn't remember what I said anyway - which is probably why I'd rather write - so that I have time to really check my words.

The part that stunned me about this statement was "with incredible patience" as I seldom recall Don ever having much patience when putting together music. All I can say is, I usually don't consider myself a liar, but this statement has some lies in it that are attributed to me. If I said all those things, then it's partly a lie and I apologize to Bill and the public for allowing that to come out of my mouth, if indeed, it did. It's really a bit unrecognizable as my speech pattern or use of words, so it could have been greatly paraphrased.

However, lies begat lies. Don told me, without giving me a moment to glance over the article myself, and with the phone being held right in my face "Hey man, Harkleroad's saying now that HE wrote *Trout Mask Replica!*" I stupidly believed him. Here's what Bill stated with my comments inserted:

"The music was put together by the band. Not by him."

For the most part - especially during *Trout Mask*, this was true. I did a lot of arranging, then Bill took the reins and did pretty much the same thing but working from tapes rather than piano transcriptions. We made many group decisions on how to get from section to section, how long each section should be, etc. So, I would say this is true.

"It was totally arranged by the band," he asserted.

The only word I would take is "totally" - Don did spend some time on arranging but not as much as he claimed.

"As a lyricist, he's one of the best I've heard in my life."

That fact is unanimously agreed upon by most MB members.

"He's not a musician... he got a lot of credit for doing a lot of music that he never did. It came from the band." [64]

This is a vague statement, and said by a person who, like myself, hadn't much experience with public speaking. I think what Zoot was trying to say is that Don never gave anyone an inkling of credit for helping with arrangements or song building. Some credit should certainly have been due, as I have repeatedly written.

Leaving For Tour

We left around the middle of Oct.1975. I had to get a passport, since my last had long since expired. Jack, our road manager, had to have us pack all the equipment we were taking with us so he could make a complete list and weigh everything. This was difficult, because we had to decide

[63] Captain Beefheart, Mike Barnes, Quartet Books Ltd., 2000, pp 233
[64] Captain Beefheart, Mike Barnes, Quartet Books Ltd., 2000, pp 232-233

right away exactly what we planned to take and pack everything up, disrupting rehearsal.

We had a black and white promotional shot taken just outside the rehearsal room at Discreet Records. I really liked everyone in the band and it was nice to be working with seasoned veterans of the road. I believe that we only were paid $300 a week, plus, of course, I would be given $1,000 bonus as musical director, which involved various responsibilities on the road. We also were given a per diem of $10, which wasn't really a lot for food on the road, but helped.

The tour would be 6 weeks or so. I was getting really happy about going to Europe. Don was prepared. I remember going out to Don and Jan's mobile home and Jan said, "look at this," opening an impeccably-packed suitcase to reveal a tiny pillow. She patted it lovingly and giggled - "Don's baby pillow" - she said gently. It was hypo-allergenic for Don, because he had so many allergies.

I drove Don and Jan in my old '63 Chevy to Discreet Records, as Don did not want to leave his car parked in Hollywood behind Discreet's office. Transportation was provided from there to LAX to board International Flight 760. I believe it was Oct 16, 1975. It was a 747 Jumbo Jet and the first in which I had been. I was absolutely stunned at the size. I sat next to Denny, and Don and Jan sat across the aisle. Don started laughing and I when I inquired as to the source of his humor, he explained simply, "I just felt my skull."

I was reading the emergency crash-landing procedures out loud, "in case of emergency landing, bend over, put your head between your knees…" and at that point Denny interjected, "and kiss your ass goodbye."

During the first hour or so of the flight Don spoke to the group - referring to playing for the Communist party in Paris. "I've played for them before, it's a great audience."

Paris

We landed safely in Paris, France and the first order of the day was to explain to our non-English-speaking driver that we wanted to buy some bottled water. This would seem like a simple thing to get across, but he must have stopped at half a dozen shops before we actually found a market where bottled water was sold. Don said, "I think the driver is playing dumb so he can jack up his fee." We were then taken to a Novotel on the edge of the city where we all spent a couple of days adjusting from the jet lag.

Amplifiers were rented in Paris for the tour. Elliot was very troubled about which amp to get, a Fender Twin, or a Fender Super Reverb. I suggested the Super Reverb, because it was a "warmer-sounding" amp. He eventually opted for the higher-powered Twin.

Walking With Walley

Denny and I took off on a walking tour of Paris the next day. We rode on the Seine, had lunch in the Eiffel tower, explored shops and generally just had a great day. We were strolling down the Champs Elysees shortly after sundown and thinking about returning to the hotel when a Mercedes pulled up. "Captain Beefheart band?" they asked. "Oui!" we replied. They immediately invited us into the car. I believe that it was two couples, one front and one back. They drove us to an apartment and we spent the next hour or so indulging in a bit of wine and there was hashish passed around, which I decided not to smoke but was breathing the smoke enough to affect me.

They then took us to a small middle-eastern restaurant where the management locked the doors and had us sit at a big table, like a picnic table with chairs. The brought out large cooking pots filled with various dishes, most of which I can't remember aside from couscous and a delicious lamb stew - probably a curry dish. It was a wonderful evening - the only down point being when I had to use the bathroom. They directed me outside and I walked down to what looked like what we would call an "outhouse" in the States. It was a small wooden shed with a footprint of one square meter. When I opened the door, it was a porcelain-lined room similar to a shower stall with two foot steps and a hole on the floor. Basically, it was "squat and shoot" time, hoping one did not lose one's balance. There was a container filled with sandpaper that I suppose was meant to be toilet paper. I can't imagine the old or infirmed using such a fixture. There was nowhere to wash hands - very unsanitary.

Sound Check

We played at the Hippodrome, which was like a giant greenhouse with no sides. We went to the sound check, and there was a fellow I had heard of setting up on stage. Don recognized him before me, and said, "there's Fred Frith." He was a guitarist working with a band called Henry Cow. I went up and introduced myself. I found Fred to be quite friendly and he carefully explained to me the function of each of his effects pedals.

Months back, I recall seeing his album at Don's house. I picked it up out of curiosity. "That guy copied me." Van Vliet said casually - a statement I had heard many times before. I borrowed the album and listened to it. I did hear a couple of rhythmic things that reminded me of the short passages from *TMR* - as though there was a possible influence. Other than that, it was very different than anything Don had written.

October 21, 1975 Hippodrome, Paris

Our spot was really late at night and it was cold. I think it was 3:00 in the morning and some rock and roll band was just finishing up as we arrived. We set up our stuff and Bruce almost immediately lost one of his contact lenses, so we immediately got down on the stage and crawled around looking for it. I don't think he ever found it, and so had to wear glasses most of the rest of the tour. The show was met with a lukewarm response, we were a little loose in places, and generally it was a bit sloppy. It didn't help that it was cold and a lot of people were lying in front of us in sleeping bags.

We had gone on after some group with a front man who kept shouting, "Is everybody ready to rock and roll?" So the crowd was more in a rebel rouser type of mood. The only thing that really bothered me about "air-bass" was the octavider was early technology and it had no punch at all. Also, he couldn't play chords. So, the beginning of *Blows It's Stacks* needed punch and it was getting none. I asked Denny, as I recall, to double the bass part softly, so as to add a percussive edge, and it worked much better.

Bordeaux, France

We then met a Danish fellow from the booking agency named Jorn (pronounced 'yorn'), which may be spelled wrong, but I believe it is Danish for "John." He wasn't too sure about us, especially Don, and I'm sure he was more used to the conventional rock band types. One morning, probably about a week after we arrived in Paris, and a day or two after our first performance, we climbed into one of two rented vehicles, a Volkswagen van and a Citroen sedan, and started a long drive to Bordeaux. Everybody seemed in great spirits and it was a very picturesque drive.

However, it was also a long drive, and the day began wearing on us by late afternoon. I was getting giddy, and had been in the car with "the guys" who were smoking a lot of pot, which I was trying my best to avoid, as it seemed to affect me in an adverse manner. I recall stopping at a small wine and cheese stand on a tree-lined road in the wine country. Bruce was collecting Trilobite fossils from a streambed, and I joined him for a few minutes.

I asked at one point if I could ride in the van with Don and Jan and they said, "fine," so I switched vehicles. I immediately found myself getting perturbed by Jorn myself. He didn't seem to know where he was going, and yet would not stop and ask directions. I finally persuaded him to pull over when I saw a beautiful young woman walking along the country road and thought I'd asked her directions. She was quite friendly, spoke perfect English, and the whole time she was leaning in the window to speak to me, Jorn was impatiently inching the Van forward, causing her to have to walk to keep up with us.

After about thirty seconds of this, I was livid, I turned, my teeth gritting, grabbed his arm and spoke very angrily, "Put your foot on the damned brake pedal and don't take it off until she's through!" The girl was able to finish her directions. Jorn was a bit tense after my outburst, however, I felt he had it coming and didn't apologize. A bit later, after dark, I started telling him about how much I loved Copenhagen and he warmed up immediately.

We played in a small club on a really narrow street. There was an African band for the warm-up act. They had a really good show and opened by marching on stage from the dressing room while playing percussion instruments. We were well accepted that night and I did a tap dance on stage - just to see the reaction of the crowd. Don was trying to get Jack to get him some water, but Jack said "Not right now, I want to see this." It went over well enough that Don left it in the show for the rest of the tour. It became part of the improvisation section and I tap-danced as part of my drum solo.

Poitiers - France

I took along a portable tape deck on this tour and occasionally used it a little like one would use a journal to record events. Unfortunately, 25 years later these cassettes have the worst sound quality you can imagine. Though I wasn't very consistent, I do have an entry on side two of tour tape 2 right at the beginning that states that we played in Poitiers, which is between Paris and Bordeaux. We then went by train from Poitiers mid morning arriving at the Paris train station that afternoon. The train station was like walking into an Agatha Christie novel for me. We then took cabs from the Paris train station directly to the Paris air terminal and boarded an Air France jet to Stockholm Sweden.

Stockholm, Sweden

Taped journal entry: *We're on a bus right now to Stockholm. Before that, we flew in from Paris. Before that we took a train to Paris from Poitiers, where we played the night before. The night before that, we played in Bordeaux. Poitiers is in between Bordeaux and Paris. We came back to Paris by train, took a cab to the air terminal, took a Jet on Air France to Stockholm, Sweden. We are riding on a specially chartered coach. We're driving to Stockholm, to our hotel. We're having the night off. The last few days I've had pretty sleepless nights. I'm pretty tired today. Tonight there'll be a press meeting for Don. Tomorrow night, we'll play in Stockholm. I took a picture today at the Paris Airport. I'm a little stuffy today, and a little tired, but so far the group has been doing better on stage each night. More electric and more positive about playing. It's not too cold here, surprisingly enough. It's about 68 or 70 degrees. Pretty good for this time of year really. I wound up in a small wood-paneled room in the hotel.*

Next day: *Morning in Stockholm, just woke up and it's 11:40. I was very tired last night. I went to bed at something like nine o'clock. It's a beautiful day, so I'm going to go out and take a walk. All the film's gone except one picture on the last of three rolls. I had three rolls when I started out. Following day: Still in Stockholm, it's ten o'clock in the morning. It's the day we leave. We leave at 1:30. We didn't play last night because the instruments didn't show up. So, we're going to come back. This is Sunday Morning. We're going to come back and play Tuesday night. There's a river that runs down the middle of the city with a huge footbridge over it. I'm going to try to get some pictures of it. It's beautiful. You can hear the church bells ringing everywhere.*

Later same day: *We're going from Stockholm, Sweden to the airport now. We had to drive here in the darkness, but as we drive back, you can see every beautiful color of tree, there's evergreens* *mixed with deciduous. I'm seeing yellows, oranges, reds, golds, and every imaginable color. Also old beautiful houses, hundreds of years old. Beside the road are farms and gardens. It's gorgeous - beautiful.*

3:40 in the afternoon, I just got a picture of Don and Elliot walking towards the plane. We're going to take off in a few minutes. In the air - heading for Helsinki from Stockholm, I'm going to try to get a picture in the cabin.

Helsinki, Finland

Landing in Helsinki, 5:30, we're on a bus, heading for the hotel. There's fourteen of us. We've been joined by violinist Jean-Luc Ponty and his group. We'll be touring together until we reach Switzerland. It's pitch black out, and it's only 5:30. It gets dark about 4:30 here. ...At the hotel, everybody is starting to get off the bus. Denny came up to tell me jokingly that my press meeting is starting in a few minutes. I told them to "stay away, I want to be alone, send them to my private diner." ...In the hotel room at Helsinki, beautiful rooms, got a shot. The color in here is amazing.

I soon discovered that I had left my beloved Capezio tap shoes in the hotel or at the club of our last show. So, in Finland, I was met at the hotel by a friendly local rep who spoke fluent English, and taken to a department store where I bought shoes, a dance studio, where I purchased taps, and a cobbler's shop, where the taps were attached.

The interesting thing about this was that it was as if I had been transported through time to the age of five, because the department store and even the fashions being sold, were very similar to what I remember as a small child in the US. The dance studio was up a few stairs off the street into a hallway lined with really cute little girls in ballet tights, toe shoes, and tutus, staring at me in wide-eyed wonder. The cobblers shop was like walking into Gepetto's shop. Shoes of all kinds lined the shelf-lined walls and the dark wood really added to the old-world feel. It was charming. The shoemaker had stayed after hours especially to do this job. I gave him the equivalent of a $10 tip. He looked at me - his face lighting up like a birthday cake - and exuberantly said "Thanks." It was nice being appreciated - for both of us.

The performance was in a sit-down stadium and the show went well. I recall tap dancing down through the audience and around the back of the middle row of seats, I tapped a rhythm with the drumsticks on the back of the chairs, people leaning forward like dominoes as I passed them.

I remember an attractive girl who was backstage before and after the show. She kept trying to hug Don. Jan was so angry that she finally smacked her if I recall. This girl had been relentless, but that seemed to cause the girl to focus her attention on me instead. She followed me back to the hotel that night. The next day, I met with her for breakfast and we were walking around the city. I'll never forget being bundled up with a thick turtleneck sweater, a heavy leather jacket, and a scarf around my neck, shivering in the bitter cold. This girl was wearing a thin tank top (like a men's undershirt) and a light open sweater, and seemed completely warm. She was laughing at me. It was embarrassing.

Tape Journal: *Took off from Helsinki, going back to Stockholm. I snapped a picture of the view of the clouds and a lake. Very beautiful, nice flight, good takeoff. I'm going to have lunch now...*
Later: We're flying over Sweden getting ready to land near Stockholm. I took a beautiful picture of the Swedish countryside on film. What a great gift God has given me to allow me to travel around like this and see all these beautiful things that he created.

October 28, 1975 Konserthuset, Stockholm, Sweden

The hotel we stayed in in Sweden had a great restaurant with a wonderful bagpipe player who came in and serenaded the crowd as they had dinner. Later that night, the whole band (minus

Don) decided to go out for a drink. We walked over a bridge and down a curvy road and suddenly a limousine pulled up and stopped. A large, drunken man came out and stood in front of me, blocking my path. He gruffly mumbled something in Swedish as I noticed an unlit cigarette in his lips, pulled out my lighter and lit it. He leaned forward, grabbed my hand to guide the flame, lit his cigarette, got back in his car without a word and sped off. "What was that all about?" Denny asked. "I thought he was going to punch you out or something!" "Nah," I said, "Sven and I go way back." We all had a laugh about this for some time.

The only thing I seem to recall about the concert is that I noticed a girl in the front, wearing a derby-like hat with a straight brim, singing along to all the songs. I found this a little incredible - especially from a female. She seemed to know every lyric. It was a stand up club and was tightly packed.

After the show, I remember going back to the hotel and Don was doing interviews so he asked me to escort Jan to their room and make sure she was all right. Jan and I got on the elevator and I was totally silent, looking at the door. "I really like the way you play drums, John," she said. I was amazingly shy and couldn't even respond, but I consider that the best compliment I ever received and her voice made me tingle. I now think I had a little crush on Jan and the feelings were pushed way down deep. She was just so beautiful, sweet, intelligent, and ... married to Don.

October 30, 1975 Oslo, Norway
I remember my first view of the fjords being breathtaking. We flew in over them and so I had a wonderful view from the air. It was an incredible place with a lot of natural beauty.

Tape Journal: *We're staying at the Hotel Bristol in Oslo, Norway. Beautiful countryside. They have a socialistic Government. The cops aren't allowed to wear guns and they aren't allowed to hit people back with very few exceptions. It's a very peaceful country. A lot of fjords, which are ocean inlets that come inland - like large lakes - for miles. It's very nice here, they have many sculptures. There's a man watching me while I speak into my tape recorder. He wanted to say a few words, but there's glass in the way.*

The hall we played in was similar to the hall in Finland, but the electricity was completely different and during the sound check, one of the monitor speakers actually burst into flames. Jack (our road manager) was holding a bottle of Coke (in fact, I have never seen anyone so addicted to sugar) that he immediately shook up and sprayed on the flames, this causing a puddle of moisture on the floor which again brought to mind visions of electrocution during the performance.

The sound crew we were traveling with was actually a bit inept. They were supposed to be doubling as sound crew and roadies, but when they weren't in the mood, the leader of the pack would arrive wearing his sourest expression to announce, "You're going to have to strike your own equipment tonight, sorry!" Sometimes this would happen with setup also. Although I don't consider myself overly filled with pride, it does take all the wind out of one's sails to have to stroll out on the stage before an audience and setup your own gear. It steals away any concept of illusion or imagination and puts audience and performer in completely the wrong perspective. The good news is that Herbie probably got a "good deal on a sound crew," and in the end, isn't that what really matters ... to Herbie?

The hotel we stayed in was ancient. I remember thinking that if I could export all the furniture to California, I could make a fortune in the antique business. I recall a really drunk and fairly attractive woman following me back to the hotel and coming up to me in the lobby as the band was having a little business meeting. She attempted to communicate, but was very drunk and slightly out of practice speaking English, that everything she said came out wrong. Jan was observing, and since I had an audience, I decided to poke a little fun.

I can't recall any of the actual conversation, but basically the woman was propositioning me, and

I kept pretending to misunderstand her and would say something that rhymed with the last word she said, but had a completely different meaning, all-the-while maintaining a cartoon-like expression of confusion and putting my hand behind my ear like I couldn't hear. She kept getting more and more confused and frustrated, and finally drifted off somewhere, totally bewildered. Jan had been silently laughing about this during the whole encounter.

October 31, 1975 Tivolis Koncertsal, København, (Copenhagen), Denmark

Tape Journal: *We're bound for Copenhagen from Oslo. Should be there in about fifty-five minutes...(later) we're in Copenhagen, Denmark on the coach. Had a great landing. I speak to Don, "That was a great landing." (Don says:) "Very good! The guy really knows what to do."It's about 2:40 in the afternoon.*

I remember nothing about the concert in Copenhagen, except that The Fugs were in Copenhagen during the same time, and Denny knew some of them. He recognized someone on the street as we were walking to lunch and they had a short conversation.

Arhus, Denmark

Arhus is very clear in my mind. The hotel was more modern and several storey's tall. The receptionist from the hotel took a break and gave several of us (about 8 if I recall) a little walking tour of the local clubs. Everything was really crowded, except this last place we went in which the lighting was quite subdued. I was standing at the bar having a soda, and I turned around and saw two guys slow-dancing together.

As my eyes adjusted to the light I looked around and quickly discovered I was in a gay club...just in time to see my prospective dance partner, a cute little Dane, strolling my way, a look of expectancy streaming from his eyes. I would swear this night that I actually teleported instantly back to the hotel. Homophobia? Nah! I just didn't want to break the poor guy's heart.

Arhus Concert

The club was narrow, being not much wider than the stage itself and the audience was wild. They loved the band and when we left the stage, they cheered and cheered yelling for "more." In particular, because of the audience reception, this was probably one of our best performances. At the bar in the hotel later, I went down to have a beer, and Don was at the bar. It was crowded, and I was afraid that someone would crash into my bottle and knock my teeth out. "Hold the bottle like this," Don suggested. The neck of the bottle was clenched in his hand, and just enough of the end was left exposed to take a drink. "That girl is interested in you," he pointed across the room. "You ought to give her your room key." I looked to see a very attractive girl in a white and red striped pullover eyeing me. She recognized me from the show. I taught her a tap dance step, but left alone.

November 2, 1975 Concertgebouw, Amsterdam, Holland

One of the most beautiful halls we played in was in Amsterdam. It's one of the most highly acclaimed halls in all of Europe and was inaugurated in 1888. We entered the hall from the rear, not actually having been there earlier for a sound check. The ceilings were twelve to fourteen feet high in the dressing rooms and the decorating was absolutely impeccable. There was a huge fireplace with a high mantle, all painted white with gold trim. A painting hung high over our heads.

A head poked in the room and someone said, "Would anyone care to inspect the stage setup?" That was my cue, as it was almost every night, to go down and make sure things were in order. I walked into the hall and realized we had to descend several flights of stairs to reach the stage. The view was breathtaking. The stage was nearly surrounded by seats. There were small individual balcony seats decorated with scarlet velvet curtains, which contrasted nicely with the pure white walls. The trim was ornate and tasteful, and I wish I could describe the period of architecture, but I am afraid I am quite ignorant of such things. Baroque perhaps?

When I reached the stage, I was really impressed by how quiet everyone was. The place was almost packed out, and yet there was barely a murmur. It was a little disconcerting (no pun intended). There was a large grand piano separating me from Bruce and Denny. This was absolutely not going to work, so I informed the stage manager, who seemed a bit frazzled by this announcement. However, he and several others moved the piano up to the next tier of the stage. The stage had about four tiers I believe, designed for orchestral performances. A grand piano has three legs, two on the keyboard end, and one opposite. These guys could not lift the entire piano, so they lifted the keyboard end up on the next tier. As soon as the bulk of the weight of the piano rested on the single front-leg, it poked through the stage like a paper punch -- phoomp! As soon as I viewed this, I left, suppressing laughter, but there was only a slight rise in the murmur of the crowd. In the US, this would have been the cue for uproarious and unbridled laughter. When I came back down to play a few minutes later, I found they had nailed a small piece of plywood over the hole.

Don told me not to worry if the crowd was silent. He said he had first thought this meant they didn't like the performance, however, he guaranteed me that if we did well, they would give us applause at the end - and they did. It's hard to tell from the stage, but from what I've read about the concert, we lost quite a few of the audience near the beginning. I hadn't really considered it before, but apparently some people who had come were only fans of Beefheart because of the more commercial Mercury recordings. I now realize that perhaps had Don continued in that direction, he possibly would have had the kind of success he was pursuing when first approached by the Di Martinos.

Museum

Our visit in Amsterdam also included one of my most memorable moments as Don and Jan invited me to the Van Gogh museum. I was really pleased and honored. However, Don had a way of dominating the visit with his overbearing personality, so I wound up going off by myself, as I prefer to just stand quietly and drink in the visions before my eyes, almost in a meditative state. Don's style is to focus on one painting and gather everyone around him saying, "Look at that! Absolutely unbelievable! He was so hip! Can you believe that, man?" To me, although I could appreciate his enthusiasm, I really became distracted and so rather than say anything, I would sort of sneak off now and then to just stand in silent awe of Van Gogh's genius. What a moment, to stand in the presence of such work!

Lausanne, Switzerland

We flew to an airport that was miles from the actual city of Lausanne. However, the lengthy bus ride to Lausanne was one of the most beautiful of the tour. Everywhere I looked I was just astounded by the beauty. You have to remember, I live in the desert, where green is a luxury. Between the greenery and the mountains here in Switzerland, I thought I was in heaven. We arrived in the afternoon, and Tom Fowler, Bruce's brother and bassist for Jean-Luc Ponty was concerned. His bass was not on the flight. Tom and I had seemed to hit it off. I really liked his personality and highly-respected his playing, as I have come to respect all the Fowler brothers.

I recall that several times during the tour, I had displayed my nasty habit of scolding waiters for not bringing me the correct food. This was a real obvious fault of mine - obvious to everyone but me. Bruce was constantly attempting to correct my manners in restaurants and I am sure I had embarrassed him more than once -having to be identified with someone so rude and intimidating. Lausanne, however, was Bruce's turn. It had been a long day, and we had to play that night. The hotel we stayed it was rather proper, and we looked for the most part like a rag tag group of hooligans to them. I came down to wait in the lobby and I saw Bruce, looking really tired and squatting by the entrance, his back against the wall. The doorman noticed him from outside and came in, requesting he kindly move to a chair in the lobby. Bruce angrily gave him the finger and said, "Fuck off." It was the only time I ever saw Bruce be rude to anyone.

I found out later that he was having some kind of emotional turmoil due to the fact that he was in love with two women, one in Europe, and one in the states whom he lived with. I believe that the European lady had been with us for a short while on the tour. I was sharing a room with him at this particular juncture of the tour (I think we switched around to avoid growing tired of someone) and he confided this to me this evening. I felt a lot closer to Bruce after that, because I could understand how this could happen. A musician's life is so fragmented. Most would like to have a home somewhere with a mate, but being gone half the time leads to sometimes unenviable situations, of which this was one.

The concert hall was a large empty television studio and I believe the performance was filmed. They had an exquisite dressing room with plenty of food and drinks. I saved a lot of money by packing lunches for the next day while I was in these various dressing rooms. I would place it in my bag and the following day as I was hiking around to see the sites, I would park myself somewhere and have fruit, cheese, sandwiches, mineral water, and an occasional small bottle of wine. You have to remember that our per diem was $10 per day, and we usually spent twice that or more for one meal.

This performance was a television taping with a live audience. There was a wide chasm on the floor between the audience and the bands, who had to perform on the floor, while the youngish audience sat on the floor on the opposite side. It was very sterile because all the house lights were turned on and the cameras were moving around. Jean-Luc played before us, and I remember seeing a very-relieved Tom Fowler, again in possession of his bass. I listened to him warm up acoustically – he is a phenomenal player.

After the concert ended, the audience rose from their uncomfortable seats and were supposed to exit through a doorway to stage left. The scheduling caused us to be cut off early. This caused several to demand "more" and the makings of a small riot ensued. The scene was subdued by armed policeman, and the crowd left in orderly fashion. Don commented as we stood there observing this and talking with a few fans, "The Swiss are a little too proud of their watches to allow themselves to have a good time."

Train Ride / Lyon, France

We boarded a train the next day. Destination: Lyon, France. The train ride was several hours, probably 8 or 10. The cars on the train had a small corridor on one side and little compartments with no doors that seated six - three to a side. It was such a long boring ride that we all kept moving around and changing seats. I walked up and down the train several times just to exercise my legs. Don approached me early afternoon and offered to buy me a drink. This was an unusual gesture for him, and I gladly accepted. Most of the time, when Don was on the road, he was constantly with Jan, and so the conversation was limited and a little uncomfortable at times, because we couldn't talk (excuse me ladies) "man to man" or "one on one" if you will.

Don said, "Follow me" and we eventually came to a coach with a bar. I'll never forget this bar. It ran along the length of the left side about two thirds of the length of the car, and then curved into the wall. There was a large thick solid plexiglass rail around the top, held in place with shiny brass brackets. The front of the bar was layered with what appeared to be quilted copper sheeting. It was very different from any bar I had ever seen. Don and I ordered drinks and he said he'd like to make a toast or give a little informal speech, I can't remember which.

But the jist of it was that he just wanted me to know that no matter whether I left again or not, he would never forget what I had done for him. He said it had saved his life and seemed very sincere. I was really touched by this. I thought back to that hug he gave me in London just after Knebworth. I started thinking that perhaps Don had truly started to change.

This tour had been extremely pleasant so far, in complete contrast to the former tours I had done with Don, this was like being in heaven. The normal problems that one encounters on the road were still there, of course, but aside from Don's maddeningly consistent habit of alienating just about every sound man he ever worked with, he had been a real pro. His performances had been really great and he seemed absolutely happy on stage, poking fun at the audience and interjecting lots of tongue-in-cheek humor.

He had been accepted almost everywhere with open arms and successful shows. He was spotlighting every member of the band and he had a great band. Elliot had really mastered the art of playing weird music. Although shaky for the first few shows, once he had "copped the licks" his playing leapt out of his amp and the notes snarled at the audience - like...winged eels.

As I stood here in this bar coach, I felt like I had made a friend and that counted more to me than all the money in the world. I felt like I had connected with Van Vliet and said with my actions, "this is what true friendship is about." I also had struggled really hard to relay the fact that though I was a Christian, all I was trying to accomplish in my relationship with him was to treat others the way I would like to be treated. Obviously, I overlooked restaurant waiters.

I had not seen Don one time verbally abuse one member of this entourage. He did the obligatory rounds of spending a little time with each member to keep spirits up and maintain a feeling of unity in the group. I felt like he was the most successful he had ever been in terms of human relationships with his band.

Lyon

Our concert was in a large, well-aged theatre with seats. I had heard Jean-Luc Ponty's group from backstage and spent time not only with him, but with his band members. Tom Fowler is the only name I recall. However, his 1975 album, *Aurora* (Atlantic SD 18163) featured the following personnel.

Jean-Luc Ponty - electric violin, violectra, acoustic violin, autoharp
Darryl Stuermer - electric and acoustic guitars
Patrice Rushen - electric piano, acoustic piano, synthesizer
Tom Fowler - bass
Norman Fearrington - drums, percussion

These names sound amazingly familiar - especially Darryl and Norman, so I have a strong hunch that this is indeed the band he toured with.

I decided that since this was the last performance I would get a chance to hear, I would go early and listen to the entire set. The soundman didn't do a very good job with the guitarist, I think probably due to a bad microphone cable. His volume was intermittent. First, you could only hear him from the stage amp, no PA at all, and then suddenly, his guitar would burst though the sound-reinforcement system and completely drown everyone out. They eventually seemed to fix this problem, as I went backstage and had someone slip Jean a note and he called to a roadie to remedy the situation. Regretfully, that was not before half the concert was over.

However, I was still very impressed by this man and his music. I had always wished to be able to play music like this at some point in my life.

I went backstage to prepare for our show to discover that there was a problem. Apparently someone had made off with all the box office returns, rendering the sponsors of the concert unable to pay us. We waited backstage for what seemed like forever and French Police showed up backstage speaking to each other in French and leaving us totally baffled as to what was up. I could hear the audience as their impatience grew. It was almost a full hour before permission was granted by the powers that be for us to walk on stage. By this time, the audience was livid. Don decided that this would be a good night to give the finger to the audience.

It was told to us afterwards that this particular audience was upset that a Frenchman should open for an American group. Who knows? Don's salute didn't help. We played a few songs, but the audience went into a near riot. I was starting to wonder if we were going to be able to finish. As I recall, we played a very short set, 35 minutes and left the stage to angry shouts of "fuck you, Beefheart." There was a large segmented door lowered in the front of the stage to keep the audience from mobbing the bandstand.

We had to stay in Lyon for a few days. It was the most boring part of the tour. We were miles from town and cab fares were prohibitive. Jack, the road manager was sick with food poisoning, and the only recreation was a pool table, and I didn't play pool. All the television was in French of course, and nothing good on to begin with.

England

I certainly recall our first night in England. Our hotel reservations didn't start until a night later, and we had to take rooms in a much fancier hotel. I remember going into the room, turning on the TV and there was a *Streets Of San Francisco* re-run - in English! I almost kneeled in prayer to give thanks. I'd just spent several incredibly boring days with nothing to do but watch *The Untouchables* with French voice-overs.

Bruce, Denny and I went into the hotel's café to have some dinner. It was a very posh little place with wrought-iron furniture painted a sparkling white while the walls were pink and white stripes - very feminine and much like an American ice cream parlor. The clientele were obviously well to do and looked at me as though I should have a begging bowl in my hands.

I remember that dessert came with the meal. It was sort of an upside down custard with syrup lightly poured on top. I had one bite, and something went down the wrong way. I wound up, coughing, spluttering and gasping for air, with pudding coming out my nose and feeling a bit embarrassed. Was this kharma? Had I been rude to one waiter too many?

When I was finally able to take a breath, it sound like a giant reverse-burp and for several minutes I made this noise with each breath. It was if I had swallowed a giant elephant-seal call. I couldn't leave as I had to pay the cheque and so there I sat, totally embarrassed, grossing-out the hoity-toities. It's hysterical as I write about it. Who said, "humor is chaos recollected in tranquility?" Thornton Wilder if I recall. I must be in tranquility, because that was certainly chaos, and I'm certainly laughing.

Unfortunately, I recall little about the individual performances in England / Britain. However, thanks to the Electricity website, I was able to copy the names and dates and some comments from eyewitnesses which have helped to spur on my memory. Thanks again to Theo Tieman for this work.

UNIVERSITY, WARWICK, ENGLAND
70 Miles NW of London
November 12, 1975

CIVIC HALL, GUILDFORD, ENGLAND
45 Miles SW of London
November 13, 1975

NEW VICTORIA THEATRE, LONDON, ENGLAND,
November 14, 1975,
Two Shows: 6:15 p.m., 10:45 p.m.

Boy, those shows are a long way apart, 4½ hours. While sitting in the dressing room a familiar female face appeared at the door. She had been one of the "band of gypsies" - the Knebworth Band's lady companions for most of the time we were in England. "Come in," I said. I can't recall her name, but she was an extremely attractive and very proper-speaking young woman barely in her twenties if that. I saw that our former visit over here had affected her in a very real way, she was, in fact expecting Jimmy Carl Black's child... The child would be born in April 1976.

I sat and spoke with her about the effect this had on her life. She had decided to have the child and raise it. Her father, especially, was extremely upset and she had to move out of her parent's home (they were quite wealthy if I recall) and live in a small flat. I really had enjoyed this girl's company on the last trip, as she rode with us in the limousine and had dinner with us several times. I would have loved to have known her better myself, as I had felt very compatible with her.

All my Christian values aside, having sex on the road is a strong probability - its very likely to happen. You find yourself in situations where it's just almost impossible to have the willpower to refuse. It's very lonely and in a sense a man is much more likely to give in. Some guys go looking for it every chance they get. I tried to avoid situations like this because I believe that sex is a special thing between two people and something spiritual passes between them. Kirlian photography revealed some kind of energy exchange between couples kissing.

I also know this bothered Jan to an extent and for some reason, on my occasional slips (I think once on this tour, although it probably looked like twice) I felt a little guilty knowing that she knew - perhaps because I always respected her so much. Also, it was just plain common sense to realize that recreational sex is to blame for bringing a lot of misery into the world in the form of unplanned babies, STDs etc. This little child that this girl was carrying might never really know his or her real father. I find that to be a tragedy in itself. However, sources have revealed that in the years before Jimmy's untimely death, a woman came to one of the Grandmothers' concerts and introduced herself as his daughter - perhaps the same child.

The shows went quite well at the New Victoria. Herbie was there. We actually had some young girl come up on stage and grab Don as he was singing. She was immediately subdued by a stage-hand, who was almost "too efficient" to make it seem believable. Don later said, "It really hurt, man, she squeezed my ribcage!" I had a feeling that Herbie was "baiting the tip jar" to see if Beefheart had any sex appeal to the female fans. He was standing to stage right, watching the show carefully. He always wore these white short-sleeved shirts with Nehru-type collars. They looked like designer doctor's dusters. He was a strange one, but there was something very likeable about him. I liked his no-nonsense approach.

It was a great night and I remember thinking to myself that Elliot had really mastered the Beefheart guitar sound that night. He was playing so relaxed and so well. The band was great, Denny was absolutely flawless. Bruce's free-form soloing always included a little of the song *Perdido*, and that was my cue to get up and tap-dance. I still have a picture of myself tap dancing on stage at New Victoria. Don and Jan gave it to me as a Christmas present. They even signed it. Don was in fine form that night. He was playing with the audience and had in fact learned all his lyrics, but would hesitate sometimes as if searching for words. Inevitably, someone would sing the next line - "prompting him" - and he would continue. I think it was less forgetting than playing with the crowd. He was smiling at the audience, and seemed totally relaxed. I think the sound system here was one of the better systems. That always helped Don tremendously.

After the show, I recall walking down a hallway with the entourage and Herb Cohen came up beside me and started speaking about Mallard - the other Magic Band. He said that if anyone were to ask me about those guys, that I was to tell them I didn't know anything about what they were doing. I think I joked with him saying something like, "Why Herbie, that would by lying and you wouldn't want me to lie now would you?" It was my gentle way of telling him that I didn't feel good about lying about my friends. In no way did I feel that they posed a threat to Don, and even if they did, maybe a little competition would make him realize it might be a good idea to learn his lyrics before he walked on stage.

A few days later, I read a little review of the show in Melody Maker by "The Raver" which said:

Captain Beefheart's concert last Friday at London's New Victoria Theatre was a painful demonstration of this artist's continuing creative decline. The current line up of the Magic Band, with the exception of slide guitarist Denny Walley, is extremely poor. Winged Eel Fingerling, particularly, proved an inept axeman.

They sounded like a K-Tel version of the Magic Band. Even Alberto Y Lost Trios Paranoias - in their justly celebrated parody of Beafheart (sic) - sounds more authentic. Big Eyed Beans From Venus - performed as an encore - redeemed matters slightly, but it was too late - the damage had been done.[65]

I found this a little disturbing, as it was the first show of which we had read a review. I thought, "could I have been that wrong in my evaluation?" Don was upset and made some inquiries on the phone. He found out that the fellow who wrote that was not even there and just had written the opinion of some friend who showed up. Also, the Raver was not a single person, but just a collective name under which a group of critics submitted short reviews. I don't know if this is true or not, but I do know that Vivien Goldman (Sounds - 2 / 11 / 75) Angus MacKinnon (sorry, have the article but no date or title of publication) and Chas De Whalley (also no publication or date) had very positive things to say about the concert, more in line with what I was perceiving from the stage. So, that's three against one.

FREE TRADE HALL, MANCHESTER, ENGLAND
Mid Island East Coast near Liverpool
November 15, 1975

THE EMPIRE, LIVERPOOL, ENGLAND
November 16, 1975

This night definitely had a wild crowd who seemed to enjoy the new Magic Band very much. After the show, in fact, when no encore was offered, people started storming the stage and they had to bring down the "iron curtain."

TOWN HALL, BIRMINGHAM, ENGLAND
November 18, 1975

I read in notes from audience participant Steve Froy that this wasn't such a good show. Hecklers had made it almost impossible for Don to get through *Orange Claw Hammer*. This happened occasionally, unfortunately. Many of the audiences seemed to expect to hear a mind-numbing hypnotic "rock" band, with guitarist skidding around on stage wagging their tongues at the crowd and a lead singer who raised the enthusiasm level by screaming the worn-out question; "is everybody ready to ROCK 'N' ROLL?" Instead, they heard something they couldn't really comprehend, and were too close-minded to accept. Their brains couldn't handle it. However, I also

[65] Melody Maker, Nov 22, 1975, Hot Licks by the Raver

think the band was weak in one respect: no bass player. Bruce is a great trombonist, but trombone is only a substitute for bass, and since much of the early material contained chords in the bass lines, the music was lacking. Trombone can only play one note at a time. Rockette Morton left a difficult pair of shoes to fill.

EDINBURGH UNIVERSITY, EDINBURGH, SCOTLAND
November 19, 1975

Note: This is a speculation on my part, as there are conflicting dates in the official records.

We were driven by coach to Edinburgh. I ate something that disagreed with me and had to call a Doctor. He checked me out and said I would live, but I was completely delirious at the show.

I had a nap before the show and a most intriguing dream that was more like a series of vivid images. I described it on tape and transcribed it for you here:

A snail crawling down through a path of dried egg yolk
On the open top of a wicker trash container
A baby; one head beautiful, another head twisted and pulled to the side
Mouth drawn with a thread pulling from the left tonsil
The stomach and torso are like a flesh chicken head
With drawn-in-ink features, not really there, but rudimentary
A beautiful girl putting on a ballet shoe in a series of pictures
A dream… Her parents applauding as I kiss the series of pictures
The phone in the top of milk with the small pointed baby nipple
Pushed up through foam, a windmill churning in water
An endless watchband painting, view of Holland's movement
The end of the watchband on a gear constantly moving.
The watch is from the fifties, square with black face
Turns into square people with black faces
Televisions, church, outline of black steeple
 With neon letters that say Baby Ben
A jig saw puzzle with lines that move like molasses
The baby takes a walk as a dog on a leash
Following a dog on a leash
Small baby, smaller dog; striped shirt.
Ends up walking in a distorted camera view
Parent's legs only visible, seamed stockings.
An empty toothpaste tube with pointed end
Drops upside down dropping yellow thick fluid into
A coyote with oil well drills for teeth
Walking through artificial snow
A plateful of dead flies dropped from several miles high
Lands and retains each fly
She's Scandinavian, but she look's Italian
Oh, God, how could you make that?
A red neon rod protruded through the eyelid
People in the backwoods united in the form of quicksand
A concave navel protrudes convex and forms a small baby's head
With a yellow cracked blonde top knot,

A man asks for help with no visitation.
This particular dog bone was buried for years
Changed into the form of a meteor
Shot up in the air, with surrounding vegetation blasting aside.
Destroyed cars, boats, houses, yachts, merry-go-rounds, schools, churches, popsicles, comic books, camera lens, luggage.
The maid came in sprayed with dark-oiled rubber.
The whites of her eyes were turned on.
Hitchcock was ready for the hitch
The Umpire did a rain dance.

Must have been something I ate…

The bandstand looked like a temporary riser type portable stage. I was on a riser in the back, and there were windows behind us, which makes the sound awful. The beginning of the show was stalled due to technical difficulties and Don said to watch him for the cue to begin *Moonlight On Vermont*. Mind you, I was really sick, though I think only Don realized that I wasn't feeling well. Don was off to my right and I just sat and stared at him, with the unending attention span one had when they want to be done with something. I was focused like a dog waiting for its master to drop a crumb under the table.

Finally, Don gave me the cue and without even looking, I started off the drum intro to *Moonlight On Vermont* only a second too late to view Bruce and Denny unplugged and talking to some audience members at the front of the stage. Elliot came in and for about one second, everyone was madly rushing for instruments. I just stopped. Elliot stopped. Bruce, really embarrassed, looked at me and asked, "What'd you do that for, asshole?"

I still have to laugh at this, because Bruce came from a large family and so this was a brotherly kind of scold more than an insult. Also, he didn't realize that I was almost hallucinating. I have no idea how the show went, but I started perking up as I played and by the end of the set, I had evidently sweated all the toxins out of my body. I felt fine. Then, when I tried to explain my mistake at the beginning, it seemed like either a big lie, or that I had been the recipient of divine healing.

A couple of young women (early twenties) had followed us to several concert performances. One of these girls spent the night in my room. The reason I mention this is because I had double beds and she slept in one, and I slept in the other. She asked me to give her a hug goodnight, like a little girl asking her father, but no sex happened between us. The next day, when we went down to breakfast, she was hanging all over me like we were on our honeymoon, evidently to impress everyone else that we had indeed frolicked all night long. She gave me a passionate kiss goodbye - the one and only kiss of our brief and public romance. It was really an odd experience.

Later, Don told me to watch out for her. She had almost filed a paternity suit against a guy in the 1974 touring band which caused him a lot of trouble. He'd never been with her, and she hadn't even been pregnant - which makes proof of paternity quite difficult I would think. From then on I avoided her like the plague.

Cardiff University, Cardiff, Wales - November 21, 1975
We were on a train all the way to Cardiff, arriving late and not actually performing until the following night. I recall nothing specific about the performance itself, although I have a lot of disjointed memories unrelated to any particular spot. On the itinerary, it just said Cardiff and I didn't realize Cardiff was in Wales at the time. We had been on a train all day the following day from Edinburgh, and checked in late the night before. As I said, I was ill in Edinburgh, and although

feeling better after the concert, I still felt weak and groggy upon my first awakening in Cardiff. I switched on the tube and watched a newscast, realizing I couldn't understand what was being said, although it sounded as it were being spoken in a British accent. For a millisecond I hilariously thought "my God, I have lost my mind and can no longer understand English." I quickly called the desk to hear, "Desk" at the other end of the phone. I was slightly relieved and asked for the time. I had a great laugh after hanging up the phone. I then realized we must be in Wales. Give me a break, I was still half-asleep, OK?

It may have been here that our road manager Jack, had received the payment for the concert in cash and had taken it to his room to count. Exhausted from the trip, he fell asleep with all the cash on the bed and his door ajar. Don and Bruce sneaked in his room and took all the money, hiding it in Don's room. When Jack awoke, I am sure he was quite surprised, and was desperate to come up with an explanation. Don relayed this story to me later, but said, "Don't say anything to Jack, I think he feels bad enough." I found this to be surprising behavior for Don, who used to be the first to publicly criticize business associates at the drop of a hat.

Friars Club, New Vale Hall, Aylesbury, England November 22, 1975

A band called The Secret Oyster joined us for the English tour. I'm not exactly sure when Jean-Luc ended and Oyster began, but I think our last stop with Ponty was Lyon, France. This is the first time Secret Oyster is mentioned in the webpage notes, however. They were a Danish group with a kind of fusion style, though I never really heard their shows. Most of the time, I was in the dressing room, tuning a guitar and warming up my tap shoes. They loved to talk. There was absolutely incessant chattering in their native tongue at high volumes, which became almost unbearable at times on the coach. Don, half-kidding, would occasionally yell out, "What's that in real money?" hoping they would take the hint and tone it down a bit. It never did any good.

I stood out in front and watched them play this one night. The venue seemed to be like a mall or something, and we were in some roped off area. The audience sort of milled around directly in front of us, which was rather distracting. The audience was rude and at the end of a very short set I got up and kicked my bass drum over in frustration. Unfortunately, I didn't realize that The Secret Oyster had miked my drums with their own personal drum mikes, the best of which got knocked off the stand, rolled into the crowd, and was immediately stolen.

When I found out about this, I made arrangements to pay for the mike. As I recall, they wouldn't hear of it, but finally settled for a partial payment.

Southampton University, Southampton, England - November 24, 1975

It seems there was a platform in front of the stage which was set up with a mike underneath for my little tap dance moment. I remember jumping down to this stage only to realize that it had been hastily assembled and lacked sufficient bracing. As a result, I almost spring-boarded myself into the audience. The stage was a temporary stage and the house lights were up a bit which ruined the atmosphere.

Dome, Brighton, England - November 25, 1975

In reading observances written by Ben Waters[66] I am reminded a bit of this concert I recall Don saying, "That clock makes me nervous," pointing to a clock facing the stage. It was a clock opposite the stage. It seems like this stage was one of the tiered types and I tap danced to the top and back down again. If I remember correctly, this is also where a group of handicapped people came to see the show, and Don was very touched by this. They were all in wheelchairs, and he watched them wheeled back into a large Van after the show. He said something like "Wow! It's really nice that they came." In fact, if I recall, he wouldn't get on the coach to leave until they were all loaded up and on their way. He was genuinely touched by their attendance.

[66] Captain Beefheart and His Magic Band Timeline, 1975, http://home.nordwest.net/dj/perf75.html

A New Wardrobe

Don would sometimes knock on the door of my room in the evening. Fortunately, he had finally learned that I don't appreciated being awakened at 3:00 a.m. out of a sound sleep and asked to record a song idea. He was constantly wearing new outfits. He would say, "I've been over here so many times, I know how to get great deals. He would be wearing pants from Yves Saint Laurant and say, "Do you know how much I paid for these, man?" and then emphatically, "TWO DOLLARS!" or some other outrageously low figure.

He had one black outfit he wore quite often. It was a wool cloak and trousers. It had an old timey vampirish look. I really thought it was a great stage costume and he wore it often during the British leg of this tour. He said that it was from Yves Saint Laurant also and gave me another outrageously low figure for price.

One day, I was walking in London on a day off. Don and Jan were in a cab and spying me, hailed to me from the open window and offered a lift into town. I went to a place that sold China. All the pieces were from broken sets, or they were "seconds" that had some small flaw. My mother had asked me to pick her up a "fancy tea cup" and so I thought this would be the perfect opportunity. Don and Jan were next door, and apparently Jan was having riding boots custom-made.

Walk Around London

I bought a china cup and saucer and headed off on foot to just walk around London for a while. I was looking for a specific drum shop, because I wanted to purchase some spare parts for my Caroline drum pedals that I couldn't get in the states. I never found the drum shop however. But it was a wonderful time. I walked around just taking in London and gazing at the sights. There was an outdoor food market, and then Piccadilly Circus. I recall as I walked through Piccadilly some bloke walking the opposite direction walked by and leaned over quickly and loudly whispering "ACID" which struck me extremely funny. I just stood there and belly-laughed, on the sidewalk, people staring at me like I was a maniac.

BRUNEL UNIVERSITY, UXBRIDGE, ENGLAND
November 26, 1975

GUILDFORD UNIVERSITY, GUILDFORD, ENGLAND
November 27, 1975

COLSTON HALL, BRISTOL, ENGLAND
November 28, 1975

LEEDS UNIVERSITY, LEEDS, ENGLAND
November 29, 1975

THE GUILDHALL, PORTSMOUTH, ENGLAND
December 1, 1975

Another place, which I am sure had to be either Warwick, Portsmouth, or Bristol, because it was about a 2 hour coach trip. Our road manager, Jack, had miscalculated how long it would take to reach the hall, and so we arrived nearly an hour late. We rushed onto stage after a few moments in the dressing room. Bruce was having trouble with his Octavider, which meant that he couldn't make "bass" tones, but would be playing an octave higher. The audience seemed quite hostile. I recall there being a tiered-stage again and I danced up to the top during my tap dance, sat on the top tiers and screamed at the top of my lungs like a wild animal.

For some reason, this seemed to actually have a calming effect on the crowd. I came down to the front and poured my whole bottle of drinking water on my head in essence saying, "Cool down." It seemed to work. Bruce finally got up and running. After the show, some rather attractive lady came up, kissed me passionately (and quite well) and asked me to come home with her. I told her I was staying in London, riding a bus etc. She then offered to drive me home the next day. I looked at the bus and back at this young lady and said, "I'm the musical director, so I may be needed, thanks anyway."

Later, I regretted this a bit, as I really liked this girl and had a very pleasant conversation with her prior to our departure. Aside from the obvious sexual implications, however, it would have been fun to stay with some locals and experience the actual lifestyles that some of our fans lived. However, my wish not to father any unknown children caused me to avoid many situations like this. I gave her my white scarf and boarded the bus. The guys rewarded me by telling me what a wimp I was.

I unfortunately cannot remember which performances match which memories. But I will attempt a few more impressions of live stage shows.

An example of my rudeness during this tour was in one town in which we stayed overnight, so it must have been quite a distance from London. I didn't know at the time that I had blood sugar problems, and so I would become like a monster when I was hungry. This one night, we had arrived early for a sound check and had to stay until the performance was over. I was desperately looking for a restaurant, a café, or anything, as I had brought no food along. I walked into a small cafeteria that was attached to the hall and was looking around for someone from whom I could glean information. A man rushed in behind me and demanded to know what I was doing in there. I tried to explain, but he very snobbily told me that I wasn't allowed in here and must leave immediately or he would call the authorities, to which I said, "Fuck you, quit being such an asshole!" and walked out.

Later, when we were actually allowed in to the restaurant, I could tell right away that the waiter found me to be "low class," probably because being on the road gives you a slightly disheveled look, plus I had the long hair. I asked about the salad bar (in the states, you can serve yourself at many) and wanted to know if I could make my own. "Of course not," he snapped, "You tell me what you want and I'll prepare it for you." By this time, Bruce had come in along with a couple others. We all sat together and the waiter brought me a salad, which not even vaguely resembled my request. "This is not what I ordered," I said, a bit impatiently.

I repeated my order and he brought me back another salad, even less similar to what I asked for. "Maybe you should write this down, because your memory and comprehension sucks," I said, and sent back yet another. Although I was not the type of person to complain in restaurants, I needed to eat well, and I was weary of restaurants.

Bruce was totally embarrassed by this. "Come on, John." He said, "Give the guy a break." My reply was: "I seem to recall being the first at this table, and if you don't like my manners, find your own damned table. If I have to send this waiter back fifty times, he is going to give me the salad I want." So, as you can see, the tour had by this time started to take a toll on my patience and health. Touring is very difficult, especially when you're dealing, as we were, with reckless or drunken (or both) coach drivers, inept road managers, and rude waiters.

As I look back, I suppose now that part of my attitude was if I stayed a bit "on edge," Don would shy away from the kind of meetings that I was fearful of seeing come to pass. None of the others had experienced the "cult version" of the Magic Band, nor seen Don rail out at someone. I had, and I wasn't about to leave myself or anyone else open for that kind of treatment.

CHAPTER THIRTY SIX:
THE TAILOR DOESN'T MEASURE UP

bo at Knebworth Festival July '75.
courtesy of Gregory Davidson.

Derek Taylor - Warner's British Office

The tour finally came to an end. There is always a certain melancholy that settles over one at the end of something like this. It's a sad moment. I think this is one reason why most people would rather work at a regular job and do the same thing every day for forty years. That's about the only way to avoid this depression, this roller coaster of emotions. I was sad. I love Europe. There is something wonderful to me about traveling - especially in Europe.

Don came to me the morning we were scheduled to leave and asked me to stay on an extra day or two. I was frustrated because I had already planned on leaving and was exhausted. He wanted me to go with him to the Warner's British office, which was headed by Derek Taylor. I had last seen a drunken Taylor in Hollywood, at his going-away party in 1967. He had been the Beatles' press agent for a time, then worked for A&M, and finally here, at Warner's UK. He was, as I recall, president of the UK branch of Warner.

We went to the Warner's office the next day. A youngish-looking man answered, and I supposed him to be Derek's assistant. "Hello, Derek, how are you?" Don greeted him. I was astounded. Derek looked ten years younger than he had looked 8 years previously. I couldn't hide my astonishment, until Derek explained that he had quit drinking several years before, and was feeling much better.

The room was furnished more like a study/library than an office, with bookshelves lining the walls and a large sectional sofa to the right. His desk was to the left. There was a coffee table in front of the sofa, and someone brought us tea. Derek said there was something he wanted to show us. He was explaining that the biggest cause of the problems in Britain at the present time was the lack of commitment to the church. I found this to be interesting, as he seemed so much more pleasant and healthy so I wondered if there was a connection. He put on a video he had recorded of some old black and white film. It was a British film and this scene depicted a boy and man talking, and the man giving the boy advice about the church. I was less impressed with the clip than Derek's insistence that we watch it. AA stresses a belief in God, though I think calling God "my higher power" is a misnomer in a sense. Very politically correct, but theologically wrong.

Don sat thumbing through royalty statements and records of sales. He actually didn't seem to have any questions, but was just checking out sales of *Clear Spot*, I believe.

We Came Back For Holidays

The plane flight back was rather uneventful. Don and Jan had bought a considerable amount of clothing contained within a big soft bag. They talked me into carrying this on the flight and checking my carry-on bag. I suspected that they asked me to stay over for this very purpose. The bag was huge, and I had to put it on the floor and set my feet on it, which made the whole flight back quite uncomfortable.

Homecoming

After the horror of hours in customs, we were "released" and hired a station wagon taxi to drive us to the parking lot in back of Discreet Records. I had left my keys there so that Dick Barber could start the car occasionally - keeping the battery charged. It was late, so when I called Herb Cohen at home, he said my keys were in an envelope in the bar next door. I retrieved them but found my car was already unlocked. I opened the door and a suffocating stench billowed out.

"What are you doing in my house?" screamed this "thing" in my car. It sounded like a man, and looked like an ugly woman. In my dazed stupor after a 12 hour flight, 2 hours in custom, and another hour driving here. I answered, "This isn't your house, it's my car." "This isn't a car," she (a gender I still guess at) cackled, "Why it doesn't even have an engine!" "Oh no," I thought, "Someone stole my engine." I actually looked under the hood. The engine was there. A bag lady

650

had taken up residence in my car. "Get OUT," I screamed angrily at this poor thing. She immediately obeyed, grabbed her shopping cart, and was on her way. The driver of the car joked with Don, "I think she wanted another month on the lease."

The car was defiled with the stench of human waste. The front seat seemed fine, she had been in the back. I looked in the trunk and found some packing quilts and laid them over the front seat. "Don't get in there, man," Don said, "Ride with us, we'll get Jan's folks to take us home." I decided however to tough it out. I put my bags in the trunk and got in, the car started. "I'll be OK." I said. Don told me later that Jan cried when she realized how badly defiled my car was.

It was really cold, but I drove with the windows down and my face outside, freezing, so that I could breathe fresh air. The next day, I looked at the car. The back floor, behind the drivers seat, had been used for a month as a bathroom. The refuse was 5 inches thick and had to be shoveled out. I took all the seats out of the car, ripped out the carpeting and threw everything away. Nothing was left but a metal floorboard. I took the hose and washed it out completely and let the water drain out holes in the bottom. The overhead and door panels were steam cleaned, and I took a front seat that was reduced to nothing but bare springs to the upholstery shop. They took a bottle of deodorizer used in cargo planes and poured the whole bottle inside the car to rid of the stench.

Don and Jan felt so badly about the car that they gave me $100 to help re-upholster the front seat and carpet the floor. The shop was done in two days and I went and picked up my $100 car sans the rear seat.

Relatives For Holidays

I remember sleeping about 12 hours a day for three days or so until I made up for jet lag. I was up half the night, and my father, who had a sleeping disorder, was usually up in the middle of the night, so I would go and talk with him. I lived diagonally to them in a small alley house. It was near Christmas time and my brother (from Wyoming) Phil, his wife Joyce and their kids Toni, Todd and Traci had come for a visit. I was able to spend time with them - for the first time in six years. The kids all got roller skates for Christmas, so I took them out to the Community College and they were able to skate around the entire campus with nary a soul around.

FZ Tour

We played four dates on a short tour with Frank Zappa between Christmas and New Year, ending up at the Inglewood Forum. My local friends all thought I was really "big-time" because I was playing the Forum. For me, at this point in time, it was like playing in the boy's gym during an assembly, and the acoustics were about as bad.

Paramount Theater, Oakland, California - December 26, 1975

We were staying in San Francisco at a Japanese style hotel near Winterland. They drove us by limousine to the concert location. It was my first time on the bay bridge. There was a steady, "bump, bump" as the tires drove across the seams in the roadway. I remember Henry Kaiser showed up at this show and brought a chart with the main chords to *One Red Rose That I Mean.* Opening my clothes bag, I discovered that I hadn't packed my stage clothes and had to wear an old pair of overalls that I wore to protect my clothes when setting up. So, I did my tap dance dressed like a car mechanic that evening.

Winterland, San Francisco, California - December 27, 1975

Denny Walley: I think Perellis was the road mangler (sic) at that time.
John French: Oh, yeah I remember him wanting to get the band downstairs when we played

Winterland, so he set off the fire alarm in the hotel.
DW: He did that to us the whole time we were on tour. That was his famous trick.
JF: Geez!
DW: That's why on one of the album covers that Calvin did, it has a fire extinguisher there labeled Perellis.

I had marked Perellis for a jerk on the plane flight up. He came and sat next to me on the flight with that "I've found my target" look on his face, and tried to frighten me with scary stories about plane crashes and severed limbs. I escalated the fear level with horror stories my nurse mother had told me from her experiences in emergency rooms. He left, disheartened.

John French: You were talking about the concert at Winterland.
Denny Walley: That was memorable to me because that was the one where the audience started booing and throwing things at us, after Don had given the finger to somebody. Somebody had given the finger to him. Frank was the headliner. We had opened for him. Frank used to give the finger a lot - to the audience - it was a way of saying "Hi!" To Don, it was a way of saying, "Fuck You!" So, he got pissed off and got right in the guys face with it and the next thing you know a lot of people were angry and they started booing and throwing shit. He left the stage and the band just played Alice In Blunderland. We played and they loved it, it was great. Elliot played the solo for the first time since they recorded it - exact. It sounded fabulous. As soon as the song ended and they saw Don coming out, the audience started up again. It was constant heckling and stuff. Don would start yelling at the audience. One of the things he meant to say was, "It's like trying to turn a jar of pickles back into a cucumbers." But he would say, "It's like trying to turn a cucumber back into a jar of pickles." At the end, when we did finish and went back in the dressing room, I went in there and Don had broken out the lights and was still breaking them, in the mirror, in the ceiling. It was just raining glass. I was just furious. I said, "Hey listen, I didn't start playing guitar and start doing all this touring just to have stuff thrown at me. He said, "Hey man, don't you know! I wanted them to do that! I like that! That's what I wanted." I told him, "I don't want any more of that shit, if this is the way it's going to be, I'm outta here!" I had a little hissy fit.
JF: Well, it sounds like it wasn't exactly unwarranted.
DW: Yeah, you know. I learned. That kind of stuff - not the audience taunting - but his temperament, it could go anywhere at any time.

I remember watching Frank's show from backstage. Terry Bozzio did a great drum solo. I envied him being able to work in a more conventional situation - that is if one can call Zappa conventional. I can, because compared to what I was involved in, he was. It seemed a good show from backstage. I tried to take pictures, but they were through a glass partition. It was a strange setup at Winterland. I recall them having some sound equipment in the backstage area and big couches and glass windows so you could sit and watch the show from behind.

Golden Hall, San Diego, California - December 28, 1975
It was a great hotel, but an uneventful concert. The audience was mostly a Zappa crowd and gave us a lukewarm response. I remember Frank had this big black guy with a shaved head who was his bodyguard. I spent some time talking to this fellow and found out that bodyguards like this go through extensive security training and are masters of martial arts. I was thinking, yeah, since Frank was thrown into an orchestra pit, he has probably been more than a little fearful in crowds.

We had breakfast with Frank and several members of the band. As I recall, it was a pleasant experience, mostly small talk. The concert was at midday if I recall. We left the next morning and arrived back in LA behind Discreet Records about 2 in the afternoon. We rode on one of two tour buses Frank had rented. It was an extremely comfortable and pleasant drive. Some of the guys played cards. I worked on *Bat Chain Puller* material on my guitar. Touring like this would have been very pleasant.

LA Forum - New Year

This was one of the last times I dated Helen. I called her up, thinking that she may enjoy seeing the show and finding out what it was like backstage at the Forum etc. She had strong ambitions to become a journalist, and I thought this might give her a good inside perspective on rock concerts. I was still very much in love with her - the bonding had never gone away. It was just good to spend some time near her.

Originally, Todd Rundgren was supposed to be on the ticket, with us opening, then Todd, then Zappa. However, Todd had to cancel for some reason and so Dr. John became the substitute. Jeff Tepper was visiting from Trinidad and had come to the concert all excited about seeing not only Don, but also Todd Rundgren. It was obvious he was a big fan, although he played it down in front of Don.

Dr. John

I had heard stories about Dr. John from Don. He said that this fellow was quite deeply immersed in black magic. Dr. John supposedly carried a bag with all kinds of herbs and potions and went around sprinkling powders on the stage and studios in order to cast good spells on his sessions and performances. Van Vliet called him a "great pianist."

Van Vliet took Helen and I backstage to meet him and as I walked through the door, I was most surprised by how much younger he looked than I had imagined. He hardly said a thing and seemed to look at me as though his whole role was to scope me out. I recall that he had two bags on his shoulder, had a cane, a top hat on, and was bent over from the weight of the bags, and that was the way he stood. I told him that I enjoyed his rhythmic approach in music and mentioned a few I'd heard. I sort of felt peculiar as we left, because he just stood and looked at me most of the time.

Concert At Forum

Our 1976 New Year's Eve performance at the forum was fine. Nothing extraordinary. Denny recalls Elliot having a date and being high on acid. He said that Elliot played a couple of songs before realizing his guitar wasn't plugged in - not the first time he had done this. I recall Bruce and Denny making a big deal about doing *Poofter's Froth Wyoming*, - the *Bongo Fury* satire on the Bicentennial Celebration. I didn't want to do it. It wasn't "Beefheart-like" and sort of flopped. It didn't appear that anyone in the crowd really "got" the lyrics. They just seem to have the reaction, "Why is this Beefheart-guy doing a country song?"

Of course, like any big room, everything you play just gets washed out in this big echo chamber and it never seems solid. It's like playing watered-down music. We did have Zappa's own personal sound and lighting system. My impression was that Zappa's crowd was not at all Beefheart's crowd. There was a small section that overlapped, sharing tastes in both styles, but they really were, for the most part, quite different.

A New Wardrobe

In early January, I went in to Herb's office to collect my $1,000 that they promised me for being musical director. Herb pulled a file out and began looking at it disapprovingly. He sat silent for a short time, reading and looking at numbers. "What's this about Don spending over $1,000 on clothes?" he asked. I thought about all those "great deals" Don had found on his Yves St. Laurent clothes - those "five-dollar" pants and Jan's custom riding boots. I had once again been duped by Don. "My musical director money was spent on clothes, right?" "Right!" Herb affirmed. A thousand dollars in 1976 money was a lot of money. You could buy an amazing amount then compared to now. In fact, you could buy several Yves St. Laurent outfits and a pair of custom-made riding boots.

I had ridden down to the Discreet Office with Don and Jan that day, and I left the office and got into the back of their Volvo sedan. I was angry but mostly disappointed, but I didn't say a word, because after years of experience with Don, I had come to understand that he would deny anything that made him look bad. I was betrayed by someone who had "posed" as my friend, and someone who I had just spent the last six months of my life helping. I reasoned to myself that I would finish this album and be done with Don for good. "How could I be such a sap? I must have "sucker" written all over me!" I thought to myself. To be fair, with the information I have now, I realize that Herbie could have been the guy who duped me. But I still remember all those Yves St. Laurent outfits and am sure that's where the money went. Plus, Don's history showed this kind of financial situation occurring constantly.

When the tour was over, and all my expenses were paid, I had cleared $78. I was told that I definitely would be paid $1,000 for being musical director of the album - plus Union studio fees.

As I think about the 1975 fall tour, it was actually the only truly pleasant Magic Band road experience (I actually did only three major tours, so my experience was limited). I confidently speculate that it was completely due to the fact that it was a "band of men" - not of boys. Denny, Bruce, Elliot and myself were all mature musicians who would never bow to the ridiculous cult-like environment that I and the former band had formerly and naively tolerated. During this tour, there wasn't a single "talk." Don would occasionally say something negative about someone else, but that was a far as it went.

This was a rather new experience for Don, and I think it was definitely a healthier environment, not only for him but for the group than having a bunch of paranoid and adoring "Fan Boys" fawning over him. Whether it was healthier or not however, Don quickly migrated back to the fan-boy environment as soon as the opportunity presented itself.

Changes
The year 1976 started with difficulty. The wind taken out of my sails, I felt I was re-living the shadows of the past. My inspiration was gone like smoke in the wind. There was a steady stream of "I told you so's" going through my mind, racing along like a tiny vehicle stuck on a mobius strip. I had hoped that Don had changed his perspective and valued the friendship I had offered. My eyes had been opened again by doing a tour and not getting paid. It was all an act: everything Van Vliet had done was just part of the same act, and that act always had the same agenda - the furthering of Van Vliet - no matter what the cost to anyone. The blinders had fallen off my eyes in a very different way.

John French to Snouffer: I kept thinking he was going to change. He was like, "Mr. Cooperative." Then I could see the crap start to happen, and when we got back from the tour, that's when I realized: this man will not change. I thought "When am I gonna learn that this guy is not any good?" and "Why am I wasting my time working with him?"
Alex Snouffer: Yeah, a chameleon can change colors, but it's still a chameleon.

Bruce Fowler Leaves
After a meeting with Fowler at the rubber room, it was decided that he would not be playing "air-bass" on the album. Bruce's reactions to the charts were, for the most part, quite negative. He

said in essence that the music "couldn't be played." I think it was a combination of the fact that the music (we focused on Seam Crooked Sam) was very unconventional and had the questionable birth of being transcribed by an ignorant drummer, which left serious doubts as to it's validity. In order to convince Bruce it could be played, I played Seam Crooked Sam on guitar from beginning to end along with the tape. Of course, I had been working on it for several months, and so had it memorized.

Bruce then attempted to play the bass tones to *Seam Crooked Sam* on the trombone, playing the bottom lines of the piano transcription. However, Bruce was at an extreme disadvantage. The bass note rhythms were difficult because Don's rhythmic perspective when playing piano caused him to play the left hand, which plays the "lower" notes or "bass" notes, on the "up beats" seldom actually on the beat. By this I mean, he plays "in-between" the right hand notes quite often. The bass notes are so rhythmically dependent on the right hand notes that they are quite awkward to play independently. It would be like having two people speak a sentence, each alternately speaking the next word in order. Also, he was dealing with my rough transcription, which I found adequate, but was probably difficult for anyone to sight-read. Bruce found it to be a pointless and frustrating exercise.

This didn't disturb me a great deal, although I knew I would greatly miss Bruce's personality in the group. He was a fun guy to be around and a man of amazing intelligence. In my mind however, the "Air-Bass" would never be an adequate replacement for a regular bass - played "Rockette" style. I looked forward to a more appropriate instrument to fill the bass position. However, emotionally, I knew it was the last time I would probably work with Bruce and he is a man I greatly enjoyed not only working with, but also with whom I spent many enjoyable hours.

Elliot Ingber Leaves

Elliot, of course, had a fear of not being able to "cop the licks" as he would often say. Once he heard the material, I think he realized it was more trouble than it was worth for him. He also left the band at this time. My reaction was mixed. I loved Elliot, yet I knew he was right. The demands this material placed on the musician were not Elliot's strongest areas as a player. The *Bat Chain Puller* material needed a totally different kind of player.

Looking Back On The '75 Tour Band

I can say with all certainty that when this band broke up, I was almost in grief. I know that the reviews on this group were mixed on the road and that we had some bad nights, but it was a fantastic mix of personalities and when the strengths of each individual player came together, it was truly an amazing group. I personally think that I had never seen Don in such fine form. The loss of the original band had forced him to do some deep introspection. Working with older, more experienced professionals kept him more in reality. He realized what he needed to do and worked harder at it than I had seen on previous tours, but he also seemed to actually enjoy performing more than ever. His usual health problems on the road never cropped up.

Jeff Tepper On Board

Don was essentially determined to get Jeff Tepper in the group - which was the reason for his visit. I was against it. Jeff was basically an amateur who had never played on a pro-level before. My take on his strong points were that he was able to grasp the concept of odd time signatures and that he did have a reasonably good ear for hearing and then duplicating parts. His weak points were his lack of experience and his adoration of Don.

He seemed to - at that point in time - practically worship Don, which I considered a point against Jeff - or more accurately against accomplishing what we needed to do. It was an unhealthy environment for Don to surround himself with fans. He needed seasoned players to keep his ego in check. Jeff didn't really understand anything about finger-picks, having used only a flat pick, although I think he had done a bit of finger-picking without picks. So, he had to be taught the whole basic Delta/Beefheart approach to guitar, slide, alternate tunings etc. from square one. As a comparison, Harkleroad and Cotton both had the rudiments of this knowledge already in tow upon joining the band, plus three to four years of performing experience each.

John Thomas On Board

One morning, I was walking through my parent's backyard to go visit them and I saw Don's car drive up to the fence encircling the side-yard. He and John Thomas, the keyboardist from Rattlesnakes And Eggs and later the (Mallard) Magic Band, got out and hailed me. "Look who I found." Don said. We all greeted and talked. I think John had shaved his head at the time.

John French: Don showed up one morning at my parent's house with you. He'd been up all night talking with you.
John Thomas: Yeah, he had called me. I remember living in a house in Lancaster, sort of going to school and not doing much. I was grieving the death of my girlfriend, Cathy Tosi, at that time. It had only been eight months or so, at that age, it's pretty heavy. I welcomed when he called and said whatever he said, it was like a ray of sunshine in my otherwise dreary life.

I hadn't spoken to John for a few months, because I had been so busy. I found out that his girlfriend, Cathy Tosi, had died of cancer. She was the daughter of Ernie Tosi, the vice-principal at Antelope Valley High School who Frank Zappa had so many run-ins with. I found it interesting to glean from this interview that Don's intention in saying "Look who I found," was to make it seem like he had just met up with John in a coincidental happenstance meeting. John makes it very clear that Don called him.

Don explained to me, after John left, that he thought John would be a good person to get in the band, he could play the bass parts on synth. I wasn't really crazy about using a synth, because I missed the Rockette Morton bass playing. Most of the synthesizers at the time were monophonic - they could only play one note at a time. Finding someone with Mark Boston's abilities would be nearly impossible. Although Roy Estrada was a dead-on player for the *Clear Spot* material, Mark was the only bass player I ever heard who played Beefheart's farther-out music with that "fire."

I wasn't really crazy about working with John and Jeff together, because they were both Beefheart fans. Was this the beginning of another cult atmosphere?

John, however, proved to be quite an asset to the album, in fact, I think he was one of Don's best players although, like Denny Walley, never really officially credited with playing on an album - as *Bat Chain Puller* was never released. John had an excellent ear. He also had several years stage experience and had mastered several styles of playing. He could read reasonably well, so I only had to spend a few days with him to bring him up to speed on the material. He was also disciplined enough to learn the material on his own.

The problems I had mentioned with Bruce's reading of the between-the-beats left-hand notes were not a problem with a keyboardist, as he played bass with his left hand and the piano part on Fender Rhodes piano with his right hand, thus coordinating the two in the same natural manner Don had originally played them.

My fears of synth bass not being strong enough on Beefheart material were quickly dissolved as I heard the bass used and realized it was a great and powerful match.

John French: I remember the first day you came to rehearsal. You asked, "Hey, John can you help me in with my Fender Rhodes." Then, you proceeded to get a ratchet and a socket out and remove your rear passenger car door. The only way you could actually get the keyboard out of the car was to take the entire door off your sedan.
John Thomas: I forgot totally about that. You're right. That is so funny.

Other Feelings On JT's Inclusion

John was more of a Zappa fan than a Beefheart fan, and he didn't seem so in awe of Don as Jeff did. This belayed a bit of my concern about the cult atmosphere developing once again. I was worried a bit about Don oppressing John in the same manner he had with the *Trout Mask* band.

John French: My reaction to you getting in the band. I was against it. I still felt protective of you. I thought that it wasn't going to be a good thing for you. I had no problem with your ability, but I was afraid that you were going to get hurt. I was against it and I argued with Don and checked him out. I said, "Look you can't ever get into the scenes again with this guy."
John Thomas: That might be one reason that I never felt like Don cornered me. I saw him corner Jeff in rehearsals, I saw him hassle you, but I always felt a little bit like Don had a different policy with me. I never understood why.
JF: I don't think he ever hassled you in that band. If he did, I took him outside and told him he better not do that. I found out that if I confronted him in front of people, he would absolutely go insane to win. He couldn't handle correction in front of others. If you got him alone, he actually would become humble and cooperate.

Material Rehearsed For Six Or Seven Weeks

John Thomas: Don was so handicapped at getting his ideas across that as soon as he knew that you knew what he meant, he shut up and let you direct the band and say, "OK, this is where we all come together."
John French: Part of my understanding with Don during this time was that if he was going to come to rehearsals, he was going to shut up and let me do the organizing. I wasn't about to let things go on forever like they did with Trout Mask. *This was an understanding that we had where I had to threaten him with violence at one point to get him to understand that I wasn't going through any more of those horrible "talks," and those endless paranoid delusions of (why) somebody (was) not getting a part "Right." I said, "It's going to sound like shit at first - let it develop. When somebody plays something for the first time, it sounds terrible, it takes them a while to get it right." The funny thing was that Don would allow Elliot to sound terrible at first and he understood, but he couldn't seem to understand other people not being able to pick up on something immediately. Yet, Don could never play anything twice the same way - so, it was a very bizarre situation.*

We began rehearsals - probably in early February, and my plan was to get everyone up and running on *The Thousandth And Tenth Day Of The Human Totem Pole*. It was the longest piece (and the longest title) and would take the most time to learn. Since neither Denny nor Jeff read music, my method was to work on about ten measures a night and then teach that to both Jeff and Denny the next day. They brought tape recorders to rehearsal and recorded each section in a very organized way. We worked on other things simultaneously.

Don didn't show up for a lot of the early rehearsals, as we were just processing information. He was home with Jan going through tapes and lyrics searching for other material for the album. We had about 12-15 minutes between these three songs and needed more material.

Don came up with *The Floppy Boot Stomp*, - lyrics he had written during *Trout Mask* period, and the basis of the original *Electricity* demo for the music, including the opening guitar riff, which was the original harp solo on the demo. More on this in track notes.

John French: Of course, there were other things that were on tape, little bits and pieces of tape. There were some things like Floppy Boot Stomp that we learned in rehearsal.
John Thomas: Right, with Don whistling parts.

He also wrote the music to *Owed T'Alecks* (a pun on "Ode To Alex" which became *Owed T' Alex*), using lyrics recorded on the same early demo tape as the original *Electricity*, but with completely different music. I remember seeing the type written lyrics at Don's mother's house on Carolside Street when I first joined the group. I have come to find out since that this almost always meant the lyrics were written by Herb Bermann.

Owed T' Alex

During the creation of *Owed T' Alex*, Jeff Tepper had a tiny taste of what it was like in the *Trout Mask* band. John Thomas appeared less of a "fawning fan" at rehearsals, and conducted himself in a very professional manner. He did observe some of Don's tactics in regards to Jeff Tepper, but didn't become the target himself.

John French: Describe a little bit about Don getting on Jeff about not being able to learn a part. I can refresh your memory if you like.
John Thomas: No, I know the part. (sings first guitar part to Ode T' Alecks)
JF: That's exactly the part I recall.
JT: It was a four-note guitar riff on ...
JF: ... Ode T' Alecks. And Don just kept saying, "No, that's not it."
JT: Yeah, for the life of me I could not figure out - from the time he was playing it right to the time that Don said he was not playing it right. Don was accusing him of trying to ruin his entire life and his career and undermine his entire existence. All because he supposedly couldn't play ... (sings part again). For the life of me, I could not hear the difference. It turned into this four hour (verbal) "pummeling" of Jeff's character and personality behind all the reasons why it could be possible why Jeff couldn't play that riff to (Don's) satisfaction. Of course, Jeff didn't see this coming at all.
JF: Yes, this was "Captain Beefheart," - his idol.
JT: It was so excruciatingly uncomfortable to be in the same room. I remember on the one level I was really grateful that it wasn't me, and wondering what day it would be my turn to get beat up by Don. I even went so far as to give him the benefit of the doubt, that what he was merely trying to get the part right. But, after the number of hours, I couldn't even really believe that anymore.
JF: The "behind the scenes stuff" that happened was that:
#1 - I wanted Jeff to get a good strong dose of Don, because he needed it, in order to be realistic and
#2: I took Don out and told him that he either apologized to Jeff and never did that again, or I was leaving that day. That's where I had to put myself on the line. Basically, it made me angry, not only because of the principle involved with human relationships, but because I was under fire from Herbie (Cohen) to get this project done.
JT: You knew where that (the "talk) would lead, too. That was just the icing on the cake.

He was playing a simple four-note part and Don kept telling him it was wrong. Actually, it was difficult even for me to grasp Don's concept on this song. When he created using the band, we were treated like "writing tools" (in his word, "paint") rather than human beings. Don kept shouting at Jeff, "That's not it, man." Jeff was exasperated. As I said to John, I allowed this to go on because I thought it would be a good idea for the "fawning fan Jeff" to get a good taste of the darker side of Don. However, I was also concerned that Don might fall back into these ridiculous time-wasting tactics and ruin this wonderful opportunity Frank was giving him. Now, I wonder at why that concerned me at all.

I privately issued him an ultimatum, either apologize or I was walking out the door immediately. Don acted semi-repentant. "You're right, John, I shouldn't have treated him that way." He told me that he apologized to Jeff and the rehearsals went along fairly smoothly after this. Ironically, Jeff later confronted me for mildly reprimanding him in front of the group when he finally showed up three hours late for rehearsal after a four-hour lunch with Don. He was very upset with me for saying something like: "Well, nice of you to show up, Jeff."

This kind of referee / musical director / drummer role was very stressful. Since I had come home with no profit from the tour thanks to Don's wardrobe, I was already drawing on earnings for the album, which meant that I was committed and had to finish the project on schedule. I was determined that Don was not going to become the tyrant I had seen him be in the past, but I was working 12-14 hour days between all the responsibilities - and spending my weekends trying to catch up.

Bat Chain Puller

I used to laugh on all the variations of descriptions of how the beat to *Bat Chain Puller* came into existence. I have read all these different accounts of trains in rain, etc. The track notes describe its actual "birth." However, I thought about it later, and I imagine that all these stories are probably true and actually just coincide with the particular musician's take on his introduction to the beat, not the actual conception thereof.

I recall the day quite clearly. John and I were in the rubber room. It was raining pretty heavily outside. Don showed up a little later - probably 10:30 - 11:00 a.m. and came in exploding in childlike excitement that would burst through during moments of extreme inspiration. "You gotta hear this, man, you GOTTA!" I wish I had a dollar for every time I had heard that phrase.

He directed us to his car, the Volvo sedan he had been driving. I sat in the passenger seat in the front, and JT sat in the back. Don turned on the windshield wipers and we just listened to the beat of them for a moment. "Can you play that?" he asked. "Sure, give me something to write on," I replied. He gave me a matchbook with a plain white cover. I opened it up and sat for a few minutes listening to the wipers and transcribed the beat in such a manner that it could be played on the drum kit.

"Got it?" he asked, and when I replied to the affirmative, he started playing with the little handle that controls the spraying of liquid window cleaner onto the windshield. The motorized pump made a little whining noise. He did it on the "and, one" beats of the windshield wipers. JT, I believe, had him record the sound of the pump - they may have even gone under the hood to get closer to the actual mechanism involved, but by this time, I had gone back in to learn the beat, which I was playing when the Captain and JT returned.

"That's it man!" Don said excitedly. John sat for a while at his mini-moog, manipulating the controls until he came up with a reasonable facsimile of the pump whinings. Jeff and Denny eventually showed up, and Don began whistling and playing harp lines for the intro of the song. The center section of the song was written later on piano. I transcribed it and transferred the information to the guys by playing the parts on guitar at rehearsal.

Slow And Laborious

If I would have only known then what I know now. Rather than me struggling through all these pieces myself, I should have made copies of the music, and copies of the piano tape and said, "Learn this stuff, if you have problems, ask me about it." I could have taught them all to read music enough to figure out the parts.

But, I chose to do it the most accurate way possible (at least for me) I would learn all the parts the night before on guitar, memorize them and teach them to the players. They had a tape, but I suggested that they not "learn ahead" as it might turn out to be incorrect (like anyone would really know) and have to be re-learned.

John Thomas: You were being very practical about it you were transcribing it, and babysitting these musicians and teaching every little guitar lick - I'm assuming that you did that on every record you worked on.
John French: Well, no, I only assumed that role of musical director during those two periods of time (TMR and BCP). You can hear the difference in the longer passages from Trout Mask to Lick My Decals, where Bill took over as musical director - working from tape.

Fortunately, John Thomas could read and so I just rehearsed with him at a separate session. He would show up a couple hours after the guitarists, and we would work together on the pieces. He played the bass parts, or left hand parts, on the mini-moog that he used back then. It was, as I explained earlier when referring to Bruce's departure, a much more natural way to play the bass part. The original mini-moog synthesizer was only capable of playing a single note at a time, but John had taken his to a technician and had it modified so that it played two notes at a time. Most of Don's left hand "chords" were fourths, fifths and octaves - two note chords.

Tepper began to surprise me. Not only was he the most enthusiastic member of the band, but he worked exceedingly hard to make up for his lack of experience. His main problems at first were technique (which I mentioned before) and intonation (keeping the guitar in tune, and playing in tune.) The technique he picked up quickly, and we started working with electronic guitar tuners (which had just recently come out at affordable prices) that helped Jeff a great deal. Though Jeff (this was in pre-Moris days) could not read music at all, he was there everyday with his guitar in tune, a fresh cassette in his tape machine, and a big enthusiastic smile on his face. It wasn't difficult for me to appreciate this guy. He was also very respectful to me.

Part of the "fan" mentality that worked in my favor was the fact that Jeff also was a fan of my playing, and so held me in high esteem. This caused him to absorb any information I passed to him like a sponge - which was obviously a win/win situation. He was also able to assimilate concepts and it was quickly apparent that this guy in his early twenties was no slouch. He also had a brilliant mind and a good sense of humor, which helped me to warm up to him quickly, and he and John Thomas, being close to the same age, seemed to get on well. Tepper was assigned the simpler, rhythmic parts, and Denny, being experienced, took over the tougher more demanding parts.

Denny shone like a star on this project. His soloing and technique so greatly enhanced Don's music that I would get goose bumps hearing songs come together. I had never heard slide played with this kind of presence and *Ode T' Alex* is still one of my favorites simply because of Walley's slide playing.

Running Out Of Money

As all my extra musical director money had been "spent" I had to draw a weekly advance against my studio fees for the album. I think it was $100 a week or something. Denny used to call it our "weekly insult." However, never having been used to actually earning money as a musician, I was just glad, like a lot of musicians, to be working and have food in my stomach. During one period,

Herb Cohen was out of town and hadn't signed any checks to be issued in his absence - probably on purpose as a motivator to get into the studio.

Dick Barber

Dick "The Knarler" Barber had been Frank's road manager, I believe. He also was probably on a retainer when Frank wasn't on the road, because he had an office at Discreet and was the person I spoke to about money. Once, when Herb was out of town for three weeks, he didn't sign any checks for us and, after I didn't eat for four days, I finally went into Dick's office. I didn't realize that I had blood sugar problems. Anyway, as I started to explain that I needed money, I burst into tears. Dick looked at me, totally shocked and went over and shut the door, because the two girls in the office were staring at me. I sat there for a minute and gained my composure, feeling absolutely like a wimp, and apologized. I explained more fully that I hadn't eaten in four days.

I have heard some negative things said about Dick, sometimes known as "The Knarler." He could be a bit forceful at times on the road, didn't seem to be "cool" or "one of the guys." However, as I sat there in his office, shaking from hunger, I experienced a person who was compassionate and sympathetic with my position. I had always been very straightforward with Dick and, like Herb Cohen, had found him to be reasonable as long as I presented him with logical facts. He said he would take care of the money problem.

I recall Denny inviting me to his house for a few days. His wife, Josie, and their son, Jaryd, were out of town, and I could stay in Jaryd's room. He fixed dinner for us and I've got to tell you, if this guy played guitar liked he cooked, he would have never gotten in a band. I think he dropped a live chicken in a pot of water, threw in some veggies, and just hoped for the best. I guess it could have been worse - it could have been eggplant... I choked down dinner, and was appreciative to have a meal in my stomach.

I enjoyed staying with Denny. He had a dog named Muddy that he "yelled" at in a faux Jackie Gleason voice and it was obviously a game between them. The dog loved him. The house was a typical North Hollywood Bungalow-type house and was cozy. I remember sleeping in Jaryd's room amongst his toys. I awoke the next morning, to a horrible wound-up wailing sound, which at first didn't register. It was the air-raid siren. Most cities in the US would run a monthly test of the air-raid sirens on the last Friday of the month, so this must have been late February. Denny was up before me and, having a touch of the sadist, knew the air-raid siren would be tested, and turned on a cassette player to catch my reaction on tape. We both had a great laugh over coffee and cereal, that, fortunately tasted better than the chicken soup we had for dinner the night before.

Herb's Interrogation

At one point, it was decided that the band was way past its deadline to go into the studio and start laying tracks. We probably had been rehearsing four or five weeks. Being used to Frank's more efficient compositional techniques, Herb wanted to know just what the hell was taking so long. Don called me outside rehearsal and said, "Man, can you talk to Herbie? He's saying we're taking too long." Probably, knowing Don, he was saying to Herbie, "I don't know what the Hell's taking John so long to teach these guys..." I walked down the corridor past Marty Perellis' office and into the reception area and Don, Dick, Herb and I had a meeting. I remember it was after the receptionists had gone home and we were all standing around their desks, which faced each other. I explained that in a way, Don's music was more complicated to learn than Frank's and that's why it was taking so long. I apologized, and this is when we decided to speed things up by having me play guitar on *Odd Jobs*. I was really not prepared to do this, and I felt like it was unfair to put this much pressure on me, but that's the way it came out. Again, I would have almost no time to spend practicing drums.

JT's Observances Of Musical Process

I asked John about the musical process and Don's creative techniques, he gave the following observance:

John Thomas: I remember feeling and being totally shocked and amazed that this is actually how he works and this is how this music that I had loved so much had come into being. Somehow, I imagined a different process. My experience was sitting in the car, listening to the windshield wipers for a drumbeat, or him whistling a bass part to me and the guitar to Jeff and then leaving it up to us as to how they fit together. I realized that there was a lot more that happened that was out of his control, than there was that was in it. I think the first eye-opener to me was that - in my expectation, me being his "worthy servant" in his band, that he would dictate every nuance. It wasn't like that at all. He would hum something, or whistle something, or point to me and say, "Make the sound of the inside of a tooth," or something like that. But then from that point on, I had to interpret it. I had to decide how many times (to play) this four-note pattern before it finished up in time to go to the next section. There was a lot more left for me, as a musician in the band, to figure out to make it work, than there was direction from him on how to make it work. I think that was the first feeling of "The Emperor's New Clothes," sort of mentality. It didn't lessen my respect for him any, or my admiration for his brilliance, but it was just that I couldn't imagine music could be made with that type of approach. I had never (experienced) something like that where ...(pause)

John French: Imagery?

JT: Yeah, imagery and randomness. Whistling a part and thinking, "He knows what the bass-line is going to sound like against the guitar part," but he didn't. It was like, "You play this, and you play that," and however we happened to get to sound together, that's "what he meant." But it wasn't like he meant it that way, or that's really what it was. I think that was a real educational thing for me to realize, that music could be made that way too as opposed to the Zappa approach wherein he knew every note that every guy was playing at any moment, Don was exactly the opposite. He really didn't know what anyone was playing, he just knew that he had started it. He knew if it "felt right" or not.

JF: It was almost like he was watering a seed and then watching it grow into whatever it cared to grow into.

JT: Right, and then he either liked the plant or he didn't.

JF: But then, there were times like I recall on, Floppy Boot Stomp *where he was pretty insistent on how he wanted it done. One of the things that I remember him telling me was to play P-K-Ro-P this beat that he played on the drums once - he said, "play it backwards." But another thing - the pulling from the past. I mean, a lot of things he did there I remember him writing during* Lick My Decals *or even before. So, he was pretty exact on the beginning of* Floppy Boot Stomp, *he wanted to Denny to play the beginning lick from the original demo of* Electricity, *that was played on harmonica. That's where Denny's first lick in* Floppy Boot Stomp *comes from. You know, sometimes, he could be very precise, sitting down with the band and starting from scratch. Humming a few things, and putting together a tune like* Ant Man Bee, *or* Sugar And Spikes. *I watched those things go together and having him be pretty specific and then saying, "repeat that again," etc.*

JT: I just think that part didn't stand out to me. The part that "stood out" to me... (was) when I saw that some of this music was put together in this other way. I couldn't believe it. I couldn't actually believe that's what he wanted. I know the first couple of times I felt at a loss - "I don't know where this starts," "Play this!" and he would whistle it to me - I'm thinking, "I don't know where this starts, I don't know how many times to play it, I don't know where it ends!"

I didn't say those things, because I didn't want to appear like a "rube," you know? But, at the same time, I was thinking, "Here I am playing with the great Captain Beefheart, but I am going to have to decide where this comes in and how many times I am going to have to play it before I go on," and I just didn't expect that.

JF: I think - you know, his first experience in a band was playing blues. Blues - the guys are looking at each other, sort of nodding their heads and going to the next change, you know there's only three chords to begin with, so how far wrong can you go? I think, in his head, he thought, "Well, you can do that with any part!"

JT: I think that was right, it was just something I learned. You don't have to be in control of everything to make it good. You can randomly throw some stuff out there, and if you like the way it lands, then it's OK - sort of like throwing paint at a canvas. If you like what it looks like, then who's to say you didn't plan it that way? It just is - what it looks like if you like that and you did it. That's how I felt with some of the stuff that he would do came together. If we liked the way we played it back to him, then on to the next thing.

JF: I always felt more like a paintbrush than a canvas. The second half of what we were talking about was that sometimes he didn't have any control. I was saying about the blues thing: I think he thought that two guys playing in different time signatures and playing in different key signatures could look at each other and hear what the other was playing, and know where to change. I don't think he realized how difficult it was and how you really had to do it mathematically, because you really couldn't concentrate on what you and the other person were doing at the same time, when you were doing two different things. You couldn't split your brain two ways or three ways. That became difficult. Anyway, as far as like trying to get those - I used to call them "touch points" - where the band actually would change to another section...

JT: And then go back off on their own...

JF: Yeah, be out there sort of counting. I remember with drum parts, as soon as I knew my drum parts well enough, I could listen to what was going on and I could hear... (pause)

JT: Hear it coming...

JF: Yeah, but not until I learned the part well. Nobody, none of us could hear that at first.

JT: Well, it takes so much familiarity, because everything appears so chaotic at any point. But, as you said, after we had done it enough times, we could see things coming "back in phase" and start to predict when it was time to make the next change. Where we could all actually count on changing together.

JF: Which is more like the way people really are. They're all thinking of different things and in different "time zones"

JT: I just never perceived of music that way. I always thought that it was something you learned, and you knew what you were doing, and if you composed music, you knew what it was going to sound like in your head maybe before you did it.

JF: Well, like John Cage used to flip a coin or toss five pennies to decide what the next note would be.

JT: I mean, that was in his art, and then some of it was an exact transcription of something he had played on the piano. So it went from one total extreme of being completely dictatorial to the other end of just letting his ideas more randomly come together.

Studio

The studio was Paramount in Hollywood, just down the street and around the corner from Discreet. I believe it was actually on Santa Monica Blvd. Just a block or two east of Vine and across from the House of Drums, one of my favorite shops. The parking was really awful - you took your car's life in your hands trying to squeeze through the tiny alley to get into the lot and then squeeze into a tiny space, if there was one. If there wasn't, you had to back out the alley and on to the street again. It was absolutely LA life at it's worst. I still to this day do not care at all for the heavy congestion of the urban environment.

The first day of recording, John Thomas showed up with all his equipment and brought a friend with him, which isn't a good idea to do in any session, as it makes for distractions. John was young and didn't realize that Don wouldn't like this, so a deal was quickly worked out whereby his friend would take the car and come back at a prescribed time. Unfortunately, after his friend, Ron Young, drove away, it was discovered that all the charts to the songs we were planning on recording that day had been left in the car, and we had no idea as to the car's location.

Obviously, it was a tough day for John Thomas, who was in turn angry with Ron, who, fortunately, showed up early because he found the music and so redeemed them both in the nick of time. I remember being set up against the back wall, facing the booth, John to my left and Denny and Jeff to my right. It was a fairly good-sized room. In the track notes, I speak more about the situation.

Everything seemed to go fine, except I never have liked the drum fill I put in *Odd Jobs*, which was an unexpected cue from Van Vliet in the booth and distracted me so it was out of time, as I first thought he wanted to cut the take and start again. One thing about almost all the sessions I have done with Captain Beefheart was the fact that I usually was unable to completely prepare for various reasons. *Safe As Milk* is actually the only album I did feel prepared for - regarding the drums, that is.

The next unexpected disaster was once I began to set up to play guitar on overdubs, Kerry McNabb (the engineer) pulled an engineer stunt. He found a small "buzz" in my guitar, probably caused by a ground wire. Although the buzz could not really be heard at the level I was playing at, he insisted that I use a different guitar. If I would have just been a bit smarter, I would have said, "Screw you and the buzz, I'm using my own guitar." However, I thought that Kerry's idea would be "best for the album."

McNabb then talked Don into recording me "direct" which means plugged directly into the board, rather than through a miked amplifier. I then had to stand in the control room, which is a very sterile environment, and play these now "squeaky clean tones" on Denny's thin strings, when I had been used to heavy strings and a bit of distortion for the last several months. It was a disaster in my mind and very stressful. I overplayed the strings until they were out of tune, and the tone stinks. Electric guitar was never made to be played straight into the board. There is no warmth at all.

John French: Any memorable thoughts about recording **Bat Chain Puller?**
Denny Walley: Other than the labor of rehearsing the stuff and getting it down. The rest of it, it seemed to be fairly frost-free once we got to the studio, things went pretty well.
JF: Do you remember JT?
DW: Yeah, I remember him well, he was very good.
JF: He's a great player. He works with Bruce Hornsby now, and I think he worked with Tracy Chapman. So, we finally got in the studio and got that out of the way. You mentioned Don having trouble on one of the songs.
DW: I think it was **Harry Irene**. *He just couldn't get the track. He had the words, but he couldn't get it in sync. I don't know why he had trouble with it. It was the easiest one. All the other stuff was impossible and he did that just fine. I think it was just too much trudging along and he just couldn't cope. He had a lot of trouble with that.*
JF: Did he seem prepared, do you think?
DW: It was always hard to tell. He would say he was over-prepared and if anything started

to mess up, it was like, "Who's thinking 'C'? Hey man, is it you?"
JF: Oh yeah, the old "psychic interference."
DW: Yeah, right, exactly.
JF: That was a theme that Vic Mortensen, the very first drummer in 1964 brought up - this thing about Don accusing people of psychic interference. It goes all the way through to the last drummer, Cliff Martinez

Vocal Overdubs

The moodiness, spontaneity, and artistic temperament of Don mixed with the sterile and non-inspirational electronic setting of a recording was always a volatile combination. Anytime I had to be in the studio with Don during vocal overdubs was a time I dreaded. He hated headphones. He wouldn't allow any reverb to be put on the tracks to warm them up a bit, he didn't understand placement of microphones or how to use them. He was not at all technically oriented. Worst of all, he never rehearsed with the band and only did a little wood shedding occasionally with the board tapes of the instrumental tracks the night before. He had to read his lyrics off lyric sheets and complained constantly "that's not my fucking voice, man!" to the engineer.

I watched Kerry go through all these same tortuous electronic acrobatics I had watched every engineer on every Beefheart album I had ever done go through. I think Don didn't consider that the album was a success unless the recording engineer was on the verge of a nervous breakdown by the end of the session. The band usually wasn't far behind. It was an uncomfortable experience for all involved.

I remember JT bringing a book and sitting in the back of the recording booth as Don sang. "Man," he would say, "How do you expect me to sing, while you're doing that?" pointing to the book. He would complain again and again of "psychic interference" and people "having too much to think." We basically were expected to sit there through the whole torturous experience like a bunch of mannerly school children with our hands folded, listening to take after take while being expected to maintain a look of unending awe on our faces. I would call this "only-child" syndrome. He needed to be the center of attention.

It was very reminiscent of *Trout Mask* days and the ridiculous mind-control methods Van Vliet used on the musicians back then.

I had already become partially convinced that the musical-director-money-for-wardrobe fiasco was a good reason to leave after the album was completed, so I wasn't much concerned about Don's thoughts or opinions concerning me. I told Don bluntly that I hated coming to his vocal over-dub sessions and that I was staying home. He said that it was "unfair" as he had been there for me in the instrumental tracking. I countered with the fact that the instrumental tracking was a lot more interesting and pleasant, whereas the vocal sessions were very unpleasant, in fact, downright miserable. Anyway, despite an uproar about my lack of interest in the band, I stayed away from the vocal overdubs.

John Thomas: By the way, there's one other thing that I really remember about the recording of that record too, it was, after we had all worked so hard to have the music and the intensity so it would be just like we rehearsed them. Of course, during this whole time, I'm imagining "Oh yeah, Don knows exactly what we're doing. He knows where the vocals are going to come in and where he's gonna play horn and where the harp is going to play." Then, when it was time for him to do his overdubs, after the first couple hours, it started to dawn on me that he could never sing anything the same way twice, he didn't know where all the entrances and all the carefully arranged things that we had worked on ... he didn't get that at all. It was purely random from take to take. I remember feeling - all the hope that I had for the record

- that it could be something great - somehow it was all shattered with the realization that the leader, whom I was following, was up there flailing. That the troops had a better sense of what was going on than the leader did. I know this sounds sort of mutinous to say it like this way. But really, my hopes that I was part of something that was special fell apart that day watching the overdubs. He didn't know where to go and he wasn't prepared at all. He was spending part of his time being blustery and trying to cover up the fact that he was so scattered and not organized. That was the day that I saw through it all. All the stuff that I loved in his records in the past. It happened that way, and it was brilliant, and it was what it was, but it didn't get there the way I imagined. It came about in a way that may be wasn't as admirable. That was a really big turning point for me, to sort of watch him come down from his pedestal.

After a long set of overdub sessions, Don invited me to the mobile home, and he, Jan and I listened to the album completely on a small cassette tape recorder. I liked what he had done and told him so. I was pleased that he had tried to "compliment" the music rather than "stepping all over" the track. This had taken hours of time in the studio punching in and out of sections, but the finished product was pleasing to hear..

JT On Bat Chain Puller

John Thomas: Well it's funny, listening to the bootleg of **Bat Chain Puller** *- the one that we did? Listening to that, I get that same feeling that Bill did. I think, "Oh, man, we played this better in rehearsal one time than we did in the studio," or, "That Rhodes sound isn't really as cool as I thought it was." It shows how your expectations play a role. I thought that being in the band at that time and doing that record, I was going to be part of something that changed music forever, you know. So when I hear it, I have to hear it in the backdrop of those expectations. While for you, you already changed music forever and it wasn't part of the thing anymore. You were being very practical about it you were transcribing it, and babysitting these musicians and teaching every little guitar lick.*

Jan Copyrights

After all the recordings were finished, the album mixed and "in the can" the only thing left to do was register the material for copyright protection. Don and Jan hired me to re-write all the transcriptions and include the lyrics. I knew the procedure, as I had previously registered a couple of songs and it was a fairly simple procedure.

After I had finished with this rather monumental task, Jan came by my house one day, with all the forms filled out asking me pertinent questions. I could never cease to be amazed at how opposite she and Don were. He was spontaneous and overly enthusiastic, she was calm and collected. He was completely unorganized and illogical, and she was totally organized and completely reasonable. Within a few hours, we had all the forms filled out, doubly checked etc. Jan then handed me a check for services rendered in an envelope, demanding that I make sure the amount was right and everything in order. I think if working with Don had been anything like working with her, I could have done a hundred more albums.

JT And Mallard

At this point, JT, who had previously played in The Magic Band in Northern California was approached by Bill Harkleroad to do the second Mallard project. I had been approached also to play drums, but I declined - while JT accepted. I was proud of him for deciding to do this project because he did it with the full understanding that Don would fire him - which is exactly what happened. John considered that his work with Captain Beefheart was a studio session in which he played a part, and now it was time to move on. He saw more clearly than I did that we were merely sidemen to be used and then discarded and saw no harm in enriching his musical experience by also playing with Mallard.

As a direct result of JT being fired, I resigned immediately. This was the little nudge I had needed. I was already upset at having been cheated out of musical director fees for the road tour, and not really that happy with Don returning to what I will refer to as his "old ways." It was time for me to move on also. I figured at this point that the next step was to replace JT

John Thomas Reflects On Expulsion

John Thomas: Also, being young and impressionable, there was one thing about working with him that scared me. After recording the album I was kind of relieved to be away. That sort of contributed to why I didn't work with him again. Remember, you know, he was mentally so powerful - So powerful that I, as a twenty-year-old found myself - even when I wasn't around him, like if I was sitting with you talking and you would say something - before I would even think myself of an answer, I would be thinking, "What would Don say?" He was with me even when he wasn't.

John French: That's a spooky feeling.

JT: Yes, it was very - once I realized that he was with me even when he wasn't. And another thing, after working on that album, that's when Bill and Mallard got their deal and started recording in Europe and I went and worked on the second album with Bill and co-wrote some songs. Once Don knew that I had done that, of course, I think he viewed me as a traitor.

JF: Well, he fired you.

JT: He fired me, yes.

JF: He fired you and as a result, I quit because I felt that it was unfair that he should dictate to you what you should do when he wasn't paying you. You're not on his payroll.

JT: Well, as an extension of this idea of him being with me. I even was immature enough to believe and to feel sometimes that - this is going to sound totally silly - that he had put a "jinx" on me. That I was actually not only fighting against my personal demons about everything that I had needed to grow and learn about. But also that - although I know for a number of years, I felt his "presence" against me in a negative way. Might be because I had done something and he had "turned" on me. Now, I'm a little skeptical about what all that meant, but at the time it was a real weight that I carried around, an extra burden that he had somehow turned that same (creative) power in (opposition) to me. ... I definitely wondered if part of - maybe it's just youthful blaming somebody else for the hassles life is bringing you - I couldn't help but feel sometimes that I was cursed or hexed.

JF: I have felt that way most of my life.

JT: It doesn't seem so strange for you to understand, then. Whether he was able to even do that consciously or it's just part of the power of his presence and personality and his ... I don't know, I don't really know how to break it down that way, all I know is that I felt him with me even when he wasn't and I felt that for a number of years. I am not sure that I could put it into those kind of "God vs. Satan" kind of terms, but I am certain that whatever sort of presence he had, it was certainly powerful enough to (affect me.) ... When I realized that I wasn't even thinking for myself, and I was pretty cocky as a twenty year-old - and even I would think, "What would Don say, or what would Don think?" - giving him preference over his ideas before my own even when he wasn't there. I knew that there was some kind of problem. So at the time when I was fired for going to Europe with Mallard, I didn't regret it. I went at a time when he had nothing going. If it would have been any other band, he wouldn't have given a damn, but because it was his "arch-rival" (laughs) Bill Harkleroad, or however he saw it, then suddenly I was a traitor.

JT's reflections on feeling "cursed" aren't that different from my own. I sometimes still find myself saying "What would Don say/do?" In Christian theology, a curse is really basically something bad being said, while a blessing is something good being said. If someone constantly says critical or negative things, it's bound to leave someone with a feeling of being "cursed," as words have a strong power. Taking this a step further, when someone who has psychic abilities is the person doing the "cursing," it stands to reason that they may have a conscious, or even a sub-conscious ability to implant thoughts within another's mind - without verbal communication taking place. If so, it also stands to reason that those thoughts could surface as negative energy, causing confusion and uncertainty about oneself.

I consulted a person I consider an expert in these matters. She is a licensed psychiatrist - formerly having several Washington D.C. politicians as clients, who is also a Christian and has had a lot of experience with "deliverance" which I write about later on. She wrote me several short emails on the subject of my experiences with Don.

One of her quotes:
"I forgot to agree with you the man you spoke of surely had a demonic hold on persons. That kind of control is Witchcraft. Also I sense you have a soul tie to him which can be broken as an act of your will..."
Perhaps my constant returning to Van Vliet had something to do with this "soul tie" that this Doctor senses. I sent her several lengthy excerpts of my book and asked for her honest opinion. I asked her if my using my Beefheart-Christened name "Drumbo" could have anything to do with this "soul tie."
"Your ideas about the name "Drumbo" are accurate. I would renounce it also."

I have had many times in my life when I found myself doing something and visualizing Don standing there watching me, and thinking "he doesn't like this." It's a very spooky feeling. So, I understand exactly what JT was referring to in his statement above. I didn't 'lead' him in the question in any way. He volunteered the information entirely as an observation of his being expelled from the band and his relief at being away from Don's mental power.

CHAPTER THIRTY SEVEN:
THE WOES OF PEARBLOSSOM

...oing his tap dance routine at The Roxy accompanied by
...harmonica, July 1975. Photo courtesy of Elliot Ingber.

Where's My House??

Alex Snouffer: Don was a good con-man.
John French: I even read somewhere, I can't remember where. They were quoting Don - that
he had bought all of us houses.
AS: (Jokingly) God, I wonder where it is, I'd like to move into it.
JF: Anyway, it was a tough time. I look back, and I regret that didn't have more of a
confrontational attitude.
AS: Yeah, you know what they say about hindsight being 20 / 20.

Mid - 1976

I decided that my best bet at this point in my life was to study piano for a while. I was able to collect unemployment from my work with Discreet for Don. I also moonlighted a little to make extra cash playing drums on the weekend in a friend's bar/café. Tom Bryden (the guy from my Rattlesnakes And Eggs days) showed up on my doorstep one day and proposed that he, a keyboardist named John Tanner, and myself play at a small place called the Llano Del Rio Outpost. His father, a retired test pilot and very successful peach rancher, had bought the Outpost and made Tom the manager. So, I started playing Friday and Saturday nights basically just winging my way through five sets a night. Tom would play guitar and then piano. John Tanner played B3 Organ and used bass pedals. It was not the kind of stuff I liked doing, but it kept me in practice and I had plenty enough money coming in to pay the bills.

Art Tripp Return July '76

Denny remembers a short stint with Art Tripp after my departure.

Denny Walley: I remember rehearsing also with Art Tripp and trying having him in the band. He came to a couple of rehearsals with the band and brought his cooler with beer and tequila but that didn't last too long. He had played with the band before, and he just couldn't handle when Don got into his rants. He'd be there for four hours and you wouldn't get to finish one song or play 8 bars. He said, "I had enough of this shit the last time - I'm outta here."

As I recall, Art had moved back out from Pittsburgh to LA, decided to go to Chiropractor school, working as a bartender in the evenings to support himself. Don would go visit him at the bar, and probably during the re-acquaintance, Don sold Art on the idea of playing drums once again. As Denny describes, it didn't last long.

Michael Traylor

Michael Traylor was playing with a guy by the name of Paul Delicato at a nightclub in Lancaster that was located in The Essex House - a hotel that was located about six blocks from where I was raised. This was mid-1976 - right after I left the group and shortly after the finish of Bat Chain Puller. Traylor used to go over to the Antelope Valley Inn coffee shop afterwards to wind down and spied who he thought was Captain Beefheart sitting in a corner booth with a drawing book.

Michael Traylor: I was there and noticed who I thought was Captain Beefheart at a table sketching and having a cup of coffee. He was looking around, being himself, rolling cigarettes. As he was getting ready to leave, he walked by and looked at me and I said, "Excuse me, are you Captain Beefheart?" His first words were, "My friends call me Don." I introduced myself to him and he sat down with me. This was about 3:00 in the morning and we probably talked a good hour and a half or two covering many subjects - about his music and how much he hated elevator music - how the Nazis created it to brainwash the assembly line workers - which I'm sure you've heard before.

The two exchanged phone numbers and about a week later, Don showed up late at the Essex house and caught the last set or two. This resulted in another late-night talk at the AVI. Don told Traylor that he liked the way he played saying: "It's sounds like you're slinging mud off the end of your sticks and it's hitting the wall." They became friends through all this talking about their ambitions and dreams.

Michael Traylor: *For some reason, Virgin Records was mentioned.*
John French: *That's because he thought about with Virgin after Herb and Frank split and went their separate ways. Don was left without a company.*
MT: *That's what I remember, it must have been after he had left Frank. I remember him talking about Virgin Records. At the same time, I was picking up a lot of Studio work, at Gold Star Studios where the "wall of sound" was created with Phil Spector, and I was working with the engineer whose name was Stan. He was teaching me engineering after sessions. I was also working with Morton Downey Junior. He started a production company and asked me to be an associate producer with his company.*
JF: *Is he the guy that had a talk show for a while?*
MT: *That was he. He was actually best man at my wedding - believe it or not - in my first marriage to Teresa. So, I was working with him and I was getting together with Don and talking mostly. It was during this same time that Paul Delicato took me over and I met you, originally. The one thing that stood out in the conversation with you was that you had told me about this set of Gon Bop drums that was made for you. I remember trying to visualize those things.*

Strangely enough, I remember nothing about this meeting, nor the place it took place.

Teresa

Michael Traylor: *I got married in December of '76 to Teresa. (Earlier) during the course of dating Teresa, Don had come out one night and Teresa met Don. I was up there playing and Don was talking to Teresa a lot. I remember after the gig her saying that he gave her an "eerie" feeling. So, that was the basis of that. The Essex House gig was coming to an end.*

Towards the end of that time, Michael thought it best to move into a rented room a friend had offered in the San Fernando Valley - in either Reseda or Van Nuys area. In one of his visits with Don, it was mentioned that the Magic Band members lived nearby. A meeting was arranged at Jeff Tepper's house in Reseda. Michael observed that Don seemed "enamoured" with Jeff's live-in girlfriend - Tina - and was fascinated with the fact that she had never eaten meat.

Michael Traylor: *(quoting Don) "Can you believe that, man? She's never had meat in her life."*
Of course, I was still dating Teresa at that time, but she didn't really come around Don very much.
John French: *So, this is still before you got married?*
MT: *This was towards the fall of '76. So, by that time you had left the band. He asked me if I would be interested in playing in the band. He said, "I've got this European tour I'm*

working on, and I got this record coming out." It sounded good to me so I accepted the offer. We went to Denny's garage. Basically, the band was Eric, Jeff, Denny and myself. We started working up stuff. I remember Don gave me - which I still have - a vinyl copy of Trout Mask Replica. He marked the songs on the back - the songs that he wanted me to learn. Of course, one of them was Moonlight On Vermont. That was the first song we started working on. I remember very distinctly Eric trying to teach me how to do the p-k-ro-p beat. He couldn't do it like you did it. I had worked it out but it wasn't near like the way it was supposed to be played. So, he was trying to show me the right feel for it. I rehearsed with them probably three or four times. At the same time, my studio schedule was getting pretty heavy. I was offered the position of musical director for Fabian. Of course, I didn't have a regular paycheck. I got paid from the production company a little bit. But the Fabian thing offered me $500 a week retainer, and a thousand dollars a week when we were out on the road. That was a pretty good gig for then. So, I accepted that gig. I called Don and said, "I can't do it. I've been offered a lot better job and I'm getting ready to get married." That was when I exited the Magic Band.

JF: What was his reaction?

MT: He actually was pretty cool. He wasn't angry at all.

JF: Well, that was in marked contrast to when I would leave, because he would really get livid with me.

MT: I think probably because I wasn't in that deep. He'd also told me that the record deal had fallen through and that there was no tour. That was part of the reason I told him. There was no record deal, there was no tour, and I needed the work. So, I think that helped kind of soften the blow.

July 1976 Gary Jaye

Gary Jaye was the drummer who eventually replaced me on a more "permanent" level, and I only saw him play once live at the Troubadour. It's the only live performance of Beefheart I have ever seen as a member of the audience. I thought Jaye did a great job. I have little recollection of him other than what he played like that evening. My date that night was a beautiful African-American woman who was a singer in a local club band. I recall her being a little intimidated by the whole evening - even as to what drink to order. There was a black waitress who, in my estimation, took my date under her wing, like a little sister, and sweetly suggested a few drinks she could try and made her feel a bit more at home.

I dressed in a light brown suit and wore a dark brown Homburg Don had given me in 1975. So, I looked completely different than my usual motorcycle-jacket-and-jeans look of the time. We met up with Lowell George next to the cigarette machine and started a conversation. He asked me what I had been doing and, as I started to answer he said, "Wait," rearranged his clothes and leaned up against the cigarette machine, and, finally satisfied that he was ready to hear a long story, said, "OK." I laughed a little at all this preparation. My answer was short, as I wanted to get a good seat and not ignore my date. We spoke 5-7 minutes. I regret I didn't spend more time with Lowell. It was the last time I ever saw him.

The tables at the Troubadour were like picnic benches set up sideways to the stage. It was amazingly uncomfortable to sit on these benches and stare sideways up at the stage, necked craned like a goose.

Feldman came out first, looking like a mad scientist. Eventually everyone appeared - Tepper, Jaye, and Walley, then Don came out to mild applause. *Lo Yo-Yo* was the only one I recall hearing. I was really impressed with Jaye's mastery of the beats and thought he was a great player. Tepper, about halfway through the set, spied me and gave a little smile of recognition. I remember Don fiddling with the microphone and having problems with it falling out of the stand. They seemed to remain a relatively foreign item in his hands throughout his entire career.

After the show, I visited the dressing room. Gail Zappa was there visiting with Don. She had a really nice camera and was taking photos. I told my date, "That's Frank Zappa's wife." She asked, "Did she go to AV too?" - referring to the High School Frank attended? I said, "No," and she immediately told me it was "probably a stupid question." I told her she was wrong and that she should quit putting herself down. Don told me later that Gail's reaction to the way I was dressed was, "I see John is in another one of his disguises." I found this quite humorous.

On the ride home, the girl slept with her head in my lap, as she worked for a mortgage loan company and had to get up early the next day. We never dated again. Relationships were difficult enough without the racial issue, but I remember her as having a great sense of humor and being great company all evening. She did say that she thought I had "strange taste in music" and I said, "I didn't write it, I just played it."

Living On Unemployment

I was astounded to find out that I was to receive the vast sum of $97 per week, which was a lot of money to me. I was only paid $100 a week for rehearsal, so I knew I could pay my bills. My expenses were extremely low. I paid $50 a month rent for my little house. My utilities were probably under $25 a month. Food was about $20 a week, and gas was under fifty cents a gallon.

I was a bachelor, so all my time was free, and this was a very happy and peaceful time for me. I was young, and I certainly didn't think about things like auto insurance, mortgages and medical insurance. Besides, I had actually gotten paid my musical director fees for this project because we were in town for recording and so Don didn't have a chance to spend all my money on clothes. It was a very meditative period for me. I used to have my breakfast outside each morning and study the ants nearby as they toiled endlessly at their tasks.

Study Piano And Dance

For a year, I studied piano four hours a day and dance twice a week just to stay limber. I should have gone to a piano instructor, but instead I was teaching myself. After about six months, I was playing Tchaikovsky's *Dance Of The Sugar Plum Fairies*, along with Scott Joplin's *Maple Leaf Rag* and *The Entertainer*. My problem is that I memorized everything and still couldn't really do what I wanted to do; which was sight-reading and improvising. I wanted to be able to transcribe my music, and then just play it back without having to struggle with reading - something I never truly accomplished.

Work In Bar With Band

I was still moonlighting by playing in my friend's bar. We did country, rock and standards. It was boring - most embarrassing at times - I made a little extra money. It also kept me busy and got me out around people, since I was in the house alone most of the time. The place I played was called The Llano Del Rio Outpost which we jokingly renamed the Gonna del Rhea Outpost. It was a very secluded spot on old Highway 138 halfway between Victorville and Palmdale. Originally built to attract long-distance travelers coming through the Mojave Desert who needed to stop and have a meal, it had survived many years as a truck stop and restaurant for the locals. On weekends, it catered to a crowd of wealthy clientele who had moved up to this area to play golf at the nearby Crystalaire Country Club. Bob "Big Boy" Wyan, who had founded the original Big Boy Hamburger stand and resulting chain, was one example. He used to keep a bass fiddle at the club. He would come up to the bandstand and grab this thing like he knew what he was doing. Since it wasn't amplified, nobody would have known that he was totally faking it and completely lacking in musical ability. Actually unbeknownst to me, everybody knew it, and it was a running joke.

There was one fellow, a Hungarian immigrant, who would bring his daughter (an attractive girl in her early twenties) out and usually every week he had a different date. He could dance up a storm. A widower ran some business in LA and always had bucks to spend. I recall seeing him with a different woman every weekend. Finally one weekend he came in with the same woman he had been with the week before. She started to become his regular date and we wound up playing at their wedding a few weeks later. The chapel was a tiny church that looked more like a Mission in the San Fernando Valley. He had a huge wedding reception. I can't remember his name as we lost touch years ago, but I greatly respected and admired this guy.

Meet Darla

There was a young woman who worked at the restaurant named Darla. I liked her immediately and we started dating. Many warned me to stay away from this girl, and so I kind of shied away for a while, but there was something about her that kept drawing me back to her. I couldn't quite understand it, because once I got to know her, it seemed we had little in common.

Harry Duncan

About May or June of 1977, Beefheart's latest manager, Harry Duncan showed up on my doorstep one day. He had a favor to ask. "Oh boy, what is it now?" I thought. Harry seemed like a very reasonable guy. He told me that he had set up a small tour of the Northwest ending with two nights at the Golden Bear in Huntington Beach. The drummer, Gary Jaye, had suddenly and unexpectedly quit the Magic Band leaving Don without a drummer. I could certainly understand how this could happen, yet I didn't mind helping out. Jeff and Denny were my war buddies and Eric seemed nice enough. Obviously, I was the first person they thought of to fill the shoes in the ten days or so they had before the tour began. I consented to fill in temporarily.

Have To Leave House

A real estate investor bought my house and demanded that I leave so that he could improve the property and then raise the rent to 350% of what it had been before. This raised several problems for me. I had to find a place to store my piano, practice for the tour, and find a place to live all within 30 days or so.

3 Days In Pearblossom 4 In Venice

I asked the girl Darla, whom I had met in the club, if she would take in a temporary boarder as I knew she had room. I also mentioned this to my dance instructor friend, Derek Bailey. Derek suggested that since I wanted to get more involved in the LA music scene, my best bet would be to stay at his apartment in Venice. He said that it was only a weekend place for him and in return for painting and maintenance and $100 a month, I could stay there for the four nights a week that he was gone. Although he was gay and I had no interest in a relationship, I took the offer, as I would only be there when he was absent.

Apartments in this area were going for far more than I could afford, so I took the offer, thinking it would be a great way for me to start making connections in Los Angeles. I moved my few belongings to Darla's house in Pearblossom. Darla had a four-year-old daughter, Shonna, of whom I was quite fond. I was nearing my twenty-ninth birthday, and I think my paternal instincts were starting to manifest.

Involved With Darla

I almost immediately became involved with Darla more than I had gambled on. I figured being there only a couple days a week, I wouldn't really have time to develop any strong ties, however, I really loved the daughter and Darla seemed like a great person. I was traveling to the San Fernando Valley to rehearse in a refurbished storage facility each day. I would travel from Venice during the week, and from Pearblossom on the weekend.

The rehearsals for the tour showed up the same problems as I had always encountered with Don. He seldom rehearsed with the group and when he did, there were always problems with the arrangements, or with the PA etc. He still didn't know his lyrics. So, I grabbed a lyric sheet at the rehearsal, put a mike next to the drums and started singing his parts to show him where to sing. I knew my parts, and everybody else knew theirs. At this point, I really didn't care what Don thought, and so I "played my hand" so to speak to actually make Don do some work. He usually showed up with his art book and drew the entire time, or talked through the entire rehearsal time, accomplishing nothing.

I knew Jeff (Moris) Tepper and Denny Walley already, of course, but the new keyboard player, Eric Feldman was a recent acquaintance. I immediately liked him and I imagine that most people do when they meet him. He was very mature in the social sense and seemed to have a reasonably balanced view of the whole band experience. He had worked as an assistant recording engineer if memory serves correctly. This had given him vast experience at working on other people's music and still keeping a good perspective. By this, I imply that it was relatively easy for Eric to take the perspective of a sideman, hired to function as nothing more than a tool for Don's creativity.

Of all the Magic Band members that I actually met, I think Eric was probably the most overall suited to the often-trying position. Because of this, there was less conflict with Don. He seemed to have a soothing effect on Don, at least during the few weeks I was there. He was extremely intelligent and always seemed to have a balanced perspective in spite of the ups and downs caused by the whims and moods of Van Vliet.

One of the songs they were doing on this tour was *Glider* that I had never performed, so I had to write a chart of the drums to give me a rough idea of the cues and how long each section of the song actually was. I remember writing out a chart at the apartment in Venice, occasionally stopping to glance out the window at the ocean. I took walks every morning and evening on the beach, and it was a nice experience.

Meet At Jeff's

We met early in the morning at Jeff's the morning we embarked on this tour, which was to be low budget, but well organized, all the way. Jeff had bought a house in the San Fernando Valley a few months after joining the band. This says something about the financial status of Mr. Tepper prior to working with Don. Prior to joining the band, I am fairly certain he had been attending Humboldt State as a pre-med student. Jeff's financial position surely enabled him to be a more "stress-free" band member. He didn't have the almost poverty-level existence of most of the former band members, and of course, he was single, so he didn't have that added responsibility as opposed to Denny, who was dealing with the responsibilities of having a wife and child.

San Francisco

The first leg of the tour was to drive with Harry Duncan to San Francisco. We then stayed at his apartment, which was roomy and comfortable. He took us to some shops where we picked up important stuff, like toiletries, toothpaste, etc.

Drive To Portland

We then drove to Portland later that day, which was quite a leap - about 650 miles. We checked in late in the evening at the Rose Hotel, a really charming older hotel that Harry knew about. I remember hearing voices coming from a door in the back of the very large room and discovered that Jeff and Eric's room was opposite mine. I tried the adjoining door and it opened. I found myself standing at the foot of Jeff's bed. Jeff was lying on his side speaking to Eric, who was standing opposite and leaning against a dresser. I was waiting until they finished what they were saying when suddenly Jeff looked at me, leaning in the doorway at the foot of his bed and screamed like someone in a black and white horror movie about to be attacked by Frankenstein. Although I felt bad that I had startled Jeff, I fell on the floor, overcome with laughter and almost unable to breathe. Jeff was quite upset, thinking I was getting joy out of scaring the wits out of him, but in fact I had thought that certainly he had noticed me and had made no attempt to conceal the fact I was standing at the foot of his bed. It was a total surprise - for both of us.

It's 175 miles from Portland Oregon to Seattle, Washington, and about another 90 or so to the U.S. / Canadian border. Vancouver lays about 20 miles north of the border, so we probably had a half days' drive, more leisurely than the 652 miles traveled the previous day.

Since Harry Duncan was a guy who liked to combine fun things with touring. He took us to a gigantic used-bookstore in Portland, where I was able to pick up a book on Tut-Ankh-Amin, a subject I was currently fascinated with, having recently gone to an exhibit at the LA County Art Museum featuring artifacts from his tomb. We also took a quick tour of the famous Portland Rose Gardens and walked through row after row of every type of conceivable rose bush or vine one could wish to see.

I had only been to Canada once before and we had flown commercially, so driving through the border was a new experience. We had to wait in long rows of cars for a long period of time to be finally allowed in the country.

Vancouver

Just before we passed over a large bridge, there was a large rock in the water to the right of the road on which sat the sculpture of a mermaid. We crossed the bridge and drove a few more miles before coming to the small two-story motel in which we would stay. The club we played in was called The Old Roller Rink and before it was a club it was probably - you guessed it; a roller rink. It was a quaint building, with an "Old Town" feeling and a sign to match. The exterior was sided in redwood and it had an old Ghost Town look.

The club layout was a little odd. The stage was actually on the left wall, and the audience area seemed wider than it was deep, which was good for visibility but could be terrible acoustically, as you would often get a nice "slapback" echo from the back wall. We set up the equipment. The soundmen were quite cooperative and actually allowed me to EQ (fancy word for "tone controls") my own drums while Eric hit each drum for me (thank you very much Eric). The dressing room was in the back and down a flight of stairs to a rather nice-sized basement.

We went to the airport (some of us, and as I recall, we had a Van plus the station wagon, although I haven't a clue as to who drove the Van up to Vancouver, it was probably Denny) went to pick up Jan and Don at the airport. It was nice to see them, and everyone seemed in good spirits. Unfortunately it soon became apparent that Don and Harry had the same kind of tension between them that I had seen between Don and so many other business associates. Harry was a little like a mother hen, telling everyone what to do and where to eat. It was a little too much of a controlled-environment, and got a bit stifling at times. Don would rebel and "put Harry in his place" so to speak. I actually found myself screaming at Harry once in the car as he tried to find us a place to eat and yet was never satisfied with any place once inside.

After we had been to about four places Harry asked everybody what kind of food they wanted. Don said, "I don't know," and turned around to say, "What do you think, John." I replied, "I don't care what I eat as long as it's soon." By this time, I knew I had all the symptoms of hypoglycemia, and when I didn't eat, I was a monster. Harry took offense at my statement and said something chastising like, "That's about enough of that, John." At this point, I came completely unglued, which I had seldom done in my life toward another person. "Fuck you, Harry," I screamed. "I am hungry and I want to eat NOW!" I was immediately ashamed of my own lack of control, but at the same time, felt I was justified enough to avoid apologizing.

Later, when Don, Jan and I were alone, Jan confided that she thought it was great the way I handled Harry - (acting like a complete lunatic). I believe I did apologize to Harry later for my outburst, but tempered it with a plea to plan out our mealtimes a little more carefully. As it turned out, I have memories of similar difficulties many times during the dates we did out of state.

For instance, we visited Chinatown, sans Don, Jan and Denny. I got hungry and wanted to go grab a bite at a Chinese Restaurant that seemed to have a nice atmosphere and Harry immediately disagreed, telling me I should wait. I just walked across, entered, grabbed a menu and ordered. The rest of the guys joined me a few minutes later when it became apparent that I wasn't about to bend. We had a great meal, but it was always a bit tense.

Another incident showed the tension between Harry and Don:

We went out to dinner, and I was sitting with Don and Jan. I'm sitting across from them next to Harry. I think we were having Chinese food. Harry had gone to numerous restaurants before he decided that he had found one that was fit for us to go into. I was starving, you know. We're getting our food, and Don had his black book that he draws in. The food comes, and Harry is looking at Don's food, and Don said, "Don't look at my food. Leave my food alone! Quit picking at my food!" finally, he ate his soup, and they bring him the main plate, whatever it was. Harry reached over to grab something off the plate and Don picked his black book up and just, "WHAP!" hit him over the head, as hard as he could! I mean, it was loud, LOUD!

Harry, with his Beatle haircut kind of went, "POOF" you know. He say's "OK, I'll see you in court on that one." Don, says, "Fine! I've got a better lawyer than you." I was just so upset after this that I went outside. I thought, "My God, I'm not even going to be able to eat my meal." I thought later about what a funny moment it was, but it caused a scene at the time and ruined the meal.

I do remember some wonderful restaurants and one which I definitely have to give credit to Harry for finding. It was a small Greek family café. I hadn't eaten much Greek food prior to this, and I found myself completely enthralled with all the delightful new tastes and smells.

Mr. Duncan, also, was quite an entertaining fellow. He had a great amount of energy and had also managed Sunnyland Slim and The Meters. His stories of Sunnyland were priceless, and he had the voice down so that all the quotes sounded totally authentic. He was a great impersonator, so all the stories were extremely entertaining. I have recently discovered that he also has a fantastically accurate (almost frightening) impersonation of Don that randomly emerges in pertinent conversation with often very humorous results.

Sunnyland used to carry spare parts for his car in the trunk. If the generator would go out, he'd get his toolbox, pull out a spare generator, and change it on the spot. Harry thought this was amazing, but I see it as the guy being a survivor. I've done similar things myself. Sunnyland hand an electric coffee pot which doubled as a pot to cook wieners. Once he was done with the wieners, he would add the coffee - not changing the water. He fixed the unknowing Don a cup of coffee this way, and Don told him, "I think this is the best cup of coffee I've ever had."

One night, after Sunnyland opened for Don, he stood in the wings, watching a little of Don's show. His observation: "That Beefheart, he got a way with words, but his music ain't for shit."

Another night, as Don was waiting for Sunnyland to finish, he told someone, "I can't follow this guy, he's the real thing."

Ye Olde Roller Rinke

I wanted to rehearse the day before the first concert. No one else in the band desired to and so I said, "Well, fine, but we need it. If the show sucks, it doesn't really matter to me anyway. After all, I'm just a substitute." Everybody got really quiet for a minute and then they all agreed to rehearse. It was a good thing we did, because there were several misconceptions about songs that were cleared up at this rehearsal. Denny later confided to me that my little "speech" had made he and the rest feel a little guilty.

I was a little surprised at this, probably because I found myself staying as aloof as possible so as to not get sucked in to the old patterns.

When we got to *Glider*, Harry Duncan played the harmonica part while Don sang. Mr. Duncan was quite a good harpist and was the only harpist I ever remember who Don allowed to accompany him on stage. It really made the song, as the recording has harp all the way through. The band did a great job on the song, and it was one of my favorites, so I remember quite well being pleased with the overall effect.

Harry also came out with a strange rubber mask on (looked like some 10 year old maniac kid from a comic book) and performed *The Blimp*. It was ironic to me to remember my ill-fated *Blimp* practice session at the Trout House, followed by hours of interrogation. Suddenly, here I am playing those very parts I rehearsed. It got a great reaction in all the concerts.

I think we did two shows a night at this club for two nights. If I remember correctly, the first night, second show Don decided to have Eric start the show with a bass solo. This would have been quite fine with me, had he told me before we began the show. The announcement had been made, and because the club was so tightly packed and the stage so small, I had to go onstage first, worming and squeezing my way to the stage. I had already been told to go onstage and had made my way to the stage when Don decided in the change of order of the beginning of the set. I sat onstage by myself for what seemed like forever. Everything was quiet and I heard this loudly whispered, "John! John! Come back!"

A few people were starting to giggle nervously as I walked back off stage and made my way through the tiny packed club to the stairwell, gritting my teeth in anger. I was angry because it brought back memories of similar tricks Don had pulled in the past that basically resulted from a combination of his being so disorganized and his endless quest to remind everyone that he was in control. After almost 11 years of similar embarrassments, I had gone past the end of the rope and into the extreme. Considering it was basically a new band and wasn't that tight, I was quite nervous about going on stage to begin with. Since, I thought, I was doing this tour as a favor to Van Vliet, the least he could do was be a little more considerate of how this last minute change would feel. Instead, I was made to look "clueless" the first night of this tour in public because of an unimportant last minute change. It was a very embarrassing moment for me, but that was only the tip of the iceberg.

I stood in the stairwell, alone, just trying to calm down. My adrenaline was racing, partially due to my anger and partially due to normal stage anticipation. Ten years of his foolish decisions raced through my mind. I watched him walking off stage at Monterey, abusing drugs, abusing band members, replacing me with Bruschele, spending funds that were reserved for me, humiliating me in the airport of this very town a few years back. I could barely contain myself and felt as though I may explode.

I was standing in the stairwell, as I said, and decided to divert my mind by attempting to climb the sides the way rock climbers climb between two large rock surfaces. I was putting my feet on one side and pressing my body against the other side - inching my way up - just to use up all this excess adrenaline. Suddenly, both my feet went through the wall! In the dark, I had conceived the walls lining the stairwell as being concrete, when in fact, they were framed and covered with plaster. So it came to be that a giant hole appeared in the wall stamped with footprints suspiciously similar to mine.

The story that the group seemed to derive from this was that I, jealous that Eric was opening the show with a bass solo (in the spirit of Mr. Rockette Morton), threw a tantrum, and kicked a hole in the wall as a result, which was far from the truth. I imagine that is what they still believe. There never seemed to be an opportunity to explain and as everyone seemed to have already made up their minds, I decided there was little use in going into it.

Aside from that, I believe that the shows at the Roller Rink went quite well. I have little remembrance of details. This was my first time onstage with either Jeff or Eric. Jeff really moved around a lot, similar to the way Rockette used to move, but more forward and back than side to side.

After the show, Jan walked up with a smile and said that from her position in the audience, when I first walked on stage dressed in black with a small white scarf around my neck someone in the audience had said, Dracula on drums. I was always a fan of those old vampire movies, so I thought that was a great compliment.

Sea Show

Don and Jan invited me to a Sea World-type show while in Vancouver. I took along an old 8mm camera and actually was able to get some footage of those whales jumping out of the water. What a beautiful sight it was. It was a very pleasant experience. The place where we went also had an exhibit of tropical birds. The weather was unusually nice that afternoon, and we spent several hours at this location.

Seattle

The next stop was Seattle. I recall this drive very clearly, as it was the last time I ever attempted a back-handspring. We were in the long line at the border, and I got out of the car just to get some air. For no particular reason, I decided to do front-handsprings on the giant lawn, having been a gymnast in high school.

Feeling loose and confident, I did a round-off back-handspring and when I landed on my hands out of the handspring, I didn't catch myself properly hit my head and fell and heard "squish" in my neck, which probably signaled the partial herniation of a disk in the cervical vertebrae. I knew this was going to be bad, and it was. My neck was totally immovable within a matter of a few minutes and I was in serious pain. Years later, I was to find that I had a very large calcium deposit in my neck - probably as a result of this injury.

Eric was kind enough to loan me an inflatable plastic headrest he had brought along for sleeping in an upright position. I was able to wrap this around my neck.

The club in Seattle was a fairly large rock club and probably held close to 1,000 people. Actually, it also was an old Roller Rink, but much larger. Once we began playing, I was fine. Even though my neck was killing me, I was relieved that I could still play effectively. As with most shows, I really don't recall whether it went well or not. It seemed to me that all the shows we did go well. Denny sounded great and Jeff was a much stronger player after his one-year tenure. Although not an exuberant showman, Eric always seemed to be very consistently precise and dependable.

Portland

Portland brought us back to the Rose Hotel. The club was a smaller place than in Seattle. We did two shows that night. One of the waitresses at the club had an apartment across the street and opened it up to the band as a place to relax in between shows. It was catered just like a dressing room during a European tour would have been. We spent about an hour there and went to play the second set.

This crowd, as I recall, really seemed to enjoy us (especially the second show). In fact, there were actually females in the audience who liked the band! I was really surprised to see this, as there was usually a majority of males in the audience. After the show, I was sitting in the station wagon waiting for everyone to get in so we could leave. Suddenly, the waitress whose room we had used between shows got in and scooted over next to me. "I was invited to come along," she said, "to the party." I'm thinking, "what party?" as everyone hopped in and we drove off.

The girl wound up coming to the room I was sharing with Harry as I think he invited her (perhaps as a favor to me), because he was with another woman, an old flame who had stirred new sparks. Suddenly, I was trying to think about what to do to entertain this poor girl who's expecting a party. So, I got out my book on King Tut. I wasn't the rocker with the weed and wine sitting around for entertaining. I was more your nerdy-type guy who just worried about performing well at the next gig.

This room was furnished with a couple of chairs and a couch if I recall, and I sat there for some time explaining some of these artifacts to this girl, who at least pretended to be interested.

About this time, Harry starting looking really annoyed behind his old flame's back and giving me these looks like "will you please get out of here" and mouthing words I couldn't quite understand. Finally, as a subtle hint, he tossed me the keys to the station wagon and when I looked up, no one saw him mouth the word "GO!" with incredible emphasis. So, we left. She finally talked me into coming to her apartment.

She was wearing a black jumpsuit, but this was in the days of "tube tops" so the top of this black jumpsuit was actually a tube top with no shoulders or sleeves. She walked up to me at her apartment, unzipped the back and let it slide to floor and was standing there in front of me wearing nothing but panties. She was probably just 21 or younger and absolutely beautiful. These were the days before AIDS, and so people weren't as cautious as they are today. Being a young healthy male with no strong sense of morals as of yet, I felt it was my responsibility - in fact my duty - to follow her lead.

I was awake all night and as the sun rose I realized that the band had to leave by 10:00 and I had no idea how to get back to the Rose Hotel. The car was almost on empty, I had no money in my pocket, and even though the girl gave me instructions, I became lost in an endless maze of one-way streets. Finally, stopping to hail a cab and ask the driver for directions, I wound up making it back just in time to see that no one else was even close to being ready.

Eugene

During the drive, Don seemed totally sociable and happy. He was less the demanding taskmaster and more the prankster during most of this tour. He was especially accommodating to me, because, unbeknownst to me, he wanted me to stay.

The club in Eugene was smaller than the one in Portland. It was right down the street, within walking distance in fact, of where we were staying, which was a fairly comfortable standard-type motel - the "U" shaped kind with the swimming pool in the middle. The club had a look that I would consider "leftover remnants of the hippy culture." Stained-glass windows, old barn wood paneling, inside and out and the quaint feeling of a ghost town saloon - much like the Olde Roller Rink in Vancouver.

There were several fans involved in Project Jonah - Don's pet environmental project - who showed up and engaged Don in conversation. He told me that a local rep had walked up to him and said, "I hear you're into whales." He looked at me with this amused grin on his face, "Into whales!" he kept repeating and grinning. "How does one get 'into' whales?"

Don patiently spent a lot of time with these people and tried to get me to stick around but unfortunately I showed them I wasn't into whales by walking out of there. I did do my bit for ecology, though, I bought a Tee Shirt that says, "What was a whale, mommy?" Though I am very saddened by the way we treat our planet, these organizations sometimes seem too obsessive. I try to do my best to recycle everything possible, not litter and conserve water. However, thousands of years of accumulated human ignorance really aided in making a mess of things.

As Denny and I were walking back to the motel after the show, Denny said, "I made a few changes to the motel marquee." I looked up to read "Free Reds and good head" and fell on the sidewalk laughing until I could barely breathe. Denny said, "It was a pretty ballsy move, as the marquee is right across from the office." As we walked in, we could see in the office, the marquee in full view of their window. No one yet had a clue.

Portland Airport

I am absolutely positive at this point that Don and Jan flew back to Los Angeles from the Portland airport. Paul Young, Harry, and the rest of the group drove back in the station wagon. I still have no idea who drove the van with our equipment.

The Golden Bear

After a long, anti-climactic drive home, we finished this short tour by playing the Golden Bear in Huntington Beach. Eric Feldman's parents came down to hear the band play. Harry Duncan, upon first meeting Eric's parents, had decided to play the role of an east-coast Jewish man. He had played the role very convincingly, but now, each time Feldman's parents showed up, he had to do this schtick and remain "in character" to keep from becoming found out. I suppose this became a bit stressful and quite a chore. Eric's parents were sweet, charming people as I recall. I lost a bit of respect for Harry, because I thought this was quite disrespectful to them. However, I think Eric and Jeff both enjoyed watching Harry sweat through these later encounters.

Ask Me To Rejoin

Darla and I had driven down to this performance and made a weekend of it. I was still considering that I should have a more committed relationship with her. I was actually so out of touch with reality that I thought I could have a meaningful marriage with a girl whom I had cheated on less than a week before. In spite of this, we had an enjoyable weekend, wandering around to various shops and taking in the beauty of the ocean.

That evening, in between shows, Don called a quick meeting in his room presumably to go over the second show. We had made no changes so far in any of the shows but I was presuming my outburst and ensuing discussions in Vancouver about last-minute changes had caused Don to be a bit more careful to announce his plans.

Darla and I were the last ones in the room, which included the entire band, Jan, and Harry.

As soon as the room was quiet, Don looked at me and said, "Are you in?" and before thinking, I replied, "Yes." I immediately bit my tongue. I had been put on the spot, hadn't thought about what I was committing to, and now, it was too late to change my mind or think about the consequences. If I were to say "no" it would have hurt feelings and felt uncomfortable, and so I chose the cowardly way out.

Pro-Beefheart Darla

Darla, having lived in the South for several years, was a big fan of the blues. She was exceedingly impressed with Don's voice, as most blues fans are. She also thought the music was absolutely great (mostly, she listened to *Safe As Milk*). I have to give her credit for being able to "hear" and have an open mind. She was overwhelmingly enthusiastic about my decision, which made it difficult for me to explain my past experiences. She would put on the albums I had at the house and say, "Listen to this! This is really great! How come you never played these albums for me before?" Mostly what she played was *Safe As Milk* and *Clear Spot*. However, she did manage to make it through *Trout Mask Replica* and *Decals*.

For a while, I made the one hundred twenty mile round trip to rehearsals, which weren't being financially compensated. I was working in a bar on weekends, as my unemployment had run out. I made $50 a week, and that was my only source of money at the time. Don would show up for about half the rehearsals and seldom if ever rehearse. Mostly, he would talk, draw incessantly, and write new song ideas when he was there. There was no plan and seemingly no work lined up.

I sat down and explained to Darla a brief history of what I had experienced thus far working with Don. I remember getting into quite a bit of detail in the talk, which went on for about two hours. The whole time, her daughter Shonna, who had never seen Van Vliet, sat opposite us drawing on a single sheet of lined paper. Usually, her attention span was quite short and her drawings consisted of two or three scribble lines and a stick figure. She would generally interrupt any conversation we had in intervals of never more than two minutes. Tonight, however, she was silent for nearly two hours.

When we finished talking, she held up her drawing. "It's a people!" she exclaimed, and when I looked, my skin crawled for a moment. It was a very detailed drawing of Don Van Vliet, dressed in black, wearing his Quaker hat and holding his soprano sax. The sax had details of keys as though she had been looking at a photo, and the whole drawing was absolutely phenomenal for anyone, much less a four-year-old to have done with no model or prior knowledge of the subject. What triggered this drawing and her absolutely unusual behavior that evening is still a mystery to me. It was as though she captured the image from my mind.

Robert Williams

I made my announcement to leave the band to Don in a phone call. He was very upset and said that I should go and apologize or at least explain myself to the "new guys" meaning Jeff and Eric, because they would think it was their fault. I went down to the rehearsal hall to pick up my drums, and Robert Williams, my replacement, was there. He was sleeping in the studio on a little pad in the corner. I recall being puzzled because one of my very wonderful foot pedals was gone from my set, as was a special rare Swiss cowbell I had had for years. Robert said that the other band that had shared the rehearsal area had just moved out and perhaps they had taken them by accident. I didn't see how this could happen, as my cowbell was on a special bracket that one would have to have a screwdriver and wrench to disassemble. The foot pedal had been attached to my left bass drum.

Robert and I spent quite a bit of time together just talking. I found out that his background was drum and bugle corps. He asked me for help on specific drum parts and so I sat with him for several hours and went over my style of playing and the Beefheart drumming in general. He was a quick studier and a good player.

Williams On Don's Control

Robert Williams: With Don, I had to hand it to him. He really had a talent for getting people to do what he wanted them to do. No one was held at gunpoint to do any of the shit that he asked them to do. But he used manipulation and brainwashing and all of that stuff ... He abused his own power - he could have been a lot cooler about it. In order to get the results he wanted I guess that's how he had to approach it. He probably didn't know any other way. But, he accomplished what he set out to do, and to get all that stuff recorded and to go out and do shows and play that music ...was cool

John French: Absolutely

But Williams enjoyed the status his Magic Band tenure brought.

Robert Williams: That was some of the better times that I had had. I was considered a "celebrity" part of the time, at least by people who had heard of him, especially in Europe.

Later in reference to Don's power over Tepper, Feldman, and Snyder:

Robert Williams: One thing that it does exemplify is the power of Beefheart over these two guys, to be so cloak-and-dagger and to be so afraid of what Don would say to the point where they would actually become fair-weather friends and spies.
John French: You know what? Bill Harkleroad and Mark Boston did the same thing. "Hey, Don wants to see you." I did go down with them and I rejoined the band, but the thing was that, it was like 2:00 a.m.
RW: With this glazed look in their eye saying, "Don - wants - to - see - you."

Williams liked the music. One of his favorites was *Dr. Dark* in which he had the challenge of coming up with parts that occasionally sounded like both Artie and I playing at the same time. Williams liked the fact that Don had such a mastery of double-entendre and could subtly denote sexual topics without drawing immediate attention and censorship. An example was "she brought an airplane down" noting the phallic symbol of the airplane being down to denote that the woman had pleased her man.

Williams said he didn't understand some of Don's art, to which I replied "He was way better with words than with a brush." RW replied, "He was way better with harmonica than he was with saxophone."

Williams On Sax

Robert Williams: We used to do Suction Prints on the Shiny Beast record. We played it live without him. I said, "Don, you know how James Brown is, he has the band come out and do all this hip stuff and all of a sudden James Brown comes out and it's like "celebrity time" and everyone stands up and starts clapping." I said, "Wouldn't it be a great idea to open the show with Suction Prints and have you come out for the next song? It would be like great. We'll kick ass and show them what your band can do, and then you walk out and people will just freak!" so we did it and it was great. That's the way it went down, we had standing ovations. We had Denny and me and Jeff and Eric. When Suction Prints came together, it was just so powerful. Then, he decided to blow saxophone over it. He saw all the attention we were getting, and thought, "Oh, I want a piece of that too." And he fucked the whole song up, and then when it was time to do the record, he blew it over the record. But there were versions I had on tape with Denny playing and you could hear the parts, you know You look at it in terms of artwork it's like someone doing a beautiful landscape and then taking a black paint brush and just scribbling over it.
John French: He did that on Japan In A Dishpan as far as I'm concerned.

French On Williams

I really enjoyed hearing Williams playing later on live recordings of tours. He was a great drummer with a good sense of time and he made the parts work well with the music. RW remarked he wasn't very happy with *Shiny Beast* but more so with *Doc* and especially the piece *Best Batch Yet* where he was able to play his own written parts. I thought he was a powerful and energetic force that really drove this incarnation of the Magic Band well.

John French: I remember that you did a great performance on Cours TV when you played **Best Batch Yet.** *Don came back and shook your hand at the end.*

Williams On Band Dynamics

Williams had asked Tepper and Feldman for Don's phone number and felt the reason they wouldn't give it to him is because they still have "that cloud of Beefheart approval" hangin' over their heads. It was a shame, as I could get neither of them to interview for this book. Asked about whether Williams had spoken with Don in recent years:

Robert Williams: Those guys won't give me his number. They like the idea of having Don as their kind of "exclusive" deal there. Like, "We have a connection with Don, but you don't." Like, I'm Cinderella and those two are the evil stepsisters.

It did seem to me that both Tepper and Feldman were very stand-offish and protective concerning Don. This is probably at Don's request and puts them in an uncomfortable position. Feldman declined an interview on the premise that there would be "hurt feelings" and Tepper just wrote an email that said I'll pass.

On the other side of this coin, I also saw more of a similarity in values with Feldman, Tepper and Van Vliet than I ever did with Williams. Williams seemed more of a party-guy, wanting to dress in contemporary fashions and hit on babes, whereas Tepper and Feldman were more conservative in the sense that pleased both Don and Jan.

East vs West

Robert was raised in a large family, which helped him to be a lot more aggressive in asking for his fair share of things and probing questionable offers and dealings with Don. Up to this point, Don's history of financial dealings definitely seemed to lean toward the shady side and this was pretty much unanimously witnessed by anyone who had business dealings with Don. The band members were only sidemen by this time, but they were young, eager to please, and happy to be associated with Beefheart, whose reputation may help later when they pursued their own careers.

John French: So, I had a real hard time standing up to Don, of course, I was a lot younger, too, I was 18 when I joined the band.
Robert Williams: And he was Beefy and strong and intimidating.
JF: Yeah, and he was even worse then. During the Doc sessions, he was a lot, lot mellower.
RW: Well, you know, there's an East Coast thing and a West Coast thing too. Look at Denny - and I'm from the East Coast too. On the East Coast, you can have fights with your brothers and sisters, pull each other's hair, break each other's toys, and say horrible things to each other, but you'd still die for each other. You get along really well. So, sometimes, that was just my personality. I'd be pissed off at him and I'd say what I thought. You know, after that, it would be like, "Hey, you wanna go out and get a beer now?" They'd be looking at me like, "YOU PSYCHO YOU!!!" Denny was the same thing you know - like "Whattaya got, a mouse in your pocket?" - a little snide jab here and there.
JF: But that's part of the culture you grew up in.
RW: Yeah. That's why it was easy for me to take some of the shit from Don too, because people back there are kind of verbally abusive and stuff.
JF: So, it kind of toughens you up, you get a thicker skin.
RW: Exactly, but you also have a softer heart. I found the difference between the East Coast

and the West Coast is the East Coast you can have bitter enemies and really close friends, but on the West Coast, your enemies are kind of lukewarm and your friends are "kinda" friends.

Married Aug. 16, 1977

In one of the worst decisions I ever made, I was married to Darla on August 16, 1977, in a civil ceremony in Las Vegas, Nevada. I was told by some of my friends and future in-laws that this marriage was "a good idea." It would serve to commit us to each other and we would be able to build on this. Moral of the story: don't go by your gut-instinct when it comes to personal relationships, especially marriage and never commit until you are certain. I knew something was lacking in my life and thought that I would find it in marriage and "instant parenthood" It wasn't meant to be and I knew it in my gut before I did it.

Happily Never After

Driving to Las Vegas, we stopped to get something to eat at The Green Tree Inn in Victorville, and I heard over the radio playing in the restaurant that Elvis Presley had been found dead that day. Now, I wasn't a big Elvis fan, but I did think he was great, and was deeply saddened to hear of his tragic death at such a young age. I wanted to turn around and go back.

We drove back the same night. The drive back was one of the scariest drives I have ever had. It was raining so hard that you could barely see the road, and trucks would barrel by and throw so much water on the windshield that it would become impossible to see the road at all for several moments at a time.

It was immediately apparent that we had a bad marriage. I couldn't sleep at night. I found out she was taking amphetamines called "black beauties" and dealing drugs from the house. This had all been hidden until after we married.

Denny Makes His Bed

Denny Walley: You know the reason I was fired out of the band was because when we came back from Europe everything was kind of falling apart and he was having rehearsals and going over the same crap again and not writing anything new in particular. Rather than play or have to come up with something, he would talk for like 3 or 4 hours. He wouldn't play a note. He was breaking in new guys. It was like 9, 12, 13 hour rehearsals and we wouldn't play one song in all that time. You know how Don can do - you take a break, you go out and have tea, and you come back two hours later. His concept of time did not exist. Mind you, at the time, I had a young son, I had a wife, and I had to generate some money. This was all wasting time. I wasn't being paid for it. I mean, we were being paid very menially. If we (could only have) expedited what had to be done, if we had a clear picture … I couldn't make appointments or anything. I couldn't do anything. I never knew when it was going to end, or where it was going to go. Having been through this a couple of times before, it was all bullshit. It was very difficult for me to stand there and keep my mouth shut. Because I knew what was going on. I liked to be involved in the writing process, you know, it is a wonderful thing, to be in on the creative process, but unfortunately, monetarily, I could not afford to do that. It wasn't something I felt I had to be there for. I felt it should happen and then you bring it in and you tell people what you want. That wasn't happening. It was like - you gotta wait ten hours before one thing would happen.
John French: Yeah, I always felt like I was being used as a paintbrush during those things. Like, my time and who I was didn't exist - it was just somebody using me.
DW: Yeah, like play this 80 times until I find out what I wanna do. I just didn't have any patience for that any longer.

And Sleeps In It

Denny received a call from one of the band members - who he recalls as being Eric - telling him that he was no longer in the group. The voice over the phone said, "You made your bed, and now you have to sleep in it."

Denny Walley: I was out - after the fatal phone call. Don couldn't even call me himself. When I approached (Van Vliet) about it later - much later, he denied that he knew anything about it. Like, "Right, your lead guitar player got fired from the band, I didn't show up (for rehearsal), and you had nothing to do with it."

RW On Denny

Robert Williams: So we go out and do all this touring and get Don's popularity up and he fucking DROPS Denny like a hot potato right after he got a deal with Warner Brothers.

Robert goes on to explain that the reason Denny was dropped was because the rest of the band members were all fans - young guys, impressionable, and easily manipulated. Van Vliet called Denny "Mr. Union. Guy."

Robert Williams: Denny had a family, and a son, Jaryd. It was like, "Hey, look, I'd love to stay, but I gotta go." At six o'clock, bam! You know, he'd wait until the song was over, but he'd have his guitar in the case. "OK guys, see ya," and he'd drive away. And you know how Don is...

This is the same trait previously frowned upon by anyone who wasn't into the "magic-band-as-total-absorption-lifestyle" approach with which Beefheart felt the most comfortable. Snouffer eventually left because of this. Artie complained about the wasted time, as did I and several others. Denny had worked with Zappa, who blocked aside specific amounts of time to do specific things. The contrast to working with Don was ridiculous. One could spend weeks and accomplish next to nothing. Another day, Don may be three hours late and just getting wound up at the prescribed end of rehearsal, railing on anyone not willing to stay because "this could mean a lot of money for you and a lot of money for me" or "man, we're gonna lose this thing if you leave now."

Robert Williams: As soon as Denny was gone, it was like, "That man, that goddamned man, that Union Guy." ... He had to get Denny out of the picture. That was a big mistake, because, even though Richard Redus is probably a good guy and everything, he's nothing compared to Denny. The solo at the end of Ode T' Alex, and the end of Bat Chain Puller? I mean, Jesus, Denny played the shit out of that. The parts are one thing, you can come up with cool parts, but if you don't have someone who knows how to execute them with feel and soul, it's not the same thing - it's a completely different part.

On The Demonization Of Denny

Richard Redus: It's all bullshit, cause there's no nicer guy in the world than Denny. But, he (Don) would have painted a picture of Denny like he was Satan. So I was convinced that he would talk the same way about me. But, he didn't and I'm not sure exactly why.

I was a little surprised by Redus' following statement, as Denny seemed to portray the opposite image to me as is stated here:

Richard Redus: Denny was a very submissive person to Don. Don and he would get into these crazy dominant / submissive little struggles.
John French: How do you know about this? Did you ever see the band rehearse?
RR: No, but I had tapes of them rehearsing, and I also heard stories from Eric and Jeff. I also talked to Denny. I went over to Denny's house a few times.
JF: So, did he help you with parts and putting things together?
RR: No, I can't remember why we were going over there. I went over there with either Jeff or Eric a couple of times. It may have just been a social thing.

This seems to fly in the face of Denny's portrayal of always standing up for himself and also what Williams remembers:

Robert Williams: He didn't take any shit from Don. He did a little bit, but there was a line and Don respected it, but he knew if Denny was going to be there, he'd never be able to bullshit, manipulate and brainwash the guys. Denny would just go "Whoa ..." he'd laugh at him.

RW On Denny Walley
Both Robert Williams and I agree on the fact that Denny Walley is one of the best slide players out there. His slide technique enhanced Don's music to a great degree - even lifting it into a more accessible level.

John French: Is it my imagination or is Denny like one of the best slide players out there?
Robert Williams: He's awesome.
JF: He made Don's music sound so good. The slide guitar parts sounded so good when he played them.
RW: Another thing is that a really hard sound to get is at the very low register of the guitar when you're doing slide. He was such a student of the blues. He knew everything about Muddy Waters and all those guys. It was a science for him. He had the savvy. He might as well have been one of them, how he played.

Denny was upset by the fact that Don was having RR learn Denny's solos - note for note - though they had, for the most part, been improvised by Denny. Richard didn't think much about it at the time:

Richard Redus: I can't believe, looking back now, that I did it, but I didn't give a darn at the time. ... That was pretty much a huge violation of Denny.
John French: Well, yeah, but it wasn't really your violation of Denny, it was Don's violation of Denny.

Richard observed that Don would bully anyone who allowed themselves to be bullied, and when they left the room, he would not hesitate to say anything about that person when they were not present in the room. The few who stood their ground, however, received good treatment from Don and he spoke respectfully of them.

John French: Most of mine (encounters with Don) were on a private level. I would get him alone and say, "Don't ever talk to me like that again." So, I learned with he and I that it was much better to approach him on a private level, get him off to himself and say, "Don, that's a no-no with me. Don't do that with me.

Richard Redus: Right, and he was much more reasonable under those circumstances. ... He didn't talk respectfully of very many people. Most people, he would say, "Aaah, they learned everything they knew from me!"

Around the end of 1976, Michael Traylor and Teresa were married. Traylor moved back to Lancaster, because his wife worked on the B-1 Bomber, which was under contract to Rockwell - one of the Aerospace companies up here at the time.

Michael Traylor: There was this biker bar - you might be able to help me remember the name - there was a biker bar right at the crossroads of Sierra Highway and ...
John French: Avenue L. Yeah, it was called the Delta Lady Saloon.
MT: That's it.
JF: Yep.
MT: My wife like to go there to play pool. She was in a woman's pool tournament. We'd go there and every once in a while I'd run into Don. I'd hang out - while she was playing pool, and I'd be chatting with Don. Apparently, Don became very enamored with my wife. She was an Apache Indian with very beautiful Indian features. The only time I was absent - like if I went to the bathroom or something - he'd always be talking to her. We lived in this little three-bedroom house near there. My wife had a daughter who was six years old at the time, so she was my stepdaughter. We had two rooms setup - one for my wife and myself, and one for my stepdaughter. The third room was a guest room. Around Christmas time, or perhaps early January, my wife and I had a big fight. She had gotten angry with me and decided to go sleep in the guest room. I rolled over and went back to sleep. A little while later, I felt the water in the waterbed rolling in there and she climbed in the bed and got up next to me. She was as cold as ice and shivering. I asked, "What's the matter." She said, "I don't know." So, I asked her again. She said, "There's a ghost in that room." She was just absolutely freezing cold and shaking. I got her calmed down. Finally, I got her to tell me what happened. She said she was in the bed and she felt this presence in the room. She looked up and really didn't see anything because it was dark. But, she felt there was a presence and it grabbed her and held her down on the bed, then laid on top of her. She could feel the presence of whatever this presence was, putting pressure against her on the bed. She said, after a few minutes, it left and that's when she came back in to where I was. So, we start thinking "Wow, maybe we've got a haunted room in this house." We really believed that, because another time my stepdaughter had gone in there and she'd had nightmares in there. We just wrote it off. It was probably not more than two or three days after that we were at the Delta Lady and Don was there. I had stepped away for a moment and Don - now I'm telling you second-party now, because this is what my wife told me - that Don came up to her and said, "Did you enjoy my visit the other night?"
JF: Ooh!
MT: She just freaked, you know? She came up to me and said, "You won't believe what he just told me."
JF: And he was referring to the night when she had this experience?
MT: Right. She asked, "That was you?" He said, "Yes, I visited you." So, I just couldn't believe it, so I went over to Don and asked, "Did you come over to the house the other night?" He said, "You'll have to ask Teresa." So, I really didn't know what to make of it, but from that night on, Teresa would never have anything to do with Don. Didn't want to be around him - nothing. I did continue to visit with him and Jan from time to time. This was in the early part of '77 - there still wasn't anything going on with him, so I continued to see him from time to

time. By the end of '77 I was pretty much entrenched in the Fabian thing in LA. I didn't see him much.

Mark Boston

Mark used to work right across the alley from where I lived. I would see him every day, driving to work, and he would look over and give a little wave. After I moved, he contacted me, by phone. There was a female singer interested in putting a group together and she wanted Mark and I in the group.

Jane Gaskill

A woman by the name of Jane Gaskill was putting together a group to do a demo. She had charts and a manager. I went to some of the rehearsals. John Thomas was also in the band. As was an English guitarist, whose name I have forgotten, his playing was even more forgettable, but he was a likeable bloke. Jane seemed to have at least adequate talent. She was a tall blonde with a real affinity for lots of makeup and high fashion. It only involved a couple rehearsals, a day in the studio, and then they would shop the tape around. Jane had hired a professional arranger, who had given her nothing imaginative at all - just stock arrangements.

John Thomas

We rehearsed in a small theatre where John Thomas was living. It was in East LA, if I remember correctly. A mutual acquaintance name Jerome was the manager, and he was trying desperately to get this place off the ground. I had met Jerome in theatre classes in late 1973 and early 1974 during the college production of *A Company Of Wayward Saints*.

Dan Dimmit

A fellow named Dan Dimmit also lived at the theatre. He was "psychic" according to some, and one of my friends, painter Mike French (no relation) said that he thought this guy was so evil he could be "The Devil Incarnate." "Devil Dan" he used to call him. I recall Dan's cousin saying that Dan had the ability to hold a camera up to his forehead , snap a picture, and when the film was developed, there would be images of his thoughts on the resulting photos.

Dan would sit during our rehearsals, on a chair placed in the middle of the empty floor and stare at me with this wild-eyed look. It was sort of a bad Bela Lugosi imitation. I had been around Don, who was mentally much more powerful than Mr. Dimmit, so I would laugh at him on purpose, just to upset him. I also knew that he was bi- or homo- sexual, and he was always coming up to give me neck rubs during breaks. Everybody would look at me like I was nuts for letting this guy touch me, but my neck really hurt after playing, and these neck rubs helped. I had been around enough gays in theatre not to be threatened any longer.

Ms Gaskill's Business Plan

I knew little about Ms. Gaskill, except that I didn't like her very much. I had to go to her apartment one day before rehearsal, and her and her female "life partner" were wearing nothing but robes, loosely undone at the waist. When answering the door, Jane casually flipped her robe open, exposing her breasts as she pulled it around her to tie the belt. Her roommate stripped to the waist and washed her hair in the kitchen sink as I sat in the dining room watching.

Jane then explained some of her business moves. The logo for her record company was the clincher to me. It was to consist of a bloody human heart tightly wrapped in several strands of barbed wire. On the front of the heart was superimposed a "cunt" (her word) and she thought that she would use "her cunt" as a model.

My thought was that her whole approach was shock value. Her music was completely boring and there was not much we could do with it to make it better. Her sordid lifestyle turned me off and depressed me.

I also noticed that cocaine was floating around at every rehearsal. I refused to indulge, but the others seemed more than willing to sniff this poison up their nose. Her manager was trying to "pay" for rehearsals with cocaine. I told her that I would only play for money, that I had bills to pay, and that I guaranteed nothing after the demo session.

The demo session was not a monumental occasion. The music was dull and unimaginative and the songs and lyrics even duller. The whole concept was kind of this "Amazon" standing on stage in big flowing garments while offstage fans blew scarves around for effect etc. She even had a theme song, *Cruising Up The Amazon* that was filled with not-so-subtle double-entendre images of oral sex.

I remember her hugging me when I showed up for the session, and I realized that her breasts, when pressed up against me, were like hardballs. She had obviously had some work done. I left the project after being told that I would be paid in cocaine.

It wasn't until several months later that I found out from a fellow musician that Ms. Gaskgill was not a Ms at all, but a Mr. I don't know how I could possibly have missed this, but apparently our tall "amazon" was a transsexual - a "man with the woman head."

Paul Delicato

Angela, one of the dance instructors I had worked with, was now married to a man named David Bates. David was a reggae-guitarist from Jamaica. He was white, and had wealthy middle class parents, so really was not a true "reggae" Rastafarian-type. He had been asked to assemble a band for a New Years performance and six-week follow-up at a local club by Paul Delicato, a local singer.

Paul had the same manager as Liberace, and was a singer of the Tom Jones / Englebert Humperdink mold. He was a guitar player and his basic love was the blues, which he could sing and play quite well. He had a couple of albums out and I had once gone to hear him perform out of curiosity as he was getting a lot of local press. However, he was a lounge act; pure and simple. He didn't write his own material, though his albums always had some of the best studio musicians one could hope for.

Essex House

So a band was formed of some of the most unlikely guys you would ever find working together. John Tanner, my keyboardist friend was hired for keys. He was a blonde longhaired guy who could have been the model for the "happy face" as he was a total optimist. Mark Boston was chosen for bass. Mark had been living in town and was still working at the local Datsun dealership (blue collar stuff). David Bates was on guitar. Now, David was a nice man, and he could play a great rhythm guitar, but he really had no affinity for soloing at all, and he was the sole guitarist in the group, as Paul just sang during his "show."

My marriage had already failed but I was struggling to make it work. I'd go to rehearsal with scratches on my face from my wife attacking me. The actual money I was to make from this gig was quite good, and I would have thought this would have made Darla happy, but instead she was trying to sabotage all my efforts. John Tanner was the guy who kept me sane through this period of time. He would always have something good to say to me.

One morning a month or so before separating from my wife, I awakened to hear men's voices in the yard. I walked out in my pajamas and found two big biker types standing in the yard. Upon inquiry, one guy answered, "I just bought the place," in a deep hoarse voice. He then turned back to his friend and continued the discussion as if I didn't exist. I walked into the house slightly stunned. I later heard rumors that the one fellow was out on bail on an attempted murder rap. I kept asking myself: "Do I lead a charmed life or what?"

While house hunting, I noticed my former landlord (the one who had made me move) over at my old house. I struck up a conversation with him and found out he was done renovating the place. Since I was working, I was able to afford to move back into the house - at three and a half times the former rate.

Peaches

Darla had brought a dog home, which Shonna named "Mr. Peachbowl" and I called "Peaches." She deserted him when moving out and so I brought him into town to live with me. He was a great dog. I had him for about ten years and we became great friends.

CHAPTER THIRTY EIGHT:
REPLACEMENT PARTS

Bat Chain Puller promo shot from 1976, L to R John Fre[...]
Don, John Thomas, Jeff Tepper and Denny Walley.

Richard Redus

Denny Walley's replacement - Richard Redus - was a twenty-one year old guitarist friend of Jeff and Eric's who was living in Colorado at the time, but at loose ends as to what to do next with his life. Redus received a letter from Jeff asking if he may be interested in playing guitar for Don. Redus was interested and they set up an audition. He describes that it was if Don had already decided to hire him before he played a note. He played a song or two from *Trout Mask Replica* with the band and that was it.

John French: What do you think Don was trusting in - the instincts of Eric and Jeff?
Richard Redus: Well I think it was partly that, and partly his hit on me as a person, because we hit it off - also partly because he was desperate to get something going. He was just -on the verge of signing that contract with Warners and was really excited to have another shot at success.

Redus, in his interview, reveals something that is, again, rather telling in light of the fact that Van Vliet claimed to have taught his band members the parts "teaspoon by teaspoon."

Richard Redus: It's funny, because I got a reputation in that band as being good at pulling parts off records? We were working up some songs off of Lick My Decals Off *- the parts are really hard to grasp. So, I did* Bellerin' Plain *and a couple other songs - guitar parts and bass parts. Then we got a chance to go into the archives and listen to the masters with total separation, and it turned out that I was totally wrong about most of the parts.*

The interviews seem to all tell the same story: the band generally learned most of the material from recordings - not from Don.
Redus also hit upon the same "xenocricity" theory Zappa had mentioned earlier, but more in the area of frequencies than tempos:

Richard Redus: You know how when frequencies blend together - they create their own new frequency?
John French: Oh yeah, well the thing is that anything that hits at the same time is going to sound like a bigger denser chord sometimes.

Redus went on to speak about how sometimes these "new frequencies" would be interpreted as the part itself - thereby causing a lot of inaccuracies in interpretation.

Baptism Of Fire

Don wanted to perform with the new lineup before going into the studio, so the band was learning material for a one-off concert opening for the new Mahavishnu Orchestra in Riverside, California in the Summer of 1978. I asked about Don's stage personae as viewed from the new member's perspective. RR observed that Don seemed to receive a certain power from being terrified and would channel that power and throw it right back out, projecting it as his own. In Redus' view, Don seemed to enjoy hitting back at the monster in front of him, but his eyes suggested that he was afraid.

Does Dark Matter?

John French: You were talking about and one of the things you mentioned was that "witch doctor" or "Obeah Man" mentality or aura. Would you care to expound on any of that?

Richard Redus: I guess what I mean when I say-especially in this culture that we live in - we prefer not to recognize darkness. However, just because we don't recognize it doesn't mean it isn't there. In fact, it's always there. It's always having its effect on reality.

JF: Are you referring to spiritual darkness here?

RR: I guess so, yeah. I guess I'm talking about spiritual darkness.

JF: As a force outside of man, a force inside of man, or both?

RR: I'd say both. Because, I guess what I'm thinking of is death, and then a compilation of things that are hovering around death, like pain, sorrow, cruelty, anguish. All those types of phenomenon are taboo for us or else they're dealt with in a totally superficial way like Terminator *(the movie), or some superficial take on them so that we can avoid looking at them any further - in our own lives.*

JF: We see them portrayed so unrealistically we can't put them into the reality of our lives.

RR: Right, and it gives us an excuse not to look further because we think we've seen them. Like, "OK, I saw fifty guys get killed in Lethal Weapon *and so therefore I understand death..."*

JF: Yeah, "I know what real stage blood is..."

RR: Right.

JF: Or, it's portrayed so ridiculously that it seems almost cartoon-like and so therefore it's not threatening. Or we view it as something that couldn't possibly be real because it is ridiculous. Like for instance, demon possession, what is the first thing you think of?

RR: I don't know, Alien?

JF: Or like The Exorcist, *which is this stupid Hollywood Movie of demon possession, which is absolutely and absurdly exaggerated in a monster movie quality.*

RR: I would say that to really profoundly understand life, one has to explore all the realms of light and darkness. That's a problem. How can Twentieth-Century Western people have a full life if half of it is considered to be taboo? The fact is - there you have it - a lot of people do have very superficial lives.

Speaking Of Superficial Lives...

When musicians are bad, they go to a place that's really hot and dry and get ordered around by someone they have nothing in common with. They have to wear really tacky clothes, play inane music, and they get to meet all kinds of people they spent their whole lives trying to avoid - like husband and wives in matching outfits. This place is called Las Vegas. The person who orders them around is an amiable lounge-singer. The people they get to meet are people who actually have such bad taste that they like it there and pay money to stay in hotels so they can lose the rest of their money gambling. I hope to never again hear the sound of slot machines roulette wheels, people gambling, and waitresses asking you if you want a half-sized, watered-down complimentary drink.

I lived (if you can call it "life") on the strip across the street from the Hacienda (which is now gone) in a motel that had silverfish the size of lobster - which is, I supposed, better than going to a restaurant that has lobster the size of silverfish. Every night, at 8:45, I would will one foot to move in front of the other until I actually found myself sitting at the drums playing the warm-up set. We were dressed in Disco outfits - white vest and white pants (so easy to keep clean) squinting under outrageously bright lights. If the PA system wasn't quite loud enough in the little lounge, we weren't legally allowed to touch the volume controls. According to the union rules, only a certified union stagehand could touch those holy knobs. If the lights were too bright, you weren't allowed to dim them. Only a certified union stagehand could fondle the holy rheostats. I changed the settings anyway - screw the unions.

Las Vegas already symbolized one bad mistake: my first marriage. Now, it symbolized so much more. Occasionally a woman from Iowa visiting on a three-day special would select me as the answer to her romantic fantasy. Eventually, all the band members were replaced and the new guys all seemed to hate me. They would all come dressed in the opposite stage outfits than we had decided upon. It made me look like I'd made the mistake.

14 Weeks Of Hell

This was probably the worst period I had in my life aside from those magical *Trout Mask* days. I was playing Disco-like music in a horrible place. My father was on his deathbed. I was going through a divorce. But, hey, it wasn't all bad. I just can't think of the good stuff right now, but tomorrow is another day!

Actually, there was a good side to this. I was getting paid for playing. It wasn't money being "advanced against my future earnings" but actual cold, hard, cash, and more money than I ever made in music per week on the best-paid Beefheart tour I ever did. Come to think of it, I was only paid for one tour I did with Don - by Herbie Cohen.

Of course, I hated the music I was playing. Paul Delicato actually wasn't a bad guy. He had a great sense of humor, was charming, and had a great set of pipes. My thought was that he shouldn't be peddling himself on the strip as "Tom Clones" (as we guys in the band used to refer to him) but pick up his Strat and sing the blues. He had a great touch on guitar, was a fantastic soloist and had a really great take on the BB King style blues.

The best night we ever had was when a party of black people came in the club. I think it was a wedding or maybe a family reunion, but there were 30-40 people - all of them African-American. Paul strapped on his Stratocaster, plugged into his vintage Fender Bassman, and wowed his crowd for two hours straight. He loved it, they loved it, and the band loved it.

The only people who didn't seem to appreciate it were the management. They complained that they did not want "those kind of people" in their lounge. A usual night in that lounge was about 7-10 people - but they were mostly white. I didn't see any lack of drinks flowing on the blues night under trial, so it was definitely a case of racist bigotry.

Mark's Father Dies

Mark's father died a few weeks after we started here. Shortly after this, Mark was fired by the bandleader. Lucky him - I had to stay.

My Father

I would occasionally make the 8-hour round trip home. We had one day when the club was "dark." I would leave immediately after playing - 3 a.m. in the morning, drive the four hours, get home at 7 a.m. and sleep until early afternoon. Then I would get up, eat something and go see my father in the hospital, spend the night, and drive back the next day, arriving about 7, with just about enough time to eat, shower and dress in those tacky outfits for the first show.

I felt like a robot. I would look in the mirror and I never liked who I saw standing there. Since I wasn't an alcoholic, I couldn't drink to escape. However, I found things to do while staying there. I jogged everyday. My usual bedtime was 4.a.m, so I would run about noon. I bought artist's paints and started painting. Actually, I found out that parts of Las Vegas were decent, it was mostly the Strip and the show-biz areas that gave me the creeps.

I had been home on Monday (my day off) and saw my father on Tuesday, before returning. My brother, Phil, was there, visiting from Maryland. I came back to play Tuesday night and Wednesday morning Phil called me to tell me our father had died. I didn't have a phone in my room, so someone had to come from the office. I found out that the funeral was on Friday. A few minutes later, I called Paul, the bandleader, who informed me that our new day off was Thursday, starting that very week. This meant I could drive home early Thursday morning, spend a day with the family, and drive back Friday after the funeral.

Kansas City

After 14 weeks in Las Vegas, I spent two weeks doing a booking in Kansas City. I drove the equipment back in a pickup truck with a cab over camper on the back. Talk about a way to get to know your country. My favorite part was pulling into a drive-in (food type) to get something to eat. I forgot about the cab over part of the pickup and....SMASH! I crashed right into the edge of the awning and neon light tube fragments rained down the windshield and the surrounding asphalt. My skating waitress (yes, roller skates folks, in Albuquerque) didn't seem to notice that she was skating through shattered neon, some of which was incriminatingly decorating my hood.

Later I got a ticket in Texas in a speed trap where they take you straight to the courthouse - just like in a movie. If you don't have the money, the guy who looks like Jackie Gleason in *Smokey And The Bandit* puts you directly in jail.

After Kansas City, I was fired at the end of the engagement by the band leader/singer for wearing a tank top while loading the equipment back in my truck at 3 in the morning. I had to laugh. It was such a classy place that the drunken manager was standing in the middle of the parking lot urinating as customers were still driving out. He looked and sounded like a low-end Mafia grunt.

The bandleader didn't realize how thankful I was to be fired and seemed puzzled by my joyous relief. He couldn't understand why I seemed so happy.

Dee McKinney

A drummer friend, Rick Lonow, who replaced me left a group that was backing a singer named Dee McKinney. Now that Dee needed a drummer, guess who was called? The same people who handled Dee's bookings later began booking Mark Boston in clubs all over California with a group fronted by two lesbians. The booking agent's favorite saying was, "Life is a shit sandwich, you either eat it or you die." I think he was quoting Emerson or Thoreau... and, of course, I found this truly inspiring.

One night we finished in Bakersfield - a deeper level of hell than Las Vegas - and the next, we played in Eureka. We packed up the gear, drove 14 hours, set up the gear, changed clothes and played, with no sleep.

It was nice being in Eureka, because I had a couple of friends up there. Bill Cody (Buffalo Bill's descendant that I mentioned earlier) still lived up there. So did my friend Tom Bryden and his ex-girlfriend, Janine. I got to visit everyone and have some interesting and fascinating talks. Bill Harkleroad's girlfriend even came down from Oregon for a visit and I was able to say "hi" to her also. Tom let me stay at his house, so I didn't have to share a room with a guitarist who smoked pot left lying on my bed in the open shoebox. He also liked to carry on conversations with a loaded stainless steel 357 Magnum in his hand, which he waved around while he talked.

The other guitarist/singer was a kind of a blowhard, insensitive jock-type who had been friends with Don for a while. This guy seemed to be oblivious to anyone else's space, and trampled on feelings like an elephant on ants. He was a great singer - in the Joe Cocker / Bob Seger category but had his own sound. I also liked his soloing, though it was simple, it reminded me of Hubert Sumlin. He told me, in front of everybody in the band "Don Van Vliet said that you were a great drummer, but that when you weren't with him, you weren't worth a shit." The last I heard, this guy was playing in cover bands in Alaska and selling jewelry. Insensitive oafs generally do well, as they are completely devoid of any sense of tromping on other's toes.

The bass player seldom took a shower, reeked of pot, and slept in the same clothes he played in for days at a time.

Paul Delicato called me around this time. He asked if I'd come back and said the drummer wasn't working out. I didn't understand why, as Rick Lonow is a great drummer and good friend.

The bass player was a friend of Rick's caught wind of what was happening and threatened to quit if I was re-hired. Paul called me back and told me the news.

Dee's Background

Dee McKinney had been a background singer for John Mayall at one time. She was a great singer and was really great at working out harmonies. In the meantime, she had a couple of kids, was on her second marriage, and things weren't going that well. I enjoyed Dee, but I told her that although there was nothing personal there was no way I was going to keep working with her. She found another drummer and we went our separate ways.

Shiny Beast Rehearsals

While this was going on, Captain Beefheart was getting ready to re-record *Bat Chain Puller*, sans a song or two with his new band and re-release it as *Shiny Beast*. Bruce was there for every rehearsal and did all the transcribing for copyright purposes.

Telepathic

John French to Richard Redus: I just wondered if you had ever seen any paranormal activity around Don?
RR: The only paranormal activity that I saw around Don would be telepathy. He constantly could start to tell you what you were thinking before you said it. That happened dozens of times to me, where I would have a thought and he would speak it for me before I did. I believe that was familiar to all the other members of the band too. I attributed it not so much to magic as to just an extension of the sensitivity I talked about. Where he could read body language.

I asked Redus about Don's ethical qualities:

Richard Redus: Well, I don't know about ethical qualities because I think Don would lie in a second. To me, ethics implies a sort of consciously - constructed view and I think Don didn't have that. I think he was really instinctive in the way he acted in the world. I think he would stab people in the back, no problem. He would lie to people just to protect his image, (yet) he was full of an artistic and human richness. It's a little bit hard for me to figure out how to describe it.
John French: Do you think that this defense mechanism, so to speak, this lying, or whatever, that Don considered this to be absolutely necessary, or it was absolutely necessary for him to survive at all?
RR: Yeah, I think it probably was absolutely necessary. I'm not sure whether he recognized it. It may very well be that when he lied, he believed he was telling the truth. On the other hand, maybe he knew he was lying, but he didn't have much choice.
JF: Did you ever hear him quote his saying? "The truth has no patterns?"
RR: Many times. That was one of the first things I heard from him that just really turned me on to him, made we want to hang out with him more.

Redus' description of Don as "instinctive in how he acted in the world" reminded me of an evening with Don back in the sixties where we went to the movies. The movie was about the life of Rasputin, the Russian mystic (for lack of a better word) who had such a strong pull on the Romanov family. Don kept saying how he identified with Rasputin, and called him a "survivalist."

He told me that he was a survivalist also, which really didn't mean much to me at age 18.

Doing a little research on survivalism which led me to the title of a book:
100 Ways To Avoid Dying (by Tim Clark April 4, 1991), which strongly led me to the question: What happens when you meet the one hundred and first way to die?

Magic Band Members Review

In the 14 or so years that Don had been in the business, he had gone through several bands and band members.

1. The original blues band through *Strictly Personal.* (Snouffer, Moon, Mortensen, Handley)
2. *The Trout Mask* through *Spotlight Kid* (Boston, Cotton, French, Harkleroad, Tripp)
3. The *Clear Spot* through *Unconditionally Guaranteed* period: (Estrada, Marcellino)
4. The "Tragic Band" (Fuscaldo, Grimes, Smith, Smotherman, Simmons, Uhrig)
5. The "Band of Gypsies" through *Bat Chain Puller* band (Black, Davidson, Fowler, Ingber, Tepper, Thomas, Walley)
6. The *Shiny Beast* band (Feldman, Redus, Williams)

There are, of course, overlaps in personnel, but counting those who didn't really stick around that long, (i.e. P.G. Blakely, Rich Hepner, Gary Marker, Ry Cooder, Gerry McGhee, Victor Hayden, Jeff Bruschele, Tom Grasso, Ian Underwood, Gary Jaye, Jimmy Carl Black), thirty-eight players so far that I recall had played in The Magic Band. Is this a reunion nightmare or what?

It was clear by now that the only common denominator was Don himself. The Magic Band members were reduced to sideman status during the Trout Mask period and never regained anything above that ever again. I am fairly certain this may have been at the suggestion of Frank, who, shortly after re-associating with Don, disbanded the Mothers of Invention for economic reasons. There was hereafter no provision made for any Magic Band member to receive any royalties or compensation other than the meager earnings they made - if they were lucky enough to get paid at all. Only two labels signed the entire group - A&M and Buddah - and both sued for breach of contract. Because of this, no royalties are due from any of those albums or any re-releases of those works.

The musical directors of each group seem to be:
1. Snouffer
2. French / Harkleroad
3. Harkleroad
4. Smotherman
5. French
6. Fowler

Bat Parts Re-Learned

The re-learning of *Bat Chain Puller* was mostly the focus of players Redus, Feldman, and Williams, as Tepper had already played the material on the original recording. The process was mostly getting the parts off an existing recording. Bruce Fowler, as described by Redus, would give him an overview of the chart, and so Bruce was possibly using the copyright transcriptions to also teach the band the songs. Fowler worked in a very non-assertive manner and was, in a sense, the unofficial musical director. The band would rehearse without Don a couple of nights a week and then Don would come down and listen, but he almost never rehearsed with the band. No surprise there...

Redus was assigned Denny's parts for the most part and he used the transcribed parts, as did Eric, to familiarize himself with the compositions. The guys were in a "total saturation" mode.

Richard Redus: We were constantly doing the Beefheart thing. Whether we were officially rehearsing or talking about parts, ...it was just eat, sleep and drink Beefheart. I don't remember anything else in that time except doing Beefheart related stuff.
John French: His music takes total absorption.

Cynical

As many other players before him had, Redus began to see in a similar manner as John Thomas that the musical process was not as he had envisioned and that there was a complex symbiosis (I use this word a lot) between the band and its leader.

Richard Redus: I became cynical about the music as I watched it being created, because I started to realize that it wasn't a grand thought-out or even a grand un-thought-out musical thunderbolt. It was just this kind of pieced-together hodge-podge of notes that half came from the band members, half came from Don. But as I saw the process where he would whistle something then he would kind of bully the player to play it and then the player might throw in his own rhythm and Don would then claim credit for doing it himself. That's how the pieces kind of grew, and at the time I felt disillusioned by that. I had imagined Don as being a guy who would just, with his great genius, make up the parts on the piano and hand them to you and you play them.

Van Vliet, as always, was the catalyst, the source of inspiration, and shaped the overall image and sound of the band, but it was obvious to Redus, as it had been to players before him, that the image portrayed to the public by Don himself of teaching his band "teaspoon by teaspoon" was a somewhat false image. The same thing that Bill Harkleroad was trying to explain in his interviews during the Mallard period was now becoming evident to Richard.

At this point, I'm wondering if a similar switch in perception and motivation happened in his motivation that happened also in my observations of the *Trout Mask* group. At some point in time, it became apparent to all of us that we were in the midst of maintaining the gap between a vast deception of who Captain Beefheart actually was as compared to how the public was perceiving him - mostly through his own interviews.

This was, as anyone who took on the task realized, a thankless job. No thanks would come from Don, who seemed to be in denial of the invisible defense being run by his band as they spanned the gap, and certainly no thanks from the public, who believed the interviews where Don claimed to teach his band note for note each and every composition. Also, the only time Don seemed to credit his present band was when he was also discrediting a former group. For instance by saying something like "this is the band that SHOULD have done *Trout Mask Replica*!"

Rehearsal Spot

John French: Where did you rehearse?
Richard Redus: It was a little storage space out in Northridge.
JF: Right, I recall rehearsing out there also.
RR: It was cool, because across the way, Fear had a storage space - the punk band? I knew them - killer drummer - we'd sometimes go and hang out and listen to Fear rehearse. That drummer was the best of all the punk drummers in my opinion. He could play so fast and just stay right on, you know, with all those crazy fills that you do in punk music.

The Err Of Tension

Redus states that, about 75% of the time, there was an "air of tension" that permeated the rehearsals. He also spoke about the "psychic interference" allegations. Redus quotes Don as saying, "I can't work under these conditions" whenever Van Vliet had a hard time focusing.

Richard Redus: He would then start spinning-out ... it would go into a tailspin and he couldn't pull out of it. He'd have to accuse other people of interrupting his flow. Then, he'd interrupt his own flow by doing that, and we'd be out of it for a while. I managed to somehow stay pretty much out of his line of fire along those lines. He would mostly pick on Robert Williams. Because of his (Don's) special personality, there was a lot that was difficult to deal with. It was well worth it, because he was such a remarkable individual.
John French: Do you feel that was part of your push-pull factor to get out of the group.
RR: It played a role, it wasn't a large role, because my personal experience was pretty positive. One thing is, I've always been a person who won't take unfounded bullshit. I would just instantly come right back in his face if he tried to accuse me of interrupting his thoughts telepathically, I would very firmly come back and tell him I wasn't doing that, and to get off my back about it. I think that he respected that.
JF: So, was that an aggressive thing that you did?
RR: Yeah, it wasn't violent or loud, but it was pretty firm. I would say it was aggressive.
JF: Good for you. Well, I was very surprised he seemed to have more tolerance for you. Even on the phone with you, he didn't seem angry. He seemed a little frustrated that he was in the position, but not that you had ruined his life or anything. It wasn't blamed on you, he was frustrated more by the position he was in, than by you personally. He and Jan both seemed to say very nice things about you.
RR: As much room as someone gave him to be a dominant bully, he would take it. Then, I think the more people were like that, the less respect he had for them and the more he would not care about trashing him.

During the Sherwood interview, Motorhead mentioned seeing the band rehearse and his description of the time may have been during this period, as he recalls that they were rehearsing in a storage facility. His comment here reveals the same old tension:

Jim Sherwood: It surprised the hell out of me when I saw Don later on and he was yelling at the guys in the band. They were rehearsing one day in a rented storage room. They had the door open and Don was yelling at those guys. I was thinking, "Jesus Christ Don, how did you (Laughs) get control of those poor little shits."

Prima Don 'Uh

The group had the hopes that this album would reclaim Don's integrity and put him back on the musical map, which should have happened two years previous with the original *Bat Chain Puller*. Glen Kolotkin, the engineer on the session, had worked on Stravinsky's last album, according to Don in interviews and what he told me later at the Doc sessions. Kolotkin was picked, rumor had it, because he was particularly good at dealing with "Prima Donnas." Van Morrison as an example - who is considered as such by some - was engineered by Kolotkin. Glen apparently impressed the brass by handling Van Morrison quite well. Don's production techniques, however, really tied Glen's hands from making this recording work better on an audiophile level. The mix is disappointing. Some of this the direct result of Don's resistance to any use of reverb, or effects in general. Zappa had mentioned that Don had little understanding of the technical aspects of recording.

Van Vliet's resistance to reverb or effects in general may have something to do with Krasnow's toying with *Strictly Personal.* It could also have developed a bit earlier, as some of the earliest demos of the original Magic Band, recorded at Gold Star Studios in Hollywood were overly-saturated in reverb, which took away from the impact of the group's sound - smoothing it over in a wash of what Don sometimes would refer to as "heavy syrup." Being an extremist, he insisted on no reverb at all - which defeats the purpose in another way, making the music experience a bit two-dimensional.

John French to Richard Redus: And, it did according to everything I have read critically about the band and the album. When I listened to it critically as with most Beefheart albums, I was a little disappointed with the mix. That was basically Don's doing. He wanted it that way. I always thought the band sounded very small and his voice was too up front in the track and things like that. ...There wasn't any warmth at all to the recordings it was very stark - no reverb at all.
RR: (Affirming my opinion throughout) *Too dry, I agree.*

Williams / Shiny Beast

Before recording the album, there was a band meeting to discuss the band's compensation. Don offered, instead of Union Scale, to give each of the players $1700 for doing the record. Williams describes Tepper and Feldman started clapping - "like they're in some kind of board meeting and they got a better stock option or something." Pete Johnson, who produced the album, said, "But we're going to give you a half point each on the record." Williams claims never to have seen a dime of royalties. Also, part of the "points" was included in the advance on royalties, which Don had received. They never received that, but Beefheart paid them seventy-five dollars a week to rehearse - out of monies that was their advance to begin with.

Robert Williams: So, he was paying us money that was already ours to rehearse every week. "You're rehearsing for free, but each week I'll give you your $75 that I already owe you."... the thing is that you have to be "on call."

Don demanded an illogical amount of availability from his band and seemed not to take into account the fact that they needed to survive, according to Williams. Finding supplemental income for a musician whose leader commanded "total saturation" was nearly impossible. Because of the nature of the music and the trickle of creativity that was slowly dished out, inefficiency seemed to reign. As usual the financial reward never came.

Robert Williams: I think Shiny Beast *got re-released on CD, (then) got released on Rhino. I never saw a dime from that.*

Shiny Beast

Gary Lucas: Anyway, they came and did a couple of gigs over the years, the early years I was (back in) New York. Redus was the guitarist, I think, at one of them. And Mary Jane Eisenberg was dancing with them on one of the times. Shiny Beast came out. I actually got an assignment. I called up the guy and Warners who I knew. He said, "I'm not going to give out copies of this, I can't unless you're going to review it." I said, "Allright, I'll review it." I wrote a really good review of it for Crawdaddy Feature Magazine, at that point.
John French: I was listening to that album the other day and I was really surprised that the

sonics - I was really disappointed that the overall sound was not very big.
GL: Yeah, I mean, I don't know Pete Johnson, so I can't really comment on it. The bands have always had complaints about the sonics on all the records. Eric, Jeff and I used to always bewail Don's production techniques. He had a justification for it. He'd say, "I want to hear it two-dimensional - flat, like a painting." It's a good theory, but as a consumer listening to this, that's not any fun.

MTV

Williams and I discussed the influence of music videos relating to *Shiny Beast* era tours.

Robert Williams: There were times when it was great and everything would click and everyone was smiling and just "into it." But I guess that's part of the visual aspect of music that has been over-emphasized in music these days. When I was doing the music with Beefheart and when you were, it was all radio, there weren't videos.
John French: So people listened to the music more ...the visual thing was secondary...
RW: ... And now it seems to be that you've gotta have a really nice pair of tits, or be really handsome and young-looking. It's really become a youth-oriented business. It's really hard for older people to make a living in music these days. I think it's so sad because a lot of the musicians who have been out there for years have just "honed their craft" are just being turned away and replaced by Britney Spears.
JF: Well, that's where the money is.
RW: It's not anything experimental though.
JF: You're right, it's a product. There's no risk!
RW: They don't want to make it that way, and they don't need to take chances. They've primed them for that.
JF: So, it's not really art.
RW: There's really not much room anywhere for anything that would be similar to Beefheart. You'd never get anywhere.
JF: I used to think, "We're paving the way for the "future music." And now the music is just a bunch of white people trying to sound like Michael Jackson.
RW: Yeah, and Michael Jackson's trying to be white while everyone else is trying to be black.

H.D. Research

In 1978, after leaving the Dee McKinney band, I was thirty years old. My only thought at that time was that I never wanted to play music - ever again - for a living. The music business had been the cause of more disappointments than I cared to think about. In early 1979, I went to work for High Desert Research - a small factory that made electrical testing units for cars and buses.

The only way I got the job was that a friend of mine, Richard Suydam, worked there and recommended me. There was a machine shop and sheet metal shop in the back section of the building. In the front, they made wire looms and did assembly of the units. A machine shop is a very dangerous place to work. All the machines had signs that read, "Do not talk to machine operator while machine is in operation." You could turn your head and be distracted for one second and instantly lose a finger, or a hand. I tried to take this in my stride, telling myself I would be all right, but I was concerned.

All I really wanted to do was practice piano and have a less-complicated life. For three months, it seemed like it was going to work out. I made a very small amount of money. I would cash my check, pay my bills, and be broke the next day. I was just starting to feel like I could see the light of day when I was laid off. The factory was moving to Illinois. I hadn't worked there long enough to acquire any kind of job record, and it was ludicrous to fill out an application. "Former Jobs, Dee McKinney Band, Paul Delicato Band, laid-off after three months in a factory." I looked like the world's biggest flake.

Williams' Silent Drum Solo

Meanwhile, the tensions in The Magic Band had been very similar to earlier experiences I had. Once, after a show, the audience wanted an encore and Don didn't come back on, so Bruce and Robert Williams, who hadn't left the stage, decided to do a silent mime improvisation. Not a sound was made, but they moved as though they were playing. It appeased the crowd, who seemed to enjoy it. Don was upset by this whole idea of the guys doing something he hadn't conceived or given permission for. Don's anger was questioned and he said "Anyone in this room know what I'm talking about." Feldman apparently raised his hand, but being unable to speak due to laryngitis, wrote on a piece of paper the words "silent drum solo." Williams felt that he was being "tattled on."

Williams and Tepper were both inclined to search the crowds of their shows for female companionship while on the road. This upset Jan, who preferred Eric, who appeared not to be interested in feminine conquest. Tepper, being on better terms with Don and Jan, was overlooked in this area, but Williams sensed that Jan "hated" him for that and thought he was a complete womanizer - ending his sentence with: "I may HAVE been, but..."

The truth is, it was none of Don's or Jan's concern what licentious behavior went on in the band member's private lives as long as they fulfilled their business commitment by showing up on time and playing the music well.

Robert Williams: I just thought to myself, "What's wrong with that?" I'm not hurting anyone. It was none of her business, but if I had been a nerd, wearing glasses and checking to see if the pens in my shirt pocket were in the right order, she would have thought that was the hippest thing in the world - and it is kind of cool and funny, but it wasn't me. I had problems with the guys in the band really. Don? Not as much, other than being ripped off and he picked on me.

Sand Sailor

The Mallard album long behind him, John Thomas was back in Lancaster playing in clubs again with former Omen's drummer Pat Prue's younger brother Marty - the guitarist from Rattlesnakes And Eggs. Marty was very prodigious at getting local club gigs and entertained a lot during the seventies in his home towns - his bands dominating the local scene. Van Vliet used to appear at the Sand Sailor as an observer, aluminum brief case in hand. He would sit by himself and draw for hours.

John Thomas: It was just very weird. But it was during that time when he was - I think he was really lonely. He was looking for friends. I don't know if he was looking for drugs? (questioningly) I don't really know, but he was on a mission.
John French: This must have been more like Shiny Beast time, right?
JT: Yeah, I think this was just around the time when he was starting to get his next record together. Again, I was never close enough to know his (moods.) I spent lots of hours with him, but it was always him blowing off steam at me. It was never me really getting underneath to see "The real Don."

Freelancing

I hated playing with copy bands, so I began doing freelance work - anything I could get. I worked for a while building pipe horse corrals. I would cut the metal, and my friend, Richard Suydam, would weld. Then, we loaded the materials onto a truck and took them onsite to install. Richard had gotten me the earlier job at HD Research. He would also occasionally hire me to cut metal for him. He was a welder who made fences, pipe corrals, and other more custom work like stair railings and custom tube fencing. He specialized in square steel tubing.

Shiny Beast Tour

It was fall 1978 and the *Shiny Beast* band was now touring. According to Teejo's "Electricity" website, there was a span from April until late October when the band did not perform. Denny probably was let go in late April, the album done and released a few months later. The Jim Jones massacre on November 18th, 1978 (also Redus' birthday) was a landmark day in which he remembers being well into the tour and on the road in Philadelphia.

"Oh Bobby"

Robert Williams continued to have strife with Don.

Robert Williams: I remember once he almost tried to kick my ass.
John French: Was that when you were getting ready to go out in Paris?

Note: Robert had finished a concert with the band, gone back to the hotel and changed into clothes of which Don didn't approve.

Robert Williams: Yeah, with my tight, bell-bottoms and my tight glitter shirt. My hair all blow-dried.

As he walked into the hallway of the hotel Don and another band member were standing in the hallway talking. Don spied Robert in his non-Beefheart-approved clothes and said in a very sarcastic voice, "Oh, Bobby!" to which Robert replied "Oh, Donny!" This antagonized Don and his posturing was as one wishing a fistfight.

Robert Williams: He was like John L. Sullivan, standing there with his fists up. "Come on, man!" ... He wanted everybody to look the way he looked. I said, "Look when I'm in 'your play' I'll slick my hair back, wear the baggy clothes. When I'm out and it's my time, I'll blow dry my hair and wear the tight clothes."

This encounter was probably enacted to show Don's disapproval of Williams' faddish stylings and to make him an example to Jeff and/or Eric. I'm sure Don had no intention of actually employing violence. It was a ploy designed to maintain control and is another example of the tight reign Beefheart still maintained over his group.

According to Redus, the Magic Band was playing a lot of stuff from *Shiny Beast*, but also worked up as much as possible from *Trout Mask* and *Decals* because: "everybody in the band was more into that stuff than into any of the more "easy listening" stuff from any of his other albums." Redus felt the set was a " good mix of his whole career."

After that, Redus became disenchanted due to the fact that there was an entire year of no activity. Everything seemed uncertain, and frustration set in.

Richard Redus: There were several months of rehearsal without a clear picture of what it was going to be for. Whether we were going to tour again, was there going to be another record. I became frustrated with it. We were making very little money...it seemed like it wasn't going anywhere.

Darla Returns

This next section is highly personal, but needs to be included in order for what happens later to make sense. In 1979 my ex-wife Darla returned to California from North Carolina. I had written her many letters about how we should try to work out our differences. After months of total silence, I got a call that she was at the LA Bus Station and needed a ride up to the desert. Her parent's called me, thinking that it would be more appropriate if she stayed with me.

I had Darla at my house for a few weeks. Her first thought was to get back together, but she quickly discarded that in favor of dating an old acquaintance, Dave B., and having him pick her up at my house. She had gone to the library and checked out several books on black magic and was incanting love spell rituals in my living room while I was gone. I would find black candle wax all over the floor and at first I was puzzled, then I realized what was going on.

One day, she brought a puppy home and left it at my house while she went out on dates. I took care of this little guy for several days, much to the chagrin of my carpet. In a nutshell, chaos ensued.

Fear Not

I started being unable to sleep in the house, and I could sense an evil presence of some kind and so I sat praying a lot and trying to figure out what to do to get this situation relieved. I was awake for five days straight and the state of my mind was definitely troubled. This was a breaking point for me, but also a time of positive change.

I went out in the desert to be alone one day and prayed and cried out. I can't explain in words the emotional low to which I had descended. I viewed myself as completely useless. All my mistakes, bad judgments, naiveté and foolish decisions flashed into my mind's eye like a giant checklist of condemnation. I wound up just crying and lying in the dirt, flat on my face. While there, I finally calmed down and relaxed, and it was at that time that I heard a whispered voice saying simply, "Fear not."

Astounded, I got up brushed myself off and drove back to my house, and when I arrived, Darla was standing outside and asked me to take her to Keith Kennedy's house. Keith was her former brother-in-law, having once been married to her sister

I consented to take her to Keith's, who lived about 40 miles away. Within about five miles or so of his house, Darla starting taunting me. I hadn't said a word the entire trip. I just wanted her away from me. She unbuttoned her dress down to her waist, pulling her dress open, laughing and saying, "You know you want me, admit it!"

I still didn't say a word. I drove her up to the house, got her bags and carried them in. I didn't say anything but, "Hi" to Keith, and then I left without another word. Keith lived in a secluded cabin in Juniper Hills that he rented from Tom Bryden.

Surprise Party

I drove back down the hill and thought that I would drop by and see the Longs, some friends of mine who had helped me through some trying times. At this point, I needed some moral support. After no one answered the front door, I walked down the driveway of the split-level house and around the back to the downstairs family room with sliding glass doors. As I came within full view of the room, I discovered, to my horror, that there was a Bible study going on in the house. I recognized about half the eight or ten people there. I wanted to run, but they had all seen me. Not wanting to face a room full of people nor appear rude, my plan was to just blend in with the wallpaper.

Then I realized that the only possible place I could sit down was right in the center of the room. In the ensuing awkwardness and after some brief introductions, Mickey Long asked me, "So, how ya been John?" - in a really friendly and exuberant voice. I was going to say, "I've been fine," but only got as far as "I" - in a gasping tone before completely losing control. Pent-up emotions just burst out of me. It was a moment of complete surrender.

Outside of my closed eyes, strangers and friends encircled me. Everyone in that room had both hands on me - some on my head or shoulders, some on my arms, while others held my hands. Nobody said a word for a long time, but I felt this wonderful peace and calmed down. After several minutes of silence one young woman I didn't know (whose name was Lisa Scudieri), put her hand right on top of my head and did what I found out later was called "prophecy." She raised her other hand up and spoke what she felt God wanted to say to me through her - sort of a "channeling God" moment.

The very first two words out her mouth were, "Fear Not" - the same exact words I had heard whispered in the desert - and an overwhelming sense of peace immediately came over me. It was as if someone had turned the pain switch off and bathed me in the essence of love. I was no longer emotional. Lisa spoke for quite some time, and though I heard every word, I can remember none of it as I was mystified at the transformation taking place inside myself. Mickey later told me that one of the things spoken by Lisa was, "I have you in the palm of my hand." I have never felt the love like I felt in that room that night - not from the people but through the people.

I believe that something happened in the spirit realm to me that night. I left that house a changed person. I was laughing and singing and acting absolutely out of my mind with happiness. I hadn't been hypnotized, I hadn't been brainwashed. It was if I was an entirely new person - same DNA, same shell of a body, but no longer the droopy melancholy pathetic person within as when I walked in. In my estimation, I was dead before - at least in the spiritual sense - and that night I came alive. Lisa, my new friend from the Bible Study persuaded me to go to a new church - the Desert Vineyard. The pastor, Brent Rue, had spoken at my father's funeral. As he spoke of Jesus, several of my family members became very angry. But, I couldn't help but admire his courage for saying what he felt committed to say. Brent was a very tall, slender blonde man, about mid-thirties. The church was a small industrial type building just outside of town. They had a small PA and brought in restaurant-style tables. There was a snack bar with coffee, doughnuts and various other snacks. It was very informal - most of the congregation wore jeans.

I don't remember much of what was said that Sunday, I just recall being impressed with the peaceful and casual atmosphere. These people weren't putting on a show for anyone, they were just gathering together to worship God and learn about the Bible. The sincerity of the people and the casual atmosphere attracted me and I started going regularly.

Shiny Beast Deterioration

Warners had released *Shiny Beast* only to have Virgin issue a lawsuit because Don was still signed to them. This caused there to be a lot of down time and setbacks - again - which Van Vliet did not need at this point. Redus was commuting to San Francisco, where he worked with other musicians and had a girlfriend. As time went on, he surmised that The Magic Band was probably going nowhere. There was little money coming in and no concerts.

Don was paying the band a minimal amount out of dwindling funds to rehearse, and he wanted to rehearse quite often. At first, everyone was enthusiastic, thinking that soon something would happen. They worked on *Human Totem Pole* and *Run Paint Run Run*.

Richard Redus: I can't remember exactly - but there may have been some blows. Like some money not coming through that was supposed to come through, or some gigs not coming through that were supposed to come through. There were some things that happened that made me believe it wasn't going anywhere. I started considering myself to be in transition well before the end of 1979.

Tiring of the holding pattern, he decided to leave the group.

Beautiful

Happy Days

Several years ago, I asked Graham Johnston of beefheart.com if I could do a question-and-answer kind of page for fans who may have a question or two. He generously obliged. There was quite a response to this, and each day, I would often spend several hours answering these questions. There were several questions about my faith - what did I believe, why, how, etc. I have always felt that this was a part of my private life and chose not to force my thoughts on the public, but I decided if so many people were interested, I would devote a bit of time to this topic. As I began writing, I realized that there was no way to tell the story and omit this aspect.

Before this spiritual awakening I had, I was miserably unhappy. Afterwards, I woke up saying all those Christian catch phrases over and over - and actually meaning it. I was amazed to find that after six months I hadn't uttered a single profanity that I could recall. I didn't lose my temper, and I had very few negative thoughts. All my life, up until this point, I had always believed in God, but I had never actually experienced a change in myself. I had seen a few things happen, but nothing that really serious had ever happened. This is why I had eventually wandered into the study of the occult.

But now, I knew something had happened. According to doctrine, it was called being "born again." It had happened in me, and skeptics be damned, they could never take away the experience. This was about the middle of 1979.

I recall that on New Year's Eve, Don showed up at my gate. I heard him outside. When I went out, he said, quite loudly and deliberately, in his best Captain Beefheart voice " Do you realize that it's NINETEEN-EIGHTY, John?" I laughed. I can't recall anything else about the night, whether he came in, what was said, nothing.

This Can't Be God

Relating to my earlier "rebirth" experience, I'd like to mention that during this time of "change" in me, absolutely nothing changed in my situation. This is the interesting point. I was happy, in fact "insanely joyous" might be a better phrase. I would go to church and stand and sing these songs in full voice and really mean every word of it. I suppose an atheist / psychiatrist would call me "delusional" but it wouldn't have changed a thing.

Actually, things got worse for me for a while before they got better. I was really broke and couldn't find a job. My truck had broken down, and I couldn't seem to get it fixed. I remember just walking somewhere one day and silently praying, asking what I was to do next when suddenly I heard a voice in my head - more like a thought pattern that wasn't my own - like telepathy. It said, "Go tell Don you want to be in his band." I stopped walking. "No! I've tried working with him too many times! This can't be God!" But, no matter how much I tried to force this idea out of my mind over the next couple of days, it remained and I became convinced that I had been instructed to do this. It may sound insane to say that I believe God "spoke" to me. However, I believe he speaks to millions everyday. It's just that most people aren't listening.

The next day, I was able to get my truck running (it was a simple thing after all, a $2.00 part) and I drove immediately out to Don's mobile home. It was a beautiful day. I apprehensively walked up to the door and he became visible through the sliding screen door. He was on the phone and waved me in with a welcoming look. I walked in as he was finishing up a discussion, saying, "Don't do this, man - not now." He finally hung up and sighed. Though he seemed a little preoccupied, he was nonetheless hospitable. "How are you, man?" he asked. We talked for only a moment, however, before he told me that his guitarist (no name was mentioned) had quit the band and he had an album to do in six weeks.

Richard Redus: I think it was really hard for me to tell Don. I wanted him to keep liking me and I didn't want to bring up that difficult subject.

John French: You didn't feel liked, it wasn't like a business thing you were ending, it was more on a personal level?
RR: Yeah, it was on a personal level. It included the business aspects but, when I finally came out and told him that I had to leave, I think it was just basically that "I can't survive under these circumstances". I wasn't asking for more, it was clear that he was without resources himself. My life was just kind of slipping away from me and nothing was happening with it.
JF: When you told him this, were you telling him face to face?
RR: I think I was on the phone.
JF: OK. And he was in Lancaster?
RR: I can't remember if he was in Lancaster or if he was in LA and I was in San Francisco.
JF: Now, was there another album in the works?
RR: Well, yeah, but as far as I recall - I want to stress how blurry it all is to me - as far as I can recall it wasn't clear when it was going to be recorded. I think it may have happened that I would hear that it was going to be happening at a certain time. Then I would find out that it had been postponed, it wasn't going to happen at that time. A couple of those things kind of demoralized me.
JF: Okay, here's my story, so we'll tie it in and see if it doesn't clarify your memory.

I told Richard the story about the telepathic urging I had to contact Don and how I had wound up at his trailer that morning while he was on the phone.

Richard Redus: He was talking to me.
John French: He was talking to you. (Redus laughs) I don't know what built up to it, but I'm trying to guess that this was your final "no." I (told Don), "I'm here to replace him!"

He pointed his finger at me and I could almost see a light bulb over his head as his face brightened, snapping out "That's a good idea, man!" He became really excited. Now, this was after not having seen him much at all since 1977 - or '78 perhaps - with the exception of the night of the "it's nineteen eighty" announcement. It was an immediate decision, no questions, thought process, nor mulling it over - it was set in stone at that moment.

Richard Redus: That's a great story. I never knew the other side of it.

I had interviewed Redus a little over 20 years after this incident. We had never met or spoken to each other up until that point, so it was quite an experience for both of us to actually hear what the other had to say about this particular event.

Fear was the first thing that attacked me. I thought about the project to which I was about to commit: I hadn't played guitar in four years, and even then I wasn't very good - at least in comparison to the guys I admired. Don's music was not easy. Maybe I would hold him back and cause him to lose his contract or something. "I don't know, Don, I don't even own a guitar," I said. This seemed to be a trait in me - to leap in faith and then start doubting while I was still flying through the air.

My beautiful Stratocaster (the Redwood guitar Tim Meyer made) had been smashed up a bit during my tumultuous marriage. Don said not to worry that he could get me a guitar. I still was apprehensive about whether I could "cut it" in six weeks. Don was sure I could and really encouraged me to give it a shot. This encouraged me.

When I mentioned to a couple of my friends at church that I needed a guitar for an album project, a guy by the name of Tim Nevins said he had a guitar I could have. He gave me a vintage

Gibson, which of course, wasn't the sound Don was looking for, but would at least get me started. I can't remember the model of this guitar, but it was a single pickup solid body, stained mahogany, single cutaway. The tuners weren't in very good shape, but I worked with them. The bridge wasn't adjustable so I bought an adjustable bridge and installed it myself: intonating the guitar with an electronic tuner.

Gary And Ling As Managers

Though I didn't know them at all, Gary Lucas and his wife Ling were co-managing the group at the time. They had just begun, apparently, and the first order of business had been to secure a recording contract with Virgin. Ling was working as a publicist for Putnam Books. I had never met Gary nor had I ever heard of him.

I do recall Don having a lot of books at his trailer - especially books about famous painters - and Don would show these to me when I came by. Gary later told me that Ling used to send him books, so I assume that these were the same.

It wasn't until years later that I found out that Gary had auditioned for Don when they had hooked up during the *Bongo Fury* tour in 1975. For Doc, Don sent Gary the tape of me playing *Flavor Bud Living* from the ill-fated *Bat Chain Puller* and assigned him the task of learning it. Gary was told by Van Vliet that my rendition was "too religious" - interesting, in lieu of the fact that I learned it from his piano tape and played it almost exactly the same in nuance.

First Rehearsal

The rehearsals were being held at Robert Williams' house. It was a house he shared with several other people, including his girlfriend, who was a model. We had a nice-sized living room in which to rehearse. Don drove me down and I carried in my little Gibson guitar. I sensed almost immediately that Tepper wasn't too happy to see me. I could be wrong about this, but it seemed like there was a friction between us almost immediately. I could understand. I was now a guitar player instead of a drummer, and that was now his area. Also I wasn't a good guitarist, which probably was a bit frustrating for him.

I had gotten a chart from Don for *The Thousandth And Tenth Day Of The Human Totem Pole* and had been working on it for a few days. I had also gotten some plastic fingerpicks and was trying to quickly learn how to use them. I had always just used my fingers before. We started going over *Totem Pole* and I realized quickly how out of shape I was as my hands cramped up.

Nevertheless, we went to work, and Jeff, after his initial reaction, seemed to warm to me. I soon became aware of the rifts in the band. Eric and Jeff implied constantly that they didn't care a lot for Robert Williams, and Don seemed to even be more critical of him than the rest. I quickly began to feel uncomfortable around Robert, because I knew that he may have felt a little insecure about my presence. Maybe I would migrate back to the drummer's chair - which wasn't my intent at all. It certainly may have been a possibility in the minds of some or all present.

Occasionally, during rehearsals, Bruce Fowler would come by. He seemed like a different person than I had known before. More like a business-person, a studio player, less friendly and more serious. I was a little disappointed, as I was looking forward to seeing him.

The house was a beautiful old place, which Williams told me was soon to be torn down. I was appalled. It had beautiful hardwood moldings and there was obviously a great deal of craftsmanship in these old places which would soon be lost forever - probably to make room for a bunch of ugly condominiums.

Daily Life In "Doc" Rehearsals

I soon settled into the routine of rehearsing with the band, catching up on all of the business stuff.

Don held a contract only with Virgin Records, no domestic companies. The album would be a fairly low-budget affair. Don was presently very interested in Chinese Opera, which he would occasionally force us to listen to for several hours during rehearsal in a sitting room behind the rehearsal room. This gave me great anxiety, as you can imagine the pressure I was under to re-learn to play guitar, learn this entire album, and get everything totally organized by album time. The time seemed to be passing by too quickly and Don was raving on about Chinese Opera for hours. Not much had changed in terms of his awareness of time.

On a few occasions, Mark Mothersbaugh, a member of Devo would show up with his girlfriend. I didn't know who he was the first time we met. "What do you do?" I asked him. He gave me some funny answer like, "I work in a bakery." It must have been refreshing to have someone not know who he was - either that or he figured I was a complete fool. Don would not allow us to play when Mark showed up, because "he was there to steal ideas." Of course, if we wanted to do that, he could have sat outside with a tape recorder.

I usually would ride down with Don, and I often wondered what possible reason I was doing this. Was I supposed to talk to Don about my spiritual experiences? I hoped not, as I had always deplored proselytizers and I certainly didn't want to become one of those thick, syrupy evangelistic types who generally turn more people off to God than on. The only other possible reason could be fame and glory... oh yeah.

We all went out one day to check out a couple of studios to see where the album would be done. I remember one day in particular driving down the street with the entire band and two attractive girls were walking down the sidewalk. Don immediately pulled the car over and started asking directions. We eventually all got out of the car and were talking with these girls. I was about to explode inside, because all I could think about was the ton of work waiting for me back at the studio. When the girls walked away, Don looked at the guys and said, "You didn't get any phone numbers? What the hell's a matter with you guys? You want women? Then ya gotta do something about it!" The guys looked dismayed. This resulted in me exploding in laughter.

Don finally picked a studio in Glendale (also home of *Trout Mask's* Whitney Studios) called Soundcastle, I believe. It was a Christian recording studio, and we would be the first non-Christian group to record there. This studio wasn't that far from Don's original home in Glendale on Waverly Drive. Occasionally, we would drive by the house and school. He'd look at the house and say, "What in the hell possessed them to move to Mojave?" referring to his parents when they made the "all artists are queers" decision. It was a beautiful two-story white house with green shutters on all the windows.

Then, he would drive by the school nearby and humorously say, "There's where I never went to school."

Our old friend Langdon Winner showed up one day for a visit. The way it worked out was that I rode down with Don to rehearsal (about 70 miles from my home) and was going to spend the night at Teppers. Don would then drive to the airport, pick up Langdon, and come back to rehearsal. I would go with Jeff and Eric to Jeff's house to work on the bass part to *Sheriff Of Hong Kong*. It was at this meeting with Langdon that I discovered his amazing talent as a tap dancer. He knew that I was at one time interested in the finer arts of "hoofing" and so proceeded to give me quite a demonstration of his abilities, which were quite impressive. I tried to pick up some pointers, but there was little time.

Don told me later that Langdon was impressed with my "invention" which was actually just a thumb pick consisting of a strap with a replaceable pick. I had found that the pick that came with the thumb picks was too thin to get the kind of gritty sound I wanted to achieve, so I found picks thicker than I needed and cut them down so they would fit in the slot of this "Thumb strap."

I never have been able to use a flat pick on a guitar, and I always found them impractical, because they tie up the thumb and first finger, where a thumb pick only needs the thumb and leaves all four fingers free. I also could never seem to get the knack of holding them.

Sherriff Of Hong Kong

So, I went with Jeff and Eric, in Eric's van to Jeff Tepper's house, where he had a spare bedroom for me. On the ride from Hollywood into the valley was the first time I really was exposed to the friendship these two had. They had really bonded, it seemed to me, and I was thinking how great it must be to have that kind of relationship with someone you work with. It also showed me that the "cult" environment was not so much in effect, though I did feel tension sometimes in the rehearsals.

After Eric dropped us off, Jeff showed me the room I'd stay in and then spent quite a bit of time feeding and showering attention on a fish he had - some kind of fighting fish in a tiny bowl. It seemed to me that it was a little cruel to put a fish in such a small bowl. "They prefer this," Jeff said.

The next day, we were having some cereal and Eric showed up to rehearse. The phone rang, and Jeff said, "I'm not going to answer it as it's probably Robert Williams, and we need to rehearse." So, there seemed to be some kind of rift or separation between these two and Williams, though I didn't really get a handle on why.

One interesting new thing for me was that I played bass on *Sherriff Of Hong Kong* and would be learning it this day. I had mentioned earlier about Bruce having a hard time reading the bass parts on the charts I had written because of all the syncopation? Well, this song had a bit of that also, but I was used to Don's rhythms. It was mostly fifths (for instance, playing a "C" and a "G" at the same time is a fifth and has a bit of an Oriental sound). As I recall, I used Eric's Danelectro bass, Eric played Jeff's piano, and Jeff stood on the opposite side of the piano as me. Eric and I read from a chart, whereas Jeff had it memorized as I recall.

I thought it would take me a long time to get this piece, but it was actually a lot simpler than I thought it would be, and once I understood the overall scope, I was able to play it fairly well within about one and a half hours. I am certain that this is a piano piece that was written during the Big Sur Suite era - post *Trout Mask* and pre-*Spotlight* - the same time *Odd Jobs* and *Seam Crooked Sam* were written. Since that was our only task for the day, Eric left and Jeff suggested that we go to the Mall. I asked why and he said, "to check out chicks." Well, I wasn't at all opposed to appreciating the fine designs of the fairer sex, so we soon found ourselves strolling through the Northridge Mall wearing sunglasses and occasionally saying, "Did you see HER???"

Jeff prepared a great meal for us that night and was, all in all, a wonderful and hospitable host. My day with Jeff and Eric was very rewarding.

Guitars

I was able to get a small advance from Don, so I bought a new neck for my Stratocaster and spent a weekend putting it together. I had learned how to mount and adjust the bridge and the nut for good intonation. The guitar went back together beautifully and sounded great.

The guitar was wired so that one could achieve 11 different combinations of sounds. Instead of having the regular switch, it had three little switches, one for each pickup, and they each had three positions, off, in phase, and out of phase. Since the guitar had vintage (the guy said 1954, but I have been told that Stratocasters weren't manufactured until 1955) pickups, it had a great sound.

Don had bought Richard Redus an older Telecaster, which I used for bottleneck on *Run Paint Run Run*. It was a turquoise color, and when I first got it, I was surprised at how difficult it was to play. The bridge was set to make the strings unusually high off the frets, even for bottleneck. "Redus must have had strong hands." I thought.

Playing Guitar

Re-learning how to play guitar, and especially while doing Beefheart music, was such an intense and insane experience for me. First of all, I had none of the calluses on my fingers, so there was a process that I had to go through just to get the physicality of the time and pain involved in that process. Then, there was the fact that I was using fingerpicks, which I had never used before. Then, there was all the muscles that needed to be re-developed for holding chords with extra-heavy strings. There was also the back and shoulder pain from the weight hanging around my neck for hours.

On the other hand, it was so much simpler to come in with a couple of cases, strap on a guitar, tune, and plug in. I still envy guitar players, because they can practice anywhere - in a hotel room, dressing room, or the corner of a studio. Drummers are stuck with making huge amounts of sound and usually annoying someone.

The most difficult and challenging piece was *Best Batch Yet.* This was a song that I am certain I remember Bill and Mark play back in the Spotlight rehearsal, and I always loved it, but it never had a second guitar part. Don decided that it needed one. Eric took his Mellotron to Jeff's house and Don and I met he and Jeff there. Eric and Jeff played the guitar and bass parts and I recorded, with a cassette player, as Don played along on the Mellotron. He'd say "turn it on," I would "click" and he would do just a bit and I'd turn it off. This happened several times, and I wound up with a bunch of bits and pieces of Mellotron parts, completely out-of-order, that were supposed to be played on guitar by me. This involved sitting with the tape for hours and charting out these bits and pieces, stringing them together in a completely different order so that they would "fit" the accompanying parts he was playing against, and then begin the task of learning this from the chart. I had to re-record all the parts onto another tape - in the correct order - so that I could hear how they sounded and pick up the nuance for interpretation.

So, it was a bit like picking up 27 pieces of film from the cutting room floor and piecing it back together to make some semblance of a finished work. Here's the interesting and amazing thing: There was exactly enough music to fit the entire song. Don had this incredible and mysterious "zen" quality, or whatever you want to call it - his instincts could be amazing.

The problem was for me to actually learn these random and strange parts. They have no relationship to the other parts and made no sense at all to me in terms of memorization or relationship to the other parts. I remember getting so frustrated by this that I would stand and pound on my bed for several minutes at a time to rid myself of pent-up energy. Being under such a deadline was bad enough without such a piece as this to deal with.

To further add to the confusion, Don decided at rehearsal to add several sections to the song. Once they were added, then he had us play them backwards and alternate high and low sections. To play them backwards, I recall actually recording them and playing the tape backwards to hear what they sounded like. So, my role in learning *Best Batch Yet* is definitely an iceberg - where ninety percent of the task is entirely invisible to the listener.

Once I learned these parts, I asked Jeff and Eric to play their parts over and over one morning at rehearsal. Williams and Van Vliet were gone somewhere. As I was struggling through this, Jeff and I became engaged in a shouting match, as he was frustrated at my slow progress. This was not a great deal of time, but it ended with me laughing at Jeff's contorted face as he screamed his last comment to me. I apologized for the incident and the shouting. Eric, the silent peacemaker, spoke up and told Jeff something to the effect of, "sometimes you do tend to incite this kind of behavior in people." Eric was and probably still is, one of the most honorable people I've ever known. This was a golden moment for him. It did seem to clear the air between Jeff and I, and we bonded a bit more after this.

I then just asked the two of them to play their parts through the length of the entire song and worked on it at home - feverishly - until I was able to memorize and play with feeling all those disconnected parts.

Interpersonal

Williams and I spent more time getting acquainted during this period. Don would sometimes leave to meet someone and be gone for hours. Most of what Williams would talk about was the horrendous relationship he had with his girlfriend. I liked him, and I understood his views. He was a very open guy and spoke honestly about what was on his mind - sometimes it was a little more information than I wanted to know. He was having problems with the fact that his girlfriend was posing for cameramen as a model and the insecurities were haunting him a bit. There was a little room upstairs in which we sat and he would sometimes make us tea and we were quite sociable.

One night as we were sitting there, I looked up to see a photo of Don holding a cowbell as if displaying it for the camera. Upon closer inspection, I noticed that it was the same cowbell, or an identical one to the cowbell that had come up missing after the Northwest tour I did in 1977. Just by chance, I looked down and there, in a cardboard box filled with percussion instruments such as shakers, guiros, and claves, was the same cowbell. I picked it up, and on close inspection, I could tell it was my missing cowbell, as I had drilled special holes in it for a bracket I fashioned myself. I looked at Robert and smiled, then walked downstairs to his set and looked at his foot pedal - it was an Asba Pedal - exactly the same pedal that had come up missing at the same time as the cowbell - which coincided exactly with when Robert first joined the group.

Robert was following me saying that Don had insisted he buy an Asba pedal because they were so good. I took the cowbell home with me that night and slipped it onto the bracket that was still on my set. It fit perfectly and so I perceived that it had to be my cowbell and kept it. My feeling on this is that Don instigated something of a "confiscation" - similar to what happened to Handley's bass. I was a little disappointed in both Van Vliet and Williams on this occasion, but quickly put it behind me - in the same little corner of my mind where I keep the little red flags.

Promo shot from the Bat Chain Puller session, 1976 with Don, John Thomas, Jeff Tepper, Denny Walley and John F...

Early Signs?

I was using a Super Reverb amp at rehearsal, which I am going to guess was Tepper's though I have no way to find out. One night, I wanted to take it home to familiarize myself with different sound possibilities and just tweak it a bit. I carried it out to the curb, but had carried it and two guitar cases from the house and realized it was a bit much, so I set it all down at the curb. Don was having a conversation with Jeff, Eric, and I, and several minutes passed.

When it was over, Don turned around, grabbed the amp and said "Let me help you with this, man." He picked up the amp very clumsily and tried to take a step with it still in front of him, lost his balance and fell hard on the hard asphalt of the street - rolling over on his back. I have seldom felt so much concern as it looked for a moment as though he had really hurt himself. "Don!" I yelled, "Are you alright?" "Yeah," he said, sitting up and grinning foolishly, "That was so stooooooopid," he said and laughed. Relieved, I looked him over and didn't see any blood or bruises at all. He seemed intact and not in pain.

His aluminum briefcase had opened and spilled all his special felt pens all over the street, along with several bags of English breakfast tea, which he always kept with him. After helping him to his feet, I quickly picked all his paraphernalia up and put it back in the case. Afterwards, I said "I think I'LL carry this amp if you don't mind." We had a little laugh. But I noticed that he was bit shaken.

I never really thought about this instance until much later when I found out about the suspicions of him having MS and being wheelchair-bound. Could it be that whatever malady he had was already affecting his coordination? I know that MS is sometimes diagnosed with no major symptoms appearing for years. I have often wondered if he had already been diagnosed before he decided to retire from the music business - and perhaps this diagnosis was part of his reason for retiring.

On the way home, he pulled off the freeway in Palmdale. "Where are we going?" I asked. "I want to buy you a drink" he answered. All I could think of was here was one more night I couldn't practice the maze of parts for *Best Batch Yet*. We had a drink and he asked if I wanted another. I declined, and he had one or two more. I started getting a little worried as he was slurring his words. Would he be able to drive? We spent about an hour and a half at the bar, he drew a dozen felt-pen drawings in his book, and then it was time to leave. I could see that he was staggering pretty heavily at this point. He handed me the keys, much to my relief, and said "You drive. Man, I'm sorry John. I can't believe it!" he said incredulously as his voice got higher and higher … "I'm drunk!"

I drove him to my house all the time thinking of the logistics of him driving home in this condition. Fifteen minutes later, we arrived at my house, and I invited him in. To my relief, he accepted, as I wasn't about to give him back his keys. I was trying to train my dog, 'Peaches' to say 'hello' - and had actually succeeded, with much coaxing to get him to say 'hello' several times that night. This took a great amount of time, during which Don did several sketches of Peaches and I.

Van Vliet had given me some drawings back in 1975-76. One framed for my birthday in 1975, and the other two just randomly. I had them all framed and hanging on my walls. The first time he came in, he looked at the walls and said, "You're the only one who ever framed them, man." He seemed really touched by this. I recall that my favorite was a black and white felt pen drawing that looked a little like a dancer in a samurai outfit. He hated it and was about to throw it away and I said, "No! Give it to me." It hung over my couch and I used to imagine when I took naps there that it came to life and danced around the room.

Don stayed at my house for about an hour, and after a cup of coffee, he drove safely home.

Journalist

There was one day that a female journalist came to interview Don. He was excited about this. I may be wrong, but I believe it was Christine McKenna. He kept talking about her in a way that made me thing he may have been attracted to her. I remember this person being there for quite some time, but they were mostly in the other part of the house as we rehearsed. After she left, he was raving about what a wonderful person she was. I often think that journalists who appreciate the arts often bond with certain artists who are, in turn, greatly intrigued by the interest.

Comrades

I enjoyed Don's company more than any other phase of our relationship during the rehearsal/recording of *Doc*. Don had mentioned that it was nice to have me there on a couple of occasions. I think that because our work had gone back nearly fourteen years to 1966, and in that time we had done seven unique albums (*Doc* being the eighth), there was a bond and a history that he was beginning to appreciate. Everyone else from the early days was out of his life and it seemed he was missing the comradeship that could develop from that kind of history.

I am in no way belittling the relationship that he had with his band - especially Jeff and Eric - which seemed to be stronger than with Williams. Fowler was seldom at rehearsal, so I didn't really get much of a take on that. On one occasion Don said to me, "It's nice to have you here because otherwise I'd be stuck with these 'kids'." - nodding toward the others jokingly. I think what he was saying was that he liked the fact that we had such a long history. I didn't take it at all to be meant as disrespect to the younger guys, because he spoke highly of them.

Although on the surface he seemed happy, there seemed to be a very prominent uneasiness riding just beneath the surface. Part of it may have been fear. The music industry had not been very kind to Don Van Vliet, and although Don surely shared in the blame of bad business dealings, the record companies themselves were quick to take advantage of his naiveté concerning contract negotiations. I tend to believe Don's statements that he hasn't received anything but publishing royalties from his albums. At the same time, he seemed to have a rather flippant and elusive way of dealing with business questions in his 1993 Mojo Magazine interview with David Di Martino.

Q: Let me ask you this: Bill Harkleroad claims he should be entitled to some record royalties from his work with you?
A: Harkleroad thinks he should get money? For what? Trout Mask? *(pause) Hmmm, sounds far out.*
Q: Do you still get your royalties for any of that?
A: For Trout Mask? *Writer's royalties.*
Q: Does it upset you that he feels that way?
A: Well, I think he should get some money. What I'm trying to figure - Harkleroad said he didn't get any money?
Q: He said the Magic Band signed a contract in which they were part of the corporation, and that they would be paid by you.
A: I owe him money? I didn't make any money myself! Jesus Christ. (pause) I can't believe that after this many years - it's been 20 years... I got beat up for money for those records as much as anybody. Yeah, I got beat. Sounds like they picked you for a target.[67]

The usual ploy that Don used when cornered like this was deflecting - to make the interviewer feel that somehow they had been duped by someone - either an ex-band-member or a disgruntled record company executive. I remembered his advice to me in the kitchen of "Trout House:" 'never think it's you' - he had warned. The more I thought about this statement, the more I realized that it was exactly this mindset that got him into the mess he was in with the music industry, and caused him to avoid rational conversations.

[67] Mojo, Issue 2, December, 1993, Heart & Soul,: Captain Beefheart pp 94

Van Dampire

There was a bartender who worked at the Sand Sailor cocktail lounge who had developed a bit of a relationship with Don. He would give Don complimentary drinks and light his cigarettes, and Don, of course, enjoyed anyone who would give him such attentive service. We stopped by one night for a drink. It was a Friday, as I recall, and no big deal as I could sleep-in the next day. I had to get Don to buy all the drinks as he was only paying me $75 a week and my rent was $175 a month, so I wasn't really rolling in cash. This fellow, whose named has long since fallen off the rolodex of my mind, was a singer - according to Don. "You should hear him, man. I'm going to start a group for him and call him 'Van Dampire'." I often wondered if this spoonerism on "Damn Vampire" was in essence what Don really thought of the fellow.

One thing led to another, and we invited him to my house - at 2:30 in the morning. He came in with a guitar case and sat on my couch, singing *Puff The Magic Dragon*. Although the guy did have a really nice voice, I was expecting blues and almost started laughing. I went to use the restroom, partially to contain myself, and when I came back, they were doing coke on a mirror in my living room.

After Van Dampire left, I gave Don a strong reprimand about doing drugs in my house. I didn't like it and didn't want it around. I had seen too many people die or ruin their life with cocaine. Don finally said, "Never, man, never again." He apologized very sincerely and left.

Eric In The Barrel

The really good thing about Doc rehearsals was that, for the most part, they were timely. Don would show up on time, rehearsal would end on time, and we'd leave. It seemed like it was from 10 a.m. to 6 p.m. Sometimes, we'd hang out for a while, sometimes we would leave shortly thereafter. I found out that Eric had a gig with some band at a club in Hollywood. He was doing it as a favor and it was a big deal for the band. Don caught wind of it and purposely decided - on that particular night - that we needed extra work on something or other and wanted to work late. I could almost see the sweat popping out on Eric's brow. Finally, Feldman said he had to leave, and Don, after finding out why (though it was evident to me that he already knew) proceeded to give Eric the worst cross-examination I have seen since Jeff Tepper caught it for playing a two-note phrase "incorrectly" at a *Bat Chain Puller* rehearsal - as described earlier.

After watching Eric melt for about twenty minutes, I interceded. "Don," I said, "Eric, Jeff and Robert all know their parts, but I'm still needing practice, so Eric really doesn't need to be here." This was just enough to break up the ill will gathering momentum in the room. Eric left for his performance, and we went home, but it was definitely an evening that left a bad taste in everyone's mouth.

Brick Bats

Speaking of leaving a bad taste in people's mouth, Robert and I got into a verbal tussle one night when learning the song *Brick Bats*. Everything was fine until we got to the center section. Don was not in the room during this argument. When we got to the center section, I played the parts as written. This was yet another "outtake" from the unreleased *Bat Chain Puller* and I had transcribed these parts. One of the rhythms was being played incorrectly and I pointed it out, playing it correctly for the other three. I was always a stickler for little details, and I didn't see any harm in correcting this, as it was only two notes!

I found the argument on one of my rehearsal tapes that I had neglected to shut off. Basically, Robert was saying that it would be easier for me, one person, to change to what the others were playing. On the other hand, I was saying that it would be more correct with respect to the composer to play it as written. This went on for five to seven minutes, and kept escalating to a point of ridiculousness - especially for a disagreement over two notes - but I held my ground because of the principle involved. At one point, I had to laugh when I heard Bruce, who was seldom at the rehearsals, say, "Yeah, but Don'll never know the difference no matter what you play." I found this to be a valid point, started laughing, and was about to concede when Jeff called Don into the room and asked him what to do. "Play it the way John says it's supposed to be," was his reply. Listening to the tape, Tepper was the ambassador of goodwill that evening.

The conflict bothered me for a while, because I have been told that I often "rub people up the wrong way" and am too harsh in my arguments. When listening back to the tape, I found that I didn't like the way I conducted myself. Even if it was the way it had been played by these three for months, I could have been more diplomatic. Don hadn't noticed, or he would have already corrected it.

Essex House

After this evening, Don wanted to go to yet another nightclub - The Essex House Lounge. The bassist in the group recognized Don as a regular and came to talk to him. I think Don just liked to be out away from that mobile home. He also was inspired, when in a group of people, to draw, and his drawings were getting better and better. One morning at Don's trailer, before the drive to rehearsal, I watched as Jan went through a huge collection of custom felt pens and picked out a few that had great color combinations for Don to use that day. He told me that she had studied art, and was instructing him in choosing colors that compliment each other.

Back to the bar, after the break, the bassist went back onstage and the band began their set. Suddenly, I noticed that fog was creeping out from the fog machine. It was too corny and I began laughing a deep belly laugh and had to run out of the place and go outside, where people in the parking lot were looking at me as though I were mad. Don eventually came out and found me, still trying to quell my laughter. He kept saying, "That girl over there keeps looking at me, man." I kept saying that maybe it was his imagination, but apparently some girl behind me was looking in our direction. I turned around and spied an attractive blonde lady standing about five cars down with a group of other relatively attractive women. "John!" she shouted, "I thought that was you! John French, right? Don seemed crestfallen.

I recognized this lady but didn't know her name. She walked over, leaving the others and introduced herself. Her name escapes me now, but she was the owner of Caravan Dance Studio, and had seen me dance years before. She wanted me to come dance at her studio in shows and even offered to pay me because "male partners are hard to come by in this ignorant red-neck town." This statement in itself brought Don completely out of his crestfallen state and I quickly introduced him as "Don Van Vliet aka Captain Beefheart." We had a nice ten minute talk and I said I'd be in touch, though I never did pursue her offer, having forgotten about it until, well, just now...where did I put those "old black cracked patent-leather shoes?"

On another occasion, we were driving to Don's trailer (where I had started parking my truck in case Don needed another drive home), and we passed the fairgrounds, where the church I went to leased a building to hold their services. I mentioned to Don "that's where I go to church." We noticed that there were cars and I figured it was a regular Tuesday night service. He, surprisingly, pulled in. We caught the tail end of a service probably went from 7 - 8:30 or so. There was singing accompanied by acoustic guitar. "I don't like the music," he said. "I don't either, but then I don't like much of any music, and neither do you." He laughed.

"The Vineyard" was a non-denominational "spirit-filled" church affiliated with Calvary Chapel. They had a leaning toward what is called "Charismatic" or, in an older term "Pentecostal." This means an occasional eruption of glossolalia or "speaking in tongues" though I seldom heard it, if ever. It also meant that people prayed for healing, and lifted up their hands when they sang worship songs. They were lifting up their hands and Don noticed this and skeptically lifted up his hands also - with an expectant, somewhat mocking-look on his face. "It doesn't work like that." I said. "What?" he replied. "It's not like you lift up your hands and a Holy Beam ascends from Heaven and you miraculously have everything you want. It's more of an acknowledgment - like a little child reaching up to their parent to be held and comforted."

A friend of mine picked me out of the crowd and also recognized Beefheart. Steve Nootenboom came over to the table. He's probably the most open-minded Christian I know. He's an accomplished artist, rock climber, hang-glider, licensed building contractor, father of four and - a harmonica player with a great admiration for Don's harp playing. We sat at the table and talked, and, as you probably know by now, Don loves to talk. They finally had to kick us out of the place. I think Van Vliet really liked Steve.

Steve Nootenboom: The last time I saw Don was when he showed up at the church. His skin was very aggravated and blotchy and he said the doctors didn't know what it was. His voice sounded shot and he sat in the back of the church with a big art tablet and large marking pens doing his art. After church I looked at his drawings and he explained each one.
They were semi-Picasso / abstracts of human figures with wolf faces snarling and drooling. The females had breasts with sharp points and the males had evil eyes and long teeth. He explained his interpretation of the church members and pastor as flirting with each other for sex. My impression at the time was that Don was insane, although as time goes on it makes a little more sense.

Sound Castle

Sound Castle, as I mentioned, had been picked by Don as the studio in which *Doc* would be recorded. We put off the session for an entire week, because I basically was barely ready in six weeks and Don, as a favor to me, postponed. I might add that had Don actually allowed me to go home at night during the first six weeks, I probably would have been prepared. I can't say I didn't enjoy the time I spent with him though, and certainly wouldn't have done it differently.

As I said, we were the first non-Christian group to record in Sound Castle studio and I was very pleased that we would be recording here because of my faith. The studio was immaculate and had great equipment. I felt like this was where this was "meant" to happen, which I'll explain more later.

Amp Blows Up

Paul Delicato had an original Fender Bassman amp, which was before the piggyback models. I think it had four ten-inch speakers in it. He offered to loan it to me for the session. I was so excited to try this amp, but it was late when I got it home, so I waited until the next day. I remember jumping out of bed at about 8:00 or so (hey, I was up late) and plugging everything in. I turned the amp on and hit a chord. All of a sudden the amp popped really loud and made a whistling buzz like "BZZZZRRRRROOOOOMPUF" sound like a whistling tea pot just being turned off, then huge amounts of smoke poured out of the back. "Oh my fucking God!" I yelled and then thinking about what I had said, looked up - half expecting a lightning bolt to come down and leave nothing but smoldering ashes of Drumbo on the shag carpet.

It was the first day of the session, and I had about an hour before I had to ride to the studio with Don. "Of all the times that amp had been turned on, why did it have to pick TODAY to do this?" I took the amp with me, although it was useless in the condition it was in, but I kept thinking that someone at some time had told me that sound I had heard meant that a capacitor had gone out. I had also heard that on the old tube amps, to find out what component was bad, just open it up and turn it on, whatever smokes is the bad component. Sounds a little crude doesn't it? I figured I had nothing more to lose, so when we got to the studio, I asked if they had a soldering iron and if there were any spare electronic parts around or if there was a store nearby.

There was a store - right across the street. They put me in a spare isolation room, furnished me with a soldering iron and a lamp along with a little tool kit.   I took the amp apart, found the smoking capacitor (I had remembered correctly) removed and replaced it, and fired up the amp. It worked great! Talk about stress out time, though. Good grief, first day of my first session playing guitar in a band after only seven weeks of rehearsal after having not played for four years and a borrowed vintage amp blows out and smokes like a bomb.

For non-musicians - the above information was included because many people requested information on equipment. Also, because I think "humor is emotional chaos recollected in tranquility" - James Thurber was right…

Don may have dropped me off and left to pick up Glen, but I do recall meeting Glen Kolotkin later that day. I wasn't aware of his involvement on *Shiny Beast* as I never pay attention to the credits on the back of albums - after not being credited on *Trout Mask Replica*, who could blame me? He seemed an amiable enough guy. I don't recall much about him. He was shorter than me, and had a mustache. He wore glasses, was a bit on the balding side, and seemed to be a really amiable fellow. After hearing what I had about his ability to work with prima donna types, it was evident that this guy not only had amazing credentials but also charismatic gift of establishing and maintaining rapport.

Our first song was *Dirty Blue Gene.* Once getting set up, sound checked, and earphone monitors balanced we struck our first note of the day.   Robert wasn't happy with his mix, so the engineer gave him his own mini-mixer so that he could control his own headphone mix.

This is the first time I had touched the guitar this day because of the repair work, and so my hands weren't yet warmed up. At the end Don said "That's a take." I said "No, it isn't, I screwed it up bad." He shot back, "Yeah, but it's got the feeling." So, I agreed to keep things moving.

Being only vaguely familiar with guitar settings, I called Don out into the studio on the beginning of each take. "This thing has eleven different settings, so help me pick one," I'd say. The other guys started making fun of me, in a playful way … like "Ooooooh wow, my guitar only has seven sounds, that's not FAIR!" It was pretty funny, but taking the hint, I started picking my own sounds after about three songs. I had written down my basic settings from rehearsal, but this was after all "The Session!"

The first day went quite well. The budget was tight and Don was rushing the session a bit, but if something wasn't right, we'd point it out. I think we did four tracks the first day.   Outside, in the parking lot, as we were saying "job well done" to each other and Glen said to me, "You know, I could have made more money on another gig in New York but … this is just so hip to be working with Beefheart." He was just like a kid, and you could tell he really liked and respected Don. Things were going well. We had dinner that night with Glen and dropped him off at the hotel.

I still didn't like *Dirty Blue Gene* and made my best plea with Don on the way to the studio for another chance. He wanted to overdub my part but I said "No, I'd feel self-conscious, and don't do well under that kind of pressure." He agreed, and we did it first thing the next day. I was ecstatic - especially when we nailed it within the first hour and a unanimous "Oh, this is SO much better" went up from the band. We still managed to get three takes a day, so things were moving along nicely.

On the day that I switched to bass for *Sheriff Of Hong Kong*, Victor Hayden showed up with Don as he drove up in his dark blue Volvo station wagon to pick me up for rehearsal. I hadn't seen The Mascara Snake for quite some time. It was really a wonderful reunion, as I liked Victor. He had a great sense of humor. Apparently he was there as official session photographer and I certainly would love to see those photos.

We changed positions in the studio, all moving over to the grand piano that was in the room. It was, as you faced the control room window, to the right. Robert sat to my left, Eric faced me on piano, looking directly opposite the window, and Jeff stood to Eric's left. Victor stayed in the room for a time, clicking away on the camera. I've never seen any of those photos, but knowing Victor's sense of composition, I imagine they are great.

Vampire

In the "Vampire" session, Jeff, Eric and I all stood very close together on small plywood squares that were miked. During the "horror" line (that starts first at 00.36 on the CD) we finalized the phrase by stomping our right foot down, as if we were vampire soldiers coming to attention. This was for the sound, but also as a visual cue to keep us together, rather than being conducted. I believe Eric played bass guitar on this piece, then overdubbed the Mellotron.

After Basic Tracks

One thing I especially enjoyed in this session was sitting in the booth listening to Jeff and Eric as they played *Sue Egypt* and *Ashtray Heart*. Five years after I first heard Tepper, he had turned into a Class A guitarist, and Feldman had loosened up and really found his niche. There was also such a wonderful rapport. Everyone seemed to be getting along well. I had never seen this kind of relaxed atmosphere. There was, of course, the urgency of getting the project done under budget, but it was such a team spirit that the fact really was never mentioned - everyone knew what needed to be done and did it. Don seemed to produce quite well in this setting.

Flavor Bud Living

Gary Lucas came out near or just after the end of the basic tracks. He played *Flavor Bud Living* and I couldn't believe how fast and sporadic it sounded.

Gary Lucas: He sent me the tape of you playing it. That's what I learned it off of - not a piano tape. He said, "I'm going to take you to England, too, and they're going to hear you, they're going to have to dust off the hands on Big Ben to be able to keep the same time that you have." He thought I had great timing. Jan would be with him and I would be talking, and he'd say, "Man, Jan, listen to his timing." I was really flattered - because I had always been an outsider all my life.

John French: It was as if you were finally validated, I bet.

GL: Yeah, and by the hippest guy I knew in the world. So, that was the big honor for me, was that he digs me.

Gary and his wife Ling had been out earlier for a visit, and somehow, I missed seeing him during this time, though I'm sure I was in town, as they came by my house, as I had built a pyramid doghouse and Don said Ling commented on it.

Gary Lucas: I went out there with Ling. We had a great magical week. We stayed at a motel in Lancaster, and hung with him and Jan and drove around. He said (Quoting Don) "I'm going to show you the exploding note theory." So I asked, "What's that?" He said, "You play every note like it has no relationship to the previous note or the one coming after it.

I had heard a lot about this "exploding note theory (ENT)" and I could see what Don meant, but I thought that the phrasing kind of trounced on the melody and took away from the beauty of the piece.

Gary Lucas: So, I said, "What, really staccato like "ak ak" or something?" He said, "Yeah." Basically, the instructions on this thing (were) - "I want you to play it much faster and jerkier." Then, he said, "We're going to be doing sessions, I'll bring you out here." So that was when I met you, they flew me in to do it.

I certainly couldn't slight his playing at all, and could see that Gary was a very powerful and precise player. I certainly wasn't at all opposed to him as a person, it just took me a while to adjust to the "ENT" version of Flavor Bud Living.

John French to Gary Lucas: I am curious about your picking style.
*GL: I think it's unorthodox. I learned it, no one showed me really. It's just my attempt with coming to grips with what I heard on the records - when I learned the first Beefheart music like, say, **Sugar And Spikes**. I find finger picks very cumbersome. I have never been able to deal with them or thumb picks. So, I just clip my nails as close as I can to the quick. I've toughened up the flesh of the fingertips to the point where I can really get a good percussive attack.*

Gary also played a little French horn part on *Best Batch Yet.* It was like something you would barely notice and is on the line that says: "You may think these are the finest pearls"... the part was whistled by Don to Gary on the phone.

Fowler
I'm not sure what songs Fowler overdubbed. *Run Paint Run Run* I can certainly hear, and the part is certainly working with the music, unlike a lot of what I heard on *Shiny Beast.* I really wished he would have played on the center section of *Brick Bats* - or maybe he did and it's low in the mix. I remember him being there the same day as Lucas played French horn and guitar, so I think he was just in and out. It was a little odd to me ... I wasn't used to the "studio musician" kind of approach with Don's music.

Sheriff Of Hong Kong / Ashtray Heart
Eric, Jeff, and I had played *Sheriff Of Hong Kong* with Robert Williams playing drum parts that were written by Don. I think Don had played them on the set, and I never liked them at all. They weren't challenging for a drummer, plus they just were ... lame. Robert played them fine, but the parts themselves just didn't cut it.

Robert Williams: It got to the point to where - instead of him kind of giving me a little bit of freedom to come up with something. He would sit behind the drums and have me play verbatim what he played.
John French: Yeah, who in the hell wants to play what an amateur plays on drums?

To clarify what I'm saying here, Don had some good ideas on drums and when he "sang" what he wanted - like he had on *Totem Pole* or *Floppy Boot Stomp* - the drummer was able to interpret what he did and still play a part that was a bit of a challenge and something that a drummer would be proud to be heard playing. During *Doc* rehearsals, I recall one particular day when Don sat at RW's drums and played some very mediocre and amateurish parts for *Sheriff Of Hong Kong* that he expected Williams to play verbatim.

*Robert Williams: But he approached **Sheriff Of Kong** and **Ashtray Heart** the same way - and the drum parts were fucked! I had played them the way he wanted. 'Cause I knew that if I* *didn't, the guys in the band would say, "Don, Robert's playing that a little bit different than you." So, I had to play it the way he did it, and it was fucked up.*

This was true - Tepper and Feldman, who seemed to have a bit of resentment for Williams - would point out any embellishment Robert added to the drum parts. Most of the time, I thought they moved better and made more sense when RW took some liberties. Since I was a drummer, I could entirely sympathize with Robert on this point. Unfortunately, Don seemed to "police" every song to make sure everything was something he had created - especially after Bill had publicly said that the band had more to do with the music than Don let on. It was an unfortunate thing, as most drummer's parts are not written by the composer. The drummer generally takes the main thrust of what the composer wants, and translates it to the drum set in a way that makes musical sense. Drum parts can't be copy written.

As we were driving home, Don told me he wanted me to play drums on *Sheriff* and I immediately said No! I hadn't touched my drums in two months, so I was out of shape, plus, from *Glider*, I knew from experience how that would make RW feel. He insisted, and turned on the cassette of the board tape he had Glen make and started telling me what he wanted - tapping on the dash board and singing as he drove. It was sort of a faux-tabla approach and he was saying "ticky ticky ta ticky ticky ta ticky ta." I hadn't mentioned this, but most of the drives home for the whole rehearsal and session time were laced with Don singing or dictating something into his tape recorder and then holding it directly to his ear with the volume full-on and saying, "Listen to THAT, man!"

Anyway, I agreed to play only if Don would just let me "respond" to the song. I said "I'm pretty familiar with this piece and with what you told me, I think I can carry it off for you, but YOU need to tell Robert I'm going to do this and I need a couple of days." Though it was all agreed upon, Don never told Robert.

He also wanted me to play drums on *Ashtray Heart* - which up to then I had assumed was like *Sue Egypt* and wasn't meant to have drums. Basically, this was tough to do, as there had been no drums to begin with which made the track waver in tempo. You can hear me groan at one point on the track after he says "Send your mother home your navel - case of the punks. (1:19)." He had me play the drum break from the end section of *Veteran's Day Poppy* and I had failed to mute the cymbal properly, but he liked the groan and left it in. The basic pattern I used on this was the first half of the P-K-RO-P beat from *Ant-Man-Bee* avoiding the cymbals. It came off well, I think, for me not having actually been in the room with the guys, and being totally unfamiliar with the structure.

When I overdubbed the drums, I tuned them really loose and Glen thought I was out of my mind but I asked him to "compress" them electronically, and it really helps my sound to do that, plus give the sound a bit of a "tabla" feel, because you can hear the tone going slightly flat at the end. He liked the idea and said "wait a minute" - for several minutes while he plugged in patch cables and tweaked knobs. Suddenly, the sound was there.

The inclusion of me drumming on two pieces here was to be a connection to the past. *Sheriff* was approached like the *Mirror Man* session era drumming mixed with *Bat Chain Puller* (not song - album) approach. *Heart* was more *Trout Mask* - simplified.

Overdubs

After the drum overdubs, I was given a very obtuse marimba part which Don played on the marimbas at my house. This was for *Making Love To A Vampire With A Monkey On My Knee*. It was unrelated, in my mind, to the music - in the same way the guitar on *Best Batch Yet* had seemed. I worked on it as Don overdubbed vocals. Finally, it was time to overdub the marimba. I walked in, and they had a beautiful set of marimbas set up. "Wow!" I said, "I hope I live up to the honor!"

I was able to knock it out by punching-in, as I had never played marimbas before. I used the chart, played a section, punched-in, played another section, etc.

As I finished and walked into the control room Tepper said "I really like your approach to marimbas, John," I jokingly said in my best old-codger voice, "It's not the approach, son, its whatcha do once ya get there!" and ended with a kind of redneck snicker. Don laughed and in the true spirit of men bonding, handed me a bottle of some alcoholic drink he'd been nursing and I took a big swig. Jeff said, "Wow, you didn't even wince." It was a very light-hearted atmosphere.

Vocal

One night during Don's vocal overdubs, I was at a neighbor's watching *The Rockford Files*. Don had actually gotten me hooked on this show, and I watched it with my friends, Mike and Gaby French - anytime I made it home in time. I had just grabbed my first handful of popcorn when their phone rang. "It's for you!" Gaby said - a little surprised. It was Don. "You gotta come with me to the studio!" he said excitedly. "You're going to sing on *Dirty Blue Gene* with me." I'm thinking "But *Rockford's* on…"

He picked me up about 10 minutes later and we drove to the studio. It was just Don, Glen, and I if memory serves. He put his lyric sheet in his own handwriting on a stand and said, "Just sing what you feel." I listened down to it a couple of times. I was starting to really appreciate what an honor this was. As far as I know, no one had ever sang with Don on a non-backup level like this. I was not backing up his voice or harmonizing with him, I was singing along with his voice, and I have to admit that for a moment I got a little lump in my throat as I thought back 14 years before when Don had said "You and I could sing together, like a really heavy version of the Righteous Brothers." So, I almost choked up, as we had come full circle. We had gone through all these ups-and-downs and I felt as though I had been wrung out and hung up to dry more times by this man, and yet, there was this bond that was so disarming, and I realized that I really, really loved the guy in spite of all the dysfunctional behavior and the pain that he had caused me.

I didn't really think about singing. I had them turn my voice completely off and just listened to Don and did my best to react instinctively. He told me not to worry about what it sounded like and he would pick and choose what went and what stayed later. So, I sort of found myself with Don's voice in the middle of my head, looking at his hand-written lyrics, and cutting loose. It was one of the most memorable moments of my relationship with the man. In a sense, that day, he paid me the highest honor he could.

… and the only way I could have appreciated it more is if I hadn't had to miss *The Rockford Files*. Later that evening, we all sang on *Run Paint Run Run*. It was interesting, as Don didn't give us lyric sheets and only wanted us to sing the words "run, paint, run run" but we had no idea when it was coming up. He kept stressing to just sing it out in as full a voice as possible. I remember Jeff's neck veins standing out he was singing so hard. If someone would start to sing and stop, he'd stop the tape and say, "Just SING it, man, don't stop like that, we'll erase it later if it's wrong." I hate working this way, but I think Don's method was to bring up the tension and capture that in the recording.

Mixing

The same atmosphere permeated the mixing session, for the most part. It was almost miraculous to have been in the studio with Don without at least one major eruption that put everyone on edge. It didn't happen here. The only thing stupid that happened was really caused by the studio. They decided, over the weekend - to re-varnish the floors! Of course, Don came in and was livid. "How am I supposed to sing when I'm breathing this carbon-laced stench?" It was tough, but he did get past it and I think they fumigated the place the next day so that the odor was minimal and also gave him some kind of discount. He had to push on through, however, because Glen was scheduled to leave soon.

The whole band was there, and when it came time to mix *Sheriff*, it was suddenly the Robert Williams hour of sorrow. Don had never mentioned that he removed his drumming and added me. This was just plain un-diplomatic of Don, and I think in a sense, he was using it as a little jab at Williams because Robert irritated him. He didn't tell me this, but I sensed a slight edge all through the Doc experience. Robert was kind of the whipping boy in a sense and Redus had even mentioned this going on prior to my re-enlistment.

Robert Williams: *I was pissed off because he had YOU come in and play drums on* Doc At The Radar Station *without telling me and having me learn that song before that. I just felt like that was a "kick in the ass."*
John French: *Oh, you mean me playing on* Sheriff Of Hong Kong?
RW: *Yeah, and* Ashtray Heart. *I had to learn those and play them live - and that was fun to play.*

Don, on one earlier occasion, kept telling Robert that he wasn't playing a part right on *Vampire* and said, quite impatiently "John, will you show him what I mean?" This had to have been like a knife in Williams' heart. I sat down and played the same thing Robert was playing and Don said, "Yeah, that's it!"

I was sitting at the console in the mixing booth. Don was on one side of Glen, and I was on the other. Anyway, when Glen brought up the drums, Robert was pretty upset as it dawned on him that not only was his drumming removed and replaced with mine, but it seemed everyone in the studio already knew about it but him. I knew how he felt, because Don had pulled me off of *Glider* and overdubbed Ty Grimes - playing essentially what I could have played - had Don allowed me. He also pulled me off of *Booglerize* by saying, rather disgustedly "Get in here John, I'll get Artie to play the fucking part," - embarrassing me in front of the entire band and the engineer in the booth.

I chose to suffer in silence through my misfortune, but not Robert. He vocalized very clearly every reason why this was unfair, he couldn't believe this had happened behind his back, it was cloke-and-dagger bullshit etc. etc. etc. ad infinitim. By the time he finished, I had a neck ache from tension. It made me feel completely uncomfortable and yet I felt that I would air my complaint to Don - about not telling Robert - at some point when the studio clock wasn't running. I both admired and disliked this about Robert. I think it's good to speak up and defend oneself, and he did so. However, I also think there's a time and a place, and this was neither.

Once mixing resumed, RW came up behind me and started rubbing my neck. "I'm sorry, man, I didn't mean to go off like that. I can really hear what a great job you did." My respect for Robert once again skyrocketed, because I knew that came from a guy with a big heart and a lot of courage. It was about twenty minutes of tension before the seismometer settled back down, but that was the only major interpersonal hitch in the session. I think I may have told him about *Ashtray Heart* out in the hallway or in the little lounge Sound Castle had set up for food and drinks, but that wasn't a big deal as he had not played on it, as I recall, to begin with.

The one regret I have is that we should have all gotten together and had a wrap party with friends, wives and girlfriends (and may they never meet). It would have been a little more of a closure. As I sit back now, all I can think of is how much respect I had for these dedicated Magic Band guys. It was obvious they all had great respect and admiration for Don.

If only I could have gotten someone to tape that episode of Rockford Files for me...

Copying A Drawing
Van Vliet always liked to go somewhere after a session or rehearsal. I could understand why to an extent. The mobile home he was living in was small, and Jan had slowly brought over box after

box and file cabinets and such to the point that the living room was a kind of office. At this point, they were leasing the trailer from Sue, who was living in a senior village called 'Mayflower Gardens.' It was very claustrophobic for Don, I believe. Almost anytime I came by, Jan was absent from the room, and Don was sitting in a chair surrounded by boxes and filing cabinets drawing in one of his black hardcover drawing books.

A woman had seen one of Don's drawings and wished to buy it. It was a drawing of a woman holding a baby. The whole purpose of the drawing was that Don saw a woman who seemed uncomfortable in her maternal role and didn't seem to be able to relax while holding her baby. Van Vliet, in his strangely humorous style, drew the woman in a cartoon-ish manner holding the baby with one finger of each hand - one on the head, and one on the behind. The mother's expression was of someone who had something suddenly appear out of nowhere, with a slightly-open mouth and wide eyes, and the baby's expression was one of puzzlement, as if asking "What in the world am I doing here?"

Don had said he would sell the woman the drawing, but he said that he had to take it home and cut it properly from the book, otherwise it would tear. He had secretly decided that he would just draw a copy of the original and give that to her. I remember him drawing this same picture over and over again, trying to get it right. "This is harder than I thought it would be," he kept saying.

I thought it was an opportune moment to make a point. "Yes, Don," I said, "so think how hard it must be for musicians to take your ideas that you have played once on piano, guitar or drums and duplicate them time after time to your satisfaction." He looked at me like a light had gone on. I went on to explain that not only did the musicians have to duplicate as closely as possible what he had done, but it had to be completely memorized. "Try putting away the original and drawing from memory, and maybe you'll get an idea why some of your stuff took so long to learn."

Bob's Big Boy

Back to Don liking to go to restaurants and bars ... he probably didn't like to go home because of the warehouse it had become. Jan was a fastidious organizer, and sitting in that trailer all day had probably caused her to focus her time on getting all Don's press clippings, cassette tapes, reel to reels, drawings, skeins of dictated prose, poetry and lyrics organized. I had been to the house and seen her with a file drawer open and her archiving was meticulous. I'll bet she even had those letters my mother sent to the band in 1968 filed away somewhere...

One particular night - it may have been after the vocal overdub session on *Dirty Blue Gene* - Don wanted to go to Bob's Big Boy just off the freeway on Avenue K in Lancaster. I remember being happy to go, as I was done with almost all my recording duties and was taking a breather for the first time in two months. I think he liked Bob's as it reminded him of happier days as a kid when his folks took him to the original in Van Nuys. Also, he loved the illuminated plastic figurine of "Bob" that sat outside. "Look at that hair," he would say, joking, "Man it would be hip if someone in the group could get their hair to go that way." I'd say "Don't look at me" - and point to my receding hairline, and we'd laugh.

When we arrived, we both had to use the restroom, and as we were washing our hands he seemed in a particularly dark state of mind. I'm not sure why. He looked in the mirror, his hat on the counter, and was "sculpting" his hair, with his eyebrows slightly raised - a bit like the expression on the outtake of the *Strictly Personal* stamp photo - and said, "You know, John - I hate myself, man."

John French to Don Aldridge: I think I said something like, "Well, I don't hate you, and there's a lot of people I know who don't hate you." I was trying to let him know that he wasn't alone. You know, his wife, and band members who worked with him during the years. Those people loved him.   They certainly didn't stay in the band because they were making good money.   For God sakes, why were they there?   They were there because they loved him, although they knew he had problems.   At the same time, it hurt their lives and (sometimes) they walked away bitter - I think we who walked away all had some bitterness - for a time.

We finally went out and sat in the southwest corner booth of the front section of the restaurant. I remember being hungry and ordering a big meal. I can't remember what Don had at all. He was quiet for a long time, drawing, and looking intently at his work. Without looking up, he said, "You know, I dig women physically, man, but I'm as queer as a three-dollar bill."

This statement made about as much sense as some of his lyrics. I didn't say anything back, as I'm not really good at quick replies. Besides, this wasn't your typical conversation, this was a deep, deep subject. I started piecing little bits together, and over the years, piecing more bits together. Both Don's cousins that I met, Victor, and later Terry, were gay. Well, Terry was gay for sure, but it was Don who kept telling me Victor was gay, so I'm going to accept that at face value. There was a rumor in high school for a while that Don was gay - the source wishes to remain anonymous, but I have it in my transcripts. Don was always calling the guys in the Trout band "closet queens." I didn't even know what that term meant when I was nineteen.

There was also the period in *Trout Mask* rehearsals when Don was talking about how women and men aren't that different and was encouraging us to wear lipstick. Bill is wearing lipstick on the back cover of *TMR* and Jeff is wearing a dress - both of which were directed by Don. He spoke also about his "feminine side" during this period, and it was, indeed a very strange but short span of time in which this particular subject was addressed.

I also wondered - especially during the *Spotlight Kid* rehearsals in the "compound" why Don would sit talking in the rehearsal room for hours to a bunch of men when he had beautiful Jan waiting upstairs. Helen was staying with me at the time and I couldn't wait to get out of rehearsal and be near her again.

It also seemed that the concerts mainly attracted guys. There were a very small percentage of females for the most part at any given concert. There was also the story of his parents moving him to Mojave when he was twelve because "all artists were queers." This is a pretty big sacrifice to make for a child. Were his parents alarmed at his behavior? Did the "famed Portuguese sculptor" exhibit homosexual traits or had the relationship between he and Don been deemed "inappropriate?"

Was Don's overly macho image with us a compensation? He claimed to have played football in high school - later proven to almost certainly be false. He claimed to be quite the "badass" - yet Jim Sherwood said "Donny was the kind of guy you could just slap around and tell him exactly what you wanted to do with him." There was, of course, the later description of Don by Vic Mortensen, "Don is the kind of guy that would rather - if you got into a fight - he would probably kill you. He's crazy enough not to quit."

I wouldn't venture to say anything beyond what went through my mind or to speculate on what was actually meant by Van Vliet. It was surely puzzling to me, and there was never an explanation offered, and I never asked.

Fred Frith, Henry Kaiser, Chris Cutler

Don mentioned to Henry Kaiser during a telephone conversation that he should hire me for a performance he, Fred Frith, and Chris Cutler were giving at UCLA. According to Don, Henry didn't think that I was "famous enough" to help draw more people. Don says he talked Henry into it. In light of what I know about Don, this seems like a highly unlikely story. Don was always very possessive of his musicians, and never wanted them seen working outside of the Magic Band. But, since I was not in the band at the time, perhaps it actually happened this way.

Anyway, I had to actually build a little lockable shell for my pickup truck (I am a cowboy at heart, I suppose, but I hate country and western music - go figure) and I drove down in pouring rain if I recall. It was about an hour and twenty minutes from my house to UCLA. I arrived and set up the drums, on the floor, next to the stage in Dickson Hall, because Fred, Henry and Chris had completely covered the stage with their equipment.

Henry came over with a newspaper called "The Reader" and told me to read the announcement on the Datebook page. It announced the show, and described everyone, who they played with etc. and didn't mention me until last, when it read, in part, the following:

...and John French, also known as Drumbo, who played drums uncredited on Captain Beefheart's **Trout Mask Replica,** *and who happens to be Datebook's favorite drummer in the whole wide world. We'll be there...*[68]

Now this may sound strange, but I had never received much attention in the press and so when I read this, I was really moved. I didn't think anybody really knew who I was or cared. It was just a line in a free newspaper, but it meant so much to me that I hung on to it for all these years.

The show was less memorable for me. I am not a true lover of improvising. I think that it's boring, pointless and often lacks discipline or focus. I enjoy improvising within a framework, such as a soloist improvising over chord changes, and of course, only when they're good, which few are. I have less interest in the style of music than the skill in which the soloist communicates through his improvisation within a framework.

Chris, Henry, and Fred were very serious about this, and they had worked together many times. I was an outsider, even physically, being forced to set up off the stage. Chris had all kinds of special percussion stuff; I just had a conventional drum set. I played sporadically, sometimes with energy, but my heart wasn't really in it. I took a couple of walks around the hall, observing. Sometimes Fred would play the bass and it was during those moments that I felt something beginning to happen.

Tim Meyer, my friend from R&E, showed up with his daughter Tansy if I remember correctly. He later told me that I seemed detached, except every now and then I seemed to take the attitude, "To hell with it! I'm going to play!" and then would come out of hiding and do some energetic burst that seemed to make a statement completely removed from anything going on onstage.

Fred's improvising consisted of him laying his guitar on a table and dropping things on it, like little finger cymbals. He had especially prepared guitars, one guitar had a pickup on the neck by the nut. That way, by "hammering" on a string (percussively "hitting" the string down on the fret) he would not only amplify the string sound from the fret to the bridge, but also the string sound from the fret to the nut (on the end of the neck,) I found many of Fred's "prepared guitar" concepts fascinating, I just didn't know what was appropriate to play along with him. What he did for the most part was based primarily on timbre and sound "effect" not on rhythm, and my whole philosophy and approach was rhythm - and the main element that seemed to be missing was exactly that: rhythm.

Henry preferred to stand holding his guitar in more conventional method. He liked using an "ebow" which was some kind of "electronic bow" (hence, the name) for the guitar. It could make strings sustain pitches indefinitely. It reminded me a bit of Don's experiments on guitar, especially during the *Mirror Man* and *Strictly Personal* sessions.

Chris was like a man doing a radio show, slamming doors, making footsteps. He used these large slapstick kind of affairs which had handles. They were like wooden "irons" and he would slap and thump them together and strike them flat on the drum heads. It was an interesting effect.

My problem was that this was the opposite end of the spectrum from my experience. I had played

[68] Reader, Los Angeles Free Weekly, Friday, October 26, 1979, pp 3.

music that was so pre-arranged as to be stifling, but so complex as to be challenging. Although there had been no room for self-expression or improvisation, it had rhythmic density and cohesiveness.

This music, was totally without form, there was little rhythm at all, and it required no discipline - in the sense that I perceived discipline. I felt that it was more "noise" than music and if it were saying something, I didn't feel I was perceiving exactly or even vaguely what that something was. However, I am probably more prone to embrace Fred Frith's concept of improvisation. One of his influences, Hans Reichel, is one of the few improvisers on guitar who ever caught my ear, partially because of the rhythmic element. On the other hand, Derek Bailey, who is one of Henry Kaiser's stronger influences, does not reach me nearly as much. His music seems less passionate and more cerebral, and definitely less rhythmic.

It was on this night that I met Scott Colby, a slide guitarist Henry had only known a short time. Scott has a unique style of slide playing that I have not personally seen anyone else employ. Henry tried to explain it to me that evening but it wasn't until much later that I actually began to understand the scope of his innovative technique. He uses "Open E" tuning exclusively. Instead of only employing the slide for major chords and single-note lines, he actually uses it more like a "reverse bar" in a bar chord. In order to achieve practically any chord he desires, he presses strings behind the slide / bar to alter the major tuning. It is a very effective and highly unusual technique, which is also difficult to master.

Shambala

Since there was no money coming in from my Beefheart tenure, through Brad Darrington, a contact at church, I wound up working for Tippi Hedren's (the actress from *The Birds*) son-in-law Joel Marshall whose father, Noel, who produced *The Exorcist*, was married to Tippi at the time. Joel made sets for movies and commercials. He had set up a shop at Shambala, which was Tippi's name for the animal preserve she and husband Noel had built in Acton, CA. Noel and she had filmed a movie called *Roar* and had somehow managed to keep all the lions and tigers bought for the filming.

Everything in Hollywood has to do with speed. If someone dreams up a commercial, they want to see the finished product immediately, because someone else might steal the idea. Therefore, it doesn't matter whether or not you have a family, or whether you haven't slept in two days and are operating heavy machinery. What matters is that these geeks - not Joel, the people who contracted him - get their stupid commercial finished as quickly as possible.

Therefore, I was being asked to take speed and stay up three and four days straight to do this job, part of which was driving a huge truck through heavy traffic to LA and picking up supplies. I finally told Joel that I would work a 10 to 12 hour day, and then I had to go sleep, and if he didn't like me working that way, then he should find someone else. He liked my work and kept me on as a "gofer."

I did help him construct some fake "flying machines" for an Australian Pepsi commercial, but most of the time, I was driving a truck.

Don Brings List For Tour

Shortly after the album was done, I had a conversation with Don about touring. I told him that since I was playing guitar, I would need a lot more time to learn tour material. Since we weren't being kept on any kind of retainer, I would be working somewhere - which turned out to be at Shambala - at a normal job. This would give me even less time to work on material. I asked Don to please give me a list of tour material as soon as possible after Doc was finished, so that I could start working on material right away. He agreed to this.

We probably finished Doc around early spring, 1980 - probably April. The tour wasn't until fall, which gave me four months of part time rehearsal (not really as much as it may seem) to really hone my skills as a guitarist and be set for the tour. The band wasn't rehearsing together at the time, but I had been going over the *Doc* repertoire a little every day.

I then became pre-occupied with work (this was during the Shambala days) and lost track of time for a while, but it was contract work, so I had some time off in between contracts. I didn't see Don much, although he would occasionally show up at the house to say "hi." Then one evening in mid-August, he came to my house to tell me we were going to start touring in three weeks and gave me a list of forty songs to learn.

First of all, tours are booked, months in advance, so he knew about this tour for months. Second of all, I had specifically asked him only one thing: to give me plenty of time to learn the tunes, so I could go on stage minus the stress and enjoy the tour. Thirdly, I had bailed him out on the album by walking into a desperate situation and putting myself under a lot of pressure.

Unfortunately, nothing had changed. There was absolutely no way I could have learned the forty songs on that list in three weeks. Just to be clear, there were nearly thirty new songs besides the twelve from *Doc* that I already knew - but it was still a huge amount of work. The guitarists on *Trout Mask* spent 9 months learning less than thirty songs.

I wasn't angry, just disappointed and disgusted. Actually, I was so exhausted from my work (I was working 12 hours a day in the summer in the desert outside in 100 degree plus weather) that I was giddy. I started laughing right in Don's face and threw the list on the floor. As I threw it on the floor, my laughing increased to a belly laugh and I just almost flipped-out as a fourteen year history with this man shot before my eyes. This was the culmination of years of madness, and I knew this was the final blow.

Gary Lucas: Well he liked to do that. It was like, "I wanted everyone around me to be thinking, eating, sleeping me to the exclusion of everything else, and I have the right to tell you how we're going to do this."

Don left, apparently deciding that I would eventually "see the light" and cave in to this ridiculous request.

I didn't.

The next day was a beautiful day, but there was a shadow cast over it by what I had to do. I loaded Don's Telecaster in the pickup and drove to the trailer park to take it back to him. I asked him to come outside, which immediately set his warning lights in gear. He came out suspiciously but tried unsuccessfully to be charming. I told him that he was going to have to find someone else to play.

We were standing on the lawn in his yard by the trailer. He was infuriated with me and I was braced for a physical confrontation and almost would have welcomed it at that point. This was, however, no screaming match. I carefully and logically explained the impossibility of me doing what he requested. I pointed out that he was being unreasonable to think that I could possibly learn this much material in three weeks.

He had the same look of fury in his eyes that used to make me cower, but I wasn't a young kid anymore - so this look was met by my own stare - right back at him. As I got into my truck to leave, he screamed at me "You're hiding behind Christ!" and slammed both opened hands into the side of the door. I just looked at him in the eyes defiantly, let out the clutch, and drove away.

I was really sad about this decision. I had the kind of mixed reactions one has when they have to have an aging pet put to sleep. I knew it was the best thing to do. I knew that Don could find a better guitarist and that he would be better off having a true guitarist than a drummer struggling to play guitar.

I also knew that I would miss all those great moments on stage with that fantastic voice and the fun of hearing Don's creative mind manifested in his conversation. I knew I would miss working with Jeff, Eric, and Robert. I knew that I had seen the last of my days as a concert musician and that anything I did after this would be anti-climactic.

I felt that the statements that Captain Beefheart and the Magic Band made were so strong and so unique that they would continue to influence music for years to come. Don was getting older and wouldn't be performing that much longer. He was ruining his health with drugs, cigarettes and alcohol. Soon, he would be moving to Northern California, because there he and Jan had been working on a custom house for years. I knew he would become an artist, because it was obvious that he had been using his albums as an art gallery for years and he spent more time drawing and painting than he did rehearsing and creating music combined.

Gary Lucas was quoted as saying the following:

"He (Van Vliet) called up, reversing the charges, two weeks before the tour. With French sitting in a bar in the desert saying, "Gary, tell French about how excited you are that he's playing." I said, "Yeah, John, it's really a thrill that you're going to play guitar and I always loved your drumming." He said, "Thank you." I said, "I've been telling the English writers that you're coming over and it's the first time Drumbo's been with Beefheart on guitar, and they're all really excited." And in the middle of it he ran out the door, Don went. "Holy shit, man. Wait a second. The goddamn guy left, hold it.' He drops the phone, I'm on a dead phone for five minutes - long distance. Then he comes back and he goes, "The guy just split. He jumped in his car. I gotta go after him, man. I'll call you back." He calls back later that day and says, "He quit, man. I snapped him like a rubber band." He gave him a list, this impossible task and French just bolted. This is what I had to worry about as the so-called manager. It was really out of my hands. I was in New York, fretting." [69]

Here's the interesting thing about this story - besides the amusing fact that Gary seemed as worried about the long distance charges as the situation - it never happened. I'm certainly not calling Mr. Lucas a liar here. What I'm saying is, I was never in a bar listening to Lucas on the phone trying to persuade me to stay in the group. The way I left the band was the way I described above. There was no other meeting. Besides, I didn't sit around in bars unless forced to because I was riding with Don from rehearsal and this was long past that era.

The only thing I can perceive is that Don had someone pose as me on the phone to make me appear less rational to Gary, as in - he just ran out, man.

From the time I first approached Don at his trailer to be in his band to the end of the recording of *Doc* was probably no more than 2¹/₂ months - which was usually still within the "honeymoon" era of a new member joining or re-joining. After that, it started going south. Gary Marker's observation about Don liking to keep everything "slightly off-kilter" is perfectly exemplified in his giving me a list of thirty new songs three weeks before a tour.

Aftermath

Later that day when I returned the guitar, Don came to my house with a list of things I owed him. I wasn't home, so he left the note with James, my house guest.

I looked at the list and decided not to give him a thing. He wanted the charts to various songs, including *Totem Pole*. He also wanted $230. This was money he had "fronted" to me to get my guitar repaired. I wanted some copies of some of the charts I had worked so hard to transcribe and I knew he had the originals.

This was all concerning such small amounts of money, and it seemed so petty to me. My anger level towards Don was low. I was mostly sad. This man who I had, to the best of my knowledge, helped so many times had stuck it to me again. Absolutely no cooperation and too many last

⁶⁹ Captain Beefheart, Mike Barnes, Quartet Books Ltd., 2000, pp 288-289

minute demands. When I was younger, I would have been so worried about what was going through his mind. Now, I had little concern because the blinders were off my eyes and I could see the truth. I knew I had done my best. I knew he was still trying to manipulate and control through maintaining his personal chaos, so I wasn't falling for it. I also knew that I had come to his rescue, in a sense, once again, by replacing Redus in such a seamless manner.

As for the $230, I wrote up an invoice "For services rendered in the position of Musical Director for the Winter Tour of 1975 - Fees: $1000, partial payment of $230 received, Balance Due: $770." I sent this to his space number at the mobile home park in which he lived.

CHAPTER FORTY:
DRAWINGS TO CROW

...her promo pic from the 1976 Bat Chain Puller session. L to R
Thomas, Don, Denny Walley, Jeff Tepper and John French

Drawings

Shortly after leaving the group for the last time, a mystifying experience happened regarding the drawings Don had given to me. I used to go to church on Tuesday night along with Sunday mornings. On Tuesdays, I often would invite a few people over for tea. It became a regular thing and people would invite friends, they would bring rolls or doughnuts, and we'd all just converse. Sometimes, it was pretty crowded in my little place. As we were leaving the meeting one night, the pastor, Brent Rue, said "Wait!" Everybody sat back down and looked a little puzzled.

Once the din had settled, he said, "I feel like I'm getting something here that I am supposed to tell. This is kind of weird. There's someone out there knows someone who was involved in the occult at some time in your life. This person has a grip on you because he has given you some things that are in your house. These are possessions that he has given you as a gift. You should get rid of those things and get them out of your house." As I drove home, I was thinking about three drawings on my wall that Don had given me and the fact that he used to be involved in the occult - according to his own words.

As usual people showed up at my house, and one new guy on a motorcycle caught my eye so I introduced myself to him. Something urged me to show him a drawing that Don had done of me and given to me as a birthday present. I asked him, "What do you think of this?" This guy took the drawing and said, "This drawing is of you," It didn't look anything like me, but Don had told me that it was a drawing of me. He went on, "The person who drew this had a power over you."

This intrigued me so much that I took him into the kitchen so I wouldn't be distracted. This guy, who I will call Jeff, described my relationship with Don vividly from this drawing. The drawing was of my head, surrounded by three or four little entities - a spider like thing, a little humanoid thing, and another little critter. These were all like stick drawings around my head. One was pressing me on the head, another was standing in front, making spider-like running movements. Jeff said that these all represented evil spirits - demons.

He went on (I paraphrase, but this is a pretty close description): "This one (pointing to one of the creatures in the drawing) is a spirit of mockery. This man used to mock you a lot, and humiliate you in front of people." Now remember, this man didn't know anything about me at all. We had just met. He said, "This other one is a spirit of manipulation, this man used to manipulate you."

Jeff then pointed to the one that had its hand upon my head and said, "That one is a spirit of intimidation because this man would intimidate you, and he knew just how far he could go. He would intimidate you, mostly mentally, and that is why his hand is on your head. It was like a spirit of familiarity that dared to be so personal in his dealing with you that it would analogically appear symbolically in the physical realm of him manipulating your head and daring to invade your space." Jeff went on for an hour detailing the relationship I had with Don and the difficulties encountered. I was awe-struck at the accuracy of his description, so much so that I burned all three drawings later that evening in my woodstove. People have said to me, "You could have sold them for lots of money." No worries, I'm glad to have them gone after that conversation and have never regretted my decision.

Richard 'Midnight Hatsize' Snyder

Richard Snyder: John French had played guitar on Doc and as he was not too keen on touring, I entered the fold as his replacement.[70]

I had left the band in August, but the band didn't actually tour until October - two months later. So, Don's information about touring in three weeks was either dis-information, or I misunderstood him. I do know that he wanted to me to learn 30 songs in three weeks - so perhaps that was when

[70] http://easyweb.easynet.co.uk/~bgwaters/hatsizejustin.html

he planned on starting rehearsals for the tour. Also, I actually was keen on touring, but Snyder was probably told otherwise. Richard Snyder was my replacement on guitar. My understanding was that he was primarily a bassist, but had played a bit of guitar.

John French: *Had you played guitar at all before joining the band as my replacement?*
Richard Snyder: *Well, considering that my mom had bought me my first guitar with Blue Chip stamps (at the tender age of 6 years old), yessir! I played mostly in cover bands over the previous years, with a repertoire that extended from garage rock to progressive to punk. I wasn't bound to make any waves with potential agents and labels, to be sure. Perhaps serendipitously, I began grabbing my brother's 1965 Fender Jazz Bass when it seemed that the local "bands-for-hire" needed bassists (being relatively few in number - and fewer in virtuosity) more often than they needed another hot-shot six-string slinger. After a while, I found myself in greater demand as a bassist and came to love its rhythmic and harmonic possibilities.*
JF: *How long after you joined was it before the band actually toured?*
RS: *Apparently it wasn't very long at all! I was searching through my admittedly messy archives - and finally came upon a piece (from the hospital where I had worked at the time) dated October 2nd, 1980 that reported that I had left the power-pop band "The Shake Shakes" and had joined Captain Beefheart's band: "Rick is headed for the road now, through Scotland and England and the rest of Europe. He may never return to work here." A news feature also ran in Los Angeles ("Eye on L.A.") that October, showing the band rehearsing for the upcoming stage-trodding. Again, I couldn't find the exact date of the original broadcast. The first gig was October 25th, 1980 at Cardiff University in Wales - so I probably had about a month to get my chops together, made all the more difficult by having to learn how to use the necessary Beefheart metal thumb and fingerpicks with some dexterity, as I'd never used them before...or since!*

I laugh as I read this because Bill Harkleroad always hated those metal finger picks, and I imagine that Snyder felt likewise, though they did help to achieve that "fingers on the chalkboard" guitar sound that Don seemed to love.

John French: *How many songs did you have to learn?*
Richard Snyder: *Unfortunately, I've yet to stumble across my "master list", which is obviously in a well-obscured box in the vast "pack rat" nest I call my garage. However, I do remember about two columns of song titles on a notepad sheet, which would approximately be about 40 entries.*

This is probably the same list Don gave to me - with the addition of the *Doc* songs that I already knew and were probably omitted from my list.

Richard Snyder: *Naturally, there was an eventual "rooting out" of some of the proposed songs to learn for the tour. One of the most salient examples was* Dachau Blues, *which proved to be too difficult to decipher both of the guitar parts from the recording (the left channel being more prominent than the right). We had looked forward to playing that one while in Europe, if only to protest the neo-Nazi twist on the now-aging punk ethos that was on the rise in that particular neck of the woods (witness the "white power skinhead" movement that culminated in the band Skrewdriver, for example).*

The "Doc" Tour

Though Lucas described himself as not being a businessman, he seemed to do a pretty good job. As manager, he accompanied the band on the road.

Gary Lucas: The first dates were October, in 1980. We started in the UK and then went to Holland on the Ferry, and into France, Belgium, back to England and then the US and I did half the dates in the US with him.

I was a bit puzzled as to whether this was as an official Magic Band member, or he was featured as a guest artist. Snyder answered the question:

John French: Were there any live gigs done with Lucas in the band?
Richard Snyder: Gary had been with us on the road for the whole worldwide slog, popping up on stage for the One Man Sentence poetry reading, the Flavor Bud Living *guitar solo and the guitar part for* Her Eyes Are A Blue Million Miles *(whilst I busied myself with the bass part). As far as any gigs with Gary putting in a full set list, there was nary a one.*

Sometimes, the composition *Making Love To A Vampire*, was included in the set and Lucas would play bass.

The early performances were loose and sloppy. The band was struggling, and Don was, as usual, forgetting his lyrics, which was obviously no help to the group. Gary noticed that Don seemed to be a "natural" but was also very sensitive to the environment, which made him a bit vulnerable.

Gary Lucas: You see, on a one on one, when he could control the mood and the situation, that's when he really could work magic. You know, like in conversation with people. And occasionally on the stage when he could forget he was on the stage and he would think he was back home or something. He was relaxed, that was when he was at his peak. It flowed out of him. Then it was effortless. When he was aware of "Gotta do this" ... there was tension and he'd get choked.

I am not surprised that the band was "loose and sloppy" with Snyder being given only a month to woodshed all that material, having never played this kind of material before. My hat's off to Snyder for his ability to jump into such an intense situation and be able to function as a guitarist at all. I also was sure that I had made the right choice in not trying to play guitar on the tour, as the band would have had more of a handicap with me than having a guitarist with experience. I have seen a few of the videos of this tour, and my assessment is that Snyder rose to the challenge surprisingly well - especially in lieu of the fact that Don seemed ill-prepared and had the usual problems with lyrics. Perhaps it had something to do with Snyder's monk-like discipline:

Richard Snyder: Unfortunately, I was not much of a glad-handing socializer out there on the road. I didn't even hang out that much with the other guys in the band, actually! After a show, my normal routine would be to rehearse my parts (with the fabulous little Zeus Mini-Amp) in the hotel room before knocking off to sleep. I was a bit disciplined in that respect - and, to be fair, I was still working hard to tighten up my parts due to the rather brief period of preparation.
If nothing else, it made me quite the "teacher's pet" (as Robert Williams would call me), inasmuch as I'd usually be the first one showered, clothed, packed and ready to head out to the next town. When the road manager told us when to be in the lobby to check out, I hit my

marks. We were in England more than anywhere else - and in London more than any other city. This, of course, afforded me the opportunity to knock around the town in search of used record shops to bequeath my per diems to. I had expressly brought an empty flat-sided suitcase with me to fill up with various vinyl purchases while out in the world. Suffice it to say that this bit of OCD behavior really put the blinders on taking in the local flavor and culture. Oh, well.

As the tour progressed, things tightened up, but Gary noticed that Don often did not fare well on the road.

Gary Lucas: *So, the tour got really better, by the time it got to London it was great. We played several sold-out shows at the Venue, which was Virgin's nightclub. They put us on an extra night for the third night. Everybody came to see it. Some of Public Image and Yes, the art-rock band, came backstage. It was quite fun. But I also have images of Don freaking out, and just the down side, where he didn't want to be around.*

By the time the band was back in the US, things were running smoothly. Beefheart appeared on Saturday Night Live performing *Hothead* and *Ashtray Heart*. Yet, Don seemed to hate being on the road. I mentioned to Gary that I liked touring.

Gary Lucas: *I like it too. I like it to this day, but he didn't. Well, we got to America. The best gig was the Beacon Theater in New York, which was quite triumphant. He was "on," and he was really good. The reviews were really good. Like I say, I'm very proud of the management job Ling and I had done. From a press standpoint, he had more press running this time out than at any time in his career. He credited me with that too - (saying) "It's better now than it's ever been. Thank you!" I got him on the cover of Musician magazine.*

Gary's admiration of Don shines through in the following statement:

Gary Lucas: *To me, he is the greatest wit in the lyrics. I showed the lyrics to Trout Mask once to Jerzy Kosinski, who wrote Being There (the movie). He's a great author and he was like, "This man is a very sophisticated lyricist."*

The Last Tour

John French: *Was there a lot of band activity after the tour of 1980?*
Richard Snyder: *Unfortunately, no! As I'd noted before, I went back to part-time employment to keep the money flowing. Having resumed my previous "day job" at the hospital on a part-time basis, I also worked at Poo-Bah Record Shop in Pasadena (for me, that's not at all unlike hiring an alcoholic to do your bartending ... I took my pay in product (vinyl, cassettes and CDs) for the most part!) ... whilst waiting for Don to make the next move - which would ultimately prove to be his last, musically speaking.*

Sadly - for Beefheart fans - the *Doc* tour proved to be the last tour Don would endeavor to make, though this wasn't actually decided upon until later. Perhaps part of the reason for the decision to do no further tours was Don's health issues.

John French: *What were your feelings when you found out Don would no longer be touring?*

Richard Snyder: Well, considering the fact that perhaps the only ambition that I'd ever actively cultivated went into the pursuit of my eventual Magic Band membership, I was both disappointed and, actually, filled with a sense of ... understanding. The subject of Don's health was not necessarily an ongoing concern, but after the announcement, I'd flash back to the increasing difficulty that he seemed to be having with his gait - becoming almost as stiff and clumsy as Frankenstein's monster when getting out of our touring van and when climbing stairways. I chalked it up to possible arthritis (we were touring in the winter, after all), but I don't remember him complaining about any pain symptoms at the time. My gut feeling is that Don was fully up to the idea of touring ICFC - and had stated so after the album was completed. He seemed to be genuinely happy with the results and had an apparent desire to bring this music to a live audience. However, time continued to pass after the album's release - and no call from either Gary or Don about tour plans. All I can offer up for conjecture is the possibility that Don's health became more of a factor as time passed - and that those health concerns played a big part in Don's eventual retirement from the music business. God bless him, though. Apparently, Michael Werner was able to net him more money on the sale of five paintings than he had in all of those years with A&M, Buddah, Blue Thumb, Straight, Reprise, Mercury, Warner Brothers and Virgin/CBS combined.

Horse Ranch/Welder

In contrast to the glories of the road, I was working on a horse ranch building pipe corrals for horses with my friend Richard Suydam, who had amazing patience with my attitude. At the end of the day, I was filthy. I made six dollars an hour, but the consistency of money coming in was far more than I ever made playing avant-garde music, and I could pay my bills and bask in autonomy.

Aloha: Henry Kaiser

Henry Kaiser called me during this period of time and asked me to play on his album *Aloha*, on a single piece, entitled *Lynn's Madd Money*. It was a rhythmic piece he had co-written with a friend, vaguely reminiscent of *Hair Pie*. I wrote the drum parts with a similar approach to the parts I wrote for *Trout Mask*. It was a fun project and took several days for me to feel comfortable with the new patterns.

The piece was recorded at Amigo Studios with Phil Brown as engineer. I was also asked to play on another previously-recorded track - a Delta Blues type jam (in the *Mirror Man* tradition) with slide guitarist Scott Colby soloing over the top. I played to it as best I could, but the time was a bit wavy. Kaiser mentioned to me later that after Don heard this, he called Kaiser saying, "MY drummer? MY music?" At this point, Henry was aware of the control issues Don had, and so wasn't that surprised at the outburst.

College: Spring 1981

I tried the dreaded college again. It just seemed like it wasn't for me. I went for a full semester and received a 3.4 grade average while working practically full time building horse corrals - even while taking a difficult pre-med anatomy class. It was a very intense period of time - I barely had time to do my laundry.

Cliff Martinez

I was first contacted by Cliff Martinez during this period. He was a Beefheart fan, a drummer, and was interested in my style of playing. I groaned. I wanted a private life and certainly didn't want to think about Beefheart any more, so I put him off.

Eventually, I wound up being talked into playing a local concert called "Laser Jam" as a favor to some of my old friends. Cliff showed up at the door of the venue. He was a very persistent guy and had transcribed meticulous charts to some of the *TMR* drum parts. They were in some kind of unconventional notation that I wasn't familiar with and since it had been over ten years since I played the parts, it was extremely difficult to actually tell whether or not he was accurate in his notation. He seemed like a nice enough guy, but I again held him at arm's length.

Starting Over

I eventually lost the job at the ranch due to refusing to do something I felt was dangerous and picked up a job delivering waterbeds, but was not able to work part time and support myself. The waterbed store soon closed and while working as a mechanic's assistant, I began a program which lasted about 27 months, and during that time, I read the Bible through three times. One hour every morning, the first hour of my day, I would get up have a cup of coffee and read. Rather than read from beginning to end, I would read sections from different parts of the Bible. This was like a meditation and did wonders to calm my anxiety.

I built a camper shell for my truck and, after selling most of my worldly goods, decided to go hobo for a while. I moved into a friend's driveway and took care of the house and landscaping in return for a place to park and have shelter. I didn't have a job, and my drums were in storage. I wanted to start over again.

Ice Cream For Crow

Richard Snyder: (writes) *Suffice it to say that nothing happened with the band after the last Golden Bear show of January 31, 1981 until well over a year later. I found a press release dated August 20, 1982 announcing the release of* ICFC, *so I'd guess that about a full 17 months passed by before we were called back into duty. I had gone back to part-time work in a psychiatric hospital and a record store in that interim period.*

After the tour, we took a break, hired Cliff Martinez as the new drummer, added our manager Gary Lucas as guitarist and put me back on bass (where I really wanted to be *anyway* - thank you, Eric, for being too busy with Snakefinger at the time...) and began rehearsals for Ice Cream For Crow *(hitherto fore to be known as* ICFC *for the sake of expediency), the last Beefheart album.*

When I saw the album cover for *ICFC* I thought it was a bit autobiographical. Here's fair-skinned, highly allergic Don, vulnerable and trapped in the burning heat of the desert. To the crows flying above, he looks like dessert: "ice cream for crow."

Mellowed With Age?

Richard Snyder: (writes) *I can be a bit of a stick in the mud? I must s'pose that this particular personality quirk may have been of some service in keeping me out of "The Barrel" (i.e., getting singled out by Don and the Band for some perceived offense). I'm fully aware, however, that the* Trout Mask*-era band had a bigger and badder "Barrel" to contend with. I have had the opportunity to meet and speak with Jeff Cotton and I've read the Zoot Horn book. 'Nuff said. We truly were blessed with a relatively "mellowed with age" Don ... though Don would probably have been the first to castigate you for any suggestion that he was "mellowing out" by anyone's yardstick. Perhaps the fury of* Ice Cream For Crow *was an attempt to invoke the "anti-mellow" Don and to commit that to vinyl for all to behold and take special notice of.*

The last Captain Beefheart album was still to be recorded. Gary was still managing Don, and was made a member of the band for the last album. Gary and Ling had separated, partly due to the stress of managing the band. Now, Gary was taking the full responsibility of the management of the band plus learning material.

Gary Lucas: I went to the head of A&R at Epic, Greg Geller. He should get a lot of credit for getting this record together. I said, "By the way, did you know that we are an active band that is still signed to Virgin, and you're the American distributor of Virgin?" He said, "Really?" None of the Virgin A&R people in England had clued him on to this. So, I said, "We really want to record!" He said, "Great! I loved Beefheart. Do your thing." He authorized it and put up half the money. I think it was a split of the US company and the English company to finance the record. It wasn't a huge budget.

Cliff Martinez, meanwhile, was pursuing his interest in Beefheart's music and had made contact with Jeff Tepper, whom he sent him a tape of himself playing "Beefheart drums." He then went on a tour with Lydia Lunch. When he returned, he called Tepper, just to get his opinion of the drum tape he had sent.

Cliff Martinez: After I had a tour with Lydia Lunch, I got back to Los Angeles, and called up Jeff. I had read an article in the Village Voice about a new Beefheart album. I called up and said, "What's going on with the new record?" He said, "Well, we're looking for a drummer and Don wanted to audition you Wednesday night." I felt like Gary Cooper in High Noon. I did not sleep for three days. I did not drink coffee, I did not do any drugs. I could not sleep. This was, for me, like working with Miles Davis or Jimi Hendrix - one of my idols. I really loved playing that music. So, for three days - I think around the clock -, I was just playing "Beefheart drums." The day of the audition, I was really getting kind of dingy. Kind of hallucinating, I was forgetting all the stuff that I had played and I was really not ... I was on another plane.
John French: Which put you in the perfect condition to be accepted as a Beefheart drummer.
CM: Yeah, plus pushed around.

Martinez got the position after auditioning in a tiny run-down rehearsal studio called the "Wilshire Fine Arts Center" (which, according to Cliff, was neither "fine" nor "artsy") where Van Vliet showed up, characteristically, two hours late, with Tepper and Victor Hayden. After having an interesting conversation about playing drums with vacuum cleaners, he auditioned. He was called three weeks later and told he had gotten the job after Ruth Underwood - Ian's wife and also the percussionist on several of Zappa's tracks, turned down the offer to drum on the album.

Van Vliet decided he wanted Gary to play a piece he had written on guitar called *Evening Bell*, and sent him a cassette recording to learn. Gary worked on this, learning five seconds a day of the rambling, discordant composition. I know how much work this must have been, having dealt with *Totem Pole*, *Odd Jobs*, *Seam-Crooked Sam*, and *Best Batch Yet*. Though shorter, this piece was much denser than any of those, and required a great amount of study and concentration, as it broke so many musical rules, which made it even more difficult to memorize. Within a month, at five to six hours a day, Gary memorized and mastered the piece, at which time Don sent him the other half - on another cassette.

Gary was still working for CBS, which put him in the unique position of having money while being in the Magic Band.

Gary Lucas: Yeah, I kept the day job. Here's the irony of it. Always, when I visited him, or recorded, it was like "leave of absence" or "vacation time." But I kept the gig, because it's just like, well, you know, what's going to happen? Am I going to be able to make enough money playing with this guy to leave the job?" NO!

There was apparently a lot of preparation by the other band members before Gary came out for the session.

Richard Snyder: (writes) *I hadn't thought about it in years, but Gary did, indeed, come into the picture well after we had been rehearsing as a "four-man band."*
When Gary came to California for the sessions, he wound up staying in California for four to five weeks. The band rehearsed at Stone Fox rehearsal studios, which was literally next door to Amigo Studios, where the album was done. He rehearsed with the band for two to three weeks, and then they moved into Amigo to record.

Gary Lucas: *I remember the first rehearsal after I got out there. He wasn't there yet. We're all hugging each other. I was happy to see Jeff again and Snyder I liked, always enjoyed him. Cliff was the new kid, but he was actually a sweet guy. I love Cliff. I mean all of them. We had a good camaraderie, that band. So, we got together and we started Semi-Multi-Colored Caucasian. It was swinging. It was rocking along. It was great, the first time we had played together; it was like, "Man, we can really play!" It was a band, right?*

Don was, as usual, late, and as they were playing the piece, according to Martinez, Don walked in and grabbed Gary by the lapels.

Gary Lucas: *Then, right in the middle of it he walked in and said, "What do you mean fucking around with my music? That isn't it man! You don't understand. Gary, you're too tanned, man. You've been sitting in the sun! You can't play my music with that suntan!" It was disastrous that I could have any fun. It was "not fair" - that was the idea of it. It was like he needed to make everybody suffer like he was suffering. "Oh my allergies, man. What are we doing in this studio?"*

Van Vliet then proceeded to re-arrange a false ending on the piece, which Jan later persuaded him to change back, saying he had ruined her favorite piece.

Richard Snyder: (writes) *There was very little actual rehearsal time prior to the recording - perhaps a month or two? We worked up the bulk of the material from old cassettes prior to entering the old Stone Fox rehearsal studio in North Hollywood:* Drink Paint Run Run *became* Ice Cream For Crow, Oat Hate *became* Cardboard Cutout Sundown, The Witch Doctor Life *got a reworking,* Semi-Multicoloured Caucasian *was revived at the behest of Jan,* Little Scratch *became* The Past Sure Is Tense, 81 Poop Hatch *and* The Thousandth And Tenth Day Of The Human Totem Pole *were rescued from* Bat Chain Puller, *and Gary had* Evening Bell *prepared well ahead of time. The* Host The Ghost The Most Holy-O, Hey Garland I Dig Your Tweed Coat, *and* Ink Mathematics *were all stitched together by the band in rehearsal.* Skeleton Makes Good *was the most impromptu track on the album, having been sprung on us during the recording. Don gave us all of our parts individually, sent us off to work them out, then had us lay it down on tape in probably no more than two passes, striving instead to capture us in a state of ... uncertainty! I used my Jordan "Boss Tone" distortion effect on the bass ... and, unfortunately, it ended up 'missing' (purloined?) shortly thereafter.*

Don also had Gary learn another piece, originally entitled *Oat Hate*, which later became *Cardboard Cutout Sundown*.

Gary Lucas: The band learned this other piece in LA that he had taught them before I got out there. Then, he hooked it up - "Start! Stop!" - the referee in the recording. The thing actually syncs up at the end. It's like this arrhythmic, staccato. It's like "We're in sync! How did he know?" To me, it was like genius.

Richard Snyder: (writes) I now distinctly recall (Gary) being a bit crestfallen at being told by Don that the guitar part that he had been working on so diligently to perfect for Oat Hate was soon to be buried underneath our newly designed setting (Cardboard Cutout Sundown). They were two independently created pieces, united by chance and random intersection - and, more often than not (and to Gary's chagrin), the intricate "exploding note theory" guitar part was buried under our collective bombast.

Cliff Martinez: It was a real chore sort of working that out. There were two sorts of "book-end parts" that almost had like an A B A sort of structure. It had an A section, a B section, then the A section repeated. The A section was worked out. The B section was this part that Don had played this kind of drum solo over. It was one of the early pieces. It wasn't derived from the tape. It was an old version of the band. I was thinking, "Man, how was this ..." I heard what the other guys were playing and what their parts were. And Don did this solo that was completely independent of the other guys parts. I thought, "How am I going to make that work with this?" What he played didn't have that much of a sense of pulse to it. Anyhow, I put it all together and tried to put a pulse to it, because what everybody else was doing was really pulse oriented, and it fit like a glove. (Laughs) When I played the last sixteenth note of that pattern (Slaps table) we were at the top of the A section again. I said to Don, "You know, Don, this is really amazing that this thing times out perfectly?" and he was, "Oh yeah!"

Gary was also learning the sax solo from *Wild Life* and the harp solos from *Click Clack* at the request of Van Vliet. Obviously, Lucas was a busy guy - still working for CBS, managing the band, and not just guesting, but playing in the band. Van Vliet purportedly spent about two weeks with the guys before Lucas showed up - though the band probably worked out much of the material beforehand from cassette tapes. The band now consisted of Tepper on guitar, Snyder was playing bass (his original instrument), and Cliff Martinez on drums. Williams had been fired, and Feldman had left to move to San Francisco.

During this period, I got a call from Cliff again, telling me about being in the band and asking me if I would give him some lessons. I really didn't want to delve back into the Beefheart repertoire, so I gave him an outrageous hourly figure and told him he'd have to drive up to my place. Much to my chagrin, he agreed. When he showed up, I decided that I would first teach him *Hair Pie*, as it had a mixture of difficult and easy sections, most of which I remembered. He wanted to get a feel for my drum style to draw from for this project, which he was quite excited about.

He only took a couple of lessons, which may have been all he could afford, but I believe he was chosen very shortly before the rehearsals began, so it may have been that he was too busy.

Epic and Virgin split the typically small budget between them for the session. Frank Zappa's management had agreed to let him include a few pieces from *Bat Chain Puller*, but this was later vetoed by Zappa, who felt the integrity and value of the album would be lost should he split it up.

Don and Gary went to confront Frank on this at Zoeotrope Studios in Hollywood. Robert

Williams was one of several people observing Frank conducting a 10-piece ensemble when Don and Gary walked in. Williams, spying Don, left immediately.

After Gary and Don confronted Frank with this issue, Frank said he thought that the whole album should be kept intact for those people out there in "Beefheartland."

Gary Lucas: So, Don just goes, "Gary?" and I go into my rap. "Listen, we called your manager about getting these tracks we have a whole fifteen minutes on this record we're doing predicated on getting these tracks. You didn't call back, what's the story? I thought we could get them." Frank won't look me in the eye. He's looking down at the ground, abashed. It's like, "Busted!" - Bad behavior on his part. He goes, "Yeah, well I thought about it. I thought there might be a higher market value out there in "Beefheartland" if I didn't split up the set." So, I asked, "Do you think with this recording budget we have with Virgin, we could afford to buy the whole record back?" Don starts going, "There ain't no Santa Claus on the evenin' stage." He started reciting his poem, which was about, among other things, the music business, and bumming Frank out - which he wanted to do. So, then I hammered Frank, "We don't have the money, what are you doing to us?" Then he asked, "How many minutes you need to fill?" I said, "aboutfifteen." He says, well, I got a track about 12 minutes long called Do You Want A Pepsi? Don sings on it. I wrote it. It's one of my tunes. I said, "You really think we want to put a Frank Zappa tune on a Captain Beefheart album?" That was it. He just said, "I don't know what to say. I've gotta go drink my coffee now. "L' herbe dangereux"- I remember him saying.[71]

Don was overjoyed that Gary had told Zappa off, commenting on how Zappa couldn't look Gary in the eye, was dejected, and it would probably "bum him out" during his entire tour. Gary was surprised at this reaction, as in his own mind, they had accomplished nothing, only had a week until the start of recording, and didn't have enough material for an album.

The idea of using tracks from the six-year-old *Bat Chain Puller* along with tracks from a band which consisted of entirely different personnel seemed to suggest that Don really wasn't that interested in music anymore. Zappa may have been upset that many of the pieces on *Bat Chain Puller* were re-recorded on *Shiny Beast* with different personnel, thus taking away from the value of the album. On the one hand, it wasn't Don's fault that the album had been tied up in litigation for years with Herbie Cohen. On the other hand, it wasn't fair to Frank that Don had re-recorded the material. Usually, there is a clause in any recording contract which forbids the re-recording of any material for a period of five years or more. Don may have been in breach of contract, and it certainly wouldn't have been the first time.

Because of this change of plans, the band had to come up with new material at the last minute. Also, they had scheduled a planned amount of rehearsal time for only the tracks they would be playing, and now there would be more to learn. This put extra pressure on the band and on Don, who had to come up with the new material on the spot.

Gary Lucas: He took a hit of pot, something he rarely did - I hardly ever saw him do this. He wrote the tune Skeleton Makes Good on the spot. (mimics) *"Snyder, you get the fuzztone going on the bass." - cause the day before I had been talking about the fuzz bass on Diddy Wah Diddy. It was in the air, you know, floating around together.* (mimics again) *" Jeff, you go -* (whistles) *- record that, here! Gary, get that steel guitar (National) out, and go* (starts singing)*." - he just constructed the whole thing. In the next few days, he wrote the rest of the tunes to make up the time.*

[71] "Grow Fins" liner notes, pp 90, Revenant Records.

Obviously Van Vliet and his fertile mind rose to the occasion, but he still used some outtakes. *Totem Pole* was a *Doc* outtake, with French's guitar and Williams' drums erased. Martinez learned the drum parts literally overnight, and Don overdubbed horns and laid a new vocal track.

Cliff Martinez: I had this inkling of what Beefheart style drums was, and I would draw upon that, when something like that came up. And then the story I told you about one of the early rehearsals when he gave me a tape to take home and said, "learn this beat," and it was he and Jan in the kitchen. It was a pretty long recording of running water with an occasional clink and clatter of dishes being put away. I thought, "Learn that beat?"
I didn't know whether he was pulling my leg or what. Being an early rehearsal, but the thing was, Jeff knew about this tape. He had heard this tape. I came to rehearsal the next day and I played something that was sort of my interpretation of what I had heard.
John French: So, it wasn't the wrong tape?
CM: No. So I played it and Don seemed very satisfied and said, "You knew that's what I wanted." Jeff (Tepper) piped in and said, "But Don, I don't hear the water thing!"

My thought here is that Don just decided to let Cliff make up a part, which he would later claim he "composed" by giving Martinez a random tape and seeing what he actually gleaned from it - more evidence to me that Don was just not that interested in doing music any longer. There were a lot of loose ends that needed to be tied up in the *ICFC* compositions. The band often secretly met at Tepper's house before rehearsal, to tie up these loose ends.

Gary Lucas: We'd get together as a band. We had a couple of meetings. They were like little rehearsals to pull a lot of the music together, because sometimes he'd walk off after trying to explain a track and it was, "Well - you know what you have to do." Like, "I'm done with this." We'd have meetings - before the official start of the rehearsals - at Jeff's house. "So, okay, how many bars of this shall we play on this motif? What did he say, was it seventeen? Or eighteen? Let's do this." You know - make sense out of the music, to try and pull it together and then he would modify it further in the rehearsal. "Ya gotta change that!" or "that's wrong!" ... It was a group thing, and we would get together saying, "Look everybody, I know that we act a certain way when we are around him" - cause we were afraid to challenge him, basically - "But, we're all friends here and we all know what the deal is, this is part of the drill. Let's hang on and make this work!"

Martinez found that drum parts were added by several means:

Cliff Martinez: You never knew - there was no one set method for writing drum parts. But he also referenced a lot of the old material. Because - that beat we were talking about earlier that was Robert Williams playing the mid section of Big Dig (Smithsonian Institute Blues). He referred to that beat, "You know that beat from the middle of Big Dig?" "Yeah!" "Play it backwards." I had a little Roland Drum machine and I would write the part out forward, play it on the drum machine backwards - cause sometimes if you played those beats mathematically backwards, the bass drum beat might be on the "a" (the last part of a 4 part division of one beat or the last sixteenth note of four is counted "a" short vowel sound). You hear it turned around, those might be down beats. It wouldn't be mathematically backwards, but it would make more musical sense. It kinda helped hearing it. I did a lot of stuff in the drum machine, playing them backwards and hearing what they sounded like. Instead of trying to write them down and learn them. So, there was some referring back to old drum patterns.

The "Christer" Buck

Gary Lucas: On **The Host, The Ghost, The Most Holy O** *- he got me and Tepper to chant in the background. He said, "I gotta put two Jews on this track." I wanna get that "Christer" buck.*
JF: The what?
GL: The Christer Buck! Yeah, Gore Vidal had some thing about people who were big on Jesus, he called them "Christers." Don was amused with that term. It was also a serious song. I dug it. He also once said to me, "Some people think it's hip to have black people play in their group. I got Jews - they understand suffering. They could really wail on guitar better. I was proud of that. Like "The Beefheart Jewish Guitar Army."

Denny Impression

Cliff Martinez: He does "Don" really well.
John French: Does he?
CM: During the rehearsal on day he stopped by, just to say, "hello." He did an outrageous Don. I think Don had just blown up. Then Denny came in and did a "Don blowing up," and it just floored everybody.

I've heard Denny's "Don" and it is pretty amusing - embellished with phrases like, "The thing is...," "Who's thinking 'C'?," "You can't leave NOW ... how are we gonna get this thing, man?," "I can't BELIEVE you didn't get that on tape!," or... my favorite "THIS is gonna mean a lot of money for YOU and a lot of money for ME!"

Carnegie With Ornette

Though he had an offer to play in New York at Carnegie Hall during this period, Don had turned it down because he would "have to learn that old vomit again" - referring to his lyrics. He hated being on the road. It's a tough life, but this would have been a very prestigious performance. This could have been another hint, however, that Don was dealing with symptoms of some degenerative condition, and perhaps these circumstances had pushed Don and Jan into deciding that it was time for him to stop performing.

He's Krass And He's Now

After the release of *Ice Cream for Crow*, Don wanted to get away from Virgin. Bob Krasnow had just been made head of Elektra, so Don flew out to meet with him, but at the same time was badmouthing him constantly. Krasnow had dinner with Van Vliet at his favorite restaurant and afterwards the champagne flowed at Don's hotel room. Krasnow told Don, "I'm not done with you yet" probably meant as reassurance that he intended to help him.

This last phrase was enough for Don. He was reminded of the earlier days with Krasnow and apparently still held resentment for things that had gone bad. In my opinion, Krasnow was one of the most ardent admirers of Don's work and had really done everything he could, in his own style of show-biz hype, to help Don achieve success as a singer/songwriter. Van Vliet, however, blamed all the past failures during the Buddah / Blue Thumb era on Krasnow, saying "he's krass and he's now."

Ice Cream Video And Art Connection

After it was discovered that Don wasn't going to tour anymore, Gary pushed Virgin for funding a video. The budget turned out to be about five thousand dollars, which is very low.

Don sang out-of-sync with the track consistently, which meant that the band had to be put out of sync in order to make the lyrics match Don's lip movements. Don would later claim that he "planned it to look like that." A simpler explanation, in my opinion, is that he simply mouthed the lyrics after hearing them on the reference track, rather than actually bothering to learn his own song. Gary called in every favor he could to get the video finished. It did go a tad over budget, but Virgin paid the additional costs.

Richard Snyder: (writes) It was quick (one day!), hot (over 110?) and, yet, a lot of fun. Again, in viewing the video now, I am taken with Don's stiff gait; he's no longer grazing around a la The Spotlight Kid tour - he's either stuck in one spot and, if he's not stationary, he's just shifting his weight back and forth from one leg to the other. Of course, Don's face and hands are very expressive - and, effectively, draw your attention away from the fact that, from time to time, Don appears to be resting his hands on his thighs as if to gain additional support. Again, I may be reading too much into this, but - as I've since become a nurse - I've learned to regard a person's body language for any clues that may betray the possible signs and symptoms of a potential disease process.

Don used the video as a tool to exhibit his paintings. His art had been more important to him than music for at least seven years, so it seemed only logical that now that he was pursuing his art career, he would use his art in the video, as he had in the past with album covers.

There was an amusing story told to me by Tepper, I believe, about the shoot. Apparently, a jogger came by as they were setting up. He was an older man, and jogged by shortly after they arrived. Don commented on how in the world anyone could jog in the heat like that. Far later in the day, the same older man jogged back by. Don looked at him in faux disgusted and humorously said something to the effect of "That's a wrap! I'm not doing anymore..." Apparently, this man had been jogging through the entire shoot.

It was Lucas who connected Van Vliet to the art world. A friend of Gary's - Brad Morrow - helped get one of Don's paintings on the cover of the second edition of a new literary magazine called *Conjunction*. The word got out that a famous painter, Julian Schnabel, was interested in meeting Don, so Gary contacted him and was successful at setting up a meeting after one of the David Letterman Show appearances made by Van Vliet in the early eighties.

Schnabel helped sponsor Don with his gallery dealer Mary Boone, wife of German gallery owner Michael Werner. The two of them arranged Van Vliet's first shows.

Steady Weekend Gig / Casuals
Around this same time, I landed a steady weekend "gig" playing swing and jazz at a restaurant lounge, called "Mr. B's" in Lake Los Angeles - 25 miles from my home. The owner played piano Friday and Saturday nights. His style was reminiscent of Eddie Duchin and he played many songs I had grown up hearing my family play. I loved these old tunes, and my enthusiasm was noticed by owner Richard Blalock aka "Mr. B." I liked him right away, and we had an uncanny ability to anticipate each other's next musical move. Thus started a seven-year steady weekend gig.

Sunday Jazz
Sunday was Jazz with a group of jazz artists of varying tastes. As they moved on, we hired others to replace them. Over the years at Mr. B's I played with some of the best players in the LA music scene. Although some players had great soul, many of these players were just involved in an intellectual exercise, with little thought at all for the audience. The general format was to play jazz interspersed with R&B i.e. *Dock Of The Bay* or something by Tom Scott's LA Express, Spyro Gyra,

Weather Report, or Return To Forever. It was really rough to find someone who was open - minded and skilled enough (especially a keyboardist) to play all the styles we needed. I was asked by Mr. B to announce tunes and talk to the audience. This intimidated me at first, but I overcame my fear and eventually relaxed into the job.

I moved into the small house that had been my friend Dan Moore's grandmother's and I made a deal with his father, Tom, to use a room next to his garage as my studio; soundproofing it. Since my gig hours were short - only four a night - I was able to get home by 12:30 at night, get up early and work in my little studio. I worked 40 hours a week writing music, practicing drums and singing. John Thomas was the second keyboardist I worked with at Mr. B's for Sunday jazz. Dalton Hagler played woodwinds, and Danny McKinney, who played Friday and Saturday nights also, played bass. For a short period, I really felt that this instrumental jazz quartet had more potential than any other group I had been in to actually succeed on a commercial level in the Fusion Jazz category. They were all great players, and Sundays were packed for the most part. However, John Thomas became busy with a band called Sparks, and started sending subs more than actually showing up. When he did show, his heart was no longer in it as he was so busy.

Prior to my inclusion, JT had played there with another group called Jazz Horizons with sax player Lee Matalon (a local college music instructor), the same bassist, and drummer Rick Lonow, who I replaced when he moved to Nashville. During this time, Don would occasionally come out and sit in with the jazz group.

John Thomas: Van Vliet would come out to Mr. B's and sit in with us sometimes. I guess, he wouldn't do it when you were there. He would do his thing and you know, it was kind of cool and you didn't know whether to laugh at him like he was a clown, or whether he was like, "Sun Ra," and heavy from the planet Venus. I'll never forget the picture: here we are up there playing and he's sitting at Mr B's bar there taking his soprano out. This is so weird. Here's this guy who I just admired the hell out of, and he's sitting there like a kid getting his horn out ready to come up and sit in with our band.

Spinnin' Round My Brain

Apparently, Don had been quite the regular at Mr. B's for a while before my inclusion in the group. He had a friend, an air traffic controller who used to frequent the place. From what I understood, the friend was heavily into cocaine as this was the buzz in the restaurant even later when I worked there. Apparently, one night while driving home from the club, the friend flipped his car going a hundred miles an hour - purportedly trying to miss a coyote - and died. Don never went to the restaurant again. Another of Don's friends, a local coke dealer, who was about one hundred thousand dollars in debt, shot himself in the head.

Hinting at his drug abuse, Don used to make jokes about getting his "noon balloon from Rangoon." It was apparent to the players that he was using and they assumed that the abuse was affecting his voice. But it could have just as easily have been the early stages of whatever nervous condition he was later reported as having, or a combination of the two factors. Perhaps the drug was used to counteract the effects of the disease.

Smokeye

I had also landed a Monday night Jazz gig at another location, called "Smokeye" which was a Disco in Lancaster built like a big barn. Lee Matalon was on woodwinds, and the rest of the band were the same personnel as Mr. B's. It was decorated in a Native American theme. Somebody really knew what they were doing because it had a great atmosphere. We usually had people sitting in with the band.

"You Were Always There"

The last time I saw Don Van Vliet in person, I was playing at the Smokeye one night with the jazz group and Van Vliet came in with Moris Tepper. I greeted them at the break. "That Lambert, Henrick and Ross tune was great," he said. I didn't know what he meant until he described Twisted, of which I'd only heard Joni Mitchell's version. They stayed a couple of sets listening to the music. Moris left, as I recall, but Don and I wound up at the old standby - the Antelope Valley Inn Coffee Shop - sitting at a booth as he drew in his book.

"Jan finally got her dream home, with the redwood shingles and all," he said, "I'm getting out of here, man." I was a little sad, because I knew that I would probably never see him again. He told me that he was going to make a lot of money painting. He stated that he had met a Jewish art dealer who loved *Dachau Blues*.

As I looked around the coffee shop, it seemed as though it hadn't changed in the twenty plus years since I sat here as a teenager to order a small dinner salad or a banana split at three in the morning, while my then future mother-in-law, Darline Blair, served the rush of drunks after the bars closed. I felt like I was in a time warp, and then I looked back at Don. He was wearing large-framed glasses that kept slipping down on his nose, giving his voice a slightly nasal quality. He seemed to be having difficulty pronouncing his words and he looked much older and weaker than the last time I had seen him. "The drug abuse is catching up with him," I thought, sadly.

"Are you going to do any more music?" I asked. He looked at me and grinned. His eyes lit up, "Of course, man! I couldn't quit doing music, I can't help but do music." About this time, there seemed to be a problem to my right. A short man dressed in a Marine uniform was verbally confronting a man and two women sitting at the table. The conversation kept escalating in conflict. The girls seemed to be egging on the conflict, pouring gasoline on the fire.

"This is great, man!" Don grinned. "I'll get four or five songs out of this." Apparently the Marine, in order to make a point, decided to bounce a glass ashtray off the table, missing my head by inches and landing in the corner booth behind us. I could feel the blood rush to my head and my temper rise. This disgrace to the Marines was doing his best to pick a fight, and my head was certainly trying it's best to stay out of this idiot's way.

Don, who could see the situation without turning his head, was calm and collected. I started shaking from anger. I said, "Look at this!" - showing him my quaking hands - "I want to take a club to that idiot's head." He said, "I don't blame you, but you know, they'd put you in jail no matter what, because HE's got a UNIFORM."

The conflict soon wound up in the parking lot. "Look at that, man, the girls are trying to get a fight started," Don observed. We could see, from the body language, that the game plan seemed to be to goad the Marine into taking a punch at their much larger and stronger-looking companion, who had taken off his shirt. Soon, the situation was quelled by the arrival of the police, who someone had obviously had the foresight to call. I was still shaking in anger. Don was completely calm.

We sat for a long time reminiscing. He would say, "Remember when..." and go on to describe something that happened on a tour when I wasn't even in the band. "I wasn't there," I would say. "You were always there, man," he would reply. He said that about three times, and would put his hand over his heart each time - his way of telling me, I suppose, that he appreciated my efforts on his behalf.

If I remember, Don picked up the tab this evening, and we shook hands for what I figured would be the last time. So far, it has been.

Last Meeting Aldridge

St. Patrick's Day 1985 was the last day Don Aldridge saw Van Vliet. Aldridge and his girlfriend, Annie mentioned being a neighbor of Captain Beefheart and Aldridge decided to pay him a 2:00 a.m. visit.

Don Aldridge: He says, "Wow man! Come on in." So, we came in and he showed me some of his paintings. He had a bunch of cigars that he claimed the A&M people gave to him. He had a disc of The Legendary A&M Sessions. *He gave me one of those. He said, "You know, I have an art show coming up in Cologne Germany - they're going to show my work. Don was looking pretty good. A lot of years had passed. I had mostly fond memories. He taught me a lot about music.*

Aldridge wanted to hear the album, but Van Vliet didn't have a stereo, so they all went to Aldridge's house.

Don Aldridge: I had a ton of speed. I got it out of the lab. So, I took this big old thing of speed and dumped it on the table, got a quart of Jack Daniels, plopped the glasses down there, started pouring, went to the stereo and put on this Legendary A&M Sessions, *it was kicking stuff.*

Van Vliet signed the album "Love Don, Love, Don."

Don Aldridge: We partied all night long. People say that Don never used drugs. Well, he used them that night. On the web, you know, you go on to the newsgroups and they'll say - One: "He's a heroin addict." Or two: "He never touched drugs."

The two Dons reviewed their experiences, and Aldridge revealed that he had met a lot of people as a result of his connection to Van Vliet - including The Lovin' Spoonful, Jackson Browne, and The Doors.

Don Aldridge: I said, "Don, you made quite an impression on me in those days, but I don't know if it was for the good." It was fun for me to be in the position of the intimidator rather than being intimidated. I felt free to say what I wanted in any way I wanted without any fear of intimidation. It was, for me, closure: I was a man.

Eventually, Aldridge took Don, then Annie, home. He told her that she would probably receive a call from Don sometime later that day figuring he'd try to drive a wedge into the middle of the relationship.

Don Aldridge: I think only maybe you and me and the guys that were in that band - guys like us - would even know what I'm talking about. Sure enough, my girlfriend got a call, - she decided not to pick up and he put (a message) on her answering machine. He called her four times that day. The girl was quite a looker. The next day, he showed up at my favorite bar - The Britisher. Don sat down at the table and we partied again, we started all over again and partied all that day and all that evening. I no longer felt like I had to "be anybody" for Don other than just who I was. He wasn't the same Don, probably just because of the passing of time and the briefness of the encounter. I said to him "Are you ever going to do it (music) again?" He said, "Oh yeah!" That was the last I ever saw Don. I think it was closure. It was appropriate.
I'm very sorry to hear that he's sick. I often wondered whether our excessiveness did not lead to whatever his ailment is now.

No Peace In New Home

Gary visited Van Vliet after his move to his present home in Northern California, overlooking the ocean swimming with whales. Lucas wanted to start working on a new music project, but by this time, Don was no longer interested. The trip was fruitless and sad for Lucas, who saw the end of an era. He was also sad because Don didn't seem to be at peace with himself in spite of his good fortune, beautiful surroundings, and profitable new art career.

Gary Lucas: I was like, "Now, what am I going to do?" I've lost this great companion, because, he was like, the funniest wit.

Zappa Dies Dec 4 1993

One day I saw a newspaper clipping. Frank Zappa had died. I had heard from Henry Kaiser that he was quite ill several years before, but it still came as a shock. Jim Sherwood relayed his feelings to me in his interview:

Jim Sherwood: I thank God for just knowing them. One of the things was that Frank's humor is probably one of the things that kept me around, because I wasn't as talented as most of the guys, but I kept him laughing all the time … Even when Frank was dying and I went to see him, he said, "Motorhead, you always make me laugh, man." That's one thing I loved about him. He kept me around because I was entertaining to him, and he had a little bit of respect there for me - even though I wasn't as talented as the rest of the guys.
John French: His death must have hit you pretty hard.
JS: Yeah, it did. I lost a good friend.

Drumbo In Retrospect

In the years that have followed my final meeting with Van Vliet, I have been approached several times for interviews. I've done some musical projects that were offered as a result of my relationship with Don. All of it was a bit rewarding musically, but never amounted to anything financially. I have struggled at different types of work and have never found a "niche" - so to speak. I wrote the liner notes for the *Grow Fins* set right after becoming an A+ Certified computer technician - which never landed me a job.

The most frustrating thing to me is to be treated like royalty by fans, but looked upon in my own town as a bum who can't hold a job. I supposed that my dysfunctional nature may have already been in place pre-Beefheart. I have an unusual and unique talent that is not really of any benefit to me in the "real world." In "Beefheartland," however, I have received mostly respect from the fans and other band members as "Drumbo."

"Drumbo" doesn't fit into the world system, however. He is a freak, associated with "that weird music." I've always felt like two people - possibly because of the name. One person is the practical guy who lives from hand to mouth doing whatever job will put food on the table. The other is "Drumbo - critically acclaimed Beefheart drummer."

It's very sad for me to have not been more of a financial success and to see my family suffer and do without. When I speak of not doing music any longer, fans and people in the business say "You can't give up - you're DRUMBO!" I should keep doing the same thing that has produced no financial reward all of these years?

I have often wondered what would have happened had I turned down Van Vliet the day he asked me to join the band in the fall of 1966. Or what would have happened had I stayed far away and never gone back after 1969. I sometimes have regrets. I also get very upset when some young record company exec calls me up for info on a "re-release" of some Beefheart material that

I worked on, and I realize that this young snot-nosed kid is going to benefit financially from something I will not - though I dedicated years of my life to the projects.

Jeff Cotton didn't turn back after some point in the seventies, and he did quite well. Bill Harkleroad seems to have a stable life. So, why do I keep going back to this music, writing liner notes and books, and arranging reunion concerts, or mixing music from reunion concerts?

There's the old story about Van Gogh having never sold a painting in his lifetime. I've read enough about his life to know that it wasn't that pleasant. He was driven - like Van Vliet - in an almost manic way, to put on canvas the world he saw. Critics have come to appreciate his work as genius, though he lived most of his life in relative obscurity.

Most of the people I meet on a daily basis have a cookie-cutter mentality. They observe their strengths, make an informed decision, conform, and play a role. They spend a lot of their spare time escaping through various forms of entertainment and hate their jobs. But they are highly responsible in the material realm, making sure every detail of life is taken care of, and planning the future well, making wise choices and making good investments.

Occasionally someone comes along and chooses to view the world from a slightly obtuse angle. Perhaps because of their rearing, or the way their brain functions, they dedicate their lives to pursuing something that seems like nonsense to those around them. Years from now - maybe after their death - there may be a new understanding of why they did what they did - like Van Gogh.

In dealing with Van Vliet, I had to closely examine my own motives because of the intensity of the situation. Was I trying to get "a piece of the action?" Was I trying to bask in his spotlight? Perhaps subconsciously it was all for selfish motives. Consciously, however, I tried to follow my basic Christian beliefs that I was raised to believe. I tried to treat Don the way I would like to be treated. I tried to be as honest as I could with him. I worked as hard as I could to achieve the highest level of excellence I could achieve.

However, I saw many others - who didn't share my belief system - do the same thing. Most of the Magic Band members worked hard on the music - some more than others. Whether or not it was "successful" or "accessible" to the world's view of what music was supposed to be - it certainly explored some unique and unusual possibilities in how sounds can be put together with lyrics.

For me, it has been a very uncomfortable fit. The lower middle-class life I've lived in contrast to the small pedestal of fame in the land of Beefheart has always been a difficult and stressful paradox between practicality and passion - between logic and desire. As I approach my later years, I find this perplexing but with an underlying peace.

Did I make the right choices? I have no idea - you have to decide that for yourselves. Some say "What difference does it make if you're recognized 50 years after your death if you lived an unfulfilled life?" I guess I would have to say, "If positive impact from what I've done in my life happens in fifty years, that is a legacy and it makes a difference to the people fifty years from now."

On the other hand, if I became rich and famous selling real estate in my lifetime - accumulating huge amounts of wealth and had never done music, what difference would it make to me fifty years from now?

Most people spend their young lives planning on how they will retire, and doing whatever it takes, no matter how difficult, to assure that they will "be able to enjoy their retirement." Then they retire and their health is shot from years of stressful work they hated, so they never actually enjoy their retirement.

There's a New Testament parable about a farmer who had a bumper crop one year and decided to tear down his storehouses and build bigger ones. Then God said to him "You fool, your soul is required of you this night." I'm paraphrasing, but the idea is, if the only reason we are here is to collect things for ourselves so that we will not be without - like the guy in the parable - then it seems like a pretty shallow view of life. Perhaps this fellow, who had more than enough for himself, should have been thinking of others less-fortunate than he.

If there is something greater than our few short years on earth - and I believe there is - then our existence here is to learn something and bless others. The thing that keeps coming back to me is that we are placed here with unique gifts which we can choose either to ignore or to embrace. The few who choose to embrace are usually scorned by the many who choose to ignore - which is why most people are scratching and fighting over who has the biggest barn rather than being concerned with who has the biggest need.

The richest man in the world could lose everything in the material realm in an instant. I once heard a man named Wurmbrand speak. He was a pastor in the former Soviet Union who was tortured for adhering to his beliefs. He spoke in his bare feet, because they used to beat the bottom of his feet with sticks until they were bloody, simply to punish him because he wanted to embrace Christianity. He was put in prison with people from all kinds of backgrounds. There were doctors, lawyers, military men, and common workers from all fields in this prison and they all had one thing in common: nothing.

Wurmbrand said that nothing is a very valuable thing to have, as the true character of a man is revealed when he has nothing to gain from any action he takes. He said that the sick in the prison were often ignored by the doctors - because the doctors had nothing to gain by treating them. The sick were often treated by people of compassion who knew nothing about medicine, but who would have made the greatest doctors because it was in their character to care for and heal others.

Perhaps nothing is the most valuable thing of all, because it makes our life like a blank canvas. Only pure motivation and true inspiration can guide the brush of one who has nothing to gain from their efforts. Unfortunately, many people are only motivated by what they will receive from what they do, and they will do just about anything to get what they desire, but will not actually take the risk to do what they desire.

Don used to say constantly "I do exactly what I want." However, he also seemed to do only what gratified him, and so, in a sense, he was motivated by getting a reward of instant gratification. I did sense in him, however, a deep passion that could not be thwarted nor discouraged. He faced many obstacles and yet clung to what he was. There are so many complicated facets to each personality, and Van Vliet is truly one of the most complex people - if not the most complex person I have ever met.

CHAPTER FORTY ONE:
ALL GOOD THINGS

~irky pic from 1977 with Eric Drew Feldman superimposed
~r Don due to accidental double exposure.

753

Dream

In the early eighties, I had a dream one night. In the dream, I had gone to visit a family, three girls and their mother. It was the Blair family, who's youngest, Donna, had been my first drum student. When I arrived at the house, I was told by the mother, Darline, that Sharon (the middle sister) was married and that her husband was in Westwood Village putting up giant letters on a marquee. I remember driving (in the dream) to Westwood (which is near UCLA) and saw a man on a huge scaffold, supervising the installment of giant letters, then I woke up.

Telephone

I hadn't talked to the Blair girls in five years. Out of curiosity, I called and the last number I had listed was still the same. The first thing that mother Darline told me was that Sharon was married. She said her husband was an artist and built props for commercials and that he had just finished building giant letters for a FORD commercial that was shot at Edwards AFB on the dry lake. "Giant letters in the dream, giant letters in reality," I wondered, "coincidence?" Darline talked to me for a while and then said that the only other person at home was Donna and asked if I wanted to speak with her.

Donna had been doing a lot of film editing, starting with commercials and gradually working her way up to major films. After several years, she became fed up with the whole industry and the shallow life one had to live to be involved in it. She was just kind of drifting at the time, trying to figure out what was next.

I told her what I was up to and the next thing I know, Darline, Barbara (oldest daughter), her friend Gloria, and Donna all showed up one Sunday for Jazz at Mr. B's. It was a great reunion. We had dinner afterwards.

Mr. B's was a great five-star restaurant that had been reviewed in several magazines. I loved the atmosphere and the people were always upbeat and friendly. The Blalock family owned land up the road that had been developed into an exclusive Country Club and exclusive housing development called Crystalaire. The restaurant catered to an elite crowd of older folks, so the music was centered around the "Frank Sinatra and the Rat Pack" crowd. Jack Grant, who was prop man for Johnny Carson of the *Tonight* show, and his wife, Peggy, were good friends with the Blalocks. I will never forget Jack in his black slacks, white shirt, and turquoise blazer walking up to the stage and saying, "Hey babe," in his deep, rumbling voice, just before dropping a generous tip into the tip jar.

Though I was able to fall into this atmosphere, it was certainly role-playing to an extent, but my heart was in it because I loved the music. It was like a little musical "enclave" - an oasis in the midst of the desert - nestled in the picturesque buttes of the Mojave Desert. People would drive over a hundred miles to come here just to swing dance to live music.

I felt that this was a good place to be for a while as it would give me time to work on original material and develop my singing. It was, as musicians say, a gig. I hadn't really understood the concept of playing just for the money, but it certainly beat putting in 40 hours a week and paid about the same. I remember a few Beefheart fans being horrified that I would do such a thing, but when I first started playing, I was one step from being homeless, so I was thankful for the income, as I couldn't live in my mother's mobile home.

Donna And I

Donna and I sensed almost immediately that we were supposed to be together. It was a very sure thing, one of the surest things I have ever known. Donna, her mother and I went out afterwards for coffee and talked. I couldn't stop thinking about her afterwards. The dream that had caused this reunion kept haunting me.

After about 4 months of dating, Donna and I lived together for about 10 months (shocking the entire Christian community), saved up some money and got married. That Christmas, it snowed a record 27 inches in about 3 days. I had just gotten home from work on Sunday, and the roads to my job were just barely cleared by the following Friday. It was the most beautiful Christmas ever, and I was in love.

10th Anniversary

Sometime later, Jack Grant, made arrangements for some of the *Tonight Show* band's players to come to Mr. B's for the 10th anniversary of his club. Back in the Johnny Carson days, Tommy Newsome was the second in command of the *Tonight Show* band, which featured some of the best jazz players in LA. Doc Severensin was the showy leader with the fancy outfits. Newsome was, however, soft-spoken, conservative and introverted but played fantastic Tenor Sax.

Maury Harris and Conte Candoli were both trumpet players. I felt like I was in the presence of royalty - every note was like gold. During the course of the evening, Candoli's girlfriend, had a temper flare-up and punched him in the mouth - which kind of broke the spell.

MIDI And Me

MIDI was a computer interface that manipulated music like a word processor manipulates words. I bought a moderately priced setup and started writing music this way. MIDI was a good writing tool for me, as I was able to write music and hear it back immediately. I worked 40-50 hours a week writing and processing music.

Married

On Feb. 19th, 1985, Donna and I were married in Boulder City, Nevada in a church that doubled as a Christian school. We invited all the children to the wedding and afterwards, the little girls all wanted Donna to throw the bouquet. We drove over the Hoover Dam, and straight to the Grand Canyon, where we were snowed in for two days. We drove through some of the Navajo reservation, stayed in Farmington (the buffet was the worst food I've ever eaten) because of the weather we were not able to view the Anasazi Indian ruins we had so been looking forward to. We then passed through Albuquerque, went through Roswell (where my wife lived as a child for a short period) and went to Carlsbad Caverns. On the way home, we hit Sea World in San Diego.

Shortly after I was married, I received a phone call from Aldridge. I hadn't seen or heard from him in years. I was completely shocked to hear from him. He was, I believe, in Bakersfield or somewhere near there. He told me, "I'm clean, man, I'm clean." I wanted to know what he meant. I didn't realize that he was such a heavy drug user. I thought he was an aircraft factory lead man and that was it. For some reason, out of all the people he knew, he decided to call me.

Mark And Bill In Town

Soon after my marriage, Harkleroad showed up for a visit. He and I had a great time just talking and getting re-acquainted. He seemed really happy and was playing a little, teaching guitar, and managing a record store in Eugene Oregon called "Face the Music." In some freak cosmic alignment Mark Boston was also in town. He was playing in a club band booked by Denny King. Bill, his girlfriend Cassia, Mark, Donna and I all had dinner at our house. As we sat, we touched on the subject of the *Trout Mask* experience. The room got really quiet for a while. Donna later told me she could tell by what was not said that it must have been a really intense experience for us all. I hadn't spoken much about this to her.

Bill had been by to see Henry Kaiser in Oakland on his way down. Henry had asked for my number and so he gave it to him.

Henry Sends Me Albums

A couple of weeks later a package arrived from Henry with a few of his latest albums. I listened briefly to several cuts. It was experimental improvised electronic guitar that as I stated earlier is not really my cup of tea. But it was nice to hear from Mr. Kaiser again.

Introduced To Andy West

A few weeks later, Henry sent me a tape of a band he had played with at a Jazz Festival (I believe in Germany). Although the material was loose, I liked the direction he was going in. One piece especially struck me. It was a Bob Adams composition called *Dropped D*, simply because it was in *Dropped D* tuning, an altered slack-key tuning on guitar.

The bassist on the tape was Andy West formerly of the Dixie Dregs, a phenomenal and unique instrumental jazz/rock group. Andy played a five string bass and used a pick, so his sound was more a rapid-fire type playing than the chordal stuff that Rockette used to crank out. Henry flew down to LA, where Andy lived, and they drove up to my house and had dinner.

Play On La Grange / Sarayushka

The drummer on the tape Henry sent me was Michael Maksemenko, a Swedish-born drummer / singer. He flew over and they did a short west coast tour and while in Los Angeles cut an album with several originals and a few Beefheart covers. They asked me to sit in on drums on La Grange (ZZ Top), sung in Russian by Michael. It was hysterical to hear the song with Russian lyrics.

Henry then asked if I would be interested in joining the group. I was very hesitant on two points. One was how could we have two drummers. He said that I would play US stuff and Michael would play European stuff. I wasn't happy about being in any group that did Beefheart covers, as I had already played in the original band, so this was like doing a parody of myself, plus I wanted to play in Europe.

Beefheart Covers Taken Off Album

I finally agreed to join if the Beefheart stuff was taken off the album and we could write some material to replace it. Henry agreed, and a band called CBA (Crazy Backwards Alphabet) was formed.

Matt Groening

While rehearsing in an LA studio, a guy whose work I had come to truly appreciate showed up to say hello. It was Matt Groening (rhymes with "complaining.") He was a cartoonist who had done a series of books called *Life In Hell* which had given him quite a bit of popularity, but in the next couple of years, he would get a much bigger break with a show called *The Simpsons*.

I also met Henry's friend named Bob Adams, and immediately liked him and the really great music he had written. He was a fan of Little Feat, so his music all had slide guitar with amazing phrasing. I wrote lyrics to one called *The Blood And The Ink*.

Scott Colby, from the Aloha session, was brought in to play guitar. Bob played bass on one piece, and guitar on another. We recorded at a strange little studio in the San Fernando Valley called "Love Productions." Henry had us lay the tracks down and then flew me up to San Francisco to coach him with his parts. We went to Mobius Studios in San Francisco, owned and operated by a great engineer named Oliver DiCicco. Oliver had built his studio himself. Everything was immaculate and there was a place for everything that gave it an overall sense of total order.

Overdubbing

It was interesting to note that Henry could play all the parts perfectly, but in the same way as Winged Eel (his first inspiration on guitar) he had a hard time finding where his part fit in relationship to the other parts. So I stood face to face with him in the control booth. I would sing and direct the part and he would follow me, barely ever looking at his guitar, and playing the part perfectly. We did one section at a time, using two tracks stair-stepped and mixing them as one. All the new tracks for CBA were recorded and mixed that day and the next.

Bob Adams

Since the jazz group was basically a dead end job that I now looked upon as just a "money gig," Bob and I started collaborating. I would take his ideas and process them into a song. Sometimes adding parts, sometimes re-arranging and writing lyrics.

Live, Love, Larf And Loaf

Kaiser called me about another project he was doing. Richard Thompson was going to do an album and Henry wanted to know if I wanted to play drums on it. At least, that was the story as I understood it. I agreed to do the project.

Fred Frith

I had already met Frith, who was scheduled for an appearance at McCabe's Guitar shop in Santa Monica. Henry talked him into having the rest of us perform as "guests." I drove down the eighty miles or so and as I walked inside, I met Richard Thompson for the first time. I liked him immediately. He was sitting on a large stool facing the stage, and as I shook his hand and started to pull away, he held my hand as though genuinely "seizing the moment." I was really touched by the depth of his being. I remember noting that he was wearing plaid pants. "They're coming back," he told me, with a twinkle in his eye. I liked him immediately.

Matt Groening showed up with the cover for Crazy Backwards Alphabet. We were all upstairs in the dressing room of McCabe's guitar shop. Fred Frith and Richard Thompson, who had just met, were playing an amazing repertoire of oldie "Garage Band" stuff they both knew and loved on acoustic guitar, laughing like schoolboys the whole time. I was really impressed with Fred's guitar abilities. After the improvisation concert, I had no idea how adept he was at "normal" playing. I had heard enough of Richard's playing to know that he was very good, but he and Fred together were just delightful to hear. As it was, CBA played a bit, Richard and Fred came up and we jammed around a bit. Andy West was there playing some of the new material. Robert Williams and Cliff Martinez showed up to listen.

Rhino Records

We were doing the record for Rhino Records, which I knew little about, as I had basically walked out of the industry years before. I hadn't known much about the industry at that time either. When I worked with the Magic Band, there were always business people handling all that. I had my hands full with the music. I was told that Rhino basically owed their success to re-issues of previously released material. This made me wonder if they actually were going to be adept at promoting us.

FFKT LLLL

A few days after the McCabe's performance, we all met at Henry's in Oakland. He lived in this great old two-story house, which was originally the gatehouse for a big estate that had contained botanical gardens. Although time and population had encroached upon the original estate transforming it into an upper middle-class neighborhood, there were still traces of the original gardens throughout the neighborhood.

I had driven up in a white 1960 Cadillac Sedan De Ville, which my wife and I had purchased from her grandmother's estate. Henry had built a beautiful but small studio on the back corner of the lot, which was highly soundproofed, but not air-conditioned, and made this spring rehearsal a bit warm. When I arrived, Fred was already there and Richard Thompson had not yet shown up.

The plan was to spend the first four days rehearsing all the material, and then play two concerts over the weekend. One would be in Davis. The other in Berkeley, at the Ashkenaz - a dance studio / concert hall which was privately run.

One of Richard's songs, *Drowned Dog Black Night*, was supposed to be a bit in the style of Neil Young. Since I hadn't listened to Neil, my style of playing didn't match their expectations. However, neither of them did much to communicate to me what it was that they wanted. I was playing very sparse and simple, just keeping time. Basically, I felt the song was strong and didn't need "Drumbo" drums.

Richard was a delightful individual and made the rehearsals fun with his quick wit and amazing playing. In the evenings in the house, Thompson would pick up an acoustic guitar and give an impromptu concert each evening that left me in awe of his abilities as a guitarist, singer, and songwriter.

We all chipped in with the housework. I did dishes, Henry cooked (he's a great cook), Fred cleared. Richard felt a little guilty, as there was nothing for him to do, so he would play guitar for us. One night, he forced me away from the dishes, saying he "rather enjoyed doing dishes."

On the day of the Davis concert, a couple of friends of Henry's had agreed to "roadie" for us to give us a bit of rest and showed up in their van. I was told by Henry at this time that I was to ride with them, as there wouldn't be enough room in the car for the four of us and all the guitars, so I had to leave several hours earlier. We actually had a great ride, and the guys were very interested in my work with Beefheart and the present project, so the time went quickly.

The place we played at in Davis was a barn - a barn on a small farm on the outskirts of town. The walls were covered with spiders and webs. After a quick sound check, we spent several hours playing cricket in the pasture out back. The lady proprietor was a real character and sort of community outcast.

We played two concerts this evening, and they went quite well. All in all, it was fun. I recall us doing a *Trout Mask* style tune I had written called *Disposable Thoughts*. At the very abrupt end, Richard played one extra note, thinking it went on another few bars, and it turned out to be a little naked "blip" at the end of the song. Fred found this extremely humorous, and having a great falsetto laugh, let loose. Richard seemed a bit embarrassed, but sheepishly grinned. The audience picked up on the comradeship and goodwill we had between us and we were complimented on this.

The performances at the Ashkenaz were a bit better, and I think there are board tapes of those concerts. The sound system was better, it was a bigger club, and I was surprised to see lines of people standing outside to see us when we arrived. The owner of the Ashekenaz, complimented us on our spirit of cooperation, not only with each other, but with him and the technicians. He commented on how many of the tempermental rock musicians seemed dedicated to belaboring petty details and ruining a perfectly good evening for the management. We sent him a "thank you" card afterward. We were obviously a "team effort."

Mobius Studios

The next day, we moved all our equipment into Mobius Studios in San Francisco. I left early to set up my drums, and the others came in a bit later. Oliver had hot coffee brewing and made me feel right at home. I was never comfortable in a studio, but Oliver made all of this seem fairly effortless and fun.

I think we did all instrumental tracks in 2½ days (first half day is getting sounds, mic placement etc.) and two days for vocal overdubs. There was a hitch in the session that involved my drumming.

John French to Robert Williams: In the studio, I was supposed to be playing "John French" drums... right? And (Richard) was trying to get me to do this "Michael Jackson" beat and I said, "Look, if you want Michael Jackson's drummer you should get him, but the thing is you guys got me because I play a weird different style and that's what you wanted on this album, so let me do it! Give me a minute here."
RW: Good for you.

I think my outspoken-ness surprised Richard, who had suggested the beat his drummer had used on the demo, but I'm glad I stood my ground. The song was *Bird In God's Garden* - which in my estimation is the best combination of our playing on the entire album. I was later "trashed" by a critic for my over-playing on *Drowned Dog Black Night* - which the guys had encouraged me to do. "Play like Elvin Jones," was what I remember hearing. The song didn't need that, it needed simple timekeeping. It was a reminder to me to be true to myself from then on.

12-Track
Henry generously gave me a 12-track recorder during this period. I could now arrange all my midi-tracks, sync the computer to the deck, and have 12 channels of analog tape to record along with the synthesizer tracks. I began having visions of production work, maybe even writing soundtracks. I began to get more interested in the technical side of recording.

Writing More
I was writing a lot of material in the Spyro Gyra / Yellowjackets type of mode - jazz fusion instrumentals. Unfortunately, no one in the jazz group at Mr. B's seemed to be interested. I eventually became disillusioned with the jazz group.

John Thomas became more involved with the group Sparks and Dalton Hagler graduated from USC and became a cruise ship entertainer for many years. The core group broke up and Danny and I were left finding replacements. It was never the same. The magic, for me, was gone, but we continued to play for several years as an empty shell of the original group.

Lyrics
Since I had been singing every weekend for years, I had found that people were now complimenting my singing, which I had never considered to be very good. I began to concentrate more on lyrics and the Bob Adams songs.

CBA II
Henry wanted to do another CBA album. He wanted to do a double album, half improvised, half songs. Half of one side (these were still Vinyl / CD days) would be the French / Adams compositions. The other half of that side would be Michael Maksemenko compositions. Then a full two sides would be more improvised instrumental music. Bob Adams' *Dropped D* would be featured in an elongated version with double drum solos etc.

Henry worked hard to make this happen, and it just never came together in the way he envisioned it. Kaiser and I, in fact, got in a huge argument that almost ruined our friendship. I had lost my famous temper once again.

The ill-fated CBA II couldn't be sold. Henry told me that there were people who perked up on the French / Adams stuff, but couldn't get into the rest and vice-versa. It was a mismatched set of music.

Marketing Half Of French Album

It was then that we first got the idea of marketing a John French album from the Adams-French collaborations. It didn't truly represent me, but CBA, which was no longer an entity.

Charles Taylor Discourages Me

Charles Taylor of Reckless Records tried to get me to go in a more avant-garde direction, which was really of no interest to me, as I had been there, and it was a financial disaster. Because I had been stereotyped, typecast, and pigeonholed, I was classified, whether I liked it or not and would never escape from the classification. There were a lot of "noise" bands coming out, just playing random patterns and trying to pass it off as music. Some of it, of course was good, some was just made by charlatans who didn't want to take the time to discipline themselves.

I didn't want to go backwards and try to become a parody of myself. I had done the avant-garde, and since there was nobody even coming close to what the Magic Band had already done, I kept thinking: "Why settle for less than the best in the field?"

Invisible Means /FFKT II

Although I was much better prepared for the second album, most people, including myself, prefer the first album. The second album comprises four distinctly different players contributing songs in which each individual's style is prevalent in their compositions. It was polarized. Fred Frith had been playing bass for John Zorn, and the machine-gun technique he had developed was very unyielding to my more "organic" rhythmic approach. A lot of the music was written in advance, and so the pre-conceptions we had before the session were more pronounced and carried through to the final product. It was as if we had recorded on separate continents.

Discouraged

I still considered myself a decent artist at that point, but it was getting very discouraging trying to break out of the mold. I was still working in a restaurant lounge to pay the bills. I started finding myself getting very depressed. I read about some guy who got a grant from the National Endowment for the Arts for suspending a crucifix in a jar of urine. I guess government subsidies for art come with only two requirements. One is to mock Christianity - the other to submit something that takes absolutely no talent.

Except to a very microscopic portion of the populace, I was a nothing. All the hours I'd spent struggling to do something that would inspire people meant absolutely nothing to most of the world. The most I would achieve in life was "he used to be Beefheart's drummer." It became clear that I would probably never be "successful" according to the world viewpoint. The later projects that I was doing were less satisfying than the earlier attempts. There always seemed to be someone imposing their will on my art, and so I can truly say that up until *City of Refuge* (Proper PRPCD024) nothing had ever been released that truly represented who I was, save parts of - ironically enough - *Trout Mask Replica*.

My thought was there was no place for me. I couldn't make a living doing music. I was, according to the world's financial measure of success (the only ruler that seems to count), a total failure. A fact which several members of my family seemed to take great joy in telling me repeatedly. I wasn't sure where to go from here.

Suicidal

It was during this period I started again becoming suicidal. I had started having these thoughts: "I could get a gun and drive out to those old ruins (a place I drove past on my way to Mr. B's) and just do myself in. One shot, and all the problems would be solved."

I had had it with negative comments about my direction in life etc. Family members in particular seemed really eager to remind me that I was relatively broke, had made all the wrong choices, and was basically a loser. Although I had battled with depression and thoughts of suicide for most of my adult life, I had never actually visualized suicide in such detail and it began to concern me. I shared my thoughts with my wife Donna, who was genuinely sympathetic, concerned, and a great comfort.

During a visit from Maryland by my brother Phill, I mentioned this to his wife, Joyce French - one of the few Christians in my family. She asked me a bunch of pertinent questions about my moods, thoughts, etc. and seemed genuinely concerned about my condition - as opposed to most family members who turned tail and ran at any mention of something uncomfortable. I remember her asking, "If I send you some books, will you actually read them?" I agreed to read any literature she sent me. The first book she sent me was entitled *On Deliverance*, and was written by Twilah A. Fox, M.D. Psychiatrist, a psychiatrist who counseled numerous politicians.

Deliverance

I could tell by the cover that this book was obviously Christian in nature. However, when I got into the book, I realized that it was addressing the rather taboo subjects of exorcism and demonism - the study of expelling evil supernatural spirit beings. I joked with Donna, saying "Joyce thinks I'm possessed!" However, I read the book and found it fascinating to find that this lady had gone through and described almost exactly the same kind of feelings I was having at this time.

After a week or two, I received another book from Joyce entitled *Pigs In The Parlor*[72] that was on the same subject and covered in detail how to deal with spiritual oppression in a step-by-step manner. After reading a number of other books on the subject, I was convinced that the doctrine was sound.

The basic theory of these books was that someone, like myself, who had been a Christian and yet willfully "backslid" (a Christian term for deserting the faith) could find their selves spiritually "chained" to certain demonic forces because of "doorways" they had created through sin in their lives. This sin could take many forms - drugs, fornication, and involvement with the occult were the main ones that I had been involved in.

Now most of the Christian community ignores this doctrine, and unbelievers only joke about it. A rather large percentage of the Christian community for the most part is a dead bunch of robots going through the motions of "being religious." They go to church on Sunday, occasionally pay their tithe, shake hands, smile and say all the right things. They listen to watered-down sermons and eventually become a useless sub-culture of spiritually impotent snobs.

I had already dealt with this type several times in my life, and it had turned me off, not only to church, but to the Bible and Christianity in general. For instance, the Bible is full of instances of God healing people and all sorts of other miracles, and yet the modern church does not seem to ever address these issues or get involved with anything involving faith. I had experienced what I considered to be a few miracles, but not so much because of church. The church seemed rabidly pre-occupied with fund-raisers, bake sales, and anything in the material realm that didn't require a leap of faith.

The Stillwells

I called on my unique friend, Steve Nootenboom, a fellow-Christian who had much the same viewpoint of the established church. I wondered if he heard of anyone who was in the ministry of deliverance. He gave me the name of an older couple in Arizona who had apparently helped a family member in a miraculous way in an incredibly short period of time.

I called the folks and the phone was answered by Bobbi Stillwell, a lady who seemed within a

[72] Pigs in the Parlor, Frank and Ida Mae Hammond, Impact Christian Books, 1990.

matter of seconds to be one of my closest friends. She knew about Deliverance (another word for exorcism). She said her and her husband would be out my way in a few weeks and would stop by. When I asked how much it would cost, I was told that there was no charge. They told me they relied upon God to supply their needs.

My Deliverance

I cringe at what I'm about to write here, because I know how much flak I'm going to get from simply telling my experience. Even from the small number of people I've told it to already (mostly Christians, mind you). I have been heckled, mocked and strongly criticized. However, I state with complete sincerity that every word is the truth.

On the day the Stillwell's came to my house, I had prepared to believe that something miraculous was about to take place. As I opened the door to greet this wonderful couple, the first words I heard from Charles Stillwell's lips was, "Believe now that you will be delivered by God." There was a surety in me that this man was indeed telling the truth and I felt confident with all my six solid weeks of reading - about seven or eight books, including checking everything out and cross referencing - that there was indeed validity to this doctrine.

The time of year was mid-October and the year was 1990. Charles pulled an envelope from his pocket, which I recognized as the letter I had sent him describing events in my life. He said very matter-of-factly that I had 17 demons and that they would all be cast out of me on this day. He said, "Please don't be offended, as I'm not telling you that you're a bad person." Suddenly, the reality of the whole thing hit me: What if I was just totally naïve and there was nothing to this? What if these people were just snake-oil salesmen and I was the sucker of the day? Then I reminded myself there was no charge for their services.

The first step was to have me forgive everyone in my life who had faulted me. I had to say out loud something like "_____ (whatever their name was), I forgive you for anything you have ever done to me in the name of Jesus." I did this with each person. There wasn't a really long list, but I must admit that Don Van Vliet was one of the first people who came to mind. A few family members made the list, along with several entertainment lawyers.

Eventually, after about 30 minutes or so, that was over. Next, I needed to go through a list of occult activities and denounce anything on the list I had been involved in. There were quite a few things that I had dabbled in at one time or another, but compared to the list, my involvement was rather minor, so this went by quickly.

Then, Charles asked me to sit on a chair in the middle of the room and stood behind me. He told me that he was going to tell these demons to leave in exactly the same way Jesus had told demons to leave; by speaking to them and commanding them in the name of Jesus to go away. I knew the procedure from my studies and so nodded in agreement.

He told me he would start with the spirit of anger, which was the "Strong Man" in my particular instance. He said that anger was the main "doorway" through which all the other demons came in. Anyone who has read this book can see that anger was a problem in my life.

With his hands on my shoulders, he then spoke out loud something to the effect of: "Spirit of Anger, I command you to come out of this man and never go back in the name of Jesus!" He spoke forcefully and with complete conviction.

Nothing happened.

I suppressed a giggle. All the fears and doubts came flooding back in; this guy and his wife were some phonies and I had invited them in my home and now I had to figure out how to get rid of them.

"Huh!" he exclaimed. "That sucker didn't even budge did he?"

At this point, I had to laugh, and then we all laughed. He then said, "This time, you say it with me, because you gave him permission to come in with your words, you have to tell him to leave with your words." Also, he instructed Donna, my wife, to sit next to me and put her hands on my shoulders because, he said, demons are repelled by love.

I went along with this and started repeating his words as he would say them, but I never had a chance to finish. Halfway through, I went into a coughing fit that practically doubled me over. It was if I had just choked while eating. My body convulsed as though I were just gasping for air or pushing something out yet I seemed totally able to breathe. It felt more as though someone had grabbed me around the chest from behind and was squeezing the air out of me like a bellows. This went on for several moments during which I could not talk or sit up straight. Eventually, I calmed down and sat up.

"Good!" said Charles, very matter-of-factly, "That one's out, now we'll go after the rest."

I was amazed at his calmness. During my period of choking and gagging, no one had gotten up to help me, and Bobbi had just sat quietly singing praise songs to God and praying for me. They knew the routine, and it was very similar to several instances I had read about in the books, so Donna was also prepared.

I looked over and saw my cassette player sitting on the desk. "Can I record this?" I asked. Charles complied, and I pushed the tape recorder "record" button. Charles then proceeded to speak to other demons in the same manner as he had addressed the spirit of anger. The first two or three manifested in the same way, with coughing and gagging and the slightly uncomfortable "squeezing" feeling around my chest.

The fourth, however, was a much stronger manifestation. I bent over double on the chair and eventually collapsed to the floor where I lay on my stomach, flopping uncontrollably like a fish out of water for several minutes. I can only describe this as similar to the "dry heaves" combined with a kind of light seizure. It was a little more uncomfortable, yet I felt no alarm. It was as though my body did not belong to me. It moved as though another force was controlling it. I wasn't afraid, but I was overwhelmed at the power being manifested each time Charles Stillwell said the words, "in the name of Jesus."

The one experience that really stuck in my mind was the manifestation of the spirit of witchcraft. I had been quite interested in witchcraft because of Van Vliet's involvement. When the spirit of witchcraft was commanded to leave, I found my self in almost a "pouting" pose - like a little kid being told it couldn't have dessert - with my lower lip stuck out. It wasn't an emotion, but I felt as though I were a puppet being made to act out the role. My arms started flailing around in front of me as though I were throwing a tantrum, although again, I felt no emotion. I did the coughing / gagging, and Charles, satisfied looked back to his list to see what was next. I told him that it hadn't left, that the spirit was still there, I could feel them leave, and this one hadn't left.

He issued the same commands and this time, I repeated them as in the beginning, and my wife repeated them. Suddenly, I began to laugh a hideously slow deep laugh. It made my diaphragm hurt and each cackle seem to take the breath completely out of me, as though I were being squeezed in a Heimlich maneuver. I bent over cackling and again fell out of the chair, collapsing helplessly on the floor choking and spitting up some frothy white matter. This was the most physically excruciating experience of the whole day. It felt as though I had all the wind knocked out of me. It took a while to recover. I lay there gasping like a marathon runner.

The interesting thing is that I read another book about deliverance shortly after this experience. The book, entitled *Deliver Us From Evil*,[73] was written by Don Basham, and contained a description of a deliverance "session" in which a person, being delivered from the spirit of witchcraft uttered a strange hair-raising cackle. The way he described it was very similar to the manifestation that had occurred in my situation. There was no way I could have known of this ahead of time, so this discounts the idea that my subconscious was just "playing out a role" - as some people suggested later.

My wife was also delivered of a spirit on this day. However, rather than it manifesting as it did

---

[73] Deliver Us From Evil, Don Basham, Chosen Books, June 1972, 228 pp.

with me, through my mouth (choking, coughing, gagging, even vomiting) she got a tingly feeling in her hands. She started shaking her hands and rubbing them to get rid of the sensation and was alarmed for a minute until the sensation vanished. She had been expecting to have a similar experience as I had.

The Stillwells took all this in stride, and when we were finished with his list, while I was still sitting on the floor choking and gagging, Charles said very matter-of-factly, "Well, that's it, I'm hungry and I'd like to take you both out to dinner." Several hours had passed since their arrival, and it was now evening. We went out for dinner at our favorite Mexican restaurant and had a wonderful time, just talking and joking.

We brought up the subject of Donna's deliverance affecting her hands and in the conversation, the Stillwell's gave a very interesting explanation. Most evil spiritual forces enter through the mouth because it is usually by our words that we become involved with them in the first place. Donna's case was a bit different, because her involvement in the occult had to do with table tilting, which I had mentioned earlier in the book. This had to do with her and her sisters putting their hands on a table and asking it questions. The table would tilt a certain number of times for "yes" and "no." Since her hands were the primary tool used in this procedure, the "doorway" for demonic influence came through her hands. She told me later than in later years, the table started moving on its own, and they all quit because it scared them.

In all, this day was one of the most exceptionally amazing days of my life. I am not easily impressed by any hocus pocus activity and most of the healing I see - especially on Christian television - leaves me doubting whether or not people are not just "doing what is expected." If I have the slightest inkling that someone is pulling strings, I am quick to remove myself from the situation. On this day I became totally convinced that there is a reality to all of this.

I Become A Father

In late 1989, I lost my steady jazz gig, so even the small flow of cash I had coming in was cut off. My wife had just started working for the school system and had just gotten medical benefits. I was suspended in "what if" land for a time. Music no longer seemed an option. I had no idea of what to do next. I had relatives telling me to start my own multi-level marketing company selling paintings and frames, which appealed to me about as much as sticking needles in my eyes.

Hear A Voice

I started thinking about how much the quality of my life improved when I was devoting an hour a day to reading the Bible and how I had slacked off in recent years. The Bible is considered to be a "living" thing - nutrition for the soul and spirit. It certainly had helped me previously, but when I got married, I got out of the habit, because of the distractions of living with someone else.

I decided that since I was at such a crossroads in my life that I would start devoting time to reading once again, in the hopes of receiving clarity of vision concerning what my next move should be. As I was reading on the fourth day, a Thursday morning, I heard a whispered voice. It said, "I'm giving you a child." I actually looked around to see who had spoken, a bit startled, because it seemed audible to me and came from my left from a person standing at the edge of the sofa. There was no one in the room, at least that I could see with my eyes.

Donna and I had chosen not to have children. We had spoken on the subject and decided that our financial situation was such that we couldn't afford children. I didn't think I would be a good father, because I was so pre-occupied with music. I also had feared that if I had to give up music because of the demands of parenthood, I might take my resentment out on the child.

Saturday night, Donna and I were watching a video and at one point I felt the strong desire to push the "pause" button and ask Donna if she was pregnant. The expression on her face was completely incredulous, because I had never asked this before in our 7 years of marriage. "No," she answered, "I don't think so."

I told her that I believed God had told me he was giving us a child and suggested that we get a home pregnancy test just to confirm or deny. The test showed overwhelmingly positive results. An ultrasound the following Tuesday confirmed the test and gave us our first picture of our daughter.

A few years before, I had written a song called *My Girl Jesse.* I received the title first while I was driving. Later, Bob Adams called me and said he had some music that needed lyrics. He said it was the best thing he had written and had a "bittersweet" feeling to it. When I received the tape, I felt instinctively that it was the music to *My Girl Jesse.* One late night, I wrote the lyrics, thinking that it was something about a guy's girlfriend. It turned out to be a song about the little girl I thought I would never have. When I finished the lyrics, I wept for hours. It was like years of pent-up emotion came forth.

As I looked at the pregnancy test results, I looked at Donna and said, "It's going to be a girl, and her name will be Jesse."

Morning Sickness

I have never been around a woman who had morning sickness before, but in the following weeks Donna's seemed unusually severe. It eventually was so bad that even water was impossible for her to keep down. Her body seemed to refuse any form of nutrition. Finally one day, I walked in to find her looking shockingly emaciated compared to just two hours before. I immediately took her to the hospital where she was admitted and put on an IV to help with her dehydration.

I took her home 24 hours later where for approximately five days she could actually function almost normally and eat food. Then, the dreaded sickness began to return, and within three days, she was as bad as she had been previously.

Don Aldridge, who was living in town with his wife Alexis, was awakened early one morning by an instinct, and our situation was immediately brought to his mind as I had told him my concerns. He said that he felt God wanted him to tell me something. Aldridge is very careful about discerning that what he receives is actually from God and not just something he's imagining. He spent about 4 hours - from 3 am until 7 am - praying and studying and thinking about our situation. At 7 am, he finally called me. I'll never forget his words. He said, "John, you don't have to take this any more." I asked, "Take what?" He answered, "This morning sickness."

He told me to get a Bible and he would show me what he meant. He first had me go to Deuteronomy 28, which contains the blessings and curses of the law. He had me read the one that said, "Cursed be the fruit of your loins." He said, "That's your children, isn't it?" I agreed. The idea of this curse was that it would come upon people who turned their back on God.

He then had me turn to Galatians 3:13, which states: "Christ has redeemed us from the curse of the law, having been made a curse for us, for it is written cursed is anyone who hangs upon a tree." He explained to me that because I was a born-again Christian, I should never tolerate any of the things being described in Deuteronomy 28 under the curses, because there was no way that God was "putting me through this." He then explained that I had a power over it and had me turn to Mark 11:23, which says: "Whoever speaks unto this mountain and says 'be removed and be cast into the sea' and does not doubt in his heart but believes that what he saith shall come to pass, he shall have whatever he saith."

He told me that I should speak directly to the morning sickness, as though it was an entity which had invaded our house, and tell it to leave in the name of Jesus. Since I had, less than four months previous to this, gone through deliverance and knew that things like this could happen, I listened closely. I also remembered something Stillwell had said. He said healing and deliverance were very similar and often the sickness had to be commanded to leave just as demonic forces are.

I hung up and told Donna, "I'm going to do something that may seem a little weird." She didn't care, she was so sick I could have called in a marching band and it wouldn't have impressed her in the slightest.

I spoke directly to the sickness, quoted the verses given, and commanded it to leave.

I told Donna, "You're healed. Get up." She carefully got out of bed. "How do you feel?" I asked. "Better!" she said. Within an hour, she was walking around cleaning the house, and she was never sick again from that day throughout her whole pregnancy except for one slight case of nausea resulting from her eating something that didn't set right. However, she ate breakfast, lunch, and dinner everyday throughout her entire pregnancy and woke up every morning with a big smile on her face. It was a total 180 turnabout from that moment forward.

I told several of my Christian friends about this, thinking that it would encourage them and they would be happy for me. Instead, for the most part, my story was met with skepticism, sarcasm, and theological argument. One woman even seemed jealous and resentful, because she had been extremely ill throughout her entire pregnancy. This same woman, however, had earlier claimed that God healed her of herpes and she'd never had an outbreak since.

Another told me that morning sickness was "good." I do think that a certain amount of morning sickness is probably indicative of nature's way of cleansing toxins out of the woman's body, and the cravings are probably some instinctual craving to replenish something needed to nourish the baby. What Donna was dealing with, however was - according to many women I have spoken with since - not normal, but quite extreme. There is a saying that Christians are the only group who shoot their own wounded. I agree.

Because we were so financially challenged, a lot of people gave us baby clothes, and we wound up with one bag of beautiful clothes, all washed and folded neatly. In the bottom of a bag was a book of baby names with the meanings of the names. I looked up Jesse, and the meaning was "God exists."

These are just a few of many experiences I had that convinced me that my faith was based upon something real.

Jesse Is Born

On August 26, 1991, Jesse Blair-French was born. I was in the room with Donna. The pregnancy had needed to be induced three weeks early due to toxemia. It was three weeks before the estimated due date, but that was still considered "full term" delivery. When Jesse was born, she was softly whining and making grunting type noises. She looked absolutely beautiful to Donna and I.

I can truly say that there had never been a musical moment, or any other moment in my life that I found more fascinating and wonderful than witnessing this miraculous moment in time.

Radical Changes

At the point I became a father, I realized that there was not much of a chance of me finding a job with benefits. My wife's job provided medical insurance and so we decided that I would take care of Jesse during the day. This was really a tough decision for me. I wanted my wife to be able to stay home with the child, but everything had happened so fast that my head was still whirling. I have been "reminded" time and time again by several people how it would have been better for my wife to stay home, however, it just couldn't work that way.

Fatherhood

As every parent knows, assuming responsibility for a completely helpless human being is a full-time occupation. It is nothing that should be taken lightly. One has to have a license to drive a car, to hunt, to fish, etc. Yet, the most important job in the world - caring for a helpless and completely dependant human being - is bequeathed upon all who exercise the ability to procreate - whether planned or not.

I found myself both taking the job completely seriously and at the same time giving up everything else that had been important prior to this. I didn't write songs. I didn't play the drums. The only music I did was play in a local bar band in the evenings (not a pleasant experience) to make a few extra bucks.

Donna Works For Schools

My wife works as a Para-Educator in Special Education and her class contains high school level high-functioning children who have various forms of mental retardation. It's called TMR (Trainable Mentally Retarded) because these people can be trained to lead meaningful lives and take care of themselves. The students vary in affliction. There are cases of downs syndrome, physical brain damage, autism, and muscular dystrophy to name a few.

It is a very difficult and stressful job that requires extreme patience and tolerance, not only with the students, but with parents who are sometimes expecting more from their children than is realistically possible to achieve. It is no easy task and I am proud of my wife's achievement - more than if she was a successful entrepreneur, supermodel, film editor, or high-achieving real estate salesperson. She is helping society in a very real and stressful way on a day-to-day basis and is quite successful at her job.

I saw a cartoon once that illustrates my feelings on this subject quite well. The cartoon was in the local paper and the caption read, "If people were actually paid what they are worth." It showed a basketball star driving a Yugo and a teacher driving a BMW. We pay our "stars" obscene amounts of money for doing something that's entertaining and fun and was motivated by selfish desire, while the people who are unselfishly dealing with harsh reality on a daily basis are getting paid so little they struggle to survive.

Van Vliet In Retrospect

The extremely gifted seem to carry heavy burdens and many seem to have tragic lives. Don seemed to me to be constantly dealing with a vast internal struggle. I always felt as though somehow I understood his struggle intuitively, but could never grasp it in a way that could be explained. A combination of extreme intelligence coupled with physical maladies, allergies, and possibly blood sugar problems may have caused his erratic and puzzling behavior at the same time accelerating his imagination to visit places most of us are unaware even exist.

No one really understands anyone else in the true sense. We can only see out of our own eyes of experience, and most of us judge others by why we would do, seldom considering that another's behavior is based on a completely different universe of atoms, making up molecules, and culminating in humans who, though we may look similar in appearance, are worlds apart.

Only when one is faced with unforgivable behavior can they learn the true meaning of forgiveness, and if Don had affected me in no other way, my association with him gave me a glimpse into a world I will never totally understand, but finally was able to accept. The frustrations, the puzzling behavior, the self-destructive actions, the cryptic conversations and intense and sometimes damaging confrontations only reinforced the clarification that we are all unique and amazing creatures living in a universe our best minds have yet to explain. There is far more that we don't know than we do. We somehow think that we are evolving and will someday merge into some kind of "universal consciousness" in which everything will be revealed.

I remember Don once holding a pair of nail nippers in his hand and saying to me, "You are looking at these right now, but don't ever forget that they are also looking at you." It was a puzzling statement for a moment, but I grasped that he was saying that there are universes within as well as without, and we are collections of matter moving around in relationship to other collections of matter (but "it doesn't matter" - sorry - I couldn't help but include one of his favorite phrases).

Whether it's kharma, or "the golden rule," it seems to be a common fact that for every action there is a reaction, and how we behave certainly affects how others around us behave. I have felt for years as though my relationship with Don "mattered" - that it wasn't just a foolish kid being manipulated. We who worked with/for Don actually did something in this world that is considered by some to be a great achievement - and the most interesting thing about it is that there was no hint of financial reward as motivation.

What motivated us, I think, was Don's obsession to create. We were fascinated with the many facets of his creative force - what was driving him so relentlessly in his pursuit. We marveled at his stream of thought and how someone's imagination could be so fruitful and wondered always what made him tick.

So, in the end, I know it was a privilege - albeit certainly wrapped in an ironic cloak - to be associated with this man. I learned how to push myself to achieve things of which I formally thought myself incapable, as did others who worked with Don. His leadership was primitive; at times miserably cruel. Yet, there seemed to be a reason for it all. He was, in a sense, reflecting the world, and because of the experience I find myself constantly thinking of people all over the world, who live entirely different lives. Some who live in dreaded fear because of war, famine, disease and a dozen other dangers that lurk just around the corner, awaiting their moment to strike.

That awareness forced me to not fall into the slumber that false comfort brings in the form of materialism. I have never been able to long sit in complacency nor considered that I've "done my share" or "paid my dues." It's driven me to keep trying, even in the face of impossible situations that seemed hopeless. In a song I wrote called *Invisible Means* (FFKT), there is a line that says, "every time I reached the end of my rope, it lengthened by *invisible means*." This has happened to me time and time again.

In a short Van Vliet poem, *Apes-Ma,* the very last line sums it up: *"Your cage isn't getting any bigger Apes-Ma."* Our earth isn't getting any bigger, but the human race continues to procreate. In *Petrified Forest* he writes; *"The rug's wearing out that we walk on, soon it will fray and we'll drop dead into yesterday."* There was always this type of urgency in Van Vliet's life. Constantly writing, drawing, creating music, or spending time in fascinating conversations that went on forever. Even in those conversations, he seemed to be drawing conclusions, assimilating information, grasping at new ideas, and searching, always searching. Life was his university. Often, the other parties in the conversation seemed drained, exhausted at the end. But Van Vliet seemed as though there was a restoration taking place, as though every moment he was alive was another moment to grasp something new to place in his collection of thoughts and images, and that collection was rejuvenation to him physically, mentally, and creatively.

A bit of him rubbed off on us all. I see characteristics, although dressed in different clothes, in almost all the Magic Band people and close-associates of Van Vliet. In myself I note that I have always carried a recording device for ideas - usually musical, sometimes lyrical. Van Vliet instilled within me the simple concept that "my thoughts are unique, and moments of inspiration may come at any time, so I should be prepared to preserve them."

Bill Harkleroad is a master of guitar, and seems intensely interested in preparing himself to be ready to play anything, with daily discipline in his practice, yet chooses ironically not to perform. Mark seems to have captured determination and never gives up. This in itself seems to be a hope in him.

Some left music altogether. Art Tripp is a successful chiropractor and doesn't play music at all. I asked him to be involved in the recent Magic Band reunion concerts and he politely declined. Jeff Cotton removed himself entirely from music and, about ten years ago, I heard he was head of his own ATM Machine company and doing quite well for himself.

I wonder what we all would have done in an alternate reality that never crossed paths with Van Vliet. Sometimes I think I would have been much better off, sometimes not. I found the best cure for calming my inner turmoil was Christianity, though I still have flare-ups, anxiety, and the feeling that disaster awaits me at any moment. My faith helps squash that into background noise, and I am able to function, even in completely alien situations that arise at times.

I still love creating music, but there is little market for my Van Vliet-influenced path. People tell me to write "normal" music, but what I write is normal to me. I find that most popular music I hear is completely beyond my grasp of understanding in terms of being taken seriously.

My wish for Van Vliet is that he is at peace with himself, and that he feels satisfied and fulfilled and has no regrets. That whatever he was pursuing he captured, and he feels satisfied that his life was lived to the fullest. I will probably never know, as it's been many years since we spoke, and I doubt we will ever speak again. I have accepted that fact, and am at peace inside with myself, and my faith is a strong assurance that somehow, some way, with God's help, I will prevail.

Final Comments

Jim Sherwood: Yeah, I'd never seen that side at all ... Before that, Donny was the kind of guy you could just slap around and tell him exactly what you wanted to do with him. I don't know, maybe somewhere along the line, he figured if he would yell at somebody it scares them off, I don't know.

Denny Walley: He was kind of notorious as a "badass." Very cool. He had a '51 blue Olds that was real tough looking.

Vic Mortensen: Don Van Vliet was fortunate to have lived in an era where his psychopathic behavior could be misconstrued as genius.

Jerry Handley: After careful thought I can positively say that Don - in the immortal words of Frank Sinatra, - "did it his way," for better or worse. I look back now at him as a kind of "sad character," who needed to control everyone around him because of his own shortcomings. He had amazing talent, but just couldn't organize it - even with your incredible patience and help. Alex and I both saw the potential but had to give up eventually. He's a strong personality. I hope he's happy doing his painting. Maybe that was always his calling. Who knows? I enjoyed the time we had traveling and making a few albums. I'm most proud of Safe As Milk. I think Alex would agree, that's when we were on the right track. Anyway my life's been great raising a family. Knowing what it's like to be shut off from the rest of the world - that was not what I had in mind as a musical career.

Doug Moon: I definitely, without any reservations, believe that Don had subjected himself to Demonic influences.

Alex Snouffer: The only thing that was holding Don back was Don. You know he can sit there and lay blame anywhere he wants but it's him, it was him, always was. Nobody, I didn't see one person ... and it didn't matter which personnel was in which band, I never saw anyone holding him back. I mean, he can make all the excuses he wants, but that's all they are; excuses.

Guy Webster: You guys - along with Zappa and his band - were the cutting edge at the time.

That intrigued me - that's where I always wanted to be. Through the years - because I became well known - anybody who had a band would want me to shoot them. I wasn't always attracted to their music. When I would do their covers, it would upset me. I was doing Andy Williams, Johnny Mathis, Liza Minnelli, and all these ... people. But, I never was excited about it like I was with avant-garde rock bands.

Don Aldridge: *Part of the sadness of this for me is that Don was a lot of fun to be around much of the time. I don't want to put him down, but my observation was that he had a very dark side as well. I thought and still do think he could be evil.*

John French: *Well, the thing is that it's bigger than Don, it's bigger than Jan, It has to do with a bunch of people who were together playing some rather important music at the time. It has historical significance. It sort of knocks the earth off its commercial axis and makes everybody stop and think! We did it because we enjoyed his company ... at times - not all the time. What was coming out - the ideas - needed to be published. I always had these visions of bygones being bygones and maybe I could sit down with him when I'm ninety years old and we could laugh about all that stuff that we did together. That was not meant to be.*

Bill Harkleroad: *As I told Don one day in a conversation, "I feel like the golden hand of God picked me up and dropped me down in the most perfect situation. I'm so lucky I can't believe it." ... That's the state of mind I was in, and I told him. I said, "This is unbelievable! I love the music. I even liked* Strictly Personal. *I liked where that was evolving to. I hadn't been freaked-out by* Trout Mask *yet. I had known you and Jeff. Unbelievable. And here's my hero, and he really worked it. I was the "special guy" the first month, right? Before I became on of the major culprits. So I was a very weakened person, and he was very good at doing that, as we all know ... like I said, it's textbook brainwashing. Sleep deprivation, food deprivation, and no contact. I mean, that's what they do at Wings seminars now. They put you in this room without any light and you're stuck in this thing separated from the world. ... Along the way,* (Lunar Notes) *became a way for - sorry for the psychobabble - but a cleansing experience. Because, as I was going back through it, I would go out of my front lawn and be ready to throw up, from the embarrassment of taking that shit for so long. For letting my self-esteem get down to such a small level. To the reverse of it is - what a tremendous learning experience. To let yourself go out that far and then "reclaim yourself." I learned a lot. I dealt with a lot of things at a very early age. So going back through it and dealing with that was quite an experience for me. So yeah, I hope* (Lunar Notes) *has an effect that would be positive, but I don't think that was my specific intent.*

Mark Boston: *... Some of it was healthy to a point ... I thought a lot of it was nitpicking after a while - bullshitting around with Don ... or each other. Some of it was good, though, for getting in contact with each other ... Trying to get people to admit things they wouldn't normally admit or whatever ... We kinda just went along with whatever, just to get through it. There was so much of it sometimes it just got old. I wanted a playing job. I didn't come down to bullshit - I wanted to play music.*

Merrel Fankhauser: *I'd drive over there (to the Trout House) at night sometimes and you know it was really ... if they would have had video camcorders back then it would have really been something because you'd drive up, (as) soon as you'd turn the engine off you'd hear this (sings). You know - that delta riff that he'd have you guys working on. It almost* transported me back to when I was a kid living in Louisville, in Kentucky. I'd met these old black blues players that lived on the other side of the railroad tracks from where we lived. They'd eat cornbread and drink wine and then I saw this old guy after he finished the wine, he just broke the end of the bottle off and stuck it on his finger and started playing. A little piece of glass got in there and cut his finger playing this, like - probably a Harmony or a Kaye guitar. Playing slide on it with his little finger bleeding and blood going all over the strings and everything. He was playing away - so that was my first introduction to southern bottleneck blues stuff. But when I walked up to you guys' house there, and heard that music coming out, it almost took me back to my childhood in a way.

Gary Marker: Had it been say 1959 or 60 with primarily acoustic instruments or electronic instruments, it would have been avant-garde beat poetry. You know, or poetry and jazz. Something like that. It's just that what he did is take this concept. Somewhere along the line he got this notion that, "We're going to take all these strange ideas and we're going to take all these images strung together and we're going to hype it up with an electronic kind of background and jarring rhythms." Once again, you see how rhythmically his personality aligns with his musical forte. You're always a little "off-kilter." The listener, the friend, the musician, he always keeps them slightly off balance. It's unpredictable. If there is any key word that describes what he does, in all phases of his life, it's unpredictability. You never know what to expect from moment to moment.

Art Tripp: Yeah, it was kinda like a "guru" situation. The guy had the "whammy" on everybody and we were all kind of - we all seem to alternate elation with intimidation and it was just really weird. ... A lot of guys have a way of putting themselves into a situation and all they have to do is say, "see ya," and take off down the road. And we don't. We linger and we stay and we put up with this shit, but basically, I think all of us were really enthused about the music that we were doing. I do think that all of us liked it. Maybe didn't understand it all the time, but we liked it and we kept - at least for my part - I tried to keep focused on the long objective, which was getting out there and doing shows and making records.

Michael Traylor: My experience with Don was indeed inspiring ... I met Don in 1976 at the AVI in Lancaster over a bran muffin and a cup of coffee at about 3 in the morning ... I loved to listen to the way he would describe things in a three dimensional way, like painting a landscape in my imagination ... He opened my mind to abstract thought in a way I never thought possible ... Although I was unable to be in the band at the time, I managed to maintain a relationship with him through 1982 ... The last time I saw him, he came to hear my band "Duck" play at the Desert Inn in Lancaster ... I played drums and sang and Mark Boston was the bass player...I do believe it was the last Mark saw him as well...I still have the vinyl copy of Trout Mask Replica he gave me and marked the songs on it he wanted me learn...I also have a colored sketch he did of me signed and dated ... on the back he wrote "to Michael love Don" - one of my prized possessions ... the years that I have been blessed to tour with you and the other Magic Band members has been the highlight of my musical career ... to honor such great music to old fans as well as an audience that was not even born when the last Beefheart album was released, has definitely made Don close to my heart again ...God bless you for writing this book and God bless Don Van Vliet.

Greg Davidson: I can only speak from my direct experiences with Don. I was with the band for only a short time. He gave me this fantastic opportunity to play in his band. He hung out a lot with me to make sure I was happy. So, he had a problem with lyric retention but that is not a malicious thing. He is a unique character and artist. I feel privileged to have known him and to have worked with him.

Cliff Martinez: It felt like a huge goal (had been achieved.) This is somebody whose music I had listened to for a long time, really admired and still admire. I got a front row seat to the process. I was always mystified by how the music was created. There was no other music like it. To be a participant was like a dream come true in a lot of ways. I worked with a lot of people before and since, and he was easily the most temperamental person I had ever worked with and that didn't make it easy, because the music was more difficult than any music I had ever done. It was around the clock. The minute you roll out of bed, you start working on the parts until you go to sleep at night.

Henry Kaiser: I recall visiting Don up in Trinidad, CA, after the Clear Spot tour. Don had been talking to Richard Perry about producing another Captain Beefheart And The Magic Band album, and Don had become obsessed with the Carly Simon track, You're So Vain, which had been recently produced by Perry. Don played it over and over and over again for me - maybe 30 times. I hate to think how many times Jan must have had to listen to it that week... Don was sure that the next album, if done with Perry, would make him rich. Unfortunately (or maybe fortunately) that production reality never came to pass and the DiMartio brothers appeared to produce Unconditionally Guaranteed instead.

John Thomas: I have to say if I ever met one true genius, it was he. I am referring to the mental things that were unlike anything. The way he could lull you into a conversation about nothing, the way he could draw, create, and poeticize constantly. It was a never-ending flow with him. It wasn't something intellectual he embraced - it was something he lived. As painful as it was for everyone around him and probably as devastating on his chance of having a grip on reality as it was for him personally, he still walked the walk and lived what he believed in that way. I always will admire that, even though I see now that maybe he had no other choice and it was out of sheer terror and paranoia about being anything else. He devoted his life to what he believed in that way. I never saw him inconsistent with that. If I saw him at 3 am in the morning in Denny's (restaurant) he had his pad out and he was drawing everybody in there. If I saw him come to a gig, he was never trying to be anyone he wasn't. He was totally in his own category. It was so amazing to me that something that could be so different and unique could leave behind a trail that could glitter. Even in our darkest hour as humans, we can still do something that has great meaning to it. That's still the puzzle to me, and it gives me hope.

Gary Lucas: I don't know, but I hope he is at peace with himself. When I quit, I thought, man, somebody going to catch it now. ... I figure he would have to take it out on somebody, you know. I hope he has conquered his demons and he's at peace with himself.

Cliff Martinez: It just felt to me like a bit of a bully mentality. Kind of like the kid at school whose idea of a good time was seeing other people in a little bit of pain. That was my only understanding of it. With me, it rarely had to do with the music directly. Learning the part, playing a part. "Psychic interference" was about as concrete as it could get. He wouldn't even call it that. It was like, "Man, he's putting tin foil in my radar again. Can you feel that, Jeff?" "Yeah, Don, I do." ... Trying to get the other band members to agree that I was "causing psychic interference." Everybody not wanting to "share the barrel" with me would agree.

"Yes, Don, I feel the interference. He's doing it to you again ..." I have no idea what it was about. Perhaps he did sense some "psychic interference," because we'd be sitting there in the room and while he was working on somebody else's part, I'd be focusing intently on whatever he was saying. So it was kind of like ... he became a little self-conscious just having people sitting there studying you waiting to see you come up with something brilliant. I think he was kind of annoyed that I was zeroing in on him or perhaps judging him as it were.

Richard Snyder: His lack of formal musical training was his own enemy and his greatest asset. It was his nemesis insofar as it presented him with little or no vocabulary with which to communicate to musicians on their terms (e.g. at one time he instructed the drummer, Cliff, to play a beat that he had just given him "as if [he] was juggling a plate full of B.B.'s". Don really meant for him to play it in free time, without concern to making the downbeats of the phrase occur at regular intervals - but he couldn't say it that way!). At no time could Don request of any of us that we play a specific note by name (e.g., "play an E flat there") - he would instead whistle it, play it on a harmonica or, in a fit of exasperation, grab the neck of your instrument and percussively hit the fret board with his hands in search of the note he was looking for. He frequently assumed the responsibility for any difficulty we were having, apologizing for not being able to tell us, in musical terms, what he was asking us to do.[74]

Richard Redus: I feel like Don is a member of this very small subclass of humanity that I've met a few other members of. They share a certain characteristic, which is that they are 100% "psychedelicised" all the time. You could look at it in terms of brain chemistry, like maybe there's something going on with him similar to schizophrenia, or you could look at it from sort of a "new age" spiritual perspective. They're like windows onto a more profound view of the cosmos. Look at it as if they were Witch Doctors, with darker forces, or more magical forces. The features that they have in common is that they are always super-sensitive people. Sensitive to everything: emotions, visual impressions, sounds, metaphors - very very sensitive people - and also people that don't feel comfortable anywhere. That was something I felt with Don is that he was rarely comfortable - always a little bit alienated. People never understood him the way he would have liked to have been understood. He always seemed like he was just a little bit of an extraterrestrial, trying to deal with these humans. A lot of his most creative and unique contributions came out of that matrix and a lot of his suffering and confusion came out of that matrix - all part of who he was.

Robert Williams: I last saw Don Van Vliet at the final show he/we ever performed live. We just finished a two day/two show run at The Golden Bear in Huntington Beach, California and it was a well executed and inspiring show. We were well rehearsed on the tale end of a European and US tour. He pulled me aside back stage before I left to show me a drawing he made of a brass ashtray suspended by springs that he wanted me to construct for a new song he was working on. It was on a metal stand, typical of a little bar room table sans the table top. Two springs held it in place so when it was stuck it would go, Boi-oi-oi-oi-oi-oi-oi-oiing. I told him I'd get to work on it soon and before I turned away, with two hands he grasped my hand and gave it a hearty shake saying, "Great job man! Great job." That was January 31st of 1980 and as I said, it was unfortunately the last time I saw him.

---

[74] http://easyweb.easynet.co.uk/~bgwaters/hatsizejustin.html

TRACK NOTES

A promo picture from the Ice Cream For Crow session 198
featuring L to R: Gary Lucas, Cliff Martinez, Don and Jeff T

SAFE AS MILK
Studio(s): Sunset Sound (*Sure 'Nuff* only), Hollywood CA, RCA Studios, (all other tracks), Hollywood, CA.
Recording Date: April, 1967
Producer(s): Richard Perry, Robert Krasnow, and unfortunately, sometimes Artie Ripp.
Engineer: Hank Cicalo
Band Personnel: Don Van Vliet, Alex St. Clair Snouffer, Ry Cooder, Jerry Handley, John French, Russ Titelman, Milt Holland, Taj Mahal, Sam Hoffman.

Intro: Of course, I was pretty excited about playing on my first album. In the spring of 1967, I was 18 and a half years old. I had dreams of becoming a "pop star." I wanted to become a famous drummer like other drummers of the time. I knew little about the workings of a band and how much "behind-the-scenes" negotiations were going on. I was in denial about a lot of what I was seeing and hearing, especially from Don. I suppose I was hoping that all these problems, complications, barriers and contradictions would just melt into a large bowl of fame and prosperity.

Pride played a large role in my still adolescent mind. I had dreams of driving up to my ex-girlfriend's door in a limousine, getting out in a very expensive suit with a copy of "my latest album," signing my name to it and handing it to her as she gazed at me with worshipful and longing eyes. Then turning and walking "out of her life forever," leaving her a broken and ruined woman, having to face herself each morning, knowing what a mistake she had made - sweet revenge for deserting me for that lifeguard!

I had visions of buying my mother, who had been deserted by my father a year or so earlier, a home. Just cashing-out the best house in town and driving her over to see it, blindfolded. Taking off the blindfold to reveal a large bow on the door, saying "Surprise, Mrs. French!" I would be an international traveler, visiting ancient archeological digs, eating in the finest restaurants, rubbing elbows with the elite. Someday, I would collaborate with other famous international stars and donate my talents to worthy causes.

These were a few of this 18-year-old's fantasies as he walked into the studio at Sunset Sound to "cut his first hit record."

I think we did somewhere near seventy takes of *Sure 'Nuff*, at Richard Perry's request. It was obvious that he was a perfectionist. Unbeknownst to me, he was also a beginner. Doug Moon played on this session, and this was the only session of *Safe As Milk*, on which he actually played. He can be heard on the demos, which were recorded a few weeks prior to this at Original Sound studios, which was upstairs from the Kama Sutra offices.

1. SURE 'NUFF 'N YES I DO - The original demo tape of this song, made on a home machine, was a much faster tempo. I felt like it was much stronger in this context than the version recorded. It still consisted of bottleneck guitar and bass, but for percussion, there was a wood block playing fast sixteenth notes, which really gave it a downbeat "train rhythm" kind of tempo. Our first rehearsal with Ry, probably late Jan. 1967 premiered the new version of this song. Ry started playing the intro lick and I had no idea it was *Sure 'Nuff*. I thought we were doing *Louisiana Blues*, similar to the Muddy Waters version. I still think it's a bit of a ripoff. I have always assumed this was Ry's arrangement, and he was a big blues fan and more conservative thereby less experimental than Don and the band. I started playing the drums, employing the same rhythm as I had heard on the demo, and Cooder suddenly suggested the half-time feel on the tonic chord. When I played the half-time feel, I was using an 8th note ride on the hi-hat, and he specifically requested I do a quarter-note (half as fast or as the musician joke goes "half-assed") ride instead. It was a little difficult to achieve for a few minutes, but I caught on, and it wound up working quite well. I could see right away that Ry knew exactly what he wanted and how to communicate his ideas. However, I still prefer the (home) demo version for originality and sheer energy, and yet I haven't heard it for over 30 years and can still remember it well. Three guitars are heard on the track. Ry is playing the intro guitar and goes into a rhythmic counterpoint based on a clave rhythm when the drums come in. Alex is playing a straighter rhythm part and no bottleneck. Moon is playing the floating bottleneck in the background that is similar in feeling to the intro. A lot of the early Beefheart live performances (pre-*SAM*) had this "feel." The lyrics are reminiscent of Jimmy Reed's *I Ain't Got You,* and the Yardbirds' cover of the same.

2. ZIG ZAG WANDERER - The piece opens with the crescendo of two 'zig zagging" notes climbing to the resolve of Milt Holland's gong, played by Alex Snouffer. This song was typical of a lot of the early pre-*SAM* style arrangements where both guitars were actually playing parts rather than one playing "lead" and one playing "rhythm." Since it was written pre-John French, I don't recall a lot of changes in the basic parts except for the bass part, which in sections I seem to recall being re-written by Cooder. The bass and drum section under the lyrics which begin, *"Zig Zag wanderer had a Zig Zag child..."* was added by Ry to break up the monotony of the riff. Milt Holland is playing log drums in this section of the tune. Mr. Holland was also playing tambourine. He laid down the tambourine during the log drum / bass riff section. I was in the studio standing near and watching. He played the log drums with his hands, then picked up the tambourine and continued. Holland was a real pro and this caught my attention. Backup vocals were Snouffer and myself and the "echo" voice singing "Zig Zag wanderer" at the end of the bass section is me alone. I was actually more excited about this vocal than all the drum parts put together, because my real love was singing. Bass marimba can be heard in the intro and even better in the outro and is probably played by Don. Lyrically, it loosely makes reference to the cigarette papers of the same name, the little man on the logo, who is probably the inspiration for "wanderer," and the hippy movement in such lines as "found his queen in nature's scene." Lyrics also denote commitment, consistency, and determination but is vague as to who this represents, perhaps the hippy counterculture, god, or just a guy who loves a woman.

3. CALL ON ME - This song was completely rearranged shortly after I joined the group. Originally, it was music by Vic Mortensen and lyrics by Don Van Vliet. The text goes into this, but it was written the night that Vic found out his father had passed away. It retains the same chord structure of the original but certainly includes a more bluesy interpretation of the lyrics in an almost Motown-like style. The little musical interjection, after the first verse, was added shortly before the actual recording and after Ry joined the group. Notice that the riff sounds very familiar to *Old Folk's Boogie*, an early blues song that had been on the original blues band's repertoire. Claves and tambourine are added percussion. Horns were arranged and conducted by Richard Perry. There were ten horns I believe. Ry Cooder added the double time ending where Don's orgasmic vocal sounds carry the song to fade out. Listen to that fancy right to left pan of the tambourine starting at 2:00 and the horn and keyboard being exposed by the guitar fade out and back in. Pretty fancy for the sixties

4. DROPOUT BOOGIE - The basic arrangement of the song is exactly as the original demo until the interjection of the 3/4 section (1:03) that was added by Don shortly before the session. This interlude has an air of comic relief because of the ballerina imagery, which it invokes in stark contrast to the angry fuzztone-centered main theme. I recall Alex dancing (faux ballet) around the room comically during the original inclusion of this section in the track. He enjoyed all this in a rather sardonic manner. The lady who played the harp was at a party when summoned and came to the session in an evening gown with her date. She had to pull the evening gown up high to straddle the harp, which didn't bother us at all. Don accused Alex of trying to look up her dress. I'm sure this session was a rather bizarre detour to their expectations of the evening. I asked her many questions about the harp, an instrument with which I was totally unfamiliar, and was fascinated by her very patient and detailed explanations. She was a very attractive lady, which added to the pleasant experience. I believe there were no percussion overdubs. I played very hard on this track and it was a difficult one because we never rehearsed it with Don, so I wasn't quite sure where the breaks were or where the phrasing changed and without the lyrics, it all sounded rather the same. With my experience now, I would just ask for the lyric sheet. Faux-Producer and Kama Sutra President Artie Ripp decided that the problem was that I lacked drive and so came into the tracking room and "coached" me through the track, like some jock (you can do it, yeah!), that actually was more distracting than anything else and made me a bit perturbed. I balanced this out by playing extremely hard (pretending I suppose that my drum was his head) to release my anger, which worked well for this particular track. Lyrics obviously denote the dilemma of adolescent sex and the resultant responsibilities incurred. Whether this song was in rebuttal to Timothy Leary's stupid and irresponsible advice, "Turn on, tune in, and drop out," I haven't a clue. I certainly hope it seemed that way. I could allude to Don's dropping out of high school years before to take over his father's Helms Bread Truck route.

5. I'M GLAD - As John Platt's notes on the CD state, this may be "the weirdest cut on the album,"- in contrast to the other material at least. It does little to even touch Beefheart's own roots, which were more Delta Blues. The original demo featured on Revenant's boxed set features Rich Hepner playing BB King style solo accompaniment during the bridge section. Don calls the contrast between the two sections the "Beauty and the Beast" approach (which is heard on many of these tracks), which may account for the ballerina interjection in *Dropout Boogie*. He also labeled guitar soloists as "solo freaks," which accounts for the lack of soloing in this version's bridge. Instead there is a repeating almost country-like guitar part. I actually prefer Rich Hepner's interjections. He was a great player and it gave the song a lot more soul. Horn parts again written and conducted by Richard Perry and done in the same session as *Call On Me*. The lyrics may have to do with a former romantic involvement Van Vliet had with a girl who lived next door to him.

6. ELECTRICITY - Development of this song is a little more complicated. This was lyrically written by Herb Bermann (Don would say that the whole thing was stolen by Herb from Van Vliet's ideas that had passed between them in a discussion at their first meeting, which I seriously doubt) and the music was probably just basically developed from a jam based on eastern raga type sounds. The idea of the song has to do with telepathy and the theoretical "radio waves" that carry thoughts through the air. It was also supposed to have the sound of voltage running through high power lines. It originally was just a tamboura-like drone over which Don sang in a similar style to what became the "verses." The vocal scale and style is heavily laden with Eastern influence. Also, and I am guessing here, but I believe this was inspired in part by the Stones' *Paint it Black*. Gary Marker takes credit for inclusion of the little 1-3-4-1 chord bridge section, and I do remember him at a more informal moment in the rehearsals previous to the album suggesting this to Don, who approved and included it in the piece. I believe the opening riff was Snouffer's idea and Don decided after that to add the bridge chord changes at the beginning slowed down. Note that the opening riff is very similar to a piece off Zappa's *Lost Episodes* CD called *Wedding Dress Song*, in fact, almost the same exact riff. The original drum part was just a straight bass drum playing pulse and a hi-hat ride in sixteenths with mallets. Don changed this beat in the official *Kama Sutra* demo that Gary Marker produced at the last minute to what became the finalized version. It was totally different, following the rhythm of Alex's guitar riff almost exactly. He asked me to follow the vocal on the bridge with the broken punctuations that worked very well, since the guitars and bass were carrying the pulse and rhythm so well. This was the beginning of my realization that drums in Beefheart's concept of music could take liberties not allowed in other groups. This in itself was an exciting prospect and opened my mind to the possibilities for innovation of new techniques that strayed away from the drummer-as-timekeeper role. I'm sure the theremin's role in the song, though Don would never admit it, was influenced by its presence in Brian Wilson's masterpiece *Good Vibrations*, which is a song with a similar theme. At (2:42) is the point of the legendary "mike breaking" where Don's voice supposedly "broke" the microphone. I was in the control room during this take, looking through the window. Don was being recorded on a Telefunken microphone, which I believe has a vacuum tube inside, so it was probably on the level of a condenser microphone (I'm not technically equipped to know if the terminology is correct, but I know the theory), really a VERY sensitive mike. Don was back away from the mike softly singing *"seeking electricity,"* and Hank Cicalo, the engineer, had the mike turned up a bit to catch it. If I am not mistaken, these mikes have "phantom power," which means they have a small bit of electrical current sent to them to feed the tube, part of which causes them to be so sensitive. Suddenly, Don moved extremely close to the mike and simultaneously sang in his pinched-trachea voice, which is very thin and mid-rangey and the tube in the microphone was overdriven for an instant. Hank went, "Oh my God my microphone!" After the take, he went running into the tracking room to check out the mike. It apparently was fine, just overdriven for a moment. This is similar to the effect of fuzztone on a guitar amplifier, and causes momentary distortion. However, from this small instance grew the l egend that Don's voice could "break" microphones. Don later confided in me that he often used this technique as a trick to blow-out speakers, to create the same type of myth. Singing softly into a mic and then suddenly moving close and singing loud will create massive distortion, which could blow out speakers.

7. YELLOW BRICK ROAD - Two songs come to mind when I hear this: the vocal is reminiscent of the song Lemon Tree, and the riff from Ike and Tina's *I Think It's Gonna Work Out Fine* happens during the *"Yellow brick, blackboard black,"* section. Taj Mahal plays washboard on this piece. I do a drum part that is basically country-esque in flavor. Lyrically it steals a little from Bob Dylan in the phrase, *"Don't look back."* Don wrote this song when seemingly swept into the "Love" movement after a performance in San Francisco. Alex once confided to me that it concerned him that Don was a "faddist" and seemed to become completely engulfed in whatever was happening at the moment, thus losing focus on what the band's image was supposed to be: a blues band. Because of his dominance over the band, this affected the entire group and weakened its commercial potential causing it to meander meaninglessly along trying to be "everyband." Don argues that the reason he had to take over the composer role was because Alex was plagiarizing already released and overly used riffs (such as the Ike and Tina riff being borrowed). The lyrics in this song seem to relate to some kind of (possibly drug-induced) religious or mystical experience, which had a strong influence on shaping his philosophies. Don himself confided to me upon my first reading of the lyrics that "bag 'o tricks" was his bag of lyrics that he carried around. He also suggested to me that "candy sticks" had to do with psychedelics, and "peppermint kite" was his nickname for marijuana. The reason I say "religious" is that the word "alter-bound" used to suggest to me love and marriage, but this song really has nothing to do with marriage, but with an experience. Don in his younger days was by reputation quite a fighter, a "hardass" as one interviewee described him. Yet here is written, *"Clouds of gray in yesterday, Dove on my shoulder says time to play."* The dove is a symbol of peace (and in the Bible, it's the symbol of the Holy Spirit of God) and has landed on his shoulder, which gives this an almost "messianic" symbolism. This does not surprise me, because Don sometimes acted as though he thought he were a God of sorts, and occasionally his fans (and band members) treated him as such.

8. ABBA ZABA - This song would have never reached a finished arrangement and been recorded had it not been for Ry Cooder's insistence and constant prodding of Don. "What's the next part, Don?" he would ask with a patient smirk on his face. The song finally came together. The center part (1:02) was borrowed from a Ravi Shankar album I owned and was listening to one afternoon in the Amor Road house. Don had me play the section (on the vinyl recording) over and over while Alex learned the section on guitar. Don called this a "figure eight" shape and since he communicated often in imagery, this helped us to begin to understand what he meant musically. In fact, I had, as a drummer tried to convey ideas in similar ways. Don asked for an African drum beat and I created this rhythm, and years later was surprised upon hearing exactly the same rhythm on an African field recording. Richard Perry insisted on joining us for backup vocals thinking his low voice would help beef up the track. He is the one singing, *"Babiddy Baboon"* instead of *"Babit Baboon."* I've heard critics call it "That Big Baboon." Don suppressed his thoughts but later confided to me how much he wanted to boot Perry out of the tracking room, "Babiddy Baboon????" he said in an incredulous tone, "What the hell kind of animal is THAT? What in the world was he THINKING man?" I remember this in amusement. This was the first song recorded at RCA studios and I had just learned the drum parts to the center section the night before. Jerry had difficulty with the bass solo (1:15), probably because of the unfamiliar drum interjections that Don had just added a few days previous. So Ry Cooder learned the part in the studio and played bass on the track, later overdubbing his guitar part. You'll notice it rushes slightly, this was a trademark of Ry's according to Gary Marker. Milt Holland added great percussion to this song, employing the whole band to play various instruments on overdubs. I played a large beaded gourd (cabasa), Ry played the cowbell part, Alex if I recall played the chimes leading into the bridges, and Milt himself chose a small pathetic-looking tambourine with only a few jingles left and a very loose head. I thought, "Why in hell doesn't he get himself a decent tambourine?" Actually, Milt probably got as much sound out of that tambourine as I did out of my whole set. By stretching the head with his fingers, he achieved the tabla-like (East Indian drum) affect heard on the bridge. He played very softly during the bridge. (1:34) introduces an instrumental section, composed purposely here to again avoid any chance of a "solo-freak lame guitar solo." It consists of two guitars playing a melodic phrase in harmony with one another. Here, it works well. This song is a perfect composition in terms of balance and form. I only wished they had turned Alex (who was playing the main notes of the melody) up a bit in the track. Ry's "fifth" harmony tends to overpower this section. It may be one of the first double harmony guitar compositions in rock music. Somebody look that up, quick. The lyrics suggest the evolution of the blues from Africa to America. I'm not sure about any specifics here, except he once later mentioned *Tobacco Sky* as symbolizing the (smoky) smog in LA. "*Two shadows at noon*" is always the image that grabbed me the most, even at nineteen. It always intrigued me. Usually two shadows are created by two separate light sources, but there is basically no shadow at noon.

9. PLASTIC FACTORY - The original demo was followed fairly closely until the center section that goes into 3/4 time. Again, as with most of the other songs, this section was added shortly before recording. Also, just before 3/4 section, Alex plays the guitar part incorrectly on the instrumental interlude. He was supposed to hit the same two high accented notes on bottleneck as Don was playing on harp. I achieved the harp sound for Don using an old stereo pre-amplifier my father had given me. The amplifier was a Fender Super Reverb probably 1964 vintage with 4 10" speakers. I believe it was Doug's amp. The microphone was an Electovoice, although I have no idea what model, it was a long shiny chrome thing. I had learned how to get this harp sound during the time I was a singer/harp player with Blues In A Bottle, the blues group I had formerly had with Jeff Cotton and Mark Boston among others. Ry is playing more straight rhythm guitar on this piece. The lyrics refer to disdain for the "rat race" mentality that conceives of working for 50 years for some company. Don, referring to the lyric "*get a fire a goin*" held thumb and finger up to his lips as though smoking a joint, when he was explaining parts of these lyrics to me. There were often references to drugs in Don's lyrics and he would often call attention to these and point them out to me, as though somehow I would be more willing to accept the song if it included a reference to drugs. Don Aldridge seems to feel this song was written in reference to his working at a "day job."

10. WHERE THERE'S WOMAN - This song was put together at the last minute because there weren't enough songs for the album. These lyrics were typed, so Herb Bermann had something to do with it. Don and I wrote the first guitar part together, which I later taught to Alex. The rest of the song was put together with the two guitarists. Jerry never had a written part and so just played a basic pattern in the studio. It didn't seem to be working and I called Don's attention to this. Jerry was unavailable and so Don called Alex, had him come to the house and wrote a bass part on the spot. We went directly to the studio and overdubbed this part, erasing Jerry's original part. So Alex should be credited for bass on this piece. Richard Perry should receive credit for the drum part in the slow section, he came up with the idea, sat down and played it to demonstrate (I played the track), and then added the echo. I only wish he would have taken the echo off during the fast sections. Milt Holland added bongos, one of the few times I've ever liked the use of the instrument because of the lack of pattern and use of understatement. This is one of my favorite songs, mainly because it was put together the way a band should work together with input from everyone, and also because the lyrics are great. I think the background vocals sound really good also, if I may say so, Alex, Don and I all sang this together. The lyrics are very good, and Don was really excited about being able to include this on the album.

11. GROWN SO UGLY - According to the liner notes by John Platt, Ry Cooder plays bass on this and I am sure that is incorrect. This performance was done live with no overdubs aside from vocal and tambourine. I never realized how much tambourine was overdubbed on this album. Ry wasn't happy with the take or the time given to this song, as it was his pet project and personal main focus for the album, and something that Don really had little interest in doing and didn't pay much attention to. Ry wrote the lyrics and music in the center section but gave all proceeds to Robert Pete Williams. (I'm sure Artie Ripp never gave him a dime, neither did he Don if I remember correctly). Ry sang it several times for Don, playing and singing in this odd time signature and brought the original recording for Don to study. Actually, Don encouraged Ry to pursue singing (not on this track, but in the future). Don did listen to the album several times and had a real respect for the artist, however, he didn't wish to emulate a blues singer, but wanted rather to create something new himself. This was part of the conflict between Ry and Don and added to other apparent areas in which Ry disapproved of Don's methodology. This arrangement is really a feather in Ry's cap and could have been played a bit stronger, but I thought the bulk of it came through the process unscathed. I believe that if Ry would have stayed with the group, this is definitely the direction (along with *Sure 'Nuff*) that he would have attempted to persuade Don to go in - to no avail, I'm sure.

12. AUTUMN'S CHILD - Dare I say it? I believe this song was Don's answer to The Rolling Stones song *Lady Jane*. It has a very similar feel and chord pattern. It was written shortly after *LJ* came out. Van Vliet claimed the Stones' tune was about pot (sometimes referred to as "mary jane"). This was definitely a band collaboration musically. The drum part idea again goes to Richard Perry who in a small way here influenced my approach to hi-hat. He again created the part by playing on the drums. I remember working on the bass part with Jerry when it was just a two chord song with no arrangement whatsoever. The intro and center section, composed by Don, were again added shortly before the session, as were many of the center sections to other songs on SAM. Doug Moon hated the new sections of the songs and felt that it took them out of the commercial realm and were superfluous additions. Krasnow argued with Don in the studio that the theramin made the song too far out and said if Don would allow him to erase it, he would hire "some opera broad to sing the fucking part." Don stood unwavering and Mr. Hoffman's part remained. Don claims he wrote the lyrics during springtime (1966) while visiting Saint Andrew's Priory in the Antelope Valley and he said the inspiration came while contemplating an apple hanging on a tree. Actually Herb Bermann wrote the lyrics, which were typewritten. Again, this is one of my favorites, and Ry Cooder said it was one of his also.

Conclusion

In a sense, it is a miracle that *Safe As Milk* actually survived the recording process. It emerges as a finished project quite a different concept from the demo presented to A&M Records. The three "Producers" of the album actually got in the way of each other and the band and caused more distraction than they did good. Richard Perry is truly the "producer" although in retrospect, it seems Marker would have done a much more professional job. Perry cut his teeth on this album, it was his "maiden voyage" and it sure shows in the mix, which is weak and thin, representing a very faded view of the true Magic Band sound. The musically unrelated "sections" that appear in many of the songs were added after Cooder became guitarist. Doug Moon was opposed to changing the songs so drastically, maintaining that they were good songs as they were.

Mirror Man Outtakes (on CD version):

Overall observations: All of the songs from the TTG sessions have certain characteristics I don't care much for. I believe they took away from the accessibility to the public. First of all, Don had been strongly influenced by Gabor Szabo and insisted on feedback sections and aleotoric slide sections at the end of nearly every song. This was in my opinion overdone and was an attempt to recapture the moment in time when Doug Moon played such an interesting bottleneck solo on the original *Mirror Man*. Don had been extremely impressed that day by the sound and the feeling in the room. Unfortunately, he fired the guitarist who inspired that, and secondly, we had all smoked a huge amount of marijuana that particular day, which distorts perception and exaggerates everything.

Also, Don insisted on everyone using huge strings on their instruments, which made some of the playing far less articulate than it could have been had players been allowed to use strings with which they were comfortable. He also insisted on playing extremely and unusually loud to match the volume levels of the "rock stars" of the day, which for me was devastating to my playing. It caused me to become muscle bound to the point where I couldn't maintain control of tempos and barely could articulate anything that required speed of any kind. There were few songs with real endings. *On Tomorrow* was such a relief to play, as it actually had a worked-out ending. Another thing is that Bob Krasnow insisted on me not using cymbals. I believe that this would have never been allowed had not Don privately made an agreement with Bob to apply this rather confining method to my playing.

On the up side (musicians always hear the bad side of the recordings and are seldom able to enjoy them from anything near an audience perspective) Don wrote some incredible pieces during a very short period of time. I believe Jeff Cotton didn't come on board until summer or late spring. From then until November, we moved into a different house in Tarzana CA, played several gigs (which meant Jeff was learning performance material and recording material) and put together all the material for this session, which I believe was in November of 1967. I would estimate that this was at the least 3 and at the most $4^{1}/_{2}$ months. It's a pretty incredible work when viewed from that perspective and quite a departure from *Safe As Milk*. It also shows how prolific Don could be. I also think the band deserves kudos for being able to assimilate all this material, rehearse it, and bring it to the level it was at in this short period of time.

I often wondered later how this album would have turned out under the guidance of a good producer, rather than Bob Krasnow, who stood in the control room loaded out of his mind shouting, "Heavy baby!" at the end of every take. A good producer would have recognized the flaw of using the same overbearing drum sound on every take. He would have also recognized the band was unprepared to perform and delayed recording until the songs were cleaned up and more recordable. He would have also insisted on hearing live tapes of rehearsals to make sure the singer knew where to sing.

Also, it comes to mind that many of these cuts have Doug Moon's fingerprints all over them, mostly the improvised cuts. He came up with the *Mirror Man* sound, which was never duplicated or simulated very accurately by Alex (with due respect, they were totally different players, which is why they worked so well together. Also, the two-guitar-part approach which partially developed from Don's total disdain of guitar solos and partially from Doug's lack of ability to really be a "lead guitarist" but abundance of ability to play riffs far above what could be labeled "rhythm" guitar.

1. SAFE AS MILK - From the drummer's point of view, this song could really have used more cymbals. When I originally started playing the drum parts with cymbals, it sounded far more rhythmically balanced. The deep toms tend to take away from the song in general. After the introduction and first verse the song seems to digress for a time into a rather monotonous rhythm and the vocal is weak and unconvincing. The upside is that some of Snouffer's bottleneck lines are totally out of character for the instrument and almost present a semi-classical stately elegance. Unfortunately, these lines are also very difficult to play on bottleneck due to the nature of the instrument, which is very limiting in some way to the overall sound and power of the lines. The lyrics are strong and rich in imagery, although the last line, *'I may be hungry but I sure ain't weird'* seems highly ironic framed by some of the weirdest music recorded by a "rock" band at that time. There is little of the clever double-entendre meanings in these lyrics that appear in later albums, however the approach is still quite sophisticated and far above anything being written in the rock genre at the time or at any time, in my estimation. After speaking with Herb Bermann, I am convinced that he should have received credit for writing the lyrics on this piece.

2. ON TOMORROW - Although this is probably my favorite piece of the section, I find that Don's amateurish and unrehearsed guitar playing being mixed louder than either of the actual "guitar-player" guitar tracks is not only a stupid mixing job on the part of Buddah, but adds nothing to the track and is actually quite distracting. I also found this distracting when playing the piece, as Don's guitar was turned up so loud in my headphones in order to accommodate his hearing himself that I could barely hear the other players. I found this particularly frustrating when I listened back and realized that I was completely out of sync with the other players and had missed a few important cues. I noticed also that no one seemed to have a clue as to where to end. The rehearsed ending would have been fine in my opinion, but due to Don's experimental guitar we wound up in a rather pointless meandering section that never seemed to really say anything significant. I would have never personally released this for public consumption in 1968, and although I can appreciate it more at the present time, it does remind me strongly of why I am a monetarily poor (thereby deemed by many as "unsuccessful") musician today. The people of 1968 were not ready for this and any producer worth his salt would have never allowed something like this to be recorded until it was a bit more refined and accessible. The lyrics reflect views of a Utopia, or perhaps Heaven, Nirvana, or some other place of religious attainment as viewed through Don's eyes. He later made fun of this song, suggesting that the lyrics were poking fun at these concepts rather than actually embracing them. However, at the time he seemed to be completely serious about the lyrics.

3. BIG BLACK BABY SHOES - I think this song was actually inspired by some young woman that Don saw wearing some rather interesting shoes. I only remember a few of the lyrics: *"She was wearing big black baby shoes, her eyes appeared swollen from crying blues."* That was all I ever heard Don sing of this piece, and I believe he had written whole sections musically without a notion of what would go on it lyrically. This is another song that could really have used cymbals. It starts out in a strong 4/4 time and that theme could have been exploited and perhaps made into an accessible piece for the time, but the tempo and time signature changes automatically put it 100% out of the realm of commerciality and out of the range of listen-ability for ninety nine percent of the unsophisticated American listening public. The ending was supposed to be faded, so that the monotony of this slow death with the drums finally ending as uncertainly as they did would have never been heard. A section of this song was used in *Alice In Blunderland* if memory serves correct. Give Cotton kudos for his quick recovery at 3:07. Also, the ending going from the 4 into the 3 count is very interesting at around 3:30.

4. FLOWER POT - Jerry McGhee (Later Gerry McGee) should probably have received writing credits for the opening theme as it was the first thing he played at the first rehearsal we had with him. The title was my idea. This piece goes through several sections until it finally winds up at the "raga" like section, momentarily taking a 3/4 time turn and then coming back to the 4/4 feel. For a moment, Alex plays a theme from *Maybe That'll Teach Ya*, which we had played once at the ill-fated Mt. Tamalpais Love-In. I cannot recall more than a vague suggestion of lyrics for this piece, I don't recall Don even writing more than a few images on a page and never was anything sung with the track that I recall. Again, Herb Bermann claims writing the lyrics, and read them to me over the phone. They definitely were the same ones Don claimed he wrote for the song.

5. DIRTY BLUE GENE - This is one of my favorites … up until the last two sections before the end. Don had taken time to rehearse background vocals for this and it had a complete set of lyrics. He actually had worked on this song from beginning to end (it actually HAD an end) and it was basically finished. I regret that the vocals were never added to the track. The lyrics are completely different than the later version recorded on *Doc At The Radar Station*, and I believe they were written by Herb Bermann, as he read his version to me over the phone and they were exactly the same.

> *What have you got after you got rich?*
> *Got a bag o' gold filled with suet and a switch.*
> *That's a lotta what cha got*
> *The gold spoon in your mouth gone,*
> *Fate gave it a pitch*
> *Now look at what cha got*
> *Yer diggin' a ditch*
> *That's a lotta what you got!*

The drum parts are reminiscent of *Moonlight On Vermont* employing counter-rhythms and the use of hi-hat. I wanted to do another take of this song, because of a major drum blunder in the center, however, it was passed over and we went to the next song. I felt that this song had the most chance of actually receiving some air play, at least until the last section of the song, which seems to go temporarily into a 40s film noir drama soundtrack and then immediately to a samba-esqe feel. My diagnosis: "What wuz u smokin' Don? Quit trying to paint so many paintings on the same canvas - get a new one!"

6. TRUST US - Months before this song was written, Don left his tape recorder with me while I lived with Fran and Alex in Hollywood. I sat down one night and came up with a guitar part that formed the basis of the intro for this song. I recorded it on Don's machine, and when he heard it, he wrote the rest of the song around it. As I have mentioned before, *Trust Us* was Don's attempt, either consciously or unconsciously, to write a song in the genre of the Beatles' *All You Need is Love* and the Stones' *We Love You*. I questioned Don on the lyrics, especially the lines, *"To find us, ya gotta look within,"* and *"There is no other way."* Also, I was troubled by *"The path is the mask of love"* and asked him why anyone would have a mask of love because it's symbolized that it wasn't really love, but just a pretense. Also *"The path is youth"* bothered me because I felt like it was making the statement that it cheapened older people's lives. I also wondered "who in the hell is the 'us' he is referring to?" I felt like this was some kind of religious connotation and it made me a bit uncomfortable as though Don thought he was writing some appendix to the Bible or something. The ideas on a spiritual level seemed a bit confusing with my own personal viewpoint. However, I came to the conclusion that Don alone was responsible for his lyrics and their eventual effect on the populace at large and just accepted these vague and confusing references as his view of spirituality that had nothing to do with me. He later applauded my probings as a responsible and cautious approach and told me that he respected me for questioning him. He wrote this song while living in his mother's apt. on Beech Ave. in Lancaster, 1½ blocks from my parent's home. Listening to the double vocal on this track confirms that Don was unsure of where the lyrics went in relationship to the arrangement. It is a poor performance to a fairly good track. This is one of the first pieces he wrote for this album and so was rehearsed a bit more and performed much better. I think I would have done a much better job had I been playing at a realistic volume level. The scream you hear as the last section comes in is my voice leaking through the drum mics. I liked the way this section came in as such a contrast to the previous rather melodramatic part. 'Let the dyin' die' is reminiscent to me of Jesus' quote, "Let the dead bury the dead." Again, I later found out the lyrics to this song were actually written by Herb Bermann, though all the discussion I had with Don seemed to indicate that he was the author.

7. KORN RING AND FINGER - The title in my estimation always related to Don's view during that time of the institution of marriage. He was a bit put out about Jerry and Alex being married and the restrictions it placed upon their time. When this song was counted off, I knew nothing about what we were playing, not the title, not a thing. It was completely improvised on my part, and not very well at that. If I were to make comparisons, it sadly reminds me musically of The Doors' *The End* because of the raga-like quality. Unfortunately I think it's a piece of self-absorbed artsy-fartsy shit. At the time, however, I thought it was the "best thing we'd ever played." I especially like the feedback when Don accidentally turned his harmonica mike towards the amp it was plugged into. This could have been mixed out, but "maybe he meant to do that." My question to myself is, "What chu was smokin' mon? Some mighty fine stuff thinks me!" Actually, I wasn't smokin' a thing, so I have no excuse at all.

From the Best Of Beefheart;

1. KANDY KORN - I love this song and always have good feelings associated with it. It is one of the few from this era that we played "live" at performances. When we lived in the Chicken Coop house in Tarzana, one evening Don, Jeff and I were sitting around the table and I was playing a guitar - if you could call it playing. I could play a little on guitar and I finger picked a bit. I started playing one of the parts of *Kandy Korn*, the fast 4 section at the where he's singing *"Kandy Korn... Yellow and Orange and"*... etc. Don really liked the little bit I was doing and immediately suggested a little "figure 8" which completed the phrase. I played it over and over a few minutes and said, "It's like a shape in three sections and pointed at one end - like Candy Corn - describing the part in a "shape." Thus the title was discovered. We had all learned to talk in imagery with Don (just in case you didn't know, Candy Corn is only an American institution, like Graham Crackers, I will say that what I am referring to is a wax-like candy that has a triangular shape. It is as though a kernel of corn has been plucked from the husk. The top is yellow, like the kernel, and then it has white and orange in the "root" part). Jeff grabbed his guitar and between Don and he they came up with Jeff's great riff. (I believe Don whistled the part in that wonderful throaty whistle he had). The next day at rehearsal, I showed Alex my part and they began playing the basic riff. The drum part came to me immediately and the bass drone was added. Don then suggested the "cut triplet" interjections just before the 3/4 section. He then worked on the intro and was becoming frustrated because no one could seem to grasp it, so he went with a simpler approach which is the intro as heard on this cut. I actually took a spare guitar outside and worked on this, coming up with one of the guitar parts for the intro. I have always wondered at Don's lyrics *"Be reborn, Be reformed, Roses thorn, Stains stains stains warn."* Don seemed to be really almost obsessed sometimes with being "reborn" and I know it wasn't in the Christian sense of becoming "saved" by saying a sinner's prayer and turning your life over to God. It was some kind of Eastern Philosophy, mixed with his own personal philosophy, and the drug philosophy at the time. I felt like he was very confused and often wished to discuss with him the simplicity of the Christian concept of "being reborn." However, at nineteen, I was very intimidated and lacked the confidence or the determination. He had lashed out at me about this more than once, and I decided reluctantly to keep my mouth shut. However, I sensed that Don was seeking for something during this time. He was unhappy and fearful and although it didn't show very often, enough of these feelings surfaced to make it apparent. I can only guess that these lyrics parallel his life in a sense. He went through a period of violence (rose's thorn) in a time of beauty (the rose) for him. I am reminded of his parents moving him to Mojave and consequently away from the beauty of his love of sculpting. He then faced the violence of the area and lost several of his teeth in frightening encounters with the Marines. This taught him to be physically strong and actually violent (stains warn). When I was in the group, he would revert to anger and threats of violence to anyone who contradicted or confronted him, yet he was writing this to the "Peace and Love Generation" and I think he was genuinely seeking inside himself for a message that could be conveyed through his lyrics. In *Yellow Brick Road*, he wrote *"Got my shield, put away my lance,"* which suggested being less offensive and more defensive. It was as though he was trying to change himself to be compatible with the more attractive elements of the cultural movement of which we were in the midst. Musically, the rest of *Kandy Korn* was Don's concept of this wall of chords with the finger picked parts, the first of which Don suggested, and much of which Alex actually composed. The overall vision of the piece was Don's, but much of this tune was a band collaboration.

2. 25th CENTURY QUAKER - Actually, this is the song that I looked up halfway through the count off and had not a clue as to what we were about to do. The original concept of 25th Century Quaker, not the song necessarily, but the concept of an actual band called 25th Century Quaker first came to Don during the *Safe As Milk* period in the house on Amor Road. I recall him coming to my room at the Amor Road house one night and speaking about this concept, which included wearing glass antennae if I recall and space-age quaker outfits. The closest thing we achieved was the normal Quaker suit which Alex wore on the Cannes Beach shot and the inside picture in the vinyl *Strictly Personal,* which suggests a band of aliens. This is one of the better of the improvised pieces and is the style we used often on stage in European performances. Note the lack of "compressed drums" on this piece, which allowed me to occasionally use cymbals without that mid range drone that accompanies compressed cymbals. I think it makes the sound a bit cleaner also. I just realized writing this that the riff that the band plays just before Don's first vocal line is from Mark IX, which was a song written at the Carolside house about a year earlier. Also, the line *"Butter lamps flutter like fire flies"* is from the lyrics of that piece. Many of the lyrics to *Mark IX* were later used in *Love Lies* from the album *Ice Cream For Crow.* I don't have a clue what this is about lyrically. It seems drug-related in a sense. The referral to being *"out picking poppies"* from which opium is derived is one hint. Often, as in *Plastic Factory,* there were these occasional subtle hints to drugs. The line *"bleu cheeze faces"* recalls hallucinations. The "me into you" theme comes up a lot as in *Mirror Man* and reminds me of the "we're all one" kind of eastern religious philosophies that seemed to be so popular then and even now, with the New Age movement. When the music becomes more delta-like, the words seem to have more of a sexual phase, interspersed with the same hallucinesque imagery so typical of much of Don's poetry. There are also times in this piece when Don makes fun of himself as in the line *"Sun just"* repeated three times and the last time sang in what I would consider Don's "mocking" voice, which he used at rehearsals occasionally to lighten up the mood. It was very tongue-in-cheek and immediately revealed that he was in a playful mood, and during these times he could be very amusing. My drums seem to fall apart for a moment and then we go back into the beginning theme fading out with what I consider to be some truly inspired moments.

3. MIRROR MAN (TTG VERSION 15:43) - This is the session in which I was told afterwards I had been given LSD in my tea by someone. Actually, it must have been a rather small amount, because I didn't find myself too far from reality, it was just as if I had a bit of extra energy and confidence this particular cut. I did come in two measures early, but one of the rules was once we started no one could stop a take. That's why there are a lot of blunders left in the recordings. Alex plays Doug's role in this version and the part, instead of coming in on the "two" count, comes in on one. I don't know if he originally conceived it that way, or just changed it accidentally. However, the rhythm interaction between the guitar and harmonica is completely different than the original and it gave me the feeling of walking down a hill in shoes with gum on the soles. It never bounced the way it should in my opinion. We "muscled" our way through this and that's the way it has always felt to me. I thought Don's performance on this was particularly good especially when he would sing into his harmonica mike and switch it on and off to get that "shattered glass" effect. Actually, this was Don in his element, because he loved to improvise and could usually come up with things spontaneously that he could never do by "rehearsal." At one point, Jeff seems to want to start the "Doug" type out-of-tempo-and-key type playing and then he just stops. I would say this piece is like trying to bring a woman to orgasm when she's watching TV. It never achieved close to the same sound as the original, nor did it even begin to capture the commitment, and was more like a tease. Afterwards, listening to the track in the studio, I thought it was the greatest thing I'd ever heard. Later, after the effects of my drug induced state, I heard all the beating around the bush by the entire band and the sections of lousy displaced drumming and, frustrated, wanted to do it again. Don's final utterance *Mirror Man* with the little cough, sums it up for me. This is a big package with a tiny gift inside.

I MAY BE HUNGRY BUT I SURE AIN'T WEIRD - THE ALTERNATE CAPTAIN BEEFHEART RECORDED NOVEMBER 1967. RELEASED JUNE 1992.

1. TRUST US (Take 6) - So, now I have to go back and listen to the *Safe As Milk* CD version of this just to see which take is which. Why didn't somebody bother to put what take was used on the *Safe As Milk* version? Maybe THAT'S why they never bothered to pay the band one penny in royalties. Oh, there it is right in front of my face on page ... good grief, number the damned pages please. Well, it's on the page with Richard Perry's picture in the little booklet included with the CD. Maybe the reason I never got the royalties is because I never forwarded my new address. Oh well, why couldn't they have done two takes of a shorter piece? Actually, both takes have their moments. I think there is more group vocal participation in the other (Yes, dummy, as I compare the two, there are NO group vocals on the other track). So, as I listen and compare, what do I hear? Well, take 6 is a little cleaner performance. I think we had trouble deciding which we liked the best even back then. I think Don's vocal is certainly better on this cut. One thing I notice is how much the drums drag throughout all the TTG sessions. I was using huge sticks on drums tuned really loose and trying to play far far too loud. This is the resultant feel and clumsy outcome. Big mistakes! Can we get the guys together and do one more take? One thing I just noticed that I had forgotten, the slowed-down *Abba Zaba* in the over dramatic no tempo section just before the end starting at 4:26. I think the 2 mins, 15 seconds outro is a little much and could have been shortened to about 40 seconds. *"Let the lyin' lie, and the dyin' die,"* and let the song end, please? When I finally do a crescendo thing on the toms and the band thinks it's a cue to end, I don't take my own cue seriously and... oh wait, that's on Take Nine. This is really confusing.

2. BEATLE BONES 'N SMOKIN' STONES - Ooh, I love those strings. I remember Bob saying at the end of the previous night's session, "OK, I got the string players coming tomorrow, so have everything written out, you know these guys are a bunch of squares." Hoo boy, he was wrong. They were very cooperative and Don just sang parts to them and they picked right up on it. The "leader" a nice older fellow in a white sweater said the music reminded him of Stravinsky. It is too bad they're mixed so low in the track, it's hard to hear them unless you know they're there. Jeff plays the beginning acoustically on his Gibson (an acoustic-electric with a mic placed in front). Then the band comes in. I played a "Ringo" type beat just for a change. I wish more of our tracks had been this easy to learn. This was written and arranged the night before by the musicians (drummers don't fall into this category do they? Actually my drums were setup in the studio) and recorded the next day. I love the String bass at the end. The voice Don is using is one he seldom used in the studio and many times was used to sing country lyrics he had made up privately. He actually wrote hysterically funny country-flavor tunes occasionally, the recording of which he never pursued. Anyway, the vocal is sung through his harmonica amp, which is probably a little Fender Super Reverb with four 10 inch speakers.

3. MOODY LIZ - This is a really pleasant surprise. I estimate that I haven't listened to this for 31 years! I totally forgot about the slow vocal that is too long for the first section of the song and so overlaps into the next part. What a weird choral effect! What are those lyrics???

> *Wee little doors open*
> *Her lunar spoon croon n' tune*
> *Rust doth thrust thru sienna slippers*
> *Through hydrangea blue meadows*
> *Babble clabber streams*
> *O' gather the children for thy keeper o' wing*

Sorry, can't hear the last line clearly enough to know for sure, but this is as much as I can recollect after all this time...

Just a supposition here, seeing this all from the other side. I think this whole choral approach and King James English had something to do with the 25th Century Quaker image which Don had conceived and was apparently still pursuing. I just saw this clearly for the first time, although there were clues all along, I never put it together before, being so wrapped up in the music. This may be totally apparent to fans looking from the outside to have seen, but for me, I just noticed the Dutch Masters approach. The fairy-tale like quality is strange indeed. I am just guessing here, but I really think that these lyrics were influenced and even perhaps partially suggested by Victor Hayden, Don's cousin. Especially "*keeper o' wing.*" The original unused lyrics to *Moody Liz* were written by Herb Bermann. Buddah used the wrong title. *Wee Little Doors* was the revised title, I believe.

4. SAFE AS MILK (Take 12) - My comments have mostly directed toward the writing and composition of the tune with the idea. So rather than going into a great amount of detail I'll just say that I think this is a better take with the exception of my completely out of time drumming at (2:32). I get a little upset at the fact that when this was mixed, no one bothered to notice that the two vocals were separate takes and the total morons just turned them both up. Perhaps I should give them the benefit of the doubt and just say that perhaps the background vocals were on the same track and so concessions had to be made (nope, Don's vocal was a separate track). On one take, Don is singing certain words in completely different places. Then on the other take occasionally, he is singing in completely the wrong key, example at (1:07), and at (2:21), when he sings one too many "*Bacon's blue, bread dog eared.*" Then there's Alex's great line followed by my great drum blunder in which I land somewhere in no-no land and have to find the tempo courageously held together by Jeff Cotton, thank you very much. At (4:22), the bouncing ball effect is something Don heard me doing one day and asked me to put in the end, then again, the little clickety rhythm at (4:35) is another beat that I just started doing one day while noodling around the kit. Don suggested that I put this at the end of the "bouncing balls." I had no idea where this came from until a few years later visiting my parents home, I discovered the rhythm was a conveyor belt at the Jacqua concrete plant two blocks from my childhood home. I must have heard it everyday and never consciously assimilated it, but it came out on drums years later.

5. GIMME DAT HARP BOY - One of Alex's favorites and probably an early band collaboration. I know this song was one of the songs on the famous "A&M says it's too negative" tape. Collected in there with *Electricity*, the original, *Sure 'Nuff N' Yes I Do*, and many others, it sat on a shelf throughout Safe As Milk. I would have rather seen this on *Safe As Milk* instead of either *Yellow Brick Road* or *I'm Glad*, because I think it fit in more with the context of those other pieces. Obviously, this song is pretty basic and somewhat reminiscent of Howlin' Wolf's *Spoonful*. Notice how at about (2:00) the harmonica plays the line out of Muddy Waters' *Louisiana Blues* that Don also used on the live version of Sure 'Nuff. The lyrics here should be credited to Herb Bermann.

6. ON TOMORROW - Not my favorite recording of this piece as far as the center section goes. The piece starts in 3/4 with Alex playing a "hammered rhythm" on guitar, something atypical for the time and something Don actually discovered on guitar one night. As far as the intro, only Jerry is not playing in 3, but actually is in 4/4. At (0:36), it goes into typical Beefheart "Delta" feel and stays there but a short time. One thing important to point out in the drumming is at (0:59). I was really proud of this little section although it doesn't sound like much, it was a very strong indication musically of where I was to later go on *Trout Mask* with the drumming. Don's influence is heard on *Trout Mask* strongly, but this was one of the first sections where I was dealing with playing hands and feet independently in a manner that evolved into a strong aspect of my later style. I like everyone's part on this section. Jeff's part beginning at (1:11) sounds like "Jeff" as a creator rather than Don. It's a simple yet obviously unique single string line, almost like a bass part played an octave higher. Brilliant playing on Mr. Cotton's part. Speaking of bass, if you notice, one of the big differences between this music and the music that followed was that Jerry was playing the traditional "single note" bass parts.

During *Trout Mask*, Jerry Handley and later Mark Boston started using finger picks and playing chords on the bass more in line with the style used by the guitarists. This makes for a big change in the sound. I'm not sure again how Don's guitar playing actually became mixed. Also, at (2:24), I always thought that the music momentarily fell apart because of my drumming, but it's actually a combination of things. One is that Jerry was quite late on one note, which put the whole thing a bit behind. This threw Jeff Cotton off, who had an echo part that makes Jerry actually sound early. The drums are actually playing what they were supposed to play, except because of all the other hesitation, I wound up slightly rushing. I feel so much better - 31 years of guilt gone through the marvel of digital technology. The song should have ended at (3:07) in my opinion. That was the original ending and one of the reasons I liked this song was because not only was it well composed, but it actually had an ending. I may have said this already on the other comments for the same song.

7. TRUST US (Take 9) - See music notes on *Safe As Milk* CD.

8. SAFE AS MILK (Take 5) - See music notes on *Safe As Milk* CD.

9. BIG BLACK BABY SHOES - See music notes on *Safe As Milk* CD.

10. FLOWER POT - See music notes on *Safe As Milk* CD.

11. DIRTY BLUE GENE - See music notes on *Safe As Milk* CD.

STRICTLY PERSONAL
Producer: Bob Krasnow
Studio: Sunset Sound
Recorded April 25th through May 2nd 1968
Band Personnel: Don Van Vliet (lead guitar and mouthharp); Alex St. Claire (guitar); Jeff Cotton (guitar); Jerry Handley (bass); John French (drums)

Introduction: I just got the CD to this album, and I am a bit excited to hear it. At the same time, I anticipate the same nauseous nostalgia to inflict me. I don't like listening to the past that much. I don't think it's healthy to live your present thinking about the past. If I didn't feel there was historical significance in submitting as accurate an account of this period as possible, I would put this away and probably not listen for years, perhaps pulling it out for a laugh now and then.

I am sitting with my only copy of the vinyl staring me in the face. It was originally a gift from my father, Thomas O. French Sr., to my mother, H. (for Huldah) Pearl French. On the cover is written:

> For my Wife
> 3 - 22 - 69
> Thomas O. French Sr.
> 530 Ivesbrook
> Lancaster Calif

It's spooky to look at this. My father has been dead for 30 years, and to see this sample of his writing, written 9 years before his death, makes me realize how much time has passed by. It's a rather frightening thought if one is convinced that this life is "all there is."

I'm looking at those stamp pictures and remembering what I can of the photo shoot, done the same day as the alien photo in the foldout. I believe this was over at a building at A&M Records. One thing I truly miss about vinyl is this wonderful space allowed for cover art - nearly six times the space of a CD. Ironically, my stamp is the unique stamp. It looks like Russian writing, and certainly is not Spanish as are the rest of the stamps. Jeff's is from Paraguay, Jerry's is from Mexico, Don's from Costa Rica, and Alex's is Argentine. It's difficult if not impossible to tell this from the CD cover, but the original vinyl can be read easily.

I had never really thought about this before, but the handwriting on the cover is of unknown origin to me. In my subconscious mind, I had always assumed it was Don's writing, and perhaps it actually is, because he did write very similarly to this. This really makes me want to contact Bob Krasnow and see if he can lay this mystery to rest. This could very well, in fact, be Don's handwriting from the actual time of the photograph session. I do know this: Don and Bob had planned to start their own record company. Don claimed credit to the concept (as he claimed credit for just about anything and everything conceivable) of not only the album cover, which I give him credit for, but also the name Blue Thumb and the company logo.

The cover was the original concept for the Buddah recordings which have been released in part and in full under various names (See track notes for *Mirror Man, Safe As Milk, The Best Beefheart, I May Be Hungry But I Sure Ain't Weird)* which I have read were supposed to be called *It Comes To You In A Plain Brown Wrapper.* This is not entirely the case as far as I can recollect. The album concept was always this idea with the cover, the postage stamps, the addresses and the stamp reading *Strictly Personal* which doubled as the title. However, I have gone back and forth on this opinion, and so throw it to the winds, as it truly doesn't matter.

I believe, and follow me on this because I think it makes more sense, that the *promotional* phrase for the album was supposed to be "It comes to you in a plain brown wrapper." The idea is covered more in the text of the book. Van Vliet may have been quoted as saying the album would be entitled with the "brown wrapper" phrase, but he often confused the facts on purpose and other times by accident, to such an extent that anything could have been said in public interviews.

We first heard the album in London, as Bob Krasnow had flown over to the British Isles supposedly to let us hear the acetate. I have to say that Don seemed immediately unhappy with the mixing and editing of the album. This could be in part due to the fact that he was not actually there giving permission to Bob's ideas, and so had to disregard them due to the fact that he couldn't lay claim to credit for Krasnow's manipulations of the tracks.

Since the one thing that bothered Van Vliet more than anything else was someone else who was linked to him or his art actually receiving credit for independent thinking, this led him into the frenzied reaction that followed. This included amusingly calling Bob's work "psychedelic bromo seltzer" when describing the phasing used to create some of the effects.

I tend to agree with Gary Marker that Krasnow's concept of the album is brilliant and timely for the early seventies. The editing makes the album more "listenable" for the average short attention span. The effects were very contemporary, and the overall effect does little to detract from the actual music. It didn't bother me at all, in fact, I liked it at the time (making me Don's temporary enemy) and still enjoy it today for what it truly is. The fact is the album was "psychedelic" in its own right. The very cover (and I am certain these were Don's addresses and words, even if I am not positive that it is his handwriting) signifies that psychedelics were being acknowledged. 5,000 mgs. is a definite reference to a "dose" (although incorrectly stated, mgs. Micrograms should have been used, I believe, as 5,000 milligrams of LSD or "acid" would have burned out the brain of Godzilla (which may be why he really destroyed Tokyo), much less a mere mortal. The return address, 25th Century Quaker, and the song, recorded not on *Strictly Personal* but during the earlier TTG sessions, is the name of the band that Don wanted to initiate and promote originally using Don Aldridge as singer (spoken of in his interview). Of course Don made many promises like this to many people over the years.

1. AH FEEL LIKE AHCID - This track is an obvious attempt to emulate Son House, the blues artist. Don was listening to his album a lot and there is actually a song *(Death Letter)* which starts out *"Got a letter this mornin'"* The voice is absolutely an imitation as is the clapping *(as on John the Revelator).* Alex is playing bottleneck in two different tunings to add the "dualing radios" sound. I do recall this track being recorded in the evening and it seems like it was the same evening we recorded *Safe As Milk.* It may have been done the first day in the studio, which according to the cover was April 25th, 1968. The first harp note (0:36) was done as a result of Don having the harmonica turned upside down by accident, there is a slight pause as he turns it over to resume playing. There isn't a lot to say about the music, which is basically Alex improvising. The guitar music itself is very reminiscent of much of the *Mirror Man*-delta-blues type improvisations. I have no recollection of this song before this night in the studio and am fairly certain it was written in the studio. Perhaps it is included in reference to postage and stamps so as to relate to the cover art in a way suddenly deemed more correct. I recall Van Vliet and Victor Hayden having a conversation about people sending LSD in the mail to each other and to keep from getting caught, they would actually use an LSD in a liquid form to moisten the glue on the envelope. The stamp was then steamed off the letter and licked *("licked the stamp saw a movie")* in order to ingest the psychedelic. Many times the phrase "I dropped acid" was used to communicate this ingestion of the psychedelic, hence the added phrase *"dropped the stamp."* The lyrics seem clearly to speak of a similar situation and the results: *"red blue and green, all through my head"* as the hallucinations began. The lyrics at (1:25) seem to be the drug itself singing, *"send me with a letter Lord, drop me with a telegram, ah-cid (acid)."*

The following lines are probably just filler, with the exception of *"walking on hard-boiled eggs,"* which seemed to be a requirement for being anyway associated with Don.

> My baby walked just like she been -
> walkin' on hard boiled eggs with a -
> mmm, there's a chicken steal an' 'uh -
> mmm, oooh.

I recall Don at this point realizing that he needed to refer to his freshly written lyrics in order to remember what was next.

> *I ain't blue no more ah-cid (laugh)*

At this point, I get the idea that the whole point of this is some comic look at an old blues guy coming on to acid and suddenly "it jes' ain't de same ol' barnyar'." Also, women don't seem to look quite the same in this new world. Don had also been listening to Lightnin' Hopkins a lot during this time, and one of the lines this seems reminiscent of is from a Lightnin' Hopkins' tune:

> *"Momma killed a chicken, thought it was a duck*
> *Put it on de table wid' it's leg's stickin' up."*
> You Got To Bottle Up And Go

2. SAFE AS MILK - Déjà vu for me. Here we go again, re-recording the same tunes in a different studio. In some ways I was more prepared for this session as we had at least had a few days rehearsal in a park recreation hall Bob had rented to get us out of Don's "volume paranoia" with the legal problems he had been dealing with. I didn't like the drum sounds as much in this studio, as I may have already mentioned (about one hundred times so far). However, I sure felt as though Don had at least a little better plan on what to do with the background vocals, and so the whole thing comes off a lot more together than TTG. Don was very upbeat during the vocal overdubs as well as the basic tracks. There seemed to be little negative energy floating through this session, and that in itself was a little difficult for me to get used to. However, once I got through the puzzlement of "Don isn't yelling at everyone, why?" I was able to enjoy the session and actually felt free to do a little experimenting and assert some of my own ideas. (1:41) is the proverbial cigarette cellophane wrapper being crinkled to achieve that "pop up toaster cracklin'" sound. Today, they would first sample the sound at a special studio. Then of course, it would have to be run through a whole rack of effects units to achieve the exact sound. Then it would carefully be layered, via hard disk recording, on the track at the precise moment which would be feverishly debated for hours because one person would want it on *"pop up"* and another on *"cracklin'."* It would then be just like the Republicans and the Democrats in debate, the album would never get released, but at least it would cost 20 times as much as originally intended to *produce* - that in itself being it's only saving grace. At (2:27) you can faintly hear Alex hitting the wrong leading note (probably because he lost his headphones and couldn't hear a damned thing because we played so loud) to go into the following phrase. His overdub covers this up to some extent. I always wondered why this was never fixed (the "wrong note" section erased). (2:56) is the beginning of the meandering final section of this song. (3:26) is the beginning of my conveyer belt replica beat and at (4:01) my bouncing balls get tingled with the psychedelic bromo seltzer (I'm having a little fun here) which did not leave me with a permanent scar of any kind, nor any erectile dysfunction. I do have a fairly clear mental image of Don playing Jeff's guitar around (4:41) and it's starts as the little high noodling which is the resulting sound of playing behind the bridge of the hollow body Gibson guitar Jeff was using at the time. Whoever is responsible, however, it does actually make for a more decent resolve to an ending, which many of the TTG session meandering endings didn't have.

3. TRUST US - As I have already stated, this was, in my humble opinion, Don's answer to the Stones' *We Love You* (which maybe should have been alternately titled, *We Love Your Money*). As I said, I was bothered by this *"the path is the mask of love"* line, because I thought love should not be worn as a mask and certainly should not be used to deceive people for commercial purposes. Here the background voices are tingling in that same psychedelic bromo seltzer (somebody's stomach must have really been upset a LOT - and I think one of them was singing background). Don accused me of sounding "too religious" on a much later recording session (more on that later) and all I can say is - this sounds like a bunch of hooded Satan worshipers candidly recorded after having eaten far too many green persimmons. If this doesn't sound religious, then I'm in an alternate universe. I keep asking myself, "Who is this 'US' the lyrics are referring to?" The band? No, 'cause "ya got ta look within." Aliens? spirit beings? - possibly - (in my best church lady voice) "Satan??" I digress. The vocals on this composition are much better and stronger and more together. I think this song does get over-baked in the phasing dept. I think Bob was "on acid" (he "dropped" man!!) during the mix down. It may be a credit to the engineer that this tape survived at all. At (2:58) the PBS (psychedelic bromo selzer) drums fizzle through another clumsily overplayed solo. One thing I do enjoy more about this take is the fact that there are actually some cymbals in there. Otherwise, in many ways it sounds little different (save the PBS) than the TTG version. At (4:28) I always picture that scene in *Gone With The Wind* as Rhett and Scarlett stand with the ruined South flaming in the background and he becomes repentant of his selfishness. He then kisses her reluctant but succulent lips goodbye to valiantly go and fight for the cause. This is so dramatic it has me on the floor in hysterics when I hear it, with its tremulous *Abba Zaba* chords. Don later made fun of this and other overly dramatic segments of *Strictly Personal,* but I remember him (and myself) as being quite sincere about all this at this particular moment. (5:09) and we go into the final fade, me screaming as I crash powerfully into the finale. At about (6:00) faint whispers rise up from nowhere. What are they saying? Oh, I hear it now, *"Just trust."* The instrumental and Don's vocal fades as these whispers crossfade to finally dominate the track ending at (6:58) … and this song was planned to be our single? Actually, I like the effect at the end.

4. RETURN OF THE "FEEL LIKE AHCID" MONSTER - Meanwhile, we have slightly over a minute of this poor old black blues singer rambling on about his psychedelic experience and the jumbled conjured images it's stirring up in his confused mind. I'm getting a little worried about this guy, is he going to make it home OK? Or, did he ever leave? I'm almost sure he doesn't know.

5. SON OF MIRROR MAN - MERE MAN - Whose idea it was to rename this is still unknown to me, however, I'm sure there is the possibility some Beefheart fans out there know more about this than I do. I think Bob just got a bit "creative" with the title of the song with this '50s monster-movie style title. This was one of the last songs we recorded. I think we had been up all night as it was sunrise outside when we finished. It took forever to get Don set up with his electric flower sifter (I had put a transducer on it), harmonica amp with Leslie speaker, and microphone, and vocal mike and musette, or simran horn, or whatever. He actually sang this one live as we recorded it, and they got the drum sound right also, which took another bit of forever. We were burned out, dead tired, drained, dehydrated. You name it. At (0:27) I hear one thing right away that makes this track work better than the TTG version. Alex is playing the riff the correct way this time, instead of "turned around" as on the TTG session. At (0:39) when Don's vocal enters, this track is cooking better than any of the stuff on the TTG session. This is more the way this was supposed to sound. At (1:24) Don actually comes in one beat late. He's supposed to sing that line on the "one" count, not on the "two." I know this because I was privy to such classified information. By his second line at (1:28) he recovers and sings on "one." At approximately (2:30), there begins a fade, which abruptly ends with a cut to the 3/4 end section of the song (later used in *Golden Birdies*). This area of the track with Jerry's orgasmic slides up the bass and Don's sudden return to the theme captures the spirit of the original recording done at the Carolside house. It also captures the fact that all of us are phrasing in completely different directions and so it is very non-musical and confusing. It sounds to me like I may have done one of my favorite tricks and jerked my head around so much I threw off my headphones, thus making me unable to hear what the hell's going on. I like Don's cock-a-doodle-doo scat ending, however.

6. ON TOMORROW - It just dawned on me that until I looked at this album cover for the first time (at the Trout House when it was first released) I never realized that the title was *On Tomorrow*, just thinking it was *Tomorrow*. I know, big deal, but I get asked questions about stuff even less interesting than this all the time. I have met people who seem to value information on every drop of pee and which location it was shaken off, oh yeah, and how many shakes did it actually take? After all this isn't just anyone's pee, this is Magic Band pee. I digress. At (0:30) is my little drum cue that in four more bars of three, we will go into four. I think I'm getting a little punch drunk, this is my third week sitting in front of a computer writing details about songs I did thirty years ago and I think I'm about to LOSE IT!!!! Anyway, now back and heavily sedated, that little cue I mentioned is also Don's (shit I dunno how I'm gonna get that in there) cue to say the line *"We're all brother's on tomorrow."* Jerry and I were recalling how when we practiced the background vocals, Don kept stressing that we sing the word "tomorrow" as though it were pronounced "tee'- ma - row" with the accent on the first syllable and sang on the downbeat. We had this hammered into our head only to discover Don sang it a completely different way on the actual recording. I wish the drum sound on this had been the same as on *Mirror Man*, which was a much warmer sound. (1:53) I always thought that this was an excellent piece of guitar work by Alex which really adds tension to the piece and sets up the next section so nicely. Is that shades of *Purple Haze* I hear at (3:11)? I always thought this song should have ended at (3:08) and I believe that's the way we rehearsed it.

7. BEATLE BONES 'N SMOKIN' STONES - I am really relieved that Bob pulled out most of the meandering bottleneck lines (we already had that on *Safe As Milk*, right?) and cut to the chase. The backwards guitar is just the same line Jeff plays forward at (0:09). At (0:51) the band comes in and I am really pleased to hear this great tone Alex is getting on his guitar. If you notice, there are some other backwards effects here. Don actually allowed me to experiment a bit in the studio. I wanted to do a backwards cymbal and I also play an electric maraca, my own little invention, just a maraca with a transducer taped to its side (philosophy students will ponder this line for years with the question: "Do maracas really have sides?") You can hear that "crunchy" kind of sound at (1:33) to accentuate "chalk man" - my favorite line in the song. This went together very well I thought. I miss the strings from the TTG session, but otherwise, this gets my vote as best take. This song also gets my vote as one of the top ten. I like it because of its simplicity and the fact that Don's words are dripping with sarcasm about the whole drug / pop-culture in such an accurate and hysterical way. The song has a sense of fun and to me reflects the best facets of Don's personality.

8. GIMME DAT HARP BOY - The timbres in this version bother me a lot. It's too big a sound for this song and the harp is just "too darned loud." It's out of the mix. The drums sound like a trash truck outside, when you can actually hear them. It's a bad sound and poorly mixed. I am going to guess that *Beatle Bones, Harp Boy,* and *Mirror Man* were all done at the same session, in that order, and that this was the last night of the session, which lasted all night. The reason I believe this is because they were all songs that actually required Don to sing as the band played, rather than him overdubbing his vocals. I love the "last word Van Vliet" cha cha ending on harp.

9. KANDY KORN - The drums on this version sound to me like a giant tin-foil balloon. Does this work? I don't think so. This is the second official recorded version of *Kandy Korn,* the third of which was supposedly done at the same session as the Zappa-produced *Moonlight / Poppy.* I would love to hear that. Now, there would be a collector's item. The drums are put through a "limiter" which has the effect of making a recording done in an expensive studio miraculously wind up sounding exactly like it was done on a cheap cassette recorder - and for 100 times the price. The laughing at the end of the intro is Don, doing his somewhat phony (we all have a phony laugh, don't we?) laugh that caused my mother to later christen him "Laughing Boy." Ha! He used to bring that up to me all the time. At first, he was quite perturbed, but in later years, it was like a running joke. The good thing about this take is that you didn't have Buddah Records morons turning up two different takes of the vocal and thinking it somehow was meant to be that way. What about those fantastic power chords that Jeff is playing at (2:10)? Somebody turn up Alex you IDIOTS. Oh, you're on acid? Sorry! Peace man! I hear two of Alex actually, and he isn't playing with himself so well in a couple of places, which shows that his part wasn't completely arranged. It wasn't planned for him to double himself, and this may be why they had him turned down.

10. MEANWHILE, BACK AT AHCID - Bob's final insult (according to Don) was to end the album with this final phrase. My comment? That guy may be saying he ain't blue no more, but I heard different.

TROUT MASK REPLICA
Studio(s): Whitney Studios, Glendale, CA and Ensenada Drive, Woodland Hills, CA
Recording Date: March / April 1969
Producer(s): Frank Zappa
Engineer: Dick Kunc
Band Personnel: Don Van Vliet (vocals, bass clarinet, tenor sax, soprano sax, simran horn, musette); **Zoot Horn Rollo / Bill Harkleroad** (glass finger guitar, guitar flute); **Antennae Jimmy Semens / Jeff Cotton** (steel appendage guitar), **The Mascara Snake / Victor Hayden** (bass clarinet, vocal); **Rockette Morton / Mark Boston** (bass and narration); **Drumbo / John French** (drums); **Doug Moon** (guitar on 11).

Van Vliet wrote a great deal of the parts for *Trout Mask Replica* on the piano, an instrument he had only recently purchased and didn't know how to play - at least in the traditional sense. But that was probably the least difficult step. Don, being an only child and slightly spoiled by his mother, had an attitude that made it difficult to achieve any level of practicality when it came to writing and learning material. I could see right away that Don's idea was to have me put a tape on the reel to reel machine and record endless hours of his struggles to nail the part. He never bought fresh tape, so I was always looking for blank spots, which takes hours. Of course, Van Vliet's inspiration could come at the drop of a hat, so this made for frustrating exchanges between he and I. I finally became extremely perturbed at his insistence that I perform the impossible task of finding a blank spot somewhere on 50 - 75 hours of used reel to reel tape. Most of these tapes were either important demo tapes or tapes that Don had already recorded on. Many of the tapes had been supplied by me and were used tapes my father had given me.

I also had visions of what a new blank tape would mean, if it were bought. Don would get an inspiration, play for an hour, pounding away. Out of that, there would be one five minute segment right in the middle of side one that he desired to use. The rest of the tape would then be useless, because one might just accidentally record over that five-minute segment. Most of the other tapes were filled with Don playing guitar or harmonica or singing for long periods with small segments that were actually used. Many times Van Vliet would play something just for fun without the slightest idea of recording in the studio, just some little funny thing he wanted on tape.

So, I decided in my dilemma to lie and shirk my responsibility as Don's "tape monitor." By this time, I had been organizing tapes for almost two years. Jeff had taken over the poetry and lyrics. So my job was a bit easier. However, with the piano, I could see that Don could easily double the amount of taped information in about two weeks with another 50 hours of tapes. Managing the tapes would then become a full-time job and I would never get a chance to drum. After considering all my options, I believe I simply took the fuse out of the tape recorder and said that it wouldn't work - which was partially true. It didn't work very well anyway, probably because it needed some simple maintenance.

My original idea was that Don would be forced to actually sit at the piano and play things for the players again and again. This would allow him the chance to discover just how difficult it was to actually play something more than once, memorize it, and be able to recall it at a later date. Unfortunately, I also had a book with some manuscript paper for writing music. One day, just on a whim, I was holding the book and started writing down what Don was playing in rudimentary notation. I then left the room and the book was probably on top of the piano. I believe I was downstairs, (the house was split-level, and so downstairs was actually the front of the house, and the second bedroom and bathroom). Don came down with my book in his hand and the ensuing conversation went something like this: "Can you actually play this back?" he asked. "Probably, don't really read piano music, but those are the notes and rhythms you played." I replied. "It looks pretty good, would you try playing what you wrote here?"

My first thought was that this would be a good learning experience for him and I. If Don actually started writing like this, it would be much easier to keep track of, reorganize and find at a later date. It could be labeled and found within a matter of moments. I also thought this would be a chance for me to actually feel like a member of the band during writing sessions. Up until now, I was always sitting for what seemed hours at a time waiting while the guitar and bass parts were created, and then suddenly the drums were added, mostly as an afterthought. It was hard to sustain an attention span. This way, I would be a participant rather than a spectator, which was a nice thought, plus it would familiarize me with the music in such a way that I would be better equipped to drum to the tracks.

To the best of my recollection (I learned that from line from some politicians) I don't recall ever consciously considering writing the music down. However, as we stood at the bottom of the stairs, it suddenly seemed like exactly the correct manner in which to approach the next project. This would limit Don, and I mean this in the best way, to not being able to play endlessly and digress. It would force him to focus a bit more musically thus actually allowing the band to tighten up arrangements. Don was constantly writing, so there was seldom time to assimilate and process what he did efficiently. What's more, trying to learn all his ideas from whistled, sung, and sometimes clumsily played guitar parts took more time than it should. Don was a natural percussionist with a great sense of time, and piano is considered a percussion instrument. It all made sense.

So it was that I climbed those narrow stairs, sat at the piano and struggled for a few moments to play what I had written as Don closely studied what I was doing. Within a minute or so, I was playing the section of music I had written down. Don had been playing an endless series of repetitive ideas, and I had only captured a measure or two here or there of the essence of what he played that seemed worth remembering.

Thus was vaguely established the new method of communication and creation. I would be the "keeper of the notes" so to speak, and would then play the parts back to the individual players. I believe the first song written was *Steal Softly Thru Snow*. I vaguely recall that particular writing session, but it seemed to be like each song took between an hour and two hours to actually complete. Thus I would imagine that Don spent between 40 and 50 hours at the piano writing the *Trout Mask* ideas rather than the fictional 8 ? - the number that appeared quite often in interviews. Sometimes, this number was the hours spent writing *Trout Mask Replica*. Sometimes, it was the number of octaves in his voice - which seemed to fluctuate considerably, from $4^1/_2$ to $8^1/_2$ depending on by whom he was being interviewed. Actually $4^1/_2$ is the number of hours we spent laying the instrumental tracks to *TMR*. I think the $8^1/_2$ hour myth was probably a misconception that grew from the fact that Fellini's $8^1/_2$, one of Don's favorite movies, was on television one evening during this period.

At first the process was slow, but then I caught on to Don's piano style and would actually sit and play along with him in a higher octave. Then, I would have him wait for a moment, and I would write down the part, playing it back to myself a couple of times. The rhythms were the difficult part, but I had been previously practicing writing down rhythms and much of what Don played fell into similar patterns after a time. I remember Bill once walking up and saying, "Wow, John, you're getting really fast at writing this stuff down!" I took this as high praise from a musician who I to this day greatly respect. As Don would play the piano, he would often "play" the sustain pedal as though it were a bass drum, like tapping his foot to keep in time. I would use his pulse to prescribe what beat a quarter note would receive. His resolution would generally be sixteenth notes or eighth note triplets over this, which I referred to as "straight time" or "shuffle time" as I taught the parts back. Also, if you notice, there was almost always conventional harmony in Don's early work. What I mean is for the most part the *Safe As Milk, Mirror Man,* and *Strictly Personal* material had a tone center. Now, often the tonal center from part to part might change.

It was my observation that this was highly dependent upon Don's attention span that particular day. One day, he might have a more centered focus on what was his vision for a composition. Other days, it seemed more scattered.

As I listen to these songs, I will probably start with *Steal Softly Thru Snow* and go to *Dali's Car,* and then to *Hair Pie* to remind myself of just how this all started. Since it was 32 years ago (at the time of this writing), it is not that easy to put it together.

Since I didn't know much about piano music, my transcripts involved a couple of strange aberrations. First, I didn't employ key signatures, because I didn't know how, first of all, and secondly, because Don wrote so atonally that the question "What key is this song in?" was never asked. I always employed the use of accidentals (flats and sharps) to indicate whether a note was a black key or a white key. Second: I had no idea of what a bass clef was or how it differed from a treble clef, so the left hand parts (which are written on a different staff) are incorrectly written in treble clef but two octaves lower. It is musically "incorrect," yet in later years Art Tripp among others, would use the *Trout Mask* charts in reading situations with no problem. Other than this, there was another series of problems which began to surface as time went on ...

One was that different length parts had to be played different numbers of times in order for the people to wind up at the same place at the same time. If I am playing a part three beats long, and you're playing a part 4 beats long, then I'm starting my second "one" on your "four," my third one your "three," and so on. In order for us to end at the same time, we must do a number of beats that has a common denominator. For instance, 3 and 4 both divide into 12 equally and so every 12 beats there is a "touch-point" as I referred to it or the end of a cycle and the beginning of another. If you're listening to the other player as is common to do in music, it's really easy to get confused and start altering your part. For instance, if Bill said, "I like dogs" at the same time and in the same tempo Jeff said "I like dogs too," it would look like this:

Bill: I   like dogs I   like dogs I   like dogs I   like dogs I ...
Jeff: I   like dogs too I   like dogs Too I   like dogs too I ...

If you look closely, you'll see that the top line says it's part four times, but the bottom part, because it is longer, only says it three times in order to wind up at the same place in time. The last "I" is the first I of the second set of parts. The cycle is completed just before this point.

This can be further complicated by adding a bass part in five...I like dogs too much!

Bill:	I	like dogs I	like	dogs	I		like	dogs	I		like	dogs	I
Jeff:	I	like dogs too I		like	dogs	too	I		like	dogs	too	I	
Mark:	I	like dogs too much I			like	dogs	too		much	I		like	dogs

As you can see, Mark's part, " I like dogs too much" is incomplete the last time as he still needs to say "too much,' which means he either has to stop after his third "dogs" or the other guys need to keep talking for a while.

To find a common denominator for this, I would just multiply the number of words (or beats) in each line times the next:

Thus: 3 times 4 times 5 equals 60.
Bill   plays 60 (total beats) divided by 3   (the length of his part) or twenty times.
Jeff   plays 60 (total beats) divided by 4   (the length of his part) or fifteen times.
Mark plays 60 (total beats) divided by 5   (the length of his part) or twelve times.

If this seems a little confusing, it is at first, but after doing it a while, it becomes easier. The basic explanation here became easy to figure out after a while, but there were constant variables that came into play. The most basic was that if someone else had a little more dominant-sounding part than yours it might make you lose your concentration, thus causing you to forget where you were. So, the guys usually first practiced their parts individually until they master them, then got together and played, basically only focusing on their part and the *pulse* or *tempo* of the piece.

Another analogy would be counting by twos to a number out loud while some one stood next to you counting by fives to a different number and someone stood next to them counting to yet a different number using sevens. All of the counters had to count out loud and with as much conviction and force as possible without getting lost.

Sounds difficult? Well, try this: as soon as your three people end their counting, they all immediately start counting to another number using a different system - and when they get to end of that section on to another with a different set of parameters. You do this for twelve different sections. All in a common pulse, without making a mistake, and each time the variables change and each one of you must memorize the order of these variables to the point that you can do them almost unconsciously and without thinking about it. This requires even more concentration

Sounds difficult? Well have about eighteen or so of these compositions that you must memorize and rehearse until they become second nature - each composition containing up to a dozen different riffs - often in different time and key signatures.

A Word About Guitar Tunings And Equipment

Because there are so many songs on this CD and I was very pre occupied with transcribing music, teaching it to the musicians, and writing and rehearsing drum parts, I can only vaguely recall the guitar tunings employed on each song. I can tell you that we used Acoustic brand amplifiers. They were, I think, part of Zappa's stage gear. Acoustic is a terrible name for these amps, as they were totally solid-state and had no warmth or acoustic tonality at all, with the exception of the bass amp, which I thought was exceptional. Bass needed a cleaner louder sound, and Acoustic amps provided that. The "house" recording of *Hair Pie* was done with those amplifiers. The same applies to the Studio recordings with the exception of Jeff Cotton, who at one point decided to switch to the little Silvertone 6-10 practice amp. It was a tube amp and had a warmer sound. I suppose a guitarist listening to the tracks closely can tell which tracks were done with which amp, but I can't.

When I mention tunings on guitar, I should explain to non-musicians that although there is a standard tuning on guitar, there are also "slack key" or "open" tunings which are usually employed when using a "slide" or "bottleneck" on the guitar (a metal or glass tube slipped over a finger and used on the strings to get a sliding sound). These tunings were usually open "D" or more commonly open "G" tuning. Sometimes a "Dropped" D tuning was used, which means that the low (fattest) E string was tuned down two half-steps to a "D."

STRING G	STANDARD	DROPPED D	OPEN D	OPEN
Sixth	E	D	D	D
Fifth	A	A	A	G
Fourth	D	D	D	D
Third	G	G	F#	G
Second	B	B	A	B
First	E	E	D	D

These are the basic tunings to the best of my knowledge that Bill and Jeff used on TMR. Notice that "open D" actually has the notes of a D major chord and "open G" has the notes of a G major chord. This is so when the slide is held across all the strings, a major chord is always formed.

One of the difficult jobs of the guitarists was constantly re-tuning their guitars to all these different tunings. To complicate matters even more, a capo was sometimes used (ex. on Moonlight On Vermont). A capo is a bar that can be temporarily fastened on the neck of the guitar to hold the strings down on any fret, acting as a "sixth" finger and allowing the guitarist to employ "open" string sounds otherwise un-achievable in certain keys. One of the reasons Bills guitar has such a bright sound on *Moonlight On Vermont* is because he is using a capo up high on the neck with an open tuning.

Often, when learning a song, the guitarists would discover halfway through the piece that Don desired them to play a slide part, which demanded a different tuning. This meant re-tuning the guitar and re-learning the entire piece up to that point - using up valuable time. Also, in the studio, the instruments had to be re-tuned after almost each take, as everybody was physically playing really hard, which stretched strings and knocked the instrument out of tune. I think we planned it out so that there would be a minimum number of re-tunings to slack-key tunings during the sessions. On stage in performance, it was best for the guitarist to have spare guitars tuned to each tuning, so that rather than re-tuning on stage, they could simply swap guitars and go directly into the next tune.

Bill's main guitar that I recall was a crème colored Fender Telecaster. Jeff's main guitar was a Gibson, the same one seen in the Cannes performance. There was also a larger Gibson guitar that Bill used for slide occasionally. Zappa's studio engineer, Dick Kunc, "souped up" all the guitars with special pickups (Gretsch, I believe) and switches that allowed them in-phase and out-of-phase positions, plus special pickup combinations not achievable on ordinary electric guitars. There were no fuzz tones or other effects units used by the guitarists, that I recall. Because of the time limit in the studio, there were barely any tonal changes on the amps.

I believe both guitarists used fairly heavy-gauge round wound strings. Ernie Ball was the brand of choice. Mark Boston used a Gretsch bass. It was a hollow-body instrument if I recall. He played through an Acoustic (brand name) bass amp, as I mentioned before.

1. FROWNLAND - A very strong statement to begin an album with, especially in 1969.
Frownland was written on the piano and was one of the very last to be written before we actually completed the creation stage and began the final rehearsal stage prior to recording. It is not only unique for being the last written and the first track, but it stands out above the cuts in an incredible manner. There is no other single cut on the CD that sounds like this, or that is arranged like this. This song affects me like being snatched from the ground by a giant hand connected to a speeding train. No apologies, no explanation, just "WE'RE GOING SOMEWHERE DIFFERENT NOW!" The first section almost reminds me of an acid-rock cover of a doo-wop song but when interlaced with Jeff's nervously persistent slide guitar and my rather non-conventional drumming, it rockets into another direction. The music was written on the piano as I said, and just from the types of phrases I was seeing, I felt this song was special and much freer. The way Don played the sections, there was hardly a hint of a similar pulse in anything. It was a cacophony of polyrhythms. It was a hundred intertwining conversations edited into under two minutes. I recall the fact that this took a long time

797

to teach to the band. It was exhausting work and I can liken it to running the last mile in a marathon - when you are running on mere will because all your resources are exhausted. You tired, you're hungry, and you need a break, but due to the very meaning of the race, you can't stop now, because everyone is depending on you to finish what you started. *Frownland* is the culmination of this group effort, the finish line, and it always seemed appropriate to me that it came first. One evening, shortly after I had finished teaching (Note: I didn't teach them how to play their instruments - just showed them the parts) everybody the final parts, I walked down the stairs and there standing at the foot were Jeff, Mark, and Bill. They were standing facing each other in a circle playing *Frownland* over and over. These three really had the chance to practice together a lot because they could do these "acoustic" rehearsals at any time without really bothering anyone. To better hear the bass, Mark used to lean the end of the neck against the wall, and the resonation would help him hear the notes. It was much more difficult for me to get time to rehearse and I certainly never went unnoticed when I *did* rehearse as there is no volume knob on an acoustic drum kit, and certainly no way to play it unplugged. The lyrics were usually written at night by dictation to Jeff while standing in the kitchen. With Don, usually the lyrics came first and then the music. I recall being "the target" of a band "talk." As Don wrote the words *"Where a man can stand by another man without an ego flyin',"* he walked over and stood next to me, as if to physically demonstrate his dilemma - causing me to feel a bit peculiar.

2. THE DUST BLOWS FORWARD 'N THE DUST BLOWS BACK - The whole band had been somewhere that evening, I believe it was Frank Zappa's. The notes for this should be the same as the notes for *Orange Claw Hammer*, which is actually my favorite of these two pieces. I can't recall which was done first. Days before, Dick Kunc had come over to visit the house and being an engineer, he spied the Ampex Two-Track tape recorder which I had "defused," sitting in the corner next to the piano. Immediately, he walked over and began to ask questions and Don's reply was "I don't know what's wrong with it, ask John." Obviously, I felt a bit foolish, as I couldn't really explain my secret sabotage of the tape recorder without giving myself away, so I chose to play dumb. "Oh, wow, it has a fuse? It can be fixed? Duhh..cool!" This was obviously close to the time when we actually began recording. Dick had probably come over to hear some of the music in order to prepare for the session. Anyway, shortly after this, and much to my chagrin, the tape recorder was repaired by Dick, who also brought over all the necessary cables to attach it to the amplifier. Back to the night of creation, we had come in from Frank's most likely and it was late. It was seldom that the whole band actually went anywhere together. Usually, it was a couple of guys going out to get groceries, or Bill driving up to the desert to get money from Marge, his mother. So, this night was a special occasion. Don asked me to run the tape recorder as he had an idea, and I groaned silently to myself, recalling my dilemma as tape-meister. However, I think due to the fact that Don had been disciplined to focus for nearly a year, I was in for a pleasant surprise. He asked me to set up a mike for him, and I set up his old Electrovoice with a cable and stand and plugged it directly into one of the preamplifiers. The unit was an old Ampex two track that we had previously gotten from Bob Krasnow. It had been in the Kama Sutra offices in pre-*Safe As Milk* days. It was actually a pretty hi-tech machine in its day. However, it still sounded great. Don signaled me to "record" and I switched on the machine. As I recall, Frank has suggested him doing a reading of *The Old Fart At Play*. Don read the entire piece into the machine and at the end, Jeff can be heard commenting, "Oh man, that's so heavy." If you listen to *The Old Fart At Play* at the end (1:37) there is an edited cut to this home session in which the faux-Shakespearian voice is heard saying, *"his excited eyes..."* I thought this was the end, however, he signaled me to switch back into "record" which took a moment, because I wanted some blank tape between the end of *Old Fart* and the beginning of whatever was coming next. I switched it on and had everybody remain quiet and then signaled him to begin, and he sang, *"There's old grey with her dove-winged hat, there's old green with her sewing machine, where's the bobbin at?"* and signaled me to shut it off. I recall that there was just one lamp on next to the tape machine in the corner and everyone was kind of gathered around on the floor, facing Don who was sitting on a chair as though he were some aging seaman telling captivating sea tales. I think we were having hot tea.

It was warm and peaceful in the house and there seemed to be no strife. Things had been going well for a day or two, and Frank's renewed friendship with Don had put him in an exceptionally pleasant state of mind this evening which created an amiable atmosphere. He signaled me to switch back to record, *"She's totin' old grain in a printed sack, the dust blows forward and the dust blows back."* Although the rest of the band really got to appreciate these lyrics at the time, I was so intent on recording and running the machine that I really didn't get to appreciate the performance at all until much later. Occasionally, during this session, Don would have me play back what he had just sung and since the machine didn't have a digital display, I would be forced to randomly rewind. This made it difficult to remember exactly where the end was at times, and so it was a bit more complex than just pushing a button. Obviously, this is a brilliant piece. Don later humorously told Frank, "Hey, I finally got to use the word 'Spam' in a song."

3. DACHAU BLUES - Definitely one of my very favorite pieces. A strong statement about the holocaust which is more relevant today than ever - in light of recent world leaders claiming it never happened. Everything about this composition is powerful except the mix, which I think puts Don's voice too far out in the track and covers some great music. You can hear the same kind of anomaly on this track as in *Electricity* at (0:11) when Don's voice temporarily overdrives the tube. It's caused by the same thing. Don was singing very softly at the beginning and then suddenly modulated to a stronger voice and, I would guess, simultaneously leaned into the mike, as was his habit, rather than away from it, as a "trained singer" would do, in order not to distort the mike. There's a lyrical misprint because at (1:01) he sings *"dancin"* and the lyric sheet reads *"danced."* I have been asked if the Mascara Snake played bass clarinet on this cut and I believe the answer is "no." First of all, Victor couldn't play that well, and second, I distinctly recall Don saying that he played Vic's clarinet on that piece. It sounds more like Don to me, because of the phrasing and the tremendous passion in the playing. This is one of those moments when everything Don practiced, he preached and delivered with extreme power. Any "trained" musician would never have found the freedom to play in such a non-musical but completely impassioned artistic manner and the playing speaks volumes about the content and subject matter. I can hear screams of suffering, the silent pains, and descriptions of the cruel environment. I can see the flames and smell the burning flesh. This is a point in our history that should never be forgotten. This piece definitely is not only an artistic achievement, it is a strong political and social statement. The fellow at the end of the piece is the Amway man who lived nearby. He was coming by to deliver some hypo-allergenic detergent, because Don was extremely sensitive to most detergents. I secretly recorded him at Don's request as Zappa loved this kind of candid conversational recording. He later included it on the album. The Amway man was describing a movie set semi-disaster a friend of his was involved in involving rats. It casts an eerie, haunting atmosphere in the context but also tends to lighten the heaviness of the subject matter and neutralize the listener for the next track.

4. ELLA GURU - *Ella Guru* was probably the fourth or fifth song written in the *Trout Mask* piano series. I always loved the opening section of this song, which seemed to have its own peculiar "groove" with the double-time bass and Bill's "dead on" rhythm guitar. The opening drum part was a suggestion by Don to open the hi hat with my foot making a clanging sound, hit it with a stick and close it tightly, giving that jerking, sucking sound. Then, he suggested I do Milt Holland's cowbell pattern from *Abba Zaba* on the toms. This was a perfect blending of patterns and is again one of my favorite moments. Most of the drum parts in the first half are Don's and in the last half are mine. The parts were written on the piano shortly after the Dali exhibit. The lyrics were always vague to me, as I didn't have much time to really think about them, being so absorbed in the music. I loved the title because it poked fun at the whole "Guru" concept. The line *"Hello Moon, Hello Moon"* may have to do with Zappa's daughter, Moon Unit Zappa. As I read the lyrics now, it seems as though it's simply saying that a child's non-pretentious ways and unaffected attitudes make them the best Guru of all. I don't get the part at the end with the Mascara Snake, maybe it wasn't supposed to have been "gotten." "Just dig it," was simply something that Victor used to say all the time. It was his "cool" phrase.

5. HAIR PIE: BAKE 1 - In a sunshine-filled bedroom lined with windows that overlooked the overgrown aloe vera on the hillside, sits a bearded slightly chubby good-humored man facing a card table. Sitting next to the mixers (no EQ, just volume controls) is a small five-inch reel-to-reel Uher tape recorder similar to the ones used for the application of live recording in film-making. Sporting headphones, Dick Kunc's magic fingers adjust the volume controls on the double set of little Shure mixers sitting on a card table in Don's room in the structure amusingly christened in later years the "Trout House" in Woodland Hills. Several plugs accommodate cables which trail from the back of the small black rectangular mixers and are quickly grouped together into a single larger cable, which snakes it's way around the queen-sized mattress and box springs, past the small night stand, out the door, past the magic bathroom door on the right, past the closet "room divider" door on the left and to the end of the room divider, where sits a set of drums, facing away at a 45 degree angle from the divider and the observer. It faces three young bizarre looking men dressed as though for an album shoot that actually won't happen for days. A window to the right of the fireplace looks out onto a covered patio area about 18 feet away, open on the sides, containing a concrete pad on whose center rests a microphone stand and microphone. Two strangely dressed men randomly walk in loosely scribed circles and random patterns around this microphone in what appears to be some bizarre ritual. These men are Victor Hayden and his cousin, Don Van Vliet warming up outside in the bushes. The younger cousin of the Captain is wearing a shower cap on his head and sunglasses on his face. He is struggling a bit with the horn, attempting and sometimes failing to push the large volume of air through the instrument that it demands. The older man is more confident in his beige top hat. There are mikes interspersed here and there in the foliage around the property, some almost hidden from view. The low tones are sometimes there and sometimes gone. Back in the bedroom, Mr. Dick Kunc sitting at his card table begins to roll tape. The horns coming through the headphones are clear, but Dick has seldom heard horns like this. (0:22) Suddenly the Captain's horn seems to be beckoning in expectation as though calling out to some recently discovered exotic animal species. The first sounds Dick hears of the band are from the perspective of being outside the house and hearing the band through the window: this is leakage through the horn microphone. Fingers begin searching for the correct knobs, and unfamiliar with the music he is unaware that he is hearing a drum break and so turns up the knob labeled Antennae Jimmy Semens. The equipment has been set up but no real mix has been achieved. Without warning, (1:57) Jeff comes in after the break at a proportionately much higher volume. The other instruments are still low in the track and the knob labeled Zoot Horn Rollo turns slowly, and more carefully until a match is made. "Perhaps" thinks he, "The drums are leaking into the guitar mikes and that accounts for their presence - no, they're up, why do they sound so dead? Oh, that's right, they're covered with cardboard. Why on earth did he want to do that? Bass is too low, but any change might overdrive the preamps, so I better just leave well enough alone and readjust later. What a bizarre sound. What's this? There's someone talking... I better leave the machine running, Frank will like this." A young Bob Sobo was one of the boys doing the talking. They both later came in and were recorded by Kunc, as Frank interviewed them about politics which they revealed themselves as shockingly precocious...

6. MOONLIGHT ON VERMONT - Through the years, a surprising number of people have said this is one of their favorite tracks. I'm not sure why, but it certainly stands out from the rest of *Trout Mask* in several ways which make it unique. First of all, it is one of the first tracks recorded for *TMR*. Second, it was done at a separate session along with *Veterans's Day Poppy* and, so I am told, yet another version of *Kandy Korn* (Here's a lost session tape I would love to hear). This session was produced by Frank Zappa at Sunset Sound studios in Hollywood in the same studio where *Sure 'Nuff 'n Yes I Do* was recorded. Also, it was NOT written on the piano, nor in the Trout House at all, but in the smaller cottage we lived in prior to the Trout House. The only other song I recall being written in that house in the same time period was *Sugar n' Spikes*, which I always relate to *Moonlight In Vermont*, though it sounds completely different because of the sound. Also interesting to note is that Gary Marker plays bass on this and *Veteran's Day Poppy*. He, of course is one of the uncredited bass players on *Trout*

Mask Replica. The other bassist I will mention on notes for *The Blimp*. At the session for *Moonlight*, when I went into the control room to listen back, I was surprised by the "brightness" of the guitars. I thought it was a bit characteristic of Zappa to make everything sound a little overdone and, if I may use the term, "toylike" at times. This is what I first thought when I heard this track and is a good example of how a producer can totally change the characteristics of a song, until it almost becomes unrecognizable to the writer. When I heard Bill's guitar part in particular, I thought it had the, "Wow gee mom, check out my new fuzztone" sound. However, the sound grew on me and after a while I really found I liked the guitar sounds. Part of the reason for Bill's sound might be because Frank was engineering from the perception that there was a "lead" guitar and a "rhythm" guitar, and simply because Bill was playing more single-string bottleneck lines, this cast the vote that he was "lead guitarist." At least on this piece. The song starts with a drum part that is basically derivative of *On Tomorrow's* opening drum part. This is the first song that we played when Frank Zappa came to the house and heard the band the first time. I can say with all surety that I don't care for the drum sound at all, and went through the same problem (at least in my head) as I did during the *Strictly Personal* sessions (also done in the same studio, as was *Alice in Blunderland* and *Booglerize You*. There's something metallic and "fake" about this sound. I like drums to sound deep and full, and these drums sound like old spittoons - tinny and shallow. However, this seemed to be a characteristic sound of this room and I blame it on the assistant engineer as much as Frank. I would have much rather had the Mirror Man sounding drums (from the *Strictly Personal* session, when they finally got it right). See notes on *Strictly Personal, Mirror Man*. Marker came to rehearsals at the house, and rather than go into all of that here, I will leave it for the context of the book. He has some interesting comments on Zappa in the studio. The lyrics I believe may be partially accredited to Victor Hayden, at least his influence. There are certain things that he found extremely "hip" at the time, and he was always talking about things to Don during his visits that had to do with funny names, a lot of which are used in this song (and also in *Sugar n' Spikes*,) eg. Mrs.Wooten and little Nitty. This song seems to be referring to the "looniness" that the full moon brings out in people. However, I always thought that this song had a bit to do with witchcraft also. The reference to *"old time religion,"* ("old time religion" is what authoress Sybil Leek claimed witchcraft was referred to by it's followers, in her book *Diary Of A Witch*) may be one clue. Another was the fact that I never heard these particular (lines at the end) until the session. Frank encouraged Don to sing this, and Don had told me on numerous occasions that at one time, both he and Frank were deeply involved in Black Magic and Witchcraft. Another is a fact that the cycles of the moon seem to play important roles in witchcraft rituals. Mostly, however, I consider it to be funny observations of the effect of the full moon on people's lives. I have seen this time and time again in myself and in others. My favorite line is *"Somebody's leavin' peanuts on the curbins (?) for uh* (instead of 'a') *white elephant escaped from zoo with love."* The vision of someone worrying about an escaped elephant's daily food requirements has always struck me as funny. Especially by leaving peanuts on the curb. Important note is that the line *"Come out to show them"* was from a Stockhausen electronic music piece. In the piece, the phrase, "Come out to show them" was spoken by a young man describing what I recall as a violent event. The recording was processed in such a way that it began to slowly "echo" itself over a period of time, the end result being something completely indiscernible as a human voice. This was one of Don's favorite things to listen to during the *Mirror Man* rehearsals. I think it is one of Don's better vocal performances, as he actually put some thought into this before the session, which was not the norm, as often he sang the track for the first time in the studio and unfortunately by then it was too late to fix any arrangement oversights to accommodate the lyrics more successfully. One thing that shocked me was that the night before we recorded this, he walked out in the living room and asked me how I would sing this to an old track we had (probably a home demo). I did, and I was surprised to hear him sing a lot of the same words and notes in the same places. As far as the song in general, I always felt a good feeling from performing it. I also thought it was one of the more accessible pieces. The drum-parts, which are mostly Don's ideas put together in part from things he heard me do in jam sessions, are unique and caught Zappa's attention immediately. The rhythms always remind me of tap dancing.

7. PACHUCO CADAVER - I can claim creation of the title here. It came from a time when Alex Snouffer came to rehearsal a little sick. He looked extremely pale, and in his younger days, he was a Pachuco, so I told Don he looked like a "pachuco cadaver" that particular day. I didn't say this to put Alex down or even in a humorous way, we were both a little concerned. However, Don's eyes lit up and he immediately wrote down this phrase. The lyrics and song didn't come until about a year later. The music starts with a pretty solid shuffle, except - what's that annoying sound - the bass? The bass seems to be taking a similar role to Jeff's guitar in the intro to *Frownland*. The first drum part is Don's famous "shuffle" rhythm, which he used to occasionally sit at the drums and play. It was an unorthodox approach in which the feet both played on the down beat along with the snare. The only thing played on the "upbeat" was the open hi-hat with the left hand. At (0:50,) the piece takes an unexpected (only if you haven't heard anything else on this album) turn into three-four tempo. At this point, I basically play what I feel and respond to the rhythms of the other players. The lyrics in this section seem to speak of a female from the pachuco era who has become an anachronism. She seems a tragic figure who lives in the past. Yet she is portrayed in a comic setting. I especially like the line *"Yellow jackets and red debbles buzzin' round 'er hair hive ho."* Because all the women used to wear these "beehive" hairdos and amphetamines were popular during this era according to what I heard from both Don and Alex. Zappa and Don seemed to particularly understand the meaning to this song more than we band members did, because we were not of that era. These descriptive lyrics seem to spill over into the next happier music section at (2:12) that happens after a short interlude. We are almost playing carnival samba-esque type music here. The first line that I recall that was actually planned for this section was *"her lovin' makes me so happy…"* in which the poem takes a sudden optimistic turn and starts bestowing virtues upon this formerly tragic figure in the guise of a love poem. Perhaps this song refers to Zappa's teenage years when he had a Mexican girlfriend who lived in Rosamond. The band used to rehearse at her parent's house, and she would make tacos for everyone. I love Don's drum suggestion here which alternates between my original part combined with his fast "shuffle" punctuated by highly muted cymbal crashes. Another thing about this piece that adds a little sparkle is the modulation to a different key at (2:48). At (3:06), it modulates back to the original key and is joined by soprano sax which was overdubbed at the vocal sessions. The band happened to be there that night and Don had trouble knowing where to come in, so Jeff (I believe) cued him. When he started playing, he was in time with the track, but slowly, he began to rush, so that he was a little ahead of the track. He came into the studio and asked, "Did I do alright?" (The humility and openness of this question was unfamiliar to all of us - and was perhaps influenced by Zappa's presence.) Of course, we didn't know what to say, should we mention it's out of time, only to have him say, "I meant it to be out of sync, you moron!"? Did he in fact actually mean for it to be "out?" I don't recall him wearing headphones and maybe this was one of the moments Zappa was referring to in the BBC Beefheart biography when he said, "He refused to wear headphones during recording, so he could only hear vague leakage from the control room, rendering him slightly out of sync with the track." Re; the ending - it is obvious to me that we knew nothing about when to stop on this piece.

8. BILLS CORPSE - This is a piano composition probably created around the fall of 1968. When Bill Harkleroad joined the band, he had come out of an LSD cult. I believe the cult-master's name was Fred. Fred had talked Bill and the other members into going on a diet that was appetizingly called "The Mucus-Free Diet" or something to that effect. It was a process by which one gradually eliminated all the foods from their diet that could promote the formation of mucus. Eventually, the lucky participant would whittle his diet down to the simple (and inexpensive for Fred) intake of one apple per day (to keep the doctor away, I suppose). This eventually had whittled Bill down to 120 pounds or so, maybe less. He was 6'4" tall and looked like a hat stand when he first joined the band. It's not hard to figure where Don came up with this title. However, as with much of Van Vliet's lyrics, I find them more puzzling than not. The irony of these lyrics is that Don created the environment in the Trout House that he surrealistically describes here. However, rather than seeing himself as a creator and contributor to this environment, he would conveniently step outside the disaster area and observe it as though entirely detached and as though we were entirely to blame for the low morale and unhappiness that resulted primarily from many of Don's indoctrination sessions. On a larger more objective perspective, he is perhaps viewing the United States (*'oh her ragged hair was streaming red, white and blue'*) and the natural beauty that it once held by portraying it in the form of a young girl. The bloated dead fish metaphor may be some horrible experience from his childhood or the loss of his pet fish, "Hotcha." The plains bleached with white skeletons suggest a nuclear war or some other holocaustic experience in an almost' Dali-esque setting. I have always been intrigued by the line *"Various species grouped together according to their past beliefs,"* because it not only seems to refer to the gathering of the Jews in Germany but seems almost prophetic. It seems to refer to an event of biblical proportions that could happen sometime in the future. I was puzzled at Don's inclusion of the out of time blundering drum part (unless he was trying to tie it into my sometimes terrible drumming on *Mirror Man*) until I heard the lyrics, "That's not the way I'd like it to get together" and realized that it was intentionally put there to emphasize the lyrics. Occasionally, he would surprise me with some little embellishment like this.

9. SWEET SWEET BULBS - Lyrically, this imagery-laden description of a simpler Utopian time and the wholesome sexuality seems to reflect upon what a mess things were in the sixties and how far from nature we'd gone. It could also be images of a child's optimism shattered by reality and it's recently discovered hostile environment. This ties into Don's experience when his sculpting world was snatched away and he was given in trade the severity and starkness of the Mojave landscape, complete with violent Marines. In a sense, it also ties in with the counterculture movement and the whole "back to nature" mentality, cleaning up the environment and living a simple more honest existence. I remember thinking that I wanted to do something unique with the drums and so I wrote the first section part out very carefully. I couldn't play it very fast at first and I recall having my drums set up in the downstairs bedroom practicing this part very slowly. During this time, we had some young visitors who used to come to the house. They were high school kids and they would show up sometimes alone, sometimes in a group. I recall that Don sent one of them downstairs to ask me, rather arrogantly, why my drumming sounded like a "marching cadence." Inside, I was really upset with Don for doing this, but I explained to the kid that a lot of things sound different when they're slowed down and when it was played up to speed it would sound quite different. I spent a lot of time explaining how I created drum beats and how I was working on a new style of drumming. He was a saxophonist, so he understood what I was talking about. I wish I could remember him and his friend's names. It seemed like this helped him to understand better what was going on and I felt good about the way I handled the situation, frustrating though it was. Most of the time, if I felt that someone was being sarcastic or arrogant I would bite their heads off. I suppose the incident bothered me the most because Don knew that I was really stressed about catching up on all the tunes, and I had very limited time to practice. On this track about (1:03) Don had me play a part using the bells of the cymbals. I remember listening back after he added his vocal and noticing that the words, *"tinkling like mercury in the wind"* were added right at this point. Another nice embellishment that surprised me. Most of the drum ideas after the first two sections are a couple of patterns Don suggested and near the end I play a counter melody similar to the beginning guitar part employing cymbals.

10. NEON MEATE DREAM OF A OCTAFISH - I only wish you could see Victor Hayden's fantastic painting that went with this piece and was supposed to be the album cover of *Trout Mask Replica*. It is done in a similar style to the *Bluejeans And Moonbeams* cover (which Don told me was the "only good thing" about the entire album). I always have wondered at the incorrect article "a" purposely used in place of "an" in the title. Lyrically? Your guess is as good as mine. I asked Don about the meaning and the answer he gave me was something akin to "an organic view of the earth." It also suggests "wet dream" to me, perhaps "wet dream on lots of LSD" might humorously be a better description. This song is filled with strange images and funny word associations. Also, what the hell is a "fedlock?" It strongly fits with John Peel's description of Don as a "verbal prankster." I think he had taken a rather non-serious approach to this particular piece and it seems childlike and playful to me. I believe that until *Frownland*, *Meate Dream* may have been considered for the opening track. Compared to *Frownland* however, the music was weak in comparison, at least the recorded version. This song had less powerful lines (than *Frownland*), and much was single-string lines as opposed to chords which didn't translate as well to the guitars. However, Mark Boston's bass lines were so good that often Don would request him to use this as his solo piece in place of *Hair Pie* during live performances. I was disappointed in the fact that the music was buried so far beneath that Simran–horn-run-through-a-Leslie-unit overdub. One of the reasons, I believe, was that I arranged this one slightly differently than most of the other piano tunes in that there are no "touch" points where everyone changes at exactly the same time into a new section. Everyone is changing randomly and at different points. This does not mean, however, that the piece was not arranged. I carefully planned each part from beginning to end so that they would begin and end together, and we are all playing to a common pulse (unlike *Frownland*, which is more a free interpretation and bordering on chaos). It's just that from point "A" to point "Z" everybody is on their own, with no touch points to let them know whether they were at the right point in the song. It required more concentration than many of the other pieces to play skillfully, and yet it was basically thrown away and buried in overdubs.

11. CHINA PIG - During the latter days of *Trout Mask* rehearsals, Doug Moon showed up for a couple of visits. I know that things were rough for him after he left the band, and it was good to see him in better times. I actually envied him. He was driving an emerald green MG fastback. It was interesting to have him walk into this environment, because it really pointed out to me the contrast of what the early days in the band were like (less than 2 years previous). This was recorded, I believe, on a portable cassette recorder (they had just recently come out) that had been loaned to Don by Dick Kunc. Doug was sitting on my "sleeping area" which was a full-size mattress folded up against the wall so half of it was a "back" to lean against. It was covered with a madras throw. He was sitting next to the fireplace and just playing guitar. I have no idea whether this was his guitar or a guitar at the house. I seem to remember him bringing a guitar with him. Years later, Doug seemed to feel that Don went to special trouble to make sure he was credited as "special guest artist" - perhaps to make up for dumping him during the *Safe As Milk* sessions. That may be true, but Captain Beefheart takes credit for writing "all songs" on the album and it certainly is an oversight to consider that "play one of those pa-chunk pa-chunk things" entitles him to musical composition credits. I point this out in spite of the fact that it's a minor point because, (to repeat myself) little pieces of all the Magic Band members creativity and influence are interspersed through all the early albums. The music here is obviously Doug Moon playing emulations of the blues artists, the most apparent influence (to me) being John Lee Hooker, whose voice Don also emulates. Aside from that technicality, I believe that the lyrics were already written as Doug and I both recall Don reading them off a sheet of paper. Once again, these lyrics are incredible. The scenario I used to suggest to Don was to write 12 songs like this with band arrangements and record an album. It would have taken no time at all for Don to write 12 great blues songs with his amazing creativity. A month later, it would have been on the stands and easy to perform on a tour promoting the album. He would have reached a larger audience, and made some money. Then, the band wouldn't have had to be supported by Sue, Don's mother and Marge, Bill's mother. I have never heard a Beefheart fan say that *China Pig* was a "commercial copout" and I believe that this would have been a "win / win" situation for Don, the band, and the listeners. One of the reasons I wished to leave the band, and did so many times, was that Don insisted (selfishly I believe) on doing music so far out from the norm, that it provided no means for us to supplement our lives and pay the rent. This did indeed make him appear a "musical genius" to the public, but did nothing for the band member's lives. *Trout Mask* set a precedent and crossed a line that could never be re-crossed successfully. Three albums later Don would attempt what I was requesting all along, and fire me from the band just prior to doing it. *Clear Spot* was an album that came as close as any to actually accomplishing what I suggested. However, it was out of order, and should have been written after *Safe As Milk*. Out of order though it was, it still provided Don with the highest commercial success of his career since *Diddy Wah Diddy*. Doug Moon's performance on this album shows the influence of the Delta Blues in the early band. His influence, as I mentioned in the musical notes to *Mirror Man*, can be widely heard and felt pre-*Trout Mask*.

12. MY HUMAN GETS ME BLUES - One of my favorites and one which got a lot of live performance mileage. This is one of the very early compositions I would refer to this as a "hybrid" composition in the sense that it was written partially on the piano, and partially from notes on the soprano sax, and partially by singing parts to the band, and partially by whistling. This song has mostly Van Vliet drum parts. The intro is Don, the next part mine, and the rest basically his. You will notice the one guitar is just playing the low / high, low / high notes and those notes were played on the sax for Bill to play, the other parts being written on the piano, along with most of the rest of the song. After the intro, the song basically stays in 4/4 until the section at (1:06) which provides a radical change and is one of my favorite sections on all of *Trout Mask*. Jeff and Bill are both in 7 while Mark is playing a long classic phrase in 3/4 with an ending in 4/4 that repeats twice. I'm playing a part in 4 that Don actually played on the drums and is simplicity in design yet ties everything together quite well. It's the perfect part. This section is like a series of small merry-go-rounds sitting on a larger one and they're all twirling at slightly different speeds and every seat is a great seat. No matter what your perspective, this whirls you around never allowing you to fixate on anything except the lyrics, which are the only thing vaguely familiar on this terrain. As the merry-go-round screeches to a halt you're suddenly back in a more blues-based riff in 4 that allows you to catch your breath, but suddenly it stops (1:33) and a single guitar modulates downward, downward, hits bottom recovers and returns to the riff. The drums fluctuate and then the listener finds himself (aren't all Beefheart fans guys?) (2:01) in a swirling, steaming blue-green clearing; a heavenly rest stop, filled with unearthly delights. At (2:19) comes the determined resolution, the amends are made, and you are invited into another land filled with promises of acceptance. I think one of Don's favorite lines is *"like an old navy fork stickin' in the sunset"* because of the surreal quality of the image.

13. DALI'S CAR - The second song written on the piano and absolutely one of the more enjoyable times writing a song. We were using a candle for light and it could have been for one of two reasons, either the electricity had gone out due to a rainstorm, or the rest of the band members were asleep on the floor. I believe, however, that during the time of *Dali's Car*, we had moved some beds downstairs and actually had a bedroom that the three of us (one slept upstairs because there was only room for three beds, I think also Mark was not yet with us) could use. Anyway, it was late at night and Don came in with a bunch of vegetables he had purchased at the Farmer's Market (I think this was our "Mucus-less Diet" phase). Don asked me to get my manuscript paper and we started in on this song. Van Vliet seemed actually very focused on this piece, as compared to other times. He would later call this a "study in dissonance" and it indeed was. Since this composition was written for two guitars playing at slower tempos, the parts don't repeat as often and also the lines are a bit longer. I believe the reason he wrote for two guitars is because Jerry had just left and had yet to be replaced. Rather than do a section by section explanation of this song, as it really explains itself and needs nothing further in the way of verbal inspection, I would rather just describe what he had seen. We had been to the LA Country Art Museum and had been privileged to view the work of Salvador Dali, an outrageous Spanish surrealist painter/sculptor. This probably influenced all of us more than any other single event. I could go into depth here, but I just wish to describe the car. It was a Model A Ford, four-door (a "Bonnie and Clyde" type twenties car) sitting on a rather large outdoor balcony, or perhaps a portion of the roof. I remember coming from an elevator and going through a glass door. The car was sitting in a giant metal pan about four or five inches deep to catch the water. The water was pumped from the pan up to the ceiling of the car when it then was allowed to "rain" down on the passengers - two female mannequins and a host of snails. The car was a rotting rusting ecosystem filled with plants of several varieties, mostly non-flowering. The vegetation had taken over the car so that the whole effect of warm, moist air with that wonderful smell of fresh soil engulfed you as you approached the car. The snails crawled uninhibited up the mannequins legs and arms, the windshield of the car (most of the other windows were rolled down) and everywhere else they could gain a foothold. Some of the snails were just shells filled with oil paint, the end was sliced off with a razor. Victor Hayden, who was with us, took great pleasure in this particular detail. "The way he just squeezed the paint into the shell and sliced it off cleanly with a razor blade," he noted. "So severe." The whole effect reminded me of one long adventurous childhood bicycle ride several miles from home. My friend and I wound up on a small dirt path behind a grove of trees that marked the rear perimeter of an alfalfa field. There, hopelessly mired in a shallow and partially dried-up irrigation ditch was a late 1940's car that had been abandoned years before. In this partially shady and unusually moist little spot in the desert, birds and other animals (mostly squirrels) along with plants had taken refuge within the half open doors. Branches of Cottonwood saplings had forced their way up through the darkness of the engine compartment, their fingers sometimes slowly prying the rusted cover up sometimes poking holes through the thin rusting sections of the hood. It was a celebration of life. The car, this carcass of an artificial alien life force, was being slowly re-assimilated back into its basic elements. Back at the museum, the warm smell that came from this car of Dali's, and the ironic smiles of ecstasy on the faces of the unknowingly endangered female mannequins who had snails crawling in very provocative areas, gave it at the same time a humorous and surreal aura. So this song, *Dali's Car*, speaks volumes to me about this day. The dissonance brings back the warmth and the smells and the expressions on the faces of the mannequins. What a great day, what a great artist, what a great composition.

14. HAIR PIE: BAKE 2 - This is the take that was done in the studio. Cardboard on the drums again, but no horns. I wish that one of these takes had drums without cardboard. I would like to focus on the drums on this song, because it was the first song where I started actually "writing" drum parts in musical notation which were far above my musical abilities and challenged me to rise to the occasion. Don's drum ideas, although good, never really posed any technical challenge to me, and as a player, I needed that challenge to help me grow. *Hair Pie* was the song on which I began to actually struggle to achieve a higher level of playing. I was very dissatisfied with my drumming on *Mirror Man* and *Strictly Personal* for the most part, but had a vision of where I wanted to go. This vision was enhanced by the influence of Salvador Dali, who, unlike Don, believed that a certain amount of technical ability must be mastered before one can actually begin to accurately express one's self. Looking at his paintings there were two things that really struck me. One was his mastery of the classical "realism" which his "surreal" objects manifested. Another was his ability to put real objects into such an other-dimensional setting that they seemed at times to actually share the same lines. I wanted to somehow achieve this on drums, putting two and three unusual rhythm patterns together and playing them simultaneously as though they were one "drum part." The only way I could envision doing this was to actually write down what I wished to attain and then struggle to learn it. As I wrote, my early parts were sometimes too dense. What I mean by this is that they actually were impossible to play because I didn't have enough arms and legs. So, I began taking out redundant or unnecessary notes and streamlining each part to the bare essentials. After a few attempts at this, I was able to develop the ability to write playable parts with little or no revision. I also started writing parts that were very sparse meaning only one drum was being played at any given moment, rather than two or three. I would usually write a part like this when the music to which I was playing was already really dense (example is *Wild Life*). I tried to write my parts with the same kind of rhythms, or complimentary patterns, as the other instruments, although sometimes I would veer off and just play something that "seemed right" although it bore little in common with the accompanying music. This composition is important to me personally in the respect that it was the beginning of me really beginning to develop a drum style that wasn't just senseless pounding or mundane and boring rhythms to "keep time," but carefully planned challenging phrases that would give me a little respect in the drumming community. One observation is that at (0:51) seconds the bass part that Mark is playing the bass part to *When it Blows It's Stacks*. More on this in *The Spotlight Kid* musical notes. The end on this performance is incorrect. Bill came in late and so played one extra section of his last part. Also I stopped early. I was supposed to end with Jeff and Mark. At (2:02), you hear Bill stop for a moment and come in after waiting a phrase. Since he is playing in 6 and the rest of us were in 4, we lost where the cycle started. I stopped early, because I felt like we needed to do another take of this piece. The sleigh bell "tin tear drop" was added by Don as a "band aid" to fix this error. He was shaking sleigh bells as Dick or Frank turned the motor off on the tape deck while leaving it in "record" mode. As the tape slowed down it continued to record, but the analog information became more compressed on gradually shorter and shorter bits of tape. When played back, it had the effect of "speeding up" because although still playing at regular speed, what had been recorded was on a shorter and shorter section of tape. Sort of a musical version of the "Doppler effect."

15. PENA (INTERLUDE; FAST 'n BULBOUS) - I found this to be a pleasant little surprise when I listened to the master tape for the first time at Zappa's house. Zappa is coaching Victor Hayden on the correct way to say the lines. Unfortunately, with The Mascara Snake (I believe "The" was his first name, was it not?) there was always an underlying current of nepotism and the natural resentments that occur as a result. Victor was obviously getting "special attention" and receiving "special privileges." However, this little dialog always made me feel happy, because it presented people having a good time. *Pena*, however, is another story. When Jeff Cotton started becoming what Bill Harkleroad refers to as "The Paper Monitor" ("The" not being *his* first name), Don would have him recite this particular poem over and over in the evenings to the rest of the band. This voice may seem obnoxiously cute the first couple of times, and the words hysterically funny. However with all respect to Jeff, after hearing this recited dozens of times over a series of several months, I could never hear this recitation again and it would be too soon. Zappa took an immediate liking to Antennae Jimmy Semens. He barely knew Jeff Cotton and certainly had not been subjected to nearly the number of readings as the rest of us, so it was more of an enjoyable experience for him, I'm sure. I believe that this recitation was at Frank's suggestion. This song (music), surprisingly enough was originally entitled *Foxanne* and I always thought the title was a little too "Jimi Hendrix." Zappa had heard Jeff recite *Pena* and thought it would be beneficial to have this on the album. After hearing Don attempting to sing the *Foxanne* lyrics, he suggested the reading of Pena by Semens. It was one of the few times he asserted "producer authority." Actually, the music to this never impressed me much aside from the first bass part, which is definitely fast 'n bulbous. The poem Pena was actually one of a series of oddball stories Don had dictated to Jeff during the rehearsals for *Trout Mask*. There were several other characters who never made it to the golden pages of fiction although the "drazy hoops" are mentioned in *The Blimp*. Most memorable to me was "the girl who smiled a lot." The only thing you knew about her was that she just smiled a lot. Don later said, after he met Jan, that she was actually "the girl that smiled a lot." Actually, Jan was a beautiful girl and DID smile a lot. There was usually some mention of *The Old Fart* in these stories also. I wish I could remember more of the characters. Big Joan was in many of them. Also, *"sorta thread with the drooped body,"* which may have been based upon tall and amazingly thin Bill. One story had Drumbo in it. In the story, Drumbo was climbing a ladder to a large pot in which he was frying the giant letters D-R-U-M-B-O out of dough. I may be wrong, but I believe I was the only band member used in this prose. At the end of most of these stories, or at some strategic spot, Pena would usually exclaim, "That's the raspberries." Most of the stories were really more like twisted children's stories, innocuous enough, but just slightly tilted. Don always said he would publish these stories, but unfortunately that hasn't happened yet. They were some of his best writings and I found them enjoyable.

16. WELL - I always thought of this as a "psychedelic field shout". Perhaps "intensely enlightened" might be a better word for now. This is definitely one of my favorites. It is another song that was done on the Ampex two track after Dick Kunc fixed it. Don was standing on the stairs of the Trout House? part of the way down on the landing (I knew so well). The mike was a ways off from him in the room.

The reason? I'm not sure, except maybe to get some room sound. However, I believe the "echo" heard on the track was added in the studio and is just reverb. The lyrical meaning is pretty clearly just a group of images and a feeling more than anything else. I strongly believe this particular poem is probably a series of images inspired by Salvador Dali's paintings. My favorite lines, *"My mind cracked like custard..."* *"The white ice horse melted like a spot of silver..."* *"thick black felt birds..."* this is phenomenal writing brought to life with an incredible voice. What it's referring to is probably best left to the listener to decide.

17. WHEN BIG JOAN SETS UP - I never really liked this piece much. In fact, I almost hate it. It has a lot of spirit, I suppose, which is why Don insisted on playing it live and playing it endlessly with a lot of jagged soprano sax. I watched him clear many auditoriums with this song on a US tour in early 1971. It's two sections and a lot of improvising and repetition to me. I found it boring to play. The words are great and I'm sure there are many out there who can empathize with poor Joan and her low self-esteem triggered by all these physical abnormalities. The words were appealing, but the music spoiled the effect by going on and on and on onstage (how's THAT for redundancy). I always felt like Big Joan was perhaps Don's view of himself *(hoy, hoy is she a boy?)*. He was always a bit uncomfortable with his weight, which sometimes fluctuated to embarrassing levels. Also, being large-boned and in an industry where rooster-thin Mick Jagger was the norm may have made Don a little insecure about his stage appearance. Big Joan was a character that showed up in the *Old Fart* series of stories mentioned above in the *Pena* notes. They were always talking to each other and doing simple childlike things. We recorded the instrumental tracks to *TMR* in 4½ hours and the longest delays we had were (1) when I broke a drum head and (2) when Don decided to play soprano sax on *Big Joan* and the snail-like setup that ensued as Dick set up a mike and Don chose just the right reed. It seemed to take forever, and I was starting to get nervous that we were going to go over Zappa's allotted time.

18. FALLIN' DITCH - Rockette Mortons's funny intro with Laurie Stone laughing in the background always perked me up on this one. This is typical "art of farting" Mark Boston. Don's humorous "on tape" cueing *"say 'laser beans'"* brings it into a very personal setting. Mark was basically the most well-balanced of us all in terms of being comfortable with who he was and I always have happy memories and good thoughts about him. He learned his parts quickly and well, and played them with phenomenal power. He was very limber and his fingers could stretch unusually far. He would try any insane non-conventional method to make a part work and never thought in terms of "conventional music." This intentionally contrived patter between Don and Mark is always fun for me to hear and brings a smile to my face. The good moments like this were few and far between in the reality of this period. Too much serious discussion and not enough fun were the norm. However, this shows the side of Don that kept us around. *Fallin' Ditch* musically is one of the more forgettable songs in most people's thoughts. I never hear anyone say *"Fallin' Ditch* is my favorite."* It wouldn't be included in any "best of" compilation. The lyrics seem to be being determined to win against the many faces of death. The different type of failures and obstacles that can stop most people who are not strong enough to persevere. Don's spirit of determination seem to really shine through here in the alter-ego guise of the personae or main character of the piece. He faces the *Fallin' Ditch* with a real thought of optimism. It is a piano composition from beginning to end. I enjoyed writing the drum parts to this, especially the end, because the rhythms the guitars played made for a "groove" and there were few in this music. Listening to this, it seems as if the end were written first in one session, and then the beginning was added later. I perceive that some of the drum parts were of the "written type" and some were more just responding to what was happening musically. If you notice, the non-melody guitar is playing a part very similar to the bridge of *Abba Zaba*. I remember hearing a tape recording of Don interrogating Jeff Cotton. One of the lines was, "are you trying to commercialize my music like John did with *Fallin' Ditch?"* That is probably why this song, out of all the others, skyrocketed in the charts...

19. SUGAR 'N SPIKES - I get the oddest associations with this song. Many of the Beefheart songs remind me of not so happy times. For some reason, *Sugar 'N Spikes* always leaves me with an air of contentment, peace, serenity. It seems like this song was written around Christmas of 1967. We were living in the little cottage before moving to the Trout House. I was writing rhythms on manuscript paper, and drinking egg nog with brandy. Don was a little more at peace with himself and so the tension level in the environment was down several points to a decent level. I always associate this song closely with *Moonlight On Vermont* because musically, the styles coincide time wise although they were recorded in completely different studios with completely different instrument timbres. I believe the lyrics were written back at the chicken coop house and the drumming is definitely a holdover from more the *Mirror Man/ Strictly Personal* era. The lyrics periodically remind me a bit of Victor's style of words and I think that his influence may be heard in phrases like "navy blue vicar." Don requested the crazy out of time drumming near the end. I love it. Aside from that, this song is relatively conventional compared to most of the rest of *TMR* and always seems like it should have been on *Mirror Man* in my mind. Note that the musical line underneath *"pies steam stale"* and the same line again under the crazy drumming is lifted straight from Miles Davis' *"Sketches Of Spain."*

20. ANT MAN BEE - This music was written at the point where Jeff had temporarily left the band and Don had persuaded Alex Snouffer to return for a short-lived reunion. We started working on this song the first evening Alex showed up. Don became very upset at the three of us (Bill, Mark and I) because we couldn't quite understand what the hell he wanted us to do. This was not unusual, as Don had a strange way of communicating his rapid fire ideas and expecting us to be able to assimilate them and put them together in such a way as to work as a unit. This was not written on the piano, at least the parts Bill, Mark and I played. This drum beat is called the P-K-Ro-P and it was played by Don on the set earlier in the day. It is a BRILLIANT perfect 4/4 balanced rhythmic delight. Probably one of the top three or four of my favorite songs because the words are so clear in meaning, and I happened to like things in those days that were more understandable. Now that I have read more, I can appreciate some of Don's more abstract lyrics. Uhuru supposedly means "Love" in Swahili according to someone. Actually, wasn't it the name of the communications person on Star Trek? Although I don't care a lot for the horns on this number for the most part, there is a soprano solo at (3:20) that is particularly good in my opinion. I say this so that the reader has a sense of what I find to be good music as opposed to just rambling, blundering nonsense. Ironically, this is just at the point where I go into an alternate drum beat which Don wrote. It doesn't have the lightness of the first beat and therefore sounds clumsy and awkward in context. I like the horns at (2:02) for a short time up to about (2:19). The line at (2.39) is nice. Don wrote Bill's and Mark's parts the night Snouffer rehearsed with us, and I know that Jeff didn't have parts for either this song or *Wild Life*. I'm not sure of Don's methodology for creating Jeff's parts. However, I always considered Jeff's parts in particular on this song as some of the best on the album. I love the wild abandon with which he played.

21. ORANGE CLAW HAMMER - I love this brilliant piece so much that I actually memorized it almost immediately after hearing it. I also requested that Don perform it in the 1975 European Tour. It was recorded as I mentioned earlier in same session as a home reading of *The Old Fart At Play and The Dust Blows Forward* and *The Dust Blows Back*. There is something so completely unique about this piece. When Don was finished with it, he seemed as surprised as the rest of us. It was totally unlike much of what Don was doing in those days. However, when he wrote, he often dictated to Jeff or someone and they would write down what he was saying. Jeff happened to be the fastest at printing, so Don would usually use his services. When finished with the last line, *"Flow out water, salt water."* I stopped the machine and he looked rather distant and said something like, "I've never done anything like THAT before." I mentioned that in the concentration of recording, I didn't get much of a chance to enjoy this piece. In fact, the band in general didn't get much of a chance to enjoy much of anything we did in the same perspective that the outside world did. We were too close to the subject matter. There's a few strange anomalies in the lyrics and one that always catches me is the contrast between *"Come little one, with your little dimpled finger, gimme one,"* and later when it says *"and here it is I'm with you, my daughter 30 years."*

22. WILD LIFE - Another favorite of mine, (how many am I allowed?). If I remember correctly, Bill's guitar and Mark's bass parts were written on the piano, and I wrote my own drum parts. The parts weren't written for Jeff as he was gone when this was written (like *Ant Man Bee*). Jeff's parts were then written later if I remember correctly either by Don singing them to him or playing them to him on the piano. I was pleasantly surprised one day as we rehearsed to find that Jeff had this whole series of parts I'd never heard. I love the way they "float" on top of the music in places, especially the opening. The horn solo that starts at (1:00) until (1:10) is one of my personal favorites along with the *Ant Man Bee* soprano solo. These to me are musical, they work with the music and they are still "out" in terms of being avant-garde. My taste is more specialized in that I don't truly care for a lot of Don's horn playing, but enjoyed these particular snippets very much. The lyrics are pretty clear in this song, portraying a man similar to the "minuteman" mentality in a sense. It's almost prophetic of the ATF fiasco at Ruby Ridge. Yet, there is a sense that this man is less paranoid and more realistic. *"They got m' mother's father n' run down all my kin,"* signifies that some kind of pogrom is actually going on here. A corrupt government, a military coup and the resulting pandemonium that is possible are all hinted at. It's also got a bit of humor in the line, *"talk the bears in tuh' takin' me in."*

23. SHE'S TOO MUCH FOR MY MIRROR - Don described the opening music to this as "a showboat kind of thing." Very odd words to me at the time. However, it describes the opening very well. I think that this song had something to do with his ties to the south, the roots of his family, and the fact that he had a hard time accepting his mother. I remember him saying things like, "I told my mother when I was young, 'I'll be Don and you be Sue'." He always called his mother by her first name and would seldom ever even refer to her as his mother. He had a really hard time accepting that I would call my mother "Mom." Didn't bother me - lots of boys call their mother more endearing terms than "Sue." Anyway, the song seems to have three sections, was mostly written on the piano, and most of the drum parts are mine except for the hi-hat rolls that go with the bass and the fact that the pick-up notes (sorry non-musicians) are left out of sync almost in a comic-way as if to make fun of them. I always got the image of dancing girls like the Rockettes on board a showboat, tripping over each other's feet and falling down, the audience in tearful laughter. Lyrically, I have always been intrigued by Don's near-obsession with mirrors and mirror images. Especially *Mirror Man* and the importance to him of that track. I am only guessing that it has to do with Don's intensity with the experience of eye contact. He would sometimes avoid it and then other times use it almost as a weapon. Frank did exact a sweet revenge here (although a different song order would have made this work better). Frank left Don's words, "Shit, I don't know how I'm going to get that in there" at the end of this take. This I believe was in retribution for Don insisting on leaving Frank's, "I gotta go back to work" line in *The Blimp* - saying "I caught ya!" Don always claimed that he "played" while Frank only "worked." It also reveals what happened quite often when Don tried to make his words fit the music in the studio and discovered to his dismay, that he was lost, which happened quite often. This was a sore point among all the bands and was pointed out especially by Artie Tripp in the studio.

24. HOBO CHANG BA - Wow! First off, what a title. This is one where I think the music and the lyrics really were in sync with each other. There is no way around the fact that this is one amazing piece. Don used to speak as a young teenager in Mojave of going down and hanging out with the hobos. He said they were really nice people and he got to know the regulars. They used to make "mulligan stew" in tin cans and he tried some once and said it was pretty good. He must have had some contact at some point, because this song talks about the experience as though he had done his homework. The solo guitar intro to this always gave Bill fits. He would practice it and practice it. It is not a comfortable thing to play on guitar, because the notes are so randomly placed. At (0:03), the band comes in with a part most likely whistled to the guitarists by Don, (and, if you are familiar with the seventies TV show *Chips*, you will notice the synthesizer is playing almost the exact same notes and getting the same effect) and then the bass and drums take off with a piano-composed section. Note Jeff's great part at (0:19). After the breaks, the part that comes in at (0:39) really gives the feel of sitting in a boxcar going about 50 mph through some country area. At (0:49) is the whistle, first done on guitar, and then joined by Don on soprano. (0:59) brings in a more "bluesy" feel. (1:20) is another new section which ends with a chordal ascension similar to one of the jazz songs we'd been listening to - a Joe Henderson piece. The voice is reminiscent of the African singer on John Coltrane's *Kulu Se Mama*. I can just imagine a hobo lying in a boxcar on the wooden straw-covered floor, being bounced around, listening to the rhythm made by the wheels thumping over the joints of the tracks.

25. THE BLIMP (mousetrapreplica) - *The Blimp* was given birth in a manner that reminded me of *Beatle Bones 'n Smokin' Stones* in that there was a sudden and clear inspiration, and it was finished that night. Don called Frank on the phone at the studio and told him that he had this thing he had to do right then. The beginning, *"Master, Master,"* was a takeoff on the lunatic librarian in the Bela Lugosi version of *Dracula* who was eating flies and going more and more insane. Since it was through the phone, it sounded a bit like someone talking through a fly's ear. My image of this song personally was that what really was going to make anyone rich in rock 'n' roll had nothing to do with intellectuality and everything to do with sexuality. The blimp, of course, being an "ultimate symbol of male virility" not unlike the Captain Beefheart name itself. I have read reviews that said this had something to do with the Hindenburg. That is ridiculous, Don knew fully well the difference between a blimp and a dirigible. However, the feel of this is a little like the famous description by the journalist of the Hindenberg disaster especially in the intensity of the voice and the telephone line cheap quality of the recording. The music on The Blimp was neither written by Don nor played by the Magic Band, but is something that Frank was working on in the studio at the time. It just happened to be the tape on the machine when Don called, from what I recall. I would guess that Artie Tripp (making his first Magic Band appearance) is on drums and Roy Estrada (likewise making his first Magic Band appearance) is on bass. At that time I believe the other drummer was Jimmy Carl Black (the Indian of the group) and he may have been playing the toms heard on the other track, or perhaps they were overdubbed by Artie. You can hear faint piano that was probably Ian Underwood. There is a voice faintly discernable under Zappa's "You ready?" which may be Art or Ian counting off again. You can hear them again at (0:31). At (0:48,) Don can be heard in the background on the phone playing his soprano like a fox-hunting call. At (1:43) Jeff says, "That's it!" in his normal voice and hands the phone to Don. The music almost sounds like a lounge act in the background. As we listened to this back in the studio, when Frank said his last words, "I gotta get back to work," Don nearly shouted, "Ah ha! Gotcha!" and laughed. Frank looked a little surprised. "What?" he inquired. "You said you gotta go back to work. I never work, I just play, man! Ya GOTTA leave that in!" Frank, rather reluctantly complied. However, see notes to *Too Much For My Mirror* to discover Frank's revenge.

26. STEAL SOFTLY THRU SNOW - This is the first song for this album that was written by Don utilizing the piano. I point out that this wasn't the first song chronologically, because that would probably be either *Moonlight On Vermont*, or *Sugar N' Spikes*, which were both written before we even moved into the Trout House. Also *Veteran's Day Poppy*, was written shortly after moving to the Trout House, however, it was also written employing the former methods and so does not qualify as a "piano" composition. First section (0:00): If you notice, even in the opening line, there is something different about this piece than anything on *Safe As Milk* and almost anything on either *Strictly Personal* or *Mirror Man* cuts. It has two guitars playing in two distinctly different time signatures. For the "musically challenged," I'll say one part is "longer" than the other. One part is 3 beats long, the other is 4 beats long. The bass part in the first section is actually Don's left hand accompaniment to one of the guitar parts, Jeff's in this instance, who is playing the part that is 3 beats long. However, the bass part is 4 beats long, because Don played an extra beat with his left hand. These two guitar parts (and the bass part) are in the same tone center (key), so it works harmonically, but tends to throw you off a bit, because there's nothing really to "groove" to in the sense of overall feeling. That's why I chose a simple "1 e", beat (if you divide a beat up into four little parts, time wise, you get a count "one-e-and-ah" and I play on the first two little parts, "one" and "e.") Mostly, this is what I played to Mark to teach him the bass rhythm (there were no drum parts to this when Jerry was in the group) and it seemed to "push" everyone just right, so the drum beat wrote itself so to speak. Since the parts are two different lengths, if you fixate on one thing, the other goes off on a tangent and this does a funny thing to the mind. It breaks a big rule in music and certainly it isn't the first example of this, as Stravinsky employed the same technique (less often and much slower) in his early works at the turn of the century. However, it was probably the first time a rock band had done this while employing electric instruments.

(0:11) The second section has everyone in the same time signature as the lyrics come in. However, the effect of that beginning, and the fact that everyone switches to a completely new section along with the first lyrics doesn't have that much of a settling effect. About the only thing normal about this section is the permutated Latin beat I am playing. However, the unsettling effect of the beginning leaves one feeling slightly out of sync and disoriented.

(0:32) The third section goes from "straight time" to shuffle time and the guitars are playing in two different keys, although the parts are in the same time signature (the same length) as is the bass part. This again has an unsettling effect on the listener.

(0:43) The fourth section goes into a double-time 3 feel. By this, I mean that Don was tapping his foot twice as fast (one beat for every two before) and also playing parts only 3 beats long again. A three feel always has an image of "rolling" and the words "a nothing wheel" precede this.

(0:54) The fifth section is harmonically and time-wise very conventional and was taken from one part which every one plays bits of at the same time. By this, I mean all three instruments are playing bits of one measure (4 beats long in this case) of music that Don wrote at once, right hand playing melody and chord and left hand alternating between tonic and fifth. He often employed either a "staggered alternate" approach, where he would play back and forth, (et. al right hand note, left hand note, right had note... etc). or he would play the same rhythms with both hands at the same time. This is an over-simplification, but these were the two methods I would employ when attempting to "replay" something that Don had just played, or created. In this case, he was mostly playing the same rhythm with both hands, with the exception of a couple of double time triplet notes on his right hand. I played a really normal type shuffle beat here. Most of these drum beats I made up on the spot and they were originally intended as time patterns to hold everyone else together, not really thinking in terms of a unique drum "part." Don referred to this section as a "Dance" and was really anxious to hear how it would sound. Now, meaning in the present, I would probably arrange this differently and make the high note line stronger by not inhibiting Bill's part with any chord, just allowing him to play single strings to pull the melody part of the line out more. Jeff is playing the "second part" so to speak and I suggested to him to use "Wes Montgomery" octaves (playing the same note on two different strings an octave apart) and this overpowered Bill's line.

(1:03) The next section, there is no Bill Harkleroad (who always got a chance to duck out for a quick smoke here). Jeff Mark and I go at it. The bass is a slow descending line repeating on a pulse of 4 and Jeffs line is punctuating and repeats every pulse. The simplification here allowed me to be a bit more complicated rhythmically. I decided to divide the pulse by two, hence two beats per pulse. Then, to take it one step further, I divided that into 3 parts played 4 times, playing 2 beats, then resting a beat, playing 2 more beats, then resting a beat, playing 2 more and resting, and playing 2 more but making the second beat on the floor tom (instead of the hi-hat) thus ending the phrase and starting again.

(1:13) This section has no bass (thus Mark's turn for a quick smoke) and the guitars are playing in what sounds like relative keys (according to Don "everything goes with everything, man" but I am referring to more traditional views of music in order to relate to a wider group) or even the same key. I decided to play more conventionally here and accent their parts.

(1:21) Next is two piano parts, Bill and Mark play right and left hand respectively, and Jeff is playing a separate part. They are all in the same time signature. The drum part is sort of a "backwards delta" beat, like if I took a measure out of *Mirror Man*, looked at it in the mirror, and play what I saw reversed in the mirror.

(1:30) The next section is two parts. Jeff and Mark are playing one part, right and left hand respectively, and Bill is playing the other. I play even more conventionally here.

(1:42) The next section: This is one of my favorite sections of the song because you have Mark playing this wonderful bass part that is almost a melody, and you have both Bill and Jeff playing these intertwining accompaniments on guitar which gives this steaming cloud effect. The lyrics refer to rain and rainbows. Everyone is in "4" here except me. I chose to play in three to keep it more consistent with the rest of the song.

(1:51) The last two sections are in 4 also and more conventionally tone centered.

(2:00) The last section at the very end, has the rapid machine gun opening and closing of the hi hats (Don's only drum contribution to this tune) which corresponds with the line, "*Man's lived a million years and still he kills.*" Don quotes the closing line in the wake of this bizarre rock composition. "*Steal softly thru sunshine, steal softly thru snow.*" What a beautiful piece of poetry in which the subject expresses his heartbreak about the rape of the natural beauty of the earth. This piece alone was worth all the trouble.

27. OLD FART AT PLAY - This song was never intended to have these lyrics. This is the only other time I saw Zappa aggressively put on his "producer's hat" and assert his will on Don. The original title to this song was *My Business Is The Truth, Your Business Is A Lie.* Don mentioned later in conversation at the house that the reason Zappa didn't like the lyrics was because it was in essence, hitting "too close to home." In other words, Zappa felt convicted by the lyrics because in Don's opinion, "Frank's business was a lie." I think the lyrics were originally inspired by Bob Krasnow, or Kama Sutra, or perhaps just by anyone in general who had power and an opinion that differed from Don's. We of course never heard the original lyrics because Don never rehearsed with the band. However, we were well-acquainted with the lyrics to *Old Fart At Play* because Don had Jeff read this innumerable times at the Trout House. The music was one of the earlier pieces done and was written shortly after Bill got in the band and possibly before Mark was in the group.

28. VETERAN'S DAY POPPY - For the benefit of those who aren't familiar with the US holiday, Veteran's Day is a day of which the veterans of the various wars are honored and appreciated for their service to the country. The Veteran's Day Poppy is a small poppy, usually an artificial flower in the form of a pin. It is sold as a fund raiser for the benefit of Vets in general. I'm not sure where the funds go or how they're distributed. The lyrics to this were written on a single sheet of paper and it very well could have been Veteran's Day, but I believe it was actually written in the spring or early summer before Bill Harkleroad joined the band. I recall that it was unusual to see lyrics written in Don's own handwriting, because he was so used to having someone else write stuff down for him. I'm talking lyrics, because Bill says that the music was written after he joined the band and he wasn't in the band until June. This is the other tune done at the session with Gary Marker on bass. It was Gary who suggested the shuffle at the end of the song just before the slow part. We were a little concerned (Gary remembers Jeff especially) that Don would be upset by us adding this section to the song. The night we rehearsed this, I had a date with a Beverly. She came to the house and Don immediately started writing drum parts that took what seemed like forever. All those weird sections in the end and the funny double time rock drum break. Frank had taught Bill a "cool" chord on guitar, and that was used in the last section of the song. I remember Don discussing the song in the house with Victor as we rehearsed in the tiny laundry shed. I came in the house for a break and he was saying something like, "Listen to that man, I'm so limited in what I can write with these guys. All I can do is this montage shit." The lyrics typify what many mothers who lost their sons in wars feel - "*It don't get me high, it can only make me cry.*" Anti-war songs were very popular during this period of the Viet-Nam conflict. However, as a Czech friend of mine once said: "Sometimes you have to pick up a gun to fight for freedom."

Conclusion

So, what does *Trout Mask Replica* mean to me personally after all these years? I'm not sure. Going track by track through this entire album was a little painful at times but mostly I am still in awe of some of the statements made here by a man who never had any formal music training. No matter the exaggerated claims on training musicians, or writing the entire thing in 8 1/2 hours, taking credits for parts he didn't write, arrangements he didn't do, etc., it still remains the overall vision of Don Van Vliet aka Captain Beefheart. It is one of the most influential groundbreaking albums ever recorded. There are textures, shapes, and colors, rhythms, chord combinations, and other departures from convention never before heard in rock music. Even if Mr. Van Vliet had been completely honest and told exactly how the music was put together, it is still an extraordinary feat on his part.

There is a sense of sadness that the psychological chemistry (or whatever the hell you want to call it) was such that the *Trout Mask* band couldn't stay together. It was like an unstable chemical formula that got bumped and suddenly erupted in a violent explosion. The actual band that recorded *Trout Mask Replica* only performed once on stage and there are only a couple of eyewitnesses that I have spoken to about what it meant to them. One was Denny Walley. He said that Frank was standing off to the side listening the whole time in direct view of the audience. Now Frank was quite famous in those days, and his approval or disapproval of something could either make or break it. He stood in strong approval of his friend "Donny's" band and this says a lot for his friendship towards Don. The other observer was Art Tripp. His thought at the time was that "this was it." Later, in spite of the fact that musically, he considered Don to know little about what he was attempting to do, and "not a true composer" in the defining sense, he still is just as impressed as ever.

Frank Zappa deserves a great deal of credit here also. Months after this album was released, Frank walked onstage in Belgium and told the audience to listen to this man's music, because "it is important." Don and the Magic Band then proceeded to play the strangest music these people had ever heard. Frank was extremely supportive of the band and especially of its leader. Frank also said that some credit should be given to the players, because they were being asked to play stuff that was "wrong" (musically breaking a lot of rules) and so had to work really hard to do it. I appreciate this comment and I am sorry I never got a chance to thank Frank personally before he left this world.

Trout Mask is a timeless work. It has little in the way of "dated" symbolism so typical of 60's rock. No bong-water boogie can be found here. The abstract quality of the music and lyrics lends mystery to this album. It will never be "explained" nor will it ever be "understood" in the traditional sense. It is an intermingling of a brilliant vision, people's unrewarded efforts, and reflects a selflessness and uniqueness which may never be matched, and its creation and birth is probably one of the strangest stories in "rock" music history. For those who "get it," it always leaves you wanting more.

LICK MY DECALS OFF, BABY
Studio(s): United Recording Corp. Sunset Boulevard, Hollywood, CA.
Recording Date: Summer 1970
Producer(s): Frank Zappa
Engineer: Dick Kunc
Band Personnel: Don Van Vliet (Vocals, bass, clarinet, tenor sax, soprano sax, chromatic harmonica) ;Zoot Horn Rollo / Harkleroad (guitar, glass finger guitar) ;Rockette Morton / Boston (bassius-o-pheilius) [sic]; Drumbo / French (percussion, broom), Art Tripp (marimba, percussion, broom)

This is where I would highly recommend Bill Harkleroad's book, *Lunar Notes*. Bill is the expert on *Lick My Decals Off, Baby* because he was the musical director of the band during that period of time. I have read critics who say that *Trout Mask Replica* is Beefheart's masterpiece and I have heard others say that it pales in comparison with *Decals*. What they're really comparing is apples and oranges. Both albums stand on their own, and both achieved greatness in their own way.

I will point out some of the major differences between *Decals* and *TMR*. Number one difference is probably the fact that while *TMR* was largely a transitional album by an artist who hadn't yet really received a great amount of attention and therefore had very limited resources, Decals was by an artist who had received prominent recognition and had some resources at his disposal. While *TMR* was composed through the more limited means of transcribing piano ideas into musical notation, *Decals* was formed by Bill Harkleroad interpreting recorded musical information from tapes made by Don. Where *TMR* was more general in its scope, *Decals* was more focused on environmental issues.

Decals was recorded at Record Plant Studios in Los Angeles at the exorbitant rate of $180 an hour over a period of several days for instrumental tracks (probably 3 or 4, which certainly was an improvement over the six hours allotted by Zappa - for a double album - *Decals* was a single album). Don's overdubs, including vocal, horn, harmonica, etc. took another four or five days. Then, there were several days more for mixing and mastering. So *Decals* had huge advantages, technically, allowing us to achieve a much better sound. Also, the implementation of the marimba cleaned up the sound somewhat, and made what was playing perhaps a bit more palatable in the timbre dept. The difference between distorted guitar and marimba allowed the listener to hear the parts more clearly and also created a less hostile audio environment in which to listen. The similarities between the albums are the fact that both are extremely abstract musically and break many of the rules of conventional music. Also, there is a lyrical content still filled with random images and free-association poetry. There is also the presence of Don's fantastic voice and those strangely disconnected horn solos. There are many *TMR*-type sections in songs, yet there are also longer musical passages on *Decals* that separate it from *TMR*.

The advent of the cassette recorder played a large role in the composition process. Suddenly, there were no longer any bothersome tape reels to wind and rewind. The tape was enclosed in a dust-free and easily manipulated cartridge. Most importantly, the cassettes were inexpensive and small, as was the machine, so this increased portability. So, rather than having a 10 - 20 pound monster and huge clumsy reels to move about, there was this tiny, book-sized machine with even tinier cassettes. Bill could record Don at the piano, and then go off to himself somewhere, undistracted, and concentrate on sorting through the mass of information I am sure he received. Don could go on for long stretches of time playing on and on. Since he didn't play in the conventional sense, analyzing and reproducing his sometimes nonsensical (in terms of conventional music) playing was stressful, time consuming work.

I didn't envy Bill this position, and it was nice for me to actually have a chance to focus on the drum parts. Bill had to learn his and Mark's parts and teach them to Mark, besides finding time to rehearse with the band and rehearse his own solo piece, *One Red Rose That I Mean*. Harkleroad seemed to have no personal life at this time, spending almost every spare minute with his ear glued to a small 4" speaker. From his *Lunar Notes* description, he had to sort through a lot of dross to find the silver at times. He was like a musical monk. Unlike Zappa, who worked just as hard at the concept of *communicating* his musical ideas to the musicians, Don spent almost all his work time (which really didn't amount to much) creating raw material, which then had to be sorted through.

I would liken it to building a house. One man has a concept for a house. He reads a few books and does a great deal of research on building houses. He goes to an architect with some rough sketches and has a plan drawn, makes a materials list, buys the materials, selects a site and carefully marks the spot on the site where the house is to be built. If there are questions, he has the answer because he daily studies the plans and the progress so as to be kept up to date. He confers with the general contractor and the sub-contractors often and keeps things rolling as seamlessly as possible. At the end of the job, everyone got paid and praised for their efforts. This is the way Zappa worked.

If Van Vliet built a house like he wrote music, the methodology would go something like this. He gets an idea for a house, but the house is sketched on the back of a Denny's placemat in such an odd fashion that when he presents it to the contractor without plans or research, the contractor says, "This structure is going to be hard to build, it's going to be tough to make it safe and stable because it is so unique in design." Van Vliet then yells at the contractor and intimidates him into doing the job anyway. The contractor builds the home, figuring out all the intricacies involved in structural integrity himself because whenever he approaches Van Vliet, he finds that he seems completely unable to comprehend technical problems and just yells *"Quit asking me this stuff and build the damned house."* If he shows up on the site, almost nothing gets done except everyone talks a lot about things that have nothing to do with finishing the house. When the house is finished no one gets paid, and Van Vliet has a housewarming party, invites none of the builders and tells his guests that he built the whole thing himself.

Bill, in this analogy, assumed the role of the general contractor for *Decals*. He was the one who sorted through tapes interpreting and assimilating the material and skimming off the dross, which was sometimes excessive. He was the one who figured out how long sections should be and how to get from one point to the next. His job description also seemed to include shuttling Don and Jan around in his old Cadillac limousine and running various errands for them. In fact, Bill seemed to almost have no "life" outside of the band. He was totally dedicated to Don, to his music, and to his own ability to play it. Did I mention he was also working on his own guitar album featuring Don's piano compositions under the title *Big Sur Suite?*

Just to clarify and repeat myself, I had been gone from the band for approximately a year. Don had shoved me down a half-flight of stairs and told me to take a walk. Then, a year later, after going through two drummers, he realized that his new drummer, Art Tripp wasn't nearly as cooperative as I had been and wasn't really interested at all in re-tracing my steps. His band basically consisted of Bill and Mark, who had loyally and faithfully learned nearly an album's worth of technically complicated material. One night, Bill and Mark showed up in my room saying that Don would like to talk to me.

I ask myself today, "What was I thinking, climbing into Bill's old Dodge and driving down there to see a man who had treated me in such a despicable manner? Answer: I have not a clue. However, after sorting through everything, I started rehearsing for yet another Beefheart album, *Lick My Decals Off, Baby.*

1. LICK MY DECALS OFF, BABY - Well, first thing you're going to hear is my opinion of the lyrics to this song. It takes off on a very low level compared to just about anything on *TMR*. I'm not really sure that it's such a great idea for a nearly 30-year-old man to be singing lyrics that are going to be heard by teenage girls that includes lines like, *"I want to lick you everywhere it's pink, in every way you think."* Don says that his statement here is to please quit putting labels on him and take off the ones you have already attached to him. I am sure it extends to and includes Frank's portrayal of Don within the same framework as Wild Man Fischer and Alice Cooper. However, these lyrics may be symbolic of such things on other levels, but there is a literal level that I find disgusting. Also, *"Rather than I wanna hold your hand"* is obviously a rebuttal the Beatles' *I Want To Hold Your Hand.* Ry Cooder mentions that Don's (actually Elliot Ingber's) black and white TV commercial for this project received "hate mail" because it was too far ahead of it's time. Actually it was supposed to be aired during the George Putnam news on Channel 11 and he thought the lyrics were "obscene" and protested, thus having the commercial banned. I respect him for his stand, actually. This song has as much to do with oral sex as unjustly labeling someone or anything else and isn't even stated that artistically. Rock stars have just as much responsibility as anyone else to say things that aren't irresponsible and to try to influence society in a positive direction. I never saw anything positive about these lyrics and was offended and embarrassed by them on a public level. If you want to talk like this in your living room, that's your business, but don't put it out for kids to listen to. Perhaps the reasons the lyrics are so sexually motivated is because Don felt like he had to appeal to women more. I didn't think it then, and time has proved that I was probably right: These lyrics are way too graphic for women, who I believe desire a more subtle approach. Don and Jan were basically still in the honeymoon stage of their marriage and so sexual feelings were probably a strong part of Don's daily experience and being the extremist he is, he took it to the limit and beyond.

Now, the music; the first way this album differs musically from *TMR* is that it has much longer lines. The intro is double drummed. I am playing a line Don actually played on the set, which I find to be a really good line that pushes the riff just right. Artie's line is basically the woodblock and probably a cross-stick on the snare. There are some elements in this song that remind me of very early Beefheart band and both the beginning riff and the line at (0:13) where the guitar and bass play the unison line are in keeping with the early band sound. I think there's a lot of Alex Snouffer influence here, believe it or not. The song switches back between time and this suspended section, and each section seems to be a bit more developed that the section before. I love Artie's extended drum fill at (1:19) as it really punctuates what Bill is playing. The piece is a power trio with extra drums basically. There's a lot of music going on here. I'm guessing that the music Don wrote on the piano is the fast sections, and the slow sections were whistled or sung to the band to break up the song and create a proper framework for the lyrics. The end section at (1:55) is a totally separate section that probably goes on a bit too long because of its repetitive nature, but works OK because there are lyrics over the top that keep it moving along.

2. DOCTOR DARK - This song kicks in at a much higher level. The first section has Bill playing a repetitive line four times with Mark playing two separate lines beneath. There are several subtle differences from part to part and Boston's playing here is as phenomenal as anything on *TMR* and more so. I'm playing a line straight from *Wild Life*, the first part, in fact, but slightly altered because I am now using two bass drums. I love the way the second section is played 3 times and then off to something new. Most people think in terms of music playing 2 or four of something - numbers. This pulls the listener to a new section at the same time slightly disorienting them. Don's voice slides in at 0:30 on top of an even more powerful section in 4/4 clicks. This is a classic "Don on piano" part and is reminiscent of many I wrote during *TMR*. The next (0:41) part is almost a *TMR* type change to $^3/_4$ time. (0:52) reveals a section reminiscent of *Frownland*, but more suspended. Mark is playing an almost country-esque riff under Bill's suspended chord, but the drums, rather than being so free-form are here playing a pattern although there doesn't seem to be any "pulse." This feeling continues on in the next section at (1:12) with a more intense dissonance on the bass and an expansion of the guitar part as if more explanation is necessary, and both parts are starting and ending together over the suspension. At (1:31) a discernable pulse returns but bass and guitar take separate time signatures. At (1:41) Artie joins Bill playing a long line that seems to be in seven over Mark's more conventional line in four. (2:00) brings in a more clearly *TMR*-type section in four then at (2:10) the bass takes leave of it's senses and explodes in emotion as the song begins to fade. I have always been amazed at the music to this piece and it never fails to move me. Part of the reason is I never heard it until the guitar and bass were finished, so I don't know the framework nearly as well. Although both instruments shine in this piece, it's really clear that Mark has had some incredible growth since *TMR* and is playing stuff I've never heard a bass player before or since achieve.

The lyrics I find that I am unqualified to approach, as with most Van Vliet lyrics. I see childlike metaphors of night coming as a scary ominous figure on horseback, perhaps thunder and lightning being imagined as horse hooves making sparks. The moon seems the only anchor of serenity here and even the music seems to set a mood of hope during the moon episodes. There are blues images, but they are taken to a supersonic level - *'The hell hounds, hell hounds, horn rim crimped.'* This is a phenomenal piece.

3. I LOVE YOU, YOU BIG DUMMY - The track again reminds me from beginning to end of the early Magic Band sound and the evolution of that sound. A lot of the parts are unison or close to conventional. It overall has a flavor of several blues riffs tied end-to-end. I liked this piece a lot until the harmonica was added like someone pouring a 40 gallon drum of paint on the floor. The harmonica itself has a definite Little Walter feel straight from Muddy Waters' recordings. It is a chromatic harmonica, but is not played chromatically, the button being opened and left opened. It has more of a minor feel to it and also a completely different sound from most blues harp sounds. It's a great sound, I just wish there were less of it and a chance for the music to breathe. I remember being in the studio when he overdubbed the harp, and the look on my face angered Don. "Sorry this is not what you were expecting, fuck off, John." - or words to that effect - was what he said to me. I left the studio that night to avoid conflict. This and Don's persistently repetitive lyrics took this right out of the range of the average listener, and yet the track had that quality of being approachable without the vocal and harp. Don always spoke of so many rock tunes having "solo freaks" on guitar, playing the same riffs over and over. Unfortunately, he didn't apply his playing to the harp, which could have been less and at the same time more complimentary to his music. All in all, it's a good statement, just overdone.

3. PEON - I can't praise this piece enough. After reading Bill's story, I am less apt to think of Don sitting down and writing this by playing it on the piano from beginning to end and more of Bill sorting through the dross to find silver. Whoever is responsible, the end product is a delight. This is such a composition that I can't even begin to describe how good it makes me feel. I find it highly underrated. It's extremely passionate in all the best ways and also has a delicate sense of balance and change. It pulls you just enough to let you know what it means, and then changes the subject at exactly the precise moment. There's not a wasted note nor a redundant line. It's one of the closest things to musical perfection I have ever witnessed. I know that Don was intensely in love with Jan at the time and this was in effect a manifestation of that experience. It is timeless and just listening to this made me think what an incredible person Jan Van Vliet must be to inspire someone to write such a beautiful piece. It also shows the human side of Don which, though seldom allowed to show, but which was present enough to keep his band enduring the other not-so pleasant facets of his personality.

5. BELLERIN' PLAIN - Originally entitled *Parapliers* (as in "pair of pliers") Don originally told me the song was about some woman who squeezed men tight while having sex with them, hence, the title. It was later changed to *Bellerin' Plain* unbeknownst to me and I didn't discover this fact until the album was released and I read the title on the sleeve. The lyrics seem to me to combine the "train song" imagery with sexual imagery in a really obtuse fashion also mixing in images of toothless hobos and vivid landscapes so that one cannot tell where one image ends and the other begins. The images are strong and at the same time confusing like quick edits in a film, little snippets that suggest, but never connect. Another incredible piece of music and poetry from beginning to end. There are only single drums on this song until the end and they are very thin and abbreviated in some sections. I can only credit this to the fact that Don had been listening to this music without drums for so long, I think he considered them only as embellishment and punctuation in sections. Most of the drum parts for this song were written by Don. The first part is mine, however, and only slightly modified by Don. The interplay between guitar and marimba, in it's first appearance on the album is a great introduction to Artie's main instrument. Don's vocal suffers from lack of preparation at (2:30), it is apparent that his second word was meant to start with an "s" and there is a hesitation as he regroups for the correct word. Also, the fact that later, Artie also appears on drums brings this piece to a strong finale.

6. WOE IS A ME BOP - I always had a feeling that this was the song meant to achieve some form of air play because of it's simple neat 4/4 arrangement. Drum parts from this song vary from the opening section where I played what Artie had already established and composed from what I recall. The next section (0:09) is a drum beat I originally wrote for one of my own songs *Reign of Pain* which seemed to fit nicely with these parts. (0:16) brings in the first drum part I wrote for *Sweet Sweet Bulbs*. (0:23) brings in Don's drum idea for the end of *Moonlight On Vermont*! The concept that Don requested was to utilize beats from *TMR* in the *Decals* pieces to tie them together a little better. That certainly happened here. The lyrics to this song always reminded me of what was worst about the hippy movement. The whole "meditation, we are one, let's take drugs, free love reigns, say 'om'" nonsense had gotten so out of hand. At (1:10) is something unusual on a Beefheart album, an actual guitar solo played by Bill. This is not Bill improvising, however, but a composed solo to fill the concept of an instrumental section. Bill was limited to playing a rehearsed solo, and I believe this solo was created by Don, as was just about any solo Bill played on a Beefheart album. Again, it typifies the lack of freedom given to the musicians in the band.

7. JAPAN IN A DISHPAN - Dare I say it? Another great composition ruined by too much meaningless horn. I wish you could hear Don's writing without him playing all over it (especially at the beginning) and basically ruining it. Although the opening phrase is good, it would have been better had he come in later in the piece and been mixed lower in the track to allow Bill's and Mark's playing to sound like more than mere scratching in the background. This was a very difficult piece for them to learn, yet it was treated with much the same carelessness in the mix as was *Neon Meate Dream Of A Octafish* on *TMR*. Artie is basically just responding as a jazz drummer would, although Don suggested he open with the P-K-Ro-P beat. Back to the horn playing; as the piece goes on; notice the monotonous short phrases with fast fingering? Does this really work or is it just someone paying no attention at all to the music they're playing to and just rambling incessantly, meaninglessly, and amateurishly? The horn playing here affects me like a gnat buzzing around my face. It won't go away, it's distracting, and I wish I could dispose of it. However, I am sure there are many listeners out there who are happy with this just as it is. Just keep in mind, you have never heard it any other way, and I have. My opinion of course. I was originally supposed to play drums on this piece, but I wasn't sure how to approach it and so tried writing "parts" for it, which really didn't work, as it changes so much and is more of a continuous flow rather than a sectioned piece. Artie was much more accustomed to playing in this style, and being older, he also carried more "weight" with Don, who allowed him liberties the rest of us weren't allowed .

8. I WANNA FIND ME WOMAN THAT'LL HOLD MY BIG TOE TILL I HAVE TO GO – I remember that Moris (then Jeff) Tepper and Eric Feldman really liked this song and wanted to perform it live. It is one of my favorites also. It is also the first song I started working on when I re-joined the group. I will focus on drums on this piece for a minute, since that's what I can explain clearly. I wrote the first section especially for this song, it seemed to work. The second section (0:12) is taken from *Hair Pie*. The next part (0:25) was written by me for this song, while the next section I believe, was Artie's original part (0:36) that I employed because it seemed to work. (0:54) is again mine, as is (1:10) which is a return to a different *Hair Pie* part which seemed to work well. The lyrics to this song are obviously meant to be humorous. I believe Don said that it had something to do with an acupressure point Jan had used to rid him of a headache. I know that it was some type of relief from pain that occurred when the big toe was squeezed. Obviously, it's much easier to have someone else squeeze your big toe than to attempt it yourself, so the primary need for a mate could be, I suppose, for this reason and nothing else. This is the kind of relationship we're all really looking for isn't it? The line, *"Cause them yams have all them eyes…"* reminds me of an old joke my parents used to say. It was: "Liza, get in here outta that potato patch and put on your panties, don't cha know them taters got eyes?" I think Don probably heard a similar joke growing up with parents whose roots were in the south and transposed it into this piece. The spoonerism (probably the wrong word - how about "transposition of words") that occurs at (1:04) is something I don't think was intentional. We all laughed in the studio as he sang it, but he looked a little disgruntled. I think he decided it worked and went along with the humor in the rest of the piece and so deigned to keep it. The faux-British pronunciation of the word "potatah" in the very last phrase punctuates the whole humorous theme of the lyrics. Interestingly enough, the music is contrastingly much more serious-sounding, and a wonderful composition, which clocks in at only (1:53). This is more of a *Trout Mask* type of composition, going from section to section, rather than the longer phrases of some of the other pieces.

9. PETRIFIED FOREST - Don had told me that part of the reason *TMR* was receiving so much attention was because of the environmental and ecological themes. In the late sixties, there was a lot of talk about cleaning up the environment, although no one really did much of anything until the mid-eighties, when "Earth Day" became popular and suddenly everyone "re-discovered" ecology. Don had decided to focus upon environmental issues on this album because it was a popular theme and he felt it was expected of him. Interestingly, *Petrified Forest* and every song following it are all focusing on these themes (with the exception of the instrumental *One Red Rose That I Mean*) while not one song before this actually did. This song almost seems Biblical in it's ominous prophetical warnings about our mistreatment of Mother Earth. Unlike many of Don's lyrics, the statement here, though filled with imagery, is quite clear. I especially am impressed by the power in the phrase, *"No flower shall grow where oil shall flow, no seed shall sow in salt water."* Almost sounds like it could be taken from the King James Bible, somewhere in Proverbs maybe. It's also scientifically accurate, and with all the offshore oil spills happening in those days, it was a warning that cried out to be heard. We, the human race, are in grave danger of creating our own extinction, if not with nuclear war, then with ecological disasters. The images in this song are apocalyptic. The fire being belched is almost imaged as the fires of hell. Musically speaking, this is one intense piece and definitely receives praise from me.

10. ONE RED ROSE THAT I MEAN - Gee, that Bill could sure play guitar back when he thought he wasn't any good, couldn't he? I think this and *Peon* are both in the same category as far as being a direct result of Don's love for Jan. I never heard Bill give a bad performance of this. What an accomplishment.

11. THE BUGGY BOOGIE WOOGIE - Orson Welles should get some thanks for inspiration on this piece. He said something to the effect of: (I paraphrase) "What this world needs is a good $2.00 cigar." Don immediately grabbed paper and penned these lyrics. It was written late in the session, probably during vocal overdubs, and Artie and I were called in to play brooms. I played mine the standard way, standing and sweeping. Artie played his the drummer's way, sitting and lightly brushing it sideways in counter rhythms (he was always such a show-off). We "broomed" on guitar cases - because they had just the right texture. The music was written on piano and Mark and Bill spent hours one day learning the entire piece. It is the *Beatle Bones N' Smokin' Stones* of this session. Inspiration, action, results ... whew! I was so tied up with sweeping that I didn't get the overpopulation theme of the song until years later. Dumb, dumb. My one criticism is that the voice is too loud in the mix.

12. THE SMITHSONIAN INSTITUTE BLUES - This was always my pick for a single until later when the center section was added. The music for this is partially recycled from a song that was part of the A&M Demos called *Sugar Honey Sugar*. That bass intro sure sounds like a dinosaur to me and it keeps playing under the *Sugar Honey Sugar* music. Artie is doubling the guitar that plays the "octave" part and Bill has overdubbed the other single string ascending line on another track. I never noticed this until the day of this writing. The drum parts start with a first part I wrote specifically for this song and I believe I used a similar beat later on in *When It Blows It's Stacks*. At (0:20) it goes into that same first *Sweet Bulbs* part again. (0:35) switches back to first part. (1:10) in the double time section sounds like a part Don would have written, but it's not the way he would ever play hi hat, so it's probably a hybrid part. At 1:10, I can't tell what I'm doing, but at (1:18) I wrote this and the following is yet another *Sweet Bulbs* part from later in the piece, followed by (you guessed it) yet another *Sweet Bulbs* part. The vocal here is tremendous and the lyrics work well with the music.

13. SPACE AGE COUPLE - This song is just as timely today as it was when it was written. I always enjoyed the fact that this song has an "up" feeling about it, while still addressing what could be considered an unpopular theme. The lyrics again need no explanation although still enhanced with enough of Don's wonderful imagery to please the poets. The music is ridiculously good. The lyrics and music in this piece fit together extremely well especially for a Beefheart song. There are a few "dead" spots where it seems like the lyrics ran out and the music kept going, however. The double drums are some of the best parts I've ever played or heard. I can barely remember what we were doing, and the drums are mixed in such a manner that it is impossible to separate them. This was completely Don's drum writing with the exception of (1:22) which is my first part on *Steal Softly Thru Snow*. Production errors: The voice way too loud again. I recall Don really being concerned about all the lyrics being heard and understood. I believe this was Phil Shier's fault as much as Don, but whoever it was, the voice is boosted ridiculously high in this and other cuts. Also, even if the lyrics were indiscernible for a fraction of a second here and there, anybody who is interested could have just read them on the sleeve. Also, why on earth, at (1:48,) is Mark Boston's wonderful solo playing not boosted in the track for that moment when he is laid bare? It's a wonderful part and believe me, when Mark played in the room, it never sounded like the toy bass this does.

14. THE CLOUDS ARE FULL OF WINE - The first forty seconds of this piece are intensely enjoyable to me. This is Don again at his best. I am just thankful he decided not to add horn to this section of music. This song happens to be the first thing I heard Artie play on marimba. I had no idea Artie could even *play marimba at all!* (After all, Jeff Bruschele was chosen to play drums, right?) So, one can imagine my surprise and delight when I discovered that not only can he play, but play really well. At forty seconds what kicks in vocally reminds me a little of some old show tune or movie theme, and also reminds me quite a bit of the band Pere Ubu, whose singer MUST have been influenced by this slightly insane piece. I believe the reason Don chose to sing these lyrics such is to mirror the image that people have of environmentalists: crackpots on the fringe. Drumbeats in this song vary from *Mirror Man* era playing to one part I recognize from *Ella Guru*. At (2:05,) the culmination of all the rubbish collects and the problem becomes apparent. Ed's marimba at the end sums up the piece quite well.

15. FLASH GORDON'S APE - I always laugh at the irony of this title which pokes a little fun at evolution, at least in my perception. The line, *"You barely know how to use your thumb"* reminds me of the aggressive and ill-mannered hitch-hikers I used to encounter in Laurel Canyon and surrounding areas. Although probably by now I've convinced everyone I dislike Don's horn playing, but I think it works here. I think the track is a little strange with the whole band mixed on one side of the stereo spectrum and the horns on the other, however, Phil Schier's idea here was to allow the listener to mix the horns out if they wanted to hear just the band. I prefer to listen to this piece with the balance control panned to the band side at least ninety percent. I can hear the horns and the band at a decent volume. The horns are at least 30% louder than the entire band. Why make the band sound like a toy all the time? The marimba interlude in this piece is incredible. Artie claims he was just improvising, but I really believe he has just forgotten listening to a piano tape of Don playing. He did take several liberties when transcribing for marimba. This is exquisite playing and shows his virtuosity. Don's vocal phrase at the end, *"You're too day"* comes from a thing he used to say back in *Trout Mask* times. Having terrible skin problems, Don was not able to go out into the sun for any prolonged period of time. He would sometimes look out side on a particularly hot, dry day, with the sun baking down and say, "It's too day." He would open the door, stick his finger outside and pull it back in. "There! I've had my daily allowance of Vitamin K for the day" and stay inside for the rest of the day, like some vampire, waiting for night to fall.

Like I wrote in the beginning, I am not the expert on this album, Bill Harkleroad is, and his book *Lunar Notes* explains this work better than anything I can offer.

THE SPOTLIGHT KID
Studio(s): The Record Plant, Los Angeles, CA.
Recording Date: Autumn, 1971
Producer(s): Don Van Vliet / Phil Schier

Engineer: Phil Schier
Band Personnel: Don Van Vliet (vocals, harmonica, jingle bells); Zoot Horn Rollo / Harkleroad (glass finger and steel appendage guitar); Ed Marimba / Tripp (marimba, piano, harpsichord); Rockette Morton / Boston (bassius ophelius) [sic]; Winged Eel Fingerling/ Elliot Ingber (guitar); Drumbo / French (drums);Ted Cactus / Tripp (drums on 1); Rhys Clark (drums on 10).

   Intro: Not unlike Bill Harkleroad, I have relatively unhappy memories about the conception, gestation and birth of this baby. As I sit looking at the album cover, I remember the first time I saw it. The picture of Don and his western-style suit with the rather gambler-esque look. His hand was carefully posed to reveal the turquoise ring. I looked at the title: *"just Captain Beefheart, no Magic Band. Hmmm."* I wasn't surprised really. He had talked of having The Magic Band do their own albums. *The Spotlight Kid* was still the same title as he had decided. I turned the cover over and looked at the back. There were the paintings of Rockette, Artie, Bill and … hmmm again … a pencil sketch of Elliot to replace the painting he did of me up in Felton which was done the same day as the other paintings. An obvious "slap in the face," similar to leaving my name off of *Trout Mask*.
   I wasn't in the band at the time of the release of *The Spotlight Kid*. I had been booted out, this time with the excuse that I was going to start my own group, a power trio, for which Don would write tunes. More on that in the text. However, I can't help feeling bad, even now 29 years later, that some of the best musicians I had ever worked with were going on tour, and I was outside looking in one more time.
   I had to go out and buy my copy off the shelf at the local Sav-On drug store. I recall having seen the commercial (originally filmed for *Lick My Decals Off, Baby*) aired on prime time television. I heard it from the other room and looked into the living room to find it there in my face. That "Ginsu-Knife announcer" enunciating, *"Captain Beefheart, The Spotlight Kid."* This prompted me to go out and buy a copy. I was delivering furniture for a company called Frontier Furniture. My friend, Don Giesen, had suggested I take a job at this company for which he worked.
   Looking at the back cover paintings I recall Don setting up some temporary easel against a redwood tree in Felton, just below the common redwood deck our cabins shared. Bill had recently gotten his hair cut and died it black. If you look closely at the painting, the first thing Don actually painted was the red shoulders and arms. Then, he painted the belt and a pocket, or whatever that red thing is on Bill's chest. If you look closely at just that section, it is like a "smiley face" with long red hair. Afterward, he proceeded to paint Bill's head sort of leaning forward and off to the side. Because of the fact Harkleroad was above average height, he used to stand with his head a bit forward and slightly hunched over, so this was a particularly accurate exaggeration of his posture.
   Ed Marimba's painting reminds me of his personality a lot. I sometimes think that Don could see auras because of the green in the painting. Artie was a tranquil, peaceful person and I would think his aura would look something like this. His poetic description contains images of his cap he wore on stage (with the embroidered Marlin on the front), the game he liked (pool) and the fact that he liked to get adjusted by chiropractors mixed with his instrument in cartoon imagery. The old skeleton xylophone that showed up in early cartoons made a cameo here. Ed went on to become Dr. Tripp, a chiropractor and for a time, Mr. & Mrs. Van Vliet's chiropractor.
   Rockette Morton's painting is alive with energy, as was Rockette. I see a lot of sadness and confusion in the painting also as though too many forces were coming against Mark at the same time. He's almost vanishing in the energy surrounding him. I'm not sure that his poetic description images are all dedicated to him. Mark was anything but catatonic but the extreme Salvador Dali catfish whiskers were still a part of his stage look. The number paintings reference reminds me of the fact that Don often told me during *Trout Mask* to "never tell him what he is playing." This was said as though Mark was somehow not hip enough to understand the music. I get the feeling from the "number paintings" line that Don is saying Mark doesn't know the difference between "real art - food for the soul" and "paint-by-numbers milk." I disagree with this vision and maintain that Mark was and is one of the deepest thinkers I know, and a true human being who played spectacular bass on Beefheart's albums and was a great showman.

"Mean E" as Elliot's sketch is titled, might have been drawn during the tour of early 71, prior to Elliot's departure from the group. I remember seeing that look on his face very few times, although for the most part, Mr. Ingber was a peaceful and good-natured individual. Elliot was one of the first people I encountered who really attempted to become a vegetarian and wear non-animal products (no leather for a time). Before the tour he had discovered mandarin oranges and ate them as often as possible. He wanted to live in some kind of harmony with nature. However, he also lived on Santa Monica Blvd in one of the worst possible sections of Hollywood. Across the street were adult bookstores, and there was a strange assortment of characters hanging out on every corner. Bill Harkleroad once said (and Elliot was quite impressed with the image in the "hip" sense) that the spirit of the adult book stores used to wind itself across the street in a snakelike fashion and try to crawl in Ingber's home. He and Don used to have some joke about lime Jello and so is the image included in the poem.

Drumbo can truly say he is sad when he hears and sees this album. Don had decided he needed to do more accessible music and suddenly, Drumbo's weird drum style wasn't such a convenient thing to have around. I attempted to play "normal," but between the terrible living conditions, the rebirth of the cultlike band "talks," the lack of normal drums (I played Gon Bops at this point), and Don's incredible 180 degree turn in an attempt to be a "commercial" success, I have to admit, I was completely uninspired. The band learned most tunes without me, and when I came in to drum, there was just a feeling that nothing I was doing worked at all. No one attempted to really communicate. It was almost like my time had come and gone: I was obsolete.

I haven't listened to this album once through in 25 years, although I have heard tracks from it occasionally, as on the BBC bio when one of my all-time favorites, *Glider* was used at the end.

1. I'M GONNA BOOGLERIZE YOU BABY - The opening statement is Winged Eel Fingerling pulling a rhythm from the air. This was a totally spontaneous track from my impression, although Don and Elliot might have cooked this up at some other point and initiated to pursue it this day. We had just finished recording *Alice in Blunderland* at Sunset Sound studios during a daytime session. I recall Don asking me to play the "Baby Beat" to this tune and impatiently ordering me out of the tracking room after about 30 seconds of my attempt to play this beat with Elliot. Art was then called into the room and the song continued without me as I sat in the control room feeling completely humiliated. I believe the lyrics to this tune were written later and overdubbed, however, as I said before, it could have been put together during the session. Don loosely directed Bill and Mark with hand cues. I always thought the lyrics were really clever with the coined phrase "booglerize." I always had the perception that this song was an attempt to "write a hit in the studio" and Elliot's natural instincts never shined through as strongly as on this. "E" as he sometimes was called, seemed to be able to persuade Don to at least "test the water" of the more commercial or accessible areas. Winged Eel's subtle soloing tastefully slinks through this rhythm track without ever becoming overbearing or obnoxious.

2. WHITE JAM - This first section was obviously written on the piano. Artie transcribed it and Bill, Mark and he learned it together. It was written near the time of *"A Carrot Is As Close As A Rabbit Gets To A Diamond"* and has a similar feel to me in a sense. As I listen now to this piece, I sense a vocal that is trying to find itself and never really does until the transition to the more blues like outro riff. The vocal is hesitant and doubtful, as though Don is trying to arrive at a feeling under laboratory conditions, then becomes confident and filled with abandon. I played "time" on this song. I had no inspiration to learn anything else, neither was there ever any ideas offered from Don. Don sang the intro part to the song in one voice, then came back and overdubbed the the raw falsetto shout voice on a separate track. This was recorded at Amigo Studios. Strange, but in most sessions, I can remember exactly where I was set up, what my view was as I looked out. In this session, as I listen to takes, I see myself facing different directions in different parts of the room. It's as though I were anaesthetized and occasionally awoke from tranquility to catch an occasional glimpse of my where-abouts. I was completely drug-free (including alcohol) during rehearsals and recording, so it can't be attributed to chemical influence. I believe it was emotional starvation and a strongly-built defense mechanism.

3. BLABBER 'N SMOKE - Highly biographical, these lyrics are credited to Jan Van Vliet who was for the most part absent from any rehearsal or band meeting and seldom came to the studio. This was when the "talks" had again erupted and apparently there was a puzzlement in Jan as to why anyone would want to sit in a room doing nothing but talking and smoking cigarettes. I believe this title is highly descriptive of Don's worst trait, which was to fritter away hours of time talking needlessly about highly negative things, which accomplished nothing constructive and amplified all the worst fears and feelings of us all. This created a highly-charged negative atmosphere at rehearsals. We were all trying to become Don's version of a "commercial" group and it wasn't working, because the music was labored and slow for the most part. The one redeeming quality of this song for me is the fact that the drum beat is a New Orleans style line beat that I enjoyed playing, even at this rather labored tempo. As you notice, there is no flow to this piece, it seems to stop and start. The tempo drags terribly and every time I listen to it I shudder. Don would absolutely go into a tirade any time a tempo seemed to creep above geriatric level, and we (especially me) were all so self conscious on the slower pieces that I cringe when I hear how badly the drums are dragging. I sometimes wish we would have used a metronome on this piece. This song has no spirit, it's like a dead thing to me. Part of the reason it may seem that way is that it was actually over rehearsed to the point that there was no way it could ever sound "fresh."

4. WHEN IT BLOWS IT'S STACKS - This piece has fire. The beginning bass part is a riff from *Hair Pie*. I remember when we were first learning Hair Pie, as I taught Mark this bass part, I thought, "This is a great riff for a more accessible blues piece." This song got its start at a rehearsal at the Trout House prior to the '71 *Decals* tour when we were supposed to be rehearsing for the tour. Elliot was at the rehearsal, and he and Don started working on this song. Ingber is largely responsible for the lyrical content, not that he wrote or created them, but as Don would write things down and read them, Elliot was standing there saying, "No man, that don't get it - that ain't the thing." (I don't have lyric sheets so I am just attempting to understand the lyrics as I hear them). I love the line about *"hand her a Ronson, say 'I'll see ya 'round."* This came from a discussion with someone where Don heard that Eskimo women who are about to die are taken to icebergs and left to die. I really thought this song had a chance to get some radio play and get us out of the category of opening for Lee Michaels etc. It has a great intro, it's a good tempo, it has a great compatability with Don's voice. The bass intro is growl-y and deep, but still accessible. At (0:09) the guitar and Marimba come it with a part that is reminiscent of Hendrix's *Are You Experienced ?* and is joined by gradually intensifying drums. At (0:26) a slightly distorted powerful guitar doubles the bass joined by a drumpart that is truly "Drumbo" yet danceable at the same time. All along, Don has been building the anticipation with his gritty trademark vocal. Bill's guitar hurls a double-time bluesy riff over the top of the powerful theme at (0:39) pushing it into high gear, going back into doubling bass at (0:48) as Don sings the first verse;

> When a wolf's claw, wear way down
> Better watch, there's a man-eater around.

So far this guy makes Bad Leroy Brown look like Truman Capote. This guy is spooky - he's a man eater, he's bad, and his voice is even scarier. The desperate fearful men of this village are running around shouting:

> Hide all the women in town!
> Hide all the women in town!
> Hide all the women in town!
> Hide all the women in town!

While Zoot's flesh-cutting slide guitar rips through the fabric of everyone's safety at (0:58) the voice is intense, growling and almost inhuman. We're not finished yet folks, now at (1:09) The bass and guitar resign themselves to an even deeper groove as a screaming solo erupts from Winged Eel Fingerling elevating the listener to an even higher plateau.

Suddenly, at (1:19) the dancers all stop and turn to the stage as one guy with long blond hair and a mustache says, "What is this - howdy doody time?" half expecting to see Van Vliet donning a rose pink tutu and toe shoes for a quick cartoon-like whirl about the stage. The guy's girl, who had been seductively dancing up until this point turns in a huff and leaves the dance floor. Don cut the song in half and added the (dare I say "stupid?") little ballet section (1:19) in order to ensure that no commercial DJ would ever consider airing the piece. This reminds me a lot of the contrasting section that was inserted in the center of *Dropout Boogie*, which had the same effect. In my opinion, this was Don's trademark of sabotaging his own pieces by inserting completely irrelevant sections. However, on its own, it's a nice piece of music and well-phrased.

He lost all the women right here. I always considered that a woman needs a lot of consistent attention and commitment to bring her to a place of satisfaction. This song starts with all the best intentions and suddenly pours gallons of ice water on its hapless unfulfilled lover. What's left of the song (and the mood) becomes a parody of going through the motions. However, for the few-remaining Beefheart fans who didn't leave the dance floor (mostly guys at this point) I will continue: (1:34) there is a slight advantage of having the contrasting section musically, in that when this section comes back in, it is heard and appreciated even more out of "context."
Probably Elliot's favorite line as I recall is the following.

> *All you girls, make no mistake*
> *He's as cold as a snake sleeping in the shade.*

(1:46) One of my few decent drum moments on *The Spotlight Kid*.
(1:50) A triple-punch as Elliot's wailing solo, Don's voice, and guitar and bass all enter at once.
(2:18) I love the vocal thing he does with his tongue here. Very powerful.
(2:24) The insistence of this riff still hasn't gotten old. You're still wanting to "hide all the women."
(2:32) This slow downhill fade is one of the most sexually powerful things I've ever heard. Don's singing on this track is one of my favorite performances of his. He nailed it, and was in great voice besides.

5. ALICE IN BLUNDERLAND - I heard this the first time around Jan. 1st 1970. Elliot was playing guitar solos on a piece that I felt was really accessible. It was instrumental and changed very little except that my drumming was very different from Artie's and employed more toms. I was told that it was a part of music from a musical, which I think was of the same name, although I may be mistaken. However, no one can seem to remember. I didn't recognize anything at the beginning, but I thought the opening line being repeated 3 times with a different tone center on the bass was nice, then the second section (0:21) seemed to work well with the first and suddenly at (0:37) I recognized an old friend from *Mirror Man* days. Don had resurrected the main section of *Big Black Baby Shoes*. Suddenly, I am hearing a guitar solo (remember, I mentioned that Don hated "solo freaks?") and I am entranced by Winged Eel's remarkable ability to say so much with six strings. "This was 'normal' music," I remember thinking to myself. "Kids can dance to this, it makes you feel good." One of the reasons I returned to the band was because of the feel of this song. Of course, here, it is crudely edited into a (3:50) neat compact radio version. The original was probably 12 - 15 minutes long and most of it was just as good as what you hear, except that it was more organic and natural sounding as it's waves and ebbs. Elliot, puzzlingly enough, learned the edited solo as closely to verbatim as humanly possible and never played it as an improvisation again (!?) beating himself over the head for hours about how he didn't quite "cop all the riffs" the night before at the show.

6. THE SPOTLIGHT KID - This song reminds me too much of Don's obnoxiously tremendous ego to actually bring back many good memories. Up to this point, Don had seldom toured, desiring instead to stay at home and challenge the band members to "who rules the roost" games. The idea of this song is Don making fun of himself for not touring and "never showing" as the lyrics relay.

> All night the village waited and the Spotlight Kid never showed
> He was up on the mountain makin' his alibis and eating his a la mode's

This was when I first became aware of Warner Brothers sort of embracing Don as their darling. Unfortunately, it had a devastating effect on ballooning his ego into an intolerably large size so that it was often difficult for him to fit into the crowded rehearsal room. I also had strong feelings at this point about how many of Don's "egocentric decisions" had taken money out of our pockets. The situation is described in the text, while living in Felton with the band.
(0:00) The intro opens with Don's "legend in his own mind" cock-a-doodle down-home concept of himself, recreated as an almost biblical (was this corn in a manger or should it have been fenced?) colorful little character who was darned loveable and golly-gee-whiz harmlessly-mischievous and wrapped-up-in-a-lovable package o' the merriment.

> Said the mama to the baby in the corn,
> You are my firstborn,
> You shall herein be known as the Spotlight Kid

Halfway between Uncle Remus and the Eddie Haskell, with the best traits of both, this darned-nice-guy had all the talent in the world and the whole village waited up for him but he never came to the concert, even though he was the unanimously-voted star o' the show. Imagine that, he was jes' so naïve that he didn't realize he had broken the hearts of nearly all the children in America. Never let it be said that this cuddly teddy bear of a man wouldn't do anything in his ever-lovin' power to mend all those millions of hearts he'd broken. Here his is, may I introduce to you, *The Spotlight Kid.* Give him all the sugar you want. Notice that expensive suit. It was a present from the band ... I think. Gee what a zany mood this beginning line sets. Then it borrows the *Pachuco Cadaver* riff (0:34) slowed down to a crawl so slow that it could be the geriatric boogie. At (0:56) we get yet an even zanier little riff. The lyrics in this section are a little out of touch with the track. However it pulls together well enough. Back to the intro and (1:32) and then a little 2 measure bass solo, then comes what might be considered loosely in conventional music as "The Bridge" at (1:50), the guitar and voice doing the same lines. Sorry folks, but I absolutely hate this piece of crap.

7. CLICK CLACK - Now, we're talking. Does this song cook like a bird all the way through or what? Unlike *I Love You, You Big Dummy*, in which Don plays all over and ruins his own track, this piece has harp that allows the music and the lyrics to shine through. It tells a story in plain English to which anyone can relate. It doesn't contain any non-related musical sections to throw the audience off. This was used in live performance often and it's no wonder. This piece of music can move anyone. Brilliant writing. Is this a "Train Song" or what?

8. GROW FINS - I never heard the words much to this song. The track was basically a bore to play without the voice, and since it was never Don's practice to rehearse with the band so we (and he) would be able to anticipate what he was going to do with the vocal. Actually, though, this one is one of my favorites lyrically. It's very funny and fits with *Booglerize*, and *Click Clack* quite well. There's not a lot to tell musically. There is a riff and a guitar hook. I'm playing the same part as in *Blabber 'n Smoke*, except this time it is done at a decent tempo and moves along. The guitar/harp hook was written by Don on the harp, and therefore was easy for him to double in the studio. One of my favorites, with great lyrics and nice riffs.

9. THERE AIN'T NO SANTA CLAUS ON THE EVENIN' STAGE - There's a lot of overdubbing on the guitar. No marimba on this baby that I can hear. Another simple track. This works fairly well for me until the end when the vocalizing becomes redundant and downright boring. It would have been nice had he decided to alternate harp and vocal and play with it a bit. The "ho ho" thing is a nice gag, but it wears thin.

10. GLIDER - If I had one song to listen to forever, this would probably be it. I won't say it's my favorite. But it appeals to me in more different moods, eras, and times than any other. My one regret is that I didn't play on this track and neither did Artie. I knew it wasn't Artie the minute I heard it. It was some outsider. I played on the original take and played it in a style similar to the *Mirror Man* session. Don never gave me a clue as to what he wanted on this. If he would have said something to the effect, "Play this like a normal drummer would play," I would have probably played something very similar to what is heard here. Perhaps the Gon Bops sound didn't work. Ironically, they achieved a much better drum sound on this song than any other on the album. Notice the nice reverb on the snare and the presence of the drums? This was another piano composition and it is in somewhat the same kind of writing style of *Sheriff Of Hong Kong* from *Doc At The Radar Station*. The area where this song loses its soul is Don's whistled, dictated, and played-to-the-note bottleneck solo as performed verbatim by Bill at Van Vliet's insistence. This leaves the song cold and lifeless, and it isn't Bill's fault. Don completely stifled all guitar soloing because he wished to take credit for everything and couldn't stand the thought of anything being on his songs that wasn't "his." It's risky standing on stage with somebody and giving them "free reign" because they may start giving you competition and even upstage you now and again. I had heard Bill play some fantastic solos when he was younger and know that had been allowed to develop as a soloist those three years and actually play on stage with a band instead of being holed up in a house with a egotistical maniac dictator of a leader, he would have been right out there with Clapton and Hendrix. I have no doubt in my mind. I will go farther and say that he and Jeff Cotton both would have SURPASSED Clapton, sorry Eric, but I heard these boys and I heard you back then, and they would have "whupped your ass" on guitar. Just for your benefit though, Eric, neither of them could sing as well. Instead, poor Bill spent most of his time huddled alone in a room with his ear to a 4" speaker listening to Don's often mindless piano banging to cull out the interesting moments. I will go a lot farther here and say that this is another reason we never had women in the audience. Guitar solos are a bold statement of free-expression, and women, especially in those days, could appreciate anything that was free. It also allowed them to be free in expressing their sexuality. Unfortunately, the oppression of the musicians, which may have gone unnoticed on the surface, was felt by these females and they felt smothered and left.

    Conclusion: Don's attempt to make a commercial record missed the mark because he didn't allow his musicians the freedom to take his ideas and run with them. His own insecurity sabotaged this album, and though it had its high points, the overall theme of the album was oppression. It covered most of the good points in dark smoke.

CLEAR SPOT
Studio(s): Amigo Studios, Los Angeles, CA
Recording Date: Autumn, 1972
Producer(s): Ted Templeman
Engineer: John Landee
Band Personnel: Don Van Vliet (vocals, harmonica, wings on singabus [sic]); Zoot Horn Rollo/Harkleroad (solo guitar, steel appendage guitar, glass finger guitar and mandolin); Rockette Morton/Boston (rhythm guitar, bass on 12); Ed Marimba/Tripp (drums, tattoos and percussion); Orejon/Roy Estrada (bass), Milt Holland (percussion); Russ Titelman (guitar on 3); The Blackberries (backing vocals on 3,8); Uncredited musicians (horns on 2, 3, 9).

Intro: *Clear Spot* is probably the closest Don ever came to commercial success. This, of course, doesn't matter to critics, who love to embrace the "hip" and "non-compromising" Van Vliet who did possess those qualities, especially in relationship to those around him who worked the hardest for him. I wasn't there for this one. Sometimes I wish I could have been. However, I must admit that Artie probably did a much better job of playing what was needed than I could have done.

Artie was a few years older than I and closer to Don in age. He had some great training and had qualifications which immediately put him in a higher quality and level of respect than I could ever hope to attain from the Captain. Also, Artie had played with Zappa, which experience gave him a fundamental perspective of music that we *Trout Mask* players could never have had. Most of the "talks" had never targeted Artie, although sometimes he found himself to be an unwilling observer as the text of the book goes into in more detail.

My point in all this is that Artie was less "self-conscious" about his playing and so more confident. Don was less likely to ever lambast Artie and steal his confidence, and so he had a freedom I had never experienced.

Technically speaking, Artie uses the more "conventional" time-keeping tools on the set and stays away from toms except in the more conventional role of "fills." Yet, I hear traces of all the influences, Milt Holland (who's back on overdubs), Don, myself, the old blues, jazz etc. I also, however, hear very strongly and clearly Art Tripp himself putting all these influences together in his usual impeccable way. There's no doubt about it, this guy could play and play very well. Much of the success of *Clear Spot* is owed to Artie's flawless sense of time. He's always on and it does make a big difference.

My first chance to listen to Clear Spot came when Bill brought a copy to my parent's house late one night. We sat in the living room, everyone asleep, and listened to it at a frustratingly low level to keep from awakening the family and spoiling the mood. He was pretty proud of the album, and I gathered from speaking with him that this was actually the first time that someone besides Don had been in full control of a recording project since *Safe As Milk*. It shows in the professional polish of the product.

I'm not talking "art" here. I'm talking accessibility to the public. Understand, unlike critics who get paid to write about starving artists, artists actually go hungry doing the products that the critic is so quick to embrace as "true art." I got into the music business to make money, and hopefully, turn out a product of which I could be proud, something which could make a positive statement. Instead of Jim Morrison waving his penis onstage and Jimi Hendrix drowning in his vomit and various other artists destroying themselves, I wanted to present a positive image. I had felt that Van Vliet would not do something degrading on stage. What I didn't know, is that he would do little to actually go onstage at all for years.

Yet, suddenly now that I was out of the band, the music was sounding like a band should sound, and the band was getting ready to tour. "Thanks a lot for doing it now!" - That's what I was thinking. Yet, I was happy to see Bill, and I was happy *for* Bill. It seemed like he had a lot more control over his life and was emanating confidence in a way I hadn't seen him do for some time.

I also noticed that it was no longer just Captain Beefheart. Apparently someone realized The Magic Band was still a valuable commodity and decided out of the goodness of their heart to acknowledge their presence.

For the most part, I can only give opinions, but I remember Bill saying that Ted Templeman took over and Don's will was overlooked in favor of making the album accessible. I recall Don having little good to say about Templeman later, and I've never met the guy, but I'm sure I would have liked him. Bill also had much more to do with the actual decision-making process and the arrangements are much tighter.

My copy of *Clear Spot* is signed by Don. I never had a copy until 1975, when he discovered I never received one (I was damned if I would buy another Beefheart album!) I think the only reason he gave it to me then was because he wanted me to teach the band *Big Eyed Beans from Venus*. He gave it to me with the following inscription on the back side:

To John, who has stood by me even when my circle was wrinkled.
Love
Don, 75
Since elaborating on this would be out of context, I'll save it for the story of the '75 tour.

1. LO YO YO - I first remember playing this during *Spotlight Kid* rehearsals, so it was written in rough form although not recorded until this session. From the intro, I recognized it immediately. However, this was a well-thought, polished, and put-in-the-display-case arrangement. From firsthand experience, I knew that I was listening to arrangements that were far above Don's ability. He never wanted to put that much thought into arrangements. (00:00) This intro grasped me immediately. Although only 10 seconds before vocal comes in, there's a lot of information here, and the guitar tones are pleasant and absolutely take command of the listener. (0:10, verse) The vocal comes in, just like I remember the first lines back during *Spotlight*. What a great drum part. It's a little of *Abba Zaba* cowbell, a nice snare punctuation, and the fill at the end brings you to a conclusion and leads almost flawlessly (the only fault is in Don's slightly sharp final "yo") into (0:23) the chorus which has a trace of my favorite *Hair Pie* drum part (one of the first I ever wrote in the *Trout* style) in combination with that wonderful buzz roll that Artie could do so flawlessly. (0:37) brings you back to that beginning groove and suggests a suspension of time in a sense. Listen to Artie's perfect fill at (0:47-0:49) never overstated or flamboyant, never draws attention away from the music. Which brings you to another *Hair Pie* groove section until (1:01) where the bass drops out and the drums do a combination of the (chorus) groove while the guitars play a riff I seem to recall Don whistling to Bill back at creation time. The song moves along fairly well until about (1:48) when the pace labors from, if I may criticize whoever made the decision to turn the beat around, the drums abandoning the afro-cuban feel and entering a "rock" feel, which just doesn't quite work and becomes a little sluggish. I feel that this in itself would have kept this off the radio, because it lost the "feel" which is the all important ingredient for the American market. What would have been nice is to have a completely freed-up Bill Harkleroad do a little short slide solo over the verse section of the song. At (2:08), however, it recovers and we get the pleasant surprise of Artie's marimba overdubbed playing the coolest little African feel along with Bill and his slightly tremolo guitar actually repeating the intro and re-introducing the song, which is an exquisite touch. (2:18, bridge) brings in the strongest section of the piece and is reminiscent and slightly suggestive of not only *Kandy Korn*, but *Big-Eyed Beans*. Bill's little guitar licks here are nice, but this would have been a good place to really let him play after the vocal ends for four more bars or so. At (2:44) it rather awkwardly goes from a stronger section to a weaker section with a build in between. It would have been good at this point to take a short pause similar to (2:08) but shorter with a quick turn-around back in to the next section. At (2:57) we go to a verse/summation and final chorus at (3:10). This wonderful guitar line repeats at (3:23) and a nice tight ending employing a line from the chorus.

2. NOWADAYS A WOMAN'S GOTTA HIT A MAN - First of all, I know Don's trying to reach the women with this album, *so how come he's still talkin' to the men?* I'm sure Jan felt like hitting Don a few times for spending so much time at supposed "rehearsals" that turned into "blabber and smoke" sessions, (which I would rename "belabor 'n smoke") in which band member's esteem was continually forced to newly discovered lows. Suddenly, in this song Don's telling all the men what he needed to know himself, - *"shut up and start rocking"* - *"enjoy yourself and allow the people around you to do the same."* Actually, I had to get "out of the magic band" to enjoy the company of women again. They sure didn't hang out around the Magic Band's doorsteps. I had more girlfriends playing in a little unknown band in the high desert for eight months than I did the entire time I worked with Don - all the years put together! I look on this the same way I do Bob Dylan's *When Ya Gonna Wake Up?* - his Christian Rock "wake up" call. Yeah, Bobby, some of us out here already knew and were saying the same thing about YOU a few months ago, so now you're the expert? What I'm saying is, I had no trouble finding women and enjoying their company once I got away from the suffocating sexually repressed Magic Band atmosphere, the only missing element of which was Don himself, who *"don't have to be hit to make him know it's there."* Yeah, sure - bullshit! OK, personal feelings aside (I have a right, you know, and if you don't like it, go get a refund!) - the track. First of all, I think the vocal is unrehearsed. It works OK 'cause the track is so good, and there's power in the vocal, but if you listen closely, it's overlapping and sometimes is not sure of where it is and the ending is really clumsy. It's starts out with Artie playing the same drum beat Don suggested for *Blabber And Smoke* and *Grow Fins*, with the addition of a couple of snare accents. You can hear them if you listen. Also, this is much faster and easier to play at this speed, so it moves really well. At (0:06) the harp comes in and I get chills, yeah, this has it. (0:33, verse) brings in the vocal with a great added guitar line that sends this into space. Don's vocal rips unhesitatingly through with power and excitement (0:58) brings us to a very sexy rhythm response between guitar on one side and bass/horns on the other. Six seconds later, the part is double timed with the rhythm section back in. (1:15) brings us back to the verse section with the added pleasure of horns playing a unison R&B rhythm that kicks this song even harder. At (1:32), the descending line repeats and descends to a suspended *Mirror Man*-esque moment before ripping into (1:38) which, I would almost put money on, was supposed to be an instrumental section featuring the horn lines. (2:06) Zoot enters with a surprisingly fluid solo that, although I am told was whistled to him note by note by Don, still has the balls to keep this piece at boogie level. There isn't anything about this solo I don't like except the tone, which I think could have been thicker and louder. This tone, however, was hard to escape being as how Don demanded the giant heavy strings on guitar, which did little to allow a soloist any sustain. This is one of the best slide solos I've ever heard on any piece of music anywhere. (3:01) has a break section that allows the music to breathe at just the right spot. An example of what I think should have happened lyrically is that Don should have waited until (3:23) to say the words: (some are re-arranged)

> *Now everywhere I go,* (first chord, 3:23)
> *...the women all know* (next chord, 3:25)
> *There ain't no other place to go but there* (guitar horn echo part, 3:26)

I'd have cut the lyrics here or at least finished up the following by (3:31) ...

> *None of my women have tear in your eyes*
> *You can ask me about them I swear*

... and then in the first two sections of the last part, starting at (3:31) the last two lines;

> *I'm talkin' bout women*
> *They don't have to hit me, to make me know it's there...*

... out by (3:37) and let song end instrumentally.

3. TOO MUCH TIME - Funny thing is, this was originally based on something that my father said when he was separated from my mother, way back in *Safe As Milk* days. He said, "I've got too much time to be without love." Don immediately wrote a song and had guitar parts worked out with Alex for the entire thing. It was more of a ballad (in the "story" sense of a ballad) and was quite long and very interesting. It could have been an hour made-for-television movie or something. I can remember almost nothing about it except a guy being stranded somewhere and being in several very bad situations and persevering until he reached his love. When I heard this, I told my father that he had written this song, and he listened for it on the radio. I think it made him feel good. The song in general is a bit out of character for Don, whose roots really go farther back into Delta Blues rather than R&B. The intro seems fine and I like the way it builds with the horns on the *Too Much Time*, because it keeps you asking "For what already?" You're curious and sucked in. (0:22) give the addition of the horns, arranged well for this type of piece. At (0:57) it loses it and the radio audience as far as I'm concerned. No one wants to hear about stale beans and sardines and *"dreaming about somebody to cook for me"* is sexist even by 1972 standards. The guitar line that backs it is awkward and unbalanced and throws the whole thing out of whack. I would have cut from (0:56) to (1:10) and left out that 14 seconds of dreck. The suspension of the beat, however, before (1:48) works really well even though it comes in later than you would expect. The 14 seconds I would have cut would have made this song (2:30), which is all it needs to be.

4. CIRCUMSTANCES - Again, here is another that was written back during *Spotlight* rehearsals. Although, I think the lyrics go back even farther to pre-*SAM* times. I love the first twenty seconds of this: the intro give you chills and has that power that leaves you dripping with anticipation. *Click Clack's* riff is re-visited here in the best of all possible ways, with a *Glider*-like harp floating along underneath. The guitar to *Click Clack* comes in at (0:34) after a simple but effective warm up, along with the lyrics. At (0:41) the drums do this wonderful assertive drop-beat punctuating the lyrics extremely effectively. At (1:08) Bill sneaks in his guitar part that soon becomes the naked theme for a moment as Don sings:

> *The sun will sunburn you but,*
> *Not as bad as those old people do…*

The guitar quickly cross-fades to Artie softly (at first) playing quads on the set which crescendo to a (1:21) half-time interpretation of the opening line and then quickly kicks into the *Click Clack* rhythm once again. The band abruptly and effectively stops at (1:47) so that Don acapella explains (to the woman this time);

> *Little girl don't you know that*
> *The stars up above,*
> *Are runnin' on love,*
> *Little girl, don't you know*
> *That they're winkin' at you?*

Bill joins in with a simple one to four chord lick that keeps the thing moving and the listener anticipating. The band comes in as Don plays a harp melody echo of what he just sang. The band stops abruptly again at (2:40) Don again acapella with just the drums doing quads this time, the band falls in at (2:54) the ending is OK. However, I wanted to hear the outro like the intro, with the slow lyrics. This would have worked better for me and I think it would have worked better live.

5. MY HEAD IS MY ONLY HOUSE UNLESS IT RAINS - The titles too long and Don is not enough in touch with his feeling to pull this off. He throws away the title in the wrong place and so makes it a forgettable piece. The lyrics are clumsily laid to a fairly well played track. Don hasn't thought this one through. He didn't arrange the lyrics to fit the music and vice versa. It just meanders around and the lyrics are lost in the muddle. He's trying to fit too much in and he doesn't know where he is, or what music section works best for what lyric. I think the line that typifies Don's feelings about this song most is the line that says;

> *I hate to have other people hear me sing this song…*

The best line in the song and the only one that really sounds like it's in the right place is the one at (2:16) which is the title line;

> *My head is my only house unless it rains…*

But I love the line that says;

> *My arms are two things in the way unless they're wrapped around you...*

6. SUN ZOOM SPARK - Definitely a favorite for me. From the over-played guitar at the beginning to the first line at (0:06), I'm sucked in. The beat moves me and it isn't rock at all. I love the way he uses his Howlin' Wolf (hey, that guy didn't influence me!) voice on the words - *Magnet draw day from Dark*. How 'bout that steam-engine harp at (0:44)? That gets it! I bet that even gets it for the "Mean E," "Winged Eel." Has this song got something to do with magic? I don't know, but this line always made me wonder:

> *I don't care who you are, or what size y'are,*
> *I'm gonna magnetize ya!*

The only thing that bugs me about this song is the zipping up and zipping down the guitar. I always want to hear it LOW the first time and HIGH the second (different octave) instead of high both times. Other than that, this works for me all the way through.

7. CLEAR SPOT - This song was originally in 5/4 time and there's a funny story about this song. But I'm not going to tell it... OK, I will. I had picked up a tube of Black Minstrel Makeup backstage at the Guthrie theatre. Ok, I STOLE IT! (That's the part I didn't want to tell, now I'll probably get a bill from them for "One Medium Tube of Mather's Minstrel Makeup) I'm not really a thief, but it was just so weird looking with the black and white minstrel picture. I had to have it. Anyway, one night in Felton, during a "band talk" in which I think Bill was the culprit, (after all, he had the nerve to devote 5 years of his life to Don's music, who does he think he is?) I snuck out of the room to take a breather from the negativity and spied this makeup in my trap case. I went into the bathroom and put it all over my face. I had a beard and rather than looking like a minstrel, I looked like some guy getting ready to do a guerilla attack on a peaceful settlement. I walked in the room and everybody saw me except Don, who had his back to me. I walked up behind him and grabbed him on the shoulders and screamed "Gotcha!" and it truly scared the holy bejabbers out of him. (Is that the correct spelling on "bejabbers?") Anyway, it ended the talk, much to Bill's relief, and blew Don's ego-ridden "cool" much to my satisfaction. We went down into the rehearsal room and played *Clear Spot*. Now, I'm talking, this is probably the only time Don "played" with the band in YEARS! I'm not kidding! Even on stage, he usually just showed up, but tonight, he performed and sang - like my hero from high school. He got out his harp, and we played *Clear Spot* (which originally was in 5/4 like I said) and the women came in voluntarily (my girlfriend, Ellen, Mark's wife Laurie, and Jan Van Vliet) and we had a party! This also goes along with my theory of women not liking the band because it was a situation filled with oppression. For that night, just for a moment. The band actually played like a band and Don acted like he was a member. It was fun for about 43 minutes. I think it was the first time I had fun playing with Don since pre-*Safe As Milk* days. I think that may be the reason this wound up being the title cut. It is a completely different arrangement, but I like it a lot. This song cooks and moves and is more reminiscent of the early band than most of the material. Art's drums on this are like a stretched-out version of what I played in the 5/4 version.

8. CRAZY LITTLE THING - I love the intro, the way it's just guitar, drums and voice and already has you moving. Then the bass and rhythm come in and just propel you. I love the way dynamics are used on this album. The instruments are not pelting you at every minute. There's taste here and thoughtful preparation (Oh, man, that's so heavy). Artie employs a Drumbo beat (modified to his needs and played on different drums) starting at (0:33) which is from *Hobo Chang Ba, TMR*. The Blackberries seem out-of-place at (0:47) but their answer;

You won't find out from me.

Works for me...

I'd love to have heard Bill's bottleneck line an octave higher at some point. One thing that bothers me about the production is that Bill's soloing should be panned center and TURNED UP you know, like a FEATURED PLAYER rather than some miniscule part on the track. It's a great solo and if eq'd properly (which is a technical term for TWEAKED) it would have sounded a lot better. This song loses its accessibility when Don (here we go again) phrases in such a way that he overlaps what should have been an instrumental part or at least a new section at (2:27).

9. LONG NECK BOTTLES - It's definitely and eccentric intro. "Where's this going?" I thought. I had to look to see what song I was listening to. Oh yeah, that one. I like the non-amplified harp. It has a totally different sound because you can do all these things with your hands to change the nuance. Bill jump starts the rhythm at (0:10) and it moves along nicely except I still maintain that Don sounds lost lyrically. Milt Holland doing some of that nice tambourine stuff that he did on *Abba Zaba* during the harmonica solo at (1:25) This song begins to sound a little like *Hit A Man* at (1:50) with a guitar solo of similar phrasings.

10. HER EYES ARE A BLUE MILLION MILES - I thought Don wrote this for Jan and when I mentioned it to him he said, "No man, Jan's eyes are brown." Oops. I know, maybe I'm completely wrong about everything else I've said here too. Anyway, he said this song was about the oceand. (It's funny, but Don always pronounced the word 'ocean' this way.) I like the way all the instruments are arranged in this, with that final tambourine beat catching each phrase. Don's vocal is pretty nice on this. I love the drooping guitar lines at (0:44) and how they don't quite release and resolve when you want them to. The bass part always struck me a little odd here. Didn't really clash, but it just seems to be another conversation entirely. Is that a mandolin playing those high double picked notes at (2:13)

11. BIG-EYED BEANS FROM VENUS - This one's right up there with *Glider* for number one spot in the John French favorites. This song always makes me feel good. I want to laugh. There's humor and strength in this song. It's making fun of itself in a sense. Greg Davidson asked Don to explain what the lyrics meant. It's all about sex, according to him. Maybe that's obvious to everyone but me, who thought it was about Aliens Concerned about Overpopulation (ACO) - an organization I've been active with for years. I was really disappointed when I found out the truth, because it was our Lodge song and we used to sing it as a group at every meeting. I made sure to bring my pitch pipe so we would get it in the right key just in case it made a difference in the "Universal Key Perspective" (UKP). All seriousness aside, to me, this is what a rock song should be about: nonesense. Having fun. I loved playing this on tour and I never walked off stage afterwards feeling like I hadn't given the audience a great uplifting moment. There's not much to say about the music. It has some great drum parts and utilizes the P-K-Ro-P beat. When Don first put it on the list I was a little apprehensive about teaching this to the band on the 1975 tour. I wasn't worried about them doing it, I was wondering, since I hadn't been there originally, if I could figure out the parts. Once I strapped on a guitar and went after it, it was simplicity. Denny and Bruce played the "Long Lunar Note" really great together, because Bruce would "circular breathe" that low note which is a way horn players can play a note seemingly without taking a breath, by storing air in their cheeks and blowing it out and then breath in by suppressing their cheeks and shutting of their throat. It's complicated, but it actually works. Denny would come in down low, and fade in. It was a great effect. (1:45) takes us into a Kandy Korn effect without using more than the two chords. It is very similar in structure, with the same drum fills at the end of each section.

12. GOLDEN BIRDIES - Another funny performance. This one is full of magic images and funny wizard like characters. *Obeah Man* was a song Don wrote in the old days and never recorded. *Obeah Man* means Witch Doctor. Elliot Ingber really has to be given credit for the whole concept of this piece. It borrows from not only *Mirror Man's* ³/₄ time bass and drum section, but also from *Clouds Are*

Full Of Wine. That wonderful introduction that should be heard 100 times. Elliot heard the poem and put it together and it became a part of the set of the 1971 Decals tour. Don strongly objected to "cutting up my music into little bits" but when he actually performed it (Elliot could be quite persuasive when inspired) he saw that it was one very interesting piece of music and had a credibility of it's own. I'm quite sure Mark's playing bass on this song, rather than guitar. The bass part is left out of the "Clouds" lines, which is rather disappointing to me, I love those lines. So, what is a Singabus? I always thought it was some kind of Demon spirit like Incubus and Succubus, which are invisible spirits that have sex with humans. What color is "acid gold?" My dictionary defines Incubus as 1. anything that tends to depress or discourage. 2. A nightmare 3. In folklore, a male demon that has sexual intercourse with sleeping women. Succubus is, in folklore, a female demon that has sexual intercourse with sleeping men. "Hush, Sookie Singabus," is almost like it could be the guy's little name. Ain't he cute? Who knows? If I think about the lyrics too much, I get a creepy feeling, so I usually just go on to something better. Like the end:

> And the pantaloon duck, white gooseneck quacked:
> Webcor, Webcor

Hard to stay serious after that line...

Clear Spot has a lot of the touches of the original Magic Band. I think it's probably my favorite album. I can put this one on and have great feeling, probably because I can't associate any negative experiences with it like with some many of the other albums. Zoot came into his own at this point, and I was really happy for him. Roy Estrada, whom I haven't mentioned at all, is a fantastic bassist. He and Artie working together formed the best foundation yet in terms of accessibility combined with Beefheart's idosyncrastic lyrics and vocals. I'm surprised it didn't do better in the charts. It did great in mine.

BAT CHAIN PULLER
(Unreleased Version 1976)
Studio(s): Paramount Studios. Los Angeles, CA
Recording Date: Spring 1975
Producer(s): Don Van Vliet, Frank Zappa
Engineer: Kerry McNab
Band Personnel: Don Van Vliet (vocals, harmonica, sax); Denny Walley (guitar); Jeff Moris Tepper (guitar); John Thomas (electric piano, synthesizer); John French (drums, guitar).

I listen to this album with a certain amount of happiness. It was a relatively good time in my relationship with Van Vliet for the most part. The recording followed a successful tour of Europe and short tour of the California West Coast ending in New Year at the LA Forum. Unfortunately, Elliot Ingber and Bruce Fowler left the band after the tour and before the session for reasons mentioned in the text. John Thomas, a keyboardist I had worked with, was then contacted by Don and became the replacement for Bruce, playing synth bass with his left hand and Fender Rhodes piano with his right. Jeff Tepper, a non-professional player who had been Don's neighbor in Trinidad, CA was contacted to replace Elliot.

I have to admit that I wasn't happy about working with Jeff. I would have rather had someone with experience in the studio and on stage. Tepper was very much a Beefheart fan in the more extreme sense. I didn't feel this was good for the project, as it became a little more cult-like because of Jeff's near-adoration of Don. It also slowed down the progress of the rehearsals, because in the beginning, Jeff barely knew how to keep a guitar in tune, plus he had to learn how to finger-pick - at least he had to learn the "Beefheart" style of fingerpicking - and Don insisted that he buy new equipment, all which took time away from rehearsals.

In the meantime, I was constantly "taking the flack" being called into Herb Cohen's office to explain why this album was taking so long. Herb was used to Frank's prolific and economic production techniques. Frank's players could put together albums more quickly because his music was not only written out, but much more within the rules of "conventional" music, and so easier to assimilate in a sense. Zappa also understood how musicians learned and comprehended music, as he was also a part of his own process, and so constantly rehearsed his players on the road and recorded much of his material live. On top of this, Denny Walley was having financial difficulties of his own. Working for Van Vliet was not nearly as prosperous as working for Zappa. Suddenly, Denny was having to hitch rides with me to rehearsal so his wife could take their car to work. He had a lot of stress and responsibility that the rest of us did not.

I was under stress to a certain extent because of being the musical director. I had transcribed three rather long and tedious pieces that were extremely difficult to teach the players. I was living in Lancaster, but the band was rehearsing every day in Hollywood, about 2 hours and 20 minutes round trip for me, plus rehearsing 6 - 8 hours a day, plus working at night on the material we would learn the next day. We basically focused on *The Thousandth And Tenth Day Of The Human Totem Pole*, which was over 7 minutes of continuously changing music. I had already mastered the two other difficult pieces on guitar, *Seam Crooked Sam*, and *Odd Jobs*, and so I concentrated on the one piece that no one yet knew.

Our daily rehearsal routine consisted of learning little pieces of *Totem Pole* and the intro to *Odd Jobs*. Other songs were easier to learn and took less time, such as *Brick Bats* and *Bat Chain Puller*. Out of necessity, and when I could put Herb off no longer (I believe we rehearsed nearly 2 months). I decided to play guitar on *Seam Crooked Sam*, and the remainder of *Odd Jobs* myself. I played without the use of picks, just using my fingers. This put a tremendous amount of pressure on me not only to learn and rehearse drum parts but to actually practice very difficult guitar parts each day and perfect them for performance. I had never considered playing guitar on the album until now - with the exception of *Flavor Bud Living*. The album was recorded at a studio not far away (I believe it was on Santa Monica Blvd). called Paramount Studios. The engineer on the session was Kerry McNabb. Herb sent Dick Barber, who I remember as a long time "roadie" of Frank's, to come to the session the first day to make sure "the boys didn't waste time," - at least this was the impression we all had of this decision. Dick knew nothing about Don's music and was immediately expelled at Don's insistence. I believe there was an effective plea made to Frank. We were all relieved to have Dick out of the session, as his comments that first day of recording seemed absolutely out of context with everything we did.

1. BAT CHAIN PULLER - I have read all the stories of how the drum beat in *Bat Chain Puller* originated with a bit of a chuckle. Although I told this story in the *Grow Fins* booklet, I will repeat it here. Don came to rehearsal one day and it was raining. It was unusual for Don to come to rehearsal as I had requested he stay away, or at least come later in the day. I recorded the progress and gave him a daily report of the progress, but this day he drove down. On the way to rehearsal, he was listening to his Volvo Windshield wipers and became very excited and inspired by the beat he perceived. He came in with a teeny portable cassette machine he carried with him everywhere. "Listen to this, can you get this, man?" he asked as he burst into the room. Don always became very excited when he was about to write something new. I listened, and what I vaguely heard over the engine noise and rain hitting the windshield was a very subtle rhythm of windshield wipers. "I can't hear it very well," I said. "Come out to my car, man, this is too good." So, we (John Thomas and I) followed him out to the car and I sat in the front passenger seat as he started the car and turned on the wipers. I could easily hear the beat he was talking about. I wrote down the idea in musical notation on a matchbook cover borrowed from Don. He then asked John Thomas to listen to the windshield cleaner pump, which squirted glass cleaner onto the windshield. I went back inside and worked on the drum beat. What I heard I interpreted thusly: The rubber wiper blades "flap over" as they get to the end of the cycle and this is just a tiny moment before they actually engage to return. I played this on the hi-hat. At the outside edge of the cycle (halfway through, when the driver's wiper is in the middle of the windshield) there is a little "click" as the gear reverses to bring the mechanism back which I played as a tom tom rim shot. As it pulls back, the window is drier, so it makes a low-pitched "rubbing" sound, which I played on a Tom tuned so that the head would have a slow decay. The kick drum was the basic mechanism cycle sound, which was lower. John's synth part was the sound of the little pump making that "wheezing" sound as the pump motor raced. Since there is no real "bass" in the song, the synth is sometimes played an octave lower than the actual sound was in order to fill in the bottom of the harmonic spectrum, and the tom with decay is eq'd (tone control) with a lot of bass and allowed to be strong in the track. This is thanks to Kerry McNabb, the engineer. It's a nice combination. I have heard a lot of rap songs in recent years that clearly seemed to have an influence that could possibly be traced back to the atonal methodology employed in this rhythm track. The rest came fairly easily, mostly from slide guitar parts Don created on the spot and whistled to the players. He also played some parts on harmonica and had Denny (primarily) "double" them on guitar. The center "polyrhythmic" section (2:00) came from a written piano part that had been written prior to this day. I recall teaching it to them in a separate section and then adding it to the rhythm track later. All in all, this went together fairly rapidly and was an enjoyable process. The lyrics have always been completely enjoyable and absolutely incomprehensible to me all at the same time. Disconnected images are sown together with the fabric of the music in such a way as to make an enjoyable whole. The title stems from Don's love of old horror movies and especially the fake Vampire Bat that always seemed to be hanging by a chain in that same window, being pulled by the "man behind the curtain." Don took a particular delight in this type of "special effect." This was in the same spirit as Zappa's *Cheepnis* in which he describes a bad horror film moment in which an already tacky special effect was marred by the momentary appearance on film of a board being used by a prop man to "animate" the featured creature out of the cave). This *Bat Chain Puller* apparently became not a song about special effects but the name of a very strange train. It is filled with images I could never hope to understand, and as I was always deeply involved with the music, I never really paid that much attention to the lyrics in those days. I do enjoy images that are created in my mind when I listen to them.

2. SEAM CROOKED SAM - One of the three difficult and lengthy piano pieces I described prior to the 1975 tour, and the first I learned on guitar. I used to take out my guitar each day of the tour and play this through. When I became completely sure of it, I then started playing it through with a blindfold so that I couldn't possibly look at the guitar, and once I mastered that, I would then play it to the tape that I had with me while on tour. I became "one" with this music, more than any other Beefheart piece. I can't remember when the decision was made for me to play guitar on this piece in the studio, but I believe it was early on, when I performed it for Don. John Thomas and I practiced this together, I playing from memory and him reading my transcript, which was several pages long and taped to a large piece of cardboard so that he would never have to turn a page. When we began to practice together, I found that after months of practice, I had interpreted about a dozen notes wrong and had to relearn small sections of the song. We spent time reviewing the tape and realized that about half these were errors in transcribing and the other half errors in my reading my own transcription and applying it to guitar. It still came together fairly quickly and when Don heard it, he felt that it did-n't need further instrumentation and I was a little disappointed because I think I could have played some really interesting drums to this. How often does a drummer first learn a really difficult piece on guitar and then play drums to it himself? It would have been a whole different concept. The lyrics I first recall hearing at the Felton cabin compound (Near Santa Cruz / Ben Lomond). It seemed like Jan actually read this to us at least once. I really get a strong set of images from the free-association poetry and especially remembered the line "architecture tincture of red arkies." I loved the coined phrases like "wrist o' fan" (wrist ah fan??). If I were to compare it to anything, it would be Tennessee Williams meets Alan Ginsberg reading Lawrence Ferlinghetti. The little vocal at the end - the "hink" sound that Don does - makes me laugh every time I hear it. These were good times in a sense that Don wasn't taking himself too seriously most of the time. This was a sound he made when he was happy. I don't know whether it was meant to be an animal sound or what, but it was a great source of fun and this era of working with Don was actually for the most part quite enjoyable.

3. HARRY IRENE - The lyrics are about the only thing Beefheartian about this piece that was first introduced to me during *Spotlight Kid* rehearsals. The tongue-in-cheek lyrics spin a rather vague, distorted yarn about exactly what, we never really know, hence the near-last line, "What does this mean?" I suppose this is Don's idea of a riddle. Of course, these lyrics are much clearer than most of Van Vliet's lyrics to begin with, so any Beefheart fan worth his salt should not be surprised by them. I do remember Don explaining that "ran a canteen" was actually the name of a "dyke" (as he referred to lesbians back in those days). I really always wondered if Harry Irene were actually one person with a sexual identity problem (two people, Harry and Irene, like you've never seen …) or actually a husband/wife team that had been pulled apart by tragic circumstances which left Harry in a strange dilemma. The important part to note about this song is the fact that this particular version includes brilliant piano work by John Thomas, who actually could PLAY this kind of music and was basically improvising through the whole piece. Also featured are the hitherto unknown accordion stylings of that MASTER of the bellows, Denny Walley, who actually COULD play the accordion and had taken lessons as a child. If I remember correctly, the accordion was borrowed from Gail Zappa - (perhaps herself a closet accordionist?). The end of this song features that great whistling that band members never quite became used to. Don whistled in his throat rather than with his lips, so he could hold a cigarette in his lips and look as though he wasn't doing a thing while whistling the most extraordinary parts. I love this ending, Don should have done more whistling in his music. What a bizarre piece for a Beefheart album, but somehow it worked.

4. BIG POOP HATCH - As I write this, I am embarrassed to say that I can't remember the title. This strongly, STRONGLY reminds me of *Howl*, the poem I had heard Ginsberg recite on an LP years earlier at Don's. This is one of the things I would have just as soon left off the album. It seemed inappropriate to me. Of course, I can't really say that I enjoy this kind of free-association poetry. Jeff Tepper was fawning over Don in what I considered the usual "Beefheart Worship Mode," that fans would take. He was young and impressionable, and the man had never pushed him down half a flight of stairs, so he was also quite naïve concerning Don's "dark side". I recall being in the control room as Don began to recite this. I didn't really like to be at any sessions Don did, because he was always relatively unprepared in my estimation. This reading was no exception. In order to save face as he stammered over the words and struggled with the lines, he began to blame Jeff and I for his inability to concentrate. Now, Jeff and I were sitting in the booth, saying nothing, and not moving around at all. However, Don would become quite self-conscious, and this is when I saw the "old Don" emerge - The *TMR* Don. It was a mild resurrection, but nonetheless made me quite uncomfortable, and I began questioning right at this point if I should continue working with him. He insisted that we had "had too much to think," as his famous quote goes and that the "fishbowl effect" (us through the window) was distracting him. We eventually wound up sitting on the floor behind him, in the tracking room, unable to make a sound or move. Imprisoned, which was a very familiar feeling to me. Jeff was just excited to be around his hero. I was pissed that I had even allowed myself to be talked into this.

5. FLAVOR BUD LIVING - Prior to the 1975 tour, Don bought an old upright piano and had it moved to his mother's trailer (which was actually a mobile home in a mobile home park). I actually found it for him through a friend, Tut Penfield, who owned a piano company and rebuilt pianos in a shop behind his home. I helped him deliver it, and it was not an easy task to get this piano up into the trailer. It sat near the front door for years, and then I bought it from him. Anyway, after Tut left, Don sat down , turned on a cassette recorder and played this piece (it's actually an octave lower on piano). This was probably July of 1975. He said, "You should play this on the guitar." So, I made a copy of the tape and took it home and began to work on it. I wound up using an alternate tuning. The tempo here is almost exactly as what was on the tape, but later Don asked Gary Lucas to play the same solo on *Doc At The Radar Station*, and when I heard it, I couldn't believe how fast he played it. More on that during Doc notes, however. I recorded this the same day that Don recited *Big Poop Hatch*. I remember Jeff Tepper really complimenting me on my playing and how good that made me feel. I was really enjoying playing guitar during those days.

6. BRICK BATS - I never quite understood why Don didn't redo the lyrics on the beginning where he stammers on "fly." The lyrics to this piece convey to me the love Don had of old horror movies once again. It also conveys the delusional visions of a paranoid watching a fire in his fireplace. It shows what a vivid and complex imagination Don has. My favorite image is "the window curtain ghost." There are three distinct sections to the music. The first theme is revisited after a more energetic middle section and then comes a third section at the end. The middle section was definitely written on the piano during this period of time, probably before the tour. The first and last, basically the same, were also written on the piano to the best of my knowledge, as was the end section, but at a different time than the center section. The center section of this actually reminds me of the center section to *Bat Chain Puller*, except that the whole band in this instance is actually playing the "other tempo." It has similar harmonic structure however. The center section was written, I believe the same day as *Flavor Bud Living*, but a few minutes later, which may be why it appears just after *FBL* in sequence. At (1:04), I am amazed by how Don could interject a part in the music and then coordinate it with his lyrics in such a manner as with *"fast, n' slow, n' every other motion."* There are moments on this album when I almost think it to be my favorite, due to the humorous approach Don takes to some of the material. This is hilariously funny and I find myself having to stop to laugh as I write these notes. If Don could have only taken his relationship to musicians as non-seriously as he took his music (which almost happened during this session), I think "a good time was had by all" could have actually applied to this situation. In this context, I really enjoy the soprano, which reinforces everything without overpowering the music. This is something we discussed before mixing. I was quite candid and frank with Don in saying that I felt he had ruined a few of his own pieces with his overdone sax solos. I wish I could have heard what he was doing when I was drumming to this track. However, the sax was overdubbed, so there is no "interplay" between the sax and drums.

7. THE FLOPPY BOOT STOMP - The title sounds like a new dance craze. I recall the lyrics to this being written during *Trout Mask* and recited by Jeff Cotton on a very rainy, rainy night. That was when Don called the tree surgeons to check out the twin eucalyptus trees that sat right next to the house. It rained a lot that winter, and neighbor's trees came crashing down all around us. Now, these trees that stood next to the house were HUGE. Unlike much of the (unpublished) material I heard recited during *Trout Mask, Floppy Boot Stomp* was one of the pieces I truly remembered. I was really happy when he pulled this one out of the proverbial hat and decided to do it. This is definitely a favorite for me from this session. It was written during the rehearsals and communicated for the most part in the old whistled/sung creation method Don would still occasionally use. The beginning is really based on the original demo of *Electricity* that A&M heard and rejected. Denny's high slide guitar solo at the beginning is the harp solo from the demo tape, almost verbatim. Don pulled out this old tape and had me teach it to him, but actually, Denny just taught it to himself. The bass part is very close to the original bass part and the rhythm guitar Jeff plays is a double-timed permutation. The drums are a combination of Don's "baby-beat" concept of drumming (feet played RLLR, while hands played double-speed RLRL on two different drums, usually hat and snare, like on *Booglerize*). Notice at (0:21) how Don suspends the word "Fear" until after the drum break, (which is a combination of baby beat and P-K-Ro-P). This was because at this point, he had become, as I mentioned earlier, much more aware of "stepping all over his own music" and allowing special moments to come through, instead of burying them in the overdubs. I also saw this as a gesture of respect to the hard work and long hours the band was putting in. After the descending guitar lines (0:22) a subdued Rhodes piano chordal (which may be in 11/4 - I'm not sure) section played by John Thomas adds another texture to the blues-like slide riffs of fourth, flatted third, and tonic. Note also that the chords are the inversion of the bridge of Electricity played in reverse order and twice as fast. At (0:48) (that little scream in the background is me) this blues-like riff becomes more accented and played by all, while the drums do a combination baby-beat / P-K-Ro-P, and background vocals pipe in with "Hoo-Doo Hoe Down." At (1:12) comes Denny's guitar break, which wasn't originally intended to be like this. He got lost as we were moving fast in the rehearsal and was struggling frantically to remember his part and actually played this totally by accident. The tape recorder was on and Don went absolutely nuts, "ARE YOU KIDDING, MAN, THAT WAS GREAT!" We turned the tape recorder back, and replayed the part and Denny learned his own "mistakes" verbatim. JT also included his bass notes. Don's ears were always open to take advantage of these kinds of moments. (1:18) reveals the band playing yet another more fragmented version of the fourth, flatted third, tonic combination. (1:43) brings the band into a "figure-eight" section which he probably just whistled to everyone. The stammering vocal line at (1:48) is left in almost as a balance to Denny's slide error at (1:12). (1:58) is the intro re-visited. In fact, although I'm not going to take time, I really believe that the entire song is repeated twice because it ends at (3:54), which is EXACTLY (1:58) time two!!! (That drummer must have been keeping pretty good time. Well, he had a lot of help from a cooking rhythm section). My favorite line is (1:41) " 'n *the horse compared his hooves,"* because I always imagined the horse looking at the devil's hooves and his own hooves, like "What the hell?" This is a very well-performed piece. The balance is slightly low between vocal and band. However, the words are really important and nothing is actually buried. I would have loved to have heard just a tad of harmonica here and there. Oh well ...

8. A CARROT IS AS CLOSE AS A RABBIT GETS TO A DIAMOND - This was Jeff and John's (Thomas) baby. I had nothing to do with it in terms of musical direction. I don't know if it was a tape or if there was an actual transcription (which would have had to have been Artie Tripp). No one seems to remember. I do recall being really worried about Jeff's guitar being out of tune with the piano. It always sounded terrible when they played it together at rehearsal. I am guessing now that it was partly the fact that the Rhodes was out with itself and therefore made the guitar sound more out. The track sounds relatively good to me. The guitar is mixed low in the track and the piano carries the song well. I am not picking on Jeff here. This was his first time in the studio and he had only been playing this style of guitar for approx 3-4 months. I know that this piece was written much earlier than this, and it always reminded me of *White Jam*. I also recall hearing it during a much earlier period. I am guessing this song was written during the period when Don lived in Woodland Hills after he and Jan moved from the Trout House into a smaller house of their own. He was writing and painting a lot during this period. I recall going over and hearing several things he had done. He had a room set up with his piano on one wall and a huge very well articulated painting of Jan's (suprisingly similar to Don's work - not the articulation part - and even reminiscent a little of Victor Hayden's) on the opposite wall. He used to look at the painting and say, "People say I can paint, but she wipes me out, man."

9. OWED T' ALECKS - I always felt that this song was a put-down to Alex Snouffer, who had a definite passion for motorcycles until he broke his wrist *(Five miles back I took uh spill ?)*. It appealed to Alex, at least the original. A demo with the same lyrics and completely different music was included on the demo submitted to A&M. I recall hearing this tape, but never playing the song. I have heard bikers say that this song actually sounds a little like the "hum" one hears on a motorcycle when riding. While learning this song for the session (Don's "sing n' whistle" composing technique) Van Vliet decided to get on Jeff Tepper's case about the way he was playing the first part. It was highly reminiscent of the "Trout House" days and the "talks" we used to have, except that no one else said much of anything or chose sides. I let it go on, but afterwards told Don in no uncertain terms that I would be gone if he ever spoke to Jeff or anyone else in that manner. I also told him he needed to apologize to Jeff, which he did. By this time, I knew that in order to keep things on track, I had to be a "cop" in a sense, or it would wind up being an everlasting "circus of terrors" and a big waste of everyone's time. Back to the music, this intro was an area where we really had to be "on our own" in a sense, because we were all playing different intertwining parts and it was a lot more difficult than it sounds. For instance, I'm playing in $3/4$ time and so is Jeff, but I am "echoing" him half a beat later. This was confusing for both he and I, as with *Trout Mask*, because we were playing to a pulse and everything everyone else played was often as not unrelated. On this, we are actually really playing similar ideas, but just staggered enough to make it confusing. The whole intro was very difficult to achieve. After we played it for a while, and Don actually "communicated" his idea, we were able to see how it worked. However, these are times I always dreaded, because although Don knew what he wanted, it was really up to us to figure out how to make it work, which was always a lot easier when he wasn't around. As soon as we started counting or trying to figure things out so that we could wind up together he would start saying, "Just play, man!" that showed his ignorance of music to the experienced musicians and scared the shit out of the inexperienced, like Jeff. I don't know if Jeff was scared that day, but I know I would have been had I been in his shoes, because he was the one Don decided to "target." Also, I would estimate that it took us 4 hours to actually get the first 23 seconds of this piece together, which was frustrating for everyone. It was a lack of Don's musical ability and his "train yourself you strain yourself" philosophy that wasted most of this 4 hours. Anyone with musical understanding would have sat down and worked this out one bit at a time. It would have been played it 20 minutes instead of 4 hours. At (1:51) I think that Don's brilliance for little touches shines through again on "took a spill" as he times it exactly with the intended drum break. Here's a guy who could get lost singing *Abba Zaba*, but could time out something like this to the exact moment. Incredible. Denny Walley is the star of this show, listen to the best slide playing ever on a Beefheart album and I remember two songs: *Alecks* and *Hit A Man*. It all depends on your taste, but I rate Denny's solo here at near top of the chart. Don't ask me to choose, but these are both damned good solos. Listen to the way Denny echoes Don's laughter and then just elevates the whole song about 15 levels as he carries it out. This makes me want to go play again. This is what is generally missing from Beefheart's music, a free-spirited independent solo from an expert guitarist. Bravo Mr. Walley.

10. ODD JOBS - A poem from the *Trout Mask* days, if I remember correctly, and music done from the *Big Sur Suite* era, when Don moved from the Trout House into his own smaller rental house with Jan shortly after their marriage in 1970, and began playing more stuff on cassettes (Note: I don't call this "composing") This was my other major guitar piece. John Thomas and I played the basic track. He played exactly what I had transcribed from the tape with his right hand on the Rhodes piano and his left hand on the Moog synth, in essence, making his left hand the "bass" part. Jeff and Denny played the introduction, which is as far as we were able to learn it as a group in the limited time we were given. I then overdubbed the guitar. More about what kind of guitar I had to use in the text. However, I will say that I was very disappointed with the "clean" guitar sound that Kerry went for on this and on *Seam Crooked Sam*. This was supposed to be a ripping piece, and this version is nothing but an anemic suggestion of what it actually could have sounded like. Re: drumming: Don started directing me as I was playing the drums and I became distracted and lost my concentration, therefore, there are some timing glitches, and because of the length of the piece and the limited funding for studio time, we had to keep this take. I was never happy with it.

11. THE THOUSANDTH AND TENTH DAY OF THE HUMAN TOTEM POLE - Nicknamed "Scrotum Pole" by Denny Walley, this song was the unending marathon of learning sessions. Neither Denny nor Jeff read music (Denny referring to written music as "fly shit on paper") but it would have been so much simpler for me and so much more productive for the project to have 3 readers instead of one. I am referring to John Thomas, who was able to take my transcribed chart and play it verbatim. He took a copy of the original piano tape home with him and worked on this song. The first time I heard him play it, it was complete, from beginning to end with very few glitches. In retrospect, I consider that perhaps I was trying too much to control the situation. However, Don was so afraid of his piano tapes being lost on the world that I actually had to secretly give John a tape and make him take a solemn oath of blood not to play it for anyone. I learned the drum parts a few days before going into the studio. Basically, I had a tape recorder and the band would play a section. In the silence following Don would then immediately "sing" drum parts to me by making "drum sounds" with his voice. I kept the parts really simple in interpretation, using many of the elements of drum vocabulary I had developed through the years of his influence. Some aspects are his and some are mine, but the basic flow of the entire drum part from beginning to end is his concept coupled with my simple interpretation. I took the tape home and listened to the sections, putting them together and had it completely memorized the next day by rehearsal. This seemed to astound Jeff Tepper - at least according to Don. However, I had been living with this song for about 7 months, listening to it nearly every day. I was so familiar with the construction of the piece that it was merely second-nature to add the drums. The lyrics to this song are absolutely and tragically hysterical. I can't think of a more fitting way in which to present the absurdity of mankind's "climb to power," whether it be for financial, political, or prideful gain.

12. APES-MA - Do I love this or what? What does this say? A million things. Three at least come to mind. There is not one human being who cannot relate to this basic sadness we all face; the aging process. The poem *Apes-Ma* faces this rather whimsically. Also, I am sure that this is one of Don's "alter egos," just as *Big Joan*, and *The Spotlight Kid*. Don may have known even back at this point in time that he was suffering from MS. I think this is a "reality check" that applies not only to his personal situation, but to all of us: to mankind. Our cage isn't getting any bigger is it? One reason I believe in God is that mankind is cumulatively too stupid to save itself. Watch the news on any given day. Who's getting all the press? murderers, thieves, rapists, corrupt politicians; morons. Where's all the good news? If there's any hope, it surely does not rest within the wisdom of man. All the money in the world will not buy us a new world if we destroy this one. I do share, in a sense, Don's disdain and disappointment with his fellow man. However, unlike Don, I have a hope in God, and this helps me make it through the daily insanity.

13. CANDLE MAMBO - Frank Zappa nixed this song, according to Don. Mr. Z's reasoning was that it "didn't match" with the rest of the cuts. Actually, there could have also been other reasons he didn't wish to express, like the fact the Van Vliet's vocal seems out of phase with the track, and sometimes hesitant and lost. I liked the music to *Candle Mambo*, and somehow, in the back of my head, I still had the misplaced hope that one day, we would actually release a song the general public would embrace. This whole arrangement if I remember correctly was begun during *The Spotlight Kid* rehearsal era and was an outtake of *Clear Spot*. There was a complete studio version, as I recall, which was duplicated as closely as possible by this band for this session. I liked the imagery of this song and I always felt that it was a great song for someone else to sing. Perhaps, Don should have shopped around and found another artist to perform this particular piece.

Conclusion

My thought was that this album would put Van Vliet back on his feet. That wasn't to happen, as a few weeks after completion of the project, Herbie Cohen locked Zappa out of his own studio and a legal battle ensued that prevented this album from being released in a timely manner. Gail Zappa is still trying to decide what to do with it as of the date of this writing. It has been remixed by Dweezil and Ahmet with the help of Denny Walley. My feelings about this, having been the musical director of the project, are fairly predictable. I was very disappointed at not being included in the remix, but at the same time I was glad that at least one participant in the project was there. I don't believe the album should have been remixed to begin with, and I think that when Gail sells it, she should consider that the original mix that Don supervised is the one he would wish to be released.

It is also quite a shame that Denny Walley was never really considered a "valid" member of the Magic Band although he played with the band for approximately 2½ years. His contributions to this album not only show his great playing ability, but also gave the music a more open appeal, to which I think more women would have been attracted.

SHINY BEAST
(BAT CHAIN PULLER)
Studio(s): Automatt, San Francisco, Wally Heider Recording, San Francisco
Recording Date: 1978
Producer(s): Don Van Vliet and Pete Johnson
Engineers: Glen Kolotkin, Jeffrey Norman
Band Personnel: Don Van Vliet (vocals, harmonica, soprano sax, whistling); Jeff Moris Tepper (slide guitar, guitar and spell guitar); Bruce Lambourne Fowler (trombone and air-bass); Eric Drew Feldman (synthesizer, [fender] rhodes, grand piano, bass); Richard Redus (slide guitar, bottleneck guitar, guitar, accordion, fretless bass); Robert Arthur Williams (drums, percussion); Art Tripp (marimba, additional percussion).

Introduction: As I obviously didn't play on this album, I can only go by interview material (which is minimal at best) and my observations of the material and how it relates in structure etc. to the original *Bat Chain Puller,* of which I was musical director.

One thing that I was surprised to learn during the interview with Richard Redus (my only connection to this album) was that Bruce Fowler played a large role as musical director, although, as usual, he received no credit for this. Redus recalls Bruce playing an integral role in the development and learning of the music.

The bass is almost non-existent in the mix. The whole album sounds very light on the bass end. It could have been the fault of the mix-down studio. Perhaps the room wasn't properly tuned and therefore the bass sounded louder than it actually was. In order for me to enjoy this album I used a graphic equalizer and adjusted as follows:

31.5hz @ +5db,
63hz @ +7.5 db
125hz @ +5 db
250hz @ -2.5db
500hz @ -2.5 db
1Khz @ 0 db
2Khz @ +2.5 db
4Khz @ +3 db
8Khz @ -2.5 db
16Khz @ -2.5 db

This is a bit of a radical curve, but definitely gave me more the sound quality I was seeking. Now the music seems a bit more in balance.

1. FLOPPY BOOT STOMP - The instrumentation sounds weaker on this version than the original. Denny definitely spoiled me for this version. The strongest thing about this track is the drums, and then the keyboard, which Eric does a nice job of duplicating. Don sounds to me like he looked one day when trying to re-create one of his own drawings. The lines just never quite fall into place. Robert Williams has a more traditional approach to the drumset and obviously had little time to really absorb the whole Beefheart sound, but for the most part, he is very strong and actually saves the track from falling apart in sections. The big difference between his playing and my playing is that he tends to favor the snare and cymbals more as a traditional drummer would and occasionally interprets parts more as "drum fills" playing them slightly different with less interplay between the hands and feet. He also plays with less dynamic range between the drums, so that everything seems more or less the same volume, which tends to "flatten" the rhythms a bit which is something Artie Tripp seemed to do. His sense of time is impeccable and his articulation also puts me in mind of Artie. Also, the drums are mixed in the more conventional manner, with the kick drum and snare mixed high and the toms a little lower. So part of what I am hearing as a difference may be in the mix rather than RW's style. At (1:12), the interplay is between two guitars as opposed to the original in which just one guitar plays the same thing. This makes the timing a little awkward and scrawly. Also, it's my opinion that the guitar sounds aren't "meaty" enough. Don's vocal sounds weak on this take and especially is off at (1:42) where he tries to duplicate a stammering that is on the original take. Here, it just takes on a staccato cerebral quality that leaves me cold. The recorded sound of his voice has a lot to do with the vocal sound, but the performance also suffers. At (2:27) the guitar is helped along by the trombone doubling the part. At (3:20), the trombone actually distracts from the composition. Especially when he begins to improvise more about (3:30).

2. TROPICAL HOT DOG NIGHT - First of all, I love the piece. The humor is appealing and I think that the instrumentation is much stronger and works better because it was *written for the musicians who are playing it!* Now, that I'm used to the thinness and difference of the tracks, I can enjoy more also. The trombone is used really well in this song. I am having a hard time for sure telling if it is "doubling" the bass in the beginning. The first guitar part on this tune is taken from the song *Odd Jobs* and probably this song was written because either *Odd Jobs* was too difficult for this band or Don just decided that this tune would be more accessible (which it is) to a larger audience. At (1:04), the song reminds me a little of *Lo Yo Yo* (What if my girlfriend back home...) except that Don is just repeating lines that he has already said. This would have been a good place to make a strong lyrical statement, instead, it just seems like it's whatever is next on the lyric sheet. Also, it sounds like he isn't having much fun with the track. There's a real Mardi Gras going on here, but that excited voice doesn't make up for the fact that there seems to be no inspiration or celebration of life behind it. Artie and Bruce are both adding wonderful embellishments to the track, and that seems to give it some lift. The first time I heard this track, I hadn't seriously been listening to Beefheart music for 3 weeks straight, so it's easier for me to notice the dramatic change in Don's level of enthusiasm. Overall, this is a wonderful, playful composition.

3. ICE ROSE - Here is a song that dates back to the *Mirror Man* sessions at TTG originally entitled *Big Black Baby Shoes*. The first thing I notice is that what Bruce is playing seems to be improvised accompaniment, and sporadic at that, and should have been (1) played in a lower octave and (2) mixed at a much lower volume in the track. It actually detracts from the track. Like the instance at (0:24) when it switches from melody to harmony and throws the whole thing off balance. Again, at (0:34) why is the original slide guitar melody covered up entirely by something that sounds like sporadic accompaniment? Whoever is playing the "picked" guitar arpeggios that the marimba is doubling certainly got the perfect tone. This is the best thing I've heard so far out of the guitars. At (0:51) is a slight improvement, but the trombone still sounds like extraneous distraction to me. I don't get it, perhaps merely because I've heard this piece so much without trombone. Robert Williams got lucky here, he was allowed to play cymbals (the original had cymbals excluded by producer Bob Krasnow), which really helps keep the slide melody in a good place in the sonic spectrum. (1:40) The trombone seems to find the right place to be, this section sounds good to me until (1:50) when the trombone takes what seems like a half-hearted attempt at a solo. Bruce could have gotten completely crazy here and made this really interesting. Instead, he sounds inhibited. As the band goes into the end section, the band sounds a little anxious - like young boys looking to get laid. It makes everything rushed - like 9 year old girls practicing their tap dancing. The title, if I remember correctly, comes from a throwaway line in the original lyrics of *When It Blows Its Stacks* - written around 1970. It was something like *"She's an ice rose that only grows in the volcanoes."* If I remember right, Elliot thought the line didn't work. The image became resurrected here.

4. HARRY IRENE - Unlike John Thomas, Eric Drew Feldman, bless his sweet heart, does not know how to play swing music at this point in his life. This John Lennon-style plunk-plunk might work for 2 bars, but it gets rather dreary after 30 seconds and maddeningly tortuous at 45. There's less life in this track than Tom Sawyer's dead frog. It's dead, it's dry, and even Don's vocal loses the whole tongue-in-cheek fun approach this song is supposed to have. At (1:00), he loses the melody of the bridge, wrongly choosing instead to stay in the same note range as the line before when he should go up. Speaking of utilization, where in hell is the trombone when you need it? This would have been the perfect song in which to have a bitchin' faux 1940's-style trombone solo to help with the ambiance. Instead, it sounds like we need to call an ambulance, or maybe pray for an avalanche). I suppose this is what happens when you hire a journalist to be your "producer." The only thing that saves this thing from being mistaken for dead and buried is the re-enactment of Denny's accordion part by Richard Redus. Even the whistling at the end, which is supposed to sound carefree, is more like, "gee, when's this thing gonna end so I can drink my Pepsi?"

5. YOU KNOW YOU'RE A MAN - Led Zeppelin meets Guy Lombardo. Don is in the wrong key for his voice trying and failing to sound like a Rod Stewart type I suppose. My main dislike of this piece is that there never seems to really be a point. Is this supposed to be rabble-rousing rock for the masses? Is this song supposed to appeal to women? Is it supposed to appeal to anybody? How about some lyrical phrasing that works with the well-played track? The low bottleneck solo is the best point in the tune although occasionally played just sharp enough to set my teeth on edge.

6. BAT CHAIN PULLER - The beginning really sets a nice mood. The mix (with the bass boosted) has a really nice quality to it. The guitar underneath is actually rushing a bit. It sets the whole thing just the teensiest bit out of balance. However, by (0:38) when Don's harsh "Bat" note comes in, everything seems to work really well. So far this is the best sounding track. Don seems in fine voice throughout. At (1:01) the harp is out-of-sync with the guitars and played half-heartedly. However at (1:59) the trombone timbre seems right at home and adds rather than detracts to the out-of-tempo guitar section. At the end, I think it would have sounded better had the trombone doubled the low slide guitar, but it certainly has a great deal going on. Though different, it definitely is a great track.

7. WHEN I SEE MOMMY, I FEEL LIKE A MUMMY - This reminds me of the original *Dirty Blue Gene* (included in the *Safe As Milk* CD). It has some of the same rhythms and feel as one section of that original take. I remember hearing these lyrics, or parts of them years before. I like the music, but again, that trombone should be playing static punchy lines. It winds up being just the wrong texture in this whole album so far with the exception of *Tropical Hot Dog Night*. I have no idea about these lyrics. Are they freudian? Or was this just Don's chance to get a bunch of (almost) grown men to sing, "Mommy, Mommy, Mommy?" I vote on the latter.

8. OWED T' ALEX - Why is the bass so low in this track? Is somebody afraid of it or something? Eric Drew Feldman has got great timbres, but boy, gotta get those thin brittle guitar sounds as exposed as possible. This could have used more bottom. Don comes in at the wrong place on harp (0:04), he's supposed to wait until (0:09) instead and of course, who noticed? And what's the trombone doing here? Interplay with the harp that doesn't work? Yes! Actually the trombone begins to work just fine at (0:24) doubling the guitar and then moving to the bass line, which could have been slid a little less or not mixed with the non-octavider part so high in the track. This is one song where the trombone could work playing low sustaining notes, but at (0:57) someone decides it might be nice to have it double the guitar part and play those octave notes which again smoothes over textures that should be left brittle. What's that, a false start at (1:20)? Sounds like a random note that someone just didn't bother to notice. It's in the same texture as the rather blandly-toned slide solo, which begins just a measure or two later. (1:50) is a nice effect with the guitars speeding by like horseflies past a dog's driven ears. Guitarists, get it together at (2:08) please. You're supposed to be playing at the same time! (2:10) is Denny Walley's solo, or a portion thereof, duplicated by Redus as closely as possible and without any of the feeling, which is probably why it's mixed so low in the track? Is that Don affecting laughter? Doesn't sound so happy to me. The harp doesn't help, it got the wrong sound, first of all, should have been through an amp. Secondly, it fights the flow of the song and takes away from the whole ambience. Should have been done more in the spirit of *Glider* to be effective. I do like what the guitars are doing on the ending.

9. CANDLE MAMBO - Where's the BASS? The track sounds good. The guitars are playing nicely, the marimba, the trombone. Everything's working pretty well. It's just that the bass player should have been allowed into the same room as the rest of the band. I like the trombone doubling the slide guitar and the rhythmic feel. The only other thing that bothers me about this track is the same thing I hear over and over in all Van Vliet's material. If Richard Perry did nothing else, he made the lyrics to *Abba Zaba* fit with the music. There's a process here called "lyrical arrangement." You don't just blindly walk into the studio, with lyrics sheets and become a singer, you have to actually know where they go! I think this was probably the number one reason why Don never had an album that sold well - even *Clear Spot* has this same flaw in places. Don is lost, and no one can tell Don he's lost. I will give him the credit of saying that his intuitive approach is flexible enough to fool the casual listener and works well in the beat-poetry approach of chaotic pieces from *Trout Mask* or *Decals*. However, here there is a piece that was actually supposed to be a romantic up-tempo piece and the singer's scrambling to make the words fit. This track is just "blurred" enough to destroy any chance of accessibility. Plus, the speed of this qualifies it as a "samba" not a "mambo."

10. LOVE LIES - This things sucks like a cheap detective novel. These lyrics were written pre-*Safe As Milk* and were slightly altered. The original title was *Mark IX* after Don's Jaguar Mark IX. The music before was very powerful but this sounds like some nightclub blues jam.
I only recall the first verse in entirety of the original (In italics)

> Stopped by your house saw your lamp lit
> *Stopped by your house saw your lamp lit*
> Not a sign of you in it
> *Looking for signs of life in it*
> Where could you go at this hour
> *Where could you go at this hour*
> Has all our love lost it's power
> *Diamond moon shine like a flower*

The first two lines of the second first break the flow of the stanza and the melody, as the second should be the answer to the first, but it's like hearing two first lines and he sounds lost after that.

> I said I'd be here with our flower
> Streetlamps flutter like fireflies:
> *Butterlamps flutter like fireflies*

What appears to be a bridge at (1:18) just repeats the last half of the first verse for the first two lines, then saying

> I miss you more hour by hour
> The roses seem to smell sour

Hmm. Maybe someone should check the expiration date on those roses…
I think this is definitely filler material - and really a bad piece of crap. About the only thing I can praise is that Robert Williams managed to hold a very slow tempo together without dying of boredom.

11. SUCTION PRINTS - Most of this was written during the Decals-era and played on stage often as *Pompadour Swamp* and I always loved doing it - especially when Elliot was playing lead lines over that great driving rhythm. It's got some of the original fire here and definitely is the second strongest "Beefheart" sounding track (*BCP* gets top billing). Bruce's snappy trombone lines help. The drum parts are a combination of mine and Don's ideas. During the *Decals* period, we hadn't been rehearsing much for a few days, so I set up my drums at Artie's Laurel Canyon "pad" in the downstairs room. I had this idea for a "Drumbo" type drum part and had just gotten the new Gon Bop drum kit. I wanted to do something that sounded like a drummer and a percussionist at the same time. I wrote this part out and worked on it until it flowed pretty well. A few days later, we had a rehearsal in Simi Valley, where Bill was living at the time. I brought in my drums and was setting up while they worked on a tune. It was this piece. It was so incredible, because the drum part I had written just "fit" the song exactly. I don't think there's another thing that would have pushed this section like this. It's the one you first hear at (1:55) though Robert Williams' version is slightly altered. He probably obtained that from a tape of Artie Tripp playing a simulation of what I played, but it still is close enough to get the idea. I always liked *Pompadour Swamp*, or *Suction Prints* as it is now called. It was fun to play and had some meat to it. At (0:16) you hear the original drumbeat that I used a lot in *Mirror Man* era songs. Williams is doing a nice bouncy job with it here.

12. APES-MA - See notes in *The Bat Chain Puller* (unreleased version) section.

Conclusion

Well, I was pretty tough on this one. Maybe I was too close to too much of this material to be able to properly judge, but I would not give this a high mark among Beefheart albums. The musicians did an average job of playing. Williams actually stands out here as the guy with the fire, taste, and professionalism. Bruce for the most part sounds misplaced, which is probably mostly Don's fault for not arranging parts for trombone that made sense. There's almost nothing new save *Tropical Hot Dog Night* and the rather dreary *Love Lies*, which is actually almost a blues jam with recycled lyrics that were better the first time around. The production value stinks. Glen Kolotkin, the only one in the control room with any savvy, should have been given equal production credits with Don (for having done the whole job of producing), Feldman, Tepper and Redus are adequate here, but no one shines overall. However, they all do a fairly good job.

DOC AT THE RADAR STATION
Studio(s): Sound Castle Recording Studios, Los Angeles
Recording Date: June 1980
Producer(s): Don Van Vliet
Engineers: Glen Kolotkin, Mitchell Gibson
Band Personnel: Don Van Vliet (vocals, Chinese gongs, harmonica, soprano sax, bass clarinet); Jeff 'Moris Tepper' (slide guitar, guitar, nerve guitar); Eric Drew Feldman (synthesizer, bass, mellotron, grand piano, electric piano); Robert Arthur Williams (drums); Bruce Lambourne Fowler (trombone); John French (slide guitar, guitar, marimba, bass and drums on 11, drums on 2); Gary Lucas (guitar on 10, French horn on 8); Whole band; background vocals on Hot Head, Run Paint, Run Run.

I'm looking at the cover of the vinyl album (does anybody miss that size like I do?) I recall first seeing that drawing before it had the black area. We were standing in the control room and Don said, "Here's the album cover drawing, but you have to imagine this blotted out with black. I think he pulled out some blackened paper and simulated the idea he had in mind. Since I don't understand art, or at least Don's art, I basically wasn't that excited. I loved the title although I didn't understand it at first. Now that I'm older, I realize I probably never will understand it, ha. The idea I get now is sort of this guy who "picks up on things" (singin' through you to me?) telepathically. He's intercepting something. Is "Doc" Don? I don't know. Part of the way he views himself metaphorically? I have no idea. I like the Dock / Doc pun. That guy on the cover looks a little worried. Is this album a message from aliens, intercepted through Van Vliet's channeling? That's the idea I get. It's all poking fun at the source of inspiration, the "muse." Don had a friend during this time who was an air traffic controller. Could this friend be "Doc?"

I turn it over and recall the photo shoot. I had to drive down to this photography studio in … I don't remember exactly where, let's say the Los Angeles basin to be safe, but Hollywood could have been the more specific area. I was there early. I was told to wear black and white. I wasn't really crazy about wearing a tie. It was supposed to be "punk." I remember Robert Williams coming in and looking at me. "I'm jealous," he said, "You look so punk." We look like a bunch of guys who work in cubicles to me. I had inadvertently left a clothes pin on my jacket pocket. Don came up and asked me to take it off, "They'll think you're copying me." I looked at his tie clip. I probably was subconsciously copying him, it was a funny idea. I used mine to attach notes to myself like a refrigerator so I wouldn't forget things. Other people read them to me, like, "You're supposed to be at …" etc. Eric is wearing a wristwatch over his cuff, arms carefully folded as to make sure this eccentricity shows in the picture. Actually, this is something I used to do in 1975, because the watch I owned (which somebody found lying in the street and gave me) hurt my wrist. Did Don suggest this to him, or did he just do that on his own? One of the deep mysteries of life that will never be solved. I wish Gary Lucas could have been in the shot.

One thing I didn't get credit for was extra vocal on *Dirty Blue Gene*, plus everyone should have received credit for singing on *Run Paint Run Run*. I'm not sure if Bruce was there, however for the vocal session.

Sound Castle Studios was actually in Glendale, not far from Waverly Drive, on which was located the house where Don spent his first years. He drove by the house a few times. It was a white two-story house with green shutters. "What kind of fools would move from here to Mojave?" he would ask. "And there's where I didn't go to school, and here's where Sue almost got us killed" (referring to his mother almost walking them out in front of a car).

This was the last project I was to be involved in with the Captain. I have heard that the album received fairly good reviews. I had to laugh at one critic who wrote, "John French win's as 'worst' Beefheart guitarist." I couldn't have agreed more. I only wish you could have heard me in 1976, through a decent amp, and not forced to play Denny's guitar. I was touching on 'good' back then.

Overall it was a fun project for me, and a couple of months to hang out with Don for the last time. The guys were great to work with, Jeff helped me a lot with guitar parts, and Eric was totally patient, very scientific, and just an all-around great guy. Robert Williams played exceptionally well. Bruce wasn't around as much as I would have expected, but he did occasionally show up at a rehearsal. He looks so serious in this shot.

1. HOT HEAD - Is this about oral sex? I don't know, probably has connotations that point in that direction. Maybe it's about some lady with a bad temper. Maybe both. This album opens up with a line from Beefheart's worst guitarist - me. Jeff is playing those spindly "nerve guitar" licks. This song actually has a groove all the way through. It was put together for this album, I believe. The lyrics are something I had never heard before. Jeff basically taught me his parts and then Don whistled and buzzed new parts to him. There may have been a few there already. Williams' drums seem to be there already. Listen to that Mellotron (Or, maybe it's the Mini Moog) being playing by Feldman like a scratchy record - way good. My favorite section on this is when Eric hits that high spooky sustained note on the Mellotron at (0:57) and the guitar plays a nonsense scale up and down the neck. What a texture that gives. There are three guitars on this tune. One of me and two of Jeff. Mine is the simple rhythm on the left and Jeff is panned right and middle. The more predominant "nerve guitar" is middle. There is no "bass" to speak of, just the "pooching" sounds on the keyboard. I think the thing that makes this song move so well is Williams' dead-on drumming.

2. ASHTRAY HEART - This track was recorded the same day as *Sheriff Of Hong Kong*, one of two tracks that was supposed to have no drums, so Williams wasn't at the studio this particular day. Unfortunately, the track was done without the drums and I was asked to overdub them, which makes for a really trashy out of sync sound, which may have been what Don was going for. I hadn't played drums at all for the whole 2 months of rehearsal, and all of a sudden, Don says, "I want you to play drums on this, man." I was appalled. "Yeah, like, thanks for the notice." Anyway, I carefully loaded up my set in Don's brand new dark-blue Volvo station wagon (I say carefully because Jan and he both seemed absolutely anal about keeping this car in pristine condition." The day after *Sheriff* and *Heart*, Glen was struggling to get a drum sound on "yet another drum set" and one that still had old beat-up heads on it at that. I thought he did considerably well. The drumbeat is a mutation of the P-K-Ro-P beat (pronounced peek'- ah - row) originally on *Ant Man Bee*. I wasn't really thrilled with either my performance or the fact that everything's just a little "off." I have seen the lyrics analyzed as having to do with many of the punk rock movement's leaders admitting Beefheart influence. If so, Don, rather than being flattered or grateful for the attention this focused on him, decided instead to revile it and accused them of using him *"Like an Ashtray Heart."* He told me that the image was like a real human heart lying on a table as an ashtray full of cigarette butts. Sort of like when the Nazis made Jew-skinned lampshades etc. My favorite line is, *"Hit me where the lover hangs out."*

3. A CARROT IS AS CLOSE AS A RABBIT GETS TO A DIAMOND - Jeff, tune your guitar please. (For more info on this track, see origninal *Bat Chain Puller* track notes.

4. RUN PAINT RUN RUN - The use of double-entendre with the idea simultaneously of paint (as in "paintings") and paint (as in "old Paint" m' horse) is about all I know about the lyrics. This may be the only track on which Bruce actually plays trombone. One of my favorites, the track was probably originally written for *Shiny Beast* and just never made it on the album. I learned my slide part (which may be the only slide guitar I play on this album) by listening to the original recording with no vocal. Redus was playing bottleneck on that piece. I chose to use a very thick solid brass slide, as it was the only thing that seemed to give me any control at all. Slide was a new experience for me and helped to appreciate Denny Walley even more. I love the way the different time signatures allow the separate phrasings to all twist together like a bunch of snakes. We all start out in 4/4 (Bruce playing low Bo Diddley-esque in the rhythm track area) and then (0:24) Bruce and I go to a line that is in 10/4 (except once or twice when I screw up and play 9/4 and thankfully Bruce joins in making me sound like I know what I'm doing) while Williams goes to 3 and Jeff and Eric stay in 4. Williams is dead on beat again and as with most of the tracks, makes this work very well. The background vocals were recorded standing in a big circle around one microphone with no lyric sheet. This made it almost impossible to know what to do, at the same time, Don is in the control room, shouting through the monitor, "Just SING, man!" To everybody. Once we had done this for about 40 days and 40 nights, and Jeff was croaking from hoarsness as the rest of us frothed at the mouth, we remembered enough just to keep singing in the right places. I think the idea he was going for here was to get us so pissed that the vocals would be INTENSE. He succeeded and was very happy with the track. As we drove home that evening, he kept playing the cassette of the board tape over and over. "Listen to that, man! I got exactly what I wanted." I have to admit, the group vocals on this are stronger than any other Beefheart album.

5. SUE EGYPT - What funny images these lyrics summon to the mind. Pith helmets, and mothers serving Pepsi's (Don's mother, Sue). This is a brilliant track and is typically Don in my favorite ways. It has humor, tongue-in-cheek mysticism, and still maintains that intensity that made Don "Captain Beefheart." Eric and Jeff both shine here in a piece I had never heard, with lyrics that were new to me. This wasn't rehearsed, so I never heard it until it was recorded, and Jeff and Eric knew it well. It was like discovering an old candid photograph no one knew existed of a funny moment no one remembers quite the same, and the photograph proves them all slightly hazy in recollection. Listen to Eric's great playing on the Moog Synth bass and the sparkling, twirling Mellotron that occasionally edges it's way in. I am intrigued by the line, "I think of all those people that ride on my bones that nobody hears, that nobody sees, that nobody knows." Is this the "demons" haunting, plaguing, inspiring and "gifting" Don? The scary ghostlike "muse" that Don used to "see" in the chicken coop house and the Trout House? Is this the roomful of people who showed up when Don was alone at the Trout House? Who are all these people who "ride on his bones." Like an ancient Egyptian Pharoah mummified, has "the Captain's" peaceful world suddenly been invaded by pith-helmeted treasure-seeker-punks? Has he suddenly found himself on "display" like some curiosity from a different time? Don's performance at (1:03) makes me wonder if he really meant to come in with "I think of all" three times in a row, or was he simply lost? At (1:43) he uses the line from the 1975 encounter with Greg Davidson, "Bring me my scissors and those hot waters." We all laughed extremely hard at this faux film-noire monster movie dialog. Here, it is in perfect context. Is the mummy being wrapped? Three minutes later, I picked myself up off the ground from laughing deeply at the humor here and the memory of the moment he first came across this line. I love the list of ingredients for the potion. Let's put this together and see if it really works.

6. BRICK BATS - Recycled from the original *Bat Chain Puller* (see those track notes). About all I should probably do is a comparison here. The beginning of the original starts a little stronger with the horn, however, the track itself is pretty strong all the way through. Jeff's contrapuntal guitar is slightly altered from the original. The vocal is quite different on the two, but they are both fairly good performances. The last part of the center section seems to fall apart for a moment. The original seems to have a little more feeling in the horn in the end sections. I also miss the "White Jam" voice that is in the end of the original that works so well with his horn playing. I miss the extended fade at the end with the drums going a little more crazy.

7. DIRTY BLUE GENE - The title suggests the "curse" on mankind, does it not? This is a recycled out-take from *Clear Spot*, with some modifications. My favorite song to play and our first song to record in the studio. However, I was not happy with the performance (especially mine) and persuaded Don (on a tight budget) to re-record it the next day. It came off much better and is the take included here. I think this is one strong take, even my guitar parts sound pretty good on this one, and Glen did such a great job of getting the sounds. The whole band is cooking. This is a far cry from the original *Dirty Blue Gene* back in *Brown Wrapper* days (November 1967). About the only line I recognize here is, *"Don't you wish you never met her."* I'm singing along (if you can call it that) with Don on this song. I was at a friends house, and he called up (detective work, how'd he know?) and said, "John, you gotta sing on this track." I didn't want to go - *Rockford Files* was on - and it was one I'd never seen before. He said, "It would be good if you and I sang on something, both our voices, you know, a tie-in from the past." I conceded and went to the studio. I had them take my voice completely out of the headphones and just looked at the lyrics and sang along with Don on every line, releasing as many inhibitions as I could. He then went back and erased all the lines he didn't want and we had a take. I walked in and they handed me a bottle of whiskey and I took a big gulp. My throat was raw. Jeff looked at me and said, "How can you DRINK like that?" "I was just faking it, Jeff, it burned, but I wasn't about to let YOU know that." Favorite line, "She's not bad, she's just genetically mean." I think there's a lot of judges out there letting serial killers back on the street with the same line.

8. BEST BATCH YET - Definitely lyrics from the *Trout Mask* era. Van Vliet wrote this in the "magic bathroom" as we called the upstairs Trout House bathroom. I recall Jeff reading them. We had just smoked hashish. We used to break off little chunks, put them on a pin, light it like incense, and suck the smoke through straws. We all had our own little hashish straw ... mine had "Drumbo" written on it ... and Jeff"s had... just kidding. (Hmm, maybe I'll put them on eBay). The music I first heard during rehearsals for *Spotlight*. But it was just guitar and bass, no marimba part. My guitar part was written by Don at a session at Jeff Tepper's house. They would play and Don would play the Mellotron as I turned the tape recorder on and off. This was a very RANDOM set of lines and was a nightmare to put together, as I had to go in and out of the parts, joining and echoing Jeff in certain places. So, here are Eric, Jeff, and Williams, playing a rather straight ahead arrangement, and I'm playing "out" somewhere in "distant cousin land." So, I first transcribed all the lines onto music paper, because they were scattered all over on the cassette. Then I learned and memorized them all. The hard part was getting them to fit the track, because there was no "reference point" for anything I played, no key signature. I was all over the neck. I remember standing in my living room for hours going over and over this, playing along with a track I had made of the band. I was SO STRESSED on this, I would take my guitar off, and stand for five minutes beating on my bed with my fists and screaming to get the accumulated anxiety out, so I could go back and stand playing this thing. It seems like it took forever, but it was only probably 4 or 5 days, before I could do a fair version with the band. I said the basic track was written during *Spotlight* rehearsals, but at (1:00) this part was added during *Radar* rehearsals. At (1:11) you hear this same part played backwards. At (1:27) you hear another part that was added. What made my part a nightmare is that Don kept adding sections, plus the part he played for me needed to be played over the same sections as he played to on the tape. When I finally got it right, there wasn't a note left over, even though it had been a totally chaotic approach, I neither had to repeat anything nor remove any passage. It all worked perfectly. This kind of thing had seldom if ever happened before. I think this is one of Williams' best performances and in the live tape from the Hippodrome, he shows not only what a great drummer, but also what a great showman he is. At the end, even the good Captain has to acknowledge that and comes back to shake his hand.

9. TELEPHONE - Another paranoia hyperbole extravaganza with an almost *Frownland*-like aura to it, except the pulse is more stable. Don's insistent gravel-falsetto works well here to convey the kind of gnat-like annoying insistency heard on *Pena* and certainly letting us know Don's attitude towards telephones. I recall calling him one night about something rather urgent (I hardly ever called him because I knew he hated phones) only to have the phone answered by a loud percussive sound and cursing in the background. Oops - musta been dinnertime. I barely remember this song with the voice on it, but I did hear a rehearsal tape a while back that called it to mind. It was one of the more difficult things for me to learn. The phrasing in the composition was more along the lines of *Trout Mask* or *Decals*. Clocking in at under two minutes, if I remember correctly, we were all playing counter point rhythms, playing the same part at different times and then trying to end together. I'm guessing that this was a piano composition by the way it's structured. Also, it was new to me, so probably was written more recently.

10. FLAVOR BUD LIVING (non-religious version) - When I heard Gary's version I was really surprised. He flew into LA, came into the studio and shook hands, walked into an isolation booth and played his ass off. This piece is a tough one to play because of the hand positions. Gary himself said that in an interview that I read somewhere. Because he was able to do it this fast and this well really made me look bad, because my version was much slower, and I've never forgiven him for that. I asked him during the interview for the Revenant set in late 1998 why he played it so differently. "Don said your version was "too religious" (paraphrased) - was his answer. This version grew on me after a while, and now I find it to be one of my favorites and it certainly has that *Peon / One Red Rose That I Mean feel to it*.

11. SHERIFF OF HONG KONG - I am playing bass on this piece - Eric's Danelectro if I recall. This one took some rehearsal with Jeff and Eric to really come together. It was a piece Don originally wrote on the piano, and the right hand is often playing on the "down beat" so the left hand (which is the bass part) is often playing on the preceding anticipated eighth note before the down beat. This makes for a tough challenge to keep the music moving as a trio with no drums. However, I enjoyed the experience of playing bass probably most of everything I did in the session. It's an easier instrument technically, but requires more strength in the hands. I was playing mostly "parallel fifths" The drums were added later. This is the other drum track Don "sprung on me" at the last minute. The piece is reminiscent of *Glider* in a sense. It is more tonally centered, and although not really a "blues" scale type of piece, it has similarities in structure and method of playing. It's also similar in that the guitar and piano and bass are effectively "doubling" everything played on the piano. I'm doubling Eric's left hand, and Jeff is doubling his right. Eric was actually "musical director" for this piece, and handled the job as well, if not better, than anyone ever had. Victor Hayden was at this session taking pictures. I'm not sure, but I think that's Eric's foot at the beginning, stomping out a tempo with his foot either to keep Jeff on time, or for effect. One thing I like about this piece is that it's the only time I ever got to play bass with myself. I recall using the chart to help me through this on drums and I am basically playing whatever I feel like playing. It's pretty tight, and the tempo is good, which is mostly due to Eric practicing with a metronome. It made it really easy to put drums to this. The style here is reminiscent of *Mirror Man* session drumming (except more in time) and is very similar to the way I played on *Glider* (before they erased me and overdubbed Rhys Clark). The only thing I regret here (aside from not having played drums for months and coming in cold) was that Glen Kolotkin was able to find a wonderful Tom sound, which got mixed too low in the tracks. One reason why there is so much space in the drums is that I was hearing these things like "tabla rockets" in the headphones and was giving them room to "breathe." All the "breath" is gone in the final mix. Don also asked me not to utilize too many cymbals, as he would be overdubbing Chinese Opera Gongs which were purchased for him by Gary Lucas' then wife, Ling. Don's Mandarin Chinese lyrics are "I love you, young lady." Probably the basic sentence a man needs to survive in China.

12. MAKING LOVE TO A VAMPIRE WITH A MONKEY ON MY KNEE - The lyrics were written at the Trout House, one evening during a beautiful lull. It was completely still outside and almost spooky. I always imagine this poem set down under the tree at the southeast corner of the property. Where the female spirit apparition once danced. Spooky stuff here. It has a minimalist approach as far as the music being very scarce in places. Castle Sound studios was a Christian studio, and Beefheart was the first non-Christian they had recorded. When the owner/ manager (I'm not sure) of the studio came in with his wife one evening, this is the track Don played him as a sample of his work. The guy listened silently, but you could see his face tensing. Finally, it ended and he said, "I am probably a sick man, but I *like* it." This song has a military sort of Armageddon feel to it. Jeff and I stood on a piece of plywood facing each other and snapped our foot to the ground (like a Nazi salute) to end all those phrases that start at (0:36). I don't know who is playing bass. Is that Eric? There is also Mellotron, properly aged with just the right amount wow and flutter. I played marimba on this piece but just barely. Untrained on the instrument, I borrowed a xylophone from Jeff, which Don wrote the part on, then wrote the part, memorized it and did it in sections on the tape - just barely. I only had a couple of days. I have no idea what this poem is really about, but I'll give it a shot. Probably how terrible it is to be in the music business, trying to make a living. The "vampire" is the industry itself - sucking away the very life juices in the music with their insistence on commerciality. The "monkey" is probably the band - probably a big responsibility for a spoiled only child.

ICE CREAM FOR CROW
Studio(s): Warner Brothers Recording Studios
North Hollywood, California
Recording Date: May/June 1982
Producer(s): Don Van Vliet, assisted by Janet Van Vliet & Jeff Moris Tepper
Engineer: Phil Brown
Band Personnel: Don Van Vliet (Vocals, harmonica, soprano saxophone, Chinese gongs, prop horn); Jeff Moris Tepper (Steel-appendage guitar, slide guitar, guitar, acoustic guitar); Gary Lucas (Glass-finger guitar, slide guitar, guitar, acoustic guitar); Richard Midnight Hatsize Snyder

(Bass guitar, marimba, viola); Cliff R. Martinez (Drums, shake bouquet, glass washboard, metal drums); Eric Drew Feldman (Rhodes piano and synthesized bass on *The Thousandth And Tenth Day Of The Human Totem Pole*).

Introduction: This is the Beefheart album that I probably know least about. By this time, I had completely lost contact with Don, who was still angry with me for leaving after the *Doc* sessions. I have never listened to this entire CD in one sitting. It leaves me with an uneasy feeling at times, probably in part because it was the "swan-song" but also because I certainly have never felt it to be one of Don's stronger albums. However, the band had little time to put it together. The cover painting, which is on a window shade, seems to be one that I recall seeing at the Trout House.

The story of the creation of this album comes from bits and pieces, but from what I understand, there was little time to rehearse. It also sounds, from listening to it, that much is recycled material from an artist who had long since lost the heart or the inspiration to write new music. It would have been even more recycled material had not Zappa nixed a suggestion to use some of the material from the unreleased *Bat Chain Puller* as "filler" for this album. There was probably little in the budget, so the Captain probably needed to conserve every penny possible.

There are titles here that I recognize. *Hey Garland, I Dig Yer Tweed Coat* was certainly poetry written during the *Trout Mask* period. I am also fairly certain that *Witch Doctor Life* comes from this period also lyrically. *81" Poop Hatch* was a recitation for the original *Bat Chain Puller* in 1976. However, I seem to recall this as a poem from the Trout House days and most assuredly heard it pre-*Spotlight Kid* recited by Jan Van Vliet as she stood on the redwood deck of the compound the band shared in Felton.

Totem Pole (excuse the abbreviation) was also recorded for the original *Bat Chain Puller* and I recall first hearing the lyrics read to me in mid or late 1974. This particular recording was almost certainly made in 1980 during the *Doc* sessions and recycled here, hence the "phantom appearance" of Eric Drew Feldman. I believe that my guitar was taken off the track and the horns and perhaps also a new vocal track were added during the *Crow* sessions.

Semi Multi-Colored Caucasian is a piece rehearsed (and possibly recorded) by *The Spotlight Kid* band originally and so is recycled here. So that is all the information I can recall from sitting and staring at the album cover.

Drummer Cliff Martinez was in contact with me during the time of this recording. I had just started playing jazz in a local lounge after being musically inactive for a time. Cliff had just joined the band to do the album and was interested in taking a few lessons from me so that he could better understand the concept of "Beefheart" drumming. Martinez had to do this in a clandestine manner as any information regarding his contact with me would be considered betrayal and probably would have resulted in his immediate dismissal from the project. I finally agreed to meet with Cliff on a couple of occasions. I had met him a couple of years previous to this, so I already knew him to be a fairly nice guy, although (my opinion only) with an extreme obsession to understand "Drumbo" drums.

Cliff came to the place I was living with my then girlfriend. It was a tiny house that had been "hippy-ized" by her and her then late husband. By this I mean the entire interior had been gutted and replaced with barnwood and old rusty tools. There was an old wood-burning stove in the corner of the living room and really ugly dark orange shag carpeting on the floor. Holes in the roof had been cut through and old glass doors positioned to become "skylights." An old Plexiglas jet-fighter cockpit became a window with a shelf holding plants. I eventually added a sprinkling system outside and also did custom brickwork around the stove.

My drum set was in the kitchen, the only place with room for them. Cliff came on two occasions and I worked with him on the parts to *Hair Pie*, which I considered to be his best place to begin. He was a little stiff, but worked really hard and mastered the parts fairly quickly.

Cliff told me that one of the tapes Don gave him to learn drum parts off of just turned out to be a tape of what sounded like someone washing dishes with running water. Cliff listened to it and did an interpretation of what he heard, and played it for Don. Van Vliet's reaction was "You knew exactly what I wanted," to which Tepper chimed in "But Don, I don't hear the water thing." Another time, the Captain asked Martinez to give him "BB's on a plate." (In 1974, we were listening to a Muddy Waters album, and I told Don the snare drum sounded like "BB Soup.")

1. ICE CREAM FOR CROW - (I scream for crow?) John Thomas (the keyboardist on the original *Bat Chain Puller*) told me that when he first heard this piece, it sounded to him like Beefheart with a disco beat. The only thing I hear that reminds me of disco is the throbbing kick drum, which is insistently on every beat. The bass is a "boogie" type approach, playing on every downbeat along with the kick drum. I hear many influences here but John Lee Hooker and the original *Mirror Man* are the two strongest. This sounds to me like a song that Don would have taught the band at a rehearsal, singing, whistling, and "sculpting the musicians" into a desired shape. There are no piano-written parts here, and the lyrics are more like a poem intermittently shouted over a musical landscape in a free and random style. The arrangement seems to consist of 3 or 4 sections or "riffs" repeated throughout with interjections of bottleneck phrases. There is no soloing (no surprise there) save Don's little harp blast at the end. The voice timbre seems reminiscent of *Tropical Hot Dog Night*, in that it is a high non-melodic shout that verges on the fringes of raspy falsetto and then creeps into the low Howlin' Wolf type sound. My impression of the track in general is that of a watered down drink, put together quickly with little thought as to quality and with the pure motive of getting it done. The musicians play well, but they weren't given much here to work with, nor long to rehearse. The lyrics are definitely inspired by the Mojave Desert. The heat waves at times distort things so much you see mirages and blurred images, like the crow with three beaks. In the early evening, when the moon first rises, it sometimes is very orange, like a pumpkin, and if it is a new crescent, you can still see enough of the moon to give the image of a white hat. I am constantly visited by ravens, which sometimes drive me nuts with their squawking. They are very interesting creatures, huge black birds (Carlos Castenada says that he was taught by his witch-doctor friend that they are actually white - *white?* When the sun hits their feathers just right, you can sometimes see that...) There seems to be a meeting of the crows in the lyrics. This generally symbolizes death. Crows are carrion and sometimes large flocks can be seen flying in the sky circling above the imminent death they smell below. It's a little spooky, but I'm glad they're around. They clean up the mess. It's certainly seems to be more natural to me to become "ice cream for crow" than be buried in an overpriced copper casket encased within concrete. That can't be good for the earth. The Tibetans have "bone breakers" who saw up their dead and feed them to the birds. The ground is frozen so hard that burial is impractical - which has absolutely nothing to do with this piece.

2. THE HOST THE GHOST THE MOST HOLY-O - Oh, these lyrics! Well, I suppose this is a good chance to give my "Christian Perspective." However, you must realize that I'm not a theologian. I am only a layman who really believes in God and has read and studied the Bible most of my life. Van Vliet here paints a very bleak portrait of the world. He speaks in metaphors of imminent disaster, morons in charge, people dying for earthly burdens. Hey! This sounds just like the six o' clock news. One of the great things about Don is his ability to "cut through the crap" and show you the real phoniness. There is an ugliness in the world that most people don't want to deal with. According to the Bible, man is in a "fallen state," hence the extreme insanity that we call civilization. Obviously, we have corrupt politicians, and lawyers who make their living by lying. One of the strongest attractions I had to Van Vliet's music is the fact that his lyrics often made extremely powerful statements about this "mess" we live in. Everywhere on earth, man seems to be a slave in one way or another, and no one seems to be really happy although some are extremely wealthy because they have learned how to use the system. We are still populating the earth in numbers growing at an absurd rate, but no one seems to look. Our environmentalists would put us into a different kind of hell, and so we live in this "denial" pretending that life is TV and we're just "watching." The lyrics here describe that "fallen state" quite well. The "mast of mercy" here seems to be part of a metaphorical ship, but I am not sure what he means. I know that "Mary's only Son" (she went on to have several other children according to the Bible) has to refer to Jesus and the next line starts with "God" which gives me the impression Don believes Jesus to be God, which is a Christian concept. However, it goes on to say that he died in vain, which is an absolute misconception. "I can't darken your dark cross no more" says to me that Don turned away from Christianity, because Jesus died and so his path must have been wrong. A lot of people don't realize that it's not the death of Jesus that is important, but the fact that he was resurrected, which is the whole cornerstone upon which Christianity is founded. I believe that Jesus is a living being who overcame what we have to overcome, Death, and did this to show us the path to Life. So all this negative stuff in the beginning of the song, and the way the images are at the end says to me that the participant stopped just shy of entrance to the road to life (the cross), and chose instead, "the light lovely one with the nothing door." Unfortunately, Lucifer means "keeper of lights" and it is said that he can "disguise himself as an angel of light." There's a lot of deception in the world about this and it is often misunderstood.

Enough said, and now the music: this music is not familiar to me at all but is reminiscent more of the Mirror Man days than of anything later. There is tremelo on one of the guitars. He told me one time, "See how smart I am? I got Jews to sing that, man!"

3. SEMI MULTI-COLORED CAUCASIAN - This seems to be an adaptation of the earlier version and has some new sections. It has a lot of the feel of the original that the Magic Band used to practice in Felton pre-Spotlight Kid. The intro seems to be the same and then it goes to an immediate faster tempo than I recall. This part I don't recall until (0:49) which is definitely part of the song as I played it back in 1971. What I'm hearing here, though, has also been modified to the extent that Gary Lucas is playing some incredibly articulate finger-picking which is probably the saving grace of the track, which seems to go on a bit too long. Overall, as many Beefheart songs go, this is desperately in need of a well-done, improvised solo to break the monotony of parts being played and again replayed. The piece is beautiful, but it doesn't really ever get a chance to "breathe."

4. HEY GARLAND, I DIG YER TWEED COAT - As I thought, this is a poem from the Trout House days set to music. The clue was the line "Pena exclaimed" near the end. I did a complete "listen-through" and, with all respect to the band, musically, there's not much there. I suppose that to an untrained ear, this might sound like a Frownland or something, with its polyrhythmic approach, but it doesn't really go anywhere. Where are all those beautiful lines Don used to write that showed up in the background? And Richard Snyder unlike, Rockette, plays a bass part that is very "single note" oriented - no chords. The whole thing becomes quite monotonous after about thirty seconds. This is a bargain basement copy of a Don Van Vliet composition, thrown together and buried underneath the alarmingly weak recitation of a recycled poem and recorded as to be sold like a discount tool. These guys were capable of so much more if they would have been given something to work with. The poem means little to me. It seems to be a street scene, a shabbily dressed tacky guy walking down a sidewalk, looking in store windows.

5. EVENING BELL - There is no way around it, Gary Lucas is a technical monster. He rips notes from a guitar like simulated machine gun fire in a movie set. There is a machine precision to his playing. Every note comes through and is clearly heard. My problem with this piece is certainly not Gary. It's the fact that I've heard Don ramble on the piano so many times like this and I just don't care for the (lack of) composition. What does this piece actually say compared to Peon or One Red Rose. I liken it more to the unreleased Seam Crooked Sam from Bat Chain Puller which I found almost equally musically disheartening until I played it so often it started actually sound like something more than it was. However, duplicating a rambling meaningless piano moment on guitar does not stamp it "valid" nor does it make it anything I like to think of as music. This, of course, is only according to my taste. This music is totally cerebral and lacks any "heart." It leaves me cold and seems pointless. Again, this is no reflection on Lucas' excellent playing.

Henry Kaiser made the following observation:

Zoot and Drumbo used to exercise some editorial judgement in transferring El Capitano's keyboard ramblings to the geetar. In the case of *Evening Bell*, Lucas was apparently still operating with the belief that lowly Magic Band members must contribute nada to the Captain's genius. So by neglecting to put his own heart and mind into the work, beyond a great deal of transcribing and practice, he ended up with a really dull clunker of a bell.

6. CARBOARD CUTOUT SUNDOWN - This poem I like. I understand that this was put together in two parts and it worked out quite well. Now, I'll give it a listen. Well, let's see, Gary is playing what appears to be a guitar solo (probably written on the piano) and the rest of the band comes in intermittently to join him. This is a pretty interesting piece and seems to have some fire to it. Lucas' playing is, as on everything he does, brilliant. Re: lyrics. We have a thing being built near where I live and it's got some stupid name like "Desert Wildlife Preserve." There's this architecturally nouveau building and a big electric fence. This is where you wanna go if you wanna see "da real desert." Right in between the rundown housing tract and the elementary school. I don't know what these morons think. "Well, lets see, before we put down asphalt on THE ENTIRE FLOOR of the Antelope Valley, we'll section off a little piece over there and save it for future generations. Maybe a jackrabbit or two'll survive inside." That's what these lyrics reminds me of. Everything artificial, cut off from nature so far that we're totally clueless as to what it's about.

7. THE PAST SURE IS TENSE - (The pasture is tents) The past sure IS tense. This is actually one of the better tracks in my opinion. I like the feel. It moves along pretty well. This is a lot like the original *Pompadour Swamp*, but is actually based on an outtake from *Clear Spot* called *Little Scratch* - another recycled piece. Don's new voice is starting to wear on me a bit. I am not very prone to enjoy hearing the same line repeated endlessly. I'm ready to hit fast forward and then the distorted guitar comes in at (2:15) and it gives me a chance to breathe. The band seems to sound exceptionally good on this one. I like the density that happens about (2:29) as though they just decided to have everyone play over the top of the basic track.

8. INK MATHEMATICS - This one has its moments. The band sounds pretty tight on this piece. Still, it seems to be more cerebral and therefore unappealing to me. There's moments here that remind me of *Bill's Corpse* from *Trout Mask Replica*. It has a bit of a lost, meandering feeling - something seems unresolved.

9. THE WITCH DOCTOR LIFE - This is obviously based on *Dirty Blue Gene* from the original *Mirror Man*. The music is played really well and the new parts improve the composition. The vocal sounds lost, out of place, and weak. The only thing missing is "Shit, I don't know how I'm going to get that in there." The lyrics were written around Trout House days. The *"Mama Kangaroo"* part loses me. Nice marimba by Snyder.

10. "81" POOP HATCH - The same exact performance as on the original *Bat Chain Puller*. See notes.

11. THE THOUSANDTH AND TENTH DAY OF THE HUMAN TOTEM POLE - An outtake from the *Doc* session. My guitar was taken off as were Williams' drums. Martinez learned the parts in a day or two. Don redid the vocal and added horns. The actual vocal, even though I have been told it was removed and replaced, really sounds more like Don sounded around the time of the "Doc" sessions. The piece is actually one of Don's best. This song doesn't make me want to get up and kick holes in the speakers like some of the other tracks, and that is mostly because of Don's voice, which is a bit more palatable here than on some of the earlier tracks. The first time I heard this, I hated the horns. The more I listen, the more I enjoy the horns. I feel like when the horns come in, I am in a big cable car on a crane being slowly hoisted up the pole in order to better observe it. The spaces that Van Vliet leaves here are like sequences of events. That little duck call creaking adds to the tension. The original version on BCP will always be my favorite, as the combination of Denny Walley and John Thomas just seemed to make it work.

12. SKELETON MAKES GOOD - This was written after it was discovered that Frank Zappa was not going to allow the use of tracks from the original *Bat Chain Puller* to be used. It's more of a theatre piece than a tune. It's claimed that Don "took a hit of pot" to write the remaining material. This is the only one that I know for certain was written after the news.

Conclusion

I may be too subjective on this material. Over the course of years, it seems to me that Van Vliet kept the elements I found least fascinating (or even sometimes most repulsive) about his music and lost more and more of the elements I found to be interesting. I am speaking mostly about taste here, but also to an extent about musicianship and the feedback a band gives their leader. There was a certain editorial task that was almost diminished to nothing by this point in time. Beefheart had surrounded himself with individuals who worshipped him to such an extent that their opinion was almost invisible. He had no perspective in such an environment. Also, he was certainly less interested in the music and in writing music in general, having been unable to really make a living, according to his public testimony at least. This accounts for the fact that he was pulling from material written as much as 13 years previous to this. The album doesn't appeal to me at all. I was attracted to Beefheart's music 17 years prior to this by elements that are all but completely vanished by this point in time. Song's like *Glider* and *Big Eyed Beans From Venus* were more to my liking. I am sure that Beefheart junkies were happy to have yet another look inside the world of Van Vliet, but to me it's like being hungry and going to the refrigerator in the middle of the night. Unfortunately, you find that everything that you really like has already been eaten, and the only thing that is left is an old jar of beets which should have been thrown out along with that baking soda months ago. Unfortunately, no one is interested enough to care. Although there are elements here that remind me of Don, I am not pleased with the way they are assembled in this package. No matter which way I pack it, I just can't seem to find a way to make it work. Of course, we are all most happy with the things we are the most comfortable with. I can listen to *Trout Mask* and for the most part enjoy it (it took me years to be able to even "hear" it close to the way I think other people do). I can do the same with most of the other albums, save the Mercury stuff (although I really haven't ever given *Unconditionally Guaranteed* a chance).

Unfortunately, the eccentric music I hear on this exaggerates and focuses on all the elements of Van Vliet's art which are unappealing to me.

GROW FINS: Rarities 1965-82
Revenant Records 1999

Introduction: This is a set I was glad to see put together for many reasons. First of all, Dean Blackwood did this as a labor of love, at least in my opinion. Second of all, he actually allowed the band to tell their story and hired me to get it. This was a big risk, as he had no idea whether I could write at all. I think he took this risk because he knew, as did many know, that the facts hadn't even gotten close to being revealed. It's nice to actually read something that tells the story from the band's perspective, though at times it is a less-than-flattering story. After the set was released and everyone had received a copy I made as much effort as possible to contact each individual and make sure they liked the story, and was able to do so with the exception of Richard Redus who I've lost contact with. I spent a lot of time researching the project and had about 3 months to actually complete it.

For the most part, I have tried to correct any errors and apologize for any other mistakes I may have overlooked.

There is so much information concerning this set that I am probably going to write the track notes over a long period of time and try to connect them in more of a timeline. This way, the listener will be able to program CD 1, for example, to play the tracks in a sequence that represents the recordings in a chronological order. That in itself can be helpful in hearing the development of the band. For instance, the first song here chronologically is *Call On Me*. I regret, however, that the early blues acetates were not included here, which actually predate *Call On Me*, or were recorded at the same session. Even these acetates, however, give little impression of the power of the original band as felt in a live setting, primarily due to recording techniques which added far too much reverb and squeezed the band into a little mid-rangy area in the aural spectrum, thereby diminishing the full impact of the band. The blues, played at such a volume with rock instruments, confronted by one of the most powerful voices ever heard, made for a sound that was sadly never truly reproduced on vinyl. The sound had changed by the time of the Avalon recordings and the "feel" was never quite the same with PG playing drums as it had been with Mortensen. Had a producer had the presence of mind to record the early Magic Band as a blues group playing covers of songs like *Evil, Somebody In My Home, St. James Infirmary*, and others, the Paul Butterfield Blues Band and Canned Heat would have had serious competition in the white blues market of the time.

One of the things the reader must keep in mind is that it was the intent of the majority of Magic Band members to actually sell records and make money by playing concerts. By this, we hoped to gain in popularity as opposed to doing an art statement that only critics would praise while the general public, at large, would shun. Yet, even Alex Snouffer, in a 1967 discussion I had with him stated that he felt Don's interjections into the *SAM* session songs were valid and "caught the public's ear." This shows that there was an "openness" to Van Vliet's obviously progressive ideas, as long as the band could support themselves through the process.

DISC 1 - JUST GOT BACK FROM THE CITY
First Three Songs
When putting together the Revenant Set, Dean Blackwood hired me to write liner notes and also search around and see if there was unreleased Beefheart material lying around in anyone's garage. Doug Moon had found an old reel-to-reel tape but didn't know what was on it. I bought a reel to reel tape deck and set it up in my tiny studio. He brought over the tape and we discovered these wonderful demos from Wally Heider Studios of the incarnation of the band that included Rich Hepner on guitar and Alex Snouffer on drums - the same band that recorded *Diddy Wah Diddy*.

1. OBEAH MAN - early 1966 demo. Just about every garage band in town - including "Patch of Blue" (Bill Harkleroad) and "Blues In A Bottle" (Boston, Cotton, and French), and "Obeah Band" (Bob Ormsby) covered this song. PG Blakely replaced Alex on drums shortly after the demos were recorded. His younger brother Bobby used to make copies of the tapes and bring them over for us to hear. We, of course, made our own copy, and from that, we learned *Obeah Man*. The song was unusual, because it was in 6/4 instead of 4/4, and it had that hoodoo-swamp mystique that appealed to our young "we're-into-the blues" minds. I don't think I can emphasize strongly enough how passionate we became about the blues and black music in general during this period.

2. JUST GOT BACK FROM THE CITY - early 1966 demo. This is a pretty simple riff-based piece. Don said that when he overdubbed the harmonica on this selection, as he walked into the control room Alex said, "That's the worst harp solo I ever heard you do, man." Don said, "Listen to it again." They did, and the phrase that starts at (0:47) completely astonished Alex - at least according to Don. I could see why. It was, I believe, a "happy accident" but that is the most interesting line I've ever heard come out of a simple cross-harp solo. At (1:53), it's a little short, and should have had a bridge and a few more lyrics to make it work.

3. I'M GLAD - early 1966 demo. I still like the vocal performance on this demo better than the *Safe As Milk* version. Hepner's question-and-answer in the bridge is still a favorite of mine. There is a certain quality to Van Vliet's voice that seems to disappear after A&M. I think he was singing too hard on the *Safe As Milk* sessions and over-driving his voice and had a hard time keeping control of the notes as a result. He seems more controlled and the quality of his "soulful" voice came through in this particular take as it did in *Diddy Wah Diddy*.

4. TRIPLE COMBINATION - early 1966 demo. This was a later home demo with Paul "PG" Blakely playing drums. It was probably right around the same timeframe as *Electricity, Yellow Brick Road*, and several other selections from *Safe As Milk* were written. In these home demos, Don sang directly into one channel using an Electrovoice 664 mic and the other mic was just a "room" mike. Don showed me these words and told me that it was about a pimp. I didn't know what a pimp was when I was 18, but I knew it wasn't a blemish.

5. HERE I AM, HERE I ALWAYS AM - early 1966 demo. Van Vliet probably couldn't hear a note he sang, so the vocal is strained and a little sharp. Alex is definitely playing the predominant guitar. I have no idea who is playing drums. It doesn't sound like PG - it sounds more like me, but I don't remember ever doing a demo of this piece. Also, the little argument at the beginning mentions a "she" that will be hearing the piece. I would guess that to be Dorothy Heard, who worked with Leonard Grant. The only thing is that I could swear in the dialogue that the guy saying "Oh yeah, boy" is me. But Alex and I used to sound suspiciously alike on tape. Jerry is the one saying, "Erase the whole bit, man…" Doug was actually an expert at editing tapes, so he knew this would all wind up on the cutting-room floor later anyway - not realizing that later it would actually wind up being released. It does show that the band was more of a unit and argued like a bunch of brothers. Alex de-fuses the situation saying, "Let's just sit down and do it, hell with it, let her hear some crap once in a while."

6. HERE I AM, HERE I ALWAYS AM - later 1966 demo. In this demo - which I am making an educated guess was done at Gold Star studios, just due to the sound - I hear that wonderful quality of Van Vliet's voice. He was in great voice here. Notice that the drum beat on the ? section is simplified. I think it's way boring compared to track 5. The song overall sounds better of course and is a little more up-tempo.

7. SOMEBODY IN MY HOME - (Live 1966) This is a fairly good example of the early band with the exception of the BIGness of the sound. The band sounded huge and Don's voice was not so "reedy" sounding as it is with this board tape from the Avalon Ballroom in San Francisco. I think the band sounded much fuller with Vic Mortensen on drums, and more "soulful." Blakely had a bit of a "marching band" sound that spilled over into his performance.

8. TUPELO - (Live 1966) This was a stunning number live and Beefheart really worked his magic on the crowd with this piece. It was a spell-binding piece that left people in awe. I loved the little falsetto swamp-howl Don used. I only wished he would have used a decent harmonica amp and mic, as the balance from voice to harp is quite different and the contrast is distracting.

9. EVIL IS GOIN' ON - (Live 1966) This song is near to my heart as it was the first time I heard Don singing in the "Wolf" style. I asked him about it after the local concert where I heard it and he told me about Howlin' Wolf. His "Wolf" voice was still developing at this time so you hear more of a throaty-quality later overcome. Also, better recording and effects later were able to bring out the quality of Don's "Wolf" voice better.

10. OLD FOLK'S BOOGIE - (Live 1967) We played the Avalon right after recording *Safe As Milk* but always seemed to resort to playing the blues live rather than the new album material. The fans loved this stuff and went crazy for it. This was probably August or September - right after Jeff Cotton joined the group, and so Alex decided it would be best to go back to the old reliable and simpler blues.

11. CALL ON ME - (1965 acetate demo) - Of course, the booklet tells the story of Mortensens's father dying and him receiving the news one night in Lancaster after or during a rehearsal. The band left and Vic was playing around with some Rickenbacker 12-string that happened to be laying around. This is an original demo for the tune that was probably done at Gold Star studios. Since Vic is playing on it, I imagine it had to be recorded before October of 1965 when he left the band. This is obviously the slower version which sounds more like a song The Byrds (a contemporary folk-rock group) might have done than a true "Beefheart" song. It was obviously re-arranged (by Don actually) shortly after I became a member of the group to sound more like a soul song.

Tracks 12-14
Gary Marker produced these songs in a demo session. The studio was above Kama Sutra's (and Buddah's) offices. It was the Original Sound studio that was designed by Paul Buff. More is written about this in the book. Marker was promised the producer's hat on *Safe As Milk* if he could persuade Ry Cooder to play on the session and, hopefully, join the group. This was my first time in an "official" demo session and was soon after Ry had taken over as musical director. So, these arrangements were slightly altered and I was very nervous. Don was busy showing all "his" (Herb Bermann's) lyrics the Artie Ripp and Bob Krasnow. It was a bit chaotic and Ry was displeased because we didn't sound like a "blues" group. Doug Moon played on these session, and later mistakenly thought that these tracks were actually included on *Safe As Milk*, but was incorrect.

12. SURE 'NUFF 'N YES I DO - (1967 acetate demo) I slightly rushed after the first "half-time" drum part, which I had just learned a few days before. Of course, I groaned when I heard it back, but everyone said, "relax, John, its only a demo." You can hear Doug playing right on the end - the high bottleneck part. He also played on *Sure 'Nuff* on the *Safe As Milk* master, and then was removed from the band before we moved production from Sunset Sound to RCA studios just down the road.

13. YELLOW BRICK ROAD - (1967 acetate demo) Wow, this is really fast. I don't know who counted it off, but ... whew. The beat was later changed to a bit more of a "Delta" rhythm. Marker recalled complaining to Don about the tempo, but said Don replied that he liked it at that speed.

14. PLASTIC FACTORY - (1967 acetate demo) It's sounds like the intro was cut off of this. The center 3/4 section was already written for this, which wasn't inserted until shortly before this demo session. The harmonica was weak on this, so we later pre-amped a special mike and got a much fatter sound.

DISC II

1. ELECTRICITY - For a live recording in 1968, this actually came off pretty well. I recognized it immediately from the bass intro, as it goes half-time for a moment, which wasn't planned. I love the falsetto howls at the end.

2. SURE 'NUFF 'N YES I DO - Well, on the demo I rushed, and on this I drag. I think I got it right about 1969. It's hard to believe that six months after this, we were starting to rehearse *Trout Mask Replica*.

Next 3 Tracks
Live at Frank Freeman's dance studio in Kidderminster. We had just posed with John Peel out front of the venue before this performance. The stage was small, Jerry kept knocking my floor tom over into my leg and I couldn't get his attention because of the volume, so I just knocked it back at him to get his attention. He was a little upset until I explained that I couldn't play the kick drum with my right foot with the tom in the way. Don brought a Simran horn and a soprano saxophone on this tour.

3. ROLLIN' N' TUMBLIN' - It seems like this piece went on forever and at 11 minutes plus that's just about right. I can't tell whether that's a Simran horn or soprano sax, but it sounds like the latter. Don would sometimes put the Simran over the mike and control the feedback with his fingers, which was an interesting effect. This tour was actually the beginning of the concept for the long drawn-out *Mirror Man / Tarotplane jams* that wound up on the *Mirror Man* sessions. Around (9:00) we start getting a little tired. Don finally returns to the form, and in a mere 2 minutes we wind up the piece. This was a pretty common length for a live performance back then. The PA system for this tour was quite inadequate - which is a shame.

4. ELECTRICITY - As this fades in, it sounds more like a Simran horn (shenai) playing the slightly-out-of-tune melodious phrases. You can also hear the feedback occasionally squawk through the speakers. Jeff's guitar sounds really out-of-tune on this. I love Don's Eastern chanting on the end of this piece.

5. ON YOUR BOND - Very odd, as the way this starts, it almost sounds like the beat "one" is in a different place. Don came in the place where "one" is and then we turn the beat around to fit his entrance. Don used to say that he heard things "backwards" and that "nothing was ever the same." He said what made life interesting to him - that "everything was always new." This ability to look at things in a completely new way probably spurred his imagination, but it was also the reason he probably often was lost in arrangements. This has a *Mirror Man* - style ending and Alex is doing some amazing stuff around (4:40). When Don came back in, I couldn't hear him at all (no monitors) I kept on with the ending.

6. KANDY KORN - Alex really shines here and gives a great performance with a wonderful tone. Jeff used to "freeze up" during live performance, sometimes not playing at all, but he is playing there. Probably mike placement causes him to be very low in the mix. We had rehearsed this material quite a bit and so we were quite seasoned at playing this song. It went well. We had shortened it by this time, it used to go twice as long.

7. KORN, RING, 'N FINGER - I'm sure this is a studio outtake from the TTG *Mirror Man* sessions that was never used, but certainly couldn't say for sure. I certainly don't recall playing at "Allegro" studios - ever. This seems to have a kind of sea chantey with Don using a voice that's similar to the one on the intro to *Electricity*. The whole thing was improvised, I believe, and I believe it is the only time we ever played it. The guitar has a bit of the Doors *The End* influence obviously. Don is singing through his harmonica mic.

DISC III

Track 1. This is a continuous track from the "Anthropological Field Recordings" that Frank Zappa was planning on using for *Trout Mask Replica*. It just keeps rolling. I will just listen and give impressions. It seems to start out with Zoot predominantly working on the intro to *Hobo Chang Ba* which was one of the latest things he'd learned and, not surprisingly, one of the more difficult sequences of notes to transpose from piano to guitar. Cotton talks about it being "loud" with Victor (The Mascara Snake). Zoot's "Is everything alright" is to Cotton who replies "Ask if we can play - through a microphone (meaning speak through one of the mics set up to record the instruments)." Since the recording equipment (Frank's portable unit that Dick Kunc used on the road) was in the bedroom and was quite primitive, with no talk back, it was hard to figure out what was going on this first day of recording. (1:16) Victor replies "Yeah, if you want to, sure" - Drumbo says, "Alright - *Dachau*," and we prepare. Finally, at (1:51), I shout "and" and we begin. The drums are not mixed well, nor is the bass drum miked and muffled correctly, so it sounds very parade-like. I remember having just learned some of these parts a few days before, as the drum parts were the last things written and almost an oversight on Don's part. Around (2:32) everything fizzles, sounding as though perhaps things were stopped by someone while balances were re-adjusted. At (2:35), balances had been adjusted but *Hair Pie* is now the song, which we are well into by the time the tape is rolling. I can tell by the transition from one part to the next that I haven't quite learned how to switch from one part to the next, so it's apparent that I wasn't as prepared as the others - especially at (3:11) where the band and I go in separate directions for a time. (3:35) finds it come back together for the last section. At (4:00) Don's suggesting I put the "cardboard on the drums." I recognize Jeff's laugh at (4:32).

Track 2. It's apparent now that the mics have been set up on the outside patio. Someone asking Don "Can you run around playing that….?" And Don replies, "I don't know…" There's a lot of extraneous noise, and the mics in the house are still live, so the combination of inside and outside add to the confusion. A plane flies over at (0.29). It sounds like a mic is being set up in the bushes also while dogs bark in the distance - probably at two boys walking down the street.

Around (2:40) or so, it sounds as though a portable cassette recorder is carried near a mic. The recording is of the Amway man who used to deliver Don's hypo-allergenic detergent. Don's favorite part is when the fellow's wife exclaims "He has records!" to her husband at (3:42). He used to quote this all the time…

(4:03) is some horn interplay, but it is difficult to perceive at first if it is another cassette tape but appears later as Don and Vic walking between two mics panned hard right and left as a large jet flies by. Someone in the house is typing - probably Laurie, most likely typing Don's lyrics because he didn't have them organized. It starts getting pretty good around (7:00) and just before (8:00) the guitars beckon from inside the house.

Track 3. Basically this is *Hair Pie Bake I*, possibly with a few edits. (1:23) hears Don hold a single note in anticipation of the band beginning. The cardboard is now on the drums. See *Trout Mask Replica* notes for more.

Track 4. Another run-through of *Hair Pie*. Don joins in a bit later after explaining to the boys he must play. Both he and Victor stay on the same mic, and you can hear talking on the other mic as the boys mess round saying "hello" on the other mic, blowing on it etc.

Track 5. Sounds like we're getting ready to do *Hobo Chang Ba* and Zoot's favorite intro. We do a relatively good take of this, but as you notice, it is instrumental. Don was supposed to be singing outside, but had never rehearsed and had no idea what he was going to do yet. He used to come up to me and confide, "I don't know how I'm going to sing to this stuff!" Another thing here that I find to be typical is the fact that he's suddenly decided that one of the guitar lines is being played incorrectly. He'd been hearing us play for months, everyday. Why pick now to tutor Antennae Jimmy Semens in how to play the part? My thought was always that he was deflecting the problem of him not knowing his vocals to someone else.

Track 6. After a couple of false takes, we made this; (0:41) - Jeff's part is a little rushed, then he comes to the section Don was singing earlier. (1:25) shows Bill playing a really fast line on slide that's tough to play. I had just learned the drums to this a few days before. Most of it was mine, but the ending was Don's.

Track 7. *Dachau Blues'* intensely dissonant line begins. I don't remember much about this except that I played less "parts" and more "time" in this piece. It really took on a different tone with the brilliant bass clarinet and vocal added later. I didn't know it well yet, as you can tell by the drums not knowing where to end.

Track 8. Tuning and Talking.

Track 9. *Pachuco Cadaver*, which was a fun one to play. It's starts out as a medium shuffle with erratic bass. When it switches to 3/4 - I originally switched with them but Don asked me to play a 4/4 after this recording. In the last section he added the embellishments where the drums would play the double time shuffle patterns and breaks. It makes it far more interesting.

Track 10. *Sugar 'n Spikes*. This doesn't sound up to speed plus the tone on Bill's guitar makes it difficult to play those low slide notes. However, not a bad version.

Track 11. *Sweet Sweet Bulbs* - false start. I have no idea who walked through and said "Sweet Sweet

Bulbs, Gentlemen." Maybe FZ.

Track 12. *Sweet Bulbs* - after this, Don added a Latin section on the drums around (1:05).

Track 13. *Frownland* - This was one of the last pieces learned by the band and I was completely unfamiliar with playing to it. Don sat at the drums and played for a while and the stuff I picked up from that allowed me to play freely but with references to the music.

Track 14. *Frownland*

Track 15. Space before *Ella Guru*.

Track 16. *Ella Guru*. I'm dragging the intro on this version and shouldn't have been. It was one of the earlier pieces we learned.

Track 17. *Too Much For My Mirror* - pretty tight.

Track 18. *Interlude*

Track 19. *Steal Softly Thru Snow* - one of the better performances, obviously we were more comfortable with this composition, having learned it months earlier.

Track 20. Interlude - a little practice of a section Jeff apparently wanted to go over or perhaps for balance.

Track 21. *My Human Gets Me Blues* - We played this one so many times at rehearsals that we could play it in our sleep. The instruments were set up quite differently, so it made it more difficult to hear each other.

Track 22. Interlude

Track 23. *Big Joan* - Since this was done without horn, it was hard to anticipate how to really pull it off. We needed something to react to. I was given the role of cueing the breaks. There was no specific idea about what to do - just follow our instincts. I had to imagine Don playing and have no idea why he didn't, as the mic's were set up outside. Notice how the bass was written to play in a different tempo at points.

Track 24. *Candy Man* - Doug Moon with Don singing comically the words to *"Candy Man."* Obviously, this goes into *China Pig* and is the cassette recording being transferred to Zappa's remote system.

DISC IV

Track 1. Starts with either a recording or a live version of *The Blimp* interrupted by the lady who always complained about the volume. Don indicates that he's not into long hair saying "It's for the kids, not for me." I think it's kind of boring actually, to listen to all of this, with Laurie or possibly Mark typing. Don is talking about Herb Alpert, saying it wasn't him playing trumpet and Frank adds, but "It's his chest when he opens his shirt for those posters."

Track 2. Story of a missing woman discovered in cesspool to which Don replies "that's really shitty."

Track 3. Don says he's going to write a song about that. *China Pig* plays in the background. Later, he mentions the fluoride in the water that breaks him out when he takes a bath. At the end FZ says "That's nice Don" referring to *China Pig*.

DISC V

Track 1. **MY HUMAN GETS ME BLUES** - recorded live at Amougies Festival, Belgium. In 1970, while at the Trout House to pick up my drums, Bill Harkleroad told me about how he had combined both guitar parts into one after Jeff left the band so as to be able to play this festival. He played this piece for me as an example. In the center section of the piece, the guitars go into two separate time signatures, but Bill combined the parts and played a single time signature, thus altering the composition, but at the same time supplying harmonic and rhythmic similarity. I was not surprised that Bill would attempt this, as he always had the desire to challenge himself and always rose to the challenge. He also had to deal with Jeff Bruschele, a non-drummer who had replaced me as drummer. Bill coached Jeff on the drum parts until he actually was able to provide a fairly-decent facsimile of the performance. Jeff dressed in my stage outfit - cape, hat, etc. and was called

"Drumbo" by Don.

Bill and Jeff B had a great rapport and enjoyed a common mindset on several points in their philosophies which Bill and myself did not have in common, so, I think that he was rooting for Jeff and encouraged him. He later told me that it took "a lot of balls" to step in and attempt to learn those parts, then play at a concert a few months later. I agree. Bruschele deserves kudos for this.

The inclusion of bass clarinet could have been better employed at filling in for the missing guitar, and could have saved Bill a mountain of trouble. My guess here is that "The Mascara Snake" was unable to play much and so doubled the bass parts and remained in the safe zone. I have no idea whether this was his call, or someone else's. Zappa was, according to Bill, "jamming" with the band at this festival, but I don't hear it on this track, which is fairly poor and probably off a cassette player. Don was reading the lyrics off a sheet. He sings with a "wolf" voice rather than a "shout" voice as on the recording. He also sings in the same key rather than ? step sharp.

Next Three Tracks 2-4

Recorded at the Detroit Tubeworks, January 1971, during US Tour. Bill Harkleroad (Zoot Horn Rollo) Gtr. - Elliot Ingber (Winged Eel Fingerling) Gtr. - Art Tripp (Ed Marimba) Marimba and drums. - Mark Boston (Rockette Morton)Bass and elastic dance - John French (Drumbo) Gon Bop drum kit.

We were taken to a TV station on a bus. There was a black and white movie being broadcast at the time. The guy wanted to interview us all, but Don (fearing one of us may say something "lame" or even worse, revealing) suggested they just have us sit at a table with our shoes off and film our naked and freezing toes (a good name for a group). I'm not sure if this was overlaid with a soundtrack of our performance or not.

Track 2. Very rushed version of *Big Joan.* Also, is that a line from *Pachuco Cadaver* that Don is singing during one of the breaks?

Track 3. It's interesting that we went from part of Mark's *Hair Pie* bass solo straight into *Woe Is A Me Bop.* This was Elliot Ingber's idea as a sort of "mini-set" designed to illustrate highlights of the show. Don, as usual, is completely lost lyrically, but always categorized as "artistic license." Artie's solo from *Flash Gordon's Ape* follows and then the band jumps directly into...

Track 4. *Bellerin' Plain.* On this last piece, the Gon Bops, which were custom drums made like Congas, really can be heard well. They are much higher in pitch and have a different timbre. They were much lower in volume and therefore I played much harder on tour.

Track 5. *Black Snake Moan I* - What a fantastic voice is all I can say. It's too bad Don never did a decent blues album. It would have sold well. He might have been able to afford to pay his band.

Track 6. *Grow Fins* - Bickershaw Festival, Lancashire. Don's voice was in great form during this period. Not even a bad recording can camouflage that fact. The harp is overbearing a bit, as it was played through the same mic as vocal.

Track 7. *Black Snake Moan II* - WBCN Radio, Boston, MA. - Don said he couldn't get it through cause the mic was to small. Maybe what really happened is that the voice was too big. But we heard enough to convince us.

Track 8. *Spitball Scalped A Baby* - Bickershaw Festival, Lancashire - this seems to start out a little slow but soon picks up steam. Artie is in great form here and his power had increased as he was now 'the drummer.' I always enjoyed these free-form improvs, as they were some of the only non-static moments of the performances, musically-speaking.

Track 9. *Harp Boogie* - WBCN Radio, Boston, MA. - The band would sometimes get a spontaneous burst of Don's harp-playing at rehearsals and this reminds me of one of those moments. He used to "pull" notes out of the harp with his hand - a bit of showmanship he rarely showed on stage. It's obvious that the nuance is great. Of course, Don apologizes for having no water on his harmonica, but we heard the fire.

Track 10. *One Red Rose That I Mean,* Town Hall, NYC. This could be late 1971. It's a great performance. I don't think he ever gave a bad one. I stood next to him several times as he performed this in 1970 and he was like a well-oiled machine.

Track 11. *Harp Boogie II* - WBCN Radio, Boston, MA. - Performed on a "Bull" harp, as Don sometimes referred to the large Marine Band harmonicas by Hohner. This is a C harmonica playing in the key of G (cross harp) and is the same type harp used on *Mirror Man.* It's an octave lower than a standard harmonica.

Track 12. *Natchez Burnin'* - Bickershaw Festival, Lancashire - The first time I played with The Magic Band, Don sang this early in the evening. I had goose bumps and chills so bad I could barely maintain. Alex and Don did a lot of interplay with Alex interjecting blues licks in between Don's lines. Spellbinding - very spellbinding.

Track 13. *Harp Boogie II* - phone-in, but great.

Track 14. *Click Clack* - Bataclan, Paris, France, 1972. This is a better performance than many I've heard - punctuated by Art Tripp's great drumming and Don's fantastic vocal.

Track 15. *Orange Claw Hammer* - this is said to be 1975, but I'm guessing 1974. I'm guessing this is NOT Frank Zappa, as he talks about how much he hates that folk-style guitar. I'm guessing this is Tragic Band guy and the year is 1974. This is 90% mundane guitar and 10% vocal, so I'm moving on as quickly as possible.

Track 16. *Odd Jobs* - I am sure this is one of the pieces Don wrote while living in Woodland Hills during the *Decals* era. It wasn't the Trout House, but a separate place. Don recorded himself playing on dozens of cassettes. This was given to me to transcribe for *Bat Chain Puller.* I think that it was originally intended for a guitar solo album planned for Zoot called 'Big Sir Suite.' Don was probably playing in G, but old pianos often happened to be tuned 1/2 step flat because they're worn-out, so I wrote it in the key of Ab and used a capo on guitar.

Track 17. This may be someone's bootleg from *Bat Chain Puller* - but it was meant to show the way a song went from piano to band.

Track 18. *Vampire Suite* - Not a room in a hotel. This just shows another way in which Don composed - whistling a part on tape, then I learned it on guitar, obviously adding a chordal note or two. It is followed by the band playing the song live at The Venue, London, UK, 1980. The credits do not include Gary Lucas, who plays bass on this piece.

Track 19. Mellotron Improv - Paradise, Boston, MA - This is actually Mellotron, Piano, and Mini Moog solo.

Track 20. *Evening Bell* - Gary Lucas supplied his piano worktape for *Evening Bell* for your listening pleasure and as yet another example of how Van Vliet composed.

Track 21. *Evening Bell* - Gary Lucas plays his interpretation of the previous piano tape in an amazing performance.

Track 22. Mellotron Improv - Stanhope, NJ 1980 Live - another keyboard improv. The crowd didn't seem to get it, but there's actually some really interesting stuff here.

Track 23. *Flavor Bud Living* - Beacon Theatre, NYC 1980. Gary Lucas performs the guitar solo piece from *Bat Chain Puller.* This is a very nice performance by Lucas, an eloquent and sensitive solo artist. Gary appeared as guest artist during this period and was managing the band at this time.